Tax Formula for Individuals

Income (broadly conceived)	$xx,xxx
Less: Exclusions	(x,xxx)
Gross income	$xx,xxx
Less: Deductions *for* adjusted gross income	(x,xxx)
Adjusted gross income	$xx,xxx
Less: The greater of—	
Total itemized deductions	
or standard deduction	(x,xxx)
Less: Personal and dependency exemptions	(x,xxx)
Taxable income	$xx,xxx
Tax on taxable income	$ x,xxx
Less: Tax credits (including Federal income tax withheld and other prepayments of Federal income taxes)	(xxx)
Tax due (or refund)	$ xxx

Basic Standard Deduction Amounts

	Standard Deduction Amount	
Filing Status	**2013**	**2014**
Single	$ 6,100	$ 6,200
Married, filing jointly	12,200	12,400
Surviving spouse	12,200	12,400
Head of household	8,950	9,100
Married, filing separately	6,100	6,200

Amount of Each Additional Standard Deduction

Filing Status	**2013**	**2014**
Single	$1,500	$1,550
Married, filing jointly	1,200	1,200
Surviving spouse	1,200	1,200
Head of household	1,500	1,550
Married, filing separately	1,200	1,200

Personal and Dependency Exemption

2013	**2014**
$3,900	$3,950

Trust the tax experts at H&R Block® to make it easy.

- ✓ A step-by-step Q&A guides you through your return.

- ✓ Automatically double-checks for errors and is guaranteed accurate.*

- ✓ Free audit support with an H&R Block enrolled agent to represent you in the event of an audit.**

H&R Block Premium & Business Tax Software. Providing students an additional tax-preparation tool, H&R Block features basic and complex problems that allow students to prepare returns for individuals, C and S corporations, partnerships, estates and trusts. Furthermore, the software's website, **www.hrblock.com,** offers useful tips, calculators, and other up-to-the-minute, relevant, tax information.

3 Simple Ways CHECKPOINT® Helps You Make Sense of All Those Taxes.

- Find what you are looking for quickly and easily online with Checkpoint

- A comprehensive collection of primary tax law, cases and rulings, along with analytical insight you simply can't find anywhere else

- Checkpoint has built-in productivity tools such as calculators to make research more efficient – a resource more tax pros use than any other

Titles that include Checkpoint Student Edition

- **Hoffman/Smith,** *South-Western Federal Taxation: Individual Income Taxes, 2015 Edition*

- **Hoffman/Raabe/Maloney/Young/Smith,** *South-Western Federal Taxation: Corporations, Partnerships, Estates & Trusts, 2015 Edition*

- **Hoffman/Maloney/Raabe/Young,** *South-Western Federal Taxation: Comprehensive Volume, 2015 Edition*

- **Smith/Raabe/Maloney/Young,** *South-Western Federal Taxation: Essentials of Taxation: Individuals and Business Entities, 2015 Edition*

- **Murphy/Higgins,** *Concepts in Federal Taxation, 2015 Edition*

IMPORTANT INFORMATION

The purchase of this textbook includes access to Thomson Reuters Checkpoint Student Edition for a 6-month duration.

To log in visit **http://checkpoint.thomsonreuters.com**
You will be asked to supply a User ID and Password. Please use the following:

USER ID: CEN14-48023

PASSWORD: CEN14-48023

PLEASE NOTE: If you have purchased a used copy of this text, the User ID and Password may have already been used. A new User ID and Password may be obtained by purchasing a new copy of this text.

SOUTH-WESTERN
FEDERAL TAXATION

INDIVIDUAL INCOME TAXES

2015 EDITION

GENERAL EDITORS

William H. Hoffman, Jr.

J.D., Ph.D., CPA

James E. Smith

Ph.D., CPA

CONTRIBUTING AUTHORS

James H. Boyd

Ph.D., CPA
Arizona State University

D. Larry Crumbley

Ph.D., CPA
Louisiana State University

Steven C. Dilley

J.D., Ph.D., CPA
Michigan State University

William H. Hoffman, Jr.

J.D., Ph.D., CPA
University of Houston

David M. Maloney

Ph.D., CPA
University of Virginia

William A. Raabe

Ph.D., CPA
University of Wisconsin-Whitewater

Boyd C. Randall

J.D., Ph.D.
Brigham Young University

W. Eugene Seago

J.D., Ph.D., CPA
Virginia Polytechnic Institute
and State University

James E. Smith

Ph.D., CPA
College of William and Mary

James C. Young

Ph.D., CPA
Northern Illinois University

CENGAGE
Learning

Australia • Brazil • Japan • Korea • Mexico • Singapore • Spain • United Kingdom • United States

**South-Western Federal Taxation:
Individual Income Taxes, 2015 Edition**

William H. Hoffman, Jr., James E. Smith

Product Director: Rob Dewey

Senior Product Manager: Sharon Oblinger

Associate Content Developer: Tristann Jones

Product Assistant: A.J. Smiley

Marketing Director: Natalie King

Associate Marketing Manager:
  Courtney Doyle Chambers

Senior Marketing Coordinator: Eileen Corcoran

Media Developer: Lysa Kosins

Content Digitization Project Manager:
  Nikkita Bankston

Manufacturing Planner: Doug Wilke

Senior Content Project Manager: Tim Bailey

Production Service: Cenveo Publisher Services

Senior Art Director: Michelle Kunkler

Cover and Internal Designer: Kim Torbeck/
  Imbue Design

Cover Image: © Dennis Flaherty/Getty Images, Inc.

Intellectual Property:

  Analyst: Christina Ciaramella

  Project Manager: Amber Hosea

For product information and technology assistance, contact us at
Cengage Learning Customer & Sales Support, 1-800-354-9706

For permission to use material from this text or product,
submit all requests online at **www.cengage.com/permissions**
Further permissions questions can be emailed to
permissionrequest@cengage.com

Unless otherwise noted, all items © Cengage Learning.

All tax forms within the text are: Source: Internal Revenue Service.

Student Edition ISBN 13: 978-1-285-43885-6
Student Edition ISBN 10: 1-285-43885-X
Student Edition with CD ISBN 13: 978-1-285-43884-9
Student Edition with CD ISBN 10: 1-285-43884-1

ISSN: 0272-0329
2015 Annual Edition

Cengage Learning
200 First Stamford Place, 4th Floor
Stamford, CT 06902
USA

Cengage Learning is a leading provider of customized learning solutions with office locations around the globe, including Singapore, the United Kingdom, Australia, Mexico, Brazil, and Japan. Locate your local office at:
www.cengage.com/global

Cengage Learning products are represented in Canada by
Nelson Education, Ltd.

To learn more about Cengage Learning Solutions, visit **www.cengage.com**

Purchase any of our products at your local college store or at our preferred online store **www.cengagebrain.com**

Printed in the United States of America
1 2 3 4 5 6 7 19 18 17 16 15 14

Preface

Committed to Educational Success

South-Western Federal Taxation (SWFT) is the most trusted and best-selling series in college **taxation.** We are focused exclusively on providing the most useful, comprehensive, and up-to-date tax texts, online study aids, tax preparation tools, and research tools to help instructors and students succeed in their tax courses and beyond.

SWFT is a comprehensive package of teaching and learning materials, significantly enhanced each edition to meet instructor and student needs and to add overall value to learning taxation.

Individual Income Taxes, 2015 Edition provides a dynamic learning experience inside and outside of the classroom. Built with resources and tools that have been identified as the most important, our complete learning system provides options for students to achieve success.

Individual Incomes Taxes, 2015 Edition provides accessible, comprehensive, and authoritative coverage of the relevant tax code and regulations as they pertain to the individual taxpayer, as well as coverage of all major developments in Federal Taxation.

In revising the 2015 Edition, we focused on:

- **Accessibility. Clarity. Substance.** The text authors and editors made this their mantra as they revised the 2015 edition. Coverage has been streamlined to make it more accessible to students, and difficult concepts have been clarified, all without losing the substance that makes up the *South-Western Federal Taxation* series.

- **CengageNOW as a complete learning system.** Cengage understands that digital learning solutions are central to the classroom. Through sustained research, we continually refine our learning solutions in CengageNOW to meet evolving student and instructor needs. CengageNOW fulfills learning and course management needs by offering a personalized study plan, video lectures, auto-graded homework, auto-graded tests, and a full eBook with features and advantages that address common challenges.

Leadership, Innovation, and Service in the Ever-Changing Tax Law Environment

LEADERSHIP

South-Western Federal Taxation leads the market in the number of instructors and students using its resources. And it leads the way in its *authoritative and comprehensive coverage* of the latest taxation practices and legislation presented in a student-accessible manner.

INNOVATION

South-Western Federal Taxation offers students and instructors the *broadest and most innovative* selection of learning and teaching solutions available:

- **CengageNOW™** is a powerful course management and online homework and learning tool that provides robust control and customization for instructors, coupled with a unique learning process for students. Together, CengageNOW's features combine to meet individual, class, departmental, and school outcomes. More than 500,000 students use CengageNOW every year!
- **Checkpoint® Student Edition** from Thomson Reuters offers career-bound students use of *true professional tax research software* to build familiarity with the Tax Code and its various administrative and judicial interpretations.*
- **H&R Block®** facilitates tax preparation practice using one of the industry's most popular tax preparation software packages.

Each of these innovative *South-Western Federal Taxation* assets helps students learn and retain with customized homework help and feedback while introducing them to the professional tools that will make them successful in their future careers.

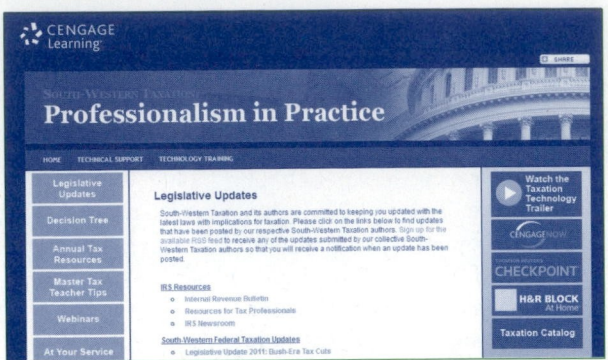

DEDICATED, ONGOING SERVICE FOR INSTRUCTORS

The South-Western Taxation Community website at **www.cengage.com/community/tax** is a *one-stop destination* for instructors' complete teaching and support needs. In addition to the Legislative Updates page shown above, instructors can access a host of other instructional materials, technology demos, annual resources, support, and training.

- Sign up for **The South-Western Taxation Annual Resources Program** and indicate which textbook you use. Upon registration, we promise to send your textbook and instructor resources automatically as they are published. This convenient service will save you time!
- **Legislative Updates** are regularly available by visiting the Community Site or simply by subscribing to our RSS feed that will link out to the newly posted updates.
- View demonstrations of the **technology products** offered with the series.
- Find **Technical Support and Training** when and how you need it.

Learning Tools and Features to Help Students Make the Connection

South-Western Federal Taxation's Individual Income Taxes, 2015 Edition includes *enhanced learning features* designed to take students beyond the usual textbook experience to a deeper understanding of the real application of tax concepts and tax law.

*Not available with the Professional Editions of South-Western Federal Taxation.

SEEING THE BIG PICTURE

Taxation comes alive at the start of each chapter. **The Big Picture: Tax Solutions for the Real World** is a glimpse into the lives, families, careers, and tax situations of typical individual filers. Each Big Picture case asks students to apply what they will learn in the upcoming chapter to develop the best tax solution to these real-life dilemmas.

At least four examples per chapter tie back to the Big Picture. This helps eliminate confusion for students by providing a more consistent application of the data and providing a tax story that spans the whole chapter.

Finally, to solidify student comprehension, each chapter concludes with a **Refocus on the Big Picture** summary and tax planning scenario. These scenarios apply the concepts and topics from the chapter in a reasonable and professional way.

THE BIG PICTURE   Tax Solutions for the Real World   © Izabela Habur/iStockphoto.com

IMPACT OF ITEMIZED DEDUCTIONS ON MAJOR PURCHASES

John and Susan Williamson, a young professional couple, have been renting an apartment in Atlanta, Georgia, since they were married. Their income has grown as they've become more established in their careers, and they now believe that the time has come to purchase their own home. In addition, their desire to buy a home now may be coming at a good time, because John's mother, Martha, needs to move in with them due to her declining health and their current apartment is too small to accommodate her. John and Susan's current monthly rent is $2,000, but they are willing to spend $2,500 per month on an after-tax basis if necessary for their first home.

After months of house hunting, they have found the perfect home, but they fear it may be too expensive. If they acquire a standard mortgage to finance the purchase of the home, the total cash outlay during the first year of ownership will be $43,000 ($2,000 principal payments, $37,000 interest payments, and $4,000 real estate taxes). Alternatively, if they use their retirement and taxable investments to secure the home financing, they can qualify for a lower interest rate and thereby reduce the interest charge from $37,000 to $35,000. They expect their Federal AGI to be $200,000 and their taxable income to range between $160,000 and $185,000 for the year. John and Susan have not itemized their deductions in prior years because the amount of their qualifying personal expenditures has fallen just short of the standard deduction amount. Assume that the Williamsons' marginal income tax rate under Georgia law is 6 percent.

MAKING THE CONNECTION

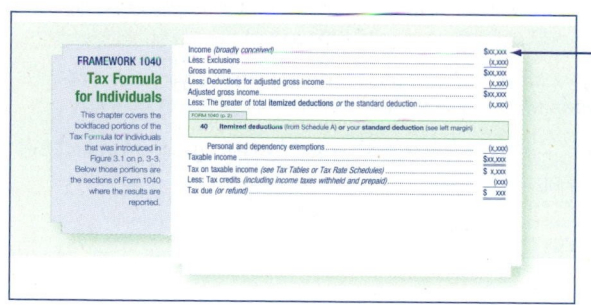

Use this chapter-opening **Framework 1040**, which shows the topics as they appear in the individual tax formula, to understand where on Form 1040 these chapter topics would appear.

FITTING IT ALL TOGETHER: FRAMEWORK 1040

This chapter-opening feature demonstrates how topics within *Individual Income Taxes* fit together, using the Income Tax Formula for Individuals as the framework. The framework helps students organize their understanding of the chapters and topics to see how they relate to the basic tax formula and then identify where these items are reported on Form 1040. Framework 1040 helps students navigate topics by explaining how tax concepts are organized.

FINANCIAL DISCLOSURE INSIGHTS

Tax professionals need to understand how taxes affect the income statement and balance sheet. **Financial Disclosure Insights,** appearing throughout the text, use current data about existing taxpayers to highlight book-tax reporting differences, effective tax rates, and trends in reporting conventions. Financial Disclosure Insights help students integrate their financial accounting knowledge with the results of state and Federal tax law. Financial Disclosure Insights help make SWFT's coverage of the role of tax data on financial statements the best in the business.

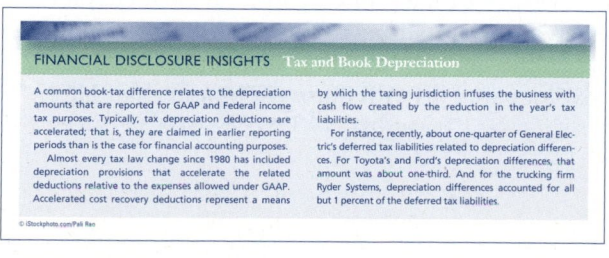

TAX IN THE NEWS

Drawn from today's business and popular press, **Tax in the News** features enliven class discussions by presenting current issues that illustrate the chapter material and applying them to real life. These plentiful and relevant news items make tax law concepts come to life.

TAX IN THE NEWS — The First Family and Itemized Deduction Phaseouts

In 2010, President Barack H. and Michelle L. Obama itemized deductions on their 2009 tax return. Because of their income level, their itemized deductions were reduced by $53,386 as required by the law at that time (see below).

Because the marginal rate of 35 percent applied to the Obamas' taxable income in 2009, the phaseout of itemized deductions cost them $18,685 in additional Federal income

tax ($53,386 reduction × 35% marginal tax rate). Over the years, phaseouts such as this have been a popular way to raise tax revenues without increasing tax rates.

Although this phaseout provision expired after 2009, Congress chose to bring it back beginning in 2013. It will be interesting to see the cost of the phaseout to the Obamas for 2013 once they release their income tax return for that year.

© iStockphoto.com/Andrey Prokhorov

ETHICS AND EQUITY

Most issues do not have just one correct answer. **Ethics & Equity** features will spark critical thinking and invite classroom discussion, enticing students to evaluate their own value system. Suggested answers to Ethics & Equity scenarios appear in the Solutions Manual.

ETHICS & EQUITY — Between a Rock and a Hard Place

Robert Ryan, a candidate for governor, has released his income tax return to the public. As Ryan's former tax adviser, you examine the return closely and realize that a considerable amount of his income was not reported on the return. You confide to a friend in the tabloid newspaper business that you are aware that a candidate for high public office has filed a fraudulent

tax return. Your friend assures you that you will be able to sell your story for at least $25,000 to a tabloid and still remain anonymous. Another friend, a CPA, argues that you should inform Ryan and give him an opportunity to correct the problem. You tell your friend that you are concerned that Ryan will be very vindictive if you approach him about the issue. Which course of action will you choose?

© iStockphoto.com/LdF

10-9 TAX PLANNING

10-9a Effective Utilization of Itemized Deductions

LO.9

Identify tax planning strategies that can maximize the benefit of itemized deductions.

Because an individual may use the standard deduction in one year and itemize deductions in another year, it is frequently possible to obtain maximum benefit by shifting itemized deductions from one year to another. For example, if a taxpayer's itemized deductions and the standard deduction are approximately the same for each year of a two-year period, the taxpayer should use the standard deduction in one year and shift itemized deductions (to the extent permitted by law) to the other year. The individual could, for example, prepay a church pledge for a particular year to shift the deduction to the current year or avoid paying end-of-the-year medical expenses to shift the deduction to the following year.

TAX PLANNING

Most chapters include a separate section, with its own Learning Objective, calling attention to how the tax law can be applied to reach the taxpayer's goals. Tax planning applications and suggestions also appear throughout each chapter.

GLOBAL TAX ISSUES

The **Global Tax Issues** feature gives insight into the ways in which taxation is affected by international concerns and illustrates the effects of various events on tax liabilities across the globe.

Global Tax Issues

© iStockphoto.com/Andrey Prokhorov

Deductibility of Foreign Taxes

Josef, a citizen of the United States who works primarily in New York, also works several months each year in Austria. He owns a residence in Austria and pays income taxes to Austria on the income he earns there. Both the property tax he pays on his Austrian residence and the income tax he pays on his Austrian income are deductible in computing U.S. taxable income. However, if Josef deducts the Austrian income tax, he may not claim the foreign tax credit with respect to this tax (see Chapter 13).

NUMEROUS REAL-WORLD EXAMPLES IN EVERY CHAPTER

An **average of over 40 examples in each chapter** use realistic situations to illustrate the complexities of the tax law and allow students to integrate chapter concepts with illustrations and examples.

Example 4

Norman has a chronic heart ailment. In October, his family decides to place Norman in a nursing home equipped to provide medical and nursing care. Total nursing home expenses amount to $35,000 during the year. Of this amount, $20,000 is directly attributable to medical and nursing care. Because Norman is in need of significant medical and nursing care and is placed in the facility primarily for this purpose, all $35,000 of the nursing home costs are deductible (subject to the AGI floor, explained earlier).

A Complete Learning System—CengageNOW

CengageNOW for Taxation takes students from motivation to mastery. Built on principles of learning, designed and created hand-in-hand with educators, Cengage Learning digital solutions focus on engagement, taking students through levels of application, analysis, and critical thinking with depth and context unmatched in the market.

CengageNOW elevates thinking by providing superior content designed with the entire student workflow in mind. Students learn move efficiently with the variety of engaging assessment and learning tools. For instructors, CengageNOW provides ultimate control and customization and a clear view into student performance that allows for the opportunity to tailor the learning experience to improve outcomes.

MOTIVATION

Many instructors find that students come to class unmotivated and unprepared. To help with engagement and preparedness, CengageNOW for SWFT offers the following features:

- **"Tell Me More" videos provide a summary of the chapter at a glance.** These videos will help students become familiar with the key terms and concepts presented in each chapter, prior to class lectures.

- **"Tax Drills" test students on key concepts and applications.** With 3 to 5 questions per learning objective, these "quick-hit" questions help students prepare for class lectures or review prior to an exam.

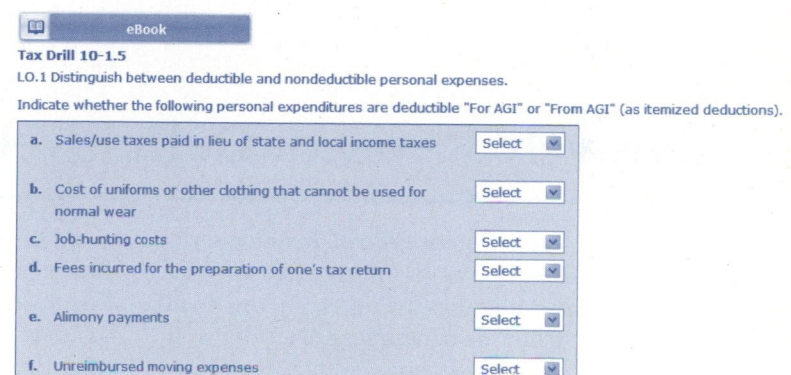

APPLICATION

Students need to learn problem-solving behavior and skills in order to complete taxation problems on their own. However, as students try to work through homework problems, sometimes they become stuck and need guidance. To help reinforce concepts and keep students on the right track, CengageNOW for SWFT offers the following:

- **End-of-chapter homework from the text** is expanded and enhanced to follow the workflow a professional would use to solve various client scenarios. These enhancements better engage students and encourage them to think like tax professionals.

- **Algorithmic versions** of end-of-chapter homework are available for at least 15 problems per chapter.

- **Detailed feedback for each homework question.** Homework questions include enhanced, immediate feedback so students can learn as they go. Levels of feedback include an option for "check my work" prior to submission of an assignment. Then, after submitting an assignment, students receive even more extensive feedback explaining why their answers were incorrect. Instructors can decide how much feedback their students receive and when, including the full solution, if they wish.

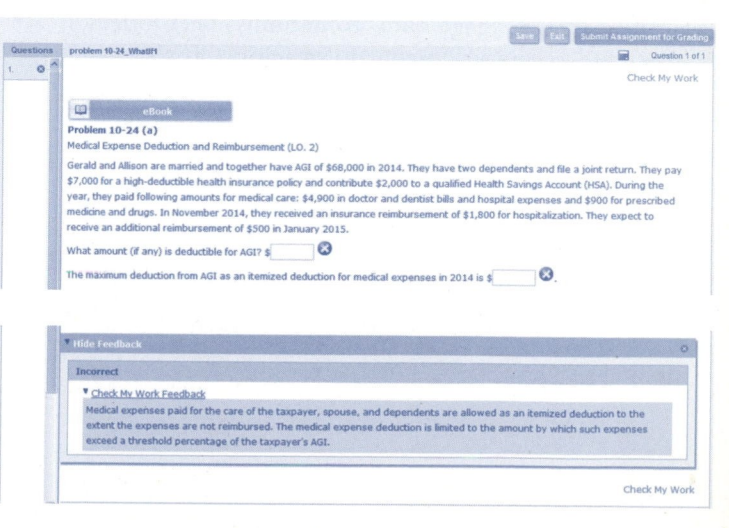

- **"Show Me How"** videos walk students step-by-step through the process of solving a problem from the end-of-chapter material. These videos focus on the more difficult problems that tie multiple learning objectives together.

- Built-in **Test Bank** for online assessment.

- For students needing additional support, CengageNOW's **Personalized Study Plan** is complete with pre-tests and post-tests, an eBook, practice quizzes, and more.

MASTERY

Finally, students need to make the leap from memorizing concepts to actual critical thinking. They need to be able to connect multiple topics and master the material. To help students grasp the big picture of taxation and achieve the end goal of mastery, CengageNOW for SWFT offers the following:

- **"What If" versions of problems** provide students with additional opportunities to practice key taxation concepts and scenarios These alternate versions allow students to work the same problem multiple times with changing tax attributes. This encourages deeper understanding of the material because students are challenged to use their prior knowledge of the tax situation and critically think through the new attributes to determine how the outcome will change.

CengageNOW Instant Access Code ISBN:
978-1-285-44167-2

Text + CengageNOW Bundle ISBN: 978-1-305-25033-8

Extensively Revised. Definitively Up to Date.

Each year the *South-Western Federal Taxation* series is updated with thousands of changes to each text. Some of these changes result from the feedback we receive from instructors and students in the form of reviews, focus groups, web surveys, and personal e-mail correspondence to our authors and team members. Other changes come from our careful analysis of the evolving tax environment. **We make sure that every tax law change relevant to the introductory taxation course was considered, summarized, and fully integrated into the revision of text and supplementary materials.**

The *South-Western Federal Taxation* community website (**www.cengage.com/community/tax**) offers immediate access to current information as soon as it is available. Instructors and students may log on and learn about the most recent tax information—including the Code and Regulations, administrative interpretations, new court rulings, and other newsworthy items.

The *South-Western Federal Taxation* authors have made every effort to keep specific chapters up to date and accurate. All chapters of *Individual Income Taxes* contain the following general changes for the 2015 Edition.

- Revised numerous materials as the result of changes caused by indexing of statutory amounts.

- Revised Problem Materials.

- Updated Tax in the News items with coverage of recent events.

- Added at least one new Ethics and Equity item per chapter.

- Updated Chapter Outlines to provide an overview of the material and to make it easier to locate specific topics.

- Revised Financial Disclosure Insights and Global Tax Issues as to current developments.

- Streamlined chapter content (where applicable) to clarify material and make it easier for students to understand.

Chapter 1

- Discussion of Social Considerations has been amplified.
- Updates made to Footnote 4 and Example 2.
- Indexation changes reflected in unified transfer tax credit and exemption amount and gift tax annual exclusion.
- FICA base amount changed.
- Interest on assessments and refunds for the first quarter of 2014 changed.

Chapter 2

- Added a Big Picture example to the beginning of the chapter and incorporated it into chapter materials.
- Added a new Ethics & Equity example related to IRS profiling of taxpayers.
- Added a new Tax in the News item comparing the length of the Affordable Care Act of 2010 to the Internal Revenue Code.
- Revised and clarified text and examples throughout the chapter.

Chapter 3

- Updated materials to reflect inflation indexation.
- Revised and clarified text and examples throughout the chapter.
- Added information on filing requirements for same-sex marriages.
- Distinguished between same-sex marriages and domestic partnerships and civil unions.
- Added a new Ethics & Equity item on the abandoned spouse rules.

Chapter 4

- Modified the factual pattern of The Big Picture example in order to clarify the key issues involved.
- Added a Global Tax Issues feature relating to the U.S. tax treatment of dividends received from foreign corporations.
- By converting to summary form, shortened the background material on the tax treatment of dividend income.
- Contrasted the ownership of community property with other forms of joint ownership.
- Clarified the tax differences between property settlements, alimony, and child support.
- Added tax planning suggestions regarding situations where discrepancies exist between a taxpayer's declared income and that reported to the IRS by a third-party payor.

Chapter 5

- Simplified the discussion of long-term care insurance and employee fringe benefits.
- Provided a new Concept Summary for employee benefits.

- Made necessary adjustments for annual indexation required by tax law.

Chapter 6

- Updated the discussion to reflect changes generated by annual indexation.
- Simplified The Big Picture factual situation to make it more meaningful.
- Added emphasis to the distinction between a deduction *for* and a deduction *from* AGI.
- Rearranged material on disallowed losses in dealings between related parties to clarify how these situations arise.
- Amplified the Tax Planning material.

Chapter 7

- Revised and clarified text and examples throughout the chapter.
- Added a new Ethics & Equity item on the validity of a casualty loss deduction when an insurance claim could have been filed.
- Modified material to reflect annual indexation for inflation.

Chapter 8

- Revised and clarified text and examples throughout the chapter.
- Reorganized depreciation materials—focusing on MACRS and splitting this discussion into a section on the basic rules (including personal property, mid-quarter convention, straight-line election, and real property) followed by a section on special rules (including bonus depreciation, the § 179 expense election, listed property, farm property, leasehold improvements, and the alternative depreciation system).
- Moved the brief discussion of ACRS to Appendix G.

Chapter 9

- Incorporated the new standard (automatic) mileage rate for 2014 as determined by the IRS.
- Added a caveat on the nondeductibility of "reciprocal entertainment."
- Reviewed the provisions of the new simplified method of determining the deduction for office in the home.
- Compared the advantages and disadvantages of the actual expense (regular) and simplified methods of determining the deduction for maintaining an office in the home.
- Added a new tax return problem.

Chapter 10

- Modified the facts in The Big Picture scenario to make it more realistic.
- Clarified the discussion relating to capital expenditures incurred for medical purposes.

- Revised the cost to the Federal government of allowing certain popular itemized deductions.
- Provided an interesting case showing the importance of having legitimate and credible evidence to support a charitable contribution deduction.

Chapter 11
- Amplified and clarified the "Tax Shelter Problem."
- Revised and simplified the coverage of the material participation requirements.
- Condensed the discussion of rental activities that are not treated as rental property for purposes of the passive loss rules.
- Reorganized and expanded the discussion of the limitation on the deduction for investment interest.
- Added a Tax in the News concerning the difficulty encountered by a full-time employee qualifying as a real estate professional.
- Enhanced the tax planning coverage to include the investment income limitation and the impact of the new surtax on net investment income.

Chapter 12
- Updated material by incorporating new indexation amounts that reflect current inflation adjustments.
- Thinned out background material to delete rules and provisions that are no longer relevant.
- Made a closer correlation between the statutory sources and IRS publications designed for taxpayer use.

Chapter 13
- Revised and clarified text and examples throughout the chapter.
- Updated chapter materials for 2014 inflation adjustments.
- Updated the coverage of the Social Security tax and the self-employment tax.
- Expanded discussion of Form W-4 along with providing a form-based example.
- Based on feedback from users, reduced coverage of employer payroll tax withholding methods.

Chapter 14
- Revised and clarified text and examples throughout the chapter.
- Eliminated redundancy of the Recovery of Capital Doctrine coverage (Learning Objective 3), as it was included with other materials in the chapter.
- Updated Tax in the News item related to cost basis reporting.
- Simplified discussion of basis adjustments for gift taxes paid given the rarity of the adjustment.
- Added new Ethics & Equity item on using IRAs to escape the wash sales rules (based on Revenue Procedure 2008-5).

Chapter 15
- Revised and clarified text and examples throughout the chapter.
- Added a new Ethics & Equity item on delayed § 1031 exchanges.
- Added Form 8824 to illustrate how like-kind exchanges are reported to the IRS.
- Updated Tax in the News item related to the use of eminent domain for nonpublic projects.
- Revised and clarified Concept Summary that lists the replacement property that qualifies to defer recognition of gain.
- Clarified and simplified the material on avoiding gain on the disposition of a "principal residence."

Chapter 16
- Revised and clarified text and examples throughout the chapter.
- Revised the chapter tax return example to include Form 8949, Schedule D (Form 1040), and the capital gains worksheet.
- Added a new Ethics & Equity item on art as a capital asset.

Chapter 17
- Revised and clarified text and examples throughout the chapter.
- Revised Concept Summary 17.1 and linked summary to chapter materials.
- Reduced the coverage of § 1250 depreciation recapture due to its limited application.
- Added a new Tax in the News item on the cost segregation of buildings and also added a related Ethics & Equity item on the same topic.

Chapter 18
- Simplified the discussion of the tax year.
- Updated the change in accounting methods rules.
- Added new Concept Summary for the economic performance test.

Chapter 19
- Adjusted amounts for inflation.

Chapter 20
- Updated comparison of individual and corporate tax attributes.
- Simplified the treatment of earnings and profits as a measure for the tax treatment of corporate distributions.
- Stressed the danger of a low salary structure in a Subchapter S setting.

Supplements Support Students and Instructors

SWFT *2015: Individual Income Taxes* provides a complete *teaching and learning experience* inside and outside of the classroom. Built around the areas students and instructors have identified as the most important, our integrated supplements package offers more flexibility than ever before to suit the way instructors teach and students learn.

ONLINE AND DIGITAL RESOURCES FOR STUDENTS

CengageNOW is a powerful course management and online homework tool that provides robust instructor control and customization to optimize the student learning experience and meet desired outcomes.

CengageNOW Instant Access Code ISBN:
978-1-285-44167-2

Text + CengageNOW Bundle ISBN:
978-1-305-25033-8

THOMSON REUTERS
CHECKPOINT®

Checkpoint® Student Edition from Thomson Reuters is the leading online tax research database used by professionals. There are three simple ways Checkpoint helps introduce students to tax research:

- Intuitive web-based design makes it fast and simple to find what you need.

- Checkpoint provides a comprehensive collection of primary tax law, cases, and rulings along with analytical insight you simply can't find anywhere else.

- Checkpoint has built-in productivity tools such as calculators to make research more efficient—a resource more tax pros use than any other.

Six months' access to Checkpoint Student Edition (after activation) is packaged automatically with every NEW copy of the textbook.*

TAX SOFTWARE

More than software: Put the experience of H&R Block tax professionals on your side.

- A step-by-step interview guides you through a customized process.

- Accurate calculations and 100% satisfaction—guaranteed.

- Worry-free Audit Support™ and tax advice from an H&R Block tax professional.

H&R Block® is offered with each NEW copy of the textbook—at no additional cost to students!*

*Checkpoint® Student Edition is not available with the Professional Editions of South-Western Federal Taxation texts. For all other editions, all NEW printed copies of the textbook are automatically packaged with Checkpoint Student Edition and H&R Block® tax software. If students purchase the eBook, they will not automatically receive access to Checkpoint Student Edition and H&R Block software. They must purchase the tax media pack offering both of these products. The ISBN is 978-1-285-44270-9 and can be purchased at **www.cengagebrain.com**.

Students save time and money. Students can use **CengageBrain.com** to select this textbook and access Cengage Learning content, empowering them to choose the most suitable format and giving them a better chance of success in the course. Buy printed materials, eBooks, and digital resources directly through Cengage Learning and save at **CengageBrain.com**.

Online Student Resources

Students can go to **www.cengagebrain.com** for free resources to help them study as well as the opportunity to purchase additional study aids. These valuable free study resources will help students earn a better grade:

- Interactive quizzes are short and auto-graded to help students brush up on important chapter topics.
- Flashcards use chapter terms and definitions to aid students in learning tax terminology for each chapter.
- Online glossary for each chapter provides terms and definitions from the text in alphabetical order for easy reference.
- Learning objectives can be downloaded for each chapter to help keep students on track.
- Tax Tips for the Recent Graduate introduce the college graduate to some common tax considerations that could be beneficial in reducing the dreaded "tax bite."
- Tax Updates provide the most recent tax information and major changes to the tax law.
- Tax tables used in the textbook are downloadable for reference.

PRINTED RESOURCES FOR STUDENTS

Looseleaf Edition (978-1-285-43887-0)

This version provides all the pages of the text in an unbound, three-hole punched format for portability and ease of use. H&R Block® is included with every NEW textbook as well as Checkpoint® Student Edition from Thomson Reuters.*

COMPREHENSIVE SUPPLEMENTS SUPPORT INSTRUCTORS' NEEDS

CengageNOW is a powerful course management and online homework tool that provides robust instructor control and customization to optimize the student learning experience and meet desired outcomes. In addition to the features and benefits mentioned earlier for students, CengageNOW includes these features for instructors:

- **Learning Outcomes Reporting** and the ability to analyze student work from the gradebook. Each exercise and problem is tagged by topic, learning objective, level of difficulty, estimated completion time, and business program standards to allow greater guidance in developing assessments and evaluating student progress.
- **Built-in Test Bank for online assessment**. The test bank files have been imported into CengageNOW so that they may be used as additional homework or tests.

Solutions Manual (978-1-305-08658-6)

Written by the South-Western Federal Taxation editors and authors, the Solutions Manual features solutions arranged in accordance with the sequence of chapter material. A matrix labels the problems by topical coverage; denotes which problems are new, modified, or unchanged from the prior edition. This matrix also references the prior edition's problem number for the unchanged and modified problems.

Solutions to all homework items are tagged with their Estimated Time to Complete, Level of Difficulty, and Learning Objective(s), as well as the AACSB's and AICPA's core competencies—giving instructors more control than ever in selecting homework to match the topics covered. **Available in print and on Instructor Companion Website at http://login .cengage.com.**

Instructor's Guide with Lecture Notes

Prepared by Kristina Zvinakis (The University of Texas at Austin), the Instructor's Guide contains resources designed to streamline and maximize the effectiveness of your course preparation. The Instructor's Guide contains lecture notes for each chapter, Big Picture integration, and solutions to Research Problems. Lecture notes present an outline the instructor can use in classroom presentation. **Available on Instructor Companion Website at http://login.cengage.com.**

PowerPoint® Lectures

Prepared by Donald R. Trippeer (SUNY College at Oneonta), the Instructor PowerPoint Lectures contain more than 30 slides per chapter, including outlines, concept definitions, alternate figures, and key points. **Available on Instructor Companion Website at http://login.cengage.com.**

Test Bank

Written by the *South-Western Federal Taxation* editors and authors, the Test Bank contains approximately 2,200 items and solutions arranged in accordance with the sequence of chapter material. To help the instructor create an exam, a matrix labels the questions by topical coverage—reflecting which are new or modified from the prior edition.

Each test item is tagged with its Estimated Time to Complete, Level of Difficulty, and Learning Objective(s), as well as the AACSB's and AICPA's core competencies—for easier instructor planning and test item selection. For the 2015 edition, the Test Bank will be available in Cengage's new test generator software, Cognero.

Cengage Learning Testing Powered by Cognero is a flexible, online system that allows you to:

- author, edit, and manage test bank content from multiple Cengage Learning solutions
- create multiple test versions in an instant
- deliver tests from your LMS, your classroom, or wherever you want
- Create tests from school, home, the coffee shop—anywhere with Internet access. (No special installs or downloads needed.)

Test Bank files in Word format, along with versions to import into your LMS, available on Instructor Companion Website. Cognero Test Banks available via Single Sign-on account at http://login.cengage.com.

For the 2015 Edition, all course materials are posted online at Cengage.com. Instructors should visit **Cengage.com** and select this textbook to access the online Instructor Resources.

- Solutions Manual
- Instructor's Guide
- Additional Test Bank items and solutions
- Solutions to Appendix E, Comprehensive Tax Return Problems
- PowerPoint Lectures

There will no longer be an Instructor's Resource CD to accompany the SWFT series, as all materials are available via the Instructor Companion Website.

Custom Solutions

Cengage Learning Custom Solutions develops personalized solutions to meet your taxation education needs. Consider the following for your adoption of *South-Western Federal Taxation 2015 Edition*:

- Remove chapters you do not cover or rearrange their order to create a streamlined and efficient text.
- Add your own material to cover new topics or information.
- Add relevance by including sections from Smith's *Internal Revenue Code and Regulations*, Raabe/Whittenburg/Sanders/Sawyers' *Federal Tax Research*, or your state's tax laws and regulations.

Acknowledgments

South-Western Federal Taxation continually polls adopters and non-adopters in a variety of ways. We are grateful to these individuals whose comments helped us in the development of the *South-Western Federal Taxation* texts:

Deborah S. Adkins, *Nperspective, LLC*

Amy An, *University of Iowa*

Susan E. Anderson, *Elon University*

Henry M. Anding, *Woodbury University*

Jennifer A. Bagwell, *Ohio University*

George Barbi, *Lanier Technical College*

Terry W. Bechtel, *Texas A&M University-Texarkana*

Chris Becker, *LeMoyne College*

John G. Bell

Tamara Berges, *UCLA*

Ellen Best, *University of North Georgia*

Tim Biggart, *Berry College*

Rachel Birkey, *Illinois State University*

Chris E. Bjornson, *Indiana University Southeast*

Patrick M. Borja, *Citrus College / California State University, Los Angeles*

Dianne H. Boseman, *Nash Community College*

Cathalene Bowler, *University of Northern Iowa*

Darryl L. Brown, *Illinois Wesleyan University*

Timothy G. Bryan, *University of Southern Indiana*

Robert S. Burdette, *Salt Lake Community College*

Lisa Busto, *William Rainey Harper College*

Julia M. Camp, *Providence College*

Al Case, *Southern Oregon University*

Machiavelli W. Chao, *Merage School of Business University of California, Irvine*

Eric Chen, *University of Saint Joseph*

James Milton Christianson, *Southwestern University and Austin Community College*

Ann Burstein Cohen, *University at Buffalo, The State University of New York*

Eric D. Schwartz, *LaRoche College*

Tony L. Scott, *Norwalk Community College*

Randy Serrett, *University of Houston – Downtown*

Paul Shoemaker, *University of Nebraska – Lincoln*

Kimberly Sipes, *Kentucky State University*

Georgi Smatrakalev, *Florida Atlantic University*

Leslie S. Sobol, *California State University Northridge*

Marc Spiegel, *University of California, Irvine*

Jason W. Stanfield, *Purdue University*

George Starbuck, *McMurry University*

Teresa Stephenson, *University of Wyoming*

Beth Stetson, *Oklahoma City University*

Frances A. Stott, *Bowling Green State University*

Todd S. Stowe, *Southwest Florida College*

Martin Stub, *DeVry University*

Kent Swift, *University of Montana*

Robert L. Taylor, *Lees-McRae College*

Francis C. Thomas, *Richard Stockton College of New Jersey*

Randall R. Thomas, *Upper Iowa University*

Ronald R. Tidd, *Central Washington University*

James P. Trebby, *Marquette University*

Donald R. Trippeer, *State University of New York College at Oneonta*

James M. Turner, *Georgia Institute of Technology*

Anthony W. Varnon, *Southeast Missouri State University*

Adria Palacios Vasquez, *Texas A&M University – Kingsville*

Terri Walsh, *Seminole State College of Florida*

Marie Wang

Natasha R. Ware, *Southeastern University*

Sarah Webber, *University of Dayton*

Bill Weispfenning, *University of Jamestown (ND)*

Andrew Whitehair

Kent Williams, *Indiana Wesleyan University*

Candace Witherspoon, *Valdosta State University*

Sheila Woods, *DeVry University, Houston, TX*

Special Thanks

We are grateful to **James C. Young** (Northern Illinois University) for providing us with his inflation adjustments, which are available prior to the release of the official amounts by the IRS. We also thank **Gregory A. Carnes** (University of North Alabama), **Annette Nellen** (San Jose State University), and **Kristina Zvinakis** (The University of Texas at Austin) for their work as chapter authors. Further thanks go to Annette Nellen who also served as editor for several chapters.

In addition, many thanks to the faculty members who have diligently worked through the problems and test questions to ensure the accuracy of the *South-Western Federal Taxation* homework, solutions manuals, test banks, comprehensive tax form problems, and practice sets. Their comments and corrections helped us focus on clarity as well as accuracy and tax law currency. They are **Sandra A. Augustine**, Hilbert College; **Chris E. Bjornson**, Indiana University Southeast; **Bradrick M. Cripe**, Northern Illinois University; **Eileen Eichler**, Farmingdale State College; **Elizabeth C. Ekmekjian**, William Paterson University; **Stephen C. Gara**, Drake University; **Mary Ann Hofmann**, Appalachian State University; **Debra M. Johnson**, Montana State University, Billings; **Timothy R. Koski**, Middle Tennessee State University; **Sandra J. Kranz**, Bemidji State University; **Stephanie Lewis**, The Ohio State University; **Joan M. Miller**, William Paterson University; **Randall Rinke**, Mercyhurst University – North East Campus; **Ray Rodriguez**, Southern Illinois University, Carbondale; **Lucia N. Smeal**, Georgia State University; **Eric Smith**, Weber State University; **Jason W. Stanfield**, Purdue University; **George R. Starbuck**, McMurry University; **Kent Swift**, University of Montana; **Ralph B. Tower**, Wake Forest University; **Donald R. Trippeer**, State University of New York College at Oneonta; **Raymond Wacker**, Southern Illinois University, Carbondale; **Sarah Webber**, University of Dayton; **Michael Weissenfluh**, Tillamook Bay Community College; **Marvin J. Williams**, University of Houston, Downtown; **Scott A. Yetmar**, Cleveland State University. We are grateful for their efforts.

We are also grateful for the assistance of **Bonnie Hoffman**, CPA who conducted a manuscript review. We also wish to thank Thomson Reuters for its permission to use Checkpoint with the text.

William H. Hoffman, Jr. / *James E. Smith*

The South-Western Federal Taxation Series

To find out more about these books, go to www.cengagebrain.com.

INDIVIDUAL INCOME TAXES, 2015 EDITION

(HOFFMAN, SMITH, Editors) provides accessible, comprehensive, and authoritative coverage of the relevant tax code and regulations as they pertain to the individual taxpayer, as well as coverage of all major developments in Federal taxation.

(ISBN 978-1-285-43884-9)

CORPORATIONS, PARTNERSHIPS, ESTATES & TRUSTS, 2015 EDITION

(HOFFMAN, RAABE, MALONEY, YOUNG, SMITH, Editors) covers tax concepts as they affect corporations, partnerships, estates, and trusts. The authors provide accessible, comprehensive, and authoritative coverage of relevant tax code and regulations, as well as all major developments in Federal income taxation. This market-leading text is intended for students who have had a previous course in tax. The text includes **Chapter 14, "Taxes on the Financial Statements."**

(ISBN 978-1-285-43829-0)

COMPREHENSIVE VOLUME, 2015 EDITION

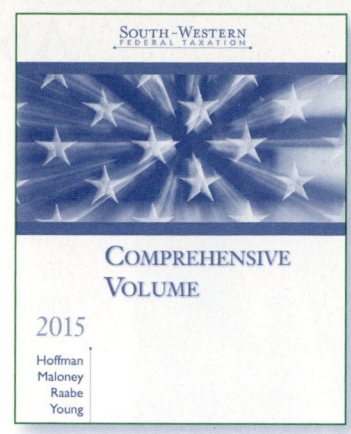

(HOFFMAN, MALONEY, RAABE, YOUNG, Editors). Combining the number one individual tax text with the number one corporations text, *Comprehensive Volume, 2015 Edition* is a true winner. An edited version of the first two **South-Western Federal Taxation** textbooks, this book is ideal for undergraduate or graduate levels. This text works for either a one-semester course in which an instructor wants to integrate coverage of individual and corporate taxation or for a two-semester sequence in which the use of only one book is desired.

(ISBN 978-1-285-43963-1)

ESSENTIALS OF TAXATION: INDIVIDUALS & BUSINESS ENTITIES, 2015 EDITION

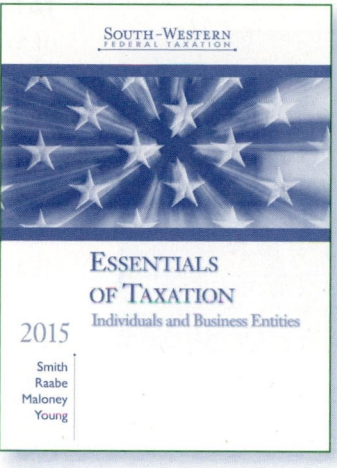

(SMITH, RAABE, MALONEY, YOUNG, Editors) emphasizes tax planning and the multidisciplinary aspects of taxation. Formerly titled *Taxation of Business Entities*, this text is designed with the AICPA Model Tax Curriculum in mind, presenting the introductory Federal taxation course from a business entity perspective. Its **Tax Planning Framework** helps users fit tax planning strategies into an innovative pedagogical framework. The text is an ideal fit for programs that offer only one course in taxation where users need to be exposed to individual taxation, as well as corporate and other business entity taxation. This text assumes no prior course in taxation has been taken.

(ISBN 978-1-285-43974-7)

INTERNAL REVENUE CODE OF 1986 AND TREASURY REGULATIONS: *Annotated and Selected, 2015 Edition*

(JAMES E. SMITH). An ideal alternative to the traditional, bulky, and expensive multivolume set of code and regulations, this single-volume reference provides a useful selection of code and regulations sections and clear annotations in the form of editorial summaries that explain, analyze, and cross-reference topics to help students fully understand the intricacies of the tax code. The text is a perfect supplement for any *South-Western Federal Taxation* text as well as an excellent primary text for a Federal taxation course that stresses a code and regulations approach.

2015 Edition coming in July 2014 (ISBN 978-1-285-44149-8)

FEDERAL TAX RESEARCH, 10E

(RAABE, WHITTENBURG, SANDERS, AND SAWYERS). *Federal Tax Research*, Tenth Edition, offers hands-on tax research analysis and fully covers computer-oriented tax research tools. The tenth edition offers a new chapter on Financial Accounting Research that, when combined with their study of tax research, will equip students with the valuable research skills they need to be marketable to future employers. Also included in this edition is coverage on international tax research, an expanded review of tax ethics, and many new real-life cases to help foster a true understanding of federal tax law.

(ISBN 978-1-285-43939-6)

About the Editors

WILLIAM H. HOFFMAN JR. earned B.A. and J.D. degrees from the University of Michigan and M.B.A. and Ph.D. degrees from The University of Texas. He is a licensed CPA and attorney in Texas. His teaching experience includes The University of Texas (1957–1961), Louisiana State University (1961–1967), and the University of Houston (1967–1999). Professor Hoffman has addressed many tax institutes and conferences and has published extensively in academic and professional journals. His articles appear in *The Journal of Taxation, The Tax Adviser, Taxes—The Tax Magazine, The Journal of Accountancy, The Accounting Review,* and *Taxation for Accountants.*

JAMES E. SMITH is the John S. Quinn Professor of Accounting at the College of William and Mary. He has been a member of the Accounting Faculty for over 30 years. He received his Ph.D. degree from the University of Arizona. Professor Smith has served as a discussion leader for Continuing Professional Education programs for the AICPA, Federal Tax Workshops, and various state CPA societies. He has conducted programs in more than 40 states for approximately 25,000 CPAs. He has been the recipient of the AICPA's Outstanding Discussion Leader Award and the American Taxation Association/Arthur Andersen Teaching Innovation Award. Among his other awards are the Virginia Society of CPAs' Outstanding Accounting Educator Award and the James Madison University's Outstanding Accounting Educator Award. He was the President of the Administrators of Accounting Programs Group (AAPG) in 1991–1992. He was the faculty adviser for the William and Mary teams that received first place in the Andersen Tax Challenge in 1994, 1995, 1997, 2000, and 2001 and in the Deloitte Tax Case Study Competition in 2002, 2004, 2005, 2006, 2008, and 2011.

Brief Contents

PART 4: SPECIAL TAX COMPUTATION METHODS, PAYMENT PROCEDURES, AND TAX CREDITS

PART 5: PROPERTY TRANSACTIONS

PART 6: ACCOUNTING PERIODS, ACCOUNTING METHODS, AND DEFERRED COMPENSATION

PART 7: CORPORATIONS AND PARTNERSHIPS

Contents

© iStockphoto.com/Pali Rao

Part 3: Deductions

Part 6: Accounting Periods, Accounting Methods, and Deferred Compensation

APPENDIXES

part 1

INTRODUCTION AND BASIC TAX MODEL

Part 1 provides an introduction to taxation in the United States. Although the primary orientation of this text is income taxation, other types of taxes are also discussed briefly. The purposes of the Federal tax law are examined, and the legislative, administrative, and judicial sources of Federal tax law, including their application to the tax research process, are analyzed. Part 1 concludes by introducing the basic tax model for the individual taxpayer and providing an overview of property transactions.

An Introduction to Taxation and Understanding the Federal Tax Law

LEARNING OBJECTIVES: *After completing Chapter 1, you should be able to:*

LO.1 Demonstrate why taxation is important.

LO.2 Describe some of the history and trends of the Federal income tax.

LO.3 Assess some of the criteria for selecting a tax structure; recognize the components of a tax structure.

LO.4 Identify the different taxes imposed in the United States at the Federal, state, and local levels.

LO.5 Explain the administration of the tax law, including the audit process utilized by the IRS.

LO.6 Evaluate some of the ethical guidelines involved in tax practice.

LO.7 Recognize the economic, social, equity, and political considerations that justify various aspects of the tax law.

LO.8 Describe the role played by the IRS and the courts in the evolution of the Federal tax system.

OUTLINE

FAMILY AND TAXES—A TYPICAL YEAR

Travis and Betty Carter are married and live in a state that imposes both a sales tax and an income tax. They have two children, April (age 17) and Martin (age 18). Travis is a mining engineer who specializes in land reclamation. After several years with a mining corporation, Travis established a consulting practice that involves a considerable amount of travel. Betty is a registered nurse who, until recently, was a homemaker. In November of this year, she decided to reenter the job market and accepted a position with a medical clinic. The Carters live only a few blocks from Ernest and Mary Walker, Betty Carter's parents. The Walkers are retired and live on interest, dividends, and Social Security benefits.

Various developments occurring during the year with possible tax ramifications are summarized below.

- The ad valorem property taxes on the Carters' residence are increased, while those on the Walkers' residence are lowered.
- When Travis registers an automobile purchased last year in another state, he is forced to pay a sales tax to his home state.
- As an anniversary present, the Carters gave the Walkers a recreational vehicle (RV).
- When Travis made a consulting trip to Chicago, the client withheld Illinois state income tax from the payment made to Travis for his services.
- Travis employs his children to draft blueprints and prepare scale models for use in his work. Both April and Martin have had training in drafting and topography.
- Early in the year, the Carters are audited by the state on an income tax return filed several years ago. Later in the year, they are audited by the IRS on a Form 1040 they filed for the same year. In each case, a tax deficiency and interest were assessed.
- The Walkers are audited by the IRS. Unlike the Carters, they did not have to deal with an agent, but settled the matter by mail.

Explain these developments and resolve the issues raised.

Read the chapter and formulate your response.

The primary objective of this chapter is to provide an overview of the Federal tax system. Among the topics discussed are the following:

- The importance and relevance of taxation.
- A brief history of the Federal income tax.
- The types of taxes imposed at the Federal, state, and local levels.
- Some highlights of tax law administration.
- Tax concepts that help explain the reasons for various tax provisions.
- The influence the Internal Revenue Service (IRS) and the courts have had in the evolution of current tax law.

1-1 LEARNING AND COPING WITH TAXATION

LO.1

Demonstrate why taxation is important.

The study of taxation is important because taxes permeate our society. Even the simplest of decisions can carry tax implications. Does it matter, for example, which son or daughter pays the medical bills when all of four adult children contribute to the support of their widowed mother? Or when you buy a new car, does it matter whether you finance the purchase through the dealership or with a home equity loan arranged by a bank?

Effectively coping with taxes often involves making decisions based on timing considerations. Does the employee who is trying to decide between a traditional Individual Retirement Account (IRA) and a Roth IRA want the tax benefit up front (i.e., traditional) or at retirement (i.e., Roth)? Timing considerations are paramount when it is deemed desirable to accelerate (or defer) income or accelerate (or defer) deductions for any one year.

Taxation is anything but stagnant. As circumstances change, so does the tax result. Consider, for example, what happens when an investor becomes a dealer— capital gains and losses on the disposition of property now convert to ordinary income and losses. Or consider an employee who becomes self-employed—the safe harbor of withholdings is lost, and new quarterly payments on income and self-employment taxes must be made. Even the purchase of a home can result in significant change—new mortgage interest and property tax deductions cause the standard deduction to be replaced by itemization on Schedule A.

One of the most common changes in circumstance that can affect the tax position of an individual is marital status. Getting married, although usually favorable, can sometimes have negative tax results. Even more diverse and pronounced, however, are the effects of a divorce. Are the payments from one ex-spouse to another ex-spouse deductible? From the standpoint of the recipient, are such payments taxable? Who can claim the children as dependents? Do these issues carry over to same-sex unions and divorces?

The study of taxation teaches us not to overlook the less obvious taxes that can block our intended objective. A grandson inherits his grandmother's personal residence. He has heard that rental property can generate significant income tax benefits. But does he realize that a change of ownership may unlock an appraised-value freeze on the property? Or that conversion from residential to income-producing use will cause an increase in ad valorem taxes on realty? Thus, an attractive income tax result could be materially diminished by adverse property tax consequences.

It is essential in working with taxation to maintain a balanced perspective. A corporation that is deciding where to locate a new factory does not automatically select the city or state that offers the most generous tax benefits. Nor does the person who is retiring to a warmer climate pick Belize over Arizona because the former has no income tax while the latter does. Tax considerations should not control decisions, but they remain one of many factors to be considered.

The study of taxation involves reviewing a multitude of rules and exceptions and, when possible, trying to understand the justification for them. But the desired goal of this learning process is the ability to recognize issues that carry tax implications. Suppose, for example, that you come upon a situation that involves a discharge of indebtedness. If you know that forgiveness of debt results in income but there are exceptions to this rule, the battle is won! The issue has been identified, and the outcome (i.e., when an exception applies) can easily be resolved by additional research.

1-2 A BRIEF HISTORY OF U.S. TAXATION

1-2a Early Periods

An income tax was first enacted in 1634 by the English colonists in the Massachusetts Bay Colony, but the Federal government did not adopt this form of taxation until 1861. In fact, both the Federal Union and the Confederate States of America used the income tax to raise funds to finance the Civil War.

When the Civil War ended, the need for additional revenue disappeared and the income tax was repealed. Once again the Federal government was able to finance its operations almost exclusively from customs duties (tariffs). It is interesting to note that the courts held that the Civil War income tax was not contrary to the Constitution.

When a new Federal income tax on individuals was enacted in 1894, its opponents were prepared and were able to successfully challenge its constitutionality. In *Pollock v. Farmers' Loan and Trust Co.*, the U.S. Supreme Court found that taxes on the income of real and personal property were the legal equivalent of a tax on the property involved and, therefore, required apportionment.[1]

A Federal corporate income tax, enacted by Congress in 1909, fared better in the judicial system. The U.S. Supreme Court found this tax to be constitutional because it was treated as an excise tax.[2] In essence, it was a tax on the right to do business in the corporate form. As such, it was likened to a form of the franchise tax.[3] Since the corporate form of doing business had been developed in the late nineteenth century, it was an unfamiliar concept to the framers of the U.S. Constitution. Because a corporation is an entity created under law, jurisdictions possess the right to tax its creation and operation. Using this rationale, many states still impose franchise taxes on corporations.

The ratification of the Sixteenth Amendment to the U.S. Constitution in 1913 sanctioned both the Federal individual and corporate income taxes and, as a consequence, neutralized the continuing effect of the *Pollock* decision.

LO.2

Describe some of the history and trends of the Federal income tax.

1-2b Revenue Acts

Following ratification of the Sixteenth Amendment, Congress enacted the Revenue Act of 1913. Under this Act, the first Form 1040 was due on March 1, 1914. The law allowed various deductions and personal exemptions of $3,000 for a single individual and $4,000 for married taxpayers. For those times, these were large exemptions that excluded all but the more wealthy taxpayers from the new income tax. Rates ranged from a low of 2 percent to a high of 6 percent. The 6 percent rate applied only to taxable income in excess of $500,000![4]

Various revenue acts were passed between 1913 and 1939. In 1939, all of these revenue laws were codified into the Internal Revenue Code of 1939. In 1954, a similar codification of the revenue law took place. The current law is entitled the Internal Revenue Code of 1986, which largely carries over the provisions of the 1954 Code. To date, the Code has been amended numerous times since 1986. This matter is discussed further in Chapter 2 under Origin of the Internal Revenue Code.

---

[1] 3 AFTR 2602, 15 S.Ct. 912 (USSC, 1895). See Chapter 2 for an explanation of the citations of judicial decisions.

[2] *Flint v. Stone Tracy Co.*, 3 AFTR 2834, 31 S.Ct. 342 (USSC, 1911).

[3] See the discussion of state franchise taxes later in the chapter.

[4] This should be contrasted with the highest 2014 tax rate of 39.6%, which applies once taxable income exceeds $406,750 for single taxpayers and $457,600 for married taxpayers.

FIGURE 1.1	Federal Budget Receipts—2014	
Individual income taxes		46%
Corporation income taxes		11
Social insurance taxes and contributions		34
Excise taxes		4
Other		5
		100%

1-2c Historical Trends

The income tax has proved to be a major source of revenue for the Federal government. Figure 1.1, which contains a breakdown of the primary sources,[5] demonstrates the importance of the income tax. *Estimated* income tax collections from individuals and corporations amount to 57 percent of the total receipts.

The need for revenues to finance the war effort during World War II converted the income tax into a *mass tax*. For example, in 1939, less than 6 percent of the U.S. population was subject to the Federal income tax. In 1945, more than 74 percent of the population was subject to the Federal income tax.[6]

Certain changes in the income tax law are of particular significance in understanding the Federal income tax. In 1943, Congress passed the Current Tax Payment Act, which provided for the first pay-as-you-go tax system. A pay-as-you-go income tax system requires employers to withhold for taxes a specified portion of an employee's wages. Persons with income from other than wages may have to make quarterly payments to the IRS for estimated taxes due for the year.

One trend that has caused considerable concern is the increasing complexity of the Federal income tax laws. In the name of tax reform, Congress has added to this complexity by frequently changing the tax laws. Most recent legislation continues this trend. Increasingly, this complexity forces many taxpayers to seek assistance. According to recent estimates, about 60 percent of all taxpayers who file a return pay a preparer, and slightly more than 32 percent purchase tax software. At this time, therefore, substantial support exists for tax law simplification.

1-3 CRITERIA USED IN THE SELECTION OF A TAX STRUCTURE

LO.3

Assess some of the criteria for selecting a tax structure; recognize the components of a tax structure.

In the eighteenth century, Adam Smith identified the following *canons of taxation*, which are still considered when evaluating a particular tax structure:[7]

- *Equality.* Each taxpayer enjoys fair or equitable treatment by paying taxes in proportion to his or her income level. Ability to pay a tax is one of the measures of how equitably a tax is distributed among taxpayers.
- *Convenience.* Administrative simplicity has long been valued in formulating tax policy. If a tax is easily assessed and collected and its administrative costs are low, it should be favored. An advantage of the existing withholding system (pay-as-you-go) is its convenience for taxpayers.
- *Certainty.* A tax structure is *good* if the taxpayer can readily predict when, where, and how a tax will be levied. Individuals and businesses need to know the likely tax consequences of a particular type of transaction.
- *Economy.* A *good* tax system involves only nominal collection costs by the government and minimal compliance costs on the part of the taxpayer.

---

[5] www.whitehouse.gov/omb.
[6] Richard Goode, *The Individual Income Tax* (Washington, D.C.: The Brookings Institution, 1964), pp. 2–4.

[7] *The Wealth of Nations* (New York: Dutton, 1910), Book V, Chapter II, Part II.

TAX IN THE NEWS   Adam Smith Stopped Too Soon

The American Institute of Certified Public Accountants (AICPA) has issued suggestions for Federal tax policy. Titled *Guiding Principles of Good Tax Policy: A Framework for Evaluating Tax Proposals*, the monograph sets forth 10 tax principles that are commonly used as indicators of desirable tax policy.

The first four principles are adapted from Adam Smith's *The Wealth of Nations*. The other six are summarized as follows:

- The tax system should be simple.
- The tax should be neutral in terms of its effect on business decisions.

- The tax system should not reduce economic growth and efficiency.
- The tax should be clear and readily understood so that taxpayers know about it and know when it applies.
- The tax should be structured so as to minimize non-compliance.
- The tax system should enable the IRS to predict the amount and timing of revenue production.

Source: Based on a Tax Policy Concept Statement issued by the Tax Division of the AICPA.

© iStockphoto.com/Andrey Prokhorov

By these canons, the Federal income tax is a contentious product. *Equality* is present as long as one accepts ability to pay as an ingredient of this component. *Convenience* exists due to a heavy reliance on pay-as-you-go procedures. *Certainty* probably generates the greatest controversy. In one sense, certainty is present because a mass of administrative and judicial guidelines exists to aid in interpreting the tax law. In another sense, however, certainty does not exist because many questions remain unanswered and frequent changes in the tax law by Congress lessen stability. Particularly troublesome in this regard are tax provisions that are given a limited life (e.g., only one year). If not extended by Congress, the provisions expire. All too often, Congress does not give the necessary approval in time, and the extension has to be applied retroactively. *Economy* is present if only the collection procedure of the IRS is considered. Although the government's cost of collecting Federal taxes amounts to less than one half of 1 percent of the revenue collected, the complexity of our current tax structure imposes substantial taxpayer compliance costs.

1-4 THE TAX STRUCTURE

1-4a Tax Base

A tax base is the amount to which the tax rate is applied. In the case of the Federal income tax, the tax base is *taxable income*. As noted later in the chapter (Figure 1.2), taxable income is gross income reduced by certain deductions (both business and personal).

1-4b Tax Rates

Tax rates are applied to the tax base to determine a taxpayer's liability. The tax rates may be proportional or progressive. A tax is *proportional* if the rate of tax remains constant for any given income level. Examples of proportional taxes include most excise taxes, general sales taxes, and employment taxes (FICA and FUTA).

> Bill has $10,000 of taxable income and pays a tax of $3,000, or 30%. Bob's taxable income is $50,000, and the tax on this amount is $15,000, or 30%. If this constant rate is applied throughout the rate structure, the tax is proportional.

Example 1

A tax is *progressive* if a higher rate of tax applies as the tax base increases. The Federal income tax, Federal gift and estate taxes, and most state income tax rate structures are progressive.

| **Example 2** | If Cora, a married individual filing jointly, has taxable income of $10,000, her tax for 2014 is $1,000 for an average tax rate of 10%. If, however, Cora's taxable income is $50,000, her tax will be $6,593 for an average tax rate of 13.2%. The tax is progressive because higher rates are applied to greater amounts of taxable income. |

1-4c Incidence of Taxation

The degree to which various segments of society share the total tax burden is difficult to assess. Assumptions must be made concerning who absorbs the burden of paying the tax. For example, because dividend payments to shareholders are not deductible by a corporation and are generally taxable to shareholders, the same income is subject to a form of double taxation. Concern over double taxation is valid to the extent that corporations are *not* able to shift the corporate tax to the consumer through higher commodity prices. Many research studies have shown a high degree of shifting of the corporate income tax, converting it into a consumption tax that is borne by the ultimate purchasers of goods.

The progressiveness of the Federal income tax rate structure for individuals has varied over the years. As late as 1986, for example, there were 15 rates, ranging from 0 to 50 percent. These later were reduced to two rates of 15 and 28 percent. Currently, there are seven rates ranging from 10 to 39.6 percent.

LO.4

Identify the different taxes imposed in the United States at the Federal, state, and local levels.

1-5 Major Types of Taxes

Why does a text devoted primarily to the Federal individual income tax discuss state and local taxes? A simple illustration shows the importance of non-Federal taxes.

| **Example 3** | Rick is employed by Flamingo Corporation in San Antonio, Texas, at a salary of $74,000. Rick's employer offers him a chance to transfer to its New York City office at a salary of $94,000. A quick computation indicates that the additional taxes (Federal, state, and local) involve approximately $12,000. |

Although Rick must consider many nontax factors before he decides on a job change, he should also evaluate the tax climate. How do state and local taxes compare? For example, neither Texas nor San Antonio imposes an income tax, but New York State and New York City do. Consequently, what appears to be a $20,000 pay increase is only $8,000 when the additional taxes of $12,000 are taken into account.

1-5a Property Taxes

Correctly referred to as **ad valorem taxes** because they are based on value, property taxes are a tax on wealth, or capital. In this regard, they have much in common with estate taxes and gift taxes discussed later in the chapter. Although property taxes do not tax income, the income actually derived (or the potential for any income) may be relevant insofar as it affects the value of the property being taxed.

Property taxes fall into *two* categories: those imposed on realty and those imposed on personalty, or assets other than land and buildings. Both have added importance because they usually generate a deduction for Federal income tax purposes (see Chapter 10).

Ad Valorem Taxes on Realty

Property taxes on realty are used exclusively by states and their local political subdivisions, such as cities, counties, and school districts. They represent a major source of revenue for *local* governments, but their importance at the *state* level has waned over the past few years. Some states, for example, have imposed freezes on upward revaluations of residential housing.

How realty is defined can have an important bearing on which assets are subject to tax. This is especially true in jurisdictions that do not impose ad valorem taxes on personalty. Primarily a question of state property law, **realty** generally includes real estate and any capital improvements that are classified as fixtures. Simply stated, a *fixture* is something so permanently attached to the real estate that its removal will cause irreparable damage. A built-in bookcase might well be a fixture, whereas a movable bookcase would not be a fixture. Certain items such as electrical wiring and plumbing cease to be personalty when installed in a building and become realty.

The following are some of the characteristics of ad valorem taxes on realty:

- Property owned by the Federal government is exempt from tax. Similar immunity usually is extended to property owned by state and local governments and by certain charitable organizations.
- Some states provide for lower valuations on property dedicated to agricultural use or other special uses (e.g., wildlife sanctuaries). Reductions in appraised valuations may also be available when the property is subject to a conservation easement (e.g., a limitation on further development).
- Some states partially exempt the homestead, or personal residence, portion of property from taxation.
- Lower taxes may apply to a residence owned by a taxpayer aged 65 or older.
- When non-income-producing property (e.g., a personal residence) is converted to income-producing property (e.g., a rental house), typically the appraised value increases.
- Some jurisdictions extend immunity from tax for a specified period of time (a *tax holiday*) to new or relocated businesses. A tax holiday can backfire, however, and cause more harm than good. If it is too generous, it can damage the local infrastructure (e.g., less funding for public works and education).

THE BIG PICTURE

Example 4

Return to the facts of *The Big Picture* on p. 1-1. Why did the Walkers' property taxes decrease while those of the Carters increased? A likely explanation is that one (or both) of the Walkers achieved senior citizen status. In the case of the Carters, the assessed value of their property was probably increased (see the following discussion). Perhaps they made significant home improvements (e.g., kitchen/bathroom renovation or addition of a sundeck).

Unlike the ad valorem tax on personalty (see the next section), the tax on realty is difficult to avoid. Because real estate is impossible to hide, a high degree of taxpayer compliance is not surprising. The only avoidance possibility that is generally available is associated with the assessed value of the property. For this reason, the assessed value of the property—particularly, a value that is reassessed upward—may be subject to controversy and litigation.

The history of the ad valorem tax on realty has been marked by inconsistent application due to a lack of competent tax administration and definitive guidelines for assessment procedures. In recent years, however, some significant improvements have occurred. Some jurisdictions, for example, have computerized their reassessment procedures so that they immediately affect all property located within the jurisdiction.

Several jurisdictions provide homeowners with a measure of protection from increased property taxes by "freezing" existing assessments and limiting future upward adjustments. Such restrictions on reassessments, however, do not carry over to the new owner when the property is sold. Thus, such measures tend to lock in ownership and restrict the mobility of those who might otherwise change residences.

Ad Valorem Taxes on Personalty

Personalty can be defined as all assets that are not realty. It may be helpful to distinguish between the *classification* of an asset (realty or personalty) and the *use* to which it is put. Both realty and personalty can be either business use or personal use property. Examples include a residence (realty that is personal use), an office building (realty that is business use), surgical instruments (personalty that is business use), and regular wearing apparel (personalty that is personal use).[8]

Personalty can also be classified as tangible property or intangible property. For ad valorem tax purposes, intangible personalty includes stocks, bonds, and various other securities (e.g., bank shares).

The following generalizations may be made concerning the ad valorem taxes on personalty:

- Particularly with personalty devoted to personal use (e.g., jewelry and household furnishings), taxpayer compliance ranges from poor to zero. Some jurisdictions do not even attempt to enforce the tax on these items. For automobiles devoted to personal use, many jurisdictions have converted from value as the tax base to arbitrary license fees based on the weight of the vehicle. Some jurisdictions also consider the vehicle's age (e.g., automobiles six years or older are not subject to the ad valorem tax because they are presumed to have little, if any, value).
- For personalty devoted to business use (e.g., inventories, trucks, machinery, equipment), taxpayer compliance and enforcement procedures are measurably better.
- Which jurisdiction possesses the authority to tax movable personalty (e.g., railroad rolling stock) always has been and continues to be a troublesome issue.
- A few states levy an ad valorem tax on intangibles such as stocks and bonds. Taxpayer compliance may be negligible if the state lacks a means of verifying security transactions and ownership.

1-5b Transaction Taxes

Transaction taxes, which characteristically are imposed at the manufacturer's, wholesaler's, or retailer's level, cover a wide range of transfers. Like many other types of taxes (e.g., income taxes, estate taxes, and gift taxes), transaction taxes usually are not within the exclusive province of any one level of taxing authority (Federal, state, or local government). As the description implies, these levies place a tax on transfers of property and normally are determined by multiplying the value involved by a percentage rate.

Federal Excise Taxes

Long one of the mainstays of the Federal tax system, Federal **excise taxes** had declined in relative importance until recently. In recent years, Congress substantially increased the Federal excise taxes on items such as tobacco products, fuel and gasoline sales, and air travel. Other Federal excise taxes include the following:

- Manufacturers' excise taxes on trucks, trailers, tires, firearms, sporting equipment, and coal and the gas guzzler tax on automobiles.[9]
- Alcohol taxes.
- Miscellaneous taxes (e.g., the tax on wagering).

---

[8]The distinction, important for ad valorem and for Federal income tax purposes, often becomes confused when personalty is referred to as "personal" property to distinguish it from "real" property. This designation does not give a complete picture of what is involved. The description "personal" residence, however, is clearer, because a residence can be identified as being realty. What is meant in this case is realty that is personal use property.

[9]The gas guzzler tax is imposed on the manufacturers of automobiles (both domestic and foreign) and increases in amount as the mileage ratings per gallon of gas decrease. For example, a 2013 Bentley Continental GTC manages 19 miles per gallon in combined city/highway driving and starts at $179,769. The gas guzzler tax is $2,100.

TAX IN THE NEWS   More Excise Taxes from the Federal Government—Good or Bad?

The increase in the Federal excise tax on tobacco (from $0.39 to $1.01 per package of cigarettes) has met with a mixed reaction. On the positive side, the increase funds a good cause—SCHIP (State Children's Health Insurance Program). Likewise, no one can take issue with a sin tax that purports to reduce smoking.

As for the negative aspects, most heavy smokers are lower-income taxpayers. Thus, this tax increase largely falls on the poor. Furthermore, various states have increased their tobacco taxes as well. Faced with a substantially higher cost for cigarettes, smokers who cannot

"kick the habit" may see the cheaper price provided by an illegal market (i.e., smuggling) as an attractive alternative. Tax increases that foster criminal activity are not a good way to raise revenue.

More importantly, does this foray into tobacco taxes portend a new trend on the part of Congress to find new sources of revenue? Note that the cigarette tax increase was followed by a new excise tax on tanning salons. Will other new excise taxes be imposed (e.g., a tax on soft drinks) or existing excise taxes increased (e.g., more taxes on alcoholic beverages)?

The list of transactions covered, although seemingly impressive, has diminished over the years. At one time, for example, there was a Federal excise tax on admission to amusement facilities (e.g., theaters) and on the sale of items such as leather goods, jewelry, furs, and cosmetics.

When reviewing the list of both Federal and state excise taxes, one should recognize the possibility that the tax laws may be trying to influence social behavior. For example, the gas guzzler tax is intended as an incentive for the automobile companies to build fuel-efficient cars.

State and Local Excise Taxes

Many state and local excise taxes parallel the Federal version. Thus, all states tax the sale of gasoline, liquor, and tobacco products; however, unlike the Federal version, the rates vary significantly. For gasoline products, for example, compare the 39.5 cents per gallon imposed by the state of California with the 4.0 cents per gallon levied by the state of Florida. For tobacco sales, contrast the 17 cents per pack of 20 cigarettes in effect in Missouri with the $4.35 per pack applicable in the state of New York. Given the latter situation, is it surprising that the smuggling of cigarettes for resale elsewhere is so widespread?

Other excise taxes found at some state and local levels include those on admission to amusement facilities, on the sale of playing cards, and on prepared foods. Most states impose a transaction tax on the transfer of property that requires the recording of documents (e.g., real estate sales).[10] Some extend the tax to the transfer of stocks and other securities.

Over the last few years, two types of excise taxes imposed at the local level have become increasingly popular: the hotel occupancy tax and the rental car "surcharge." Because they tax the visitor who cannot vote, they are a political windfall and are often used to finance special projects that generate civic pride (e.g., convention centers and state-of-the-art sports arenas). These levies can be significant, as demonstrated by Houston's hotel tax of 17 percent and the car rental tax and fees of 37 percent in Minneapolis.

---

[10]This type of tax has much in common with the stamp tax levied by Great Britain on the American colonies during the pre-Revolutionary War period in U.S. history.

TAX IN THE NEWS   A 'Sin Tax' That Needs Fixing!

Ideally, a good sin tax discourages certain types of behavior and generates revenue. But any such tax should be properly structured to be fully effective. In this regard, the taxes on tobacco products leave much to be desired. Consider, for example, the tax on conventional cigarettes, which in some states has reached the level of $4, $5, or more per pack. From 2000 to 2011, the result was a 33 percent decline in consumption. But for those who craved nicotine, the usage of other *less heavily taxed* forms of tobacco increased by 123 percent. First, it was the smokeless variety; then it was roll-your-own cigarettes;

and lately it has been "little cigars." For about $1.40 a pack, a user can purchase a package of little cigars that look similar to conventional cigarettes (except for a brown wrapper). For the younger consumer, some of these products come in flavors such as grape, vanilla, and chocolate.

If the use of tobacco is to be discouraged, all loopholes must be closed. This can only be done effectively by equalizing the taxes on all forms of tobacco products.

Source: Based on Liz Szabo, "CDC: Littler Cigars are Cheaper, Not Safer," *USA TODAY*, August 3–5, 2012, p. 3A.

General Sales Taxes

The distinction between an excise tax and a general **sales tax** is easy to make. One is restricted to a particular transaction (e.g., the 18.4 cents per gallon Federal excise tax on the sale of gasoline), while the other covers a multitude of transactions (e.g., a 5 percent tax on *all* retail sales). In actual practice, however, the distinction is not always that clear. Some state statutes exempt certain transactions from the application of the general sales taxes (e.g., sales of food to be consumed off the premises and sales of certain medicines and drugs). Also, it is not uncommon to find that rates vary depending on the commodity involved. Many states, for example, allow preferential rates for the sale of agricultural equipment or apply different rates (either higher or lower than the general rate) to the sale of automobiles. With many of these special exceptions and classifications of rates, a general sales tax can take on the appearance of a collection of individual excise taxes.

A **use tax** is an ad valorem tax, usually at the same rate as the sales tax, on the use, consumption, or storage of tangible property purchased outside the state but used in the state. The purpose of a use tax is to prevent the avoidance of a sales tax. Every state that imposes a general sales tax levied on the consumer also has a use tax. Alaska, Delaware, Montana, New Hampshire, and Oregon have neither tax. There is no Federal general sales or use tax.

THE BIG PICTURE

Example 5

Return to the facts of *The Big Picture* on p. 1-1. The payment Travis made when he registered the car is probably a use tax. When the car was purchased in another state, likely no (or a lesser) sales tax was levied. The current payment makes up for the amount of sales tax he would have paid had the car been purchased in his home state.

The use tax is difficult to enforce for many purchases; therefore, the purchaser often does not pay it. In some cases, for example, it may be worthwhile to make purchases through an out-of-state mail-order business or the websites of certain vendors. In spite of shipping costs, the avoidance of the local sales tax that otherwise might be incurred can lower the cost of such products as computer components. Some states are taking steps to curtail this loss of revenue. For items such as automobiles (refer to Example 5), the use tax probably will be collected when the purchaser registers the item in his or her home state.

ETHICS & EQUITY   *Making Good Use of Out-of-State Relatives*

Marcus, a resident of Texas, has found the ideal gift for his wife in celebration of their upcoming wedding anniversary—a $22,000 diamond tennis bracelet. However, Marcus is appalled at the prospect of paying the state and local sales tax of $1,815 (combined rate of 8.25 percent). He, therefore, asks his aunt, a resident of Montana, to purchase the bracelet. The jewelry store lists the aunt as the buyer and ships the bracelet to her. Prior to the anniversary, Marcus receives the bracelet from his aunt. Is Marcus able to save $1,815 on the present for his wife? What can go wrong?

© iStockphoto.com/LdF

Local general sales taxes, over and above those levied by the state, are common. It is not unusual to find taxpayers living in the same state but paying different general sales taxes due to the location of their residence.

Pete and Sam both live in a state that has a general sales tax of 3%. Sam, however, resides in a city that imposes an additional general sales tax of 2%. Even though Pete and Sam live in the same state, one is subject to a rate of 3%, while the other pays a tax of 5%.	**Example 6**

For various reasons, some jurisdictions will suspend the application of a general sales tax. Frequently, the "sales tax holiday" occurs in late summer when it applies to back-to-school clothing and supplies. Some states use sales tax holidays to encourage the purchase of energy-conserving appliances and hurricane preparedness items.

Severance Taxes

Severance taxes are transaction taxes that are based on the notion that the state has an interest in its natural resources (e.g., oil, gas, iron ore, or coal). Therefore, a tax is imposed when the natural resources are extracted.

For some states, severance taxes can be a significant source of revenue. Due to the severance tax on oil production, Alaska has been able to avoid both a state income tax and a state general sales tax.

1-5c Taxes on Transfers at Death

The right to transfer property or to receive property upon the death of the owner may be subject to estate and/or inheritance taxes. Consequently, such taxes fall into the category of excise taxes. If the tax is imposed on the right to pass property at death, it is classified as an **estate tax**. If it taxes the right to receive property from a decedent, it is termed an **inheritance tax**. As is typical of other types of excise taxes, the value of the property transferred provides the base for determining the amount of the tax.

The Federal government imposes only an estate tax. Many state governments, however, levy inheritance taxes, estate taxes, or both. Some states (e.g., Florida and Texas) levy neither tax. An estate tax is levied on the estate of the decedent, whereas an inheritance tax is paid from the property received by the heir.

At the time of her death, Wilma lived in a state that imposes an inheritance tax but not an estate tax. Mary, one of Wilma's heirs, lives in the same state. Wilma's estate is subject to the Federal estate tax, and Mary is subject to the state inheritance tax.	**Example 7**

The Federal Estate Tax

The Revenue Act of 1916 incorporated the estate tax into the tax law. The tax was originally intended to prevent large concentrations of wealth from being kept in a family for many generations. Whether this objective has been accomplished is debatable. Like the income tax, estate taxes can be reduced through various planning procedures.

The gross estate includes property the decedent owned at the time of death. It also includes property interests, such as life insurance proceeds paid to the estate or to a beneficiary other than the estate if the deceased-insured had any ownership rights in the policy. Quite simply, the gross estate represents property interests subject to Federal estate taxation.[11] All property included in the gross estate is valued as of the date of death or, if the alternate valuation date is elected, six months later.[12]

Deductions from the gross estate in arriving at the taxable estate include funeral and administration expenses; certain taxes; debts of the decedent; casualty losses[13] incurred during the administration of the estate; transfers to charitable organizations; and, in some cases, the marital deduction. The *marital deduction* is available for amounts actually passing to a surviving spouse (a widow or widower).

Once the taxable estate has been determined and certain taxable gifts made by the decedent during life have been added to it, the estate tax can be computed. From the amount derived from the appropriate tax rate schedules, various credits should be subtracted to arrive at the tax, if any, that is due.[14] Although many other credits are also available, probably the most significant is the *unified transfer tax credit*. The main reason for this credit is to eliminate or reduce the estate tax liability for certain estates. For 2014, the amount of the credit is $2,081,800. Based on the estate tax rates, the credit exempts a tax base of up to $5.34 million.

Example 8	Ned made no taxable gifts before his death in 2014. If Ned's taxable estate amounts to $5.34 million or less, no Federal estate tax is due because of the application of the unified transfer tax credit. Under the tax law, the estate tax on a taxable estate of $5.34 million is $2,081,800.

State Taxes on Transfers at Death

As noted earlier, some states levy an inheritance tax, an estate tax, or both. The two forms of taxes on transfers at death differ according to whether the tax is imposed on the heirs or on the estate.

Characteristically, an inheritance tax divides the heirs into classes based on their relationship to the decedent. The more closely related the heir, the lower the rates imposed and the greater the exemption allowed. Some states completely exempt from taxation amounts passing to a surviving spouse.

1-5d Gift Taxes

Like taxes on transfers at death, a **gift tax** is an excise tax levied on the right to transfer property. In this case, however, the tax is imposed on transfers made during the owner's life and not at death. A gift tax applies only to transfers that are not offset by full and adequate consideration.

Example 9	Carl sells property worth $50,000 to his daughter for $1,000. Although property worth $50,000 has been transferred, only $49,000 represents a gift, because this is the portion not supported by full and adequate consideration.

The Federal Gift Tax

First enacted in 1932, the Federal gift tax was intended to complement the estate tax. If lifetime transfers by gift were not taxed, it would be possible to avoid the estate tax and escape taxation entirely.

---

[11]For further information on these matters, see *South-Western Federal Taxation: Corporations, Partnerships, Estates, & Trusts.*

[12]See the discussion of the alternate valuation date in Chapter 14.

[13]For a definition of *casualty losses*, see the Glossary in Appendix C.

[14]For tax purposes, it is crucial to appreciate the difference between a deduction and a credit. A *credit* is a dollar-for-dollar reduction of tax liability. A *deduction*, however, benefits the taxpayer only to the extent of his or her tax bracket. An estate in a 50% tax bracket, for example, would need $2 of deductions to prevent $1 of tax liability. In contrast, $1 of credit neutralizes $1 of tax liability.

Only taxable gifts are subject to the gift tax. For this purpose, a taxable gift is measured by the fair market value of the property on the date of transfer less the *annual exclusion per donee* and, in some cases, less the *marital deduction*, which allows tax-free transfers between spouses. In 2013 and 2014, each donor is allowed an annual exclusion of $14,000 for each donee.[15]

On December 31, 2013, Louise (a widow) gives $14,000 to each of her four married children, their spouses, and her eight grandchildren. On January 2, 2014, she repeats the procedure, again giving $14,000 to each recipient. Due to the annual exclusion, Louise has not made a taxable gift, although she transferred $224,000 [$14,000 (annual exclusion) × 16 (donees)] in 2013 and $224,000 [$14,000 (annual exclusion) × 16 (donees)] in 2014, for a total of $448,000 ($224,000 + $224,000).	**Example 10**

A married couple may make a special election that allows one-half of the gift made by the donor-spouse to a third party to be treated as being made by the non-donor-spouse. This *gift splitting* effectively allows the annual exclusion to double. Also, it allows the use of the nondonor-spouse's unified transfer tax credit and may lower the tax rates that will apply.

THE BIG PICTURE

Return to the facts of *The Big Picture* on p. 1-1. Although the value of the RV is not stated, it is highly likely to exceed the annual exclusion allowed of $56,000 [$14,000 (annual exclusion) × two donees (the Walkers) × two donors (the Carters)]. Thus, a taxable gift results, and a Form 709 (Gift Tax Return) must be filed. Whether any gift tax is due depends on what past taxable gifts the Carters have made and how much of their unified transfer tax credit (see the following discussion) is still available.	**Example 11**

The gift tax rate schedule is the same as that applicable to the estate tax. The schedule is commonly referred to as the *unified transfer tax rate schedule.*

The Federal gift tax is *cumulative* in effect. What this means is that the tax base for current taxable gifts includes past taxable gifts. Although a credit is allowed for prior gift taxes, the result of adding past taxable gifts to current taxable gifts could be to force the donor into a higher tax bracket.[16] Like the Federal estate tax rates, the Federal gift tax rates are progressive (see Example 2 earlier in this chapter).

The unified transfer tax credit is available for all taxable gifts. As was the case with the Federal estate tax, the credit for 2013 is $2,045,800 (which covers taxable gifts up to $5,250,000) and for 2014 is $2,081,800 (which covers taxable gifts up to $5,340,000). There is, however, only one unified transfer tax credit, and it applies to both taxable gifts and the Federal estate tax. In a manner of speaking, therefore, once the unified transfer tax credit has been exhausted for Federal gift tax purposes, it is no longer available to insulate a decedent's transfers from the Federal estate tax, except to the extent of the excess of the credit amount for estate tax purposes over that for gift tax purposes.

Making lifetime gifts of property carries several tax advantages over passing the property at death. If income-producing property is involved (e.g., marketable securities and rental real estate), a gift may reduce income taxes for the family unit by shifting subsequent income to lower-bracket donees. If the gift involves property that is expected to appreciate in value (e.g., life insurance policies, real estate, and artwork), future increases in value will be assigned to the donee and will not be included in the donor's estate. Also important is that due to the annual exclusion

---

[15]The purpose of the annual exclusion is to avoid the need to report and pay a tax on *modest* gifts. Without the exclusion, the IRS could face a real problem of taxpayer noncompliance. The annual exclusion is indexed as the level of inflation warrants. The exclusion was $13,000 from 2009 through 2012.

[16]For further information on the Federal gift tax, see *South-Western Federal Taxation: Corporations, Partnerships, Estates & Trusts*, 2015 Edition, Chapter 18.

($14,000 per donee in 2014), some of the gift is not subject to any gift tax. Recall that the gift-splitting election enables married donors to double up on the annual exclusion.

Neither the receipt of a gift nor an inheritance will cause income tax consequences to the donee or heir.

1-5e Income Taxes

Income taxes are levied by the Federal government, most states, and some local governments. The trend in recent years has been to place greater reliance on this method of taxation. This trend is not consistent with what is happening in other countries, and in this sense, our system of taxation is somewhat different.

Income taxes generally are imposed on individuals, corporations, and certain fiduciaries (estates and trusts). Most jurisdictions attempt to ensure the collection of income taxes by requiring pay-as-you-go procedures, including withholding requirements for employees and estimated tax prepayments for all taxpayers.

Federal Income Taxes

The Federal income tax imposed on individuals follows the formula set forth in Figure 1.2. The formula for the individual income tax establishes the framework followed in the text. Beginning with Chapter 3, each component of the formula is illustrated and explained. In large part, the text coverage of individual taxpayers follows the same order as the components in the formula.

Like its individual counterpart, the Federal corporate income tax is progressive in nature. But its application does not require the computation of adjusted gross income (AGI) and does not provide for the standard deduction and personal and dependency exemptions. All allowable deductions of a corporation fall into the business-expense category. In effect, therefore, the taxable income of a corporation is the difference between gross income and deductions. While Chapters 3 through 19 cover the Federal income tax applicable to individuals, Chapter 20 summarizes the rules relating to corporations and partnerships.[17]

FIGURE 1.2	Formula for Federal Income Tax on Individuals
Income (broadly conceived)	$xx,xxx
Less: Exclusions (income that is not subject to tax)	(x,xxx)
Gross income (income that is subject to tax)	$xx,xxx
Less: Certain deductions (usually referred to as deductions *for* adjusted gross income)	(x,xxx)
Adjusted gross income	$xx,xxx
Less: The greater of certain personal and employee deductions (usually referred to as *itemized deductions*)	
or	
The standard deduction (including any additional standard deduction)	(x,xxx)
and	
Less: Personal and dependency exemptions	(x,xxx)
Taxable income	$xx,xxx
Tax on taxable income (see the Tax Tables and Tax Rate Schedules in Appendix A)	$ x,xxx
Less: Tax credits (including Federal income tax withheld and other prepayments of Federal income taxes)	(xxx)
Tax due (or refund)	$ xxx

---

[17]For an in-depth treatment of the Federal income tax as it affects corporations, partnerships, estates, and trusts, see *South-Western Federal Taxation:* *Corporations, Partnerships, Estates & Trusts,* 2015 Edition, Chapters 2 through 9, 12, and 20.

State Income Taxes

All but the following states impose an income tax on individuals: Alaska, Florida, Nevada, South Dakota, Texas, Washington, and Wyoming. New Hampshire and Tennessee impose an individual income tax only on interest and dividends.

Some of the characteristics of state income taxes are summarized as follows:

- With few exceptions, all states require some form of withholding procedures.
- Most states use as the tax base the income determination made for Federal income tax purposes.
- A minority of states go even further and impose a flat rate on AGI as computed for Federal income tax purposes. Several apply a rate to the Federal income tax liability. This is often referred to as the piggyback approach to state income taxation. Although the term *piggyback* does not lend itself to a precise definition, in this context, it means making use, for state income tax purposes, of what was done for Federal income tax purposes.
- Some states are somewhat eroding the piggyback approach by "decoupling" from selected recent tax reductions passed by Congress. The purpose of the decoupling is to retain state revenue that would otherwise be lost. In other words, the state cannot afford to allow its taxpayers the same deductions for state purposes that are allowed for Federal purposes.
- Because of the tie-ins to the Federal return, a state may be notified of any changes made by the IRS upon audit of a Federal return. In recent years, the exchange of information between the IRS and state taxing authorities has increased. Lately, some states (e.g., California) are playing a major role in revealing tax shelter abuses to the IRS.
- Most states allow a deduction for personal and dependency exemptions. Some states substitute a tax credit for a deduction.
- A diminishing minority of states allow a deduction for Federal income taxes.
- Virtually all state income tax returns provide checkoff boxes for donations to various causes. Many are dedicated to medical research and wildlife programs, but special projects are not uncommon. For example, Oklahoma had one to retire the debt incurred for its new capitol dome, while Wisconsin uses one for maintenance and operating costs of Lambeau Field (home of the Green Bay Packers). These checkoff boxes have been criticized as adding complexity to the returns and misleading taxpayers.[18]
- Most states allow their residents some form of tax credit for income taxes paid to other states.

THE BIG PICTURE

Example 12

Return to the facts of *The Big Picture* on p. 1-1. Because the income earned by Travis on his Chicago trip will be subject to tax by his home state, he probably will be able to claim an offsetting tax credit. Whether this negates the double taxation of the same income depends on the amount of credit allowed.

- The objective of most states is to tax the income of residents and those who regularly conduct business in the state (e.g., nonresidents who commute to work). These states also purport to tax the income of nonresidents who earn income in the state on an itinerant basis. Usually, however, the only visitors actually taxed are highly paid athletes and entertainers. This so-called *jock tax* has been much criticized as being discriminatory due to its selective imposition.
- The due date for filing generally is the same as for the Federal income tax (the fifteenth day of the fourth month following the close of the tax year).

---

[18]Many taxpayers do not realize that they are paying for the checkoff donation (usually with some of their income tax refund). Unlike the presidential election campaign fund available for Federal income tax purposes ($3 in this case), the contribution is *not made* by the government.

FINANCIAL DISCLOSURE INSIGHTS   What Do You Mean by "Income" Anyway?

Most business taxpayers keep at least "two sets of books," in that they report one amount of "income" for financial accounting purposes and another amount of "taxable income" as required by various taxing jurisdictions—the definition that will be used throughout this book. In fact, "income" might be defined in many different ways, as required by the recipients of the income reports of the enterprise. For instance, a business entity might prepare markedly different income reports for lenders, employee unions, managers in operating divisions, and international agencies.

Financial accounting income guidance is provided for U.S. businesses by the **Financial Accounting Standards Board (FASB)**, using the accumulated **Generally Accepted Accounting Principles (GAAP)** for the reporting period. When an entity conducts business outside the United States, the **International Financial Reporting Standards (IFRS)** of the **International Accounting Standards Board (IASB)** also may apply.

Throughout this book, we will point out some of the effects that Federal income tax provisions can have on the taxpayer's financial accounting results for the tax year. The vast majority of an entity's business transactions receive identical treatment under GAAP, IFRS, and the Federal tax law. But when the applicable provisions differ, "income" can be reported as different amounts—accounting professionals often refer to these as "book-tax differences." A tax professional must be able to identify and explain the various constructs of "income" so that the business entity's operating results will be accurately reflected in its stock price, loan covenants, and cash-flow demands.

© iStockphoto.com/Pali Rao

- Some states have occasionally instituted amnesty programs that allow taxpayers to pay back taxes (and interest) on unreported income with no (or reduced) penalty. In many cases, the tax amnesty has generated enough revenue to warrant the authorization of follow-up programs covering future years.[19] Amnesties usually include other taxes as well (e.g., sales, franchise, and severance). One major advantage of amnesty programs is that they uncover taxpayers who were previously unknown to the taxing authority.
- Because many consumers do not pay state and local sales taxes on out-of-state purchases, state income tax returns often contain a separate line for the reporting of the use tax that is due. The instructions to the form may provide tables of suggested amounts based on income levels for those who lack records on the purchases not previously taxed. Thus, the income tax return serves as a means of collecting use taxes.

Nearly all states have an income tax applicable to corporations. It is difficult to determine those that do not because a state franchise tax (discussed later in the chapter) sometimes is based in part on the income earned by the corporation.

Local Income Taxes

Cities imposing an income tax include, but are not limited to, Baltimore, Cincinnati, Cleveland, Detroit, Kansas City (Missouri), New York, Philadelphia, and St. Louis. The application of a city income tax is not limited to local residents.

1-5f Employment Taxes

Classification as an employee usually leads to the imposition of **employment taxes** and to the requirement that the employer withhold specified amounts for income taxes. The rules governing the withholding for income taxes are discussed in Chapter 13. The material that follows concentrates on the two major employment taxes: FICA (Federal Insurance Contributions Act—commonly referred to as the Social Security tax) and FUTA (Federal Unemployment Tax Act). Both taxes can be justified by social and public welfare considerations: FICA offers some measure of

---

[19]Although the suggestion has been made, no comparable amnesty program has been offered for the Federal income tax. The IRS has, however, offered exemption from certain penalties for taxpayers who disclose offshore bank accounts and participation in certain tax shelters.

TAX IN THE NEWS   Something to Consider

Aaron is a successful football player—a two-time Pro-Bowler—who is currently a free agent. He is considering major offers, all in the realm of $4 million, from the following teams: Green Bay Packers (WI), Pittsburgh Steelers (PA), and Dallas Cowboys (TX). State and local income tax rates applicable in these jurisdictions are 7.75% (WI), 3.07% (PA), and 0% (TX).

Regardless of Aaron's choice, some of his salary will be subject to the jock tax (when an away game is played in a state that imposes an income tax). What about the considerable income that might result from endorsements? This will be assigned to Aaron's place of residence, which may well be the state where the chosen team is located.

Aaron's ultimate selection should not be controlled by tax implications. Nevertheless, regarding only the salary, the difference between an expense of $310,000 (WI), $122,800 (PA), and $0 (TX) has to be considered in any decision that Aaron makes.

retirement security, and FUTA provides a modest source of income in the event of loss of employment.

Employment taxes come into play only if two conditions are satisfied. First, is the individual involved an *employee* (as opposed to *self-employed*)? The differences between an employee and a self-employed person are discussed in Chapter 9. Second, if the individual involved is an employee, is he or she covered under FICA or FUTA or both? The coverage of both of these taxes is summarized in Exhibit 13.3 in Chapter 13.[20]

FICA Taxes

The **FICA tax** rates and wage base have increased steadily over the years. It is difficult to imagine that the initial rate in 1937 was only 1 percent of the first $3,000 of covered wages. Thus, the maximum tax due was only $30.

The FICA tax has two components: Social Security tax (old age, survivors, and disability insurance) *and* Medicare tax (hospital insurance). The Social Security tax rate is 6.2 percent for 2014 and generally does not change each year.[21] The base amount does vary and is $117,000 for 2014 ($113,700 for 2013).

The Medicare portion of FICA is applied at a rate of 1.45 percent and, unlike Social Security, is not subject to any dollar limitation. Beginning in 2013, an additional .9 percent is imposed on earned income (including self-employment income) *above* $200,000 (single filers) or $250,000 (married filing jointly).[22] Unlike the Social Security tax of 6.2 percent and the regular Medicare portion of 1.45 percent, an employer does not have to match the employees' .9 percent.

A spouse employed by another spouse is subject to FICA. However, children under the age of 18 who are employed in a parent's unincorporated trade or business are exempted.

THE BIG PICTURE

Example 13

Return to the facts of *The Big Picture* on p. 1-1. Presuming that April and Martin perform meaningful services for Travis (which the facts seem to imply), they are legitimate employees. April is not subject to Social Security tax because she is under the age of 18. However, Martin is 18 and needs to be covered. Furthermore, recall that Betty Carter is now working at a medical clinic and will likewise be subject to Social Security tax. Travis, as an independent contractor, is subject to self-employment tax.

---

[20]Chapter 13 includes coverage of the self-employment tax (the Social Security and Medicare taxes for self-employed persons). See also Circular E, *Employer's Tax Guide*, issued by the IRS as Publication 15.

[21]To help stimulate consumer activity by making more spendable funds available, an employees' contribution was reduced from 6.2% to 4.2% during 2011 and 2012. The 2% reduction was not extended beyond 2012.

[22]Enacted as part of the Patient Protection and Affordable Care Act (one of several health care acts passed in 2010).

Taxpayers who are not employees (e.g., sole proprietors and independent contractors) may also be subject to Social Security taxes. Known as the self-employment tax, the rates are 12.4 percent for Social Security and 2.9 percent for Medicare, or twice that applicable to an employee. The additional .9 percent Medicare tax also covers situations involving high net income from self-employment. The Social Security tax is imposed on net self-employment income up to a base amount of $117,000 for 2014. The Medicare portion of the self-employment tax is not subject to any dollar limitation.

To defray the cost of extended medical care, Congress enacted a special tax on investment income.[23] For this purpose, "investment income" is often referred to as "unearned income" because it is not generated by the performance of services. A tax of 3.8 percent is imposed on investment income when a taxpayer's modified adjusted gross income (MAGI) exceeds certain threshold amounts.[24] The threshold amounts are $250,000 for married taxpayers and $200,000 for single taxpayers. Investment income generally includes passive income (e.g., taxable interest, dividends, and capital gains). The tax is effective beginning in 2013. For an in-depth discussion, see Chapter 13.

FUTA Taxes

The purpose of the **FUTA tax** is to provide funds the states can use to administer unemployment benefits. This leads to the somewhat unusual situation of one tax being handled by both Federal and state governments. The end result of such joint administration is to compel the employer to observe two sets of rules. Thus, state and Federal returns must be filed and payments made to both governmental units.

In 2014, FUTA is 6 percent on the first $7,000 of covered wages paid during the year to each employee. The Federal government allows a credit for FUTA paid (or allowed under a merit rating system) to the state. The credit cannot exceed 5.4 percent of the covered wages. Thus, the amount required to be paid to the IRS could be as low as .6 percent (6.0% − 5.4%).

States follow a policy of reducing the unemployment tax on employers who experience stable employment. Thus, an employer with little or no employee turnover might find that the state rate drops to as low as .1 percent or, in some states, even to zero. The reason for the merit rating credit is that the state has to pay fewer unemployment benefits when employment is steady.

FUTA, unlike FICA, is paid entirely by the employer. A few states, however, levy a special tax on employees to provide either disability benefits or supplemental unemployment compensation or both.

1-5g Other U.S. Taxes

To complete the overview of the U.S. tax system, some missing links need to be covered that do not fit into the classifications discussed elsewhere in this chapter.

Federal Customs Duties

One tax that has not yet been mentioned is the tariff on certain imported goods.[25] Generally referred to as customs duties or levies, this tax, together with selective excise taxes, provided most of the revenues needed by the Federal government during the nineteenth century. In view of present times, it is remarkable that tariffs and excise taxes alone paid off the national debt in 1835 and enabled the U.S. Treasury to pay a surplus of $28 million to the states.

In recent years, tariffs have served the nation more as an instrument for carrying out protectionist policies than as a means of generating revenue. Thus, a particular U.S. industry might be saved from economic disaster, so the argument goes, by imposing customs duties on the importation of foreign goods that can be sold at lower prices. Protectionists contend that the tariff thereby neutralizes the competitive edge held by the producer of the foreign goods. History shows that tariffs often lead to retaliatory action on the part of the nation or nations affected.

---

[23]Enacted as part of the Health Care and Education Reconciliation Act of 2010.

[24]MAGI is adjusted gross income (see Figure 1.2 and the bottom of page 1 of Form 1040) plus any foreign income or excluded foreign housing costs.

[25]Less-developed countries that rely principally on one or more major commodities (e.g., oil or coffee) are prone to favor *export* duties as well.

Miscellaneous State and Local Taxes

Most states impose a franchise tax on corporations. Basically, a **franchise tax** is levied on the right to do business in the state. The base used for the determination of the tax varies from state to state. Although corporate income considerations may come into play, this tax most often is based on the capitalization of the corporation (either with or without certain long-term indebtedness).

Closely akin to the franchise tax are **occupational fees** applicable to various trades or businesses (e.g., a liquor store license; a taxicab permit; or a fee to practice a profession such as law, medicine, or accounting). Most of these are not significant revenue producers and fall more into the category of licenses than taxes. The revenue derived is used to defray the cost incurred by the jurisdiction in regulating the business or profession in the interest of the public good.

THE BIG PICTURE

Example 14

Return to the facts of *The Big Picture* on p. 1-1. Although the facts do not mention the matter, both Travis and Betty will almost certainly pay occupational fees—Travis for engineering and Betty for nursing.

1-5h Proposed U.S. Taxes

Considerable dissatisfaction with the U.S. Federal income tax has led to several recent proposals that, to say the least, are rather drastic in nature. One proposal would retain the income tax but with substantial change. Two other proposals would replace the Federal income tax with an entirely different system of taxation.

The Flat Tax

One proposal is for a **flat tax** that would replace the current graduated income tax with a single rate of 17 percent. Large personal exemptions (e.g., approximately $30,000 for a family of four) would allow many low- and middle-income taxpayers to pay no tax. All other deductions would be eliminated, and no tax would be imposed on income from investments.

Various other versions of the flat tax have been suggested that would retain selected deductions (e.g., interest on home mortgages and charitable contributions) and not exclude all investment income from taxation.

The major advantage of the flat tax is its simplicity. Everyone agrees that the current Federal income tax is inappropriately complex. Consequently, compliance costs are disproportionately high. Proponents of the flat tax further believe that simplifying the income tax will significantly reduce the current "tax gap" (i.e., the difference between the amount of taxes that *should be paid* and what is *actually paid*).

Political considerations are a major obstacle to the enactment of a flat tax in its pure form. Special interest groups, such as charitable organizations and mortgage companies, are likely to strongly oppose the elimination of a tax deduction that benefits their industry. In addition, there is uncertainty as to the economic effects of a flat tax.

Value Added Tax

The **value added tax (VAT)** is one of two proposals that would replace the Federal income tax. Under the VAT, a business would pay the tax (approximately 17 percent) on all of the materials and services required to manufacture its product. In effect, the VAT taxes the increment in value as goods move through production and manufacturing stages to the marketplace. Moreover, the VAT paid by the producer will be reflected in the selling price of the goods. Thus, the VAT is a tax on consumption. In fact, the VAT has been described by some as a "layered sales tax."

Global Tax Issues

VAT in USA? Not Likely!

The United States is the only country in the OECD (Organization of Economic Cooperation and Development) that does not have a value added tax (VAT). Approximately 80 countries around the world use a VAT, ranging from 5 percent in Japan to 27 percent in Hungary.

Although the adoption of a VAT by the United States has been suggested, such a move seems unlikely. Because the VAT is an effective generator of revenue, many fear that it would fuel big government and lead to the expansion of entitlements available to certain sectors of the general public. Also, the VAT is regressive in its effect and, in practice, does not alleviate the burden of the income tax.

Source: United States Council for International Business, **www.uscib.org/index.asp**, and based on Ernest Christian and Gary Robbins, "A Value-Added Tax Fuels Big Government," *Wall Street Journal*, August 24, 2011, p. A13.

In spite of its extensive use by other countries (including Canada), the adoption of a VAT by the United States appears doubtful (see comments under "Global Tax Issues" above).

National Sales Tax

A **national sales tax** differs from a VAT in that it would be collected on the final sale of goods and services. Consequently, it is collected from the consumer, not from businesses that add value to the product. Like the VAT, the national sales tax is intended to replace the Federal income tax.

A current proposal for a national sales tax, called the "Fair Tax," would tax all purchases, including food and medicine, at approximately 23 percent. Exempt items include business expenses, used goods, and the costs of education. The "Fair Tax" would replace not only the income tax (both individual and corporate) but also payroll taxes (including the self-employment tax) and the gift and estate taxes.

Critics contend that both forms of consumption taxes, a VAT and a national sales tax, are regressive. They impose more of a burden on low-income taxpayers who must spend larger proportions of their incomes on essential purchases. The proposals attempt to remedy this inequity by granting some sort of credit, rebate, or exemption to low-income taxpayers.

In terms of taxpayer compliance, a VAT is preferable to a national sales tax. Without significant collection efforts, a national sales tax could easily be circumvented by resorting to a barter system of doing business. Its high rate would also encourage smuggling and black market activities.

1-6 TAX ADMINISTRATION

LO.5

Explain the administration of the tax law, including the audit process utilized by the IRS.

1-6a Internal Revenue Service

The responsibility for administering the Federal tax laws rests with the Treasury Department. The IRS is part of the Department of the Treasury and is responsible for enforcing the tax laws. The Commissioner of Internal Revenue is appointed by the President and is responsible for establishing policy and supervising the activities of the IRS.

1-6b The Audit Process

Selection of Returns for Audit

Due to budgetary limitations, only a small number of tax returns are audited. While an audit may be conducted on any taxpayer, those with higher income, $1 million or more, are more likely than lower income taxpayers to be audited.

The IRS utilizes mathematical formulas and statistical sampling techniques to select tax returns that are most likely to contain errors and to yield substantial amounts of additional tax revenues upon audit. The mathematical formula yields what is called a Discriminant Index Formula (DIF) score. It is the DIF score given to a particular return that may lead to its selection for audit. Periodically, the IRS updates the DIF components by auditing a cross section of returns to determine the most likely areas of taxpayer noncompliance.

Although the IRS does not openly disclose all of its audit selection techniques, the following observations may be made concerning the probability of selection for audit:

- Certain groups of taxpayers are subject to audit much more frequently than others. These groups include individuals with large amounts of gross income, self-employed individuals with substantial business income and deductions, and taxpayers with prior tax deficiencies. Also vulnerable are businesses that receive a large proportion of their receipts in cash (e.g., cafés and small service businesses) and thus have a high potential for tax avoidance.

Example 15

Jack owns and operates a liquor store on a cash-and-carry basis. Because all of Jack's sales are for cash, he might well be a prime candidate for an audit by the IRS. Cash transactions are easier to conceal than those made on credit.

- If information returns (e.g., Form 1099 or Form W–2) are not in substantial agreement with reported income, an audit can be anticipated.
- If an individual's itemized deductions are in excess of norms established for various income levels, the probability of an audit is increased.
- Filing of a refund claim by the taxpayer may prompt an audit of the return.
- Information obtained from other sources (e.g., informants and news items) may lead to an audit. Recently, for example, the IRS advised its agents to be on the alert for newspaper accounts of large civil court judgments. The advice was based on the assumption that many successful plaintiffs were not reporting as income the taxable punitive damages portion of awards.

The tax law permits the IRS to pay rewards to persons who provide information that leads to the detection and punishment of those who violate the tax laws. The rewards may not exceed 30 percent of the taxes, fines, and penalties recovered as a result of such information.

Example 16

After 15 years of service, Rita is discharged by her employer, Dr. Smith. Shortly thereafter, the IRS receives an anonymous letter stating that Dr. Smith keeps two separate sets of books and that the one used for tax reporting substantially understates his cash receipts.

Example 17

During a divorce proceeding, it is revealed that Leo, a public official, kept large amounts of cash in a shoe box at home. This information is widely disseminated by the news media and comes to the attention of the IRS. Needless to say, the IRS is interested in knowing whether these funds originated from a taxable source and, if so, whether they were reported on Leo's income tax returns.

Types of Audits

Once a return is selected for audit, the taxpayer is notified. If the issue involved is minor, the matter often can be resolved simply by correspondence (a **correspondence audit**) between the IRS and the taxpayer.

Other examinations are generally classified as either office audits or field audits. An **office audit** usually is restricted in scope and is conducted in the facilities of the IRS. In contrast, a **field audit** involves an examination of numerous items reported on the return and is conducted on the premises of the taxpayer or the taxpayer's representative.

TAX IN THE NEWS   Pay or Shame!

States and local jurisdictions are learning that the threat of public humiliation can be rewarding. When someone owes taxes but does not pay, the prospect of having his or her name listed on a public website may make a difference. Often payment is made to avoid the cybershame that comes from being exposed as a tax deadbeat. Numerous states are publishing the names of tax delinquents online. Some taxing jurisdictions have found the shaming procedure so productive that they maintain separate lists for different types of taxes (e.g., sales taxes and income taxes) or different types of delinquents (e.g., personal and business). As of yet, the IRS has not considered this approach for Federal tax scofflaws. Perhaps the length of the list would be too overwhelming!

© iStockphoto.com/Andrey Prokhorov

THE BIG PICTURE

Example 18

Return to the facts of *The Big Picture* on p. 1-1. The audit of the Walkers by the IRS obviously was a correspondence type. The reason for the audit was probably a minor oversight, such as the omission of some interest or dividend income. The audit of the Carters, however, was more serious—probably a field or office type. Because the Federal audit followed a state audit that was productive (i.e., led to the assessment of a deficiency), there may have been an exchange of information between the two taxing authorities—see p. 1-15 in this chapter.

Upon the conclusion of the audit, the examining agent issues a Revenue Agent's Report (RAR) that summarizes the findings. The RAR will result in a refund (the tax was overpaid), a deficiency (the tax was underpaid), or a no change (the tax was correct) finding. If, during the course of an audit, a special agent accompanies (or takes over from) the regular auditor, this means the IRS suspects fraud. If the matter has progressed to an investigation for fraud, the taxpayer should retain competent counsel.

Settlement Procedures

If an audit results in an assessment of additional tax and no settlement is reached with the IRS agent, the taxpayer may attempt to negotiate a settlement with a higher level of the IRS. If an appeal is desired, an appropriate request must be made to the Appeals Division of the IRS. The Appeals Division is authorized to settle all disputes based on the *hazard of litigation* (the probability of favorable resolution of the disputed issue or issues if litigated). In some cases, a taxpayer may be able to obtain a percentage settlement or a favorable settlement of one or more disputed issues.

If a satisfactory settlement is not reached in the administrative appeal process, the taxpayer can litigate the case in the Tax Court, a Federal District Court, or the Court of Federal Claims. However, litigation is recommended only as a last resort because of the legal costs involved and the uncertainty of the final outcome. Tax litigation considerations are discussed more fully in Chapter 2.

1-6c Statute of Limitations

A **statute of limitations** is a provision in the law that offers a party a defense against a suit brought by another party after the expiration of a specified period of time. The purpose of a statute of limitations is to preclude parties from prosecuting stale claims. The passage of time makes the defense of such claims difficult because witnesses may no longer be available or evidence may have been lost or destroyed. Found at the state and Federal levels, such statutes cover a multitude of suits, both civil and criminal.

For our purposes, the relevant statutes deal with the Federal income tax. The two categories involved cover both the period of limitations applicable to the assessment of additional tax deficiencies by the IRS and the period applicable to claims for refunds by taxpayers.

Assessment by the IRS

Under the general rule, the IRS may assess an additional tax liability against a taxpayer within *three years* of the filing of the income tax return. If the return is filed early, the three-year period begins to run from the due date of the return (usually April 15 for a calendar year individual taxpayer). If the taxpayer files the return late (i.e., beyond the due date), the three-year period begins to run on the date filed.

If a taxpayer omits an amount of gross income in excess of 25 percent of the gross income reported on the return, the statute of limitations is increased to six years.

For 2014, Mark, a calendar year taxpayer, reported gross income of $400,000 on a timely filed income tax return. If Mark omitted more than $100,000 (25% × $400,000), the six-year statute of limitations would apply to the 2014 tax year.

Example 19

The six-year provision on assessments by the IRS applies only to the omission of income and does not cover other factors that might lead to an understatement of tax liability, such as overstatement of deductions and credits.

There is *no* statute of limitations on assessments of tax if *no return* is filed or if a *fraudulent* return is filed.

Limitations on Refunds

If a taxpayer believes that an overpayment of Federal income tax was made, a claim for refund should be filed with the IRS. A *claim for refund*, therefore, is a request to the IRS that it return to the taxpayer excessive income taxes paid.[26]

A claim for refund generally must be filed within *three years* from the date the return was filed *or* within *two years* from the date the tax was paid, whichever is later. Income tax returns that are filed early are deemed to have been filed on the date the return was due.

1-6d Interest and Penalties

Interest rates are determined quarterly by the IRS based on the existing Federal short-term rate. Currently, the rates for tax refunds (overpayments) for individual taxpayers are the same as those applicable to assessments (underpayments). For the first quarter (January 1–March 31) of 2014, the rates are 3 percent for refunds and assessments.[27]

For assessments of additional taxes, the interest begins running on the unextended due date of the return. With refunds, however, no interest is allowed if the overpayment is refunded to the taxpayer within 45 days of the date the return is filed. For this purpose, returns filed early are deemed to have been filed on the due date.

In addition to interest, the tax law provides various penalties for lack of compliance by taxpayers. Some of these penalties are summarized as follows:

- For *failure to file* a tax return by the due date (including extension—see Chapter 3), a penalty of 5 percent per month up to a maximum of 25 percent is imposed on the amount of tax shown as due on the return. Any fraction of a month counts as a full month.
- A penalty for *failure to pay* the tax due as shown on the return is imposed in the amount of .5 percent per month up to a maximum of 25 percent. Again, any fraction of a month counts as a full month. During any month in which

---

[26]Generally, an individual filing a claim for refund should use Form 1040X.

[27]The rates applicable after March 31, 2014 were not available when this text went to press.

both the failure to file penalty and the failure to pay penalty apply, the failure to file penalty is reduced by the amount of the failure to pay penalty.

Example 20

Adam files his tax return 18 days after the due date of the return. Along with the return, he remits a check for $1,000, which is the balance of the tax he owed. Disregarding the interest element, Adam's total penalties are as follows:

Failure to pay penalty (0.5% × $1,000)		$ 5
Plus:		
Failure to file penalty (5% × $1,000)	$50	
Less failure to pay penalty for the same period	(5)	
Failure to file penalty		45
Total penalties		$50

Note that the penalties for one full month are imposed even though Adam was delinquent by only 18 days. Unlike the method used to compute interest, any part of a month is treated as a whole month.

- A *negligence* penalty of 20 percent is imposed if any of the underpayment was for intentional disregard of rules and regulations without intent to defraud. The penalty applies to just that portion attributable to the negligence.

Example 21

Cindy underpaid her taxes for 2012 in the amount of $20,000, of which $15,000 is attributable to negligence. Cindy's negligence penalty is $3,000 (20% × $15,000).

- Various penalties may be imposed in the case of *fraud*. Fraud involves specific intent on the part of the taxpayer to evade a tax. In the case of *civil* fraud, the penalty is 75 percent of the underpayment attributable to fraud. In the case of *criminal* fraud, the penalties can include large fines as well as prison sentences. The difference between civil and criminal fraud is one of degree. Criminal fraud involves the presence of willfulness on the part of the taxpayer. Also, the burden of proof, which is on the IRS in both situations, is more stringent for criminal fraud than for civil fraud. The negligence penalty is not imposed when the fraud penalty applies. For possible fraud situations, refer to Examples 16 and 17.

1-6e Tax Practice

If a practitioner is a member of a profession such as law or public accounting, he or she must abide by certain ethical standards. Furthermore, the Internal Revenue Code imposes penalties upon the preparers of Federal tax returns who violate proscribed acts and procedures.

Ethical Guidelines

LO.6

Evaluate some of the ethical guidelines involved in tax practice.

The American Institute of CPAs has issued numerous pronouncements, called the "Statements on Standards for Tax Services," dealing with CPAs engaged in tax practice. These pronouncements are *enforceable* as part of its Code of Professional Conduct. They include the following summarized provisions:

- Do not take questionable positions on a client's tax return in the hope that the return will not be selected for audit by the IRS. Any positions taken should be supported by a good-faith belief that they have a realistic possibility of being sustained if challenged. The client should be fully advised of the risks involved and of the penalties that will result if the position taken is not successful.
- A practitioner can use a client's estimates if they are reasonable under the circumstances. If the tax law requires receipts or other verification, the client should be so advised. In no event should an estimate be given the appearance of greater accuracy than is the case. For example, an estimate of $1,000 should not be deducted on a return as $999.

Outsourcing of Tax Return Preparation

Global Tax Issues

© iStockphoto.com/Andrey Prokhorov

The use of foreign nationals to carry out certain job assignments for U.S. businesses is an increasingly popular practice. Outsourcing such activities as telemarketing to India, for example, usually produces the same satisfactory result as having the work done in the United States but at a much lower cost.

Outsourcing is also being applied to the preparation of tax returns. Not only can this practice be expected to continue, but it probably will increase in volume. Outsourcing tax return preparation does not violate Federal law and is compatible with accounting ethical guidelines as long as three safeguards are followed: First, the practitioner must make sure client confidentiality is maintained. Second, the practitioner must verify the accuracy of the work that has been outsourced. Third, the practitioner must inform clients, preferably in writing, when any third-party contractor is used to provide professional services.

Practitioners justify outsourcing as a means of conserving time and effort that can be applied toward more meaningful tax planning on behalf of their clients.

Source: AICPA Ethics Ruling No. 1 (under Rule 301), see **www.aicpa.org/research/standards/ codeofconduct/pages/et_391.aspx**.

- Every effort should be made to answer questions appearing on tax returns. A question need not be answered if the information requested is not readily available, the answer is voluminous, or the question's meaning is uncertain. The failure to answer a question on a return cannot be justified on the grounds that the answer could prove disadvantageous to the taxpayer.
- Upon learning of an error on a past tax return, advise the client to correct it. Do not, however, inform the IRS of the error. If the error is material and the client refuses to correct it, consider withdrawing from the engagement. This will be necessary if the error has a carryover effect and prevents the current year's tax liability from being determined correctly.

ETHICS & EQUITY   Let Bygones Be Bygones

Arturo is a new client who wants you to prepare his Federal income tax return for 2014. In the past, he has prepared his own returns, but has become overwhelmed by the time and effort involved. In your first meeting with Arturo, you learn that he inherited some foreign rental property several years ago. As of yet, however, he has not reported on his tax returns any transactions regarding the property. He is not averse to including the rent income on his 2014 return, but wants to avoid the hassle of filing amended returns. He prefers to "let bygones be bygones."

Under these circumstances, do you accept the engagement? Why or why not?

© iStockphoto.com/LdF

Statutory Penalties Imposed on Tax Return Preparers

In addition to ethical constraints, a tax return preparer may be subject to certain statutorily sanctioned penalties, including the following:

- Various penalties involving procedural matters. Examples include failing to furnish the taxpayer with a copy of the return, endorsing a taxpayer's refund check, failing to sign the return as a preparer, failing to furnish one's identification number, and failing to keep copies of returns or maintain a client list.

- Penalty for understatement of a tax liability based on a position that lacks any realistic possibility of being sustained. If the position is not frivolous, the penalty can be avoided by disclosing it on the return.
- Penalty for any willful attempt to understate taxes. This usually results when a preparer disregards or makes no effort to obtain pertinent information from a client.
- Penalty for failure to exercise due diligence in determining eligibility for, or the amount of, an earned income tax credit.

1-7 UNDERSTANDING THE FEDERAL TAX LAW

LO.7

Recognize the economic, social, equity, and political considerations that justify various aspects of the tax law.

The Federal tax law is a mosaic of statutory provisions, administrative pronouncements, and court decisions. Anyone who has attempted to work with this body of knowledge would have to admit to its complexity. For the person who has to trudge through a mass of rules to find the solution to a tax problem, it may be of some consolation to know that the law's complexity can generally be explained. Whether sound or not, there is a reason for the formulation of every rule. Knowing these reasons, therefore, is a considerable step toward understanding the Federal tax law.

The Federal tax law has as its *major objective* the raising of revenue. But although the fiscal needs of the government are important, other considerations explain certain portions of the law. Economic, social, equity, and political factors also play a significant role. Added to these factors is the marked impact the IRS and the courts have had and will continue to have on the evolution of Federal tax law. These matters are treated in the remainder of the chapter, and wherever appropriate, the discussion is referenced to subjects covered later in the text.

1-7a Revenue Needs

The foundation of any tax system has to be the raising of revenue to cover the cost of government operations. Ideally, annual outlays should not exceed anticipated revenues, thereby leading to a balanced budget with no resulting deficit.

When enacting tax legislation, a deficit-conscious Congress often has been guided by the concept of **revenue neutrality**. Also referred to as "pay-as-you-go" ("paygo"), the concept means that every new tax law that lowers taxes must include a revenue offset that makes up for the loss. Revenue neutrality does not mean that any one taxpayer's tax liability will remain the same. Because the circumstances involved will differ, one taxpayer's increased tax liability could be another's tax savings. Although revenue-neutral tax reform does not reduce deficits, at least it does not aggravate the problem.

In addition to making revenue neutral changes in the tax law, several other procedures can be taken to mitigate any revenue loss. When tax reductions are involved, the full impact of the legislation can be phased in over a period of years. Or as an alternative, the tax reduction can be limited to a period of years. When the period expires, the prior law is reinstated through a **sunset provision**. Most of the major tax bills recently passed by Congress have contained numerous sunset provisions. They provide some semblance of revenue neutrality as some of the bills include tax cuts that were not offset by new sources of revenue. It remains to be seen, however, whether Congress will allow the sunset provisions to take effect and, thereby, kill the tax cuts that were enacted.

1-7b Economic Considerations

Using the tax system in an effort to accomplish economic objectives has become increasingly popular in recent years. Generally, proponents of this goal use tax legislation to amend the Internal Revenue Code in ways designed to help control the economy or encourage certain activities and businesses.

Control of the Economy

Congress has used depreciation write-offs as a means of controlling the economy. Theoretically, shorter asset lives and accelerated methods should encourage additional investment in depreciable property acquired for business use. Conversely, longer asset lives and the required use of the straight-line method of depreciation dampen the tax incentive for capital outlays.

Another approach that utilizes depreciation as a means of controlling capital investment is the amount of write-off allowed upon the acquisition of assets. This is the approach followed by the § 179 election to expense assets.

A change in the tax rate structure has a more immediate impact on the economy. With lower tax rates, taxpayers are able to retain additional spendable funds. If lower tax rates are accompanied by the elimination of certain deductions, exclusions, and credits, however, the overall result may not be lower tax liabilities.

Encouragement of Certain Activities

Without passing judgment on the wisdom of any such choices, it is quite clear that the tax law encourages certain types of economic activity or segments of the economy. For example, providing favorable treatment for research and development expenditures can be explained by the desire to foster technological progress. Under the tax law, such expenditures can be either deducted in the year incurred or capitalized and amortized over a period of 60 months or more. In terms of the timing of the tax savings, these options usually are preferable to capitalizing the cost with a write-off over the estimated useful life of the asset created. If the asset developed has an indefinite useful life, no write-off would be available without the two options allowed by the tax law.

Part of the tax law addresses the energy crisis—in terms of both our reliance on foreign oil and the need to ease the problem of climate change. For example, a tax credit is allowed for installation of solar and small wind energy equipment. In addition, tax credits are available to those who purchase new plug-in electric drive motor vehicles. Residential energy credits are allowed for home improvements that conserve energy or make its use more efficient (e.g., solar hot water and geothermal heat pumps). Ecological considerations justify a tax provision that permits a more rapid expensing of the costs of installing pollution control facilities. Measures such as these that aid in maintaining a clean air environment and conserving energy resources can also be justified under social considerations.

Is it wise to stimulate U.S. exports of services? Along this line, Congress has deemed it advisable to establish incentives for U.S. citizens who accept employment overseas. Such persons receive generous tax breaks through special treatment of their foreign-source income.

Is saving desirable for the economy? Saving leads to capital formation and thereby makes funds available to finance home construction and industrial expansion. The tax law encourages saving by according preferential treatment to private retirement plans. Besides contributions to Keogh (H.R. 10) plans and certain IRAs being deductible, income from the contributions accumulates free of tax. The encouragement of private-sector pension plans can also be justified under social considerations.

Encouragement of Certain Industries

Because a sound agricultural base is necessary for a well-balanced national economy, farmers are accorded special treatment under the Federal tax system. Among the benefits are the election to expense rather than capitalize certain soil and water conservation expenditures and fertilizers and the election to defer the recognition of gain on the receipt of crop insurance proceeds.

To stimulate the manufacturing industry, Congress enacted a domestic production activities deduction. The provision provides a tax benefit in the form of a deduction for profits derived from manufacturing activities conducted in the

United States. By restricting the deduction to manufacturing income attributable to wages reportable to the IRS, new U.S. jobs will result and the outsourcing of labor is discouraged. Thus, the tax system is used to encourage both domestic manufacturing and job growth.

Encouragement of Small Business

At least in the United States, a consensus exists that what is good for small business is good for the economy as a whole. Whether valid or not, this assumption has led to a definite bias in the tax law favoring small business.

In the corporate tax area, several provisions can be explained by the desire to benefit small business. One provision permits the shareholders of a small business corporation to make a special election that generally avoids the imposition of the corporate income tax.[28] Furthermore, such an election enables the corporation to pass through its operating losses to its shareholders.

1-7c Social Considerations

Some provisions of the Federal tax law, particularly those dealing with the income tax of individuals, can be explained by social considerations. Some notable examples and their rationales include the following:

- Certain benefits provided to employees through accident and health plans financed by employers are nontaxable to employees. Encouraging such plans is considered socially desirable because they provide medical benefits in the event of an employee's illness or injury.
- Most premiums paid by an employer for group term insurance covering the life of the employee are nontaxable to the employee. These arrangements can be justified on social grounds in that they provide funds for the family unit to help it adjust to the loss of wages caused by the employee's death.
- A contribution made by an employer to a qualified pension or profit sharing plan for an employee may receive special treatment. The contribution and any income it generates are not taxed to the employee until the funds are distributed. Such an arrangement also benefits the employer by allowing a tax deduction when the contribution is made to the qualified plan. Private retirement plans are encouraged to supplement the subsistence income level the employee otherwise would have under the Social Security system.[29]
- A deduction is allowed for contributions to qualified charitable organizations. The deduction attempts to shift some of the financial and administrative burden of socially desirable programs from the public (the government) to the private (the citizens) sector.
- A tax credit is allowed for amounts spent to furnish care for certain minor or disabled dependents to enable the taxpayer to seek or maintain gainful employment. For those employees who do not choose home care for their children, employers are allowed a credit for child care provided at the workplace. Who could deny the social desirability of encouraging taxpayers to provide care for their children while they work?
- To encourage taxpayers to join the workforce even though their wages may be marginal, an earned income tax credit can be claimed. The credit varies depending on the number of qualifying children being claimed and the level of wages earned. Because it stimulates employment, the earned income tax credit can also be justified on economic grounds.
- Due to the usual impairment in earning potential, certain credits are made available to elderly and disabled persons. Credits also are allowed to businesses that incur expenditures to make their facilities more accessible to the disabled.

---

[28]Known as the S election, it is discussed in Chapter 20.

[29]The same rationale explains the availability of similar arrangements for self-employed persons (the H.R. 10, or Keogh, plan). See Chapter 19.

- Various tax credits, deductions, and exclusions are designed to encourage taxpayers to obtain additional education.[30]
- A tax deduction is not allowed for certain expenditures deemed to be contrary to public policy. This disallowance extends to such items as fines, penalties, illegal kickbacks, bribes to government officials, and gambling losses in excess of gains. Social considerations dictate that the tax law should not encourage these activities by permitting a deduction.

Many other examples could be cited, but the conclusion would be unchanged. Social considerations do explain a significant part of the Federal tax law.

1-7d Equity Considerations

The concept of equity is relative. Reasonable persons can, and often do, disagree about what is fair or unfair. In the tax area, moreover, equity is most often tied to a particular taxpayer's personal situation. To illustrate, compare the tax positions of those who rent their personal residences with those who own their homes. Renters receive no Federal income tax benefit from the rent they pay. For homeowners, however, a large portion of the house payments they make may qualify for the Federal interest and property tax deductions. Although renters may have difficulty understanding this difference in tax treatment, the encouragement of home ownership can be justified on both economic and social grounds.

In the same vein, compare the tax treatment of a corporation with that of a partnership. Although the two businesses may be equal in size, similarly situated, and competitors in the production of goods or services, they are not treated comparably under the tax law. The corporation is subject to a separate Federal income tax; the partnership is not. Whether the differences in tax treatment can be justified logically in terms of equity is beside the point. The point is that the tax law can and does make a distinction between these business forms.

Equity, then, is not what appears fair or unfair to any one taxpayer or group of taxpayers. Some recognition of equity does exist, however, and explains part of the law. The concept of equity appears in tax provisions that alleviate the effect of multiple taxation and postpone the recognition of gain when the taxpayer lacks the ability or wherewithal to pay the tax. Provisions that mitigate the effect of the application of the annual accounting period concept and help taxpayers cope with the eroding results of inflation also reflect equity considerations.

Alleviating the Effect of Multiple Taxation

The income earned by a taxpayer may be subject to taxes imposed by different taxing authorities. If, for example, the taxpayer is a resident of New York City, income might generate Federal, state of New York, and city of New York income taxes. To compensate for this apparent inequity, the Federal tax law allows a taxpayer to claim a deduction for state and local income taxes. The deduction does not, however, neutralize the effect of multiple taxation because the benefit derived depends on the taxpayer's Federal income tax rate. Only a tax credit, not a deduction, would eliminate the effects of multiple taxation on the same income.

Equity considerations can explain the Federal tax treatment of certain income from foreign sources. Because double taxation results when the same income is subject to both foreign and U.S. income taxes, the tax law permits the taxpayer to choose between a credit and a deduction for the foreign taxes paid.

The Wherewithal to Pay Concept

The **wherewithal to pay** concept recognizes the inequity of taxing a transaction when the taxpayer lacks the means with which to pay the tax. It is particularly

---

[30]These provisions can also be justified under the category of economic considerations because a better-educated workforce carries a positive economic impact.

suited to situations in which the taxpayer's economic position has not changed significantly as a result of the transaction.

An illustration of the wherewithal to pay concept is the provision of the tax law dealing with the treatment of gain resulting from an involuntary conversion. An involuntary conversion occurs when property is destroyed by a casualty or taken by a public authority through condemnation. If gain results from the conversion, it need not be recognized if the taxpayer replaces the property within a specified period of time. The replacement property must be similar or related in service or use to that involuntarily converted.

Example 22	Some of the pasture land belonging to Ron, a rancher, is condemned by the state for use as a game preserve. The condemned pasture land cost Ron $120,000, but the state pays him $150,000 (its fair market value). Shortly thereafter, Ron buys more pasture land for $150,000.

In Example 22, Ron has a realized gain of $30,000 [$150,000 (condemnation award) − $120,000 (cost of land)]. It would be inequitable to force Ron to pay a tax on this gain for two reasons. First, without disposing of the property acquired (the new land), Ron would be hard-pressed to pay the tax. Second, his economic position has not changed.

A warning is in order regarding the application of the wherewithal to pay concept. If the taxpayer's economic position changes in any way, tax consequences may result.

Example 23	Assume the same facts as in Example 22, except that Ron reinvests only $140,000 of the award in new pasture land. Now, Ron has a taxable gain of $10,000. Instead of ending up with only replacement property, Ron has $10,000 in cash.

Mitigating the Effect of the Annual Accounting Period Concept

For purposes of effective administration of the tax law, all taxpayers must report to and settle with the Federal government at periodic intervals. Otherwise, taxpayers would remain uncertain as to their tax liabilities, and the government would have difficulty judging revenues and budgeting expenditures. The period selected for final settlement of most tax liabilities, in any event an arbitrary determination, is one year. At the close of each year, therefore, a taxpayer's position becomes complete for that particular year. Referred to as the annual accounting period concept, its effect is to divide each taxpayer's life, for tax purposes, into equal annual intervals.

The finality of the annual accounting period concept could lead to dissimilar tax treatment for taxpayers who are, from a long-range standpoint, in the same economic position.

Example 24	José and Alicia, both sole proprietors, have experienced the following results during the past three years:

	Profit (or Loss)	
Year	**José**	**Alicia**
2012	$50,000	$150,000
2013	60,000	60,000
2014	60,000	(40,000)

Although José and Alicia have the same profit of $170,000 over the period from 2012 to 2014, the finality of the annual accounting period concept places Alicia at a definite disadvantage for tax purposes. The net operating loss procedure offers Alicia some relief by allowing her to apply some or all of her 2014 loss to the earlier profitable years (in this case, 2012). Thus, with a net operating loss carryback, Alicia is in a position to obtain a refund for some of the taxes she paid on the $150,000 profit reported for 2012.

The same reasoning used to support the deduction of net operating losses can explain the special treatment the tax law accords to excess capital losses and excess charitable contributions.[31] Carryback and carryover procedures help mitigate the effect of limiting a loss or a deduction to the accounting period in which it was realized. With such procedures, a taxpayer may be able to salvage a loss or a deduction that might otherwise be wasted.

The installment method of recognizing gain on the sale of property allows a taxpayer to spread tax consequences over the payout period.[32] The harsh effect of taxing all of the gain in the year of sale is thereby avoided. The installment method can also be explained by the wherewithal to pay concept because recognition of gain is tied to the collection of the installment notes received from the sale of the property. Tax consequences, then, tend to correspond to the seller's ability to pay the tax.

Coping with Inflation

Because of the progressive nature of the income tax, a wage adjustment to compensate for inflation can increase the income tax bracket of the recipient. Known as *bracket creep*, its overall impact is an erosion of purchasing power. Congress recognized this problem and began to adjust various income tax components, such as tax brackets, standard deduction amounts, and personal and dependency exemptions, through an indexation procedure. **Indexation** is based upon the rise in the consumer price index over the prior year.

1-7e Political Considerations

A large segment of the Federal tax law is made up of statutory provisions. Because these statutes are enacted by Congress, is it any surprise that political considerations influence tax law? For purposes of discussion, the effect of political considerations on the tax law is divided into the following topics: special interest legislation, political expediency situations, and state and local government influences.

Special Interest Legislation

There is no doubt that certain provisions of the tax law can largely be explained by the political influence some pressure groups have had on Congress. Is there any other realistic reason that, for example, prepaid subscription and dues income is not taxed until earned while prepaid rents are taxed to the landlord in the year received?

A recent provision, sponsored by a senator from Georgia, suspended the import duties on ceiling fans. The nation's largest seller of ceiling fans is Home Depot, which is based in Atlanta, Georgia. Another provision, sponsored by a congressman from Illinois, reduced the excise taxes on fishing tackle boxes. The representative's district includes Plano Molding, a major manufacturer of tackle boxes. The justification for this change was that it placed tackle boxes on a more level playing field with toolboxes (which are not subject to tax). Allegedly, fishermen had been buying and converting toolboxes to avoid the excise tax.

Special interest legislation is not necessarily to be condemned if it can be justified on economic, social, or some other utilitarian grounds. In most cases, however, it is objectionable in that it adds further complexity to an already cluttered tax law. At any rate, it is an inevitable product of our political system.

Political Expediency Situations

Various tax reform proposals rise and fall in favor with the shifting moods of the American public. That Congress is sensitive to popular feeling is an accepted fact. Therefore, certain provisions of the tax law can be explained by the political climate at the time they were enacted.

---

[31]The tax treatment of these items is discussed in Chapters 7, 10, and 16.

[32]Under the installment method, each payment received by the seller represents both a recovery of capital (the nontaxable portion) and profit from the sale (the taxable portion). The tax rules governing the installment method are discussed in Chapter 18.

Measures that deter more affluent taxpayers from obtaining so-called preferential tax treatment have always had popular appeal and, consequently, the support of Congress. A direct approach bars the benefit completely and explains such provisions as the imputed interest rules and the limitations on the deductibility of interest on investment indebtedness. More subtle are provisions that phase out tax breaks as income rises. Because taxpayers may be unaware of what is causing the shift to higher marginal tax rates, these phaseouts are often called "stealth taxes." The tax law contains several dozen such phaseout provisions. Examples include the earned income credit, the child tax credit, the lifetime learning credit, and the credit for first-time home purchases. At least for the immediate future, the use of these stealth taxes can be expected to increase.

Other changes, explained at least partially by political expediency, include the lowering of individual income tax rates, the increase in the personal and dependency exemptions, and the increase in the amount of the earned income credit.

State and Local Government Influences

Political considerations have played a major role in the nontaxability of interest received on state and local obligations. In view of the furor that state and local political figures have raised every time any modification of this tax provision has been proposed, one might well regard it as next to sacred.

Somewhat less apparent has been the influence that state law has had in shaping our present Federal tax law. Such was the case with community property systems. The nine states with community property systems are Louisiana, Texas, New Mexico, Arizona, California, Washington, Idaho, Nevada, and Wisconsin. The rest of the states are classified as common law jurisdictions.[33] The difference between common law and community property systems centers around the property rights possessed by married persons. In a common law system, each spouse owns whatever he or she earns. Under a community property system, one-half of the earnings of each spouse is considered owned by the other spouse.

Example 25	Al and Fran are husband and wife, and their only income is the $80,000 annual salary Al receives. If they live in New Jersey (a common law state), the $80,000 salary belongs to Al. If, however, they live in Arizona (a community property state), the $80,000 is divided equally, in terms of ownership, between Al and Fran.

At one time, the tax position of the residents of community property states was so advantageous that many common law states adopted community property systems. Needless to say, the political pressure placed on Congress to correct the disparity in tax treatment was considerable. To a large extent, this was accomplished in the Revenue Act of 1948, which extended many of the community property tax advantages to residents of common law jurisdictions.

The major advantage extended was the provision allowing married taxpayers to file joint returns and compute their tax liability as if one-half of the income had been earned by each spouse. This result is automatic in a community property state, because half of the income earned by one spouse belongs to the other spouse. The income-splitting benefits of a joint return are now incorporated as part of the tax rates applicable to married taxpayers. See Chapter 3.

1-7f Influence of the Internal Revenue Service

LO.8

Describe the role played by the IRS and the courts in the evolution of the Federal tax system.

The influence of the IRS is apparent in many areas beyond its role in issuing the administrative pronouncements that make up a considerable portion of our tax law. In its capacity as the protector of the national revenue, the IRS has been instrumental in securing the passage of much legislation designed to curtail the most flagrant tax avoidance practices (to close *tax loopholes*). As the administrator of the tax law, the IRS has sought and obtained legislation to make its job easier (to attain administrative feasibility).

---

[33]In Alaska, spouses can choose to have the community property rules apply. Otherwise, property rights are determined under common law rules.

The IRS as Protector of the Revenue

Innumerable examples can be given of provisions in the tax law that stem from the direct influence of the IRS. Usually, such provisions are intended to prevent a loophole from being used to avoid the tax consequences intended by Congress. Working within the letter of existing law, ingenious taxpayers and their advisers devise techniques that accomplish indirectly what cannot be accomplished directly. As a consequence, legislation is enacted to close the loopholes that taxpayers have located and exploited. Some tax law can be explained in this fashion and is discussed in the chapters to follow.

In addition, the IRS has secured from Congress legislation of a more general nature that enables it to make adjustments based on the substance, rather than the formal construction, of what a taxpayer has done. For example, one such provision permits the IRS to make adjustments to a taxpayer's method of accounting when the method used by the taxpayer does not clearly reflect income.[34]

Example 26

Tina, a cash basis taxpayer, owns and operates a pharmacy. All drugs and other items acquired for resale, such as cosmetics, are charged to the purchases account and written off (expensed) for tax purposes in the year of acquisition. As this procedure does not clearly reflect income, it would be appropriate for the IRS to require that Tina establish and maintain an ending inventory account.

ETHICS & EQUITY   It All Washes Out

Mason owns and operates a pharmacy as a sole proprietor. He manages to compete with the national chains because of the personalized service he provides to his customers. Also, he maintains a large and varied assortment of medical equipment and supplies (e.g., wheelchairs, walkers, and bath aids). He uses the cash method of accounting and expenses all purchases. He sees no need to keep inventory accounts, as it "all washes out" over time—last year's ending inventory becoming this year's beginning inventory. Thus, any misstatement of income in one year is offset in the following year.

Comment on Mason's rationalization and the propriety of his approach.

Administrative Feasibility

Some tax law is justified on the grounds that it simplifies the task of the IRS in collecting the revenue and administering the law. With regard to collecting the revenue, the IRS long ago realized the importance of placing taxpayers on a pay-as-you-go basis. Elaborate withholding procedures apply to wages, while the tax on other types of income may be paid at periodic intervals throughout the year. The IRS has been instrumental in convincing the courts that accrual basis taxpayers should, in most cases, pay taxes on prepaid income in the year received and not when earned. The approach may be contrary to generally accepted accounting principles, but it is consistent with the wherewithal to pay concept.

Of considerable aid to the IRS in collecting revenue are the numerous provisions that impose interest and penalties on taxpayers for noncompliance with the tax law. Provisions such as the penalties for failure to pay a tax or to file a return that is due, the negligence penalty for intentional disregard of rules and regulations, and various penalties for civil and criminal fraud serve as deterrents to taxpayer noncompliance.

One of the keys to an effective administration of our tax system is the audit process conducted by the IRS. To carry out this function, the IRS is aided by provisions that reduce the chance of taxpayer error or manipulation and therefore simplify the audit effort that is necessary. An increase in the amount of the standard

---

[34]See Chapter 18.

deduction, for example, reduces the number of individual taxpayers who will choose the alternative of itemizing their personal deductions.[35] With fewer deductions to check, the audit function is simplified.[36]

1-7g Influence of the Courts

In addition to interpreting statutory provisions and the administrative pronouncements issued by the IRS, the Federal courts have influenced tax law in two other respects.[37] First, the courts have formulated certain judicial concepts that serve as guides in the application of various tax provisions. Second, certain key decisions have led to changes in the Internal Revenue Code.

Judicial Concepts Relating to Tax

A leading tax concept developed by the courts deals with the interpretation of statutory tax provisions that operate to benefit taxpayers. The courts have established the rule that these relief provisions are to be narrowly construed if there is any doubt about their application.

Important in this area is the *arm's length* concept. Particularly in dealings between related parties, transactions may be tested by looking to whether the taxpayers acted in an arm's length manner. The question to be asked is: Would unrelated parties have handled the transaction in the same way?

Example 27

Rex, the sole shareholder of Silver Corporation, leases property to the corporation for a yearly rent of $60,000. To test whether the corporation should be allowed a rent deduction for this amount, the IRS and the courts will apply the arm's length concept. Would Silver Corporation have paid $60,000 a year in rent if it had leased the same property from an unrelated party (rather than from Rex)? Suppose it is determined that an unrelated third party would have charged an annual rent for the property of only $50,000. Under these circumstances, Silver Corporation will be allowed a deduction of only $50,000. The other $10,000 it paid for the use of the property represents a nondeductible dividend. Accordingly, Rex will be treated as having received rent income of $50,000 and dividend income of $10,000.

Judicial Influence on Statutory Provisions

Some court decisions have been of such consequence that Congress has incorporated them into statutory tax law. For example, many years ago the courts found that stock dividends distributed to the shareholders of a corporation were not taxable as income. This result was largely accepted by Congress, and a provision in the tax statutes now covers the issue.

On occasion, however, Congress has reacted negatively to judicial interpretations of the tax law.

Example 28

Nora leases unimproved real estate to Wade for 20 years. At a cost of $400,000, Wade erects a building on the land. The building is worth $150,000 when the lease terminates and Nora takes possession of the property. Does Nora have any income either when the improvements are made or when the lease terminates? In a landmark decision, a court held that Nora must recognize income of $150,000 upon the termination of the lease.

Congress belived that the result reached in Example 28 was inequitable in that it was not consistent with the wherewithal to pay concept. Consequently, the tax law was amended to provide that a landlord does not recognize any income either when the improvements are made (unless made in lieu of rent) or when the lease terminates.

---

[35]For a discussion of the standard deduction, see Chapter 3.

[36]The same justification was given by the IRS when it proposed to Congress the $100 limitation on personal casualty and theft losses. Imposition of the limitation eliminated many casualty and theft loss deductions and, as a consequence, saved the IRS considerable audit time. Later legislation, in addition to retaining the $100 feature, limits deductible losses to those in excess of 10% of a taxpayer's adjusted gross income. See Chapter 7.

[37]A great deal of case law is devoted to ascertaining congressional intent. The courts, in effect, ask: What did Congress have in mind when it enacted a particular tax provision?

1-8 SUMMARY

In addition to its necessary revenue-raising objective, the Federal tax law has developed in response to several other factors:

- *Economic considerations.* The emphasis here is on tax provisions that help regulate the economy and encourage certain activities and types of businesses.
- *Social considerations.* Some tax provisions are designed to encourage (or discourage) certain socially desirable (or undesirable) practices.
- *Equity considerations.* Of principal concern in this area are tax provisions that alleviate the effect of multiple taxation, recognize the wherewithal to pay concept, mitigate the effect of the annual accounting period concept, and recognize the eroding effect of inflation.
- *Political considerations.* Of significance in this regard are tax provisions that represent special interest legislation, reflect political expediency, and exhibit the effect of state and local law.
- *Influence of the IRS.* Many tax provisions are intended to aid the IRS in the collection of revenue and the administration of the tax law.
- *Influence of the courts.* Court decisions have established a body of judicial concepts relating to tax law and have, on occasion, led Congress to enact statutory provisions to either clarify or negate their effect.

These factors explain various tax provisions and thereby help in understanding why the tax law developed to its present state. The next step involves learning to work with the tax law, which is the subject of Chapter 2.

REFOCUS ON THE BIG PICTURE

FAMILY AND TAXES—A TYPICAL YEAR

The explanation given for the difference in the ad valorem property taxes—the Carters' increase and the Walkers' decrease—seems reasonable (see Example 4). It is not likely that the Carters' increase was due to a *general* upward assessment in valuation, as the Walkers' taxes on their residence (located nearby) dropped. More business use of the Carters' residence (presuming that Travis conducts his consulting practice from his home) might be responsible for the increase, but capital improvements appear to be a more likely cause.

The imposition of the use tax when Travis registered the new automobile illustrates one of the means by which a state can preclude the avoidance of its sales tax (see Example 5).

When gifts between family members are material in amount (e.g., an RV) and exceed the annual exclusion, a gift tax return needs to be filed (see Example 11). Even though no gift tax may be due because of the availability of the unified transfer tax credit, the filing of a return starts the running of the statute of limitations.

The imposition of the "jock tax" on nonathletes is unusual but not improper. The Carters must recognize that some of their income is subject to income taxes in two states and take advantage of whatever relief is available to mitigate the result (see Example 12).

Employment within and by the family group (e.g., children, other relatives, and domestics) has become a priority item in the enforcement of Social Security tax and income tax withholdings. Thus, the Carters must be aware of the need to cover their son, Martin (see Example 13).

Because of the double audit (i.e., both state and Federal) and the deficiency assessed, the Carters need to make sure that future returns do not contain similar errors (see Example 18). As the text suggests, taxpayers with prior deficiencies are among those whose returns may be selected for audit.

© Corbis/SuperStock

Key Terms

Ad valorem taxes, 1-6

Correspondence audit, 1-21

Employment taxes, 1-16

Estate tax, 1-11

Excise taxes, 1-8

FICA tax, 1-17

Field audit, 1-21

Financial Accounting Standards Board (FASB), 1-16

Flat tax, 1-19

Franchise tax, 1-19

FUTA tax, 1-18

Generally Accepted Accounting Principles (GAAP), 1-16

Gift tax, 1-12

Indexation, 1-31

Inheritance tax, 1-11

International Accounting Standards Board (IASB), 1-16

International Financial Reporting Standards (IFRS), 1-16

National sales tax, 1-20

Occupational fees, 1-19

Office audit, 1-21

Personality, 1-8

Realty, 1-7

Revenue neutrality, 1-26

Sales tax, 1-10

Severance taxes, 1-11

Statute of limitations, 1-22

Sunset provision, 1-26

Use tax, 1-10

Value added tax (VAT), 1-19

Wherewithal to pay, 1-29

Discussion Questions

1. **LO.1** In the following independent situations, is the tax position of the taxpayer likely to change? Explain why or why not.
   a. John used to make casual purchases and sales of real estate as an investor. Currently, he does so on a regular basis and has obtained a license as a dealer.
   b. Theresa quit her job as a staff accountant and has established her own practice as a CPA.
   c. After saving enough for a down payment, Paul has purchased a personal residence.

   Issue ID 2. **LO.1** Marvin is the executor and sole heir of his aunt's estate. The estate includes her furnished home, which Marvin is considering converting to rental property to generate additional cash flow. What are some of the tax problems Marvin may confront?

3. **LO.2** The Sixteenth Amendment to the U.S. Constitution was passed to overturn a Supreme Court decision that had invalidated the Federal income tax. Do you agree? Why or why not?

4. **LO.2** World War II converted the Federal income tax into a *mass tax*. Explain.

5. **LO.2** How does the pay-as-you-go procedure apply to wage earners? To persons who have income from sources other than wages?

6. **LO.3** Using Adam Smith's canon on *economy*, evaluate the Federal income tax.

7. **LO.3** Distinguish between taxes that are *proportional* and those that are *progressive*.

   Issue ID 8. **LO.4** Several years ago Ethan purchased the former parsonage of St. James Church to use as a personal residence. To date, Ethan has not received any ad valorem property tax bills from either the city or the county tax authorities.
   a. What is a reasonable explanation for this oversight?
   b. What should Ethan do?

   Issue ID 9. **LO.4** The Adams Independent School District wants to sell a parcel of unimproved land that it does not need. Its three best offers are as follows: from the state's Department of Public Safety (DPS), $2.3 million; from the Second Baptist Church, $2.2 million; and from Baker Motors, $2.1 million. DPS would use the property for a new state highway patrol barracks; Second Baptist would start a church school; and Baker would open a car dealership. If you are the financial adviser for the school district, which offer would you prefer? Why?

10. **LO.4** The commissioners for Walker County are actively negotiating with Falcon Industries regarding the location of a new manufacturing plant in the area. As Falcon is considering several other sites, a "generous tax holiday" may be needed to influence the final choice. The local school district is opposed to any "generous tax holiday."
    a. What would probably be involved in a generous tax holiday?
    b. Why would the school district be opposed?

11. **LO.4** Sophia lives several blocks from her parents in the same residential subdivision. Sophia is surprised to learn that her ad valorem property taxes for the year were raised, while those of her parents were lowered. What is a possible explanation for the difference?

12. **LO.4** The Morgan family lives in Massachusetts. They moor their sailboat in Rhode Island. What might be a plausible reason for the possible inconvenience?

13. **LO.4** Is the breadth and number of Federal excise taxes increasing or decreasing? Explain.

14. **LO.4** After his first business trip to a major city, Herman is alarmed when he reviews his credit card receipts. Both the hotel bill and the car rental charge are in excess of the price he was quoted. Was Herman overcharged, or is there an explanation for the excess amounts?

15. **LO.4** What is the difference between an excise tax and a general sales tax?
    a. Do all states impose a general sales tax?
    b. Does the Federal government impose a general sales tax?

16. **LO.4** The Grays live in Clay County, which is adjacent to Jackson County. Although the retail stores in both counties are comparable, the Grays usually drive a few extra miles to shop in Jackson County. As to why the Grays might do this, consider the following:
    a. Clay County is in a different state than Jackson County.
    b. Clay County and Jackson County are in the same state.

17. **LO.4** During a social event, Muriel and Earl are discussing the home computer each recently purchased. Although the computers are identical makes and models, Muriel is surprised to learn that she paid a sales tax, while Earl did not. Comment as to why this could happen.   Issue ID

18. **LO.4** Distinguish between an estate tax and an inheritance tax.
    a. Do some states impose both? Neither?
    b. Which, if either, does the Federal government impose?

19. **LO.4** Jake (age 72) and Jessica (age 28) were recently married. To avoid any transfer taxes, Jake has promised to leave Jessica all of his wealth when he dies. Is Jake under some misconception about the operation of the Federal gift and estate taxes? Explain.   Issue ID

20. **LO.4** Address the following issues:
    a. What is the purpose of the unified transfer tax credit?
    b. Is the same amount available for both the Federal gift tax and the estate tax? Explain.
    c. Does the use of the credit for a gift affect the amount of credit available for the estate tax? Explain.

21. **LO.4** Elijah and Anastasia are husband and wife who have five married children and nine minor grandchildren. For 2014, what is the maximum amount they can give to their family (including the sons- and daughters-in-law) without using any of their unified transfer tax credit?

22. **LO.4** What is the difference between the Federal income tax on individuals and that imposed on corporations?

23. **LO.4** As to those states that impose an income tax, comment on the following:
    a. "Piggyback" approach and possible "decoupling" from this approach.
    b. Deductibility of Federal income taxes.
    c. Credit for taxes paid to other states.

24. **LO.4** In May 2014, Hernando, a resident of California, has his 2012 Federal income tax return audited by the IRS. An assessment of additional tax is made because he had inadvertently omitted some rental income. In October 2014, California audits his state return for the same year. Explain the coincidence.

Issue ID

25. **LO.4** Mike Barr was an outstanding football player in college and expects to be drafted by the NFL in the first few rounds. Mike has let it be known that he would prefer to sign with a club located in Florida, Texas, or Washington. Mike sees no reason why he should have to pay state income tax on his player's salary. Is Mike under any delusions? Explain.

Issue ID

26. **LO.4, 5** A question on a state income tax return asks the taxpayer if he or she made any out-of-state Internet or mail-order catalog purchases during the year. The question requires a yes or no answer, and if the taxpayer answers yes, the amount of such purchases is to be listed.
    a. Does such an inquiry have any relevance to the state income tax? If not, why is it being asked?
    b. Your client, Harriet, wants to leave the question unanswered. As the preparer of her return, how do you respond?

27. **LO.4** Many state income tax returns contain checkoff boxes that allow taxpayers to make donations to a multitude of local charitable causes. On what grounds has this procedure been criticized?

28. **LO.4** Many states have occasionally adopted amnesty programs that allow taxpayers to pay back taxes with reduced penalties.
    a. Besides the revenue generated, how are these programs advantageous?
    b. Could an amnesty program be used by a state that does not levy an income tax?
    c. Does the IRS utilize this approach?

29. **LO.4** Contrast FICA and FUTA as to the following:
    a. Purpose of the tax.
    b. Upon whom imposed.
    c. Governmental administration of the tax.
    d. Reduction of tax based on a merit rating system.

30. **LO.4** In connection with the Medicare component of FICA, comment on the following:
    a. Any dollar limitation imposed.
    b. The applicability of the .9 % increase in the 1.45% regular tax rate.

31. **LO.4** One of the tax advantages of hiring family members to work in your business is that FICA taxes are avoided. Do you agree with this statement? Explain.

32. **LO.4** Describe the nature and purpose of the following taxes:
    a. Severance taxes.
    b. Franchise taxes.
    c. Occupational fees.
    d. Customs duties.
    e. Export duties.

33. **LO.4** Regarding the value added tax (VAT), comment on the following:
    a. Popularity of this type of tax.
    b. Nature of the tax.
    c. Effect on government spending.

34. **LO.4** Both a value added tax (VAT) and a national sales tax have been criticized as being *regressive* in their effect.
    a. Explain.
    b. How could this shortcoming be remedied in the case of a national sales tax?

Issue ID

35. **LO.4, 5** Serena operates a lawn maintenance service in Southern California. As most of her employees are itinerant, they are paid on a day-to-day basis. Because of cash-flow problems, Serena requires her customers to pay cash for the services she provides.
    a. What are some of the tax problems Serena might have?
    b. Assess Serena's chances of audit by the IRS.

36. **LO.5** Assess the probability of an audit in each of the following independent situations:
    a. As a result of a jury trial, Linda was awarded $3.5 million because of job discrimination. The award included $3 million for punitive damages.
    b. Mel operates a combination check-cashing service and pawnshop.
    c. Jayden, a self-employed trial lawyer, routinely files a Schedule C (Form 1040) that, due to large deductions, reports little (if any) profit from his practice.
    d. Bernard is the head server at an upscale restaurant and recently paid $1.8 million for a residence in an exclusive gated community.

    e. Homer has yearly AGI of around $70,000 and always claims the standard deduction. He works for a builder installing wallboard in new homes.

    f. Gloria lost a Form 1099–DIV that she received from a corporation that paid her a dividend.

    g. Cindy, a former vice president of a bank, has been charged with embezzling large sums of money.

    h. Giselle is a cocktail waitress at an upscale nightclub. She has been audited several times in past years.

    i. Marcus was recently assessed a large *state* income tax deficiency by the state of California for his utilization of an abusive tax shelter.

    j. Guy, a professional gambler, recently broke up with his companion of 10 years and married her teenage daughter.

37. **LO.5** With regard to the IRS audit process, comment on the following:
    a. The audit is resolved by mail.
    b. The audit is conducted at the office of the IRS.
    c. A "no change" RAR results.
    d. A special agent joins the audit team.

38. **LO.5** Aldo has just been audited by the IRS. He does not agree with the agent's findings but believes that he has only two choices: pay the proposed deficiency or resort to the courts. Do you agree with Aldo's conclusion? Why or why not?

39. **LO.5** What purpose is served by a statute of limitations? How is it relevant in the case of tax controversies?

40. **LO.5** Regarding the statute of limitations on additional assessments of tax by the IRS, determine the applicable period in each of the following situations. Assume a calendar year individual with no fraud or substantial omission involved.
    a. The income tax return for 2013 was filed on February 21, 2014.
    b. The income tax return for 2013 was filed on June 25, 2014.
    c. The income tax return for 2013 was prepared on April 4, 2014, but was never filed. Through some misunderstanding between the preparer and the taxpayer, each expected the other to file the return.
    d. The income tax return for 2013 was never filed because the taxpayer thought no additional tax was due.

41. **LO.5** Brianna, a calendar year taxpayer, files her income tax return for 2013 on February 3, 2014. Although she makes repeated inquiries, she does not receive her refund from the IRS until May 28, 2014. Is Brianna entitled to interest on the refund? Explain.

42. **LO.5, 6** On a Federal income tax return filed five years ago, Andy inadvertently omitted a large amount of gross income.
    a. Andy seeks your advice as to whether the IRS is barred from assessing additional income tax in the event he is audited. What is your advice?
    b. Would your advice differ if you were the person who prepared the return in question? Explain.
    c. Suppose Andy asks you to prepare his current year's return. Would you do so? Explain.

43. **LO.5** Isabella files her income tax return 35 days after the due date of the return without obtaining an extension from the IRS. Along with the return, she remits a check for $40,000, which is the balance of the tax she owes. Disregarding the interest element, what are Isabella's penalties for failure to file and for failure to pay?

44. **LO.5** For tax year 2011, the IRS assesses a deficiency against David for $500,000. Disregarding the interest component, what is David's penalty if the deficiency is attributable to:
    a. Negligence?
    b. Fraud?

45. **LO.5, 6** In March 2014, Jim asks you to prepare his Federal income tax returns for tax years 2011, 2012, and 2013. In discussing this matter with him, you discover that he also has not filed for tax year 2010. When you mention this fact, Jim tells you that the statute of limitations precludes the IRS from taking any action as to this year.
    a. Is Jim correct about the application of the statute of limitations? Why or why not?
    b. If Jim refuses to file for 2010, should you prepare returns for 2011 through 2013? Explain.

46. **LO.5, 6** The Benson CPA firm is considering utilizing an offshore service provider to prepare many of its tax returns. In this regard, what ethical considerations must be taken into account?

47. **LO.7** In terms of tax policy, what do the following mean?
    a. Revenue neutrality.
    b. Pay-as-you-go, or "paygo."
    c. Sunset provision.
    d. Indexation.

48. **LO.7** Some tax rules can be justified on multiple grounds (e.g., economic and social). In this connection, comment on the possible justification for the rules governing the following:
    a. Pension plans.
    b. Education.
    c. Home ownership.

49. **LO.7** Discuss the probable justification for each of the following provisions of the tax law:
    a. A tax credit allowed for electricity produced from renewable sources.
    b. A tax credit allowed for the purchase of a motor vehicle that operates on an alternative fuel source (i.e., nonfossil fuels).
    c. A deduction for state and local income taxes.
    d. The deduction for personal casualty losses is subject to dollar and percentage limitations.
    e. Favorable treatment accorded to research and development expenditures.
    f. A deduction allowed for income resulting from U.S. production (manufacturing) activities.
    g. The deduction allowed for contributions to qualified charitable organizations.
    h. An election that allows certain corporations to avoid the corporate income tax and pass losses through to their shareholders.

50. **LO.7, 8** Discuss the probable justification for each of the following aspects of the tax law:
    a. A tax credit is allowed for amounts spent to furnish care for minor children while the parent works.
    b. Deductions for interest on home mortgage and property taxes on personal residence.
    c. The income splitting benefits of filing a joint return.
    d. Gambling losses in excess of gambling gains.
    e. Net operating losses of a current year can be carried back to profitable years.
    f. A taxpayer who sells property on an installment basis can recognize gain on the sale over the period the payments are received.
    g. The exclusion from Federal tax of certain interest income from state and local bonds.
    h. Prepaid income is taxed to the recipient in the year received and not in the year it is earned.

51. **LO.7** Mia owns a warehouse that has a cost basis to her of $80,000. The city condemns the warehouse to make room for a new fire station. It pays Mia $400,000 for the property, its agreed-to fair market value. Shortly after the condemnation, Mia purchases another warehouse as a replacement. What is her recognized gain if the new property cost:
    a. $280,000?
    b. $444,000?
    c. $80,000?
    d. What, if any, is the justification for deferring the recognition of gain on the involuntary conversion?

52. **LO.8** A mother sells a valuable collection of antiques to her daughter for $1,000. What judicial concept might the IRS invoke to question this transaction?

53. **LO.8** Edward leases real estate to Janet for a period of 20 years. Janet makes capital improvements to the property. When the lease expires, Edward reclaims the property, including the improvements made by Janet.
    a. Under current law, at what point does Edward recognize income as a result of Janet's improvements?
    b. Has the law in part (a) always been the rule?
    c. What is the justification, if any, for the current rule?

Working with the Tax Law

LEARNING OBJECTIVES: *After completing Chapter 2, you should be able to:*

LO.1 **Distinguish between the statutory, administrative, and judicial sources of the tax law and understand the purpose of each source.**

LO.2 **Locate and work with the appropriate tax law sources.**

LO.3 **Develop an awareness of tax research tools.**

LO.4 **Describe the tax research process.**

LO.5 **Communicate the results of the tax research process in a client letter and a tax file memorandum.**

LO.6 **Apply tax research techniques and planning procedures.**

LO.7 **Be aware of taxation on the CPA examination.**

CHAPTER OUTLINE

IMPORTANCE OF TAX RESEARCH

Early in December 2014, Fred and Megan Samuels review their financial and tax situation with their son, Sam, and daughter-in-law, Dana, who live with them. Fred and Megan are in the 28% tax bracket in 2014. Both Sam and Dana are age 21. Sam, a student at a nearby university, owns some publicly traded stock that he inherited from his grandmother. A current sale would result in approximately $8,000 of gross income ($19,000 amount realized − $11,000 adjusted basis). At this point, Fred and Megan provide about 55% of Sam and Dana's support. Although neither is now employed, Sam has earned $960 and Dana has earned $900. The problem: Should the stock be sold, and would the sale prohibit Fred and Megan from claiming Sam and Dana as dependents? Would the stock sale in 2014 result in a tax liability for Sam and Dana?

Read the chapter and formulate your responses.

F ederal tax law is a mixture of statutory provisions, administrative pronounce-ments, and court decisions. Anyone who has attempted to work with this body of knowledge is familiar with its complexity. Tax research provides the vehicle by which one makes sense out of this complexity.

2-1 TAX SOURCES

LO.1

Distinguish between the statutory, administrative, and judicial sources of the tax law and understand the purpose of each source.

Understanding taxation requires a mastery of the sources of the *rules of tax law.* These sources include not only legislative provisions in the form of the Internal Revenue Code but also congressional Committee Reports, Treasury Department Regulations, other Treasury Department pronouncements, and court decisions. Thus, the *primary sources* of tax information include pronouncements from all three branches of government: legislative, executive, and judicial.

In addition to being able to locate and interpret the sources of the tax law, a tax professional must understand the relative weight of authority within these sources. The tax law is of little significance, however, until it is applied to a set of facts and circumstances. This chapter, therefore, both introduces the statutory, administrative, and judicial sources of tax law and explains how the law is applied to individ-ual and business transactions. It also explains how to apply research techniques and use planning procedures effectively. A large part of tax research focuses on determining the intent of Congress.

Frequently, uncertainty in the tax law causes disputes between the Internal Revenue Service (IRS) and taxpayers. Due to these *gray areas* and the complexity of the tax law, a taxpayer may have more than one alternative for structuring a financial transaction. In structuring financial transactions and engaging in other tax planning activities, the tax adviser must be cognizant that the objective of tax planning is not necessarily to minimize the tax liability. Instead, a taxpayer should maximize his or her after-tax return, which may include maximizing nontax as well as noneconomic benefits.

2-1a Statutory Sources of the Tax Law

Statutory sources of law include the Constitution (Article I, Sections 7, 8, and 10), tax treaties (agreements between countries to mitigate the double taxation of tax-payers subject to the tax laws of those countries), and the Internal Revenue Code. The Constitution grants Congress the power to impose and collect taxes and author-izes the creation of treaties with other countries. The power of Congress to imple-ment and collect taxes is summarized in the Internal Revenue Code, the official title of U.S. tax law, and it is the basis for arriving at solutions to all tax questions.

Origin of the Internal Revenue Code

Before 1939, the statutory provisions relating to Federal taxation were contained in the individual revenue acts enacted by Congress. Because dealing with many sepa-rate acts was inconvenient and confusing, Congress codified all of the Federal tax laws in 1939. Known as the Internal Revenue Code of 1939, the codification arranged all Federal tax provisions in a logical sequence and placed them in a sepa-rate part of the Federal statutes. A further rearrangement took place in 1954 and resulted in the Internal Revenue Code of 1954, which continued in effect until 1986, when it was replaced by the Internal Revenue Code of 1986. Although Con-gress did not recodify the law in the Tax Reform Act (TRA) of 1986, the magnitude of the changes made by TRA of 1986 did provide some rationale for renaming the Federal tax law the Internal Revenue Code of 1986.

The following observations help clarify the codification procedure:

- Neither the 1939 nor the 1954 Code substantially changed the tax law existing on the date of its enactment. Much of the 1939 Code, for example, was incor-porated into the 1954 Code; the major change was the reorganization and renumbering of the tax provisions.

TAX IN THE NEWS   Tax Freedom Day

In income tax history, 1913 was an important year. In that year, the Sixteenth Amendment to the Constitution was ratified:

The Congress shall have power to tax and collect taxes on incomes, from whatever source derived, without apportionment among the several States, and without regard to any census or enumeration.

The first income tax legislation that definitely was constitutional was passed that same year.

According to the Tax Foundation, in 2013, Tax Freedom Day fell on April 18, five days later than in 2012. Tax Freedom Day is the date on which an average taxpayer through working has paid off his or her taxes for the year. Nevertheless, Americans still paid more in taxes in 2013 than they spent on food, clothing, and shelter combined. Of course, if you lived in Connecticut with the heaviest total tax burden, Tax Freedom Day fell on May 13. Mississippi celebrated Tax Freedom Day the earliest—on March 29, the 88th day of the year.

Source: Tax Foundation, "America Celebrates Tax Freedom Day," **www.taxfoundation.org/taxfreedomday.html**

- Although the 1986 Code resulted in substantial changes, only a minority of the statutory provisions were affected.[1]
- Statutory amendments to the tax law are integrated into the Code. For example, over the past few years, the Hiring Incentives to Restore Employment Act of 2010, the Patient Protection and Affordable Care Act of 2010, and the American Taxpayer Relief Act of 2012, as well as several other Acts, all became part of the Internal Revenue Code of 1986. In view of the frequency with which tax legislation has been enacted in recent years, it appears that the tax law will continue to be amended frequently.

The Legislative Process

Federal tax legislation generally originates in the House of Representatives, where it is first considered by the House Ways and Means Committee. It is also possible for tax bills to originate in the Senate when they are attached as riders to other legislative proposals.[2] If acceptable to the House Ways and Means Committee, the proposed bill is referred to the entire House of Representatives for approval or disapproval. Approved bills are sent to the Senate, where they are considered by the Senate Finance Committee.

The next step is referral from the Senate Finance Committee to the entire Senate. Assuming no disagreement between the House and Senate, passage by the Senate results in referral to the President for approval or veto. If the bill is approved or if the President's veto is overridden, the bill becomes law and part of the Internal Revenue Code of 1986.

House and Senate versions of major tax bills frequently differ. One reason bills are often changed in the Senate is that each senator has considerable latitude to make amendments when the Senate as a whole is voting on a bill referred to it by the Senate Finance Committee.[3] In contrast, the entire House of Representatives either accepts or rejects what is proposed by the House Ways and Means Committee, and changes from the floor are rare. When the Senate version of the bill

---

[1]This point is important in assessing judicial decisions interpreting provisions of the Internal Revenue Code of 1939 and the Internal Revenue Code of 1954. If the same provision was included in the Internal Revenue Code of 1986 and has not been subsequently amended, the provision and the related judicial decision have continuing validity.

[2]The Tax Equity and Fiscal Responsibility Act of 1982 originated in the Senate, and its constitutionality was unsuccessfully challenged in the courts. The Senate version of the Deficit Reduction Act of 1984 was attached as an amendment to the Federal Boat Safety Act.

[3]During the passage of the Tax Reform Act of 1986, Senate leaders tried to make the bill *amendment proof* to avoid the normal amendment process.

FIGURE 2.1	Legislative Process for Tax Bills

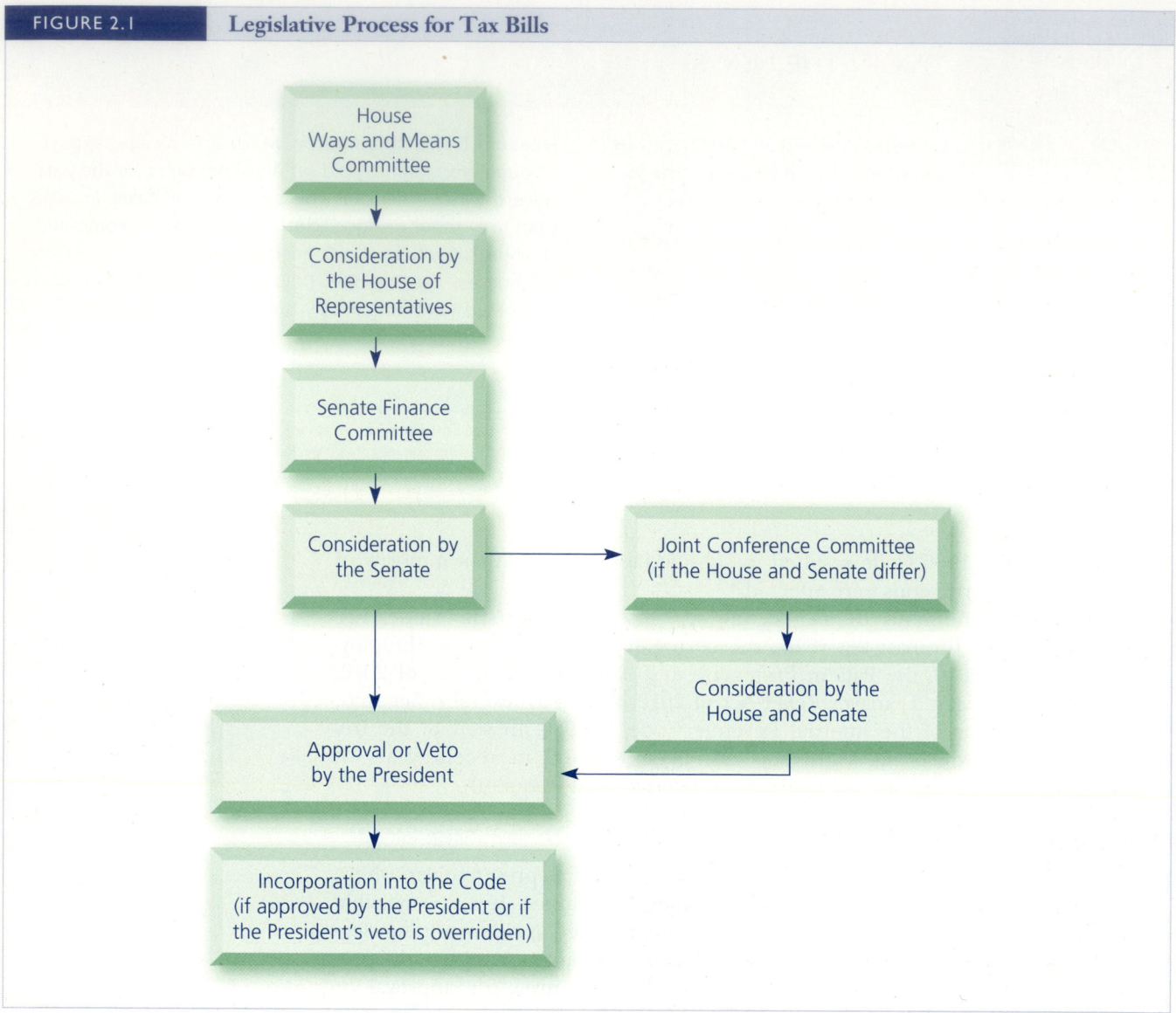

differs from that passed by the House, the Joint Conference Committee, which includes members of both the House Ways and Means Committee and the Senate Finance Committee, is called upon to resolve the differences. The deliberations of the Joint Conference Committee usually produce a compromise between the two versions, which is then voted on by both the House and the Senate. If both bodies accept the bill, it is referred to the President for approval or veto. Former Senator Daniel Patrick Moynihan observed that in the last hours of Congress, the White House and lawmakers often agree on a "1,200-page monster, we vote for it; nobody knows what is in it." Figure 2.1 summarizes the typical legislative process for tax bills.

The role of the Joint Conference Committee indicates the importance of compromise in the legislative process. As an example of the practical effect of the compromise process, consider Figure 2.2, which shows what happened with amendments to the first-time homebuyer credit in the American Recovery and Reinvestment Tax Act of 2009.

Referrals from the House Ways and Means Committee, the Senate Finance Committee, and the Joint Conference Committee are usually accompanied by Committee Reports. These Committee Reports often explain the provisions of the proposed legislation and are a valuable source for ascertaining the *intent of Congress*. What Congress had in mind when it considered and enacted tax legislation is, of course, the

| FIGURE 2.2 | Example of Compromise in the Joint Conference Committee |

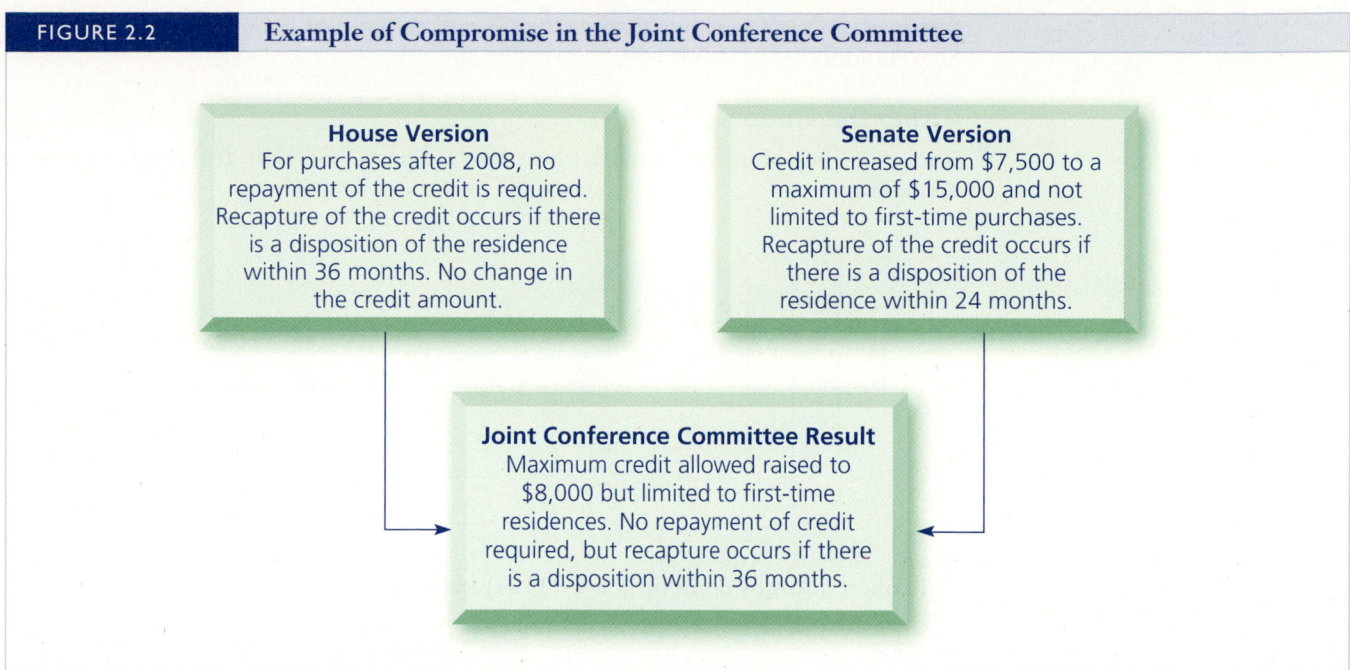

House Version
For purchases after 2008, no repayment of the credit is required. Recapture of the credit occurs if there is a disposition of the residence within 36 months. No change in the credit amount.

Senate Version
Credit increased from $7,500 to a maximum of $15,000 and not limited to first-time purchases. Recapture of the credit occurs if there is a disposition of the residence within 24 months.

Joint Conference Committee Result
Maximum credit allowed raised to $8,000 but limited to first-time residences. No repayment of credit required, but recapture occurs if there is a disposition within 36 months.

key to interpreting such legislation by taxpayers, the IRS, and the courts. Because Regulations normally are not issued immediately after a statute is enacted, taxpayers often look to Committee Reports to determine congressional intent.

Arrangement of the Code

The Internal Revenue Code of 1986 is found in Title 26 of the U.S. Code. In working with the Code, it helps to understand the format. Note, for example, the following partial table of contents:

> Subtitle A. Income Taxes
>   Chapter 11. Normal Taxes and Surtaxes
>   Subchapter A. Determination of Tax Liability
>   Part I. Tax on Individuals
>   Sections 1–5
>   Part II. Tax on Corporations
>   Sections 11–12

In referring to a provision of the Code, the *key* is usually the Section number. In citing Section 2(a) (dealing with the status of a surviving spouse), for example, it is unnecessary to include Subtitle A, Chapter 1, Subchapter A, Part I. Merely mentioning Section 2(a) will suffice, because the Section numbers run consecutively and do not begin again with each new Subtitle, Chapter, Subchapter, or Part. Not all Code Section numbers are used, however. Notice that Part I ends with Section 5 and Part II starts with Section 11 (at present, there are no Sections 6, 7, 8, 9, and 10).[4]

Tax practitioners commonly refer to some specific areas of income tax law by their Subchapters. Some of the more common Subchapter designations include Subchapter C ("Corporate Distributions and Adjustments"), Subchapter K ("Partners and Partnerships"), and Subchapter S ("Tax Treatment of S Corporations and Their Shareholders"). In the last situation in particular, it is much more convenient to describe the subject of the applicable Code provisions (Sections 1361–1379) as

---

[4]When the 1954 Code was drafted, some Section numbers were intentionally omitted so that later changes could be incorporated into the Code without disrupting its organization. When Congress does not leave enough space, subsequent Code Sections are given A, B, C, etc., designations. A good example is the treatment of §§ 280A through 280H.

S corporation status rather than as the "Tax Treatment of S Corporations and Their Shareholders."

Citing the Code

Code Sections often are broken down into subparts.[5] Section 2(a)(1)(A) serves as an example.

Broken down by content, § 2(a)(1)(A) becomes:

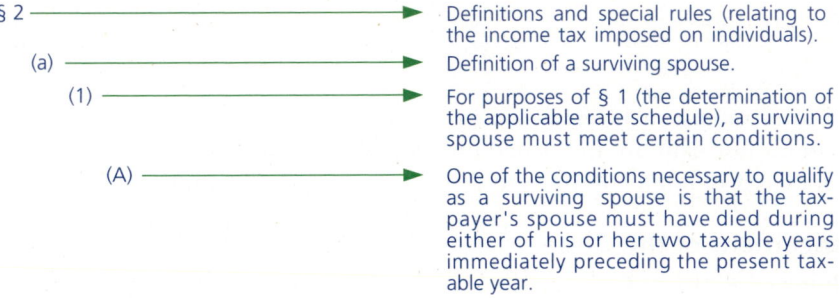

§ 2	→	Definitions and special rules (relating to the income tax imposed on individuals).
(a)	→	Definition of a surviving spouse.
(1)	→	For purposes of § 1 (the determination of the applicable rate schedule), a surviving spouse must meet certain conditions.
(A)	→	One of the conditions necessary to qualify as a surviving spouse is that the taxpayer's spouse must have died during either of his or her two taxable years immediately preceding the present taxable year.

Throughout the text, references to the Code Sections are in the form given above. The symbols "§" and "§§" are used in place of "Section" and "Sections," respectively. Unless otherwise stated, all Code references are to the Internal Revenue Code of 1986. The following table summarizes the format that will be used:

Complete Reference	Text Reference
Section 2(a)(1)(A) of the Internal Revenue Code of 1986	§ 2(a)(1)(A)
Sections 1 and 2 of the Internal Revenue Code of 1986	§§ 1 and 2
Section 2 of the Internal Revenue Code of 1954	§ 2 of the Internal Revenue Code of 1954
Section 12(d) of the Internal Revenue Code of 1939[7]	§ 12(d) of the Internal Revenue Code of 1939

2-1b Administrative Sources of the Tax Law

The administrative sources of the Federal tax law can be grouped as follows: Treasury Department Regulations, Revenue Rulings and Revenue Procedures, and various other administrative pronouncements (see Exhibit 2.1). All are issued by either the U.S. Treasury Department or the IRS.

---

[5]Some Code Sections do not require subparts. See, for example, §§ 211 and 241.

[6]Some Code Sections omit the subsection designation and use the paragraph designation as the first subpart. See, for example, §§ 212(1) and 1222(1).

[7]Section 12(d) of the Internal Revenue Code of 1939 is the predecessor to § 2 of the Internal Revenue Code of 1954 and the Internal Revenue Code of 1986. Keep in mind that the 1954 Code superseded the 1939 Code and the 1986 Code has superseded the 1954 Code. Footnote 1 of this chapter explains why references to the 1939 or 1954 Code are included.

EXHIBIT 2.1	Administrative Sources	
Source	**Location**	**Authority****
Regulations	*Federal Register**	Force and effect of law.
Temporary Regulations	*Federal Register** *Internal Revenue Bulletin* *Cumulative Bulletin*	May be cited as a precedent.
Proposed Regulations	*Federal Register** *Internal Revenue Bulletin* *Cumulative Bulletin*	Preview of final Regulations.
Revenue Rulings Revenue Procedures Treasury Decisions Actions on Decisions	*Internal Revenue Bulletin* *Cumulative Bulletin*	Do not have the force and effect of law.
General Counsel Memoranda Technical Advice Memoranda	Tax Analysts' *Tax Notes;* RIA's *Internal Memoranda of the IRS;* CCH's *IRS Position Reporter*	May not be cited as a precedent.
Letter Rulings	Research Institute of America and Commerce Clearing House tax services	Applicable only to taxpayer addressed. No precedential force.

* Finalized, Temporary, and Proposed Regulations are published in soft-cover form by several publishers.

** Each of these sources may be substantial authority for purposes of the accuracy-related penalty in § 6662 (discussed on pages 2-27 and 2-30; Notice 90–20, 1990–1 C.B. 328).

Treasury Department Regulations

Regulations are issued by the U.S. Treasury Department under authority granted by Congress.[8] Interpretive by nature, they provide taxpayers with considerable guidance on the meaning and application of the Code. Regulations, which may be issued in *proposed, temporary,* or *final* form, carry considerable authority as the official interpretation of tax statutes. They are an important factor to consider in complying with the tax law.

Because Regulations interpret the Code, they are arranged in the same sequence as the Code. A number is added at the beginning, however, to indicate the type of tax or administrative, procedural, or definitional matter to which they relate. For example, the prefix 1 designates the Regulations under the income tax law. Thus, the Regulations under Code § 2 are cited as Reg. § 1.2, with subparts added for further identification. The numbering patterns of these subparts often have no correlation with the Code subsections. The prefix 20 designates estate tax Regulations, 25 covers gift tax Regulations, 31 relates to employment taxes, and 301 refers to procedure and administration. This list is not all-inclusive.

ETHICS & EQUITY Is It Ethical for the IRS to Ideologically Profile Nonprofit Advocacy Groups?

In 2013, the Treasury Department Inspector General issued a report that concluded that the IRS scrutinized nonprofit advocacy groups in different ways, with some advocacy groups targeted for additional scrutiny based on their political views. Is this type of scrutiny appropriate for the IRS? Why or why not?

---

[8]§ 7805.

New Regulations and changes to existing Regulations are usually issued in proposed form before they are finalized. The interval between the proposal of a Regulation and its finalization permits taxpayers and other interested parties to comment on the propriety of the proposal. **Proposed Regulations** under Code § 2, for example, are cited as Prop.Reg. § 1.2. The Tax Court indicates that Proposed Regulations carry little weight. **Finalized Regulations** have the force and effect of law.[9]

Sometimes the Treasury Department issues **Temporary Regulations** relating to matters where immediate guidance is important. These Regulations are issued without the comment period required for Proposed Regulations. Temporary Regulations have the same authoritative value as final Regulations and may be cited as precedents. However, Temporary Regulations must also be issued as Proposed Regulations and automatically expire within three years after the date of issuance.[10] Temporary Regulations and the simultaneously issued Proposed Regulations carry more weight than traditional Proposed Regulations. An example of a Temporary Regulation is Temp.Reg. § 1.956–2T, which provides a definition of a U.S. property.

Proposed, Temporary, and final Regulations are published in the *Federal Register*, in the *Internal Revenue Bulletin* (I.R.B.), and by major tax services. Final Regulations are issued as Treasury Decisions (TDs).

Regulations may also be classified as *legislative, interpretive,* or *procedural.* This classification scheme is discussed under Assessing the Validity of a Treasury Regulation later in the chapter.

Revenue Rulings and Revenue Procedures

Revenue Rulings are official pronouncements of the National Office of the IRS.[11] They typically provide one or more examples of how the IRS would apply a law to specific fact situations. Like Regulations, Revenue Rulings are designed to provide interpretation of the tax law. However, they do not carry the same legal force and effect as Regulations and usually deal with more restricted problems. Regulations are approved by the Secretary of the Treasury, whereas Revenue Rulings generally are not.

Although letter rulings (discussed in the next section) are not the same as Revenue Rulings, a Revenue Ruling often results from a specific taxpayer's request for a letter ruling. If the IRS believes that a taxpayer's request for a letter ruling deserves official publication because of its widespread impact, the letter ruling will be converted into a Revenue Ruling and issued for the information and guidance of taxpayers, tax practitioners, and IRS personnel. Names, identifying descriptions, and money amounts are changed to conceal the identity of the requesting taxpayer. Revenue Rulings also arise from technical advice to District Offices of the IRS, court decisions, suggestions from tax practitioner groups, and various tax publications.

Revenue Procedures are issued in the same manner as Revenue Rulings but deal with the internal management practices and procedures of the IRS. Familiarity with these procedures can increase taxpayer compliance and help the IRS administer the tax laws more efficiently. A taxpayer's failure to follow a Revenue Procedure can result in unnecessary delay or, in a discretionary situation, can cause the IRS to decline to act on behalf of the taxpayer.

Both Revenue Rulings and Revenue Procedures serve an important function by providing *guidance* to IRS personnel and taxpayers in handling routine tax matters. For example, one recent Revenue Procedure provided inflation-adjusted amounts for various Code provisions. Revenue Rulings and Revenue Procedures generally apply retroactively and may be revoked or modified by subsequent rulings or procedures, Regulations, legislation, or court decisions.

Revenue Rulings and Revenue Procedures are published weekly by the U.S. Government in the *Internal Revenue Bulletin* (I.R.B.).

---

[9]*F. W. Woolworth Co.,* 54 T.C. 1233 (1970); *Harris M. Miller,* 70 T.C. 448 (1978); and *James O. Tomerlin Trust,* 87 T.C. 876 (1986).

[10]§ 7805(e).
[11]§ 7805(a).

The proper form for citing Revenue Rulings is as follows. Revenue Procedures are cited in the same manner, except that "Rev.Proc." is substituted for "Rev.Rul."

Rev.Rul. 2013–10, 2013–26 I.R.B. 1257.

Explanation: Revenue Ruling Number 10, appearing on page 1257 of the 26th weekly issue of the *Internal Revenue Bulletin* for 2013.

Revenue Rulings and other tax resources may be found in the *Tax Almanac*, a free online resource from Intuit at **www.taxalmanac.org**.[12]

Letter Rulings

Letter rulings are issued for a fee upon a taxpayer's request and describe how the IRS will treat a *proposed* transaction for tax purposes. They apply only to the taxpayer who asks for and obtains the ruling, but post-1984 letter rulings may be substantial authority for purposes of the accuracy-related penalty.[13] Letter rulings can be useful to taxpayers who want to be certain of how a transaction will be taxed before proceeding with it. Letter rulings also allow taxpayers to avoid unexpected tax costs. Although the procedure for requesting a ruling can be quite cumbersome, sometimes requesting a ruling is the most effective way to carry out tax planning. Nevertheless, the IRS limits the issuance of individual rulings to restricted, preannounced areas of taxation. The main reason the IRS will not rule in certain areas is that they involve fact-oriented situations. Thus, a ruling may not be obtained on many of the problems that are particularly troublesome for taxpayers.[14] The IRS issues more than 2,000 letter rulings each year.

The law now requires the IRS to make individual rulings available for public inspection after identifying details are deleted.[15] Published digests of private letter rulings can be found in *Private Letter Rulings* (published by RIA), BNA's *Daily Tax Reports,* and Tax Analysts' *Tax Notes.* In addition, computerized databases of letter rulings are available through several private publishers.

Letter rulings are issued multidigit file numbers that indicate the year and week of issuance as well as the number of the ruling during that week. Consider, for example, Ltr.Rul. 201314038, which determines that income derived by a

---

[12]Commercial sources for Revenue Rulings and Revenue Procedures are available, usually requiring a subscription fee. Older Revenue Rulings and Revenue Procedures are often cited as being published in the *Cumulative Bulletin* (C.B.) rather than in the *Internal Revenue Bulletin* (I.R.B.).

[13]See pages 2-27 and 2-30; Notice 90–20, 1990–1 C.B. 328. In this regard, letter rulings differ from Revenue Rulings, which are applicable to *all* taxpayers. A letter ruling may later lead to the issuance of a Revenue Ruling if the holding affects many taxpayers. In its Agents' Manual, the IRS

indicates that letter rulings may be used as a guide with other research materials in formulating a District Office position on an issue. The IRS is required to charge a taxpayer a fee for letter rulings, determination letters, etc.

[14]Rev.Proc. 2014–3, 2014–1 I.R.B. 111 contains a list of areas in which the IRS will not issue advance rulings. From time to time, subsequent Revenue Procedures are issued that modify or amplify Rev.Proc. 2014–3.

[15]§ 6110.

master limited partnership from processing natural gas into dimethyl ether is qualified income for a real estate investment trust.

2013	14	038
Year 2013	14th week of issuance	38th ruling issued during the 14th week

Other Administrative Pronouncements

Treasury Decisions (TDs) are issued by the Treasury Department to promulgate new Regulations, amend or otherwise change existing Regulations, or announce the position of the Government on selected court decisions. Like Revenue Rulings and Revenue Procedures, TDs are published in the *Internal Revenue Bulletin* and subsequently transferred to the *Cumulative Bulletin*.

The IRS also publishes other administrative communications in the *Internal Revenue Bulletin*, such as Announcements, Notices, IRs (News Releases), Legal Memoranda (ILMs), Chief Counsel Notices (CC), and Prohibited Transaction Exemptions.

Like letter rulings, **determination letters** are issued at the request of taxpayers and provide guidance on the application of the tax law. They differ from letter rulings in that the issuing source is the Area Director rather than the National Office of the IRS. Also, determination letters usually involve *completed* (as opposed to proposed) transactions. Determination letters are not published and are made known only to the party making the request.

The following examples illustrate the distinction between letter rulings and determination letters:

Example 1

The shareholders of Red Corporation and Green Corporation want assurance that the consolidation of the corporations into Blue Corporation will be a nontaxable reorganization. The proper approach is to request that the National Office of the IRS issue a letter ruling concerning the income tax effect of the proposed transaction.

Example 2

Chris operates a barbershop in which he employs eight barbers. To comply with the rules governing income tax and payroll tax withholdings, Chris wants to know whether the barbers working for him are employees or independent contractors. The proper procedure is to request a determination letter on their status from the appropriate Area Director.

Several internal memoranda that constitute the working law of the IRS are released. These General Counsel Memoranda (GCMs), Technical Advice Memoranda (TAMs), Internal Legal Memorandum (ILM), and Field Service Advices (FSAs) are not officially published, and the IRS indicates that they may not be cited as precedents by taxpayers.[16] However, these working documents do explain the IRS's position on various issues.

The National Office of the IRS releases **Technical Advice Memoranda (TAMs)** weekly. TAMs resemble letter rulings in that they give the IRS's determination of an issue. However, they differ in several respects. Letter rulings deal with proposed transactions and are issued to taxpayers at their request. In contrast, TAMs deal with completed transactions. Furthermore, TAMs arise from questions raised by IRS personnel during audits and are issued by the National Office of the IRS to its field personnel. TAMs are often requested for questions relating to exempt organizations and employee plans. TAMs are not officially published and may not be cited or used as precedent.[17] They are assigned file numbers according to the same procedure used for letter rulings. For example, TAM 201314021 refers to the 21st TAM issued during the 14th week of 2013.

---

[16]These are unofficially published by the publishers listed in Exhibit 2.1. Such internal memoranda for post-1984 transactions may be substantial authority for purposes of the accuracy-related penalty (see pages 2-27 and 2-30; Notice 90–20, 1990–1 C.B. 328).

[17]§ 6110(j)(3). Post-1984 TAMs may be substantial authority for purposes of avoiding the accuracy-related penalty. Notice 90–20, 1990–1 C.B. 328.

The Office of Chief Counsel prepares Field Service Advice (FSAs) to help IRS employees. They are issued in response to requests for advice, guidance, and analysis on difficult or significant tax issues. FSAs are not binding on either the taxpayer to whom they pertain or the IRS. For example, FSA 200233016 states that § 269 may be used to disallow foreign tax credits and deductions that arise from a series of reorganizations if the underlying transaction's principal purpose is to secure tax benefits.

Field Service Advices are being replaced by a new form of field guidance called Technical Expedited Advice Memoranda (TEAMs). The purpose of TEAMs is to expedite legal guidance to field agents as disputes are developing. FSAs are reverting to their original purpose of case-specific development of facts.

A TEAM guidance differs from a TAM in several ways, including a mandatory presubmission conference involving the taxpayer. In the event of a tentatively adverse conclusion for the taxpayer or the field agent, a conference of right is offered to the taxpayer and to the field agent; once the conference of right is held, no further conferences are offered.

2-1c Judicial Sources of the Tax Law

Five Federal courts have jurisdiction over tax disputes between the IRS and taxpayers: the U.S. Tax Court, the U.S. District Court, the U.S. Court of Federal Claims, the U.S. Court of Appeals, and the U.S. Supreme Court.

The Judicial Process in General

After a taxpayer has exhausted some or all of the remedies available within the IRS (i.e., no satisfactory settlement has been reached at the agent or at the Appeals Division level), the dispute can be taken to the Federal courts. The dispute is first considered by a **court of original jurisdiction** (known as a trial court) with any appeal (either by the taxpayer or the IRS) taken to the appropriate appellate court. In most situations, the taxpayer has a choice of any of *four trial courts:* a **Federal District Court**, the **U.S. Court of Federal Claims**, the **U.S. Tax Court**, or the **Small Cases Division** of the U.S. Tax Court. The trial and appellate court system for Federal tax litigation is illustrated in Figure 2.3.

The broken line between the U.S. Tax Court and the Small Cases Division indicates that there is no appeal from the Small Cases Division. The jurisdiction of the Small Cases Division is limited to cases involving amounts of $50,000 or less. The proceedings of the Small Cases Division are informal (e.g., no necessity for the taxpayer to be represented by a lawyer or other tax adviser). Special trial judges rather than Tax Court judges preside over these proceedings. The decisions of the Small Cases Division are not precedents for any other court decision and are not reviewable by any higher court. Proceedings can be more timely and less expensive in the Small Cases Division. Some of these cases can now be found on the U.S. Tax Court website.

American law, following English law, is frequently *created* by judicial decisions. Under the doctrine of *stare decisis*, each case (except in the Small Cases Division) has precedential value for future cases with the same controlling set of facts. Most Federal and state appellate court decisions and some decisions of trial courts are published. Published court decisions are organized by jurisdiction (Federal or state) and level of court (trial or appellate).

A decision of a particular court is called its holding. Sometimes a decision includes *dicta* or incidental opinions beyond the current facts. Such passing remarks, illustrations, or analogies are not essential to the current holding. Although the holding has precedential value under *stare decisis*, dicta are not binding on a future court.

Knowledge of several terms is important in understanding court decisions. The term *plaintiff* refers to the party requesting action in a court, and the *defendant* is the party against whom the suit is brought. Sometimes a court uses the terms *petitioner* and *respondent*. In general, *petitioner* is a synonym for *plaintiff*, and *respondent* is a synonym for *defendant*. At the trial court level, a taxpayer is normally the plaintiff

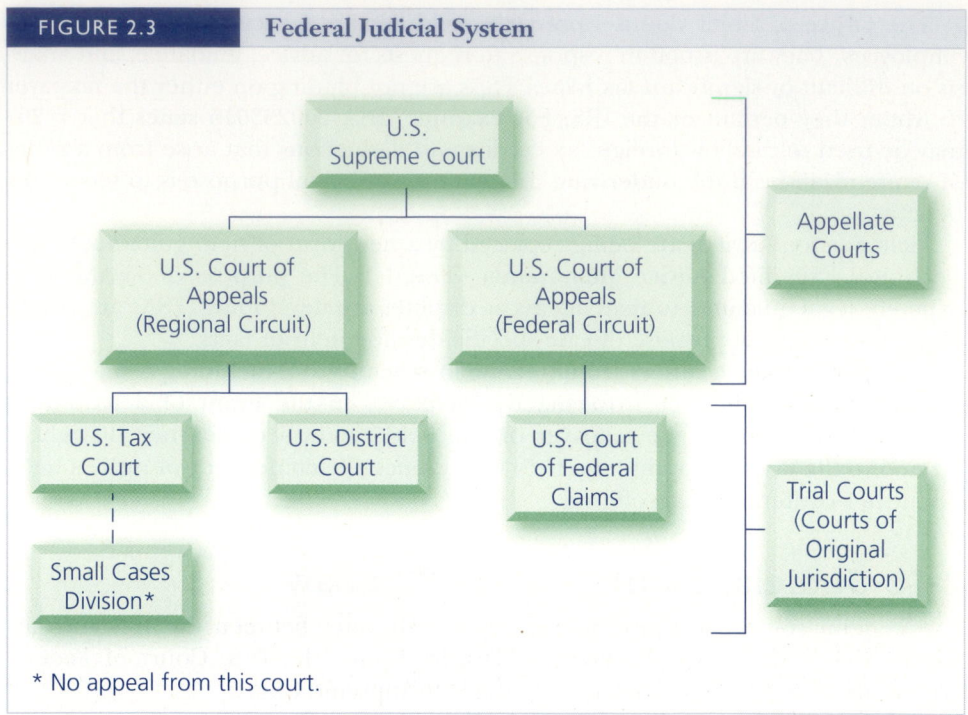

FIGURE 2.3 **Federal Judicial System**

* No appeal from this court.

(or petitioner), and the Government is the defendant (or respondent). If the taxpayer wins and the Government appeals as the new petitioner (or appellant), the taxpayer becomes the new respondent.

Trial Courts

The differences among the various trial courts (courts of original jurisdiction) can be summarized as follows:

- *Number of courts.* There is only one Court of Federal Claims and only one Tax Court, but there are many Federal District Courts. The taxpayer does not select the District Court that will hear the dispute, but must sue in the one that has jurisdiction where the taxpayer resides.
- *Number of judges.* District Courts have various numbers of judges, but only one judge hears a case. The Court of Federal Claims has 16 judges, and the Tax Court has 19 regular judges. The entire Tax Court, however, reviews a case (the case is sent to court conference) only when more important or novel tax issues are involved. Many cases will be heard and decided by one of the 19 regular judges. If a case is reviewed by the full Tax Court, such an *en banc* decision has compelling authority.
- *Location.* The Court of Federal Claims meets most often in Washington, D.C., whereas a District Court meets at a prescribed seat for the particular district. Each state has at least one District Court, and many of the more populous states have more than one. Choosing the District Court usually minimizes the inconvenience and expense of traveling for the taxpayer and his or her counsel. Although the Tax Court is officially based in Washington, D.C., the various judges travel to different parts of the country and hear cases at predetermined locations and dates. This procedure eases the distance problem for the taxpayer, but it can mean a delay before the case comes to trial and is decided.
- *Jurisdiction of the Court of Federal Claims.* The Court of Federal Claims has jurisdiction over any claim against the United States that is based upon the Constitution, any Act of Congress, or any regulation of an executive department. Thus, the Court of Federal Claims hears nontax litigation as well as tax cases. This forum appears to be more favorable for issues having an equitable or

TAX IN THE NEWS   **Dispute Alternatives within the IRS**

If a taxpayer disagrees with the findings of a Revenue Agent, the taxpayer may appeal to the Appeals Division. This Appeals Division is an independent division within the IRS that provides a forum for a taxpayer to contest a compliance action by any part of the IRS.

If the taxpayer decides not to go to the Appeals Division, the taxpayer may take advantage of several arbitration and mediation alternatives. Under a Fast Track Mediation option, an Appeals Officer or team case leader trained in mediation techniques will help speed up the IRS settlement process. A Fast Track Settlement attempts to resolve disputes through a mediated settlement within 170 days.

Source: Based on Leeah Fontaine, Tax Clinic, "Overview of IRS Pre-Appeals Alternative Dispute Resolution Methods," *The Tax Adviser*, April 2012, pp. 229–231.

pro-business orientation (as opposed to purely technical issues) and for those requiring extensive discovery of evidence.[18]

- *Jurisdiction of the Tax Court and District Courts.* The Tax Court hears only tax cases and is the most popular forum. The District Courts hear a wide variety of nontax cases, including drug crimes and other Federal violations, as well as tax cases. Some Tax Court judges have been appointed from IRS or Treasury Department positions. For these reasons, some people suggest that the Tax Court has more expertise in tax matters.

- *Jury trial.* The only court in which a taxpayer can obtain a jury trial is a District Court. But because juries can decide only questions of fact and not questions of law, even taxpayers who choose the District Court route often do not request a jury trial. In that event, the judge will decide all issues. Note that a District Court decision applies only in the district in which the court has jurisdiction.

- *Payment of deficiency.* For the Court of Federal Claims or a District Court to have jurisdiction, the taxpayer must pay the tax deficiency assessed by the IRS and sue for a refund. A taxpayer who wins (assuming no successful appeal by the Government) recovers the tax paid plus appropriate interest. For the Tax Court, however, jurisdiction is usually obtained without first paying the assessed tax deficiency. In the event the taxpayer loses in the Tax Court (and does not appeal or an appeal is unsuccessful), the deficiency must be paid with appropriate interest. With the elimination of the deduction for personal (consumer) interest (see Chapter 10), the Tax Court route of delaying payment of the deficiency can become expensive. By paying the tax, a taxpayer limits underpayment interest and penalties on the underpayment.

- *Termination of running of interest.* A taxpayer who selects the Tax Court may deposit a cash bond to stop the running of interest. The taxpayer must deposit both the amount of the tax and any accrued interest. If the taxpayer wins and the deposited amount is returned, the Government does not pay interest on the deposit.

- *Appeals.* Appeals from a District Court or a Tax Court decision are to the U.S. Court of Appeals for the circuit in which the taxpayer resides. Appeals from the Court of Federal Claims go to the Court of Appeals for the Federal Circuit. Few Tax Court cases are appealed, and when appeals are made, most are filed by the taxpayer rather than the IRS.

- *Bankruptcy.* When a taxpayer files a bankruptcy petition, the IRS, like other creditors, is prevented from taking action against the taxpayer. Sometimes a bankruptcy court may settle a tax claim.

For a summary of various attributes of the Federal trial courts, see Concept Summary 2.1.

---

[18]T. D. Peyser, "The Case for Selecting the Claims Court to Litigate a Federal Tax Liability," *The Tax Executive* (Winter 1988): 149.

CONCEPT SUMMARY 2.1

Federal Judicial System: Trial Courts

Issue	U.S. Tax Court	U.S. District Court	U.S. Court of Federal Claims
Number of judges per court	19*	Varies	16
Payment of deficiency before trial	No	Yes	Yes
Jury trial available	No	Yes	No
Types of disputes	Tax cases only	Most criminal and civil issues	Claims against the United States
Jurisdiction	Nationwide	Location of taxpayer	Nationwide
IRS acquiescence policy	Yes	Yes	Yes
Appeal route	U.S. Court of Appeals	U.S. Court of Appeals	U.S. Court of Appeals for the Federal Circuit

* Normally; there are also 5 special trial judges and 13 senior judges.

Appellate Courts

The losing party can appeal a trial court decision to a **Circuit Court of Appeals**. The 11 geographic circuits, the circuit for the District of Columbia, and the Federal Circuit[19] appear in Figure 2.4. The appropriate circuit for an appeal depends on where the litigation originated. For example, an appeal from New York goes to the Second Circuit.

If the Government loses at the trial court level (District Court, Tax Court, or Court of Federal Claims), it need not (frequently does not) appeal. The fact that an appeal is not made, however, does not indicate that the IRS agrees with the result and will not litigate similar issues in the future. The IRS may decide not to appeal for a number of reasons. First, if the current litigation load is heavy, the IRS may decide that available personnel should be assigned to other more important cases. Second, the IRS may determine that this case is not a good one to appeal. Perhaps the taxpayer is in a sympathetic position or the facts are particularly strong in his or her favor. In that event, the IRS may wait to test the legal issues involved with a taxpayer who has a much weaker case. Third, if the appeal is from a District Court or the Tax Court, the Court of Appeals of jurisdiction could have some bearing on whether the IRS chooses to go forward with an appeal. Based on past experience and precedent, the IRS may conclude that the chance for success on a particular issue might be more promising in another Court of Appeals. If so, the IRS will wait for a similar case to arise in a different jurisdiction.

The Federal Circuit at the appellate level provides the taxpayer with an alternative forum to the Court of Appeals for his or her home circuit. Appeals from both the Tax Court and the District Court go to a taxpayer's home circuit. When a particular circuit has issued an adverse decision in a similar case, the taxpayer may prefer the Court of Federal Claims route, because any appeal will be to the Federal Circuit.

The Appellate Process

The *role* of the appellate court is limited to a review of the trial record compiled by the trial court. Thus, the appellate process usually involves a determination of whether the trial court applied the proper law in arriving at its decision. Rarely will an appellate court question a lower court's fact-finding determination.

---

[19] The Court of Appeals for the Federal Circuit was created, effective October 1, 1982, by P.L. No. 97-164 (4/2/82) to hear decisions appealed from the Claims Court (now the Court of Federal Claims).

FIGURE 2.4	The Federal Courts of Appeals

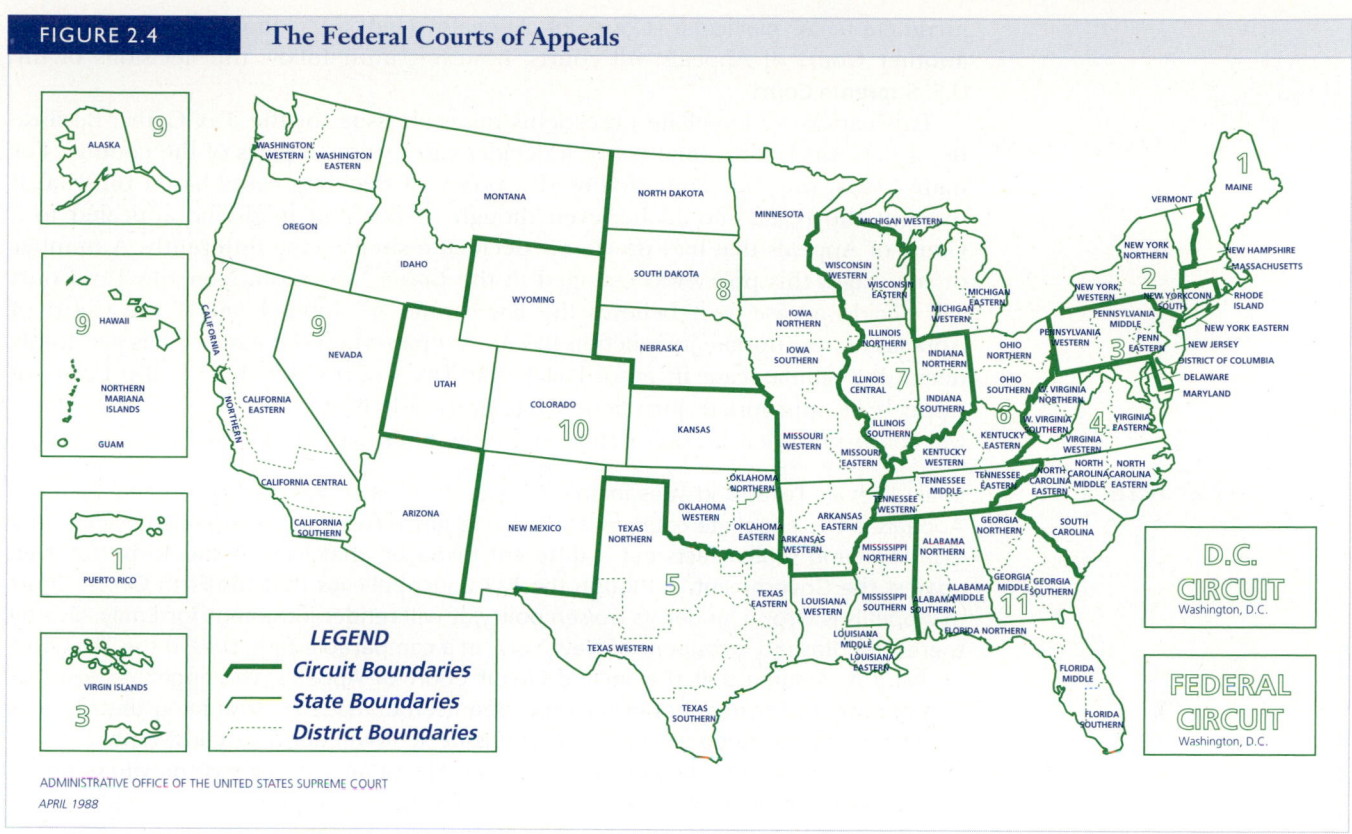

ADMINISTRATIVE OFFICE OF THE UNITED STATES SUPREME COURT
APRIL 1988

Both the Code and the Supreme Court indicate that Federal appellate courts are bound by findings of facts unless they are clearly erroneous.[20] This aspect of the appellate process is illustrated by a decision of the Court of Appeals for the District of Columbia involving whether a taxpayer was engaged in an activity for profit under § 183.[21] This appeals court specifically held that the "Tax Court's findings of facts are binding on Federal courts of appeals unless clearly erroneous." The court applauded the Tax Court for the thoroughness of its factual inquiry but could "not place the stamp of approval upon its eventual legal outcome." In reversing and remanding the decision to the Tax Court, the appellate court said that "the language of § 183, its legislative history and the applicable Treasury Regulation combine to demonstrate that the court's [Tax Court's] standard is erroneous as a matter of law." The appeals court held that this taxpayer's claims of deductibility were to be evaluated by proper legal standards.

An appeal can have any of a number of possible outcomes. The appellate court may approve (*affirm*) or disapprove (*reverse*) the lower court's finding, or it may send the case back for further consideration (*remand*). When many issues are involved, a mixed result is not unusual. Thus, the lower court may be affirmed (*aff'd*) on Issue A and reversed (*rev'd*) on Issue B, while Issue C is remanded (*rem'd*) for additional fact finding.

When more than one judge is involved in the decision-making process, disagreements are not uncommon. In addition to the majority view, one or more judges may concur (agree with the result reached but not with some or all of the reasoning) or dissent (disagree with the result). In any one case, of course, the majority view controls. But concurring and dissenting views can have an influence on other courts or at some subsequent date when the composition of the court has changed.

Appellate Precedents and the Tax Court District Courts, the Tax Court, and the Court of Federal Claims must abide by the **precedents** set by the Court of Appeals of

---

[20]§§ 7482(a) and (c). *Comm. v. Duberstein*, 60–2 USTC ¶9515, 5 AFTR 2d 1626, 80 S.Ct. 1190 (USSC, 1960). See Rule 52(a) of the Federal Rules of Civil Procedure.

[21]*Dreicer v. Comm.*, 81–2 USTC ¶9683, 48 AFTR 2d 5884, 665 F.2d 1292 (CA–DC, 1981).

jurisdiction. A particular Court of Appeals need not follow the decisions of another Court of Appeals. All courts, however, must follow the decisions of the **U.S. Supreme Court**.

This pattern of appellate precedents raises an issue for the Tax Court. Because the Tax Court is a national court, it decides cases from all parts of the country. For many years, the Tax Court followed a policy of deciding cases based on what it thought the result should be, even though its decision might be appealed to a Court of Appeals that had previously decided a similar case differently. A number of years ago, this policy was changed in the *Golsen*[22] decision. Now the Tax Court will decide a case as it believes the law should be applied *only* if the Court of Appeals of appropriate jurisdiction has not yet passed on the issue or has previously decided a similar case in accord with the Tax Court's decision. If the Court of Appeals of appropriate jurisdiction has previously held otherwise, the Tax Court will conform under the *Golsen* rule even though it disagrees with the holding.

Example 3	Emily lives in Texas and sues in the Tax Court on Issue A. The Fifth Circuit Court of Appeals is the appellate court of appropriate jurisdiction. It has already decided, in a case involving similar facts but a different taxpayer, that Issue A should be resolved against the Government. Although the Tax Court believes that the Fifth Circuit Court of Appeals is wrong, under its *Golsen* policy, it will render judgment for Emily. Shortly thereafter, Rashad, a resident of New York, in a comparable case, sues in the Tax Court on Issue A. Assume that the Second Circuit Court of Appeals, the appellate court of appropriate jurisdiction, has never expressed itself on Issue A. Presuming that the Tax Court has not reconsidered its position on Issue A, it will decide against Rashad. Thus, it is entirely possible for two taxpayers suing in the same court to end up with opposite results merely because they live in different parts of the country.

Appeal to the U.S. Supreme Court   Appeal to the U.S. Supreme Court is by **Writ of Certiorari**. If the Court agrees to hear the case, it will grant the Writ (*Cert. granted*). Most often, it will deny jurisdiction (*Cert. denied*). For whatever reason or reasons, the Supreme Court rarely hears tax cases. The Court usually grants certiorari to resolve a conflict among the Courts of Appeals (e.g., two or more appellate courts have assumed opposing positions on a particular issue) or where the tax issue is extremely important. The granting of a Writ of Certiorari indicates that at least four of the nine members of the Supreme Court believe that the issue is of sufficient importance to be heard by the full Court.

Judicial Citations

LO.2

Locate and work with the appropriate tax law sources.

Having briefly described the judicial process, it is appropriate to consider the more practical problem of the relationship of case law to tax research. As previously noted, court decisions are an important source of tax law. The ability to cite and locate a case is, therefore, a must in working with the tax law. Judicial citations usually follow a standard pattern: case name, volume number, reporter series, page or paragraph number, court (where necessary), and year of the decision (see Concept Summary 2.2).

Judicial Citations—The U.S. Tax Court   A good starting point is with the Tax Court, which issues two types of decisions: Regular and Memorandum, based on the Chief Judge's determination. The distinction between the two involves both substance and form. In terms of substance, *Memorandum* decisions deal with situations necessitating only the application of already established principles of law. *Regular* decisions involve novel issues not previously resolved by the court. In actual practice, however, this distinction is not always preserved. Not infrequently, Memorandum decisions will be encountered that appear to warrant Regular status and vice versa. At any rate, do not conclude that Memorandum decisions possess no value as precedents. Both represent the position of the Tax Court and, as such, can be relied on.

---

[22]*Jack E. Golsen*, 54 T.C. 742 (1970).

CONCEPT SUMMARY 2.2

Judicial Sources

Court	Location	Authority
U.S. Supreme Court	S.Ct. Series (West)	Highest authority
	U.S. Series (U.S. Gov't.)	
	L.Ed.2d (Lawyer's Co-op.)	
	AFTR (RIA)	
	USTC (CCH)	
U.S. Courts of Appeal	Federal 3d (West)	Next highest appellate court
	AFTR (RIA)	
	USTC (CCH)	
Tax Court (Regular decisions)	U.S. Gov't. Printing Office	Highest trial court*
	RIA/CCH separate services	
Tax Court (Memorandum decisions)	RIA T.C.Memo. (RIA)	Less authority than Regular T.C. decision
	TCM (CCH)	
U.S. Court of Federal Claims**	Federal Claims Reporter (West)	Similar authority as Tax Court
	AFTR (RIA)	
	USTC (CCH)	
U.S. District Courts	F.Supp.2d Series (West)	Lowest trial court
	AFTR (RIA)	
	USTC (CCH)	
Small Cases Division of Tax Court	U.S. Tax Court website***	No precedent value

*Theoretically, the Tax Court, Court of Federal Claims, and District Courts are on the same level of authority. But some people believe that because the Tax Court hears and decides tax cases from all parts of the country (i.e., it is a national court), its decisions may be more authoritative than a Court of Federal Claims or District Court decision.

**Before October 29, 1992, the U.S. Claims Court.

***Starting in 2001.

The Regular and Memorandum decisions issued by the Tax Court also differ in form. Memorandum decisions are made available but are not published by the government. Regular decisions are published by the U.S. Government in a series entitled *Tax Court of the United States Reports* (T.C.). Each volume of these *Reports* covers a six-month period (January 1 through June 30 and July 1 through December 31) and is given a succeeding volume number. But there is usually a time lag between the date a decision is rendered and the date it appears in bound form. A temporary citation may be necessary to help the researcher locate a recent Regular decision. Consider, for example, the temporary and permanent citations for *B.V. Belk, Jr.,* a decision filed on January 28, 2013:

Temporary Citation   { *B.V. Belk, Jr.,* 140 T.C. ___, No. 1 (2013).
                      { *Explanation:* Page number left blank because not yet known.

Permanent Citation   { *B.V. Belk, Jr.,* 140 T.C. 1 (2013).
                     { *Explanation:* Page number now available.

Both citations tell us that the case will ultimately appear in Volume 140 of the *Tax Court of the United States Reports.* But until this volume is bound and made available to the general public, the page number must be left blank. Instead, the temporary citation identifies the case as being the 1st Regular decision issued by the Tax Court since Volume 139 ended. With this information, the decision can easily be located in either of the special Tax Court services published by Commerce Clearing House (CCH) or Research Institute of America (RIA). Once Volume 140 is released, the permanent citation can be substituted and the number of the case dropped. Starting in 1999, both Regular decisions and Memorandum decisions are published on the U.S. Tax Court website (**www.ustaxcourt.gov**).

Before 1943, the Tax Court was called the Board of Tax Appeals, and its decisions were published as the *United States Board of Tax Appeals Reports* (B.T.A.). These 47 volumes cover the period from 1924 to 1942. For example, the citation *Karl Pauli*, 11 B.T.A. 784 (1928), refers to the 11th volume of the *Board of Tax Appeals Reports*, page 784, issued in 1928.

If the IRS loses in a decision, it may indicate whether it agrees or disagrees with the results reached by the court by publishing an **acquiescence** ("A" or "*Acq.*") or **nonacquiescence** ("NA" or "*Nonacq.*"), respectively. Until 1991, acquiescences and nonacquiescences were published only for certain Regular decisions of the Tax Court, but the IRS has expanded its acquiescence program to include other civil tax cases where guidance is helpful. The acquiescence or nonacquiescence is published in the *Internal Revenue Bulletin* and the *Cumulative Bulletin* as an *Action on Decision*. The IRS can retroactively revoke an acquiescence.

Most often, the IRS issues nonacquiescences to adverse decisions that are not appealed. In this manner, the Government indicates that it disagrees with the result reached, despite its decision not to seek review of the matter in an appellate court. A nonacquiescence provides a warning to taxpayers that a similar case cannot be settled administratively. A taxpayer will incur fees and expenses while the case moves through the IRS even though the IRS may be unwilling to litigate a fact pattern similar to a nonacquiescence decision.[23]

Although Memorandum decisions were not published by the U.S. Government until recently, they have been and are published by CCH and RIA. Consider, for example, the three different ways the *Nick R. Hughes* case can be cited:

> *Nick R. Hughes*, T.C.Memo. 2009–94
>
> *Explanation:* The 94th Memorandum decision issued by the Tax Court in 2009.

> *Nick R. Hughes*, 97 TCM 1488
>
> *Explanation:* Page 1488 of Vol. 97 of the CCH *Tax Court Memorandum Decisions*.

> *Nick R. Hughes*, 2009 RIA T.C.Memo. ¶2009,094
>
> *Explanation:* Paragraph 2009,094 of the RIA *T.C. Memorandum Decisions*.

Note that the third citation contains the same information as the first. Thus, ¶2009,094 indicates the following information about the case: year 2009, 94th T.C.Memo. decision. Before the Prentice Hall Information Services division was incorporated into Research Institute of America, PH was used instead of RIA for the third citation.[24]

U.S. Tax Court Summary Opinions relate to decisions of the Tax Court's Small Cases Division.[25] These opinions are published commercially, and on the U.S. Tax Court website, with the warning that they may not be treated as precedent for any other case. For example, *Martin Toombs*, filed on June 25, 2013, is cited as follows:

> *Martin Toombs*, T.C. Summary Opinion 2013–51.

Judicial Citations—The U.S. District Court, Court of Federal Claims, and Courts of Appeals   District Court, Court of Federal Claims, Court of Appeals, and Supreme Court decisions dealing with Federal tax matters are reported in both the CCH *U.S. Tax Cases* (USTC) and the RIA *American Federal Tax Reports* (AFTR) series. Federal District Court decisions, dealing with *both* tax and nontax issues, also are published by West in its *Federal Supplement Series* (F.Supp.). Volume 999, published in 1998, is the last volume of the *Federal Supplement Series*. It is followed by the *Federal*

---

[23]G. W. Carter, "Nonacquiescence: Winning by Losing," *Tax Notes* (September 19, 1988): 1301–1307.

[24]In this text, the RIA citation for Memorandum decisions of the U.S. Tax Court is omitted. Thus, *Nick R. Hughes* will be cited as 97 TCM 1488, T.C. Memo. 2009–94.

[25]In 2005, the U.S. Supreme Court held that decisions of the Small Cases Division must be made public.

Supplement Second Series (F.Supp.2d). The following examples illustrate three different ways of citing a District Court case:

> *Turner v. U.S.,* 2004–1 USTC ¶60,478 (D.Ct. Tex., 2004).
>
> *Explanation:* Reported in the first volume of the *U.S. Tax Cases* published by
>   Commerce Clearing House for calendar year 2004 (2004–1) and located at
>   paragraph 60,478 (¶60,478).
>
> *Turner v. U.S.,* 93 AFTR 2d 2004–686 (D.Ct. Tex., 2004).
>
> *Explanation:* Reported in the 93rd volume of the second series of the *American
>   Federal Tax Reports* (AFTR 2d) published by RIA and beginning on page 686.
>
> *Turner v. U.S.,* 306 F.Supp.2d 668 (D.Ct. Tex., 2004).
>
> *Explanation:* Reported in the 306th volume of the *Federal Supplement Second Series*
>   (F.Supp.2d) published by West and beginning on page 668.

In all of the preceding citations, note that the name of the case is the same
(Turner being the taxpayer), as is the reference to the Federal District Court of
Texas (D.Ct. Tex.) and the year the decision was rendered (2004).[26]

Decisions of the Court of Federal Claims[27] and the Courts of Appeals are published in the USTCs, AFTRs, and a West reporter called the *Federal Second Series*
(F.2d). Volume 999, published in 1993, is the last volume of the *Federal Second Series.*
It is followed by the *Federal Third Series* (F.3d). Beginning with October 1982, the
Court of Federal Claims decisions are published in another West reporter entitled
the *Claims Court Reporter* (abbreviated Cl.Ct.). Beginning with Volume 27 on October 30, 1992, the name of the reporter changed to the *Federal Claims Reporter*
(abbreviated as Fed.Cl.). The following examples illustrate the different forms:

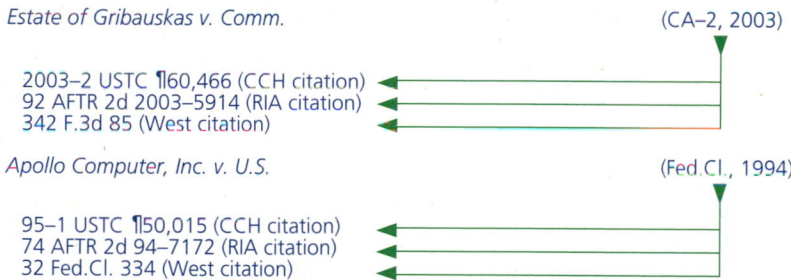

Note that *Estate of Gribauskas v. Comm.* is a decision rendered by the Second Circuit Court of Appeals in 2003 (CA–2, 2003), while *Apollo Computer, Inc.* was issued
by the Court of Federal Claims in 1994 (Fed.Cl., 1994).

Judicial Citations—The U.S. Supreme Court   Like all other Federal tax decisions
(except those rendered by the Tax Court), Supreme Court decisions are published
by CCH in the USTCs and by RIA in the AFTRs. The U.S. Government Printing
Office also publishes these decisions in the *United States Supreme Court Reports* (U.S.)
as does West in its *Supreme Court Reporter* (S.Ct.) and the Lawyer's Co-operative Publishing Company in its *United States Reports, Lawyer's Edition* (L.Ed.). The following
illustrates the different ways the same decision can be cited:

---

[26]In this text, the case would be cited in the following form: *Turner v. U.S.,*
2004–1 USTC ¶60,478, 93 AFTR 2d 2004–686, 306 F.Supp.2d 668 (D.Ct.
Tex., 2004).

[27]Before October 29, 1992, the Court of Federal Claims was called the
Claims Court. Before October 1, 1982, the Court of Federal Claims was
called the Court of Claims.

The parenthetical reference (USSC, 1969) identifies the decision as having been rendered by the U.S. Supreme Court in 1969. In this text, the citations of Supreme Court decisions will be limited to the CCH (USTC), RIA (AFTR), and West (S.Ct.) versions.

2-1d Other Sources of the Tax Law

Other sources of tax information that a tax practitioner may need to consult include tax treaties and tax periodicals.

Tax Treaties

The United States signs certain tax treaties (sometimes called tax conventions) with foreign countries to render mutual assistance in tax enforcement and to avoid double taxation. Tax legislation enacted in 1988 provided that neither a tax law nor a tax treaty takes general precedence. Thus, when there is a direct conflict between the Code and a treaty, the most recent item takes precedence. A taxpayer must disclose on the tax return any position where a treaty overrides a tax law.[28] There is a $1,000 penalty per failure to disclose for individuals and a $10,000 per failure penalty for corporations.[29]

Tax Periodicals

The use of tax periodicals can often shorten the research time needed to resolve a tax issue. If the article is relevant to the issue at hand, it may provide the references needed to locate the primary sources of the tax law that apply (e.g., citations to judicial decisions, Regulations, and other IRS pronouncements). Thus, the researcher obtains a "running start" in arriving at a solution to the problem.

Among the many indexes available for locating tax articles pertinent to a tax problem is CCH's *Federal Tax Articles*. This multivolume service includes a subject index, a Code Section number index, and an author's index.

Another is the *Index to Federal Tax Articles* (published by Warren, Gorham, and Lamont). Both of these indexes are updated periodically, but are available only in print form.

The following are some of the more useful tax periodicals:

Journal of Taxation
Journal of International Taxation
Practical Tax Strategies
Estate Planning
Corporate Taxation
Business Entities
Taxation of Exempts
Real Estate Taxation
ria.thomsonreuters.com/journals

The Tax Executive
www.tei.org

The Tax Adviser
aicpa.org/pubs/taxadv

Tax Law Review
www.law.nyu.edu/tax/ taxlawreview/index.htm

Journal of the American Taxation Association
aaahq.org/ata/_atamenu/ atapubjata.html

The ATA Journal of Legal Tax Research
aaahq.org/ata/_atamenu/ atapubjltr.html

Oil, Gas & Energy Quarterly
www.bus.lsu.edu/accounting/ faculty/lcrumbley/oilgas.html

Trusts and Estates
trustsandestates.com

Journal of Passthrough Entities
TAXES—The Tax Magazine
tax.cchgroup.com/books

Tax Notes
taxanalysts.com

---

[28]§ 7852(d).

[29]Reg. §§ 301.6114–1, 301.6712–1, and 301.7701(b)(7).

Tax Treaties

The United States has entered into treaties with most of the major countries of the world to eliminate possible double taxation. For example, nonresident alien students wanting to claim exemption from taxation are required to provide an information statement as set forth in several Revenue Procedures. The withholding agent must also certify the form.

Chinese students are required to prepare a four-part statement. Part 3 of the student's statement is as follows:

I will receive compensation for personal services performed in the United States. This compensation qualifies for exemption from withholding of Federal income tax under the tax treaty between the United States and the People's Republic of China in an amount not in excess of $5,000 for any taxable year.

Global Tax Issues

© iStockphoto.com/Andrey Prokhorov

2-2 WORKING WITH THE TAX LAW— TAX RESEARCH TOOLS

Tax law consists of a body of legislative (e.g., Code Sections and tax treaties), administrative (e.g., Regulations and Rulings), and judicial (e.g., court cases) pronouncements. Working with the tax law requires being able to effectively locate and use these sources. A key consideration is the time required to carry out this research and finding activity.

Unless the problem is simple (e.g., the Code Section is known and there is a Regulation on point), the research process should begin with a tax service.

LO.3

Develop an awareness of tax research tools.

2-2a Commercial Tax Services

Due to various changes, categorizing tax services has become an almost impossible task. Previously, services could be classified as *annotated* (i.e., organized by Internal Revenue Code) or *topical* (i.e., organized by major topics), but this classification system is no longer appropriate for many tax services as their format has been modified. Often, the change is due to the acquisition of what was a competing tax service. For example, the *United States Tax Reporter* (annotated) now has a version that contains the *Federal Tax Coordinator 2d* (topical).

Tax services also can no longer be distinguished based on whether they are available only in hard copy or online versions. Previously, for example, *Tax Management Portfolios* was solely a print publication. Now, like most other tax services, it is also accessible online.

A partial list of the available commercial tax services includes:

- *Standard Federal Tax Reporter*, Commerce Clearing House.
- *CCH IntelliConnect*, Commerce Clearing House Internet service.
- *United States Tax Reporter*, Research Institute of America.
- RIA *Checkpoint*, Research Institute of America. The online version of *United States Tax Reporter* also can include the *Federal Tax Coordinator 2d*.
- ATX/Kleinrock *Tax Expert*, CCH/Wolters Kluwer Business services.
- *Tax Management Portfolios*, Bloomberg BNA.
- *Mertens Law of Federal Income Taxation*, West Group.
- Westlaw services—compilations include access to *Tax Management Portfolios*, *Federal Tax Coordinator 2d*, and *Mertens*.
- *TaxCenter*, LexisNexis compilation of primary sources and various materials taken from CCH, Matthew Bender, Kleinrock, and Bloomberg BNA.
- *Federal Research Library*, Tax Analysts (a nonprofit organization) databases dealing with explanations and commentaries on primary source materials.

Possible Penalty on Banks for Offshore Tax Evasion

American taxpayers with overseas bank accounts and foreign assets are required to file special disclosures with the IRS each year. The top penalty for failure to file is 50 percent of the account balance for each year of violation. Thus, a tax evader can owe multiples of what may be in the account. The Justice Department is exploring how and whether the penalty can be applied to banks should they violate American tax laws.

Source: Based on Lynnley Browning, "U.S. Considers Novel Penalty on Banks That Have Aided Offshore Tax Evasion," *New York Times*, April 13, 2011, p. B3.

2-2b Using Online Tax Services

Instructions on how to use a tax service are not particularly worthwhile unless a specific service is involved. Even here, instructions need to be followed by hands-on experience to be effective. For online versions of a tax service, however, following certain procedures can simplify the research process. Because a practitioner's time is valuable and several research services base usage charges on time spent, time is of the essence.

When the principal emphasis is on time, every shortcut helps. The following suggestions (most of which are familiar to any user of the Internet) may be helpful:[30]

- Choose keywords for the search carefully. Words with a broad usage, such as *income*, are worthless when standing alone. If the researcher is interested in qualified dividend income, even *dividend income* is too broad because it will call up stock dividends, constructive dividends, liquidating dividends, and more. By using *qualified dividend income* at the outset, the search is considerably narrowed. In RIA *Checkpoint*, for example, these two modifications narrowed the search from over 10,000 items to 3,824 and finally to 884. From that point, further contraction will be needed.
- Take advantage of *connectors*, such as "+" and quotation marks, to place parameters on the search and further restrict the output. Although each service has its own set of connectors, many are used by several services. Thus, quotation marks around a phrase mean "exact phrase" in both RIA *Checkpoint* and CCH *IntelliConnect* (e.g., "personal service corporation").
- Be selective in choosing a database. For example, if the research project does not involve case law, there is no point in including the judicial decision component in the search database. Doing so just adds to the output items and will necessitate further screening through a search modification.
- Use a table of contents, index, or citation approach when appropriate. Although the keyword approach is most frequently used, databases can be searched in other ways. Using the table of contents or index is the usual approach with print versions of a tax service. With the citation route, access may be through a statutory (e.g., Code Section), administrative (e.g., Rev.Rul.), or judicial citation (e.g., Tax Court), depending on the tax service. Using just a Code Section number or the taxpayer's last name, however, can require a significant amount of screening to narrow the information.

2-2c Noncommercial Online Tax Services

The Internet provides a wealth of tax information in several popular forms, sometimes at no direct cost to the researcher. Using so-called browser software that often is distributed with new computer systems and their communication devices, the tax professional can access information provided around the world that aids the research process.

---

[30]For a more complete discussion of the use of RIA *Checkpoint* and CCH *IntelliConnect* and Internet research in taxation, see Raabe, Whittenburg, Sanders, and Sawyers, *South-Western's Federal Tax Research*, 9th ed. (Cengage Learning South-Western, 2012), Chapters 6 and 7.

EXHIBIT 2.2   **The IRS's Home Page**

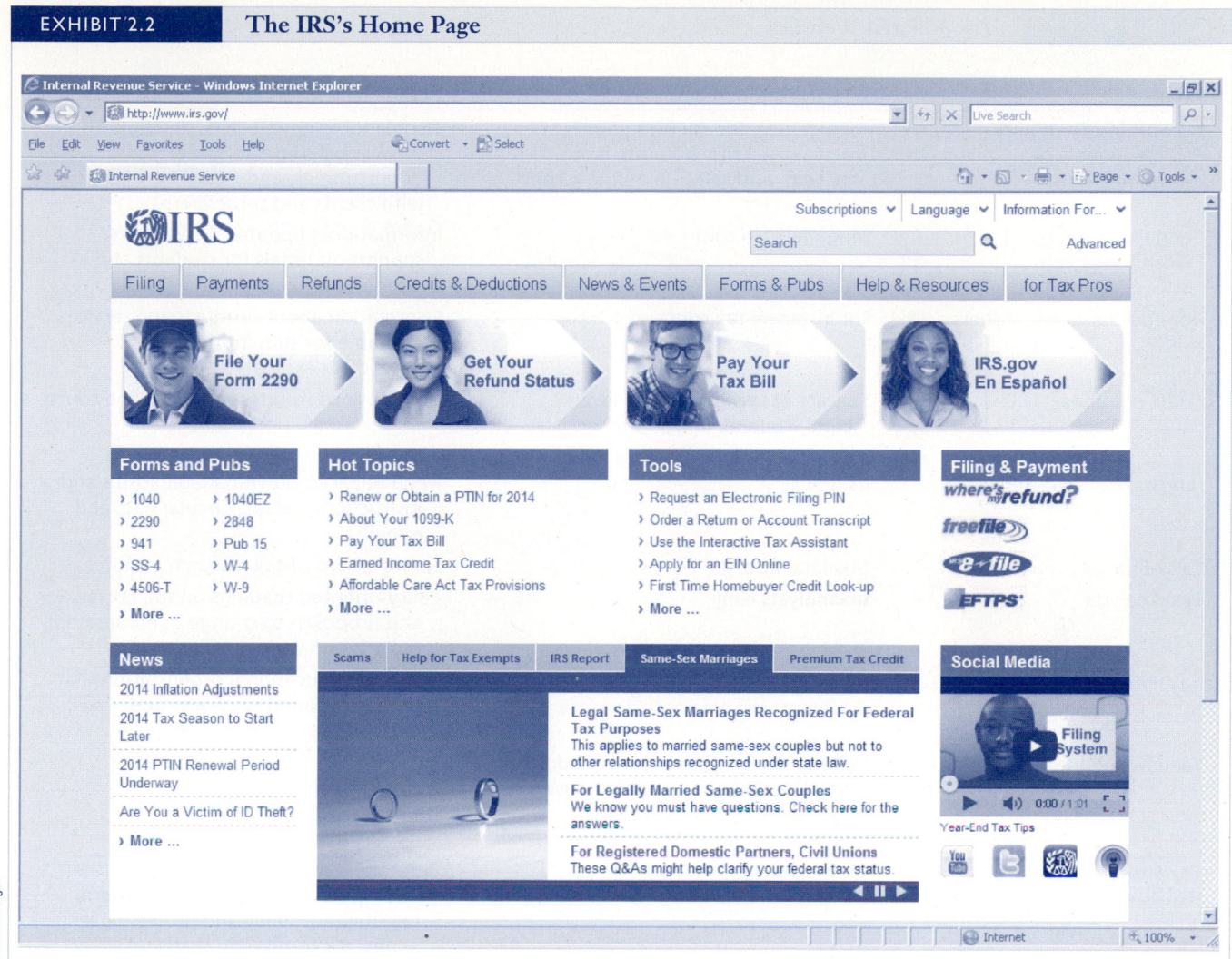

- *Home pages (sites) on the Web* are provided by accounting and consulting firms, publishers, tax academics and libraries, and governmental bodies as a means of making information widely available or of soliciting subscriptions or consulting engagements. The best sites offer links to other sites and direct contact to the site providers. One of the best sites available to the tax practitioner is the Internal Revenue Service's home page, illustrated in Exhibit 2.2. This site offers downloadable forms and instructions, "plain English" versions of Regulations, and news update items. Exhibit 2.3 lists some of the websites and their Internet addresses as of press date that may be most useful to tax researchers. Particularly useful is the directory at **taxsites.com**, which provides links to accounting and tax sources (including international as well as payroll).
- *Newsgroups* provide a means by which information related to the tax law can be exchanged among taxpayers, tax professionals, and others who subscribe to the group's services. Newsgroup members can read the exchanges among other members and offer replies and suggestions to inquiries as desired. Discussions address the interpretation and application of existing law, analysis of proposals and new pronouncements, and reviews of tax software.

In many situations, solutions to research problems benefit from or require the use of various electronic tax research tools. A competent tax professional must become familiar and proficient with these tools and be able to use them to meet the expectations of clients and the necessities of work in the modern world.[31]

---

[31] For a more detailed discussion of the use of electronic tax research in tax practice, see Raabe, Whittenburg, Sanders, and Sawyers, *South-* *Western's Federal Tax Research*, 9th ed. (Cengage Learning South-Western, 2012).

EXHIBIT 2.3	Tax-Related Websites

Website	Web Address	Description
Accounting firms and professional organizations	For instance, the AICPA's page is at **aicpa.org**, Ernst & Young is at **ey.com**, and KPMG is at **kpmg.com**	Tax planning newsletters, descriptions of services offered and career opportunities, and exchange of data with clients and subscribers
Cengage Learning South-Western	**cengagebrain.com**	Informational updates, newsletters, support materials for students and adopters, and continuing education
Commercial tax publishers	For instance, **tax.com** and **cch.com**	Information about products and services available for subscription and newsletter excerpts
Court opinions	The site at **law.justia.com** covers state, Federal, and Supreme Court decisions but not the Tax Court	A synopsis of results reached by the court
Internal Revenue Service	**irs.gov**	News releases, downloadable forms and instructions, tables, Circular 230, and e-mail
Tax Almanac	**taxalmanac.org**	Smorgasbord of tax research resources
Tax Analysts	**taxanalysts.com**	Policy-oriented readings on the tax law and proposals to change it, moderated bulletins on various tax subjects
Tax Foundation	**taxfoundation.org**	Nonprofit educational organization that promotes sound tax policy and measures tax burdens
Tax laws online	Regulations are at **law.cornell.edu/cfr** and the Code is at **uscode.house .gov/search/criteria.shtml** and **www.law.cornell.edu/uscode**	
Tax Sites Directory	**taxsites.com**	References and links to tax sites on the Internet, including state and Federal tax sites, academic and professional pages, tax forms, and software
U.S. Tax Court decisions	**ustaxcourt.gov**	Recent U.S. Tax Court decisions

Note: Web addresses change frequently.

2-3 WORKING WITH THE TAX LAW— TAX RESEARCH

LO.4

Describe the tax research process.

Tax research is the method used to determine the best available solution to a situation that possesses tax consequences. In other words, it is the process of finding a competent and professional conclusion to a tax problem. The problem may originate from completed or proposed transactions. In the case of a completed transaction, the objective of the research is to determine the tax result of what has already taken place. For example, was the expenditure incurred by the taxpayer deductible or not deductible for tax purposes? When dealing with proposed transactions, the tax research process is directed toward the determination of possible alternative tax consequences. To the extent that tax research leads to a choice of alternatives or otherwise influences the future actions of the taxpayer, it becomes the key to effective tax planning.

Tax research involves the following procedures:

- Identifying and refining the problem.
- Locating the appropriate tax law sources.
- Assessing the validity of the tax law sources.

FIGURE 2.5 **Tax Research Process**

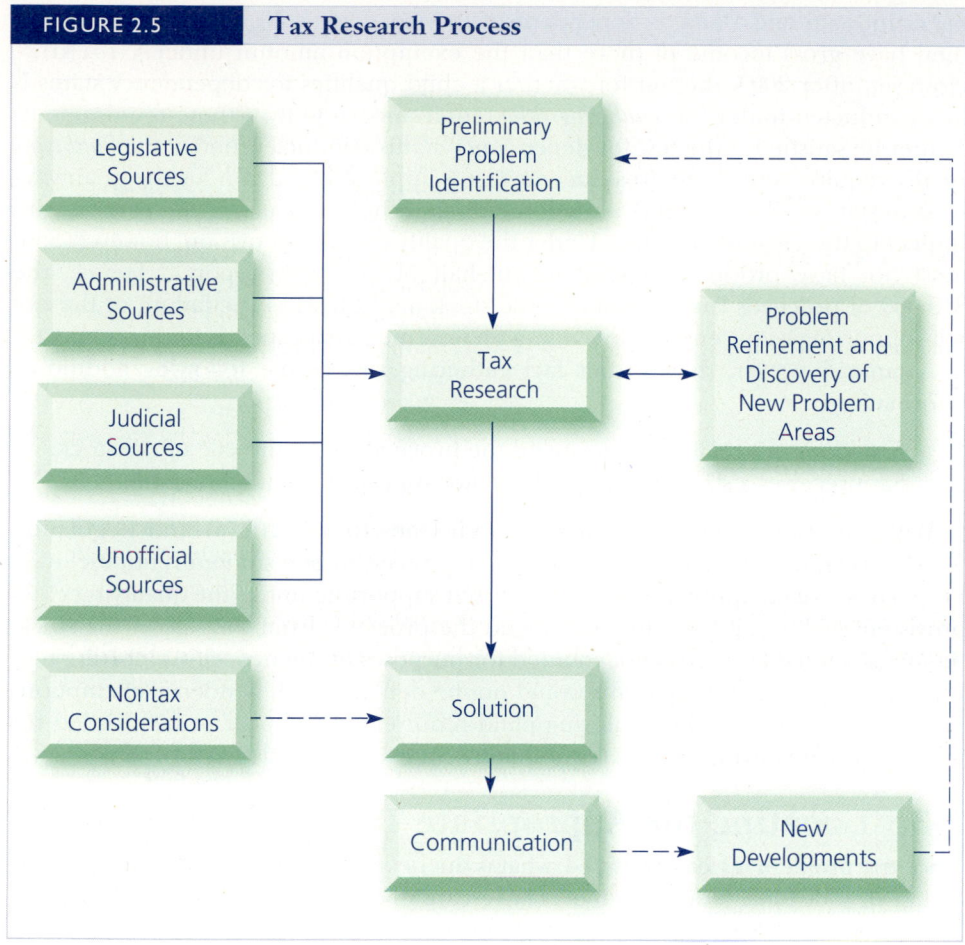

- Arriving at the solution or at alternative solutions with due consideration given to nontax factors.
- Effectively communicating the solution to the taxpayer or the taxpayer's representative.
- Following up on the solution (where appropriate) in light of new developments.

This process is depicted schematically in Figure 2.5. The broken lines reflect the steps of particular interest when tax research is directed toward proposed, rather than completed, transactions.

2-3a Identifying the Problem

Problem identification must start with a compilation of the relevant facts involved.[32] In this regard, *all* of the facts that may have a bearing on the problem must be gathered because any omission could modify the solution reached. To illustrate, return to the facts of *The Big Picture* on page 2-1 and consider what appears to be a very simple problem: Can Fred and Megan claim Sam and Dana as dependents?

2-3b Refining the Problem

Returning to the facts of *The Big Picture* on page 2-1, the simple question of whether Fred and Megan can claim Sam and Dana as dependents becomes more complicated with the potential stock sale. Initially, it appears that Fred and Megan could

---

[32]For an excellent discussion of the critical role of facts in carrying out tax research, see R. L. Gardner, D. N. Stewart, and R. G. Worsham, *Tax* *Research Techniques*, 8th ed. (New York: The American Institute of Certified Public Accountants, 2008), Chapter 2.

not claim Sam and Dana as dependents if the stock was sold, because Sam would then have gross income of more than the exemption amount under § 151(d).[33] However, after 2004, the test for whether a child qualifies for dependency status is first conducted under the *qualifying child* requirements. Only if these requirements cannot be satisfied is the test for dependency status conducted under the *qualifying relative* requirements. The gross income test is applicable only under the qualifying relative status.[34] Thus, Sam could sell the stock without penalizing the parents with respect to the gross income test. Under the qualifying child provision, however, Sam must not have provided more than one-half of his own support.[35] Hence, the $19,000 of proceeds from the sale of the stock might lead to the failure of the not self-supporting requirement, depending on how much Sam spends for his support.

Assume, however, that further fact gathering reveals the following additional information:

- Sam does not really need to spend the proceeds from the sale of the stock.
- Sam receives a sizable portion of his own support from a scholarship.

With these new facts, additional research leads to § 152(f)(5) and Regulation § 1.152–1(c), which indicate that a scholarship received by a student is not included for purposes of computing whether Sam is self-supporting under the qualifying child provision. Further, if Sam does not spend the proceeds from the sale of the stock, the unexpended amount is not counted for purposes of the not self-supporting test. Thus, it appears that the parents would not be denied the dependency exemptions for Sam and Dana, as the qualifying child requirements appear to be satisfied for Sam and the qualifying relative requirements appear to be satisfied for Dana.

2-3c Locating the Appropriate Tax Law Sources

Once the problem is clearly defined, what is the next step? Although the next step is a matter of individual judgment, most tax research begins with the index volume of a hard copy tax service or a keyword search on an online tax service as described earlier. If the problem is not complex, the researcher may bypass the hard copy tax service or online service and turn directly to the Internal Revenue Code and Treasury Regulations. For the beginner, the latter procedure saves time and solves many of the more basic problems. If the researcher does not have a personal copy of the Code or Regulations, resorting to the appropriate volume(s) of a tax service will be necessary.[36]

2-3d Assessing the Validity of the Tax Law Sources

Once a source has been located, the next step is to assess it in light of the problem at hand. Proper assessment involves careful interpretation of the tax law with consideration given to its relevance and validity. In connection with validity, an important step is to check for recent changes in the tax law.

Interpreting the Internal Revenue Code

The language of the Code often is difficult to comprehend fully. Contrary to many people's suspicions, the Code is not written deliberately to confuse. Unfortunately, though, it often has that effect. The Code is intended to apply to more than 200 million taxpayers, many of whom are willing to exploit any linguistic imprecision to their benefit—to find a "loophole" in popular parlance. Many of the Code's provisions are limitations or restrictions involving two or more variables. Expressing such concepts algebraically would be more direct; using words to accomplish this task instead is often quite cumbersome. Among the worst such attempts was former

---

[33]§ 152(d)(2). See the related discussion in Chapter 3.

[34]Compare § 152(c) for qualifying child with § 152(d) for qualifying relative.

[35]§ 152(c)(1)(D).

[36]Several of the major tax services publish paperback editions of the Code and Treasury Regulations that can be purchased at modest prices. These editions are usually revised twice each year. For an annotated and abridged version of the Code and Regulations that is published annually, see James E. Smith, *South-Western Federal Taxation: Internal Revenue Code of 1986 and Treasury Regulations: Annotated and Selected* (Cengage Learning South-Western, 2015).

TAX IN THE NEWS   The Difficult Language of the Code

The language of the Code often is extremely difficult to comprehend. For example, a former subsection [§ 341(e)] relating to collapsible corporations contained one sentence of more than 450 words (twice as many as in the Gettysburg Address). Within this same subsection was another sentence of 300 words.

The Code must be read carefully for restrictive language such as "at least 80 percent" and "more than 80 percent" or "less than 50 percent" and "exceeds 50 percent." It also makes a significant difference, for example, whether two or more clauses are connected by "or" or "and."

If an answer is not in the Code, it may be necessary to resort to the Regulations and judicial decisions. In 1969, Congress directed the Treasury Department to promulgate Regulations under § 385 to distinguish corporate debt from corporate equity. As of yet, there are no Regulations under § 385. The researcher, therefore, must resort to past judicial decisions for a definition of debt.

Sometimes the Code directs the researcher elsewhere for the answer. For example, § 162(c) refers to the Foreign Corrupt Practices Act for purposes of determining when payments to foreign officials are deductible.

Cross-referencing between Code Sections is often poor or nonexistent. Code Sections are enacted at different times by Congresses that are operating under stringent deadlines. Consequently, a certain lack of integration within the Code is frequently apparent.

Definitions vary from one Code Section to another. For example, § 267 disallows losses between related parties and includes brothers and sisters in the definition of related parties. Not so with § 318, which deals with the definition of related parties as to certain stock redemptions.

§ 341(e) relating to so-called collapsible corporations. One sentence had more than 450 words (twice as many as in Abraham Lincoln's Gettysburg Address). Within this same subsection was another sentence of 300 words. Research has shown that in one-third of the conflicts reaching the Tax Court, the court could not discern the intent of Congress by simply reading the statute. Yet the overriding attitude of the Tax Court judges is that the statute comes first. Even when the statute is unworkable, the court will not rewrite the law.[37]

Assessing the Validity of a Treasury Regulation

Treasury Regulations are the official interpretation of the Code and are entitled to great deference. Occasionally, however, a court will invalidate a Regulation or a portion thereof on the grounds that the Regulation is contrary to the intent of Congress. Usually, the courts do not question the validity of Regulations because of the belief that "the first administrative interpretation of a provision as it appears in a new act often expresses the general understanding of the times or the actual understanding of those who played an important part when the statute was drafted."[38]

Keep the following observations in mind when assessing the validity of a Regulation:

- IRS agents must give the Code and any related Regulations equal weight when dealing with taxpayers and their representatives.
- Proposed Regulations provide a preview of future final Regulations, but they are not binding on the IRS or taxpayers.
- In a challenge, the burden of proof is on the taxpayer to show that the Regulation varies from the language of the statute and has no support in the Committee Reports.
- If the taxpayer loses the challenge, a 20 percent negligence penalty may be imposed.[39] This accuracy-related penalty applies to any failure to make a

---

[37]T. L. Kirkpatrick and W. B. Pollard, "Reliance by the Tax Court on the Legislative Intent of Congress," *The Tax Executive* (Summer 1986): 358–359.

[38]*Augustus v. Comm.*, 41–1 USTC ¶9255, 26 AFTR 612, 118 F.2d 38 (CA–6, 1941).

[39]§§ 6662(a) and (b)(1).

reasonable attempt to comply with the tax law and any disregard of rules and Regulations.[40]

- Final Regulations can be classified as procedural, interpretive, or legislative. **Procedural Regulations** neither establish tax laws nor attempt to explain tax laws. Procedural Regulations are *housekeeping-type instructions* indicating information that taxpayers should provide the IRS, as well as information about the internal management and conduct of the IRS itself.

- Some **interpretive Regulations** rephrase and elaborate what Congress stated in the Committee Reports that were issued when the tax legislation was enacted. Such Regulations are *hard* and *solid* and almost impossible to overturn because they clearly reflect the intent of Congress. An interpretive Regulation is given less deference than a legislative Regulation, however. The Supreme Court has told lower courts to analyze Treasury Regulations carefully before accepting the Treasury's interpretation.[41]

- In some Code Sections, Congress has given the *Treasury Secretary or his delegate* the authority to prescribe Regulations to carry out the details of administration or to otherwise complete the operating rules. Under such circumstances, Congress effectively is delegating its legislative powers to the Treasury Department. Regulations issued pursuant to this type of authority possess the force and effect of law and are often called **legislative Regulations** (e.g., consolidated return Regulations).

- Courts tend to apply a legislative reenactment doctrine. A particular Regulation is assumed to have received congressional approval if the Regulation was finalized many years earlier and Congress has not amended the Code Section pertaining to that Regulation.

Assessing the Validity of Other Administrative Sources of the Tax Law

Revenue Rulings issued by the IRS carry less weight than Treasury Department Regulations. Revenue Rulings are important, however, in that they reflect the position of the IRS on tax matters. In any dispute with the IRS on the interpretation of tax law, therefore, taxpayers should expect agents to follow the results reached in any applicable Revenue Rulings. A 1986 Tax Court decision, however, indicated that Revenue Rulings "typically do not constitute substantive authority for a position."[42] Most Revenue Rulings apply retroactively unless a specific statement indicates the extent to which a ruling is to be applied without retroactive effect.[43]

Actions on Decisions further tell the taxpayer the IRS's reaction to certain court decisions. Recall that the IRS follows a practice of either acquiescing (agreeing) or nonacquiescing (not agreeing) with selected judicial decisions. A nonacquiescence does not mean that a particular court decision is of no value, but it does indicate that the IRS may continue to litigate the issue involved.

Assessing the Validity of Judicial Sources of the Tax Law

The judicial process as it relates to the formulation of tax law has already been described. How much reliance can be placed on a particular decision depends upon the following variables:

- The higher the level of the court that issued a decision, the greater the weight accorded to that decision. A decision rendered by a trial court (e.g., a Federal District Court) carries less weight than one issued by an appellate court (e.g., the Fifth Circuit Court of Appeals). Unless Congress changes the Code, decisions by the U.S. Supreme Court represent the last word on any tax issue.

---

[40]§ 6662(c). The term *reasonable* is not defined in the Code; the IRS looks at all the facts and circumstances surrounding the effort of the taxpayer to report the correct tax liability.

[41]*U.S. v. Vogel Fertilizer Co.*, 82–1 USTC ¶9134, 49 AFTR 2d 82–491, 102 S.Ct. 821 (USSC, 1982); *National Muffler Dealers Assn., Inc.*, 79–1 USTC ¶9264, 43 AFTR 2d 79–828, 99 S.Ct. 1304 (USSC, 1979).

[42]*Nelda C. Stark*, 86 T.C. 243 (1986). See also *Ann R. Neuhoff*, 75 T.C. 36 (1980). For a different opinion, however, see *Industrial Valley Bank & Trust Co.*, 66 T.C. 272 (1976).

[43]Rev.Proc. 87–1, 1987–1 C.B. 503.

TAX IN THE NEWS ObamaCare Law Is Massive

The Patient Protection and Affordable Care Act (known as Obama-Care) grants at least 46 new responsibilities to the IRS. In testimony before the House Appropriations Committee, J. Russell George, Inspector General for Tax Administration, indicated that the sweeping changes are unprecedented. The amount of responsibility being given to the IRS will cause taxpayers to have "more questions about their taxes because of health care penalties or credits, flooding already busy call-in and walk-in tax help centers."

The Patient Protection and Affordable Care Act is about 1,000 pages long, and more than 10,000 pages of Regulations have already been issued. In comparison, the Internal Revenue Code is about 9,000 pages long and has more than 4 million words.

Sources: "Patient Protection and Affordable Care Act: IRS Should Expand Its Strategic Approach to Implementation," Government Accountability Office, June 2011, **www.gao.gov/new.items/d11719.pdf**; Ryan Ellis, "The IRS and Its 46 New Powers to Enforce ObamaCare," Gallen Institute, June 5, 2013, **www.galen.org/2013/46-new-irs-powers-to-enforce-obamacare**; 2012 National Taxpayer Advocate Annual Report to Congress, **www.taxpayeradvocate.irs.gov/2012-Annual-Report/tax-code-complexity**.

- More reliance is placed on decisions of courts that have jurisdiction in the area where the taxpayer's legal residence is located. If, for example, a taxpayer lives in Texas, a decision of the Fifth Circuit Court of Appeals (which would hear an appeal from a Texas trial court) means more than one rendered by the Second Circuit Court of Appeals.[44]
- A Tax Court Regular decision carries more weight than a Memorandum decision because the Tax Court does not consider Memorandum decisions to be binding precedents.[45] Furthermore, a Tax Court *reviewed* decision carries even more weight. All of the Tax Court judges participate in a reviewed decision.
- A Circuit Court decision where certiorari has been requested and denied by the U.S. Supreme Court carries more weight than a Circuit Court decision that was not appealed. A Circuit Court decision heard *en banc* (all of the judges participate) carries more weight than a normal Circuit Court case.
- A decision that is supported by cases from other courts carries more weight than a decision that is not supported by other cases.
- The weight of a decision also can be affected by its status on appeal. For example, was the decision affirmed or overruled?

In connection with the last two variables, the use of a citator is invaluable to tax research.[46] A **citator** provides the history of a case, including the authority relied on (e.g., other judicial decisions) in reaching the result. Reviewing the references listed in the citator discloses whether the decision was appealed and, if so, with what result (e.g., affirmed, reversed, or remanded). It also reveals other cases with the same or similar issues and how they were decided. Thus, a citator reflects on the validity of a case and may lead to other relevant judicial material.[47] If one intends to rely on a judicial decision to any significant degree, "running" the case through a citator is imperative.

Assessing the Validity of Other Sources

Primary sources of tax law include the Constitution, legislative history materials, statutes, treaties, Treasury Regulations, IRS pronouncements, and judicial decisions. In general, the IRS considers only primary sources to constitute substantial authority. However, a researcher might want to refer to *secondary materials* such as legal

---

[44]Before October 1, 1982, an appeal from the then-named U.S. Court of Claims (the other trial court) was directly to the U.S. Supreme Court.

[45]*Severino R. Nico, Jr.,* 67 T.C. 647 (1977).

[46]The major citators are published by CCH; RIA; Westlaw; and Shepard's Citations, Inc.

[47]The CCH version is available online through the CCH *IntelliConnect* service; for RIA, use *Checkpoint*. Shepard's Internet version is part of LexisNexis.

FINANCIAL DISCLOSURE INSIGHTS   Where Does GAAP Come From?

As this chapter has described, the tax law is developed by many entities, including Congress, and the legislators of other countries, the courts, and the IRS. Accounting principles also have many sources. Consequently, in reconciling the tax and financial accounting reporting of a transaction, the tax professional will need to know the hierarchy of authority of accounting principles—in particular, the level of importance to assign to a specific GAAP document. The diagram below presents the sources of GAAP arranged in a general order of authority from highest to lowest.

Professional research is conducted to find and analyze the sources of accounting reporting standards in much the same way a tax professional conducts research on an open tax question. In fact, many of the publishers that provide tax research materials also can be used to find GAAP and International Financial Reporting Standards (IFRS) documents. These include the Research Institute of America (RIA) and the Commerce Clearing House (CCH). The Financial Accounting Standards Board (FASB) also makes its standards and interpretations available by subscription.

Highest Authority
- Financial Accounting Standards and Interpretations of the FASB.
- Pronouncements of bodies that preceded the FASB, such as the Accounting Principles Board (APB).

- FASB Technical Bulletins.
- Audit and Accounting Guides, prepared by the American Institute of CPAs (AICPA) and cleared by the FASB.
- Practice Bulletins, prepared by the American Institute of CPAs (AICPA) and cleared by the FASB.

- Interpretation Guides of the FASB Staff.
- Accounting Interpretations of the AICPA.
- IASB Accounting Standards
- FASB Concepts Standards.
- Widely accepted accounting practices, professional journals, accounting textbooks, and treatises.

© iStockphoto.com/Pali Rao

periodicals, treatises, legal opinions, General Counsel Memoranda, and written determinations. In general, secondary sources are not authority.

Although the statement that the IRS regards only primary sources as substantial authority generally is true, there is one exception. In Notice 90–20,[48] the IRS expanded the list of substantial authority *for purposes of* the accuracy-related penalty in § 6662 to include a number of secondary materials (e.g., letter rulings, General Counsel Memoranda, and the Bluebook). "Authority" does not include conclusions reached in treatises, legal periodicals, and opinions rendered by tax professionals.

A letter ruling or determination letter is substantial authority *only* for the taxpayer to whom it is issued, except as noted previously with respect to the accuracy-related penalty.

Upon the completion of major tax legislation, the staff of the Joint Committee on Taxation (in consultation with the staffs of the House Ways and Means and Senate Finance Committees) often will prepare a General Explanation of the Act, commonly known as the Bluebook because of the color of its cover. The IRS will not accept this detailed explanation as having legal effect, except as noted previously with respect to the accuracy-related penalty. The Bluebook does, however, provide

---

[48]1990–1 C.B. 328; see also Reg. § 1.6661–3(b)(2).

valuable guidance to tax advisers and taxpayers until Regulations are issued. Some letter rulings and General Counsel Memoranda of the IRS cite Bluebook explanations.

2-3e   Arriving at the Solution or at Alternative Solutions

The Big Picture on page 2-1 raised the question of whether a taxpayer would be denied dependency exemptions for a son and a daughter-in-law if the son sold some stock near the end of the year. A refinement of the problem supplies additional information:

- Sam and Dana anticipate filing a joint return.

Section 152(b)(2) indicates that a taxpayer is not permitted a dependency exemption for a married dependent if the married individual files a joint return. An initial reaction is that a joint return by Sam and Dana would be problematic to the parents. However, more research uncovers two Revenue Rulings that provide an exception if neither the dependent nor the dependent's spouse is required to file a return but does so solely to claim a refund of tax withheld. The IRS asserts that each spouse must have gross income of less than the exemption amount.[49] Therefore, if Sam sells the stock and he and Dana file a joint return, the parents will lose the dependency exemption for both Sam and Dana.

If the stock is not sold until January 2015, both dependency exemptions are available to the parents in 2014 even if Sam and Dana file a joint return. However, under § 151(d)(2), a personal exemption is not available to a taxpayer who can be claimed as a dependent by another taxpayer (whether actually claimed). Thus, if the parents can claim Sam and Dana as dependents, Sam and Dana would lose their personal exemptions on their tax return.

2-3f   Communicating Tax Research

Once the problem has been researched adequately, the researcher may need to prepare a memo, a letter, or an oral presentation setting forth the result. The form such a communication takes could depend on a number of considerations. For example, does the employer or professor recommend a particular procedure or format for tax research memos? Is the memo to be given directly to the client, or will it first go to the researcher's employer? Who is the audience for the oral presentation? How long should you talk? Whatever form it takes, a good tax research communication should contain the following elements:

- A clear statement of the issue.
- In more complex situations, a short review of the facts that raise the issue.
- A review of the pertinent tax law sources (e.g., Code, Regulations, Revenue Rulings, and judicial authority).
- Any assumptions made in arriving at the solution.
- The solution recommended and the logic or reasoning supporting it.
- The references consulted in the research process.

In short, a good tax research communication should tell the audience what was researched, the results of that research, and the justification for the recommendation made.[50]

Illustrations of the memos for the tax file and the client letter associated with the facts of *The Big Picture* appear in Figure 2.6, Figure 2.7, and Figure 2.8.

LO.5

Communicate the results of the tax research process in a client letter and a tax file memorandum.

---

[49]Rev.Rul. 54–567, 1954–2 C.B. 108; Rev.Rul. 65–34, 1965–1 C.B. 86.

[50]See Chapter 6 of the publication cited in Footnote 32. For oral presentations, see W. A. Raabe and G. E. Whittenburg, "Talking Tax: How to Make a Tax Presentation," *The Tax Adviser* (March 1997): 179–182.

FIGURE 2.6	Tax File Memorandum

August 16, 2014

TAX FILE MEMORANDUM

FROM: John J. Jones
SUBJECT: Fred and Megan Samuels
          Engagement: Issues

Today I talked to Fred Samuels about his August 12, 2014 letter requesting tax assistance. He wants to know if his son, Sam, can sell stock worth $19,000 (basis = $11,000) without the parents losing the dependency exemptions for Sam and Sam's wife, Dana. Fred would also like to know the effect on Sam and Dana's tax liability in 2014 if the stock is sold.

Fred Samuels is married to Megan, and Sam is a full-time student at a local university. Sam inherited the stock from his grandmother about five years ago. If he sells the stock, he will save the proceeds from the sale rather than spend them because he receives a $5,500 scholarship that he uses for his own support (i.e., to pay for tuition, books, and fees). Although neither Sam nor Dana is currently employed, Sam has earned income of $960 and Dana has earned income of $900. Fred and Megan are in the 28% tax bracket and furnish approximately 55% of Sam and Dana's support.

ISSUES: If the stock is sold, would the sale prohibit Fred and Megan from claiming Sam and Dana as dependents? What is the effect on Sam and Dana's tax liability if the stock is sold in 2014? Fred would like an answer within two weeks.

FIGURE 2.7	Tax File Memorandum

August 26, 2014

TAX FILE MEMORANDUM

FROM: John J. Jones
SUBJECT: Fred and Megan Samuels
          Engagement: Conclusions

See the Tax File Memorandum dated August 16, 2014, which contains the facts and identifies the tax issues.

Section 152(a) provides that for a taxpayer to take a dependency exemption, the potential dependent must satisfy either the qualifying child requirements or the qualifying relative requirements [see Chapter 3]. Fred and Megan provide about 55% of the support of their son, Sam, and their daughter-in-law, Dana. If Sam should sell the stock in 2014, he would not need to spend the proceeds for support purposes (i.e., would save the proceeds). Thus, the stock sale would not affect his qualifying as not self-supporting under § 152(c)(1)(D). In calculating the percentage of support provided by Fred and Megan, a $5,500 scholarship received by Sam is not counted in determining the amount of support Sam provides for himself [see § 152(f)(5) and Reg. § 1.152–1(c)]. Note, however, that if the $5,500 had been provided by student loans, it would have been included in calculating support [*Philip J. McCauley*, 56 T.C. 48 (1971)].

Section 152(d)(1)(B) provides that to qualify for a dependency exemption as a qualifying relative, the potential dependent's gross income must be less than the exemption amount (i.e., $3,950 in 2014). Without the stock sale, the gross income of both Sam ($960) and Dana ($900) will be below the exemption amount in 2014. The $5,500 Sam receives as a scholarship is excluded from his gross income under § 117(a) because he uses the entire amount to pay for his tuition, books, and fees at a local university.

Although the gross income test is not applicable to Sam (he is a qualifying child), it is applicable to Dana, the daughter-in-law (she is a qualifying relative) [see Concept Summary 3.1]. A key issue is whether the stock sale that produces $8,000 of recognized gain for Sam and Dana will cause the gross income test to be violated for Dana. Because the $8,000 recognized gain is from the sale of Sam's separately owned asset and they do not live in a community property state, Dana should qualify as a dependent because her gross income would be only $900.

The stock sale would result in the parents' loss of the dependency exemptions for Sam and Dana if they file a joint return for 2014 [see § 152(b)(2)]. The joint return requirement does not apply, however, if the dependent files a joint return solely to claim a refund and neither spouse had a tax liability on a separate return (Rev.Rul. 65–34, 1965–1 C.B. 86). However, sale of the stock would keep this exception from applying.

From a tax planning perspective, Sam can choose to sell the stock in 2014. However, if this choice is made, Sam and Dana need to file separate returns so as not to violate the absence of a joint return provision. Under these circumstances, the sale will not interfere with Fred and Megan's ability to claim dependency exemptions for Sam and Dana on their 2014 return. Note, however, that neither Sam nor Dana will be permitted to take a personal exemption deduction on their 2014 tax return because they are claimed as dependents on someone else's return [see § 151(d)(2)]. This disallowance of the personal exemption deduction will not produce any significant negative tax consequences for Dana because her tax liability would be $0. However, Sam's tax liability would now be $900 [see the kiddie tax discussion in Chapter 3]. Alternatively, Sam could delay the sale of the stock until 2015. In this case, Sam and Dana's tax liability in 2014 would be $0. The disallowance of the personal exemption deductions by Sam and Dana will not produce any negative tax consequences because both Sam and Dana's tax liability would be $0.

FIGURE 2.8	Client Letter

Hoffman and Smith, CPAs
5191 Natorp Boulevard
Mason, OH 45040

August 30, 2014

Mr. and Ms. Fred Samuels
111 Boulevard
Williamsburg, VA 23185

Dear Mr. and Ms. Samuels:

This letter is in response to your request for us to review your family's financial and tax situation. Our conclusions are based upon the facts as outlined in your August 12 letter. Any change in the facts may affect our conclusions.

You provide over 50% of the support for your son, Sam, and his wife, Dana. The scholarship Sam receives is not included in determining support. If the stock is not sold, you will qualify for a dependency exemption for both Sam and Dana.

If the stock is sold, a gain of approximately $8,000 will result. If Sam and Dana then file a joint return, you will lose the dependency exemption for Sam as a qualifying child and will lose the dependency exemption for Dana as a qualifying relative. You can avoid the loss of these two dependency exemptions if Sam and Dana file separate returns. This would result in a tax liability of $0 for Dana and $900 for Sam.

From a family tax planning and tax avoidance perspective, Sam should not sell the stock in 2014. Delaying the stock sale will enable you to claim dependency exemptions for both Sam and Dana and will enable Sam and Dana to have a $0 tax liability for 2014.

Should you need more information or need to clarify our conclusions, do not hesitate to contact me.

Sincerely yours,

John J. Jones, CPA
Partner

2-4 WORKING WITH THE TAX LAW— TAX PLANNING

Tax research and tax planning are inseparable. The *primary* purpose of effective *tax planning* is to reduce the taxpayer's total tax bill. This statement does not mean that the course of action selected must produce the lowest possible tax under the circumstances. The minimization of tax liability must be considered in context with the legitimate business goals of the taxpayer.

A *secondary* objective of effective tax planning is to reduce or defer the tax in the current tax year. Specifically, this objective aims to accomplish one or more of the following: eradicating the tax entirely; eliminating the tax in the current year; deferring the receipt of income; converting ordinary income into capital gains; converting active income to passive income; converting passive expense to active expense; proliferating taxpayers (i.e., forming partnerships and corporations or making lifetime gifts to family members); eluding double taxation; avoiding ordinary income; or creating, increasing, or accelerating deductions. However, this second objective should be approached with considerable reservation and moderation. For example, a tax election in one year may reduce taxes currently, but saddle future years with a disadvantageous tax position.

LO.6

Apply tax research techniques and planning procedures.

2-4a Nontax Considerations

There is an honest danger that tax motivations may take on a significance that does not correspond to the true values involved. In other words, tax considerations may impair the exercise of sound business judgment by the taxpayer. Thus, the tax planning process can become a medium through which to accomplish ends that are socially and economically objectionable. All too often, planning seems to lean toward the opposing extremes of placing either too little or too much emphasis on tax considerations. The goal should be a balance that recognizes the significance of taxes, but not beyond the point where planning detracts from the exercise of good business judgment.

The remark is often made that a good rule is to refrain from pursuing any course of action that would not be followed were it not for certain tax considerations. This statement is not entirely correct, but it does illustrate the desirability of preventing business logic from being *sacrificed at the altar of tax planning.*

2-4b Components of Tax Planning

The popular perception of tax planning often is restricted to the adage "defer income and accelerate deductions." Although this timing approach does hold true and is important, meaningful tax planning involves considerably more.

Preferable to deferring income is complete *avoidance.* Consider, for example, the corporate employee who chooses nontaxable fringe benefits (e.g., group term life insurance and health insurance) over a fully taxable future pay increase.[51] Complete avoidance of gain recognition also occurs when the owner of appreciated property transfers it by death. If this "step-up" in basis to fair market value occurs, the built-in appreciation escapes the income tax forever.[52]

If the recognition of income cannot be avoided, its deferral will postpone income tax consequences. *Deferral* of income can take many forms. Besides like-kind exchanges and involuntary conversions, most retirement plans put off income tax consequences until the payout period. Deferral of gain recognition also can occur when appreciated property is transferred to a newly formed corporation or partnership.[53]

A corollary to the deferral of income is the acceleration of deductions. For example, an accrual basis, calendar year corporation wants an additional charitable deduction for 2014 but has a cash-flow problem. If the corporation authorizes the contribution in 2014 and pays it on or before March 15, 2015, the deduction can be claimed for 2014.[54] Taxes can be saved by *shifting* income to lower-bracket taxpayers. Gifts of appreciated property to lower-bracket family members can reduce the applicable capital gain rate on a later sale by 15 percentage points (from 15 percent to 0 percent).[55] For certain high-income taxpayers, the reduction is 20 percentage points (from 20 percent to 0 percent).

If income cannot be avoided, deferred, or shifted, the nature of the gain can be *converted.* By changing the classification of property, income taxes can be reduced.[56] Thus, a taxpayer who transfers appreciated inventory to a controlled corporation has converted ordinary income property to a capital asset. When the taxpayer's stock is later sold, preferential capital gain rates apply.

The conversion approach also can work in tax planning for losses. Properly structured, a loan to a corporation that becomes worthless can be an ordinary loss rather than the less desirable capital loss. Likewise, planning with § 1244 permits an investor in qualified small business stock to convert what would be a capital loss into an ordinary loss.[57]

Effective tax planning requires that careful consideration be given to the *choice of entity* used for conducting a business. The corporate form results in double taxation but permits shareholder-employees to be covered by fringe benefit programs. Partnerships and S corporations allow a pass-through of losses and other tax

---

[51]See Section 5-6 and Example 23 in Chapter 5.

[52]See Examples 22 and 24 in Chapter 14.

[53]See Examples 22 and 43 in Chapter 20 and Chapter 19 in general.

[54]See Example 7 in Chapter 20.

[55]See Section 14-3b in Chapter 14.

[56]See Example 48 in Chapter 4.

[57]See Example 9 in Chapter 7.

attributes, but transferring ownership interests as gifts to family members may be difficult.[58]

Although the substance of a transaction, rather than its form, generally controls, this rule is not always the case with tax planning. *Preserving formalities*, particularly clear documentation, often is crucial to the result. Is an advance to a corporation a loan or a contribution to capital? The answer may well depend on the existence of a note. Along with preserving formalities, the taxpayer should keep records that support a transaction. Returning to the issue of loan versus contribution to capital, how is the advance listed on the books of the borrower? What do the corporate minutes say about the advance?

Finally, effective tax planning requires *consistency* on the part of taxpayers. A shareholder who treats a corporate distribution as a return of capital cannot later avoid a stock basis adjustment by contending that the distribution was really a dividend.

In summary, the key components of tax planning include the following:

- *Avoid* the recognition of income (usually by resorting to a nontaxable source or nontaxable event).
- *Defer* the recognition of income (or accelerate deductions).
- *Convert* the classification of income (or deductions) to a more advantageous form (e.g., ordinary income into capital gain).
- *Choose* the business *entity* with the desired tax attributes.
- Preserve *formalities* by generating and maintaining supporting documentation.
- Act in a manner *consistent* with the intended objective.

2-4c Tax Avoidance and Tax Evasion

A fine line exists between legal tax planning and illegal tax planning—tax avoidance versus tax evasion. **Tax avoidance** is merely tax minimization through legal techniques. In this sense, tax avoidance is the proper objective of all tax planning. Tax evasion, while also aimed at the elimination or reduction of taxes, connotes the use of subterfuge and fraud as a means to an end. Popular usage—probably because of the common goals involved—has so linked these two concepts that many individuals are no longer aware of the true distinctions between them. Consequently, some taxpayers have been deterred from properly taking advantage of planning possibilities. The now classic words of Judge Learned Hand in *Commissioner v. Newman* reflect the true values the taxpayer should have:

> Over and over again courts have said that there is nothing sinister in so arranging one's affairs as to keep taxes as low as possible. Everybody does so, rich or poor; and all do right, for nobody owes any public duty to pay more than the law demands: taxes are enforced extractions, not voluntary contributions. To demand more in the name of morals is mere cant.[59]

As Denis Healy, a former British Chancellor, once said, "The difference between tax avoidance and tax evasion is the thickness of a prison wall."

The Government Accountability Office estimates that U.S. taxpayers spend at least $107 billion each year on tax compliance costs. The Treasury Department estimates that individuals spend at least 6.4 billion hours preparing Federal income tax returns. Small businesses, self-employed persons, and taxpayers with the highest marginal tax rates have the highest levels of tax evasion.[60]

[58]See Sections 20-4 and 20-6c in Chapter 20.

[59]*Comm. v. Newman*, 47–1 USTC ¶9175, 35 AFTR 857, 159 F.2d 848 (CA–2, 1947).

[60]Adapted from J. A. Tackett, Joe Antenucci, and Fran Wolf, "A Criminological Perspective of Tax Evasion," *Tax Notes* (February 6, 2006): 654–658;

L. E. Burman, "Tax Evasion, IRS Priorities, and the EITC," *Statement before the United States House of Representatives Committee on the Budget; On Waste, Fraud, and Abuse in Federal Mandatory Programs* (July 9, 2003).

ETHICS & EQUITY   Global Poverty Saint Should Pay Up!

Bono's band U2 moved its music and publishing business, worth millions of pounds, from Ireland to Holland in 2006 to avoid taxes as a result of tax breaks for artists. In 2010, U2 was the highest-paid music group, earning around 80 million pounds.

The protest group Art Uncut had a massive inflatable sign with the message "Bono Pay Up" at its Glastonbury performance. Although Bono has been nominated for a Nobel Peace prize, Irish politicians complain that Bono urges governments to give more money to relieve poverty, but the band denies the Irish government the funds to do so. Also, some contend that only about 1.2 percent of his 2008 contributions of 9.6 million pounds was given to good causes. What are your thoughts?

Sources: Based on George Arbuthnott, "'Saint Bono' The Anti-poverty Campaigner Facing Huge Glastonbury Protest—For Avoiding Taxes," Mail Online, June 5, 2011, **www.dailymail.co.uk/news/article-1394422/saint-bono-facing-huge-glastonbury-protest-avoiding-tax.html**.

2-4d Follow-Up Procedures

Because tax planning usually involves a proposed (as opposed to a completed) transaction, it is predicated upon the continuing validity of the advice based upon the tax research. A change in the tax law (legislative, administrative, or judicial) could alter the original conclusion. Additional research may be necessary to test the solution in light of current developments (refer to the broken lines at the right in Figure 2.5).

2-4e Tax Planning—A Practical Application

Returning to the facts of *The Big Picture* on page 2-1, what could be done to protect the dependency exemptions for the parents? If Sam and Dana refrain from filing a joint return, both could be claimed by the parents.

Another tax planning tool is the installment method. Could the securities be sold using the installment method so that most of the gain is deferred into the next year? Under the installment method (§ 453), certain gains may be postponed and recognized as the cash proceeds are received. The problem is that the installment method is not available for stock traded on an established securities market.[61]

A little more research, however, indicates that Sam might be able to sell the stock and postpone the recognition of gain until the following year by selling short an equal number of substantially identical shares and covering the short sale in the subsequent year with the shares originally held. Selling short means that Sam sells borrowed stock (substantially identical) and repays the lender with the stock held on the date of the short sale. This *short against the box* technique would allow Sam to protect his $8,000 profit and defer the closing of the sale until the following year.[62] However, additional research indicates that 1997 tax legislation provides that the short against the box technique will no longer produce the desired postponement of recognized gain. That is, at the time of the short sale, Sam will have a recognized gain of $8,000 from a constructive sale. Note the critical role of obtaining the correct facts in attempting to resolve the proper strategy for the taxpayers.

Throughout this text, most chapters include observations on tax planning. Such observations are not all-inclusive, but are intended to illustrate some of the ways in which the material covered can be effectively utilized to minimize taxes.

---

[61]See Chapter 18 for a discussion of installment sales.
[62]§§ 1233(a) and 1233(b)(2). See Chapter 16 for a discussion of short sales.

2-5 TAXATION ON THE CPA EXAMINATION

The CPA examination has changed from a paper-and-pencil exam to a computer-based exam with increased emphasis on information technology and general business knowledge. The 14-hour exam has four sections, and taxation is included in the 3-hour Regulations section.

In January 2011, the CPA examination was reorganized, with all written communication tasks now concentrated in the Business Environment & Concepts section. Shorter simulations have replaced the longer simulations.

Each exam section includes multiple-choice questions and two other sections that have short task-based simulation (TBS) questions. The Regulations section is 60 percent Taxation and 40 percent Law & Professional Responsibilities (all areas other than Business Structure). The three-hour Regulations section has a new format. It now contains:

- Three multiple-choice question (MCQ) testlets consisting of 72 questions.
- One testlet (i.e., a group of questions prepared to appear together) containing six short task-based simulations with the research question in a new format.

A candidate may review and change answers within each testlet but cannot go back after exiting a testlet. Candidates take different but equivalent exams.

Simulations are small case studies designed to test a candidate's tax knowledge and skills using real-life work-related situations. Simulations include a four-function pop-up calculator, a blank spreadsheet with some elementary functionality, and authoritative literature appropriate to the subject matter. The taxation database includes authoritative excerpts that are necessary to complete the tax case study simulations (e.g., Internal Revenue Code, Regulations, IRS publications, and Federal tax forms). Examples of such simulations follow.

LO.7

Be aware of taxation on the CPA examination.

> **Example 4**
>
> The *tax citation type* simulation requires the candidate to research the Internal Revenue Code and enter a Code Section and subsection. For example, Amber Company is considering using the simplified dollar-value method of pricing its inventory for purposes of the LIFO method that is available to certain small businesses. What Code Section is the relevant authority in the Internal Revenue Code to which you should turn to determine whether the taxpayer is eligible to use this method? To be successful, the candidate needs to find § 474.

> **Example 5**
>
> A *tax form completion* simulation requires the candidate to fill out a portion of a tax form. For example, Red Company is a limited liability company (LLC) for tax purposes. Complete the income section of the IRS Form 1065 for Red Company using the values found and calculated on previous tabs along with the following data:
>
> | | |
> |---|---|
> | Ordinary income from other partnerships | $ 5,200 |
> | Net gain (loss) from Form 4797 | 2,400 |
> | Management fee income | 12,000 |
>
> The candidate is provided with page 1 of Form 1065 on which to record the appropriate amounts.
>
> Any field that requires an entry is a shaded rectangular cell. Some white rectangular cells will automatically calculate based on the entries in the shaded cell.

Candidates can learn more about the CPA examination at **www.cpa-exam.org**. This online tutorial site's topics include:

- Common tools.
- Navigation.
- Form completion.
- Numeric entry.
- Research questions.
- Authoritative literature search.
- Written communication.

TAX IN THE NEWS   Did Honest Abe Have to Pay Taxes?

When Congress passed a comprehensive income tax in 1862 because of the Civil War, the lawmakers included themselves as taxpayers. However, the law did not include President Abraham Lincoln and Federal judges.

Although some observers insisted that the President was excluded from the tax, President Lincoln apparently made voluntary payments to the Treasury equal to the taxes he might have owed. Whether the payments were voluntary, $92 per month was withheld from his paycheck.

Eventually, the courts held that Lincoln did not have to pay the taxes, and the administrator of his estate filed for a refund. The Treasury refunded $3,556 to his estate in 1872.

———————
Source: J. J. Thorndike, "Abraham Lincoln Paid Income Taxes—But He Didn't Have To," *Tax Notes*, July 8, 2013, pp. 122–123.

The common tools are a calculator, a spreadsheet, reminder flags, and an examination clock. A 30- to 60-minute sample exam will familiarize a candidate with the types of questions on the examination.

Key Terms

Acquiescence, 2-18

Circuit Court of Appeals, 2-14

Citator, 2-29

Court of original jurisdiction, 2-11

Determination letters, 2-10

Federal District Court, 2-11

Finalized Regulations, 2-8

Interpretive Regulations, 2-28

Legislative Regulations, 2-28

Letter rulings, 2-9

Nonacquiescence, 2-18

Precedents, 2-15

Procedural Regulations, 2-28

Proposed Regulations, 2-8

Revenue Procedures, 2-8

Revenue Rulings, 2-8

Small Cases Division, 2-11

Tax avoidance, 2-35

Tax research, 2-24

Technical Advice Memoranda (TAMs), 2-10

Temporary Regulations, 2-8

U.S. Court of Federal Claims, 2-11

U.S. Supreme Court, 2-16

U.S. Tax Court, 2-11

Writ of Certiorari, 2-16

Discussion Questions

1. **LO.1** A large part of tax research consists of determining what?

2. **LO.1** Why do taxpayers often have more than one alternative for structuring a business transaction?

3. **LO.1** To what date in 2013 did an average taxpayer have to work in order to pay his or her taxes for the year?

4. **LO.1** Where does the Federal tax legislation generally originate?

5. **LO.1** In which title and subtitle of the U.S. Code is the income tax portion of the *Internal Revenue Code of 1986* found?

Communications   6. **LO.2, 5** Butch Bishop operates a small international firm named Tile, Inc. A new treaty between the United States and Spain conflicts with a Section of the Internal Revenue Code. Butch asks you for advice. If he follows the treaty position, does he need to disclose this on his tax return? If he is required to disclose, are there any penalties for failure to disclose? Prepare a letter in which you respond to Butch. Tile's address is 100 International Drive, Tampa, FL 33620.

7. **LO.I, 2** Interpret this Regulation citation: Reg. § 1.163–10(a)(2).

8. **LO.I, 2** Explain how Regulations are arranged. How would the following Regulations be cited?
   a. Finalized Regulations under § 152.
   b. Proposed Regulations under § 274.
   c. Temporary Regulations under § 163.
   d. Legislative Regulations under § 1501.

9. **LO.I, 4** Distinguish between legislative, interpretive, and procedural Regulations.

10. **LO.I** In the citation Notice 90–20, 1990–1 C.B. 328, to what do the 20 and the 328 refer?

11. **LO.I, 4** Rank the following items from the lowest to the highest authority in the Federal tax law system:
    a. Interpretive Regulation.
    b. Legislative Regulation.
    c. Letter ruling.
    d. Revenue Ruling.
    e. Internal Revenue Code.
    f. Proposed Regulation.

12. **LO.I** Interpret each of the following citations:
    a. Temp.Reg. § 1.956–2T.
    b. Rev.Rul. 2012–15, 2012–23 I.R.B. 975.
    c. Ltr.Rul. 200204051.

13. **LO.I, 5** Sally Andrews calls you on the phone. She says that she has found a 2007 letter ruling that agrees with a position she wants to take on her tax return. She asks you about the precedential value of a letter ruling. Draft a memo for the tax files outlining what you told Sally.   Communications

14. **LO.I** Sri is considering writing the IRS to find out whether a possible stock redemption would be a qualified stock redemption. Outline some relevant tax issues Sri faces in determining whether to request a letter ruling.   Issue ID

15. **LO.I** Where may private letter rulings be found?

16. **LO.I** What are the differences between Technical Advice Memoranda (TAMs) and Technical Expedited Advice Memoranda (TEAMs)?

17. **LO.I** Dwain receives a 90-day letter after his discussion with an appeals officer. He is not satisfied with the $101,000 settlement offer. Identify the relevant tax research issues facing Dwain.   Issue ID

18. **LO.I** Which of the following would be considered advantages of the Small Cases Division of the Tax Court?
    a. Appeal to the U.S. Tax Court is possible.
    b. A hearing of a deficiency of $65,000 is considered on a timely basis.
    c. Taxpayer can handle the litigation without using a lawyer or certified public accountant.
    d. Taxpayer can use other Small Cases Division decisions for precedential value.
    e. The actual hearing is conducted informally.
    f. Travel time will probably be reduced.

19. **LO.I** List an advantage and a disadvantage of using the U.S. Court of Federal Claims as the trial court for Federal tax litigation.

20. **LO.I, 5** Eddy Falls is considering litigating a tax deficiency of approximately $229,030 in the court system. He asks you to provide him with a short description of his alternatives indicating the advantages and disadvantages of each. Prepare your response to Eddy in the form of a letter. His address is 200 Mesa Drive, Tucson, AZ 85714.   Communications

21. **LO.I** List an advantage and a disadvantage of using the U.S. Tax Court as the trial court for Federal tax litigation.

22. **LO.1** A taxpayer lives in Michigan. In a controversy with the IRS, the taxpayer loses at the trial court level. Describe the appeal procedure under the following different assumptions:
    a. The trial court was the Small Cases Division of the U.S. Tax Court.
    b. The trial court was the U.S. Tax Court.
    c. The trial court was a U.S. District Court.
    d. The trial court was the U.S. Court of Federal Claims.

23. **LO.1** What is meant by the term *petitioner*?

24. **LO.1** An appellate court will often become involved in fact-finding determination. Discuss the validity of this statement.

25. **LO.1** For the U.S. Tax Court, U.S. District Court, and U.S. Court of Federal Claims, indicate the following:
    a. Number of regular judges per court.
    b. Availability of a jury trial.
    c. Whether the deficiency must be paid before the trial.

26. **LO.1** A taxpayer living in the following states would appeal a decision of the U.S. District Court to which Court of Appeals?
    a. Wyoming.
    b. Nebraska.
    c. Idaho.
    d. Louisiana.
    e. Illinois.

27. **LO.1** What precedents must each of these courts follow?
    a. U.S. Tax Court.
    b. U.S. Court of Federal Claims.
    c. U.S. District Court.

28. **LO.1** What determines the appropriate Circuit Court of Appeals for a particular taxpayer?

29. **LO.1, 4** In assessing the validity of a prior court decision, discuss the significance of the following on the taxpayer's issue:
    a. The decision was rendered by the U.S. District Court of Wyoming. Taxpayer lives in Wyoming.
    b. The decision was rendered by the U.S. Court of Federal Claims. Taxpayer lives in Wyoming.
    c. The decision was rendered by the Second Circuit Court of Appeals. Taxpayer lives in California.
    d. The decision was rendered by the U.S. Supreme Court.
    e. The decision was rendered by the U.S. Tax Court. The IRS has acquiesced in the result.
    f. Same as (e) except that the IRS has issued a nonacquiescence as to the result.

30. **LO.2** In the citation *Schuster's Express, Inc.*, 66 T.C. 588 (1976), *aff'd* 562 F.2d 39 (CA–2, 1977), *nonacq.*, to what do the 66, 39, and *nonacq.* refer?

31. **LO.2** Is there an automatic right to appeal to the U.S. Supreme Court? If so, what is the process?

32. **LO.2** Referring to the citation only, determine which court issued these decisions.
    a. 716 F.2d 693 (CA–9, 1983).
    b. 92 T.C. 400 (1998).
    c. 70 U.S. 224 (1935).
    d. 3 B.T.A. 1042 (1926).
    e. T.C.Memo. 1957–169.
    f. 50 AFTR2d 92–6000 (Ct. Cl., 1992).
    g. Ltr.Rul. 9046036.
    h. 111 F.Supp.2d 1294 (S.D. N.Y., 2000).
    i. 98–50, 1998–1 C.B. 10.

33. **LO.2** Interpret each of the following citations:
    a. 14 T.C. 74 (1950).
    b. 592 F.2d 1251 (CA–5, 1979).
    c. 95–1 USTC ¶50,104 (CA–6, 1995).
    d. 75 AFTR2d 95–110 (CA–6, 1995).
    e. 223 F.Supp. 663 (W.D. Tex., 1963).

34. **LO.1, 2** Explain the following abbreviations:
    a. CA–2.
    b. Fed.Cl.
    c. *aff'd.*
    d. *rev'd.*
    e. *rem'd.*
    f. *Cert. denied.*
    g. *acq.*
    h. B.T.A.
    i. USTC.
    j. AFTR.
    k. F.3d.
    l. F.Supp.
    m. USSC.
    n. S.Ct.
    o. D.Ct.

35. **LO.2** Give the Commerce Clearing House citation for the following courts:
    a. Small Cases Division of the Tax Court.
    b. Federal District Court.
    c. U.S. Supreme Court.
    d. U.S. Court of Federal Claims.
    e. Tax Court Memorandum decision.

36. **LO.2** Where can you locate a published decision of the U.S. Court of Federal Claims?

37. **LO.1, 2** Which of the following items can probably be found in the *Internal Revenue Bulletin?*
    a. Action on Decision.
    b. Small Cases Division of the U.S. Tax Court decision.
    c. Letter ruling.
    d. Revenue Procedure.
    e. Finalized Regulation.
    f. U.S. Court of Federal Claims decision.
    g. Acquiescences to Tax Court decisions.
    h. U.S. Circuit Court of Appeals decision.

38. **LO.3** For her tax class, Yvonne has to prepare a research paper discussing the tax aspects of child support payments. Explain to Yvonne how she can research this topic using various tax research resources.   Issue ID

39. **LO.4** Where can a researcher find the current Internal Revenue Code of 1986?

40. **LO.2, 4** You inherit a tax problem that was researched five months ago. You believe the answer is correct, but you are unfamiliar with the general area. How would you find recent articles dealing with the subject area? How do you evaluate the reliability of the authority cited in the research report? How do you determine the latest developments pertaining to the research problem?   Decision Making

41. **LO.6** What is the primary purpose of effective tax planning? Explain.

42. **LO.7** Describe simulation questions on the CPA exam.

Problems

43. **LO.1** In which Subchapter of the Internal Revenue Code would one find information about corporate distributions?
    a. Subchapter S.
    b. Subchapter C.
    c. Subchapter P.
    d. Subchapter K.
    e. Subchapter M.

44. **LO.1** To locate an IRS Revenue Procedure that was issued during the past week, which source would you consult?
    a. *Federal Register.*
    b. *Internal Revenue Bulletin.*
    c. Internal Revenue Code.
    d. Some other source.

45. **LO.1** Which of the following items can be found in the *Federal Register*?
    a. Letter Ruling.
    b. Action on Decision.
    c. Revenue Procedure.
    d. Temporary Regulation.
    e. Technical Advice Memorandum.

46. **LO.1, 4** Rank the items below from most reliable to least reliable:
    a. Letter Ruling.
    b. Legislative Regulation.
    c. Code Section.
    d. Revenue Ruling.
    e. Proposed Regulation.
    f. Interpretive Regulation.
    g. Recent Temporary Regulation.

47. **LO.4** Using the legend provided, classify each of the following tax sources:

Legend
P = Primary tax source
S = Secondary tax source
B = Both
N = Neither

    a. Sixteenth Amendment to the U.S. Constitution.
    b. Tax treaty between the United States and India.
    c. Revenue Procedure.
    d. General Counsel Memoranda (1989).
    e. U.S. District Court decision.
    f. *Yale Law Journal* article.
    g. Temporary Regulations (issued 2013).
    h. U.S. Tax Court Memorandum decision.
    i. Small Cases Division of the U.S. Tax Court decision.
    j. House Ways and Means Committee report.

48. **LO.1, 2** Using the legend provided, classify each of the following citations as to publisher:

Legend
RIA = Research Institute of America
CCH = Commerce Clearing House
W = West
U.S. = U.S. Government
O = Others

   a. 83–2 USTC ¶9600.
   b. 52 AFTR 2d 83–5954.
   c. 67 T.C. 293 (1976).
   d. 39 TCM 32 (1979).
   e. 416 U.S. 938.
   f. RIA T.C. Memo. ¶80,582.
   g. 89 S.Ct. 501.
   h. 2 Cl.Ct. 600.
   i. 415 F.2d 488.
   j. 592 F.Supp. 18.
   k. 77–37, 1977–2 C.B. 568.
   l. S. Rep. No. 1622, 83rd Cong., 2d Sess. 42 (1954).

49. **LO.6** Using the legend provided, classify each of the following statements:

Legend

A = Tax avoidance
E = Tax evasion
N = Neither

---

   a. Sue writes a $707 check for a charitable contribution on December 28, 2014, but does not mail the check to the charitable organization until January 10, 2015. She takes a deduction in 2014.
   b. Sam decides not to report interest income from a bank because the amount is only $19.75.
   c. Harry pays property taxes on his home in December 2014 rather than waiting until February 2015.
   d. Variet switches her investments from taxable corporate bonds to tax exempt municipal bonds.
   e. Mel encourages his mother to save most of her Social Security benefits so that he will be able to claim her as a dependent.

Research Problems

Note: Solutions to Research Problems can be prepared by using the **Checkpoint®** **Student Edition** online research product, which is available to accompany this text. It is also possible to prepare solutions to the Research Problems by using tax research materials found in a standard tax library.

THOMSON REUTERS
CHECKPOINT®

Research Problem 1. Under Code § 274(a), are lunches with lawyers and accountants to build up goodwill deductible?

Research Problem 2. Describe the IRC sections that are found in Subtitle E of the IRC. Would you expect these provisions not to be addressed anywhere else in the IRC? Explain.

Research Problem 3. Locate the following items and give a brief summary of the results.
   a. *Charles Y. Choi*, T.C. Memo. 2002–183.
   b. Ltr.Rul. 200231003.
   c. Action on Decision, 2000–004, May 10, 2000.

Research Problem 4. Determine the missing data in these court decisions and rulings.
   a. *Higgens v. Comm.*, 312 U.S._____ (1941).
   b. *Talen v. U.S.*, 355 F.Supp.2d 22 (D.Ct. D.C., _____).
   c. Rev.Rul. 2008–18, 2008–13 I.R.B._____.
   d. *Pahl v. Comm.*, 150 F.3d 1124 (CA–9, _____).
   e. *Veterinary Surgical Consultants PC*, 117 T.C._____(2001).
   f. *Yeagle Drywall Co.*, T.C.Memo. 2001_____.

Research Problem 5. Locate the following Tax Court case: *Thomas J. Green, Jr.*, 59 T.C. 456 (1972). Briefly describe the issue in the case and explain what the Tax Court said about using IRS publications to support a research conclusion.

Research Problem 6. Can a Tax Court Small Case Decision be treated as a precedent for other cases? Explain.

Partial list of research aids:
IRC § 7463(b).
Maria Antionette Walton Mitchell, T.C. Summ. 2004–160.

Research Problem 7. In the following tax publications matrix, place an X if a court decision can be found in the publication. There may be more than one X in a row for a particular court.

Court	U.S. Govt. Printing Office	West				Research Institute of America			Commerce Clearing House	
		Federal Supp.2d	Federal 3d	Federal Claims Reporter	S.Ct.	BTA Memo.	T.C. Memo.	AFTR	T.C. Memo.	USTC
U.S. Supreme Court										
Circuit Court of Appeals										
Court of Federal Claims										
District Court										
Tax Court (Regular decisions)										
Tax Court (Memo decisions)										
Board of Tax Appeals										
BTA Memo.										

Decision Making

Research Problem 8. When Oprah gave away Pontiac G6 sedans to her TV audience, was the value of the cars taxable? On Labor Day weekend in 2006, World Furniture Mall in Plano, Illinois, gave away $275,000 of furniture because the Chicago Bears shut out the Green Bay Packers in the team's football season opener at Lambeau Field in Green Bay (26–0). Was the free furniture in the form of a discount or rebate taxable, or should the furniture company have handed the customers a Form 1099–MISC?

Decision Making

Research Problem 9. You are interviewing a client before preparing his tax return. He indicates that he did not list as income $96,000 received as a recovery for false imprisonment. What should you do with respect to this significant recovery?

Partial list of research aids:
CCA 200809001.
Daniel and Brenda Stadnyk, T.C.Memo. 2008–289.
Rev.Rul. 2007–14, 2007–1 C.B. 747.
§ 104.

Internet Activity

Use the tax resources of the Internet to address the following questions. Do not restrict your search to the Web, but include a review of newsgroups and general reference materials, practitioner sites and resources, primary sources of the tax law, chat rooms and discussion groups, and other opportunities.

Research Problem 10. (1) Go to **www.taxalmanac.org** and use the website to find § 61(a). What is defined in this Code Section? Is the definition broad or narrow?

(2) Go to **www.legalbitstream.com** and find the case in which Mark Spitz, the former Olympic gold medalist, is the petitioner. Answer the following questions about the case:

a. What tax years are at issue in the case?
b. In what year was the case decided?
c. Did the court decide in favor of Mr. Spitz or the IRS?
d. Were any penalties imposed on Mr. Spitz? Why or why not?

Research Problem 11. Go to the U.S. Tax Court website (**www.ustaxcourt.gov**).

a. What different types of cases can be found on the site?
b. What is a Summary Opinion? Find one.
c. What is a Memorandum Opinion? Find one.
d. Find the "Rules of Practice and Procedure."

CHAPTER

3

Tax Formula and Tax Determination; An Overview of Property Transactions

LEARNING OBJECTIVES: *After completing Chapter 3, you should be able to:*

LO.1 Recognize and apply the components of the Federal income tax formula.

LO.2 Explain the standard deduction and evaluate its choice in arriving at taxable income.

LO.3 Apply the rules for arriving at personal exemptions.

LO.4 Explain the rules for determining dependency exemptions.

LO.5 List the filing requirements and choose the proper filing status.

LO.6 Demonstrate the proper procedures for determining the tax liability.

LO.7 Identify and report kiddie tax situations.

LO.8 Formulate the fundamentals of property transactions.

LO.9 Evaluate tax planning opportunities associated with the individual tax formula.

THE BIG PICTURE   Tax Solutions for the Real World

A DIVIDED HOUSEHOLD

Polly maintains a household in which she lives with her unemployed husband (Nick), stepdaughter (Paige), and a family friend (Maude). She provides more than one-half of the support for both Paige and Maude. Maude was fatally injured in an automobile accident in February, and Polly paid for her hospitalization and funeral expenses. Paige, an accomplished gymnast, graduated from high school last year. Paige has a part-time job but spends most of her time training and looking for an athletic scholarship to the "right" college. In March, Nick left for parts unknown and has not been seen or heard from since. Polly was more surprised than distressed over Nick's unexpected departure. One reaction, however, was to sell her wedding rings to a cousin who was getting married. The rings cost $11,800 and were sold for their approximate value of $9,000.

Based on these facts, what are Polly's income tax concerns for the current year?

Read the chapter and formulate your response.

FRAMEWORK 1040
Tax Formula for Individuals

This chapter covers the boldfaced portions of the Tax Formula for Individuals that is introduced in Figure 3.1 on p. 3-3. Below those portions are the sections of Form 1040 where the results are reported.

Income *(broadly conceived)*	$xx,xxx
Less: Exclusions	(x,xxx)
Gross income	$xx,xxx
Less: Deductions for adjusted gross income	(x,xxx)

FORM 1040 (p.1)

1 ☐ Single
2 ☐ Married filing jointly (even if only one had income)
3 ☐ Married filing separately. Enter spouse's SSN above and full name here. ▶

4 ☐ Head of household (with qualifying person). (See instructions.) If the qualifying person is a child but not your dependent, enter this child's name here. ▶
5 ☐ Qualifying widow(er) with dependent child

Adjusted gross income	$xx,xxx
Less: The greater of total **itemized deductions** *or* the standard deduction	(x,xxx)

FORM 1040 (p.2)

39a Check if: ☐ **You** were born before January 2, 1949, ☐ Blind. ☐ **Spouse** was born before January 2, 1949, ☐ Blind. } **Total boxes checked** ▶ **39a** ☐

b If your spouse itemizes on a separate return or you were a dual-status alien, check here ▶ 39b ☐

40 **Itemized deductions** (from Schedule A) **or** your **standard deduction** (see left margin) . .

42 **Exemptions.** If line 38 is $150,000 or less, multiply $3,900 by the number on line 6d. Otherwise, see instructions

Personal and dependency exemptions	(x,xxx)
Taxable income	$xx,xxx
Tax on taxable income *(see Tax Tables or Tax Rate Schedules)*	$ x,xxx
Less: Tax credits *(including income taxes withheld and prepaid)*	(xxx)
Tax due *(or refund)*	$ xxx

The framework for the application of the Federal income tax to individuals is the tax formula. As Chapter 1 mentioned, the tax formula is an integral part of our U.S. tax system (i.e., local, state, and Federal), and Chapter 3 provides a summary of its components. In addition, several of its key components—the standard deduction, personal and dependency exemptions, and tax determination—are discussed at length in Chapter 3.

By introducing the tax formula, therefore, Chapter 3 establishes the framework for almost all of the rest of the text (i.e., Chapters 4 through 19). The formula and its impact on the chapters to follow are reflected in Figure 3.1. In integrating the formula with the chapters in the text, however, some liberties were taken. In the interest of simplicity, Figure 3.1 omits references to several chapters for the following reasons:

- Chapter 18 deals with the more sophisticated aspects of accounting periods and methods. The main consideration in this area is the distinction between the cash and accrual methods of accounting. The method used controls the recognition *or* deferral of *income* and *deductions* and, therefore, is discussed in Chapters 4 and 6.
- Chapter 19 deals with deferred compensation and cuts across several parts of the tax formula. Depending on the type of arrangement involved, gross income may be recognized (or deferred) or a deduction can materialize.

Chapter 3 also provides an overview of property transactions. When property is sold or otherwise disposed of, a gain or loss may result, which can affect the determination of taxable income. Although property transactions are covered in detail in Chapters 14 through 17, an understanding of certain basic concepts helps in working with some of the materials to follow. The chapter concludes by

FIGURE 3.1	Tax Formula for Individuals (Components Integrated into the Text)	
		Text Discussion
Income (broadly conceived)	$xx,xxx	Chs. 3, 4
Less: **Exclusions**	(x,xxx)	Ch. 5
Gross income	$xx,xxx	Chs. 4, 16, 17
Less: **Deductions** *for* adjusted gross income	(x,xxx)	Chs. 6–9, 11, 16, 17
Adjusted gross income	$xx,xxx	
Less: The greater of—		
Total **itemized deductions** *or* **standard deduction**	(x,xxx)	Chs. 6, 9, 10, 11 Ch. 3
Less: **Personal** and **dependency exemptions**	(x,xxx)	Ch. 3
Taxable income	$xx,xxx	Chs. 3, 12, 13
Tax on taxable income	$ x,xxx	Chs. 3, 12, 13
Less: **Tax credits**	(xxx)	Ch. 13
Tax due (or refund)	$ xxx	Chs. 3, 12, 13

addressing the difference between realized and recognized gain or loss and the classification of such gain or loss (ordinary or capital) for income tax purposes.

3-1 TAX FORMULA

Given that the tax formula establishes the framework for the Federal income tax on individuals, a brief review of its components will be helpful in understanding the in-depth discussion that follows in this and subsequent chapters.

LO.1

Recognize and apply the components of the Federal income tax formula.

3-1a Components of the Tax Formula

Income (Broadly Conceived)

In the tax formula, "income" is broadly conceived and includes all of the taxpayer's income, both taxable and nontaxable. Although it is essentially equivalent to gross receipts, it does not include a return of capital or receipt of borrowed funds.

Example 1

Dan decides to quit renting and move into a new house. Consequently, the owner of the apartment building returns to Dan the $600 damage deposit he previously made. To make a down payment on the house, Dan sells stock for $20,000 (original cost of $8,000) and borrows $50,000 from a bank. Only the $12,000 gain from the sale of the stock is income to Dan. The $600 damage deposit and the $8,000 cost of the stock are a return of capital. The $50,000 bank loan is not income as Dan has an obligation to repay that amount.

Exclusions

For various reasons, Congress has chosen to exclude certain types of income from the income tax base. The principal income exclusions are discussed in Chapter 5. A partial list of these exclusions is shown in Exhibit 3.1.

Gross Income

The Internal Revenue Code defines gross income broadly as "except as otherwise provided ..., all income from whatever source derived."[1] The "except as otherwise

---

[1]§ 61(a).

EXHIBIT 3.1	Partial List of Exclusions from Gross Income

Accident insurance proceeds	Life insurance paid upon death
Annuities (cost element)	Meals and lodging (if furnished for employer's
Bequests	convenience)
Child support payments	Military allowances
Cost-of-living allowance (for military)	Minister's dwelling rental value allowance
Damages for personal injury or sickness	Railroad retirement benefits (to a limited extent)
Gifts received	Scholarship grants (to a limited extent)
Group term life insurance, premium paid by employer	Social Security benefits (to a limited extent)
(for coverage up to $50,000)	Veterans' benefits
Inheritances	Welfare payments
Interest from state and local (i.e., municipal) bonds	Workers' compensation benefits

provided" refers to exclusions. Gross income includes, but is not limited to, the items in the partial list in Exhibit 3.2. It does not include unrealized gains. Gross income is discussed in Chapters 4 and 5.

Example 2

Beth received the following amounts during the year:

Salary	$30,000
Interest on savings account	900
Gift from her aunt	10,000
Prize won in state lottery	1,000
Alimony from ex-husband	12,000
Child support from ex-husband	6,000
Damages for injury in auto accident	25,000
Ten $50 bills in an unmarked envelope found in an airport lounge (airport authorities could not locate anyone who claimed ownership)	500
Federal income tax refund for last year's tax overpayment	120
Increase in the value of stock held for investment	5,000

Review Exhibits 3.1 and 3.2 to determine the amount Beth must include in the computation of taxable income and the amount she may exclude. Then check your answer in footnote 2.[2]

Deductions for Adjusted Gross Income

Individual taxpayers have two categories of deductions: (1) deductions *for* adjusted gross income (deductions to arrive at adjusted gross income) and (2) deductions *from* adjusted gross income.

Deductions *for* adjusted gross income (AGI) are sometimes known as *above-the-line* deductions because on the tax return they are taken before the "line" designating AGI. They are also referred to as *page 1 deductions* because they are claimed, either directly or indirectly (i.e., through supporting schedules), on page 1 of Form 1040. Deductions *for* AGI include, but are not limited to, the following:[3]

- Expenses incurred in a trade or business.
- Part of the self-employment tax.
- Unreimbursed moving expenses.
- Contributions to traditional Individual Retirement Accounts (IRAs) and certain other retirement plans.

[2]Beth must include $44,400 in computing taxable income ($30,000 salary + $900 interest + $1,000 lottery prize + $12,000 alimony + $500 found property). She can exclude $41,000 ($10,000 gift from aunt + $6,000 child support + $25,000 damages). The $120 Federal income tax refund is excluded because it represents an adjustment (i.e., overpayment) of a non-deductible expenditure made in the previous year. The unrealized gain on the stock held for investment also is not included in gross income. Such gain will be included in gross income only when it is realized upon disposition of the stock.

[3]§ 62.

EXHIBIT 3.2	Partial List of Gross Income Items

Alimony	Hobby income
Annuities (income element)	Interest
Awards	Jury duty fees
Back pay	Living quarters, meals (unless furnished for employer's
Bargain purchase from employer	convenience)
Bonuses	Mileage allowance
Breach of contract damages	Military pay (unless combat pay)
Business income	Notary fees
Clergy fees	Partnership income
Commissions	Pensions
Compensation for services	Prizes
Death benefits	Professional fees
Debts forgiven	Punitive damages
Director's fees	Rents
Dividends	Rewards
Embezzled funds	Royalties
Employee awards (in certain cases)	Salaries
Employee benefits (except certain fringe benefits)	Severance pay
Estate and trust income	Strike and lockout benefits
Farm income	Supplemental unemployment benefits
Fees	Tips and gratuities
Gains from illegal activities	Travel allowance (in certain cases)
Gains from sale of property	Treasure trove (found property)
Gambling winnings	Wages
Group term life insurance, premium paid by employer (for coverage over $50,000)	

- Fees for college tuition and related expenses.
- Contributions to Health Savings Accounts (HSAs).
- Penalty for early withdrawal from savings.
- Interest on student loans.
- Excess capital losses.
- Alimony payments.

The effect on AGI of deductions *for* AGI is illustrated below.

Example 3

Mason, age 45, earned a salary of $78,000 in the current year. He contributed $4,000 to his traditional Individual Retirement Account (IRA), sold stock held as an investment for a short-term capital loss of $2,000, and paid $4,600 in alimony to his ex-wife. His AGI is determined as follows:

Gross income		
Salary		$ 78,000
Less: Deductions *for* AGI		
IRA contribution	$4,000	
Capital loss	2,000	
Alimony paid	4,600	(10,600)
AGI		$ 67,400

The principal deductions *for* AGI are discussed in Chapters 6, 7, 8, 9, 11, 16, and 17.

Deductions from Adjusted Gross Income

As a general rule, personal expenditures are disallowed as deductions in arriving at taxable income. However, Congress allows specified personal expenses as deductions from AGI (commonly referred to as **itemized deductions**).

Global Tax Issues

© iStockphoto.com/Andrey Prokhorov

Citizenship Is Not Tax-Free

Gross income from "whatever source derived" includes income from both U.S. and foreign sources. This approach to taxation, where the government taxes its citizens and residents on their worldwide income regardless of where earned, is referred to as a *global system*. Income earned by U.S. citizens outside the United States can be subject to additional taxes, however, because all countries maintain the right to tax income earned within their borders. Consequently, the U.S. tax law includes various mechanisms to alleviate the double taxation that arises when income is subject to tax in multiple jurisdictions. These mechanisms include the foreign tax deduction, the foreign tax credit, the foreign earned income exclusion for U.S. citizens and residents working abroad, and various tax treaty provisions.

Most industrialized countries use variants of the global system. An alternative approach is the *territorial system*, where a government taxes only the income earned within its borders. Hong Kong and Guatemala, for example, use a territorial approach.

AGI is an important subtotal that serves as the basis for computing percentage limitations on certain itemized deductions such as medical expenses, charitable contributions, and certain casualty losses. For example, medical expenses are deductible only to the extent they exceed 10 percent (7.5 percent if at least age 65) of AGI, and charitable contribution deductions may not exceed 50 percent of AGI. These limitations might be described as a 10 percent (or 7.5 percent) *floor* under the medical expense deduction and a 50 percent *ceiling* on the charitable contribution deduction.

> **Example 4**
>
> Assume the same facts as in Example 3 and assume that Mason had medical expenses of $8,000. Medical expenses may be included in itemized deductions to the extent they exceed 10% of AGI. In computing his itemized deductions, Mason may include medical expenses of $1,260 [$8,000 medical expenses − $6,740 (10% × $67,400 AGI)].

In addition to these personal expenses, taxpayers are allowed itemized deductions for expenses related to (1) the production or collection of income and (2) the management of property held for the production of income.[4] These expenses, sometimes referred to as *nonbusiness expenses*, differ from trade or business expenses. Trade or business expenses, which are deductions *for* AGI, must be incurred in connection with a trade or business. Nonbusiness expenses, on the other hand, are expenses incurred in connection with an income-producing activity that does not qualify as a trade or business. Such expenses are itemized deductions.

> **Example 5**
>
> Leo is the owner and operator of a video game arcade. All allowable expenses that he incurs in connection with the arcade business are deductions *for* AGI. In addition, Leo has an extensive portfolio of stocks and bonds. Leo's investment activity is not treated as a trade or business. All allowable expenses that Leo incurs in connection with these investments are itemized deductions.

Itemized deductions include, but are not limited to, the expenses listed in Exhibit 3.3. See Chapters 9 and 10 for a detailed discussion of itemized deductions.

---

[4]§ 212.

EXHIBIT 3.3	**Partial List of Itemized Deductions**

Medical expenses in excess of 10% (7.5% if at least age 65) of AGI
State and local income or sales taxes
Real estate taxes
Personal property taxes
Interest on home mortgage
Investment interest (to a limited extent)
Charitable contributions (within specified percentage limitations)
Casualty and theft losses in excess of 10% of AGI
Miscellaneous expenses (to the extent such expenses exceed 2% of AGI)
  Union dues
  Professional dues and subscriptions
  Certain educational expenses
  Tax return preparation fee
  Investment counsel fees
  Unreimbursed employee business expenses (after a percentage reduction for meals
    and entertainment)

Nondeductible Expenditures

Many expenditures are not deductible and, therefore, provide no tax benefit. Examples include, but are not limited to, the following:

- Personal living expenses, including any losses on the sale of personal use property.
- Hobby losses.
- Life insurance premiums.
- Expenses incident to jury duty.
- Gambling losses (in excess of gains).
- Child support payments.
- Fines and penalties.
- Political contributions.
- Certain passive losses.
- Funeral expenses.
- Expenses paid on another's behalf.
- Capital expenditures.

If an expenditure is classified as nondeductible, the component of the tax formula affected will be either the deduction *for* AGI or the deduction *from* AGI. Thus, a traffic fine for speeding is nondeductible whether the taxpayer was using the automobile on a business trip (normally a deduction *for* AGI) or participating in a Habitat for Humanity project (normally a deduction *from* AGI).[5] Most of the nondeductible items in the preceding list are discussed in Chapter 6. Passive loss limitations, however, are addressed in Chapter 11.

Standard Deduction

In lieu of claiming itemized deductions, taxpayers will use the **standard deduction**. As discussed later in the chapter, the standard deduction varies depending on filing status, age, and blindness. The standard deduction is adjusted (i.e., indexed) each year for inflation.

---

[5]The use of a personal automobile in connection with a charitable activity would probably qualify for the charitable contribution deduction—a deduction *from* AGI.

Personal and Dependency Exemptions

Exemptions are allowed for the taxpayer, the taxpayer's spouse, and each dependent of the taxpayer. Like the standard deduction, personal and dependency exemptions (discussed later) are adjusted each year for inflation. The exemption amount for 2014 is $3,950 (up from $3,900 in 2013).

Taxable Income

The determination of taxable income is illustrated in Example 6.

Example 6	Grace, age 25, is single and has her disabled and dependent mother living with her. This qualifies Grace for head-of-household filing status and a standard deduction of $9,100 in 2014. In 2014, Grace earned a $42,000 salary as a high school teacher. Her other income consisted of $1,000 interest on a certificate of deposit (CD) and $500 interest on nontaxable municipal bonds that she had received as a graduation gift in 2009. During 2014, she sustained a deductible capital loss of $1,000. Her itemized deductions are $9,500. Grace's taxable income for the year is computed as follows:

Income (broadly conceived)	
Salary	$42,000
Interest on a CD	1,000
Interest on municipal bonds	500
	$43,500
Less: Exclusion—Interest on municipal bonds	(500)
Gross income	$43,000
Less: Deduction *for* adjusted gross income—capital loss	(1,000)
Adjusted gross income	$42,000
Less: The greater of total itemized deductions ($9,500) *or* the standard deduction for head of household ($9,100)	(9,500)
Personal and dependency exemptions (2 × $3,950)	(7,900)
Taxable income	$24,600

Note that the exclusion of $500 (i.e., interest from municipal bonds) is subtracted in determining gross income. The loss of $1,000 from a property transaction is classified as a deduction *for* AGI. Grace chose to itemize her deductions *from* AGI as they exceed the standard deduction (see Table 3.1 for the derivation of the $9,100 amount). Grace's income tax is determined later in this chapter in Example 42.

Tax Due (or Refund)

The last step in applying the tax formula is the determination of tax due (or refund). Ascertain the appropriate filing status (e.g., single, head of household, etc.) and then apply the appropriate set of rates (i.e., Tax Rate Schedules or Tax Tables) to taxable income. Once the tax is derived, adjust for the various tax credits allowed (e.g., withholdings, earned income, research, or foreign) to arrive at the additional tax due or any overpayment (i.e., refund) involved. Filing status and the use of the tax rates are discussed later in this chapter; tax credits are the subject of Chapter 13.

3-1b Tax Formula—Correlation with Form 1040

The structure of individual income tax returns (Forms 1040, 1040A, or 1040EZ) parallels the tax formula in Figure 3.1. Like the formula, the tax return places major emphasis on adjusted gross income (AGI), which appears on the bottom of page 1 and at the top of page 2 of Form 1040. In arriving at gross income (referred to as *total income*), *most* exclusions are not reported on the tax return. Deductions *for* AGI are summarized on page 1 of Form 1040. Deductions *from* AGI (referred to as "itemized deductions") are carried over from Schedule A to page 2 of Form 1040. The choice between the standard deduction and itemized deductions is made on page 2. This is followed by the deduction for personal and dependency exemptions to arrive at taxable income. Page 2 contains the tax determination aspects of the tax

TABLE 3.1	Basic Standard Deduction Amounts	

	Standard Deduction Amount	
Filing Status	2013	2014
Single	$ 6,100	$ 6,200
Married, filing jointly	12,200	12,400
Surviving spouse	12,200	12,400
Head of household	8,950	9,100
Married, filing separately	6,100	6,200

formula, including any reduction allowed for available tax credits. The format of Form 1040 and its tie-in to the various supporting schedules containing components of the tax formula is graphically illustrated in Figure 6.1 of Chapter 6.

3-2 STANDARD DEDUCTION

A major component of the tax formula is the standard deduction. The effect of the standard deduction is to exempt part of a taxpayer's income from Federal income tax liability. In the past, Congress has attempted to set the tax-free amount represented by the standard deduction approximately equal to an estimated poverty level,[6] but it has not always been consistent in doing so.

LO.2

Explain the standard deduction and evaluate its choice in arriving at taxable income.

3-2a Basic and Additional Standard Deduction

The standard deduction is the sum of two components: the *basic* standard deduction and the *additional* standard deduction.[7] Table 3.1 lists the basic standard deduction allowed for taxpayers in each filing status. All taxpayers allowed a *full* standard deduction are entitled to the applicable amount listed in Table 3.1. The standard deduction amounts are subject to adjustment for inflation each year.

Certain taxpayers are not allowed to claim *any* standard deduction, and the standard deduction is *limited* for others. These provisions are discussed later in the chapter.

A taxpayer who is age 65 or over *or* blind in 2014 qualifies for an *additional standard deduction* of $1,200 or $1,550, depending on filing status (see amounts in Table 3.2). Two additional standard deductions are allowed for a taxpayer who is age 65 or over *and* blind. The additional standard deduction provisions also apply for a qualifying spouse who is age 65 or over or blind, but a taxpayer may not claim an additional standard deduction for a dependent.

To determine whether to itemize, the taxpayer compares the *total* standard deduction (the sum of the basic standard deduction and any additional standard deductions) with total itemized deductions. Taxpayers are allowed to deduct the *greater* of itemized deductions or the standard deduction. The choice is elective. Undoubtedly, some taxpayers claim the standard deduction because they do not want to bother completing the Schedule A required for itemizing deductions *from* AGI. Likewise, the choice is an annual one, and a taxpayer is not bound by what was done on returns filed for past years. For example, many taxpayers who have previously claimed the standard deduction will switch to itemizing after purchasing a home (because of the mortgage interest and property tax deductions). In other circumstances, the reverse could be true—the taxpayer will switch from itemizing to the standard deduction. As illustrated in the next example, age can make a difference.

---

[6]S.Rep. No. 92–437, 92nd Cong., 1st Sess., 1971, p. 54. Another purpose of the standard deduction was discussed in Chapter 1 under Influence of the Internal Revenue Service—Administrative Feasibility. The size of the standard deduction has a direct bearing on the number of taxpayers who

are in a position to itemize deductions. Reducing the number of taxpayers who itemize also reduces the audit effort required from the IRS.
[7]§ 63(c)(1).

TABLE 3.2	Amount of Each Additional Standard Deduction		
Filing Status		**2013**	**2014**
Single		$1,500	$1,550
Married, filing jointly		1,200	1,200
Surviving spouse		1,200	1,200
Head of household		1,500	1,550
Married, filing separately		1,200	1,200

Example 7

Prior to 2014, Sara, who is single, had always chosen to itemize. In 2014, however, she reaches age 65. Her itemized deductions for 2014 are $6,500, but her total standard deduction is $7,750 [$6,200 (basic standard deduction) + $1,550 (additional standard deduction)]. Sara should compute her taxable income for 2014 using the standard deduction ($7,750), because it exceeds her itemized deductions ($6,500).

3-2b Individuals Not Eligible for the Standard Deduction

Although almost two-thirds of individuals choose the standard deduction in preference to itemizing their deductions *from* AGI, some taxpayers do not qualify. The following individual taxpayers are ineligible to use the standard deduction and must therefore itemize:[8]

- A married individual filing a separate return where either spouse itemizes deductions.
- A nonresident alien.
- An individual filing a return for a period of less than 12 months because of a change in the annual accounting period.

The death of an individual does not eliminate the standard deduction for the year of death; nor does the deduction have to be allocated to the pre-death portion of the year. If, for example, Sandy (age 80 and single) died on January 14, 2014, his executor would be able to claim a standard deduction of $7,750 [$6,200 (basic standard deduction) + $1,550 (additional standard deduction for age)] on his final income tax return (covering the period from January 1 to January 14, 2014). This presumes, of course, that the standard deduction is preferable to itemizing.

3-2c Special Limitations on the Standard Deduction for Dependents

Special rules apply to the standard deduction and personal exemption of an individual who can be claimed as a dependent on another person's tax return.

When filing his or her own tax return, a *dependent's* basic standard deduction in 2014 is limited to the greater of $1,000 or the sum of the individual's earned income for the year plus $350.[9] However, if the sum of the individual's earned income plus $350 exceeds the normal standard deduction, the standard deduction is limited to the appropriate amount shown in Table 3.1. These limitations apply only to the basic standard deduction. A dependent who is 65 or over or blind

---

[8]§ 63(c)(6).

[9]§ 63(c)(5). Both the $1,000 amount and the $350 amount are subject to adjustment for inflation each year. In 2013, the amounts were $1,000 and $350; in 2012, the amounts were $950 and $300.

or both is also allowed the additional standard deduction amount on his or her own return (refer to Table 3.2). These provisions are illustrated in Examples 8 through 11.

Susan, who is 17 years old and single, is claimed as a dependent on her parents' tax return. During 2014, she received $1,200 interest (unearned income) on a savings account. She also earned $400 from a part-time job. When Susan files her own tax return, her standard deduction is $1,000 (the greater of $1,000 or the sum of earned income of $400 plus $350).	**Example 8**

Assume the same facts as in Example 8, except that Susan is 67 years old and is claimed as a dependent on her son's tax return. In this case, when Susan files her own tax return, her standard deduction is $2,550 [$1,000 (the greater of $1,000 or the sum of earned income of $400 plus $350) + $1,550 (the additional standard deduction allowed because Susan is 65 or over)].	**Example 9**

Peggy, who is 16 years old and single, earned $700 from a summer job and had no unearned income during 2014. She is claimed as a dependent on her parents' tax return. Her standard deduction is $1,050 (the greater of $1,000 or the sum of $700 earned income plus $350).	**Example 10**

Jack, who is a 20-year-old, single, full-time college student, is claimed as a dependent on his parents' tax return. He worked as a musician during the summer of 2014, earning $6,400. Jack's standard deduction is $6,200 (the greater of $1,000 or the sum of $6,400 earned income plus $350, but limited to the $6,200 standard deduction for a single taxpayer).	**Example 11**

3-3 PERSONAL EXEMPTIONS

The use of exemptions in the tax system is based in part on the idea that a taxpayer with a small amount of income should be exempt from income taxation. An exemption frees a specified amount of income from tax ($3,950 in 2014 and $3,900 in 2013). The exemption amount is adjusted (i.e., indexed) annually for inflation.

Exemptions that are allowed for the taxpayer and spouse are designated as **personal exemptions**. Those exemptions allowed for the care and maintenance of other persons are called dependency exemptions and are discussed in the next section.

An individual cannot claim a personal exemption if he or she is claimed as a dependent by another.

LO.3

Apply the rules for arriving at personal exemptions.

Assume the same facts as in Example 11. On his own income tax return,[10] Jack's taxable income is determined as follows: Gross income $ 6,400 Less: Standard deduction (6,200) Personal exemption (–0–) Taxable income $ 200 Note that Jack is not allowed a personal exemption because he is claimed as a dependent by his parents.	**Example 12**

When a husband and wife file a joint return, they may claim two personal exemptions. However, when separate returns are filed, a married taxpayer cannot claim an exemption for his or her spouse *unless* the spouse has no gross income and is not claimed as the dependent of another taxpayer.[11]

[10]As noted on p. 3-21, Jack's situation is such that he will be required to file an income tax return.

[11]§ 151(b).

The determination of marital status generally is made at the end of the taxable year, except when a spouse dies during the year. Spouses who enter into a legal separation under a decree of divorce or separate maintenance before the end of the year are considered to be unmarried at the end of the taxable year.

The amount of the exemption is not reduced due to the taxpayer's death. The same rule applies to dependency exemptions. As long as an individual qualified as a dependent at the time of death, the full amount of the exemption can be claimed.

3-4 DEPENDENCY EXEMPTIONS

LO.4

Explain the rules for determining dependency exemptions.

As is the case with personal exemptions, a taxpayer is permitted to claim an exemption of $3,950 in 2014 ($3,900 in 2013) for each person who qualifies as a dependent. A **dependency exemption** is available for either a qualifying child or a qualifying relative and must not run afoul of certain other rules (i.e., joint return or nonresident alien prohibitions).

3-4a Qualifying Child

In the interest of uniformity, Congress has tried to establish a uniform definition of a qualifying child. The qualifying child definition applies to the following tax provisions:

- Dependency exemption.
- Head-of-household filing status.
- Earned income tax credit.
- Child tax credit.
- Credit for child and dependent care expenses.

A **qualifying child** must meet the relationship, abode, age, and support tests.[12] For dependency exemption purposes, a qualifying child must also satisfy the joint return test and the citizenship or residency test.

Relationship Test

The relationship test includes a taxpayer's child (son or daughter), adopted child, stepchild, eligible foster child, brother, sister, half brother, half sister, stepbrother, stepsister, or a *descendant* of any of these parties (e.g., grandchild, nephew, niece). Note that *ancestors* of any of these parties (e.g., uncles and aunts) and in-laws (e.g., son-in-law and brother-in-law) *are not included.*

An adopted child includes a child lawfully placed with the taxpayer for legal adoption even though the adoption is not final. An eligible foster child is a child who is placed with the taxpayer by an authorized placement agency or by a judgment decree or other order of any court of competent jurisdiction.

Example 13

Maureen's household includes her mother, grandson, stepbrother, stepbrother's daughter, uncle, and sister. All meet the relationship test for a qualifying child except the mother and uncle.

Abode Test

A qualifying child must live with the taxpayer for more than half of the year. For this purpose, temporary absences (e.g., school, vacation, medical care, military service, detention in a juvenile facility) are disregarded. Special rules apply in the case of certain kidnapped children.[13]

---

[12]§ 152(c).   [13]§ 152(f)(6).

Age Test

A qualifying child must be under age 19 or under age 24 in the case of a student. A student is a child who, during any part of five months of the year, is enrolled full-time at a school or government-sponsored on-farm training course.[14] The age test does not apply to a child who is disabled during any part of the year.[15] Also, an individual cannot be older than the taxpayer claiming him or her as a qualifying child (e.g., a brother cannot claim his older sister as a qualifying child).

THE BIG PICTURE

Example 14

Return to the facts of *The Big Picture* on p. 3-1. Does Paige meet the requirements of a qualifying child as to Polly? Paige satisfies the relationship and abode tests, but the answer to the age test remains unclear. Because she is not a full-time student or disabled, she must be under 19 to meet the age test. Unfortunately, the facts given do not provide Paige's age.

Support Test

To be a qualifying child, the individual must not be self-supporting (i.e., provide more than one-half of his or her own support). In the case of a child who is a full-time student, scholarships are not considered to be support.[16]

Example 15

Shawn, age 23, is a full-time student and lives with his parents and an older cousin. During 2014, Shawn receives his support from the following sources: 30% from a part-time job, 30% from a scholarship, 20% from his parents, and 20% from the cousin. Shawn is not self-supporting and can be claimed by his parents as a dependent even though his parents only contribute 20% of his support. (Note: Shawn cannot be a qualifying child as to his cousin due to the relationship test.)

Tiebreaker Rules

In some situations, a child may be a qualifying child to more than one person. In this event, the tax law specifies which person has priority in claiming the dependency exemption.[17] Called "tiebreaker rules," these rules are summarized in Table 3.3 and are illustrated in the examples that follow.

TABLE 3.3	Tiebreaker Rules for Claiming Qualified Child
Persons Eligible to Claim Exemption	**Person Prevailing**
One of the persons is the parent.	Parent
Both persons are the parents, and the child lives longer with one parent.	Parent with the longer period of residence
Both persons are the parents, and the child lives with each the same period of time.	Parent with the higher adjusted gross income (AGI)
None of the persons is the parent.	Person with highest AGI

---

[14]§ 152(f)(2).
[15]Within the meaning of § 22(e)(3). See the discussion of the credit for the elderly or disabled in Chapter 13.

[16]§ 152(f)(5).
[17]§ 152(c)(4).

Example 16   Tim, age 15, lives in the same household with his mother and grandmother. As the parent, the mother has priority as to the dependency exemption.

Example 17   Jennifer, age 17, lives in the same household with her parents during the entire year. If her parents file separate returns, the one with the higher AGI has priority as to the dependency exemption.

Example 18   Assume the same facts as in Example 17, except that the father moves into an apartment in November (Jennifer remains with her mother). The mother has priority as to the dependency exemption (see Table 3.3).

Resorting to the tiebreaker rules in Table 3.3 is not necessary if the person who would prevail does not claim the exemption. Thus, in Example 16, the mother can allow the grandmother to claim Tim as a dependent by not claiming him on her own return.

3-4b Qualifying Relative

Besides the category of a qualifying child, there is a second category of dependency exemption designated as the **qualifying relative**.

A qualifying relative must meet the relationship, gross income, and support tests.[18] As in the case of the qualifying child category, qualifying relative status also requires that the joint return and nonresident alien restrictions be avoided (see Other Rules for Dependency Exemptions later in the chapter).

Relationship Test

The relationship test for a qualifying relative is more expansive than for a qualifying child. Also included are the following relatives:

- Lineal ascendants (e.g., parents and grandparents).
- Collateral ascendants (e.g., uncles and aunts).
- Certain in-laws (e.g., son-, daughter-, father-, mother-, brother-, and sister-in-law).[19]

Children who do not satisfy the qualifying child definition may meet the qualifying relative criteria.

The relationship test also includes unrelated parties who live with the taxpayer all year (i.e., are members of the household). Member-of-the-household status is not available for anyone whose relationship with the taxpayer violates local law or anyone who was a spouse during any part of the year.[20] However, an ex-spouse can qualify as a member of the household in a year following that of the divorce.

As the relationship test indicates, the category designation of "qualifying relative" is somewhat misleading. As just noted, persons other than relatives can qualify as dependents. Furthermore, not all relatives will qualify—notice the absence of the "cousin" grouping.

THE BIG PICTURE

Example 19   Return to the facts of *The Big Picture* on p. 3-1. Although Maude is unrelated to Polly, she qualifies as Polly's dependent by being a member of the household. Because Maude is a dependent, Polly can also claim the medical expenses she paid on Maude's behalf. The funeral expenses are not deductible. Although Maude lived for only two months, the full amount of the dependency exemption is allowed and does not have to be apportioned.

---

[18] § 152(d).

[19] Once established by marriage, in-law status continues to exist and survives divorce.

[20] §§ 152(d)(2)(H) and (f)(3).

Gross Income Test

A dependent's gross income must be *less* than the exemption amount—$3,950 in 2014 and $3,900 in 2013. Gross income is determined by the income that is taxable. In the case of scholarships, for example, include the taxable portion (e.g., amounts received for room and board) and exclude the nontaxable portion (e.g., amounts received for books and tuition).

> **Example 20**
>
> Elsie provides more than half of the support of her son, Tom, who does not live with her. Tom, age 26, is a full-time student in medical school, earns $3,000 from a part-time job, and receives a $12,000 scholarship covering his tuition. Elsie may claim Tom as a dependent because he meets the gross income test and is a qualifying relative. (Note: Tom is not a qualifying child due to either the abode or the age test.)

> **Example 21**
>
> Aaron provides more than half of the support of his widowed aunt, Myrtle, who does not live with him. Myrtle's income for the year is as follows: dividend income of $1,100, earnings from pet sitting of $1,200, nontaxable Social Security benefits of $6,000, and nontaxable interest from City of Milwaukee bonds of $8,000. Because Myrtle's gross income is only $2,300 ($1,100+$1,200), she meets the gross income test and can be claimed as Aaron's dependent.

THE BIG PICTURE

> **Example 22**
>
> Return to the facts of *The Big Picture* on p. 3-1. Assuming that Paige is not a qualifying child (see Example 14), can she be a qualifying relative for dependency exemption purposes? She meets the relationship and support tests, but what about the gross income test? If her income from her part-time job is less than $3,950, she does qualify and can be claimed by Polly as a dependent.

Support Test

Over one-half of the support of the qualifying relative must be furnished by the taxpayer. Support includes food, shelter, clothing, toys, medical and dental care, education, and the like.[21] However, a scholarship (both taxable and nontaxable portions) received by a student is not included for purposes of computing whether the taxpayer furnished more than half of the child's support.

> **Example 23**
>
> Hal contributed $3,400 (consisting of food, clothing, and medical care) toward the support of his nephew, Sam, who lives with him. Sam earned $1,300 from a part-time job and received $2,000 from a student loan to attend a local university. Assuming that the other dependency tests are met, Hal can claim Sam as a dependent because Hal has contributed more than half of Sam's support.

If the individual does not spend funds that have been received from any source, the unexpended amounts are not counted for purposes of the support test.

> **Example 24**
>
> Emily contributed $3,000 to her father's support during the year. In addition, her father received $2,400 in Social Security benefits, $200 of interest, and wages of $600. Her father deposited the Social Security benefits, interest, and wages in his own savings account and did not use any of the funds for his support. Thus, the Social Security benefits, interest, and wages are not considered as support provided by Emily's father. Emily may claim her father as a dependent if the other tests are met.

An individual's own funds, however, must be taken into account if applied toward support. In this regard, the source of the funds so used is immaterial.

---

[21]A worksheet for determining support is provided in IRS Publication 501 (*Exemptions, Standard Deduction, and Filing Information*).

Example 25

Frank contributes $8,000 toward his parents' total support of $20,000. The parents, who do not live with Frank, obtain the other $12,000 from savings and a home equity loan on their residence. Although the parents have no income, their use of savings and borrowed funds are counted as part of their support. Because Frank does not satisfy the support test, he cannot claim his parents as dependents.

Capital expenditures for items such as furniture, appliances, and automobiles are included in total support if the item does, in fact, constitute support.

Example 26

Norm purchased a television set costing $950 and gave it to his mother who lives with him. The television set was placed in the mother's bedroom and was used exclusively by her. Norm should include the cost of the television set in determining the support of his mother.

Multiple Support Agreements An exception to the support test involves a **multiple support agreement**. A multiple support agreement permits one of a group of taxpayers who furnish support for a qualifying relative to claim a dependency exemption for that individual even if no one person provides more than 50 percent of the support.[22] The group together must provide more than 50 percent of the support. Any person who contributed *more than 10 percent* of the support is entitled to claim the exemption if each person in the group who contributed more than 10 percent files a written consent. This provision frequently enables one of the children of aged dependent parents to claim an exemption when none of the children meets the 50 percent support test.

Each person who is a party to the multiple support agreement must meet all other requirements (except the support requirement) for claiming the exemption. A person who does not meet the relationship or member-of-the-household requirement, for instance, cannot claim the dependency exemption under a multiple support agreement. It does not matter if he or she contributes more than 10 percent of the individual's support.

Example 27

Wanda, who resides with her son, Adam, received $12,000 from various sources during the year. This constituted her entire support for the year. She received support from the following:

	Amount	Percentage of Total
Adam, a son	$ 5,760	48
Bob, a son	1,200	10
Carol, a daughter	3,600	30
Diane, a friend	1,440	12
	$12,000	100

If Adam and Carol file a multiple support agreement, either may claim the dependency exemption for Wanda. Bob may not claim Wanda because he did not contribute *more than 10%* of her support. Bob's consent is not required for Adam and Carol to file a multiple support agreement. Diane does not meet the relationship or member-of-the-household test and cannot be a party to the agreement. The decision as to who claims Wanda rests with Adam and Carol. It is possible for Carol to claim Wanda, even though Adam furnished more of Wanda's support.

The individual claiming the exemption must complete Form 2120 (Multiple Support Declaration) and file it with his or her tax return. In addition, each person who qualifies under the more-than-10 percent rule (except for the person claiming the exemption) must submit a signed statement waiving his or her right to the exemption to the person who is claiming the exemption. The person claiming the exemption must retain these written statements for his or her records.

---

[22]§ 152(d)(3).

ETHICS & EQUITY   Discovering Lost Dependency Exemptions

For the six years prior to his death in late 2014, Jesse lived with his daughter, Hannah. Because he had no source of income, Jesse was supported by equal contributions from Hannah and his two sons, Bill and Bob. At Jesse's funeral, his surviving children are amazed to discover that none of them has been claiming Jesse as a dependent. Upon the advice of the director of the funeral home, they decide to divide among themselves the dependency exemptions for the past six years. Multiple Forms 2120 are executed, and each of the three children files amended returns for different past years. As Jesse died before the end of the current year, no deduction is planned for 2014.

Comment on the tax expectations of the parties involved.

© iStockphoto.com/LdF

Children of Divorced or Separated Parents Another exception to the support test applies when parents with children are divorced or separated under a decree of separate maintenance. For unmarried parents, living apart (for the last six months of the year) will suffice. Special rules apply if the parents meet the following conditions:

- They would have been entitled to the dependency exemption(s) had they been married and filed a joint return.
- They have custody (either jointly or singly) of the child (or children) for more than half of the year.

Under the general rule, the parent having custody of the child (children) for the greater part of the year (i.e., the custodial parent) is entitled to the dependency exemption(s).[23] The general rule does not apply if a multiple support agreement is in effect. It also does not apply if the custodial parent issues a waiver in favor of the noncustodial parent.[24]

The waiver, Form 8332 (Release/Revocation of Release of Claim to Exemption for Child by Custodial Parent), can apply to a single year, a number of specified years, or all future years. The noncustodial parent must attach a copy of Form 8332 to his or her return.

3-4c Other Rules for Dependency Exemptions

In addition to fitting into either the qualifying child or the qualifying relative category, a dependent must meet the joint return and the citizenship or residency tests.

Joint Return Test

If a dependent is married, the supporting taxpayer (e.g., the parent of a married child) generally is not permitted a dependency exemption if the married individual files a joint return with his or her spouse.[25] The joint return rule does not apply, however, if the following conditions are met:

- The reason for filing is to claim a refund for tax withheld.
- No tax liability would exist for either spouse on separate returns.
- Neither spouse is required to file a return (tested using the married, filing separately rules).

See Table 3.4 later in the chapter and the related discussion concerning income level requirements for filing a return.

---

[23]Reg. § 1.152–4T.
[24]§§ 152(e)(2) and (5).

[25]§ 152(b)(2).

CONCEPT SUMMARY 3.1

Tests for Dependency Exemption

Category	
Qualifying Child	**Qualifying Relative**
Relationship[1]	Support
Abode	Relationship[2] or member of household
Age	Gross income
Support	Joint return[3]
Joint return[3]	Citizenship or residency[3]
Citizenship or residency[3]	

[1] Children and their descendants, and siblings and stepsiblings and their descendants.
[2] Children and their descendants, siblings and their children, parents and their ascendants, uncles and aunts, stepparents and stepsiblings, and certain in-laws.
[3] The joint return rules and the citizenship or residency rules are the same for each category.

© iStockphoto.com/Andrey Prokhorov

Example 28

Paul provides over half of the support of his son, Quinn. He also provides over half of the support of Vera, who is Quinn's wife. During the year, both Quinn and Vera had part-time jobs. To recover the taxes withheld, they file a joint return. If Quinn and Vera are not required to file a return, Paul is allowed to claim both as dependents.

Citizenship or Residency Test

To be a dependent, the individual must be a U.S. citizen, a U.S. resident, or a resident of Canada or Mexico for some part of the calendar year in which the taxpayer's tax year begins.[26]

Under an exception, an adopted child need not be a citizen or resident of the United States (or a contiguous country) as long as his or her principal abode is with a U.S. citizen.

Example 29

Esther is a U.S. citizen who lives and works in Spain. She has adopted Benito, a 4-year-old Italian national, who lives with her and is a member of her household. Although Benito does not meet the usual citizenship or residency test, he is covered by the exception. Benito is a qualifying child, and Esther can claim him as a dependent.

3-4d Comparison of Categories for Dependency Exemptions

Concept Summary 3.1 sets forth the tests for the two categories of dependency exemptions. In contrasting the two categories, the following observations are in order:

- As to the relationship tests, the qualifying relative category is considerably more expansive. Besides including those prescribed under the qualifying child grouping, other relatives are added. Nonrelated persons who are members of the household are also included.
- The support tests are entirely different. In the case of a qualifying child, support is not necessary. What is required is that the child not be self-supporting.
- The qualifying child category has no gross income limitation, whereas the qualifying relative category has no age restriction.

---

[26]§ 152(b)(3).

TAX IN THE NEWS   How to Subtly Pluck the Chicken

No government likes to admit that it is enacting new taxes or even raising the rates on existing taxes. Needless to say, this is particularly true of the U.S. Congress. But there are more subtle ways to raise revenue (or to curtail revenue loss). The most popular way is to use a so-called *stealth tax*. A stealth tax is not really a tax at all. Instead, it is a means of depriving higher-income taxpayers of the benefits of certain tax provisions thought to be available to all.

The heart and soul of the stealth tax is the phaseout approach. Thus, as income increases, the tax benefit thought to be derived from a particular relief provision decreases. Because the phaseout usually is gradual and not drastic, many affected taxpayers are unaware of what has happened.

The tax law is rampant with phaseouts. The two most prominent phaseouts limit the deductibility of personal and dependency exemptions (discussed in this chapter) and itemized deductions (discussed in Chapter 10). In addition to these, here are some other examples of these stealth taxes, along with where each is discussed in the text:

- Earned income credit (Chapter 13).
- Spousal IRA deduction (Chapter 19).
- Child tax credit (Chapter 13).
- College tuition deduction (Chapter 9).
- Interest deduction on student loans (Chapter 10).
- American Opportunity college credit (Chapter 13).
- Social Security benefits (Chapter 4).
- Medicare tax on investment income (Chapter 13).

© iStockphoto.com/Andrey Prokhorov

3-4e Phaseout of Exemptions

Several provisions of the tax law are intended to increase the tax liability of more affluent taxpayers who might otherwise enjoy some benefit from having some of their taxable income subject to the lower income tax brackets (e.g., 10 percent, 15 percent, 25 percent). One such provision phases out certain itemized deductions and is discussed in Chapter 10. Another provision phases out personal and dependency exemptions.[27] The exemption phaseout occurs as AGI exceeds specified threshold amounts (indexed annually for inflation). The phaseout begins when AGI exceeds the following amounts:

Filing Status	2013	2014
Married, filing jointly	$300,000	$305,050
Head of household	275,000	279,650
Single	250,000	254,200
Married, filing separately	150,000	152,525

Exemptions (both personal and dependency) are phased out by 2 percent for each $2,500 (or fraction thereof) by which the taxpayer's AGI exceeds the threshold amounts. For a married taxpayer filing separately, the phaseout is 2 percent for each $1,250 (or fraction thereof). The allowable exemption amount can be determined with the following steps:

1. AGI − threshold amount = excess amount.
2. Excess amount ÷ $2,500 = reduction factor [rounded up to the next whole number (e.g., 18.1 = 19)] × 2 = phaseout percentage.
3. Phaseout percentage × exemption amount = phaseout amount.
4. Exemption amount − phaseout amount = allowable exemption deduction.

Example 30

Brad files as a single individual in 2014. His AGI is $286,850. He is entitled to one personal exemption. Brad's allowable exemption amount is determined as follows:

1. $286,850 − $254,200 = $32,650 excess amount.
2. [($32,650 ÷ $2,500) = 13.06; rounded to 14]; 14 × 2 = 28% (phaseout percentage).
3. 28% × $3,950 = $1,106 phaseout amount.
4. $3,950 − $1,106 = $2,844 allowable exemption deduction.

---

[27] § 151(d)(3); this provision did not apply in 2010, 2011, or 2012.

ETHICS & EQUITY   Whose Qualifying Child Is He?

The Rands are successful professionals and have combined AGI of approximately $400,000. Their household includes two children: Henry (age 16) and Belinda (age 22). Belinda is not a student and has a job where she earns $15,000 a year. After a short family meeting in early April 2014, the parties decide that Belinda should claim Henry as her qualifying child. As a result, Belinda is able to deduct a full dependency exemption and claim a child tax credit and an earned income tax credit for a tax savings of more than $3,000. Had the Rands claimed Henry on their joint return, no child tax credit or earned income credit would have been available. As noted in Chapter 13, these credits are phased out for higher-bracket taxpayers. Further, only a partial dependency exemption would have been allowed. Has the Rand family acted properly?

© iStockphoto.com/LdF

Note that the exemption amount is completely phased out when the taxpayer's AGI exceeds the threshold amount by more than $122,500 ($61,250 for a married taxpayer filing a separate return). With an excess amount of $122,501, the phase-out percentage is 100 percent, calculated as follows:

$$\$122,501 \div \$2,500 = 49.0004, \text{ rounded to 50 and multiplied by } 2 = 100\%$$

Example 31

Bill and Carol file a joint return in 2014 claiming two personal exemptions and two dependency exemptions for their children. Their AGI equals $438,600.

$$\$438,600 - \$305,050 = \$133,550 \text{ excess amount}$$

Since the excess amount exceeds $122,500, their exemptions are completely phased out.

3-4f Child Tax Credit

In addition to providing a dependency exemption, a child of the taxpayer may also generate a tax credit. Called the **child tax credit**, the amount allowed is $1,000 for each dependent child (including stepchildren and eligible foster children) under the age of 17.[28] For a more complete discussion of the child tax credit, see Chapter 13.

3-5 TAX DETERMINATION—FILING CONSIDERATIONS

LO.5

List the filing requirements and choose the proper filing status.

Once taxable income has been ascertained, a two-step process is used in determining income tax due (or refund available). First, certain procedural matters must be resolved. Second, the tax has to be computed and adjusted for available tax credits—see Figure 3.1 and the tax formula. This section deals with the procedural aspects—designated as filing considerations. The next section covers the computation procedures.

Under the category of filing considerations, the following questions need to be resolved:

- Is the taxpayer required to file an income tax return?
- If so, which form should be used?
- When and how should the return be filed?
- What is the taxpayer's filing status?

---

[28]§ 24(a). Absent Congressional intervention, the credit will decrease to $500 per child in 2018.

3-5a Filing Requirements

General Rules

An individual must file a tax return if certain minimum amounts of gross income have been received. The general rule is that a tax return is required for every individual who has gross income that equals or exceeds the sum of the exemption amount plus the applicable standard deduction.[29] For example, a single taxpayer under age 65 must file a tax return in 2014 if gross income equals or exceeds $10,150 ($3,950 exemption plus $6,200 standard deduction). Table 3.4 lists the income levels[30] that require tax returns under the general rule and under certain special rules.

The additional standard deduction for being age 65 or older is considered in determining the gross income filing requirements. For example, note in Table 3.4 that the 2014 filing requirement for a single taxpayer age 65 or older is $11,700 ($6,200 basic standard deduction + $1,550 additional standard deduction + $3,950 exemption). Except in the case of dependents (see below), the additional standard deduction for blindness is not taken into account in determining whether a taxpayer must file a tax return.

A self-employed individual with net earnings of $400 or more from a business or profession must file a tax return regardless of the amount of gross income.

Even though an individual has gross income below the filing level amounts and therefore does not owe any tax, he or she must file a return to obtain a tax refund of amounts withheld. A return is also necessary to obtain the benefits of the earned income credit allowed to taxpayers with little or no tax liability. Chapter 13 discusses the earned income credit.

TABLE 3.4	Filing Requirements for Most Taxpayers	
Filing Status	**2013 Gross Income**	**2014 Gross Income**
Single		
Under 65	$10,000	$10,150
65 or older	11,500	11,700
Married, filing joint return		
Both spouses under 65	$20,000	$20,300
One spouse 65 or older	21,200	21,500
Both spouses 65 or older	22,400	22,700
Married, filing separate return		
All	$ 3,900	$ 3,950
Head of household		
Under 65	$12,850	$13,050
65 or older	14,350	14,600
Qualifying widow(er)		
Under 65	$16,100	$16,350
65 or older	17,300	17,550

---

[29]Because the exemption and standard deduction amounts are subject to an annual inflation adjustment, the gross income amounts for determining whether a tax return must be filed normally change each year.

[30]§ 6012(a)(1).

Filing Requirements for Dependents

Computation of the gross income filing requirement for an individual who can be claimed as a dependent on another person's tax return is subject to more complex rules. Such an individual must file a return if he or she has *any* of the following:

- Earned income only and gross income that is more than the total standard deduction (including any additional standard deduction) the individual is allowed for the year.
- Unearned income only and gross income of more than $1,000 plus any additional standard deduction the individual is allowed for the year.
- Both earned and unearned income and gross income of more than the larger of $1,000 or the sum of earned income plus $350 (but limited to the applicable basic standard deduction) plus any additional standard deduction the individual is allowed for the year.

Thus, the filing requirement for a dependent who has no unearned income is the total of the *basic* standard deduction plus any *additional* standard deduction, which includes *both* the additional deduction for blindness and the deduction for being age 65 or older. For example, the 2014 filing requirement for a single dependent who is under age 65 and not blind is $6,200, the amount of the basic standard deduction. The filing requirement for a single dependent under age 65 and blind is $7,750 ($6,200 basic standard deduction + $1,550 additional standard deduction).

Selecting the Proper Form

The 2014 tax forms had not been released at the date of publication of this text. The following comments apply to the 2013 forms. It is possible that some provisions will change for the 2014 forms.

Although a variety of forms are available to individual taxpayers, the use of some of these forms is restricted. For example, Form 1040EZ cannot be used if:

- Taxpayer claims any dependents;
- Taxpayer (or spouse) is 65 or older or blind; or
- Taxable income is $100,000 or more.

Taxpayers who want to itemize deductions *from* AGI cannot use Form 1040A, but must file Form 1040 (the long form).

The E-File Approach

In addition to traditional paper returns, the **e-file** program is an increasingly popular alternative. Here, the required tax information is transmitted to the IRS electronically either directly from the taxpayer (i.e., an "e-file online return") or indirectly through an electronic return originator (ERO). EROs are tax professionals who have been accepted into the electronic filing program by the IRS. Such parties hold themselves out to the general public as "authorized IRS e-file providers." Providers often are the preparers of the return as well.

Through prearrangement with the IRS, approximately 15 software providers offer free e-filing services. These services are generally available only to taxpayers who have AGI of $57,000 or below. A list of these providers and their eligibility requirements can be obtained through the IRS website. Regardless of income, any taxpayer can use Free File Fillable Forms, which are an electronic version of IRS paper forms and can be e-filed. Fillable Forms are best for those taxpayers experienced in preparing their own tax returns.

For direct online e-filing, a taxpayer must have a personal computer and purchase commercial tax preparation software with the capability of conveying the information via modem to an electronic return transmitter. Otherwise, a taxpayer must use an authorized provider who makes the e-file transmission. Except as previously noted, the provider charges a fee for the e-filing service.

All taxpayers and tax return preparers must attest to the returns they file. For most taxpayers, this attesting can be done through an electronic return signature

TAX IN THE NEWS   IRS Toughens Procedures for Issuing Individual Taxpayer Identification Numbers

Foreign persons who earn income in the United States may need to file a Federal income tax return but may not have a Social Security number for filing purposes. If not, they can use a nine-digit Individual Tax Identification Number (ITIN) instead. The IRS issues ITINs upon the submission of an application [Form W–7 and proof of identification (e.g., a driver's license)]. As the IRS does not require an applicant to show that he or she is in the United States legally, the ITINs are freely available to undocumented persons (i.e., illegal immigrants). The use of an ITIN also can enable the holder to carry out other financial transactions (e.g., establish a bank account, secure a credit card, and obtain a loan).

Through its lax procedures in issuing ITINs, is the IRS indirectly encouraging, or at least condoning, the status of undocumented persons? Along this line, should the IRS require proof of legal presence in the United States before issuing an ITIN? Because the IRS and USCIS (U.S. Citizenship and Immigration Services) do not collaborate on the issuance of ITINs, is this another example of one Federal agency not cooperating with another?

The position of the IRS is that the current ITIN procedure brings in revenue that otherwise would not be forthcoming. Some undocumented workers want to comply with the law and pay the income taxes they owe. This practice should not be discouraged, as the tax law applies with equal force to legal and illegal residents of the United States. Although a breakdown between legal and illegal residents is not available, the tax liability of ITIN filers from 1996 to 2003 was $50 billion.

The aforementioned describes the IRS policy prior to the IRS announcement in June 2012 that the IRS was making changes in the procedure for issuing ITINs. The IRS now will issue ITINs when applications (typically on Form W–7) include the original documentation needed to confirm the identity of the applicant, such as passports and birth certificates or certified copies of these documents from the issuing agency. ITINs will no longer be issued based on applications supported by notarized copies of such documents.

using a personal identification number (a Self-Select PIN). Information on establishing a Self-Select PIN can be found in the instructions to Form 1040, Form 1040A, or Form 1040EZ or at **www.irs.gov/efile**. If certain paper documents must be submitted, a one-page form must be completed and filed when the return is e-filed. Form 8453 (U.S. Individual Income Tax Transmittal for an IRS *e-file* Return) is used to submit required attachments for both self- and practitioner-prepared electronic returns. Or a practitioner PIN method may be used whereby the taxpayer authorizes a tax preparer to generate a PIN by signing Form 8879 (IRS e-file Signature Authorization).

The e-file approach has two major advantages. First, compliance with the format required by the IRS eliminates many errors that would otherwise occur. Second, the time required for processing a refund usually is reduced to three weeks or less.

When and Where to File

Tax returns of individuals are due on or before the fifteenth day of the fourth month following the close of the tax year. For the calendar year taxpayer, the usual filing date is on or before April 15 of the following year.[31] When the due date falls on a Saturday, Sunday, or legal holiday, the last day for filing falls on the next business day. If the return is mailed to the proper address with sufficient postage and is postmarked on or before the due date, it is deemed timely filed. The Code enables the IRS to prescribe rules governing the filing of returns using various private parcel delivery services (e.g., FedEx, UPS).[32]

If a taxpayer is unable to file the return by the specified due date, a six-month extension of time can be obtained by filing Form 4868 (Application for Automatic Extension of Time to File U.S. Individual Income Tax Return) on or before the specified due date. Certain taxpayers who are members of the Armed Forces are allowed additional time for filing their Federal income tax returns.[33]

---

[31]§ 6072(a).
[32]§ 7502(f).

[33]Reg. § 1.6081–4. See also *Your Federal Income Tax* (IRS Publication 17), Chapter 1.

TAX IN THE NEWS   IRS Goes Mobile

Several years ago, the IRS launched its first mobile device application, IRS2Go, and has continued to update it. This app is available free at the iTunes app store for Apple iPhone, iPad, or iTouch devices and at the Android Marketplace for Android devices. The IRS2Go app allows taxpayers to check their refund and to get tax updates daily during tax filing season and periodically during the rest of the year, as well as to order their tax return transcript.

And taxpayers can sign up to follow the IRS Twitter news feed, @IRSnews. The IRSnews tweets provide the latest Federal tax law changes and other important information. The IRS also uses tools such as YouTube at www.youtube.com/irsvideos and other social media channels to share the latest information.

© iStockphoto.com/Andrey Prokhorov

Although obtaining an extension excuses a taxpayer from a penalty for failure to file, it does not insulate against the penalty for failure to pay. If more tax is owed, the filing of Form 4868 should be accompanied by an additional remittance to cover the balance due. The failure to file and failure to pay penalties are discussed in Chapter 1.

The return should be sent or delivered to the Regional Service Center listed in the instructions for each type of return or contained in software applications.[34] Because of an IRS reorganization that began in October 2000 and is still ongoing, some taxpayers may be required to file at a different Service Center than in the past.

If an individual taxpayer needs to file an amended return (e.g., because of a failure to report income or to claim a deduction or tax credit), Form 1040X is filed. The form generally must be filed within three years of the filing date of the original return or within two years from the time the tax was paid, whichever is later.

Mode of Payment

Usually, payment is made by check. In that event, the check should be made out to "United States Treasury."

The IRS has approved the use of MasterCard, American Express, Discover, and Visa to pay Federal taxes through a card service provider. The use of a credit card or debit card to pay taxes will result in a charge against the cardholder by the credit card company and service provider.

Also available is the Electronic Federal Tax Payment System (EFTPS) through the Internet or by phone. This service is provided free, and enrollment in the program can be accomplished through the IRS website.

3-5b Filing Status

The amount of tax will vary considerably depending on which Tax Rate Schedule is used. This is illustrated in the following example.

Example 32

The following amounts of tax are computed using the 2014 Tax Rate Schedules for a taxpayer (or taxpayers in the case of a joint return) with $60,000 of taxable income (see Appendix A).

Filing Status	Amount of Tax
Single	$10,856
Married, filing joint return	8,093
Married, filing separate return	10,856
Head of household	9,413

---

[34]The Regional Service Centers and the geographic area each covers can also be found at www.irs.gov/file.

TAX IN THE NEWS "Charge It"—Convenient but Not Cheap!

When a consumer uses a credit card to buy goods, the merchant pays a fee to the credit card company. When a credit card is used to pay income taxes, however, the law prevents the IRS from paying any such fee. Instead, the credit card company charges the user a "convenience fee" equal to 2.5 percent of the tax paid. The fee must be paid even if the user pays the credit card bill in full when it arrives. If, for example,

John uses his Visa card to pay the $10,000 in taxes that he owes, he will be charged $250 (2.5% × $10,000) as a convenience fee. John will have to pay the $250 fee even if he pays Visa the $10,000 when billed. Furthermore, regular credit card interest (usually 15 percent or more) will be charged on extended time payments.

Clearly, then, using credit cards to pay income taxes, although convenient, is not without cost.

Besides the effect on the tax rates that will apply, filing status also has an impact on the amount of the standard deduction that is allowed—see Tables 3.1 and 3.2 earlier in the chapter.

Single Taxpayers

A taxpayer who is unmarried or separated from his or her spouse by a decree of divorce or separate maintenance and does not qualify for another filing status must use the rates for single taxpayers. Marital status is determined as of the last day of the tax year, except when a spouse dies during the year. In that case, marital status is determined as of the date of death.

Under a special relief provision, however, married persons who live apart may be able to qualify as single. Married taxpayers who are considered single under the *abandoned spouse rules* are allowed to use the head-of-household rates. See the discussion of this filing status under Abandoned Spouse Rules later in the chapter.

Married Individuals

The joint return [Tax Rate Schedule Y, Code § 1(a)] was originally enacted in 1948 to establish equity between married taxpayers in common law states and those in community property states. Before the joint return rates were enacted, taxpayers in community property states were in an advantageous position relative to taxpayers in common law states because they could split their income. For instance, in a community property state, if one spouse earned $100,000 and the other spouse was not employed, each spouse could report $50,000 of income. Splitting the income in this manner caused the total income to be subject to lower marginal tax rates. Each spouse would start at the bottom of the rate structure.

Taxpayers in common law states did not have this income-splitting option, so their taxable income was subject to higher marginal rates. This inconsistency in treatment was remedied by the joint return provisions. The progressive rates in the joint return Tax Rate Schedule are constructed based on the assumption that income is earned equally by the two spouses.

Same-sex couples that are legally married in a state or jurisdiction that recognizes same-sex marriages will be treated as married for Federal tax purposes (no matter where they live). According to the IRS, registered domestic partners are not "spouses" under Federal law. Therefore, they cannot file Federal tax returns using married filing jointly or married filing separately status. The same rule applies to same-sex partners in civil unions.[35]

If married individuals elect to file separate returns, each reports only his or her own income, exemptions, deductions, and credits, and each must use the Tax Rate Schedule applicable to married taxpayers filing separately. It is generally

---

[35]Rev.Rul. 2013–17, 2013–38 I.R.B. 201 and *U.S. v. Windsor*, 111 AFTR 2d 2013–2385, 133 S.Ct. 2675; **www.irs.gov/uac/Answers-to-Frequently-Asked- Questions-for-Registered-Domestic-Partners-and-Individuals-in-Civil- Unions.**

Global Tax Issues

Filing a Joint Return

John Garth is a U.S. citizen and resident, but he spends a lot of time in London, where his employer sends him on frequent assignments. John is married to Victoria, a citizen and resident of the United Kingdom.

Can John and Victoria file a joint return for U.S. Federal income tax purposes? Although § 6013(a)(1) specifically precludes the filing of a joint return if one spouse is a nonresident alien, another Code provision permits an exception. Under § 6013(g), the parties can elect to treat the nonqualifying spouse as a "resident" of the United States. This election would allow John and Victoria to file jointly.

But should John and Victoria make this election? If Victoria has considerable income of her own (from non-U.S. sources), the election could be ill-advised. As a nonresident alien, Victoria's non-U.S. source income *would not* be subject to the U.S. income tax. If she is treated as a U.S. resident, however, her non-U.S. source income *will be subject to U.S. tax.* Under the U.S. global approach to taxation, all income (regardless of where earned) of anyone who is a *resident* or *citizen* of the United States is subject to tax.

advantageous for married individuals to file a joint return, because the combined amount of tax is lower. However, special circumstances (e.g., significant medical expenses incurred by one spouse subject to the 10 percent limitation) may warrant the election to file separate returns. It may be necessary to compute the tax under both assumptions to determine the most advantageous filing status. Filing a joint return carries the potential disadvantage of joint and several liability.[36] This means that the IRS can pursue the collection of the tax due for that year against either spouse.

Once a joint return has been filed and the due date has passed, the spouses cannot switch to separate returns for that year. However, if married persons file separately, they can change later to a joint return.

Marriage Penalty   When Congress enacted the rate structure available to those filing joint returns, it generally favored married taxpayers. In certain situations, however, the parties would incur less tax if they were not married and filed separate returns. The additional tax that a joint return caused, commonly called the **marriage penalty**, usually developed when *both* spouses had large taxable incomes. Long aware of the inequity of the marriage penalty, Congress reduced the effect of the problem in 2003. Beginning in 2003, the standard deduction available to married filers increased to 200 percent of that applicable to single persons. Furthermore and also beginning in 2003, the 15 percent bracket for joint filers increased to 200 percent of the size of that applicable to single filers.

Although changes in the tax rates and the standard deduction have reduced the marriage penalty, the Code places some limitations on married persons who file separate returns. Some examples of these limitations are as follows:

- If either spouse itemizes deductions, the other spouse must also itemize.
- The earned income credit and the credit for child and dependent care expenses cannot be claimed (see Chapter 13).
- No deduction is allowed for interest paid on qualified education loans (see Chapter 10).
- Only $1,500 of excess capital losses can be claimed by each spouse (see Chapter 16).

In such cases, being single would be preferable to being married and filing separately.

---

[36]§ 6013(d)(3).

TAX IN THE NEWS   Same-Sex Couples Face a Tax Filing Nightmare

In *U.S. v. Windsor*, the Supreme Court struck down portions of the Defense of Marriage Act. Specifically, this decision invalidated a Federal definition of marriage as between one man and one woman. Recent guidance from the IRS (Rev.Rul. 2013–17) provides that a same-sex couple possessing a marriage license from any U.S. state will be considered married for Federal income tax purposes (no matter where they live). However, this interpretation of marriage does not extend to "domestic partnerships" or "civil unions." Couples in these relationships are still regarded as *single* by the IRS.

As far as income taxes are concerned, have these new rules resolved the prior difficulties of same-sex couples? The answer depends on where they live and whether such location imposes an income tax. Consider the following possibilities as to residence.

1. No state or local income taxes imposed.
2. State and local income taxes imposed and jurisdiction recognizes same-sex marriages.
3. State and local income taxes imposed but jurisdiction does not recognize same-sex marriages.

Category (1) was never a problem and category (2) has largely been resolved. Thus, the filing status used for state and local purposes (e.g., married filing jointly) will also be available for Federal purposes. Category (3), moreover, continues to yield divergent results. For example, married persons for Federal purposes are "single" under state law.

For persons who are in a domestic partnership or civil union, a different inconsistency comes about. They could be treated as married for state purposes but single in terms of Federal tax law.

Surviving Spouse The joint return rates also apply for two years following the death of one spouse if the surviving spouse maintains a household for a dependent child. The child must be a son, stepson, daughter, or stepdaughter who qualifies as a dependent of the taxpayer. This is referred to as **surviving spouse** status.[37]

Example 33

Fred dies in 2013, leaving Ethel with a dependent child. For the year of Fred's death (2013), Ethel files a joint return with Fred (presuming the consent of Fred's executor is obtained). For the next two years (2014 and 2015), Ethel, as a surviving spouse, may use the joint return rates. In subsequent years, Ethel may use the head-of-household rates if she continues to maintain a household as her home that is the domicile of the child.

Keep in mind, however, that for the year of death, the surviving spouse is treated as being married. Thus, a joint return can be filed if the deceased spouse's executor agrees. If not, the surviving spouse is forced into the status of married, filing separately.

Head of Household

Unmarried individuals who maintain a household for a dependent (or dependents) are generally entitled to use the **head-of-household** rates.[38] The tax liability using the head-of-household rates falls between the liability using the joint return Tax Rate Schedule and the liability using the Tax Rate Schedule for single taxpayers.

To qualify for head-of-household rates, a taxpayer must pay more than half the cost of maintaining a household as his or her home. The household must also be the principal home of a dependent. Except for temporary absences (e.g., school, hospitalization), the dependent must live in the taxpayer's household for over half the year.

---

[37]§ 2(a). The IRS label for surviving spouse status is "qualifying widow(er) with dependent child."

[38]§ 2(b).

A dependent must be either a qualifying child or a qualifying relative who meets the relationship test (other than a member-of-the-household test).

Example 34

Return to the facts of *The Big Picture* on p. 3-1. Assuming that Polly can be treated as single (i.e., not married), can Maude qualify Polly for head-of-household filing status? The answer is no. Even though Maude can be claimed as Polly's dependent (see Example 19), she does not meet the relationship test.

Example 35

Emma, a widow, maintains a household in which she and her aunt live. If the aunt qualifies as a dependent, Emma may file as head of household. Note that an aunt meets the relationship test.

A special rule allows taxpayers to avoid having to live with their parents. Head-of-household status still may be claimed if the taxpayer maintains a *separate home* for his or her *parent or parents* if at least one parent qualifies as a dependent of the taxpayer.[39]

Example 36

Rick, an unmarried individual, lives in New York City and maintains a household in Detroit for his dependent parents. Rick may use the head-of-household rates even though his parents do not reside in his New York home.

ETHICS & EQUITY   Temporary or Permanent Absence?

For several years, Minerva, a widow, has maintained a household in which she and her uncle, Luther, live. Because Luther has no income, he is supported by Minerva and claimed by her as a dependent. In June 2014, Luther is admitted to a medical facility for treatment of a mental disorder. In January 2015, Luther unexpectedly dies while still at the facility.

In completing her Federal income tax returns for both 2014 and 2015, Minerva intends to file as head of household and claim Luther as her dependent. Comment on the propriety of what Minerva plans to do.

Head-of-household status is not changed during the year by the death of the dependent. As long as the taxpayer provided more than half of the cost of maintaining the household prior to the dependent's death, head-of-household status is preserved.

Abandoned Spouse Rules

When married persons file separate returns, several unfavorable tax consequences result. For example, the taxpayer must use the Tax Rate Schedule for married taxpayers filing separately. To mitigate such harsh treatment for some taxpayers, Congress enacted provisions commonly referred to as the **abandoned spouse** rules. The IRS does not use the "abandoned spouse" terminology but

---

[39]§ 2(b)(1)(B).

considers the taxpayer to be treated as *not married* if the following conditions are satisfied:[40]

- The taxpayer does not file a joint return.
- The taxpayer paid more than one-half the cost of maintaining his or her home for the tax year.
- The taxpayer's spouse did not live in the home during the last six months of the tax year.
- The home was the principal residence of the taxpayer's son, daughter, stepson, stepdaughter, foster child, or adopted child for more than half the year, and the child can be claimed as a dependent.[41]

Thus, the net effect of being treated as unmarried and having the specified dependents is that the abandoned spouse qualifies for head-of-household filing status.

ETHICS & EQUITY   Abandoned Spouse?

Bob and Carol have been in and out of marital counseling for the past few years. Early in 2014, they decide to separate. However, because they are barely able to get by on their current incomes, they cannot afford separate housing or the legal costs of a divorce. So Bob moves out of their house in March and takes up residence in their detached garage (which has an enclosed workshop and bathroom). Carol stays in the house with their two children and pays more than half of the costs of maintaining their residence. Bob does not enter the house for the remainder of the year. Can Carol qualify as an abandoned spouse?

© iStockphoto.com/LdF

THE BIG PICTURE

Example 37

Return to the facts of *The Big Picture* on p. 3-1. Can Polly qualify as an abandoned spouse? Yes, if she can claim Paige as a dependent—either as a qualifying child (see Example 14) or as a qualifying relative (see Example 22). If so, Polly can use head-of-household filing status. If not, her filing status is married person filing separately.

3-6 TAX DETERMINATION—COMPUTATION PROCEDURES

The computation of income tax due (or refund) involves applying the proper set of tax rates to taxable income and then adjusting for available credits. In certain cases, however, the application of the kiddie tax will cause a modification of the means by which the tax is determined.

LO.6

Demonstrate the proper procedures for determining the tax liability.

3-6a Tax Rates

The basic tax rate structure is progressive, with current rates ranging from 10 percent to 39.6 percent.[42] By way of comparison, the lowest rate structure, which was

---

[40]§ 7703(b).

[41]§ 152(f)(1). The dependency requirement does not apply, however, if the taxpayer could have claimed a dependency exemption except for the fact that the exemption was claimed by the noncustodial parent under a written agreement.

[42]The Tax Relief Reconciliation Act of 2001 as amended by the American Taxpayer Relief Act of 2012.

in effect in 1913–1915, ranged from 1 to 7 percent, and the highest, in effect during 1944–1945, ranged from 23 to 94 percent.

Tax Table Method

The tax liability is computed using either the Tax Table method or the Tax Rate Schedule method. Most taxpayers compute their tax using the **Tax Table**. Eligible taxpayers compute taxable income (as shown in Figure 3.1) and *must* determine their tax by reference to the Tax Table. The following taxpayers, however, may not use the Tax Table method:

- An individual who files a short period return (see Chapter 18).
- Individuals whose taxable income exceeds the maximum (ceiling) amount in the Tax Table. The 2013 Tax Table applies to taxable income below $100,000 for Form 1040.
- An estate or a trust.

The IRS does not release the Tax Tables until late in the year to which they apply. The Tax Rate Schedules, however, are released at the end of the year preceding their applicability. To illustrate, the Tax Table for 2014 will be available at the end of 2014. The Tax Rate Schedules for 2014, however, were released at the end of 2013.[43] For purposes of estimating tax liability and making quarterly prepayments, the Tax Rate Schedules usually need to be consulted. Based on its availability, the 2013 Tax Table will be used to illustrate the tax computation using the Tax Table method.

Although the Tax Table is derived by using the Tax Rate Schedules (discussed next), the tax calculated using the two methods may vary slightly. This variation occurs because the tax for a particular income range in the Tax Table is based on the midpoint amount.

Example 38

Linda is single and has taxable income of $30,000 for calendar year 2013. To determine Linda's tax using the Tax Table (see Appendix A), find the $30,000 to $30,050 income line. The tax of $4,058 is actually the tax the Tax Rate Schedule for 2013 would yield on taxable income of $30,025 (i.e., the midpoint amount between $30,000 and $30,050).

Tax Rate Schedule Method

As previously noted, the **Tax Rate Schedules** have undergone several reductions since 1970. The American Taxpayer Relief Act of 2012 made these reductions permanent while adding a 39.6% tax bracket for high-income taxpayers.[44]

The 2014 tax rate schedule for single taxpayers is reproduced in Table 3.5. This schedule is used to illustrate the tax computations in Examples 39 and 40.

Example 39

Pat is single and had $5,870 of taxable income in 2014. His tax is $587 ($5,870 × 10%).

Several terms are used to describe tax rates. The rates in the Tax Rate Schedules are often referred to as *statutory* (or nominal) rates. The *marginal* rate is the highest rate that is applied in the tax computation for a particular taxpayer. In Example 39, the statutory rate and the marginal rate are both 10 percent.

Example 40

Chris is single and had taxable income of $90,000 in 2014. Her tax is $18,375.75 [$18,193.75 + 28%($90,000 − $89,350)].

The *average* rate is equal to the tax liability divided by taxable income. In Example 40, Chris has statutory rates of 10 percent, 15 percent, 25 percent, and 28 percent and a marginal rate of 28 percent. Chris's average rate is 20.4 percent ($18,375.75 tax liability ÷ $90,000 taxable income).

---

[43]The 2014 Tax Table was not available from the IRS at the date of publication of this text. The Tax Table for 2013 and the Tax Rate Schedules for 2013 and 2014 are reproduced in Appendix A. For quick reference, the rate schedules are also reproduced inside the front cover of this text.

[44]§ 1(i).

TABLE 3.5		2014 Tax Rate Schedule for Single Taxpayers	

If Taxable Income Is			
Over	**But Not Over**	**The Tax Is:**	**Of the Amount Over**
$ –0–	$ 9,075	10%	$ –0–
9,075	36,900	$ 907.50 + 15%	9,075
36,900	89,350	5,081.25 + 25%	36,900
89,350	186,350	18,193.75 + 28%	89,350
186,350	405,100	45,353.75 + 33%	186,350
405,100	406,750	117,541.25 + 35%	405,100
406,750		118,118.75 + 39.6%	406,750

A tax is *progressive* (or graduated) if a higher rate of tax applies as the tax base increases. The progressive nature of the Federal income tax on individuals is illustrated by computing the tax in Example 40 utilizing each rate bracket.

Tax on first $9,075 at 10%	$ 907.50
Tax on $36,900 – $9,075 at 15%	4,173.75
Tax on $89,350 – $36,900 at 25%	13,112.50
Tax on $90,000 – $89,350 at 28%	182.00
Total tax on taxable income of $90,000	$18,375.75

A special computation limits the effective tax rate on qualified dividends (see Chapter 4) and net long-term capital gain (see Chapter 16).

3-6b Computation of Net Taxes Payable or Refund Due

The pay-as-you-go feature of the Federal income tax system requires payment of all or part of the taxpayer's income tax liability during the year. These payments take the form of Federal income tax withheld by employers or estimated tax paid by the taxpayer or both.[45] The payments are applied against the tax from the Tax Table or Tax Rate Schedules to determine whether the taxpayer will get a refund or pay additional tax.

Employers are required to withhold income tax on compensation paid to their employees and to pay this tax to the government. The employer notifies the employee of the amount of income tax withheld on Form W–2 (Wage and Tax Statement). The employee should receive this form by January 31 after the year in which the income tax is withheld.

If taxpayers receive income that is not subject to withholding or income from which not enough tax is withheld, they may have to pay estimated tax. These individuals must file Form 1040–ES (Estimated Tax for Individuals) and pay in quarterly installments the income tax and self-employment tax estimated to be due (see Chapter 13 for a thorough discussion).

The income tax from the Tax Table or the Tax Rate Schedules is reduced first by the individual's tax credits. There is an important distinction between tax credits and tax deductions. Tax credits reduce the tax liability dollar for dollar. Tax deductions reduce taxable income on which the tax liability is based.

---

[45]§ 3402 for withholding; § 6654 for estimated payments.

Example 41

Gail is a taxpayer in the 25% tax bracket. As a result of incurring $1,000 in child care expenses (see Chapter 13 for details), she is entitled to a $200 child care credit ($1,000 child care expenses × 20% credit rate). She also contributed $1,000 to the American Cancer Society and included this amount in her itemized deductions. The child care credit results in a $200 reduction of Gail's tax liability for the year. The contribution to the American Cancer Society reduces taxable income by $1,000 and results in a $250 reduction in Gail's tax liability ($1,000 reduction in taxable income × 25% tax rate).

Tax credits are discussed in Chapter 13. Following are several of the more common credits:

- Earned income credit.
- Credit for child and dependent care expenses.
- Credit for the elderly.
- Foreign tax credit.
- Child tax credit.

The computation of net taxes payable or refund due can be illustrated by returning to the facts of Example 6.

Example 42

Grace is single and has her disabled and dependent mother living with her. Recall that Example 6 established that Grace has taxable income of $24,600. Further assume that she has the following: income tax withheld, $2,500; estimated tax payments, $600; and credit for dependent care expenses, $200. Grace's net tax payable is computed as follows:

Income tax (from 2014 Tax Rate Schedule, for head of household, Appendix A)		$ 3,043 (rounded)
Less: Tax credits and prepayments—		
Credit for dependent care expenses	$ 200	
Income tax withheld	2,500	
Estimated tax payments	600	(3,300)
Net taxes payable or (refund due if negative)		$ (257)

Note that because Grace maintains a home for a qualifying dependent relative, she can utilize head-of-household filing status. Her tax was computed using the Tax Rate Schedules. In actual practice, she would have used the Tax Tables—see footnote 43 as to why the rate schedules were used.

3-6c Kiddie Tax—Unearned Income of Children Taxed at Parents' Rate

LO.7

Identify and report kiddie tax situations.

At one time, a dependent child could claim an exemption on his or her own return even if claimed as a dependent by the parents. This enabled a parent to shift investment income (such as interest and dividends) to a child by transferring ownership of the assets producing the income. The child would pay no tax on the income to the extent that it was sheltered by the child's exemption and standard deduction amounts.

Also, an additional tax motivation existed for shifting income from parents to children. Although a child's unearned income in excess of the exemption and standard deduction amounts was subject to tax, it was taxed at the child's rate, rather than the parents' rate.

To reduce the tax savings that result from shifting income from parents to children, the net **unearned income** (commonly called investment income) of certain children is taxed as if it were the parents' income. Unearned income includes income such as taxable interest, dividends, capital gains, rents, royalties, pension and annuity income, and income (other than earned income) received as the beneficiary of a trust. This provision, commonly referred to as the **kiddie tax**, applies to any child who is under age 19 (or under age 24 if a full-time student) and has unearned income of more than $2,000 (in 2014 or 2013).[46] The kiddie tax does not apply if the child has earned income that exceeds half of his or her support, if the child is married and files a joint return, or if both parents are deceased.

Net Unearned Income

In 2014, net unearned income of a dependent child is computed as follows:

Unearned income
Less: $1,000
Less: The greater of
- $1,000 of the standard deduction *or*
- The amount of allowable itemized deductions directly connected with the production of the unearned income

Equals: Net unearned income

If net unearned income is zero (or negative), the child's tax is computed without using the parents' rate. If the amount of net unearned income (regardless of source) is positive, the net unearned income is taxed at the parents' rate. The child's remaining taxable income (known as nonparental source income) is taxed at the child's rate. The $1,000 amounts in the preceding formula are subject to adjustment for inflation each year (these amounts were $1,000 in 2013 and $950 in 2012).

Tax Determination

If a child is subject to the kiddie tax, there are two options for computing the tax on the income. A separate return may be filed for the child, or the parents may elect to report the child's income on their own return. If a separate return is filed for the child, the tax on net unearned income (referred to as the *allocable parental tax*) is computed as though the income had been included on the parents' return. Form 8615 is used to compute the tax. The steps required in this computation are illustrated in Example 43.

Olaf and Olga have a child, Hans (age 10). In 2014, Hans received $3,100 of interest income and paid investment-related fees of $200. Olaf and Olga had $70,000 of taxable income, not including their child's investment income. The parents have no qualified dividends or capital gains. Olaf and Olga do not make the parental election (discussed below).		**Example 43**

1. Determine Hans's net unearned income

Gross income (unearned)	$ 3,100
Less: $1,000	(1,000)
Less: The greater of	
• $1,000 or	
• Investment expense ($200)	(1,000)
Equals: Net unearned income	$ 1,100

2. Determine allocable parental tax

Parents' taxable income	$70,000
Plus: Hans's net unearned income	1,100
Equals: Revised taxable income	$71,100
Tax on revised taxable income	$ 9,758
Less: Tax on parents' taxable income	(9,593)
Allocable parental tax	$ 165

---

[46]§ 1(g)(2).

3. Determine Hans's nonparental source tax

Hans's AGI	$ 3,100
Less: Standard deduction	(1,000)
Less: Personal exemption	(–0–)
Equals: Taxable income	$ 2,100
Less: Net unearned income	(1,100)
Nonparental source taxable income	$ 1,000
Equals: Tax ($1,000 × 10% rate)	$ 100

4. Determine Hans's total tax liability

Nonparental source tax (step 3)	$ 100
Allocable parental tax (step 2)	165
Total tax	$ 265

Election to Claim Certain Unearned Income on Parent's Return

If a child who is subject to the kiddie tax is required to file a tax return and meets all of the following requirements, the parent may elect to report the child's unearned income that exceeds $2,000 on the parent's own tax return.

- Gross income is from interest and dividends only.
- Gross income is more than $1,000 but less than $10,000.
- No estimated tax has been paid in the name and Social Security number of the child, and the child is not subject to backup withholding (see Chapter 13).

If the parental election is made, the child is treated as having no gross income and is not required to file a tax return. In this case, Form 8814 (Parents' Election to Report Child's Interest and Dividends) must be filed as part of the parents' tax return.

The parent(s) must also pay an additional tax equal to the smaller of $100 or 10 percent of the child's gross income over $1,000. Parents who have substantial itemized deductions based on AGI (see Chapter 10) may find that making the parental election increases total taxes for the family unit. Taxes should be calculated both with and without the parental election to determine the appropriate choice.

Other Provisions

If parents have more than one child subject to the tax on net unearned income, the tax for the children is computed as shown in Example 43 and then allocated to the children based on their relative amounts of income. For children of divorced parents, the taxable income of the custodial parent is used to determine the allocable parental tax. This parent is the one who may elect to report the child's unearned income. For married individuals filing separate returns, the individual with the greater taxable income is the applicable parent.[47]

3-7 GAINS AND LOSSES FROM PROPERTY TRANSACTIONS—IN GENERAL

LO.8

Formulate the fundamentals of property transactions.

Gains and losses from property transactions are discussed in detail in Chapters 14 through 17. Because of their importance in the tax system, however, they are introduced briefly at this point.

When property is sold or otherwise disposed of, gain or loss may result. Such gain or loss has an effect on the income tax position of the party making the sale or other disposition when the *realized* gain or loss is *recognized* for tax purposes.

---

[47]See Chapter 31 of *Your Federal Income Tax* (IRS Publication 17).

Without realized gain or loss, there generally can be no recognized gain or loss. The concept of realized gain or loss is expressed as follows:

$$\text{Amount realized from the sale} - \text{Adjusted basis of the property} = \text{Realized gain (or loss)}$$

The amount realized is the selling price of the property less any costs of disposition (e.g., brokerage commissions) incurred by the seller. The adjusted basis of the property is determined as follows:

Cost (or other original basis) at date of acquisition[48]
Add: Capital additions
Subtract: Depreciation (if appropriate) and other capital recoveries
               (see Chapter 8)
Equals: Adjusted basis at date of sale or other disposition

All realized gains are recognized (taxable) unless some specific part of the tax law provides otherwise (see Chapter 15 dealing with certain nontaxable exchanges). Realized losses may or may not be recognized (deductible) for tax purposes, depending on the circumstances involved. Generally, losses realized from the disposition of personal use property (property neither held for investment nor used in a trade or business) are not recognized.

During the current year, Ted sells his sailboat (adjusted basis of $4,000) for $5,500. Ted also sells one of his personal automobiles (adjusted basis of $8,000) for $5,000. Ted's realized gain of $1,500 from the sale of the sailboat is recognized. On the other hand, the $3,000 realized loss on the sale of the automobile is not recognized and will not provide Ted with any deductible tax benefit.	**Example 44**

In terms of the tax formula, net gains from property transactions that are recognized will affect the gross income component. If the gain is deferred (e.g., like-kind exchanges or involuntary conversions—see Chapter 15) or not recognized (e.g., sale of a residence—see Chapter 15), there is no immediate tax effect. Recognized losses from property transactions are treated as deductions *for* adjusted gross income (AGI).

Once it has been determined that the disposition of property results in a recognized gain or loss, the next step is to classify the gain or loss as capital or ordinary. Although ordinary gain is fully taxable and ordinary loss is fully deductible, the same may not hold true for capital gains and capital losses.

3-8 GAINS AND LOSSES FROM PROPERTY TRANSACTIONS—CAPITAL GAINS AND LOSSES

To obtain a good perspective on how the Federal income tax functions, some overview of property transactions is needed. This is particularly the case with capital gains and losses, which can generate unique tax consequences. For in-depth treatment of property transactions (including capital gains and losses), refer to Chapters 14 through 17. For now, the overview appearing below should suffice.

3-8a Definition of a Capital Asset

Capital assets are defined in the Code as any property held by the taxpayer *other than* property listed in § 1221. The list in § 1221 includes inventory, accounts

---

[48]Cost usually means purchase price plus expenses related to the acquisition of the property and incurred by the purchaser (e.g., brokerage commissions). For the basis of property acquired by gift or inheritance and other basis rules, see Chapter 14.

receivable, and depreciable property or real estate used in a business. Thus, the sale or exchange of assets in these categories usually results in ordinary income or loss treatment (see Chapter 17).

Example 45	Kelly owns a pizza parlor. During the current year, he sells an automobile that had been used as a pizza delivery car for three years. The sale resulted in a loss of $1,000. Because this automobile is property used in his business, Kelly has an ordinary loss deduction of $1,000, rather than a capital loss deduction.

The principal capital assets held by an individual taxpayer include assets held for personal (rather than business) use, such as a personal residence or an automobile, and assets held for investment purposes (e.g., corporate securities and land). Capital assets generally include collectibles, which are subject to somewhat unique tax treatment. **Collectibles** include art, antiques, gems, metals, stamps, some coins and bullion, and alcoholic beverages that are held as investments.

3-8b Taxation of Net Capital Gain

Net capital gains are classified and taxed as follows:

Classification	Maximum Rate
Short-term gains (held for one year or less)	39.6%
Long-term gains (held for more than one year)—	
Collectibles	28%
Certain depreciable property used in a trade or business (known as unrecaptured § 1250 gain and discussed in Chapter 17)	25%
All other long-term capital gains	20%, 15%, or 0%

The special tax rate applicable to long-term capital gains is called the alternative tax computation. It is to be used only when the taxpayer's regular tax rate *exceeds* the applicable alternative tax rate. The 0 percent rate, noted above, applies only when the taxpayer's regular tax bracket is 15 percent or less. The 20 percent rate applies beginning in 2013 when the taxpayer's regular tax bracket is 39.6 percent.[49]

Example 46	During 2014, Polly is in the 15% tax bracket and has the following capital gains for the year:

Robin Corporation stock (held for 6 months)	$1,000
Crow Corporation stock (held for 13 months)	1,000

Polly's tax on these transactions is $150 ($1,000 × 15%) as to Robin and $0 ($1,000 × 0%) as to Crow.

Example 47	Assume the same facts as in Example 46, except that Polly's regular tax bracket for the year is 33% (not 15%). Polly's tax on these transactions now becomes $330 ($1,000 × 33%) as to Robin and $150 ($1,000 × 15%) as to Crow.

3-8c Determination of Net Capital Gain

To arrive at a net capital gain, capital losses must be taken into account. The capital losses are aggregated by holding period (short-term and long-term) and applied against the gains in that category. If excess losses result, they are then shifted to the category carrying the *highest* tax rate. A *net capital gain* will occur if

---

[49]§ 1(h)(1) as amended by JGTRRA of 2003, further amended by TIPRA of 2005 and extended by TRA of 2010 and ATRA of 2012. For recognized gains prior to May 6, 2003, the maximum rates were 20% and 10%. A 5% rate applied to recognized gains from May 7, 2003, through December 31, 2007, for taxpayers in the 10% or 15% marginal tax bracket.

the net long-term capital gain (NLTCG) exceeds the net short-term capital loss (NSTCL).

	Example 48

In the current year, Colin is in the 35% tax bracket and has the following capital transactions and resulting gains (losses):

Penguin Corporation stock (held for 8 months)	$ 1,000
Owl Corporation stock (held for 10 months)	(3,000)
Stamp collection (held for 5 years)	2,000
Land (held as an investment for 3 years)	4,000

The Penguin Corporation short-term capital gain (STCG) of $1,000 is offset by the Owl Corporation short-term capital loss (STCL) of $3,000, resulting in a net STCL of $2,000. This $2,000 net STCL is then applied against the stamp collection gain—a collectible long-term capital gain (LTCG) with the *highest* tax rate (28%). Because there is no remaining STCL, Colin has a net LTCG of $4,000 from the land sale. This is Colin's net capital gain, and it is taxed at a 15% rate.

3-8d Treatment of Net Capital Loss

For individual taxpayers, net capital loss can be used to offset ordinary income of up to $3,000 ($1,500 for married persons filing separate returns). If a taxpayer has both short- and long-term capital losses, the short-term category is used first to arrive at the $3,000. Any remaining net capital loss is carried over indefinitely until exhausted. When carried over, the excess capital loss retains its classification as short- or long-term.

	Example 49

In 2014, Tina has a short-term capital loss of $2,000, a long-term capital loss of $2,500, and no capital gains. She can deduct $3,000 ($2,000 short-term + $1,000 long-term) of this amount as an ordinary loss. The remaining $1,500 is carried over to 2015 as a long-term capital loss.

THE BIG PICTURE

	Example 50

Return to the facts of *The Big Picture* on p. 3-1. Polly's sale of her wedding rings resulted in a realized capital loss of $2,800 [$9,000 (selling price) − $11,800 (cost basis)]. However, because they were personal use property, Polly cannot deduct the loss.

3-9 TAX PLANNING

3-9a Maximizing the Use of the Standard Deduction

LO.9

Evaluate tax planning opportunities associated with the individual tax formula.

In most cases, the choice between using the standard deduction and itemizing deductions *from* AGI is a simple matter—pick whichever yields the larger tax benefit. Families in the initial stages of home ownership, for example, will invariably make the itemization choice due to the substantial mortgage interest and property tax payments involved. Older taxpayers, however, may have paid for their homes and are enjoying senior citizen property tax exemptions. For them, the more attractive benefit is the additional standard deduction that can accompany the standard deduction choice.

In some cases, the difference between using the standard deduction and itemizing may not be a significant amount. Here, taxes might be saved by alternating between the two options. The taxpayer does this by using the cash method to concentrate multiple years' deductions in a single year (e.g., church pledges for several years can be paid in one year). Then the standard deduction is used in alternate years.

3-9b Dependency Exemptions

The Joint Return Test

A married person can be claimed as a dependent only if that individual does not file a joint return with his or her spouse. If a joint return has been filed, the damage may be undone if separate returns are substituted on a timely basis (on or before the due date of the return).

Example 51	While preparing a client's 2013 income tax return on April 2, 2014, the tax practitioner discovered that the client's daughter filed a joint return with her husband in late January 2014. Presuming that the daughter otherwise qualifies as the client's dependent, the exemption is not lost if she and her husband file separate returns on or before April 15, 2014.

An initial election to file a joint return must be considered carefully in any situation in which the taxpayers might later decide to amend their return and file separately. As indicated previously, separate returns may be substituted for a joint return only if the amended returns are filed on or before the normal due date of the return. If the taxpayers in Example 51 attempt to file separate returns after April 15, 2014, the returns will not be accepted and the joint return election is binding.[50]

Keep in mind that the filing of a joint return is not fatal to the dependency exemption if the parties are filing solely to recover all income tax withholdings, they are not required to file a return, and no tax liability would exist on separate returns.

Support Considerations

The support of a qualifying child becomes relevant only if the child is self-supporting. In cases where the child has an independent source of funds, planning could help prevent an undesirable result. When a qualifying relative is involved, meeting the support test is essential, as the dependency exemption is not otherwise available.

Example 52	In 2014, Imogene maintains a household that she shares with her son and mother. The son, Barry, is 23 years of age and a full-time student in law school. The mother, Gladys, is 68 years of age and active in charitable causes. Barry works part-time for a local law firm, while Gladys has income from investments. In resolving the support issue (or self-support in the case of Barry), compare Imogene's contribution with that made by Barry and Gladys.[51] In this connection, what Barry and Gladys do with their funds becomes crucial. The funds that are used for nonsupport purposes (e.g., purchase of investments) or not used at all (e.g., deposited in a bank) should not be considered. To the extent possible, control how much Barry and Gladys contribute to their own support. Records should be maintained showing the amount of support and its source.

Example 52 does not mention the possible application of the gross income test. Presuming that Barry is a qualifying child, the amount he earns does not matter, as the gross income test does not apply. Gladys, however, comes under the qualifying relative category, where the gross income test applies. Therefore, for her to be claimed as a dependent, her income that is taxable will have to be less than $3,950.

Community Property Ramifications

In certain cases, state law can have an effect on the availability of a dependency exemption.

---

[50]Reg. § 1.6013–1(a)(1).

[51]As part of her support contribution to Barry and Gladys, Imogene can count the fair market value of the meals and lodging she provides.

During the year, Mitch provides more than half of the support of his son, Ross, and daughter-in-law, Connie, who live with him. Ross, age 22, is a full-time student, while Connie earns $4,000 from a part-time job. Ross and Connie do not file a joint return. All parties live in New York, a common law state. Mitch can claim Ross as a dependent, as he is a qualifying child. Connie is not a dependent because she does not meet the gross income test under the qualifying relative category.

Example 53

Assume the same facts as in Example 53, except that all parties live in Arizona, a community property state. Now Connie also qualifies as a dependent. Because Connie's gross income is only $2,000 (one-half of the community income), she satisfies the gross income test.

Example 54

Relationship to the Deduction for Medical Expenses

Generally, medical expenses are deductible only if they are paid on behalf of the taxpayer, his or her spouse, and their dependents. Because deductibility may rest on dependency status, planning is important in arranging multiple support agreements.

During the year, Zelda will be supported by her two sons (Vern and Vito) and her daughter (Maria). Each will furnish approximately one-third of the required support. If the parties decide that the dependency exemption should be claimed by the daughter under a multiple support agreement, any medical expenses incurred by Zelda should be paid by Maria.

Example 55

In planning a multiple support agreement, take into account which of the parties is most likely to exceed the 10 percent (7.5 percent if at least age 65) limitation (see Chapter 10). In Example 55, for instance, Maria might be a poor choice if she and her family do not expect to incur many medical and drug expenses of their own.

One exception permits the deduction of medical expenses paid on behalf of someone who is not a spouse or a dependent. If the person could be claimed as a dependent *except* for the gross income or joint return test, the medical expenses are, nevertheless, deductible. For additional discussion, see Chapter 10.

3-9c Taking Advantage of Tax Rate Differentials

It is natural for taxpayers to be concerned about the tax rates they are paying. How does a tax practitioner communicate information about rates to clients? There are several possibilities.

The marginal rate (refer to Examples 39 and 40) provides information that can help a taxpayer evaluate a particular course of action or structure a transaction in the most advantageous manner. For example, a taxpayer who is in the 15 percent bracket this year and expects to be in the 28 percent bracket next year should, if possible, defer payment of deductible expenses until next year to maximize the tax benefit of the deduction.

A note of caution is in order with respect to shifting income and expenses between years. Congress has recognized the tax planning possibilities of such shifting and has enacted many provisions to limit a taxpayer's ability to do so. Some of these limitations on the shifting of income are discussed in Chapters 4, 5, and 18. Limitations that affect a taxpayer's ability to shift deductions are discussed in Chapters 6 through 11 and in Chapter 18.

A taxpayer's *effective rate* can be an informative measure of the effectiveness of tax planning. The effective rate is computed by dividing the taxpayer's tax liability by the total amount of income. A low effective rate can be considered an indication of effective tax planning.

One way of lowering the effective rate is to exclude income from the tax base. For example, a taxpayer might consider investing in tax-free municipal bonds rather than taxable corporate bonds. Although pre-tax income from corporate bonds is usually higher, after-tax income may be higher if the taxpayer invests in tax-free municipals.

Another way of lowering the effective rate is to make sure the taxpayer's expenses and losses are deductible. For example, losses on investments in passive activities may not be deductible (see Chapter 11). Therefore, a taxpayer who plans to invest in an activity that will produce a loss in the early years should take steps to ensure that the business is treated as active rather than passive. Active losses are deductible, while passive losses are not.

3-9d Income of Certain Children

Taxpayers can use several strategies to avoid or minimize the effect of the rules that tax the unearned income of certain children at the parents' rate. With the cutoff age being 19 (under 24 for full-time students), many children are vulnerable to the application of the kiddie tax. Parents should consider giving a younger child assets that defer taxable income until the child reaches a nonvulnerable age. For example, U.S. government Series EE savings bonds can be used to defer income until the bonds are cashed in (see Chapter 4).

Growth stocks typically pay little in the way of dividends. However, the profit on an astute investment may more than offset the lack of dividends. The child can hold the stock until he or she reaches a safe age. If the stock is sold then at a profit, the profit is taxed at the child's low rates.

Taxpayers in a position to do so can employ their children in their business and pay them a reasonable wage for the work they actually perform (e.g., light office help such as filing). The child's earned income is sheltered by the standard deduction, and the parents' business is allowed a deduction for the wages. The kiddie tax rules have no effect on earned income, even if it is earned from the parents' business.

REFOCUS ON THE BIG PICTURE

A DIVIDED HOUSEHOLD

© Michael DeFreitas Caribbean/Alamy

Of major concern to Polly is her filing status. If she qualifies as an abandoned spouse, she is entitled to file as head of household. If not, she is considered to be a married person filing separately. Moreover, to be an abandoned spouse, Polly must be able to claim Paige as a dependent. To be a dependent, Paige must meet the requirements of a qualifying child *or* a qualifying relative.

For qualifying child purposes, Paige must meet either the age (i.e., under age 19) or the full-time student (under age 24) test. (A disabled child exception seems highly unlikely.) Because Paige currently is not a full-time student, is she under age 19? If so, she is a qualifying child (see Example 14). If Paige is not a qualifying child, is she a qualifying relative? Here, the answer depends on meeting the gross income test (see Example 22). How much did Paige earn from her part-time job? If her earnings are under $3,950, she satisfies the gross income test. Thus, if Paige can be claimed as a dependent under either the qualifying child or the qualifying relative category, Polly is an abandoned spouse entitled to head-of-household filing status (see Example 37). If not, she is a married person filing separately.

Maude can be claimed as Polly's dependent because she is a member of the household. It does not matter that she died in February, and the dependency exemption amount need not be apportioned and is allowed in full. Because Maude is her dependent, Polly can claim the medical expenses she paid on Maude's behalf. The funeral expenses, however, are not deductible (see Example 19).

Does Maude qualify Polly for head-of-household filing status? No—although she is a dependent, Maude does not meet the relationship test (see Example 34).

The sale of the wedding rings results in a capital loss of $2,800 ($9,000 − $11,800). Because the loss is for personal use property, it cannot be claimed for tax purposes (see Example 50).

What If?

Assume that Nick left for parts unknown in August (not March). Now Polly cannot qualify as an abandoned spouse. Her spouse lived in the home during part of the last six months of the year. Consequently, Polly is treated as married and cannot qualify for head-of-household filing status. She must file as a married person filing separately. The change in when Nick left will not affect the dependency issue regarding Paige, however.

Key Terms

Abandoned spouse, 3-28	Itemized deductions, 3-5	Qualifying relative, 3-14
Child tax credit, 3-20	Kiddie tax, 3-32	Standard deduction, 3-7
Collectibles, 3-36	Marriage penalty, 3-26	Surviving spouse, 3-27
Dependency exemption, 3-12	Multiple support agreement, 3-16	Tax Rate Schedules, 3-30
E-file, 3-22	Personal exemptions, 3-11	Tax Table, 3-30
Head-of-household, 3-27	Qualifying child, 3-12	Unearned income, 3-32

Discussion Questions

1. **LO.1** Rearrange the following items to show the correct formula for arriving at *taxable income* of individuals under the Federal income tax:
   a. Deductions *for* AGI.
   b. Income (broadly conceived).
   c. Taxable income.
   d. Adjusted gross income.
   e. Personal and dependency exemptions.
   f. Gross income.
   g. Exclusions.
   h. The greater of the standard deduction or itemized deductions.

2. **LO.1, 5, 8, 9** During the year, Addison is involved in the following transactions: Issue ID

   - Lost money gambling on a recent trip to a casino.
   - Helped pay for her neighbor's dental bills. The neighbor is a good friend who is unemployed.
   - Received from the IRS a tax refund due to Addison's overpayment of last year's Federal income taxes.
   - Paid a traffic ticket received while double parking to attend a business meeting.
   - Contributed to the mayor's reelection campaign. The mayor had promised Addison to have some of her land rezoned. The mayor was reelected and got Addison's land rezoned.
   - Borrowed money from a bank to make a down payment on an automobile.
   - Sold a houseboat and a camper on eBay. Both were personal use items, and the gain from one offset the loss from the other.
   - Her dependent grandfather died on June 3 of the year.
   - Paid for dependent grandfather's funeral expenses.
   - Paid premiums on her dependent son's life insurance policy.

   What are the possible income tax ramifications of these transactions?

3. **LO.1** Which of the following items are *inclusions* in gross income?
   a. During the year, stock the taxpayer purchased as an investment doubled in value.
   b. Amount an off-duty motorcycle police officer received for escorting a funeral procession.
   c. While his mother was in the hospital, the taxpayer sold her jewelry and gave the money to his girlfriend.
   d. Child support payments received.
   e. A damage deposit the taxpayer recovered when he vacated the apartment he had rented.
   f. Interest received by the taxpayer on an investment in general purpose bonds issued by IBM.
   g. Amounts received by the taxpayer, a baseball "Hall of Famer," for autographing sports equipment (e.g., balls and gloves).
   h. Tips received by a bartender from patrons. (Taxpayer is paid a regular salary by the cocktail lounge that employs him.)
   i. Taxpayer sells his Super Bowl tickets for three times what he paid for them.
   j. Taxpayer receives a new BMW from his grandmother when he passes the CPA exam.

4. **LO.1** Which of the following items are *exclusions* from gross income?
   a. Alimony payments received.
   b. Damages award received by the taxpayer for personal physical injury—none were for punitive damages.
   c. A new golf cart won in a church raffle.
   d. Amount collected on a loan previously made to a college friend.
   e. Insurance proceeds paid to the taxpayer on the death of her uncle—she was the designated beneficiary under the policy.
   f. Interest income on City of Chicago bonds.
   g. Jury duty fees.
   h. Stolen funds the taxpayer had collected for a local food bank drive.
   i. Reward paid by the IRS for information provided that led to the conviction of the taxpayer's former employer for tax evasion.
   j. An envelope containing $8,000 found (and unclaimed) by the taxpayer in a bus station.

5. **LO.1** To save on U.S. income taxes, Lucas (a U.S. citizen and resident of Vermont) invests in foreign stocks and bonds. Is Lucas correct in his approach? Explain.

6. **LO.1** One class of deductions is variously described as *deductions for AGI, above-the-line deductions*, and *page 1 deductions*. Explain the meaning of the various designations.

Decision Making   7. **LO.1, 8, 9** In late 2014, the Polks come to you for tax advice. They are considering selling some stock investments for a loss and making a contribution to a traditional IRA. In reviewing their situation, you note that they have large medical expenses and a casualty loss, neither of which is covered by insurance. What advice would you give the Polks?

Issue ID   8. **LO.2** In choosing between the standard deduction and itemizing deductions *from* AGI, what effect, if any, does each of the following have?
   a. The age of the taxpayer(s).
   b. The health (i.e., physical condition) of the taxpayer.
   c. Whether taxpayers rent or own their residence.
   d. Taxpayer's filing status (e.g., single, married, filing jointly).
   e. Whether married taxpayers decide to file separate returns.
   f. The taxpayer's uninsured personal residence was recently destroyed by fire.
   g. The number of personal and dependency exemptions the taxpayer can claim.

9. **LO.2** In connection with the standard deduction alternative, comment on the following:
   a. Percentage of taxpayers who chose the standard deduction rather than itemize.
   b. Status of a taxpayer who dies before year-end.
   c. Types of standard deductions available.
   d. Special limitations on standard deduction for dependents.
   e. When not available.

10. **LO.2, 3, 5** David is age 78, is a widower, and is being claimed as a dependent by his son. How does this situation affect the following?
    a. David's own individual filing requirement.
    b. David's personal exemption.
    c. The standard deduction allowed to David.
    d. The availability of any additional standard deduction.

11. **LO.2** Sam and Abby are dependents of their parents, and each has income of $2,100 for the year. Sam's standard deduction for the year is $1,000, while Abby's is $2,450. As their income is the same, what causes the difference in the amount of the standard deduction?   Issue ID

12. **LO.4** Kirby, age 18, lives with her parents in a household maintained by them. As an actress, she earns $600,000 during the year, which, after taxes, is placed in a trust for her. Can Kirby be claimed as a dependent by her parents? Explain.   Issue ID

13. **LO.4** Patsy maintains a household that includes a son (age 30) and a cousin (age 28). She can claim the cousin as a dependent but not her son. Explain.   Issue ID

14. **LO.4** Heather, age 12, lives in the same household with her mother, grandmother, and uncle.
    a. Who can qualify for the dependency exemption?
    b. Who takes preference?

15. **LO.4** Caden and Lily are divorced on March 3, 2013. For financial reasons, however, Lily continues to live in Caden's apartment and receives her support from him. Caden does not claim Lily as a dependent on his 2013 Federal income tax return but does so on his 2014 return. Explain.

16. **LO.4** Isabella, Emma, and Jacob share equally in the support of their parents. Jacob tells his sisters to split the dependency exemptions between the two of them. Explain what Jacob means.

17. **LO.4** Mark and Lisa were divorced in 2013. In 2014, Mark has custody of their children, but Lisa provides nearly all of their support. Who is entitled to claim the children as dependents?   Issue ID

18. **LO.4** Mario, who is single, is a U.S. citizen and resident. He provides almost all of the support of his parents and two aunts, who are citizens and residents of Guatemala. Mario's parents and aunts are seriously considering moving to and becoming residents of Mexico. Would such a move have any impact on Mario? Why or why not?   Issue ID

19. **LO.3, 4** What are stealth taxes? What purpose do they serve, and why are they used?

20. **LO.5, 9** Paul and Sonja, who are married, had itemized deductions of $8,200 and $400, respectively, during 2014. Paul suggests that they file separately—he will itemize his deductions *from* AGI, and she will claim the standard deduction.   Issue ID
    a. Evaluate Paul's suggestion.
    b. What should they do?

21. **LO.5** Oliver is a U.S. citizen employed by a multinational corporation at its London office. Oliver is married to Regina, a British citizen, and they reside in England. Regina receives substantial rent income from real estate she owns in western Europe.   Issue ID
    a. Must Oliver file a U.S. income tax return?
    b. Under what circumstances might Regina be considered a resident of the United States? Would such a classification be advantageous? Disadvantageous? Explain.

22. **LO.4, 5** Comment on the availability of head-of-household filing status for 2014 in each of the following independent situations:
    a. Taxpayer lives alone but maintains the household of his parents. In July 2014, the parents use their savings to purchase a Lexus automobile for $62,000.
    b. Taxpayer maintains a home in which she and her dependent father live. The father enters a nursing facility for treatment for a mental disorder.
    c. Taxpayer, a single parent, maintains a home in which she and her unmarried son live. The son, age 18, earns $5,000 from a part-time job.
    d. Assume the same facts as in (c), except that the son is age 19, not 18.

e. Taxpayer is married and maintains a household in which he and his dependent step-son live.

f. Taxpayer lives alone but maintains the household where her dependent daughter lives.

g. Taxpayer maintains a household that includes an unrelated friend who qualifies as his dependent.

23. **LO.5** In many cases, a surviving spouse ultimately becomes a head of household for filing status purposes. Explain this statement.

24. **LO.6** Jayden calculates his 2014 income tax by using both the Tax Tables and the Tax Rate Schedules. Because the Tax Rate Schedules yield a slightly lower tax liability, he plans to pay this amount.
    a. Why is there a difference?
    b. Is Jayden's approach permissible? Why or why not?

25. **LO.7** In connection with the application of the kiddie tax, comment on the following:
    a. The child has only earned income.
    b. The child has a modest amount of unearned income.
    c. The child is age 20, not a student, and not disabled.
    d. The child is married.
    e. Effect of the parental election.
    f. The result when the parental election is made and the married parents file separate returns.

26. **LO.8** During the year, Hernando has the following transactions:

    - Gain on the sale of stock held as an investment for 10 months.
    - Gain on the sale of land held as an investment for 4 years.
    - Gain on the sale of a houseboat owned for 2 years and used for family vacations.
    - Loss on the sale of a reconditioned motorcycle owned for 3 years and used for recreational purposes.

    How should Hernando treat these transactions for income tax purposes?

Issue ID

27. **LO.8** In 2012, Randy, Sarah, and Tori inherited an equal share in their grandmother's art collection. In 2014, they sold the collection to an art dealer. When they filed their tax returns, Randy's tax rate on the gain was 28%, while Sarah's was 25% and Tori's was 10%. How is this possible when each of the grandchildren had the same amount of gain?

28. **LO.8** During the year, Brandi had the following transactions: a long-term capital gain from the sale of land, a short-term capital loss from the sale of stock, and a long-term capital gain from the sale of a gun collection.
    a. How are these transactions treated for income tax purposes?
    b. Does this treatment favor the taxpayer or the IRS? Explain.

Problems

29. **LO.1** Compute the taxable income for 2014 in each of the following independent situations:
    a. Drew and Meg, ages 40 and 41, respectively, are married and file a joint return. In addition to four dependent children, they have AGI of $65,000 and itemized deductions of $15,000.
    b. Sybil, age 40, is single and supports her dependent parents who live with her, as well as her grandfather who is in a nursing home. She has AGI of $80,000 and itemized deductions of $8,000.
    c. Scott, age 49, is a surviving spouse. His household includes two unmarried stepsons who qualify as his dependents. He has AGI of $75,000 and itemized deductions of $10,100.
    d. Amelia, age 33, is an abandoned spouse who maintains a household for her three dependent children. She has AGI of $58,000 and itemized deductions of $9,500.
    e. Dale, age 42, is divorced but maintains the home in which he and his daughter, Jill, live. Jill is single and qualifies as Dale's dependent. Dale has AGI of $64,000 and itemized deductions of $9,900.

Note: Problems 30 and 31 can be solved by referring to Figure 3.1, Exhibits 3.1 through 3.3, Tables 3.1 and 3.2, and the discussion under Deductions for Adjusted Gross Income in this chapter.

30. **LO.1, 8** Compute the taxable income for 2014 for Emily on the basis of the following information. Her filing status is single.

Salary	$85,000
Interest income from bonds issued by Xerox	1,100
Alimony payments received	6,000
Contribution to traditional IRA	5,500
Gift from parents	25,000
Short-term capital gain from stock investment	2,000
Amount lost in football office pool (sports gambling is against the law where Emily lives)	500
Number of potential dependents (two cousins, who live in Canada)	?
Age	40

31. **LO.1** Compute the taxable income for 2014 for Aiden on the basis of the following information. Aiden is married but has not seen or heard from his wife since 2012.

Salary	$ 80,000
Interest on bonds issued by City of Boston	3,000
Interest on CD issued by Wells Fargo Bank	2,000
Cash dividend received on Chevron common stock	2,200
Life insurance proceeds paid upon death of aunt (Aiden was the designated beneficiary of the policy)	200,000
Inheritance received upon death of aunt	100,000
Jackson (a cousin) repaid a loan Aiden made to him in 2008 (no interest was provided for)	5,000
Itemized deductions (state income tax, property taxes on residence, interest on home mortgage, and charitable contributions)	9,400
Number of dependents (children, ages 17 and 18, and mother-in-law, age 70)	3
Age	43

32. **LO.2** Determine the amount of the standard deduction allowed for 2014 in the following independent situations. In each case, assume that the taxpayer is claimed as another person's dependent.
    a. Curtis, age 18, has income as follows: $700 interest from a certificate of deposit and $6,000 from repairing cars.
    b. Mattie, age 18, has income as follows: $600 cash dividends from a stock investment and $4,700 from handling a paper route.
    c. Mel, age 16, has income as follows: $800 interest on a bank savings account and $700 for painting a neighbor's fence.
    d. Lucy, age 15, has income as follows: $400 cash dividends from a stock investment and $500 from grooming pets.
    e. Sarah, age 67 and a widow, has income as follows: $500 from a bank savings account and $3,200 from babysitting.

33. **LO.4** Using the legend provided below, classify each statement as to the taxpayer for dependency exemption purposes.

Legend
QC = Could be a qualifying child
QR = Could be a qualifying relative
B   = Could satisfy the definition of *both* a qualifying child *and* a qualifying relative
N   = Could not satisfy the definition of *either* a qualifying child *or* a qualifying relative

a. Taxpayer's son has gross income of $7,000.
b. Taxpayer's niece has gross income of $3,000.
c. Taxpayer's uncle lives with him.
d. Taxpayer's daughter is age 25 and disabled.
e. Taxpayer's daughter is age 18, has gross income of $8,000, and does not live with him.
f. Taxpayer's cousin does not live with her.
g. Taxpayer's brother does not live with her.
h. Taxpayer's sister has dropped out of school, is age 17, and lives with him.
i. Taxpayer's older nephew is age 23 and a full-time student.
j. Taxpayer's grandson lives with her and has gross income of $7,000.

34. **LO.3, 4** For tax year 2014, determine the number of personal and dependency exemptions in each of the following independent situations:
    a. Leo and Amanda (ages 48 and 46, respectively) are husband and wife and furnish more than 50% of the support of their two children, Elton (age 18) and Trista (age 24). During the year, Elton earns $4,500 providing transportation for elderly persons with disabilities, and Trista receives a $5,000 scholarship for tuition at the law school she attends.
    b. Audry (age 45) was divorced this year. She maintains a household in which she, her ex-husband (Clint), and his mother (Olive), live and furnishes more than 50% of their support. Olive is age 91 and blind.
    c. Crystal, age 45, furnishes more than 50% of the support of her married son, Andy (age 18), and his wife, Paige (age 19), who live with her. During the year, Andy earned $8,000 from a part-time job. All parties live in Iowa (a common law state).
    d. Assume the same facts as in (c), except that all parties live in Washington (a community property state).

35. **LO.3, 4** Compute the number of personal and dependency exemptions in each of the following independent situations:
    a. Reginald, a U.S. citizen and resident, contributes 100% of the support of his parents who are citizens of Canada and live there.
    b. Pablo, a U.S. citizen and resident, contributes 100% of the support of his parents who are citizens of Panama. Pablo's father is a resident of Panama, and his mother is a legal resident of the United States.
    c. Gretchen, a U.S. citizen and resident, contributes 100% of the support of her parents, who are U.S. citizens but residents of Germany.
    d. Elena is a U.S. citizen and a resident of Italy. Her household includes Carlos, a 4-year-old adopted son who is a citizen of Spain.

36. **LO.3, 4** Determine how many personal and dependency exemptions would be available in each of the following independent situations. Specify whether any such exemptions would come under the qualifying child or the qualifying relative category.
    a. Andy maintains a household that includes a cousin (age 12), a niece (age 18), and a son (age 26). All are full-time students. Andy furnishes all of their support.
    b. Minerva provides all of the support of a family friend's son (age 20) who lives with her. She also furnishes most of the support of her stepmother, who does not live with her.
    c. Raul, a U.S. citizen, lives in Costa Rica. Raul's household includes a friend, Helena, who is age 19 and a citizen of Costa Rica. Raul provides all of Helena's support.
    d. Karen maintains a household that includes her ex-husband, her mother-in-law, and her brother-in-law (age 23 and not a full-time student). Karen provides more than half of all of their support. Karen is single and was divorced last year.

37. **LO.4** During 2014, Jenny, age 14, lives in a household with her father, uncle, and grandmother. The household is maintained by the uncle. The parties, all of whom file separate returns, have AGI as follows: father ($30,000), uncle ($50,000), and grandmother ($40,000).
    a. Who is eligible to claim Jenny as a dependent?
    b. Who has preference as to the exemption?

38. **LO.3, 4** Sam and Elizabeth Jefferson file a joint return and have three children—all of whom qualify as dependents. If the Jeffersons have AGI of $327,000, what is their allowable deduction for personal and dependency exemptions for 2014?

39. **LO.4, 9** Wesley and Myrtle (ages 90 and 88, respectively) live in an assisted care facility and for 2013 and 2014 received their support from the following sources:

	Percentage of Support
Social Security benefits	16%
Son	20
Niece	29
Cousin	12
Brother	11
Family friend (not related)	12

a. Which persons are eligible to claim the dependency exemptions under a multiple support agreement?

b. Must Wesley and Myrtle be claimed by the same person(s) for both 2013 and 2014? Explain.

c. Who, if anyone, can claim their medical expenses?

40. **LO.3, 7** Taylor, age 18, is claimed as a dependent by her parents. For 2014, she has the following income: $4,000 wages from a summer job, $1,800 interest from a money market account, and $2,000 interest from City of Boston bonds.

a. What is Taylor's taxable income for 2014?

b. What is Taylor's tax for 2014? [Her parents file a joint return and have taxable income of $130,000 (no dividends or capital gains).]

41. **LO.4, 9** Walter and Nancy provide 60% of the support of their daughter (age 18) and son-in-law (age 22). The son-in-law (John) is a full-time student at a local university, while the daughter (Irene) holds various part-time jobs from which she earns $11,000. Walter and Nancy engage you to prepare their tax return for 2014. During a meeting with them in late March 2015, you learn that John and Irene have filed a joint return. What tax advice would you give based on the following assumptions:

Issue ID

Decision Making

a. All parties live in Louisiana (a community property state).

b. All parties live in New Jersey (a common law state).

42. **LO.1, 2, 3, 4, 5, 6** Charlotte (age 40) is a surviving spouse and provides all of the support of her four minor children who live with her. She also maintains the household in which her parents live and furnished 60% of their support. Besides interest on City of Miami bonds in the amount of $5,500, Charlotte's father received $2,400 from a part-time job. Charlotte has a salary of $80,000, a short-term capital loss of $2,000, a cash prize of $4,000 from a church raffle, and itemized deductions of $10,500. Using the Tax Rate Schedules, compute the 2014 tax liability for Charlotte.

43. **LO.1, 2, 3, 4, 5, 6** Morgan (age 45) is single and provides more than 50% of the support of Rosalyn (a family friend), Flo (a niece, age 18), and Jerold (a nephew, age 18). Both Rosalyn and Flo live with Morgan, but Jerold (a French citizen) lives in Canada. Morgan earns a salary of $95,000, contributes $5,000 to a traditional IRA, and receives sales proceeds of $15,000 for an RV that cost $60,000 and was used for vacations. She has $8,200 in itemized deductions. Using the Tax Rate Schedules, compute the 2014 tax liability for Morgan.

44. **LO.5** Which of the following individuals are required to file a tax return for 2014? Should any of these individuals file a return even if filing is not required? Why or why not?

a. Patricia, age 19, is a self-employed single individual with gross income of $5,200 from an unincorporated business. Business expenses amounted to $4,900.

b. Mike is single and is 67 years old. His gross income from wages was $10,800.

c. Ronald is a dependent child under age 19 who received $6,500 in wages from a part-time job.

d. Sam is married and files a joint return with his spouse, Lana. Both Sam and Lana are 67 years old. Their combined gross income was $22,750.

e. Quinn, age 20, is a full-time college student who is claimed as a dependent by his parents. For 2014, Quinn has taxable interest and dividends of $2,500.

Decision Making

45. **LO.5, 6, 9** Roy and Brandi are engaged and plan to get married. During 2014, Roy is a full-time student and earns $9,000 from a part-time job. With this income, student loans, savings, and nontaxable scholarships, he is self-supporting. For the year, Brandi is employed and has wages of $61,000. How much income tax, if any, can Brandi save if she and Roy marry in 2014 and file a joint return?

46. **LO.5** In each of the following independent situations, determine Winston's filing status for 2014. Winston is not married.
    a. Winston lives alone, but he maintains a household in which his parents live. The mother qualifies as Winston's dependent, but the father does not.
    b. Winston lives alone but maintains a household in which his married daughter, Karin, lives. Both Karin and her husband (Winston's son-in-law) qualify as Winston's dependents.
    c. Winston maintains a household in which he and a family friend, Ward, live. Ward qualifies as Winston's dependent.
    d. Winston maintains a household in which he and his mother-in-law live. Winston's wife died in 2013.
    e. Same as (d), except that Winston's wife disappeared (i.e., she did not die) in 2012.

47. **LO.4, 5** Christopher died in 2012 and is survived by his wife, Chloe, and their 18-year-old son, Dylan. Chloe is the executor of Christopher's estate and maintains the household in which she and Dylan live. All of their support is furnished by Chloe while Dylan saves his earnings. Dylan's status for 2012 to 2014 is as follows:

Year	Earnings	Student Status
2012	$5,000	Yes
2013	7,000	No
2014	6,000	Yes

What is Chloe's filing status for:
a. 2012?
b. 2013?
c. 2014?

48. **LO.3, 4, 5** Nadia died in 2013 and is survived by her husband, Jerold (age 44), her married son, Travis (age 22), and her daughter-in-law, Macy (age 18). Jerold is the executor of his wife's estate. He maintains the household where he, Travis, and Macy live and furnishes all of their support. During 2013 and 2014, Travis is a full-time student, while Macy earns $7,000 each year from a part-time job. Travis and Macy do not file jointly during either year. What is Jerold's filing status for 2013 and 2014 if all parties reside in:
    a. Idaho (a community property state)?
    b. Kansas (a common law state)?

49. **LO.1, 3, 7** Paige, age 17, is claimed as a dependent on her parents' 2014 return, on which they report taxable income of $120,000 (no qualified dividends or capital gains). Paige earned $3,900 pet sitting and $4,000 in interest on a savings account. What are Paige's taxable income and tax liability for 2014?

50. **LO.1, 3, 7** Terri, age 16, is claimed as a dependent on her parents' 2014 return. During the year, Terri earned $5,000 in interest income and $3,000 from part-time jobs.
    a. What is Terri's taxable income?
    b. How much of Terri's income is taxed at her rate? At her parents' rate?
    c. Can the parental election be made? Why or why not?

51. **LO.8** During the year, Inez had the following transactions involving capital assets:

Gain on the sale of unimproved land (held as an investment for 3 years)	$ 3,000
Loss on the sale of a camper (purchased 2 years ago and used for family vacations)	(5,000)
Gain on the sale of ADM stock (purchased 9 months ago as an investment)	4,000
Gain on the sale of a fishing boat and trailer (acquired 18 months ago at an auction and used for recreational purposes)	1,000

    a. If Inez is in the 35% bracket, how much income tax results?
    b. If Inez is in the 15% bracket and 2014 is the year when these sales occurred?

52. **LO.8** During the year, Chester had the following transactions involving capital assets:

Gain on the sale of an arrowhead collection (acquired as an investment at different times but all pieces have been held for more than one year) $ 6,000

Loss on the sale of IBM Corporation stock (purchased 11 months ago as an investment)   (4,000)

Gain on the sale of a city lot (acquired 5 years ago as an investment)   2,000

a. If Chester is in the 33% bracket, how much income tax results?
b. If Chester is in the 15% bracket and 2014 is the year involved?

53. **LO.9** Each year, Tom and Cindy Bates normally have itemized deductions of $10,000, including a $4,000 pledge payment to their church. Upon the advice of a friend, they do the following: in early January 2014, they pay their pledge for 2013; during 2014, they pay the pledge for 2014; and in late December 2014, they prepay their pledge for 2015.
a. Explain what the Bates are trying to accomplish.
b. What will be the tax saving if their marginal tax bracket is 25% for all three years? (Assume that the standard deduction amounts for 2014 and 2015 are the same.)
c. Write a letter to Tom and Cindy Bates (8212 Bridle Court, Reston, VA 20194) summarizing your analysis.

Decision Making

Communications

Cumulative Problems

Tax Return Problem

54. Lance H. and Wanda B. Dean are married and live at 431 Yucca Drive, Santa Fe, NM 87501. Lance works for the convention bureau of the local Chamber of Commerce, while Wanda is employed part-time as a paralegal for a law firm.

During 2013, the Deans had the following receipts:

H&R BLOCK
TAX SOFTWARE

Salaries ($60,000 for Lance, $41,000 for Wanda)		$101,000
Interest income—		
City of Albuquerqe general purpose bonds	$1,000	
Ford Motor company bonds	1,100	
Ally Bank certificate of deposit	400	2,500
Child support payments from John Allen		7,200
Annual gifts from parents		26,000
Settlement from Roadrunner Touring Company		90,000
Lottery winnings		600
Federal income tax refund (for tax year 2012)		400

Wanda was previously married to John Allen. When they divorced several years ago, Wanda was awarded custody of their two children, Penny and Kyle. (Note: Wanda has never issued a Form 8332 waiver.) Under the divorce decree, John was obligated to pay alimony and child support—the alimony payments were to terminate if Wanda remarried.

In July, while going to lunch in downtown Santa Fe, Wanda was injured by a tour bus. As the driver was clearly at fault, the owner of the bus, Roadrunner Touring Company, paid her medical expenses (including a one-week stay in a hospital). To avoid a lawsuit, Roadrunner also transferred $90,000 to her in settlement of the personal injuries she sustained.

The Deans had the following expenditures for 2013:

Medical expenses (not covered by insurance)		$7,200
Taxes—		
Property taxes on personal residence	$3,600	
State of New Mexico income tax (includes amount withheld from wages during 2013)	4,200	7,800
Interest on home mortgage		6,000
Paid church pledge		3,600
Life insurance premiums (policy on Lance's life)		1,200
Contribution to traditional IRA (on Wanda's behalf)		5,000

Traffic fines	$ 300
Contribution to the reelection campaign fund of the mayor of Santa Fe	500
Funeral expenses for Wayne Boyle	6,300

The life insurance policy was taken out by Lance several years ago and designates Wanda as the beneficiary. As a part-time employee, Wanda is excluded from coverage under her employer's pension plan. Consequently, she provides for her own retirement with a traditional IRA obtained at a local trust company. Because the mayor is a member of the local Chamber of Commerce, Lance felt compelled to make the political contribution.

The Deans' household includes the following, for whom they provide more than half of the support:

	Social Security Number	Birth Date
Lance Dean (age 42)	123-45-6786	12/16/1971
Wanda Dean (age 40)	123-45-6787	08/08/1973
Penny Allen (age 19)	123-45-6788	10/09/1994
Kyle Allen (age 17)	123-45-6789	05/03/1996
Wayne Boyle (age 75)	123-45-6785	06/15/1937

Penny graduated from high school on May 9, 2013, and is undecided about college. During 2013, she earned $8,500 (placed in a savings account) playing a harp in the lobby of a local hotel. Wayne is Wanda's widower father who died on January 20, 2013. For the past few years, Wayne qualified as a dependent of the Deans.

Federal income tax withheld is $5,200 (Lance) and $3,100 (Wanda). The proper amount of Social Security and Medicare tax was withheld.

Determine the Federal income tax for 2013 for the Deans on a joint return by completing the appropriate forms. They do not want to contribute to the Presidential Election Campaign Fund. If an overpayment results, it is to be refunded to them. Suggested software: H&R BLOCK Tax Software.

Tax Return Problem

Decision Making

Communications

55. Logan B. Taylor is a widower whose wife, Sara, died on June 6, 2011. He lives at 4680 Dogwood Lane, Springfield, MO 65801. He is employed as a paralegal by a local law firm. During 2013, he had the following receipts:

Salary		$ 80,000
Interest income—		
Money market account at Omni Bank	$ 300	
Savings account at Boone State Bank	1,100	
City of Springfield general purpose bonds	3,000	4,400
Inheritance from Daniel		60,000
Life insurance proceeds		200,000
Amount from sale of St. Louis lot		80,000
Proceeds from estate sale		9,000
Federal income tax refund (for 2012 tax overpayment)		700

Logan inherited securities worth $60,000 from his uncle, Daniel, who died in 2013. Logan also was the designated beneficiary of an insurance policy on Daniel's life with a maturity value of $200,000. The lot in St. Louis was purchased on May 2, 2008, for $85,000 and held as an investment. As the neighborhood has deteriorated, Logan decided to cut his losses and sold the lot on January 5, 2013, for $80,000. The estate sale consisted largely of items belonging to Sara and Daniel (e.g., camper, boat, furniture, and fishing and hunting equipment). Logan estimates that the property sold originally cost at least twice the $9,000 he received and has declined or stayed the same in value since Sara and Daniel died.

Logan's expenditures for 2013 include the following:

Medical expenses (including $10,500 for dental)		$11,500
Taxes—		
State of Missouri income tax (includes withholdings during 2013)	$3,200	
Property taxes on personal residence	4,500	7,700
Interest on home mortgage		4,600
Contribution to church (paid pledges for 2013 and 2014)		4,800

Logan and his dependents are covered by his employer's health insurance policy. However, he is subject to a deductible, and dental care is not included. The $10,500 dental charge was for Helen's implants. Helen is Logan's widowed mother, who lives with him (see below). Logan normally pledges $2,400 ($200 per month) each year to his church. On December 5, 2013, upon the advice of his pastor, he prepaid his pledge for 2014.

Logan's household, all of whom he supports, includes the following:

	Social Security Number	Birth Date
Logan Taylor (age 48)	123-45-6787	08/30/1965
Helen Taylor (age 70)	123-45-6780	01/13/1943
Asher Taylor (age 23)	123-45-6783	07/18/1990
Mia Taylor (age 22)	123-45-6784	02/16/1991

Helen receives a modest Social Security benefit. Asher, a son, is a full-time student in dental school and earns $4,500 as a part-time dental assistant. Mia, a daughter, does not work and is engaged to be married.

Part 1—Tax Computation
Using the appropriate forms and schedules, compute Logan's income tax for 2013. Federal income tax of $5,500 was withheld from his wages. If Logan has any overpayment on his income tax, he wants the refund sent to him. Assume that the proper amounts of Social Security and Medicare taxes were withheld. Logan does not want to contribute to the Presidential Election Campaign Fund. Suggested software: H&R BLOCK Tax Software.

Part 2—Follow-Up Advice
In early 2014, the following take place:

- Helen decides she wants to live with one of her daughters and moves to Arizona.
- Asher graduates from dental school and joins an existing practice in St. Louis.
- Mia marries, and she and her husband move in with his parents.
- Using the insurance proceeds he received on Daniel's death, Logan pays off the mortgage on his personal residence.

Logan believes these events may have an effect on his tax position for 2014. Therefore, he requests your advice.

Write a letter to Logan explaining in general terms the changes that will occur for tax purposes. Assume that Logan's salary and other factors not mentioned (e.g., property and state income taxes) will remain the same. Use the Tax Rate Schedules in projecting Logan's tax for 2014.

Research Problems

Note: Solutions to Research Problems can be prepared by using the **Checkpoint®** **Student Edition** online research product, which is available to accompany this text. It is also possible to prepare solutions to the Research Problems by using tax research materials found in a standard tax library.

THOMSON REUTERS
CHECKPOINT®

Communications

Research Problem 1. Kathy and Brett Ouray married in 1996. They began to experience marital difficulties in 2010 and, in the current year, although they are not legally separated, consider themselves completely estranged. They have contemplated getting a divorce. However, because of financial concerns and because they both want to remain involved in the lives of their three sons, they have not yet filed for divorce. In addition, their financial difficulties have meant that Kathy and Brett cannot afford to live in separate residences. So although they consider themselves emotionally estranged, they and their three sons all reside in a single-family home in Chicago, Illinois.

Although Brett earns significantly more than Kathy, both contribute financially to maintaining their home and supporting their teenage sons. In one of their few and brief conversations this year, they determined that Brett had contributed far more than Kathy to the maintenance of their home and the support of their sons. Thus, Brett has decided that for the current tax year, they will file separate Federal income tax returns and that he will claim head-of-household filing status. While they live under the same roof, Brett believes that he and Kathy should maintain separate households. Given this fact and the fact that he provides significantly more for the support of their sons, he believes he is eligible for head-of-household filing status. Advise Brett on which filing status is most appropriate for him in the current year.

Communications

Research Problem 2. Sophia Durbin maintains a household in which she, her son (Ryan), and her widowed mother-in-law (Isabella) live. Since 2012, she also has provided more than half of their support. Sophia's husband, Karl, left for parts unknown in April 2012 and, except for one postcard, has not been heard from since. In the postcard (no return address included) that Sophia received in March 2013, Karl announced that he planned to claim both Ryan and Isabella as dependents on his own tax return.

Ryan (age 19 in December 2012) graduated from high school on May 6, 2012, and plans to start college in 2014. Until then, he is working as much as possible to save for college expenses. He earned $8,000 in 2012 and $17,000 in 2013. Isabella's income is negligible and originates from nontaxable sources (e.g., Social Security benefits and interest on municipal bonds).

For tax year 2012, Sophia filed her Federal income tax return as married filing separately and claimed no exemptions for dependents. She has not yet filed for 2013. Being somewhat perplexed with her situation, she comes to you for advice in early March 2014.

a. Write a letter to Sophia Durbin addressing her concerns. She lives at 1310 Ash Street, Kearney, NE 68849.

b. Prepare a memo for your firm's client files that lists and discusses the legal basis for the advice rendered.

Decision Making

Research Problem 3. John and Janet Baker are husband and wife and maintain a household in which the following persons live: Calvin and Florence Carter and Darin, Andrea, and Morgan Baker.

- Calvin and Florence are Janet's parents, who are retired. During the year, they receive $19,000 in nontaxable funds (e.g., disability income, interest on municipal bonds, and Social Security benefits). Of this amount, $8,000 is spent equally between them for clothing, transportation, and recreation (e.g., vacation) and the balance of $11,000 is invested in tax-exempt securities. Janet paid $1,000 for her mother's dental work and paid the $1,200 premium on an insurance policy her father owned on his own life. Calvin also had medical expenses, but he insisted on paying for them with his own funds.

- Darin is the Bakers' 18-year-old son who is not a student but operates a pool-cleaning service on a part-time basis. During the year, he earns $14,000 from the business, which he places in a savings account for later college expenses.

- Andrea is the Bakers' 19-year-old daughter who does not work or go to school. Tired of the inconvenience of borrowing and sharing the family car, during the year, she purchased a Camaro for $21,000. Andrea used funds from a savings account she had established several years ago with an inheritance from her paternal grandfather.

- Morgan is the Bakers' 23-year-old daughter. To attend graduate school at a local university, she applied for and obtained a student loan of $20,000. She uses the full amount to pay her college tuition.

The Bakers' fair rental value of their residence, including utilities, is $14,000, while their total food expense for the household is $10,500.

a. How many dependency exemptions are the Bakers entitled to claim for the year? Explain your answer.

b. From a planning standpoint, how might the Bakers have improved the tax result?

Partial list of research aids:
Reg. §§ 1.152–1(a) and –1(c).
Your Federal Income Tax (IRS Publication 17), Chapter 3.

Research Problem 4. Tom and Sandy were divorced on July 7, 2014. Under the divorce decree, Sandy received full custody of their three children, and Tom was awarded the dependency exemptions for them. After the trial was over, Tom had Sandy sign a Form 8332 (Release/Revocation of Release of Claim to Exemption for Child by Custodial Parent), releasing her rights to the dependency exemptions for the next five years. In early April 2014, Sandy realizes the tax costs of losing the deduction for the dependency exemptions. Besides contacting Tom, who is already delinquent in his child support payments, does she have any way out? Explain.

Use the tax resources of the Internet to address the following questions. Do not restrict your search to the Web, but include a review of newsgroups and general reference materials, practitioner sites and resources, primary sources of the tax law, chat rooms and discussion groups, and other opportunities.

Internet Activity

Research Problem 5. Locate IRS Form 2120 (at **www.irs.gov**) and answer the following questions.
a. Who must sign the form?
b. Who must file the form?
c. Can it be used for someone who is not related to the taxpayer? Explain.

Research Problem 6. What purpose is served by Form 8857? Read the directions for the form and see IRS Publication 971 for additional information.

Research Problem 7. A nonresident alien earns money in the United States that is subject to Federal income tax. What guidance does the IRS provide about what tax form needs to be used and when it should be filed? In terms of the proper filing date, does it matter whether the earnings were subject to income tax withholding? Explain.

Research Problem 8. When taxpayers pay their income taxes by means of a credit or debit card, they are charged "convenience fees" by the issuer of the card. Are these fees deductible for income tax purposes? Explain. [See the instructions for Schedule A (Form 1040), line 23.]

Research Problem 9. Locate Forms 8615 and 8814 (at **www.irs.gov**). What do these forms have in common? What purpose is served by each?

part 2

GROSS INCOME

Part 2 presents the income component of the basic tax model. Included in this presentation are the determination of what is income and the statutory exclusions that are permitted in calculating gross income. Because the taxpayer's accounting method and accounting period affect when income is reported, an introductory discussion of these topics is also included.

Dennis Flaherty/Photographer's Choice/Getty Images

CHAPTER

4

Gross Income: Concepts and Inclusions

LEARNING OBJECTIVES: *After completing Chapter 4, you should be able to:*

LO.1 Explain the concepts of gross income and realization and distinguish between the economic, accounting, and tax concepts of gross income.

LO.2 Describe the cash and accrual methods of accounting and the related effects of the choice of taxable year.

LO.3 Identify who should pay the tax on a particular item of income in various situations.

LO.4 Apply the Internal Revenue Code provisions on alimony, loans made at below-market interest rates, annuities, prizes and awards, group term life insurance, unemployment compensation, and Social Security benefits.

LO.5 Identify tax planning strategies for minimizing gross income.

Dennis Flaherty/Photographer's Choice/Getty Images

THE BIG PICTURE   Tax Solutions for the Real World

CALCULATION OF GROSS INCOME

In 2014, Dr. Cliff Payne, age 27, opened his dental practice as a sole proprietorship with a December 31 year-end. By the beginning of February, construction on his medical building was completed. He also leased an office building and entered into a contract to make improvements. In addition, early in the year, he used $12,000 of extra money to purchase some stock.

The following financial information shows the results of Dr. Payne's first year of operation. The accounts receivable represent the amounts billed to patients.

Revenues (amounts billed patients for dental services)	$385,000
Accounts receivable: January 1	–0–
Accounts receivable: December 31	52,000

During the year, Sam Jones, a contractor who owed Dr. Payne $4,000 for dental services, satisfied the account by installing solar panels on the roof of Dr. Payne's new medical building.

As an undergraduate student, Cliff took an accounting course in which he learned that the accrual method of accounting provides a better measure of the correct income and expenses of a business. Therefore, based on the above financial information, Cliff concludes that the gross income for Federal income tax purposes is the $385,000 he billed his patients for the dental services rendered.

Has Dr. Payne correctly calculated the gross income of this dental practice?

Read the chapter and formulate your response.

FRAMEWORK 1040

Tax Formula for Individuals

This chapter covers the boldfaced portions of the Tax Formula for Individuals that was introduced in Figure 3.1 on p. 3-3. Below those portions are the sections of Form 1040 where the results are reported.

Income *(broadly conceived)*		$xx,xxx
Less: Exclusions		(x,xxx)
Gross income		$xx,xxx

FORM 1040 (p. 1)

7	Wages, salaries, tips, etc. Attach Form(s) W-2	
8a	**Taxable** interest. Attach Schedule B if required	
b	**Tax-exempt** interest. **Do not** include on line 8a	**8b**
9a	Ordinary dividends. Attach Schedule B if required	
b	Qualified dividends	**9b**
11	Alimony received	
12	Business income or (loss). Attach Schedule C or C-EZ	
20a	Social security benefits **20a**	**b** Taxable amount
21	Other income. List type and amount	

Less: Deductions for adjusted gross income	(x,xxx)
Adjusted gross income	$xx,xxx
Less: The greater of total **itemized deductions** *or* the standard deduction	(x,xxx)
Personal and dependency exemptions	(x,xxx)
Taxable income	$xx,xxx
Tax on taxable income *(see Tax Tables or Tax Rate Schedules)*	$ x,xxx
Less: Tax credits *(including income taxes withheld and prepaid)*	(xxx)
Tax due *(or refund)*	$ xxx

This chapter is concerned with the first step in the computation of taxable income—the determination of gross income. Questions that are addressed include the following:

- What is income?
- When is the income recognized?
- Who must include the gross income?

The Code provides an all-inclusive definition of gross income in § 61. Chapter 5 presents items of income that are specifically excluded from gross income (exclusions).

4-1 GROSS INCOME—WHAT IS IT?

LO.1

Explain the concepts of gross income and realization and distinguish between the economic, accounting, and tax concepts of gross income.

4-1a Definition

Section 61(a) of the Internal Revenue Code defines the term **gross income** as follows:

> Except as otherwise provided in this subtitle, gross income means all income from whatever source derived.

This definition is based on the language of the Sixteenth Amendment to the Constitution.

Supreme Court decisions have made it clear that all sources of income are subject to tax unless Congress specifically excludes a type of income.[1]

Congress left it to the judicial and administrative branches to specifically determine the meaning of *income*.

---

[1]*James v. U.S.*, 61–1 USTC ¶9449, 7 AFTR 2d 1361, 81 S.Ct. 1052 (USSC, 1961).

Global Tax Issues

© iStockphoto.com/Andrey Prokhorov

4-1b Recovery of Capital Doctrine

While the Constitution grants Congress the power to tax income, it does not define the term. Thus, it would seem that Congress could simply tax gross receipts. Although Congress does allow certain deductions, none are constitutionally required. On the other hand, the Supreme Court has held that there is no income subject to tax until the taxpayer has recovered the capital invested.[2] This concept is known as the **recovery of capital doctrine**.

In its simplest application, this doctrine means that sellers can reduce their gross receipts (selling price) by the adjusted basis of the property sold to determine the amount of gross income.[3]

THE BIG PICTURE

Example 1

Return to the facts of *The Big Picture* on p. 4-1. Assume Dr. Payne receives $15,000 when he sells the common stock he had purchased for $12,000. His gross receipts are $15,000, which consist of a $12,000 recovery of capital and $3,000 of gross income.

4-1c Economic and Accounting Concepts

The term **income** is used in the Code but is not separately defined. Thus, the courts were required to interpret "the commonly understood meaning of the term which must have been in the minds of the people when they adopted the Sixteenth Amendment to the Constitution."[4] Early in the development of the income tax law, a choice had to be made between two competing models: economic income and accounting income. In determining the definition of income, the Supreme Court rejected the economic concept of income.

Economists measure income (**economic income**) by first determining the fair market value of the individual's net assets (assets minus liabilities) at the beginning and end of the year (change in net worth). Then to arrive at economic income, this change in net worth is increased by the value of the goods and services that person actually consumed during the period. Economic income also includes imputed values for such items as the rental value of an owner-occupied home and the value of food a taxpayer might grow for personal consumption.[5]

---

[2]*Doyle v. Mitchell Bros. Co.*, 1 USTC ¶17, 3 AFTR 2979, 38 S.Ct. 467 (USSC, 1916).

[3]For a definition of *adjusted basis*, see the Glossary in Appendix C.

[4]*Merchants Loan and Trust Co. v. Smietanka*, 1 USTC ¶42, 3 AFTR 3102, 41 S.Ct. 386 (USSC, 1921).

[5]See Henry C. Simons, *Personal Income Taxation* (Chicago: University of Chicago Press, 1933), Chapters 2–3.

Example 2	Helen has economic income as follows:		
	Fair market value of Helen's assets on		
	December 31, 2014	$220,000	
	Less liabilities on December 31, 2014	(40,000)	
	Net worth on December 31, 2014		$ 180,000
	Fair market value of Helen's assets on		
	January 1, 2014	$200,000	
	Less liabilities on January 1, 2014	(80,000)	
	Net worth on January 1, 2014		(120,000)
	Increase in net worth		$ 60,000
	Consumption		
	Food, clothing, and other personal expenditures		25,000
	Imputed rental value of the home Helen owns		
	and occupies		12,000
	Economic income		$ 97,000

The need to value assets annually would make compliance with the tax law burdensome and would cause numerous controversies between the taxpayer and the IRS over valuation. In addition, using market values to determine income for tax purposes could result in liquidity problems. The taxpayer's assets may increase in value even though they are not readily convertible into the cash needed to pay the tax (e.g., commercial real estate). Thus, the IRS, Congress, and the courts have rejected the economic concept of income as impractical.

In contrast, the accounting concept of income is founded on the realization principle.[6] According to this principle, income (**accounting income**) is not recognized until it is realized. For realization to occur, (1) an exchange of goods or services must take place between the accounting entity and some independent, external group and (2) in the exchange, the accounting entity must receive assets that are capable of being objectively valued. Thus, income is recognized when an employee embezzles his or her employer's funds, when the income from an illegal business is realized, and when a person discovers buried treasure.[7] On the other hand, the appreciation in the market value of an asset owned is not realized and thus is not included in gross income until the asset is sold. Income is not realized when an individual creates assets for his or her own use (e.g., vegetables grown in a personal garden) because there is no exchange transaction with another party.

The Supreme Court expressed an inclination toward the accounting concept of income when it adopted the realization requirement in *Eisner v. Macomber*.[8]

In summary, *income* represents an increase in wealth recognized for tax purposes only upon realization.

4-1d Comparison of the Accounting and Tax Concepts of Income

Although income tax rules frequently parallel financial accounting measurement concepts, differences do exist. Of major significance, for example, is the fact that unearned (prepaid) income received by accrual basis taxpayer often is taxed in the year of receipt. For financial accounting purposes, such prepayments are not treated as income until earned.[9] Because of this and other differences, many corporations report financial accounting income that is substantially different from the amounts reported for tax purposes (see Reconciliation of Corporate Taxable Income and Accounting Income in Chapter 20).

---

[6]See the American Accounting Association Committee Report on the "Realization Concept," *The Accounting Review* (April 1965): 312–322.

[7]*Rutkin v. U.S.*, 52–1 USTC ¶9260, 41 AFTR 2d 596, 72 S.Ct. 571 (USSC, 1952); Rev.Rul. 61, 1953–1 C.B. 17.

[8]1 USTC ¶32, 3 AFTR 3020, 40 S.Ct. 189 (USSC, 1920).

[9]Similar differences exist in the deduction area.

TAX IN THE NEWS Bartering Gets Organized

Bartering was the only way to conduct commerce before money was invented. But bartering has experienced a revival as a result of the creation of "barter trade exchanges." Advertisements appear on the Internet encouraging individuals to form "barter trade exchanges," which operate like a local eBay, except services are exchanged (rather than sold for cash) among members.

Bartering is a part of the "underground economy." The individuals who exchange services informally often do not report their income from these transactions, and it is very difficult for the IRS to discover the unreported income. However, the organized exchanges should provide the IRS with a source for discovering the taxable income from bartering.

Source: See, for example, Start Your Own Barter Trade Exchange Using Tom McDowell's Proven Barter System, **www.bartertrainer. com/clubs.asp**.

© iStockphoto.com/Andrey Prokhorov

The Supreme Court provided an explanation for some of the variations between accounting and taxable income in a decision involving inventory and bad debt adjustments:

> The primary goal of financial accounting is to provide useful information to management, shareholders, creditors, and others properly interested; the major responsibility of the accountant is to protect these parties from being misled. The primary goal of the income tax system, in contrast, is the equitable collection of revenue…. Consistently with its goals and responsibilities, financial accounting has as its foundation the principle of conservatism, with its corollary that 'possible errors in measurement [should] be in the direction of understatement rather than overstatement of net income and net assets.' In view of the Treasury's markedly different goals and responsibilities, understatement of income is not destined to be its guiding light.
>
> … Financial accounting, in short, is hospitable to estimates, probabilities, and reasonable certainties; the tax law, with its mandate to preserve the revenue, can give no quarter to uncertainty.[10]

4-1e Form of Receipt

Gross income is not limited to cash received. "It includes income realized in any form, whether in money, property, or services. Income may be realized [and recognized], therefore, in the form of services, meals, accommodations, stock or other property, as well as in cash."[11]

Ostrich Corporation allows Bill, an employee, to use a company car for his vacation. Bill realizes income equal to the rental value of the car for the time and mileage.	**Example 3**

Terry owes $10,000 on a mortgage. The creditor accepts $8,000 in full satisfaction of the debt. Terry realizes income of $2,000 from retiring the debt.[12]	**Example 4**

Sam began his law practice in a building in need of repairs. Sam decided to list his services on a barter exchange. He offered to provide an hour of legal services in exchange for building repairs. A qualified carpenter performed the repairs in eight hours. The carpenter normally charges $50 an hour. Sam formed a corporation for the carpenter in exchange for the carpenter's services. Sam realized $400 (8 hours × $50) in gross income for his services.	**Example 5**

---

[10]*Thor Power Tool Co. v. Comm.,* 79–1 USTC ¶9139, 43 AFTR 2d 79–362, 99 S.Ct. 773 (USSC, 1979).

[11]Reg. § 1.61–1(a).

[12]Reg. § 1.61–12. See *U.S. v. Kirby Lumber Co.,* 2 USTC ¶814, 10 AFTR 458, 52 S.Ct. 4 (USSC, 1931). Exceptions to this general rule are discussed in Chapter 5.

4-2 YEAR OF INCLUSION

LO.2

Describe the cash and accrual methods of accounting and the related effects of the choice of taxable year.

4-2a Taxable Year

The annual accounting period, or **taxable year**, is a basic component of our tax system.[13] Generally, an entity must use the *calendar year* to report its income. However, a *fiscal year* (a period of 12 months ending on the last day of any month other than December) can be elected if the taxpayer maintains adequate books and records. This fiscal year option generally is not available to partnerships, S corporations, and personal service corporations, as discussed in Chapter 18.[14]

In determining a person's tax liability, it is important that the income be placed in the correct tax year. The tax on the income is dependent on the applicable tax rates. The applicable rates can change between years for the following reasons:

- With a progressive rate system, a taxpayer's marginal tax rate can change from year to year.
- Congress may change the tax rates.
- The relevant rates may change because of a change in the entity's status (e.g., a person may marry or a business may be incorporated).
- Several provisions in the Code are dependent on the taxpayer's gross income for the year (e.g., whether the person can be claimed as a dependent, as discussed in Chapter 3).

Even when the rates do not change between tax years, the longer payment of the tax can be postponed, the lower the present value of the tax.

4-2b Accounting Methods

The year an item of income is subject to tax often depends upon which acceptable **accounting method** the taxpayer regularly employs.[15] The three primary methods of accounting are (1) the cash receipts and disbursements method, (2) the accrual method, and (3) the hybrid method. Most individuals use the cash receipts and disbursements method of accounting, while most larger corporations use the accrual method. The Regulations require the accrual method for determining purchases and sales when inventory is an income-producing factor.[16] Some businesses use a hybrid method that is a combination of the cash and accrual methods of accounting.

In addition to these overall accounting methods, a taxpayer may choose to spread the gain from an installment sale of property over the collection periods by using the *installment method* of income recognition. Contractors may either spread profits from contracts over the periods in which the work is done (the *percentage of completion method*) or defer all profit until the year in which the project is completed (the *completed contract method*, which can be used only in limited circumstances).[17]

The IRS has the power to prescribe the accounting method to be used by the taxpayer. Section 446(b) grants the IRS broad powers to determine whether the accounting method used *clearly reflects income.*

> If no method of accounting has been regularly used by the taxpayer, or *if the method used does not clearly reflect income, the computation of taxable income shall be made under such method as, in the opinion of the Secretary … does clearly reflect income.*

A change in the accounting method of accounting requires the consent of the IRS.[18]

---

[13]See Accounting Periods in Chapter 18.

[14]§§ 441(a) and (d).

[15]See Accounting Methods in Chapter 18.

[16]Reg. § 1.446–1(c)(2)(i). Other circumstances in which the accrual method must be used are presented in Chapter 18. For the small busi-ness exception to the inventory requirement, see Rev.Proc. 2002–28, 2002–1 C.B. 815.

[17]§§ 453 and 460. See Chapter 18 for limitations on the use of the install-ment method and the completed contract method.

[18]§ 446(e).

Cash Receipts Method

Under the **cash receipts method**, property or services received are included in the taxpayer's gross income in the year of actual or constructive receipt by the taxpayer or agent, regardless of whether the income was earned in that year.[19] The income received need not be reduced to cash in the same year. All that is necessary for income recognition is that property or services received have a fair market value—a cash equivalent.[20] Thus, a cash basis taxpayer who receives a note in payment for services has income in the year of receipt equal to the fair market value of the note. However, a creditor's mere promise to pay (e.g., an account receivable), with no supporting note, usually is not considered to have a fair market value.[21] Thus, the cash basis taxpayer defers income recognition until the account receivable is collected.

| | | **Example 6** |

Dana, an accountant, reports her income by the cash method. In 2014, she performed an audit for Orange Corporation and billed the client for $5,000, which was collected in 2015. In 2014, Dana also performed an audit for Blue Corporation. Because of Blue's precarious financial position, Dana required Blue to issue an $8,000 secured negotiable note in payment of the fee. The note had a fair market value of $6,000. Dana collected $8,000 on the note in 2015. Dana's gross income for the two years is as follows:

	2014	2015
Fair market value of note received from Blue	$6,000	
Cash received		
From Orange on account receivable		$ 5,000
From Blue on note receivable		8,000
Less: Recovery of capital		(6,000)
Total gross income	$6,000	$ 7,000

Generally, a check received is considered a cash equivalent and, upon receipt, must be recognized as income by a cash basis taxpayer. An exception to this rule is if the person paying with the check requests that the check not be cashed until a subsequent date, the income is deferred until that later date.[22]

Accrual Method

Under the **accrual method**, an item is generally included in gross income for the year in which it is earned, regardless of when it is collected. The income is earned when (1) all events have occurred that fix the right to receive such income and (2) the amount to be received can be determined with reasonable accuracy.[23]

Generally, the taxpayer's rights to the income accrue when title to property passes to the buyer or the services are performed for the customer or client.[24] If the rights to the income have accrued but are subject to a potential refund claim (e.g., under a product warranty), the income is reported in the year of sale and a deduction is allowed in subsequent years when actual claims accrue.[25]

Where the taxpayer's rights to the income are being contested (e.g., when a contractor fails to meet specifications), the year in which the income is subject to tax depends upon whether payment has been received. If payment has not been received, no income is recognized until the claim is settled. Only then is the right to the income established.[26] However, if the payment is received before the dispute is settled, a **claim of right doctrine** requires the taxpayer to recognize the income in the year of receipt.[27]

---

[19] *Julia A. Strauss,* 2 B.T.A. 598 (1925). See the Glossary in Appendix C for a discussion of the terms *cash equivalent doctrine* and *constructive receipt.*

[20] Reg. §§ 1.446–1(a)(3) and (c)(1)(i).

[21] *Bedell v. Comm.,* 1 USTC ¶359, 7 AFTR 8469, 30 F.2d 622 (CA–2, 1929).

[22] *Charles F. Kahler,* 18 T.C. 31 (1952); *Bright v. U.S.,* 91–1 USTC ¶50,142, 67 AFTR 2d 91–673, 926 F.2d 383 (CA–5, 1991).

[23] Reg. § 1.451–1(a).

[24] *Lucas v. North Texas Lumber Co.,* 2 USTC ¶484, 8 AFTR 10276, 50 S.Ct. 184 (USSC, 1930).

[25] *Brown v. Helvering,* 4 USTC ¶1222, 13 AFTR 851, 54 S.Ct. 356 (USSC, 1933).

[26] *Burnet v. Sanford and Brooks,* 2 USTC ¶636, 9 AFTR 603, 51 S.Ct. 150 (USSC, 1931).

[27] *North American Oil Consolidated Co. v. Burnet,* 3 USTC ¶943, 11 AFTR 16, 52 S.Ct. 613 (USSC, 1932).

Example 7

Return to the facts of *The Big Picture* on p. 4-1. On completing the construction improvements to Dr. Payne's medical office building in 2014, the contractor, who uses the accrual method, submitted a bill. Dr. Payne refused to pay the bill, however, claiming that the contractor had not met specifications. The contractor did not reach a settlement with Dr. Payne until 2015. No income accrues to the contractor until 2015. If Dr. Payne had paid for the work and then filed suit for damages, the contractor could not defer the income (the income would be taxable in 2014).

The measure of accrual basis income is generally the amount the taxpayer has a right to receive. Unlike the cash basis, the fair market value of the customer's obligation is irrelevant in measuring accrual basis income.

Example 8

Assume the same facts as in Example 6, except that Dana is an accrual basis taxpayer. Dana must recognize $13,000 ($8,000 + $5,000) gross income in 2014, the year her rights to the income accrued.

Hybrid Method

The **hybrid method** is a combination of the accrual method and the cash method. Generally, when the hybrid method is used, inventory is a material income-producing factor. Therefore, the Regulations require that the accrual method be used for determining sales and cost of goods sold. In this circumstance, to simplify record keeping, the taxpayer accounts for inventory using the accrual method and uses the cash method for all other income and expense items (e.g., dividend and interest income). The hybrid method is primarily used by small businesses.

4-2c Exceptions Applicable to Cash Basis Taxpayers

Constructive Receipt

Income that has not actually been received by the taxpayer is taxed as though it had been received—the income is constructively received—under the following conditions:

- The amount is made readily available to the taxpayer.
- The taxpayer's actual receipt is not subject to substantial limitations or restrictions.[28]

The rationale for the **constructive receipt** doctrine is that if the income is available, the taxpayer should not be allowed to postpone the income recognition. For instance, a taxpayer is not permitted to defer income for December services by refusing to accept payment until January. However, determining whether the income is *readily available* and whether *substantial limitations or restrictions exist* necessitates a factual inquiry that leads to a judgment call.[29] Following are some examples of the application of the constructive receipt doctrine.

Example 9

Ted is a member of a barter club. In 2014, Ted performed services for other club members and earned 1,000 points. Each point entitles him to $1 in goods and services sold by other members of the club; the points can be used at any time. In 2015, Ted exchanged his points for a new high-definition TV. Ted must recognize $1,000 gross income in 2014 when the 1,000 points were credited to his account.[30]

---

[28]Reg. § 1.451–2(a).

[29]*Baxter v. Comm.*, 87–1 USTC ¶9315, 59 AFTR 2d 87–1068, 816 F.2d 493 (CA–9, 1987).

[30]Rev.Rul. 80–52, 1980–1 C.B. 100.

Example 10

Return to the facts of *The Big Picture* on p. 4-1. On December 31, Dr. Payne has $10,000 in patients' checks that have not been deposited. They include a check for $3,000 from a patient who asked Dr. Payne not to deposit the check until after January 4 of next year because her account did not contain sufficient funds to pay the debt. Under the cash method, Dr. Payne must recognize $7,000 income from the $7,000 in checks on hand in the current year because the checks are a cash equivalent that is actually received. The income from the $3,000 check is neither actually nor constructively received in the current year because an insufficient account means that the funds are not available.[31]

Example 11

Rick has a savings account with Eagle Savings and Loan Association. Under the terms of the account, interest accrues monthly and the depositor can withdraw the funds (including accrued interest) at any time. The interest for the year is constructively received by Rick even though he does not withdraw the funds.[32]

The constructive receipt doctrine does not reach income the taxpayer is not yet entitled to receive even though the taxpayer could have contracted to receive the income at an earlier date.

Example 12

Return to the facts of *The Big Picture* on p. 4-1. Assume that Dr. Payne elected to use the cash basis of accounting. If he allowed patients to pay by credit card, Dr. Payne would receive immediate credit in his bank account for 96% of the charge. The other 4% would be retained by the credit card issuer. To avoid the 4% charge, Dr. Payne chose not to accept credit card payments. Instead, he established a policy of requiring all bills to be paid within 30 days after the dental services were provided. He communicated this policy to patients before he performed the services. At the end of the year, several patients who owed a combined $2,000 offered to pay with credit cards, but his office rejected their offers.

The $2,000 was not constructively received at the end of the year. Although Dr. Payne could have received payment by credit card in the current year before the dental services were performed, he contracted to receive payment at a later date. Moreover, the 4% charge by the credit card company would be a "substantial limitation."[33]

Income set apart or made available is not constructively received if its actual receipt is subject to *substantial restrictions*. The life insurance industry has used substantial restrictions as a cornerstone for designing life insurance contracts with favorable tax features. Ordinary life insurance policies provide (1) current protection—an amount payable in the event of death—and (2) a savings feature—a cash surrender value payable to the policyholder if the policy is terminated during the policyholder's life. The annual increase in cash surrender value is not taxable because the policyholder must cancel the policy to actually receive the increase in value. Because the cancellation requirement is a substantial restriction, the policyholder does not constructively receive the annual increase in cash surrender value.[34] Employees often receive from their employers property subject to substantial restrictions. Generally, no income is recognized until the restrictions lapse.[35]

---

[31]*L. M. Fischer*, 14 T.C. 792 (1950).

[32]Reg. § 1.451–2(a).

[33]*Cowden v. Comm.*, 61–1 USTC ¶9382, 7 AFTR 2d 1160, 289 F.2d 20 (CA–5, 1961).

[34]*Theodore H. Cohen*, 39 T.C. 1055 (1963).

[35]§ 83(a). See also Restricted Property Plans in Chapter 19.

Example 13	Carlos is a key employee of Red, Inc. The corporation gives stock with a value of $10,000 to Carlos. The stock cannot be sold, however, for five years. Carlos is not required to recognize income until the restrictions lapse at the end of five years.

Original Issue Discount

Lenders frequently make loans that require a payment at maturity of more than the amount of the original loan. The difference between the amount due at maturity is actually interest but is referred to as **original issue discount**. In such an arrangement, the Code requires the original issue discount to be reported when it is earned, regardless of the taxpayer's accounting method.[36] The interest "earned" is calculated by the effective interest rate method.

Example 14	On January 1, 2014, Mark, a cash basis taxpayer, pays $82,645 for a 24-month certificate. The certificate is priced to yield 10% (the effective interest rate) with interest compounded annually. No interest is paid until maturity, when Mark receives $100,000. Thus, Mark's gross income from the certificate is $17,355 ($100,000 − $82,645). Mark's income earned each year is calculated as follows:

2014 (.10 × $82,645) =	$ 8,264
2015 [.10 × ($82,645 + $8,264)] =	9,091
	$17,355

The original issue discount rules do not apply to U.S. savings bonds (discussed in the following paragraphs) or to obligations with a maturity date of one year or less from the date of issue.[37] See Chapter 16 for additional discussion of the tax treatment of original issue discount.

Series E and Series EE Bonds

Certain U.S. government savings bonds (Series E before 1980 and Series EE after 1979) are issued at a discount and are redeemable for fixed amounts that increase at stated intervals. No interest payments are actually made. The difference between the purchase price and the amount received on redemption is the bondholder's interest income from the investment.

The income from these savings bonds is generally deferred until the bonds are redeemed or mature. Furthermore, Series E bonds previously could be exchanged within one year of their maturity date for Series HH bonds, and the interest on the Series E bonds could be further deferred until maturity of the Series HH bonds.[38] Thus, U.S. savings bonds have attractive income deferral features not available with corporate bonds and certificates of deposit issued by financial institutions.

Of course, the deferral feature of government bonds issued at a discount is not an advantage if the investor has insufficient income to be subject to tax as the income accrues. In fact, the deferral may work to the investor's disadvantage if the investor has other income in the year the bonds mature or the bunching of the bond interest into one tax year creates a tax liability. Fortunately, U.S. government bonds have a provision for these investors. A cash basis taxpayer can elect to include in gross income the annual increment in redemption value.[39]

Example 15	Kate purchases Series EE U.S. savings bonds for $500 (face value of $1,000) on January 2 of the current year. If the bonds are redeemed during the first six months, no interest is paid. At December 31, the redemption value is $519.60. If Kate elects to report the interest income annually, she must report interest income of $19.60 for the current year. If she does not make the election, she will report no interest income for the current year.

---

[36]§§ 1272(a)(3) and 1273(a).

[37]§ 1272(a)(2).

[38]Treas. Dept. Circulars No. 1–80 and No. 2–80, 1980–1 C.B. 714, 715. Note that interest is paid at semiannual intervals on the Series HH bonds and must be included in income as received. Refer to Chapter 5 for a discussion of the savings bond interest exclusion. This exchange opportunity applied through August 31, 2004.

[39]§ 454(a).

When a taxpayer elects to report the income from the bonds on an annual basis, the election applies to all such bonds the taxpayer owns at the time of the election and to all such securities acquired subsequent to the election. A change in the method of reporting the income from the bonds requires permission from the IRS.

ETHICS & EQUITY Should the Tax Treatment of Government Bonds and Corporate Bonds Be Different?

Taxpayers are permitted to defer the original issue discount earned on U.S. Government Series EE bonds until the bonds mature, but the original issue discount on a corporate bond must be taken into gross income each year the bond is held. Is this difference in the tax treatment of income government and corporate bonds defensible in terms of equity? Why or why not?

© iStockphoto.com/LdF

Amounts Received under an Obligation to Repay

The receipt of funds with an obligation to repay that amount in the future is the essence of borrowing. Because the taxpayer's assets and liabilities increase by the same amount, no income is realized when the borrowed funds are received. Thus, unless no obligation to repay the funds exists, the receipt of deposited or borrowed funds is not a taxable event.

> A landlord receives a damage deposit from a tenant. The landlord does not recognize income until the deposit is forfeited because the landlord has an obligation to repay the deposit if no damage occurs.[40] However, if the deposit is in fact a prepayment of rent, it is taxed in the year of receipt.

Example 16

4-2d Exceptions Applicable to Accrual Basis Taxpayers

Prepaid Income

For financial reporting purposes under accrual accounting, advance payments received from customers are reflected as prepaid income and as a liability of the seller. However, for tax purposes, the prepaid income often is taxed in the year of receipt.

> In December 2014, a tenant pays his January 2015 rent of $1,000. The accrual basis landlord must include the $1,000 in her 2014 gross income for tax purposes, although the unearned rent income is reported as a liability on the landlord's December 31, 2014 financial accounting balance sheet.

Example 17

Taxpayers have repeatedly argued that deferral of income until it is actually earned properly matches revenues and expenses. Moreover, a proper matching of income with the expenses of earning the income is necessary to clearly reflect income, as required by the Code. The IRS responds that § 446(b) grants it broad powers to determine whether an accounting method clearly reflects income. The IRS further argues that generally accepted financial accounting principles should not dictate tax accounting for prepaid income because of the practical problems of collecting Federal revenues. Collection of the tax is simplest in the year the taxpayer receives the cash from the customer or client.

After a number of years of continual disputes between the IRS and taxpayers, the IRS relented and modified its rules on the prepaid income issue in some situations, as explained below.

---

[40]*John Mantell*, 17 T.C. 1143 (1952).

Global Tax Issues

Tax Credit Neutralizes Foreign Income Taxes

When a U.S. taxpayer invests in a foreign country, that investment income is subject to tax in the United States and may also be subject to tax in the foreign country. However, the taxpayer is allowed a credit on his or her U.S. Federal income tax return for income taxes paid to the foreign country. The credit system allows the taxpayer to treat the taxes paid to the foreign country as though they were paid to the United States. If the foreign taxes paid are less than the U.S. tax on the income, the foreign taxes have cost the taxpayer nothing. On the other hand, if the foreign taxes are greater than the U.S. tax on the income, the credit is limited to the amount of the U.S. tax on the income. In this case, the taxes paid by the taxpayer will exceed what they would have been if the income had been earned in the United States.

Deferral of Advance Payments for Goods

Generally, a taxpayer can elect to defer recognition of income from *advance payments for goods* if the method of accounting for the sale is the same for tax and financial reporting purposes.[41]

Example 18

Brown Company will ship goods only after payment for the goods has been received. In December 2014, Brown received $10,000 for goods that were not shipped until January 2015. Brown can elect to report the income for tax purposes in 2015, assuming the company reports the income in 2015 for financial reporting purposes.

Deferral of Advance Payments for Services

Revenue Procedure 2004–34[42] permits an accrual basis taxpayer to defer recognition of income for *advance payments for services* to be performed after the end of the tax year of receipt. The portion of the advance payment that relates to services performed in the tax year of receipt is included in gross income in the tax year of receipt. The portion of the advance payment that relates to services to be performed after the tax year of receipt is included in gross income in that *tax year*.

Example 19

Yellow Corporation, an accrual basis calendar year taxpayer, sells its services under 12-month, 24-month, and 36-month contracts. The corporation provides services to each customer every month. On May 1, 2014, Yellow Corporation sold the following customer contracts:

Length of Contract	Total Proceeds
12 months	$3,000
24 months	4,800
36 months	7,200

Yellow may defer until 2015 all of the income that will be earned after 2014.

Length of Contract	Income Recorded in 2014	Income Recorded in 2015
12 months	$2,000 ($3,000 × 8/12)	$1,000 ($3,000 × 4/12)
24 months	1,600 ($4,800 × 8/24)	3,200 ($4,800 × 16/24)
36 months	1,600 ($7,200 × 8/36)	5,600 ($7,200 × 28/36)

---

[41]Reg. § 1.451–5(b). See Reg. § 1.451–5(c) for exceptions to this deferral opportunity. The financial accounting conformity requirement is not applicable to contractors who use the completed contract method.

[42]2004–1 C.B. 991.

Revenue Procedure 2004–34 *does not* apply to prepaid rent or prepaid interest. Advance payments for these items are always taxed in the year of receipt.

4-3 INCOME SOURCES

4-3a Personal Services

LO.3

Identify who should pay the tax on a particular item of income in various situations.

It is a well-established principle of taxation that income from personal services must be included in the gross income of the person who performs the services. This principle was first established in a Supreme Court decision, *Lucas v. Earl*.[43] Mr. Earl entered into a binding agreement with his wife under which Mrs. Earl was to receive one-half of Mr. Earl's salary. Justice Holmes used the celebrated **fruit and tree metaphor** to explain that the fruit (income) must be attributed to the tree from which it came (Mr. Earl's services). A mere **assignment of income** does not shift the liability for the tax.

Services of an Employee

Services performed by an employee for the employer's customers are considered performed by the employer. Thus, the employer is taxed on the income from the services provided to the customer, and the employee is taxed on any compensation received from the employer.[44]

THE BIG PICTURE

Example 20

Return to the facts of *The Big Picture* on p. 4-1. Assume that instead of operating his dental practice as a sole proprietorship, Dr. Payne incorporated his dental practice in an attempt to limit his liability. He entered into an employment contract with his corporation and was to receive a salary. All patients contract to receive their services from the corporation, and those services are provided through the corporation's employee, Dr. Payne. Thus, the corporation earned the income from patients' services and must include the patients' fees in its gross income. Dr. Payne must include his salary in his gross income. The corporation is allowed a deduction for the reasonable salary paid to Dr. Payne. (See the discussion of unreasonable compensation in Chapter 6.)

Services of a Child

In the case of a child, the Code specifically provides that amounts earned from personal services must be included in the child's gross income. This result applies even though the income is paid to other persons (e.g., the parents).[45]

4-3b Income from Property

The courts have used the fruit and tree metaphor to determine who should pay the tax on the income from property. The "tree" is the property, and income is its "fruit." The owner of the tree has control over the fruit; therefore, the owner of the property should pay tax on the income the property produces. Thus, if a father clips interest coupons shortly before the interest payment date and gives the coupons to his son, the interest will still be taxed to the father. And a father who assigns to his daughter the right to collect the rent from his rental property will be taxed on the rent because he retains ownership of the property.[46]

---

[43]2 USTC ¶496, 8 AFTR 10287, 50 S.Ct. 241 (USSC, 1930).

[44]*Sargent v. Comm.*, 91–1 USTC ¶50,168, 67 AFTR 2d 91–718, 929 F.2d 1252 (CA–8, 1991).

[45]§ 73. For circumstances in which the child's unearned income is taxed at the parents' rate, see Kiddie Tax—Unearned Income of Children Taxed at Parents' Rate in Chapter 3.

[46]*Galt v. Comm.*, 54–2 USTC ¶9457, 46 AFTR 633, 216 F.2d 41 (CA–7, 1954); *Helvering v. Horst*, 40–2 USTC ¶9787, 24 AFTR 1058, 61 S.Ct. 144 (USSC, 1940).

Interest

According to the IRS, interest accrues daily. Therefore, the interest for the period that includes the date of the transfer is allocated between the transferor and transferee based on the number of days during the period that each owned the property.

| Example 21 | Floyd, a cash basis taxpayer, gave his son, Ethan, corporate bonds with a face amount of $12,000 and a 5% stated annual interest rate. The gift was made on February 28, 2014, and the interest was paid on the last day of each quarter. Floyd must recognize $100 in interest income (5% × $12,000 × 3/12 × 2/3) accrued at the time of the gift. |

For the transferor, the timing of the recognition of the income from the property depends upon the accounting method and the manner in which the property was transferred. In the case of a gift of income-producing property, the donor must recognize his or her share of the accrued income at the time it would have been recognized had the donor continued to own the property.[47] However, if the transfer is a sale, the transferor must recognize the accrued income at the time of the sale. This results because the accrued interest will be included in the sales proceeds.

| Example 22 | Mia purchased a corporate bond at its face amount of $10,000 on January 1, 2013. The bond pays 5% interest on each December 31. On March 31, 2014, Mia sold the bond for $10,600. Mia must recognize $125 interest income in 2014 (5% × $10,000 × 3/12). She must also recognize a $475 capital gain from the sale of the bond: |

Amount received from sale	$ 10,600
Less, accrued interest income	(125)
Selling price of bond, less interest	$ 10,475
Less cost of the bond	(10,000)
Gain on sale	$ 475

Dividends

A corporation is taxed on its earnings, and the shareholders are taxed on the dividends paid to them from the corporation's after-tax earnings.

Partial relief from the double taxation of dividends has been provided in the Code since 2003. Generally, dividends received are taxed at the same marginal rate as is applied to net long-term capital gains.[48] Thus, individuals otherwise subject to the 10 or 15 percent marginal tax rate are eligible for a 0 percent tax on qualified dividends received. Individuals subject to the 25, 28, 33, or 35 percent marginal tax rate pay a 15 percent tax on qualified dividends received. Beginning in 2013, the maximum tax rate applied to qualified dividends increased from 15 percent to 20 percent for high-income taxpayers—those subject to the 39.6 percent marginal tax rate.

A holding period requirement must be satisfied for the special rates to apply: The stock must have been held for more than 60 days during the 121-day period beginning 60 days before the ex-dividend date.[49] The purpose of this requirement is to prevent the taxpayer from buying the stock shortly before the dividend is paid, receiving the dividend, and then selling the stock at a loss (a short-term capital loss) after the stock goes ex-dividend. A stock's price often declines after the stock goes ex-dividend.

Note that qualified dividends are not included as capital gains in the gains and losses netting process; thus, they are *not* reduced by capital losses. Qualified dividend income is merely taxed at the rates that would apply to the taxpayer if he or she had an excess of net long-term capital gain over net short-term capital loss.

---

[47]Rev.Rul. 72–312, 1972–1 C.B. 22.
[48]§ 1(h)(11).

[49]The ex-dividend date is the date before the record date on which the corporation finalizes the list of shareholders who will receive the dividends.

Do Dividends from Foreign Corporations Warrant Special Treatment?

Global Tax Issues

© iStockphoto.com/Andrey Prokhorov

The special rates on dividends are intended to mitigate the double-tax burden—taxing income at the corporate level then taxing the dividends to the shareholder. The United States taxes foreign corporations only on the income the corporation earns in this country. Therefore, if the corporation does no business in the United States but pays dividends to shareholders subject to U.S. taxes, the corporation's income is only taxed once.

Nevertheless, special rates apply to the foreign corporation's dividends if (1) the foreign corporation's stock is traded on an established U.S. securities market or (2) the foreign corporation is eligible for the benefits of an income tax treaty between its country of incorporation and the United States. The apparent reason for the first exception is that if the corporation is listed on an established U.S. securities market, it probably does enough business in the United States to be subject to its tax. The second exception is a reciprocal arrangement: The United States confers a benefit to corporations formed in countries that exempt U.S. corporations from taxes.

Example 23

In June 2014, Green Corporation pays a dividend of $1.50 on each share of its common stock. Madison and Daniel, two unrelated shareholders, each own 1,000 shares of the stock. Consequently, each receives a dividend of $1,500 (1,000 shares × $1.50). Assume that Daniel satisfies the 60/121-day holding period rule but Madison does not. The $1,500 that Daniel receives is subject to preferential 0%/15%/20% treatment in 2014. The $1,500 that Madison receives, however, is not. Because Madison did not comply with the holding period rule, her dividend is not a *qualified dividend* and is taxed at ordinary income rates.

Example 24

Assume that both Madison and Daniel in Example 23 are in the 35% tax bracket. Consequently, Madison pays a tax of $525 (35% × $1,500) on her dividend, while Daniel pays a tax of $225 (15% × $1,500) on his. The $300 saving that Daniel enjoys underscores the advantages of qualified dividend treatment.

Unlike interest, dividends do not accrue on a daily basis because the declaration of a dividend is at the discretion of the corporation's board of directors. Generally, dividends are taxed to the person who is entitled to receive them—the shareholder of record as of the corporation's record date.[50] Thus, if a taxpayer sells stock after a dividend has been declared but before the record date, the dividend generally will be taxed to the purchaser.

This rule differs in the case of a gift of stock. If a donor makes a gift of stock to someone (e.g., a family member) after the declaration date but before the record date, the Tax Court has held that the donor does not shift the dividend income to the donee. The *fruit* has sufficiently ripened as of the declaration date to tax the dividend income to the donor of the stock.[51] In a similar set of facts, the Fifth Circuit Court of Appeals concluded that the dividend income should be included in the gross income of the donee (the owner at the record date). In this case, the taxpayer gave stock to a qualified charity (a charitable contribution) after the declaration date and before the record date.[52] Thus, gifts to charities and gifts to family members are treated differently.

---

[50]Reg. § 1.61–9(c). The record date is the cutoff for determining the shareholders who are entitled to receive the dividend.

[51]*M. G. Anton*, 34 T.C. 842 (1960).

[52]*Caruth Corp. v. U.S.*, 89–1 USTC ¶9172, 63 AFTR 2d 89–716, 865 F.2d 644 (CA–5, 1989).

Example 25	On June 20, the board of directors of Black Corporation declares a $10 per share dividend. The dividend is payable on June 30 to shareholders of record on June 25. As of June 20, Maria owned 200 shares of Black Corporation's stock. On June 21, Maria sold 100 of the shares to Norm for their fair market value and gave 100 of the shares to Sam (her son). Both Norm and Sam are shareholders of record as of June 25. Norm (the purchaser) will be taxed on $1,000 because he is entitled to receive the dividend. However, Maria (the donor) will be taxed on the $1,000 received by Sam (the donee) because the gift was made after the declaration date but before the record date of the dividend.

4-3c Income Received by an Agent

Income received by the taxpayer's agent is considered to be received by the tax-payer. A cash basis principal must recognize the income at the time it is received by the agent.[53]

Example 26	Jack, a cash basis taxpayer, delivered cattle to the auction barn in late December. The auctioneer, acting as the farmer's agent, sold the cattle and collected the proceeds in December. The auctioneer did not pay Jack until the following January. Jack must include the sales proceeds in his gross income for the year the auctioneer received the funds.

4-3d Income from Partnerships, S Corporations, Trusts, and Estates

A **partnership** is not a separate taxable entity. Rather, the partnership merely files an information return (Form 1065), which serves to provide the data necessary for determining the character and amount of each partner's distributive share of the partnership's income and deductions. Each partner must then report his or her distributive share of the partnership's income and deductions for the partnership's tax year ending in or with the partner's tax year. The income must be reported by each partner in the year it is earned, even if such amounts are not actually distributed to the partners. Because a partner pays tax on income as the partnership earns it, a distribution by the partnership to the partner is treated under the recovery of capital rules.[54]

Example 27	Tara owns a one-half interest in the capital and profits of T & S Company (a calendar year partnership). For tax year 2014, the partnership earned revenue of $150,000 and had operating expenses of $80,000. During the year, Tara withdrew from her capital account $2,500 per month (for a total of $30,000). For 2014, Tara must report $35,000 as her share of the partnership's profits [$1/2 \times ($150,000 - $80,000)$] even though she received distributions of only $30,000.

Contrary to the general provision that a corporation must pay tax on its income, a *small business corporation* may elect to be taxed similarly to a partnership. Thus, the shareholders rather than the corporation pay the tax on the corporation's income.[55] The electing corporation is referred to as an **S corporation**. The shareholders report their proportionate shares of the corporation's income and deductions for the year, regardless of whether the corporation actually makes any distributions to the shareholders.

---

[53]Rev.Rul. 79–379, 1979–2 C.B. 204.

[54]§ 706(a) and Reg. § 1.706–1(a)(1). For further discussion, see Chapter 20.

[55]§§ 1361(a) and 1366. For further discussion, see Chapter 20.

The *beneficiaries of estates and trusts* generally are taxed on the income earned by the estates or trusts that is actually distributed or required to be distributed to them.[56] Any income not taxed to the beneficiaries is taxable to the estate or trust.

4-3e Income in Community Property States

General

State law in Louisiana, Texas, New Mexico, Arizona, California, Washington, Idaho, Nevada, and Wisconsin is based upon a community property system. In Alaska, spouses can choose to have the community property rules apply. All other states have a common law property system. The basic difference between common law and community property systems centers around the property rights of married persons. Questions about community property income most frequently arise when the husband and wife file separate returns.

Under a **community property** system, all property is deemed either to be separately owned by the spouse or to belong to the marital community. Property may be held separately by a spouse if it was acquired before marriage or received by gift or inheritance following marriage. Otherwise, any property is deemed to be community property. For Federal tax purposes, each spouse is taxed on one-half of the income from property belonging to the community.

The laws of Texas, Louisiana, Wisconsin, and Idaho distinguish between separate property and the income it produces. In these states, the income from separate property belongs to the community. Accordingly, for Federal income tax purposes, each spouse is taxed on one-half of the income. In the remaining community property states, separate property produces separate income that the owner-spouse must report on his or her Federal income tax return.

What appears to be income, however, may really represent a recovery of capital. A recovery of capital and gain realized on separate property retain their identity as separate property. Items such as nontaxable stock dividends, royalties from mineral

---

[56] §§ 652(a) and 662(a). For further discussion of the taxation of income from partnerships, S corporations, trusts, and estates, see *South-Western* *Federal Taxation: Corporations, Partnerships, Estates, & Trusts,* Chapters 10, 11, 12, and 20.

interests, and gains and losses from the sale of property take on the same classification as the assets to which they relate.

Example 28

Bob and Jane are husband and wife who reside in California. Among other transactions during the year, the following occurred:

- Nontaxable stock dividend received by Jane on stock that was given to her by her mother after Jane's marriage.
- Gain of $10,000 on the sale of unimproved land purchased by Bob before his marriage.
- Oil royalties of $15,000 from a lease Jane acquired with her separate funds after marriage.

Because the stock dividend was distributed on stock held by Jane as separate property, it also is her separate property. The same result occurs for the oil royalties Jane receives. All of the proceeds from the sale of the unimproved land (including the gain of $10,000) are Bob's separate property.

In all community property states, income from personal services (e.g., salaries, wages, and income from a professional partnership) is generally treated as if one-half is earned by each spouse.

Example 29

Fred and Wilma are married but file separate returns. Fred received $25,000 of salary and $300 of taxable interest on a savings account he established in his name. All deposits to the savings account were made from Fred's salary that he earned since the marriage. Wilma collected $2,000 taxable dividends on stock she inherited from her father. Wilma's gross income is computed as follows under three assumptions as to the state of residency of the couple:

	California	Texas	Common Law States
Dividends	$ 2,000	$ 1,000	$2,000
Salary	12,500	12,500	–0–
Interest	150	150	–0–
	$14,650	$13,650	$2,000

Note that the savings account is a community asset because it was created with community funds (i.e., Fred's salary).

Do not confuse community property with jointly owned property, as a number of differences can exist.

- Jointly owned property (i.e., tenants in common, joint tenants) is not limited to husband and wife.
- More than two owners can be involved. Thus, three brothers can be joint owners of a tract of land.

Ownership interests need not be equal. Of the three brothers who own a tract of land, one can hold a one-half interest, while each of the other two brothers owns a one-quarter interest.

Community Property Spouses Living Apart

The general rules for taxing the income from services performed by residents of community property states can create complications and even inequities for spouses who are living apart.

Example 30

Mason and Lily, husband and wife, have always lived in a community property state. After a bitter argument in December 2013, Lily moves in with her parents, where she remains for all of 2014. When Lily files her separate return for 2014, must she include one-half of Mason's salary? No, if she meets the requirements set forth below.

Congress has developed a simple solution to this problem. A spouse (or former spouse) is taxed only on his or her actual earnings from personal services if the following conditions are met:[57]

- The individuals live apart for the entire year.
- They do not file a joint return with each other.
- No portion of the earned income is transferred between the individuals.

4-4 ITEMS SPECIFICALLY INCLUDED IN GROSS INCOME

As discussed earlier, the general principles of gross income determination have occasionally yielded results that Congress found unacceptable. Thus, Congress has provided more specific rules for determining the gross income from certain sources. Some of these special rules appear in §§ 71–90 of the Code.

LO.4

Apply the Internal Revenue Code provisions on alimony, loans made at below-market interest rates, annuities, prizes and awards, group term life insurance, unemployment compensation, and Social Security benefits.

4-4a Alimony and Separate Maintenance Payments

When a married couple divorce or become legally separated, state law generally requires a division of the property accumulated during the marriage. In addition, one spouse may have a legal obligation to support the other spouse. The Code distinguishes between the support payments (alimony or separate maintenance) and the property division in terms of the tax consequences.

Alimony and separate maintenance payments are *deductible* by the party making the payments and are *includible* in the gross income of the party receiving the payments.[58] Thus, income is shifted from the income earner to the income beneficiary, who is better able to pay the tax on the amount received.

Example 31

Pete and Tina are divorced, and Pete is required to pay Tina $15,000 of alimony each year. Pete earns $61,000 a year. The tax law presumes that because Tina receives the $15,000, she is better able than Pete to pay the tax on that amount. Therefore, Tina must include the $15,000 in her gross income, and Pete is allowed to deduct $15,000 from his gross income.

---

[57]§ 66. See Form 8958.   [58]§§ 71 and 215.

Property Settlements

A transfer of property *other than cash* to a former spouse under a divorce decree or agreement is not a taxable event. The transferor is not entitled to a deduction and does not recognize gain or loss on the transfer. The transferee does not recognize income and has a cost basis equal to the transferor's basis.[59]

Example 32

Paul transfers stock to Rosa as part of a divorce settlement. The cost of the stock to Paul is $12,000, and the stock's value at the time of the transfer is $15,000. Rosa later sells the stock for $16,000. Paul is not required to recognize gain from the transfer of the stock to Rosa, and Rosa has a realized and recognized gain of $4,000 ($16,000 − $12,000) when she sells the stock.

Requirements for Alimony

To clarify whether payments are classified as support obligation (alimony) or as property of the other spouse (property settlement), Congress developed the following objective rules. Payments made under agreements and decrees are *classified as alimony* only if the following conditions are satisfied:

1. The payments are in cash. (This clearly distinguishes alimony from property division.)
2. The agreement or decree does not specify that the payments are not alimony. (This allows the parties to determine by agreement whether the payments will be alimony.)
3. The payor and payee are not members of the same household at the time the payments are made. (This ensures the payments are for maintaining two households.)
4. There is no liability to make the payments for any period after the death of the payee.

Front-Loading

As a further safeguard against a property settlement being disguised as alimony, special rules apply to post-1986 agreements if payments in the first or second year exceed $15,000. If the change in the amount of the payments exceeds statutory limits, **alimony recapture** results to the extent of the excess alimony payments. In the *third* year, the payor must include the excess alimony payments for the first and second years in gross income, and the payee is allowed a deduction for these excess alimony payments. The mechanics involved in computing recapture are unduly complex and beyond the scope of this text. Worksheets for computing the recapture are provided in *Divorced or Separated Individuals* (IRS Publication 504).

Child Support

A taxpayer does not realize income from the receipt of child support payments made by his or her former spouse. This result occurs because the money is received subject to the duty to use the money for the child's benefit. The payor is not allowed to deduct the child support payments because the payments are made to satisfy the payor's legal obligation to support the child.

In many cases, it is difficult to determine whether an amount received is alimony or child support. If the amount of the payments would be reduced upon the happening of a contingency related to a child (e.g., the child attains age 21 or dies), the amount of the future reduction in the payment is deemed child support.[60]

---

[59]§ 1041, added to the Code in 1984 to repeal the rule of *U.S. v. Davis*, 62–2 USTC ¶9509, 9 AFTR 2d 1625, 82 S.Ct. 1190 (USSC, 1962). Under the *Davis* rule, which applied to pre-1985 divorces, a property transfer incident to divorce was a taxable event.

[60]§ 71(c)(2).

CONCEPT SUMMARY 4.1

Tax Treatment of Payments and Transfers Pursuant to Divorce Agreements and Decrees

	Payor	Recipient
Alimony	Deduction from gross income.	Included in gross income.
Alimony recapture	Included in gross income of the third year.	Deducted from gross income of the third year.
Child support	Not deductible.	Not includible in gross income.
Property settlement	No income or deduction.	No income or deduction; basis for the property is the same as the transferor's basis.

© iStockphoto.com/Andrey Prokhorov

> **Example 33**
>
> Under the divorce agreement, Matt is required to make periodic alimony payments of $500 per month to Grace. However, when Matt and Grace's child reaches age 21, marries, or dies (whichever occurs first), the payments will be reduced to $300 per month. Grace has custody of the child. Because the required contingency is the cause for the reduction in the payments, from $500 to $300, child support payments are $200 per month and alimony is $300 per month.

The tax rules relating to marital disputes are reviewed in Concept Summary 4.1.

4-4b Imputed Interest on Below-Market Loans

As discussed earlier in the chapter, generally no income is recognized unless it is realized. Realization usually occurs when the taxpayer performs services or sells goods, thus becoming entitled to a payment from the other party. It follows that no income is realized if the goods or services are provided at no charge. Under this interpretation of the realization requirement, before 1984, interest-free loans were used to shift income between taxpayers.

> **Example 34**
>
> Veneia (daughter) is in the 20% (combined Federal and state rates) tax bracket and has no investment income. Kareem (father) is in the 50% (combined Federal and state rates) tax bracket and has $400,000 in a money market account earning 5% interest. Kareem would like Veneia to receive and pay tax on the income earned on the $400,000. Because Kareem would also like to have access to the $400,000 should he need the money, he does not want to make an outright gift of the money, nor does he want to commit the money to a trust.
>
> Before 1984, Kareem could achieve his goals as follows: He could transfer the money market account to Veneia in exchange for her $400,000 non-interest-bearing note, payable on Kareem's demand. As a result, Veneia would receive the income, and the family's taxes would be decreased by $6,000 [$400,000 × 5% × (50% − 20%)].

Under the 1984 amendments to the Code, Kareem in Example 34 is required to recognize **imputed interest** income.[61] Veneia is deemed to have incurred interest expense equal to Kareem's imputed interest income. Veneia's interest may be deductible on her return as investment interest if she itemizes deductions (see Chapter 10). In addition, Kareem is then deemed to have given Veneia the amount of the imputed interest she did not pay. The gift received by Veneia is not subject to income tax (see Chapter 5), although Kareem may be subject to the gift tax (unified transfer tax) on the amount deemed given to Veneia (refer to Chapter 1).

Imputed interest is calculated using the rate the Federal government pays on new borrowings and is compounded semiannually. This Federal rate is adjusted monthly and is published by the IRS.[62] Actually, there are three Federal rates:

---

[61]§ 7872(a)(1).

[62]§§ 7872(b)(2) and (f)(2).

CONCEPT SUMMARY 4.2

Effect of Certain Below-Market Loans on the Lender and Borrower

Type of Loan	Lender	Borrower
Gift	Interest income	Interest expense
	Gift made	Gift received
Compensation-related	Interest income	Interest expense
	Compensation expense	Compensation income
Corporation to shareholder	Interest income	Interest expense
	Dividend paid	Dividend income

© iStockphoto.com/Andrey Prokhorov

short-term (not over three years and including demand loans), mid-term (over three years but not over nine years), and long-term (over nine years).[63]

Example 35

Assume that the Federal rate applicable to the loan in Example 34 is 3.5% through June 30 and 4% from July 1 through December 31. Kareem made the loan on January 1, and the loan is still outstanding on December 31. Kareem must recognize interest income of $15,140, and Veneia has interest expense of $15,140. Kareem is deemed to have made a gift of $15,140 to Veneia.

Imputed interest calculations:

January 1–June 30—.035($400,000) ($\frac{1}{2}$ year)	$ 7,000
July 1–December 31—.04($400,000 + $7,000) ($\frac{1}{2}$ year)	8,140
	$15,140

If interest is charged on the loan but is less than the Federal rate, the imputed interest is the difference between the amount that would have been charged at the Federal rate and the amount actually charged.

Example 36

Assume the same facts as in Example 35, except that Kareem charged 3% interest, compounded annually.

Interest at the Federal rate	$ 15,140
Less interest charged (.03 × $400,000)	(12,000)
Imputed interest	$ 3,140

The imputed interest rules apply to the following *types* of below-market loans:[64]

1. Gift loans (made out of love, affection, or generosity, as in Example 34).
2. Compensation-related loans (employer loans to employees).
3. Corporation-shareholder loans (a corporation's loans to its shareholders).

The effects of these loans on the borrower and lender are summarized in Concept Summary 4.2.

Exceptions and Limitations

No interest is imputed on total outstanding *gift loans* of $10,000 or less between individuals, unless the loan proceeds are used to purchase income-producing property.[65] This exemption eliminates immaterial amounts that do not result in apparent shifts of income. However, if the proceeds of such a loan are used to purchase

[63]§ 1274(d).
[64]§ 7872(c).
[65]§ 7872(c)(2).

income-producing property, the limitations discussed in the following paragraphs apply instead.

On loans of $100,000 or less between individuals, the imputed interest cannot exceed the borrower's net investment income for the year (gross income from all investments less the related expenses).[66] Thus, the income imputed to the lender is limited to the borrower's net investment income. In addition, if the borrower's net investment income for the year does not exceed $1,000, no interest is imputed on loans of $100,000 or less. However, these limitations for loans of $100,000 or less do not apply if a principal purpose of a loan is tax avoidance.[67]

Example 37

Vicki made interest-free gift loans as follows:

Borrower	Amount	Borrower's Net Investment Income	Purpose
Susan	$ 8,000	$ –0–	Education
Dan	9,000	500	Purchase of stock
Bonnie	25,000	–0–	Purchase of a business
Megan	90,000	15,000	Purchase of a residence
Olaf	120,000	–0–	Purchase of a residence

Assume that tax avoidance is not a principal purpose of any of the loans. The loan to Susan is not subject to the imputed interest rules because the $10,000 exception applies. The $10,000 exception does not apply to the loan to Dan because the proceeds were used to purchase income-producing assets. However, under the $100,000 exception, the imputed interest is limited to Dan's investment income ($500). Because the $1,000 exception also applies to this loan, no interest is imputed.

No interest is imputed on the loan to Bonnie because the $100,000 exception applies. Interest is imputed on the loan to Megan based on the lesser of (1) the borrower's $15,000 net investment income or (2) the interest as calculated by applying the Federal rate to the outstanding loan. None of the exceptions apply to the loan to Olaf because the loan was for more than $100,000.

Assume that the relevant Federal rate is 10% and that the loans were outstanding for the entire year. Vicki would recognize interest income, compounded semiannually, as follows:

Loan to Megan:
First 6 months (.10 × $90,000 × ½ year) $ 4,500
Second 6 months (.10 × $94,500 × ½ year)   4,725
$ 9,225

Loan to Olaf:
First 6 months (.10 × $120,000 × ½ year) $ 6,000
Second 6 months (.10 × $126,000 × ½ year)   6,300
$12,300

Total imputed interest ($9,225 + $12,300) $21,525

As with gift loans, there is a $10,000 exemption for *compensation-related loans* and *corporation-shareholder loans*. However, the $10,000 exception does not apply if tax avoidance is one of the principal purposes of a loan.[68] This vague tax avoidance standard makes practically all compensation-related and corporation-shareholder loans suspect. Nevertheless, the $10,000 exception should apply when an employee's borrowing was necessitated by personal needs (e.g., to meet unexpected expenses) rather than tax considerations.

These exceptions to the imputed interest rules are summarized in Concept Summary 4.3.

[66]§ 7872(d).
[67]*Deficit Reduction Tax Bill of 1984: Explanation of the Senate Finance Committee* (April 2, 1984), p. 484.
[68]§ 7872(c)(3).

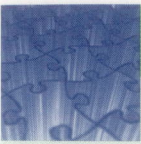

CONCEPT SUMMARY 4.3

Exceptions to the Imputed Interest Rules for Below-Market Loans

Exception	Eligible Loans	Ineligible Loans and Limitations
De minimis—aggregate loans of $10,000 or less	Gift loans	Proceeds used to purchase income-producing assets.
	Employer-employee	Principal purpose is tax avoidance.
	Corporation-shareholder	Principal purpose is tax avoidance.
Aggregate loans of $100,000 or less	Between individuals	Principal purpose is tax avoidance. For all other loans, interest is imputed to the extent of the borrower's net investment income if that income exceeds $1,000.

© iStockphoto.com/Andrey Prokhorov

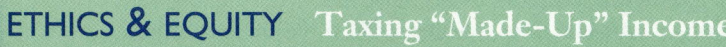

ETHICS & EQUITY Taxing "Made-Up" Income

Under the imputed interest rules, the taxpayer who makes a below-market loan may be required to recognize income he or she did not actually receive. For example, assume that Christian loans $200,000 to Mia, his daughter, to start a business (income-producing property). Christian does not charge interest because Mia needs the funds to operate a struggling startup business. Why should Christian be required to pay tax on a "made-up" number (i.e., the interest he did not charge)?

© iStockphoto.com/LdF

4-4c Income from Annuities

Annuity contracts generally require the purchaser (the annuitant) to pay a fixed amount for the right to receive a future stream of payments. Typically, the issuer of the contract is an insurance company and will pay the annuitant a cash value if the annuitant cancels the contract. The insurance company invests the amounts received from the annuitant, and the income earned serves to increase the cash value of the annuity. No income is recognized by the annuitant at the time the cash value of the annuity increases because the taxpayer has not actually received any income. The income is not constructively received because, generally, the taxpayer must cancel the policy to receive the increase in value (the increase in value is subject to substantial restrictions).

Example 38

Jean, age 50, pays $30,000 for an annuity contract that is to pay her $500 per month beginning when she reaches age 65 and continuing until her death. If Jean should cancel the policy after one year, she would receive $30,200 and would include $200 ($30,200 − $30,000) in her gross income. However, if she does not cancel the policy, the $200 increase in value is not includible in her gross income, as long as she does not actually receive the $200.

The tax accounting problem associated with receiving payments under an annuity contract is one of apportioning the amounts received between recovery of capital and income. The statutory solution to this problem depends upon whether the payments began before or after the annuity starting date and upon when the policy was acquired.

Computing the Exclusion Amount

The annuitant can exclude from income (as a recovery of capital) the proportion of each payment that the investment in the contract bears to the expected return under the contract. The *exclusion amount* is calculated as follows:

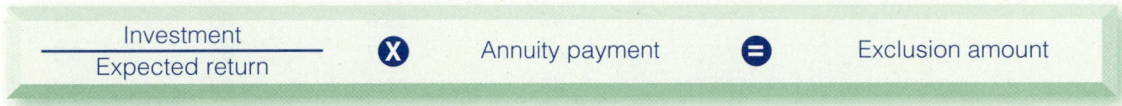

$$\frac{\text{Investment}}{\text{Expected return}} \quad \mathbf{X} \quad \text{Annuity payment} \quad \mathbf{=} \quad \text{Exclusion amount}$$

The *expected return* is the annual amount to be paid to the annuitant multiplied by the number of years the payments will be received. The payment period may be fixed (a *term certain*) or for the life of one or more individuals. When payments are for life, the taxpayer generally must use the annuity table published by the IRS to determine the expected return (see Table 4.1). This is an actuarial table that contains life expectancies.[69] The expected return is calculated by multiplying the appropriate multiple (life expectancy) by the annual payment.

> **Example 39**
>
> A taxpayer, age 60, purchases an annuity from an insurance company for $90,000. She is to receive $500 per month for life. Her life expectancy (from Table 4.1) is 24.2 years from the annuity starting date. Thus, her expected return is $500 × 12 × 24.2 = $145,200, and the exclusion amount is $3,719 [($90,000 investment/$145,200 expected return) × $6,000 annual payment]. The $3,719 is a nontaxable return of capital, and $2,281 ($6,000 − $3,719) is included in gross income.

The *exclusion ratio* (investment ÷ expected return) applies until the annuitant has recovered his or her investment in the contract. Once the investment is recovered, the entire amount of subsequent payments is taxable. If the annuitant dies before recovering the investment, the unrecovered cost (adjusted basis) is deductible in the year the payments cease (usually the year of death).[70]

> **Example 40**
>
> Assume that the taxpayer in Example 39 receives annuity payments for 25.2 years (302 months). For the last 12 months [302 − (12 × 24.2) = 12], the taxpayer will include $500 each month in gross income. If instead the taxpayer dies after 36 months, she is eligible for a $78,843 deduction on her final tax return.
>
> | | |
> |---|---:|
> | Cost of the contract | $ 90,000 |
> | Cost previously recovered $90,000/$145,200 × 36($500) = | (11,157) |
> | Deduction | $ 78,843 |

Simplified Method for Annuity Distributions from Qualified Retirement Plans

A simplified method is required for allocating basis to the annuity payments received under a qualified retirement plan.[71] The portion of each annuity payment that is excluded as a return of capital is the employee's investment in the contract divided by the number of anticipated monthly payments determined in accordance with Table 4.2.[72]

> **Example 41**
>
> Andrea, age 62, receives an annuity distribution of $500 per month for life from her qualified retirement plan beginning in January 2014. Her investment in the contract is $100,100. The excludible amount of each payment is $385 ($100,100 investment/260 monthly payments). Thus, $115 ($500 − $385) of each annuity payment is included in Andrea's gross income.

[69]The life expectancies in Table 4.1 apply for annuity investments made on or after July 1, 1986. See *General Rules for Pensions and Annuities*, IRS Publication 939 (Rev. April 2003), p. 25. See also *Pension and Annuity Income*, IRS Publication 575 (Rev. 2012).

[70]§ 72(b).
[71]See Chapter 19.
[72]§ 72(d).

TABLE 4.1			Ordinary Life Annuities: One Life—Expected Return Multiples		
Age	**Multiple**	**Age**	**Multiple**	**Age**	**Multiple**
5	76.6	42	40.6	79	10.0
6	75.6	43	39.6	80	9.5
7	74.7	44	38.7	81	8.9
8	73.7	45	37.7	82	8.4
9	72.7	46	36.8	83	7.9
10	71.7	47	35.9	84	7.4
11	70.7	48	34.9	85	6.9
12	69.7	49	34.0	86	6.5
13	68.8	50	33.1	87	6.1
14	67.8	51	32.2	88	5.7
15	66.8	52	31.3	89	5.3
16	65.8	53	30.4	90	5.0
17	64.8	54	29.5	91	4.7
18	63.9	55	28.6	92	4.4
19	62.9	56	27.7	93	4.1
20	61.9	57	26.8	94	3.9
21	60.9	58	25.9	95	3.7
22	59.9	59	25.0	96	3.4
23	59.0	60	24.2	97	3.2
24	58.0	61	23.3	98	3.0
25	57.0	62	22.5	99	2.8
26	56.0	63	21.6	100	2.7
27	55.1	64	20.8	101	2.5
28	54.1	65	20.0	102	2.3
29	53.1	66	19.2	103	2.1
30	52.2	67	18.4	104	1.9
31	51.2	68	17.6	105	1.8
32	50.2	69	16.8	106	1.6
33	49.3	70	16.0	107	1.4
34	48.3	71	15.3	108	1.3
35	47.3	72	14.6	109	1.1
36	46.4	73	13.9	110	1.0
37	45.4	74	13.2	111	.9
38	44.4	75	12.5	112	.8
39	43.5	76	11.9	113	.7
40	42.5	77	11.2	114	.6
41	41.5	78	10.6	115	.5

The rules for annuity payments received after the basis has been recovered by the annuitant and for the annuitant who dies before the basis is recovered are the same as under the exclusion ratio method discussed earlier.

4-4d Prizes and Awards

The fair market value of prizes and awards (other than scholarships exempted under § 117, to be discussed subsequently) must be included in gross income.[73] Therefore, TV giveaway prizes, magazine publisher prizes, door prizes, and awards from an employer to an employee in recognition of performance are fully taxable to the recipient.

[73]§ 74.

TABLE 4.2	Number of Anticipated Monthly Annuity Payments under the Simplified Method	

Age	Number of Anticipated Monthly Payments
55 and under	360
56–60	310
61–65	260
66–70	210
71 and over	160

A narrow exception permits a prize or an award to be excluded from gross income if *all* of the following requirements are satisfied:

- The prize or award is received in recognition of religious, charitable, scientific, educational, artistic, literary, or civic achievement (e.g., Nobel Prize, Pulitzer Prize, or faculty teaching award).
- The recipient transfers the prize or award to a qualified governmental unit or nonprofit organization.
- The recipient was selected without any action on his or her part to enter the contest or proceeding.
- The recipient is not required to render substantial future services as a condition for receiving the prize or award.[74]

Because the transfer of the property to a qualified governmental unit or nonprofit organization ordinarily would be a charitable contribution (an itemized deduction as presented in Chapter 10), the exclusion produces beneficial tax consequences in the following situations:

- The taxpayer does not itemize deductions and thus would receive no tax benefit from the charitable contribution.
- The taxpayer's charitable contributions exceed the annual statutory ceiling on the deduction.
- Including the prize or award in gross income would reduce the amount of deductions the taxpayer otherwise would qualify for because of gross income limitations (e.g., the gross income test for a dependency exemption or the adjusted gross income limitation in calculating the medical expense deduction).

The taxpayer can avoid including prizes and awards in gross income by refusing to accept the prize or award.

Another exception is provided for certain *employee achievement awards* in the form of tangible personal property (e.g., a gold watch). The awards must be made in recognition of length of service or safety achievement. Generally, the ceiling on the excludible amount for an employee is $400 per taxable year. However, if the award is a qualified plan award, the ceiling on the exclusion is $1,600 per taxable year.[75]

4-4e Group Term Life Insurance

For many years, the IRS did not attempt to tax the value of life insurance protection provided to an employee by the employer. Some companies took undue advantage of the exclusion by providing large amounts of insurance protection for executives. Therefore, Congress enacted § 79, which created a limited exclusion for **group term life insurance**. The premiums on the first $50,000 of group term life insurance protection are excludible from the employee's gross income.

The benefits of this exclusion are available only to employees. Proprietors and partners are not considered employees. The Regulations generally require broad-

[74]§ 74(b).

[75]§ 74(c). Qualified plan awards are defined in § 274(j) and explained in Business Expenses, Chapter 2 (IRS Publication 535).

TAX IN THE NEWS   Olympic Gold and Taxes

An Olympic gold medal is worth $650, and the Olympic Committee pays $25,000 to the gold medal recipient. Both the medal and the cash is income realized, and no provision in the Code exempts the winnings. Therefore, the winner is subject to tax.

Michael Phelps, as a result of his fame as an Olympic champion, received $1,000,000 for endorsing a product and donated the funds to a charity. Although the charity was the beneficiary, Michael Phelps earned the income and thus was subject to tax on the endorsement fee. If swimming fast was considered "artistic," an exclusion would have been available under § 74(b).

_____

Source: Based on Meredith Bennett-Smith, "Olympians Could Owe the IRS Thousands in Taxes On Medals, Cash Bonuses," *Huffington Post,* **www.huffingtonpost.com**, August 1, 2012.

scale coverage of employees to satisfy the *group* requirement (e.g., shareholder-employees would not constitute a qualified group). The exclusion applies only to term insurance (protection for a period of time but with no cash surrender value) and not to ordinary life insurance (lifetime protection plus a cash surrender value that can be drawn upon before death).

As mentioned, the exclusion applies to the first $50,000 of group term life insurance protection. For each $1,000 of coverage in excess of $50,000, the employee must include the amounts indicated in Table 4.3 in gross income.[76]

Example 42

Finch Corporation has a group term life insurance policy with coverage equal to the employee's annual salary. Keith, age 52, is president of the corporation and receives an annual salary of $350,000. Keith must include $828 in gross income from the insurance protection for the year.

$$\frac{\$350,000 - \$50,000}{\$1,000} \times \$.23 \times 12 \text{ months} = \$828$$

Generally, the amount that must be included in gross income, computed from Table 4.3, is much less than the price an individual would pay an insurance company for the same amount of protection. Thus, even the excess coverage provides some tax-favored income for employees when group term life insurance coverage in excess of $50,000 is desirable.

If the plan discriminates in favor of certain key employees (e.g., officers), the key employees are not eligible for the exclusion. In such a case, the key employees must include in gross income the *greater* of actual premiums paid by the employer or the amount calculated from the Uniform Premiums in Table 4.3. The other employees are still eligible for the $50,000 exclusion and continue to use the Uniform Premiums table to compute the income from excess insurance protection.[77]

4-4f Unemployment Compensation

The unemployment compensation program is sponsored and operated by the states and Federal government to provide a source of income for people who have been employed and are temporarily (hopefully) out of work. In a series of rulings over a period of 40 years, the IRS exempted unemployment benefits from tax. These payments were considered social benefit programs for the promotion of the general welfare. After experiencing dissatisfaction with the IRS's treatment of unemployment compensation, Congress amended the Code to make the benefits taxable.[78]

4-4g Social Security Benefits

If a taxpayer's income exceeds a specified base amount, as much as 85 percent of Social Security retirement benefits must be included in gross income. The taxable

_____

[76]Reg. § 1.79–3(d)(2).
[77]§ 79(d).
[78]§ 85.

TABLE 4.3	Uniform Premiums for $1,000 of Group Term Life Insurance Protection
Attained Age on Last Day of Employee's Tax Year	**Cost per $1,000 of Protection for One-Month Period***
Under 25	$ .05
25–29	.06
30–34	.08
35–39	.09
40–44	.10
45–49	.15
50–54	.23
55–59	.43
60–64	.66
65–69	1.27
70 and above	2.06

*Reg. § 1.79–3, effective for coverage after June 30, 1999.

amount of benefits is determined through the application of one of two formulas that utilize a unique measure of income—*modified adjusted gross income (MAGI)*.[79] MAGI is, for this purpose, the taxpayer's adjusted gross income from all sources (other than Social Security) plus the foreign earned income exclusion and any tax-exempt interest income.

In the formulas, two sets of base amounts are established. The first set is as follows:

- $32,000 for married taxpayers who file a joint return.
- $0 for married taxpayers who do not live apart for the entire year but file separate returns.
- $25,000 for all other taxpayers.

The second set of base amounts is as follows:

- $44,000 for married taxpayers who file a joint return.
- $0 for married taxpayers who do not live apart for the entire year but file separate returns.
- $34,000 for all other taxpayers.

If MAGI plus one-half of Social Security benefits exceeds the first set of base amounts but not the second set, the taxable amount of Social Security benefits is the *lesser* of the following:

- .50(Social Security benefits).
- .50[MAGI + .50(Social Security benefits) − first base amount].

Example 43

A married couple with adjusted gross income of $30,000, no tax-exempt interest, and $11,000 of Social Security benefits who file jointly must include $1,750 of the benefits in gross income. This works out as the lesser of the following:

1. .50($11,000) = $5,500.
2. .50[$30,000 + .50($11,000) − $32,000] = .50($3,500) = $1,750.

If instead the couple had adjusted gross income of $15,000 and their Social Security benefits totaled $5,000, none of the benefits would be taxable because .50[$15,000 + .50($5,000) − $32,000] is not a positive number.

---

[79]§ 86. The rationale for taxing 85% of the Social Security benefits is as follows: For the average Social Security recipient, 15% of the amount received is a recovery of amounts that the individual paid into the program, and the remainder of the benefits is financed by the employer's contribution and interest earned by the Social Security trust fund.

TAX IN THE NEWS   Social Security Benefits as a Source of Federal Revenue

Recipients' Social Security benefits are indexed for inflation, but the base amounts used in the formula to calculate the taxable portion of the benefits are not indexed. The $25,000 and $32,000 base amounts were established in 1984. If they were indexed for inflation, these nontaxable amounts would have doubled by 2010. Thus, as income and Social Security benefits rise with inflation, taxable income increases more than the related increase in "real" benefits.

If MAGI plus one-half of Social Security benefits exceeds the second set of base amounts, the taxable amount of Social Security benefits is the *lesser* of 1 or 2 below:

1. .85(Social Security benefits).
2. Sum of:
   a. .85[MAGI + .50(Social Security benefits) − second base amount], and
   b. Lesser of:
      - Amount included through application of the first formula.
      - $4,500 ($6,000 for married filing jointly).

Example 44

A married couple who file jointly have adjusted gross income of $72,000, no tax-exempt interest, and $12,000 of Social Security benefits. Their includible Social Security benefits will be $10,200.

Include the lesser of the following:

1. .85($12,000) = $10,200.
2. Sum of:
   a. .85[$72,000 + .50($12,000) − $44,000] = $28,900, and
   b. Lesser of:
      - Amount calculated by the first formula, which is the lesser of:
         - .50($12,000) = $6,000.
         - .50[$72,000 + .50($12,000) − $32,000] = $23,000.
      - $6,000.

The sum equals $34,900 ($28,900 + $6,000). Because 85% of the Social Security benefits received is less than this amount, $10,200 is included in the couple's gross income.[80]

4-5 TAX PLANNING

LO.5

Identify tax planning strategies for minimizing gross income.

The materials in this chapter have focused on the following questions:

- What is income?
- When is the income recognized?
- Who is the taxpayer?

Planning strategies suggested by these materials include the following:

- Maximize economic benefits that are not included in gross income.
- Defer the recognition of income.
- Shift income to taxpayers who are in a lower marginal tax bracket.

Some specific techniques for accomplishing these strategies are discussed in the following paragraphs.

---

[80]To compute taxable benefits, a worksheet is provided in the instructions to Form 1040 at lines 20a and 20b and to Form 1040A at lines 14a and 14b, as well as in *Social Security and Railroad Retirement Benefits* (IRS Publication 915).

4-5a Tax Deferral

General

Because deferred taxes are tantamount to interest-free loans from the government, the deferral of taxes is a worthy goal of the tax planner. However, the tax planner must also consider the tax rates for the years the income is shifted from and to. For example, a one-year deferral of income from a year in which the taxpayer's tax rate was 28 percent to a year in which the tax rate will be 35 percent would not be advisable if the taxpayer expects to earn less than a 7 percent after-tax return on the deferred tax dollars.

The taxpayer can often defer the recognition of income from appreciated property by postponing the event triggering realization (the final closing on a sale or exchange of property). If the taxpayer needs cash, obtaining a loan by using the appreciated property as collateral may be a less costly alternative than selling the property.

> **Example 45**
>
> Ira owns 100 shares of Pigeon Company common stock with a cost of $20,000 and a fair market value of $50,000. Although the stock's value has increased substantially in the past three years, Ira thinks the growth days are over. If he sells the Pigeon stock, Ira will invest the proceeds from the sale in other common stock. Assuming that Ira's marginal tax rate on the sale is 15%, he will have only $45,500 [$50,000 − .15($50,000 − $20,000)] to reinvest. The alternative investment must substantially outperform Pigeon in the future for the sale to be beneficial.

Selection of Investments

Because no tax is due until a gain has been recognized, the law favors investments that yield appreciation rather than annual income.

> **Example 46**
>
> Vera can buy a corporate bond or an acre of land for $10,000. The bond pays $1,000 of interest (10%) each year, and Vera expects the land to increase in value 10% each year for the next 10 years. She is in the 40% (combined Federal and state) tax bracket for ordinary income and 26% for qualifying capital gains. Assuming that the bond would mature or the land would be sold in 10 years and Vera would reinvest the interest at a 10% before-tax return, she would accumulate the following amount at the end of 10 years:
>
> | | | Bond | Land |
> | --- | --- | --- | --- |
> | Original investment | | $10,000 | $10,000 |
> | Annual income | $1,000 | | |
> | Less tax | (400) | | |
> | | $ 600 | | |
> | Compound amount reinvested for | | | |
> | 10 years at 6% after-tax | × 13.18 | 7,908 | |
> | | | $17,908 | |
> | Compound amount, 10 years at 10% | | | × 2.59 |
> | | | | $25,900 |
> | Less tax on sale: | | | |
> | 26%($25,900 − $10,000) | | | (4,134) |
> | | | | $21,766 |
>
> Therefore, the value of the deferral that results from investing in the land rather than in the bond is $3,858 ($21,766 − $17,908).

Series EE bonds can also be purchased for long-term deferrals of income. In situations where the taxpayer's goal is merely to shift income one year into the future, bank certificates of deposit are useful tools. If the maturity period is one year or less, all interest is reported in the year of maturity. Bank certificates of deposit are especially useful for a taxpayer who realizes an unusually large gain from the sale of property in one year (and thus is in a high tax bracket) but expects his or her gross income to be less the following year.

Cash Basis

The timing of income from services can often be controlled through the use of the cash method of accounting. Although taxpayers are somewhat constrained by the constructive receipt doctrine (they cannot turn their backs on income), seldom will customers and clients offer to pay before they are asked. The usual lag between billings and collections (e.g., December's billings collected in January) will result in a continuous deferring of some income until the last year of operations. A salaried individual approaching retirement may contract with the employer before the services are rendered to receive a portion of compensation in the lower tax bracket retirement years.

Prepaid Income

For the accrual basis taxpayer who receives advance payments from customers, the transactions should be structured to avoid payment of tax on income before the time the income is actually earned. Revenue Procedure 2004–34 provides the guidelines for deferring the tax on prepayments for services, and Regulation § 1.451–5 provides the guidelines for deferrals on sales of goods. In addition, both cash and accrual basis taxpayers can sometimes defer income by stipulating that the payments are deposits rather than prepaid income. For example, a landlord should require an equivalent damage deposit rather than prepayment of the last month's rent under the lease.

4-5b Reporting Conflicts

The IRS relies upon businesses to report the amounts they paid to individuals for services. Employees receive a Form W–2, and independent contractors receive a Form 1099–MISC. The IRS attempts to match the forms they receive to the individual's income tax return. If the form submitted by the business and the individual's tax return are not in agreement, the individual has a problem, but innocent differences can occur.

Example 47	Dr. Anders, a college professor on a cash basis, performs consulting services for Dove Corporation in early December 2014. In late December, Dove mailed a check in payment, but Anders did not receive and cash the check until early January 2015. Dove sent Anders a Form 1099–MISC showing the payment date as 2014. If Anders did not report the income on his 2014 return, he could have a problem. Dr. Anders should attach a note to his tax return explaining the discrepancy.

4-5c Shifting Income to Relatives

The tax liability of a family can be minimized by shifting income from higher- to lower-bracket family members. This can be accomplished through gifts of income-producing property. Furthermore, in many cases, income can be shifted with no negative effect on the family's investment plans.

Example 48	Adam, who is in the 28% tax bracket, would like to save for his children's education. All of the children are under 19 years of age and are dependents of Adam. Adam could transfer income-producing properties to the children, and the children could each receive up to $1,000 of income each year (refer to Chapter 3) with no tax liability. The next $1,000 would be taxed at the child's tax rate. After a child has more than $2,000 of unearned income, there is no tax advantage to shifting more income to the child (because the income will be taxed at the parents' rate) until the child is 19 years old (or age 24 if a full-time student), when all income will be taxed according to the child's tax rate.

The Uniform Gifts to Minors Act, a model law adopted by all states (but with some variations among the states), facilitates income shifting. Under the Act, a gift of intangibles (e.g., bank accounts, stocks, bonds, and life insurance contracts) can be made to a minor but with an adult serving as custodian. Usually, a parent who makes the gift is also named as custodian. The state laws allow the custodian to sell or redeem and reinvest the principal and to accumulate or distribute the income, practically at the custodian's discretion provided there is no commingling of the child's income with the parent's property. Thus, the parent can give appreciated securities to the child, and the donor custodian can then sell the securities and reinvest the proceeds, thereby shifting both the gain and the annual income to the child. Such planning is limited by the tax liability calculation provision for a child under the age of 19 (or age 24 if a full-time student) (refer to Chapter 3).

U.S. government bonds (Series EE) can be purchased by parents for their children. When this is done, the children generally should file a return and elect to report the income on the accrual basis.

> **Example 49**
>
> Abby pays $7,500 for Series EE bonds in 2014 and immediately gives them to Wade (her son), who will enter college the year of original maturity of the bonds. The bonds have a maturity value of $10,000. Wade elects to report the annual increment in redemption value as income for each year the bonds are held. The first year the increase is $250, and Wade includes that amount in his gross income. If Wade has no other income, no tax will be due on the $250 bond interest because such an amount will be more than offset by his available standard deduction. The following year, the increment is $260, and Wade includes this amount in income. Thus, over the life of the bonds, Wade will include $2,500 in income ($10,000 − $7,500), none of which will result in a tax liability, assuming he has no other income. However, if the election had not been made, Wade would have been required to include $2,500 in income on the bonds in the year of original maturity, if they had been redeemed as planned. This amount of income might result in a tax liability.

In some cases, it may be advantageous for the child not to make the accrual election. For example, a child under age 19 (or age 24 if a full-time student) with investment income of more than $2,000 each year and parents in the 25, 28, 33, 35, or 39.6 percent tax bracket would probably benefit from deferring the tax on the savings bond interest. The child would also benefit from the use of the usually lower tax rate (rather than subjecting the income to the parents' tax rate) if the bonds mature after the child is age 19 or older (or age 24 or older if a full-time student).

4-5d Accounting for Community Property

The classification of income as community or separate property becomes important when either of two events occurs:

- Husband and wife, married taxpayers, file separate income tax returns for the year.
- Husband and wife obtain a divorce and therefore have to file separate returns for the year (refer to Chapter 3).

For planning purposes, it behooves married persons to keep track of the source of income (community or separate). To be in a position to do this effectively when income-producing assets are involved, it may be necessary to distinguish between separate and community property.[81]

---

[81]Being able to distinguish between separate and community property is crucial to the determination of a property settlement incident to a divorce. It also is vital in the estate tax area (refer to Chapter 1) because the surviving wife's or husband's share of the community property is not included in the gross estate of the deceased spouse.

4-5e Alimony

The person making the alimony payments favors a divorce settlement that includes a provision for deductible alimony payments. On the other hand, the recipient prefers that the payments not qualify as alimony. If the payor is in a higher tax bracket than the recipient, both parties may benefit by increasing the payments and structuring them so that they qualify as alimony.

Example 50

Carl and Polly are negotiating a divorce settlement. Carl has offered to pay Polly $10,000 each year for 10 years, but payments would cease upon Polly's death. Polly is willing to accept the offer if the agreement will specify that the cash payments are not alimony. Carl is in the 35% tax bracket, and Polly's marginal rate is 15%.

If Carl and Polly agree that Carl will pay Polly $12,000 of alimony each year, both will have improved after-tax cash flows.

	Annual Cash Flows	
	Carl	**Polly**
Nonalimony payments	($10,000)	$10,000
Alimony payments	($12,000)	$12,000
Tax effects		
.35($12,000)	4,200	
.15($12,000)		(1,800)
After-tax cash flows	($ 7,800)	$10,200
Benefit of alimony option	$ 2,200	$ 200

Both parties benefit at the government's expense if the $12,000 alimony option is used.

REFOCUS ON THE BIG PICTURE

© Bob Daemmrich/PhotoEdit

CALCULATION OF GROSS INCOME

Using the accrual method of accounting, Dr. Cliff Payne has correctly calculated the gross income of his sole proprietorship. He will report the $385,000 amount on his tax return (Schedule C of Form 1040).

What If?

From a tax planning perspective, what can Dr. Payne do to decrease his gross income from the first year of operating his dental practice and thereby produce better financial results for him?

Rather than electing to use the accrual method of accounting, Dr. Payne should elect the cash method of accounting because his dental practice is a service entity rather than a merchandising entity. His gross income for Federal income tax purposes under the cash method is calculated as follows:

Revenues	$385,000
Plus: Accounts receivable: January 1	–0–
Less: Accounts receivable: December 31	(52,000)
Gross income	$333,000

Electing to use the cash method of accounting enables Dr. Payne to defer paying Federal income taxes on the unpaid accounts receivable. Furthermore, each year that Dr. Payne has accounts receivable at the end of the tax year, that income is continuously deferred. Thus, if his accounts receivable remain at $52,000 at the end of each tax year, by using the cash method of accounting rather than the accrual method, he will defer that amount of income until he terminates his practice.

Key Terms

Accounting income, 4-4

Accounting method, 4-6

Accrual method, 4-7

Alimony and separate maintenance payments, 4-19

Alimony recapture, 4-20

Annuity, 4-24

Assignment of income, 4-13

Cash receipts method, 4-7

Claim of right doctrine, 4-7

Community property, 4-17

Constructive receipt, 4-8

Economic income, 4-3

Fruit and tree metaphor, 4-13

Gross income, 4-2

Group term life insurance, 4-27

Hybrid method, 4-8

Imputed interest, 4-21

Income, 4-3

Original issue discount, 4-10

Partnership, 4-16

Recovery of capital doctrine, 4-3

S corporation, 4-16

Taxable year, 4-6

Discussion Questions

1. **LO.1** According to the Supreme Court, would it be good tax policy to use income as computed by financial accounting principles as the correct measure of income for Federal income tax purposes? Explain.

2. **LO.1** Compare and contrast the economist's concept used to recognize income with the concept employed in measuring taxable income.

3. **LO.1** Allen visits Reno, Nevada, once a year to gamble. This year his gambling loss was $25,000. He commented to you, "At least I didn't have to pay for my airfare and hotel room. The casino paid that because I am such a good customer. That was worth at least $3,000." What are the relevant tax issues for Allen? **Issue ID**

4. **LO.1** Ben lost his job when his employer moved its plant. During the year, he collected unemployment benefits for three months, a total of $1,800. While he was waiting to hear from prospective employers, he painted his house. If Ben had paid someone else to paint his house, the cost would have been $3,000. The cost of the paint Ben used was $800. What is Ben's gross income for tax purposes from the above events?

5. **LO.1** Howard buys wrecked cars and stores them on his property. Recently, he purchased a 1990 Ford Taurus for $400. If he can sell all of the usable parts, his total proceeds from the Taurus will be over $2,500. As of the end of the year, he has sold only the radio for $75 and he does not know how many, if any, of the remaining parts will ever be sold. What are Howard's income recognition issues? **Issue ID**

6. **LO.2, 3** On December 29, 2014, an employee received a $5,000 check from her employer's client. The check was payable to the employer. The employee did not remit the funds to the employer until December 30, 2014. The employer deposited the check on December 31, 2014, but the bank did not credit the employer's bank account until January 2, 2015. When is the cash basis employer required to include the $5,000 in gross income?

7. **LO.2** What is the purpose of the constructive receipt doctrine?

8. **LO.2** How does the hybrid method of accounting differ from the cash method and the accrual method? **Issue ID**

9. **LO.2** Sandra, a cash basis taxpayer, purchased a certificate of deposit for $970 on July 1, 2014, that matures on June 30, 2015, with the maturity value being $1,000. Also on July 1, 2014, she purchased a certificate of deposit for $940 that matures on June 30, 2016, with the maturity value being $1,000. Is Sandra required to recognize any income from the certificates in 2014, 2015, or 2016? Explain.

10. **LO.2** A Series EE U.S. government savings bond accrues 3.5% interest each year. The bond matures in three years, at which time the principal and interest will be paid. The bank will pay the taxpayer at a 3.5% interest rate each year if he agrees to leave money on deposit for three years. What tax advantage does the Series EE bond offer that is not available with the bank deposit?

WWW **For the latest in changes to tax legislation, visit www.cengagebrain.com**

11. **LO.2** The taxpayer performs services with payment due from the customer within 30 days. All customers pay within the time limit. What would be the benefit to the taxpayer using the cash method of accounting rather than the accrual method?

12. **LO.3, 5** Wade paid $7,000 for an automobile that needed substantial repairs. He worked nights and weekends to restore the car and spent $2,400 on parts for it. He knows that he can sell the car for $13,000, but he is very wealthy and does not need the money. On the other hand, his daughter, who has very little income, needs money to make the down payment on a house.
    a. Would it matter, after taxes, whether Wade sells the car and gives the money to his daughter or whether he gives the car to his daughter and she sells it for $13,000? Explain.
    b. Assume Wade gave the car to his daughter after he had arranged for another person to buy it from his daughter. The daughter then transferred the car to the buyer and received $13,000. Who is taxed on the gain?

13. **LO.3** Anita, a cash basis taxpayer, sued her former employer for wage discrimination. Her attorney agreed to pursue the case on a contingent fee basis—the attorney would receive one-third of any settlement or court award. The parties reached a settlement, and the attorney for Anita's former employer wrote a check payable to Anita for $320,000 and a check payable to her attorney for $160,000. Anita reasons that she and the attorney were partners in the lawsuit who shared profits two-thirds and one-third, respectively. Therefore, she includes $320,000 in her gross income. Is Anita's analysis correct? Explain.

14. **LO.3** Rex became a partner with a 30% interest in the partnership profits when he invested $200,000. In 2014, the partnership generated $400,000 of taxable income, and Rex withdrew $100,000. In 2015, the partnership had $600,000 of taxable income, and Rex withdrew $200,000. What is Rex's gross income from the partnership in 2014 and 2015?

Issue ID   15. **LO.3, 5** Mark and Del were residents of Texas. In 2014, Del left Mark, and he has been unable to find her even though he hired a private investigator to do so. Mark and Del are still married at year-end. Both Del and Mark were employed. Mark is aware of the fact that Del inherited dividend-paying stocks in early 2014. They did not have any children. How will Del's absence complicate Mark's 2014 income tax return?

16. **LO.4** The divorce agreement requires Alice to pay her former spouse $50,000 a year for the next ten years. Will the payments qualify as alimony? Why or why not?

17. **LO.4** Evaluate the following statement: "In dividing up assets when a couple divorces, the *basis* of the assets is *not* relevant because the property division is nontaxable."

Issue ID   18. **LO.4, 5** William and Abigail, who live in San Francisco, have been experiencing problems with their marriage. They have a 3-year-old daughter, April, who stays with William's parents during the day because both William and Abigail are employed. Abigail worked to support William while he attended medical school, and now she has been accepted by a medical school in Mexico. Abigail has decided to divorce William and attend medical school. April will stay in San Francisco because of her strong attachment to her grandparents and because they can provide her with excellent day care. Abigail knows that William will expect her to contribute to the cost of raising April. Abigail also believes that to finance her education, she must receive cash for her share of the property they accumulated during their marriage. In addition, she believes that she should receive some reimbursement for her contribution to William's support while he was in medical school. She expects the divorce proceedings to take several months. Identify the relevant tax issues for Abigail.

Decision Making   19. **LO.4, 5** Patrick and Eva are planning to divorce. Patrick has offered to pay Eva $12,000 each year until their 11-year-old daughter reaches age 21. Alternatively, Patrick will transfer to Eva common stock that he owns with a fair market value of $100,000. What factors should Eva and Patrick consider in deciding between these two options?

20. **LO.4, 5** Brenda loaned her son Bart $250,000 to purchase a new home. Brenda did not charge interest on the loan. Brenda was required to recognize imputed interest income, and Bart had imputed home mortgage interest expense that he deducted as an itemized deduction. Would Brenda's and Bart's combined total income taxes likely increase or decrease as a result of the imputed interest? Explain.

21. **LO.4** In the current year, the Rose Corporation made a $400,000 interest-free loan to John Rose, the corporation's controlling shareholder. Mr. Rose is also the corporation's chief executive officer and receives a salary of $300,000 a year. What are the tax consequences of classifying the loan as a compensation-related loan rather than as a corporation-shareholder loan?

22. **LO.2, 4** Brad is the president of Yellow Corporation. He and other members of his family control the corporation. Brad has a temporary need for $50,000, and the corporation has excess cash. He could borrow the money from a bank at 9%, and Yellow is earning 6% on its temporary investments. Yellow has made loans to other employees on several occasions. Therefore, Brad is considering borrowing $50,000 from the corporation. He will repay the loan principal in two years plus interest at 5%. Identify the relevant tax issues for Brad and Yellow Corporation.   *Issue ID*

23. **LO.4** Connor purchased an annuity that was to pay him a fixed amount each month for the remainder of his life. He began receiving payments in 1998, when he was 65 years old. In 2014, Connor was killed in an automobile accident. What are the effects of the annuity on Connor's final tax return?

24. **LO.4** An employer provides all of his employees with life insurance protection equal to twice the employee's annual salary. Melba, age 42, has an annual salary of $70,000. Is Melba required to recognize income even though she is still alive at the end of the year and thus nothing has been collected on the life insurance policy? Explain.

25. **LO.4** For a person who receives Social Security benefits, what effect, if any, can an increase in other income have on that person's taxable income?   *Issue ID*

26. **LO.1, 5** Andy recently completed medical school and is beginning his medical practice. Most of his patients are covered by health insurance with a co-pay requirement (e.g., the patient pays $10, and the insurance company is billed for the remainder). It takes approximately two months to collect from the health insurance plan. What advice can you provide Andy regarding the selection of a tax accounting method?   *Issue ID*

Problems

27. **LO.1** Determine the taxpayer's current-year (1) economic income and (2) gross income for tax purposes from the following events:
    a. Sam's employment contract as chief executive of a large corporation was terminated, and he was paid $500,000 not to work for a competitor of the corporation for five years.
    b. Elliot, a 6-year-old child, was paid $5,000 for appearing in a television commercial. His parents put the funds in a savings account for the child's education.
    c. Valery found a suitcase that contained $100,000. She could not determine who the owner was.
    d. Winn purchased a lottery ticket for $5 and won $750,000.
    e. Larry spent $1,000 to raise vegetables that he and his family consumed. The cost of the vegetables in a store would have been $2,400.
    f. Dawn purchased an automobile for $1,500 that was worth $3,500. The seller was in desperate need of cash.

28. **LO.1, 2, 5** Harper is considering three alternative investments of $10,000. Assume that the taxpayer is in the 28% marginal tax bracket for ordinary income and 15% for qualifying capital gains in all tax years. The selected investment will be liquidated at the end of five years. The alternatives are: *Decision Making*

    • A taxable corporate bond yielding 5% before tax, and the interest can be reinvested at 5% before tax.
    • A Series EE bond that will have a maturity value of $12,200 (a 4% before-tax rate of return).
    • Land that will increase in value.

The gain on the land will be classified and taxed as a long-term capital gain. The income from the bonds is taxed as ordinary income. How much must the land increase in value to yield a greater after-tax return than either of the bonds?

Given: Compound amount of $1 and compound value of annuity payments at the end of five years:

Interest Rate	$1 Compounded for 5 Years	$1 Annuity Compounded for 5 Years
5%	$1.28	$5.53
4%	1.22	5.42
3.6%	1.19	5.37

29. **LO.I** Determine the taxpayer's gross income for tax purposes in each of the following situations:
    a. Deb, a cash basis taxpayer, traded a corporate bond with accrued interest of $300 for corporate stock with a fair market value of $12,000 at the time of the exchange. Deb's cost of the bond was $10,000. The value of the stock had decreased to $11,000 by the end of the year.
    b. Deb needed $10,000 to make a down payment on her house. She instructed her broker to sell some stock to raise the $10,000. Deb's cost of the stock was $3,000. Based on her broker's advice, instead of selling the stock, she borrowed the $10,000 using the stock as collateral for the debt.
    c. Deb's boss gave her two tickets to the Rabid Rabbits rock concert because she met her sales quota. At the time she received the tickets, each ticket had a face price of $200 and was selling on eBay for $300. On the date of the concert, the tickets were selling for $250 each. Deb and her son attended the concert.

30. **LO.I, 2** Determine Amos's gross income in each of the following cases:
    a. In the current year, Amos purchased an automobile for $25,000. As part of the transaction, Amos received a $1,500 rebate from the manufacturer.
    b. Amos sold his business. In addition to the selling price of the stock, he received $50,000 for a covenant not to compete—an agreement that he will not compete with his former business for five years.
    c. Amos owned some land he held as an investment. As a result of a change in the zoning rules, the property increased in value by $20,000.

Decision Making

31. **LO.2, 5** Al is a medical doctor who conducts his practice as a sole proprietor. During 2014, he received cash of $280,000 for medical services. Of the amount collected, $40,000 was for services provided in 2013. At the end of 2014, Al had accounts receivable of $60,000, all for services rendered in 2014. In addition, at the end of the year, Al received $12,000 as an advance payment from a health maintenance organization (HMO) for services to be rendered in 2015. Compute Al's gross income for 2014:
    a. Using the cash basis of accounting.
    b. Using the accrual basis of accounting.
    c. Advise Al on which method of accounting he should use.

32. **LO.2** Selma operates a contractor's supply store. She maintains her books using the cash method. At the end of the year, her accountant computes her accrual basis income that is used on her tax return. For 2014, Selma had cash receipts of $1.4 million, which included $200,000 collected on accounts receivable from 2013 sales. It also included the proceeds of a $100,000 bank loan. At the end of 2014, she had $250,000 in accounts receivable from customers, all from 2014 sales.
    a. Compute Selma's accrual basis gross receipts for 2014.
    b. Selma paid cash for all of the purchases. The total amount paid for merchandise in 2014 was $1.3 million. At the end of 2013, she had merchandise on hand with a cost of $150,000. At the end of 2014, the cost of merchandise on hand was $300,000. Compute Selma's gross income from merchandise sales for 2014.

Decision Making

Communications

33. **LO.2, 3, 5** Your client is a new partnership, ARP Associates, which is an engineering consulting firm. Generally, ARP bills clients for services at the end of each month. Client billings are about $50,000 each month. On average, it takes 45 days to collect the receivables. ARP's expenses are primarily for salary and rent. Salaries are paid on the last day of each month, and rent is paid on the first day of each month. The partnership has a line of credit with a bank, which requires monthly financial statements. These must be

prepared using the accrual method. ARP's managing partner, Amanda Sims, has suggested that the firm also use the accrual method for tax purposes and thus reduce accounting fees by $600. Assume that the partners are in the 35% (combined Federal and state) marginal tax bracket. Write a letter to your client explaining why you believe it would be worthwhile for ARP to file its tax return on the cash basis even though its financial statements are prepared on the accrual basis. ARP's address is 100 James Tower, Denver, CO 80208.

34. **LO.2** Trip Garage, Inc. (459 Ellis Avenue, Harrisburg, PA 17111), is an accrual basis taxpayer that repairs automobiles. In late December 2014, the company repaired Samuel Mosley's car and charged him $1,000. Samuel did not think the problem had been fixed and refused to pay; thus, Trip refused to release the automobile. In early January 2015, Trip made a few adjustments and convinced Samuel that the automobile was working properly. At that time, Samuel agreed to pay only $900 because he did not have the use of the car for a week. Trip said "fine," accepted the $900, and released the automobile to Samuel. An IRS agent thinks Trip, as an accrual basis taxpayer, should report $1,000 of income in 2014, when the work was done, and then deduct a $100 loss in 2015. Prepare a memo to Susan Apple, the treasurer of Trip, with the recommended treatment for the disputed income.

Communications

35. **LO.2** Determine the effects of the following on a cash basis taxpayer's gross income for 2014 and 2015.
    a. On the morning of December 31, 2014, the taxpayer received a $1,500 check from a customer. The taxpayer did not cash the check until January 3, 2015.
    b. The same as part (a), except the customer asked the taxpayer not to cash the check until January 3, 2015, after the customer's salary check could be deposited.
    c. The same as part (a), except the check was not received until after the bank had closed on December 31, 2014.

36. **LO.2** Marlene, a cash basis taxpayer, invests in Series EE U.S. government savings bonds and bank certificates of deposit (CDs). Determine the tax consequences of the following on her 2014 gross income:
    a. On September 30, 2014, she cashed in Series EE bonds for $10,000. She purchased the bonds in 2004 for $7,090. The yield to maturity on the bonds was 3.5%.
    b. On July 1, 2013, she purchased a CD for $10,000. The CD matures on June 30, 2015, and will pay $10,816, thus yielding a 4% annual return.
    c. On July 1, 2014, she purchased a CD for $10,000. The maturity date on the CD was June 30, 2015, when Marlene would receive $10,300.

37. **LO.2** Drake Appliance Company, an accrual basis taxpayer, sells home appliances and service contracts. Determine the effect of each of the following transactions on the company's 2014 gross income assuming that the company uses any available options to defer its taxes.
    a. In December 2013, the company received a $1,200 advance payment from a customer for an appliance that Drake special ordered from the manufacturer. The appliance did not arrive from the manufacturer until January 2014, and Drake immediately delivered it to the customer. The sale was reported in 2014 for financial accounting purposes.
    b. In October 2014, the company sold a 6-month service contract for $240. The company also sold a 36-month service contract for $1,260 in July 2014.
    c. On December 31, 2014, the company sold an appliance for $1,200. The company received $500 cash and a note from the customer for $700 and $260 interest, to be paid at the rate of $40 a month for 24 months. Because of the customer's poor credit record, the fair market value of the note was only $600. The cost of the appliance was $750.

38. **LO.2, 5** Freda is a cash basis taxpayer. In 2014, she negotiated her salary for 2015. Her employer offered to pay her $21,000 per month in 2015 for a total of $252,000. Freda countered that she would accept $10,000 each month for the 12 months in 2015 and the remaining $132,000 in January 2016. The employer accepted Freda's terms for 2015 and 2016.
    a. Did Freda actually or constructively receive $252,000 in 2015?
    b. What could explain Freda's willingness to spread her salary over a longer period of time?

c. In December 2015, after Freda had earned the right to collect the $132,000 in 2016, the employer offered $133,000 to Freda at that time, rather than $132,000 in January 2016. The employer wanted to make the early payment so as to deduct the expense in 2015. Freda rejected the employer's offer. Was Freda in constructive receipt of the income in 2015? Explain.

Decision Making

39. **LO.2, 5** The Bluejay Apartments, a new development, is in the process of structuring its lease agreements. The company would like to set the damage deposits high enough that tenants will keep the apartments in good condition. The company is actually more concerned about damage than about tenants not paying their rent.
   a. Discuss the tax effects of the following alternatives:
      • $1,000 damage deposit with no rent prepayment.
      • $500 damage deposit and $500 rent for the final month of the lease.
      • $1,000 rent for the final two months of the lease and no damage deposit.
   b. Which option do you recommend? Why?

40. **LO.3** Rusty has been experiencing serious financial problems. His annual salary was $100,000, but a creditor garnished his salary for $20,000; so the employer paid the creditor (rather than Rusty) the $20,000. To prevent creditors from attaching his investments, Rusty gave his investments to his 21-year-old daughter, Rebecca. Rebecca received $5,000 in dividends and interest from the investments during the year. Rusty transferred some cash to a Swiss bank account that paid him $6,000 interest during the year. Rusty did not withdraw the interest from the Swiss bank account. Rusty also hid some of his assets in his wholly owned corporation that received $150,000 rent income but had $160,000 in related expenses, including a $20,000 salary paid to Rusty. Rusty reasons that his gross income should be computed as follows:

Salary received	$ 80,000
Loss from rental property ($150,000 − $160,000)	(10,000)
Gross income	$ 70,000

   Compute Rusty's correct gross income for the year and explain any differences between your calculation and Rusty's.

41. **LO.2, 3** Troy, a cash basis taxpayer, is employed by Eagle Corporation, also a cash basis taxpayer. Troy is a full-time employee of the corporation and receives a salary of $60,000 per year. He also receives a bonus equal to 10% of all collections from clients he serviced during the year. Determine the tax consequences of the following events to the corporation and to Troy:
   a. On December 31, 2014, Troy was visiting a customer. The customer gave Troy a $10,000 check payable to the corporation for appraisal services Troy performed during 2014. Troy did not deliver the check to the corporation until January 2015.
   b. The facts are the same as in (a), except that the corporation is an accrual basis taxpayer and Troy deposited the check on December 31, but the bank did not add the deposit to the corporation's account until January 2015.
   c. The facts are the same as in (a), except that the customer told Troy to hold the check until January 2015 when the customer could make a bank deposit that would cover the check.

42. **LO.3, 4** Faye, Gary, and Heidi each have a one-third interest in the capital and profits of the FGH Partnership. Each partner had a capital account of $50,000 at the beginning of the tax year. The partnership profits for the tax year were $270,000. Changes in their capital accounts during the tax year were as follows:

	Faye	Gary	Heidi	Total
Beginning balance	$ 50,000	$ 50,000	$ 50,000	$150,000
Withdrawals	(20,000)	(35,000)	(10,000)	(65,000)
Additional contributions	–0–	–0–	5,000	5,000
Allocation of profits	90,000	90,000	90,000	270,000
Ending balance	$120,000	$105,000	$135,000	$360,000

In arriving at the $270,000 of partnership profits, the partnership deducted $2,400 ($800 for each partner) in premiums paid for group term life insurance on the partners.

Faye and Gary are 39 years old, and Heidi is 35 years old. Other employees are also eligible for group term life insurance equal to their annual salary. These premiums of $10,000 have been deducted in calculating the partnership profits of $270,000. Compute each partner's gross income from the partnership for the tax year.

43. **LO.3, 5** In 2014, Alva received dividends on her stocks as follows:

Amur Corporation (a French corporation whose stock is traded on an established U.S. securities market)	$60,000
Blaze, Inc., a Delaware corporation	40,000
Grape, Inc., a Virginia corporation	22,000

a. Alva purchased the Grape stock three years ago, and she purchased the Amur stock two years ago. She purchased the Blaze stock 18 days before it went ex-dividend and sold it 20 days later at a $5,000 loss. Alva had no other capital gains and losses for the year. She is in the 35% marginal tax bracket. Compute Alva's tax on her dividend income for 2014.

b. Alva's daughter, who is 25 and not Alva's dependent, had taxable income of $6,000, which included $1,000 of dividends on Grape, Inc. stock. The daughter had purchased the stock two years ago. Compute the daughter's tax liability on the dividends.

c. Alva can earn 5% before-tax interest on a corporate bond or a 4% dividend on a preferred stock. Assuming that the appreciation in value is the same, which investment produces the greater after-tax income?

d. The same as part (c), except that Alva's daughter is to make the investment.

44. **LO.3** Liz and Doug were divorced on December 31 of the current year after 10 years of marriage. Their current year's income received before the divorce was as follows:

Doug's salary	$41,000
Liz's salary	55,000
Rent on apartments purchased by Liz 15 years ago	8,000
Dividends on stock Doug inherited from his mother 4 years ago	1,900
Interest on a savings account in Liz's name funded with her salary	2,400

Allocate the income to Liz and Doug assuming that they live in:
a. California.
b. Texas.

45. **LO.4** Nell and Kirby are in the process of negotiating their divorce agreement. What should be the tax consequences to Nell and Kirby if the following, considered individually, became part of the agreement?

a. In consideration for her one-half interest in their personal residence, Kirby will transfer to Nell stock with a value of $200,000 and $50,000 of cash. Kirby's cost of the stock was $150,000, and the value of the personal residence is $500,000. They purchased the residence three years ago for $300,000.

b. Nell will receive $1,000 per month for 120 months. If she dies before receiving all 120 payments, the remaining payments will be made to her estate.

c. Nell is to have custody of their 12-year-old son, Bobby. She is to receive $1,200 per month until Bobby (1) dies or (2) attains age 21 (whichever occurs first). After either of these events occurs, Nell will receive only $300 per month for the remainder of her life.

46. **LO.4** Alicia and Rafel are in the process of negotiating a divorce agreement. They both worked during the marriage and contributed an equal amount to the marital assets. They own a home with a fair market value of $400,000 (cost of $300,000) that is subject to a mortgage for $250,000. They have lived in the home for 12 years. They also have investment assets with a cost of $160,000 and a fair market value of $410,000. Thus, the net worth of the couple is $560,000 ($400,000 − $250,000 + $410,000). The holding period for the investments is longer than one year. Alicia would like to continue to live in the house. Therefore, she has proposed that she receive the residence subject to the mortgage, a net value of $150,000. In addition, she would receive $17,600 each year for the next 10 years, which has a present value (at 6% interest) of $130,000. Rafel would

Decision Making

receive the investment assets. If Rafel accepts this plan, he must sell one-half of the investments so that he can purchase a home. Assume that you are counseling Alicia. Explain to Alicia whether the proposed agreement would be "fair" on an after-tax basis.

Decision Making

47. **LO.4, 5** Roy decides to buy a personal residence and goes to the bank for a $150,000 loan. The bank tells him that he can borrow the funds at 4% if his father will guarantee the debt. Roy's father, Hal, owns a $150,000 CD currently yielding 3.5%. The Federal rate is 3%. Hal agrees to either of the following:

- Roy borrows from the bank with Hal's guarantee to the bank.
- Cash in the CD (with no penalty) and lend Roy the funds at 2% interest.

Hal is in the 33% marginal tax bracket. Roy, whose only source of income is his salary, is in the 15% marginal tax bracket. The interest Roy pays on the mortgage will be deductible by him. Which option will maximize the family's after-tax wealth?

48. **LO.2, 4** Ridge is a generous individual. During the year, he made interest-free loans to various family members when the Federal rate was 3%. What are the tax consequences of the following loans by Ridge:

a. On June 30, 2014, Ridge loaned $12,000 to his cousin, Jim, to buy a used truck. Jim's only source of income was his wages on various construction jobs during the year.

b. On August 1, 2014, Ridge loaned $8,000 to his niece, Sonja. The loan was to enable her to pay her college tuition. Sonja had $1,200 interest income from CDs her parents had given her.

c. On September 1, 2014, Ridge loaned $25,000 to his brother, Al, to start a business. Al had $220 of dividends and interest for the year.

d. On September 30, 2014, Ridge loaned $150,000 to his mother so that she could enter a nursing home. His mother's only income was $9,000 of Social Security benefits and $500 of interest income.

49. **LO.4** Indicate whether the imputed interest rules should apply in the following situations. Assume that all of the loans were made at the beginning of the tax year unless otherwise indicated.

a. Mike loaned his sister $90,000 to buy a new home. Mike did not charge interest on the loan. The Federal rate was 5%. Mike's sister had $900 of investment income for the year.

b. Sam's employer maintains an emergency loan fund for its employees. During the year, Sam's wife was very ill, and he incurred unusually large medical expenses. He borrowed $8,500 from his employer's emergency loan fund for six months. The Federal rate was 5.5%. Sam and his wife had no investment income for the year.

c. Jody borrowed $25,000 from her controlled corporation for six months. She used the funds to pay her daughter's college tuition. The corporation charged Jody 4% interest. The Federal rate was 5%. Jody had $3,500 of investment income for the year.

d. Kait loaned her son, Jake, $60,000 for six months. Jake used the $60,000 to pay off college loans. The Federal rate was 5%, and Kait did not charge Jake any interest. Jake had dividend and interest income of $2,100 for the tax year.

50. **LO.4** Vito is the sole shareholder of Vito, Inc. He is also employed by the corporation. On June 30, 2014, Vito borrowed $8,000 from Vito, Inc., and on July 1, 2015, he borrowed an additional $10,000. Both loans were due on demand. No interest was charged on the loans, and the Federal rate was 4% for all relevant dates. Vito used the money to purchase a boat, and he had $2,500 of investment income. Determine the tax consequences to Vito and Vito, Inc., in each of the following situations:

a. The loans are considered employer-employee loans.

b. The loans are considered corporation-shareholder loans.

51. **LO.4** Pam retires after 28 years of service with her employer. She is 66 years old and has contributed $42,000 to her employer's qualified pension fund. She elects to receive her retirement benefits as an annuity of $3,000 per month for the remainder of her life.

a. Assume that Pam retires in June 2014 and collects six annuity payments this year. What is her gross income from the annuity payments in the first year?

b. Assume that Pam lives 25 years after retiring. What is her gross income from the annuity payments in the twenty-fourth year?

c. Assume that Pam dies after collecting 160 payments. She collected eight payments in the year of her death. What are Pam's gross income and deductions from the annuity contract in the year of her death?

52. **LO.4** For each of the following, determine the amount that should be included in gross income:
    a. Peyton was selected the most valuable player in the Super Bowl. In recognition of this, he was awarded an automobile with a value of $60,000. Peyton did not need the automobile, so he asked that the title be put in his parents' names.
    b. Jacob was awarded the Nobel Peace Prize. When he was presented the check for $1.4 million, Jacob said, "I do not need the money. Give it to the United Nations to use toward the goal of world peace."
    c. Linda won the Craig County Fair beauty pageant. She received a $10,000 scholarship that paid her $6,000 for tuition and $4,000 for meals and housing for the academic year.

53. **LO.4** The LMN Partnership has a group term life insurance plan. Each partner has $150,000 of protection, and each employee has protection equal to twice his or her annual salary. Employee Alice (age 32) has $90,000 of insurance under the plan, and partner Kay (age 47) has $150,000 of coverage. Because the plan is a "group plan," it is impossible to determine the cost of coverage for an individual employee or partner.
    a. Assuming that the plan is nondiscriminatory, how much must Alice and Kay each include in gross income as a result of the partnership paying the insurance premiums?
    b. Assume that the partnership is incorporated. Kay becomes a shareholder and an employee who receives a $75,000 annual salary. The corporation provides Kay with $150,000 of group term life insurance coverage under a nondiscriminatory plan. What is Kay's gross income as a result of the corporation paying the insurance premiums?

54. **LO.2, 4** Herbert was employed for the first six months of 2014 and earned $90,000 in salary. During the next six months, he collected $8,800 of unemployment compensation, borrowed $12,000 (using his personal residence as collateral), and withdrew $2,000 from his savings account (including $60 of interest). He received dividends of $550. His luck was not all bad, for in December, he won $1,500 in the lottery on a $5 ticket. Calculate Herbert's gross income.

55. **LO.4, 5** Linda and Don are married and file a joint return. In 2014, they received $12,000 in Social Security benefits and $35,000 in taxable pension benefits and interest.   **Decision Making**
    a. Compute the couple's adjusted gross income on a joint return.
    b. Don would like to know whether they should sell for $100,000 (at no gain or loss) a corporate bond that pays 8% in interest each year and use the proceeds to buy a $100,000 nontaxable State of Virginia bond that will pay $6,000 in interest each year.
    c. If Linda in (a) works part-time and earns $30,000, how much will Linda and Don's adjusted gross income increase?

56. **LO.4** Melissa, who is 70 years old, is unmarried and has no dependents. Her annual income consists of a taxable pension of $17,000, $14,000 in Social Security benefits, and $3,000 of dividend income. She does not itemize her deductions. She is in the 15% marginal income tax bracket. She is considering getting a part-time job that would pay her $5,000 a year.
    a. What would be Melissa's after-tax income from the part-time job, considering Social Security and Medicare tax (7.65%) as well as Federal income tax on the earnings of $5,000?
    b. What would be the effective tax rate (increase in tax/increase in income) on the additional income from the part-time job?

57. **LO.3, 4** Donna does not think she has an income tax problem but would like to discuss her situation with you just to make sure there is no unexpected tax liability. Base your suggestions on the following relevant financial information:
    a. Donna's share of the SAT Partnership income is $150,000, but none of the income can be distributed because the partnership needs the cash for operations.
    b. Donna's Social Security benefits totaled $8,400, but Donna loaned the cash received to her nephew.
    c. Donna assigned to a creditor the right to collect $1,200 of interest on some bonds she owned.
    d. Donna and her husband lived together in California until September, when they separated. Donna has heard rumors that her husband has substantial gambling winnings since they separated.

Cumulative Problems

58. Daniel B. Butler and Freida C. Butler, husband and wife, file a joint return. The Butlers live at 625 Oak Street in Corbin, KY 40701. Dan's Social Security number is 111-11-1111, and Freida's is 123-45-6789. Dan was born on January 15, 1963, and Freida was born on August 20, 1964.

During 2013, Dan and Freida furnished over half of the total support of each of the following individuals, all of whom still live at home:

a. Gina, their daughter, age 22, a full-time student, who married on December 21, 2013, has no income of her own and for 2013 did not file a joint return with her husband, Casey, who earned $10,600 during 2013. Gina's Social Security number is 123-45-6788.

b. Sam, their son, age 20, who had gross income of $6,300 in 2013, dropped out of college in October 2013. He had graduated from high school in May 2013. Sam's Social Security number is 123-45-6787.

c. Ben, their oldest son, age 26, is a full-time graduate student with gross income of $5,200. Ben's Social Security number is 123-45-6786.

Dan was employed as a manager by WJJJ, Inc. (employer identification number 11-1111111, 604 Franklin Street, Corbin, KY 40702), and Freida was employed as a salesperson for Corbin Realty, Inc. (employer identification number 98-7654321, 899 Central Street, Corbin, Ky 40701). Selected information from the W–2 Forms provided by the employers is presented below. Dan and Freida use the cash method.

Line	Description	Dan	Freida
1	Wages, tips, other compensation	$74,000	$86,000
2	Federal income tax withheld	$11,000	$12,400
17	State income tax withheld	$2,960	$3,440

Freida sold a house on December 30, 2013, and will be paid a commission of $3,100 (not included in the $86,000 reported on the W–2) on the January 10, 2014 closing date.

Other income (as reported on 1099 Forms) for 2013 consisted of the following:

Dividends on CSX stock (qualified)	$4,200
Interest on savings at Second Bank	1,600
Interest on City of Corbin bonds	900
Interest on First Bank CD	382

The $382 from First Bank was original issue discount. Dan and Freida collected $16,000 on the First Bank CD that matured on September 30, 2013. The CD was purchased on October 1, 2011, for $14,995, and the yield to maturity was 3.3%.

Dan received a Schedule K–1 from the Falcon Partnership, which showed his distributive share of income as $7,000. In addition to the above information, Dan and Freida's itemized deductions included the following:

Paid on 2013 Kentucky income tax	$ 700
Personal property tax paid	600
Real estate taxes paid	1,800
Interest on home mortgage (Corbin S&L)	4,900
Cash contributions to the Boy Scouts	800

Sales tax from the sales tax table is $1,860. Dan and Freida made Federal estimated tax payments of $8,000. The Kentucky income tax rate is 4%.

Part 1—Tax Computation

Compute Dan and Freida's 2013 Federal income tax payable (or refund due). If you use tax forms for your computations, you will need Form 1040 and Schedules A, B, and E. Suggested software: H&R BLOCK Tax Software.

Part 2—Tax Planning

Dan plans to reduce his work schedule and work only half-time for WJJJ in 2014. He has been writing songs for several years and wants to devote more time to developing a career as a songwriter. Because of the uncertainty in the music business, however, he would like you to make all computations assuming that he will have no income from songwriting in 2014. To make up for the loss of income, Freida plans to increase the amount of time she spends selling real estate. She estimates that she will be able to earn $90,000 in 2014. Assume that all other income and expense items will be approximately the same as they were in 2013. Assume that Sam will be enrolled in college as a full-time student for the summer and fall semesters. Will the Butlers have more or less disposable income (after Federal income tax) in 2014? Write a letter to the Butlers that contains your advice and prepare a memo for the tax files.

59. Cecil C. Seymour is a 64-year-old widower. He had income for 2014 as follows:

Tax Computation Problem

Pension from former employer	$39,850
Interest income from Alto National Bank	5,500
Interest income on City of Alto bonds	4,500
Dividends received from IBM	2,000
Collections on annuity contract he purchased from Great Life Insurance	5,400
Social Security benefits	14,000
Rent income on townhouse	9,000

The cost of the annuity was $46,800, and Cecil was expected to receive a total of 260 monthly payments of $450. Cecil has received 22 payments through 2014.

Cecil's 40-year-old daughter, Sarah C. Seymour, borrowed $60,000 from Cecil on January 2, 2014. She used the money to start a new business. Cecil does not charge her interest because she could not afford to pay it, but he does expect to eventually collect the principal. Sarah is living with Cecil until the business becomes profitable. Except for housing, Sarah provides her own support from her business and $1,600 in dividends on stocks that she inherited from her mother.

Other relevant information is presented below:

- Cecil's Social Security number: 123-45-6785
- Address: 3840 Springfield Blvd., Alto, GA 30510
- Sarah's Social Security number: 123-45-6784
- Expenses on rental townhouse:

Utilities	$2,800
Maintenance	1,000
Depreciation	2,000
Real estate taxes	750
Insurance	700

- State income taxes paid: $3,500
- County personal property taxes paid: $2,100
- Payments on estimated 2014 Federal income tax: $5,900
- Charitable contributions of cash to Alto Baptist Church: $6,400
- Federal interest rate: 6%
- Sales taxes paid: $912

Compute Cecil's 2014 Federal income tax payable (or refund due).

Research Problems

Note: Solutions to Research Problems can be prepared by using the **Checkpoint®** **Student Edition** online research product, which is available to accompany this text. It is also possible to prepare solutions to the Research Problems by using tax research materials found in a standard tax library.

THOMSON REUTERS
CHECKPOINT®

Research Problem 1. Tranquility Funeral Home, Inc., your client, is an accrual basis taxpayer that sells preneed funeral contracts. Under these contracts, the customer pays in advance for goods and services to be provided at the contract beneficiary's death. These payments are refundable at the contract purchaser's request, pursuant to state law, any time until the goods and services are furnished. Tranquility, consistent with its financial accounting reporting, includes the payments in income for the year the funeral service is provided.

Communications

The IRS agent insists that the payments be prepaid income subject to tax in the year of receipt. Your client believes that the amounts involved are customer deposits. Write a letter to Tranquility that contains your advice about how the issue should be resolved. The client's address is 400 Rock Street, Memphis, TN 38152.

Research Problem 2. Your client was the beneficiary of an annuity contract purchased by her stepmother. When the stepmother died, the insurance company paid the client $400,000 and sent her a Form 1099 indicating that the taxable portion (i.e., the amount in excess of the investment in the contract) was $50,000. However, according to the client, her father fraudulently convinced her that he was the intended beneficiary. She gave her father a check equal to the amount she had received from the insurance company. She did not report any of the annuity proceeds in her income tax return. She later discovered the fraud and filed a lawsuit to collect from her father. The IRS has examined your client's return and has taken the position that she must include the $50,000 in her gross income.
    Evaluate the IRS's position.

Research Problem 3. Your client owns a life insurance policy on his life. He has paid $6,800 in premiums, and the cash surrender value of the policy is $30,000. He borrowed $30,000 from the insurance company, using the cash surrender value as collateral. He is considering canceling the policy in payment of the loan. He would like to know the tax consequences of canceling his policy.

Research Problem 4. Your client is a new retailer who often issues store gift (debit) cards to customers in lieu of a cash refund. You recall that the IRS issued a Revenue Procedure that provided that the prepaid income rules in Revenue Procedure 2004–34 could be applied to the income from the gift cards. Locate the Revenue Procedure authorizing the deferral of the income from gift cards.

Internet Activity

Use the tax resources of the Internet to address the following questions. Do not restrict your search to the Web, but include a review of newsgroups and general reference materials, practitioner sites and resources, primary sources of the tax law, chat rooms and discussion groups, and other opportunities.

Research Problem 5. Lottery winnings are taxable for Federal income tax purposes. What many lottery hopefuls forget to factor into their tax considerations are that lottery winnings are also taxable in many states. Search the Internet to see whether you can determine if lottery winnings are taxable for California residents.

Communications

Research Problem 6. Go to the web page of a consulting firm that offers counseling services to individuals as they negotiate the terms of a divorce. What specific tax-related services do these firms offer? Suggest a new tax-related service the consulting firm could offer.

CHAPTER 5

Gross Income: Exclusions

LEARNING OBJECTIVES: *After completing Chapter 5, you should be able to:*

LO.1 Be aware that statutory authority is required to exclude an item from gross income.

LO.2 Identify the circumstances under which various items are excludible from gross income.

LO.3 Determine the extent to which receipts can be excluded under the tax benefit rule.

LO.4 Describe the circumstances under which income must be reported from the discharge of indebtedness.

LO.5 Identify tax planning strategies for obtaining the maximum benefit from allowable exclusions.

CHAPTER OUTLINE

© Andrew Shurtleff/ZUMA Press/Corbis

EXCLUSIONS

Paul is a graduate student in the last semester of an accounting program at State University. This past summer he was an intern with a CPA firm, working in the compliance area. Paul was paid well enough for his work as an intern that he was able to pay for his meals and lodging and to save some for school. The CPA firm was so pleased with Paul's work that at the conclusion of his internship, he was given a bonus of $1,500 more than the firm had agreed to pay him. The extra amount was intended to help with his graduate school expenses. The CPA firm has offered him a full-time job after he completes his graduate program in December.

Because of his excellent academic record, the university has awarded Paul a graduate assistantship that waives his tuition of $6,000 per semester and pays him $400 per month. Paul is required to teach a principles of accounting course each semester. Paul has used the $400 per month for books and for room and board.

In November, Paul was crossing a street in the pedestrian crosswalk when a delivery van struck him. The driver of the truck had a blood alcohol level of .12. Paul suffered a severe injury to his right arm that has delayed his starting date for work by three months. The delivery company's insurance company settled the case by paying damages, itemized as follows:

Compensatory damages:	
Medical expenses	$ 30,000
Injury to Paul's right arm	100,000
Pain and suffering	50,000
Loss of income	15,000
Legal fees	25,000
Punitive damages	160,000
	$380,000

Paul's mother was with him in the crosswalk. Fortunately, the van did not hit her, and she was not physically injured. But she did suffer emotional distress and received $25,000 in the settlement.

Besides being Paul's friend, you also are a senior accounting major and have a keen interest in taxation. You tell Paul that you will look into the tax consequences of the settlement.

Read the chapter and formulate your response.

FRAMEWORK 1040
Tax Formula for Individuals

This chapter covers the boldfaced portions of the Tax Formula for Individuals that was introduced in Figure 3.1 on p. 3-3. Below those portions are the sections of Form 1040 where the results are reported.

Income *(broadly conceived)*	$xx,xxx
Less: Exclusions	(x,xxx)

FORM 1040 (p. 1)

8b	**Tax-exempt** interest. **Do not** include on line 8a	**8b**	

Gross income	

FORM 1040 (p. 1)

10	Taxable refunds, credits, or offsets of state and local income taxes
19	Unemployment compensation
21	Other income. List type and amount

Less: Deductions for adjusted gross income	(x,xxx)
Adjusted gross income	$xx,xxx
Less: The greater of total itemized deductions *or* the standard deduction	(x,xxx)
Personal and dependency exemptions	(x,xxx)
Taxable income	$xx,xxx
Tax on taxable income *(see Tax Tables or Tax Rate Schedules)*	$ x,xxx
Less: Tax credits *(including income taxes withheld and prepaid)*	(xxx)
Tax due *(or refund)*	$ xxx

Chapter 4 discussed the concepts and judicial doctrines that affect the determination of gross income. If an income item is within the all-inclusive definition of gross income, the item can be excluded only if the taxpayer can locate specific authority for doing so. Chapter 5 focuses on the exclusions Congress has authorized.

5-1 STATUTORY AUTHORITY

LO.1

Be aware that statutory authority is required to exclude an item from gross income.

Sections 101 through 150 provide the authority for excluding specific items from gross income. In addition, other exclusions are scattered throughout the Code. Each exclusion has its own legislative history and reason for enactment. Certain exclusions are intended as a form of indirect welfare payments. Other exclusions prevent double taxation of income or provide incentives for socially desirable activities (e.g., nontaxable interest on certain U.S. government bonds where the owner uses the funds for educational expenses).

In some cases, Congress has enacted exclusions to rectify the effects of judicial decisions or IRS pronouncements.[1] For example, in the past, the IRS and some courts interpreted gross income to include payments the taxpayer received from his or her insurance policy to cover temporary living expenses after the person's residence was destroyed by fire. Although the IRS's and the courts' reasoning may have been a sound interpretation of the meaning of gross income, Congress determined that taxing the person under such dire circumstances was bad policy. Therefore, in 1969, Congress enacted § 123, which exempts from tax the insurance proceeds received for extraordinary living expenses when the taxpayer's home has been destroyed by fire or other casualty.[2]

---

[1]See Chapter 1, Example 28.

[2]P.L. 91–172, Tax Reform Act of 1969, Senate Report No. 91–552.

At times, Congress responds to specific events. For example, in 2001, Congress enacted § 139 to ensure that victims of a *qualified disaster* (disaster resulting from a terrorist attack, presidentially declared disaster, or common carrier accident of a catastrophic nature) would not be required to include in gross income payments received for living expenses, funeral expenses, and property damage resulting from the disaster.

5-2 GIFTS AND INHERITANCES

5-2a Legislative Intent

LO.2

Identify the circumstances under which various items are excludible from gross income.

Beginning with the Income Tax Act of 1913 and continuing to the present, Congress has allowed the recipient of a gift to exclude the value of the property from gross income. The exclusion applies to gifts made during the life of the donor (*inter vivos* gifts) and transfers that take effect upon the death of the donor (bequests and inheritances).[3] However, as discussed in Chapter 4, the recipient of a gift of income-producing property is subject to tax on the income subsequently earned from the property. Also, as discussed in Chapter 1, the donor or the decedent's estate may be subject to gift or estate taxes on the transfer.

In numerous cases, gifts are made in a business setting. For example, a salesperson gives a purchasing agent free samples, an employee receives cash from his or her employer on retirement, or a corporation makes payments to employees who were victims of a natural disaster. In these and similar instances, it is frequently unclear whether the payment was a gift or represents compensation for past, present, or future services.

The courts have defined a gift as "a voluntary transfer of property by one to another without adequate [valuable] consideration or compensation therefrom."[4] If the payment is intended to be for services rendered, it is not a gift, even though the payment is made without legal or moral obligation and the payor receives no economic benefit from the transfer. To qualify as a gift, the payment must be made "out of affection, respect, admiration, charity or like impulses."[5] Thus, the cases on this issue have been decided on the basis of the donor's intent.

In a landmark case, *Comm. v. Duberstein*,[6] the taxpayer (Duberstein) received a Cadillac from a business acquaintance. Duberstein had supplied the businessman with the names of potential customers with no expectation of compensation. The Supreme Court concluded:

> . . . despite the characterization of the transfer of the Cadillac by the parties [as a gift] and the absence of any obligation, even of a moral nature, to make it, it was at the bottom a recompense for Duberstein's past service, or an inducement for him to be of further service in the future.

Duberstein was therefore required to include the fair market value of the automobile in gross income.

5-2b Gifts to Employees

In the case of cash or other property *received by an employee* from his or her employer, Congress has eliminated any ambiguity. Transfers from an employer to an employee cannot be excluded as a gift.[7]

---

[3]§ 102.

[4]*Estate of D. R. Daly*, 3 B.T.A. 1042 (1926).

[5]*Robertson v. U.S.*, 52–1 USTC ¶9343, 41 AFTR 1053, 72 S.Ct. 994 (USSC, 1952).

[6]60–2 USTC ¶9515, 5 AFTR 2d 1626, 80 S.Ct. 1190 (USSC, 1960).

[7]§ 102(c). But see § 139 for qualified disaster situations.

TAX IN THE NEWS Begging as a Tax-Disfavored Occupation

The Tax Court has ruled that amounts received from begging are nontaxable gifts. In a reversal of the normal roles, the beggars contended that the amounts received were earned income while the IRS argued that the taxpayers had merely received gifts. The beggars wanted the fruit of their efforts to be treated as earned income to qualify

them for the earned income credit (see Chapter 13). In all cases addressing the issue, the taxpayers were incarcerated and received the money from relatives and friends who had few prospects for being repaid.

Source: John Walter Wolf, 78 TCM 488, T.C.Memo. 1990–320.

THE BIG PICTURE

Example 1

Return to the facts of *The Big Picture* on p. 5-1. The $1,500 paid to Paul by his summer employer was compensation for his services rather than a gift, even though the employer had not contracted to pay this additional amount. This results because the payment was most likely not motivated by the employer's generosity, but rather was made as a result of business considerations. Even if the payment had been made out of generosity, because the payment was received from his employer, Paul could not exclude the "gift."

5-2c Employee Death Benefits

Frequently, an employer makes payments (**death benefits**) to a deceased employee's surviving spouse, children, or other beneficiaries. If the decedent had a nonforfeitable right to the payments (e.g., the decedent's accrued salary), the amounts are generally taxable to the recipient as if the employee had lived and collected the payments. But when the employer makes voluntary payments, the gift issue arises. Generally, the IRS considers such payments to be compensation for prior services rendered by the deceased employee.[8] However, some courts have held that payments to an employee's surviving spouse or other beneficiaries are gifts if the following are true:[9]

- The payments were made to the surviving spouse and children rather than to the employee's estate.
- The employer derived no benefit from the payments.
- The surviving spouse and children performed no services for the employer.
- The decedent had been fully compensated for services rendered.
- Payments were made pursuant to a board of directors' resolution that followed a general company policy of providing payments for families of deceased employees (but not exclusively for families of shareholder-employees).

When all of the above conditions are satisfied, the payment is presumed to have been made *as an act of affection or charity*. When one or more of these conditions is not satisfied, the surviving spouse and children may still be deemed the recipients of a gift if the payment is made in light of the survivors' financial needs.[10]

Income earned by an employee that was not received by the employee prior to his or her death is not an employee death benefit. These earnings are referred to

[8]Rev.Rul. 62–102, 1962–2 C.B. 37.
[9]*Estate of Sydney J. Carter v. Comm.*, 72–1 USTC ¶9129, 29 AFTR 2d 332, 453 F.2d 61 (CA–2, 1972), and the cases cited there.

[10]*Simpson v. U.S.*, 58–2 USTC ¶9923, 2 AFTR 2d 6036, 261 F.2d 497 (CA–7, 1958), *cert. denied* 79 S.Ct. 724 (USSC, 1958).

as "income in respect of a decedent" and, according to § 691, are generally taxable income to the decedent's beneficiary. This is another rare instance (see Alimony in Chapter 4) where the beneficiary of the income, rather than the person who earned the income, is subject to tax.

5-3 LIFE INSURANCE PROCEEDS

5-3a General Rule

Life insurance proceeds paid to the beneficiary because of the death of the insured are exempt from income tax.[11]

> **Example 2**
>
> Mark purchases an insurance policy on his life and names his wife, Linda, as the beneficiary. Mark pays $45,000 in premiums. When he dies, Linda collects the insurance proceeds of $200,000. The $200,000 is exempt from Federal income tax.

Congress chose to exempt life insurance proceeds for the following reasons:

- For family members, life insurance proceeds serve much the same purpose as a nontaxable inheritance.
- In a business context (as well as in a family situation), life insurance proceeds replace an economic loss suffered by the beneficiary.

> **Example 3**
>
> Gold Corporation purchases a life insurance policy to cover its key employee. If the proceeds were taxable, the corporation would require more insurance coverage to pay the tax as well as to cover the economic loss of the employee.

Thus, in general, Congress concluded that making life insurance proceeds exempt from income tax was a good policy.

5-3b Accelerated Death Benefits

Generally, if the owner of a life insurance policy cancels the policy and receives the cash surrender value, the taxpayer must recognize gain equal to the excess of the amount received over premiums paid on the policy (a loss is not deductible). The gain is recognized because the general exclusion provision for life insurance proceeds applies only to life insurance proceeds paid upon the death of the insured. If the taxpayer cancels the policy and receives the cash surrender value, the life insurance policy is treated as an investment by the insured.

[11]§ 101(a).

In a limited circumstance, however, the insured is permitted to receive the benefits of the life insurance contract without having to include the gain in gross income. Under the **accelerated death benefits** provisions, exclusion treatment is available for insured taxpayers who are either terminally ill or chronically ill.[12] A terminally ill taxpayer can collect the cash surrender value of the policy from the insurance company or assign the policy proceeds to a qualified third party. The resultant gain, if any, is excluded from the insured's gross income. A *terminally ill* individual is a person whom a medical doctor certifies as having an illness that is reasonably expected to cause death within 24 months.

In the case of a chronically ill patient, no gain is recognized if the proceeds of the policy are used for the long-term care of the insured. A person is *chronically ill* if he or she is certified as being unable to perform without assistance certain activities of daily living. These exclusions for the terminally ill and the chronically ill are available only to the insured. Thus, a person who purchases a life insurance policy from the insured does not qualify.

Example 4	Tom owned a term life insurance policy at the time he was diagnosed as having a terminal illness. After paying $5,200 in premiums, he sold the policy to Amber Benefits, Inc., a company that is authorized by the state of Virginia to purchase such policies. Amber paid Tom $50,000. When Tom died six months later, Amber collected the face amount of the policy, $75,000. Tom is not required to include the $44,800 gain ($50,000 − $5,200) on the sale of the policy in his gross income.

Example 5	Assume that Amber in Example 4 paid additional premiums of $4,000 during the six months it owned the policy. When Amber collects the life insurance proceeds of $75,000, it must include the $21,000 gain [$75,000 proceeds − ($50,000 cost + $4,000 additional premiums paid)] in gross income.

ETHICS & EQUITY   Should the Terminally Ill Pay Social Security Taxes?

The rationale for excluding accelerated death benefits from the gross income of the terminally ill is that they often use the funds to pay medical expenses and other costs associated with dying and do not have the ability to pay tax on the gain from the accelerated receipt of the life insurance proceeds. Yet the wages of a terminally ill person who is employed (or profits of a self-employed person) are subject to Social Security taxes. The Social Security taxes are intended to pay for retirement benefits, but a terminally ill person is unlikely to collect any Social Security benefits.

Several bills have been introduced in Congress to exempt the terminally ill from the Social Security tax. Evaluate the equity of the current tax treatment versus that in the proposed legislation.

© iStockphoto.com/LdF

5-3c Transfer for Valuable Consideration

A life insurance policy (other than one associated with accelerated death benefits) may be transferred after it is issued by the insurance company. If the policy is *transferred for valuable consideration*, the insurance proceeds are includible in the gross income of the transferee to the extent the proceeds received exceed the amount paid for the policy by the transferee plus any subsequent premiums paid.

Example 6	Adam pays premiums of $4,000 for an insurance policy in the face amount of $10,000 upon the life of Beth and subsequently transfers the policy to Carol for $6,000. Upon Beth's death, Carol receives the proceeds of $10,000. The amount Carol can exclude from gross income is limited to $6,000 plus any premiums she paid subsequent to the transfer.

---

[12]§ 101(g).

The Code, however, provides four exceptions to the rule illustrated in the preceding example. These exceptions permit exclusion treatment for transfers to the following:

1. The insured under the policy.
2. A partner of the insured.
3. A partnership in which the insured is a partner.
4. A corporation in which the insured is an officer or a shareholder.
5. A transferee whose basis in the policy is determined by reference to the transferor's basis.

> **Example 7**
>
> When Logan's daughter Emily was born, he purchased an insurance policy on her life. Twenty-four years later after Emily graduated from college and married, Logan sold her the policy for its fair value. When Emily dies, the transfer for consideration rules will not apply. Because the transfer was to the insured, the policy proceeds will be excluded from the recipient's gross income. The results would be the same if Logan gave (rather than sold) the policy to Emily.

The fifth exception applies to policies that were transferred pursuant to a tax-free exchange or were received by gift.[13]

Investment earnings arising from the reinvestment of life insurance proceeds are generally subject to income tax. Often the beneficiary will elect to collect the insurance proceeds in installments. The annuity rules (discussed in Chapter 4) are used to apportion the installment payment between the principal element (excludible) and the interest element (includible).[14]

5-4 SCHOLARSHIPS

5-4a General Information

Payments or benefits received by a student at an educational institution may be (1) compensation for services, (2) a gift, or (3) a scholarship. If the payments or benefits are received as compensation for services (past or present), the fact that the recipient is a student generally does not render the amounts received nontaxable.[15] Thus, a university teaching or research assistant is generally considered an employee, and his or her stipend is taxable compensation for services rendered. On the other hand, athletic scholarships generally are nontaxable when the individual is not required to participate in the sport.[16] In general, amounts received to be used for educational purposes (other than amounts received from family members) cannot be excluded as gifts because conditions attached to the receipt of the funds mean that the payments were not made out of "detached generosity."

The **scholarship** rules are intended to provide exclusion treatment for education-related benefits that cannot qualify as gifts but are not compensation for services. According to the Regulations, "a scholarship is an amount paid or allowed to, or for the benefit of, an individual to aid such individual in the pursuit of study or research."[17] The recipient must be a candidate for a degree at an educational institution.[18]

> **Example 8**
>
> Terry enters a contest sponsored by a local newspaper. Each contestant is required to submit an essay on local environmental issues. The prize is one year's tuition at State University. Terry wins the contest. The newspaper has a legal obligation to Terry (as contest winner). Thus, the benefits are not a gift. However, because the tuition payment aids Terry in pursuing her studies, the payment is a scholarship.

---

[13]See the discussion of gifts in Chapter 14 and tax-free exchanges in Chapters 15 and 20. In the case of a gift, the donor's basis becomes the donee's basis.

[14]Reg. §§ 1.72–7(c)(1) and 1.101–7T.

[15]Reg. § 1.117–2(a). See *C. P. Bhalla*, 35 T.C. 13 (1960), for a discussion of the distinction between a scholarship and compensation. See also *Bingler v.*

Johnson, 69–1 USTC ¶9348, 23 AFTR 2d 1212, 89 S.Ct. 1439 (USSC, 1969). For potential exclusion treatment, see the subsequent discussion of qualified tuition reductions.

[16]Rev. Rul. 77–263, 1977–2 C.B. 47.

[17]§ Prop.Reg. § 117–6(c)(3)(i).

[18]§ 117(a).

As an exception to the compensation for services, nonprofit educational institutions can provide qualified tuition reduction plans for their employees and the employees can exclude the tuition from their gross income. The exclusion also applies to tuition reductions granted to the employee's spouse and the employee's dependent children.[19]

A scholarship recipient may exclude from gross income the amount used for tuition and related expenses (fees, books, supplies, and equipment required for courses), provided the conditions of the grant do not require that the funds be used for other purposes.[20]

Example 9

Kelly receives a scholarship of $9,500 from State University to be used to pursue a bachelor's degree. She spends $4,000 on tuition, $3,000 on books and supplies, and $2,500 for room and board. Kelly may exclude $7,000 ($4,000 + $3,000) from gross income. The $2,500 spent for room and board is includible in Kelly's gross income.

5-4b Timing Issues

Frequently, the scholarship recipient is a cash basis taxpayer who receives the money in one tax year but pays the educational expenses in a subsequent year. The amount eligible for exclusion may not be known at the time the money is received. In that case, the transaction is held *open* until the educational expenses are paid.[21]

Example 10

In August 2014, Sanjay received $10,000 as a scholarship for the academic year 2014–2015. Sanjay's expenditures for tuition, books, and supplies were as follows:

August–December 2014	$3,000
January–May 2015	4,500
	$7,500

Sanjay's gross income for 2015 includes $2,500 ($10,000 − $7,500) that is not excludible as a scholarship. None of the scholarship is included in his gross income in 2014.

5-4c Disguised Compensation

Some employers make scholarships available solely to the children of key employees. The tax objective of these plans is to provide a nontaxable fringe benefit to the executives by making the payment to the child in the form of an excludible scholarship. However, the IRS has ruled that the payments are generally includible in the gross income of the parent-employee.[22]

THE BIG PICTURE

Example 11

Return to the facts of *The Big Picture* on p. 5-1. Paul was paid $400 a month by the university for teaching. This is reasonable compensation for his services. Although he received the assistantship because of his excellent academic record, the monthly pay of $400 must be included in his gross income because it is compensation for his services. However, the $6,000 graduate tuition reduction can be excluded from gross income.

---

[19]§ 117(d).
[20]§ 117(b).
[21]Prop.Reg. § 1.117–6(b)(2).

[22]Rev.Rul. 75–448, 1975–2 C.B. 55; *Richard T. Armantrout*, 67 T.C. 996 (1977).

5-5 COMPENSATION FOR INJURIES AND SICKNESS

5-5a Damages

A person who suffers harm caused by another is often entitled to compensatory damages. The tax consequences of the receipt of damages depend on the type of harm the taxpayer has experienced. The taxpayer may seek recovery for (1) a loss of income, (2) expenses incurred, (3) property destroyed, or (4) personal injury.

Generally, reimbursement for a loss of income is taxed the same as the income replaced (see the exception under Personal Injury below). The recovery of an expense is not income unless the expense was deducted. Damages that are a recovery of the taxpayer's previously deducted expenses are generally taxable under the tax benefit rule, discussed later in this chapter.

A payment for damaged or destroyed property is treated as an amount received in a sale or exchange of the property. Thus, the taxpayer has a realized gain if the damages payments received exceed the property's basis. Damages for personal injuries receive special treatment under the Code.

Personal Injury

The legal theory of personal injury damages is that the amount received is intended "to make the plaintiff [the injured party] whole as before the injury."[23] It follows that if the damages payments received were subject to tax, the after-tax amount received would be less than the actual damages incurred and the injured party would not be "whole as before the injury." In terms of personal injury damages, a distinction is made between compensatory damages and punitive damages.

---

[23] *C. A. Hawkins*, 6 B.T.A. 1023 (1928).

CONCEPT SUMMARY 5.1

Taxation of Damages

Type of Claim	Taxation of Award or Settlement
Breach of contract (generally loss of income)	Taxable.
Property damages	Recovery of cost; gain to the extent of the excess over basis. A loss is deductible for business property and investment property to the extent of basis over the amount realized. A loss may be deductible for personal use property (see discussion of casualty losses in Chapter 7).
Personal injury	
Physical	All compensatory amounts are excluded unless previously deducted (e.g., medical expenses). Amounts received as punitive damages are included in gross income.
Nonphysical	Compensatory damages and punitive damages are included in gross income.

Compensatory damages are intended to compensate the taxpayer for the damages incurred. Only those compensatory damages received on account of *physical personal injury or physical sickness* can be excluded from gross income.[24] Such exclusion treatment includes amounts received for loss of income associated with the physical personal injury or physical sickness. Compensatory damages awarded on account of emotional distress are not received on account of physical injury or physical sickness and thus cannot be excluded (except to the extent of any amount received for medical care) from gross income. Likewise, any amounts received for age discrimination or injury to one's reputation cannot be excluded.

Punitive damages are amounts the person who caused the harm must pay to the victim as punishment for outrageous conduct. Punitive damages are not intended to compensate the victim, but rather to punish the party who caused the harm. Thus, it follows that amounts received as punitive damages may actually place the victim in a better economic position than before the harm was experienced. Thus, punitive damages are included in gross income.

These rules are set forth in Concept Summary 5.1.

THE BIG PICTURE

Example 12

Return to the facts of *The Big Picture* on p. 5-1. The damages Paul received were awarded as a result of a physical personal injury. Therefore, all of the compensatory damages can be excluded. Note that even the compensation for the loss of income of $15,000 can be excluded. The punitive damages Paul received, however, must be included in his gross income.

Paul's mother did not suffer a personal physical injury or sickness. Therefore, the $25,000 she received must be included in her gross income.

---

[24]§ 104(a)(2).

ETHICS & EQUITY   Classifying the Amount of the Claim

Lee was injured in an automobile accident caused by a negligent driver of a commercial vehicle. Lee threatened to file a lawsuit against the company for $100,000 damages for his physical injury and $100,000 punitive damages. The company's insurer would not pay punitive damages. Therefore, the company advised Lee to revise his claim for $150,000 physical damages and no punitive damages. Should Lee accept the offer?

5-5b Workers' Compensation

State workers' compensation laws require the employer to pay fixed amounts for specific job-related injuries. The state laws were enacted so that the employee will not have to go through the ordeal of a lawsuit (and possibly not collect damages because of some defense available to the employer) to recover the damages. Although the payments are intended, in part, to compensate for a loss of future income, Congress has specifically exempted workers' compensation benefits from inclusion in gross income.[25]

5-5c Accident and Health Insurance Benefits

The income tax treatment of accident and health insurance benefits depends on whether the policy providing the benefits was purchased by the taxpayer or the taxpayer's employer. Benefits collected under an accident and health insurance policy *purchased by the taxpayer* are excludible even though the payments are a substitute for income.[26]

Bonnie purchases a medical and disability insurance policy. The insurance company pays Bonnie $1,000 per week to replace wages she loses while in the hospital. Although the payments serve as a substitute for income, the amounts received are tax-exempt benefits collected under Bonnie's insurance policy.	**Example 13**

Joe's injury results in a partial paralysis of his left foot. He receives $20,000 for the injury from his accident insurance company under a policy he had purchased. The $20,000 accident insurance proceeds are tax-exempt.	**Example 14**

A different set of rules applies if the accident and health insurance protection was *purchased by the individual's employer*, as discussed in the following section.

5-6 EMPLOYER-SPONSORED ACCIDENT AND HEALTH PLANS

Congress encourages employers to provide employees, retired former employees, and their dependents with **accident and health benefits**, disability insurance, and long-term care plans. The *premiums* are deductible by the employer and excluded from the employee's income.[27] Although § 105(a) provides the general rule that the employee has includible income when he or she collects the insurance *benefits*, two exceptions are provided.

Section 105(b) generally excludes payments received for medical care of the employee, spouse, and dependents. However, if the payments are for expenses that do not meet the Code's definition of medical care,[28] the amount received must be included in gross income. In addition, the taxpayer must include in gross income

---

[25]§ 104(a)(1).
[26]§ 104(a)(3).

[27]§ 106, Reg. § 1.106–1, and Rev.Rul. 82–196, 1982–1 C.B. 106.
[28]See the discussion of medical care in Chapter 10.

Global Tax Issues

When Jobs Leave the Country, So Do the Health Insurance Benefits

Firms in the textile industry generally provided health insurance coverage for their employees. As textile mills in the United States close and production is moved to foreign countries, often the U.S. employees lose their health insurance as well as their jobs. If and when the former textile worker finds new employment, the new employer may not provide health insurance. In addition, the pay on the new job is often so low that the worker cannot afford to purchase health insurance, which may cost over $500 per month.

Among the factors contributing to increased foreign competition for the domestic textile industry are the North American Free Trade Agreement of 1993, the Caribbean Basin Initiative of 2000, and the opening of trade with China.

any amounts received for medical expenses that were deducted by the taxpayer on a prior return.

Example 15

In 2014, Tab's employer-sponsored health insurance plan pays $4,000 for hair transplants that do not meet the Code's definition of medical care. Tab must include the $4,000 in his gross income for 2014.

Section 105(c) excludes payments for the permanent loss or the loss of the use of a member or function of the body or the permanent disfigurement of the employee, the spouse, or a dependent. Payments that are a substitute for salary (e.g., related to the period of time absent) are includible.

Example 16

Jill loses an eye in an automobile accident unrelated to her work. As a result of the accident, Jill incurs $2,000 of medical expenses, which she deducts on her return. She collects $10,000 from an accident insurance policy carried by her employer. The benefits are paid according to a schedule of amounts that vary with the part of the body injured (e.g., $10,000 for loss of an eye and $20,000 for loss of a hand). Because the payment is for loss of a *member or function of the body*, the $10,000 is excluded from gross income. Jill is absent from work for a week as a result of the accident. Her employer provides her with insurance for the loss of income due to illness or injury. Jill collects $500, which is includible in gross income.

5-6a Medical Reimbursement Plans

In lieu of providing the employee with insurance coverage for hospital and medical expenses, the employer may agree to reimburse the employee for these expenses. The amounts received through the insurance coverage (insured plan benefits) are excluded from income under § 105 (as previously discussed). Unfortunately, in terms of cost considerations, the insurance companies that issue this type of policy usually require a broad coverage of employees. An alternative is to have a plan that is not funded with insurance (a self-insured arrangement). The benefits received under a self-insured plan can be excluded from the employee's income if the plan does not discriminate in favor of highly compensated employees.[29]

There is also an alternative means of accomplishing a medical reimbursement plan. The employer can purchase a medical insurance plan with a high deductible (e.g., the employee is responsible for the first $2,200 of the family's medical expenses) and then make contributions to the employee's **Health Savings Account (HSA)**.[30] The employer can make contributions each month up to the maximum contribution of 100 percent of the deductible amount. The monthly deductible amount is limited to one-twelfth of $4,350 under a high-deductible plan for self-only coverage. The monthly amount for an individual who has family coverage is

---

[29]§ 105(h).

[30]§§ 106(d) and 223. See additional coverage in Chapter 10.

TAX IN THE NEWS Same-Sex Marriage and Employer-Provided Health Insurance

Now that same-sex marriages are recognized in some states, those marriages are recognized for Federal income tax purposes. As a result of the recent Supreme Court decision in *United States v. Windsor* [133 S.Ct. 2675 (USSC, 2013)], the IRS recognizes marriages validly entered into in a state whose laws authorize the marriage of two individuals of the same sex even if the married couple is domiciled in a state that does not recognize the validity of same-sex marriages. As a result, when a same-sex spouse is provided coverage under a spouse's employee health insurance, the premiums may be excluded from the employee's gross income.

Source: Rev.Rul. 2013–17, 2013–38 I.R.B. 201.

limited to one-twelfth of $6,550 under a high-deductible plan. Withdrawals from the HSA must be used to reimburse the employee for the medical expenses paid by the employee that are not covered under the high-deductible plan. The employee is not taxed on the employer's contributions to the HSA, the earnings on the funds in the account, or the withdrawals made for medical expenses.[31]

5-6b Long-Term Care Insurance Benefits

Generally, **long-term care insurance**, which covers expenses such as the cost of care in a nursing home, is treated the same as accident and health insurance benefits. Thus, the employee does not recognize income when the employer pays the premiums. Also, the individual who purchases his or her own policy can exclude the benefits from gross income. However, statutory limitations (indexed for inflation) exist for the following amounts:

* Premiums paid by the employer.
* Benefits collected under the employer's plan.
* Benefits collected from the individual's policy.

The employer or insurance company generally provides the employee with information on the amount of his or her taxable benefits.

The maximum amount excluded must be reduced by any amount received from third parties (e.g., Medicare, Medicaid).[32]

Example 17

Hazel, who suffers from Alzheimer's disease, is a patient in a nursing home for the last 30 days of 2014. While in the nursing home, she incurs total costs of $7,600. Medicare pays $3,200 of the costs. Hazel receives $7,000 from her long-term care insurance policy, which pays while she is in the facility.

The amount Hazel may exclude is calculated as follows:

Greater of:		
Daily statutory amount in 2014 ($330 × 30 days)	$9,900	
Actual cost of the care	7,600	$ 9,900
Less: Amount received from Medicare		(3,200)
Amount of exclusion		$ 6,700

Therefore, Hazel must include $300 ($7,000 − $6,700) of the long-term care benefits received in her gross income.

The exclusion for long-term care insurance is not available if it is provided as part of a cafeteria plan or a flexible spending plan (explained later in the chapter).

---

[31]§§ 106(d), 223(b), and 223(d). The amounts for 2012 were $3,250 and $6,450.

[32]§§ 7702B and § 213(d)(10). See IRS Publication 525 for the taxable and nontaxable amounts that the employer is required to report on the employee's W–2.

5-7 MEALS AND LODGING

5-7a General Rules for the Exclusion

As discussed in Chapter 4, income can take any form, including meals and lodging. However, § 119 excludes from income the value of meals and lodging provided to the employee and the employee's spouse and dependents under the following conditions:[33]

- The meals and/or lodging are *furnished* by the employer on the employer's *business premises* for the *convenience of the employer*.
- In the case of lodging, the *employee is required* to accept the lodging as a condition of employment.

The courts have interpreted both of these requirements strictly.

Furnished by the Employer

The following two questions have been raised with regard to the *furnished by the employer* requirement:

- Who is considered an *employee?*
- What is meant by *furnished?*

The IRS and some courts have reasoned that because a partner is not an employee, the exclusion does not apply to a partner. However, the Tax Court and the Fifth Circuit Court of Appeals have ruled in favor of the taxpayer on this issue.[34]

The Supreme Court held that a cash meal allowance was ineligible for the exclusion because the employer did not actually furnish the meals.[35] Similarly, one court denied the exclusion where the employer paid for the food and supplied the cooking facilities but the employee prepared the meal.[36]

On the Employer's Business Premises

The *on the employer's business premises* requirement, applicable to both meals and lodging, has resulted in much litigation. The Regulations define business premises as simply "the place of employment of the employee."[37] Thus, the Sixth Circuit Court of Appeals held that a residence, owned by the employer and occupied by an employee, two blocks from the motel that the employee managed was not part of the business premises.[38] However, the Tax Court considered an employer-owned house across the street from the hotel that was managed by the taxpayer to be on the business premises of the employer.[39] Apparently, the closer the lodging is to the business operations, the more likely the convenience of the employer is served.

For the Convenience of the Employer

The *convenience of the employer* test is intended to focus on the employer's motivation for furnishing the meals and lodging rather than on the benefits received by the employee. If the employer furnishes the meals and lodging primarily to enable the employee to perform his or her duties properly, it does not matter that the employee considers these benefits to be a part of his or her compensation.

[33] § 119(a). The meals and lodging are also excluded from FICA and FUTA tax. *Rowan Companies, Inc. v. U.S.*, 81–1 USTC ¶9479, 48 AFTR 2d 81–5115, 101 S.Ct. 2288 (USSC, 1981).

[34] Rev.Rul. 80, 1953–1 C.B. 62; *Comm. v. Doak*, 56–2 USTC ¶9708, 49 AFTR 1491, 234 F.2d 704 (CA–4, 1956); but see *G. A. Papineau*, 16 T.C. 130 (1951); *Armstrong v. Phinney*, 68–1 USTC ¶9355, 21 AFTR 2d 1260, 394 F.2d 661 (CA–5, 1968).

[35] *Comm. v. Kowalski*, 77–2 USTC ¶9748, 40 AFTR 2d 6128, 98 S.Ct. 315 (USSC, 1977).

[36] *Tougher v. Comm.*, 71–1 USTC ¶9398, 27 AFTR 2d 1301, 441 F.2d 1148 (CA–9, 1971).

[37] Reg. § 1.119–1(c)(1).

[38] *Comm. v. Anderson*, 67–1 USTC ¶9136, 19 AFTR 2d 318, 371 F.2d 59 (CA–6, 1966).

[39] *J. B. Lindeman*, 60 T.C. 609 (1973).

The Regulations give the following examples in which the tests for excluding meals are satisfied:[40]

- A restaurant requires its service staff to eat their meals on the premises during the busy lunch and breakfast hours.
- A bank furnishes meals on the premises for its tellers to limit the time the employees are away from their booths during the busy hours.
- A worker is employed at a construction site in a remote part of Alaska. The employer must furnish meals and lodging due to the inaccessibility of other facilities.

Required as a Condition of Employment

The *employee is required to accept* test applies only to lodging. If the employee's use of the housing would serve the convenience of the employer but the employee is not required to use the housing, the exclusion is not available.

Example 18

Khalid is the manager of a large apartment complex. The employer requires Khalid to live on the premises but does not charge him rent. The rental value of his apartment is $9,600 a year. Although Khalid considers the rent-free housing a significant benefit, he is not required to include the value of the housing in his gross income.

5-7b Other Housing Exclusions

An employee of an educational institution may be able to exclude the value of campus housing provided by the employer. Generally, the employee does not recognize income if he or she pays annual rents equal to or greater than 5 percent of the appraised value of the facility. If the rent payments are less than 5 percent of the value of the facility, the deficiency must be included in gross income.[41]

Ministers of the gospel and other religious leaders can exclude (1) the rental value of a home furnished as compensation; (2) a rental allowance paid to them as compensation, to the extent the allowance is used to rent, buy, or provide a home; or (3) the rental value of a home owned by the minister.[42] The housing or housing allowance must be provided as compensation for the conduct of religious worship, the administration and maintenance of religious organizations, or the performance of teaching and administrative duties at theological seminaries.

Military personnel are allowed housing exclusions under various circumstances. Authority for these exclusions generally is found in Federal laws that are not part of the Internal Revenue Code.[43]

5-8 EMPLOYEE FRINGE BENEFITS

Benefits other than wages and salary that are provided to employees by the employer are often referred to as **fringe benefits**. Generally, Congress decided that

---

[40]Reg. § 1.119–1(f).

[41]§ 119(d).

[42]§ 107 and Reg. § 1.107–1.

[43]H. Rep. No. 99–841, 99th Cong., 2d Sess., p. 548 (1986). See § 134 and *Armed Forces Tax Guide* (IRS Publication 3).

the availability of these benefits serve social goals. Moreover, the income tax exclusion will provide an incentive for employees to bargain for these fringe benefits in lieu of cash, thus increasing the use of this form of compensation. For example, if the employee is in the 25 percent marginal tax bracket, $1.00 of nontaxable fringe benefits is equivalent to $1.33 ($1.00/(1 − .25) = $1.33) in taxable compensation. From the employer's perspective then, it costs only $1.00 to provide $1.33 in value to that employee in the form of a tax-favored fringe benefit.

In Chapter 4 and earlier in this chapter, various fringe benefits were discussed (e.g., group term life insurance, accident and health insurance, and meals and lodging). Other employee benefits are discussed below.

5-8a Specific Benefits

Congress has dealt specifically with some other fringe benefits, which are summarized below.

- The employee does not have to include in gross income the value of child and dependent care services paid for by the employer and incurred to enable the employee to work. The exclusion cannot exceed $5,000 per year ($2,500 if married and filing separately). For a married couple, the annual exclusion cannot exceed the earned income of the spouse who has the lesser amount of earned income. For an unmarried taxpayer, the exclusion cannot exceed the taxpayer's earned income.[44]

- The value of the use of a gymnasium or other athletic facilities by employees, their spouses, and their dependent children may be excluded from an employee's gross income. The facilities must be on the employer's premises, and substantially all of the use of the facilities must be by employees and their family members.[45]

- Qualified employer-provided educational assistance (tuition, fees, books, and supplies) at the undergraduate and graduate level is excludible from gross income. The exclusion does not cover meals, lodging, and transportation costs. In addition, it does not cover educational payments for courses involving sports, games, or hobbies. The exclusion is subject to an annual employee statutory ceiling of $5,250.[46]

- The employee can exclude from gross income up to $13,190 of expenses incurred to adopt a child where the adoption expenses are paid or reimbursed by the employer under a qualified adoption assistance program.[47] The limit on the exclusion is the same even if the child has special needs (is not physically or mentally capable of caring for himself or herself). However, for a child with special needs, the $13,190 exclusion from gross income applies even if the actual adoption expenses are less than that amount. The exclusion is phased out as adjusted gross income increases from $197,880 to $237,880.

5-8b Cafeteria Plans

Generally, if an employee is offered a choice between cash and some other form of compensation, the employee is deemed to have constructively received the cash even when the noncash option is elected. Thus, the employee has gross income regardless of the option chosen.

An exception to this constructive receipt treatment is provided under the **cafeteria plan** rules. Under such a plan, the employee is permitted to choose between cash and nontaxable benefits (e.g., group term life insurance, health and accident protection, child care). If the employee chooses the otherwise nontaxable benefits, the cafeteria plan rules enable the benefits to remain nontaxable.[48] Cafeteria plans provide tremendous flexibility in tailoring the employee pay package to

---

[44]§ 129. The exclusion applies to the same types of expenses that, if paid by the employee (and not reimbursed by the employer), would be eligible for the credit for child and dependent care expense discussed in Chapter 13.

[45]§ 132(j)(4).

[46]§ 127.

[47]§ 137. A credit is also available under § 23, as discussed in Chapter 13.

[48]§ 125.

fit individual needs. Some employees (usually the younger group) prefer cash, while others (usually the older group) will opt for the fringe benefit program.

Example 19

Hawk Corporation offers its employees (on a nondiscriminatory basis) a choice of any one or all of the following benefits:

Benefit	Cost
Group term life insurance	$ 200
Hospitalization insurance for family members	2,400
Child care payments	1,800
	$4,400

If a benefit is not selected, the employee receives cash equal to the cost of the benefit. Kay, an employee, has a spouse who works for another employer that provides hospitalization insurance but no child care payments. Kay elects to receive the group term life insurance, the child care payments, and $2,400 of cash. Only the $2,400 must be included in Kay's gross income.

5-8c Flexible Spending Plans

Flexible spending plans (often referred to as flexible benefit plans) operate much like cafeteria plans. Under these plans, the employee accepts lower cash compensation (as much as $2,500) in return for the employer agreeing to pay certain costs that the employer can pay without the employee recognizing gross income. For example, assume that the employer's health insurance policy does not cover dental expenses. The employee could estimate his or her dental expenses for the upcoming year and agree to a salary reduction equal to the estimated dental expenses. The employer then pays or reimburses the employee for the actual dental expenses incurred, with a ceiling of the amount of the salary reduction. If the employee's actual dental expenses are less than the reduction in cash compensation, the employee cannot recover the difference. Hence, these plans are often referred to as *use or lose* plans. To avoid forfeiture of unpaid amounts, the IRS allows a payment until March 15 of the following year to count. As is the case for cafeteria plans, flexible spending plans cannot be used to pay long-term care insurance premiums.

5-8d General Classes of Excluded Benefits

An employer can confer numerous forms and types of economic benefits on employees. Under the all-inclusive concept of income, the benefits are taxable unless one of the provisions previously discussed specifically excludes the item from gross income. The amount of the income is the fair market value of the benefit.

Example 20

Ryan is employed in New York as a ticket clerk for Trans National Airlines. He has a sick mother in Miami, Florida, but has no money for plane tickets. Trans National has daily flights from New York to Miami that often leave with empty seats. The cost of a round-trip ticket is $400. If Trans National allows Ryan to fly without charge to Miami, under the general gross income rules, Ryan has income equal to the value of a ticket. Therefore, Ryan must include $400 in gross income on a trip to Miami.

Because Congress believed that taxing fringe benefits often yielded harsh results, Code § 132 was enacted to provide exclusion treatment. This provision established seven broad classes of nontaxable employee benefits:[49]

- No-additional-cost services.
- Qualified employee discounts.
- Working condition fringes.

---

[49]See, generally, § 132.

TAX IN THE NEWS   Patient Protection and Affordable Care Act of 2010 to Affect Flexible Spending Plans

Determining all of the tax ramifications of the 2010 health care law will take time. But already it is clear that companies will be modifying their flexible spending plans as a result of the legislation. Beginning in 2013, the annual income exclusion under flexible benefit plans are limited to $2,500. Also, with respect to medicines, only prescription drugs and insulin are eligible for reimbursement.

———————

Source: Internal Revenue Code §§ 125(i) and 106(f).

- *De minimis* fringes.
- Qualified transportation fringes.
- Qualified moving expense reimbursements.
- Qualified retirement planning services.

The value of the services that the employer provides its employees are nontaxable under certain circumstances.

No-Additional-Cost Services

Return to Example 20 above. This illustrates the reason for the **no-additional-cost service** type of fringe benefit. The services will be nontaxable if all of the following conditions are satisfied:

- The employee receives services, as opposed to property.
- The employer does not incur substantial additional cost, including forgone revenue, in providing the services to the employee.
- The services are offered to customers in the ordinary course of the business in which the employee works.[50]

Example 21

In Example 20, although the airplane may burn slightly more fuel because Ryan is on board and he may receive the same snacks and meals as paying customers, the additional costs to the airline would not be substantial. Thus, the trip could qualify as a no-additional-cost service, and the value of Ryan's flight can be excluded from his gross income.

The no-additional-cost exclusion extends to the employee's spouse and dependent children and to retired and disabled former employees.[51] However, the exclusion is not allowed to highly compensated employees unless the benefit is available on a nondiscriminatory basis.

Qualified Employee Discounts

When the employer sells goods or services (other than no-additional-cost benefits just discussed) to the employee for a price that is less than the price charged regular customers, the employee realizes income equal to the discount. However, the discount, referred to as a **qualified employee discount**, can be excluded from the gross income of the employee, subject to the following conditions and limitations:

- The exclusion is not available for real property (e.g., a house) or for personal property of the type commonly held for investment (e.g., common stocks).
- The property or services must be from the same line of business in which the employee works.
- In the case of *property*, the exclusion is limited to the *gross profit component* of the price to customers.
- In the case of *services*, the exclusion is limited to 20 percent of the customer price.

---

[50]Reg. § 1.132–2.

[51]Reg. § 1.132–1(b).

Example 22

Silver Corporation, which operates a department store, sells a television set to a store employee for $300. The regular customer price is $500, and the gross profit rate is 25%. The corporation also sells the employee a service contract for $120. The regular customer price for the contract is $150. The employee must include $75 in gross income.

Customer price for property	$ 500
Less: Gross profit (25%)	(125)
	$ 375
Employee price	(300)
Income	$ 75
Customer price for service	$ 150
Less: 20 percent	(30)
	$ 120
Employee price	(120)
Income	$ –0–

As in the case of no-additional-cost benefits, the exclusion applies to employees (including service partners), employees' spouses and dependent children, and retired and disabled former employees.

Working Condition Fringes

Generally, an employee is not required to include in gross income the cost of property or services provided by the employer if the employee could deduct the cost of those items if he or she had actually paid for them. These benefits are called **working condition fringes**.

Example 23

Mitch is a CPA employed by an accounting firm. The employer pays Mitch's annual dues to professional organizations. Mitch is not required to include the payment of the dues in gross income because if he had paid the dues, he would have been allowed to deduct the amount as an employee business expense (as discussed in Chapter 9).[52]

Unlike the other fringe benefits discussed previously, working condition fringes can be made available on a discriminatory basis and still qualify for the exclusion.

De Minimis Fringes

As the term suggests, *de minimis* **fringe** benefits are so small that accounting for them is impractical. The House Report contains the following examples of *de minimis* fringes:

- The typing of a personal letter by a company secretary, occasional personal use of a company copying machine, occasional company cocktail parties or picnics for employees, occasional supper money or taxi fare for employees because of overtime work, and certain holiday gifts of property with a low fair market value are excluded.
- Subsidized eating facilities (e.g., an employees' cafeteria) operated by the employer are excluded if located on or near the employer's business premises, if revenue equals or exceeds direct operating costs, and if nondiscrimination requirements are met.

When taxpayers venture beyond the specific examples contained in the House Report and the Regulations, there is obviously much room for disagreement as to what is *de minimis*.

In Notice 2011–72, the IRS addressed the question of whether cell phones provided by the employer could be excluded from gross income as a working condition fringe benefit. Generally, the value of the cell phone can be excluded if it is

---

[52]In many cases, this exclusion merely avoids reporting income and an off-setting deduction.

provided for business reasons such as to enable the employee to be in contact with clients when the employee is away from the office. When the primary purpose test is satisfied, any personal use of the employer-provided cell phone will be excluded as a *de minimis* fringe benefit.

Qualified Transportation Fringes

The intent of the exclusion for **qualified transportation fringes** is to encourage the use of mass transit for commuting to and from work. Qualified transportation fringes encompass the following transportation benefits provided by the employer to the employee:

1. Transportation in a commuter highway vehicle between the employee's residence and the place of employment.
2. A transit pass.
3. Qualified parking.
4. Qualified bicycle commuting reimbursement.

Statutory dollar limits are placed on the amount of the exclusion. Categories (1) and (2) above are combined for purposes of applying the limit. In this case, the limit on the exclusion for 2013 was $145 and for 2014 is $130. Category (3) has a separate limit. For qualified parking, the limit on the exclusion for 2014 is $250 per month ($245 in 2013). Both of these dollar limits are indexed annually for inflation.

A *commuter highway vehicle* is any highway vehicle with a seating capacity of at least six adults (excluding the driver). In addition, at least 80 percent of the vehicle's use must be for transporting employees between their residences and place of employment.

Qualified parking includes the following:

- Parking provided to an employee on or near the employer's business premises.
- Parking provided to an employee on or near a location from which the employee commutes to work via mass transit, in a commuter highway vehicle, or in a carpool.

The *qualified bicycle commuting reimbursement* enables an employee to exclude up to $20 per month received from an employer as reimbursement for the cost of commuting by bicycle (i.e., bicycle purchase, improvement, repair, and storage).

Qualified transportation fringes may be provided directly by the employer or may be in the form of cash reimbursements.

| **Example 24** | Gray Corporation's offices are located in the center of a large city. The company pays for parking spaces to be used by the company officers. Steve, a vice president, receives $300 of such benefits each month. The parking space rental qualifies as a qualified transportation fringe. Of the $300 benefit received each month by Steve, $250 is excludible from gross income. The balance of $50 is included in his gross income. The same result would occur if Steve paid for the parking and was reimbursed by his employer. |

Qualified Moving Expense Reimbursements

Qualified moving expenses that are reimbursed or paid by the employer are excludible from gross income. A qualified moving expense is an expense that would be deductible under § 217. See the discussion of moving expenses in Chapter 9.

Qualified Retirement Planning Services

Qualified retirement planning services include any retirement planning advice or information that an employer who maintains a qualified retirement plan provides to an employee or the employee's spouse. Congress decided to exclude the value of such services from gross income because they are a key part of retirement income planning. Such an exclusion should motivate more employers to provide retirement planning services to their employees.

Nondiscrimination Provisions

For no-additional-cost services, qualified employee discounts, and qualified retirement planning services that are discriminatory in favor of highly compensated employees, exclusion treatment is denied. However, for the discriminatory plans, the exclusion treatment for non-highly compensated employees remains.[53]

Example 25

Dove Company's officers are allowed to purchase goods from the company at a 25% discount. All other employees are allowed only a 15% discount. The company's gross profit margin on these goods is 30%. Because the officers receive more favorable discounts, the plan is discriminatory in favor of the officers. In regard to all other employees, the discount is "qualified" because it is available to all employees (other than the officers who receive a more favorable discount) and the discount is less than the company's gross profit.

Peggy, an officer in the company, purchased goods from the company for $750 when the price charged to customers was $1,000. Peggy must include $250 in gross income because the plan is discriminatory.

Mason, an employee of the company who is not an officer, purchased goods for $850 when the customer price was $1,000. Mason is not required to recognize gross income because he received a qualified employee discount.

De minimis (except in the case of subsidized eating facilities) and working condition fringe benefits can be provided on a discriminatory basis. The *de minimis* benefits are not subject to tax because the accounting problems that would be created are out of proportion to the amount of additional tax that would result. A nondiscrimination test would simply add to the compliance problems. In the case of working condition fringes, the types of services required vary with the job. Therefore, a nondiscrimination test probably could not be satisfied, although usually there is no deliberate plan to benefit a chosen few. Likewise, the qualified transportation fringe and the qualified moving expense reimbursement can be provided on a discriminatory basis.

A review of employee fringe benefits is set forth in Concept Summary 5.2.

5-9 FOREIGN EARNED INCOME

The United States uses a global tax system as opposed to a territorial system. Under this global system, a U.S. citizen is generally subject to tax on his or her income regardless of its economic origin. Some other countries use a territorial system; that is, a person's income is taxed only in the country in which the income was earned. Under this global system, a U.S. citizen who earns income in another country could experience double taxation: the same income would be taxed in the United States and in the foreign country. Out of a sense of fairness and to encourage U.S. citizens to work abroad (so that exports might be increased), Congress has provided alternative forms of relief from taxes on foreign earned income. The taxpayer can elect *either* (1) to include the foreign income in his or her taxable income and then claim a credit for foreign taxes paid or (2) to exclude the foreign earnings from his or her U.S. gross income (the **foreign earned income exclusion**).[54] The foreign tax credit option is discussed in Chapter 13, but as is apparent from the following discussion, most taxpayers will choose the exclusion.

Foreign earned income consists of the earnings from the individual's personal services rendered in a foreign country (other than as an employee of the U.S. government). To qualify for the exclusion, the taxpayer must be either of the following:

- A bona fide resident of the foreign country (or countries).
- Present in a foreign country (or countries) for at least 330 days during any 12 consecutive months.[55]

---

[53]§§ 132(j)(1) and 132(m)(2).
[54]§ 911(a). The exclusion for 2014 is limited to $99,200.

[55]§ 911(d). For the definition of *resident*, see Reg. § 1.871–2(b). Under the Regulations, a taxpayer is not a resident if he or she is there for a definite period (e.g., until completion of a construction contract).

CONCEPT SUMMARY 5.2

Employee Fringe Benefits

Type of Benefit	Exclusion
Group term life insurance (§ 74)	Premiums on up to $50,000 protection
Employee achievement awards (§ 74)	Up to $1,600 in a year
Accident, health, and long-term care insurance and medical reimbursement (§§ 105 and 106)	Insurance premiums paid by the employer and benefits collected
High-deductible health insurance and contributions to employee's Health Savings Account (§§ 106 and 223)	Employer premiums on high-deductible medical insurance plus contributions to Health Savings Account (statutory limits, indexed for inflation).
Meals and lodging furnished for the convenience of the employer (§ 119)	Value of meals and lodging on the employer's premises
Child care provided by the employer or reimbursement for employee's cost (§ 129)	Services provided or reimbursement of expenses up to $5,000 a year
Athletic facilities on the employer's premises (§ 132)	Value of services
Educational assistance for tuition, fees, books, and supplies (§ 127)	Limited to $5,250 per year
No-additional-cost services [e.g., use of employer's facilities (§ 132)]	Value of the use
Employee discount on purchase of goods from employer at employer's cost (§ 132)	Employer's normal profit margin
Employee discount for purchases of employer's services (§ 132)	Maximum of 20% of employer's normal price
Working condition fringes [e.g., the mechanic's tools (§ 132)]	Employer's cost
De minimis items so small that the accounting effort is not warranted [e.g., use of employer telephone (§ 132)]	Value of the goods or services
Qualified transportation [e.g, transit passes and parking (§ 132)]	Statutory amounts, adjusted for inflation
Moving expense reimbursement (§ 132)	Reimbursement to the extent otherwise deductible by employee
Retirement planning services (§ 132)	Reasonable cost of services

Example 26

Sandra's trip to and from a foreign country in connection with her work were as follows:

Arrived in Foreign Country	Returned to United States
March 10, 2013	February 15, 2014

During the 12 consecutive months ending on March 10, 2014, Sandra was present in the foreign country for at least 330 days (365 days less 13 days in February and 10 days in March 2014). Therefore, all income earned in the foreign country through March 10, 2014, is eligible for the exclusion.

Example 27

Keith qualifies for the foreign earned income exclusion. He was present in France for all of 2014. Keith's salary for 2014 is $100,000. Because all of the days in 2014 are qualifying days, Keith can exclude $99,200 of his $100,000 salary.

Assume instead that only 335 days were qualifying days. Then Keith's exclusion is limited to $91,047, computed as follows:

$$\$99,200 \times \frac{335 \text{ days in foreign country}}{365 \text{ days in the year}} = \$91,047$$

U.S. Taxpayers Abroad Are Gone but Not Forgotten

U.S. citizens and residents working and living abroad create unique compliance issues for the IRS. These individuals are potentially liable for U.S. taxes and must file U.S. tax returns, even if they earn less than the § 911 foreign earned income exclusion amount. However, in practical terms, many of these individuals are outside the enforcement net of the IRS. In recent years, the IRS has taken several steps to improve compliance, including taxpayer education, simplification of the filing burden, and increased enforcement efforts.

Global Tax Issues

© iStockphoto.com/Andrey Prokhorov

Example 28

In 2014, Carol, who is not married, had taxable income of $30,000 after excluding $99,200 of foreign earned income. Without the benefit of the exclusion, Carol's taxable income would have been $129,200 ($30,000 + $99,200). The tax on the taxable income of $30,000 is calculated using the marginal rate applicable to income between $99,200 and $129,200, which is 28%. Therefore, Carol's tax liability is $8,400 (.28 × $30,000).

As previously mentioned, the taxpayer may elect to include the foreign earned income in gross income and claim a credit (an offset against U.S. tax) for the foreign tax paid. The credit alternative may be advantageous if the individual's foreign earned income far exceeds the excludible amount so that the foreign taxes paid exceed the U.S. tax on the amount excluded. However, once an election is made, it applies to all subsequent years unless affirmatively revoked. A revocation is effective for the year of the change and the four subsequent years.

The foreign earned income is not excluded in computing modified adjusted gross income (e.g., $250,000 for married filing a joint return, see Chapter 13) for purposes of the net investment income tax.

5-10 INTEREST ON CERTAIN STATE AND LOCAL GOVERNMENT OBLIGATIONS

At the time the Sixteenth Amendment was ratified by the states, there was some question as to whether the Federal government possessed the constitutional authority to tax interest on state and local government obligations. Taxing such interest was thought to violate the doctrine of intergovernmental immunity in that the tax would impair the state and local governments' ability to finance their operations.[56] Thus, interest on state and local government obligations was specifically exempted from Federal income taxation.[57] However, the Supreme Court has concluded that there is no constitutional prohibition against levying a nondiscriminatory Federal income tax on state and local government obligations.[58] Nevertheless, currently, the statutory exclusion still exists.

Obviously, the exclusion of the interest reduces the cost of borrowing for state and local governments. A taxpayer in the 35 percent tax bracket requires only a 5.2 percent yield on a tax-exempt bond to obtain the same after-tax income as a taxable bond paying 8 percent interest [5.2% ÷ (1 − .35) = 8%].

The current exempt status applies solely to state and local government bonds. Thus, income received from the accrual of interest on a condemnation award or an overpayment of state income tax is fully taxable.[59] Nor does the exemption apply to gains on the sale of tax-exempt securities.

---

[56]*Pollock v. Farmer's Loan & Trust Co.,* 3 AFTR 2602, 15 S.Ct. 912 (USSC, 1895).

[57]§ 103(a).

[58]*South Carolina v. Baker III,* 88–1 USTC ¶9284, 61 AFTR 2d 88–995, 108 S.Ct. 1355 (USSC, 1988).

[59]*Kieselbach v. Comm.,* 43–1 USTC ¶9220, 30 AFTR 370, 63 S.Ct. 303 (USSC, 1943); *U.S. Trust Co. of New York v. Anderson,* 3 USTC ¶1125, 12 AFTR 836, 65 F.2d 575 (CA–2, 1933).

Example 29	Megan purchases State of Virginia bonds for $10,000 on July 1, 2013. The bonds pay $400 interest each June 30 and December 31. On March 31, 2014, Megan sells the bonds for $10,500 plus $200 accrued interest. Megan must recognize a $500 gain ($10,500 − $10,000), but the $200 accrued interest is exempt from taxation.

Although the Internal Revenue Code excludes from Federal gross income the interest on state and local government bonds, the interest on U.S. government bonds is not excluded from the Federal tax base. Congress has decided, however, that if the Federal government is not to tax state and local bond interest, the state and local governments are prohibited from taxing interest on U.S. government bonds.[60] While this parity between the Federal and state and local governments exists in regard to taxing each other's obligations, the states are free to tax one another's obligations. Thus, some states exempt the interest on the bonds they issue, but tax the interest on bonds issued by other states.[61]

5-11 DIVIDENDS

5-11a General Information

A *dividend* is a payment to a shareholder with respect to his or her stock (see Chapter 4). Dividends to shareholders are taxable only to the extent the payments are made from *either* the corporation's *current earnings and profits* (similar to net income per books) or its *accumulated earnings and profits* (similar to retained earnings per books).[62] Distributions that exceed earnings and profits are treated as a nontaxable recovery of capital and reduce the shareholder's basis in the stock. Once the shareholder's basis is reduced to zero, any subsequent distributions are taxed as capital gains (see Chapters 14 and 20).[63]

Some payments are frequently referred to as dividends but are not considered dividends for tax purposes:

- Dividends received on deposits with savings and loan associations, credit unions, and banks are actually interest (a contractual rate paid for the use of money).
- Patronage dividends paid by cooperatives (e.g., for farmers) are rebates made to the users and are considered reductions in the cost of items purchased from the association. The rebates are usually made after year-end (after the cooperative has determined whether it has met its expenses) and are apportioned among members on the basis of their purchases.
- Mutual insurance companies pay dividends on unmatured life insurance policies that are considered rebates of premiums.
- Shareholders in a mutual investment fund are allowed to report as capital gains their proportionate share of the fund's gains realized and distributed. The capital gain and ordinary income portions are reported on the Form 1099 that the fund supplies its shareholders each year.

5-11b Stock Dividends

When a corporation issues a simple stock dividend (e.g., common stock issued to common shareholders), the shareholder has merely received additional shares that represent the same total investment. Thus, the shareholder does not realize income.[64] However, if the shareholder has the *option* of receiving either cash or

[60]31 U.S.C.A. § 742.
[61]The practice of a state exempting interest on its bonds from tax but taxing the interest on bonds issued by other states has been upheld by the Supreme Court. See *Department of Revenue of Kentucky v. Davis*, 128 S.Ct. 1801 (USSC, 2008).
[62]§ 316(a). Refer to the discussion of the beneficial tax rates for qualified dividends in Chapter 4.
[63]§ 301(c). See Chapter 5, *South-Western Federal Taxation: Corporations, Partnerships, Estates, & Trusts*, for a detailed discussion of corporate distributions.
[64]*Eisner v. Macomber*, 1 USTC ¶32, 3 AFTR 3020, 40 S.Ct. 189 (USSC, 1920); § 305(a).

stock in the corporation, the individual realizes gross income whether he or she receives stock or cash.[65] A taxpayer who elects to receive the stock could be deemed to be in constructive receipt of the cash he or she has rejected.[66] However, the amount of the income in this case is the value of the stock received, rather than the cash the shareholder has rejected. See Chapter 14 for a detailed discussion of stock dividends.

5-12 EDUCATIONAL SAVINGS BONDS

The cost of a college education has risen dramatically during the past 15 years. According to U.S. Department of Education estimates, the cost of attending a publicly supported university for four years now commonly exceeds $60,000. For a private university, the cost often exceeds $200,000. Consequently, Congress has attempted to assist low- to middle-income parents in saving for their children's college education.

One of the ways Congress assists such families is through an interest income exclusion on **educational savings bonds**.[67] The interest on Series EE U.S. government savings bonds may be excluded from gross income if the bond proceeds are used to pay qualified higher education expenses. The exclusion applies only if both of the following requirements are satisfied:

* The savings bonds are issued after December 31, 1989.
* The savings bonds are issued to an individual who is at least 24 years old at the time of issuance.

The exclusion is not available for a married couple who file separate returns.

The redemption proceeds must be used to pay qualified higher education expenses. *Qualified higher education expenses* consist of tuition and fees paid to an eligible educational institution for the taxpayer, spouse, or dependent. In calculating qualified higher education expenses, the tuition and fees paid are reduced by excludible scholarships and veterans' benefits received. If the redemption proceeds (both principal and interest) exceed the qualified higher education expenses, only a pro rata portion of the interest will qualify for exclusion treatment.

Example 30

Tracy's redemption proceeds from qualified savings bonds during the taxable year are $6,000 (principal of $4,000 and interest of $2,000). Tracy's qualified higher education expenses are $5,000. Because the redemption proceeds exceed the qualified higher education expenses, only $1,667 [($5,000/$6,000) × $2,000] of the interest is excludible.

The exclusion is limited by the application of the wherewithal to pay concept. That is, once the modified adjusted gross income exceeds a threshold amount, the phaseout of the exclusion begins. *Modified adjusted gross income (MAGI)* is adjusted gross income prior to the § 911 foreign earned income exclusion and the educational savings bond exclusion. The threshold amounts are adjusted for inflation each year. For 2014, the phaseout begins at $76,000 ($113,950 on a joint return).[68] The phaseout is completed when MAGI exceeds the threshold amount by more than $15,000 ($30,000 on a joint return). The otherwise excludible interest is reduced by the amount calculated as follows:

$$\frac{\text{MAGI} - \$76,000}{\$15,000} \times \begin{array}{c}\text{Excludible interest}\\ \text{before phaseout}\end{array} = \begin{array}{c}\text{Reduction in}\\ \text{excludible interest}\end{array}$$

On a joint return, $113,950 is substituted for $76,000 (in 2014), and $30,000 is substituted for $15,000.

---

[65]§ 305(b).
[66]Refer to the discussion of constructive receipt in Chapter 4.

[67]§ 135.
[68]The indexed amounts for 2013 were $74,700 and $112,050.

Example 31   Assume the same facts as in Example 30, except that Tracy's MAGI for 2014 is $80,000. The phaseout results in Tracy's interest exclusion being reduced by $445 {[($80,000 − $76,000)/$15,000] × $1,667}. Therefore, Tracy's exclusion is $1,222 ($1,667 − $445).

5-13 QUALIFIED TUITION PROGRAMS (§ 529 PLANS)

Nearly all, if not all, states have created programs whereby parents can in effect prepay their child's college tuition. The prepayment serves as a hedge against future increases in tuition. Generally, if the child does not attend college, the parents are refunded their payments plus interest. Upon first impression, these prepaid tuition programs resemble the below-market loans discussed in Chapter 4. That is, assuming that the tuition increases, the parent receives a reduction in the child's tuition in exchange for the use of the funds. However, Congress has created an exclusion provision for these programs.[69]

Under a **qualified tuition program (§ 529 plan)**, the amounts contributed must be used for qualified higher education expenses. These expenses include tuition, fees, books, supplies, room and board, and equipment required for enrollment or attendance at a college, a university, or certain vocational schools. The allowable expenses include computers and computer technology, including software that provides access to the Internet. Qualified higher education expenses also include the expenses for special needs services that are incurred in connection with the enrollment and attendance of special needs students.

The earnings of the contributed funds, including the discount on tuition charged to participants, are not included in Federal gross income provided the contributions and earnings are used for qualified higher education expenses. Some states also exclude these educational benefits from state gross income.

Example 32   Agnes paid $20,000 into a qualified tuition program to be used for her son's college tuition. When her son graduated from high school, the fund balance had increased to $30,000 as a result of interest credited to the account. The interest was not included in Agnes's gross income. During the current year, $7,500 of the balance in the fund was used to pay the son's tuition and fees. None of this amount is included in either Agnes's or the son's gross income.

If the parent receives a refund (e.g., child does not attend college), the excess of the amount refunded over the amount contributed by the parent is included in the parent's gross income.

Qualified tuition programs have been expanded to apply to private educational institutions as well as public educational institutions.

LO.3

Determine the extent to which receipts can be excluded under the tax benefit rule.

5-14 TAX BENEFIT RULE

Generally, if a taxpayer obtains a deduction for an item in one year and in a later year recovers all or a portion of the prior deduction, the recovery is included in gross income in the year received.[70]

Example 33   A taxpayer deducted as a loss a $1,000 receivable from a customer when it appeared the amount would never be collected. The following year, the customer paid $800 on the receivable. The taxpayer must report the $800 as gross income in the year it is received.

---

[69]§ 529. For another way to beneficially fund educational costs, see the discussion of Coverdell Education Savings Accounts (CESAs) in Chapter 19 (§ 530).

[70]§ 111(a).

However, the § 111 **tax benefit rule** provides that no income is recognized upon the recovery of a deduction, or the portion of a deduction, that did not yield a tax benefit in the year it was taken. If the taxpayer in Example 33 had no tax liability in the year of the deduction (e.g., itemized deductions and personal exemptions exceeded adjusted gross income), the recovery would be partially or totally excluded from gross income in the year of the recovery.[71]

Example 34

Ali filed his 2013 income tax return as a single individual. His AGI for 2013 was $48,000. He had $6,350 in itemized deductions, including $1,200 in state income tax. His personal exemption was $3,900. In 2014, he received a $700 refund of the state income taxes that he paid in 2013. Because the standard deduction in 2013 was $6,100, the $1,200 of state income taxes Ali paid in 2013 yielded a tax benefit of only $250 ($6,350 itemized deduction − $6,100 standard deduction) in 2013. Under the tax benefit rule, only $250 of the state income tax refund is included in gross income in 2014.

5-15 INCOME FROM DISCHARGE OF INDEBTEDNESS

A transfer of appreciated property (fair market value is greater than adjusted basis) in satisfaction of a debt is an event that triggers the realization of income. The transaction is treated as a sale of the appreciated property followed by payment of the debt.[72] Foreclosure by a creditor is also treated as a sale or exchange of the property.[73]

LO.4

Describe the circumstances under which income must be reported from the discharge of indebtedness.

Example 35

Juan owes State Bank $50,000 on a note secured by land. When Juan's basis in the land is $20,000 and the land's fair market value is $50,000, the bank forecloses on the loan and takes title to the land. Juan must recognize a $30,000 gain on the foreclosure.

In some cases, creditors will not exercise their right of foreclosure and will even forgive a portion of the debt to ensure the vitality of the debtor. In such cases, the debtor realizes income from discharge of indebtedness.

Example 36

Kayla is unable to meet the mortgage payments on her office building. Both Kayla and the mortgage holder are aware of the depressed market for real estate in the area. Foreclosure would only result in the creditor's obtaining unsalable property. The creditor agrees to forgive all amounts past due and to reduce the principal amount of the mortgage. Kayla must recognize income equal to the amount of the forgiven debt, unless one of the exceptions discussed below apply.

The following discharge of indebtedness situations are subject to special treatment:[74]

1. Creditors' gifts.
2. Discharges under Federal bankruptcy law.
3. Discharges that occur when the debtor is insolvent.
4. Discharge of the farm debt of a solvent taxpayer.
5. Discharge of **qualified real property business indebtedness**.
6. A seller's cancellation of the buyer's indebtedness.
7. A shareholder's cancellation of the corporation's indebtedness.
8. Forgiveness of certain loans to students.
9. Discharge of indebtedness on the taxpayer's principal residence that occurs between January 1, 2007, and January 1, 2014, and is the result of the financial condition of the debtor.

If the creditor reduces the debt as an act of *love, affection,* or *generosity,* the debtor has simply received a nontaxable gift (situation 1). Rarely will a gift be found to have occurred in a business context. A businessperson may settle a debt for less

---

[71]Itemized deductions are discussed in Chapter 10.
[72]Reg. § 1.1001–2(a).

[73]*Estate of Delman,* 73 T.C. 15 (1979).
[74]§§ 108 and 1017.

than the amount due, but as a matter of business expediency (e.g., high collection costs or disputes as to contract terms) rather than generosity.[75]

In situations 2, 3, 4, 5, and 9, the Code allows the debtor to reduce his or her basis in the assets by the realized gain from the discharge.[76] Thus, the realized gain is merely deferred until the assets are sold (or depreciated). Similarly, in situation 6 (a price reduction), the debtor reduces the basis in the specific assets financed by the seller.[77]

A shareholder's cancellation of the corporation's indebtedness to him or her (situation 7) usually is considered a tax-free contribution of capital to the corporation by the shareholder. Thus, the corporation's paid-in capital is increased, and its liabilities are decreased by the same amount.[78]

Many states make loans to students on the condition that the loan will be forgiven if the student practices a profession in the state upon completing his or her studies. The amount of the loan that is forgiven (situation 8) is excluded from gross income.[79]

5-16 TAX PLANNING

LO.5

Identify tax planning strategies for obtaining the maximum benefit from allowable exclusions.

The present law excludes certain types of economic gains from taxation. Therefore, taxpayers may find tax planning techniques helpful in obtaining the maximum benefits from the exclusion of such gains. Following are some of the tax planning opportunities made available by the exclusions described in this chapter.

5-16a Life Insurance

Life insurance offers several favorable tax attributes. As discussed in Chapter 4, the annual increase in the cash surrender value of the policy is not taxable (because no income has been actually or constructively received). By borrowing on the policy's cash surrender value, the owner can actually receive the policy's increase in value in cash without recognizing income.

5-16b Employee Fringe Benefits

Generally, employees view accident and health insurance, as well as life insurance, as necessities. Employees can obtain group coverage at much lower rates than individuals would have to pay for the same protection. Premiums paid by the employer can be excluded from the employees' gross income. Because of the exclusion, employees will have a greater after-tax and after-insurance income if the employer pays a lower salary but also pays the insurance premiums.

Example 37

Pat receives a salary of $30,000. The company has group insurance benefits, but Pat is required to pay his own premiums as follows:

Hospitalization and medical insurance	$1,400
Term life insurance ($30,000 coverage)	200
Disability insurance	400
	$2,000

To simplify the analysis, assume that Pat's tax rate on income is 25%. After paying taxes of $7,500 (.25 × $30,000) and $2,000 for insurance, Pat has $20,500 ($30,000 − $7,500 − $2,000) for his other living needs.

---

[75]*Comm. v. Jacobson*, 49–1 USTC ¶9133, 37 AFTR 516, 69 S.Ct. 358 (USSC, 1949).

[76]§§ 108(a), (c), (e), and (g). Note that § 108(b) provides that other tax attributes (e.g., net operating loss) will be reduced by the realized gain

from the debt discharge prior to the basis adjustment unless the taxpayer elects to apply the basis adjustment first.

[77]§ 108(e)(5).

[78]§ 108(e)(6).

[79]§ 108(f).

If Pat's employer reduced Pat's salary by $2,000 (to $28,000) but paid his insurance premiums, Pat's tax liability would be only $7,000 ($28,000 × .25). Thus, Pat would have $21,000 ($28,000 − $7,000) to meet his other living needs. The change in the compensation plan would save Pat $500 ($21,000 − $20,500), which is the marginal tax times the value of the insurance benefits, .25 × $2,000 = $500.

Similarly, employees must often incur expenses for child care and parking. The employee can have more income for other uses if the employer pays these costs for the employee but reduces the employee's salary by the cost of the benefits.

The use of cafeteria plans has increased dramatically in recent years. These plans allow employees to tailor their benefits to meet their individual situations. Thus, where both spouses in a married couple are working, duplications of benefits can be avoided and other needed benefits can often be added. If less than all of the employee's allowance is spent, the employee can receive cash.

The meals and lodging exclusion enables employees to receive from their employer what they ordinarily must purchase with after-tax dollars. Although the requirements that the employee live and take his or her meals on the employer's premises limit the tax planning opportunities, the exclusion is an important factor in the employee's compensation in certain situations (e.g., hotels, motels, restaurants, farms, and ranches).

The employees' discount provision is especially important for manufacturers and wholesalers. Employees of manufacturers can avoid tax on the manufacturer's, wholesaler's, and retailer's markups. The wholesaler's employees can avoid tax on an amount equal to the wholesale and retail markups.

It should be recognized that the exclusion of benefits is generally available only to employees. Proprietors and partners must pay tax on the same benefits their employees receive tax-free. By incorporating and becoming an employee of the corporation, the former proprietor or partner can also receive these tax-exempt benefits. Thus, the availability of employee benefits is a consideration in the decision to incorporate.

5-16c Investment Income

Tax-exempt state and local government bonds are almost irresistible investments for high-income taxpayers, who may be subject to a 39.6 percent regular tax rate plus a 3.8 percent rate on their net investment income. To realize the maximum benefit from the exemption, the investor can purchase zero-coupon bonds. Like Series EE U.S. government savings bonds, these investments pay interest only at maturity. The advantage of the zero-coupon feature for a tax-exempt bond is that the investor can earn tax-exempt interest on the accumulated principal and interest. If the investor purchases a bond that pays the interest each year, the interest received may be such a small amount that an additional tax-exempt investment cannot be made. In addition, reinvesting the interest may entail transaction costs (brokers' fees). The zero-coupon feature avoids these problems.

Series EE U.S. government savings bonds can earn tax-exempt interest if the bond proceeds are used for qualified higher education expenses. Many taxpayers can foresee these expenditures being made for their children's educations. In deciding whether to invest in the bonds, however, the investor must take into account the income limitations for excluding the interest from gross income.

REFOCUS ON THE BIG PICTURE

EXCLUSIONS

© Andrew Shurtleff/ZUMA Press/Corbis

You have looked into Paul's tax situation and have the following information for him:

- *Compensation.* The amount Paul was paid for his internship is compensation for services rendered and must be included in his gross income. This includes both his base pay and the $1,500 bonus (Example 1).
- *Graduate assistantship.* The tuition waiver of $6,000 is excluded from Paul's gross income. The related payments of $400 per month are intended as a form of compensation. So Paul must include the $400 per month in his gross income (Example 11).
- *Damages.* Damages awards that relate to personal physical injury or sickness can be excluded from gross income if the payments are for compensatory damages. So all of the compensatory damages of $220,000 can be excluded from gross income. The punitive damages of $160,000 must be included in Paul's gross income. Likewise, the compensatory damages of $25,000 received by Paul's mother must be included in her gross income because emotional distress does not qualify as personal physical injury or sickness (Example 12).

What If?

From a tax planning perspective, can Paul do anything to reduce the amount of the punitive damages settlement that he must include in his gross income?

As things now stand (i.e., a completed settlement), Paul cannot reduce the $160,000 punitive damages amount he must include in gross income. However, proper tax planning might have enabled Paul to reduce the amount includible in gross income. Note that both the amount of the damages and the labels attached to the damages are negotiated. If a larger portion of the settlement had been assigned to compensatory damages rather than punitive damages, Paul could have reduced the amount he must include in his gross income.

Key Terms

Accelerated death benefits, 5-6

Accident and health benefits, 5-11

Cafeteria plan, 5-16

Compensatory damages, 5-10

Death benefits, 5-4

De minimis fringe, 5-19

Educational savings bonds, 5-25

Flexible spending plans, 5-17

Foreign earned income exclusion, 5-21

Fringe benefits, 5-15

Health Savings Account (HSA), 5-12

Life insurance proceeds, 5-5

Long-term care insurance, 5-13

No-additional-cost service, 5-18

Punitive damages, 5-10

Qualified employee discount, 5-18

Qualified real property business indebtedness, 5-27

Qualified transportation fringes, 5-20

Qualified tuition program (§ 529 plan), 5-26

Scholarship, 5-7

Tax benefit rule, 5-27

Working condition fringes, 5-19

Discussion Questions

1. **LO.2** Fred specified in his will that his nephew John should serve as executor of Fred's estate. John received $10,000 for serving as executor. Can John exclude the $10,000 from his gross income? Explain.

2. **LO.2** Leonard's home was damaged by a fire. He also had to be absent from work for several days to make his home habitable. Leonard's employer paid Leonard his regular salary, $2,500, while he was absent from work. In Leonard's pay envelope was the following note from the employer: To help you in your time of need. Leonard's fellow

employees also took up a collection and gave him $900. Leonard spent over $4,000 repairing the fire damage.

   Based on the above information, how much is Leonard required to include in his gross income?

3. **LO.1, 2** Twenty college fraternity brothers each placed $2,500 in a mutual fund account. They agreed that upon the death of a fraternity brother, his beneficiary would receive $20,000 that was to be paid from the mutual fund account. The beneficiary of the last remaining fraternity brother would receive the balance remaining in the account. The mutual fund did very well. Earl was the last to die, at age 92, and his beneficiary received $250,000. Can the $250,000 be excluded from the beneficiary's gross income? Why or why not?

4. **LO.2** Janice was a cash basis taxpayer. At the time of her death, she was owed $100,000 in accrued salary. Upon Janice's death, the employer was required to pay Wayne, Janice's brother, her accrued salary. Janice was a key employee, and her employer had purchased a $1,000,000 insurance policy on her life, with the proceeds payable to the employer. Her employer had paid $300,000 in premiums when it collected the face amount of the policy. What amount must be included in the gross income of Janice, Wayne, and Janice's employer?

5. **LO.2** Dolly is a college student who works as a part-time server in a restaurant. Her usual tip is 20% of the price of the meal. A customer ordered a piece of pie and said that he would appreciate prompt service. Dolly abided with the customer's request. The customer's bill was $8, but the customer left a $100 bill on the table and did not ask for a receipt. Dolly gave the cashier $8 and pocketed the $100 bill. Dolly concludes that the customer thought that he had left a $10 bill, although the customer did not return to correct the apparent mistake. The customer had commented about how much he appreciated Dolly's prompt service. Dolly thinks that a $2 tip would be sufficient and that the other $98 is like "found money." How much should Dolly include in her gross income?

6. **LO.2** Carey is a waiter at a restaurant that pays a small hourly amount plus tips. Customers are not required to tip the waiter. Carey is especially attentive and friendly, and her tips average 25% of the restaurant charges. Is Carey required to include any of her tips in gross income when the customer has no legal obligation to make the payment? Explain the basis for your conclusion.

7. **LO.2** Lime Finance Company requires its customers to purchase a credit life insurance policy associated with the loans it makes. Lime is the beneficiary of the policy to the extent of the remaining balance on the loan at the time of the customer's death. In 2013, Lime wrote off as uncollectible a $5,000 account receivable from Wally, which included $1,500 of accrued interest. When Wally died in 2014, the life insurance policy was still in force and Lime received $3,500. Is the $3,500 of life insurance proceeds received by Lime included in its gross income? Explain.

8. **LO.2** Sarah, who has a terminal illness (i.e., one year or less), cashed in her life insurance policy (cost of $24,000 and proceeds of $50,000) to go on an around-the-world cruise (recommended by her physician). Ed paid $24,000 of life insurance premiums before cashing in his life insurance policy for the $50,000 cash surrender value. He decided he could invest the money and earn a higher rate of return. Tom's wife died, and Tom collected $50,000 as the beneficiary on a group term life insurance policy purchased by her employer. Determine the amounts that Sarah, Ed, and Tom should include in their gross income.

9. **LO.2** Joe is a graduate student who works as a resident adviser (RA) in the college dormitory. As compensation for serving as an RA, he is not charged the $2,200 other students pay for their dormitory rooms for the fall 2014 semester. As an RA, he is required to live in the dormitory. He is also paid $1,500 for being available to dormitory residents at all hours during the fall semester. Joe also has a scholarship that pays him $12,000 to be used for his tuition for the academic year. He uses the scholarship proceeds to pay $6,000 of tuition in August 2014. In January 2015, he pays $6,000 for his spring semester tuition. What is Joe's gross income for 2014?

10. **LO.2** Billy fell off a bar stool and hurt his back. As a result, he was unable to work for three months. He sued the bar owner and collected $100,000 for the physical injury and $50,000 for the loss of income. Billy also collected $15,000 from an income replacement insurance policy he purchased. Amber was away from work for three months following heart bypass surgery. Amber collected $30,000 under an income replacement insurance policy purchased by her employer. Are the amounts received by Billy and Amber treated the same under the tax law? Explain.

11. **LO.2** Wes was a major league baseball pitcher who earned $10 million for his 20 wins this year. Sam was also a major league baseball pitcher before a career-ending injury caused by a negligent driver. Sam sued the driver and collected $6 million as compensation for lost estimated future income as a pitcher and $4 million as punitive damages. Do the amounts that Wes and Sam receive have the same effect on their gross income? Explain.

12. **LO.2** Holly was injured while working in a factory and received $12,000 as workers' compensation while she was unable to work because of the injury. Jill, who was self-employed, was also injured and unable to work. Jill collected $12,000 on an insurance policy she had purchased to replace her loss of income while she was unable to work. How much are Holly and Jill each required to include in their gross income?

13. **LO.2** Melba's employer provides a flexible spending plan for medical and dental expenses not covered by insurance. Melba contributed $1,500 during 2014, but by the end of December 2014, she still had $300 remaining in the account. Melba intended to get new eyeglasses, but was too busy during the holiday season. Is Melba required to forfeit the balance in her flexible spending account? Explain.

Decision Making 14. **LO.2, 5** Casey is in the 15% marginal tax bracket, and Jean is in the 35% marginal tax bracket. Their employer is experiencing financial difficulties and cannot continue to pay for the company's health insurance plan. The annual premiums are approximately $8,000 per employee. The employer has proposed to either (1) require the employee to pay the premiums or (2) reduce each employee's pay by $10,000 per year with the employer paying the premium. Which option is less objectionable to Casey, and which is less objectionable to Jean?

15. **LO.2** What is the difference between a cafeteria plan and an employee flexible spending plan?

16. **LO.2** Ted works for Azure Motors, an automobile dealership. All employees can buy a car at the company's cost plus 2%. The company does not charge employees the $300 dealer preparation fee that nonemployees must pay. Ted purchased an automobile for $29,580 ($29,000 + $580). The company's cost was $29,000. The price for a nonemployee would have been $33,900 ($33,600 + $300 preparation fee). What is Ted's gross income from the purchase of the automobile?

17. **LO.2, 5** Wilbur has been offered a job at a salary that would put him in the 25% marginal tax bracket. In addition to his salary, he would receive health insurance coverage. Another potential employer does not offer health insurance but has agreed to match the first offer on an after-tax and insurance basis. The cost of health insurance comparable to that provided by the other potential employer is $9,000 per year. How much more in salary must the second potential employer pay so that Wilbur's financial status will be the same under both offers?

18. **LO.2, 5** Eagle Life Insurance Company pays its employees $.30 per mile for driving their personal automobiles to and from work. The company reimburses each employee who rides the bus $100 a month for the cost of a pass. Tom collected $100 for his automobile mileage, and Mason received $100 as reimbursement for the cost of a bus pass.
   a. What are the effects of the above on Tom's and Mason's gross income?
   b. Assume that Tom and Mason are in the 28% marginal tax bracket and the actual before-tax cost for Tom to drive to and from work is $.30 per mile. What are Tom's and Mason's after-tax costs of commuting to and from work?

Issue ID 19. **LO.2** Several of Egret Company's employees have asked the company to create a hiking trail that employees could use during their lunch hours. The company owns vacant land that is being held for future expansion but would have to spend approximately

$50,000 if it were to make a trail. Nonemployees would be allowed to use the facility as part of the company's effort to build strong community support. What are the relevant tax issues for the employees?

20. **LO.2** The Sage Company has the opportunity to purchase a building located next to its office. Sage would use the building as a day care center for the children of its employees and an exercise facility for the employees. Occasionally, portions of the building could be used for employees' family events such as reunions, birthday parties, and anniversaries. The company would like to know if the planned uses of the building would fit into a beneficially taxed employee compensation plan.

21. **LO.2** Brad is a single individual with $25,000 in taxable interest income and a salary of $86,000 from working in a foreign country for the past 12 months. What tax rate is applied to Brad's salary in 2014?

22. **LO.2, 5** Tammy, a resident of Virginia, is considering purchasing a North Carolina bond that yields 4.6% before tax. She is in the 35% Federal marginal tax bracket and the 5% state marginal tax bracket. She is aware that State of Virginia bonds of comparable risk are yielding 4.5%. However, the Virginia bonds are exempt from Virginia tax, but the North Carolina bond interest is taxable in Virginia. Which of the two options will provide the greater after-tax return to Tammy? Tammy can deduct any state taxes paid on her Federal income tax return.

Decision Making

23. **LO.3** Zack is a farmer who buys his feed and fertilizer from a farmer's cooperative. In 2013, Zack purchased $300,000 in feed and fertilizer for the farm and $10,000 of household goods. Because the cooperative made a profit in 2013, it distributed to its members 2% of their purchases. Zack received his share of the distribution, $6,200, in March 2014. What is Zack's gross income from the distribution?

24. **LO.2** Andrea entered into a § 529 qualified tuition program for the benefit of her daughter, Joanna. Andrea contributed $15,000 to the fund. The fund balance had accumulated to $25,000 by the time Joanna was ready to enter college. However, Joanna received a scholarship that paid for her tuition, fees, books, supplies, and room and board. Therefore, Andrea withdrew the funds from the § 529 plan and bought Joanna a new car.
   a. What are the tax consequences to Andrea of withdrawing the funds?
   b. Assume instead that Joanna's scholarship did not cover her room and board, which cost $7,500 per academic year. During the current year, $7,500 of the fund balance was used to pay for Joanna's room and board. The remaining amount was left in the § 529 plan to cover her room and board for future academic years. What are the tax consequences to Andrea and to Joanna of using the $7,500 to pay for the room and board?

25. **LO.3** Dolly is a cash basis taxpayer. In 2014, she filed her 2013 South Carolina income tax return and received a $2,200 refund. Dolly took the standard deduction on her 2013 Federal income tax return, but will itemize her deductions in 2014. Molly, a cash basis taxpayer, also filed her 2013 South Carolina income tax return in 2014 and received a $600 refund. Molly had $12,000 in itemized deductions on her 2013 Federal income tax return, but will take the standard deduction in 2014. How does the tax benefit rule apply to Dolly's and Molly's situations? Explain.

26. **LO.4** Harry purchased equipment for his business and gave the seller cash and a note due in two years. Larry also purchased business equipment, but financed the transaction with a bank loan. Because Harry and Larry were having financial difficulty, the creditors reduced the balance due on each mortgage by $50,000. What are the tax effects of the debt adjustments experienced by Harry and Larry?

27. **LO.4** Ralph has experienced financial difficulties as a result of his struggling business. He has been behind on his mortgage payments for the last six months. The mortgage holder, who is a friend of Ralph's, has offered to accept $80,000 in full payment of the $100,000 owed on the mortgage and payable over the next 10 years. The interest rate of the mortgage is 7%, and the market rate is now 8%. What tax issues are raised by the creditor's offer?

Issue ID

Problems

28. **LO.2** Ed, an employee of the Natural Color Company, suffered from a rare disease that was very expensive to treat. The local media ran several stories about Ed's problems, and the family received more than $10,000 in gifts from individuals to help pay the medical bills. Ed's employer provided hospital and medical insurance for its employees, but the policy did not cover Ed's illness. When it became apparent that Ed could not pay all of his medical expenses, the hospital canceled the $25,000 Ed owed at the time of his death. After Ed's death, his former employer paid Ed's widow $12,000 in "her time of need." Ed's widow also collected $50,000 on a group term life insurance policy paid for by Ed's employer. What are Ed's and his widow's gross income?

29. **LO.2** Determine the gross income of the beneficiaries in the following cases:
    a. Justin's employer was downsizing and offered employees an amount equal to one year's salary if the employee would voluntarily retire.
    b. Trina contracted a disease and was unable to work for six months. Because of her dire circumstances, her employer paid her one-half of her regular salary while she was away from work.
    c. Coral Corporation collected $1 million on a key person life insurance policy when its chief executive died. The corporation had paid the premiums on the policy of $77,000, which were not deductible by the corporation.
    d. Juan collected $40,000 on a life insurance policy when his wife, Leona, died in 2014. The insurance policy was provided by Leona's employer, and the premiums were excluded from Leona's gross income as group term life insurance. In 2015, Juan collected the $3,500 accrued salary owed to Leona at the time of her death.

Decision Making

30. **LO.2, 5** Laura was recently diagnosed with cancer and has begun chemotherapy treatments. A cancer specialist has stated that Laura has less than one year to live. She has incurred a lot of medical bills and other general living expenses and is in need of cash. Therefore, she is considering selling stock that cost $35,000 and has a fair market value of $50,000. This amount would be sufficient to pay her medical bills. However, she has read about a company (the Vital Benefits Company) that would purchase her life insurance policy for $50,000. She has paid $30,000 in premiums on the policy.
    a. Considering only the tax effects, would selling the stock or selling the life insurance policy result in more beneficial tax treatment?
    b. Assume that Laura is a dependent child and that her mother owns the stock and the life insurance policy, which is on the mother's life. Which of the alternative means of raising the cash would result in more beneficial tax treatment?

31. **LO.2** What is the taxpayer's gross income in each of the following situations?
    a. Darrin received a salary of $50,000 in 2014 from his employer, Green Construction.
    b. In July 2014, Green gave Darrin an all-expense-paid trip to Las Vegas (value of $3,000) for exceeding his sales quota.
    c. Megan received $10,000 from her employer to help her pay medical expenses not covered by insurance.
    d. Blake received $15,000 from his deceased wife's employer "to help him in his time of greatest need."
    e. Clint collected $50,000 as the beneficiary of a group term life insurance policy when his wife died. The premiums on the policy were paid by his deceased wife's employer.

32. **LO.2** Donald was killed in an accident while he was on the job in 2014. Darlene, Donald's wife, received several payments as a result of Donald's death. What is Darlene's gross income from the items listed below?
    a. Donald's employer paid Darlene an amount equal to Donald's three months' salary ($60,000), which is what the employer does for all widows and widowers of deceased employees.
    b. Donald had $20,000 in accrued salary that was paid to Darlene.
    c. Donald's employer had provided Donald with group term life insurance of $480,000 (twice his annual salary), which was payable to his widow in a lump sum. Premiums on this policy totaling $12,500 had been included in Donald's gross income under § 79.
    d. Donald had purchased a life insurance policy (premiums totaled $250,000) that paid $600,000 in the event of accidental death. The proceeds were payable to Darlene,

who elected to receive installment payments as an annuity of $30,000 each year for a 25-year period. She received her first installment this year.

33. **LO.2** Ray and Carin are partners in an accounting firm. The partners have entered into an arm's length agreement requiring Ray to purchase Carin's partnership interest from Carin's estate if she dies before Ray. The price is set at 120% of the book value of Carin's partnership interest at the time of her death. Ray purchased an insurance policy on Carin's life to fund this agreement. After Ray had paid $45,000 in premiums, Carin was killed in an automobile accident and Ray collected $800,000 of life insurance proceeds. Ray used the life insurance proceeds to purchase Carin's partnership interest.

    a. What amount should Ray include in his gross income from receiving the life insurance proceeds?

    b. The insurance company paid Ray $16,000 interest on the life insurance proceeds during the period Carin's estate was in administration. During this period, Ray had left the insurance proceeds with the insurance company. Is this interest taxable?

    c. When Ray paid $800,000 for Carin's partnership interest, priced as specified in the agreement, the fair market value of Carin's interest was $1 million. How much should Ray include in his gross income from this bargain purchase?

34. **LO.2** Sally was an all-state soccer player during her junior and senior years in high school. She accepted an athletic scholarship from State University. The scholarship provided the following:

Tuition and fees	$15,000
Housing and meals	6,000
Books and supplies	1,500
Transportation	1,200

    a. Determine the effect of the scholarship on Sally's gross income.

    b. Sally's brother, Willy, was not a gifted athlete, but he received $8,000 from their father's employer as a scholarship during the year. The employer grants the children of all executives a scholarship equal to one-half of annual tuition, fees, books, and supplies. Willy also received a $6,000 scholarship (to be used for tuition) as the winner of an essay contest related to bioengineering, his intended field of study. Determine the effect of the scholarships on Willy's and his father's gross income.

35. **LO.2** Adrian was awarded an academic scholarship to State University for the 2014–2015 academic year. He received $6,500 in August and $7,200 in December 2014. Adrian had enough personal savings to pay all expenses as they came due. Adrian's expenditures for the relevant period were as follows:

Tuition, August 2014	$3,700
Tuition, January 2015	3,750
Room and board	
August–December 2014	2,800
January–May 2015	2,500
Books and educational supplies	
August–December 2014	1,000
January–May 2015	1,200

Determine the effect on Adrian's gross income for 2014 and 2015.

36. **LO.2** Leigh sued an overzealous bill collector and received the following settlement:

Damage to her automobile that the collector attempted to repossess	$ 3,300
Physical damage to her arm caused by the collector	15,000
Loss of income while her arm was healing	6,000
Punitive damages	80,000

    a. What effect does the settlement have on Leigh's gross income?

    b. Assume that Leigh also collected $25,000 of damages for slander to her personal reputation caused by the bill collector misrepresenting the facts to Leigh's employer and other creditors. Is this $25,000 included in Leigh's gross income? Explain.

37. **LO.2** Determine the effect on gross income in each of the following cases:
    a. Eloise received $150,000 in settlement of a sex discrimination case against her former employer.
    b. Nell received $10,000 for damages to her personal reputation. She also received $40,000 in punitive damages.
    c. Orange Corporation, an accrual basis taxpayer, received $50,000 from a lawsuit filed against its auditor who overcharged for services rendered in a previous year.
    d. Beth received $10,000 in compensatory damages and $30,000 in punitive damages in a lawsuit she filed against a tanning parlor for severe burns she received from using its tanning equipment.
    e. Joanne received compensatory damages of $75,000 and punitive damages of $300,000 from a cosmetic surgeon who botched her nose job.

38. **LO.2** Rex, age 55, is an officer of Blue Company, which provides him with the following nondiscriminatory fringe benefits in 2014:

    - Hospitalization insurance premiums for Rex and his dependents. The cost of the coverage for Rex is $2,900 per year, and the additional cost for his dependents is $3,800 per year. The plan has a $2,000 deductible, but his employer contributed $1,500 to Rex's Health Savings Account (HSA). Rex withdrew only $800 from the HSA, and the account earned $50 of interest during the year.
    - Insurance premiums of $840 for salary continuation payments. Under the plan, Rex will receive his regular salary in the event he is unable to work due to illness. Rex collected $4,500 on the policy to replace lost wages while he was ill during the year.
    - Rex is a part-time student working on his bachelor's degree in engineering. His employer reimbursed his $5,200 tuition under a plan available to all full-time employees.

    Determine the amount Rex must include in gross income.

Communications

39. **LO.2** The UVW Union and HON Corporation are negotiating contract terms. Assume that the union members are in the 25% marginal tax bracket and that all benefits are provided on a nondiscriminatory basis. Write a letter to the UVW Union members explaining the tax consequences of the options discussed below. The union's address is 905 Spruce Street, Washington, D.C. 20227.
    a. The company would eliminate the $250 deductible on medical insurance benefits. Most employees incur more than $250 each year in medical expenses.
    b. Employees would get an additional paid holiday with the same annual income (the same pay but less work).
    c. An employee who did not need health insurance (because the employee's spouse works and receives family coverage) would be allowed to receive the cash value of the coverage.

Decision Making

40. **LO.2, 5** Mauve Corporation has a group hospitalization insurance plan that has a $200 deductible amount for hospital visits and a $15 deductible for doctor visits and prescriptions. The deductible portion paid by employees who have children has become substantial for some employees. The company is considering adopting a medical reimbursement plan or a flexible benefits plan to cover the deductible amounts. Either of these plans can be tailored to meet the needs of the employees. What are the cost considerations to the employer that should be considered in choosing between these plans?

41. **LO.2** Belinda spent the last 60 days of 2014 in a nursing home. The cost of the services provided to her was $18,000 ($300 per day). Medicare paid $8,500 toward the cost of her stay. Belinda also received $5,500 of benefits under a long-term care insurance policy she purchased. What is the effect on Belinda's gross income?

42. **LO.2** Tim is the vice president of western operations for Maroon Oil Company and is stationed in San Francisco. He is required to live in an employer-owned home, which is three blocks from his company office. The company-provided home is equipped with high-speed Internet access and several telephone lines. Tim receives telephone calls and e-mails that require immediate attention any time of day or night because the company's business is spread all over the world. A full-time administrative assistant resides in the house to assist Tim with the urgent business matters. Tim often uses the home for entertaining customers, suppliers, and employees. The fair market value of comparable housing is $9,000 per month. Tim is also provided with free parking at his company's office.

The value of the parking is $350 per month. Calculate the amount associated with the company-provided housing and free parking that Tim must include in his gross income.

43. **LO.2** Does the taxpayer recognize gross income in the following situations?

   a. Ava is a filing clerk at a large insurance company. She is permitted to leave the premises for lunch, but she usually eats in the company's cafeteria because it is quick and she is on a tight schedule. On average, she pays $2 for a lunch that would cost $12 at a restaurant. However, if the prices in the cafeteria were not so low and the food was not so delicious, she would probably bring her lunch at a cost of $3 per day.

   b. Scott is an executive for an international corporation located in New York City. Often he works late, taking telephone calls from the company's European branch. Scott often stays in a company-owned condominium when he has a late-night work session. The condominium is across the street from the company office.

   c. Ira recently moved to take a job. For the first month on the new job, Ira was searching for a home to purchase or rent. During this time, his employer permitted Ira to live in an apartment the company maintains for customers during the buying season. The month that Ira occupied the apartment was not during the buying season, and the apartment would not otherwise have been occupied.

44. **LO.2, 5** Bertha is considering taking an early retirement offered by her employer. She would receive $3,000 per month, indexed for inflation. However, she would no longer be able to use the company's health facilities, and she would be required to pay her hospitalization insurance premiums of $8,000 each year. Bertha and her husband will file a joint return and take the standard deduction. She currently receives a salary of $55,000 a year. If she retires, she will spend approximately $300 less each month for commuting and clothing. Bertha and her husband have other sources of income and are in and will remain in the 25% marginal tax bracket. She currently pays Social Security and Medicare taxes of 7.65% on her salary, but her retirement pay would not be subject to this tax. According to Bertha, she and her husband could live well if her after-tax retirement income was at least 50% of her current income. Provide Bertha with information she will need to make her decision.   *Decision Making*

45. **LO.2, 5** Finch Construction Company provides the carpenters it employs with all of the required tools. However, the company believes that this practice has led to some employees not taking care of the tools and to the mysterious disappearance of some tools. The company is considering requiring all of its employees to provide their own tools. Each employee's salary would be increased by $1,500 to compensate for the additional cost. Write a letter to Finch's management explaining the tax consequences of this plan to the carpenters. Finch's address is 300 Harbor Drive, Vermillion, SD 57069.   *Communications*

46. **LO.2, 5** Bluebird, Inc., does not provide its employees with any tax-exempt fringe benefits. The company is considering adopting a hospital and medical benefits insurance plan that will cost approximately $9,000 per employee. To adopt this plan, the company may have to reduce salaries and/or lower future salary increases. Bluebird is in the 35% (combined Federal and state rates) bracket. Bluebird is also responsible for matching the Social Security and Medicare taxes withheld on employees' salaries (at the full 7.65% rate). The hospital and medical benefits insurance plan will not be subject to the Social Security and Medicare taxes, and the company is not eligible for the small business credit for health insurance. The employees generally fall into two marginal tax rate groups:

Income Tax	Social Security and Medicare Tax	Total
.15	.0765	.2265
.35	.0145	.3645

The company has asked you to assist in its financial planning for the hospital and medical benefits insurance plan by computing the following:

   a. How much taxable compensation is the equivalent of $9,000 of exempt compensation for each of the two classes of employees?

   b. What is the company's after-tax cost of the taxable compensation computed in part (a)?

   c. What is the company's after-tax cost of the exempt compensation?

   d. Briefly explain your conclusions from the preceding analysis.

Decision Making

47. **LO.2, 5** Rosa's employer has instituted a flexible benefits program. Rosa will use the plan to pay for her daughter's dental expenses and other medical expenses that are not covered by health insurance. Rosa is in the 28% marginal tax bracket and estimates that the medical and dental expenses not covered by health insurance will be within the range of $4,000 to $5,000. Her employer's plan permits her to set aside as much as $5,000 in the flexible benefits account. Rosa does not itemize her deductions.

   a. Rosa puts $4,000 into her flexible benefits account, and her actual expenses are $5,000. What is her cost of underestimating the expenses?

   b. Rosa puts $5,000 into her flexible benefits account, and her actual expenses are only $4,000. What is her cost of overestimating her expenses?

   c. What is Rosa's cost of underfunding as compared to the cost of overfunding the flexible benefits account?

   d. Does your answer in part (c) suggest that Rosa should fund the account closer to the low end or to the high end of her estimates?

48. **LO.2** Sparrow Corporation would like you to review its employee fringe benefits program with regard to the tax consequences of the plan for the company's president (Polly), who is also the majority shareholder.

   a. The company has a qualified retirement plan. The company pays the cost of employees attending a retirement planning seminar. The employee must be within 10 years of retirement, and the cost of the seminar is $1,500 per attendee.

   b. The company owns a parking garage that is used by customers, employees, and the general public. Only the general public is required to pay for parking. The charge to the general public for Polly's parking for the year would have been $3,600 (a $300 monthly rate).

   c. All employees are allowed to use the company's fixed charge long-distance telephone services, as long as the privilege is not abused. Although no one has kept track of the actual calls, Polly's use of the telephone had a value (what she would have paid on her personal telephone) of approximately $600.

   d. The company owns a condominium at the beach, which it uses to entertain customers. Employees are allowed to use the facility without charge when the company has no scheduled events. Polly used the facility 10 days during the year. Her use had a rental value of $1,000.

   e. The company is in the household moving business. Employees are allowed to ship goods without charge whenever there is excess space on a truck. Polly purchased a dining room suite for her daughter. Company trucks delivered the furniture to the daughter. Normal freight charges would have been $750.

   f. The company has a storage facility for household goods. Officers are allowed a 20% discount on charges for storing their goods. All other employees are allowed a 10% discount. Polly's discounts for the year totaled $900.

49. **LO.2** George is a U.S. citizen who is employed by Hawk Enterprises, a global company. Beginning on June 1, 2014, George began working in London. He worked there until January 31, 2015, when he transferred to Paris. He worked in Paris the remainder of 2015. His salary for the first five months of 2014 was $100,000, and it was earned in the United States. His salary for the remainder of 2014 was $175,000, and it was earned in London. George's 2015 salary from Hawk was $300,000, with part being earned in London and part being earned in Paris. What is George's gross income in 2014 and 2015? (Assume that the 2015 indexed amount is the same as the 2014 indexed amount.)

50. **LO.2, 3** Determine Hazel's gross income from the following receipts for the year:

Gain on sale of Augusta County bonds	$800
Interest on U.S. government savings bonds	400
Interest on state income tax refund	200
Interest on Augusta County bonds	700
Patronage dividend from Potato Growers Cooperative	350

The patronage dividend was received in March of the current year for amounts paid for her (nondeductible) garden and lawn supplies.

51. **LO.2** In January 2014, Ezra purchased 2,000 shares of Gold Utility Mutual Fund for $20,000. In June, Ezra received an additional 100 shares as a dividend, in lieu of receiving $1,000 in cash dividends. In December, the company declared a two-for-one stock split. Ezra received an additional 2,100 shares, but there was no option to receive cash.

At the time of the stock dividend in December and at the end of the year, the fund shares were trading for $5 per share. Also, at the end of the year, the fund offered to buy outstanding shares for $4.50. Ezra did not sell any shares during the year.

a. What is Ezra's gross income from the 100 shares received in June?

b. What is Ezra's gross income from the receipt of the 2,100 shares as a two-for-one stock split in December?

c. Should Ezra be required to recognize gross income in 2014 even though the fair market value of his investment at the end of the year was less than the fair market value at the beginning of the year? Explain.

52. **LO.2** Tonya, who lives in California, inherited a $100,000 State of California bond in 2014. Her marginal Federal tax rate is 35%, and her marginal state tax rate is 5%. The California bond pays 3.3% interest, which is not subject to California income tax. She can purchase a corporate bond of comparable risk that will yield 5.2% or a U.S. government bond that pays 4.6% interest. Which investment will provide the greatest after-tax yield?

Decision Making

53. **LO.2** Lynn Swartz's husband died three years ago. Her parents have an income of over $200,000 a year and want to ensure that funds will be available for the education of Lynn's 8-year-old son Eric. Lynn is currently earning $45,000 a year. Lynn's parents have suggested that they start a savings account for Eric. They have calculated that if they invest $4,000 a year for the next 8 years, at the end of 10 years, sufficient funds will be available for Eric's college expenses. Lynn realizes that the tax treatment of the investments could significantly affect the amount of funds available for Eric's education. She asked you to write a letter to her advising about options available to her parents and to her for Eric's college education. Lynn's address is 100 Myrtle Cove, Fairfield, CT 06824.

Decision Making

Communications

54. **LO.2** Starting in 2003, Chuck and Luane have been purchasing Series EE bonds in their name to use for the higher education of their daughter Susie, who currently is age 18. During the year, they cash in $12,000 of the bonds to use for freshman year tuition, fees, and room and board. Of this amount, $5,000 represents interest. Of the $12,000, $8,000 is used for tuition and fees, and $4,000 is used for room and board. Chuck and Luane's AGI, before the educational savings bond exclusion, is $120,000.

a. Determine the tax consequences for Chuck and Luane, who will file a joint return, and for Susie.

b. Assume that Chuck and Luane purchased the bonds in Susie's name. Determine the tax consequences for Chuck and Luane and for Susie.

c. How would your answer to (a) change if Chuck and Luane filed separate returns?

55. **LO.2** Albert established a qualified tuition program for each of his twins, Kim and Jim. He started each fund with $20,000 when the children were 5 years old. Albert made no further contributions to his children's plans. Thirteen years later, both children have graduated from high school. Kim's fund has accumulated to $45,000, while Jim's has accumulated to $42,000. Kim decides to attend a state university, which will cost $60,000 for four years (tuition, fees, room and board, and books). Jim decides to go to work instead of going to college. During the current year, $7,500 is used from Kim's plan to pay the cost of her first semester in college. Because Jim is not going to college now or in the future, Albert withdraws the $42,000 plan balance and gives it to Jim to start his new life after high school.

a. During the period since the plans were established, should Albert or the twins have been including the annual plan earnings in gross income? Explain.

b. What are the tax consequences to Kim and Albert of the $7,500 being used for the first semester's higher education costs?

c. Because of her participation in the qualified tuition program, Kim received a 10% reduction in tuition charges, so less than $7,500 was withdrawn from her account. Is either Albert or Kim required to include the value of this discount in gross income? Explain.

d. What are the tax consequences to Albert and Jim of Jim's qualified tuition program being closed?

56. **LO.3** How does the tax benefit rule apply in the following cases?

a. In 2012, the Orange Furniture Store, an accrual method taxpayer, sold furniture on credit for $1,000 to Sammy. The cost of the furniture was $600. In 2013, Orange took a bad debt deduction for the $1,000. In 2014, Sammy inherited some money and paid Orange the $1,000 he owed. Orange was in the 35% marginal tax bracket in 2012, the 15% marginal tax bracket in 2013, and the 35% marginal tax bracket in 2014.

b. In 2013, Marvin, a cash basis taxpayer, took a $2,000 itemized deduction for state income taxes paid. This increased his itemized deductions to a total that was $800 more than the standard deduction. In 2014, Marvin received a $1,600 refund when he filed his 2013 state income tax return. Marvin was in the 15% marginal tax bracket in 2013, but was in the 35% marginal tax bracket in 2014.

c. In 2013, Barb, a cash basis taxpayer, was in an accident and incurred $8,000 in medical expenses, which she claimed as an itemized deduction for medical expenses. Because of the 10%-of-AGI reduction, the expense reduced her taxable income by only $3,000. In 2014, Barb successfully sued the person who caused the physical injury and collected $8,000 to reimburse her for the cost of her medical expenses. Barb was in the 15% marginal tax bracket in both 2013 and 2014.

Decision Making

57. **LO.4, 5** Fran, who is in the 35% tax bracket, recently collected $100,000 on a life insurance policy she carried on her father. She currently owes $120,000 on her personal residence and $120,000 on business property. National Bank holds the mortgage on both pieces of property and has agreed to accept $100,000 in complete satisfaction of either mortgage. The interest rate on the mortgages is 8%, and both mortgages are payable over 10 years. What would be the tax consequences of each of the following alternatives assuming that Fran currently deducts the mortgage interest on her tax return?

a. Retire the mortgage on the residence.

b. Retire the mortgage on the business property.

Which alternative should Fran select?

58. **LO.4** Vic, who was experiencing financial difficulties, was able to adjust his debts as follows:

a. Vic is an attorney. Vic owed his uncle $25,000. The uncle told Vic that if he serves as the executor of the uncle's estate, Vic's debt will be canceled in the uncle's will.

b. Vic borrowed $80,000 from First Bank. The debt was secured by land that Vic purchased for $100,000. Vic was unable to pay, and the bank foreclosed when the liability was $80,000, which was also the fair market value of the property.

c. The Land Company, which had sold land to Vic for $80,000, reduced the mortgage on the land by $12,000.

Determine the tax consequences to Vic.

Cumulative Problems

Tax Return Problem

H&R BLOCK

TAX SOFTWARE

59. Alfred E. Old and Beulah A. Crane, each age 42, married on September 7, 2011. Alfred and Beulah will file a joint return for 2013. Alfred's Social Security number is 111-11-1111. Beulah's Social Security number is 123-45-6789, and she adopted "Old" as her married name. They live at 211 Brickstone Drive, Atlanta, GA 30304.

Alfred was divorced from Sarah Old in March 2011. Under the divorce agreement, Alfred is to pay Sarah $1,250 per month for the next 10 years or until Sarah's death, whichever occurs first. Alfred pays Sarah $15,000 in 2013. In addition, in January 2013, Alfred pays Sarah $50,000, which is designated as being for her share of the marital property. Also, Alfred is responsible for all prior years' income taxes. Sarah's Social Security number is 123-45-6788.

Alfred's salary for 2013 is $150,000, and his employer, Cherry, Inc. (Federal I.D. No. 98-7654321), provides him with group term life insurance equal to twice his annual salary. His employer withheld $24,900 for Federal income taxes and $8,000 for state income taxes. The proper amounts were withheld for FICA taxes.

Beulah recently graduated from law school and is employed by Legal Aid Society, Inc. (Federal I.D. No. 11-1111111), as a public defender. She receives a salary of $40,000 in 2013. Her employer withheld $7,500 for Federal income taxes and $2,400 for state income taxes. The proper amounts were withheld for FICA taxes.

Beulah has $2,500 in qualified dividends on Yellow Corporation stock she inherited. Alfred and Beulah receive a $1,900 refund on their 2012 state income taxes. They itemized deductions on their 2012 Federal income tax return (total of $15,000). Alfred and Beulah pay $4,500 interest and $1,450 property taxes on their personal residence in

2013. Their charitable contributions total $2,400 (all to their church). They paid sales taxes of $1,400, for which they maintain the receipts.

Compute the Olds's net tax payable (or refund due) for 2013. If you use tax forms for your solution, you will need Form 1040 and Schedules A and B. Suggested software: H&R BLOCK Tax Software.

60. Martin S. Albert (Social Security number 111-11-1111) is 39 years old and is married to Michele R. Albert (Social Security number 123-45-6789). The Alberts live at 512 Ferry Road, Newport News, VA 23601. They file a joint return and have two dependent children, Charlene, age 17, and Jordan, age 18. Charlene's Social Security number is 123-45-6788, and Jordan's Social Security number is 123-45-6787. In 2014, Martin and Michele had the following transactions:

   a. Martin received $120,000 in salary from Red Steel Corporation, where he is a construction engineer. Withholding for Federal income tax was $10,750. The amounts withheld for FICA taxes were as follows: $7,049 ($113,700 × 6.2%) for Social Security and $1,740 ($120,000 × 1.45%) for Medicare. Martin worked in Mexico from January 1, 2013, until February 15, 2014. His $120,000 salary for 2014 includes $18,000 he earned for January and one-half of February 2014 while working in Mexico.

   b. Martin and Michele received $800 in qualified dividends on Green, Inc. stock and $400 interest on Montgomery County (Virginia) school bonds.

   c. Martin received $2,300 interest from a Bahamian bank account.

   d. Michele received 50 shares of Applegate Corporation common stock as a stock dividend. The shares had a fair market value of $2,500 at the time Michele received them, and she did not have the option of receiving cash.

   e. Martin and Michele received a $1,200 refund on their 2013 Virginia income taxes. Their itemized deductions in 2013 totaled $14,000.

   f. Martin paid $6,600 alimony to his former wife, Rose T. Morgan (Social Security number 123-45-6786).

   g. Martin and Michele kept the receipts for their sales taxes paid of $1,100.

   h. Martin and Michele's itemized deductions were as follows:

   - State income tax paid and withheld totaled $5,100.
   - Real estate taxes on their principal residence were $3,700.
   - Mortgage interest on their principal residence was $2,500.
   - Cash contributions to the church totaled $2,800.

Tax Computation Problem

Decision Making

Communications

Part 1—Tax Computation
Compute the Alberts's net tax payable (or refund due) for 2014.

Part 2—Tax Planning
The Alberts are considering buying another house. Their house mortgage payments would increase by $500 (to $1,500) per month, which includes a $250 increase in interest and a $100 increase in property tax. The Alberts would like to know how much the mortgage payments would increase net of any change in their income tax. Write a letter to the Alberts that contains your advice.

Research Problems

Note: Solutions to Research Problems can be prepared by using the **Checkpoint®** **Student Edition** online research product, which is available to accompany this text. It is also possible to prepare solutions to the Research Problems by using tax research materials found in a standard tax library.

THOMSON REUTERS
CHECKPOINT®

Research Problem 1. Murray reported to the Environmental Protection Agency that his employer was illegally dumping chemicals into a river. His charges were true, and Murray's employer was fined. In retaliation, Murray's employer fired him and made deliberate efforts to prevent Murray from obtaining other employment. Murray sued the employer, claiming that his reputation had been damaged. Murray won his lawsuit and received an award for "damages to his personal and professional reputation and for his mental suffering." Now he would like to know whether the award is taxable. He argues that he was awarded damages as a recovery of his human capital and that a recovery of capital is not income. Therefore, the Federal government does not have the power to tax the award.

Research Problem 2. The employees of the city of Greenville must make mandatory contributions to the city's postretirement health benefit plan. The employees' contributions are placed in a trust and are used exclusively for the employees' benefits. The employees believe that because they are required to make the contributions from their base salaries, the result should be the same as if the employer made the contribution and had reduced their salaries by the amount of the contributions. Therefore, the employees believe they should be permitted to exclude the payments from gross income. The employees have asked you to research the issue.

Research Problem 3. Your client, John Butler, is an avid Houston Astros fan. Last March at the Astros' home opener, as a result of a random drawing of those in attendance at the game, John won 300 Shipley Do-Nut coupons. Each coupon entitled him to a cup of coffee and a free doughnut or a dozen doughnut holes.

John used some of the coupons (approximately 20), but he found that eating so many doughnuts directly conflicted with his goal of losing weight. The unused coupons expired on January 1, 2014. Thus, John was surprised when he received a Form 1099 in February 2014 that valued his prize at $900. John would like to know whether the value of the doughnut coupons should be included in income and asks you to research his question. If you conclude that their value should be included in income, John also would like to know if he can reduce his gross income by including in income only the value of the coupons that he used. He has the unused coupons as documentation that neither he nor anyone else used them.

Research Problem 4. Aubrey Brown is a decorated veteran of the Vietnam War. As a result of his exposure to Agent Orange during the war, Aubrey developed lung cancer and is unable to work. He received $12,000 of Social Security disability payments in the current year. He reasons that the payments should be excluded from his gross income because the payments are compensation for the physical injury he suffered as a result of his service in the armed forces. Is Aubrey correct? Explain.

Partial list of research aids:
Rev.Rul. 77–318, 1977–2 C.B. 45.
Reimels v. Comm., 2006–1 USTC ¶50,147, 97 AFTR 2d 2006–820, 436 F.3d 344 (CA–2, 2006).

Research Problem 5. Your client works for a defense contractor and was assigned to work on a military base in Australia. As a condition of his employment, he was required to live in housing that was provided to military personnel. The housing provided was a condominium located in a civilian neighborhood that was 20 miles from the military base where he performed his services. The employer paid over $6,000 of rent while the employee was living there. Your client would like to know whether the value of the housing can be excluded from his gross income. He read an article that indicated that employees who are required to live in a "camp" in a foreign country can exclude the cost of the housing from gross income. What is the result of your research?

Internet Activity

Communications

Use the tax resources of the Internet to address the following questions. Do not restrict your search to the Web, but include a review of newsgroups and general reference materials, practitioner sites and resources, primary sources of the tax law, chat rooms and discussion groups, and other opportunities.

Research Problem 6. The parsonage allowance in Code § 107(2) allows clergymen and clergywomen to exclude from gross income any rental allowance paid to them as compensation, as long as that allowance is used to rent or buy a home. In a recent court case [*Freedom From Religion Foundation, Inc. v. Lew*, 112 AFTR 2d 2013–7103 (D.Ct. Wis., 2013)], a District Court judge in Wisconsin ruled that this exclusion from income was unconstitutional. What rationale underlies the judge's conclusion that this benefit is unconstitutional?

Research Problem 7. Employers often use the Internet as a means of attracting applications from potential employees. Locate an Internet site offering employment opportunities, ideally one provided by a well-known corporation. How does the employer promote its fringe benefit and cafeteria plan packages? Compare and contrast several such sites.

part 3

DEDUCTIONS

Part 3 presents the deduction component of the basic tax model. Deductions are classified as business versus nonbusiness, "for" AGI versus "from" AGI, employee versus employer, active versus passive, and reimbursed versus unreimbursed. The effect of each of these classifications is analyzed. The presentation includes not only the deductions that are permitted, but also limitations and disallowances associated with deductions. A separate chapter is included dealing with the special tax treatment accorded to losses resulting from investment activities.

Dennis Flaherty/Photographer's Choice/Getty Images

Deductions and Losses: In General

LEARNING OBJECTIVES: *After completing Chapter 6, you should be able to:*

LO.1 Differentiate between deductions *for* and *from* adjusted gross income and describe the relevance of the differentiation.

LO.2 Describe the cash and accrual methods of accounting with emphasis on the deduction aspects.

LO.3 Apply the Internal Revenue Code deduction disallowance provisions associated with the following: public policy limitations, political activities, excessive executive

compensation, investigation of business opportunities, hobby losses, vacation home rentals, payment of others' expenses, personal expenditures, capital expenditures, related-party transactions, and expenses related to tax-exempt income.

LO.4 Identify tax planning opportunities for maximizing deductions and minimizing the disallowance of deductions.

CHAPTER OUTLINE

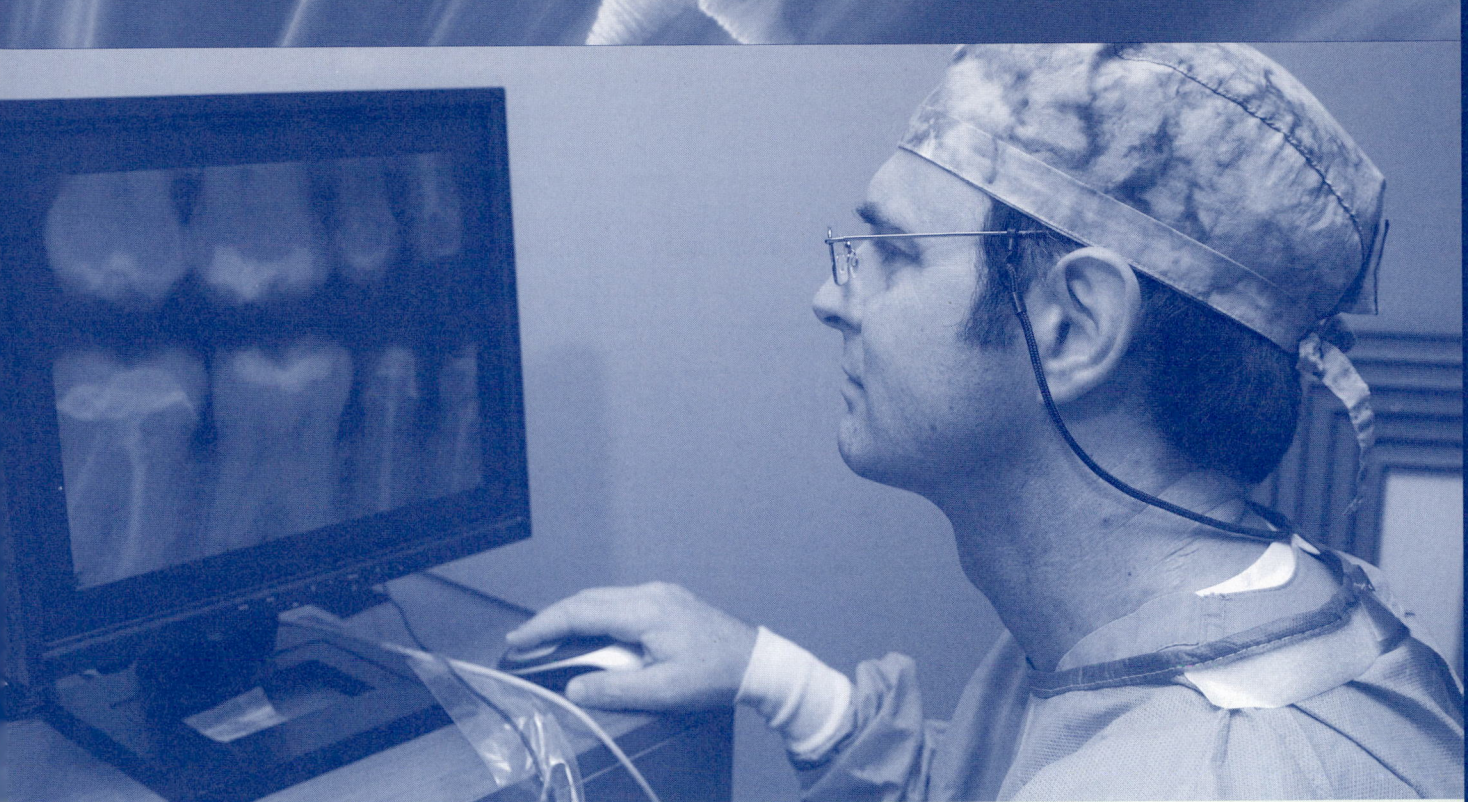

CALCULATION OF DEDUCTIBLE EXPENSES

Dr. Cliff Payne determines that his deductible expenses associated with his dental practice are as follows:

Salaries including FICA (unpaid at year-end of $5,000)	$120,000
Building rent	24,000
Depreciation of dental equipment and office furnishings and equipment	52,000
Insurance (malpractice and of dental equipment and office furnishings and equipment)	22,000
Dental supplies	16,000
Office supplies	3,000
Investigation expenses	6,000
Contribution to the State Senate campaign fund of Tom Smith	1,000
Contribution to the State Senate campaign fund of Virginia White	1,000
Legal expenses associated with patient lawsuit (jury decision for defendant)	4,000
Fine imposed by city for improper disposal of medical waste	3,000
Draw by Dr. Payne for living expenses ($5,000 monthly)	60,000

Has Dr. Payne correctly calculated the business expenses for his dental practice?

Read the chapter and formulate your response.

FRAMEWORK 1040
Tax Formula for Individuals

This chapter covers the boldfaced portions of the Tax Formula for Individuals that was introduced in Figure 3.1 on p. 3-3. Below those portions are the sections of Form 1040 where the results are reported.

Income *(broadly conceived)*	$xx,xxx
Less: Exclusions	(x,xxx)
Gross income	$xx,xxx
Less: Deductions for adjusted gross income	(x,xxx)

FORM 1040 (p. 1)

12	Business income or (loss). Attach Schedule C or C-EZ	

Adjusted gross income	$xx,xxx
Less: The greater of total **itemized deductions** *or* the standard deduction	(x,xxx)

FORM 1040 (p. 2)

40	Itemized deductions (from Schedule A) **or** your **standard deduction** (see left margin) . .	

Personal and dependency exemptions	(x,xxx)
Taxable income	$xx,xxx
Tax on taxable income *(see Tax Tables or Tax Rate Schedules)*	$ x,xxx
Less: Tax credits *(including income taxes withheld and prepaid)*	(xxx)
Tax due *(or refund)*	$ xxx

The tax law has an all-inclusive definition of income; that is, income from whatever source derived is includible in gross income. Income cannot be excluded unless there is a specific statement to that effect in the Internal Revenue Code.

Similarly, deductions are disallowed unless a specific provision in the tax law permits them. The inclusive definition of income and the exclusive definition of deductions may not seem fair to taxpayers, but it is the structure of the tax law.

The courts have held that whether and to what extent deductions are allowed depends on legislative grace.[1] In other words, any exclusions from income and all deductions are gifts from Congress.

6-1 CLASSIFICATION OF DEDUCTIBLE EXPENSES

LO.1

Differentiate between deductions *for* and *from* adjusted gross income and describe the relevance of the differentiation.

It is important to classify deductible expenses as **deductions for adjusted gross income** (AGI) or **deductions from adjusted gross income**. Deductions *for* AGI can be claimed whether or not the taxpayer itemizes. Deductions *from* AGI result in a tax benefit only if they exceed the taxpayer's standard deduction. If itemized deductions (*from* AGI) are less than the standard deduction, they provide no tax benefit. As Example 1 illustrates, whether a deduction is classified as *for* AGI or *from* AGI can affect the benefit the taxpayer receives from the deduction.

[1] *New Colonial Ice Co. v. Helvering*, 4 USTC ¶1292, 13 AFTR 1180, 54 S.Ct. 788 (USSC, 1934).

Example 1

Steve is a self-employed CPA. Ralph is one of Steve's employees. During the year, Steve and Ralph incur the following expenses:

	Steve	Ralph
Dues to American Institute of CPAs and State Society of CPAs	$ 400	$ 300
Subscriptions to professional journals	500	200
Registration fees for tax conferences	800	800
	$1,700	$1,300

Steve does not reimburse any of his employees for dues, subscriptions, or educational programs.

Steve's expenses are classified as a deduction *for* AGI because they are considered business expenses since he is a sole proprietor. Therefore, he can deduct the $1,700 on his Federal income tax return. Ralph's unreimbursed employee business expenses are classified as deductions *from* AGI. Ralph will be able to benefit from the $1,300 of expenses on his Federal income tax return only if his itemized deductions exceed his standard deduction. If he takes the standard deduction instead, the $1,300 of expenses will have no effect on the calculation of his taxable income. Even if Ralph does itemize deductions, he still may not benefit from the deduction because of the 2 percent-of-AGI phaseout rule for certain itemized deductions.

Concept Summary 6.3 shows the classification of deductions as deductions *for* AGI or as deductions *from* AGI.

It is important to understand that deductions *for* AGI may directly affect the *amount* of itemized deductions. The impact arises because many itemized deductions are limited to amounts in excess of specified percentages of AGI. Examples of such itemized deductions are medical expenses; personal casualty losses; and, as shown in Example 1, unreimbursed employee expenses.

Example 2

Tina, age 36, earns a salary of $80,000 and has no other income. She itemizes her deductions during 2014. Unreimbursed medical expenses for the year are $12,000. Tina's medical expense deduction is $4,000, as computed below. Alternatively, assume that Tina receives a $10,000 bonus from her employer in 2014. Her AGI would then be $90,000 ($80,000 + $10,000), and her medical expense is reduced by $1,000 to $3,000.

	No Bonus	Bonus
Qualified medical expenses	$12,000	$12,000
Reduction: AGI × 10%	(8,000)	(9,000)
Deductible medical expenses	$ 4,000	$ 3,000

When Tina's income increased by $10,000, this reduced her medical expense deduction; so the total effect on taxable income is an increase of $11,000.[2]

6-1a Classifying Deductions

It is important to understand that two key issues must be resolved for any potential deduction. First, it must be determined whether the item is deductible, as

---

[2]Example 4 in Chapter 3 illustrates this same point!

discussed in Section 6-1b. If the item is deductible, then the second issue is to determine if the deduction is classified as *for* AGI or *from* AGI. To understand how deductions of individual taxpayers are classified, it is necessary to examine the role of § 62. The purpose of § 62 is to classify various deductions as deductions *for* AGI. It does not provide the statutory authority for taking the deduction.

If a deduction is not listed in § 62, it is an itemized deduction, not a deduction *for* AGI. Following is a *partial* list of the items classified as deductions *for* AGI by § 62:

- Expenses attributable to a trade or business carried on by the taxpayer. A trade or business does not include the performance of services by the taxpayer as an employee (refer to Chapter 9).
- Expenses incurred by a taxpayer in connection with the performance of services as an employee if the expenses are reimbursed and other conditions are satisfied (refer to Chapter 9).
- Deductions that result from losses on the sale or exchange of property by the taxpayer (refer to Chapters 14 and 16).
- Deductions attributable to property held for the production of rents and royalties (discussed in this chapter).
- The deduction for payment of alimony (refer to Chapter 4).
- The deduction for part of the self-employment tax paid by a self-employed taxpayer (refer to Chapter 13).
- The deduction for the medical insurance premiums paid by a self-employed taxpayer for coverage of the taxpayer, a spouse, and any dependents (refer to Chapter 10).
- Certain contributions to pension, profit sharing, and annuity plans of self-employed individuals (refer to Chapters 9 and 19).
- The deduction for certain retirement savings allowed by § 219 (e.g., traditional IRAs) (refer to Chapters 9 and 19).
- The penalty imposed on premature withdrawal of funds from time savings accounts or deposits (refer to Chapter 19).
- The deduction for moving expenses (refer to Chapter 9).
- The deduction for interest paid on student loans (refer to Chapters 9 and 10).
- The deduction for qualified tuition and related expenses under § 222 if extended to 2014 by Congress. (refer to Chapter 9).
- The deduction for up to $250 for teacher supplies for elementary and secondary school teachers if extended to 2014 by Congress. (refer to Chapter 9).

6-1b Authority for Deductions

The specific authority for deductions is provided in many different Code sections. However, two of the most important are § 212 and § 162. To determine the proper authority for claiming a deduction, first determine what type of activity the expenditure relates to. All activities can be divided into one of the following mutually exclusive categories:

1. Investment/production of income (§ 212)
2. Trade or business (§ 162)
3. Personal (various sections)

For example, are legal expenses deductible? To make that determination, first determine whether the legal expense relates to an investment, trade or business or to personal activity.

Section 212 Expenses

Section 212 allows deductions for ordinary and necessary expenses paid or incurred for the following:

- The production or collection of income.
- The management, conservation, or maintenance of property held for the production of income.
- Expenses paid in connection with the determination, collection, or refund of any tax.

Section 212 expenses may be *for* AGI or *from* AGI. Common examples of deductions *for* AGI are expenses related to rent and royalty income (reported on Schedule E) and professional fees paid to determine tax liability for a sole proprietor (reported on Schedule C), a farmer (Schedule F), or one that has rent or royalties (Schedule E). All other § 212 expenses are itemized deductions (deductions *from* AGI). For example, investment-related expenses (e.g., safe deposit box rentals) are deductible as itemized deductions attributable to the production of investment income.[3]

Section 162 Trade or Business Expenses

Section 162(a) permits a deduction for all ordinary and necessary expenses paid or incurred in carrying on a trade or business. These include reasonable salaries paid for services, expenses for the use of business property, and part of self-employment taxes paid (see Chapter 13). Such expenses are deducted *for* AGI.

It is sometimes difficult to determine whether an expenditure is deductible as a trade or business expense. The term *trade or business* is not defined in the Code or Regulations, and the courts have not provided a satisfactory definition. It is usually necessary to ask one or more of the following questions to determine whether an item qualifies as a trade or business expense:

- Was the use of the particular item related to a business activity? For example, if funds are borrowed for use in a business, the interest is deductible as a business expense.
- Was the expenditure incurred with the intent to realize a profit or to produce income? For example, expenses in excess of the income from raising horses are not deductible if the activity is classified as a personal hobby rather than a trade or business.
- Were the taxpayer's operation and management activities extensive enough to indicate the carrying on of a trade or business?

Section 162 *excludes* the following items from classification as trade or business expenses:

- Charitable contributions or gifts.
- Illegal bribes and kickbacks and certain treble damage payments.
- Fines and penalties.

6-1c Deduction Criteria for § 162 and § 212

The terms **ordinary and necessary** are found in both § 162 and § 212. To be deductible, any trade or business expense must be "ordinary and necessary." In addition, compensation for services must be "reasonable" in amount.

Many expenses that are necessary may not be ordinary. Neither "ordinary" nor "necessary" is defined in the Code or Regulations. The courts have held that an expense is *necessary* if a prudent businessperson would incur the same expense and the expense is expected to be appropriate and helpful in the taxpayer's business.[4] But as Example 3 shows, no deduction will be allowed unless the expense is also ordinary.

---

[3]§ 62(a)(4) and Reg. § 1.212–1(g).

[4]*Welch v. Helvering*, 3 USTC ¶1164, 12 AFTR 1456, 54 S.Ct. 8 (USSC, 1933).

Example 3	Pat purchased a business that had just been adjudged bankrupt. Because the business had a poor financial rating, Pat wanted to restore its financial reputation. Consequently, he paid off some of the debts owed by the former owners that had been cancelled by the bankruptcy court. Because Pat had no legal obligation to make these payments, the U.S. Supreme Court found he was trying to generate goodwill. Although the payments were necessary (i.e., appropriate and helpful), they were *not* ordinary and their deduction *was not* allowed.[5]

An expense is *ordinary* if it is normal, usual, or customary in the type of business conducted by the taxpayer and is not capital in nature.[6] However, an expense need not be recurring to be deductible as ordinary. For example, a business may be in a situation that is a very rare occurrence and incur an expense. If other businesses in a similar situation are likely to incur a similar expense, then the expense can be ordinary, even though it it not recurring.

Example 4	Albert engaged in a mail-order business. The post office judged that his advertisements were false and misleading. Under a fraud order, the post office stamped "fraudulent" on all letters addressed to Albert's business and returned them to the senders. Albert spent $30,000 on legal fees in an unsuccessful attempt to force the post office to stop. The legal fees (although not recurring) were ordinary business expenses because they were normal, usual, or customary in the circumstances.[7]

For § 212 deductions, the law requires that expenses bear a reasonable and proximate relationship to (1) the production or collection of income or to (2) the management, conservation, or maintenance of property held for the production of income.[8]

Example 5	Debbye is a retired pilot who owns a small portfolio of investments, including 10 shares of Robin, Inc., a publicly traded company, worth $1,000. She incurred $350 in travel expenses to attend the annual shareholders' meeting where she voted her 10 shares against the current management group. No deduction is permitted because a 10-share investment is insignificant in value in relation to the travel expenses incurred.[9]

The Code refers to **reasonableness** solely with respect to salaries and other compensation for services.[10] But the courts have held that for any business expense to be ordinary and necessary, it must also be reasonable in amount.[11]

What constitutes reasonableness is a question of fact. If an expense is unreasonable, the excess amount is not allowed as a deduction. The question of reasonableness generally arises with respect to closely held corporations where there is no separation of ownership and management.

Transactions between the shareholders and the closely held company may result in the disallowance of deductions for excessive salaries and rent expense paid by the corporation to the shareholders. The courts will view an unusually large salary in light of all relevant circumstances and may find that the salary is reasonable despite its size.[12] If excessive payments for salaries and rents are closely related to the percentage of stock owned by the recipients, the payments are generally treated as dividends.[13] Because dividends are not deductible by the corporation, the disallowance results in an increase in the corporate taxable income. Deductions for reasonable salaries will not be disallowed *solely* because the corporation has paid insubstantial portions of its earnings as dividends to its shareholders.

[5]*Welch v. Helvering,* cited in footnote 4. But compare, *Dunn and McCarthy, Inc. v. Comm.,* 43–2 USTC ¶9688, 31 AFTR 1043, 139 F.2d 242 (CA–2, 1943) where a deduction was allowed. In *Dunn,* most of the creditors were unpaid creditor-employees. As they continued to work for the new owner, paying their loans was maintaining *existing* goodwill—not creating *new* goodwill.

[6]*Deputy v. DuPont,* 40–1 USTC ¶9161, 23 AFTR 808, 60 S.Ct. 363 (USSC, 1940).

[7]*Comm. v. Heininger,* 44–1 USTC ¶9109, 31 AFTR 783, 64 S.Ct. 249 (USSC, 1943).

[8]Reg. § 1.212–1(d).

[9]*J. Raymond Dyer,* 36 T.C. 456 (1961).

[10]§ 162(a)(1).

[11]*Comm. v. Lincoln Electric Co.,* 49–2 USTC ¶9388, 38 AFTR 411, 176 F.2d 815 (CA–6, 1949).

[12]*Kennedy, Jr. v. Comm.,* 82–1 USTC ¶9186, 49 AFTR 2d 82–628, 671 F.2d 167 (CA–6, 1982), *rev'g* 72 T.C. 793 (1979).

[13]Reg. § 1.162–8.

Example 6

Sparrow Corporation, a closely held corporation, is owned equally by Lupe, Carlos, and Ramon. The company has been highly profitable for several years and has not paid dividends. Lupe, Carlos, and Ramon are key officers of the company, and each receives a salary of $200,000. Salaries for similar positions in comparable companies average only $100,000. Amounts paid the owners in excess of $100,000 may be deemed unreasonable; if so, a total of $300,000 in salary deductions by Sparrow is disallowed. The disallowed amounts are treated as dividends rather than salary income to Lupe, Carlos, and Ramon because the payments are proportional to stock ownership. Salaries are deductible by the corporation, but dividends are not. Note that the shareholders may benefit from this reclassification. Salaries would be taxed at ordinary income rates and are subject to payroll taxes. However, dividend income would be taxed at long-term capital rates if qualified.

6-1d Personal Expenses

Expenditures that are incurred in one's personal life are not deductible unless a specific Code section authorizes the deduction. These expenses, which generally are not related to the production of income, are usually deductions *from* AGI and, in some cases, must be less than (or greater than) a certain percentage of the AGI. Some of the more frequently encountered deductions in this category include the following:

- Contributions to qualified charitable organizations.
- Medical expenses.
- Certain state and local taxes.
- Personal casualty losses.
- Certain personal interest.
- Legal fees, but only if they relate to the determination of a tax liability.

Itemized deductions are discussed in detail in Chapter 10.

6-1e Business and Nonbusiness Losses

Section 165 provides for a deduction for losses not compensated for by insurance. As a general rule, deductible losses of individual taxpayers are limited to those incurred in a trade or business or in a transaction entered into for profit. Individuals also are allowed to deduct losses that are the result of a casualty. Casualty losses include, but are not limited to, those caused by fire, storm, shipwreck, and theft. See Chapter 7 for a further discussion of this topic. A personal casualty loss is an itemized deduction.

6-1f Reporting Procedures

All deductions *for* AGI are ultimately reported on page 1 of Form 1040. Most of the deductions *for* AGI originate on supporting schedules. Examples include business expenses (Schedule C); rent, royalty, partnership, and fiduciary deductions (Schedule E); and farming expenses (Schedule F). Other deductions *for* AGI, such as traditional IRAs, Keogh retirement plans, and alimony, are entered directly on page 1 of Form 1040.

Adjusted gross income appears on the last line of page 1 and, again, on the first line of page 2. The total of all itemized deductions, which is carried over from Schedule A, is then subtracted *from* AGI. After that, personal and dependency exemptions are deducted to arrive at taxable income.

As indicated in Figure 6.1, some Schedule A deductions originate on other forms. Form 1040 incorporates the deductible amounts for many expenses that are computed on other schedules and forms. Also, see Concept Summary 6.3 later in the chapter for the classification of deductions as *for* AGI or *from* AGI.

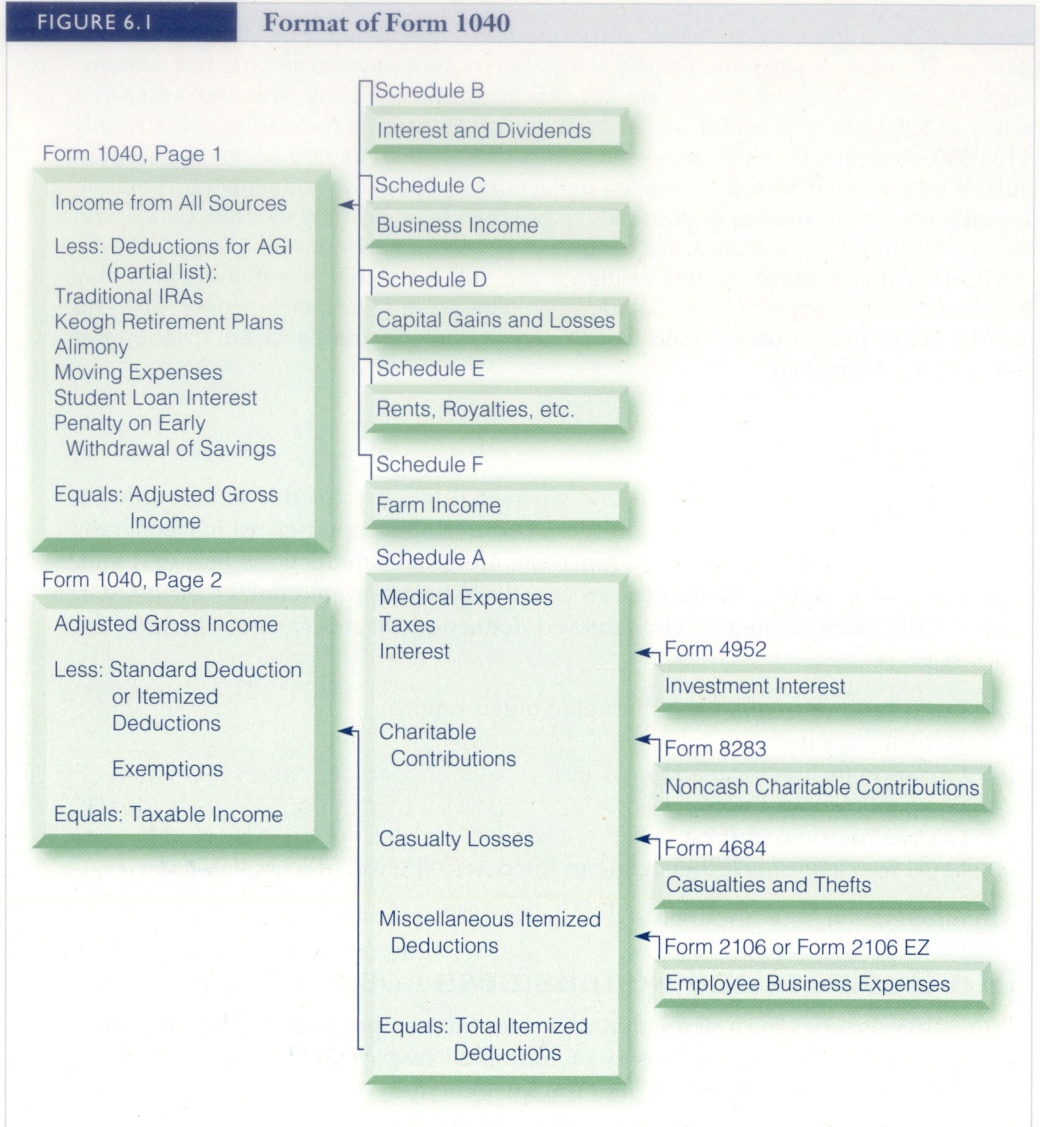

| FIGURE 6.1 | Format of Form 1040 |

6-2 DEDUCTIONS AND LOSSES—TIMING OF EXPENSE RECOGNITION

LO.2

Describe the cash and accrual methods of accounting with emphasis on the deduction aspects.

6-2a Importance of Taxpayer's Method of Accounting

A taxpayer's **accounting method** is a major factor in determining taxable income. The method used determines when an item is includible in income and when an item is deductible on the tax return. Usually, the taxpayer's regular method of record keeping is used for income tax purposes.[14] The taxing authorities do not require uniformity among all taxpayers. They do require that the method used clearly reflect income and that items be handled consistently.[15] The most common methods of accounting are the cash method and the accrual method. If a taxpayer owns multiple businesses, it may be possible to use the cash method for some and the accrual method for others.

---

[14]§ 446(a).   [15]§§ 446(b) and (e); Reg. § 1.446–1(a)(2).

Throughout the portions of the Code dealing with deductions, the phrase *paid or incurred* is used. *Paid* refers to the cash basis taxpayer who gets a deduction only in the year of payment. *Incurred* concerns the accrual basis taxpayer who obtains the deduction in the year in which the liability for the expense becomes certain (refer to Chapter 4).

6-2b Cash Method Requirements

The expenses of cash basis taxpayers are deductible only when they are actually paid with cash or other property. Promising to pay or issuing a note does not satisfy the actually paid requirement.[16] However, the payment can be made with borrowed funds. At the time taxpayers charge expenses on their credit cards, they are allowed to claim the deduction. They are deemed to have simultaneously borrowed money from the credit card issuer and constructively paid the expenses.[17]

Although the cash basis taxpayer must have actually or constructively paid the expense, payment does not ensure a current deduction. Cash basis and accrual basis taxpayers cannot take a current deduction for capital expenditures except through amortization, depletion, or depreciation over the life (actual or statutory) of the asset. The Regulations set forth the general rule that an expenditure that creates an asset having a useful life that extends substantially beyond the end of the tax year must be capitalized.[18] Examples 7 and 8 illustrate how this rule applies to prepaid expenses.

> **Example 7**
>
> John, a calendar year and cash basis taxpayer, rents property from Carl. On July 1, 2014, John pays $24,000 rent for the 24 months ending June 30, 2016. The prepaid rent extends 18 months after the close of the tax year—substantially beyond the year of payment. Therefore, John must capitalize the prepaid rent and amortize the expense on a monthly basis. His deduction for 2014 is $6,000.

The Tax Court and the IRS took the position that an asset that will expire or be consumed by the end of the tax year following the year of payment must be prorated. The Ninth Circuit Court of Appeals held that such expenditures are currently deductible, however, and the Supreme Court apparently concurs (the one-year rule for prepaid expenses).[19]

> **Example 8**
>
> Assume the same facts as in Example 7, except that John is required to pay only 12 months' rent in 2014. He pays $12,000 on July 1, 2014. The entire $12,000 is deductible in 2014 as the benefit does not extend beyond the end of 2015.

The payment must be required, not a voluntary prepayment, to obtain the current deduction under the one-year rule.[20] The taxpayer must also demonstrate that allowing the current deduction will not result in a material distortion of income. Generally, the deduction will be allowed if the item is recurring or was made for a business purpose rather than to manipulate income.[21]

As Chapter 18 explains, not all taxpayers are allowed to use the cash method.[22] For example, in most cases, the taxpayer is required to use the accrual method for sales and cost of goods sold if inventories are an income-producing factor of the business.

---

[16]*Page v. Rhode Island Trust Co., Exr.*, 37–1 USTC ¶9138, 19 AFTR 105, 88 F.2d 192 (CA–1, 1937).

[17]Rev.Rul. 78–39, 1978–1 C.B. 73. See also Rev.Rul. 80–335, 1980–2 C.B. 170, which applies to pay-by-phone arrangements.

[18]Reg. § 1.461–1(a).

[19]*Zaninovich v. Comm.*, 80–1 USTC ¶9342, 45 AFTR 2d 80–1442, 616 F.2d 429 (CA–9, 1980), *rev'g* 69 T.C. 605 (1978). Cited by the Supreme Court

in *Hillsboro National Bank v. Comm.*, 83–1 USTC ¶9229, 51 AFTR 2d 83–874, 103 S.Ct. 1134 (USSC, 1983).

[20]*Bonaire Development Co. v. Comm.*, 82–2 USTC ¶9428, 50 AFTR 2d 82–5167, 679 F.2d 159 (CA–9, 1982).

[21]*Keller v. Comm.*, 84–1 USTC ¶9194, 53 AFTR 2d 84–663, 725 F.2d 1173 (CA–8, 1984), *aff'g* 79 T.C. 7 (1982).

[22]§ 448.

6-2c Accrual Method Requirements

The period in which an accrual basis taxpayer can deduct an expense is determined by applying the *all events test* and the *economic performance test*. That is, a deduction cannot be claimed until (1) all of the events have occurred to create the taxpayer's liability and (2) the amount of the liability can be determined with reasonable accuracy. Once these requirements are satisfied, the deduction is permitted only if economic performance has occurred. The economic performance test is met only when the service, property, or use of property giving rise to the liability is actually performed for, provided to, or used by the taxpayer.[23]

Example 9

Chris's entertainment business sponsored a jazz festival in a rented auditorium at a local college. His business is responsible for cleaning up after the festival, which took place on December 22, 2014, and reinstalling the auditorium seats. Because the college is closed over the Christmas holidays, the company hired by Chris to perform the work did not begin these activities until January 2, 2015. Chris's business cannot deduct its $1,200 labor cost until 2015, when the services are performed.

An exception to the economic performance requirements allows certain *recurring items* to be deducted if all of the following conditions are met:

- The item is recurring in nature and is treated consistently by the taxpayer.
- Either the accrued item is not material or accruing it results in better matching of income and expenses.
- All of the events have occurred that determine the fact of the liability, and the amount of the liability can be determined with reasonable accuracy.
- Economic performance occurs within a reasonable period (but not later than $8\frac{1}{2}$ months after the close of the taxable year).[24]

Example 10

Rick, an accrual basis, calendar year taxpayer, entered into a monthly maintenance contract during the year. He makes a monthly accrual at the end of every month for this service and pays the fee sometime between the first and fifteenth of the following month when services are performed. The amount involved is immaterial, and all of the other tests are met. The December 2014 accrual is deductible in 2014 even though the service is performed on January 12, 2015.

Example 11

Rita, an accrual basis, calendar year taxpayer, shipped merchandise sold on December 30, 2014, via Greyhound Van Lines on January 2, 2015, and paid the freight charges at that time. Because Rita reported the sale of the merchandise in 2014, the shipping charge should also be deductible in 2014. This procedure results in a better matching of income and expenses.

Reserves for estimated expenses (frequently employed for financial accounting purposes) generally are not allowed for tax purposes because the economic performance test cannot be satisfied.

Example 12

Blackbird Airlines is required by Federal law to test its engines after 3,000 flying hours. Aircraft cannot return to flight until the tests have been conducted. An unrelated aircraft maintenance company does all of the company's tests for $1,500 per engine. For financial reporting purposes, the company accrues an expense based upon $.50 per hour of flight and credits an allowance account. The actual amounts paid for maintenance are offset against the allowance account. For tax purposes, the economic performance test is not satisfied until the work has been done. Therefore, the reserve method cannot be used for tax purposes.

---

[23]§ 461(h).   [24]§ 461(h)(3)(A).

6-3 DISALLOWANCE POSSIBILITIES

The tax law provides for the disallowance of certain types of expenses. Without specific restrictions in the tax law, taxpayers might attempt to deduct items that, in reality, are personal expenditures. For example, specific tax rules are provided to determine whether an expenditure is for trade or business purposes or related to a personal hobby.

6-3a Public Policy Limitation

Certain disallowance provisions are a codification or extension of prior court decisions. For example, after the courts denied deductions for payments considered to be in violation of public policy, the tax law was changed to provide specific authority for the disallowance of these deductions. Discussions of specific disallowance provisions in the tax law follow.

Justification for Denying Deductions

The courts developed the principle that a payment in violation of public policy is not a necessary expense and is not deductible.[25] Although a bribe or fine may be helpful, and may even contribute to the profitability of an activity, the courts held that to allow such expenses would be contrary to public policy. A deduction would, in effect, be indirectly subsidizing a taxpayer's wrongdoing.

Because tax law did not explain which actions violated public policy, the IRS and taxpayers had no clear guidance as to whether an expense was contrary to public policy. To solve these problems, Congress enacted legislation that attempts to better define the use of the public policy doctrine. Under the legislation, the following deductions are disallowed for certain specific types of expenditures that are considered contrary to public policy:

- Bribes and kickbacks, including those associated with Medicare or Medicaid (in the case of foreign bribes and kickbacks, only if the payments violate the U.S. Foreign Corrupt Practices Act of 1977).
- Fines and penalties paid to a government for violation of law.

LO.3

Apply the Internal Revenue Code deduction disallowance provisions associated with the following: public policy limitations, political activities, excessive executive compensation, investigation of business opportunities, hobby losses, vacation home rentals, payment of others' expenses, personal expenditures, capital expenditures, related-party transactions, and expenses related to tax-exempt income.

THE BIG PICTURE

Example 13

Refer to the facts of *The Big Picture* on p. 6-1. Dr. Payne had not instituted proper procedures for disposing of medical waste from his laboratory. During the current tax year, he was fined $3,000 by the city. Dr. Payne believes the fine should be deducted as an ordinary business expense. However, because the fine was due to a violation of public policy, the $3,000 is not deductible.

- Two-thirds of the treble damage payments made to claimants resulting from violation of the antitrust law.[26]

To be disallowed, the bribe or kickback must be illegal under either Federal or state law and must also subject the payor to a criminal penalty or the loss of a license or privilege to engage in a trade or business. For a bribe or kickback that is illegal under state law, a deduction is denied if the state law is generally enforced.

Example 14

During the year, Keith, an insurance salesperson, paid $5,000 to Karen, a real estate broker. The payment represented 20% of the commissions Keith earned from customers referred by Karen. Under state law, the splitting of commissions by an insurance salesperson is an act of misconduct that could warrant a revocation of the salesperson's license. Keith's $5,000 payments to Karen are not deductible if the state law is generally enforced.

---

[25]*Tank Truck Rentals, Inc. v. Comm.*, 58–1 USTC ¶9366, 1 AFTR 2d 1154, 78 S.Ct. 507 (USSC, 1958).

[26]§§ 162(c), (f), and (g).

Global Tax Issues

High Fashion? At What Price?

The Foreign Corrupt Practices Act (FCPA) is intended to punish taxpayers who make illegal payments to foreign officials to obtain economic advantages. Not only are such payments (usually improperly recorded as business expenses) nondeductible for income tax purposes, but serious and consistent violations can lead to the imposition of fines. Severe consequences can result from violating the bribery provisions of the FCPA, as Ralph Lauren recently discovered.

Ralph Lauren Corporation is known for its high-quality and expensive merchandise. To remove some of the bureaucratic hurdles that could significantly delay the time it takes to get merchandise into Argentina, Ralph Lauren employees had been providing dresses, perfume, and cash to Argentine customs officials. The bribes, which occurred over a five-year period, were labeled as "loading and delivery expenses" to disguise them. An internal investigation at Ralph Lauren uncovered this illegal activity, and company officials reported the crimes to the Department of Justice and the Securities and Exchange Commission. The company was required to pay over $1.5 million in penalties due to violation of the FCPA. Note that companies spend large amounts of money to conduct investigations such as the one performed by Ralph Lauren to ensure compliance with the FCPA.

While the Ralph Lauren managers in Argentina were willing to violate the law to attempt to increase their business sales, the efforts had little success. Besides resulting in large penalties for Ralph Lauren (which are not deductible), the company decided to leave the Argentina market in 2012 due to economic and currency issues.

Source: Based on Chad Bray, "Perfume, Dresses and Cash in Ralph Lauren Bribe Case," *Wall Street Journal*, April 23, 2013, pp. B1 and B2.

Legal Expenses Incurred in Defense of Civil or Criminal Penalties

To deduct legal expenses, the taxpayer must be able to show that the origin and character of the claim are directly related to a trade or business; an income-producing activity; or the determination, collection, or refund of a tax. Personal legal expenses are not deductible. Thus, legal fees incurred in connection with a criminal defense are deductible only if the crime is associated with the taxpayer's trade or business or income-producing activity.[27]

Example 15

Debra, a financial officer of Blue Corporation, incurs legal expenses in connection with her defense in a criminal indictment for evasion of Blue's income taxes. Debra may deduct her legal expenses because she is deemed to be in the trade or business of being an executive. The legal action impairs her ability to conduct this business activity.[28]

Deductible legal expenses associated with the following are deductible *for* AGI:

* Ordinary and necessary expenses incurred in connection with a trade or business.
* Ordinary and necessary expenses incurred in conjunction with rental or royalty property held for the production of income.

All other deductible legal expenses are deductible *from* AGI. For example, legal expenses generally are deductible *from* AGI if they are for fees for tax advice relative to the preparation of an individual's income tax return. Contrast this with the *for* AGI classification of legal fees for tax advice relative to the preparation of the portion of the tax return for a sole proprietor's trade or business (Schedule C) or an individual's rental or royalty income (Schedule E).

---

[27]*Comm. v. Tellier,* 66–1 USTC ¶9319, 17 AFTR 2d 633, 86 S.Ct. 1118 (USSC, 1966).

[28]Rev.Rul. 68–662, 1968–2 C.B. 69.

Expenses Relating to an Illegal Business

The usual expenses of operating an illegal business (e.g., a gambling operation) are deductible.[29] While allowing deductions for illegal activity may seem inappropriate, recall that the law taxes net income from a business operation, not gross revenue. However, § 162 disallows a deduction for fines, bribes to public officials, illegal kickbacks, and other illegal payments whether these payments are part of a legal or illegal business.

Example 16

Sam owns and operates an illegal gambling establishment. In connection with this activity, he has the following expenses during the year:

Rent	$ 60,000
Payoffs to the police	40,000
Depreciation on equipment	100,000
Wages	140,000
Interest	30,000
Criminal fines	50,000
Illegal kickbacks	10,000
Total	$430,000

All of the usual expenses (rent, depreciation, wages, and interest) are deductible; payoffs, fines, and kickbacks are not deductible. Of the $430,000 spent, $330,000 is deductible and $100,000 is not.

An exception applies to expenses incurred in illegal trafficking in drugs.[30] *Drug dealers* are not allowed a deduction for ordinary and necessary business expenses incurred in their business. In arriving at gross income from the business, however, dealers may reduce total sales by the cost of goods sold.[31]

ETHICS & EQUITY   Medical Marijuana: Trade or Business Activity or Illegal Operation?

Cole England operates Herbal Medical Center in Sacramento, California, as a sole proprietorship. The distribution of marijuana for medical purposes is legal in California, as follows:

Medical patients and their designated primary caregivers may legally possess and cultivate (but not distribute or sell) marijuana under Health and Safety Code 11362.5 (Prop 215) if they have a physician's recommendation or approval.

This is Cole's first year of business operations. All of his patients have signed statements indicating that he is their designated primary caregiver. He also has on file physician's recommendations for all marijuana that was provided to his patients. Tax information for this year is as follows:

Revenues	$200,000
Cost of goods sold	120,000
Other expenses	50,000

Cole reported $30,000 of net income on Schedule C this year for Herbal Medical Center. Is this position appropriate?

6-3b Political Contributions and Lobbying Activities

Generally, no business deduction is permitted for direct or indirect payments for political purposes.[32] Historically, the government has been reluctant to accord favorable tax treatment to business expenditures for political purposes. Allowing deductions might encourage abuses and enable businesses to have undue influence on the political process.

---

[29]*Comm. v. Sullivan,* 58–1 USTC ¶9368, 1 AFTR 2d 1158, 78 S.Ct. 512 (USSC, 1958).

[30]§ 280E.

[31]Reg. § 1.61–3(a). Gross income is defined as sales minus cost of goods sold. Thus, while § 280E prohibits any deductions for drug dealers, it does not modify the normal definition of gross income.

[32]§ 276.

THE BIG PICTURE

Example 17

Refer to the facts of *The Big Picture* on p. 6-1. Dr. Payne had made political contributions to the State Senate campaigns of Tom Smith and Virginia White. Dr. Payne made these contributions to encourage these senators to support a new bill that is beneficial to the state's dental profession. Therefore, he assumed that these would be deductible business expenses. However, political contributions are not deductible, so he will receive no tax benefit from them.

Lobbying expenses incurred in attempting to influence state or Federal legislation or the actions of certain high-ranking public officials are not deductible.[33] The disallowance also applies to a pro rata portion of the membership dues of trade associations and other groups that are involved in lobbying activities.

Example 18

Egret Company pays a $10,000 annual membership fee to the Free Trade Group, a trade association for plumbing wholesalers. The trade association estimates that 70% of its dues are allocated to lobbying activities. Thus, Egret Company's deduction is limited to $3,000 ($10,000 × 30%).

There are three exceptions to the disallowance of lobbying expenses. First, an exception is provided for influencing local legislation (e.g., city and county governments). Second, the disallowance provision does not apply to activities devoted solely to monitoring legislation. Third, a *de minimis* exception is provided for annual in-house expenditures (lobbying expenses other than those paid to professional lobbyists or any portion of dues used by associations for lobbying) if such expenditures do not exceed $2,000. If the in-house expenditures exceed $2,000, none of the in-house expenditures can be deducted.

6-3c Excessive Executive Compensation

The deduction of executive compensation normally is subject to two limitations. As discussed earlier in this chapter, the compensation of shareholder-employees of closely held corporations is subject to the reasonableness requirement. The second limitation, the so-called millionaires' provision, applies to publicly held corporations (a corporation that has at least one class of stock registered under the Securities Exchange Act of 1934).[34]

The millionaires' provision does not limit the amount of compensation that can be paid to an employee. Instead, it limits the amount the employer can deduct for the compensation of a covered executive to $1 million annually. Covered employees as defined by the SEC are the principal executive officer (PEO), the principal financial officer (PFO), and the three other most highly compensated executives.

Employee compensation *excludes* the following:

- Commissions based on individual performance.
- Certain performance-based compensation tied to company performance using a formula approved by a board of directors compensation committee (composed solely of two or more outside directors) and by shareholder vote. The performance attainment must be certified by this compensation committee.
- Payments to tax-qualified retirement plans.
- Payments that are excludible from the employee's gross income (e.g., certain fringe benefits).

---

[33]§ 162(e).   [34]§ 162(m).

6-3d Investigation of a Business

Investigation expenses are expenses paid or incurred to determine the feasibility of entering a new business or expanding an existing business. They include such costs as travel, engineering and architectural surveys, marketing reports, and various legal and accounting services. How such expenses are treated for tax purposes depends on a number of variables, including the following:

- The current business, if any, of the taxpayer.
- The nature of the business being investigated.
- The extent to which the investigation has proceeded.
- Whether the acquisition actually takes place.

If the taxpayer is in a business that is the *same as or similar to* that being investigated, all investigation expenses are deductible in the year paid or incurred. The tax result is the same whether or not the taxpayer acquires the business being investigated.[35]

THE BIG PICTURE

Example 19

Refer to the facts of *The Big Picture* on p. 6-1. Dr. Payne believes that his administrative and business skills can be used to turn around dental practices whose revenues have been declining. He investigates Teeth Restoration, LLC, a local dental practice that is for sale. Expenses paid to consultants and accountants as part of this investigation totaled $6,000. He determined that Teeth Restoration would not be a good investment, so he did not buy it. The $6,000 spent to investigate this business is deductible as a business expense because Dr. Payne is already in the dental business. Investigating new business opportunities in one's current trade or business is an ordinary and necessary business expense.

---

[35]§ 195. *York v. Comm.*, 58–2 USTC ¶9952, 2 AFTR 2d 6178, 261 F.2d 421 (CA–4, 1958).

When the taxpayer is *not* in a business that is the same as or similar to the one being investigated, the tax result depends on whether the new business is acquired. If the business is not acquired, all investigation expenses generally are nondeductible.[36]

Example 20	Lynn, a retired merchant, incurs expenses in traveling from Rochester, New York, to California to investigate the feasibility of acquiring several auto care centers. If no acquisition takes place, none of the expenses are deductible.

If the taxpayer is *not* in a business that is the same as or similar to the one being investigated and actually acquires the new business, the expenses must be capitalized as **startup expenditures**. Startup costs are not deductible under § 162 because they are incurred *before* a business begins rather than in the course of operating a trade or business. The first $5,000 of the expenses is immediately deducted. Any excess of expenses is amortized over a period of 180 months (15 years). In arriving at the $5,000 immediate deduction allowed, a dollar-for-dollar reduction must be made for those expenses in excess of $50,000.[37] An election can be made by the taxpayer to not deduct or amortize any portion of the startup costs. In that case, this intangible asset will remain on the balance sheet until the business is sold.

Example 21	Tina owns and operates 10 restaurants located in various cities throughout the Southeast. She travels to Atlanta to discuss the acquisition of an auto dealership. In addition, she incurs legal and accounting costs associated with the potential acquisition. After incurring total investigation costs of $52,000, she acquires the auto dealership on October 1, 2014.
	Tina may immediately deduct $3,000 [$5,000 − ($52,000 − $50,000)] and amortize the balance of $49,000 ($52,000 − $3,000) over a period of 180 months. For calendar year 2014, therefore, Tina can deduct $3,817 [$3,000 + ($49,000 × 3/180)].

ETHICS & EQUITY   Business Investigation or Vacation?

Jacob owns and operates several small motels throughout cities in Kentucky that are located near an interstate highway. The motel business is reported on Schedule C as a sole proprietorship. Jacob is married and has three children, two boys and one girl, who are in elementary school. Jacob's wife has wanted to take the children to Disney World in Orlando, Florida, for the last two years. This year she has suggested that they drive to Orlando during the Christmas holiday break in December. After discussing this at length with his wife one night, Jacob reads an article in a trade publication that describes the benefits of owning motels across multiple states. He also notices that several motels are for sale in Orlando. Jacob decides that if the family went to Orlando for 10 days in December, he could plan a trip for his family and investigate the potential purchase of a motel in Orlando.

The family had a great trip. Total expenses are as follows:

Airfare ($300 each)	$1,500
Hotel	1,200
Meals	1,000
Theme Park tickets	1,300

During one afternoon during the trip, Jacob visited a motel that was for sale. The owners were asking $350,000 for the motel. Jacob walked around the property and inspected a few rooms. He then offered the owners $125,000, which they rejected.

When Jacob prepares his tax return for the current year, he deducts the cost of the trip to Orlando as the investigation of a business. He realizes that the theme park tickets were an optional expense during the time in Orlando, so he deducts $3,700. Is this position appropriate?

© iStockphoto.com/LdF

---

[36]Rev.Rul. 57–418, 1957–2 C.B. 143; *Morton Frank*, 20 T.C. 511 (1953); and *Dwight A. Ward*, 20 T.C. 332 (1953).

[37]§ 195(b).

CONCEPT SUMMARY 6.1

Costs of Investigating a Business

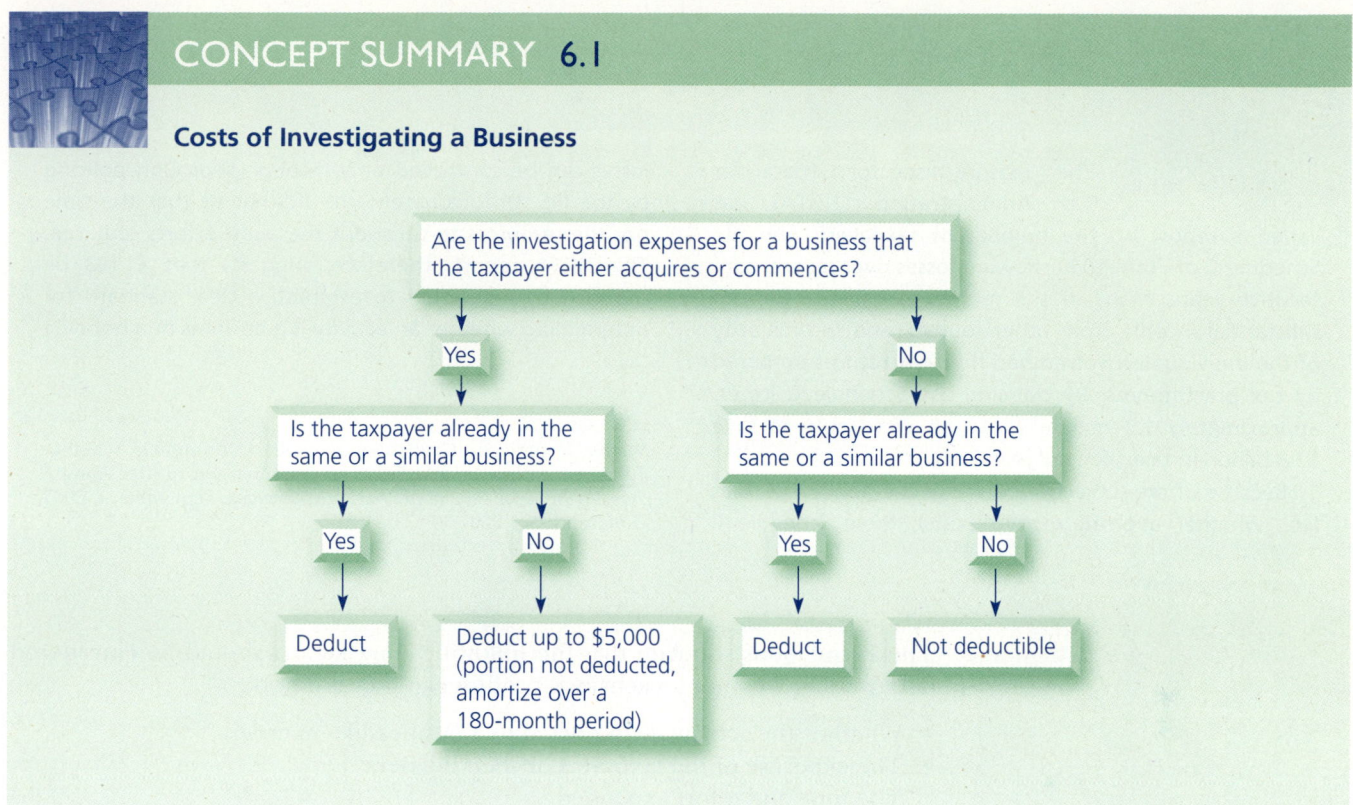

© iStockphoto.com/Andrey Prokhorov

Concept Summary 6.1 sets forth the tax rules applicable to the costs involved in investigating a business.

6-3e Hobby Losses

Business or investment expenses are deductible only if the taxpayer can show that the activity was entered into for the purpose of making a profit. Certain activities can have attributes that make it difficult to determine if the primary motivation for the activity is to make a profit or is for personal pleasure. Examples include raising horses and operating a farm used as a weekend residence. While personal losses are not deductible, losses attributable to profit-seeking activities may be deducted and used to offset a taxpayer's other income. Activities that have both personal and profit-seeking motives are classified as hobbies, and the tax law limits the deductibility of **hobby losses**.

The income and deductions from a hobby are reported separately on the tax return. Whether deductions related to a hobby generate a tax benefit, the revenue for the hobby is always reported as other income on page 1 of Form 1040. The reporting of deductions is discussed below.

General Rules

If an individual can show that an activity has been conducted with the intent to earn a profit, losses from the activity are fully deductible. The hobby loss rules apply only if the activity is not engaged in for profit. Hobby expenses are deductible only to the extent of hobby income.[38]

---

[38]§ 183(b)(2).

TAX IN THE NEWS   IRS Doing Poorly in Policing Hobby Loss Deductions

The Treasury Inspector General for Tax Administration (TIGTA) has issued a report on the number of taxpayers who file Schedule C of Form 1040 showing losses over several consecutive years. Many of the returns examined reported substantial income from other sources, and the majority of the individuals involved had their tax returns prepared by tax practitioners. By claiming the Schedule C losses, approximately 1.2 million taxpayers were able to save $2.8 billion in taxes for tax year 2005.

Because of the subjective nature of the hobby loss rules (i.e., whether a profit motive exists), these Schedule C losses can be controlled only through thorough policing by the IRS. Unfortunately, the IRS has neither the time nor the resources to carry out the audit efforts required. The TIGTA report, therefore, suggests that § 183 be changed by legislation to establish a clear standard for determining whether an activity is a business or a hobby.

Source: "Significant Challenges Exist in Determining Whether Taxpayers with Schedule C Losses Are Engaged in Tax Abuse," *Treasury Inspector General for Tax Administration,* September 7, 2007 (Reference No. 2007-30-173).

The Regulations stipulate that the following nine factors should be considered in determining whether an activity is profit-seeking or is a hobby:[39]

- Whether the activity is conducted in a businesslike manner.
- The expertise of the taxpayers or their advisers.
- The time and effort expended.
- The expectation that the assets of the activity will appreciate in value.
- The taxpayer's previous success in conducting similar activities.
- The history of income or losses from the activity.
- The relationship of profits earned to losses incurred.
- The financial status of the taxpayer (e.g., if the taxpayer does not have substantial amounts of other income, this may indicate that the activity is engaged in for profit).
- Elements of personal pleasure or recreation in the activity.

The presence or absence of a factor is not by itself determinative of whether the activity is profit-seeking or is a hobby. Rather, the decision is a subjective one that is based on an analysis of the facts and circumstances.

Presumptive Rule of § 183

The Code provides a rebuttable presumption that an activity is profit-seeking if the activity shows a profit in at least three of the previous five tax years.[40] If the activity involves horses, a profit in at least two of the previous seven tax years meets the presumptive rule. If these profitability tests are met, the activity is presumed to be a trade or business rather than a personal hobby. In this situation, the IRS bears the burden of proving that the activity is personal rather than trade- or business-related. On the other hand, if the three-year test (two for horses) is not met, then the activity is presumed to be a hobby and the taxpayer has the burden to prove that it is profit-seeking.

Example 22

Camille and Walter are married taxpayers who enjoy a busy lifestyle. Camille, who is an executive for a large corporation, is paid a salary of $800,000. Walter is a collector of antiques. Several years ago he opened an antique shop in a local shopping center and spends most of his time buying and selling antiques. He occasionally earns a small profit from this activity but more frequently incurs substantial losses. If Walter's losses are business-related, they are fully deductible

---

[39]Reg. §§ 1.183–2(b)(1) through (9).   [40]§ 183(d).

against Camille's salary income on a joint return. In resolving this issue, consider the following:

- Initially determine whether Walter's antique activity has met the three-out-of-five years profit test.
- If the presumption is not met, the activity may nevertheless qualify as a business if Walter can show that the intent is to engage in a profit-seeking activity. It is not necessary to show actual profits.
- Attempt to fit the operation within the nine criteria prescribed in the Regulations listed previously.

Determining the Amount of the Deduction

If an activity is deemed to be a hobby, the expenses are deductible only to the extent of the gross income from the hobby. These expenses must be deducted in the following order:

- Amounts deductible under other Code sections without regard to the nature of the activity, such as property taxes and home mortgage interest.
- Amounts deductible under other Code sections if the activity had been engaged in for profit, but only if those amounts do not affect adjusted basis. Examples include maintenance, utilities, and supplies.
- Amounts for depreciation, amortization, and depletion.[41]

The last two categories of deductions are deductible *from* AGI as itemized deductions to the extent they exceed 2 percent of AGI.[42] If the taxpayer uses the standard deduction rather than itemizing, the hobby loss deductions generate no tax benefit. Even if this is the case, the revenue from a hobby still must be reported on page 1 of Form 1040.

		Example 23

Jim, the vice president of an oil company, has AGI of $80,000. He decides to pursue painting in his spare time. He uses a home studio comprising 10% of the home's square footage. During the current year, Jim incurs the following expenses:

Frames	$ 1,800
Art supplies	900
Fees paid to models	4,000
Home studio expenses:	
Total home property taxes	2,000
Total home mortgage interest	10,000
Total home maintenance and utilities	4,600
Calculated depreciation on 10% of home	500

During the year, Jim sold paintings for a total of $8,660. If the activity is held to be a hobby, Jim is allowed deductions as follows:

Gross income		$ 8,660
Deduct: Taxes and interest (10% of $12,000)		(1,200)
Remainder		$ 7,460
Deduct: Frames	$1,800	
Art supplies	900	
Models' fees	4,000	
Maintenance and utilities (10%)	460	(7,160)
Remainder		$ 300
Deduct: Depreciation ($500, but limited to $300)		(300)
Net income		$ –0–

---

[41]Reg. § 1.183–1(b)(1). [42]Reg. § 1.67–1T(a)(1)(iv) and Rev.Rul. 75–14, 1975–1 C.B. 90.

Jim includes the $8,660 of income in AGI, making his AGI $88,660. The taxes and interest are itemized deductions, deductible in full. The remaining $7,460 of expenses are reduced by 2% of his AGI (2% × $88,660 = $1,773), so the net deduction is $5,687. All of these deductions are reported as itemized deductions on Schedule A. Because the property taxes and home mortgage interest are deductible even without the hobby, the net effect is a $2,973 ($8,660 less $5,687) increase in taxable income.

Example 24

Assume that Jim's activity in Example 23 is held to be a business. The business is located in a small office building he owns. Expenses are property taxes of $200, mortgage interest of $1,000, frames of $1,800, art supplies of $900, models' fees of $4,000, maintenance and utilities of $460, and depreciation of $500. Under these circumstances, Jim could deduct expenses totaling $8,860. All of these expenses would be trade or business expenses deductible *for* AGI and reported on Schedule C. His reduction in AGI would be as follows:

Gross income		$ 8,660
Less: Taxes and interest	$1,200	
Other business expenses	7,160	
Depreciation	500	(8,860)
Reduction in AGI		($ 200)

6-3f Rental of Vacation Homes

Restrictions on the deductions allowed for part-year rentals of personal **vacation homes** were written into the law to prevent taxpayers from deducting essentially personal expenses as rental losses. Many taxpayers who own vacation homes use the property for personal use during a portion of the year and rent the property at other times. For example, a summer cabin would be rented for 2 months per year, used for vacationing for 1 month, and left vacant the rest of the year. If the taxpayer could then deduct 11 months' depreciation, utilities, maintenance, etc., as rental expenses, resulting in a rental loss, the taxpayer would have converted into rental expenses personal expenses from the time the property was vacant. Section 280A eliminates this treatment by not allowing a loss for property that is not used primarily for rental purposes. Only a break-even situation is allowed; no losses can be deducted.

There are three possible tax treatments for residences used for both personal and rental purposes. The treatment depends upon the *relative time* the residence is used for personal purposes versus rental use. These rules are summarized in Concept Summary 6.2.

Primarily Personal Use

If the residence is *rented* for *fewer than 15 days* in a year, it is treated as a personal residence. The rent income is excluded from gross income, and mortgage interest and real estate taxes are allowed as itemized deductions, as with any personal residence.[43] No other expenses (e.g., depreciation, utilities, and maintenance) are deductible.

Example 25

Catherine owns a vacation cottage on the lake. During the current year, she rented it for $1,600 for two weeks, lived in it two months, and left it vacant the remainder of the year. The year's expenses amounted to $6,000 mortgage interest expense, $500 property taxes, $1,500 utilities and maintenance, and $2,400 depreciation. Because the property was not rented for at least 15 days, the income is excluded, the mortgage interest and property tax expenses are itemized deductions, and the remaining expenses are nondeductible personal expenses.

---

[43]§ 280A(g).

CONCEPT SUMMARY 6.2

Vacation/Rental Home

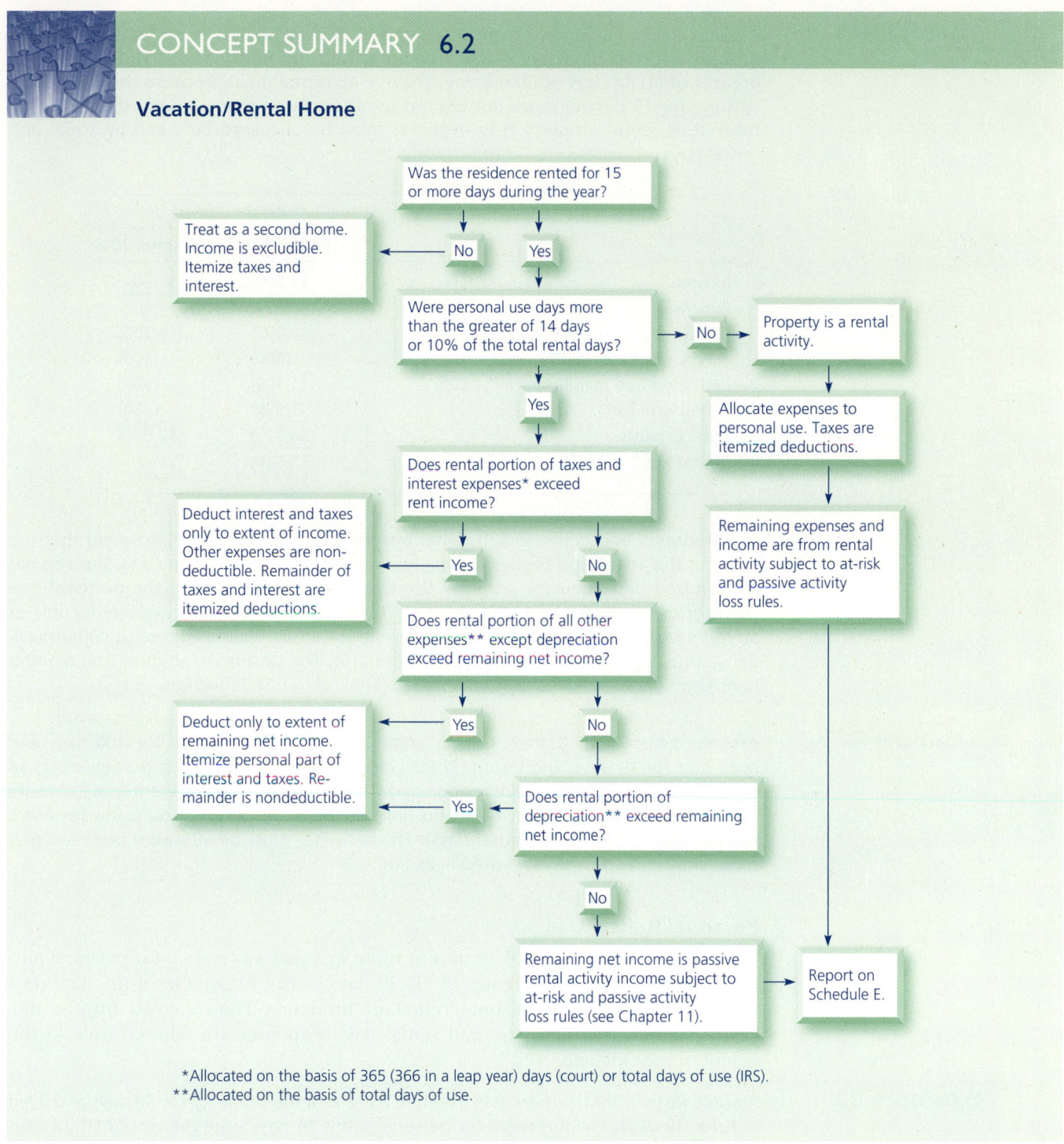

*Allocated on the basis of 365 (366 in a leap year) days (court) or total days of use (IRS).
**Allocated on the basis of total days of use.

© iStockphoto.com/Andrey Prokhorov

Primarily Rental Use

If the residence is *rented* for 15 days or more in a year and is *not used* for personal purposes for more than the greater of (1) 14 days or (2) 10 percent of the total days rented, the residence is treated as rental property.[44] The expenses must be allocated between personal and rental days if there are any personal use days during the year. The deduction of the expenses allocated to rental days can exceed rent income and result in a rental loss. The loss may be deductible, subject to the at-risk and passive activity loss rules (discussed in Chapter 11).

---

[44]§ 280A(d) and Prop.Reg. § 1.280A–3(c).

Example 26

Assume instead that Catherine in Example 25 used the cottage for 12 days and rented it for 48 days for $4,800. The threshold for personal use is 14 days—the greater of (1) 14 days or (2) 4.8 days (10% × 48 rental days). Because she rented the cottage for 15 days or more but did not use it for more than 14 days, the cottage is treated as rental property. The expenses must be allocated between personal and rental days.

	Percentage of Use	
	Rental 80%	**Personal 20%**
Income	$4,800	$ –0–
Expenses		
Mortgage interest ($6,000)	($4,800)	($1,200)
Property taxes ($500)	(400)	(100)
Utilities and maintenance ($1,500)	(1,200)	(300)
Depreciation ($2,400)	(1,920)	(480)
Total expenses	($8,320)	($2,080)
Rental loss	($3,520)	$ –0–

Catherine deducts the $3,520 rental loss *for* AGI on Schedule E (assuming that she satisifies the at-risk and passive activity loss rules, discussed in Chapter 11). She also has an itemized deduction for property taxes of $100 associated with the personal use. The mortgage interest of $1,200 associated with the personal use is not deductible as an itemized deduction because the cottage is not a qualified residence (qualified residence interest) for this purpose (see Chapter 10). The portion of utilities and maintenance and depreciation attributable to personal use is not deductible.

Example 27

Assume instead that Catherine in Example 25 rented the cottage for 200 days and lived in it for 19 days. The threshold for personal use is 20 days—the greater of (1) 14 days or (2) 20 days (10% × 200 rental days). The cottage is primarily rental use because she rented it for 15 days or more and did not use it for personal purposes for more than 20 days (10% of the rental days). The expenses must be allocated between personal and rental days as illustrated in Example 26.

Personal/Rental Use

If the residence is rented for 15 days or more in a year *and* is used for personal purposes for more than the greater of (1) 14 days or (2) 10 percent of the total days rented, it is treated as a personal/rental use residence. The expenses must be allocated between personal days and rental days. Expenses are allowed only to the extent of rent income.

Example 28

Assume instead that Catherine in Example 25 rented the property for 30 days and lived in it for 30 days. The threshold for personal use is 14 days—the greater of (1) 14 days or (2) 3 days (10% × 30 rental days). The residence is classified as personal/rental use property because she used it more than 14 days and rented it for 15 days or more. The expenses must be allocated between rental use and personal use, and the rental expenses are allowed only to the extent of rent income.

If a residence is classified as personal/rental use property, the expenses that are deductible anyway (e.g., real estate taxes and mortgage interest) must be deducted first. If a positive net income results, expenses, other than depreciation, that are deductible for rental property (e.g., maintenance, utilities, and insurance) are allowed next. Finally, if any positive balance remains, depreciation is allowed. Any disallowed expenses allocable to rental use are carried forward and used in future years subject to the same limitations. Note that these ordering rules for deductions are the same as for hobby expenses.

Expenses must be allocated between personal and rental days before the limits are applied. The courts have held that real estate taxes and mortgage interest, which accrue ratably over the year, are allocated on the basis of 365 days.[45] The IRS, however, disagrees and allocates real estate taxes and mortgage interest on the basis of total days of use.[46] Other expenses (utilities, maintenance, depreciation, etc.) are allocated on the basis of total days used.

Example 29

Jason rents his vacation home for 60 days and lives in the home for 30 days. The property is classified as personal/rental because it is rented for 15 days or more, and personal use (30 days) is greater than 14 [greater of 14 days or 6 days (10% × 60 rental days)]. Jason's gross rent income is $10,000. For the entire year, the real estate taxes are $2,190, his mortgage interest expense is $10,220, utilities and maintenance expense equals $2,400, and depreciation is $9,000. Using the IRS approach, these amounts are deductible in this specific order:

Gross income	$10,000
Deduct: Taxes and interest ($^{60}/_{90}$ × $12,410)	(8,273)
Remainder to apply to rental operating expenses and depreciation	$ 1,727
Deduct: Utilities and maintenance ($^{60}/_{90}$ × $2,400)	(1,600)
Balance	$ 127
Deduct: Depreciation ($^{60}/_{90}$ × $9,000 = $6,000 but limited to above balance)	(127)
Net rent income	$ –0–

The nonrental use portion of real estate taxes and mortgage interest ($4,137 in this case) is deductible if the taxpayer elects to itemize (see Chapter 10). The personal use portion of utilities, maintenance, and depreciation is not deductible in any case. Jason has a carryover of $5,873 ($6,000 − $127) of the unused depreciation, which he may be able to deduct in future years. Also note that the basis of the property is only reduced by the $127 depreciation allowed because of the above limitation. (See Chapter 14 for a discussion of the reduction in basis for depreciation allowed or allowable.)

Example 30

Using the court's approach in allocating real estate taxes and mortgage interest, Jason, in Example 29, would have this result:

Gross income	$10,000
Deduct: Taxes and interest ($^{60}/_{365}$ × $12,410)	(2,040)
Remainder to apply to rental operating expenses and depreciation	$ 7,960
Deduct: Utilities and maintenance ($^{60}/_{90}$ × $2,400)	(1,600)
Balance	$ 6,360
Deduct: Depreciation ($^{60}/_{90}$ × $9,000 but limited to above balance.)	(6,000)
Net rent income	$ 360

Jason can deduct $10,370 ($12,410 paid − $2,040 deducted as expense in computing net rent income) of personal use mortgage interest and real estate taxes as itemized deductions.

Note the contrasting results in Examples 29 and 30. The IRS's approach (Example 29) results in no rental gain or loss and an itemized deduction for real estate taxes and mortgage interest of $4,137. In Example 30, Jason has net rent income of $360 and $10,370 of itemized deductions. The court's approach decreases his taxable income by $10,010 ($10,370 itemized deductions less $360 net rent income). The IRS's approach reduces his taxable income by only $4,137.

---

[45]*Bolton v. Comm.*, 82–2 USTC ¶9699, 51 AFTR 2d 83–305, 694 F.2d 556 (CA–9, 1982). For leap years, the allocation is on the basis of 366 days.

[46]Prop.Reg. § 1.280A–3(d)(4).

TAX IN THE NEWS — Vacation Home Location: Times Are Changing

The purchase of vacation homes is on the upswing. This has probably resulted from an oversupply and the lower prices caused by the housing slump. But unlike the past, when the vacation homes usually were out-of-state, this new activity involves homes located nearby and in state. The driving distance from the primary residence to the vacation home is being reduced because of transportation costs.

Also, more buyers are looking for second homes that eventually will become the primary residence at retirement. Quite often, vacation homes are rented during the period between purchase and conversion from rental property to the principal residence use at retirement.

Source: Based on "Getting Away—But Not Too Far," *Wall Street Journal,* May 2, 2012, p. A3.

Conversion to Rental Property

A related issue is whether a taxpayer's *primary residence* is subject to the preceding rules if it is converted to rental property. If the vacation home rules apply, a taxpayer who converts a personal residence to rental property during the tax year, without any tax avoidance motive, could have the allowable deductions limited to the rent income. This would occur if the personal use exceeded the greater of 14 days or 10 percent of rental days test (a likely situation). To prevent this from occurring, the personal use days will not cause the property to be treated as personal/rental if once the rental period begins, the property is rented for at least 12 consecutive months at a fair rental price (a *qualified rental period*). The 12-month period could begin in the current tax year or end in the current tax year. In other words, the personal use of the property could occur before the qualified rental period or after the qualified rental period.

There are two exceptions to this rule. First, if the property is sold before the end of the 12-month period, the qualified rental period is shortened to the actual time the property is rented. Second, if the property is rented to a related party, this relief measure is not available and the property will be treated as personal/ rental.[47]

Example 31

Rhonda converts her residence to rental property on May 1 and rents it for the remainder of 2014 for $5,600 and for all of 2015 for $8,400. The house would be classified as personal/rental use property (personal use days during 2014 are greater than both 14 days and 10% of rental days). However, because a rental period of more than 12 months began in 2014, this is treated as a qualified rental period. Therefore, Rhonda's deduction for rental expenses is not limited to the gross income of $5,600 in 2014.

6-3g Expenditures Incurred for Taxpayer's Benefit or Taxpayer's Obligation

To be deductible, an expense must be incurred for the taxpayer's benefit or arise from the taxpayer's obligation. An individual cannot claim a tax deduction for the payment of the expenses of another individual.

Example 32

During the current year, Fred pays the property taxes on his son Jayden's home. Neither Fred nor Jayden can take a deduction for the amount paid for Jayden's property taxes. Fred is not entitled to a deduction because the property taxes are not his obligation. Jayden cannot claim a deduction because he did not pay the property taxes. The tax result would have been more favorable had Fred made a cash gift to Jayden and let him pay the property taxes. Then Jayden could have deducted the property taxes. Fred likely would not be liable for any gift taxes depending upon the amount involved due to the annual exclusion (see Chapter 1). A deduction would have been created with no cash difference to the family.

---

[47]§ 280A(d)(4)(A).

One exception to this disallowance rule is the payment of medical expenses for a dependent. Such expenses are deductible by the payor subject to the normal rules that limit the deductibility of medical expenses (see Chapters 3 and 10).[48]

6-3h Disallowance of Personal Expenditures

Section 262 states that "except as otherwise expressly provided in this chapter, no deduction shall be allowed for personal, living, or family expenses." To justify a deduction, an individual must be able to identify a particular section of the Code that sanctions the deduction (e.g., charitable contributions and medical expenses). Sometimes the character of a particular expenditure is not easily determined. For example, the legal fee associated with a property settlement that results in one party retaining ownership of a family business is not deductible.

The IRS has clarified the issue of the deduction of legal fees incurred in connection with a divorce.[49] To be deductible, an expense must relate solely to tax advice in a divorce proceeding. For example, legal fees attributable to the determination of dependency exemptions of children are deductible if the fees are distinguishable from the general legal fees incurred in obtaining a divorce. Therefore, it is advisable to request an itemization of attorney's fees to substantiate a deduction for the tax-related amounts.

ETHICS & EQUITY   Personal or Business Expenses?

For the last eight years, Jaynice and her family have lived in a large Victorian house in New England. In the current year, Jaynice and her husband decide to convert the home into a "bed-and-breakfast." The family (including the two children and the dog) moves into the basement, which accounts for 30 percent of the square footage of the house. The basement has two bedrooms, two baths, a den, and a small kitchen. The upper two floors of the house are used for the bed–and–breakfast, which is operated as a sole proprietorship.

Jaynice hires two employees to help her run the business. Total expenses for the first year of operation are as follows:

Mortgage interest	$18,000
Real estate taxes	3,000
Salaries for two employees	40,000
Groceries for breakfast and snacks	7,000
Depreciation	10,000

For breakfast, all of the family members eat the same food that is prepared for the guests. They usually also share in the homemade cookies and cakes in the evening.

On Jaynice's Schedule C for the business, she deducts $78,000 of expenses for the current tax year. Discuss whether these deductions are appropriate.

© iStockphoto.com/LdF

Example 33

Terry and Jack are divorced near the end of the current tax year. They had been married for 28 years and have two dependent children, Pauline (age 17) and Neal (age 18). As part of the divorce agreement, Jack paid all of the legal fees, which amounted to $24,300. The invoice from the divorce lawyer listed the following charges:

Child custody agreement and determination of amount of monthly child support	$ 3,000
Divorce decree proceedings	10,000
County court filing costs	1,800
Property settlement determination	6,000
Tax consequences of property settlement	2,000
Tax consequences of child custody and child support payments and tax filing status	1,500

Only the $3,500 ($2,000 + $1,500) paid by Jack for the charges relating to tax advice is deductible.

[48]§ 213(a).   [49]Rev.Rul. 72–545, 1972–2 C.B. 179.

6-3i Disallowance of Deductions for Capital Expenditures

The Code specifically disallows a deduction for "any amount paid out for new buildings or for permanent improvements or betterments made to increase the value of any property or estate."[50] The Regulations further define capital expenditures to include those expenditures that add to the value or prolong the life of property or adapt the property to a new or different use.[51] Incidental repairs and maintenance of the property are not capital expenditures and can be deducted as ordinary and necessary business expenses. Repairing a roof is a deductible expense, but replacing a roof is a capital expenditure subject to depreciation deductions over its recovery period. The tune-up of a delivery truck is an expense; a complete overhaul probably is a capital expenditure. Adding new gravel to a gravel parking lot is a repair, but paving the parking lot is a capital expenditure because this is doing more than restoring the asset to its original condition.

New temporary Regulations take effect January 1, 2014, which provide additional guidance on whether expenditures to acquire, produce, or improve tangible property must be capitalized or deducted.[52]

Capitalization versus Expense

When an expenditure is capitalized rather than expensed, the deduction is at best deferred and at worst lost forever. Although an immediate tax benefit for a large cash expenditure is lost, the cost may be deductible in increments over a longer period of time as the asset is depreciated, amortized, or depleted.

If the expenditure is for a tangible asset that has an ascertainable life, it is capitalized and may be deducted as depreciation (or cost recovery) over its depreciable life. Land is not subject to depreciation (or cost recovery) because it does not have an ascertainable life. [See Chapter 8 for a discussion of depreciation (cost recovery).]

Example 34

Stan purchased a prime piece of land located in an apartment-zoned area. Stan paid $500,000 for the property, which had an old but usable apartment building on it. He immediately had the building demolished at a cost of $100,000. The $500,000 purchase price and the $100,000 demolition costs must be capitalized, and the basis of the land is $600,000. Because land is a nondepreciable asset, no deduction is allowed.

If the expenditure is for an intangible asset (e.g., copyright, patent, covenant not to compete, and goodwill), the capitalized expenditure can be amortized regardless of whether the intangible asset has an ascertainable life. Intangible assets, referred to as § 197 intangibles, are amortized over a 15-year statutory period using the straight-line method. See Chapter 8 for additional discussion of the amortization of intangibles.

6-3j Transactions between Related Parties

The Code places restrictions on the recognition of gains and losses from **related-party transactions**. Without these restrictions, relationships created by birth, marriage, and business would provide endless possibilities for engaging in financial transactions that produce tax savings with no real economic substance or change. For example, to create an artificial loss, a wife could sell investment property to her husband at a loss and deduct the loss on their joint return. Her husband could then hold the asset indefinitely, and the family would sustain no real economic loss. A complex set of laws has been designed to eliminate such possibilities.

[50]§ 263(a)(1).
[51]Reg. § 1.263(a)–1(b).
[52]Reg. § 1.263(a)–1T(a).

Relationships and Constructive Ownership

Before reviewing the tax consequences of related party sales, it is important to know the individuals and business entities that are considered to be related parties. *Related parties* include the following:

- Brothers and sisters (whether whole, half, or adopted), spouse, ancestors (parents and grandparents), and lineal descendants (children and grandchildren) of the taxpayer.
- A corporation owned more than 50 percent (directly or indirectly) by the taxpayer.
- Two corporations that are members of a controlled group.
- A series of other complex relationships between trusts, corporations, and individual taxpayers.

Constructive ownership provisions are applied to determine whether the taxpayers are related. Under these provisions, stock owned by certain relatives or related entities is *deemed* to be owned by the taxpayer for purposes of applying the loss and expense deduction disallowance provisions. For example, a taxpayer is deemed to own not only his or her stock but also the stock owned by lineal descendants, ancestors, brothers and sisters or half-brothers and half-sisters, and spouse.

The stock of Sparrow Corporation is owned 20% by Ted, 30% by Ted's father, 30% by Ted's mother, and 20% by Ted's sister. On July 1 of the current year, Ted loaned $10,000 to Sparrow Corporation at 6% annual interest, principal and interest payable on demand. For tax purposes, Sparrow uses the accrual basis and Ted uses the cash basis. Both are on a calendar year. Through constructive ownership, Ted is deemed also to own the 80% held by his parents and sister. Thus, he directly and constructively owns 100% of Sparrow Corporation. If the corporation accrues the interest within the taxable year, no deduction can be taken until payment is made to Ted.	**Example 35**

Losses

The Code provides for the disallowance of any "losses from sales or exchanges of property . . . directly or indirectly" between related parties.[53] A right of offset is created equal to the disallowed loss. When the property is subsequently sold to a nonrelated party, any gain recognized is reduced by the right of offset. However, the right of offset cannot create or increase a loss. Any right of offset is permanently lost if it is not used by the related-party buyer to offset some or all of the recognized gain on a subsequent sale or exchange to an unrelated party.

Freida sells common stock with a basis of $10,000 to her son, Bill, for its fair market value of $8,000. The $2,000 realized loss is not recognized, which creates a $2,000 right of offset. Bill sells the stock several years later for $11,000. Freida's $2,000 loss is disallowed upon the sale to Bill, and only $1,000 of gain ($11,000 selling price − $8,000 basis − $2,000 right of offset) is taxable to him upon the subsequent sale.	**Example 36**

Assume the same facts as in Example 36, except that Bill sells the stock for $9,000. Bill's gain of $1,000 ($9,000 selling price − $8,000 basis) is not recognized because of the right of offset of $2,000 from Freida's sale. Note that the offset may result in only partial tax benefit upon the subsequent sale (as in this case). If Freida had sold the stock to an unrelated party rather than to Bill, she could have recognized a $2,000 loss. However, as a family unit, Freida and Bill recognized only $1,000 of loss.	**Example 37**

A loss can also be disallowed even if the asset is sold to an unrelated party. This occurs if a related party repurchases the asset on or near the same day and the two sales were prearranged.[54]

---

[53] § 267(a)(1).

[54] *McWilliams v. Comm.*, 47-1 USTC ¶9289, 35 AFTR 1184, 67 S.Ct. 1477 (USSC, 1947).

Example 38   Pete sells common stock with a basis of $10,000 to an unrelated third party for its fair market value of $8,000. Pete's son repurchased the same stock in the market on the same day for $8,000. The $2,000 loss is not allowed because the transaction is an indirect sale between related parties.

Unpaid Expenses and Interest

The law prevents related taxpayers from engaging in tax avoidance schemes where one related taxpayer uses the accrual method of accounting and the other uses the cash basis. An accrual basis, closely held corporation, for example, could borrow funds from a cash basis individual shareholder. At the end of the year, the corporation would accrue and deduct the interest, but the cash basis lender would not recognize interest income because no interest had been paid. Section 267 specifically defers the deduction of the accruing taxpayer until the recipient taxpayer must include it in income; that is, when it is actually paid to the cash basis taxpayer. This *matching* provision applies to interest as well as other expenses, such as salaries and bonuses. While this provision applies to related parties as previously defined, note that it also applies to transactions between any partner (shareholder) and a partnership (S corporation), regardless of the ownership interest held by the partner or shareholder.

This deduction deferral provision does not apply if both of the related taxpayers use the accrual method or both use the cash method. Likewise, it does not apply if the related party reporting income uses the accrual method and the related party taking the deduction uses the cash method.

6-3k Substantiation Requirements

The tax law is built on a voluntary compliance system. Taxpayers file their tax returns, report income and take deductions to which they are entitled, and pay their taxes through withholding or estimated tax payments during the year. The taxpayer has the burden of proof for substantiating expenses deducted on the returns and must retain adequate records. Upon audit, the IRS can disallow any undocumented or unsubstantiated deductions. These requirements have resulted in numerous conflicts between taxpayers and the IRS.

For example, in the case of charitable contributions, Congress has enacted stringent substantiation requirements. One of these requires all cash contributions to be supported by receipts (e.g., canceled checks).[55] Single donations of $250 or more of cash and/or property value require an acknowledgment from the charity. Substantial donations of property (i.e., $500 or more in fair market value) necessitate the filing of Form 8283 and may have to be supported by appraisals (see Chapter 10 for further details).

Another example involves *specific* and *more stringent* rules for deducting travel, entertainment, and gift expenses, which are discussed in Chapter 9. Certain mixed-use (both personal and business use) and listed property are also subject to the adequate records requirement (see Chapter 8).

6-3l Expenses and Interest Relating to Tax-Exempt Income

Certain income, such as interest on municipal bonds, is tax-exempt.[56] The law also allows the taxpayer to deduct expenses incurred for the production of income.[57] However, the law does not permit a taxpayer to profit at the expense of the government by excluding interest income and deducting interest expense.[58] The Code

---

[55]Rev.Proc. 92–71, 1992–2 C.B. 437, addresses circumstances where checks are not returned by a financial institution or where electronic transfers are made.

[56]§ 103.

[57]§ 212.

[58]§ 265.

specifically disallows as a deduction the expenses of producing tax-exempt income. Interest on any indebtedness used to purchase or hold tax-exempt obligations also is disallowed.

Example 39

Sandy, a taxpayer in the 35% bracket, purchased $100,000 of 6% municipal bonds. At the same time, she used the bonds as collateral on a bank loan of $100,000 at 8% interest. A positive cash flow would result from the tax benefit as follows:

Cash paid out on loan	($8,000)
Cash received from bonds	6,000
Net negative cash flow	($2,000)

Had the deduction of $8,000 been allowed for interest expense, this would have resulted in a tax benefit of $2,800 (35% of $8,000). In that case, a positive cash flow of $800 ($6,000 + $2,800 − $8,000) would have resulted.

To eliminate the possibility illustrated in Example 39, the Code specifically disallows as a deduction the expenses of producing tax-exempt income. Interest on any indebtedness incurred or continued to purchase or carry tax-exempt obligations also is disallowed.

Example 40

In January of the current year, Alan borrowed $100,000 at 8% interest. He used the loan proceeds to purchase 5,000 shares of stock in White Corporation. In July, he sold the stock for $120,000 and reinvested the proceeds in City of Denver bonds, the income from which is tax-exempt. Assuming that the $100,000 loan remained outstanding throughout the entire year, Alan cannot deduct the interest attributable to the period in which he held the bonds.

Judicial Interpretations

It is often difficult to show a direct relationship between borrowings and investment in tax-exempt securities. Suppose, for example, a taxpayer borrows money, adds it to existing funds, buys inventory and stocks, and later sells the inventory and buys municipal bonds. A series of transactions such as these can completely obscure any connection between the loan and the tax-exempt investment. One solution would be to disallow interest on any debt to the extent that the taxpayer holds any tax-exempt securities. This approach would preclude individuals from deducting part of their home mortgage interest if they owned any municipal bonds. The law was not intended to go to such extremes. As a result, judicial interpretations have tried to be reasonable in disallowing interest deductions.

In one case, a company used municipal bonds as collateral on short-term loans to meet seasonal liquidity needs.[59] The court disallowed the interest deduction on the grounds that the company could predict its seasonal liquidity needs. The company could anticipate the need to borrow the money to continue to carry the tax-exempt securities. The same company *was* allowed an interest deduction on a building mortgage, even though tax-exempt securities it owned could have been sold to pay off the mortgage. The court reasoned that short-term liquidity needs would have been impaired if the tax-exempt securities were sold. Furthermore, the court ruled that carrying the tax-exempt securities bore no relationship to the long-term financing of a construction project.

The classification of various expenses in terms of their deductibility and nondeductibility is reflected in Concept Summary 6.3.

---

[59]*The Wisconsin Cheeseman, Inc. v. U.S.*, 68–1 USTC ¶9145, 21 AFTR 2d 383, 388 F.2d 420 (CA–7, 1968).

CONCEPT SUMMARY 6.3

Classification of Expenses

Expense Item	Deductible		Not Deductible	Applicable Code §
	For AGI	**From AGI**		
Investment expenses				
Rent and royalty	X			§ 62(a)(4)
All other investments		X[4]		§ 212
Employee expenses				
Commuting expenses			X	§ 262
Travel and transportation[1]		X[4,5]		§ 162(a)(2)
Reimbursed expenses[1]	X			§ 62(a)(2)(A)
Moving expenses	X			§ 62(a)(15)
Entertainment[1]		X[4,5]		§ 162(a)
Teacher supplies	X[11]	X[4]		§ 62(a)(2)(D)
All other employee expenses[1]		X[4,5]		§ 162(a)
Certain expenses of performing artists	X			§ 62(a)(2)(B)
Trade or business expenses	X			§§ 162 and 62(a)(1)
Casualty losses				
Business	X			§ 165(c)(1)
Personal		X[6]		§ 165(c)(3)
Tax determination				
Collection or refund expenses	X[8]	X		§§ 212 and 62(a)(1) or (4)
Bad debts	X			§§ 166 and 62(a)(1) or (3)
Medical expenses		X[7]		§ 213
Charitable contributions		X		§ 170
Taxes				
Trade or business	X			§§ 162, 164, and 62(a)(1)
Personal taxes				
Real property		X		§ 164(a)(1)
Personal property		X		§ 164(a)(2)
State and local income *or* sales		X		§§ 164(a)(3) and (b)(5)
Investigation of a business[2]	X			§§ 162 and 62(a)(1)
Interest				
Business	X			§§ 162, 163, and 62(a)(1)
Personal	X[9]	X[3]	X[10]	§§ 163(a), (d), and (h)
Qualified tuition and related expenses	X			§§ 62(a)(18) and 222
All other personal expenses			X	§ 262

[1]Deduction *for* AGI if reimbursed, an adequate accounting is made, and employee is required to repay excess reimbursements.
[2]Provided certain criteria are met.
[3]Subject to the excess investment interest and the qualified residence interest provisions.
[4]Subject (in the aggregate) to a 2%-of-AGI floor imposed by § 67.
[5]Only 50% of meals and entertainment are deductible.
[6]Subject to a $100 floor per event and a 10%-of-AGI floor per tax year.
[7]Subject to a 7.5%- or 10%-of-AGI floor.
[8]Only the portion relating to business, rental, or royalty income or losses.
[9]Only the portion relating to student loans.
[10]Other personal interest is disallowed.
[11]Subject to a statutory limit of $250.

6-4 Tax Planning

6-4a Time Value of Tax Deductions

Cash basis taxpayers often have the ability to make early payments for their expenses at the end of the tax year. This may permit the payments to be deducted currently instead of in the following tax year. In view of the time value of money, a tax deduction this year may be worth more than the same deduction next year. Before employing this strategy, the taxpayer must consider what next year's expected income and tax rates will be and whether a cash-flow problem may develop from early payments. Thus, the time value of money as well as tax rate changes must be considered when an expense can be paid and deducted in either of two years.

LO.4

Identify tax planning opportunities for maximizing deductions and minimizing the disallowance of deductions.

> **Example 41**
>
> Jena pledged $50,000 to her church's special building fund. She can make the contribution in December 2014 or January 2015. Jena is in the 35% tax bracket in 2014 and in the 28% bracket in 2015. She itemizes in both years. Assume that Jena's discount rate is 8%. If she takes the deduction in 2014, she saves $4,536 ($17,500 − $12,964) due to the decrease in the tax rates and the time value of money.
>
> | | 2014 | 2015 |
> |---|---|---|
> | Contribution | $50,000 | $50,000 |
> | Tax bracket | × .35 | × .28 |
> | Tax savings | $17,500 | $14,000 |
> | Discounted @ 8% | × 1.0 | × .926 |
> | Savings in present value | $17,500 | $12,964 |

6-4b Vacation Homes

As previously discussed in this chapter, homes that are used for both personal and rental use can fall into one of three categories, all of which have different tax consequences. Therefore, careful tax planning often ensures that the home is classified into the category that provides the optimal tax result. For example, if a taxpayer is planning to rent a home for 15 or more days, this will subject the net income from the rental activity to taxation. If the homeowner could rent the home for 14 days or less (possibly just one less day), then all of the rental income received would escape taxation. This strategy is particularly attractive to individuals who live in areas where major sporting or entertainment events are held if there is a lack of hotel accommodations in the area.

In addition, assume that a taxpayer intends to use a home for 150 rental days and 16 personal days. Because the personal days exceed 15 (the greater of 14 days or 10% × the number of rental days), the property will be classified as *rental/personal* and a rental loss will not be allowed. However, if the owner can reduce the personal use days by only one day to 15, then the property will be classified as *rental*, and a rental loss can be allowed (subject to the passive loss rules).

6-4c Excessive Executive Compensation

With the $1 million limit on the deduction of compensation of covered employees, many corporations and their executives must engage in additional tax planning. The $1 million limit applies specifically to publicly held corporations. To deduct more than $1 million in compensation, these companies must structure compensation packages so that the excess income meets the exceptions to this rule. Opportunities include compensation payable on a commission basis, certain other performance-based compensation, payments to qualified retirement plans, and payments that are excludible fringe benefits.

6-4d Shifting Deductions

To the extent possible, taxpayers should time their deductions to provide the maximum possible tax benefit. Planning opportunities arise when tax rates vary across tax years.

Example 42

Referring to the facts of *The Big Picture* on p. 6-1, assume that Dr. Payne's marginal tax rate in 2014 is 25% but that he estimates his rate in 2015 to be 40%. In this case, he should consider deferring the charitable contribution to UNA College until 2015. His tax benefit in 2015 will be $2,000 (40% × $5,000) but would be only $1,250 in 2014 (25% × $5,000).

6-4e Hobby Losses

To demonstrate that an activity has been entered into for the purpose of making a profit, a taxpayer should treat the activity as a business. The business should engage in advertising, use business letterhead stationery, and maintain a business phone.

If a taxpayer's activity earns a profit in three out of five consecutive years, the presumption is that the activity is engaged in for profit. It may be possible for a cash basis taxpayer to meet these requirements by timing the payment of expenses or the receipt of revenues. The payment of certain expenses incurred before the end of the year might be made in the following year. The billing of year-end sales might be delayed so that collections are received in the following year.

Keep in mind that the three-out-of-five-years rule under § 183 is not absolute. All it does is shift the burden of proof. If a profit is not made in three out of five years, the losses may still be allowed if the taxpayer can show that they are due to the nature of the business. For example, success in artistic or literary endeavors can take a long time, so losses for several years in a row could occur even for a legitimate business. Also, depending on the state of the economy, full-time farmers and ranchers may have losses for several consecutive years.

Merely satisfying the three-out-of-five-years rule does not guarantee that a taxpayer is automatically home free. If the three years of profits are insignificant relative to the losses of other years or if the profits are not from the ordinary operation of the business, the taxpayer is vulnerable. The IRS may still be able to establish that the taxpayer is not engaged in an activity for profit.

Example 43

Ashley had the following gains and losses in an artistic endeavor:

2010	($50,000)
2011	(65,000)
2012	400
2013	200
2014	125

Under these circumstances, the IRS might try to overcome the presumption that this is a business because it has profits in three of the last five years. To do this, the IRS would focus on the nine factors from the Regulations discussed in Section 6-3e.

On the other hand, if Ashley could show conformity with the factors enumerated in the Regulations or could show evidence of business hardships (e.g., injury, death, or illness), the government might have difficulty overriding the presumption.[60]

6-4f Substantiation

This chapter has emphasized the laws that provide the authority for deducting losses and other expenditures. However, a properly authorized deduction will be

---

[60]*Faulconer, Sr. v. Comm.*, 84–2 USTC ¶9955, 55 AFTR 2d 85–302, 748 F.2d 890 (CA–4, 1984), *rev'g* 45 TCM 1084, T.C.Memo. 1983–165.

disallowed if the taxpayer cannot provide adequate substantiation. Deductions are a matter of legislative grace, and the taxpayer has the burden of proving that a deduction is justified. Although all deductions must be substantiated, taxpayers often tend to be lax in their record keeping for activities that have a mixed personal/business use, such as vacation homes, a home office (see Chapter 9), and business use of an automobile. Taxpayers must be vigilant in maintaining all business receipts and in documenting the business purpose of the deduction. Time, date, place, and individuals in attendance must also be documented, as appropriate. A contemporaneous mileage log must be maintained to support the business use of an automobile. Numerous substantiation rules exist for charitable contributions (see Chapter 10).

Substantiation is also extremely important for establishing the basis of an asset (see Chapter 14). An asset's basis includes all costs incurred to place an asset in service, which includes transportation, sales tax, setup, testing, unpaid property taxes of the previous owner, and other purchase costs. Basis is used to determine gain or loss on a sale of the asset and to compute depreciation for depreciable assets. The taxpayer has the burden of substantiating all expenditures included in basis.

REFOCUS ON THE BIG PICTURE

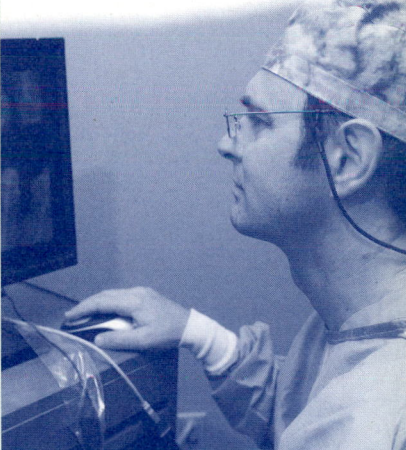

CALCULATION OF DEDUCTIBLE BUSINESS EXPENSES AND TAX PLANNING

Of the expenses incurred by Dr. Payne, several comments need to be made. Being personal in nature, none of the $5,000 monthly draw is deductible. Nor is the amount involved subject to the reasonableness test (see Example 6). Dr. Payne is a sole proprietor and not in an employment relationship. The fine paid for violating waste control rules comes under the public policy limitations (see Example 13) and is specifically made nondeductible by Code § 162(f). Along the same line are the political contributions (Example 17) made nondeductible by § 162(e). However, Dr. Payne's investigation of the practice of another dental firm (Example 19) appears reasonable and the expense incurred deductible. Although not specifically discussed in the text as to Dr. Payne, his legal fees incurred in connection with a lawsuit filed by a patient appear related to his practice (Example 15). As such, they are ordinary and necessary to his trade or business.

What If?

From a tax planning perspective, should Dr. Payne calculate his deductible business expenses using the accrual method of accounting or the cash method?

In Chapter 4, we concluded that Dr. Payne could minimize his Federal income tax liability if he used the cash method of accounting. If the cash method is used for reporting the gross income of a Schedule C business, the cash method must be used for reporting the deductible business expenses that will appear on Schedule C of Form 1040.

Key Terms

Accounting method, 6-8	Hobby losses, 6-17	Related-party transactions, 6-26
Deductions for adjusted gross income, 6-2	Ordinary and necessary, 6-5	Startup expenditures, 6-16
Deductions from adjusted gross income, 6-2	Reasonableness, 6-6	Vacation homes, 6-20

Discussion Questions

1. **LO.I** "All income must be reported, and all deductions are allowed unless specifically disallowed in the Code." Discuss.

2. **LO.I** Aaron has AGI of $85,000 and deductions of $9,500. Does it matter to Aaron whether the deductions are *for* or *from* AGI? Why or why not?

3. **LO.I** Michael earned $20,000 at the K-M Resort Golf Club during the summer prior to his senior year in college. He wants to make a contribution to a traditional IRA, but the amount is dependent on whether it reduces his taxable income. If Michael is going to claim the standard deduction, how much should he contribute to a traditional IRA?

4. **LO.I** Classify each of the following expenditures as a deduction *for* AGI, a deduction *from* AGI, or not deductible:
   a. Sam gives cash to his father as a birthday gift.
   b. Sandra gives cash to her church.
   c. Albert pays Dr. Dafashy for medical services rendered.
   d. Mia pays alimony to Bill.
   e. Rex, who is self-employed, contributes to his pension plan.
   f. April pays expenses associated with her rental property.

5. **LO.I** Classify each of the following expenditures as a deduction *for* AGI, a deduction *from* AGI, or not deductible:
   a. Amos contributes to his H.R. 10 plan (i.e., a retirement plan for a self-employed individual).
   b. Keith pays child support to his former wife, Renee, for the support of their son, Chris.
   c. Judy pays professional dues that are reimbursed by her employer.
   d. Ted pays $500 as the monthly mortgage payment on his personal residence. Of this amount, $100 represents a payment on principal, and $400 represents an interest payment.
   e. Lynn pays a moving company for moving her household goods to Detroit, where she is starting a new job. She is not reimbursed by her employer.
   f. Ralph pays property taxes on his personal residence.

6. **LO.I** Larry and Susan each invest $10,000 in separate investment activities. They each incur deductible expenses of $800 associated with their respective investments. Explain why Larry's expenses might be properly classified as deductions *from* AGI (itemized deductions) and Susan's expenses might be appropriately classified as deductions *for* AGI.

7. **LO.I** Nanette is a first-grade teacher. Potential deductions are charitable contributions of $800, personal property taxes on her car of $240, and various supplies purchased for use in her classroom of $225 (none reimbursed by her school). How will these items affect Nanette's Federal income tax return for 2013?

8. **LO.I** List three items that § 162 specifically excludes from classification as a trade or business expense.

9. **LO.I** In the determination of whether a business expense is deductible, the reasonableness requirement applies only to salaries. Evaluate this statement.

10. **LO.I** Dave uses the second floor of a building for his residence and the first floor for his business. The uninsured building is destroyed by fire. Are the tax consequences the same for each part of the building? Explain.

11. **LO.I** Mary Kate owns a building that she leases to an individual who operates a grocery store. Rent income is $10,000, and rental expenses are $6,000. On what Form 1040 schedule or schedules are the income and expenses reported?

12. **LO.2** What is the "actually paid" requirement for the deduction of an expense by a cash basis taxpayer? Does actual payment ensure a deduction? Explain.

13. **LO.2** Aubry, a cash basis and calendar year taxpayer, decides to reduce his taxable income for 2014 by buying $65,000 worth of supplies for his business on December 27, 2014. The supplies will be used up in 2015.
    a. Can Aubry deduct the expenditure for 2014?
    b. Would your answer in part (a) change if Aubry bought the supplies because the seller was going out of business and offered a large discount on the price? Explain.

14. **LO.2** What is the significance of the all events and economic performance tests?

15. **LO.2** Why is the reserve method not allowed to be used for Federal income tax purposes?

16. **LO.3** Clear, Inc., is a bottled water distributor. Clear's delivery trucks frequently are required to park in no-parking zones to make their deliveries. If the trucks are occasionally ticketed, can Clear deduct the fines that it pays? Explain.

17. **LO.3** Ted, an agent for an airline manufacturer, is negotiating a sale with a representative of the U.S. government and with a representative of a developing country. Ted's company has sufficient capacity to handle only one of the orders. Both orders will have the same contract price. Ted believes that if his employer authorizes a $500,000 payment to the representative of the foreign country, he can guarantee the sale. He is not sure that he can obtain the same result with the U.S. government. Identify the relevant tax issues for Ted.

Issue ID

18. **LO.3** Stuart, an insurance salesperson, is arrested for allegedly robbing a convenience store. He hires an attorney who is successful in getting the charges dropped. Is the attorney's fee deductible? Explain.

19. **LO.3** Linda operates an illegal gambling operation. Which of the following expenses that she incurs can reduce taxable income?
    a. Bribes paid to city employees.
    b. Salaries to employees.
    c. Security cameras.
    d. Kickbacks to police.
    e. Rent on an office.
    f. Depreciation on office furniture and equipment.
    g. Tenant's casualty insurance.
    h. Utilities.

20. **LO.3** Gordon anticipates that being positively perceived by the individual who is elected mayor will be beneficial for his business. Therefore, he contributes to the campaigns of both the Democratic and the Republican candidates. The Republican candidate is elected mayor. Can Gordon deduct any of the political contributions he made?

21. **LO.3** Melissa, the owner of a sole proprietorship, does not provide health insurance for her 20 employees. She plans to spend $1,500 lobbying in opposition to legislation that would require her to provide such insurance. Discuss the tax advantages and disadvantages of paying the $1,500 to a professional lobbyist rather than spending the $1,500 on in-house lobbying expenditures.

22. **LO.3** What limits exist on the deductibility of executive compensation? Do the limits apply to all types of business entities? Are there any exceptions to the limitations? Explain.

23. **LO.3** Paul operates a restaurant in Cleveland. He travels to Columbus to investigate acquiring a business. He incurs expenses as follows: $1,500 for travel, $2,000 for legal advice, and $3,500 for a market analysis. Based on the different tax consequences listed below, describe the circumstances that were involved in Paul's investigation of the business.
    a. Paul deducts the $7,000 of expenses.
    b. Paul cannot deduct any of the $7,000 of expenses.
    c. Paul deducts $5,000 of the expenses and amortizes the $2,000 balance over a period of 180 months.

24. **LO.3** Under what circumstances may a taxpayer deduct a rental loss associated with a vacation home?

25. **LO.3** Karen and Andy own a beach house. They have an agreement with a rental agent to rent it up to 200 days per year. For the past three years, the agent has been successful in renting it for 200 days. Karen and Andy use the beach house for one week during the summer and one week during Thanksgiving. Their daughter, Sarah, a college student, has asked if she and some friends can use the beach house for the week of spring break. Advise Karen and Andy how they should respond and identify any relevant tax issues.

Issue ID

26. **LO.3** Hank was transferred from Arizona to North Dakota on March 1 of the current year. He immediately put his home in Phoenix up for rent. The home was rented May 1 to November 30 and was vacant during the month of December. It was rented again on January 1 for six months. What expenses related to the home, if any, can Hank deduct on his return? Which deductions are *for* AGI, and which ones are *from* AGI?

Decision Making

27. **LO.3** Ray loses his job as a result of a corporate downsizing. Consequently, he falls behind on the mortgage payments on his personal residence. His friend Ted would like to make the delinquent mortgage payments for him.
   a. Could the payments be structured so that Ray can deduct the mortgage interest?
   b. Could the payment arrangement deny both Ray and Ted a mortgage interest deduction?
   c. Could the payments be structured so that Ted could deduct the mortgage interest?

28. **LO.3** Edna incurs various legal fees in obtaining a divorce. Which types of expenses associated with the divorce are deductible by Edna, and which are not?

Issue ID

29. **LO.3** Ella owns 60% of the stock of Peach, Inc. The stock has declined in value since she purchased it five years ago. She is going to sell 5% of the stock to a relative. Ella is also going to make a gift of 10% of the stock to another relative. Identify the relevant tax issues for Ella.

30. **LO.3** Jarret owns City of Charleston bonds with an adjusted basis of $190,000. During the year, he receives interest payments of $3,800. Jarret partially financed the purchase of the bonds by borrowing $100,000 at 5% interest. Jarret's interest payments on the loan this year are $4,900, and his principal payments are $1,100.
   a. Should Jarret report any interest income this year? Explain.
   b. Can Jarret deduct any interest expense this year? Explain.

Problems

31. **LO.1** Amos is a self-employed tax attorney. He and Monica, his employee, attend a conference in Dallas sponsored by the American Institute of CPAs. The following expenses are incurred during the trip:

	Amos	Monica
Conference registration	$ 900	$900
Airfare	1,200	700
Taxi fares	100	–0–
Lodging in Dallas	750	300

   a. Amos pays for all of these expenses. Calculate the effect of these expenses on Amos's AGI.
   b. Would your answer to part (a) change if the American Bar Association had sponsored the conference? Explain.

Decision Making

32. **LO.1** Daniel, age 38, is single and has the following income and expenses in 2014.

Salary income	$60,000
Net rent income	6,000
Dividend income	3,500
Payment of alimony	12,000
Mortgage interest on residence	4,900
Property tax on residence	1,200
Contribution to traditional IRA	5,000
Contribution to United Church	2,100
Loss on the sale of real estate (held for investment)	2,000
Medical expenses	3,250
State income tax	300
Federal income tax	7,000

   a. Calculate Daniel's AGI.
   b. Should Daniel itemize his deductions *from* AGI or take the standard deduction?

33. **LO.1** Janice, age 22, is a student who earns $10,000 working part-time at the college ice cream shop in 2014. She has no other income. Her medical expenses for the year total $3,000. During the year, she suffers a casualty loss of $3,500 when her apartment catches on fire. Janice contributes $1,000 to her church. On the advice of her parents, Janice is trying to decide whether to contribute $1,000 to the traditional IRA her parents set up for her. What effect would the IRA contribution have on Janice's itemized deductions?

34. **LO.1** A list of the items that Peggy sold and the losses she incurred during the current tax year is as follows:

Yellow, Inc. stock	$ 1,600
Peggy's personal use SUV	8,000
Peggy's personal residence	10,000
City of Newburyport bonds	900

She also had a theft loss of $1,500 on her uninsured business use car. Calculate Peggy's deductible losses.

35. **LO.2** Falcon, Inc., paid salaries of $500,000 to its employees during its first year of operations. At the end of the year, Falcon had unpaid salaries of $45,000.
   a. Calculate the salary deduction if Falcon is a cash basis taxpayer.
   b. Calculate the salary deduction if Falcon is an accrual basis taxpayer.

36. **LO.2** Maud, a calendar year taxpayer, is the owner of a sole proprietorship that uses the cash method. On February 1, 2014, she leases an office building to use in her business for $120,000 for an 18-month period. To obtain this favorable lease rate, she pays the $120,000 at the inception of the lease. How much rent expense may Maud deduct on her 2014 tax return?

37. **LO.2** Duck, an accrual basis corporation, sponsored a rock concert on December 29, 2014. Gross receipts were $300,000. The following expenses were incurred and paid as indicated:

Expense		Payment Date
Rental of coliseum	$ 25,000	December 21, 2014
Cost of goods sold:		
Food	30,000	December 30, 2014
Souvenirs	60,000	December 30, 2014
Performers	100,000	January 5, 2015
Cleaning of coliseum	10,000	February 1, 2015

Because the coliseum was not scheduled to be used again until January 15, the company with which Duck had contracted did not perform the cleanup until January 8–10, 2015.
   Calculate Duck's net income from the concert for tax purposes for 2014.

38. **LO.3** Doug incurred and paid the following expenses during the year:

   • $50 for a ticket for running a red light while he was commuting to work.
   • $100 for a ticket for parking in a handicapped parking space.
   • $200 to an attorney to represent him in traffic court as to the two tickets.
   • $500 to an attorney to draft an agreement with a tenant for a one-year lease on an apartment that Doug owns.
   • $1,000 to an attorney to negotiate a reduction in his child support payments.
   • $2,500 to an attorney to negotiate a reduction in his qualified alimony payments to a former spouse.

   Calculate the amount of Doug's deductible expenses.

39. **LO.3** Trevor, a friend of yours from high school, works as a server at the ST Café. He asks you to help him prepare his Federal income tax return. When you inquire about why his bank deposits substantially exceed his tip income, he confides to you that he is a

bookie on the side. Trevor then provides you with the following documented income and expenses for the year:

Tip income	$16,000
Gambling income	52,000
Gambling expenses	
Payouts to winners	29,000
Employee compensation	8,000
Bribe to police officer who is aware of Trevor's	
bookie activity	7,500

a. How will these items affect Trevor's AGI?
b. His taxable income?

Decision Making

Communications

40. **LO.3, 4** Amber, a publicly held corporation, currently pays its president an annual salary of $900,000. In addition, it contributes $20,000 annually to a defined contribution pension plan for him. As a means of increasing company profitability, the board of directors decides to increase the president's compensation. Two proposals are being considered. Under the first proposal, the salary and pension contribution for the president would be increased by 30%. Under the second proposal, Amber would implement a performance-based compensation program that is projected to provide about the same amount of additional compensation and pension contribution for the president.
a. Evaluate the alternatives from the perspective of Amber, Inc.
b. Prepare a letter to Amber's board of directors that contains your recommendations. Address the letter to the board chairperson, Agnes Riddle, whose address is 100 James Tower, Cleveland, OH 44106.

41. **LO.3** Vermillion, Inc., a publicly held corporation, pays the following salaries to its executives:

	Salary	Bonus	Retirement Plan Contribution
CEO	$2,000,000	$100,000	$80,000
CFO	1,800,000	90,000	72,000
Treasurer	1,600,000	–0–	64,000
Marketing vice president	1,500,000	75,000	60,000
Operations vice president	1,400,000	70,000	56,000
Distribution vice president	1,200,000	60,000	48,000
Research vice president	1,100,000	–0–	44,000
Controller	800,000	–0–	32,000

Vermillion normally does not pay bonuses, but after reviewing the results of operations for the year, the board of directors decided to pay a 5% bonus to selected executives. What is the amount of these payments that Vermillion may deduct?

42. **LO.3** Nancy, the owner of a very successful hotel chain in the Southeast, is exploring the possibility of expanding the chain into a city in the Northeast. She incurs $35,000 of expenses associated with this investigation. Based on the regulatory environment for hotels in the city, she decides not to expand. During the year, she also investigates opening a restaurant that will be part of a national restaurant chain. Her expenses for this are $53,000. The restaurant begins operations on September 1. Determine the amount that Nancy can deduct in the current year for investigating these two businesses.

43. **LO.3** Terry traveled to a neighboring state to investigate the purchase of two hardware stores. His expenses included travel, legal, accounting, and miscellaneous expenses. The total was $52,000. He incurred the expenses in June and July 2014. Under the following circumstances, what can Terry deduct in 2014?
a. Terry was in the hardware store business and did not acquire the two hardware stores.
b. Terry was in the hardware store business and acquired the two hardware stores and began operating them on October 1, 2014.
c. Terry did not acquire the two hardware stores and was not in the hardware store business.
d. Terry acquired the two hardware stores but was not in the hardware store business when he acquired them. Operations began on October 1, 2014.

44. **LO.3** Harold conducts a business with the following results for the year:

Revenue	$20,000
Depreciation on car	3,960
Operating expenses of car	3,100
Rent	6,000
Wages	8,200
Amortization of intangibles	680

Harold estimates that due to a depressed real estate market, the value of land owned by the business declined by $5,200.

a. Calculate the effect of Harold's business on his AGI.

b. How would your answer in part (a) change if the activity was a hobby?

45. **LO.3** Alex, who is single, conducts an activity in 2014 that is appropriately classified as a hobby. The activity produces the following revenues and expenses:

Revenue	$18,000
Property taxes	3,000
Materials and supplies	4,500
Utilities	2,000
Advertising	5,000
Insurance	750
Depreciation	4,000

Without regard to this activity, Alex's AGI is $42,000. Determine the amount of income Alex must report, the amount of the expenses he is permitted to deduct, and his taxable income.

46. **LO.3** Samantha, an executive, has AGI of $100,000 before considering income or loss from her miniature horse business. Her outside income comes from prizes for winning horse shows, stud fees, and sales of yearlings. Samantha's home is on 20 acres, half of which she uses for the horse activity (i.e., stables, paddocks, fences, tack houses, and other related improvements).

Samantha's office in her home is 10% of the square footage of the house. She uses the office exclusively for maintaining files and records on the horse activities. Her books show the following income and expenses for the current year:

Income from fees, prizes, and sales		$22,000
Expenses		
Entry fees		1,000
Feed and veterinary bills		4,000
Supplies		900
Publications and dues		500
Travel to horse shows (no meals)		2,300
Salaries and wages of employees		8,000
Depreciation —		
Horse equipment	$3,000	
Horse farm improvements	7,000	
On 10% of personal residence	1,000	11,000
Total home mortgage interest		24,000
Total property taxes on home		2,200
Total property taxes on horse farm improvements		800

The mortgage interest is only on her home because the horse farm improvements are not mortgaged.

a. What are Samantha's tax consequences if the miniature horse activity is a hobby?

b. If it is a business?

47. **LO.3** Sarah owns a vacation cabin in the Tennessee mountains. Without considering the cabin, she has gross income of $65,000. During the year, she rents the cabin for two weeks for $2,500 and uses it herself for four weeks. The total expenses for the year are

$10,000 mortgage interest; $1,500 property tax; $2,000 utilities, insurance, and mainte-nance; and $3,200 depreciation.

a. What effect does the rental of the vacation cabin have on Sarah's AGI?

b. What expenses can Sarah deduct, and how are they classified (i.e., *for* or *from* AGI)?

48. **LO.3** Adelene, who lives in a winter resort area, rented her personal residence for 14 days while she was visiting Brussels. Rent income was $5,000. Related expenses for the year were as follows:

Real property taxes	$ 3,800
Mortgage interest	7,500
Utilities	3,700
Insurance	2,500
Repairs	2,100
Depreciation	15,000

Determine the effect on Adelene's AGI.

49. **LO.3** During the year (not a leap year), Anna rented her vacation home for 30 days, used it personally for 20 days, and left it vacant for 315 days. She had the following income and expenses:

Rent income	$ 7,000
Expenses	
Real estate taxes	2,500
Interest on mortgage	9,000
Utilities	2,400
Repairs	1,000
Roof replacement (a capital expenditure)	12,000
Depreciation	7,500

a. Compute Anna's net rent income or loss and the amounts she can itemize on her tax return, using the court's approach to allocating property taxes and interest.

b. How would your answer in part (a) differ using the IRS's method of allocating property taxes and interest?

50. **LO.3** How would your answer to Problem 49 differ if Anna had rented the house for 87 days and had used it personally for 13 days?

51. **LO.1, 3** Chee, single, age 40, had the following income and expenses during 2014:

Income	
Salary	$43,000
Rental of vacation home (rented 60 days, used personally 60 days, vacant 245 days)	4,000
Municipal bond interest	2,000
Dividend from General Electric	400
Expenses	
Interest on home mortgage	8,400
Interest on vacation home	4,758
Interest on loan used to buy municipal bonds	3,100
Property tax on home	2,200
Property tax on vacation home	1,098
State income tax	3,300
State sales tax	900
Charitable contributions	1,100
Tax return preparation fee	300
Utilities and maintenance on vacation home	2,600
Depreciation on rental 50% of vacation home	3,500

Calculate Chee's taxable income for the year before personal exemptions.

52. **LO.1, 3, 4** Elisa and Clyde operate a retail sports memorabilia shop. For the current year, sales revenue is $55,000 and expenses are as follows:

Cost of goods sold	$21,000
Advertising	1,000
Utilities	2,000
Rent	4,500
Insurance	1,500
Wages to Boyd	8,000

Decision Making

Elisa and Clyde pay $8,000 in wages to Boyd, a part-time employee. Because this amount is $1,000 below the minimum wage, Boyd threatens to file a complaint with the appropriate Federal agency. Although Elisa and Clyde pay no attention to Boyd's threat, Chelsie (Elisa's mother) gives Boyd a check for $1,000 for the disputed wages. Both Elisa and Clyde ridicule Chelsie for wasting money when they learn what she has done. The retail shop is the only source of income for Elisa and Clyde.
   a. Calculate Elisa and Clyde's AGI.
   b. Can Chelsie deduct the $1,000 payment on her tax return? Explain.
   c. How could the tax position of the parties be improved?

53. **LO.3, 4** Brittany Callihan sold stock (basis of $184,000) to her son, Ridge, for $160,000, the fair market value.
   a. What are the tax consequences to Brittany?
   b. What are the tax consequences to Ridge if he later sells the stock for $190,000? For $152,000? For $174,000?
   c. Write a letter to Brittany in which you inform her of the tax consequences if she sells the stock to Ridge for $160,000. Explain how a sales transaction could be structured that would produce better tax consequences for her. Brittany's address is 32 Country Lane, Lawrence, KS 66045.

Decision Making

Communications

54. **LO.3** The Robin Corporation is owned as follows:

Isabelle	26%
Peter, Isabelle's husband	19%
Sonya, Isabelle's mother	15%
Reggie, Isabelle's father	25%
Quinn, an unrelated party	15%

Robin is on the accrual basis, and Isabelle and Peter are on the cash basis. Isabelle and Peter each loaned the Robin Corporation $40,000 out of their separate funds. On December 31, 2014, Robin accrued interest at 7% on both loans. The interest was paid on February 4, 2015. What is the tax treatment of this interest expense/income to Isabelle, Peter, and Robin?

55. **LO.3** For each of the following independent transactions, calculate the recognized gain or loss to the seller and the adjusted basis to the buyer.
   a. Bonnie sells Parchment, Inc. stock (adjusted basis $17,000) to Phillip, her brother, for its fair market value of $12,000.
   b. Amos sells land (adjusted basis $85,000) to his nephew, Boyd, for its fair market value of $70,000.
   c. Susan sells a tax-exempt bond (adjusted basis $20,000) to her wholly owned corporation for its fair market value of $19,000.
   d. Ron sells a business truck (adjusted basis $20,000) that he uses in his sole proprietorship to his cousin, Agnes, for its fair market value of $18,500.
   e. Martha sells her partnership interest (adjusted basis $175,000) in Pearl Partnership to her adult daughter, Kim, for $220,000.

56. **LO.3** Murphy has a brokerage account and buys on the margin, which resulted in an interest expense of $20,000 during the year. Income generated through the brokerage account was as follows:

Municipal interest	$ 50,000
Taxable dividends and interest	350,000

How much investment interest can Murphy deduct?

Decision Making

57. **LO.I, 3, 4** During the current year, Robert pays the following amounts associated with his own residence:

Property taxes	$3,000
Mortgage interest	8,000
Repairs	1,200
Utilities	2,700
Replacement of roof	4,000

In addition, Robert paid $1,500 of property taxes on the home that is owned and used by Anne, his daughter.
a. Which of these expenses can Robert deduct?
b. Can Anne deduct the $1,500 of property taxes?
c. Are the deductions *for* AGI or *from* AGI (itemized)?
d. How could the tax consequences be improved?

Cumulative Problems

Tax Return Problem

H&R BLOCK

TAX SOFTWARE

58. Roberta Santos, age 41, is single and lives at 120 Sanborne Avenue, Springfield, IL 60781. Her Social Security number is 123-45-6789. Roberta has been divorced from her former husband, Wayne, for three years. She has a son, Jason, who is 17, and a daughter, June, who is 18. Jason's Social Security number is 111-11-1111, and June's is 123-45-6788. Roberta does not want to contribute $3 to the Presidential Election Campaign Fund.

Roberta, an advertising executive, earned a salary of $80,000 in 2013. Her employer withheld $9,000 in Federal income tax and $3,100 in state income tax.

Roberta has legal custody of Jason and June. The divorce decree provides that Roberta is to receive the dependency deductions for the children. Jason lives with his father during summer vacation. Wayne indicates that his expenses for Jason are $10,500. Roberta can document that she spent $6,500 for Jason's support during 2013. In prior years, Roberta gave a signed Form 8332 to Wayne regarding Jason. For 2013, she has decided not to do so. Roberta provides all of June's support.

Roberta's mother died on January 7, 2013. Roberta inherited assets worth $625,000 from her mother. As the sole beneficiary of her mother's life insurance policy, Roberta received insurance proceeds of $300,000. Her mother's cost basis for the life insurance policy was $120,000. Roberta's favorite aunt gave her $13,000 for her birthday in October.

On November 8, 2013, Roberta sells for $22,000 Amber stock that she had purchased for $24,000 from her first cousin, Walt, on December 5, 2008. Walt's cost basis for the stock was $26,000, and the stock was worth $23,000 on December 5, 2008. On December 1, 2013, Roberta sold Falcon stock for $13,500. She had acquired the stock on July 2, 2010, for $8,000.

An examination of Roberta's records reveals that she received the following:

- Interest income of $2,500 from First Savings Bank.
- Groceries valued at $750 from a local grocery store for being the 100,000th customer.
- Qualified dividend income of $1,800 from Amber.
- Interest income of $3,750 on City of Springfield school bonds.
- Alimony of $16,000 from Wayne.
- Distribution of $4,800 from ST Partnership. Her distributive share of the partnership passive taxable income was $5,300. She had no prior passive losses.

From her checkbook records, she determines that she made the following payments during 2013:

- Charitable contributions of $4,500 to First Presbyterian Church and $1,500 to the American Red Cross (proper receipts obtained).
- Mortgage interest on her residence of $7,800.
- Property taxes of $3,200 on her residence and $1,100 (ad valorem) on her car.
- Estimated Federal income taxes of $3,800 and estimated state income taxes of $1,000.
- Medical expenses of $5,000 for her and $800 for Jason. In December, her medical insurance policy reimbursed $1,500 of her medical expenses.
- A $1,000 ticket for parking in a handicapped space.

- Attorney's fees of $500 associated with unsuccessfully contesting the parking ticket.
- Contribution of $250 to the campaign of a candidate for governor.
- Because she did not maintain records of the sales tax she paid, she calculates the amount from the sales tax table to be $994.

Calculate Roberta's net tax payable or refund due for 2013. If you use tax forms, you will need Form 1040 and Schedules A, B, D, and E. Suggested software: H&R BLOCK Tax Software.

59. John and Mary Jane Diaz are married, filing jointly. Their address is 204 Shoe Lane, Blacksburg, VA 24061. John is age 35, and Mary Jane is age 30. They are expecting their first child in early 2015. John's salary in 2014 was $105,000, from which $20,800 of Federal income tax and $4,700 of state income tax were withheld. Mary Jane made $52,000 and had $3,000 of Federal income tax and $3,100 of state income tax withheld. The appropriate amounts of FICA tax and Medicare tax were withheld for John and for Mary Jane. John's Social Security number is 111-11-1111, and Mary Jane's Social Security number is 123-45-6789.

    John and Mary Jane are both covered by their employer's medical insurance policies with four-fifths of the premiums being paid by the employers. The total premiums were $10,000 for John and $6,200 for Mary Jane. Mary Jane received medical benefits of $7,300 under the plan. John was not ill during 2014. Mary Jane paid noncovered medical expenses of $1,300.

    John makes child support payments of $15,000 for his son, Rod, who lives with June, John's former spouse, except for two months in the summer when he visits John and Mary Jane. At the time of the divorce, John worked for a Fortune 500 company and received a salary of $225,000. As a result of corporate downsizing, he lost his job.

    Mary Jane's father lived with them until his death in November. His only sources of income were salary of $2,800, unemployment compensation benefits of $3,500, and Social Security benefits of $4,100. Of this amount, he deposited $6,000 in a savings account. The remainder of his support of $9,500, which included funeral expenses of $4,500, was provided by John and Mary Jane.

    Other income received by the Diazes was as follows:

Interest on certificates of deposit	$3,500
Share of S corporation taxable income (distributions from the S corporation to Mary Jane were $1,100)	1,500
Award received by Mary Jane from employer for an outstanding suggestion for cutting costs	4,000

    John has always wanted to operate his own business. In October 2014, he incurred expenses of $15,000 in investigating the establishment of a retail computer franchise. With the birth of their child expected next year, however, he decides to forgo self-employment for at least a couple of years.

    John and Mary Jane made charitable contributions of $3,700 during the year and paid an additional $1,800 in state income taxes in 2014 upon filing their 2013 state income tax return. Their deductible home mortgage interest was $8,200, and their property taxes came to $4,800. They paid sales taxes of $2,000, for which they have receipts. They paid a ticket of $150 that Mary Jane received for running a red light (detected by a red light camera).

Part 1—Tax Computation
Calculate John and Mary Jane's tax (or refund) due for 2014.

Part 2—Tax Planning
Assume that the Diazes come to you for advice in December 2014. John has learned that he will receive a $30,000 bonus. He wants to know if he should take it in December 2014 or in January 2015. Mary Jane will quit work on December 31 to stay home with the baby. Their itemized deductions will decrease by $3,100 because Mary Jane will not have state income taxes withheld. Mary Jane will not receive the employee award in 2015. She expects the medical benefits received to be $9,000. The Diazes expect all of their other income items to remain the same in 2015. Write a letter to John and Mary Jane that contains your advice and prepare a memo for the tax files.

Tax Computation Problem

Decision Making

Communications

Research Problems

THOMSON REUTERS
CHECKPOINT®

Note: Solutions to Research Problems can be prepared by using the **Checkpoint®** **Student Edition** online research product, which is available to accompany this text. It is also possible to prepare solutions to the Research Problems by using tax research materials found in a standard tax library.

Communications

Research Problem 1. Gray Chemical Company manufactured pesticides that were toxic. Over the course of several years, the toxic waste contaminated the air and water around the company's plant. Several employees suffered toxic poisoning, and the Environmental Protection Agency cited the company for violations. In court, the judge found Gray guilty and imposed fines of $15 million. The company voluntarily set up a charitable fund for the purpose of bettering the environment and funded it with $8 million. The company incurred legal expenses in setting up the foundation and defending itself in court. The court reduced the fine from $15 million to $7 million.

Gray Chemical Company deducted the $8 million paid to the foundation and the legal expenses incurred. The IRS disallowed both deductions on the grounds that the payment was, in fact, a fine and in violation of public policy.

Gray's president, Ted Jones, has contacted you regarding the deductibility of the $7 million fine, the $8 million payment to the foundation, and the legal fees. Write a letter to Mr. Jones that contains your advice and prepare a memo for the tax files. Gray's address is 200 Lincoln Center, Omaha, NE 68182.

Partial list of research aids:
§§ 162(a) and (f).
Reg. § 1.162–21(b).

Research Problem 2. Rex and Agnes Harrell purchased a beach house at Duck, North Carolina, in early 2012. Although they intended to use the beach house occasionally for recreational purposes, they also planned to rent it through the realty agency that had handled the purchase to help pay the mortgage payments, property taxes, and maintenance costs. Rex is a surgeon, and Agnes is a counselor.

The beach house was in need of substantial repairs. Rather than hiring a contractor, Rex and Agnes decided they would make the repairs themselves. During both high school and college, Rex had worked summers in construction. In addition, he had taken an advanced course in woodworking and related subjects from a local community college several years ago.

During 2012, according to a log maintained by the Harrells, they occupied the beach house 38 days and rented it 49 days. The log also indicated that on 24 of the 38 days they occupied the beach house, one or both of them were engaged in work on the beach house. Their two teenage children were with them on all of these days but did not help with the work being done. On their 2012 income tax return, Rex and Agnes, who filed a joint return, treated the beach house as a rental property and deducted a pro rata share of the property taxes, mortgage interest, utilities, maintenance and repairs, and depreciation in determining their net loss from the beach home. In the current year, after examining their return, an IRS agent has limited the deductions to the rent income. He contends that the 14-day personal use provision was exceeded and that many of the alleged repairs were capital expenditures. Advise the Harrells on how they should respond to the IRS.

Research Problem 3. In early 2012, Walter Hodges began investigating the real estate market with the intention of acquiring real estate for investment or rental. He had not previously been involved in any real estate rental or investment ventures.

Walter started marketing his business via business cards, flyers, and word of mouth in spring 2012. At the same time, he completed a business plan for buying, remodeling, and renting property.

In October 2012, Walter paid $25,000 for training classes designed to provide real estate investment skills. He obtained a loan for his business of $45,000 from the U.S. Small Business Administration in November 2012. During the same month, he obtained an employer ID number from the IRS. In December 2012, he opened a checking account and obtained a credit card in the name of the business.

Walter attempted to purchase several properties during the last half of 2012, but he was unsuccessful until he acquired property on December 30, 2012. He listed the property for rent in early January 2013 and was successful in renting it in March 2013.

On his Form 1040 for 2012, Walter prepared a Schedule C on which he showed a business loss of $29,000. He included the cost of the training classes, automobile expenses, meals and entertainment, computer and software expenses, and supplies.

Walter asked a friend, who is a CPA, to review his Schedule C calculations. His friend suggested that Walter should not be able to deduct the $29,000 on his 2012 return as he did not believe that Walter was in a trade or business during 2012. Evaluate whether Walter's trade or business activity began in 2012 or 2013.

Research Problem 4. Mona viewed herself as a creative individual who had chosen to go to law school for economic reasons. Mona's undergraduate majors were creative writing and American Indian studies.

Mona was very successful as an attorney and eventually was admitted to partnership in her law firm, having an expertise in negotiating settlements involving Indian water rights.

While practicing law, Mona continued her interest in the arts. She had directed plays in high school and maintained her involvement in the theater, even during law school. She belonged to local theater organizations while she practiced law. She took several courses in filmmaking and read extensively in the area. She even took several months off from her legal practice to enroll in NYU's filmmaking program. Her enrollment in the program provided her with hands-on experience and taught her about the technical aspects of filmmaking and allowed her to meet individuals who would later work with her on her documentary.

When she discovered that her husband had similar interests, she decided to create a documentary about Way to Sing America. After acquiring the rights to all of the archival footage of Way to Sing America, she hired a video production company to film interviews that she conducted with Way to Sing America alumni (over 400 hours of such interviews). She spent weekends and nights over a three-year period working on the documentary.

Once the documentary was completed, Mona began marketing it at film festivals. At some of these festivals, her documentary received awards. At the same time, she developed a business plan, hired a bookkeeper to manage the finances, and hired an accounting firm to provide tax advice.

During this three-year period, she reported the following losses:

2010	$ 30,000
2011	400,000
2012	200,000

On her tax returns for the three-year period, she offset these amounts against her law firm income of approximately $1 million in each year.

Upon audit by the IRS, the agent concluded that her filmmaking activity is a hobby and therefore the losses cannot be deducted except to the extent of the income generated.

Who is correct? Explain.

Research Problem 5. Sam Adams is a CPA who is also an aspiring actor. In 2013, his AGI (before any deductions for performing arts expenses) was $42,000 and was from the following sources:

CPA practice	$30,000
Acting jobs (4 employers)	12,000

Expenses associated with his acting career were $9,000. Sam is uncertain of the proper tax treatment for these expenses. One alternative is to deduct these expenses under § 162 and classify them as deductions *for* AGI under § 62(a)(2)(B).

Another alternative is to classify these expenses as miscellaneous itemized deductions (subject to the 2%-of-AGI floor). Sam's uncertainty arises because he is unsure about how to calculate the AGI ceiling referenced in § 62(b)(1)(C). Advise Sam on the appropriate tax treatment.

Use the tax resources of the Internet to address the following questions. Do not restrict your search to the Web, but include a review of newsgroups and general reference materials, practitioner sites and resources, primary sources of the tax law, chat rooms and discussion groups, and other opportunities.

Internet Activity

Research Problem 6. Sarah was contemplating making a contribution to her traditional IRA in 2013. She determined she would contribute $5,000 in December 2013, but forgot about making the contribution until she was preparing her 2013 tax return in February

2014. Use the website of any well-known IRA provider (e.g., Fidelity, Vanguard, T. Rowe Price) to determine if Sarah can make a 2013 contribution to her IRA after the tax year has ended.

Research Problem 7. The $1 million maximum compensation deduction does not seem to have deterred large corporations from remunerating their executives at very high levels. What techniques are being used to work around the millionaires' provision? Are executives taking pay cuts, or are their salaries being deferred or changed in nature due to § 162(m)?

CHAPTER

7

Deductions and Losses: Certain Business Expenses and Losses

LEARNING OBJECTIVES: *After completing Chapter 7, you should be able to:*

LO.1 Determine the amount, classification, and timing of the bad debt deduction.

LO.2 State and illustrate the tax treatment of worthless securities, including § 1244 stock.

LO.3 Distinguish between deductible and nondeductible losses of individuals.

LO.4 Identify a casualty and determine the amount, classification, and timing of casualty and theft losses.

LO.5 State and apply the alternative tax treatments for research and experimental expenditures.

LO.6 Calculate the domestic production activities deduction.

LO.7 Determine the amount of the net operating loss and review the impact of the carryback and carryover provisions on previous and subsequent years' taxable income.

LO.8 Identify tax planning opportunities in deducting certain business expenses, business losses, and personal losses.

CHAPTER OUTLINE

© Tetra Images/Jupiter Images

Losses

Martha, a cash basis taxpayer, is nearing the end of a year that she would like to forget. Several years ago, she loaned a friend $25,000 to enable him to start a business. The friend had made scheduled payments of $7,000 ($1,000 of this was interest) when he unexpectedly died in January. At the time of his death, he was insolvent. Martha's attempts to collect on the debt were fruitless.

Last October, Martha invested $50,000 in the stock of a pharmaceutical company that previously had been profitable. However, as a result of losing a patent infringement suit, the company declared bankruptcy in May of this year. Martha is notified by the bankruptcy trustee that she can expect to receive nothing from the company.

Martha has owned and operated a bookstore as a sole proprietorship for the past 10 years. The bookstore previously produced annual profits of about $75,000. Due to a chain bookstore opening down the street, Martha's bookstore sustained a net loss of $180,000 this year.

In September, a hurricane caused a large oak tree to blow over onto Martha's house. The cost of removing the tree and making repairs was $32,000. Martha received a check for $25,000 from her insurance company in final settlement of the claim. Her adjusted basis for the house was $280,000.

Martha purchased what she believes to be § 1244 stock. Unfortunately, the stock's value began to decline significantly soon after its purchase (see Example 10).

Can you help relieve Martha's feeling of despair by making her aware of beneficial loss provisions in the tax law?

Read the chapter and formulate your response.

Income *(broadly conceived)*	$xx,xxx
Less: Exclusions	(x,xxx)
Gross income	$xx,xxx
Less: Deductions for adjusted gross income	(x,xxx)

FORM 1040 (p. 1)

| 12 | Business income or (loss). Attach Schedule C or C-EZ . . . . |
| 35 | Domestic production activities deduction. Attach Form 8903 |

Adjusted gross income	$xx,xxx
Less: The greater of total **itemized deductions** *or* the standard deduction	(x,xxx)

FORM 1040 (p. 2)

| 40 | **Itemized deductions** (from Schedule A) **or** your **standard deduction** (see left margin) . . |

Personal and dependency exemptions	(x,xxx)
Taxable income	$xx,xxx
Tax on taxable income *(see Tax Tables or Tax Rate Schedules)*	$ x,xxx
Less: Tax credits *(including income taxes withheld and prepaid)*	(xxx)
Tax due *(or refund)*	$ xxx

Working with the tax formula for individuals requires the proper classification of items that are deductible *for* adjusted gross income (AGI) and items that are deductions *from* AGI (itemized deductions). Business expenses and losses, discussed in this chapter, are reductions of gross income to arrive at the taxpayer's AGI. Expenses and losses incurred in connection with a transaction entered into for profit and attributable to rents and royalties are deducted *for* AGI. All other expenses and losses incurred in connection with a transaction entered into for profit are deducted *from* AGI. The determination of the taxpayer's activity (i.e., whether the taxpayer is engaged in a trade or business, an investment, or a personal activity) is crucial in this classification process.[1]

Deductible losses on personal use property are deducted as an itemized deduction. Itemized deductions are deductions *from* AGI. While the general coverage of itemized deductions is in Chapter 10, casualty and theft losses on personal use property are discussed in this chapter.

In determining the amount and timing of the deduction for bad debts, proper classification is again important. A business bad debt is classified as a deduction *for* AGI, and a nonbusiness bad debt is classified as a short-term capital loss.

Other topics discussed in Chapter 7 are research and experimental expenditures, the domestic production activities deduction, and the net operating loss deduction.

7-1 BAD DEBTS

LO.1

Determine the amount, classification, and timing of the bad debt deduction.

If a taxpayer sells goods or provides services on credit and the account receivable subsequently becomes worthless, a **bad debt** deduction is permitted only if income arising from the creation of the account receivable was previously included in income.[2] No deduction is allowed, for example, for a bad debt arising from the sale

---

[1]See, for example, *Groetzinger v. Comm.*, 85–2 USTC ¶9622, 56 AFTR 2d 85–5683, 771 F.2d 269 (CA–7, 1985), aff'd in 87–1 USTC ¶ 9191. 59 AFTR 2d 87–532, 107 S.Ct. 980 (USSC, 1987), discussed later in the chapter.

[2]Reg. § 1.166–1(e).

of a product or service when the taxpayer is on the cash basis because no income is reported until the cash has been collected. Permitting a bad debt deduction for a cash basis taxpayer would amount to a double deduction because the expenses of the product or service rendered are deducted when payments are made to suppliers and to employees, or at the time of the sale.

Example 1

Tracy, an individual, is a sole proprietor. She operates a business named Executive Accounting and Tax Services. Last year, Pat hired Tracy to help him with the accounting for his small business. Tracy also prepared the S corporation income tax return for the business and Pat's personal income tax return. Tracy billed Pat $8,000 for the services she performed. Pat has never paid the bill, his business no longer exists, and his whereabouts are unknown.

If Tracy is an accrual basis taxpayer, she includes the $8,000 in income when the services are performed. When she determines that Pat's account will not be collected, she deducts the $8,000 as a bad debt expense.

If Tracy is a cash basis taxpayer, she does not include the $8,000 in income until payment is received. When she determines that Pat's account will not be collected, she cannot deduct the $8,000 as a bad debt expense because it was never recognized as income.

THE BIG PICTURE

Example 2

Return to the facts of *The Big Picture* on p. 7-1. Because Martha is a cash basis taxpayer, she cannot take as a bad debt deduction any unpaid accrued interest on the loan to her friend because it was never recognized as income.

A bad debt can also result from the nonrepayment of a loan made by the taxpayer or from purchased debt instruments.

7-1a Specific Charge-Off Method

Taxpayers (other than certain financial institutions) may use only the **specific charge-off method** in accounting for bad debts. Certain financial institutions are allowed to use the **reserve method** for computing deductions for bad debts.

A taxpayer using the specific charge-off method may claim a deduction when a specific business debt becomes either partially or wholly worthless or when a specific nonbusiness debt becomes wholly worthless.[3] For the business debt, the taxpayer must satisfy the IRS that the debt is partially worthless and must demonstrate the amount of worthlessness.

If a business debt previously deducted as partially worthless becomes totally worthless in a future year, only the remainder not previously deducted can be deducted in the future year.

In the case of total worthlessness, a deduction is allowed for the entire amount in the year the debt becomes worthless. The amount of the deduction depends on the taxpayer's basis in the bad debt. If the debt arose from the sale of services or products and the face amount was previously included in income, that amount is deductible. If the taxpayer purchased the debt, the deduction is equal to the amount the taxpayer paid for the debt instrument.

One of the more difficult tasks is determining if and when a bad debt is worthless. The loss is deductible only in the year of partial or total worthlessness for business debts and only in the year of total worthlessness for nonbusiness debts. Legal proceedings need not be initiated against the debtor when the surrounding facts indicate that such action will not result in collection.

---

[3]§ 166(a).

TAX IN THE NEWS   Impact of Funding Cuts on Skilled Nursing Facilities

A so-called "bad debt" provision contained in the Middle Class Tax Relief and Job Creation Act of 2012 is having a negative impact on skilled nursing facilities (SNFs). An analysis shows that Medicare funding cuts to SNFs in the states of Florida, Ohio, Illinois, Pennsylvania, North Carolina, Louisiana, Indiana, Tennessee, Georgia, and New Jersey will reduce payments by a least $3 billion over the period 2012–2021. It has been pointed out that the term *bad debt* is a complete misnomer. The Federal government prevents SNFs from collecting as much as 90 percent of SNF debts from state Medicaid agencies. The bad debt is more accurately described as "uncollectible debt" as mandated by Federal law.

Source: Based on "New Avalere Health Analysis Details State Impact of 'Bad Debt' SNF Medicare Funding Cuts," *PR Newswire Association LLC*, April, 3, 2012.

Example 3

In 2012, Ross loaned $1,000 to Kay, who agreed to repay the loan in two years. In 2014, Kay disappeared after the note became delinquent. If a reasonable investigation by Ross indicates that he cannot find Kay or that a suit against Kay would not result in collection, Ross can deduct the $1,000 in 2014.

Bankruptcy is generally an indication of at least partial worthlessness of a debt. Bankruptcy may create worthlessness before the settlement date. If this is the case, the deduction may be taken in the year of worthlessness.

Example 4

In Example 3, assume that Kay filed for personal bankruptcy in 2013 and that the debt is a business debt. At that time, Ross learned that unsecured creditors (including Ross) were ultimately expected to receive 20 cents on the dollar. In 2014, settlement is made, and Ross receives only $150. He should deduct $800 ($1,000 loan − $200 expected settlement) in 2013 and $50 in 2014 ($200 balance − $150 proceeds).

If a receivable has been written off as uncollectible during the current tax year and is subsequently collected during the current tax year, the write-off entry is reversed. If a receivable has been written off (deducted) as uncollectible, the collection of the receivable in a later tax year may result in income being recognized. Income will result if the deduction yielded a tax benefit in the year it was taken. See Examples 33 and 34 in Chapter 5.

See Concept Summary 7.1.

7-1b Business versus Nonbusiness Bad Debts

A **nonbusiness bad debt** is a debt unrelated to the taxpayer's trade or business either when it was created or when it became worthless. The nature of a debt depends upon whether the lender was engaged in the business of lending money or whether there is a proximate relationship between the creation of the debt and the lender's trade or business. The use to which the borrowed funds are put by the debtor is of no consequence. Loans to relatives or friends are the most common type of nonbusiness bad debt.

THE BIG PICTURE

Example 5

Return to the facts of *The Big Picture* on p. 7-1. Martha loaned her friend, Jamil, $25,000. Jamil used the money to start a business, which subsequently failed. When Jamil died after having made payments of $7,000 on the loan, he was insolvent. Even though the proceeds of the loan were used in a business, the loan is a nonbusiness bad debt because the business was Jamil's, not Martha's.

CONCEPT SUMMARY 7.1

Specific Charge-Off Method

Expense deduction and account write-off	The expense arises and the write-off takes place when a specific business account becomes either partially or wholly worthless or when a specific nonbusiness account becomes wholly worthless.
Recovery of accounts previously written off	If the account recovered was written off during the current taxable year, the write-off entry is reversed. If the account recovered was written off during a previous taxable year, income is created subject to the tax benefit rule.

The distinction between a business bad debt and a nonbusiness bad debt is important. A **business bad debt** is deductible as an ordinary loss in the year incurred, whereas a nonbusiness bad debt is always treated as a short-term capital loss. Thus, regardless of the age of a nonbusiness bad debt, the deduction may be of limited benefit due to the limitations on capital loss deductibility in any one year. The maximum amount of a net short-term capital loss that an individual can deduct against ordinary income in any one year is $3,000 (see Chapter 16 for a detailed discussion). Although no deduction is allowed when a nonbusiness bad debt is partially worthless, the taxpayer is entitled to deduct the net amount of the loss upon final settlement.

The following example is an illustration of business bad debts adapted from the Regulations.[4]

> **Example 6**
>
> In 2013, Leif sold his business but retained a claim (note or account receivable) against Bob. The claim became worthless in 2014. Leif's loss is treated as a business bad debt because the debt was created in the conduct of his former trade or business. Leif is accorded business bad debt treatment even though he was holding the note as an investor and was no longer in a trade or business when the claim became worthless.

The nonbusiness bad debt provisions are *not* applicable to corporations. It is assumed that any loans made by a corporation are related to its trade or business. Therefore, any bad debts of a corporation are business bad debts.

7-1c Loans between Related Parties

Loans between related parties (especially family members) raise the issue of whether the transaction was a *bona fide* loan or a gift. The Regulations state that a bona fide debt arises from a debtor-creditor relationship based on a valid and enforceable obligation to pay a fixed or determinable sum of money. Thus, individual circumstances must be examined to determine whether advances between related parties are gifts or loans. Some considerations are these:

- Was a note properly executed?
- Was there a reasonable rate of interest?
- Was collateral provided?
- What collection efforts were made?
- What was the intent of the parties?

> **Example 7**
>
> Lana loans $2,000 to her widowed mother for an operation. Lana's mother owns no property and is not employed, and her only income consists of Social Security benefits. No note is issued for the loan, no provision for interest is made, and no repayment date is mentioned. In the current year, Lana's mother dies, leaving no estate. Assuming that the loan is not repaid, Lana cannot take a deduction for a nonbusiness bad debt because the facts indicate that no debtor-creditor relationship existed.

See Concept Summary 7.2 for a review of the bad debt deduction rules.

---

[4]Reg. § 1.166–5(d).

TAX IN THE NEWS   Denial of Bad Debt Deduction

What is the relationship between sales tax paid and a bad debt deduction? What is the identity of the corporation for which litigation occurred at the state level on this issue?

Home Depot had a contractual arrangement with finance companies to allow Home Depot customers to use private label credit cards to pay for their purchases. When a customer used the credit card for a purchase, the finance company paid Home Depot the amount of the purchase (which included Alabama sales tax) less a service fee. The finance company took a bad debt deduction if the Home Depot customer failed to pay.

Home Depot wanted to take a deduction for sales taxes paid on uncollectible accounts. The court denied the deduction because the bad debt was not that of Home Depot.

Source: Based on "Ryan; Alabama Court of Civil Appeals Denies Home Depot's Attempt to Take Bad Debt Deduction," *NewsRx*, January 20, 2012.

© iStockphoto.com/Andrey Prokhorov

CONCEPT SUMMARY 7.2

Bad Debt Deductions

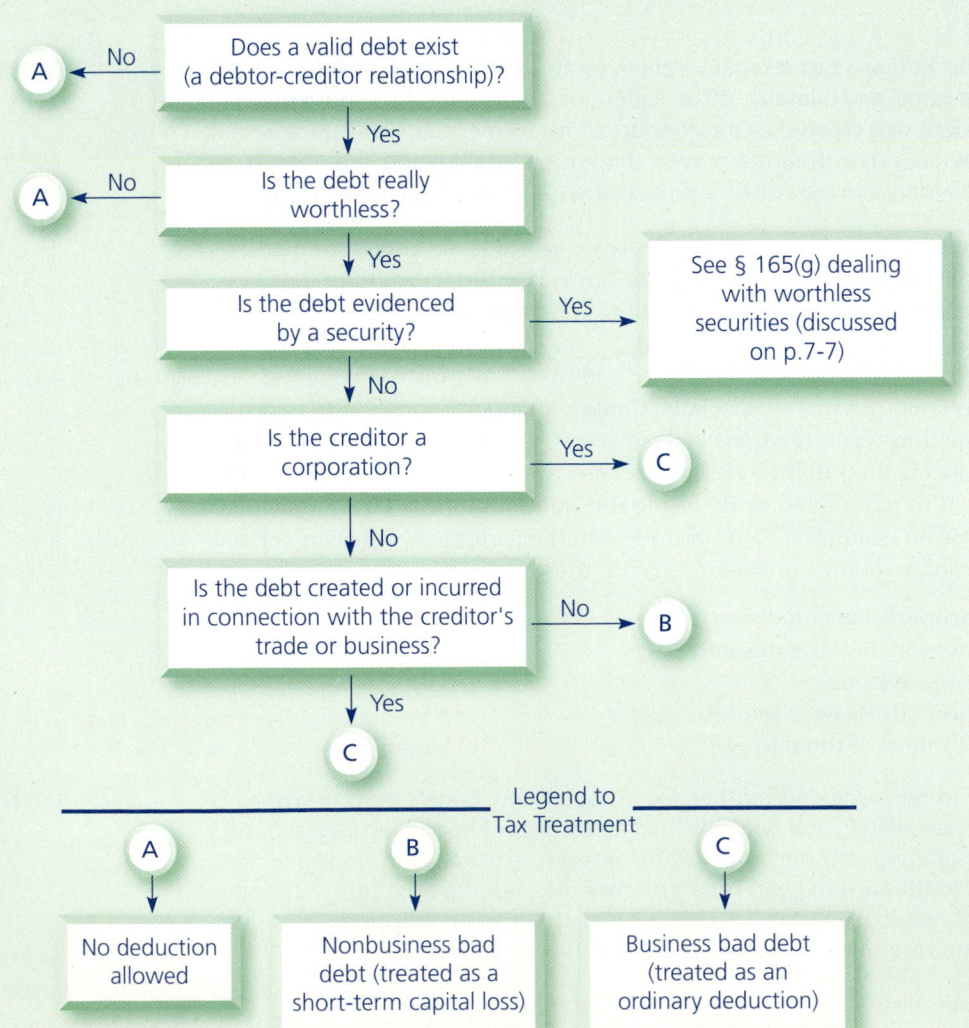

© iStockphoto.com/Andrey Prokhorov

7-2 WORTHLESS SECURITIES

A loss is allowed for securities that become *completely* worthless during the year (**worthless securities**).[5] Such securities are shares of stock, bonds, notes, or other evidence of indebtedness issued by a corporation or government. The losses generated are treated as capital losses deemed to have occurred on the *last day* of the taxable year. By treating the loss as having occurred on the last day of the taxable year, a loss that would otherwise have been classified as short-term (if the date of worthlessness was used) may be classified as a long-term capital loss. Capital losses may be of limited benefit due to the $3,000 capital loss limitation.[6]

LO.2

State and illustrate the tax treatment of worthless securities, including § 1244 stock.

THE BIG PICTURE

Example 8

Return to the facts of *The Big Picture* on p. 7-1. Assume that Martha is a calendar year taxpayer. She owned stock in Owl Corporation (a publicly held company). She acquired the stock as an investment on October 1, 2013, at a cost of $50,000. On May 31, 2014, the stock became worthless when the company declared bankruptcy. Because the stock is deemed to have become worthless as of December 31, 2014, Martha has a capital loss from an asset held for 15 months (a long-term capital loss).

7-2a Small Business Stock (§ 1244)

The general rule is that shareholders receive capital gain or loss treatment upon the sale or exchange of stock. However, it is possible to receive an ordinary loss deduction if the loss is sustained on **small business stock (§ 1244 stock)**. This loss could arise from a sale of the stock or from the stock becoming worthless. Only *individuals*[7] who acquired the stock *from* the corporation are eligible to receive ordinary loss treatment under § 1244. The ordinary loss treatment is limited to $50,000 ($100,000 for married individuals filing jointly) per year. Losses on § 1244 stock in excess of the statutory limits receive capital loss treatment.

The corporation must meet certain requirements for the loss on § 1244 stock to be treated as an *ordinary*—rather than a capital—loss. The major requirement is that the total amount of money and other property received by the corporation for stock as a contribution to capital (or paid-in surplus) does not exceed $1 million. The $1 million test is made at the time the stock is issued. Section 1244 stock can be common or preferred stock. Section 1244 applies only to losses. If § 1244 stock is sold at a gain, the Section is not applicable and the gain is capital gain.

Example 9

Iris, a single individual, was looking for an investment that would give some diversity to her stock portfolio. A friend suggested she acquire some stock in Eagle Corporation, a new startup company. On July 1, 2012, Iris purchased 100 shares of Eagle Corporation for $100,000. At the time Iris acquired her stock from Eagle Corporation, the corporation had $700,000 of paid-in capital. Hence, the stock qualified as § 1244 stock. On June 20, 2014, Iris sold all of her Eagle stock for $20,000. Because the Eagle stock is § 1244 stock, Iris has $50,000 of ordinary loss and $30,000 of long-term capital loss.

---

[5]§ 165(g).
[6]§ 1211(b).

[7]The term *individuals* for this purpose does not include a trust or an estate (but could include a partnership or an LLC).

Example 10

Return to the facts of *The Big Picture* on p. 7-1. On March 8, 2014, Martha purchases what she believes is § 1244 stock from her friend Janice for $20,000. On November 2, 2014, she sells the stock in the marketplace for $12,000. Because Martha purchases the stock from Janice and not the corporation, the stock is not § 1244 stock to Martha. Hence, Martha has an $8,000 short-term capital loss.

7-3 LOSSES OF INDIVIDUALS

LO.3

Distinguish between deductible and nondeductible losses of individuals.

An individual may deduct the following losses under § 165(c):

- Losses incurred in a trade or business.
- Losses incurred in a transaction entered into for profit.
- Losses caused by fire, storm, shipwreck, or other casualty or by theft.

Examples of losses in the first two categories include a loss on property used in a proprietorship, a loss on property held for rent, or a loss on stolen bearer bonds. Note that losses in these two categories are not limited to losses caused by fire, storm, shipwreck, or other casualty or by theft.

An individual taxpayer suffering losses from damage to *nonbusiness* property can deduct only those losses attributable to fire, storm, shipwreck, or other casualty or theft. Although the meaning of the terms *fire, storm, shipwreck,* and *theft* is relatively free from dispute, the term *other casualty* needs further clarification. It means casualties analogous to fire, storm, or shipwreck. The term also includes accidental loss of property provided the loss qualifies under the same rules as any other casualty. These rules are that the loss must result from an event that is (1) identifiable; (2) damaging to property; and (3) sudden, unexpected, and unusual in nature.

A *sudden event* is an event that is swift and precipitous and not gradual or progressive. An *unexpected event* is an event that is ordinarily unanticipated and occurs without the intent of the individual who suffers the loss. An *unusual event* is an event that is extraordinary and nonrecurring and does not commonly occur during the activity in which the taxpayer was engaged when the destruction occurred.[8] Examples include hurricanes, tornadoes, floods, storms, shipwrecks, fires, auto accidents, mine cave-ins, sonic booms, and vandalism. Weather that causes damage (e.g., drought) must be unusual and severe for the particular region. Damage must be to the taxpayer's property to qualify as a **casualty loss**.

A taxpayer can take a deduction for a casualty loss from an automobile accident only if the damage was not caused by the taxpayer's willful act or willful negligence.

Example 11

Ted parks his car on a hill and fails to set the brake properly and to curb the wheels. As a result of Ted's negligence, the car rolls down the hill and is damaged. The repairs to Ted's car should qualify for casualty loss treatment because Ted's act of negligence appears to be simple rather than willful.

7-3a Events That Are Not Casualties

LO.4

Identify a casualty and determine the amount, classification, and timing of casualty and theft losses.

Not all acts of God are treated as casualty losses for income tax purposes. Because a casualty must be sudden, unexpected, and unusual, progressive deterioration (such as erosion due to wind or rain) is not a casualty because it does not meet the suddenness test.

Examples of nonsudden events that generally do not qualify as casualties include disease and insect damage. When the damage was caused by termites over a period

---

[8]Rev.Rul. 72–592, 1972–2 C.B. 101.

of several years, some courts have disallowed a casualty loss deduction.[9] On the other hand, some courts have held that termite damage over periods of up to 15 months after infestation constituted a sudden event and was, therefore, deductible as a casualty loss.[10] Despite the existence of some judicial support for the deductibility of termite damage as a casualty loss, the current position of the IRS is that termite damage is not deductible.[11]

Other examples of events that are not casualties are losses resulting from a decline in value rather than an actual loss of the property. No loss was allowed where the taxpayer's home declined in value as a result of a landslide that destroyed neighboring homes but did no actual damage to the taxpayer's home.[12] Similarly, a taxpayer was allowed a loss for the actual flood damage to his property but not for the decline in market value due to the property being flood-prone.[13]

7-3b Theft Losses

Theft includes, but is not necessarily limited to, larceny, embezzlement, and robbery.[14] Theft does not include misplaced items.[15]

Theft losses are computed like other casualty losses (discussed in the following section), but the *timing* for recognition of the loss differs. A theft loss is deducted in the year of discovery, not the year of the theft (unless, of course, the discovery occurs in the same year as the theft). If, in the year of the discovery, a claim exists (e.g., against an insurance company) and there is a reasonable expectation of recovering the adjusted basis of the asset from the insurance company, no deduction is permitted.[16] If, in the year of settlement, the recovery is less than the asset's adjusted basis, a partial deduction may be available. If the recovery is greater than the asset's adjusted basis, gain may be recognized.

Keith's new sailboat, which he uses for personal purposes, was stolen from the storage marina in December 2013. He discovered the loss on June 3, 2014, and filed a claim with his insurance company that was settled on January 30, 2015. Assuming that there is a reasonable expectation of full recovery, no deduction is allowed in 2014. A partial deduction may be available in 2015 if the actual insurance proceeds are less than the lower of the fair market value or the adjusted basis of the asset. (Loss measurement rules are discussed later in this chapter.)	**Example 12**

7-3c When to Deduct Casualty Losses

General Rule

Generally, a casualty loss is deducted in the year the loss occurs. However, no casualty loss is permitted if a reimbursement claim with a *reasonable prospect of full recovery* exists.[17] If the taxpayer has a partial claim, only part of the loss can be claimed in the year of the casualty, and the remainder is deducted in the year the claim is settled.

Brian's new sailboat was completely destroyed by fire in 2014. Its cost and fair market value were $15,000. Brian's only claim against the insurance company was on a $10,000 policy and was not settled by year-end. The following year, 2015, Brian settled with the insurance company for $8,000. He is entitled to a $5,000 deduction in 2014 ($15,000 less $10,000) and a $2,000 deduction in 2015. If Brian held the sailboat for personal use, the $5,000 deduction in 2014 is reduced first by $100 and then by 10% of his 2014 AGI. The $2,000 deduction in 2015 is reduced by 10% of his 2015 AGI (see the following discussion on the $100 and 10% floors).	**Example 13**

[9]*Fay v. Helvering,* 41–2 USTC ¶9494, 27 AFTR 432, 120 F.2d 253 (CA–2, 1941); *U.S. v. Rogers,* 41–1 USTC ¶9442, 27 AFTR 423, 120 F.2d 244 (CA–9, 1941).

[10]*Rosenberg v. Comm.,* 52–2 USTC ¶9377, 42 AFTR 303, 198 F.2d 46 (CA–8, 1952); *Shopmaker v. U.S.,* 54–1 USTC ¶9195, 45 AFTR 758, 119 F.Supp. 705 (D.Ct. Mo., 1953).

[11]Rev.Rul. 63–232, 1963–2 C.B. 97.

[12]*H. Pulvers v. Comm.,* 69–1 USTC ¶9222, 23 AFTR 2d 69–678, 407 F.2d 838 (CA–9, 1969).

[13]*S. L. Solomon,* 39 TCM 1282, T.C.Memo. 1980–87.

[14]Reg. § 1.165–8(d).

[15]*Mary Francis Allen,* 16 T.C. 163 (1951).

[16]Reg. §§ 1.165–1(d)(2) and 1.165–8(a)(2).

[17]Reg. § 1.165–1(d)(2)(i).

If a taxpayer receives reimbursement for a casualty loss sustained and deducted in a previous year, an amended return is not filed for that year. Instead, the taxpayer must include the reimbursement in gross income on the return for the year in which it is received to the extent the previous deduction resulted in a tax benefit.

Example 14

Fran had a deductible casualty loss of $4,000 on her 2013 tax return. Fran's taxable income for 2013 was $60,000. In June 2014, Fran is reimbursed $2,750 for the prior year's casualty loss. Fran includes the entire $2,750 in gross income for 2014 because the deduction in 2013 produced a tax benefit.

Disaster Area Losses

An exception to the general rule for the time of deduction is allowed for **disaster area losses**, which are casualties sustained in an area designated as a disaster area by the President of the United States.[18] In such cases, the taxpayer may *elect* to treat the loss as having occurred in the taxable year immediately *preceding* the taxable year in which the disaster actually occurred. The rationale for this exception is to provide immediate relief to disaster victims in the form of accelerated tax benefits.

If the due date, plus extensions, for the prior year's return has not passed, a taxpayer makes the election to claim the disaster area loss on the prior year's tax return. If the disaster occurs after the prior year's return has been filed, it is necessary to file either an amended return or a refund claim. In any case, the taxpayer must show clearly that such an election is being made.

Disaster loss treatment also applies in the case of a personal residence that has been rendered unsafe for use as a residence because of a disaster. This provision applies when, within 120 days after the President designates the area as a disaster area, the state or local government where the residence is located orders the taxpayer to demolish or relocate the residence.[19]

THE BIG PICTURE

Example 15

Return to the facts of *The Big Picture* on p. 7-1. On September 28, 2014, Martha's personal residence was damaged when a hurricane caused an oak tree to fall onto the house. The amount of her uninsured loss was $7,000. Because of the extent of the damage in the area, the President of the United States designated the area a disaster area. Because Martha's loss is a disaster area loss, she may elect to file an amended return for 2013 and take the loss in that year. If Martha elects this course of action, the amount of the loss will be reduced first by $100 (the materiality amount in 2013) and then by 10% of her 2013 AGI. If Martha forgoes the election, she may take the loss on her 2014 income tax return. The amount of the loss will be reduced first by $100 (the materiality amount in 2014) and then by 10% of her 2014 AGI.

7-3d Measuring the Amount of Loss

Amount of Loss

The rules for determining the amount of a loss depend in part on whether business use, income-producing use, or personal use property was involved. Another factor that must be considered is whether the property was partially or completely destroyed.

---

[18]§ 165(h).   [19]§ 165(k).

If business property or property held for the production of income (e.g., rental property) is *completely destroyed*, the loss is equal to the adjusted basis of the property at the time of destruction.

> **Example 16**
>
> Vicki's automobile, which was used only for business purposes, was destroyed by fire. Vicki had unintentionally allowed her insurance coverage to expire. The fair market value of the automobile was $9,000 at the time of the fire, and its adjusted basis was $10,000. Vicki is allowed a loss deduction of $10,000 (the basis of the automobile). The $10,000 loss is a deduction *for* AGI.

A different measurement rule applies for *partial destruction* of business property and income-producing property and for *partial* or *complete destruction* of personal use property. In these situations, the loss is the *lesser* of the following:

- The adjusted basis of the property.
- The difference between the fair market value of the property before the event and the fair market value immediately after the event.

> **Example 17**
>
> Kelly's uninsured automobile, which was used only for business purposes, was damaged in an accident. On the date of the accident, the fair market value of the automobile was $12,000, and its adjusted basis was $9,000. After the accident, the automobile was appraised at $4,000. Kelly's loss deduction is $8,000 (the lesser of the adjusted basis or the decrease in fair market value). The $8,000 loss is a deduction *for* AGI.

The deduction for the loss of property that is part business and part personal must be computed separately for the business portion and the personal portion.

Any insurance recovery reduces the loss for business, production of income, and personal use losses. In fact, a taxpayer may realize a gain if the insurance proceeds exceed the amount of the loss. Chapter 17 discusses the treatment of net gains and losses on business property and income-producing property.

A taxpayer is not permitted to deduct a casualty loss for damage to insured personal use property unless a *timely insurance claim* is filed with respect to the damage to the property. This rule applies to the extent that any insurance policy provides for full or partial reimbursement for the loss.[20]

Generally, an appraisal before and after the casualty is needed to measure the amount of the loss. However, the *cost of repairs* to the damaged property is acceptable as a method of establishing the loss in value provided the following criteria are met:

- The repairs are necessary to restore the property to its condition immediately before the casualty.
- The amount spent for such repairs is not excessive.
- The repairs do not extend beyond the damage suffered.
- The value of the property after the repairs does not, as a result of the repairs, exceed the value of the property immediately before the casualty.[21]

ETHICS & EQUITY   Is Policy Cancellation an Escape Hatch?

Noah's house is burglarized for the third time and he knows that if he files a claim, the insurance company will cancel his homeowner's policy or impose a prohibitive premium. Noah does not file a claim, yet he deducts the loss on his tax return. Is his loss allowed?

© iStockphoto.com/LdF

---

[20]§ 165(h)(5)(E).   [21]Reg. § 1.165–7(a)(2)(ii).

Reduction for $100 and 10 Percent-of-AGI Floors

The amount of the loss for personal use property must be further reduced by a $100 *per event* floor and a 10 percent-of-AGI *aggregate* floor.[22] The $100 floor applies separately to each casualty and applies to the entire loss from each casualty (e.g., if a storm damages both a taxpayer's residence and automobile, only $100 is subtracted from the total amount of the loss). The losses are then added together, and the total is reduced by 10 percent of the taxpayer's AGI. The resulting loss is the taxpayer's itemized deduction for casualty and theft losses.

Example 18	Rocky, who had AGI of $30,000, was involved in a motorcycle accident in 2014. His motorcycle, which was used only for personal use and had a fair market value of $12,000 and an adjusted basis of $9,000, was completely destroyed. He received $5,000 from his insurance company. Rocky's casualty loss deduction is $900 [$9,000 basis − $5,000 insurance recovery − $100 floor − $3,000 (.10 × $30,000 AGI)]. The $900 casualty loss is an itemized deduction (*from* AGI).

When a nonbusiness casualty loss is spread between two taxable years because of the *reasonable prospect of recovery* doctrine, the loss in the second year is not reduced by the $100 floor. This result occurs because this floor is imposed per event and has already reduced the amount of the loss in the first year. However, the loss in the second year is still subject to the 10 percent floor based upon the taxpayer's second-year AGI (refer to Example 13). For taxpayers who suffer qualified disaster area losses, the 10 percent-of-AGI floor is determined by using the AGI of the year for which the deduction is claimed.[23]

Multiple Losses

The rules for computing loss deductions where multiple losses have occurred are explained in Examples 19 and 20.

Example 19	During the year, Tim had the following casualty losses:

Asset	Adjusted Basis	Fair Market Value of Asset Before the Casualty	Fair Market Value of Asset After the Casualty	Insurance Recovery
A	$900	$600	$−0−	$400
B	300	800	250	100

Assets A and B were used in Tim's business at the time of the casualty. The following losses are allowed:

Asset A: $500. The complete destruction of a business asset results in a deduction of the adjusted basis of the property (reduced by any insurance recovery), regardless of the asset's fair market value.

Asset B: $200. The partial destruction of a business (or personal use) asset results in a deduction equal to the lesser of the adjusted basis ($300) or the decline in value ($550), reduced by any insurance recovery ($100).

Both the Asset A and Asset B losses are deductions *for* AGI. The $100 floor and the 10%-of-AGI floor do not apply because the assets are business assets.

---

[22]§ 165(c)(3).   [23]§ 165(i).

In 2014, Emily had AGI of $20,000 and the following casualty losses:

Example 20

Asset	Adjusted Basis	Fair Market Value of Asset		Insurance Recovery
		Before the Casualty	After the Casualty	
A	$1,900	$1,400	$ –0–	$200
B	2,500	4,000	1,000	–0–
C	800	400	100	250

Assets A, B, and C were held for personal use, and the losses to these three assets are from three different casualties. The loss for each asset is computed as follows:

Asset A: $1,100. The lesser of the adjusted basis of $1,900 or the $1,400 decline in value, reduced by the insurance recovery of $200, minus the $100 floor.

Asset B: $2,400. The lesser of the adjusted basis of $2,500 or the $3,000 decline in value, minus the $100 floor.

Asset C: $0. The lesser of the adjusted basis of $800 or the $300 decline in value, reduced by the insurance recovery of $250, minus the $100 floor.

Emily's itemized casualty loss deduction for the year is $1,500:

Asset A loss	$ 1,100
Asset B loss	2,400
Asset C loss	–0–
Total loss	$ 3,500
Less: 10% of AGI (10% × $20,000)	(2,000)
Itemized casualty loss deduction	$ 1,500

7-3e Statutory Framework for Deducting Losses of Individuals

Casualty and theft losses incurred by an individual in connection with a trade or business are deductible *for* AGI.[24] These losses are not subject to the $100 per event and the 10 percent-of-AGI limitations. Casualty and theft losses incurred by an employee in connection with a trade or business are deductible *for* AGI if the loss is reimbursed by the employer (with the net loss being deductible). If the loss is not reimbursed, the loss is deductible *from* AGI as a miscellaneous itemized deduction subject to the 2 percent-of-AGI floor. However, because these are business-related losses, they are not subject to the $100 per event and the 10 percent-of-AGI limitations.

Casualty and theft losses incurred by an individual in a transaction entered into for profit are not subject to the $100 per event and the 10 percent-of-AGI limitations. If these losses are attributable to rents or royalties, the deduction is *for* AGI.[25] However, if these losses are not connected with property held for the production of rents and royalties, they are deductions *from* AGI. More specifically, these losses are classified as other miscellaneous itemized deductions. An example of this type of loss would be the theft of a security. However, theft losses of investment property are not subject to the 2 percent-of-AGI floor on certain miscellaneous itemized deductions (explained in Chapters 9 and 10).

Casualty and theft losses attributable to personal use property are subject to the $100 per event and the 10 percent-of-AGI limitations. These losses are itemized deductions, but they are not subject to the 2 percent-of-AGI floor.[26]

---

[24]§ 62(a)(1).
[25]§ 62(a)(4).

[26]§ 67(b)(3).

7-3f Personal Casualty Gains and Losses

If a taxpayer has personal casualty and theft gains as well as losses, a special set of rules applies for determining the tax consequences. A **personal casualty gain** is the recognized gain from a casualty or theft of personal use property. A **personal casualty loss** for this purpose is a casualty or theft loss of personal use property after the application of the $100 floor. A taxpayer who has both gains and losses for the taxable year must first net (offset) the personal casualty gains and personal casualty losses. If the gains exceed the losses, the gains and losses are treated as gains and losses from the sale of capital assets. The capital gains and losses are short-term or long-term, depending on the period the taxpayer held each of the assets. In the netting process, personal casualty and theft gains and losses are not netted with the gains and losses on business and income-producing property.

Example 21

During the year, Cliff had the following personal casualty gains and losses (after deducting the $100 floor):

Asset	Holding Period	Gain or (Loss)
A	Three months	($ 300)
B	Three years	(2,400)
C	Two years	3,200

Cliff computes the tax consequences as follows:

Personal casualty gain	$ 3,200
Personal casualty loss ($300 + $2,400)	(2,700)
Net personal casualty gain	$ 500

Cliff treats all of the gains and losses as capital gains and losses and has the following:

Short-term capital loss (Asset A)	$ 300
Long-term capital loss (Asset B)	2,400
Long-term capital gain (Asset C)	3,200

If personal casualty losses exceed personal casualty gains, all gains and losses are treated as ordinary items. The gains—and the losses to the extent of gains—are treated as ordinary income and ordinary loss in computing AGI. Losses in excess of gains are deducted as itemized deductions to the extent the losses exceed 10 percent of AGI.[27]

Example 22

During the year, Hazel had AGI of $20,000 and the following personal casualty gain and loss (after deducting the $100 floor):

Asset	Holding Period	Gain or (Loss)
A	Three years	($2,700)
B	Four months	200

Hazel computes the tax consequences as follows:

Personal casualty loss	($2,700)
Personal casualty gain	200
Net personal casualty loss	($2,500)

Hazel treats the gain and the loss as ordinary items. The $200 gain and $200 of the loss are included in computing AGI. Hazel's itemized deduction for casualty losses is computed as follows:

Casualty loss in excess of gain ($2,700 − $200)	$ 2,500
Less: 10% of AGI (10% × $20,000)	(2,000)
Itemized deduction	$ 500

---

[27]§ 165(h).

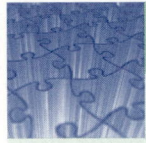

CONCEPT SUMMARY 7.3

Casualty Gains and Losses

	Business Use or Income-Producing Property	Personal Use Property
Event creating the loss	Any event.	Casualty or theft.
Amount	The lesser of the decline in fair market value or the adjusted basis, but always the adjusted basis if the property is totally destroyed.	The lesser of the decline in fair market value or the adjusted basis.
Insurance	Insurance proceeds received reduce the amount of the loss.	Insurance proceeds received (or for which there is an unfiled claim) reduce the amount of the loss.
$100 floor	Not applicable.	Applicable per event.
Gains and losses	Gains and losses are netted (see detailed discussion in Chapter 17).	Personal casualty and theft gains and losses are netted.
Gains exceeding losses		The gains and losses are treated as gains and losses from the sale of capital assets.
Losses exceeding gains		The gains—and the losses to the extent of gains—are treated as ordinary items in computing AGI. The losses in excess of gains, to the extent they exceed 10% of AGI, are itemized deductions.

© iStockphoto.com/Andrey Prokhorov

See Concept Summary 7.3 for a review of the tax treatment of casualty gains and losses.

ETHICS & EQUITY   Improper Redemption of Savings Bonds

In Nancy's divorce settlement two years ago, Nancy's daughter, April, was awarded savings bonds that Nancy had purchased for April's education. Nancy's former husband redeemed the bonds and gambled away the money. He has not paid the money from the redemption to April, and under his current circumstances, he is unlikely to pay her. Nancy is preparing April's tax return and is considering claiming the amount that is owed to April as a nonbusiness bad debt on April's tax return. April has capital gains that will offset the nonbusiness bad debt. Evaluate Nancy's plan.

© iStockphoto.com/LdF

7-4 RESEARCH AND EXPERIMENTAL EXPENDITURES

Section 174 covers the treatment of research and experimental expenditures. The Regulations define **research and experimental expenditures** as follows:

> all such costs incident to the development of an experimental or pilot model, a plant process, a product, a formula, an invention, or similar property, and the improvement of already existing property of the type mentioned. The term does not include expenditures such as those for the ordinary testing or inspection of materials or products for quality control or those for efficiency surveys, management studies, consumer surveys, advertising, or promotions.[28]

LO.5

State and apply the alternative tax treatments for research and experimental expenditures.

---

[28]Reg. § 1.174–2(a)(1).

Expenses in connection with the acquisition or improvement of land or depreciable property are not research and experimental expenditures. Rather, they increase the basis of the land or depreciable property. However, depreciation on a building used for research may be a research and experimental expense. Only the depreciation that is a research and experimental expense (not the cost of the asset) is subject to the three alternatives discussed below.

The law permits the following *three alternatives* for the handling of research and experimental expenditures:

- Expensed in the year paid or incurred.
- Deferred and amortized.
- Capitalized.

If the costs are capitalized, a deduction is not available until the research project is abandoned or is deemed worthless. Because many products resulting from research projects do not have a definite and limited useful life, a taxpayer should ordinarily elect to write off the expenditures immediately or to defer and amortize them. It is generally preferable to elect an immediate write-off of the research expenditures because of the time value of the tax deduction.

The law also provides for a research activities credit. The credit amounts to 20 percent of certain research and experimental expenditures.[29]

7-4a Expense Method

A taxpayer can elect to expense all of the research and experimental expenditures incurred in the current year and all subsequent years. The consent of the IRS is not required if the method is adopted for the first taxable year in which such expenditures were paid or incurred. Once the election is made, the taxpayer must continue to expense all qualifying expenditures unless a request for a change is made to, and approved by, the IRS. In certain instances, a taxpayer may incur research and experimental expenditures before actually engaging in any trade or business activity. In such instances, the Supreme Court has applied a liberal standard of deductibility and permitted a deduction in the year of incurrence.[30]

7-4b Deferral and Amortization Method

Alternatively, research and experimental expenditures may be deferred and amortized if the taxpayer makes an election.[31] Under the election, research and experimental expenditures are amortized ratably over a period of not less than 60 months. A deduction is allowed beginning with the month in which the taxpayer first realizes benefits from the experimental expenditure. The election is binding, and a change requires permission from the IRS.

Example 23

Gold Corporation decides to develop a new line of adhesives. The project begins in 2014. Gold incurs the following expenses in 2014 in connection with the project:

Salaries	$25,000
Materials	8,000
Depreciation on machinery	6,500

Gold incurs the following expenses in 2015 in connection with the project:

Salaries	$18,000
Materials	2,000
Depreciation on machinery	5,700

---

[29]§ 41. The research activities credit expired on December 31, 2013 but is expected to be reinstated on a retroactive basis. See Chapter 13 for additional details.

[30]*Snow v. Comm.,* 74–1 USTC ¶9432, 33 AFTR 2d 74–1251, 94 S.Ct. 1876 (USSC, 1974).

[31]§ 174(b)(2).

The benefits from the project will be realized starting in March 2016. If Gold Corporation elects a 60-month deferral and amortization period, there is no deduction prior to March 2016, the month benefits from the project begin to be realized. The deduction for 2016 is $10,867, computed as follows:

Salaries ($25,000 + $18,000)	$43,000
Materials ($8,000 + $2,000)	10,000
Depreciation ($6,500 + $5,700)	12,200
Total	$65,200
$65,200 × (10 months/60 months)	$10,867

The option to treat research and experimental expenditures as deferred expense is usually employed when a company does not have sufficient income to offset the research and experimental expenses. Rather than create net operating loss carryovers that might not be utilized because of the 20-year limitation on such carryovers, the deferral and amortization method may be used. The deferral of research and experimental expenditures should also be considered if the taxpayer expects higher tax rates in the future.

7-5 DOMESTIC PRODUCTION ACTIVITIES DEDUCTION

The American Jobs Creation Act of 2004 was enacted to replace certain tax provisions that our world trading partners regarded as allowing unfair advantage to U.S. exports. Among other changes, the Act created a deduction based on the income from manufacturing activities (designated as *production activities*).[32] The **domestic production activities deduction (DPAD)** is contained in § 199. Form 8903 is used to report the calculation of the domestic production activities deduction.

LO.6

Calculate the domestic production activities deduction.

7-5a Operational Rules

Calculation of the Domestic Production Activities Deduction

The DPAD is based on the following formula:[33]

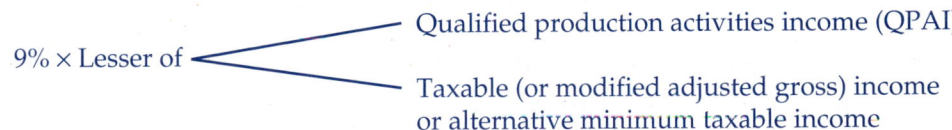

$$9\% \times \text{Lesser of} \begin{cases} \text{Qualified production activities income (QPAI)} \\ \text{Taxable (or modified adjusted gross) income or alternative minimum taxable income} \end{cases}$$

Taxable income is determined without regard to the DPAD. In the case of an individual (a sole proprietorship or an owner of a flow-through entity), **modified adjusted gross income** is substituted for taxable income.[34]

The taxable income limitation is determined after the application of any net operating loss (NOL) deduction for the tax year (NOLs are explained in detail later in the chapter). Thus, a company with an NOL carryforward for a tax year is ineligible for the DPAD if the carryforward eliminates current taxable income. Further, a taxpayer that has an NOL carryback may lose part or all of the DPAD benefit for that year. As taxable income is reduced by the NOL carryback, there is a corresponding reduction in the DPAD. If qualified production activities income (QPAI) cannot be used in a particular year due to the taxable income limitation

---

[32]Section 101 of the *American Jobs Creation Act of 2004*, Public Law No. 108-357 (October 22, 2004).

[33]§ 199(a). For tax years beginning in 2005 or 2006, the 9 percent factor was 3 percent. For tax years beginning in 2007, 2008, and 2009, the 9 percent factor was 6 percent.

[34]§ 199(d)(2). Generally, modified AGI is AGI prior to the effect of § 199.

(see the preceding formula), it is lost forever. (The calculation of QPAI is explained in the next section.)

Example 24

Opal, Inc., manufactures and sells costume jewelry. It also sells costume jewelry purchased from other manufacturers. During 2014, Opal had a *profit* of $200,000 (QPAI) from the sale of its own manufactured jewelry and a *loss* of $50,000 from the sale of the purchased jewelry. Based on this information, Opal's QPAI is $200,000 and its taxable income is $150,000 ($200,000 − $50,000). Opal's DPAD becomes $13,500 [9% of the lesser of $200,000 (QPAI) or $150,000 (taxable income)].

Example 25

Assume the same facts as in Example 24, except that Opal also has an NOL carryover from 2013 of $300,000. As taxable income for 2014 is zero ($200,000 − $50,000 − $300,000), there is no DPAD.

Another important limitation is that the amount of the DPAD cannot exceed 50 percent of certain **W–2 wages** paid by the taxpayer during the tax year.[35] If no W–2 wages are paid, no DPAD will be allowed. So part of the rationale behind this limitation is to preserve U.S. manufacturing jobs and to discourage their outsourcing. An employer's W–2 wages include the sum of the aggregate amount of wages and elective deferrals required to be included on the W–2 wage statements for certain employees during the employer's taxable year. Elective deferrals include those amounts deferred under § 457 plans and Roth contributions (see Chapter 19). An employer previously included wages paid to all workers during a tax year and not just the wages of the employees engaged in qualified production activities. However, as a result of a recent statutory change, an employer is permitted to include only those W–2 wages paid to employees engaged in qualified production activities.

Example 26

In 2014, Red, Inc., a calendar year taxpayer, has QPAI of $2 million and taxable income of $2.1 million. Because Red outsources much of its work to independent contractors, its W–2 wage base, which for Red is related entirely to production activities, is $80,000. Although Red's DPAD normally would be $180,000 [9% of the lesser of $2 million (QPAI) or $2.1 million (taxable income)], it is limited to $40,000 [50% of $80,000 (W–2 wages)].

Example 27

Assume the same facts as in Example 26, except that Red also pays salaries of $50,000 related to its *nonproduction* activities. Because these wages are not paid to employees engaged in production activities, the wage limitation on the DPAD remains at $40,000 [50% of $80,000 ($80,000 + $0)].

Calculation of Qualified Production Activities Income

Qualified production activities income (QPAI) is the excess of **domestic production gross receipts (DPGR)** over the sum of:

- The cost of goods sold allocated to such receipts.
- Other deductions, expenses, or losses directly allocated to such receipts.
- The ratable portion of deductions, expenses, and losses not directly allocable to such receipts or another class of income.[36]

QPAI is determined on an item-by-item basis—not on a division-by-division or a transaction-by-transaction basis. Because all items must be netted in the calculation, the final QPAI amount can be either positive or negative. The effect of the netting rule is to preclude taxpayers from selecting only profitable product lines or profitable transactions when calculating QPAI.

Example 28

A taxpayer manufactures pants and shirts with the following QPAI results: $5 for one pair of pants and a negative $2 for one shirt. Because the two items are netted, the QPAI amount that controls is $3 ($5 − $2).

---

[35]§ 199(b).   [36]§ 199(c).

FINANCIAL DISCLOSURE INSIGHTS Tax Losses and the Deferred Tax Asset

To some people, a current-year net operating loss (NOL) represents a failure of an entity's business model, but others see it as an immediate tax refund. But when an NOL hits the balance sheet as a deferred tax asset, the story is not over. The NOL creates or increases a deferred tax asset that may or may not be used in future financial accounting reporting periods: the key question for a financial analyst is whether the entity will generate enough net revenue in future years that can be offset by the NOL carryover amount.

When a business entity holds a loss carryforward, for every reporting period, its management must assess whether the loss is likely to be used to create cash flow in the future, as the loss carryforward offsets operating or other profits from future years. When it is more likely than not that a loss carryforward *will not be realized*, GAAP requires that a valuation allowance be created to reduce the deferred tax asset to a lower amount that is expected to be realized in the future. The valuation allowance is a contra-asset account (like accumulated depreciation on a fixed asset) against the deferred tax asset.

A valuation allowance against an NOL carryforward might be created when there is doubt as to the level of the entity's future net profits. The valuation allowance is reduced or eliminated, though, when it appears that the NOL will be fully realized due to any of the following:

- Future years' net income from operations or other activities.
- New product orders or contracts for the business.
- The reversal of other temporary book-tax differences.
- An effective use of tax planning strategies.

Evidence that a loss carryforward might not be realized in the future includes the following:

- A series of operating losses in previous years for the reporting entity.
- A history of the entity's tax losses expiring unused.
- Open transactions, such as lawsuits and regulatory challenges, that might reduce the business's future profits.

The current version of IFRS does not allow for a valuation allowance. Under IAS 12, a deferred tax asset is recorded only when it is "probable" (a higher standard than GAAP's "more likely than not") that the deferred tax amount will be realized, and then only to the extent of that probable amount. Thus, no offsetting valuation allowance is needed.

Five specific categories of DPGR qualify for the DPAD:[37]

- The lease, license, sale, exchange, or other disposition of qualified production property (QPP) that was manufactured, produced, grown, or extracted (MPGE) in the United States.
- Qualified films largely created in the United States.
- The production of electricity, natural gas, or potable water.
- Construction (but not self-construction) performed in the United States.
- Engineering and architectural services for domestic construction.

The sale of food and beverages prepared by a taxpayer at a retail establishment and the transmission or distribution of electricity, natural gas, or potable water are specifically excluded from the definition of DPGR.

7-5b Eligible Taxpayers

The deduction is available to a variety of taxpayers, including individuals, partnerships, S corporations, C corporations, cooperatives, estates, and trusts. For a pass-through entity (e.g., partnerships and S corporations), the deduction flows through to the individual owners. In the case of a sole proprietor, a deduction *for* AGI results and is claimed on Form 1040, line 35 on page 1. A Form 8903 must be attached to support the deduction.

For additional information on the DPAD, see Chapter 3 in *South-Western Federal Taxation: Corporations, Partnerships, Estates & Trusts.*

---

[37]§ 199(c)(4).

7-6 NET OPERATING LOSSES

LO.7

Determine the amount of the net operating loss and review the impact of the carryback and carryover provisions on previous and subsequent years' taxable income.

The requirement that every taxpayer file an annual income tax return (whether on a calendar year or a fiscal year) may result in certain inequities for taxpayers who experience cyclical patterns of income or expense. Inequities result from the application of a progressive rate structure to taxable income determined on an annual basis. A **net operating loss (NOL)** in a particular tax year would produce no tax benefit if the Code did not provide for the carryback and carryforward of such losses to profitable years.

Example 29

Juanita has a business and realizes the following taxable income or loss over a five-year period: year 1, $50,000; year 2, ($30,000); year 3, $100,000; year 4, ($200,000); and year 5, $380,000. She is married and files a joint return. Hubert also has a business and has a taxable income pattern of $60,000 every year. He, too, is married and files a joint return. Note that both Juanita and Hubert have total taxable income of $300,000 over the five-year period. Assume that there is no provision for carryback or carryover of NOLs. Juanita and Hubert would have the following five-year tax bills:

Year	Juanita's Tax	Hubert's Tax
1	$ 6,593	$ 8,093
2	–0–	8,093
3	16,713	8,093
4	–0–	8,093
5	101,305	8,093
	$124,611	$40,465

Note: The computation of tax is made without regard to any NOL benefit. Rates applicable to 2014 (ignoring the additional 3.8% Medicare tax) are used to compute the tax.

Even though Juanita and Hubert realized the same total taxable income ($300,000) over the five-year period, Juanita had to pay taxes of $124,611, while Hubert paid taxes of only $40,465.

To provide partial relief from this inequitable tax treatment, a deduction is allowed for NOLs.[38] This provision permits NOLs for any one year to be offset against taxable income of other years. The NOL provision is intended as a form of relief for business income and losses. Thus, only losses from the operation of a trade or business (or profession), casualty and theft losses, or losses from the confiscation of a business by a foreign government can create an NOL. In other words, a salaried individual with itemized deductions and personal exemptions in excess of gross income is not permitted to deduct the excess amounts as an NOL. On the other hand, a personal casualty loss is treated as a business loss and can therefore create (or increase) an NOL for an individual.

7-6a Carryback and Carryover Periods

General Rules

An NOL generally must be applied initially to the two taxable years preceding the year of the loss (unless an election is made not to carry the loss back at all). It is carried first to the second prior year and then to the immediately preceding tax year (or until used up). If the loss is not fully used in the carryback period, it must be carried forward to the first year after the loss year and then forward to the second, third, etc., year after the loss year. The carryover (i.e., carryforward) period is 20 years. A loss sustained in 2014 is used in this order: 2012, 2013, 2015 through 2034.

---
[38]§ 172.

A three-year carryback period is available for any portion of an individual's NOL resulting from a casualty or theft loss. The three-year carryback rule also applies to NOLs that are attributable to presidentially declared disasters that are incurred by a small business. A small business is a business whose average annual gross receipts for a three-year period are $5 million or less.

A 5-year carryback period and a 20-year carryover period are allowed for a farming loss. A taxpayer may elect to waive the special five-year carryback period. If this election is made, the general two-year carryback period applies. A farming loss is the amount of the NOL for the taxable year if only income and deductions attributable to the farming business are taken into account. However, the amount of the farming loss cannot exceed the amount of the taxpayer's NOL for the taxable year. To determine the amount of the carryback and carryover, a farming loss for any taxable year is treated as a separate NOL for such year and applied after the remaining portion of the NOL for the year is taken into account.

Example 30

For 2014, the taxpayer and spouse have an NOL of $50,000. The $50,000 NOL includes a $40,000 loss that is attributable to a farming business. Only the $40,000 loss attributable to the farming business can be carried back five years. The loss not attributable to the farming business can be carried back only two years.

If the loss is being carried to a preceding year, an amended return is filed on Form 1040X or a quick refund claim is filed on Form 1045. In either case, a refund of taxes previously paid is requested. Form 1045 is an application for a tentative refund. The IRS normally will process Form 1045 and pay the refund within 90 days of the date it is filed. When the loss is carried forward, the current return shows an NOL deduction for the prior year's loss.

Sequence of Use of NOLs

When the taxpayer has NOLs in two or more years, the rule is always to use the earliest year's loss first until it is completely absorbed. The later years' losses can then be used until they also are absorbed or lost. Thus, one year's return could show NOL carryovers from two or more years. Each loss is computed and applied separately.

Election to Forgo Carryback

A taxpayer can *irrevocably elect* not to carry back an NOL to any of the prior years. In that case, the loss is available as a carryover for 20 years. The election is made if it is to the taxpayer's tax advantage. For example, a taxpayer might be in a low marginal tax bracket in the carryback years but expect to be in a high marginal tax bracket in future years. Therefore, it would be to the taxpayer's advantage to use the NOL to offset income in years when the tax rate is high rather than use it when the tax rate is relatively low.

Example 31

For 2014, taxpayer and spouse have an NOL of $10,000. The NOL may be carried back and applied against taxable income first in 2012 and then in 2013. Any remaining NOL is carried forward to 2015 through 2034. If, however, the taxpayer and spouse elect to forgo the carryback period, the NOL initially is carried to 2015 and forward through 2034, until it's completely applied.

7-6b Computation of the Net Operating Loss

Because the NOL provisions apply solely to business-related losses, certain adjustments must be made so that the loss more closely resembles the taxpayer's *economic* loss. The required adjustments for corporate taxpayers are usually insignificant because a corporation's tax loss is generally similar to its economic loss. However, in computing taxable income, individual taxpayers are allowed deductions for such items as personal and dependency exemptions and itemized deductions that do not reflect actual business-related economic losses.

To arrive at the NOL for an individual, taxable income must be adjusted by adding back the following items:[39]

1. No deduction is allowed for personal and dependency exemptions. These amounts do not reflect economic, or business, outlays and hence must be added back.
2. The NOL carryover or carryback from another year is not allowed in the computation of the current year's NOL.
3. Capital losses and nonbusiness deductions are limited in determining the current year's NOL. These limits are as follows:
   a. The excess of nonbusiness capital losses over nonbusiness capital gains must be added back.
   b. The excess of nonbusiness deductions over the sum of nonbusiness income and *net* nonbusiness capital gains must be added back. *Net nonbusiness capital gains* are the excess of nonbusiness capital gains over nonbusiness capital losses. *Nonbusiness income* is income that is not attributable to, or derived from, a taxpayer's trade or business. It includes items such as dividends, investment interest, alimony received, and Social Security income. *Nonbusiness deductions* are those deductions that are not attributable to, or derived from, a taxpayer's trade or business. Examples are Individual Retirement Account (IRA) deductions, alimony paid deductions, most itemized deductions except for personal casualty and theft losses and losses incurred in a transaction entered into for profit, and employee business expense deductions.

      A taxpayer who does not itemize deductions computes the excess of nonbusiness deductions over nonbusiness income by substituting the standard deduction for total itemized deductions.
   c. The excess of business capital losses over the sum of business capital gains and the excess of nonbusiness income and net nonbusiness capital gains over nonbusiness deductions must be added back.
   d. The add-back for net nonbusiness capital losses and excess business capital losses does not include net capital losses not included in the current-year computation of taxable income because of the capital loss limitation provisions (discussed in Chapter 16).

---

[39]§ 172(d); Reg. § 1.172–3(a).

CONCEPT SUMMARY 7.4

Computation of Net Operating Loss

Taxable income shown on the return
Add back:

1. Personal and dependency exemptions.
2. Net operating loss carryover or carryback from another year.
3. The excess of nonbusiness capital losses over nonbusiness capital gains.
4. The excess of nonbusiness deductions over the sum of nonbusiness income plus *net* nonbusiness capital gains.

5. The excess of business capital losses over the sum of business capital gains plus the excess of nonbusiness income and *net* nonbusiness capital gains over nonbusiness deductions. The add-back from the total of items 3 and 5 will not exceed $3,000 because of the capital loss limitation rules.

Equals the net operating loss

© iStockphoto.com/Andrey Prokhorov

For a review of the computation of the net operating loss for individuals, see Concept Summary 7.4.

The capital loss and nonbusiness deduction limits are illustrated in Examples 32 through 35.

For 2014, taxpayer and spouse have $6,000 of nonbusiness capital losses and $4,000 of nonbusiness capital gains. They must add back $2,000 ($6,000–$4,000), which is the excess of nonbusiness capital losses over nonbusiness capital gains.	**Example 32**

For 2014, taxpayer and spouse have $2,600 of nonbusiness capital gains, $1,000 of nonbusiness capital losses, $2,000 of interest income, and no itemized deductions. They must add back $8,800 {$12,400 standard deduction – [$2,000 interest income + $1,600 ($2,600 – $1,000) net nonbusiness capital gains]}. Note that in this example, there is no excess of nonbusiness capital losses over nonbusiness capital gains.	**Example 33**

For 2014, taxpayer and spouse have $2,600 of nonbusiness capital gains, $1,000 of nonbusiness capital losses, $15,000 of interest income, $14,500 of itemized deductions (none of which are personal casualty and theft losses), $4,000 of business capital losses, and $1,000 of business capital gains. They must add back $900 {$4,000 business capital losses – [$1,000 business capital gains + ($15,000 nonbusiness income + $1,600 net nonbusiness capital gains – $14,500 nonbusiness deductions)]}. Note that in this example, there is no excess of nonbusiness capital losses over nonbusiness capital gains, nor is there an excess of nonbusiness deductions over the sum of nonbusiness income and net nonbusiness capital gains.	**Example 34**

For 2014, taxpayer and spouse have $2,600 of nonbusiness capital gains, $3,000 of nonbusiness capital losses, $13,000 of interest income, $15,000 of itemized deductions (none of which are personal casualty and theft losses), $8,000 of business capital losses, and $4,000 of business capital gains. They must add back $2,000 ($15,000 – $13,000), which is the excess of nonbusiness deductions over nonbusiness income, and $3,000, which is the excess of combined capital losses because the capital loss limitation caps the loss at $3,000 in computing taxable income for the year.	**Example 35**

Example 36 illustrates the computation of an NOL.

Example 36

James opened a retail store in 2013 and experienced an NOL of $185 for that year. James had no taxable income for 2011 or 2012. James is married, has no dependents, and files a joint return. For 2014, James and his wife have the following taxable income:

Gross income from the business	$ 67,000	
Less: Business expenses	(73,000)	($ 6,000)
Salary from a part-time job		875
Interest on savings account		525
Nonbusiness long-term capital gain		1,000
NOL carryover from 2013		(185)
Net loss on rental property		(100)
Adjusted gross income		($ 3,885)
Less: Itemized deductions		
Interest expense	$ 4,600	
Taxes	7,300	
Casualty loss	2,000	
Total itemized deductions		(13,900)
Exemptions (2 × $3,950)		(7,900)
Taxable income		($25,685)

James's 2014 NOL is computed as follows:

Taxable income				($25,685)
Add:				
Net operating loss from 2013			$ 185	
Personal exemptions (2)			7,900	
Excess of nonbusiness deductions over nonbusiness income				
Total itemized deductions		$13,900		
Less: Casualty loss		(2,000)		
		$11,900		
Less: Interest	$ 525			
Less: Long-term capital gain	1,000	(1,525)	10,375	18,460
Net operating loss				($ 7,225)

The NOL can be thought of as follows:

Business loss	($ 6,000)
Rental loss	(100)
Casualty loss	(2,000)
Salary income	875
Net operating loss	($ 7,225)

7-6c Recomputation of Tax Liability for Year to Which Net Operating Loss Is Carried

When an NOL is carried back to a nonloss year, the taxable income and income tax for the carryback year must be recomputed by including the NOL as a deduction *for* AGI. Several deductions (such as medical expenses and charitable contributions) are based on the amount of AGI. When an NOL is carried back, all such deductions *except* the charitable contributions deduction must be recomputed on the basis of the new AGI after the NOL has been applied. The deduction for charitable contributions is determined without regard to any

NOL carryback but with regard to any other modification affecting AGI. Furthermore, any tax credits limited by or based upon the tax must be recomputed, based on the recomputed tax.

Example 37

Peggy sustains an NOL of $11,000 in 2014. Because Peggy had no taxable income in 2012, the loss is carried back to 2013. For 2013, the joint income tax return of Peggy and her husband was as follows:

Salary income		$ 15,000
Dividends (not qualified dividends)		4,000
Net short-term capital gain		1,600
Adjusted gross income		$ 20,600
Itemized deductions		
Charitable contributions	$3,810	
Medical [$2,130 − ($20,600 × 10%)]	70	
Interest	5,700	
Taxes	2,420	(12,000)
Exemptions (2 × $3,900)		(7,800)
Taxable income		$ 800
Tax (married filing jointly)		$ 80

Peggy's new tax liability for the carryback year is computed as follows:

Adjusted gross income		$ 20,600
Less: Net operating loss		(11,000)
Recomputed adjusted gross income		$ 9,600
Itemized deductions		
Charitable contributions	$3,810	
Medical [$2,130 − ($9,600 × 10%)]	1,170	
Interest	5,700	
Taxes	2,420	(13,100)
Exemptions (2 × $3,900)		(7,800)
Recomputed taxable income		($ 11,300)
Tax		$ –0–
Tax originally paid and refund claim		$ 80

7-6d Calculation of the Remaining Net Operating Loss

After computing the amount of the refund claim for the initial carryback year, it is then necessary to determine the extent to which any NOL remains to carry over to future years. The amount of this carryover loss is the excess of the NOL over the taxable income of the year to which the loss is being applied. However, the taxable income of the year to which the loss is being applied must be determined with the following *modifications*:

- No deduction is allowed for excess capital losses over capital gains.
- No deduction is allowed for the NOL that is being carried back. However, deductions are allowed for NOLs occurring before the loss year.
- Any deductions claimed that are based on or limited by AGI must be determined after making the preceding adjustments. However, charitable contributions do not take into account any NOL carryback.
- No deduction is allowed for personal and dependency exemptions.

Example 38

Referring to the facts in Example 37, the NOL carryover from 2013 available for future years is ($2,400), computed as follows:

Salary income		$ 15,000
Dividends (not qualified dividends)		4,000
Net short-term capital gain		1,600
Adjusted gross income		$ 20,600
Itemized deductions		
Charitable contributions	$3,810	
Medical [$2,130 − ($20,600 × 10%)]	70	
Interest	5,700	
Taxes	2,420	(12,000)
Exemptions (not allowed)		–0–
Modified taxable income		$ 8,600
Net operating loss		($ 11,000)
Modified taxable income		8,600
Net operating loss to carry forward		($ 2,400)

Because the ending figure is negative, it represents the NOL remaining to carry over to 2015 or later years.

7-7 TAX PLANNING

7-7a What Is a "Trade or Business"? The Tax Consequences of the *Groetzinger* Case

LO.8

Identify tax planning opportunities in deducting certain business expenses, business losses, and personal losses.

In the case of Robert P. Groetzinger,[40] the court was asked to decide whether a taxpayer who had quit his job and spent virtually all his time betting on dog races was in a trade or business. The taxpayer spent 60 to 80 hours each week at the track and had no other source of employment. The court established that the appropriate tests for determining whether an activity (in this case, gambling) is a trade or business are whether an individual engages in the activity full-time in good faith, with regularity, and for the production of income as a livelihood, and not as a mere hobby. The court held that Robert Groetzinger satisfied the tests because of his constant and large-scale effort. Skill was required and was applied. He did what he did for a livelihood, although with less than successful results (during the year in question, his net losses amounted to about $2,200). His gambling was not a hobby, a passing fancy, or an occasional bet for amusement. Therefore, his gambling was a trade or business, and hence, he was able to deduct his gambling losses *for* AGI. If the court had ruled that Groetzinger's gambling was not a trade or business, his gambling losses would have been limited to his gambling winnings and would have been classified as itemized deductions.

7-7b Documentation of Related-Taxpayer Loans, Casualty Losses, and Theft Losses

Because non-bona fide loans between related taxpayers may be treated as gifts, adequate documentation is needed to substantiate a bad debt deduction if the loan subsequently becomes worthless. Documentation should include proper execution of the note (legal form) and the establishment of a bona fide purpose for the loan. In addition, it is desirable to stipulate a reasonable rate of interest and a fixed maturity date.

---

[40]*Groetzinger v. Comm.*, cited in Footnote 1.

© iStockphoto.com/Andrey Prokhorov

TAX IN THE NEWS   When Is a Security Worthless?

Usually, losses that have not been documented by the marketplace cannot be deducted (i.e., unrealized losses). An exception exists for securities that are completely worthless. But proving complete worthlessness can sometimes be difficult. Just because a company declares bankruptcy does not necessarily prove that its stock is completely worthless because in some cases the stock can recover. Determining whether this can happen requires an analysis of the relevant facts and circumstances. Even though a stock may be selling for a fraction of a penny (i.e., it has some value), some tax advisers argue that if the stock's selling price would be less than the broker's commission for selling the stock, a deduction can be taken at that time.

Because a theft loss is not permitted for misplaced items, a loss should be documented by a police report and evidence of the value of the property (e.g., appraisals, pictures of the property, and newspaper clippings). Similar documentation of the value of property should be provided to support a casualty loss deduction because the amount of loss is measured, in part, by the decline in fair market value of the property.

Casualty loss deductions must be reported on Form 4684.

7-7c Worthless Securities

To be deductible, a security must be completely worthless. To obtain the deduction, the taxpayer must prove that the security was not worthless in a prior year and that the security was worthless in the year claimed. Because of the subjectivity associated with this burden of proof, the only safe practice is to claim a loss for the earliest year when it may be allowed and to renew the claim in subsequent years if there is any reasonable chance that it will be applicable to the income for those years.[41] Fortunately, the statute of limitations for worthless securities is seven years.[42]

7-7d Small Business Stock (§ 1244)

Because § 1244 limits the amount of loss classified as ordinary loss on a yearly basis, a taxpayer might maximize the benefits of § 1244 by selling the stock in more than one taxable year. The result could be that the losses in any one taxable year would not exceed the § 1244 limits on ordinary loss.

> **Example 39**
>
> Mitch, a single individual, purchased small business stock in 2012 for $150,000 (150 shares at $1,000 per share). On December 20, 2014, the stock is worth $60,000 (150 shares at $400 per share). Mitch wants to sell the stock at this time. Mitch earns a salary of $80,000 a year, has no other capital transactions, and does not expect any in the future. If Mitch sells all of the small business stock in 2014, his recognized loss will be $90,000 ($60,000 − $150,000). The loss will be characterized as a $50,000 ordinary loss and a $40,000 long-term capital loss. In computing taxable income for 2014, Mitch could deduct the $50,000 ordinary loss but could deduct only $3,000 of the capital loss. The remainder of the capital loss could be carried over and used in future years subject to the $3,000 limitation if Mitch has no capital gains. If Mitch sells 82 shares in 2014, he will recognize an ordinary loss of $49,200 [82 × ($1,000 − $400)]. If Mitch then sells the remainder of the shares in 2015, he will recognize an ordinary loss of $40,800 [68 × ($1,000 − $400)]. Mitch could deduct the $49,200 ordinary loss in computing 2014 taxable income and the $40,800 ordinary loss in computing 2015 taxable income.

---

[41]*Young v. Comm.*, 41–2 USTC ¶9744, 28 AFTR 365, 123 F.2d 597 (CA–2, 1941).

[42]§ 6511(d)(1).

FINANCIAL DISCLOSURE INSIGHTS Valuation Allowances for NOLs

Financial analysts use the valuation allowance system to help them determine the entity's expected future cash flows. Some critics of the GAAP rules for valuation allowances maintain that they enable management to manipulate profits and earnings per share in an arbitrary fashion.

Only a few of the largest business entities, supported by going-concern assumptions and access to worldwide debt and equity capital, need to record sizable valuation allowances. But smaller entities and those in volatile industries are more likely to present questions as to their future profitability, and the valuation allowances may be found in those financial reports somewhat more often.

In a recent reporting year, for instance, the following telecommunications businesses reported valuation allowances related to expectations that their NOLs (for Federal and/or state taxing jurisdictions) would expire unused.

	Deferred Tax Assets ($000)	Valuation Allowance ($000)
Verizon	$10,750	$2,700
Bell South	2,100	1,100
AT&T	11,400	1,050
SBC Communications	3,900	150

Establishing a valuation allowance does not affect the entity's internal cash balances, but it might have an effect on the stock price. Valuation allowances can be "released" by management when evidence develops that the carryforwards are likely to be used in the future, for example, if profitability has improved and appears to be sustainable. For instance, the homebuilder Toll Brothers created a large valuation allowance when the real estate market collapsed, but it will release the allowance when housing prices stabilize and increase.

Several corporations estimated that the Patient Protection and Affordable Care Act of 2010 would force them to create sizable valuation allowances, because the mandated expenditures would reduce future profitability.

Reduction in Deferred Tax Assets Due to the Patient Protection and Affordable Care Act of 2010 ($ million): Estimate	
AT&T	$1,000
John Deere	150
Caterpillar	100
3M	90
Norfolk Southern	27

© iStockphoto.com/Pali Rao

7-7e Casualty Losses

A special election is available for taxpayers who sustain casualty losses in an area designated by the President as a disaster area. This election affects only the *timing*, not the calculation, of the deduction. The deduction can be taken in the year before the year in which the loss occurred. Thus, for a loss occurring between January 1 and December 31, 2014, an individual can take the deduction on the 2013 return. The benefit, of course, is a faster refund (or reduction in tax). It will also be advantageous to carry the loss back if the taxpayer's tax rate in the carry-back year is higher than the tax rate in the year of the loss.

To find out if an event qualifies as a disaster area loss, one can look in any of the major tax services, the Weekly Compilation of Presidential Documents, or the *Internal Revenue Bulletin*.

7-7f Net Operating Losses

In certain instances, it may be advisable for a taxpayer to elect not to carry back an NOL. For an individual, the benefits from the loss carryback could be scaled down or lost due to the economic adjustments that must be made to taxable income for the year to which the loss is carried. For example, a taxpayer should attempt to minimize the number of taxable years to which an NOL is carried. The more years to which the NOL is applied, the more benefits are lost from adjustments for items such as personal and dependency exemptions.

The election not to carry back the loss might also be advantageous if there is a disparity in marginal tax rates applicable to different tax years.

Abby sustained an NOL of $10,000 in year 3. Her marginal tax bracket in year 1 was 15%. In year 4, however, she expects her bracket to be 35% due to a large profit she will make on a business deal. If Abby carries her loss back, her refund will be $1,500 (15% × $10,000). If she elects not to carry it back to year 1 but chooses, instead, to carry it forward, her savings will be $3,500 (35% × $10,000). Even considering the time value of an immediate tax refund, Abby appears to be better off using the carryover approach.

Example 40

REFOCUS ON THE BIG PICTURE

LOSSES

Martha can receive tax benefits associated with her unfortunate occurrences during the current tax year. Some of the losses, however, will provide a greater tax benefit than others as a result of different tax provisions governing the amount and the classification of the losses.

Bad Debt

Based on the facts provided, it appears that Martha's loan to her friend was a bona fide debt. Otherwise, nothing would be deductible. The amount of the deduction is the unpaid principal balance of $19,000 ($25,000 − $6,000). Unfortunately, because the bad debt is a nonbusiness bad debt, it is classified as a short-term capital loss (see Example 5).

Loss from Investment

The $50,000 loss is deductible. However, it appears that the loss should be classified as a long-term capital loss rather than as a short-term capital loss. Although the actual holding period was not greater than one year (October through May), the disposal date for the stock (qualifies as a worthless security) is deemed to be the last day of the tax year (October of last year through end of December of the current year). The loss does not appear to qualify for ordinary loss treatment under § 1244 (see Example 8).

Loss from Bookstore

The $180,000 loss from the bookstore is reported on Schedule C of Form 1040. It is an ordinary loss, and it qualifies for NOL treatment. Therefore, Martha can carry the $180,000 net loss back and offset it against the net income of the bookstore for the past two years. Any amount not offset (probably about $30,000) can be carried forward for the next 20 years. The carryback will produce a claim for a tax refund.

Casualty Loss

The loss on the damage to Martha's personal residence is classified as a personal casualty loss. Using the cost of repairs method, the amount of the casualty loss is $7,000 ($32,000 − $25,000). However, this amount must be reduced by the statutory materiality amounts of $100 and 10 percent of AGI.

If the President classified the area in which Martha's house is located as a disaster area, Martha has the option of deducting the casualty loss on the prior year's tax return (see Example 15).

© Tetra Images/Jupiter Images

Key Terms

Bad debt, 7-2

Business bad debt, 7-5

Casualty loss, 7-8

Disaster area losses, 7-10

Domestic production activities deduction (DPAD), 7-17

Domestic production gross receipts (DPGR), 7-18

Modified adjusted gross income, 7-17

Net operating loss (NOL), 7-20

Nonbusiness bad debt, 7-4

Personal casualty gain, 7-14

Personal casualty loss, 7-14

Qualified production activities income (QPAI), 7-18

Research and experimental expenditures, 7-15

Reserve method, 7-3

Small business stock (§ 1244 stock), 7-7

Specific charge-off method, 7-3

Theft losses, 7-9

W–2 wages, 7-18

Worthless securities, 7-7

Discussion Questions

1. **LO.1** Explain how an account receivable can give rise to a bad debt deduction.

2. **LO.1** Ron, a cash basis taxpayer, sells his business accounts receivable of $100,000 to Mike for $70,000 (70% of the actual accounts receivable). Discuss the amount and classification of Ron's bad debt deduction.

3. **LO.1** Discuss when a bad debt deduction can be taken for a nonbusiness debt.

4. **LO.1** During the past tax year, Jane identified $50,000 as a nonbusiness bad debt. In that tax year, Jane had $100,000 of taxable income, of which $5,000 consisted of short-term capital gains. During the current tax year, Jane collected $10,000 of the amount she had previously identified as a bad debt. Discuss Jane's tax treatment of the $10,000 received in the current tax year.

5. **LO.1** Bob owns a collection agency. He purchases uncollected accounts receivable from other businesses at 60% of their face value and then attempts to collect these accounts. During the current year, Bob collected $60,000 on an account with a face value of $80,000. Discuss the amount of Bob's bad debt deduction.

6. **LO.1** Discuss the treatment of a business bad debt when the business also has long-term capital gains.

Issue ID 7. **LO.1** Many years ago, Jack purchased 400 shares of Canary stock. During the current year, the stock became worthless. It was determined that the company "went under" because several corporate officers embezzled a large amount of company funds. Identify the relevant tax issues for Jack.

8. **LO.2** Sean is in the business of buying and selling stocks and bonds. He has a bond of Green Corporation for which he paid $200,000. The bond is currently worth only $50,000. Discuss whether Sean can take a $150,000 loss for a business bad debt or for a worthless security.

9. **LO.2** Discuss the tax treatment of the sale of § 1244 stock at a gain.

10. **LO.3, 4** Jim discovers that his residence has extensive termite damage. Discuss whether he may take a deduction for the damage to his residence.

11. **LO.3, 4** The value of Mary's personal residence has declined significantly because of a recent forest fire in the area where she lives. Mary's house suffered no actual damage during the fire, but because much of the surrounding area was destroyed, the value of all of the homes in the area declined substantially. Discuss whether Mary can take a casualty loss for the decline in value of her residence caused by the fire.

12. **LO.4** Discuss at what point in time a theft loss generally is recognized.

13. **LO.4** Mary's diamond ring was stolen in 2013. She originally paid $8,000 for the ring, but it was worth considerably more at the time of the theft. Mary filed an insurance claim for the stolen ring, but the claim was denied. Because the insurance claim was denied, Mary took a casualty loss for the stolen ring on her 2013 tax return. In 2013, Mary had AGI of $40,000. In 2014, the insurance company had a "change of heart" and

sent Mary a check for $5,000 for the stolen ring. Discuss the proper tax treatment of the $5,000 Mary received from the insurance company in 2014.

14. **LO.4** Discuss the measurement rule for the theft of property used in a transaction entered into for profit.

15. **LO.4** Discuss the tax consequences of not making an insurance claim when insured business use property is subject to a loss.

16. **LO.4** Discuss the circumstances under which the cost of repairs to the damaged property can be used to measure the amount of a casualty loss.

17. **LO.4** Discuss the treatment of a loss on rental property under the following facts:

Basis	$650,000
FMV before the loss	800,000
FMV after the loss	200,000

18. **LO.4** Hazel sustained a loss on the theft of a painting. She had paid $20,000 for the painting, but it was worth $40,000 at the time of the theft. Evaluate the tax consequences of treating the painting as investment property or as personal use property.

19. **LO.4** Discuss the tax treatment when personal casualty gains exceed personal casualty losses.

20. **LO.4** Kelly decided to invest in Lime, Inc. common stock after reviewing Lime's public disclosures, including recent financial statements and a number of press releases issued by Lime. On August 7, 2012, Kelly purchased 60,000 shares of Lime for $210,000. In May 2013, Lime entered into a joint venture with Cherry, Inc. In November 2013, the joint venture failed, and Lime's stock began to decline in value. In December 2013, Cherry filed a lawsuit against Lime for theft of corporate opportunity and breach of fiduciary responsibility. In February 2014, Lime filed a countersuit against Cherry for fraud and misappropriation of funds. At the end of December 2014, Kelly's stock in Lime was worth $15,000. Identify the relevant tax issues for Kelly. *Issue ID*

21. **LO.3, 4** In 2011, John opened an investment account with Randy Hansen, who held himself out to the public as an investment adviser and securities broker. John contributed $200,000 to the account in 2011. John provided Randy with a power of attorney to use the $200,000 to purchase and sell securities on John's behalf. John instructed Randy to reinvest any gains and income earned. In 2011, 2012, and 2013, John received statements of the amount of income earned by his account and included these amounts in his gross income for these years. In 2014, it was discovered that Randy's purported investment advisory and brokerage activity was in fact a fraudulent investment arrangement known as a Ponzi scheme. In reality, John's account balance was zero, the money having been used by Randy in his scheme. Identify the relevant tax issues for John. *Issue ID*

22. **LO.5** Discuss the tax treatment of capitalized research and experimental expenditures.

23. **LO.5** Discuss under what circumstances a company would elect to amortize research and experimental expenditures rather than use the expense method.

24. **LO.6** Amos began a business, Silver, Inc., on July 1, 2011. The business extracts and processes silver ore. During 2014, Amos becomes aware of the domestic production activities deduction (DPAD) and would like to take advantage of this deduction. Identify the relevant tax issues for Silver, Inc. *Issue ID*

25. **LO.6** The DPAD is unlike other deductions and is designed to provide a tax benefit in a somewhat unique manner. Explain this statement.

26. **LO.6** Discuss the impact of an NOL on the DPAD.

27. **LO.7** Discuss whether unreimbursed employee business expenses can create an NOL for an individual taxpayer.

28. **LO.7** Discuss whether deductions *for* AGI can be treated as nonbusiness deductions in computing an individual's NOL.

29. **LO.7** Discuss whether the theft of a painting held for investment can create an NOL.

30. **LO.7** Discuss the effect of an NOL carryback on medical deductions.

Issue ID   31. **LO.7** Thomas believes that he has an NOL for the current year and wants to carry it back to a previous year and receive a tax refund. In determining his NOL, Thomas offset his business income by alimony payments he made to his ex-wife, contributions he made to his traditional Individual Retirement Account (IRA), and moving expenses he incurred. His reason for using these items in the NOL computation is that each item is a deduction *for* AGI. Identify the relevant tax issues for Thomas.

Problems

Communications   32. **LO.1** Several years ago, John Johnson, who is in the lending business, loaned Sara $30,000 to purchase an automobile to be used for personal purposes. In August of the current year, Sara filed for bankruptcy, and John was notified that he could not expect to receive more than $4,000. As of the end of the current year, John has received $1,000. John has contacted you about the possibility of taking a bad debt deduction for the current year.

Write a letter to John that contains your advice as to whether he can claim a bad debt deduction for the current year. Also prepare a memo for the tax files. John's address is 100 Tyler Lane, Erie, PA 16563.

33. **LO.1** Monty loaned his friend Ned $20,000 three years ago. Ned signed a note and made payments on the loan. Last year, when the remaining balance was $11,000, Ned filed for bankruptcy and notified Monty that he would be unable to pay the balance on the loan. Monty treated the $11,000 as a nonbusiness bad debt. Last year, Monty had capital gains of $4,000 and taxable income of $20,000. During the current year, Ned paid Monty $10,000 in satisfaction of the debt. Determine Monty's tax treatment for the $10,000 received in the current year.

34. **LO.1** Sally is in the business of purchasing accounts receivable. Last year, Sally purchased an account receivable with a face value of $80,000 for $60,000. During the current year, Sally settled the account, receiving $65,000. Determine the maximum amount of the bad debt deduction for Sally for the current year.

35. **LO.1, 2** Mable and Jack file a joint return. For the current year, they had the following items:

Salaries	$120,000
Loss on sale of § 1244 stock acquired two years ago	105,000
Gain on sale of § 1244 stock acquired six months ago	20,000
Nonbusiness bad debt	19,000

Determine their AGI for the current year.

Decision Making   36. **LO.2, 8** Mary, a single taxpayer, purchased 10,000 shares of § 1244 stock several years ago at a cost of $20 per share. In November of the current year, Mary received an offer to sell the stock for $12 per share. She has the option of either selling all of the stock now or selling half of the stock now and half of the stock in January of next year. Mary will receive a salary of $80,000 for the current year and $90,000 next year. Mary will have long-term capital gains of $8,000 for the current year and $10,000 next year. If Mary's goal is to minimize her AGI for the two years, determine whether she should sell all of her stock this year or half of her stock this year and half next year.

37. **LO.4** During 2014, someone broke into Jacob's personal residence and took the following items:

Asset	Adjusted Basis	FMV before	FMV after	Insurance Recovery
Business computer	$12,000	$10,000	–0–	$ 7,000
Bearer bonds	30,000	25,000	–0–	–0–
Silverware	7,000	20,000	–0–	18,000
Cash	8,000	8,000	–0–	–0–

Jacob is an employee and used the computer 100% of the time in his employment. Although his homeowner's insurance policy paid Jacob $7,000 for the stolen computer,

Jacob's employer did not reimburse Jacob for any of the remainder of his loss. Jacob's AGI for the year, before considering any of the above items, is $50,000. Determine the total deduction for the stolen items on Jacob's 2014 tax return.

38. **LO.3, 4, 8** Olaf lives in the state of Minnesota. A tornado hit the area and damaged his home and automobile. Applicable information is as follows:

Decision Making

Item	Adjusted Basis	FMV before	FMV after	Insurance Proceeds
Home	$350,000	$500,000	$100,000	$280,000
Auto	60,000	40,000	10,000	20,000

Because of the extensive damage caused by the tornado, the President designated the area a disaster area.

Olaf and his wife, Anna, always file a joint return. Their return for last year shows AGI of $180,000 and taxable income of $140,000. For the current year, their return shows AGI of $300,000 and taxable income (exclusive of the casualty loss deduction) of $215,000.

Determine the amount of Olaf and Anna's loss and the year in which they should take the loss.

39. **LO.3, 4** Heather owns a two-story building. The building is used 40% for business use and 60% for personal use. During 2014, a fire caused major damage to the building and its contents. Heather purchased the building for $800,000 and has taken depreciation of $100,000 on the business portion. At the time of the fire, the building had a fair market value of $900,000. Immediately after the fire, the fair market value was $200,000. The insurance recovery on the building was $600,000. The contents of the building were insured for any loss at fair market value. The business assets had an adjusted basis of $220,000 and a fair market value of $175,000. These assets were totally destroyed. The personal use assets had an adjusted basis of $50,000 and a fair market value of $65,000. These assets were also totally destroyed. If Heather's AGI is $100,000 before considering the effects of the fire, determine her itemized deduction as a result of the fire. Also determine Heather's AGI.

40. **LO.3, 4** On July 24 of the current year, Sam Smith was involved in an accident with his business use automobile. Sam had purchased the car for $30,000. The automobile had a fair market value of $20,000 before the accident and $8,000 immediately after the accident. Sam has taken $20,000 of depreciation on the car. The car is insured for the fair market value of any loss. Because of Sam's history, he is afraid that if he submits a claim, his policy will be canceled. Therefore, he is considering not filing a claim. Sam believes that the tax loss deduction will help mitigate the loss of the insurance reimbursement. Sam's current marginal tax rate is 35%.

Decision Making

Communications

Write a letter to Sam that contains your advice with respect to the tax and cash-flow consequences of filing versus not filing a claim for the insurance reimbursement for the damage to his car. Also prepare a memo for the tax files. Sam's address is 450 Colonel's Way, Warrensburg, MO 64093.

41. **LO.5** Blue Corporation, a manufacturing company, decided to develop a new line of merchandise. The project began in 2014. Blue had the following expenses in connection with the project:

	2014	2015
Salaries	$500,000	$600,000
Materials	90,000	70,000
Insurance	8,000	11,000
Utilities	6,000	8,000
Cost of inspection of materials for quality control	7,000	6,000
Promotion expenses	11,000	18,000
Advertising	–0–	20,000
Equipment depreciation	15,000	14,000
Cost of market survey	8,000	–0–

The new product will be introduced for sale beginning in July 2016. Determine the amount of the deduction for research and experimental expenditures for 2014, 2015, and 2016 if:

a. Blue Corporation elects to expense the research and experimental expenditures.

b. Blue Corporation elects to amortize the research and experimental expenditures over 60 months.

42. **LO.6** Sarah Ham, operating as a sole proprietor, manufactures printers in the United States. For 2014, the proprietorship has QPAI of $400,000. Sarah's modified AGI was $350,000. The W–2 wages paid by the proprietorship to employees engaged in the qualified domestic production activity were $60,000. Calculate Sarah's DPAD for 2014.

43. **LO.6** Barbara, a calendar year taxpayer, owns and operates a company that manufactures toys. For 2014, she has modified AGI of $500,000 and QPAI of $550,000. Ignoring the W–2 wage limitation, calculate Barbara's DPAD.

44. **LO.6** Red Corporation manufactures hand tools in the United States. For the current year, the QPAI derived from the manufacture of hand tools was $1 million. Red's taxable income for the current year was $2.0 million. Last year, Red had an NOL of $800,000, which Red elected to carry forward. Calculate Red's DPAD for the current year.

45. **LO.6** Green Corporation manufactures skirts and blouses in the United States. The DPGR derived from the manufacture of one skirt is $12, and the DPGR from one blouse is $10. The cost of goods sold is $5 for one skirt and $6 for one blouse. Other allocated costs are $1 for one skirt and $5 for one blouse. What amount of QPAI is available to Green for calculating the DPAD?

Decision Making

46. **LO.6** In 2014, Rose, Inc., has QPAI of $4 million and taxable income of $3 million. Rose pays independent contractors $500,000. Rose's W–2 wages are $600,000, but only $400,000 of the wages are paid to employees engaged in qualified domestic production activities.

a. Calculate the DPAD for Rose, Inc., for 2014.

b. What suggestions could you make to enable Rose to increase its DPAD?

47. **LO.7** Sam, age 45, is single. For 2014, he has the following items:

Business income	$70,000
Business expenses	75,000
Alimony paid	12,000
Interest income	3,000
Itemized deductions	8,000

a. Determine Sam's taxable income for 2014.

b. Determine Sam's NOL for 2014.

48. **LO.7** Mary, a single taxpayer with two dependent children, has the following items of income and expense during 2014:

Gross receipts from business	$144,000
Business expenses	180,000
Alimony received	22,000
Interest income	3,000
Itemized deductions (no casualty or theft)	24,000

a. Determine Mary's taxable income for 2014.

b. Determine Mary's NOL for 2014.

49. **LO.7** Gus, who is married and files a joint return, owns a grocery store. In 2014, his gross sales were $276,000, and operating expenses were $320,000. Other items on his 2014 return were as follows:

Nonbusiness capital gains (short term)	$20,000
Nonbusiness capital losses (long term)	9,000
Itemized deductions (no casualty or theft)	18,000
Ordinary nonbusiness income	8,000
Salary from part-time job	10,000

During 2012, Gus had no taxable income. In 2013, Gus had taxable income of $21,300 computed as follows:

Net business income		$ 60,000
Interest income		2,000
Adjusted gross income		$ 62,000
Less: Itemized deductions		
Charitable contributions of $40,000, limited to 50% of AGI	$31,000	
Medical expenses of $8,100, limited to the amount in excess of 10% of AGI ($8,100 − $6,200)	1,900	
Total itemized deductions		(32,900)
Exemptions (2 × $3,900)		(7,800)
Taxable income		$ 21,300

a. What is Gus's 2014 NOL?
b. Determine Gus's recomputed taxable income for 2013.
c. Determine the amount of Gus's 2014 NOL to be carried forward to 2015.

50. **LO.7** During 2014, Rick and his wife, Sara, had the following items of income and expense to report:

Gross receipts from farming business	$400,000
Farming expenses	525,000
Interest income from bank savings accounts	8,000
Sara's salary	50,000
Long-term capital gain on stock held as an investment	4,000
Itemized deductions (no casualty or theft)	15,000

a. Assuming that Rick and Sara file a joint return, what is their taxable income for 2014?
b. What is the amount of Rick and Sara's farming loss for 2014?
c. What is the amount of Rick and Sara's NOL for 2014?
d. To what years can Rick and Sara's NOL be carried?

51. **LO.7** Assume that in addition to the information in Problem 50, Rick and Sara had no taxable income for 2009, 2010, 2011, and 2012 and $3,900 of taxable income for 2013 computed as follows:

Salary		$ 25,000
Capital loss		(1,000)
Adjusted gross income		$ 24,000
Less: Itemized deductions		
Charitable contributions of $20,000, limited to 50% of AGI	$12,000	
Medical expenses of $2,700, limited to the amount in excess of 10% of AGI ($2,700 − $2,400)	300	
Total itemized deductions		(12,300)
Exemptions (2 × $3,900)		(7,800)
Taxable income		$ 3,900

a. Determine Rick and Sara's recomputed taxable income for 2013.
b. Determine the amount of Rick and Sara's 2014 NOL to be carried forward to 2015.

52. **LO.7** During 2014, Ron and his wife, Sue, had the following items of income and expense to report:

Farming income	$300,000
Farming expenses	350,000
Interest income	30,000
Taxes	15,000
Casualty loss (after $100 reduction and 10%-of-AGI reduction)	20,000

a. Determine Ron and Sue's taxable income for 2014.
b. Determine Ron and Sue's NOL for 2014.
c. Determine Ron and Sue's farming loss for 2014.
d. To what years can Ron and Sue's NOL be carried?

Communications

53. **LO.7** Robert and Susan Reid had an NOL of $30,000 in 2014. They had no taxable income for 2012 and $14,450 of taxable income for 2013 computed as follows:

Salary		$ 50,000
Capital loss		(4,000)
Adjusted gross income		$ 46,000
Less: Itemized deductions		
Charitable contributions of $24,000, limited to 50% of AGI	$23,000	
Medical expenses of $5,350, limited to the amount in excess of 10% of AGI ($5,350 − $4,600)	750	
Total itemized deductions		(23,750)
Exemptions (2 × $3,900)		(7,800)
Taxable income		$ 14,450

Write a letter to Robert and Susan informing them of the amount of the remaining NOL to be carried forward if the loss is applied against the 2013 taxable income. Also prepare a memo for the tax files. Their address is 201 Jerdone Avenue, Conway, SC 29526.

54. **LO.7** Pete and Polly are married and file a joint return. They had the following income and deductions for 2014:

Salary	$50,000
Interest from savings account	5,000
Itemized deductions (no casualty or theft)	15,000
2013 NOL carried to 2014	60,000

a. What is Pete and Polly's taxable income for 2014?
b. What is Pete and Polly's NOL for 2014?
c. What is Pete and Polly's NOL to be carried to 2015?

55. **LO.1, 2, 7** Soong, single and age 32, had the following items for the tax year 2014:

- Salary of $30,000.
- Interest income from U.S. government bonds of $2,000.
- Dividends from a foreign corporation of $500.
- Sale of small business § 1244 stock on October 20, 2014, for $20,000. The stock had been acquired two years earlier for $65,000.
- Business bad debt of $4,000.
- Nonbusiness bad debt of $5,000.
- Sale of small business § 1244 stock on November 12, 2014, for $4,000. The stock had been acquired on June 5, 2014, for $800.
- Sale of preferred stock on December 4, 2014, for $40,000. The stock was acquired four years ago for $18,000.
- Total itemized deductions of $25,000 (no casualty or theft).

a. Determine Soong's NOL for 2014.
b. Assuming that Soong had taxable income for each of the last five years, determine the carryback year to which the 2014 NOL should be applied.

56. **LO.1, 3** Nell, single and age 38, had the following income and expense items in 2014:

Nonbusiness bad debt	$ 6,000
Business bad debt	2,000
Nonbusiness long-term capital gain	4,000
Nonbusiness short-term capital loss	3,000
Salary	50,000
Interest income	3,000

Determine Nell's AGI for 2014.

57. **LO.1, 4** Assume that in addition to the information in Problem 56, Nell had the following items in 2014:

Personal casualty gain on an asset held for four months	$10,000
Personal casualty loss on an asset held for two years	1,000

Determine Nell's AGI for 2014.

58. **LO.1, 4, 7** Assume that in addition to the information in Problems 56 and 57, Nell had the following items in 2014:

Personal casualty loss on an asset held for five years	$60,000
Interest expense on home mortgage	15,000

Determine Nell's taxable income and NOL for 2014.

59. **LO.1, 2, 3, 4, 7** Jed, age 55, is married with no children. During 2014, Jed had the following income and expense items:
   a. Three years ago, Jed loaned a friend $10,000 to help him purchase a new car. In June of the current year, Jed learned that his friend had been declared bankrupt and had left the country. There is no possibility that Jed will ever collect any of the $10,000.
   b. In April of last year, Jed purchased some stock for $5,000. In March of the current year, the company was declared bankrupt, and Jed was notified that his shares of stock were worthless.
   c. Several years ago, Jed purchased some § 1244 stock for $120,000. This year, he sold the stock for $30,000.
   d. In July of this year, Jed sold some land that he had held for two years for $60,000. He had originally paid $42,000 for the land.
   e. Jed received $40,000 of interest income from State of Minnesota bonds.
   f. In September, Jed's home was damaged by an earthquake. Jed's basis in his home was $430,000. The value of the home immediately before the quake was $610,000. After the quake, the home was worth $540,000. Because earthquake damage was an exclusion on Jed's homeowner's insurance policy, he received no insurance recovery.
   g. Jed received a salary of $80,000.
   h. Jed paid home mortgage interest of $14,000.

If Jed files a joint return for 2014, determine his NOL for the year.

Cumulative Problems

60. Jane Smith, age 40, is single and has no dependents. She is employed as a legal secretary by Legal Services, Inc. She owns and operates Typing Services located near the campus of Florida Atlantic University at 1986 Campus Drive. Jane is a material participant in the business. She is a cash basis taxpayer. Jane lives at 2020 Oakcrest Road, Boca Raton, FL 33431. Jane's Social Security number is 123-45-6789. Jane indicates that she wants to designate $3 to the Presidential Election Campaign Fund. During 2013, Jane had the following income and expense items:
   a. $100,000 salary from Legal Services, Inc.
   b. $20,000 gross receipts from her typing services business.
   c. $700 interest income from Acme National Bank.
   d. $1,000 Christmas bonus from Legal Services, Inc.
   e. $60,000 life insurance proceeds on the death of her sister.
   f. $5,000 check given to her by her wealthy aunt.
   g. $100 won in a bingo game.
   h. Expenses connected with the typing service:

Office rent	$7,000
Supplies	4,400
Utilities and telephone	4,680
Wages to part-time typists	5,000
Payroll taxes	500
Equipment rentals	3,000

Tax Return Problem

Decision Making

Communications

TAX SOFTWARE

    i. $9,500 interest expense on a home mortgage (paid to San Jose Savings and Loan).

    j. $15,000 fair market value of silverware stolen from her home by a burglar on October 12, 2013. Jane had paid $14,000 for the silverware on July 1, 2004. She was reimbursed $1,500 by her insurance company.

    k. Jane had loaned $2,100 to a friend, Joan Jensen, on June 3, 2010. Joan declared bankruptcy on August 14, 2013, and was unable to repay the loan. Assume that the loan is a bona fide debt.

    l. Legal Services, Inc., withheld Federal income tax of $16,000 and the appropriate amount of FICA tax from her wages.

    m. Alimony of $10,000 received from her former husband, Ted Smith.

    n. Interest income of $800 on City of Boca Raton bonds.

    o. Jane made estimated Federal tax payments of $1,000.

    p. Sales taxes from the sales tax table of $946.

    q. Property taxes on her residence of $1,100.

    r. Charitable contributions of $2,500.

    s. In November 2013, Jane was involved in an automobile accident. At the time of the accident, Jane's automobile had an FMV of $45,000. After the accident, the automobile's FMV was $38,000. Jane's basis in the car was $52,000. Jane's car was covered by insurance, but because the policy had a $5,000 deduction clause, Jane decided not to file a claim for the damage.

Part 1—Tax Computation

Compute Jane Smith's 2013 Federal income tax payable (or refund due). If you use tax forms for your computations, you will need Forms 1040 and 4684 and Schedules A, C, and D. Suggested software: H&R BLOCK Tax Software.

Part 2—Tax Planning

In 2014, Jane plans to continue her job with Legal Services, Inc. Therefore, items a, d, and l will recur in 2014. Jane plans to continue her typing services business (refer to item b) and expects gross receipts of $26,000. She projects that all business expenses (refer to item h) will increase by 10%, except for office rent, which, under the terms of her lease, will remain the same as in 2013. Items e, f, g, j, k, and s will not recur in 2014. Items c, i, m, n, p, q, and r will be approximately the same as in 2013.

    Jane would like you to compute the minimum amount of estimated tax she will have to pay for 2014 so that she will not have to pay any additional tax upon filing her 2014 Federal income tax return. Write a letter to Jane that contains your advice and prepare a memo for the tax files.

Tax Computation Problem

61. Mason Phillips, age 45, and his wife, Ruth, live at 230 Wood Lane, Salt Lake City, UT 84101. Mason's Social Security number is 111-11-1111. Ruth's Social Security number is 123-45-6789. Mason and Ruth are cash basis taxpayers and had the following items for 2014:

- Salary of $140,000.
- Bad debt of $30,000 from uncollected rent.
- Collection of unpaid rent from a prior year of $6,000.
- Sale of § 1244 stock resulting in a loss of $105,000. The stock was acquired eight months ago.
- Rental income of $60,000.
- Rental expenses of $33,000.
- Casualty loss on rental property of $10,000.
- Personal casualty loss (from one event) of $20,000.
- Theft loss of $5,000 on a computer used 100% associated with their jobs.
- Theft loss of $8,000 on a painting held for investment.
- Other itemized deductions of $18,000.
- Federal income tax withheld of $3,000.

Compute Mason and Ruth's 2014 Federal income tax payable (or refund due).

Research Problems

CHECKPOINT

THOMSON REUTERS

Note: Solutions to Research Problems can be prepared by using the **Checkpoint®** **Student Edition** online research product, which is available to accompany this text. It is also possible to prepare solutions to the Research Problems by using tax research materials found in a standard tax library.

Research Problem 1. During 2014, John was the chief executive officer and a shareholder of Maze, Inc. He owned 60% of the outstanding stock of Maze. In 2011, John and Maze, as co-borrowers, obtained a $100,000 loan from United National Bank. This loan was secured by John's personal residence. Although Maze was listed as a co-borrower, John repaid the loan in full in 2014. On Maze's Form 1120 tax returns, no loans from shareholders were reported. Discuss whether John is entitled to a bad debt deduction for the amount of the payment on the loan.

Partial list of research aids:
U.S. v. Generes, 405 U.S. 93 (1972).
Dale H. Sundby, T.C.Memo. 2003–204.
Arrigoni v. Comm., 73 T.C. 792 (1980).
Estate of Herbert M. Rapoport, T.C.Memo. 1982–584.
Clifford L. Brody and Barbara J. DeClerk, T.C. Summary Opinion, 2004–149.

Research Problem 2. Henry Hansen is a real estate developer. He was successful for many years. Three years ago, however, the real estate market crashed, and Henry reported losses for the two following tax years. The IRS disputed these losses and assessed tax deficiencies of $300,000 and $200,000 for the two years in question. In March of the current year, Henry offered to resolve all issues relating to those two years by paying the IRS $250,000, or $125,000 for each year. In April of the current year, the Commissioner accepted Henry's offer without discussion or negotiation. Henry now finds that he has an NOL for last year. If he carries the NOL back to the two years for which he reached a settlement with the IRS, the stipulated tax deficiency will be eliminated. Discuss whether Henry will be allowed to carry his NOL back to the two prior years for which he reached a settlement.

Research Problem 3. Jeb Simmons operated an illegal gambling business out of his home. While executing a search warrant, the local sheriff seized gambling paraphernalia and $200,000 in cash. Subsequently, Jeb voluntarily consented to forfeit to the state the cash that had been seized in connection with the execution of the search warrant. Write a letter to Jeb advising him as to whether he can claim a loss under § 165 for the seized cash. Also prepare a memo for the tax files. Jeb's address is 100 Honey Lane, Macon, GA 31208.

Communications

Research Problem 4. Mary Marble took out a homeowner's insurance policy on her residence. One of the policy provisions listed the insured's duties with respect to a loss. This provision required the policyholder to give notice and required an inventory of damaged personal property within 60 days of the insurance company's request and to supply proof of loss.

   In November of the current year, Mary's home was damaged by a fire. Shortly after the fire, Mary reported the loss to the insurance company. In December, the insurance company generated a claim report sheet with a claim number and sent Mary a proof of loss form. Mary failed to provide the insurance company with the proof of loss form within the required 60-day period; hence, the insurance company denied Mary's claim for damages. Discuss whether Mary is entitled to a casualty loss deduction for the damage to her home caused by the fire.

Research Problem 5. Esther owns a large home on the East Coast. Her home is surrounded by large, mature oak trees that significantly increase the value of her home. In August 2013, a hurricane damaged many of the trees surrounding her home. In September 2013, Esther engaged a local arborist to evaluate and treat the trees, but five of the largest trees were seriously weakened by the storm. These trees died from disease in 2014. Esther has ascertained that the amount of the casualty loss from the death of the five trees is $25,000; however, she is uncertain in which year to deduct this loss. Discuss whether the casualty loss should be deducted in the calculation of Esther's 2013 or 2014 taxable income.

Partial list of research aids:
Reg. § 1.165-1.
Oregon Mesabi Corporation, 39 B.T.A. 1033 (1939).

Internet Activity

Use the tax resources of the Internet to address the following questions. Do not restrict your search to the Web, but include a review of newsgroups and general reference materials, practitioner sites and resources, primary sources of the tax law, chat rooms and discussion groups, and other opportunities.

Research Problem 6. Find a newspaper article that discusses tax planning for casualty losses when a disaster area designation is made. Does the article convey the pertinent tax rules correctly? Then list all of the locations identified by the President as Federal disaster areas in the last two years.

Communications

Research Problem 7. Many states that have corporate income taxes "piggyback" onto the Federal corporate income tax calculation. In other words, these states' corporate income tax calculations incorporate many of the Federal calculations and deductions to make both compliance and verification of tax liability easier. However, some state legislatures were concerned that the domestic production activities deduction, if allowed for state tax purposes, would result in significant revenue losses. Determine whether states with corporate income taxes allow or disallow the domestic production activities deduction in the calculation of the state's corporate income tax liability.

CHAPTER

8

Depreciation, Cost Recovery, Amortization, and Depletion

LEARNING OBJECTIVES: *After completing Chapter 8, you should be able to:*

LO.1 State the rationale for the cost consumption concept and identify the relevant time periods for depreciation, ACRS, and MACRS.

LO.2 Determine the amount of cost recovery under MACRS.

LO.3 Recognize when and how to make the § 179 expensing election, calculate the amount of the deduction, and apply the effect of the election in making the MACRS calculation.

LO.4 Identify listed property and apply the deduction limitations on listed property and on luxury automobiles.

LO.5 Determine when and how to use the alternative depreciation system (ADS).

LO.6 Report cost recovery deductions appropriately.

LO.7 Identify intangible assets that are eligible for amortization and calculate the amount of the deduction.

LO.8 Determine the amount of depletion expense, including being able to apply the alternative tax treatments for intangible drilling and development costs.

LO.9 Identify tax planning opportunities for cost recovery, amortization, and depletion.

CHAPTER OUTLINE

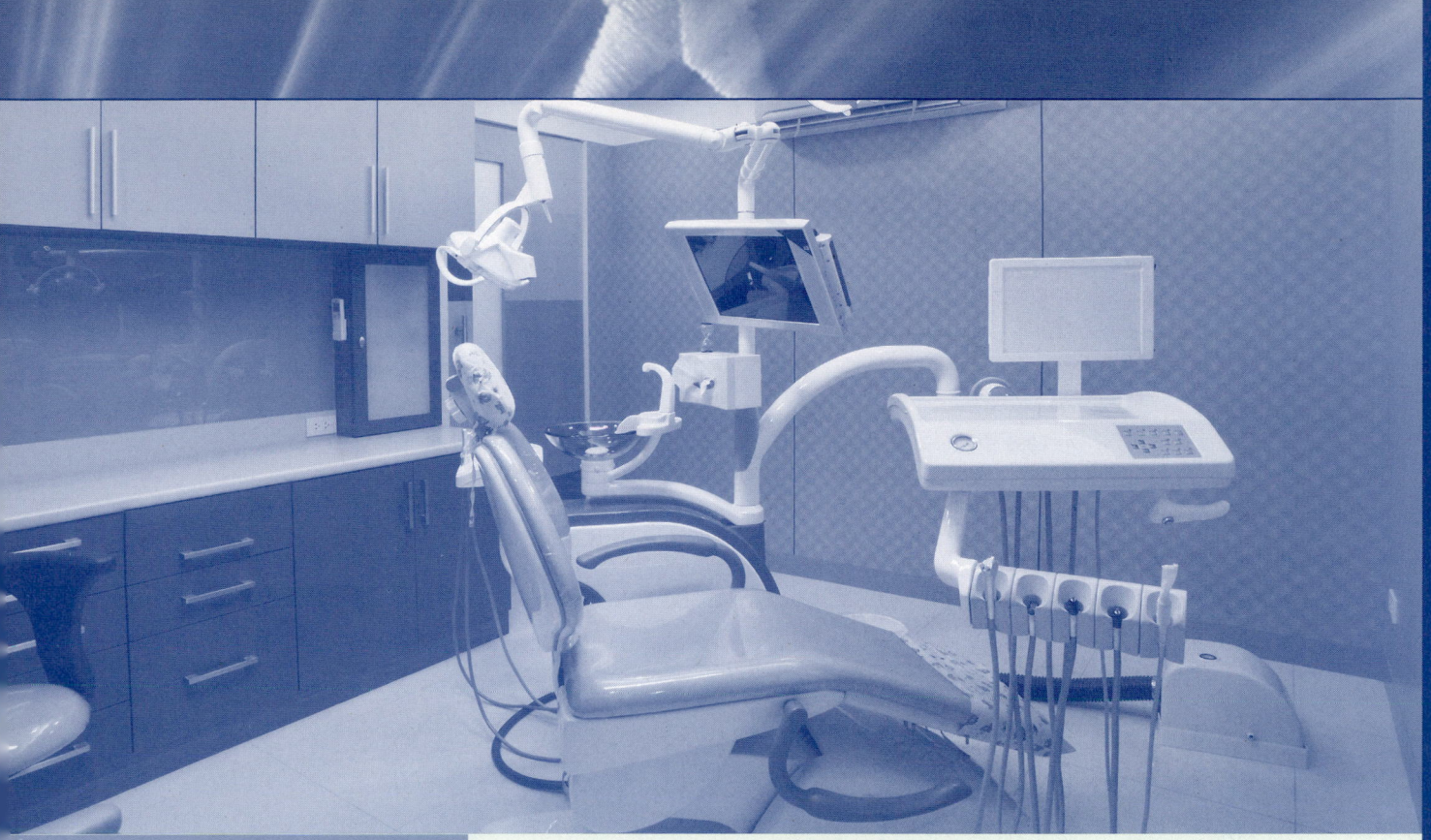

THE BIG PICTURE — Tax Solutions for the Real World

© Ersler Dmitry/Shutterstock.com

CALCULATING COST RECOVERY DEDUCTIONS

Dr. Cliff Payne purchased and placed in service in his dental practice the following new fixed assets during the current year.

Office furniture and fixtures	$ 70,000
Computers and peripheral equipment	67,085
Dental equipment	475,000

Using his financial reporting system, he concludes that the depreciation expense on Schedule C of Form 1040 is $91,298.

Office furniture and fixtures ($70,000 × 14.29%)	$10,003
Computers and peripheral equipment ($67,085 × 20%)	13,417
Dental equipment ($475,000 × 14.29%)	67,878
	$91,298

In addition, this year Dr. Payne purchased another personal residence for $300,000 and converted his original residence to rental property. He also purchased a condo in the prior year for $170,000 near his office that he is going to rent to a third party.

Has Dr. Payne correctly calculated the depreciation expense for his dental practice? Will he be able to deduct any depreciation expense for his rental properties?

Read the chapter and formulate your response.

FRAMEWORK 1040
Tax Formula for Individuals

This chapter covers the boldfaced portions of the Tax Formula for Individuals that was introduced in Figure 3.1 on p. 3-3. Below those portions are the sections of Form 1040 where the results are reported.

Income *(broadly conceived)*..	$xx,xxx
Less: Exclusions	(x,xxx)
Gross income...	$xx,xxx
Less: Deductions for adjusted gross income..	(x,xxx)

FORM 1040 (p.1)

12   Business income or (loss). Attach Schedule C or C-EZ . . . .

Adjusted gross income...	$xx,xxx
Less: The greater of total itemized deductions *or* the standard deduction..............................	(x,xxx)
Personal and dependency exemptions	(x,xxx)
Taxable income	$xx,xxx
Tax on taxable income *(see Tax Tables or Tax Rate Schedules)*	$ x,xxx
Less: Tax credits *(including income taxes withheld and prepaid)*................................	(xxx)
Tax due *(or refund)*	$ xxx

The Internal Revenue Code allows a depreciation, cost recovery, amortization, or depletion deduction based on an asset's cost. These deductions are applications of the recovery of capital doctrine (discussed in Chapter 4). Cost recovery deductions are based on the premise that the asset acquired (or improvement made) benefits more than one accounting period. Otherwise, the expenditure is deducted in the year incurred.[1]

Congress completely overhauled the **depreciation** rules in 1981 by creating the **accelerated cost recovery system (ACRS)**, which shortened depreciable lives and allowed accelerated depreciation methods. In 1986, Congress made substantial modifications to ACRS, which resulted in the **modified accelerated cost recovery system (MACRS)**. Tax professionals use the terms *depreciation* and **cost recovery** interchangeably. Concept Summary 8.1 provides an overview of the various depreciation systems and the time frames involved.

The statutory changes that have taken place since 1980 have widened the gap that exists between the accounting and tax versions of depreciation. The tax rules that existed prior to 1981 were much more compatible with generally accepted accounting principles.

This chapter focuses on the MACRS rules because they cover more recent property acquisitions (i.e., after 1986).[2] The ACRS rules and the pre-1981 rules are covered in Appendix G of this text. The chapter concludes with a discussion of the amortization of intangible property and startup expenditures and the depletion of natural resources.

Taxpayers may "write off" (deduct) the cost of certain assets that are used in a trade or business or held for the production of income. A write-off may take the form of depreciation (or cost recovery), depletion, or amortization. Tangible

---

[1]See Chapter 6 and the discussion of capitalization versus expense.

[2]§ 168. The terms *depreciation* and *cost recovery* are used interchangeably in the text and in § 168.

CONCEPT SUMMARY 8.1

Depreciation and Cost Recovery: Relevant Time Periods

System	Date Property Is Placed in Service
Pre-1981 depreciation	Before January 1, 1981, and *certain* property placed in service after December 31, 1980.
Accelerated cost recovery system (ACRS)	After December 31, 1980, and before January 1, 1987.
Modified accelerated cost recovery system (MACRS)	After December 31, 1986.

© iStockphoto.com/Andrey Prokhorov

assets, other than natural resources, are *depreciated*. Natural resources, such as oil, gas, coal, and timber, are *depleted*. Intangible assets, such as copyrights and patents, are *amortized*. Generally, no write-off is allowed for an asset that does not have a determinable useful life.

8-1 DEPRECIATION AND COST RECOVERY

8-1a Nature of Property

Property includes both realty (real property) and personalty (personal property). Realty generally includes land and buildings permanently affixed to the land. Personalty is defined as any asset that is not realty.[3] Do not confuse personalty (or personal property) with *personal use* property. Personal use property is any property (realty or personalty) that is held for personal use rather than for use in a trade or business or an income-producing activity. Cost recovery deductions are not allowed for personal use assets.

In summary, both realty and personalty can be either business use/income-producing property or personal use property. Examples include:

- a residence (realty that is personal use),
- an office building (realty that is business use),
- a dump truck (personalty that is business use), and
- common wearing apparel (personalty that is personal use).

It is imperative that this distinction between the *classification* of an asset (realty or personalty) and the *use* to which the asset is put (business or personal) be understood.

Assets used in a trade or business or for the production of income are eligible for cost recovery if they are subject to wear and tear, decay or decline from natural causes, or obsolescence (e.g., an automobile that the taxpayer rents to third parties). Assets that do not decline in value on a predictable basis or that do not have a determinable useful life (e.g., land, stock, and antiques) are not eligible for cost recovery.

8-1b Placed in Service Requirement

The key date for the commencement of depreciation is the date an asset is placed in service. This date, and not the purchase date of an asset, is relevant. This distinction is particularly important for an asset that is purchased near the end of the tax year, but not placed in service until after the beginning of the following tax year.

LO.1

State the rationale for the cost consumption concept and identify the relevant time periods for depreciation, ACRS, and MACRS.

---

[3]Refer to Chapter 1 (pp. 6–8) for further discussion.

8-1c Cost Recovery Allowed or Allowable

The basis of cost recovery property is reduced by the cost recovery allowed, and by not less than the allowable amount. The *allowed* cost recovery is the cost recovery actually deducted, whereas the *allowable* cost recovery is the amount that could have been taken under the applicable cost recovery method. If the taxpayer does not claim any cost recovery on property during a particular year, the basis of the property still is reduced by the amount of cost recovery that should have been deducted (the allowable cost recovery).

Example 1

On March 15, 2014, Jack purchased a copier, to use in his business, for $10,000. The copier is 5-year property, and Jack elected to use the straight-line method of cost recovery. Jack made the election because the business was a new undertaking and he reasoned that in the first few years of the business, a large cost recovery deduction was not needed.

Because the business was doing poorly, Jack did not even claim any cost recovery deductions in years 3 and 4. In years 5 and 6, Jack deducted the proper amount of cost recovery. Therefore, the allowed cost recovery (cost recovery actually deducted) and the allowable cost recovery are computed as follows.

	Cost Recovery Allowed	Cost Recovery Allowable
Year 1	$1,000	$1,000
Year 2	2,000	2,000
Year 3	–0–	2,000
Year 4	–0–	2,000
Year 5	2,000	2,000
Year 6	1,000	1,000

If Jack sold the copier for $800 in year 7, he would recognize an $800 gain ($800 amount realized – $0 adjusted basis); the adjusted basis of the copier is zero ($10,000 cost – $10,000 total allowable cost recovery in years 1 through 6).

8-1d Cost Recovery Basis for Personal Use Assets Converted to Business or Income-Producing Use

If personal use assets are converted to business or income-producing use, the basis for cost recovery and for loss is the *lower* of the adjusted basis or the fair market value at the time the property was converted. As a result of this lower-of basis rule, losses that occurred while the property was personal use property are not recognized for tax purposes through the cost recovery of the property.

THE BIG PICTURE

Example 2

Return to the facts of *The Big Picture* on p. 8-1. Five years ago, Dr. Payne purchased a personal residence for $250,000. In the current year, with the housing market down, Payne found a larger home that he acquired for his personal residence. Because of the downturn in the housing market, however, he was not able to sell his original residence and recover his purchase price of $250,000. The residence was appraised at $180,000.

Instead of continuing to try to sell the original residence, Dr. Payne converted it to rental property. The basis for cost recovery of the rental property is $180,000 because the fair market value is less than the adjusted basis. The $70,000 decline in value is deemed to be personal (because it occurred while the property was held for personal use by Payne) and therefore nondeductible.

8-2 MODIFIED ACCELERATED COST RECOVERY SYSTEM (MACRS): GENERAL RULES

Under the modified accelerated cost recovery system (MACRS), the cost of an asset is recovered over a predetermined period that generally is shorter than the useful life of the asset or the period that the asset is used to produce income. The MACRS rules were designed to encourage investment, improve productivity, and simplify the pertinent law and its administration.

MACRS provides separate cost recovery tables for realty and personalty. Cost recovery allowances for real property, other than land, are based on recovery lives specified in the law. The IRS provides tables that specify cost recovery allowances for personalty and for realty. Excerpts from those tables are provided in Section 8-7d of this chapter.

LO.2

Determine the amount of cost recovery under MACRS.

8-2a Personalty: Recovery Periods and Methods

Classification of Property

MACRS provides that the cost recovery basis of eligible personalty (and certain realty) is recovered over 3, 5, 7, 10, 15, or 20 years. Property is classified by recovery period under MACRS as follows. See Exhibit 8.1 for examples of assets in each class.[4]

3-year 200% class.........	ADR midpoints of 4 years and less.[5] Excludes automobiles and light trucks. Includes racehorses more than 2 years old and other horses more than 12 years old.
5-year 200% class.........	ADR midpoints of more than 4 years and less than 10 years, adding automobiles, light trucks, qualified technological equipment, renewable energy and biomass properties that are small power production facilities, research and experimentation property, semiconductor manufacturing equipment, and computer-based central office switching equipment.
7-year 200% class.........	ADR midpoints of 10 years and more and less than 16 years, adding property with no ADR midpoint not classified elsewhere. Includes railroad track and office furniture, fixtures, and equipment.
10-year 200% class.......	ADR midpoints of 16 years and more and less than 20 years, adding single-purpose agricultural or horticultural structures, any tree or vine bearing fruits or nuts.
15-year 150% class.......	ADR midpoints of 20 years and more and less than 25 years, including sewage treatment plants and telephone distribution plants and comparable equipment used for the two-way exchange of voice and data communications.
20-year 150% class.......	ADR midpoints of 25 years and more, other than real property with an ADR midpoint of 27.5 years and more and including sewer pipes.

Accelerated depreciation is allowed for these six MACRS classes of property. Two hundred percent declining-balance is used for the 3-, 5-, 7-, and 10-year

---

[4]§ 168(e).

[5]Rev.Proc. 87–56, 1987–2 C.B. 674 is the source for the ADR midpoint lives.

EXHIBIT 8.1	Cost Recovery Periods: MACRS Personalty

Class of Property	Examples
3-year	Tractor units for use over the road.
	Any horse that is not a racehorse and is more than 12 years old at the time it is placed in service.
	Any racehorse that is more than 2 years old at the time it is placed in service.
	Breeding hogs.
	Special tools used in the manufacturing of motor vehicles such as dies, fixtures, molds, and patterns.
5-year	Automobiles and taxis.
	Light and heavy general-purpose trucks.
	Buses.
	Trailers and trailer-mounted containers.
	Typewriters, calculators, and copiers.
	Computers and peripheral equipment.
	Breeding and dairy cattle.
	Rental appliances, furniture, and carpets.
7-year	Office furniture, fixtures, and equipment.
	Breeding and work horses.
	Agricultural machinery and equipment.
	Railroad track.
10-year	Vessels, barges, tugs, and similar water transportation equipment.
	Assets used for petroleum refining or for the manufacture of grain and grain mill products, sugar and sugar products, or vegetable oils and vegetable oil products.
	Single-purpose agricultural or horticultural structures.
15-year	Land improvements.
	Assets used for industrial steam and electric generation and/or distribution systems.
	Assets used in the manufacture of cement.
	Assets used in pipeline transportation.
	Electric utility nuclear production plant.
	Municipal wastewater treatment plant.
20-year	Farm buildings except single-purpose agricultural and horticultural structures.
	Gas utility distribution facilities.
	Water utilities.
	Municipal sewer.

classes, with a switchover to straight-line depreciation when the latter computation yields a larger amount. One hundred and fifty percent declining-balance is allowed for the 15- and 20-year classes, with an appropriate straight-line switchover.[6] The appropriate computation methods and conventions are built into the tables, so it is not necessary to calculate the appropriate percentages.

To determine the amount of the cost recovery allowances, simply identify the asset by class and go to the appropriate table for the percentage. The MACRS percentages for personalty appear in Table 8.1 (see Section 8-7d). Concept Summary 8.2 provides an overview of the various conventions that apply under the MACRS statutory percentage method.

---

[6]§ 168(b).

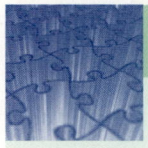

CONCEPT SUMMARY 8.2

Statutory Percentage Method under MACRS

	Personal Property	Real Property*
Convention	Half-year or mid-quarter	Mid-month
Cost recovery deduction in the year of disposition	Half-year for year of disposition or half-quarter for quarter of disposition	Half-month for month of disposition

*Straight-line method must be used.

© iStockphoto.com/Andrey Prokhorov

Taxpayers may *elect* the straight-line method to compute cost recovery allowances for each of these classes of property. Certain property is not eligible for accelerated cost recovery and must be depreciated under an alternative depreciation system (ADS). Both the straight-line election and ADS are discussed later in the chapter.

MACRS views property as placed in service in the middle of the asset's first year (the **half-year convention**).[7] Thus, for example, the statutory recovery period for property with a life of three years begins in the middle of the year an asset is placed in service and ends three years later. In practical terms, this means that taxpayers must wait an extra year to recover the full cost of depreciable assets. That is, the actual write-offs are claimed over 4, 6, 8, 11, 16, and 21 years. MACRS also allows for a half-year of cost recovery in the year of disposition or retirement.

> **Example 3**
>
> Kareem acquires a 5-year class asset on April 10, 2014, for $30,000. Kareem's cost recovery deduction for 2014 is computed as follows.
>
> MACRS cost recovery [$30,000 × .20 (Table 8.1)] $6,000

> **Example 4**
>
> Assume the same facts as in Example 3. Kareem disposes of the asset on March 5, 2016. Kareem's cost recovery deduction for 2016 is $2,880 [$30,000 × ½ × .192 (Table 8.1)].

Classification of Property

Global Tax Issues

In New Zealand, it is important for tax depreciation purposes to know the difference between a dairy shed and a fence. Dairy sheds are classified as buildings with an expected life of 25 years and a straight-line depreciation rate of 4 percent. If a fenced holding yard is built next to the shed and deemed to be part of the shed, the depreciation rate for the pipe railings and the gate are the same as for the shed. If the holding yard is deemed not to be part of the shed, the costs associated with the holding yard can be expensed.

© iStockphoto.com/Andrey Prokhorov

Source: Based on "Tax Deductions Can be Tricky," *Taranaki Daily News*, July 12, 2012, p. 14.

---

[7]§ 168(d)(4)(A).

FINANCIAL DISCLOSURE INSIGHTS   Tax and Book Depreciation

A common book-tax difference relates to the depreciation amounts that are reported for GAAP and Federal income tax purposes. Typically, tax depreciation deductions are accelerated; that is, they are claimed in earlier reporting periods than is the case for financial accounting purposes.

Almost every tax law change since 1980 has included depreciation provisions that accelerate the related deductions relative to the expenses allowed under GAAP. Accelerated cost recovery deductions represent a means by which the taxing jurisdiction infuses the business with cash flow created by the reduction in the year's tax liabilities.

For instance, recently, about one-quarter of General Electric's deferred tax liabilities related to depreciation differences. For Toyota's and Ford's depreciation differences, that amount was about one-third. And for the trucking firm Ryder Systems, depreciation differences accounted for all but 1 percent of the deferred tax liabilities.

© iStockphoto.com/Pali Rao

Mid-Quarter Convention

The half-year convention arises from the simplifying presumption that assets generally are acquired at an even pace throughout the tax year. However, Congress was concerned that taxpayers might defeat that presumption by placing large amounts of property in service during the last quarter of the taxable year (and, by doing so, receive a half-year's depreciation on those large, fourth-quarter acquisitions).

To inhibit this behavior, Congress added the **mid-quarter convention** that applies if more than 40 percent of the value of property other than eligible real estate (discussed in a later section) is placed in service during the last quarter of the year.[8] Under this convention, property acquisitions are grouped by the quarter they were acquired for cost recovery purposes. Acquisitions during the first quarter are allowed 10.5 months (three and one-half quarters) of cost recovery; the second quarter, 7.5 months (two and one-half quarters); the third quarter, 4.5 months (one and one-half quarters); and the fourth quarter, 1.5 months (one-half quarter). The percentages are shown in Table 8.2.

Example 5

Silver Corporation acquires the following new 5-year class property in 2014.

Property Acquisition Dates	Cost
February 15	$ 200,000
July 10	400,000
December 5	600,000
Total	$1,200,000

Under the statutory percentage method, Silver's cost recovery allowances for the first two years are computed below. Because more than 40% ($600,000/$1,200,000 = 50%) of the acquisitions are in the last quarter, the mid-quarter convention applies.

2014	Mid-Quarter Convention Depreciation (Table 8.2)	Total Depreciation
February 15	$200,000 × .35	$ 70,000
July 10	$400,000 × .15	60,000
December 5	$600,000 × .05	30,000
		$160,000

[8]§ 168(d)(3).

2015

	Mid-Quarter Convention Depreciation (Table 8.2)	Total Depreciation
February 15	$200,000 × .26	$ 52,000
July 10	$400,000 × .34	136,000
December 5	$600,000 × .38	228,000
		$416,000

Without the mid-quarter convention, Silver's 2014 MACRS deduction would have been $240,000 [$1,200,000 × .20 (Table 8.1)]. The mid-quarter convention slows down the taxpayer's available cost recovery deductions.

When property to which the mid-quarter convention applies is disposed of, the property is treated as though it were disposed of at the midpoint of the quarter. Hence, in the quarter of disposition, cost recovery is allowed for one-half of the quarter.

Example 6

Assume the same facts as in Example 5, except that Silver Corporation sells the $400,000 asset on November 30, 2015. The cost recovery allowance for 2015 is computed as follows (Table 8.2).

February 15	$200,000 × .26	$ 52,000
July 10	$400,000 × .34 × (3.5/4)	119,000
December 5	$600,000 × .38	228,000
Total		$399,000

THE BIG PICTURE

Example 7

Return to the facts of *The Big Picture* on p. 8-1. If the placed-in-service date for the office furniture and fixtures and computers and peripheral equipment is September 29 and the placed-in-service date for the dental equipment is October 3, Dr. Payne's total cost recovery is computed as follows.

Office furniture and fixtures:	
MACRS cost recovery $70,000 × .1071 (Table 8.2)	$ 7,497
Computers and peripheral equipment:	
MACRS cost recovery $67,085 × .15 (Table 8.2)	10,063
Dental equipment:	
MACRS cost recovery $475,000 × .0357 (Table 8.2)	16,958
Total cost recovery	$ 34,518

Note the implications of the mid-quarter convention. If the dental equipment had been placed in service before October 1 (the beginning of the fourth quarter), the total cost recovery deduction would have been $91,298 (p. 8-1).

Accelerated Depreciation for Wind Power Producers

The government of India has extended accelerated depreciation for wind power producers. Accelerated depreciation has been a major support to producers trying to achieve energy independence and freeze power costs.

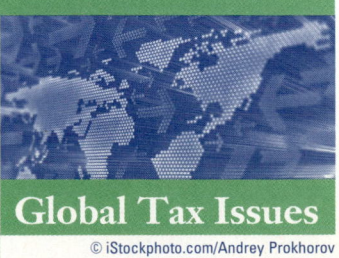

Global Tax Issues

© iStockphoto.com/Andrey Prokhorov

Source: Based on Shreya Jai, "Government Extends Popular Accelerated Depreciation Scheme for Wind Power Producers," *The Economic Times,* March 28, 2012.

TAX IN THE NEWS Cost Segregation

Cost segregation identifies certain assets within a commercial property that can qualify for shorter depreciation schedules than the building itself. The identified assets are classified as 5-, 7-, or 15-year property, rather than 39-year property, as part of the building. This allows for greater accelerated deprecia-tion, which reduces taxable income and hence the tax liability.

For instance, a telecommunications system might be segregated from the building in which it is installed. This allows the system to be depreciated over 5 or 7 years, instead of 39 years.

8-2b Realty: Recovery Periods and Methods

Under MACRS, the cost recovery period for residential rental real estate is 27.5 years, and the straight-line method is used for computing the cost recovery allow-ance. **Residential rental real estate** includes property where 80 percent or more of the gross rental revenues are from nontransient dwelling units (e.g., an apart-ment building). Hotels, motels, and similar establishments are not residential rental property. Low-income housing is classified as residential rental real estate. Non-residential real estate uses a recovery period of 39 years; it also is depreciated using the straight-line method.[9]

Some items of real property are not treated as real estate for purposes of MACRS. For example, single-purpose agricultural structures are in the 10-year MACRS class. Land improvements are in the 15-year MACRS class.

All eligible real estate is depreciated using the **mid-month convention**.[10] Regardless of when the property is placed in service, it is deemed to have been placed in service at the middle of the month. This allows for one-half month's cost recovery for the month the property is placed in service. If the property is disposed of before the end of the recovery period, one-half month's cost recovery is permitted for the month of disposition regardless of the specific date of disposition.

Cost recovery is computed by multiplying the applicable rate (Table 8.6) by the cost recovery basis.

Example 8	Alec acquired a building on April 1, 1996, for $800,000. If the building is classified as residential rental real estate, the cost recovery deduction for 2014 is $29,088 (.03636 × $800,000). If the building is sold on October 7, 2014, the cost recovery deduction for 2014 is $23,028 [.03636 × (9.5/12) × $800,000]. (See Table 8.6 for percentage.)

Example 9	Jane acquired a building on March 2, 1993, for $1 million. If the building is classified as nonresidential real estate, the cost recovery deduction for 2014 is $31,740 (.03174 × $1,000,000). If the building is sold on January 5, 2014, the cost recovery deduction for 2014 is $1,323 [.03174 × (.5/12) × $1,000,000]. (See Table 8.6 for percentage.)

Example 10	Mark acquired a building on November 19, 2014, for $1.2 million. If the building is classified as nonresidential real estate, the cost recovery deduction for 2014 is $3,852 [.00321 × $1,200,000 (Table 8.6)]. The cost recovery deduction for 2015 is $30,768 [.02564 × $1,200,000 (Table 8.6)]. If the building is sold on May 21, 2015, the cost recovery deduction for 2015 is $11,538 [.02564 × (4.5/12) × $1,200,000 (Table 8.6)].

---

[9]§§ 168(b), (c), and (e). A 31.5-year life is used for such property placed in service before May 13, 1993.

[10]§ 168(d)(1).

CONCEPT SUMMARY 8.3

Straight-Line Election under MACRS

	Personal Property	Real Property*
Convention	Half-year or mid-quarter	Mid-month
Cost recovery deduction in the year of disposition	Half-year for year of disposition or half-quarter for quarter of disposition	Half-month for month of disposition
Elective or mandatory	Elective	Mandatory
Breadth of election	Class by class	

*Straight-line method must be used.

© iStockphoto.com/Andrey Prokhorov

8-2c Straight-Line Election

Although MACRS requires straight-line depreciation for all eligible real estate, the taxpayer may *elect* to use the straight-line method for depreciable personal property.[11] The property is depreciated using the class life (recovery period) of the asset with a half-year convention or a mid-quarter convention, whichever applies. The election is available on a class-by-class and year-by-year basis (see Concept Summary 8.3). The percentages for the straight-line election with a half-year convention appear in Table 8.3.

THE BIG PICTURE
Example 11

Return to the facts of *The Big Picture* on p. 8-1. If Dr. Payne elects the straight-line method of cost recovery, his total cost recovery is computed as follows.

Office furniture and fixtures ($70,000 × .0714) (Table 8.3)	$ 4,998
Computers and peripheral equipment ($67,085 × .10) (Table 8.3)	6,709
Dental equipment ($475,000 × .0714) (Table 8.3)	33,915
Total cost recovery	$45,622

If Payne does not elect the straight-line cost recovery method, his cost recovery deduction is $91,298 (as detailed on p. 8-1).

THE BIG PICTURE
Example 12

Assume the same facts as in Example 11, except that Dr. Payne sells the computers and peripheral equipment on November 21, 2015. His cost recovery deduction for 2015 is $6,709 ($67,085 × .20 × 1/2) (Table 8.3).

---

[11]§ 168(b)(5).

8-3 MODIFIED ACCELERATED COST RECOVERY SYSTEM (MACRS): SPECIAL RULES

8-3a Additional First-Year Depreciation

As noted in Chapter 1, Congress uses the tax system to stimulate the economy—especially in times of recession. Such is the case with **additional first-year depreciation** (also referred to as bonus depreciation). In 2012 and 2013, taxpayers were allowed to take an additional 50 percent cost recovery in the year qualified property is placed in service. Although the provision was written to expire at the end of 2013, Congress may extend this provision during 2014.

The term *qualified property* includes most *new* depreciable assets other than buildings. The term *new* means the original or first use of the property. Property that is used but "new to the taxpayer" does not qualify.[12]

The additional first-year depreciation is taken in the year in which the qualifying property is placed in service; it may be claimed in addition to the otherwise available depreciation deduction. For property placed in service in 2012 or 2013, after the additional first-year depreciation is calculated, the standard MACRS cost recovery allowance is calculated by multiplying the cost recovery basis (original cost recovery basis less additional first-year depreciation) by the percentage that reflects the applicable cost recovery method and convention. A taxpayer may elect *not* to take additional first-year depreciation.

Examples 13 and 14 reflect the tax treatment for 2013.

Example 13

Morgan acquires, for $50,000, and places in service a 5-year class asset on March 20, 2013. Morgan's total 2013 cost recovery deduction is:

50% additional first-year depreciation ($50,000 × .50)	$25,000
MACRS cost recovery [($50,000 − $25,000) × .20 (Table 8.1)]	5,000
Total cost recovery	$30,000

Example 14

Assume the same facts as in Example 13. Morgan disposes of the asset on October 22, 2014. Morgan's 2014 cost recovery deduction for the asset is $4,000 [$25,000 basis for MACRS recovery × ½ year convention × .32 (Table 8.1)].

THE BIG PICTURE

Example 15

Return to the facts of *The Big Picture* on p. 8-1 and assume that the tax year is 2013. If Dr. Payne takes additional first-year depreciation, his total cost recovery is computed as follows.

Office furniture and fixtures	
Additional first-year depreciation ($70,000 × .50)	$ 35,000
MACRS cost recovery [($70,000 − $35,000) × .1429 (Table 8.1)]	5,002
Computers and peripheral equipment	
Additional first-year depreciation ($67,085 × .50)	33,543
MACRS cost recovery [($67,085 − $33,543) × .20 (Table 8.1)]	6,708
Dental equipment	
Additional first-year depreciation ($475,000 × .50)	237,500
MACRS cost recovery [($475,000 − $237,500) × .1429 (Table 8.1)]	33,939
Total cost recovery	$351,692

---

[12]§ 168(k). The 50 percent additional first-year depreciation is allowed for qualified property placed in service after 2011 and before 2014; different rules applied between 2008 and 2011.

8-3b Election to Expense Assets (§ 179)

Section 179 (Election to Expense Certain Depreciable Business Assets) permits the taxpayer to elect to write off up to $25,000 in 2014 ($500,000 in 2013) of the acquisition cost of *tangible personal property* used in a trade or business. Amounts that are expensed under § 179 may not be capitalized and depreciated.

The **§ 179 expensing** election is an annual election that applies to the acquisition cost of property placed in service that year. The immediate expense election generally is not available for real property or for property used for the production of income.[13]

Any elected § 179 expense is taken *before* additional first-year depreciation is computed. The base for calculating the remaining standard MACRS deduction is net of the § 179 expense and any additional first-year depreciation (50 percent for assets placed in service in 2013).

LO.3

Recognize when and how to make the § 179 expensing election, calculate the amount of the deduction, and apply the effect of the election in making the MACRS calculation.

Example 16

Kelly acquires equipment (5-year class asset) on February 1, 2013, at a cost of $525,000 and elects to expense $500,000 under § 179. Kelly takes the statutory percentage cost recovery for 2013 (see Table 8.1). As a result, the total deduction for the year is calculated as follows.

§ 179 expense	$500,000
50% additional first-year depreciation [($525,000 − $500,000) × 50%]	12,500
Standard MACRS calculation [($525,000 − $500,000 − $12,500) × .20]	2,500
	$515,000

Annual Limitations

Two additional limitations apply to the amount deductible under § 179. First, the ceiling amount on the deduction is reduced dollar for dollar when § 179 property placed in service during the taxable year exceeds a maximum amount ($200,000 in 2014; $2 million in 2013). Second, the § 179 deduction cannot exceed the taxpayer's trade or business taxable income, computed without regard to the § 179 amount.

Any § 179 amount in excess of taxable income is carried forward to future taxable years and added to other amounts eligible for expensing. The § 179 amount eligible for expensing in a carryforward year is limited to the *lesser* of (1) the statutory dollar amount ($25,000 in 2014; $500,000 in 2013) reduced by the cost of § 179 property placed in service in excess of $200,000 in 2014 ($2 million in 2013) in the carryforward year, or (2) business taxable income in the carryforward year.

Example 17

Continue with the facts of Example 16. If Congress does not extend bonus depreciation and makes no changes to the scheduled 2014 § 179 expense limitation and related phaseout amounts, Kelly's cost recovery deduction is much different if the equipment is acquired in 2014.

§ 179 expense (assets placed in service exceed phaseout)	$ –0–
50% additional first-year depreciation (provision expired)	–0–
Standard MACRS calculation ($525,000 × .20)	105,000
	$105,000

---

[13]The § 179 amount allowed is per taxpayer, per year. On a joint return, the statutory amount applies to the couple. If the taxpayers are married and file separate returns, each spouse is eligible for 50% of the statutory amount. During 2014, Congress may retroactively apply the modifications to the entire year.

Example 18

Jill owns a computer service and operates it as a sole proprietorship. In 2014, taxable income is $12,500 before considering any § 179 deduction. If Jill spends $204,000 on new equipment, her § 179 expense deduction is computed as follows.

§ 179 deduction before adjustment	$25,000
Less: Dollar limitation reduction ($204,000 − $200,000)	(4,000)
Remaining § 179 deduction	$21,000
Business income limitation	$12,500
§ 179 deduction allowed	$12,500
§ 179 deduction carryforward ($21,000 − $12,500)	$ 8,500

Effect on Basis

The basis of the property for cost recovery purposes is reduced by the § 179 amount after accounting for the current-year amount of property placed in service in excess of $200,000 in 2014 ($2 million in 2013). This adjusted amount does not reflect any business income limitation.

Conversion to Personal Use

Conversion of the expensed property to personal use at any time results in recapture income (see Chapter 17). A property is converted to personal use if it is not used predominantly in a trade or business.[14]

ETHICS & EQUITY   Section 179 Limitation

Joe Moran worked in the construction business throughout most of his career. In June of the current year, he sold his interest in Ajax Enterprises, LLC, for a profit of $300,000. Shortly thereafter, Joe started his own business, which involves the redevelopment of distressed residential real estate.

In connection with his new business venture, Joe purchased a dump truck at a cost of $70,000. The new business struggled and showed a net operating loss for the year. Joe is considering expensing the $70,000 cost of the truck under §179 on this year's tax return. Evaluate Joe's plan.

© iStockphoto.com/LdF

8-3c Business and Personal Use of Automobiles and Other Listed Property

LO.4

Identify listed property and apply the deduction limitations on listed property and on luxury automobiles.

Limits exist on MACRS deductions for automobiles and other listed property that are used for both personal and business purposes.[15] If the listed property is *predominantly used* for business, the taxpayer can use the MACRS tables to recover the cost. In cases where the property is *not predominantly used* for business, the cost is recovered using the *straight-line method*.

Listed property includes:

- Any passenger automobile.
- Any other property used as a means of transportation.
- Any property of a type generally used for purposes of entertainment, recreation, or amusement.
- Any computer or peripheral equipment, with the exception of equipment used exclusively at a regular business establishment, including a qualifying home office.
- Any other property specified in the Regulations.

---

[14]See Reg. § 1.179–1(e) and related examples.   [15]§ 280F.

Automobiles and Other Listed Property Used Predominantly in Business

For listed property to be considered as *predominantly used in business*, its *business usage* must exceed 50 percent.[16] The use of listed property for production of income does not qualify as business use for purposes of the more-than-50 percent test. However, both production of income and business use percentages are used to compute the cost recovery deduction.

On September 1, 2014, Emma places in service listed 5-year recovery property. The property cost $10,000. She elects not to take any available additional first-year depreciation. If Emma uses the property 40% for business and 25% for the production of income, the property is not considered as predominantly used for business. The cost is recovered using straight-line cost recovery. Emma's cost recovery allowance for the year is $650 ($10,000 × 10% × 65%). If, however, Emma uses the property 60% for business and 25% for the production of income, the property is considered as used predominantly for business. Therefore, she may use the statutory percentage method. Emma's cost recovery allowance for the year is $1,700 ($10,000 × .200 × 85%).	**Example 19**

In determining the percentage of business usage for listed property, a mileage-based percentage is used for automobiles. For other listed property, one employs the most appropriate unit of time (e.g., hours) for which the property actually is used (rather than its availability for use).[17]

Limits on Cost Recovery for Automobiles

The law places special limitations on cost recovery deductions for passenger automobiles. These statutory dollar limits were imposed on passenger automobiles because of the belief that the tax system was being used to underwrite automobiles whose cost and luxury far exceeded what was needed for the taxpayer's business use.

A *passenger automobile* is any four-wheeled vehicle manufactured for use on public streets, roads, and highways with an unloaded gross vehicle weight (GVW) rating of 6,000 pounds or less.[18] This definition specifically excludes vehicles used directly in the business of transporting people or property for compensation, such as taxicabs, ambulances, hearses, and trucks and vans as prescribed by the Regulations.

The following "luxury auto" depreciation limits apply.[19]

Date Placed in Service	First Year	Second Year	Third Year	Fourth and Later Years
2013*	$3,160	$5,100	$3,050	$1,875
2012	$3,160	$5,100	$3,050	$1,875
2010–2011	$3,060	$4,900	$2,950	$1,775
2009	$2,960	$4,800	$2,850	$1,775

*Because the 2014 indexed amounts were not available at the time of this writing, the 2013 amounts are used in the Examples and problem materials.

For an automobile placed in service prior to 2009, the limitation for subsequent years' cost recovery is based on the limits for the year the automobile was placed in service.[20]

In the event a passenger automobile used predominantly for business qualifies for additional first-year depreciation (i.e., new property), the first-year recovery limitation is increased by $8,000. Therefore, for acquisitions made in 2013, the initial-year cost recovery limitation increases from $3,160 to $11,160 ($3,160 + $8,000).

---

[16]§ 280F(b)(3).

[17]Reg. § 1.280F–6T(e).

[18]§ 280F(d)(5).

[19]§ 280F(a)(1); Rev.Proc. 2013-21 (2013–12 I.R.B.660).

[20]Cost recovery limitations for years prior to 2009 are found in IRS Publication 463.

There are also separate cost recovery limitations for trucks and vans and for electric automobiles. Because these limitations are applied in the same manner as those imposed on passenger automobiles, these additional limitations are not discussed further in this chapter.

The luxury auto limits are imposed before any percentage reduction for personal use. In addition, the limitation in the first year includes any amount the taxpayer elects to expense under § 179.[21] If the passenger automobile is used partly for personal use, the personal use percentage is ignored for the purpose of determining the unrecovered cost available for deduction in later years.

Example 20

On July 1, 2014, Dan places in service a new automobile that cost $40,000. He does not elect § 179 expensing, and he elects not to take any available additional first-year depreciation. The car is used 80% for business and 20% for personal use in each tax year. Dan chooses the MACRS 200% declining-balance method of cost recovery (the auto is a 5-year asset).

The depreciation computation for 2014 through 2019 is summarized in the table below. The cost recovery allowed is the lesser of the MACRS amount or the recovery limitation.

Year	MACRS Amount	Recovery Limitation	Depreciation Allowed
2014	$6,400 ($40,000 × 20% × 80%)	$2,528 ($3,160 × 80%)	$2,528
2015	$10,240 ($40,000 × 32% × 80%)	$4,080 ($5,100 × 80%)	$4,080
2016	$6,144 ($40,000 × 19.2% × 80%)	$2,440 ($3,050 × 80%)	$2,440
2017	$3,686 ($40,000 × 11.52% × 80%)	$1,500 ($1,875 × 80%)	$1,500
2018	$3,686 ($40,000 × 11.52% × 80%)	$1,500 ($1,875 × 80%)	$1,500
2019	$1,843 ($40,000 × 5.76% × 80%)	$1,500 ($1,875 × 80%)	$1,500

If Dan continues to use the car after 2019, his cost recovery is limited to the lesser of the recoverable basis or the recovery limitation (i.e., $1,875 × business use percentage). For this purpose, the recoverable basis is computed as if the full recovery limitation was allowed even if it was not. Thus, the recoverable basis as of January 1, 2020, is $23,065 ($40,000 − $3,160 − $5,100 − $3,050 − $1,875 − $1,875 − $1,875).

If Dan placed the car in service in 2013 and took additional first-year depreciation, the calculated amount of additional first-year depreciation would have been $16,000 ($40,000 × 50% × 80%). However, the deduction would have been limited to $8,928 [($8,000 + $3,160) × 80%].

The cost recovery limitations are maximum amounts. If the regular MACRS calculation produces a lesser amount of cost recovery, the lesser amount is used.

Example 21

On April 2, 2014, Gail places in service a used automobile that cost $10,000. The car is always used 70% for business and 30% for personal use. Therefore, the cost recovery allowance for 2014 is $1,400 ($10,000 × 20% MACRS table factor × 70%), and not $2,212 ($3,160 passenger auto maximum × 70%).

The luxury auto limitations apply *only* to passenger automobiles and not to other listed property.

---

[21]§ 280F(d)(1).

First-Time Car Buyers

Thailand uses a tax cut policy for first-time car buyers. The law allows taxpayers who purchase cars for less than 1 million baht to deduct 20,000 baht each year for five years, much like the depreciation deduction, from their taxable income.

Source: Based on "Gov't to Launch Tax Cut Policy for First-Time Car Buyers," *Thai Press Reports,* September 1, 2011.

Global Tax Issues

© iStockphoto.com/Andrey Prokhorov

Special Limitation

A $25,000 limit applies for the § 179 deduction when the luxury auto limits do not apply. The limit is in effect for sport utility vehicles (SUVs) with an unloaded GVW rating of more than 6,000 pounds and not more than 14,000 pounds.[22]

> **Example 22**
>
> During 2013, Jay acquires and places in service a new SUV that cost $70,000 and has a GVW of 8,000 pounds. Jay uses the vehicle 100% of the time for business use. The total deduction for 2013 with respect to the SUV is computed as follows.
>
> | | |
> |---|---:|
> | § 179 expense | $25,000 |
> | 50% additional first-year depreciation [($70,000 − $25,000) × 50%] | 22,500 |
> | Standard MACRS calculation [($70,000 − $25,000 − $22,500) × .20 (Table 8.1)] | 4,500 |
> | | $52,000 |

Automobiles and Other Listed Property Not Used Predominantly in Business

For automobiles and other listed property not used predominantly in business in the year of acquisition (i.e., 50 percent or less), the straight-line method under the alternative depreciation system (see Section 8-3f) is required.[23] Under this system, the straight-line recovery period for automobiles is five years. However, the cost recovery allowance for any passenger automobile cannot exceed the luxury auto amount.

> **Example 23**
>
> On July 27, 2014, Fred places in service an automobile that cost $20,000. The auto is used 40% for business and 60% for personal use. The cost recovery allowance for 2014 is $800 [$20,000 × 10% (Table 8.5) × 40%].

> **Example 24**
>
> Assume the same facts as in Example 23, except that the automobile cost $50,000. The cost recovery allowance for 2014 is $1,264 [$50,000 × 10% (Table 8.5) = $5,000 (limited to $3,160) × 40%].

The straight-line method is used even if, at some later date, the business usage of the property increases to more than 50 percent. In that case, the amount of cost recovery reflects the increase in business usage.

> **Example 25**
>
> Assume the same facts as in Example 23, except that in 2015, Fred uses the automobile 70% for business and 30% for personal use. Fred's cost recovery allowance for 2015 is $2,800 [$20,000 × 20% (Table 8.5) × 70%], which is less than 70% of the second-year limit.

---

[22]§ 179(b)(6).   [23]§ 280F(b)(1).

Change from Predominantly Business Use

If the business use percentage of listed property falls to 50 percent or less after the year the property is placed in service, the property is subject to *cost recovery recapture*. The amount required to be recaptured and included in the taxpayer's return as ordinary income is the excess cost recovery.

Excess cost recovery is the excess of the cost recovery deduction taken in prior years using the statutory percentage method over the amount that would have been allowed if the straight-line method had been used since the property was placed in service.[24]

Example 26	Seth purchased a new car on January 22, 2014, at a cost of $20,000. Business usage was 80% in 2014, 70% in 2015, 40% in 2016, and 60% in 2017. Seth elects not to take any available additional first-year depreciation. Seth's excess cost recovery to be recaptured as ordinary income in 2016 is:

2014	
MACRS [($20,000 × .20 × 80%) (limited to $3,160 × 80%)]	$ 2,528
Straight-line [($20,000 × .10 × 80%) (limited to $3,160 × 80%)]	(1,600)
Excess	$ 928

2015	
MACRS [($20,000 × .32 × 70%) (limited to $5,100 × 70%)]	$ 3,570
Straight-line [($20,000 × .20 × 70%) (limited to $5,100 × 70%)]	(2,800)
Excess	$ 770

2016	
2014 excess	$ 928
2015 excess	770
Ordinary income recapture	$ 1,698

After the business usage of the listed property drops below the more-than-50 percent level, the straight-line method is used for the remaining life of the property.

Example 27	Assume the same facts as in Example 26. Seth's cost recovery deduction for 2016 and 2017 is:
	2016 $1,220 [($20,000 × .20 × 40%) limited to $3,050 × 40%]
	2017 $1,125 [($20,000 × .20 × 60%) limited to $1,875 × 60%]

Concept Summary 8.4 illustrates the cost recovery rules for various types of listed property.

Leased Automobiles

A taxpayer who leases a passenger automobile reports an *inclusion amount* in gross income. The inclusion amount is computed from an IRS table for each taxable year for which the taxpayer leases the automobile. The purpose of this provision is to prevent taxpayers from circumventing the luxury auto and other limitations by leasing, instead of purchasing, an automobile.

---

[24]§ 280F(b)(2).

CONCEPT SUMMARY 8.4

Listed Property Cost Recovery

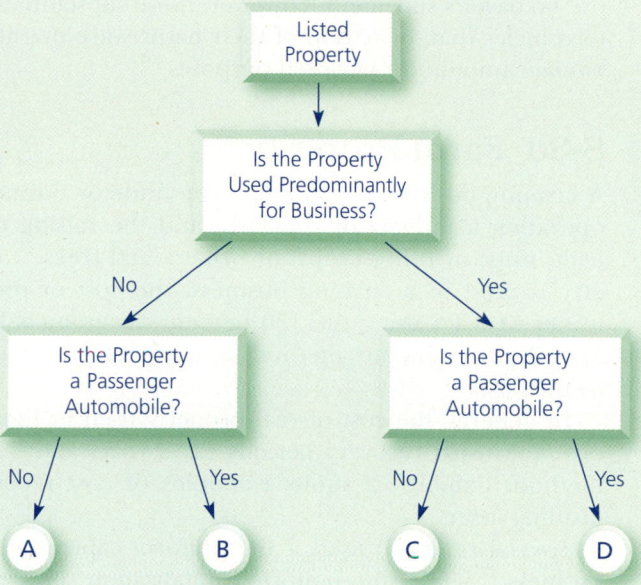

Legend to Tax Treatment

A   Straight-line cost recovery reduced by the personal use percentage.

B   Straight-line cost recovery subject to the recovery limitations that apply (based on the year placed in service) and reduced by the personal use percentage.

C   Statutory percentage cost recovery reduced by the personal use percentage.

D   Statutory percentage cost recovery subject to the recovery limitations that apply (based on the year placed in service) and reduced by the personal use percentage.

The inclusion amount is based on the fair market value of the automobile; it is prorated for the number of days the auto is used during the taxable year. The prorated dollar amount then is multiplied by the business and income-producing usage percentage.[25] The taxpayer deducts the lease payments, multiplied by the business and income-producing usage percentage. In effect, the taxpayer's annual deduction for the lease payment is reduced by the inclusion amount.

Example 28

On April 1, 2014, Jim leases and places in service a passenger automobile worth $52,400. The lease is to be for a period of five years. During the taxable years 2014 and 2015, Jim uses the automobile 70% for business and 30% for personal use.

Assuming that the dollar amounts from the IRS table for 2014 and 2015 are $20 and $43, respectively, Jim includes in gross income:

2014 $20 × (275/365) × 70% = $11
2015 $43 × (365/365) × 70% = $30

In each year, Jim still can deduct 70% of the lease payments made, related to his business use of the auto.

---

[25]Reg. § 1.280F–7(a).

Substantiation Requirements

Listed property is subject to the substantiation requirements of § 274. This means that the taxpayer must prove for any business usage the amount of expense or use, the time and place of use, the business purpose for the use, and the business relationship to the taxpayer of persons using the property.

Substantiation requires adequate records or sufficient evidence corroborating the taxpayer's statement. However, these substantiation requirements do not apply to vehicles that, by reason of their nature, are not likely to be used more than a *de minimis* amount for personal purposes.[26]

8-3d Farm Property

A farming business is defined as the trade or business of farming, which includes operating a nursery or sod farm and the raising or harvesting of trees bearing fruit, nuts, or other crops, or ornamental trees.[27] When tangible personal property is used in a farming business, the cost of the asset generally is recovered under MACRS using the 150 percent declining-balance method.[28] However, the MACRS straight-line method is required for any tree or vine bearing fruits or nuts.[29]

In general, the cost of real property used in the farming business is recovered over the usual recovery periods (27.5 years and 39 years) using the straight-line method. Exhibit 8.2 shows examples of cost recovery periods for some typical farming assets.

Special rules are used if the uniform capitalization rules apply to the farming business.[30] Under the uniform capitalization rules, the costs of property produced or acquired for resale must be capitalized.

Alternatively, the farmer can elect to apply the alternative depreciation system (ADS) straight-line method (discussed in Section 8-3f). Section 179 expensing can be used even when the ADS is in effect.[31]

Example 29	James purchased new farm equipment on July 10, 2014, for $80,000. If James does not elect to expense any of the cost under § 179, his cost recovery deduction for 2014 is $8,568 [(.1071 × $80,000) (Table 8.4)].

Example 30	Assume the same facts as in Example 29, except that James has made an election not to have the uniform capitalization rules apply. His 2014 cost recovery deduction is $4,000 [(.05 × $80,000) (Table 8.5)].

8-3e Leasehold Improvement Property

When the lessor is the owner of leasehold improvement property, the cost recovery period is the statutorily prescribed life. The recovery period for residential rental real estate is 27.5 years, and the recovery period for nonresidential real estate is 39 years. For these real property leasehold improvements, the straight-line method is used. If the improvement is tangible personal property, the shorter MACRS lives and accelerated methods are used.

---

[26]§§ 274(d) and (i).
[27]§ 263A(e)(4).
[28]§ 168(b)(2)(B).

[29]§§ 168(b)(3)(E) and 168(e)(3)(D)(ii).
[30]§ 263A(d)(3)(A).
[31]Reg. § 1.263A–4(d)(4)(ii).

EXHIBIT 8.2	**Cost Recovery Periods for Farming Assets**	

	Recovery Period in Years	
Assets	**MACRS**	**ADS**
Agricultural structures (single purpose)	10	15
Cattle (dairy or breeding)	5	7
Farm buildings	20	25
Farm machinery and equipment	7	10
Fences (agricultural)	7	10
Horticultural structures (single purpose)	10	15
Trees or vines bearing fruit or nuts	10	20
Truck (heavy-duty, unloaded weight 13,000 pounds or more)	5	6
Truck (actual weight less than 13,000 pounds)	5	5

When lessor-owned leasehold improvements are disposed of or abandoned by the lessor because of the termination of the lease, the property is treated as disposed of by the lessor; hence, a loss can be deducted relative to any unrecovered basis.[32]

> **Example 31**
>
> On April 7, 2014, Mary signed a 10-year lease with John on a building to be used for her business. The lease period begins on May 1, 2014, and ends on April 30, 2024. Prior to the signing of the lease, John paid $300,000 to have a unique storefront added to the building. John's cost recovery deduction for 2014 for the addition is $4,815 [(.01605 × $300,000) (Table 8.6)].

> **Example 32**
>
> Assume the same facts as in Example 31. John's cost recovery deduction for 2024 is $2,244 {[.02564 × (3.5/12) × $300,000] (Table 8.6)}. At the end of the lease, John must remove the unique storefront so that he can lease the building to other tenants. John's loss as a result of the termination of the lease and removal of the unique storefront is computed as follows.
>
> | | |
> |---|---|
> | Cost | $300,000 |
> | Less: Cost recovery | |
> | 2014 (see Example 31) | (4,815) |
> | 2015–2023 (.02564 × $300,000 × 9 years) | (69,228) |
> | 2024 | (2,244) |
> | Loss (unrecovered cost) | $223,713 |

The costs of improvements made to leased property and owned by the lessee are recovered in accordance with the general cost recovery rules. This means that the cost recovery period is determined without regard to the lease term. Any unrecovered basis in the leasehold improvement property not retained by the lessee is deducted in the year the lease is terminated.

---

[32]§ 163(i)(8)(B).

8-3f Alternative Depreciation System (ADS)

LO.5

Determine when and how to use the alternative depreciation system (ADS).

The **alternative depreciation system (ADS)** must be used:[33]

- To calculate the portion of depreciation treated as an alternative minimum tax (AMT) adjustment for purposes of the corporate and individual AMT (see Chapters 12 and 20).[34]
- To compute depreciation allowances for property for which any of the following is true.
  - Used predominantly outside the United States.
  - Leased or otherwise used by a tax-exempt entity.
  - Financed with the proceeds of tax-exempt bonds.
  - Imported from foreign countries that maintain discriminatory trade practices or otherwise engage in discriminatory acts.
- To compute depreciation allowances for earnings and profits purposes (see Chapter 20).

In general, ADS depreciation is computed using straight-line recovery. However, for purposes of the AMT, depreciation of personal property is computed using the 150 percent declining-balance method with an appropriate switch to the straight-line method.

The taxpayer must use the half-year or the mid-quarter convention, whichever is applicable, for all property other than eligible real estate. The mid-month convention is used for eligible real estate. The applicable ADS rates are found in Tables 8.4, 8.5, and 8.7.

The recovery periods under ADS are determined as follows.[35]

- The ADR midpoint life for property that does not fall into any of the following listed categories.
- Five years for qualified technological equipment, automobiles, and light-duty trucks.
- Twelve years for personal property with no class life.
- Forty years for all residential rental property and all nonresidential real property.

Taxpayers may *elect* to use the 150 percent declining-balance method to compute the regular income tax rather than the 200 percent declining-balance method that is available for personal property. Hence, when the election is made, there is no difference between the cost recovery for computing the regular income tax and the AMT.[36]

Example 33

On March 1, 2014, Abby purchases computer-based telephone central office switching equipment for $80,000. Abby elects not to take any available additional first-year depreciation. If Abby uses statutory percentage cost recovery (assuming no § 179 election), the cost recovery allowance for 2014 is $16,000 [$80,000 × 20% (Table 8.1, 5-year class property)]. If Abby elects to use ADS 150% declining-balance cost recovery for the regular income tax (assuming no § 179 election), the cost recovery allowance for 2014 is $12,000 [$80,000 × 15% (Table 8.4, 5-year class property)].

In lieu of depreciation under the regular MACRS method, taxpayers may *elect* straight-line under ADS for property that qualifies for the regular MACRS method. One reason for making this election is to avoid a difference between deductible

---

[33]§ 168(g).

[34]This AMT adjustment applies for real and personal property placed in service before 1999. However, it also applies for personal property placed in service after 1998 if the taxpayer uses the 200% declining-balance method for regular income tax purposes. See Chapter 12.

[35]The class life for certain properties described in § 168(e)(3) is specially determined under § 168(g)(3)(B).

[36]For personal property placed in service before 1999, taxpayers making the election use the ADS recovery periods in computing cost recovery for the regular income tax. The ADS recovery periods generally are longer than the regular recovery periods under MACRS.

depreciation and earnings and profits depreciation, thereby reducing the number of cost recovery computations that must be made.[37]

> **Example 34**
>
> Polly acquires an apartment building on March 17, 2014, for $700,000. She takes the maximum cost recovery allowance for determining taxable income. Polly's cost recovery allowance for computing 2014 taxable income is $20,153 [$700,000 × .02879 (Table 8.6)]. However, Polly's cost recovery for computing her earnings and profits is only $13,853 [$700,000 × .01979 (Table 8.7)].

8-4 REPORTING PROCEDURES

Sole proprietors engaged in a business file a Schedule C, Profit or Loss from Business, to accompany Form 1040. The 2014 Schedule C was not available at our press date, so a 2013 Schedule C is illustrated.

The top part of page 1 requests certain key information about the taxpayer (e.g., name, address, Social Security number, principal business activity, and accounting method used). Part I provides for the reporting of items of income. If the business requires the use of inventories and the computation of cost of goods sold (see Chapter 18 for when this is necessary), Part III must be completed and the cost of goods sold amount transferred to line 4 of Part I.

Part II allows for the reporting of deductions. Some of the deductions discussed in this chapter and their location on the form are depletion (line 12) and depreciation (line 13). Other expenses (line 27) include those items not already covered (see lines 8–26). An example is research and experimental expenditures.

If depreciation is claimed, it should be supported by completing Form 4562. The 2014 Form 4562 was not available at our press date, so a 2013 Form 4562 is illustrated. The amount listed on line 22 of Form 4562 is transferred to line 13 of Part II of Schedule C.

LO.6

Report cost recovery deductions appropriately.

> **Example 35**
>
> Thomas Andrews, Social Security number 111-11-1111, was employed as an accountant until May 2013, when he opened his own practice. His address is 279 Mountain View, Ogden, UT 84201. Andrews keeps his books on the cash basis and reported the following revenue and business expenses in 2013.
>
> a. Revenue from accounting practice, $192,000.
> b. Insurance, $5,000.
> c. Office supplies, $4,000.
> d. Office rent, $16,000.
> e. Copier lease payments, $3,000.
> f. Licenses, $2,000.
> g. New furniture and fixtures were acquired on May 10, for $142,000. Thomas elects § 179 expensing and uses the statutory percentage cost recovery method.
>
> Andrews reports the above information on Schedule C and Form 4562 as illustrated on the following pages.

8-5 AMORTIZATION

Taxpayers can claim an **amortization** deduction on intangible assets called "amortizable § 197 intangibles." The amount of the deduction is determined by amortizing the adjusted basis of such intangibles ratably over a 15-year period beginning in the month in which the intangible is acquired.[38]

LO.7

Identify intangible assets that are eligible for amortization and calculate the amount of the deduction.

---

[37]This straight-line election is made on a year-by-year basis. For property other than real estate, the election is made by MACRS class and applies to all assets in that MACRS class. So, for example, the election could be made for 7-year MACRS property and not for 5-year MACRS property placed in service during the same year. For real estate, the election is made on a property-by-property basis.

[38]§ 197(a).

Form **4562**	**Depreciation and Amortization** (Including Information on Listed Property)	OMB No. 1545-0172 **2013**
Department of the Treasury Internal Revenue Service (99)	▶ See separate instructions. ▶ Attach to your tax return.	Attachment Sequence No. **179**

Name(s) shown on return	Business or activity to which this form relates	Identifying number
Thomas Andrews	*Accounting services*	*111-11-1111*

Part I   Election To Expense Certain Property Under Section 179

Note: *If you have any listed property, complete Part V before you complete Part I.*

1 Maximum amount (see instructions)	**1**	
2 Total cost of section 179 property placed in service (see instructions)	**2**	*142,000*
3 Threshold cost of section 179 property before reduction in limitation (see instructions)	**3**	
4 Reduction in limitation. Subtract line 3 from line 2. If zero or less, enter -0-	**4**	*-0-*
5 Dollar limitation for tax year. Subtract line 4 from line 1. If zero or less, enter -0-. If married filing separately, see instructions	**5**	*142,000*

6	**(a)** Description of property	**(b)** Cost (business use only)	**(c)** Elected cost	
	Furniture and Fixtures	*142,000*	*142,000*	

7 Listed property. Enter the amount from line 29	**7**		
8 Total elected cost of section 179 property. Add amounts in column (c), lines 6 and 7	**8**	*142,000*
9 Tentative deduction. Enter the **smaller** of line 5 or line 8	**9**	*142,000*
10 Carryover of disallowed deduction from line 13 of your 2012 Form 4562	**10**	*-0-*
11 Business income limitation. Enter the smaller of business income (not less than zero) or line 5 (see instructions)	**11**	*142,000*
12 Section 179 expense deduction. Add lines 9 and 10, but do not enter more than line 11	**12**	*142,000*
13 Carryover of disallowed deduction to 2014. Add lines 9 and 10, less line 12 ▶	**13**	

Note: *Do not use Part II or Part III below for listed property. Instead, use Part V.*

Part II   Special Depreciation Allowance and Other Depreciation (Do not include listed property.) (See instructions.)

14 Special depreciation allowance for qualified property (other than listed property) placed in service during the tax year (see instructions)	**14**	
15 Property subject to section 168(f)(1) election	**15**	
16 Other depreciation (including ACRS)	**16**	

Part III   MACRS Depreciation (Do not include listed property.) (See instructions.)

Section A

17 MACRS deductions for assets placed in service in tax years beginning before 2013	**17**	
18 If you are electing to group any assets placed in service during the tax year into one or more general asset accounts, check here . . . . ▶ ☐		

Section B—Assets Placed in Service During 2013 Tax Year Using the General Depreciation System

(a) Classification of property	**(b)** Month and year placed in service	**(c)** Basis for depreciation (business/investment use only—see instructions)	**(d)** Recovery period	**(e)** Convention	**(f)** Method	**(g)** Depreciation deduction
19a 3-year property						
b 5-year property						
c 7-year property						
d 10-year property						
e 15-year property						
f 20-year property						
g 25-year property			25 yrs.		S/L	
h Residential rental property			27.5 yrs.	MM	S/L	
			27.5 yrs.	MM	S/L	
i Nonresidential real property			39 yrs.	MM	S/L	
				MM	S/L	

Section C—Assets Placed in Service During 2013 Tax Year Using the Alternative Depreciation System

20a Class life					S/L	
b 12-year			12 yrs.		S/L	
c 40-year			40 yrs.	MM	S/L	

Part IV   Summary (See instructions.)

21 Listed property. Enter amount from line 28	**21**	
22 **Total.** Add amounts from line 12, lines 14 through 17, lines 19 and 20 in column (g), and line 21. Enter here and on the appropriate lines of your return. Partnerships and S corporations—see instructions .	**22**	*142,000*
23 For assets shown above and placed in service during the current year, enter the portion of the basis attributable to section 263A costs	**23**	

For Paperwork Reduction Act Notice, see separate instructions.   Cat. No. 12906N   Form **4562** (2013)

SCHEDULE C
(Form 1040)

Department of the Treasury
Internal Revenue Service (99)

Profit or Loss From Business
(Sole Proprietorship)

▶ For information on Schedule C and its instructions, go to *www.irs.gov/schedulec*.
▶ Attach to Form 1040, 1040NR, or 1041; partnerships generally must file Form 1065.

OMB No. 1545-0074

20**13**

Attachment
Sequence No. **09**

Name of proprietor	Social security number (SSN)
Thomas Andrews	*111–11–1111*

A Principal business or profession, including product or service (see instructions)

B Enter code from instructions
▶

C Business name. If no separate business name, leave blank.
Andrews Accounting Services

D Employer ID number (EIN), (see instr.)

E Business address (including suite or room no.) ▶ *279 Mountain View*
City, town or post office, state, and ZIP code *Ogden, UT 84201*

F Accounting method: **(1)** ☒ Cash **(2)** ☐ Accrual **(3)** ☐ Other (specify) ▶

G Did you "materially participate" in the operation of this business during 2013? If "No," see instructions for limit on losses . ☒ **Yes** ☐ **No**

H If you started or acquired this business during 2013, check here . . . . ▶ ☐

I Did you make any payments in 2013 that would require you to file Form(s) 1099? (see instructions) . . . . ☐ **Yes** ☐ **No**

J If "Yes," did you or will you file required Forms 1099? . . . . ☐ **Yes** ☐ **No**

Part I Income

1	Gross receipts or sales. See instructions for line 1 and check the box if this income was reported to you on Form W-2 and the "Statutory employee" box on that form was checked . . . . ▶ ☐	**1**	*192,000*
2	Returns and allowances	**2**	
3	Subtract line 2 from line 1	**3**	*192,000*
4	Cost of goods sold (from line 42)	**4**	
5	**Gross profit.** Subtract line 4 from line 3	**5**	*192,000*
6	Other income, including federal and state gasoline or fuel tax credit or refund (see instructions) . . .	**6**	
7	**Gross income.** Add lines 5 and 6 . . . . ▶	**7**	*192,000*

Part II Expenses Enter expenses for business use of your home only on line 30.

8	Advertising	**8**		18	Office expense (see instructions)	**18**	*4,000*
9	Car and truck expenses (see instructions)	**9**		19	Pension and profit-sharing plans	**19**	
10	Commissions and fees .	**10**		20	Rent or lease (see instructions):		
11	Contract labor (see instructions)	**11**		a	Vehicles, machinery, and equipment	**20a**	*3,000*
12	Depletion	**12**		b	Other business property . . .	**20b**	*16,000*
13	Depreciation and section 179 expense deduction (not included in Part III) (see instructions)	**13**	*142,000*	21	Repairs and maintenance . . .	**21**	
				22	Supplies (not included in Part III) .	**22**	
				23	Taxes and licenses	**23**	*2,000*
				24	Travel, meals, and entertainment:		
14	Employee benefit programs (other than on line 19) . .	**14**	*5,000*	a	Travel	**24a**	
15	Insurance (other than health)	**15**		b	Deductible meals and entertainment (see instructions) .	**24b**	
16	Interest:			25	Utilities	**25**	
a	Mortgage (paid to banks, etc.)	**16a**		26	Wages (less employment credits) .	**26**	
b	Other	**16b**		27a	Other expenses (from line 48) . .	**27a**	
17	Legal and professional services	**17**		b	**Reserved for future use** . . .	**27b**	

28	**Total expenses** before expenses for business use of home. Add lines 8 through 27a . . . . ▶	**28**	*172,000*
29	Tentative profit or (loss). Subtract line 28 from line 7	**29**	*20,000*
30	Expenses for business use of your home. Do not report these expenses elsewhere. Attach Form 8829 unless using the simplified method (see instructions). **Simplified method filers only:** enter the total square footage of: (a) your home: _____ and (b) the part of your home used for business: _____ . Use the Simplified Method Worksheet in the instructions to figure the amount to enter on line 30	**30**	
31	**Net profit or (loss).** Subtract line 30 from line 29. • If a profit, enter on both **Form 1040, line 12** (or **Form 1040NR, line 13**) and on **Schedule SE, line 2.** (If you checked the box on line 1, see instructions). Estates and trusts, enter on **Form 1041, line 3.** • If a loss, you **must** go to line 32.	**31**	*20,000*
32	If you have a loss, check the box that describes your investment in this activity (see instructions). • If you checked 32a, enter the loss on both **Form 1040, line 12,** (or **Form 1040NR, line 13**) and on **Schedule SE, line 2.** (If you checked the box on line 1, see the line 31 instructions). Estates and trusts, enter on **Form 1041, line 3.** • If you checked 32b, you **must** attach **Form 6198.** Your loss may be limited.	**32a** ☐ All investment is at risk. **32b** ☐ Some investment is not at risk.	

For Paperwork Reduction Act Notice, see the separate instructions.   Cat. No. 11334P   **Schedule C (Form 1040) 2013**

TAX IN THE NEWS   Amortizing a Franchise

The Ricketts family purchased the Chicago Cubs for $845 million from the Tribune Company. The deal makes sense for the Ricketts because the tax breaks will enable them to save $100 million.

Section 197 of the Internal Revenue Code allows the cost of a franchise to be amortized over 15 years. Dividing the $845 million purchase price by 15 years produces a $56.3 million deduction against income each year for the next 15 years. If the projected income for the Cubs of about $45 million a year is realized, the $56 million amortization deduction will offset all of the team's gross income, and a zero tax will be due.

Source: Based on Josh Peter, "Buying Cubs Could Be a Steal for Ricketts," *Yahoo! Sports,* September 16, 2010.

An *amortizable § 197 intangible* is any § 197 intangible acquired after August 10, 1993, and held in connection with the conduct of a trade or business or for the production of income. Section 197 intangibles include goodwill and going-concern value, franchises, trademarks, and trade names. Covenants not to compete, copyrights, and patents also are included if they are acquired in connection with the acquisition of a business. Generally, self-created intangibles are not § 197 intangibles.

The 15-year amortization period applies regardless of the actual useful life of an amortizable § 197 intangible. No other depreciation or amortization deduction is permitted with respect to any amortizable § 197 intangible except those permitted under the 15-year amortization rules.

Example 36

On June 1, 2014, Neil purchased and began operating the Falcon Café. Of the purchase price, $90,000 is allocated to goodwill. The 2014 § 197 amortization deduction is $3,500 [($90,000/15) × (7/12)].

ETHICS & EQUITY   Allocation of Purchase Price to Covenant Not to Compete

Red Corporation and Bernie Jones, an officer of the corporation, signed an agreement that called for $400,000 to be paid to Bernie for the redemption of his Red stock and for a covenant not to compete.

When Bernie and Red negotiated the agreement, neither side called for the $400,000 to be allocated between the stock and the covenant not to compete. The agreement itself specifically stated that the amount to be paid was for the purchase of Bernie's stock. Nothing in the agreement allocated a portion of the payment to the covenant not to compete.

Now that the transaction has been completed, Red unilaterally is considering allocating a portion of the payment to the covenant not to compete, so that theallocated amount can be capitalized and amortized under § 197. Evaluate the appropriateness of this plan.

Startup expenditures are partially amortizable, by using a § 195 election.[39] A taxpayer must make this election no later than the due date of the return for the taxable year in which the trade or business begins.[40] If no election is made, the startup expenditures are capitalized.[41]

The amortization election for startup expenditures allows the taxpayer to deduct the lesser of (1) the amount of startup expenditures with respect to the trade or business or (2) $5,000, reduced, but not below zero, by the amount by which the startup expenditures exceed $50,000. Any startup expenditures not deducted are

---

[39]§ 195(b).
[40]§ 195(d).

[41]§ 195(a).

amortized ratably over a 180-month period, beginning in the month in which the trade or business begins.[42]

Example 37

Green Corporation begins business on August 1, 2014. The corporation incurs startup expenditures of $47,000. If Green elects amortization under § 195, the total startup expenditures that Green may deduct in 2014 is computed as follows.

Deductible amount	$5,000
Amortizable amount {[($47,000 − $5,000)/180] × 5 months}	1,167
Total deduction	$6,167

Example 38

Assume the same facts as in Example 37, except that the startup expenditures total $53,000. The 2014 deduction is computed as follows.

Deductible amount [$5,000 − ($53,000 − $50,000)]	$2,000
Amortizable amount {[($53,000 − $2,000)/180] × 5 months}	1,417
Total deduction	$3,417

Amortizable startup expenditures generally must satisfy two requirements.[43] First, the expenditures must be paid or incurred in connection with:

- The creation of an active trade or business,
- The investigation of the creation or acquisition of an active trade or business, or
- Any activity engaged in for profit in anticipation of such activity becoming an active trade or business.

Second, the expenditures must involve costs that the taxpayer could deduct if they were paid or incurred to operate a business currently in existence (in the same field that the taxpayer is entering).

The startup costs of creating a new active trade or business could include advertising; salaries and wages; travel and other expenses incurred in lining up prospective distributors, suppliers, or customers; and salaries and fees for executives, consultants, and professional services. Costs that relate to either created or acquired businesses could include expenses incurred for the analysis or survey of potential markets, products, labor supply, transportation facilities, and the like. Startup expenditures do not include allowable deductions for interest, taxes, and research and experimental costs.[44]

Amortization deductions also can be claimed for organizational expenses (see Chapter 20) and research and experimental expenditures(see Chapter 7).

ETHICS & EQUITY   **Business Expense or Startup Expense?**

Jim became interested in the real estate industry and decided to start an apartment rental business. In March of year 1, he purchased a duplex house comprising two side-by-side one-bedroom apartments. Because the property was in a severe state of disrepair, Jim began making extensive renovations in year 1. He intended to rent the property to third parties once the renovations were complete.

Jim completed the renovations early in year 2, after which he began to rent the property. Jim is considering deducting the renovation costs fully in year 1 as business expenses. Evaluate Jim's plan.

© iStockphoto.com/LdF

---

[42]§§ 195(b)(1)(A) and (B).
[43]§§ 195(c)(1)(A) and (B).

[44]§ 195(c).

TAX IN THE NEWS   Depletion of Air Space

Landfill operators are allowed a depletion allowance, which is a deduction in computing Federal taxable income. The depletion deduction is the value of the air space that is being filled up. The value of the air space is the product of some of the goodwill costs; some of the land costs; and all of the engineering, siting, and construction costs.

8-6 DEPLETION

LO.8

Determine the amount of depletion expense, including being able to apply the alternative tax treatments for intangible drilling and development costs.

Natural resources (e.g., oil, gas, coal, gravel, and timber) are subject to **depletion**, which can be seen as a form of depreciation applicable to natural resources. Land generally cannot be depleted.

The owner of an interest in the natural resource is entitled to deduct depletion. An owner is one who has an economic interest in the property.[45] An economic interest requires the acquisition of an interest in the resource in place and the receipt of income from the extraction or severance of that resource. Like depreciation, depletion is a trade or business deduction *for* adjusted gross income.

Although all natural resources are subject to depletion, oil and gas wells are used as an example in the following paragraphs to illustrate the related costs and issues.

In developing an oil or gas well, the producer typically makes four types of expenditures.

- Natural resource costs.
- Intangible drilling and development costs.
- Tangible asset costs.
- Operating costs.

Natural resources are physically limited, and the costs to acquire them (e.g., oil under the ground) are, therefore, recovered through depletion. Costs incurred in making the property ready for drilling, such as the cost of labor in clearing the property, erecting derricks, and drilling the hole, are **intangible drilling and development costs (IDCs)**. These costs generally have no salvage value and are a lost cost if the well is dry.

Costs for tangible assets such as tools, pipes, and engines are capital in nature. These costs must be capitalized and recovered through depreciation (cost recovery). Costs incurred after the well is producing are operating costs. These costs include expenditures for such items as labor, fuel, and supplies. Operating costs are deductible when incurred (on the accrual basis) or when paid (on the cash basis).

The expenditures for depreciable assets and operating costs pose no unusual problems for producers of natural resources. The tax treatment of depletable costs and intangible drilling and development costs is quite a different matter.

8-6a Intangible Drilling and Development Costs (IDCs)

Intangible drilling and development costs can be handled in one of two ways at the option of the taxpayer. They can be *either* charged off as an expense in the year in which they are incurred *or* capitalized and written off through depletion. The taxpayer makes the election in the first year such expenditures are incurred, either by taking a deduction on the return or by adding them to the depletable basis.

Once made, the election is binding on both the taxpayer and the IRS for all such expenditures in the future. If the taxpayer fails to elect to expense IDCs on

---

[45]Reg. § 1.611–1(b).

the original timely filed return for the first year in which such expenditures are incurred, an irrevocable election to capitalize them has been made.

As a general rule, it is more advantageous to expense IDCs. The obvious benefit of an immediate write-off (as opposed to a deferred write-off through depletion) is not the only advantage. Because a taxpayer can use percentage depletion, which is calculated without reference to basis (see Example 40), the IDCs may be completely lost as a deduction if they are capitalized.

8-6b Depletion Methods

There are two methods of calculating depletion. *Cost depletion* can be used on any wasting asset (and is the only method allowed for timber). *Percentage depletion* is subject to a number of limitations, particularly for oil and gas deposits. Depletion should be calculated both ways, and the method that results in the larger deduction should be used. The choice between cost depletion and percentage depletion is an annual decision; the taxpayer can use cost depletion in one year and percentage depletion in the following year.

Cost Depletion

Cost depletion is determined by using the adjusted basis of the asset.[46] The basis is divided by the estimated recoverable units of the asset (e.g., barrels and tons) to arrive at the depletion per unit. This amount then is multiplied by the number of units sold (*not* the units produced) during the year to arrive at the cost depletion allowed. Cost depletion, therefore, resembles the units-of-production method of calculating depreciation.

> **Example 39**
>
> On January 1, 2014, Pablo purchases the rights to a mineral interest for $1 million. At that time, the remaining recoverable units in the mineral interest are estimated to be 200,000. The depletion per unit is $5 ($1,000,000 adjusted basis ÷ 200,000 estimated recoverable units).
>
> If 60,000 units are mined and 25,000 are sold this year, the cost depletion is $125,000 ($5 depletion per unit × 25,000 units sold).

If the taxpayer later discovers that the original estimate was incorrect, the depletion per unit for future calculations is redetermined, using the revised estimate.[47]

> **Example 40**
>
> Assume the same facts as in Example 39. In 2015, Pablo realizes that an incorrect estimate was made as to the capacity of the mine. The remaining recoverable units now are determined to be 400,000. Based on this new information, the revised depletion per unit is $2.1875 ($875,000 adjusted basis ÷ 400,000 estimated recoverable units). The $875,000 adjusted basis is the original cost ($1,000,000) reduced by the depletion claimed in 2014 ($125,000).
>
> If 30,000 units are sold in 2015, the depletion for the year is $65,625 ($2.1875 depletion per unit × 30,000 units sold).

Percentage Depletion

Percentage depletion (also referred to as statutory depletion) uses a specified percentage provided by the Code. The percentage varies according to the type of mineral interest involved. A sample of these percentages is shown in Exhibit 8.3. The rate is applied to the gross income from the property, but in no event may percentage depletion exceed 50 percent of the taxable income from the property before the allowance for depletion.[48]

---

[46]§ 612.

[47]§ 611(a).

[48]§ 613(a). Special rules apply for certain oil and gas wells (e.g., the 50% ceiling is replaced with a 100% ceiling, and the percentage depletion

may not exceed 65% of the taxpayer's taxable income from all sources before the allowance for depletion). § 613A.

EXHIBIT 8.3	Sample of Percentage Depletion Rates

22% Depletion

Cobalt	Sulfur
Lead	Tin
Nickel	Uranium
Platinum	Zinc

15% Depletion

Copper	Oil and gas
Gold	Oil shale
Iron	Silver

14% Depletion

Borax	Magnesium carbonates
Calcium carbonates	Marble
Granite	Potash
Limestone	Slate

10% Depletion

Coal	Perlite
Lignite	Sodium chloride

5% Depletion

Gravel	Pumice
Peat	Sand

Example 41

CarrollCo reports gross income of $100,000, a depletion rate of 22%, and other property-related expenses of $60,000. CarrollCo's depletion allowance is determined as follows.

Gross income	$100,000
Less: Other expenses	(60,000)
Taxable income before depletion	$ 40,000
Depletion allowance [the lesser of $22,000 (22% × $100,000) or $20,000 (50% × $40,000)]	(20,000)
Taxable income after depletion	$ 20,000

The adjusted basis of CarrollCo's property is reduced by $20,000, the depletion deduction allowed. If the other expenses had been only $55,000, the full $22,000 could have been deducted, and the adjusted basis would have been reduced by $22,000.

Note that percentage depletion is based on a percentage of the gross income from the property and makes no reference to cost. Thus, when percentage depletion is used, it is possible to claim aggregate depletion deductions that exceed the original cost of the property. If percentage depletion is used, however, the adjusted basis of the property (for computing cost depletion in a future tax year) is reduced by the amount of percentage depletion taken until the adjusted basis reaches zero. See Example 45.

Effect of Intangible Drilling Costs on Depletion

The treatment of IDCs has an effect on the depletion deduction in two ways. If the costs are capitalized, the basis for cost depletion is increased. As a consequence, the cost depletion deductions can be increased. If IDCs are expensed, they reduce the taxable income from the property. This reduction may trigger the provision that limits depletion to 50 percent (100 percent for certain oil and gas wells) of taxable income before depletion is deducted.

Example 42

Iris purchased the rights to an oil interest for $1 million. The recoverable barrels were estimated to be 200,000. During the year, 50,000 barrels were sold for $2 million. Other business expenses amounted to $800,000, and IDCs totaled $650,000. If the IDCs are capitalized, the depletion per unit is $8.25 [($1,000,000 + $650,000) ÷ 200,000 barrels], and the following taxable income results.

Gross income	$2,000,000
Less: Expenses	(800,000)
Taxable income before depletion	$1,200,000
Cost depletion ($8.25 × 50,000) = $412,500	
Percentage depletion (15% × $2,000,000) = $300,000	
Greater of cost or percentage depletion	(412,500)
Taxable income	$ 787,500

If the IDCs are expensed, taxable income is calculated as follows.

Gross income	$ 2,000,000
Less: Expenses, including IDCs	(1,450,000)
Taxable income before depletion	$ 550,000
Cost depletion [($1,000,000 ÷ 200,000 barrels) × 50,000 barrels] = $250,000	
Percentage depletion (15% × $2,000,000 = $300,000, limited to 100% of $550,000 taxable income before depletion) = $300,000	
Greater of cost or percentage depletion	(300,000)
Taxable income	$ 250,000

8-7 TAX PLANNING

LO.9

Identify tax planning opportunities for cost recovery, amortization, and depletion.

8-7a Cost Recovery

Cost recovery schedules should be reviewed annually for possible retirements, abandonments, and obsolescence.

Example 43

An examination of the cost recovery schedule of Eagle Company reveals:

- Asset A was abandoned when it was discovered that the cost of repairs would be in excess of the cost of replacement. Asset A had an adjusted basis of $3,000.
- Asset J became obsolete this year, at which point its adjusted basis was $8,000.

Assets A and J should be written off, resulting in deductions of $11,000.

Because of the deductions for cost recovery, interest, and ad valorem property taxes, investments in real estate can be highly attractive. In examining the economics of such investments, one should take into account any tax savings that result.

THE BIG PICTURE

Example 44

Return to the facts of *The Big Picture* on p. 8-1. In early January 2013, Dr. Payne purchased residential rental property for $170,000 (of which $20,000 was allocated to the land and $150,000 to the building). He made a down payment of $25,000 and assumed the seller's mortgage for the balance. Under the mortgage agreement, monthly payments of $1,000 are required and are applied toward interest, taxes, insurance, and principal.

Because the property was already occupied, Payne continued to receive rent income of $1,200 per month from the tenant. He actively participates in this activity and so comes under the special rule for a rental real estate activity with respect to the limitation on passive activity losses (refer to Chapter 11). He is in the 28% tax bracket.

During 2014, Payne's expenses were determined to include:

Interest	$10,000
Taxes	800
Insurance	1,000
Repairs and maintenance	2,200
Depreciation ($150,000 × .03636)	5,454
Total expenses	$19,454

The deductible loss from the rental property is:

Rent income ($1,200 × 12 months)	$ 14,400
Less total expenses (see above)	(19,454)
Net loss	($ 5,054)

But what is Dr. Payne's net cash position for the year when the tax benefit of the loss is taken into account?

Intake—		
Rent income	$14,400	
Tax savings [28% (income tax bracket) × $5,054		
(loss from the property)]	1,415	$ 15,815
Outlay—		
Mortgage payments ($1,000 × 12 months)	$12,000	
Repairs and maintenance	2,200	(14,200)
Net cash benefit		$ 1,615

Should Payne cease to be an active participant in the rental activity, the passive activity loss rules would apply and he could lose the current period benefit of the loss.

Another consideration when making decisions with respect to cost recovery is whether fast or slow cost recovery will be more beneficial for the taxpayer. If the taxpayer's goal is to recover the cost of fixed assets as quickly as possible, the following strategies should be used.

- When constructing a facility, keep in mind any resulting property tax implications. Refer to the discussion in Chapter 1 on p. 1-7.
- When electing § 179 expensing, choose assets with longer lives.
- Choose accelerated cost recovery methods where available.

If a taxpayer has a new business with little income or a business with a net operating loss carryover, the taxpayer's goal may be to slow down cost recovery. In such a situation, the taxpayer should:

- Elect not to take additional first-year depreciation, if available.
- Choose the straight-line cost recovery method.
- Make no election under § 179.
- Defer placing assets in service in the current tax year or postpone capital outlays until future tax years.

Section 179 and the Mid-Quarter Convention

The mid-quarter convention generally results in smaller depreciation deductions in the asset's acquisition year. However, the basis of property used to determine whether the mid-quarter convention applies is derived *after* any § 179 immediate expense election.[49] As a result, a taxpayer may be able to avoid the mid-quarter convention by designating § 179 treatment for assets placed in service during the last quarter of the taxable year.

---

[49]Reg. § 1.168(d)–1(b)(4).

Tim Dimond places the following assets in service during 2014. All are 5-year class assets, and they are the only assets that Tim placed in service during the year.

Asset 1 (April 3, 2014)	$34,000
Asset 2 (July 17, 2014)	18,000
Asset 3 (October 22, 2014)	45,000
Total	$97,000

Example 45

As Tim has placed more than 40% of the assets in service during the last quarter of the taxable year, the mid-quarter convention applies ($45,000/$97,000 = 46.4%). As a result, his MACRS deduction for the year is computed as follows (see Table 8.2).

Asset 1	$34,000 × .25	$ 8,500
Asset 2	$18,000 × .15	2,700
Asset 3	$45,000 × .05	2,250
Total		$13,450

However, if Tim elects to expense $25,000 of the October 22 acquisition under § 179, the mid-quarter convention would not apply.

Asset 1 (April 3, 2014)	$34,000
Asset 2 (July 17, 2014)	18,000
Asset 3 (October 22, 2014; $45,000 − $25,000)	20,000
Total	$72,000

Now, Tim has placed only 27.8% ($20,000/$72,000) of the assets in service during the last quarter of the taxable year. As a result, the mid-quarter convention does not apply, and Tim's MACRS deduction for the year (including the § 179 expense election) is:

MACRS depreciation ($72,000 × .20; Table 8.1)	$14,400
Section 179 expense (Asset 3)	25,000
Total	$39,400

As a result of his effective use of § 179, Tim has increased his 2014 MACRS deduction and simplified his reporting and record keeping related to these assets.

8-7b Amortization

When a business is purchased, goodwill and covenants not to compete are both subject to a statutory amortization period of 15 years. Therefore, the purchaser does not derive any tax benefits when part of the purchase price is assigned to a covenant rather than to goodwill.

Thus, from the purchaser's perspective, bargaining for a covenant should be based on legal rather than tax reasons. Note, however, that from the seller's perspective, goodwill is a capital asset, and the covenant is an ordinary income asset.

Because the amortization period for both goodwill and a covenant is 15 years, the purchaser may want to attempt to minimize these amounts if the purchase price can be assigned to assets with shorter lives (e.g., inventory, receivables, and personalty). Conversely, the purchaser may want to attempt to maximize these amounts if part of the purchase price will otherwise be assigned to assets with longer recovery periods (e.g., realty) or to assets not eligible for cost recovery (e.g., land).

8-7c Depletion

As long as the basis of a depletable asset remains above zero, cost depletion or percentage depletion, whichever method produces the larger deduction, will be used. When the basis of the asset is exhausted, percentage depletion still can be taken.

Example 46

Melissa reports the following related to her sulfur mine.

Remaining depletable basis	$ 11,000
Gross income (10,000 units)	100,000
Expenses (other than depletion)	30,000

Because cost depletion is limited to the remaining depletable basis of $11,000, Melissa would choose percentage depletion of $22,000 (a 22% depletion rate is used for sulfur). Her basis in the mine then becomes zero. In future years, however, she can continue to take percentage depletion; percentage depletion is computed without reference to the remaining basis.

The election to expense intangible drilling and development costs is a one-time election. Once the election is made to either expense or capitalize the IDCs, it is binding on all future expenditures. The permanent nature of the election makes it extremely important for the taxpayer to determine which treatment will provide the greater tax advantage. (Refer to Example 42 for an illustration of the effect of using the two alternatives for a given set of facts.)

8-7d Cost Recovery Tables

Summary of Tables

Table 8.1	Modified ACRS statutory percentage table for personalty.
	Applicable depreciation methods: 200 or 150 percent declining-balance switching to straight-line.
	Applicable recovery periods: 3, 5, 7, 10, 15, 20 years.
	Applicable convention: half-year.
Table 8.2	Modified ACRS statutory percentage table for personalty.
	Applicable depreciation method: 200 percent declining-balance switching to straight-line.
	Applicable recovery periods: 3, 5, 7 years.
	Applicable convention: mid-quarter.
Table 8.3	Modified ACRS optional straight-line table for personalty.
	Applicable depreciation method: straight-line.
	Applicable recovery periods: 3, 5, 7, 10, 15, 20 years.
	Applicable convention: half-year.
Table 8.4	Alternative minimum tax declining-balance table for personalty.
	Applicable depreciation method: 150 percent declining-balance switching to straight-line.
	Applicable recovery periods: 3, 5, 7, 9.5, 10, 12 years.
	Applicable convention: half-year.
Table 8.5	Alternative depreciation system straight-line table for personalty.
	Applicable depreciation method: straight-line.
	Applicable recovery periods: 5, 10, 12 years.
	Applicable convention: half-year.
Table 8.6	Modified ACRS straight-line table for realty.
	Applicable depreciation method: straight-line.
	Applicable recovery periods: 27.5, 31.5, 39 years.
	Applicable convention: mid-month.
Table 8.7	Alternative depreciation system straight-line table for realty.
	Applicable depreciation method: straight-line.
	Applicable recovery period: 40 years.
	Applicable convention: mid-month.

TABLE 8.1	MACRS Accelerated Depreciation for Personal Property Assuming Half-Year Convention

For Property Placed in Service after December 31, 1986

Recovery Year	3-Year (200% DB)	5-Year (200% DB)	7-Year (200% DB)	10-Year (200% DB)	15-Year (150% DB)	20-Year (150% DB)
1	33.33	20.00	14.29	10.00	5.00	3.750
2	44.45	32.00	24.49	18.00	9.50	7.219
3	14.81*	19.20	17.49	14.40	8.55	6.677
4	7.41	11.52*	12.49	11.52	7.70	6.177
5		11.52	8.93*	9.22	6.93	5.713
6		5.76	8.92	7.37	6.23	5.285
7			8.93	6.55*	5.90*	4.888
8			4.46	6.55	5.90	4.522
9				6.56	5.91	4.462*
10				6.55	5.90	4.461
11				3.28	5.91	4.462
12					5.90	4.461
13					5.91	4.462
14					5.90	4.461
15					5.91	4.462
16					2.95	4.461
17						4.462
18						4.461
19						4.462
20						4.461
21						2.231

*Switchover to straight-line depreciation.

TABLE 8.2	MACRS Accelerated Depreciation for Personal Property Assuming Mid-Quarter Convention

For Property Placed in Service after December 31, 1986 (Partial Table*)

Recovery Year	First Quarter	3-Year Second Quarter	Third Quarter	Fourth Quarter
1	58.33	41.67	25.00	8.33
2	27.78	38.89	50.00	61.11

Recovery Year	First Quarter	5-Year Second Quarter	Third Quarter	Fourth Quarter
1	35.00	25.00	15.00	5.00
2	26.00	30.00	34.00	38.00

Recovery Year	First Quarter	7-Year Second Quarter	Third Quarter	Fourth Quarter
1	25.00	17.85	10.71	3.57
2	21.43	23.47	25.51	27.55

*The figures in this table are taken from the official tables that appear in Rev.Proc. 87–57, 1987–2 C.B. 687. Because of their length, the complete tables are not presented.

TABLE 8.3 **MACRS Straight-Line Depreciation for Personal Property Assuming Half-Year Convention***

For Property Placed in Service after December 31, 1986

MACRS Class	% First Recovery Year	Other Recovery Years		Last Recovery Year	
		Years	%	Year	%
3-year	16.67	2–3	33.33	4	16.67
5-year	10.00	2–5	20.00	6	10.00
7-year	7.14	2–7	14.29	8	7.14
10-year	5.00	2–10	10.00	11	5.00
15-year	3.33	2–15	6.67	16	3.33
20-year	2.50	2–20	5.00	21	2.50

*The official table contains a separate row for each year. For ease of presentation, certain years are grouped in this table. In some instances, this will produce a difference of .01 for the last digit when compared with the official table.

TABLE 8.4 **Alternative Minimum Tax: 150% Declining-Balance Assuming Half-Year Convention**

For Property Placed in Service after December 31, 1986 (Partial Table*)

Recovery Year	3-Year 150%	5-Year 150%	7-Year 150%	9.5-Year 150%	10-Year 150%	12-Year 150%
1	25.00	15.00	10.71	7.89	7.50	6.25
2	37.50	25.50	19.13	14.54	13.88	11.72
3	25.00**	17.85	15.03	12.25	11.79	10.25
4	12.50	16.66**	12.25**	10.31	10.02	8.97
5		16.66	12.25	9.17**	8.74**	7.85
6		8.33	12.25	9.17	8.74	7.33**
7			12.25	9.17	8.74	7.33
8			6.13	9.17	8.74	7.33
9				9.17	8.74	7.33
10				9.16	8.74	7.33
11					4.37	7.32
12						7.33
13						3.66

*The figures in this table are taken from the official table that appears in Rev.Proc. 87–57, 1987–2 C.B. 687. Because of its length, the complete table is not presented.
**Switchover to straight-line depreciation.

TABLE 8.5	ADS Straight-Line for Personal Property Assuming Half-Year Convention

For Property Placed in Service after December 31, 1986 (Partial Table)*

Recovery Year	5-Year Class	10-Year Class	12-Year Class
1	10.00	5.00	4.17
2	20.00	10.00	8.33
3	20.00	10.00	8.33
4	20.00	10.00	8.33
5	20.00	10.00	8.33
6	10.00	10.00	8.33
7		10.00	8.34
8		10.00	8.33
9		10.00	8.34
10		10.00	8.33
11		5.00	8.34
12			8.33
13			4.17

*The figures in this table are taken from the official table that appears in Rev.Proc. 87–57, 1987–2 C.B. 687. Because of its length, the complete table is not presented. The tables for the mid-quarter convention also appear in Rev.Proc. 87–57.

TABLE 8.6	MACRS Straight-Line Depreciation for Real Property Assuming Mid-Month Convention*

For Property Placed in Service after December 31, 1986: 27.5-Year Residential Real Property

Recovery Year(s)	The Applicable Percentage Is (Use the Column for the Month in the First Year the Property Is Placed in Service):											
	1	2	3	4	5	6	7	8	9	10	11	12
1	3.485	3.182	2.879	2.576	2.273	1.970	1.667	1.364	1.061	0.758	0.455	0.152
2–18	3.636	3.636	3.636	3.636	3.636	3.636	3.636	3.636	3.636	3.636	3.636	3.636
19–27	3.637	3.637	3.637	3.637	3.637	3.637	3.637	3.637	3.637	3.637	3.637	3.637
28	1.970	2.273	2.576	2.879	3.182	3.485	3.636	3.636	3.636	3.636	3.636	3.636
29	0.000	0.000	0.000	0.000	0.000	0.000	0.152	0.455	0.758	1.061	1.364	1.667

For Property Placed in Service after December 31, 1986, and before May 13, 1993: 31.5-Year Nonresidential Real Property

Recovery Year(s)	The Applicable Percentage Is (Use the Column for the Month in the First Year the Property Is Placed in Service):											
	1	2	3	4	5	6	7	8	9	10	11	12
1	3.042	2.778	2.513	2.249	1.984	1.720	1.455	1.190	0.926	0.661	0.397	0.132
2–19	3.175	3.175	3.175	3.175	3.175	3.175	3.175	3.175	3.175	3.175	3.175	3.175
20–31	3.174	3.174	3.174	3.174	3.174	3.174	3.174	3.174	3.174	3.174	3.174	3.174
32	1.720	1.984	2.249	2.513	2.778	3.042	3.175	3.175	3.175	3.175	3.175	3.175
33	0.000	0.000	0.000	0.000	0.000	0.000	0.132	0.397	0.661	0.926	1.190	1.455

For Property Placed in Service after May 12, 1993: 39-Year Nonresidential Real Property

Recovery Year(s)	The Applicable Percentage Is (Use the Column for the Month in the First Year the Property Is Placed in Service):											
	1	2	3	4	5	6	7	8	9	10	11	12
1	2.461	2.247	2.033	1.819	1.605	1.391	1.177	0.963	0.749	0.535	0.321	0.107
2–39	2.564	2.564	2.564	2.564	2.564	2.564	2.564	2.564	2.564	2.564	2.564	2.564
40	0.107	0.321	0.535	0.749	0.963	1.177	1.391	1.605	1.819	2.033	2.247	2.461

*The official tables contain a separate row for each year. For ease of presentation, certain years are grouped in these tables. In some instances, this will produce a difference of .001 for the last digit when compared with the official tables.

TABLE 8.7		ADS Straight-Line for Real Property Assuming Mid-Month Convention										

For Property Placed in Service after December 31, 1986

Recovery Year	Month Placed in Service											
	1	2	3	4	5	6	7	8	9	10	11	12
1	2.396	2.188	1.979	1.771	1.563	1.354	1.146	0.938	0.729	0.521	0.313	0.104
2–40	2.500	2.500	2.500	2.500	2.500	2.500	2.500	2.500	2.500	2.500	2.500	2.500
41	0.104	0.312	0.521	0.729	0.937	1.146	1.354	1.562	1.771	1.979	2.187	2.396

REFOCUS ON THE BIG PICTURE

CALCULATING COST RECOVERY DEDUCTIONS

Regardless of whether the accrual method or the cash method of accounting is used, MACRS must be used in calculating the depreciation expense for fixed assets for tax purposes. Evidently, Dr. Payne's financial reporting system uses MACRS, because $91,298 is the correct amount of depreciation expense. The computers and peripheral equipment are 5-year property. The office furniture and fixtures and the dental equipment are 7-year property.

Based on the IRS cost recovery tables, the following percentages are used in calculating depreciation expense for the first year of each asset's life.

5-year property	20.00%
7-year property	14.29%

Payne can deduct depreciation on the house he converted from personal use to rental use, and on the rental house he purchased.

What If?

From a tax planning perspective, what can Dr. Payne do to increase the depreciation deductions associated with the purchase of these fixed assets and thereby reduce the amount of the business net income reported on Schedule C of Form 1040 for his dental practice?

In addition to the standard MACRS deduction using the percentages for 2014, § 179 provides for the limited expensing of fixed assets. This provision applies to personalty, but does not apply to realty (e.g., buildings). The maximum amount that can be deducted under this limited expensing provision is subject to several overall limits. First, the total amount deducted cannot exceed $25,000. Second, the $25,000 amount is reduced dollar for dollar for § 179 asset purchases placed in service during the tax year once such purchases exceed $200,000. Finally, the § 179 deduction for a tax year cannot exceed the taxable income from the trade or business. Unfortunately, given that Dr. Payne has placed more than $225,000 of assets in service in 2014, § 179 is not available to him. In addition, unless Congress makes a law change during 2014, additional first-year depreciation ceased at the end of 2013.

For future reference associated with similar fixed asset purchases for his business, the sequence of calculating the deduction is as follows.

- § 179 limited expensing.
- Additional first-year depreciation, if available.
- Standard MACRS cost recovery.

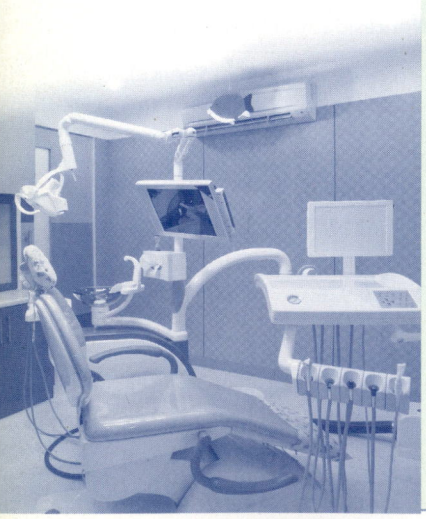

Key Terms

Accelerated cost recovery system (ACRS), 8-2

Additional first-year depreciation, 8-12

Alternative depreciation system (ADS), 8-22

Amortization, 8-23

Cost depletion, 8-29

Cost recovery, 8-2

Depletion, 8-28

Depreciation, 8-2

Half-year convention, 8-7

Intangible drilling and development costs (IDCs), 8-28

Listed property, 8-14

Mid-month convention, 8-10

Mid-quarter convention, 8-8

Modified accelerated cost recovery system (MACRS), 8-2

Percentage depletion, 8-29

Residential rental real estate, 8-10

Section 179 expensing, 8-13

Startup expenditures, 8-26

Discussion Questions

1. **LO.1** Discuss whether property that is classified as personal use is subject to cost recovery.

2. **LO.1** Discuss the difference between personal property and personal use property.

3. **LO.1** Discuss whether land improvements are eligible for cost recovery.

4. **LO.2** At the beginning of the current year, Henry purchased a ski resort for $10 million. Henry does not own the land on which the resort is located. The Federal government owns the land, and Henry has the right to operate the resort on the land pursuant to Special Use Permits, which are terminable at will by the Federal government, and Term Special Use Permits, which allow the land to be used for a fixed number of years.

   In preparing the income tax return for the current year, Henry properly allocated $2 million of the purchase price to the costs of constructing mountain roads, slopes, and trails. Since the acquisition, Henry has spent an additional $1 million on maintaining the mountain roads, slopes, and trails. Identify the relevant tax issues for Henry.

   Issue ID

5. **LO.2** Discuss whether the date that an asset is placed in service is important in determining whether the mid-quarter convention applies for personalty.

6. **LO.2** Identify the three factors reflected in the MACRS tables when the amount of cost recovery is determined.

7. **LO.2** Discuss the computation of cost recovery in the year an asset is placed in service when the mid-quarter convention is being used.

8. **LO.2** Discuss what property qualifies for additional first-year depreciation.

9. **LO.2** Discuss the computation of cost recovery in the year of sale of an asset when the mid-quarter convention is being used.

10. **LO.2** Discuss the definition of residential rental real estate.

11. **LO.2** Robert purchased and placed in service $100,000 of 7-year class assets on August 10 of the current year. He also purchased and placed in service $500,000 of 5-year class assets on November 15 of the current year. He does not claim any available additional first-year depreciation. If Robert elects to use the MACRS straight-line method of cost recovery on the 7-year class assets, discuss the calculation of cost recovery for the 5-year class assets.

12. **LO.2** Discuss the general cost recovery method for farming assets.

13. **LO.2** Discuss whether § 179 is applicable when a farmer uses ADS computations for depreciable assets.

14. **LO.2** Jim owns a very large ranch. A large part of his business is the production and raising of breeding cattle. Jim understands that he is entitled to use MACRS cost recovery on breeding cattle. Identify the relevant tax issues for Jim with respect to taking cost recovery on his self-produced breeding cattle.

    Issue ID

15. **LO.2** Discuss the cost recovery periods and methods to be used on leasehold improvement property owned by the lessor.

16. **LO.2** Discuss the cost recovery periods and methods to be used on leasehold improvement property owned by the lessee.

17. **LO.3** Discuss whether § 179 expensing may be taken on qualified property used in a transaction entered into for profit.

18. **LO.3** Discuss when § 179 expense must be recaptured.

19. **LO.3** Explain how the § 179 limited expensing deduction affects the computation of MACRS cost recovery.

20. **LO.3** Discuss the treatment of a § 179 expensing carryforward.

21. **LO.3** Discuss the definition of *taxable income* as it is used in limiting the § 179 expensing amount.

Issue ID 22. **LO.2, 3** A professional consulting business sells professional tools and equipment and provides associated services, such as repair and maintenance, to its customer base. The company's employees include technicians, who are required to provide and maintain their own tools and equipment for performing the repairs and maintenance work. The company will reimburse a technician for amounts spent to purchase tools and equipment eligible for a § 179 deduction up to a set amount each year. Any costs for tools and equipment that exceed the set amount will not be reimbursed.

   John is a technician for the company. During the current year, he purchased equipment that qualifies for the § 179 deduction. John paid $50,000 for the equipment and was reimbursed the set amount of $40,000. Identify the relevant tax issues for John with respect to § 179 and the computation of his taxable income.

23. **LO.3, 4** Discuss the implications of an automobile that is used in a trade or business and has a gross vehicle weight (GVW) exceeding 6,000 pounds.

24. **LO.4** Discuss how the limits on cost recovery apply to listed property.

25. **LO.4** Discuss the tax consequences if the business use percentage of listed property falls to 50% or lower after the year the property is placed in service.

26. **LO.7** Explain the amortization period of a § 197 intangible if the actual useful life is less than 15 years.

Issue ID 27. **LO.7** Harold and Bart own 75% of the stock of Orange Motors. The other 25% of the stock is owned by Jeb. Orange Motors entered into an agreement with Harold and Bart to acquire all of their Orange stock.

   In addition, Harold and Bart signed a noncompete agreement with Orange Motors. Under the terms of the noncompete agreement, Orange will pay Harold and Bart $15,000 each per year for four years. Identify the relevant tax issues for Orange Motors.

28. **LO.7** Discuss the amortization of startup expenditures.

Issue ID 29. **LO.7** In May 2014, George began searching for a trade or business to acquire. In anticipation of finding a suitable aquisition, George hired an investment banker to evaluate three potential businesses. He also hired a law firm to begin drafting regulatory approval documents for a target company. Eventually, George decided to purchase all of the assets of Brash Corporation. Brash and George entered into an acquisition agreement on December 1, 2014. Identify the relevant tax issues for George.

30. **LO.8** Discuss how the cost of mineral rights enters into the calculation of cost depletion.

Problems

31. **LO.1, 2** On November 4, 2012, Blue Company acquired an asset (27.5-year residential real property) for $200,000 for use in its business. In 2012 and 2013, respectively, Blue took $642 and $5,128 of cost recovery. These amounts were incorrect; Blue applied the wrong percentages (i.e., those for 39-year rather than 27.5-year assets). Blue should have taken $910 and $7,272 cost recovery in 2012 and 2013, respectively. On January 1, 2014, the asset was sold for $180,000. Calculate the gain or loss on the sale of the asset in 2014.

32. **LO.1, 2** José purchased a house for $300,000 in 2011. He used the house as his personal residence. In March 2014, when the fair market value of the house was $400,000, he converted the house to rental property. What is José's cost recovery for 2014?

33. **LO.2** Orange Corporation acquired new office furniture on August 15, 2014, for $210,000. Orange elects immediate expensing under § 179. Orange does not claim any available additional first-year depreciation. Determine Orange's cost recovery for 2014.

34. **LO.2** Weston acquires a new office machine (7-year class asset) on November 2, 2013, for $75,000. This is the only asset Weston acquired during the year. He does not elect immediate expensing under § 179. He claims the maximum additional first-year depreciation deduction. On September 15, 2014, Weston sells the machine.
    a. Determine Weston's cost recovery for 2013.
    b. Determine Weston's cost recovery for 2014.

35. **LO.2** Juan acquires a new 5-year class asset on March 14, 2014, for $200,000. This is the only asset Juan acquired during the year. He does not elect immediate expensing under § 179. He does not claim any available additional first-year depreciation. On July 15, 2015, Juan sells the asset.
    a. Determine Juan's cost recovery for 2014.
    b. Determine Juan's cost recovery for 2015.

36. **LO.2** Debra acquired the following new assets during 2014.

Date	Asset	Cost
April 11	Furniture	$40,000
July 28	Trucks	40,000
November 3	Computers	70,000

Determine Debra's cost recovery deductions for the current year. Debra does not elect immediate expensing under § 179. She does not claim any available additional first-year depreciation.

37. **LO.2** On August 2, 2014, Wendy purchased a new office building for $3.8 million. On October 1, 2014, she began to rent out office space in the building. On July 15, 2018, Wendy sold the office building.
    a. Determine Wendy's cost recovery deduction for 2014.
    b. Determine Wendy's cost recovery deduction for 2018.

38. **LO.2** On April 3, 2014, Terry purchased and placed in service a building. The building cost $2 million. An appraisal determined that 25% of the total cost was attributed to the value of the land. The bottom floor of the building is leased to a retail business for $32,000. The other floors of the building are rental apartments with an annual rent of $160,000. Determine Terry's cost recovery deduction for 2014.

39. **LO.2** On May 5, 2014, Christy purchased and placed in service a hotel. The hotel cost $10.8 million. Calculate Christy's cost recovery deductions for 2014 and for 2024.

40. **LO.2** Janice acquired an apartment building on June 4, 2014, for $1.6 million. The value of the land is $300,000. Janice sold the apartment building on November 29, 2020.
    a. Determine Janice's cost recovery deduction for 2014.
    b. Determine Janice's cost recovery deduction for 2020.

41. **LO.2** On April 20, 2014, Ralph purchased used equipment to be used in his farming business. The cost of the equipment is $150,000. Ralph does not elect immediate expensing under § 179, nor does he elect not to have the uniform capitalization rules apply. Compute Ralph's cost recovery deduction for 2014.

42. **LO.2** During March 2014, Sam constructed new agricultural fences on his farm. The cost of the fencing was $80,000. Sam does not elect immediate expensing under § 179, and he does not claim any available additional first-year depreciation. However, an election not to have the uniform capitalization rules apply is in effect. Compute Sam's cost recovery deduction for 2014. Sam wants to maximize his cost recovery deductions.

43. **LO.2** As a condition of leasing a 10-year-old warehouse, Martha was required to make capital improvements to the interior of the building to accommodate the lessee. These improvements cost Martha $300,000. The improvements were completed, and the 10-year lease commenced on October 28, 2014. Martha does not claim any available additional first-year depreciation. Determine Martha's cost recovery for 2014 with respect to the leasehold improvement.

44. **LO.2** On January 1, 2006, Jim leased a building to be used in his business as an office building. The lease will terminate on December 31, 2014. On February 2, 2008, Jim made a capital improvement to the exterior of the building. The cost of the leasehold improvement to Jim was $80,000. Jim has no legal rights in the capital improvement after the termination of the lease. Determine Jim's 2014 loss deduction for unrecovered costs, if any, with respect to the leasehold improvement as a result of the termination of the lease.

Decision Making   45. **LO.2, 3, 9** Lori, who is single, purchased 5-year class property for $31,000 and 7-year class property for $42,000 on May 20, 2014. Lori expects the taxable income derived from her business (without regard to the amount expensed under § 179) to be about $100,000. Lori wants to elect immediate § 179 expensing, but she doesn't know which asset she should expense under § 179. She does not claim any available additional first-year depreciation.
    a. Determine Lori's total deduction if the § 179 expense is first taken with respect to the 5-year class asset.
    b. Determine Lori's total deduction if the § 179 expense is first taken with respect to the 7-year class asset.
    c. What is your advice to Lori?

46. **LO.2, 3** Olga is the proprietor of a small business. In 2014, the business's income, before consideration of any cost recovery or § 179 deduction, is $104,000.
    Olga spends $40,000 on new 7-year class assets and elects to take the § 179 deduction on them. She does not claim any available additional first-year depreciation. Olga's cost recovery deduction for 2014, except for the cost recovery with respect to the new 7-year assets, is $86,000. Determine Olga's total cost recovery for 2014 with respect to the 7-year class assets and the amount of any § 179 carryforward.

47. **LO.2, 3, 9** On June 5, 2013, Dan purchased and placed in service a 7-year class asset costing $550,000. Determine the maximum deductions that Dan can claim with respect to this asset in 2013 and 2014.

Communications   48. **LO.3, 4** John Johnson is considering acquiring an automobile at the beginning of 2014 that he will use 100% of the time as a taxi. The purchase price of the automobile is $35,000. John has heard of cost recovery limits on automobiles and wants to know how much of the $35,000 he can deduct in the first year.
    Write a letter to John in which you present your calculations. Also prepare a memo for the tax files, summarizing your analysis. John's address is 100 Morningside, Clinton, MS 39058.

49. **LO.2, 4** On October 15, 2014, Jon purchased and placed in service a used car. The purchase price was $25,000. This was the only business use asset Jon acquired in 2014. He used the car 80% of the time for business and 20% for personal use. Jon used the MACRS statutory percentage method. Calculate the total deduction Jon may take for 2014 with respect to the car.

50. **LO.4** On June 5, 2013, Leo purchased and placed in service a new car that cost $20,000. The business use percentage for the car is always 100%. Leo claims any available additional first-year depreciation. Compute Leo's cost recovery deductions for 2013 and 2014.

51. **LO.2, 3, 4** On March 15, 2014, Helen purchased and placed in service a new Escalade. The purchase price was $62,000, and the vehicle had a rating of 6,500 GVW. The vehicle was used 100% for business. Calculate the maximum total depreciation deduction that Helen may take with respect to the vehicle in 2014.

52. **LO.2, 4** On May 28, 2014, Mary purchased and placed in service a new $20,000 car. The car was used 60% for business, 20% for production of income, and 20% for personal use in 2014. In 2015, the usage changed to 40% for business, 30% for production of income, and 30% for personal use. Mary did not elect immediate expensing under § 179. She did not claim any available additional first-year depreciation. Compute Mary's cost recovery deduction and any cost recovery recapture in 2015.

53. **LO.2, 4, 9** Sally purchased a new computer (5-year property) on June 1, 2014, for $4,000. Sally could use the computer 100% of the time in her business, or she could allow her family to use the computer as well. Sally estimates that if her family uses the computer, the business use will be 45% and the personal use will be 55%.

    Determine the tax cost to Sally, in the year of acquisition, of allowing her family to use the computer. Assume that Sally would not elect § 179 limited expensing and that her marginal tax rate is 28%. She does not claim any available additional first-year depreciation.

    Decision Making

54. **LO.2, 4, 9** Dennis Harding is considering acquiring a new automobile that he will use 100% for business. The purchase price of the automobile would be $48,500. If Dennis leased the car for five years, the lease payments would be $375 per month. Dennis will acquire the car on January 1, 2014. The inclusion dollar amounts from the IRS table for the next five years are $19, $42, $63, $75, and $87.

    Dennis wants to know the effect on his adjusted gross income of purchasing versus leasing the car for the next five years. He does not claim any available additional first-year depreciation. Write a letter to Dennis and present your calculations. Also prepare a memo for the tax files. His address is 150 Avenue I, Memphis, TN 38112.

    Decision Making

    Communications

55. **LO.2, 5** In 2014, Muhammad purchased a new computer for $16,000. The computer is used 100% for business. Muhammad did not make a § 179 election with respect to the computer. He does not claim any available additional first-year depreciation. If Muhammad uses the MACRS statutory percentage method, determine his cost recovery deduction for 2014 for computing taxable income, and for computing his alternative minimum tax.

56. **LO.2, 5, 9** Jamie purchased $100,000 of new office furniture for her business in June of the current year. Jamie understands that if she elects to use ADS to compute her regular income tax, there will be no difference between the cost recovery for computing the regular income tax and the AMT. Jamie wants to know the *regular* income tax cost, after three years, of using ADS rather than MACRS. Assume that Jamie does not elect § 179 limited expensing and that her marginal tax rate is 28%. She does not claim any available additional first-year depreciation.

    Decision Making

57. **LO.2, 7, 9** Mike Saxon is negotiating the purchase of a business. The final purchase price has been agreed upon, but the allocation of the purchase price to the assets is still being discussed. Appraisals on a warehouse range from $1.2 million to $1.5 million. If a value of $1.2 million is used for the warehouse, the remainder of the purchase price, $800,000, will be allocated to goodwill. If $1.5 million is allocated to the warehouse, goodwill will be $500,000.

    Mike wants to know what effect each alternative will have on cost recovery and amortization during the first year. Under the agreement, Mike will take over the business on January 1 of next year. Write a letter to Mike in which you present your calculations and recommendation. Also prepare a memo for the tax files. Mike's address is 200 Rolling Hills Drive, Shavertown, PA 18708.

    Decision Making

    Communications

58. **LO.7** Oleander Corporation, a calendar year entity, begins business on March 1, 2014. The corporation incurs startup expenditures of $64,000. If Oleander elects § 195 treatment, determine the total amount of startup expenditures that it may deduct in 2014.

59. **LO.7** Martha was considering starting a new business. During her preliminary investigations related to the new venture, she incurred the following expenditures.

Salaries	$22,000
Travel	18,000
Interest on short-term note	4,000
Professional fees	13,000

    Martha begins the business on July 1 of the current year. If Martha elects § 195 treatment, determine her startup expenditure deduction for the current year.

60. **LO.8** Wes acquired a mineral interest during the year for $10 million. A geological survey estimated that 250,000 tons of the mineral remained in the deposit. During the year, 80,000 tons were mined, and 45,000 tons were sold for $12 million. Other related expenses amounted to $5 million. Assuming that the mineral depletion rate is 22%, calculate Wes's lowest taxable income, after any depletion deductions.

Decision Making

61. **LO.8, 9** Chris purchased an oil interest for $2 million. Recoverable barrels were estimated to be 500,000. During the year, 120,000 barrels were sold for $3.84 million, other business expenses (including cost recovery) were $1.24 million, and IDCs were $1 million. Calculate Chris's taxable income under the expensing and capitalization methods of accounting for IDCs.

Cumulative Problems

Tax Return Problem

TAX SOFTWARE

62. Janice Morgan, age 32, is single and has no dependents. She is a freelance writer. In January 2013, Janice opened her own office located at 2751 Waldham Road, Pleasant Hill, NM 88135. She called her business Writers Anonymous. Janice is a cash basis taxpayer. She lives at 132 Stone Avenue, Pleasant Hill, NM 88135. Her Social Security number is 123-45-6789. Janice wants to contribute to the Presidential Election Campaign Fund.

During 2013, Janice reported the following income and expense items connected with her business.

Income from sale of articles	$85,000
Rent	16,500
Utilities	7,900
Supplies	1,800
Insurance	5,000
Travel (including meals of $1,200)	3,500

Janice purchased and placed in service the following fixed assets for her business. Janice wants to elect immediate expensing under § 179.

- Furniture and fixtures (new) costing $21,000 on January 10.
- Computer equipment (new) costing $12,400 on July 28.

Janice's itemized deductions include:

State income tax	$3,000
Home mortgage interest paid to First Bank	6,000
Property taxes on home	1,500
Charitable contributions	1,200

Janice did not keep a record of the sales tax she paid. The pertinent amount from the sales tax table is $437.

Janice reports interest income of $4,000 on certificates of deposit at Second Bank. Janice makes estimated tax payments of $3,000 for 2013.

Compute Janice Morgan's 2013 Federal income tax payable (or refund due). If you use tax forms for your computations, you will need Forms 1040 and 4562 and Schedules A, B, and C. Suggested software: H&R BLOCK Tax Software.

Tax Computation Problem

Decision Making

Communications

63. John Smith, age 31, is single and has no dependents. At the beginning of 2014, John started his own excavation business and named it Earth Movers. John lives at 1045 Center Street, Lindon, UT, and his business is located at 381 State Street, Lindon, UT. The ZIP Code for both addresses is 84042. John's Social Security number is 111-11-1111, and the business identification number is 11-1111111. John is a cash basis taxpayer.

During 2014, John reports the following items in connection with his business.

Fee income for services rendered	$460,000
Building rental expense	36,000
Office furniture and equipment rental expense	9,000
Office supplies	2,500
Utilities	4,000
Salary for secretary	34,000
Salary for equipment operators	42,000
Payroll taxes	7,000
Fuel and oil for the equipment	21,000
Purchase of three new front-end loaders on January 15, 2014, for $550,000.	550,000
Purchase of a new dump truck on January 18, 2014	80,000

During 2014, John recorded the following additional items.

Interest income from First National Bank	$10,000
Dividends from ExxonMobil	9,500
Quarterly estimated tax payments	11,500

John does not claim any available additional first-year depreciation.

On October 8, 2014, John inherited IBM stock from his Aunt Mildred. John had been her favorite nephew. According to the data provided by the executor of Aunt Mildred's estate, the stock was valued for estate tax purposes at $110,000. John is considering selling the IBM stock for $125,000 on December 29, 2014, and using $75,000 of the proceeds to purchase an Acura ZDX. He would use the car 100% for business. John wants to know what effect these transactions would have on his 2014 adjusted gross income.

Write a letter to John in which you present your calculations, and prepare a memo for the tax files. Ignore any Federal self-employment tax implications.

Research Problems

Note: Solutions to Research Problems can be prepared by using the **Checkpoint®** **Student Edition** online research product, which is available to accompany this text. It is also possible to prepare solutions to the Research Problems by using tax research materials found in a standard tax library.

THOMSON REUTERS
CHECKPOINT®

Research Problem 1. Your client, Dave's Sport Shop, sells sports equipment and clothing in three retail outlets in New York City. Earlier this year, the CFO decided that keeping track of inventory using a combination of QuickBooks and Excel was not an efficient way to manage the stores' inventories. So Dave's purchased an inventory management system for $9,000 that allowed the entity to keep track of inventory, as well as automate ordering and purchasing, without replacing QuickBooks for its accounting function.

The CFO would like to know whether the cost of the inventory management program can be expensed in the year of purchase. Write a letter to the CFO, Cassandra Martin, that addresses the tax treatment of purchased software. Cassandra's mailing address is 867 Broadway, New York, NY 10003.

Communications

Research Problem 2. Acme Motors sells and leases automobiles. Acme administers a leasing program for its employees. The lease terminates automatically if the employee (lessee) ceases to be employed by Acme. The leases make autos available solely for the lessee's personal use; they do not involve use of the automobile in the employee's employment-related activities for Acme. The leased vehicles are registered and titled in Acme's name, and Acme pays all registration fees, insurance, and maintenance costs.

Acme wants to know whether the leased vehicles are exempt from the depreciation limitations of § 280F for purposes of computing its taxable income.

Research Problem 3. In 2010, Jed James began planting a vineyard. The costs of the land preparation, labor, rootstock, and planting were capitalized. The land preparation costs do not include any nondepreciable land costs. In 2014, when the plants became viable, Jed placed the vineyard in service. Jed wants to know whether he can claim a deduction under § 179 on his 2014 income tax return for the costs incurred in 2010 with respect to planting the vineyard.

Research Problem 4. Juan owns a business that acquires exotic automobiles that are high-tech, state-of-the-art vehicles with unique design features or equipment. The exotic automobiles are not licensed or set up to be used on the road. Rather, the cars are used exclusively for car shows or related promotional photography. With respect to the exotic automobiles, Juan would like to know whether he can take a cost recovery deduction on his Federal income tax return.

Partial list of research aids:
Bruce Selig, 70 TCM 1125, T.C.Memo. 1995–519.

Research Problem 5. Green Corporation is in the business of providing consulting and management services to insolvent companies. George Jones, one of the founders of the company, entered into a buyout agreement with Green Corporation whereunder Green agreed to acquire all of George's stock, which represents 30% of Green's outstanding stock. Green also paid George $600,000 for signing a noncompetition and nonsolicitation agreement prohibiting George from engaging in competitive activities for two years. Green would like to know how the $600,000 should be treated for tax purposes.

Internet Activity

Use the tax resources of the Internet to address the following questions. Do not restrict your search to the Web, but include a review of newsgroups and general reference materials, practitioner sites and resources, primary sources of the tax law, chat rooms and discussion groups, and other opportunities.

Research Problem 6. Locate a financial calculator program that assesses the wisdom of buying versus leasing a new car. Install the program on your computer and become familiar with it. Use the program to work through Problem 54 in this chapter.

Communications

Research Problem 7. Changes to depreciation systems often are discussed by policymakers and observers of the tax system. Outline the terms and policy objectives of one of the changes currently proposed by the Treasury, a member of Congress, or a tax policy think tank.

Deductions: Employee and Self-Employed-Related Expenses

LEARNING OBJECTIVES: *After completing Chapter 9, you should be able to:*

LO.1 Distinguish between employee and self-employed status.

LO.2 Recognize deductible transportation expenses.

LO.3 Describe how travel expenses are treated.

LO.4 Determine the moving expense deduction.

LO.5 Differentiate between deductible and nondeductible education expenses.

LO.6 Explain how entertainment and meal expenses are treated.

LO.7 Identify other employee expenses.

LO.8 Compare various deductions for contributions to retirement accounts.

LO.9 Demonstrate the difference between accountable and nonaccountable employee plans.

LO.10 Apply the limitations on miscellaneous itemized deductions.

LO.11 List and evaluate tax planning ideas related to employee business expenses.

CHAPTER OUTLINE

THE BIG PICTURE   Tax Solutions for the Real World

© iStockphoto.com/Svetikd

THE FIRST JOB

After an extensive search, Morgan, a recent college graduate with a major in finance, has accepted a job with Kite Corporation. The job is in sales and will require travel and some entertainment (i.e., business lunches). She will be based in a major metropolitan area in another state. Kite has no available space in the locale, so Morgan will have to maintain her own work facility. In addition to her salary, Morgan will receive a travel allowance. However, Kite has made it clear that the allowance *will not* cover all of her travel expenses.

Morgan is delighted with the new job because it will enable her to maintain a flexible work schedule. Furthermore, working out of her own apartment avoids a time-consuming and costly commute.

What are some of the income tax problems presented by this situation?

Read the chapter and formulate your response.

FRAMEWORK 1040
Tax Formula for Individuals

This chapter covers the boldfaced portions of the Tax Formula for Individuals that was introduced in Figure 3.1 on p. 3-3. Below those portions are the sections of Form 1040 where the results are reported.

Income *(broadly conceived)*		$xx,xxx
Less: Exclusions		(x,xxx)
Gross income		$xx,xxx
Less: Deductions for adjusted gross income		(x,xxx)

FORM 1040 (p. 1)

12	Business income or (loss). Attach Schedule C or C-EZ	
23	Educator expenses	**23**
24	Certain business expenses of reservists, performing artists, and fee-basis government officials. Attach Form 2106 or 2106-EZ	**24**
26	Moving expenses. Attach Form 3903	**26**
32	IRA deduction	**32**
34	Tuition and fees. Attach Form 8917.	**34**

Adjusted gross income		$xx,xxx
Less: The greater of total **itemized deductions** *or* the standard deduction		(x,xxx)

FORM 1040 (p. 2)

40	**Itemized deductions** (from Schedule A) **or** your **standard deduction** (see left margin)

Personal and dependency exemptions		(x,xxx)
Taxable income		$xx,xxx
Tax on taxable income *(see Tax Tables or Tax Rate Schedules)*		$ x,xxx
Less: Tax credits *(including income taxes withheld and prepaid)*		(xxx)
Tax due *(or refund)*		$ xxx

Considering the large number of taxpayers affected, the tax treatment of job-related expenses is unusually complex. To resolve this matter in a systematic fashion, a number of key questions must be asked:

- Is the taxpayer an *employee* or *self-employed?*
- If an employee, what expenses *qualify* as deductions?
- How are the expenses that qualify *classified* for tax purposes?
- To the extent the expenses are classified as deductions *from* AGI, are they subject to any *limitation?*

Once these questions have been posed and answered, the chapter considers various planning procedures available to maximize the deductibility of employee and self-employed expenses.

9-1 EMPLOYEE VERSUS SELF-EMPLOYED

LO.1

Distinguish between employee and self-employed status.

When one person performs services for another, the person performing the service either is an employee or is self-employed (an **independent contractor**). Failure to recognize one's work status correctly can have serious consequences. Tax deficiencies as well as interest and penalties may result.

Unlike employees, self-employed persons do not have to be included in various fringe benefit programs (e.g., group term life insurance and retirement plans). Because they are not covered by FICA and FUTA (see Chapter 1), these payroll costs are avoided. The IRS is very much aware of the tendency of businesses to wrongly classify workers as self-employed rather than as employees.

In terms of tax consequences, employment status makes a great deal of difference to the persons who perform the services. Expenses of self-employed taxpayers, to the extent allowable, are classified as deductions *for* AGI and are reported on

Schedule C (Profit or Loss From Business) of Form 1040.[1] With the exception of reimbursement under an accountable plan (see later in the chapter), expenses of employees are deductions *from* AGI. They are reported on Form 2106 (Employee Business Expenses) and Schedule A (Itemized Deductions) of Form 1040.[2]

Most persons classified as employees are common law employees. The common law employee classification originated in judicial case law and is summarized in various IRS pronouncements.[3] Revenue Ruling 87–41, for example, lists 20 factors that can be used in determining whether a worker is a common law employee or an independent contractor (and, thus, self-employed).[4]

A common law employee-employer relationship exists when the employer has the right to specify the end result and the ways and means by which that result is to be attained.[5] An employee is subject to the will and control of the employer with respect not only to what shall be done but also to how it shall be done. If the individual is subject to the direction or control of another only to the extent of the end result but not as to the means of accomplishment, an employee-employer relationship does not exist.

Certain factors indicate a common law employee-employer relationship. These include the performance of the following by the employer:

- Furnishing tools or equipment and a place to work.
- Providing support services, including the hiring of assistants to help do the work.
- Making training available to provide needed job skills.
- Allowing participation in various workplace fringe benefits (e.g., accident and health plans, group life insurance, and retirement plans).
- Paying for services based on time rather than the task performed.

For their part, independent contractors are more likely than employees to have unreimbursed business expenses, a significant investment in tools and work facilities, and less permanency in their business relationships. Independent contractors, moreover, anticipate a profit from their work, make their services available to the relevant marketplace, and are paid a flat fee on a per-job basis.

In resolving employment status, each case must be tested on its own merits. Keep in mind, however, that the right to control the means and methods of accomplishment is the definitive test that leads to a common law employee result. Compare Examples 1 and 2.

Example 1

Arnold is a lawyer whose major client accounts for 60% of his billings. He does the routine legal work and income tax returns at the client's request. He is paid a monthly retainer in addition to amounts charged for extra work. Arnold is a self-employed individual. Even though most of his income comes from one client, he still has the right to determine how the end result of his work is attained.

Example 2

Ellen is a lawyer hired by Arnold to assist him in the performance of services for the client mentioned in Example 1. Ellen is under Arnold's supervision; he reviews her work and pays her an hourly fee. Ellen is an employee of Arnold.

When one taxpayer holds multiple jobs, it is possible to have dual status as both an employee and an independent contractor (i.e., self-employed).

Example 3

Dr. Davis, DDS, is a full-time employee at the Robin University Health Center. In the evenings and on weekends, he shares a practice with another dentist who works the Monday through Friday daytime shifts. Dr. Davis is both employed and self-employed.

---

[1] In simple situations, a Schedule C–EZ can be substituted. Also, a Schedule SE (Self-Employment Tax) must be filed.

[2] In simple situations, a Form 2106–EZ (Unreimbursed Employee Business Expenses) can be substituted.

[3] See, for example, *Employer's Supplemental Tax Guide* (IRS Publication 15-A).

[4] 1987–1 C.B. 296.

[5] Reg. § 31.3401(c)–(1)(b).

Certain workers who *are not* common law employees are treated as employees for employment tax purposes. Known as **statutory employees**, this group includes certain drivers (e.g., nondairy beverage distributors and laundry and dry cleaning pickup service), life insurance sales agents, home workers, and other salespersons. These employees are allowed to claim their business-related expenses as deductions *for* AGI by using Schedule C. The wages or commissions paid to statutory employees are not subject to Federal income tax withholding but are subject to Social Security tax.[6]

To avoid the confusion that might otherwise result in their classification, the tax law categorically treats certain categories of workers as independent contractors. Included in this group are licensed real estate agents and direct sellers. Such persons are treated as self-employed for all Federal purposes, including income and employment taxes.[7]

If a taxpayer wants clarification as to whether employee or independent contractor status exists, a ruling from the IRS can be obtained by filing Form SS–8 (Determination of Worker Status for Purposes of Federal Employment Taxes and Income Tax Withholding). An adverse ruling is appealable to the U.S. Tax Court.[8]

9-2 EMPLOYEE EXPENSES—IN GENERAL

Once the employment relationship is established, employee expenses fall into one of the following categories:

- Transportation.
- Travel.
- Moving.
- Education.
- Entertainment.
- Other.

These expenses are discussed below in the order presented.

Keep in mind, however, that these expenses are not necessarily limited to employees. A deduction for business transportation, for example, is equally available to taxpayers who are self-employed.

9-3 TRANSPORTATION EXPENSES

9-3a Qualified Expenditures

LO.2

Recognize deductible transportation expenses.

An employee may deduct unreimbursed employment-related transportation expenses as an itemized deduction *from* AGI. **Transportation expenses** include only the cost of transporting the employee from one place to another in the course of employment when the employee is *not* away from home *in travel status*. Such costs include taxi fares, automobile expenses, tolls, and parking.

Commuting Expenses

Commuting between home and one's place of employment is a personal, nondeductible expense. The fact that one employee drives 30 miles to work and another employee walks six blocks is of no significance.

Example 4

Geraldo is employed by Sparrow Corporation. He drives 22 miles each way to work. The 44 miles he drives each workday are nondeductible commuting expenses.

---

[6]§ 3121(d)(3). See Circular E, *Employer's Tax Guide* (IRS Publication 15), for further discussion of statutory employees.

[7]§ 3508. See *Employer's Supplemental Tax Guide* (IRS Publication 15–A).
[8]§ 7436.

The rule that disallows a deduction for commuting expenses has several exceptions. An employee who uses an automobile to transport heavy tools to work and who otherwise would not drive to work is allowed a deduction, but only for the additional costs incurred to transport the work implements. Additional costs are those exceeding the cost of commuting by the same mode of transportation without the tools. For example, the rental of a trailer for transporting tools is deductible, but the expenses of operating the automobile generally are not deductible. The Supreme Court has held that a deduction is permitted only when the taxpayer can show that the automobile would not have been used without the necessity to transport tools or equipment.[9]

Another exception is provided for an employee who has a second job. The expenses of getting from one job to another are deductible. If the employee goes home between jobs, the deduction is based on the distance between jobs.

In the current year, Cynthia holds two jobs, a full-time job with Blue Corporation and a part-time job with Wren Corporation. Cynthia customarily leaves home at 7:30 A.M. and drives 30 miles to the Blue Corporation plant, where she works until 5:00 P.M. After dinner at a nearby café, Cynthia drives 20 miles to Wren Corporation and works from 7:00 to 11:00 P.M. The distance from the second job to Cynthia's home is 40 miles. Her deduction is based on 20 miles (the distance between jobs).	**Example 5**

If the taxpayer is required to incur a transportation expense to travel between workstations, that expense is deductible.

Norman is the local manager for a national chain of fast-food outlets. Each workday, he drives from his home to his office to handle administrative matters. Most of his day, however, is then spent making the rounds of the retail outlets, after which he drives home. The costs incurred in driving to his office and driving home from the last outlet are nondeductible commuting expenses. The other transportation costs are deductible.	**Example 6**

Likewise, the commuting costs from home to a temporary workstation and from the temporary workstation to home are deductible.

Vivian works for a firm in downtown Denver and commutes to work. She occasionally works in a customer's office. On one such occasion, Vivian drove directly to the customer's office, a round-trip distance from her home of 40 miles. She did not go into her office, which is a 52-mile round-trip. Her mileage for going to and from the temporary workstation is deductible.	**Example 7**

Also deductible is the reasonable travel cost between the general working area and a temporary workstation outside that area.

Sam, a building inspector in Minneapolis, regularly inspects buildings for building code violations for his employer, a general contractor. During one busy season, the St. Paul inspector became ill, and Sam was required to inspect several buildings in St. Paul. The expenses for transportation for the trips to St. Paul are deductible.	**Example 8**

What constitutes the general working area depends on the facts and circumstances of each situation. Furthermore, if an employee customarily works on several temporary assignments in a localized area, that localized area becomes the regular place of employment. Transportation from home to these locations becomes a personal, nondeductible commuting expense.

If a taxpayer has an office in the home that qualifies as a principal place of business, the transportation between home and various work locations is not a commuting expense.

---

[9]*Fausner v. Comm.*, 73–2 USTC ¶9515, 32 AFTR 2d 73–5202, 93 S.Ct. 2820
(USSC, 1973).

Example 9

Return to the facts of *The Big Picture* on p. 9-1. Because Morgan will have an office in her home, the apartment will be her principal place of business. Thus, any transportation from her home to business sites is *not* a commuting expense.[10]

9-3b Computation of Automobile Expenses

A taxpayer has two choices in determining automobile expenses: the automatic mileage method and the actual cost method. If a mixed-use automobile is involved, only the expenses attributable to the business use are deductible. The percentage of business use is usually arrived at by comparing the business mileage with total mileage—both business and personal.

Automatic Mileage Method

Also called the standard mileage method, the **automatic mileage method** is convenient in that it simplifies record keeping. The rate allowed per mile takes into account average operating expenses (such as gas and oil, repairs, and depreciation). Consequently, the taxpayer only has to multiply the automatic mileage rate by the miles driven to compute the deduction for business transportation.

For 2014, the deduction is based on 56 cents per mile for business miles.[11] This represents a one-half cent decrease from the rate of 56.5 cents applicable to 2013. Although the mileage rate usually remains constant for an entire year, such is not always the case. In the past and due to the extreme variation in the cost of fuel, the IRS has made mid-year changes in the rate. The possibility of such a change makes it important that the taxpayer be able to identify when the mileage took place.

The automatic mileage rate for deductible education expenses is the same as for business; 23.5 cents per mile is allowed for moving (discussed later in this chapter) and medical purposes, and the rate for the charitable contribution deduction is 14 cents a mile (as to medical and charitable deductions, see Chapter 10). Parking fees and tolls are allowed in addition to expenses computed using the automatic mileage method.

Generally, a taxpayer may elect either method for any particular year. However, the following restrictions apply:

- The vehicle must be owned or leased by the taxpayer.
- The vehicle is not used for hire (e.g., taxicab).
- If five or more vehicles are in use (for business purposes) at the *same* time (not alternately), a taxpayer may not use the automatic mileage method.
- A basis adjustment is required if the taxpayer changes from the automatic mileage method to the actual operating cost method. Depreciation is considered allowed for the business miles in accordance with the following schedule for the most recent five years:

Year	Rate per Mile
2014	23 cents
2013	23 cents
2012	23 cents
2011	22 cents
2010	23 cents

---

[10] *Walter K. Strohmalter*, 113 T.C. 106 (1999).

[11] Notice 2013–80, 2013–52 I.R.B. 821 and Rev.Proc. 2010–51, 2010–51 I.R.B. 883.

Example 10

Tim purchased his automobile in 2011 for $36,000. It is used 90% for business purposes. Tim drove the automobile for 10,000 business miles in 2013, 8,500 business miles in 2012, and 6,000 business miles in 2011. At the beginning of 2014, the basis of the business portion is $26,825.

Depreciable basis ($36,000 × 90%)	$32,400
Less depreciation:	
2013 (10,000 miles × 23 cents)	(2,300)
2012 (8,500 miles × 23 cents)	(1,955)
2011 (6,000 miles × 22 cents)	(1,320)
Adjusted business basis 1/1/2014	$26,825

- Use of the automatic mileage method in the first year the auto is placed in service is considered an election to exclude the auto from the MACRS method of depreciation (discussed in Chapter 8).
- A taxpayer may not switch to the automatic mileage method if the MACRS statutory percentage method or the election to expense under § 179 has been used.

Actual Cost Method

Under this method, the actual cost of operating the automobile is used to compute the deduction. Actual costs include the following expenses:

- Gas and oil, lubrication.
- Depreciation (or lease payments).
- Insurance.
- Dues to auto clubs.
- Repairs.
- Tires and other parts.
- Licenses and registration fees.
- Parking and tolls.

As noted in Chapter 8, the allowance for depreciation (or lease payments) is subject to limitations when mixed-use vehicles are involved. Interest on car loans is not deductible if the taxpayer is an employee, but it can qualify as a business expense if the taxpayer is self-employed. Sales taxes paid on the purchase of a car are added to the cost of the car and recovered by means of the depreciation deduction. In mixed-use situations, the portion of the sales tax attributable to personal use may, in some cases, be claimed as a deduction *from* AGI (see Chapter 10 and the choice required between state and local income and sales taxes).

Except for parking and tolls, none of the expenses noted previously can be separately claimed under the automatic mileage method. A deduction for parking tickets and other traffic violations is not allowed under either method due to the public policy limitation (see Chapter 6).

THE BIG PICTURE

Example 11

Return to the facts of *The Big Picture* on p. 9-1. During Morgan's senior year in college, her parents gave her one of the family cars—a 2009 Chevrolet Impala. Morgan has no idea as to the car's original cost or the odometer reading at the time the car was registered in her name. She has, however, kept track of the miles driven for business since she accepted her new job. Morgan should use the automatic mileage method in claiming business use of the car.

9-4 TRAVEL EXPENSES

LO.3

Describe how travel expenses are treated.

9-4a Definition of Travel Expenses

An itemized deduction is allowed for unreimbursed travel expenses related to a taxpayer's employment. **Travel expenses** are more broadly defined in the Code than are transportation expenses. Travel expenses include transportation expenses and meals and lodging while away from home in the pursuit of a trade or business. Meals cannot be lavish or extravagant under the circumstances. Transportation expenses (as previously discussed) are deductible even though the taxpayer is not away from home. A deduction for travel expenses is available only if the taxpayer is away from his or her tax home. Travel expenses also include reasonable laundry and incidental expenses.

9-4b Away-from-Home Requirement

The crucial test for the deductibility of travel expenses is whether the employee is away from home overnight. "Overnight" need not be a 24-hour period, but it must be a period substantially longer than an ordinary day's work and must require rest, sleep, or a relief-from-work period.[12] A one-day business trip is not travel status, and meals and lodging for such a trip are not deductible.

Temporary Assignments

The employee must be away from home for a temporary period. If the taxpayer-employee is reassigned to a new post for an indefinite period of time, that new post becomes his or her tax home. *Temporary* indicates that the assignment's termination is expected within a reasonably short period of time. The position of the IRS is that the tax home is the business location, post, or station of the taxpayer. Thus, travel expenses are not deductible if a taxpayer is reassigned for an indefinite period and does not move his or her place of residence to the new location.

Example 12

Malcolm's employer opened a branch office in San Diego. Malcolm was assigned to the new office for three months to train a new manager and to assist in setting up the new office. He tried commuting from his home in Los Angeles for a week and decided that he could not continue driving several hours a day. He rented an apartment in San Diego, where he lived during the week. He spent weekends with his wife and children at their home in Los Angeles. Malcolm's rent, meals, laundry, incidentals, and automobile expenses in San Diego are deductible. To the extent that Malcolm's transportation expense related to his weekend trips home exceeds what his cost of meals and lodging would have been, the excess is personal and nondeductible.

Example 13

Assume that Malcolm in Example 12 was transferred to the new location to become the new manager permanently. His wife and children continued to live in Los Angeles until the end of the school year. Malcolm is no longer "away from home" because the assignment is not temporary. His travel expenses are not deductible.

To curtail controversy in this area, the Code specifies that a taxpayer "*shall not* be treated as *temporarily* away from home during any period of employment if such period exceeds 1 year."[13]

Local Lodging—Special Circumstances

Under the away-from-home rule, the cost of local lodging would not qualify as a deductible travel expense.[14] However, recent rules proposed by the IRS will allow

---

[12] *U.S. v. Correll*, 68–1 USTC ¶9101, 20 AFTR 2d 5845, 88 S.Ct. 445 (USSC, 1967); Rev.Rul. 75–168, 1975–1 C.B. 58.

[13] § 162(a).

[14] Reg. § 1.262–1(b)(5) provides that local lodging is a personal expense. Thus, if paid for by an employer, it would be income to the employee. If not paid for by an employer but the cost is absorbed by the employee, it would be a nondeductible expense.

TAX IN THE NEWS Turning a Saturday Leisure Day into a Business Day

The high cost of air travel together with the substantial discount allowed for a Saturday night stayover may offer travelers an opportunity to do some sightseeing or shopping on business trips. The extra meals and lodging expenses for the nonbusiness day are deductible if the cost is less than the additional cost of flying without a Saturday stay. For the employee, any reimbursement for such costs is nontaxable. Thus, the Saturday is treated as a business day even though no business activity takes place.

_____

Source: Private Letter Ruling (Ltr.Rul.) 9237014.

such expenses in appropriate circumstances. A safe harbor for deductibility is provided if the following conditions are met:

- The lodging is necessary to accomplish the business objective.
- The lodging period does not exceed five calendar days.
- The individual is an employee, and the employer requires the overnight stay.
- The lodging is not lavish or extravagant and provides no significant personal pleasure.[15]

Henderson Associates, a large CPA firm located in Houston, provides a four-day training session for recent hires. For this purpose, it rents meeting rooms and overnight facilities at a local motel. To foster team building, evening exercises are planned and all participants are required to stay at the motel. The overnight-stay requirement maximizes training time by avoiding the distraction of having to commute.	**Example 14**

The Regulations contain other examples of when local lodging qualifies as an exception to the away-from-home rule.[16]

Determining the Tax Home

Under ordinary circumstances, determining the location of a taxpayer's tax home does not present a problem. The tax home is the area in which the taxpayer derives his or her source of income.

It is possible for a taxpayer never to be away from his or her tax home. In other words, the tax home follows the taxpayer. Thus, all meals and lodging remain personal and are not deductible.

Jim is single and works full-time as a long-haul truck driver. He lists his mother's home as his address and stays there during holidays. However, he contributes nothing toward its maintenance. Because Jim has no regular place of duty or place where he regularly lives, his tax home is where he works (i.e., on the road). As an itinerant (transient), he is never away from home, and all of his meals and lodging while on the road are personal and not deductible.	**Example 15**

The result reached in Example 15 is justified on the grounds that there is no duplication of living expenses in the case of itinerant taxpayers.[17]

When a taxpayer has more than one place of business or work, the main one is considered to be the tax home. This is determined by considering the time spent, the level of activity involved, and the income earned at each job.

---

[15]REG–137589–07, 2012–21 I.R.B. 942, adding new Reg. § 1.162–31.
[16]Reg. § 1.162–31(c).

[17]Rev.Rul. 73–539, 1973–2 C.B. 37 and *James O. Henderson,* 70 TCM 1407, T.C.Memo. 1995–559, *aff'd* by 98–1 USTC ¶50,375, 81 AFTR 2d 98–1748, 143 F.3d 497 (CA–9, 1998).

Example 16

Art, a physical therapist, lives with his family in Lancaster, Pennsylvania. For seven months of each year, he is employed by the New Orleans Saints football team at a salary of $150,000. During this period, he rents an apartment in New Orleans. In the off-season, he works for the Lancaster YMCA at a salary of $15,000. Art's tax home is clearly New Orleans and not Lancaster. Consequently, his living expenses while in New Orleans (i.e., food and lodging) are not deductible.

9-4c Restrictions on Travel Expenses

The possibility always exists that taxpayers will attempt to treat vacation or pleasure travel as deductible business travel. To prevent such practices, the law contains restrictions on certain travel expenses.

Conventions

For travel expenses to be deductible, a convention must be directly related to the taxpayer's trade or business.[18] Compare Examples 17 and 18.

Example 17

Dr. Hill, a pathologist who works for a hospital in Ohio, travels to Las Vegas to attend a two-day session on recent developments in estate planning. No deduction is allowed for Dr. Hill's travel expenses.

Example 18

Assume the same facts as in Example 17, except that the convention deals entirely with recent developments in pathology. Now a travel deduction is allowed.

If the proceedings of the convention are videotaped, the taxpayer must attend convention sessions to view the videotaped materials along with other participants. However, a deduction will be allowed for costs (other than travel, meals, and entertainment) of renting or using videotaped materials related to business.

Example 19

A CPA is unable to attend a convention at which current developments in taxation are discussed. She pays $300 for videotapes of the lectures and views them at home later. The $300 is an itemized deduction if the CPA is an employee. If she is self-employed, the $300 is a deduction *for* AGI.

The Code places stringent restrictions on the deductibility of travel expenses of the taxpayer's spouse or dependent.[19] Generally, the accompaniment by the spouse or dependent must serve a bona fide business purpose, and the expenses must be otherwise deductible.

Example 20

Assume the same facts as in Example 18 with the additional fact that Dr. Hill is accompanied by Mrs. Hill. Mrs. Hill is not employed, but possesses secretarial skills and takes notes during the proceedings. No deduction is allowed for Mrs. Hill's travel expenses. If, however, Mrs. Hill is a nurse trained in pathology and is employed by Dr. Hill as his assistant, her travel expenses become deductible.

Education

Travel as a form of education is not deductible.[20] If, however, the education qualifies as a deduction, the travel involved is allowed. Compare Examples 21 and 22.

Example 21

Greta, a German teacher, travels to Germany to maintain general familiarity with the language and culture. No travel expense deduction is allowed.

---

[18]§ 274(h)(1).
[19]§ 274(m)(3).

[20]§ 274(m)(2).

Jean-Claude, a scholar of French literature, travels to Paris to do specific library research that cannot be done elsewhere and to take courses that are offered only at the Sorbonne. The travel costs are deductible, assuming that the other requirements for deducting education expenses (discussed later in the chapter) are met.

Example 22

9-4d Combined Business and Pleasure Travel

To be deductible, travel expenses need not be incurred in the performance of specific job functions.

Domestic Travel for Business and Pleasure

In order to limit the possibility of a taxpayer claiming a tax deduction for what is essentially a personal vacation, several provisions have been enacted to govern deductions associated with combined business and pleasure trips. If the business/pleasure trip is from one point in the United States to another point in the United States, the transportation expenses are deductible only if the trip is *primarily for business*.[21] Meals, lodging, and other expenses are allocated between business and personal days. If the trip is primarily for pleasure, no transportation expenses qualify as a deduction. Compare Examples 23 and 24.

In the current year, Hana travels from Seattle to New York primarily for business. She spends five days conducting business and three days sightseeing and attending shows. Her plane and taxi fare amounts to $1,160. Her meals amount to $200 per day, and lodging and incidental expenses are $350 per day. She can deduct the transportation charges of $1,160, because the trip is primarily for business (five days of business versus three days of sightseeing). Meals are limited to five days and are subject to the 50% cutback (discussed later in the chapter), for a total of $500 [5 days × ($200 × 50%)], and other expenses are limited to $1,750 (5 days × $350). If Hana is an employee, the unreimbursed travel expenses are miscellaneous itemized deductions.

Example 23

Assume that Hana goes to New York for a two-week vacation. While there, she spends several hours renewing acquaintances with people in her company's New York office. Her transportation expenses are not deductible.

Example 24

Foreign Travel for Business and Pleasure

When the trip is *outside the United States*, special rules apply. Transportation expenses must be allocated between business and personal unless (1) the taxpayer is away from home for seven days or less *or* (2) less than 25 percent of the time was for personal purposes. No allocation is required if the taxpayer has no substantial control over arrangements for the trip or the desire for a vacation is not a major factor in taking the trip. If the trip is primarily for pleasure, no transportation charges are deductible. Days devoted to travel are considered business days. Weekends, legal holidays, and intervening days are considered business days, provided both the preceding and succeeding days were business days.[22] Compare Examples 25 and 26.

In the current year, Robert takes a trip from New York to Japan primarily for business purposes. He is away from home from June 10 through June 19. He spends three days vacationing and seven days (including two travel days) conducting business. His airfare is $4,000, his meals amount to $200 per day, and lodging and incidental expenses are $300 per day. Because Robert is away from home for more than seven days and more

Example 25

---

[21]Reg. § 1.162–2(b)(1).

[22]§ 274(c) and Reg. § 1.274–4. For purposes of the seven-days-or-less exception, the departure travel day is not counted.

than 25% of his time is devoted to personal purposes, only 70% (7 days business/10 days total) of the transportation is deductible. His deductions are as follows:

Transportation (70% × $4,000)		$2,800
Lodging ($300 × 7)		2,100
Meals ($200 × 7)	$1,400	
Less: 50% cutback (discussed later)	(700)	700
Total		$5,600

Example 26   Assume the same facts as in Example 25. Robert is gone the same period of time but spends only two days (rather than three) vacationing. Now no allocation of transportation is required. Because the pleasure portion of the trip is less than 25% of the total, all of the airfare qualifies for the travel deduction.

9-5 MOVING EXPENSES

LO.4

Determine the moving expense deduction.

Moving expenses are deductible for moves in connection with the commencement of work at a new principal workplace.[23] Both employees and self-employed individuals can deduct these expenses. To be eligible for a moving expense deduction, a taxpayer must meet two basic tests: distance and time.

9-5a Distance Test

To meet the distance test, the taxpayer's new job location must be at least 50 miles farther from the taxpayer's old residence than the old residence was from the former place of employment. In this regard, the location of the new residence is not relevant. This eliminates a moving deduction for taxpayers who purchase a new home in the same general area without changing their place of employment. Those who accept a new job in the same general area as the old job location are also eliminated.

Example 27   Harry is permanently transferred to a new job location. As the following diagram shows, the distance from Harry's former home to his new job (80 miles) exceeds the distance from his former home to his old job (30 miles) by at least 50 miles. Harry has met the distance test for a moving expense deduction.

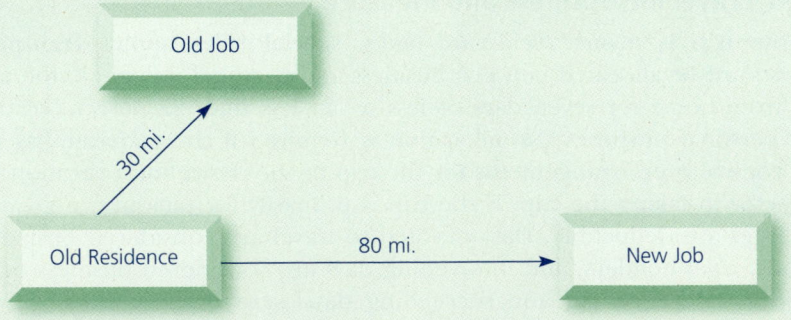

If an individual is not employed before the move, the new job must be at least 50 miles from the former residence. Thus, in Example 27, Harry's move has met the distance test even if he was not previously employed.

9-5b Time Test

To meet the time test, an employee must be employed on a full-time basis at the new location for 39 weeks in the 12-month period following the move. If the taxpayer is a self-employed individual, he or she must work in the new location for

---

[23] § 217(a).

78 weeks during the next two years. The first 39 weeks must be in the first 12 months. The time test is disregarded if the taxpayer dies, becomes disabled, or is discharged (other than for willful misconduct) or transferred by the employer.

A taxpayer might not be able to meet the 39-week test by the due date of the tax return for the year of the move. For this reason, two alternatives are allowed. The taxpayer can take the deduction in the year the expenses are incurred, even though the 39-week test has not been met. If the taxpayer later fails to meet the test, either (1) the income of the following year is increased by an amount equal to the deduction previously claimed for moving expenses or (2) an amended return is filed for the year of the move. The second alternative is to wait until the test is met and then file an amended tax return for the year of the move.

9-5c Treatment of Moving Expenses

What Is Included

"Qualified" moving expenses include *reasonable* expenses of:

- Moving household goods and personal effects.
- Traveling from the former residence to the new place of residence.

For this purpose, *traveling* includes lodging, but not meals, for the taxpayer and members of the household.[24] The taxpayer can elect to use actual auto expenses (no depreciation is allowed) or the automatic mileage method. In this case, moving expense mileage is limited in 2014 to 23.5 cents per mile for each car. The automatic mileage rate for 2013 was 24 cents. These expenses are also limited by the reasonableness standard. For example, if one moves from Texas to Florida via Maine and takes six weeks to do so, the transportation and lodging must be allocated between personal and moving expenses.

Example 28	

Jill is transferred by her employer from the Atlanta office to the San Francisco office. In this connection, she spends the following amounts:

Cost of moving furniture	$4,800
Transportation	700
Meals	450
Lodging	600

Jill's total qualified moving expense is $6,100 ($4,800 + $700 + $600).

The moving expense deduction is allowed regardless of whether the employee is transferred by the existing employer or is employed by a new employer. It is allowed if the employee moves to a new area and obtains employment or switches from self-employed status to employee status (and vice versa). The moving expense deduction is also allowed if an individual is unemployed before obtaining employment in a new area.

What Is Not Included

In addition to meals while en route, the moving expense deduction does *not* include the following costs:

- New car tags and driver's licenses.
- Loss on the sale of a residence or penalty for breaking a lease.
- Forfeiture of security deposits and loss from disposing of club memberships.
- Pre-move house-hunting expenses.
- Temporary living expenses.

Also not deductible are the costs of moving servants and others who are not members of the household.

---

[24]§ 217(b).

How Treated

Qualified moving expenses that are paid (or reimbursed) by the employer are not reported as part of the gross income of the employee.[25] Moving expenses that are paid (or reimbursed) by the employer and are not qualified moving expenses are included in the employee's gross income and are not deductible.

The employer is responsible for allocating the reimbursement between the qualified and nonqualified moving expenses. Reimbursed qualified moving expenses are separately stated on the Form W–2 given to the employee for the year involved. Qualified moving expenses that are not reimbursed and those of self-employed taxpayers are deductions *for* AGI.[26]

THE BIG PICTURE

Example 29

Return to the facts of *The Big Picture* on p. 9-1. Even though this is her first job, Morgan will be entitled to a moving expense deduction. This presumes that she is not reimbursed by Kite Corporation for these expenses. She should not forget that the mileage on her auto also is allowed. Her deduction is *for* AGI and can be claimed even if she chooses the standard deduction option.

Form 3903 is used to report the details of the moving expense deduction if the employee is not reimbursed or a self-employed person is involved.

9-6 EDUCATION EXPENSES

LO.5

Differentiate between deductible and nondeductible education expenses.

9-6a General Requirements

An employee can deduct expenses incurred for education (**education expenses**) as ordinary and necessary business expenses provided the expenses are incurred for either of two reasons:

- To meet the express requirements of the employer or the requirements imposed by law to retain his or her employment status.
- To maintain or improve existing skills required in the present job.

Education expenses are *not* deductible if the education is for either of the following purposes (except as discussed under A Limited Deduction Approach, which follows):

- To meet the minimum educational standards for qualification in the taxpayer's existing job.
- To qualify the taxpayer for a new trade or business.[27]

Fees incurred for professional qualification exams (the bar exam, for example) and fees for review courses (such as a CPA review course) are not deductible.[28] If the education incidentally results in a promotion or raise, the deduction still can be taken as long as the education maintained and improved existing skills and did not qualify a person for a new trade or business. A change in duties is not always fatal to the deduction if the new duties involve the same general work. For example, the IRS has ruled that a practicing dentist's education expenses incurred to become an orthodontist are deductible.[29]

---

[25]§§ 132(a)(6) and (g).
[26]§ 62(a)(15).
[27]Reg. §§ 1.162–5(b)(2) and (3).

[28]Reg. § 1.212–1(f) and Rev.Rul. 69–292, 1969–1 C.B. 84.
[29]Rev.Rul. 74–78, 1974–1 C.B. 44.

Expatriates and the Moving Expense Deduction

Expatriates, U.S. persons who accept work assignments overseas, enjoy several favorable tax advantages regarding foreign moves. First, the cost of storing household goods qualifies as a moving expense. This could lead to a major tax saving because expatriates do not ship most of their household effects to the foreign location. Furthermore, the cost of storage, particularly in a climate-controlled facility, is not insignificant.

The second advantage expatriates could enjoy is an exemption from the time test. Those who return to the United States to retire are absolved from the 39-week or 78-week work requirement. Thus, the return home expenses are treated as qualified moving expenses.

Global Tax Issues

© iStockphoto.com/Andrey Prokhorov

Source: Internal Revenue Code § 217(i).

9-6b Requirements Imposed by Law or by the Employer for Retention of Employment

Taxpayers are permitted to deduct education expenses if additional courses are required by the employer or are imposed by law. Many states require a minimum of a bachelor's degree and a specified number of additional courses to retain a teaching job. In addition, some public school systems have imposed a master's degree requirement and require teachers to make satisfactory progress toward a master's degree to keep their positions. If the required education is the minimum degree required for the job, no deduction is allowed.

A taxpayer classified as a staff accountant who went back to school to obtain a bachelor's degree in accounting was not allowed to deduct the expenses. Although some courses tended to maintain and improve his existing skills in his entry-level position, the degree was the minimum requirement for his job.[30]

Expenses incurred for education required by law for various professions will also qualify for deduction.

To satisfy the State Board of Public Accountancy rules for maintaining her CPA license, Nancy takes an auditing course sponsored by a local college. The cost of the education is deductible.

Example 30

9-6c Maintaining or Improving Existing Skills

The "maintaining or improving existing skills" requirement in the Code has been difficult for both taxpayers and the courts to interpret. For example, a business executive may be permitted to deduct the costs of obtaining an MBA on the grounds that the advanced management education is undertaken to maintain and improve existing management skills. The executive is eligible to deduct the costs of specialized, nondegree management courses that are taken for continuing education or to maintain or improve existing skills. Expenses incurred by the executive to obtain a law degree are not deductible, however, because the education constitutes training for a new trade or business. The Regulations specifically deny a self-employed accountant a deduction for expenses relating to law school.[31]

9-6d Classification of Specific Items

Education expenses include books and supplies, tuition, and transportation (e.g., from the office to night school) and travel (e.g., meals and lodging while away from home at summer school).

---

[30]Reg. § 1.162–5(b)(2)(iii) Example (2); *Collin J. Davidson*, 43 TCM 743, T.C.Memo. 1982–119. But see the subsequent discussion of § 222 (i.e., the deduction for higher education qualified tuition and related expenses).

[31]Reg. § 1.162–5(b)(3)(ii) Example (1).

TAX IN THE NEWS   Is an MBA Degree Deductible?

Education that maintains or improves existing skills is deductible, but education that qualifies a taxpayer for a new field is not. But how do these basic rules apply to a conventional (i.e., nonspecialized) MBA degree? Does being a manager or a consultant require an MBA degree? Generally, the answer has always been that it does not. In this regard, therefore, the education does not create a new skill; so its cost should be deductible.

Several recent holdings, however, have found that an MBA degree can lead to qualifying for a new trade or business. But these holdings involved situations where the education resulted in a job change and satisfied different minimum requirements set by the employer. In one case, for example, the taxpayer moved from the position of investment analyst to become an investment banker, and the latter position required an MBA degree. Under these circumstances, the cost of the education was held to be nondeductible.

But barring a change to a job where the degree is required, the cost of an MBA degree should be deductible as merely improving existing managerial skills.

———————

Source: Daniel R. Allemeier, Jr., 90 TCM 197, T.C.Memo. 2005–207.

Example 31

Bill, who holds a bachelor of education degree, is a secondary education teacher in the Charleston school system. The school board recently raised its minimum education requirement for new teachers from four years of college training to five. A grandfather clause allows teachers with only four years of college to continue to qualify if they show satisfactory progress toward a graduate degree. Bill enrolls at the University of South Carolina and takes two graduate courses. His unreimbursed expenses for this purpose are as follows:

Books and tuition	$3,600
Lodging while in travel status (June–August)	2,150
Meals while in travel status	1,100
Laundry while in travel status	220
Transportation	900

Bill has an itemized deduction as follows:

Books and tuition	$3,600
Lodging	2,150
Meals less 50% cutback (see below)	550
Laundry	220
Transportation	900
	$7,420

9-6e A Limited Deduction Approach

One of the major shortcomings of the education deduction, previously discussed, is that it is unavailable for taxpayers obtaining a basic skill (i.e., to meet the minimum standards required for the taxpayer's current job). This shortcoming has been partly resolved with the **deduction for qualified tuition and related expenses**.

A deduction *for* AGI is allowed for qualified tuition and related expenses involving higher education (i.e., postsecondary). The deduction is the lesser of the qualifying amount spent or the maximum amount allowed by § 222. The maximum deductions allowed are shown in Table 9.1. Note that the limitations are based on the taxpayer's MAGI and filing status.[32] Although a phaseout is provided for, note its short and drastic effect. Only two steps are involved ($65,000/$80,000 for single

———————

[32]MAGI is modified adjusted gross income as defined in § 222(b)(2)(C). Examples of some of these modifications include the adding back to regular AGI of the foreign earned income exclusion and the domestic pro- duction activities deduction. See *Tax Benefits for Education* (IRS Publication 970).

TABLE 9.1	Limitations for Qualified Tuition Deduction	
Filing Status	**MAGI Limit**	**Maximum Deduction Allowed**
Single	$ 65,000 ⎫	$4,000
Married	130,000 ⎭	
Single	65,001 to 80,000* ⎫	2,000
Married	130,001 to 160,000* ⎫	2,000

*No deduction at all is available if MAGI exceeds this amount.

and $130,000/$160,000 for married), and the benefit of § 222 *disappears completely* after the second step. Thus, a married couple with MAGI of $160,000 would lose the entire deduction if they earned an additional $1. The § 222 limitations are not indexed for inflation.[33]

Various aspects of the higher education tuition deduction are summarized below:

- *Qualified tuition and related expenses* include whatever is required for enrollment at the institution. Usually, student activity fees, books, and room and board are not included.[34]
- The expense need not be employment related, although it can be.
- The deduction is available for a taxpayer's spouse or anyone who can be claimed as a dependent and is an eligible student.
- The deduction is not available for married persons who file separate returns.
- To avoid a "double benefit," the deduction must be coordinated with other education provisions (e.g., American Opportunity and lifetime learning credits). Along this same line, no deduction is allowed for a taxpayer who qualifies as another's dependent.[35]
- The deduction *for* AGI classification avoids the 2 percent-of-AGI floor on miscellaneous itemized deductions. As noted later in the chapter, this is the fate suffered by other education-related employee expenses.

The deduction for qualified tuition and related expenses can be determined by completing Form 8917 (Tuition and Fees Deduction). The form should be attached to Form 1040 (or Form 1040–A).

THE BIG PICTURE

Example 32

Return to the facts of *The Big Picture* on p. 9-1. After starting her new job, Morgan enrolls in the night program of a local law school and begins attending classes. Although Morgan does not plan to practice law, she thinks that a law degree will advance her career. Except for the tuition she pays (see the discussion of § 222), none of her expenses relating to the education will be deductible.[36]

---

[33]Section 222 expired on December 31, 2013, but is expected to be extended.

[34]Section 222(d) refers to § 25A(f), which deals with the American Opportunity and lifetime learning credits (see Chapter 13). Student activity fees

and prescribed course-related books may be allowed if they are a condition for enrollment.

[35]§ 222(c).

[36]*Steven Galligan*, 83 TCM 1859, T.C.Memo. 2002–150.

ETHICS & EQUITY   Maximizing the Tuition Deduction

Blake maintains a household that includes his daughter Bianca, who is 23 years old and a full-time student. Using funds from a savings account she inherited from her aunt, Bianca pays for her $5,000 college tuition. For the year, Blake properly claims Bianca as a dependent (under the qualifying child category) and, making use of § 222, deducts $4,000 of the tuition. On her own income tax return, Bianca also uses § 222 to deduct the $1,000 balance of the $5,000 tuition. What are the parties trying to accomplish? Have they acted properly? Explain.

© iStockphoto.com/LdF

9-6f Other Provisions Dealing with Education

Although this chapter deals with employment-related expenses, mention should be made of various other tax provisions that deal with education. Because the encouragement of education is a desirable social goal, Congress continues to enact laws that provide tax incentives. The incentives come in the form of income exclusions, deductions (both *for* AGI and *from* AGI), and various credits. The paragraphs that follow summarize these benefits.

Similar to the § 222 deduction for qualified tuition and related expenses just discussed is a deduction for interest on student loans.[37] The interest is a deduction *for* AGI, with an allowable maximum of up to $2,500 per year.

Two types of education savings plans, both created to help pay for a beneficiary's (including a dependent family member's) education, may help reduce the cost of education. Although each plan does not allow a deduction for any contribution to the plan, earnings on these funds accumulate free of tax, thus excluding them from gross income. The Coverdell Education Savings Accounts (CESAs)[38] allow a maximum annual contribution of $2,000. Under these plans, distributions also are nontaxable if used for tuition and related expenses and are not limited to postsecondary education. In addition, income limits apply to the contributors. The second type is a qualified tuition program (known as "§ 529 plans") that must be sponsored by a state or private university.[39] Thus, the terms and conditions set forth in the plan vary accordingly.

Another exclusion from gross income comes in the form of educational assistance programs.[40] Sponsored by employers, such programs cover up to $5,250 per year of an employee's education costs (e.g., tuition, fees, books, and supplies), which can be at the undergraduate or graduate level.

Finally, exclusion treatment is available for scholarships covering tuition and related expenses but not for those providing room and board.[41]

In the area of tax credits, taxpayers benefit significantly from two provisions: the American Opportunity credit (formerly the HOPE scholarship credit) and the lifetime learning credit.[42] Both cover tuition and related expenses but not room and board costs. The American Opportunity credit allows no more than $2,500 per year for the first four years of college, while the lifetime learning credit permits up to $2,000 (20 percent of qualifying costs up to $10,000) per year with no time constraints. Concept Summary 9.1 reviews the tax consequences of the various provisions dealing with education and indicates where they are discussed in the text.

---

[37]§ 221.

[38]§ 530.

[39]The major advantage of one of the two types of § 529 plans is protection against increasing tuition cost. The plan freezes the tuition that will be charged to the current amount.

[40]§ 127.

[41]§ 117.

[42]§ 25A.

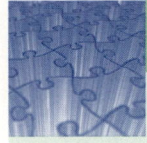

CONCEPT SUMMARY 9.1

Tax Consequences of Provisions Dealing with Education

Provision	Tax Effect	Income Phaseout[a]	Reference Code	Reference Text
Educational savings bonds	*Exclusion* for interest on U.S. Series EE bonds used for higher education	Yes	§ 135	Ch. 5, p. 5-25
Qualified tuition program	No deduction; *exclusion* for distributions	No	§ 529	Ch. 5, p. 5-26
Educational assistance plans	*Exclusion* of up to $5,250 for employer-provided assistance	No[b]	§ 127	Ch. 5, p. 5-16
Scholarships	*Exclusion* allowed for education costs (excluding room and board)	No	§ 117	Ch. 5, p. 5-7
Qualified tuition reduction plan	*Exclusion* as to tuition waivers for employees (and dependents) of nonprofit educational institutions	No[b]	§ 117(d)	Ch. 5, p. 5-8
Coverdell Education Savings Account (CESA)	No deduction; *exclusion* for distributions	Yes	§ 530	Ch. 19, p. 19-23
Premature distributions from IRAs	If used for qualified higher education, income recognized but penalty waived	—	§ 72(t)	Ch. 19, p. 19-26
Qualified tuition and related expenses	*Deduction for* AGI; up to $4,000	Yes	§ 222	Ch. 9, p. 9-16
Educator expenses	*Deduction for* AGI; up to $250	No	§ 62(a)(2)(D)	Ch. 9, p. 9-26
Interest on student loans	*Deduction for* AGI; up to $2,500 per year	Yes	§ 221	Ch. 10, p. 10-15
Job-related education expenses	*Deduction from* AGI for an *employee* and subject to 2%-of-AGI floor; *deduction for* AGI for *self-employed*	No	§ 162	Ch. 9, p. 9-14
American Opportunity credit	Formerly the HOPE credit; extended to 4 years of postsecondary education; up to $2,500 per year	Yes	§ 25A(i)	Ch. 13, p. 13-24
Lifetime learning credit	20% of qualifying expenses (not to exceed $10,000 per year)	Yes	§ 25(A)(c)	Ch. 13, p. 13-24

[a] The phaseout of benefits occurs when income reaches a certain level. The phaseout amounts vary widely, depend on filing status (i.e., single or married filing jointly), and are based on MAGI (modified AGI).

[b] The availability of the benefit cannot be discriminatory (i.e., cannot favor higher-income taxpayers).

9-7 ENTERTAINMENT AND MEAL EXPENSES

Many taxpayers attempt to deduct personal entertainment expenses as business expenses. For this reason, the tax law restricts the deductibility of entertainment expenses. The Code contains strict record-keeping requirements and provides restrictive tests for the deduction of certain types of **entertainment expenses**.

LO.6

Explain how entertainment and meal expenses are treated.

9-7a Cutback Adjustment

During the administration of Jimmy Carter, considerable controversy arose regarding the "three martini" business lunch. By virtue of allowing a tax deduction, should the tax law be subsidizing a practice that contained a significant element of personal pleasure? One possible remedy for the situation was to disallow any deduction for business entertainment, but this option was regarded as being too harsh. Instead the *cutback* rule was instituted. Rather than disallowing *all* of the deduction, only a certain percentage would be allowed, and the rest of the expenditure would be cut back. Currently, only 50 percent of meal and entertainment expenses are allowed as a deduction.[43] The limitation applies in the context of both employment and self-employment status. Although the 50 percent cutback can apply to either the employer or the employee, it will not apply twice. The cutback applies to the one who really pays (economically) for the meals or entertainment.

Example 33

Jane, an employee of Pato Corporation, entertains one of her clients. If Pato Corporation does not reimburse Jane, she is subject to the cutback adjustment. If, however, Pato Corporation reimburses Jane (or pays for the entertainment directly), Pato suffers the cutback.

In certain situations, however, a full 50 percent cutback seems unfair. If, for example, the hours of service are regulated (by the U.S. Department of Transportation) and away-from-home meals are frequent and necessary, the "three martini" business lunch type of abuse is unlikely. Consequently, the cutback rule is mitigated for the following types of employees:

- Certain air transportation employees, such as flight crews, dispatchers, mechanics, and control tower operators.
- Interstate truck and bus drivers.
- Certain railroad employees, such as train crews and dispatchers.
- Certain merchant mariners.

In these situations, 80 percent of the cost of meals is allowed as a deduction.

What Is Covered

Transportation expenses are not affected by the cutback rule—only meals and entertainment. The cutback also applies to taxes and tips relating to meals and entertainment. Cover charges, parking fees at an entertainment location, and room rental fees for a meal or cocktail party are also subject to the 50 percent rule.

Example 34

Joe pays a $40 cab fare to meet his client for dinner. The meal costs $150, and Joe leaves a $30 tip. His deduction is $130 [($150 + $30) × 50% + $40 cab fare].

What Is Not Covered

The cutback rule has a number of exceptions. One exception covers the case where the full value of the meals or entertainment is included in the compensation of the employee (or independent contractor).

Example 35

Myrtle wins an all-expense-paid trip to Europe for selling the most insurance for her company during the year. Her employer treats this trip as additional compensation to Myrtle. The cutback adjustment does not apply to the employer.

Another exception applies to meals and entertainment in a subsidized eating facility or where the *de minimis* fringe benefit rule is met (see Chapter 5).

Example 36

General Hospital has an employee cafeteria on the premises for its doctors, nurses, and other employees. The cafeteria operates at cost. The cutback rule does not apply to General Hospital.

Example 37

Canary Corporation gives a ham, a fruitcake, and a bottle of wine to each employee at year-end. Because the *de minimis* fringe benefit exclusion applies to business gifts of packaged foods and beverages, their *full* cost is deductible by Canary.

A similar exception applies to employer-paid recreational activities for employees (e.g., the annual Christmas party or spring picnic).[44]

---

[43]§ 274(n).   [44]§ 274(e)(4).

9-7b Classification of Expenses

Entertainment expenses are categorized as follows: those *directly related* to business and those *associated with* business.[45] Directly related expenses are related to an actual business meeting or discussion. These expenses are distinguished from entertainment expenses that are incurred to promote goodwill, such as maintaining existing customer relations. To obtain a deduction for directly related entertainment, it is not necessary to show that actual benefit resulted from the expenditure as long as there was a reasonable expectation of benefit. To qualify as directly related, the expense should be incurred in a clear business setting. If there is little possibility of engaging in the active conduct of a trade or business due to the nature of the social facility, it is difficult to qualify the expenditure as directly related to business.

Expenses associated with, rather than directly related to, business entertainment must serve a specific business purpose, such as obtaining new business or continuing existing business. These expenditures qualify only if the expenses directly precede or follow a bona fide business discussion. Entertainment occurring on the same day as the business discussion meets the test.

9-7c Restrictions upon Deductibility

Business Meals

Any business meal is deductible only if all of the following are true:[46]

- The meal is directly related to or associated with the active conduct of a trade or business.
- The expense is not lavish or extravagant under the circumstances.
- The taxpayer (or an employee) is present at the meal.

A business meal with a business associate or customer is not deductible unless business is discussed before, during, or after the meal. This requirement is not intended to disallow the deduction for a meal consumed while away from home on business.

Example 38
Lacy travels to San Francisco for a business convention. She pays for dinner with three colleagues and is not reimbursed by her employer. They do not discuss business. She can deduct 50% of the cost of her meal. However, she cannot deduct the cost of her colleagues' meals.

The taxpayer or an employee must be present at the business meal for the meal to be deductible. An independent contractor who renders significant services to the taxpayer is treated as an employee.

Example 39
Lance, a party to a contract negotiation, buys dinner for other parties to the negotiation but does not attend the dinner. No deduction is allowed.

ETHICS & EQUITY   *Your Turn or Mine?*

Natalie (a CPA), Mathew (an attorney), Jacob (a banker), and Avery (an insurance agent) all live and work in the same community. They have been friends since college. Every Friday, they have lunch together and make it a point to discuss some business matters. They take turns paying for the group's lunches, and each deducts the amount he or she paid for the lunch as an entertainment expense. Presuming that one of the four is audited, do you anticipate any difficulty with the IRS? Explain.

© iStockphoto.com/LdF

---

[45]§ 274(a)(1)(A).   [46]§ 274(k).

Club Dues

The Code provides: "No deduction shall be allowed … for amounts paid or incurred for membership in any club organized for business, pleasure, recreation, or other social purpose."[47] Although this prohibition seems quite broad, the IRS does allow a deduction for dues to clubs whose primary purpose is public service and community volunteerism (e.g., Kiwanis, Lions, and Rotary).

Even though dues are not deductible, actual entertainment at a club may qualify.

Example 40

During the current year, Vincent spent $1,400 on business lunches at the Lakeside Country Club. The annual membership fee was $6,000, and Vincent used the facility 60% of the time for business. Presuming that the lunches meet the business meal test, Vincent may claim $700 (50% × $1,400) as a deduction. None of the club dues are deductible.

Ticket Purchases for Entertainment

A deduction for the cost of a ticket for an entertainment activity is limited to the face value of the ticket.[48] This limitation is applied before the 50 percent rule. The face value of a ticket includes any tax. Under this rule, the excess payment to a scalper for a ticket is not deductible. Similarly, the fee to a ticket agency for the purchase of a ticket is not deductible.

Expenditures for the rental or use of a luxury skybox at a sports arena in excess of the face value of regular tickets are disallowed as deductions. If a luxury skybox is used for entertainment that is directly related to or associated with business, the deduction is limited to the face value of nonluxury box seats. All seats in the luxury skybox are counted, even when some seats are unoccupied.

The taxpayer may also deduct stated charges for food and beverages under the general rules for business entertainment. The deduction for skybox seats, food, and beverages is limited to 50 percent of cost.

Example 41

In the current year, Jay Company pays $12,000 to rent a 10-seat skybox at City Stadium for three football games. Nonluxury box seats at each event range in cost from $55 to $120 a seat. In September, a Jay representative and eight clients use the skybox for the first game. The entertainment follows a bona fide business discussion, and Jay spends $490 for food and beverages during the game. The deduction for the first sports event is as follows:

Food and beverages	$ 490
Deduction for seats ($120 × 10 seats)	1,200
Total entertainment expense	$1,690
50% limitation	× .50
Deduction	$ 845

Business Gifts

Although not subject to a cutback adjustment, business gifts are deductible only to the extent of $25 per donee per year.[49] An exception is made for gifts costing $4 or less (e.g., pens with the employee's or company's name on them) or promotional materials. Such items are not treated as business gifts subject to the $25 limitation. In addition, incidental costs such as engraving of jewelry and nominal charges for gift-wrapping, mailing, and delivery are not included in the cost of the gift in applying the limitation. Gifts to superiors and employers are not deductible.

The $25 limitation on business gifts cannot be circumvented by having the donor's spouse join in the gift or by making multiple gifts that include the customer's family.

An activity that can be considered either a gift or entertainment generally will be classified as entertainment. However, packaged food or beverages intended for

---

[47] § 274(a)(3).
[48] § 274(l).

[49] § 274(b)(1).

later consumption are treated as a gift. Tickets to a theater performance or sporting event can be treated as *either* entertainment or a gift if the taxpayer *does not* accompany the client. However, if the taxpayer also attends (see Example 41), the gift option is not available.

Records must be maintained to substantiate business gifts.

9-8 OTHER EMPLOYEE EXPENSES

9-8a Office in the Home

LO.7

Identify other employee expenses.

Employees and self-employed individuals are not allowed a deduction for **office in the home expenses** unless a portion of the residence is used *exclusively* on a *regular basis* as either of the following:

- The principal place of business for any trade or business of the taxpayer.
- A place of business used by clients, patients, or customers.

Employees must meet an additional test: The use must be for the *convenience of the employer* rather than merely being "appropriate and helpful."[50]

The precise meaning of "principal place of business" has been the subject of considerable controversy.[51] Congress ultimately resolved the issue by amending the Code.[52] The term *principal place of business* now includes a place of business that satisfies the following requirements:

- The office is used by the taxpayer to conduct administrative or management activities of a trade or business.
- There is no other fixed location of the trade or business where the taxpayer conducts these activities.

Dr. Smith is a self-employed anesthesiologist. During the year, he spends 30 to 35 hours per week administering anesthesia and postoperative care to patients in three hospitals, none of which provides him with an office. He also spends two or three hours per day in a room in his home that he uses exclusively as an office. He does not meet patients there, but he performs a variety of tasks related to his medical practice (e.g., contacting surgeons, bookkeeping, and reading medical journals). A deduction will be allowed because Dr. Smith uses the office in the home to conduct administrative or management activities of his trade or business and there is no other fixed location where these activities can be carried out.

Example 42

The exclusive use requirement means that part of the home must be used solely for business purposes. An exception allows mixed use (both business and personal) of the home if a licensed day-care business is involved.

Troy is self-employed and maintains an office in his home for business purposes. The office is also used by his wife to pay the family bills and by his children to do homework assignments. Troy does not satisfy the exclusive use requirement, and no office in the home deduction is allowed.

Example 43

Muriel operates a licensed day-care center in her home. The children use the living room as a play area during the day, and Muriel and her family use it for personal purposes in the evening and on weekends. The mixed use of the living room does not disqualify Muriel from an office in the home deduction.

Example 44

The office in the home deduction can be determined in either of two ways: the regular (actual expense) method or the simplified (safe harbor) method.

---

[50]§ 280A(c)(1).

[51]See the restrictive interpretation arrived at in *Comm. v. Soliman*, 93-1 USTC ¶50,014, 71 AFTR 2d 93–463, 113 S.Ct. 701 (USSC, 1993).

[52]§ 280A(c)(1) as modified by the Tax Reform Act of 1997.

Regular Method

In arriving at the office in the home deduction, relevant expenses are categorized as direct or indirect. Direct expenses benefit only the business part of the home (e.g., the office is repainted) and are deducted in full. Indirect expenses are for maintaining and operating the home. Because they benefit both business and personal use, an allocation between the two is necessary. The allocation is made based on the floor space involved—divide the business area by the total home area to arrive at the business percentage.

The allowable home office expenses cannot exceed the gross income from the business less all other business expenses attributable to the activity. Furthermore, the home office expenses that are allowed as itemized deductions anyway (e.g., mortgage interest and real estate taxes) must be deducted first. All home office expenses of an employee are miscellaneous itemized deductions, except those (such as interest and taxes) that qualify as other personal itemized deductions. Home office expenses of a self-employed individual are trade or business expenses and are deductible *for* AGI.

Any disallowed home office expenses are *carried forward* and used in future years subject to the same limitations.

Example 45

Rick is a certified public accountant employed by a regional CPA firm as a tax manager. He operates a separate business in which he refinishes furniture in his home. For this business, he uses two rooms in the basement of his home exclusively and regularly. The floor space of the two rooms is 240 square feet, which constitutes 10% of the total floor space of his 2,400-square-foot residence. Gross income from the business totals $8,000. Expenses of the business (other than home office expenses) are $6,500. Rick incurs the following home office expenses:

Real property taxes on residence	$ 4,000
Interest expense on residence	7,500
Operating expenses of residence (including homeowners insurance)	2,000
Depreciation on residence (based on 10% business use)	350

Rick's deductions are determined as follows:

Business income		$ 8,000
Less: Other business expenses		(6,500)
Net income from the business (before the office in the home deduction)		$ 1,500
Less: Allocable taxes ($4,000 × 10%)	$400	
Allocable interest ($7,500 × 10%)	750	(1,150)
		$ 350
Allocable operating expenses of the residence ($2,000 × 10%)		(200)
		$ 150
Allocable depreciation ($350, limited to remaining income)		(150)
		$ –0–

Rick has a carryover of $200 (the unused excess depreciation). Because he is self-employed, the allocable taxes and interest ($1,150), the other deductible office expenses ($200 + $150), and $6,500 of other business expenses are deductible *for* AGI.

As noted in Example 45, the office in the home deduction includes an allocable portion of the depreciation on the personal residence. To arrive at this depreciation, taxpayers use the MACRS percentage for 39-year nonresidential real property. Except for the first and last years (i.e., 1 and 40), the applicable percentage is 2.564 percent—see Table 8.6 in Chapter 8. Office furnishings are handled separately and are either expensed under § 179 or depreciated in accordance with the rules discussed in Chapter 8—see Exhibit 8.1 and Table 8.1.

TAX IN THE NEWS   Has the Trend Toward Working From Home Changed?

Is the recent decision by Yahoo, Inc., to end work-from-home arrangements and require job-site presence likely to reverse the home-based work trend? That is unlikely, according to the U.S. Census Bureau. Although much depends on the industry involved, the home-based workforce keeps increasing. Driven by employers' cost savings, employees' savings in commute time, and documented productivity increases, the mutual benefits are too strong to overlook. All indicators support a continued emphasis on home-based work assignments.

Source: Based on Neil Shaw, "More Americans Working Remotely," *Wall Street Journal*, March 6, 2013, p. A4.

An office in the home deduction is also available to those who rent (rather than own) their home. If the taxpayer does not own the property, the applicable percentage of business use is applied to the rent being paid.

The office in the home deduction as computed under the regular method can be claimed using Form 8829 (Expenses for Business Use of Your Home).

Simplified Method

Because of the complexity involved in using the regular method and, in particular, the difficulty in working with Form 8829, the IRS has established an optional simplified method for the office in the home deduction.[53] Presuming the taxpayer has met the requirements for the deduction (e.g., business purpose, exclusive use requirements), the amount allowed is $5 per square foot of space devoted to the office. However, as no more than 300 square feet can be counted, the maximum deduction is limited to $1,500. The various rules governing the use of the simplified method are summarized below.

* No depreciation on the residence can be claimed.
* Actual expenses of maintaining and operating the home (e.g., qualified residence interest, property taxes, homeowners insurance, utilities) are ignored. Some of these expenses (e.g., qualified residence interest, property taxes) might otherwise be claimed elsewhere on the return. Further, these expenses can be claimed in full without any reduction due to a home office deduction being claimed.
* No unused deduction (e.g., in excess of the net income from the business) can be carried over to a future year. Nor can an unused deduction from a prior year be carried to a simplified method year.

Taxpayers who claim an office in the home deduction are allowed an annual choice between the regular method and the simplified method. Although the choice of the simplified method once made is binding for that year, it is not binding on future years. Care should be taken in making the choice because the simplified method may yield a smaller deduction.

Example 46

Assume the same facts as in Example 45 except that Rick does not choose the regular method for determining the office in the home deduction. He chooses the simplified method with the following results:

Net income from the business (before the office in the home deduction)	$ 1,500
Simplified office in the home deduction ($5 × 240 square feet)	1,200
Net income from the business	$ 300

---

[53]Rev.Proc. 2013–13, 2013–6 I.R.B. 478.

In comparing the results of Examples 45 and 46, note that the use of the simplified method left Rick with $500 less in deductions (counting the $200 unused carryover). However, Rick can now restore the nonallocated property taxes ($400) and interest ($750) to his itemized deductions on Schedule A.

9-8b Miscellaneous Employee Expenses

Miscellaneous employee expenses include those costs that are job-related and are not otherwise covered elsewhere. As the focus here is on their deductibility, this discussion presumes that such expenses have not been reimbursed by the employer under an accountable plan arrangement (discussed later in the chapter).

Expenses related to maintaining job status make up a significant category of miscellaneous expenses. They include such costs as union dues, membership dues to professional organizations, subscriptions to trade publications and professional journals, and various license fees paid to government agencies and other regulatory bodies.

Special Clothing

To be deductible, special clothing must be both specifically required as a condition of employment and not adaptable for regular wear. For example, a police officer's uniform must be worn when "on duty" but is not suitable for "off-duty" activities. Its cost, therefore, is deductible. When special clothing qualifies for deductibility, so does the cost of its maintenance (i.e., alterations, laundry, and dry cleaning).

Whether the out-of-pocket cost of military uniforms is deductible depends on the duty status of the taxpayer. If a member of the National Guard (or reserves) is not on active duty, then the cost of the uniform qualifies for deductibility. For those on active duty, the cost of regular uniforms does not qualify because the uniforms are suitable for ordinary street wear. Even for those on active duty, some apparel, such as ceremonial attire (dress blues) or combat gear, will qualify because it is not adaptable for regular wear.

The cost of clothing possessing *safety* features to prevent workplace injuries will qualify. This includes such items as safety glasses, shoes (e.g., "steel-toed"), special gloves, lab coats, and hard hats. The tolerance of the IRS in the area of safety clothing is partially attributable to its lack of suitability for personal use.

Job Hunting

The expenses incurred in seeking employment can be deductible under certain conditions. The search must involve the same trade or business as the taxpayer's current position. No deduction is allowed for the cost of obtaining the first job. An unemployed person, however, can qualify for the deduction if there has not been a significant time lapse since the last job. In terms of deductibility, it does not matter whether the job search is successful. Nor does a change in jobs have to result. Costs that qualify include job counseling, compilation and distribution of biographical data (such as work history), and unreimbursed travel for job interviews.

THE BIG PICTURE

Example 47

Return to the facts of *The Big Picture* on p. 9-1. Recall that Morgan conducted an extensive job search before obtaining her position with Kite Corporation. Because this is her first job, the expenses she incurred in the search are not deductible.

Educator Expenses

Many teachers purchase school supplies for classroom use and are not reimbursed by their employer. These out-of-pocket expenses can be deducted only if the teacher itemizes his or her deductions *from* AGI, and even then they are subject to the 2 percent-of-AGI floor (see later in this chapter). Thus, these restrictions can reduce or eliminate any tax benefit available to the teacher. *Modest* relief is provided for such out-of-pocket expenses by allowing elementary and secondary school teachers to claim up to $250 for school supplies as a deduction *for* AGI.[54] Eligible educators must work at least 900 hours during a school year as a teacher, an instructor, a counselor, a principal, or an aide at either public or private elementary and secondary schools. Covered costs include unreimbursed expenses for books, supplies, computer and other equipment, and supplementary materials used in the classroom.

> **Example 48**
>
> Hortense is a full-time teacher at Hoover Elementary. During the year, she spends $1,200 for school supplies for her fourth-grade class. Under an accountable plan (see later in the chapter), Hoover reimburses her for $400 of these supplies. As to the $800 balance, Hortense may claim $250 as a deduction *for* AGI and $550 as a miscellaneous itemized deduction (subject to the 2%-of-AGI floor).

9-9 CONTRIBUTIONS TO RETIREMENT ACCOUNTS

Pension considerations are an essential feature of any compensation arrangement. As noted in Chapter 1, providing retirement security for employees can be justified on both economic and social grounds. Because the public sector (i.e., Social Security) will not provide sufficient retirement security for recipients, the private sector must fill the need. Congress has given the private sector the necessary incentive by enacting various measures that provide significant tax advantages for retirement plans. These plans fall into two major classifications: those available to employees and those available to self-employed persons.

LO.8

Compare various deductions for contributions to retirement accounts.

9-9a Employee IRAs

Pension plans covering employees follow one of two income tax approaches. Most plans allow an *exclusion* for the contributions the employee makes to the plan. The employee's income tax return shows nothing regarding the contribution—no income, exclusion, or deduction. This is the case even if the contribution is funded entirely (or partially) by means of a salary reduction.[55]

The other income tax approach is followed by the **traditional IRA**. Here, the contributing employee is allowed a deduction *for* AGI. The amount, a maximum of $5,500 in 2014 or 2013 ($5,000 in 2012) or $6,500 in 2014 or 2013 ($6,000 in 2012) for those age 50 and older, is reported as a deduction on Form 1040.[56] As with the exclusion variety of pension plan, nothing is taxed to the employee-participant until distributions from the traditional IRA occur. Consequently, all of these types of retirement plans carry the advantage of deferring the taxation of income. As described in Chapter 19, all retirement plans are subject to various rules regarding coverage requirements, degree of vesting, excessive contributions, and premature distributions. Generally, these rules are less stringent for traditional IRAs.

The traditional IRA is to be distinguished from the **Roth IRA**, which takes a radically different tax approach. No tax benefit (i.e., exclusion or deduction) results from the initial contribution to a Roth IRA. Instead, later distributions (including postcontribution earnings) are recovered tax-free.[57]

9-9b Self-Employed Keogh (H.R. 10) Plans

Self-employed taxpayers can also participate in retirement plans with tax-favored benefits. Known as Keogh (or H.R. 10) plans, these arrangements follow the deduction approach of traditional IRAs.[58] The amount contributed under a plan is a

---

[54]§ 62(a)(2)(D). This provision expired on December 31, 2013, but is expected to be extended.

[55]See, for example, §§ 401(k), 403(b), and 457.

[56]§§ 219 and 408.

[57]§ 408A.

[58]§ 401(c).

deduction *for* AGI and is reported as a deduction on Form 1040. The plan established by a self-employed taxpayer who has employees must meet stringent requirements to ensure that it provides similar retirement benefits for the group. The law is structured to ensure that employees share an owner-employer's ability to defer taxes.

Retirement plans for self-employed taxpayers and other small businesses are not restricted to H.R. 10 plans. Other options include solo or individual § 401(k) plans, simplified employee pension (SEP) plans, and savings incentive match plans for employees (SIMPLEs).[59] The operational rules governing all of these plans are covered in Chapter 19.

9-10 CLASSIFICATION OF EMPLOYEE EXPENSES

LO.9

Demonstrate the difference between accountable and nonaccountable employee plans.

The classification of employee expenses depends on whether they are reimbursed by the employer under an accountable plan. If so, then they are not reported by the employee at all. In effect, therefore, this result is equivalent to treating the expenses as deductions *for* AGI. If the expenses are reimbursed under a nonaccountable plan or are not reimbursed at all, then they are classified as deductions *from* AGI and can be claimed only if the employee-taxpayer itemizes. An exception is made for moving expenses and the employment-related expenses of a qualified performing artist.[60] Here, deduction *for* AGI classification is allowed.

For classification purposes, therefore, the difference between accountable and nonaccountable plans is significant.

ETHICS & EQUITY   A Sanitized Expense Account

Jacob is the top traveling salesperson for Heron Aquatics, a wholesaler of pool equipment and supplies. He has a reputation with management of being very conservative in his use of company funds. Because of these traits—salesmanship and frugality—Jacob has received frequent promotions and bonuses.

Unknown to Heron, Jacob is quite generous when entertaining customers. He believes that his high level of "wine and dine" is largely the reason for his outstanding sales record. In the expense account he submits to Heron, Jacob omits the excessive portion. He is not sure whether the company would reimburse him for the extra costs, and he wants to maintain his reputation for frugality. On his own tax return, however, Jacob deducts the portion of the expenses that were not included in the expense account he submitted to Heron.

What difficulties, if any, do you anticipate with what Jacob is doing?

© iStockphoto.com/LdF

9-10a Accountable Plans

An **accountable plan** requires the employee to satisfy these two requirements:

- Adequately account for (substantiate) the expenses. An employee renders an *adequate accounting* by submitting a record, with receipts and other substantiation, to the employer.[61]
- Return any excess reimbursement or allowance. An "excess reimbursement or allowance" is any amount the employee does not adequately account for as an ordinary and necessary business expense.

Substantiation

The law provides that no deduction is allowed for any travel, entertainment, business gift, or listed property (automobiles and computers) expenditure unless

---

[59]Relevant Code Sections are § 408(k) for SEPs and § 408(p) for SIMPLEs.   [61]Reg. § 1.162–17(b)(4).
[60]As defined in § 62(b).

properly substantiated by adequate records. The records should contain the following information:[62]

- The amount of the expense.
- The time and place of travel or entertainment (or date of gift).
- The business purpose of the expense.
- The business relationship of the taxpayer to the person entertained (or receiving the gift).

This means that the taxpayer must maintain an account book or diary in which the above information is recorded at the time of the expenditure. Documentary evidence, such as itemized receipts, is required to support any expenditure for lodging while traveling away from home and for any other expenditure of $75 or more. If a taxpayer fails to keep adequate records, each expense must be established by a written or oral statement of the exact details of the expense and by other corroborating evidence.[63]

Bertha has travel expenses substantiated only by canceled checks. The checks establish the date, place, and amount of the expenditure. Because neither the business relationship nor the business purpose is established, the deduction is disallowed.[64]	**Example 49**

Dwight has travel and entertainment expenses substantiated by a diary showing the time, place, and amount of the expenditure. His oral testimony provides the business relationship and business purpose. However, because he has no receipts, any expenditures of $75 or more are disallowed.[65]	**Example 50**

Deemed Substantiation

In lieu of reimbursing actual expenses for travel away from home, many employers reduce their paperwork by adopting a policy of reimbursing employees with a *per diem* allowance, a flat dollar amount per day of business travel. Of the substantiation requirements listed previously, the *amount* of the expense is proved, or *deemed substantiated*, by using such a per diem allowance or reimbursement procedure. The amount of expenses that is deemed substantiated is equal to the lesser of the per diem allowance or the amount of the Federal per diem rate.

The regular Federal per diem rate is the highest amount the Federal government will pay to its employees for lodging, meals, and incidental expenses[66] while in travel status away from home in a particular area. The rates are different for different locations.[67]

The use of the standard Federal per diem rates for meals and incidental expenses constitutes an adequate accounting. Employees and self-employed persons can use these standard allowances instead of deducting the actual cost of daily meals and incidental expenses, even if not reimbursed. There is no standard lodging allowance, however.

Only the amount of the expense is considered substantiated under the deemed substantiated method. The other substantiation requirements must be provided: place, date, business purpose of the expense, and the business relationship of the parties involved.

9-10b Nonaccountable Plans

A **nonaccountable plan** is a plan in which an adequate accounting or return of excess amounts, or both, is not required. All reimbursements of expenses are reported in full as wages on the employee's Form W–2. Any allowable expenses are deductible in the same manner as unreimbursed expenses.

---

[62]§ 274(d).

[63]Reg. § 1.274–5T(c)(3).

[64]*William T. Whitaker*, 56 TCM 47, T.C.Memo. 1988–418.

[65]*W. David Tyler*, 43 TCM 927, T.C.Memo. 1982–160.

[66]Incidental expenses include tips and fees to porters, bellhops, hotel maids, etc. For travel away from home, the term does *not* include expenses for laundry and dry cleaning of clothing, lodging taxes, and telephone calls.

[67]*Per Diem Rates* (IRS Publication 1542) contains the list and amounts for the year. This publication is available only on the Internet at **www.irs.gov**. Links to per diem rates can also be found at **www.gsa.gov**.

Unreimbursed Employee Expenses

Unreimbursed employee expenses are treated in a straightforward manner. Meals and entertainment expenses are subject to the 50 percent limit. Total unreimbursed employee business expenses are usually reported as miscellaneous itemized deductions subject to the 2 percent-of-AGI floor (see next page). If the employee could have received, but did not seek, reimbursement for whatever reason, none of the employment-related expenses are deductible.

Failure to Comply with Accountable Plan Requirements

An employer may have an accountable plan and require employees to return excess reimbursements or allowances, but an employee may fail to follow the rules of the plan. In that case, the expenses and reimbursements are subject to nonaccountable plan treatment.

9-10c Reporting Procedures

The reporting requirements range from no reporting at all (accountable plans when all requirements are met) to the use of some or all of the following forms: Form W–2 (Wage and Tax Statement), Form 2106 (Employee Business Expenses) or Form 2106–EZ (Unreimbursed Employee Business Expenses), and Schedule A (Itemized Deductions) for nonaccountable plans and unreimbursed employee expenses.

Reimbursed employee expenses that are adequately accounted for under an accountable plan are deductible *for* AGI on Form 2106. Allowed excess expenses, expenses reimbursed under a nonaccountable plan, and unreimbursed expenses are deductible *from* AGI on Schedule A, subject to the 2 percent-of-AGI floor.

When a reimbursement under an accountable plan is paid in separate amounts relating to designated expenses such as meals or entertainment, no problem arises. The reimbursements and expenses are reported as such on the appropriate forms. If the reimbursement is made in a single amount, an allocation must be made to determine the appropriate portion of the reimbursement that applies to meals and entertainment and to other employee expenses.

Example 51

Sophia, who is employed by Garnet Company, had AGI of $60,000 during the year. She incurred employment-related expenses as follows: $4,000 (transportation), $3,000 (lodging), $2,000 (meals), and $1,000 (entertainment). Under an accountable plan, Sophia received partial reimbursement from Garnet of $6,000. Because Sophia was not fully reimbursed, she must make an allocation to determine the portion attributable to the expenses subject to the cutback adjustment.

$$\frac{\$2,000 \text{ (meals)} + \$1,000 \text{ (entertainment)}}{\$10,000 \text{ (total expenses)}} = 30\%$$

Thus, 30% of the reimbursement, or $1,800, relates to meals and entertainment, while the balance of $4,200 applies to transportation and lodging. Further computations follow to account for the reimbursement (treated, in effect, as a deduction *for* AGI), apply the cutback adjustment, and deduct the 2% floor.

	No Cutback Adjustment	Cutback Adjustment
Transportation and lodging ($4,000 + $3,000)	$ 7,000	
Meals and entertainment ($2,000 + $1,000)		$ 3,000
Less reimbursement		
(70% × $6,000)	(4,200)	
(30% × $6,000)		(1,800)
	$ 2,800	$ 1,200
Cutback adjustment (50% × $1,200)		(600)
Unreimbursed portion	$ 2,800	$ 600

The unreimbursed portion of $3,400 ($2,800 + $600) is reported on Schedule A and is reduced by 2% of AGI. Thus, $3,400 − $1,200 [2% × $60,000 (AGI)] yields a deduction *from* AGI of $2,200. Sophia does not have to report any of the $6,000 reimbursement.

9-11 LIMITATIONS ON ITEMIZED DEDUCTIONS

Many itemized deductions, such as medical expenses and charitable contributions, are subject to limitations expressed as a percentage of AGI. These limitations may be expressed as floors or ceilings and are discussed in Chapter 10.

LO.10

Apply the limitations on miscellaneous itemized deductions.

9-11a Miscellaneous Itemized Deductions Subject to the 2 Percent Floor

Certain miscellaneous itemized deductions, including most *unreimbursed employee business expenses*, are aggregated and then reduced by 2 percent of AGI.[68] Expenses subject to the 2 percent floor include the following:

- All § 212 expenses, except expenses of producing rent and royalty income (refer to Chapter 6).
- All unreimbursed employee expenses (after the 50 percent reduction, if applicable) except moving expenses.
- Professional dues and subscriptions.
- Union dues and work uniforms.
- Employment-related education expenses (except § 222 qualified tuition and related expenses).
- Malpractice insurance premiums.
- Expenses of job hunting (including employment agency fees and résumé-writing expenses).
- Home office expenses of an employee or outside salesperson.
- Legal, accounting, and tax return preparation fees.
- Hobby expenses (up to hobby income).
- Investment expenses, including investment counsel fees, subscriptions, and safe deposit box rental.
- Custodial fees relating to income-producing property or a traditional IRA or a Keogh plan.
- Any fees paid to collect interest or dividends.
- Appraisal fees establishing a casualty loss or charitable contribution.

9-11b Miscellaneous Itemized Deductions Not Subject to the 2 Percent Floor

Certain miscellaneous itemized deductions, including the following, are not subject to the 2 percent floor:

- Impairment-related work expenses of handicapped individuals.
- Gambling losses to the extent of gambling winnings.
- Certain terminated annuity payments.

---

[68]§ 67.

TAX IN THE NEWS   Relief for Members of the Armed Forces Reserves

In the Military Family Tax Relief Act of 2003, Congress provided various tax benefits for reservists, one of which deals with the classification of travel expenses. Members of the Reserves or National Guard who travel to drills and other service-related activities may claim the expenses as deductions *for* AGI. Previously, the expenses were not deductible unless the taxpayer itemized. (As miscellaneous itemized deductions, they were subject to the 2 percent-of-AGI floor.) To qualify for the deduction *for* AGI classification, the trip must be more than 100 miles from home and include an overnight stay. Any deduction is limited to the Federal per diem rates applicable to the area involved.

Source: *Armed Forces' Tax Guide* (IRS Publication 3), p. 5.

Example 52

Ted, who has AGI of $40,000, has the following miscellaneous itemized deductions:

Gambling losses (to extent of gains)	$2,200
Tax return preparation fees	500
Unreimbursed employee transportation	600
Professional dues and subscriptions	360
Safe deposit box rental	90

Ted's itemized deductions are as follows:

Deduction not subject to 2% floor (gambling losses)		$2,200
Deductions subject to 2% floor ($500 + $600 + $360 + $90)	$1,550	
Less 2% of AGI	(800)	750
Total miscellaneous itemized deductions		$2,950

If instead Ted's AGI is $80,000, the floor is $1,600 (2% of $80,000); in this case, he can only deduct the $2,200 because his expenses subject to the 2% floor do not exceed $1,600.

9-12 TAX PLANNING

9-12a Employment Status

LO.11

List and evaluate tax planning ideas related to employee business expenses.

When considering the merits of employee or independent contractor status, much depends on which party is involved. If it is the worker, being self-employed carries the obvious advantage of a deduction *for* AGI category of job-related expenses and the avoidance of the 2 percent limitation applicable to any unreimbursed excess.

However, a self-employed individual may have other costs, such as local gross receipts taxes, license fees, franchise fees, personal property taxes, and occupation taxes. In addition, the record-keeping and filing requirements can be quite burdensome.

One of the most expensive considerations is the Social Security tax versus the self-employment tax. For an employee in 2014, for example, the Social Security tax applies at a rate of 6.2 percent on a base amount of wages of $117,000 ($113,700 in 2013) and the Medicare tax applies at a rate of 1.45 percent with no limit on the base amount. Further, a .9 percent additional Medicare tax applies to certain high earners. For self-employed persons, the rate, but not the base amount, for each tax doubles. Even though a deduction *for* AGI is allowed for part of the self-employment tax paid, an employee and a self-employed individual are not in the same tax position on equal amounts of earnings. The self-employment tax is explained in Chapter 13. For the applicability of these taxes to employees, see Chapter 1.

TAX IN THE NEWS The i's Were Dotted But the t's Weren't Crossed

In two recent cases, the taxpayers sincerely believed that their workers were independent contractors and applied for Section 530 relief (see text discussion) against their reclassification as employees. The relief was denied because they did not file Form 1099–MISC for any of the workers and, therefore, did not meet one of the three requirements.

Source: *John Keller* (103 TCM 1298, T.C.Memo. 2012–62); *Atlantic Coast Masonry, Inc.* (104 TCM 189, T.C.Memo. 2012–233).

9-12b Misclassification Danger

From an employer's perspective, moreover, there are many reasons to favor classifying workers as independent contractors rather than as employees. Besides avoiding payroll taxes and income tax withholdings the employer circumvents a myriad of state and local laws. Examples include vacation pay obligations, unemployment tax and workers' compensation requirements, and overtime and minimum wage restrictions. Because complying with these rules is costly and burdensome, many employers are motivated to misclassify their workers as independent contractors.

In the event of misclassification, two remedies are available—one legislative and one administrative. The legislative option, known as Section 530 relief, completely absolves the employer of the employment taxes that should have been paid.[69] To obtain Section 530 relief, *all* three of the following requirements must be met:

- The employer has a reasonable basis for *not* treating the workers as employees. Reasonable basis means reliance on any of the following:
  - A judicial precedent, a published ruling, or technical advice.
  - A past IRS audit that resulted in no employment tax assessment.
  - A longstanding practice of independent contractor status in the same industry.
- The employer has consistently treated the workers as independent contractors.
- The employer has filed Form 1099–MISC (Miscellaneous Income) for each worker (when such filing was required).

As noted in the "Tax in the News" (see above), a common hurdle to securing Section 530 relief is the failure to file the required Forms 1099–MISC.

The administrative remedy for employers who are misclassifying workers is the recently promulgated Voluntary Classification Settlement Program (VCSP).[70] A type of amnesty arrangement, the VCSP allows the applicant to be absolved from all employment taxes that should have been paid plus any interest and penalties that would be due. To be accepted, Form 8952 [Application for Voluntary Classification Settlement Program (VCSP)] must be filed and certain conditions met.[71] A major condition is the payment of about 1 percent of the wages paid to reclassified workers in the past year.

9-12c Improving the Tax Position of Employees

For an employee with job-related expenses who receives reimbursement from the employer, the ideal tax position results from the following arrangement:

- Render an adequate accounting to the employer.
- Be fully reimbursed.
- Return any excess reimbursement.

---

[69]This safe harbor for withholding purposes originated in Section 530 of the Revenue Act of 1978. See IRS *Headliner*, vol. 152 (March 27, 2006).

[70]Announcement 2011–64, 2011–4 I.R.B. 503.

[71]The conditions to be met are set forth in the instructions for Form 8952. Many of these conditions are the same as those required for Section 530 relief.

If these conditions exist, the employee will avoid any cutback adjustment (for meals and entertainment) and will completely eliminate the 2 percent floor on employee expenses. As all of the employee expenses are shifted to the employer, the employee may even be able to claim the standard deduction rather than itemize.

Even if the reimbursement of expenses is partial (not full), some planning is possible. Consider what happens in Example 51 if Garnet's reimbursement states that it specifically covers the $2,000 meals and $1,000 entertainment expenditures. Sophia now has no cutback adjustment, and her deduction is increased.

These considerations should be taken into account when an employee enters into an employment agreement. In some cases, it may even be worthwhile to accept a lower base salary in order to obtain a favorable expense reimbursement arrangement.

9-12d Transportation and Travel Expenses

Adequate detailed records of all transportation and travel expenses should be kept. Because the automatic (standard) mileage allowance often is modest in amount, a new, expensive automobile used primarily for business may generate a higher expense based on actual cost. In using the actual cost method, include the business portion of depreciation, repairs and maintenance, automobile club dues, insurance, gasoline and oil, and other related costs. The cost of gasoline, when coupled with the poor mileage performance of some vehicles, can be a significant factor. If the taxpayer is located in a metropolitan area, automobile insurance is more expensive. For the self-employed taxpayer, the business portion of finance charges (i.e., interest on car loans) can be included under the actual cost method.

Once a method is chosen, a later change may be possible. Conversion from the automatic mileage method to the actual cost method is allowed if a basis adjustment is made for depreciation deemed taken (see Example 10). Conversion from the actual cost method to the automatic mileage method is possible only if the taxpayer has not used the MACRS statutory percentage method or claimed § 179 limited expensing.

If a taxpayer wants to sightsee or vacation on a business trip, it would be beneficial to schedule business on both a Friday and a Monday to turn the weekend into business days for allocation purposes. It is especially crucial to schedule appropriate business days when foreign travel is involved.

ETHICS & EQUITY   Walking to Soccer Practice

Mel Wilson is married and has three children, ages 9, 12, and 14. Mel works in the city of Houston, and he and his family live in the suburbs. Mrs. Wilson does not work outside the home. The Wilsons own only one automobile and for tax purposes classify it as being used 95 percent for business use and 5 percent for personal use. Do you envision any problems with this allocation? Would it matter whether the Wilsons base their deduction on the actual cost method or the automatic mileage method? Explain.

9-12e Moving Expenses

Persons who retire and move to a new location incur personal nondeductible moving expenses. If the retired person accepts a full-time job in the new location, the moving expenses are deductible.

Example 53

At the time of his retirement from the national office of a major accounting firm, Gordon had an annual salary of $420,000. He moves from New York City to Seattle to retire. To qualify for the moving expense deduction, Gordon accepts a full-time teaching position at a Seattle junior college at an annual salary of $15,000. If Gordon satisfies the 39-week test, his moving expenses are deductible. The disparity between the two salaries (previous and current) is of no consequence.

9-12f Education Expenses

Education expenses are treated as nondeductible personal items unless the individual is employed or is engaged in a trade or business. A temporary leave of absence for further education is one way to reasonably ensure that the taxpayer is still qualified, even if a full-time student. An individual was permitted to deduct education expenses even though he resigned from his job, returned to school full-time for two years, and accepted another job in the same field upon graduation. The court held that the student had merely suspended active participation in his field.[72]

If the time out of the field is too long, educational expense deductions will be disallowed. For example, a teacher who left the field for four years to raise her child and curtailed her employment searches and writing activities was denied a deduction. She was not actively engaged in the trade or business of being an educator.[73]

To secure the deduction, an individual should arrange his or her work situation to preserve employee or business status.

The deduction for qualified tuition and related expenses provides some relief from the current restrictions on the deduction of education expenses by employees. First, the education expense does not have to be work-related. Second, it is a deduction *for* (not *from*) AGI. Unfortunately, the deduction possesses severe shortcomings: not only is the annual amount allowed quite modest, but it may be unavailable to certain taxpayers. It is not available, for example, to those who exceed an AGI ceiling or to someone who can be claimed as a dependent of another.

Before selecting the § 222 deduction approach, however, consider the possible availability of the American Opportunity (formerly the HOPE) credit or the lifetime learning credit under § 25A.[74] As credits provide a dollar-for-dollar reduction of tax liability, these provisions could yield a greater tax benefit than deductions *for* AGI. But these credits may not be available to higher-income taxpayers.

9-12g Entertainment and Meal Expenses

Proper documentation of expenditures is essential because of the strict record-keeping requirements and the restrictive tests that must be met. For example, documentation that consists solely of credit card receipts and canceled checks may be inadequate to substantiate the business purpose and business relationship.[75] Taxpayers should maintain detailed records of amounts, time, place, business purpose, and business relationships. A credit card receipt details the place, date, and amount of the expense. A notation made on the receipt of the names of the person(s) attending, the business relationship, and the topic of discussion should constitute proper documentation.

Associated with or goodwill entertainment is not deductible unless a business discussion is conducted immediately before or after the entertainment. Furthermore, a business purpose must exist for the entertainment. Taxpayers should arrange for a business discussion before or after such entertainment. They must provide documentation of the business purpose, such as obtaining new business from a prospective customer.

Unreimbursed meals and entertainment are subject to the 50 percent cutback rule in addition to the 2 percent floor. Consequently, the procedure of negotiating a salary reduction, as discussed in a prior section, is even more valuable to the taxpayer.

[72]*Stephen G. Sherman*, 36 TCM 1191, T.C.Memo. 1977–301.

[73]*Brian C. Mulherin*, 42 TCM 834, T.C.Memo. 1981–454; *George A. Baist*, 56 TCM 778, T.C.Memo. 1988–554.

[74]These credits are briefly mentioned on p. 19 in this chapter and are discussed at greater length in Chapter 13.

[75]*Kenneth W. Guenther*, 54 TCM 382, T.C.Memo. 1987–440.

9-12h Office in the Home

The availability of the simplified method under Rev.Proc. 2013–13 presents another decision that a taxpayer will have to make each year. In arriving at which method to use for computing the office in the home deduction, here are some factors to consider:

- The simplified method requires fewer calculations and less record keeping.
- Because no depreciation is allowed, the simplified method will avoid recapture on the disposition of the residence.
- Even though the simplified method frees up certain home-related expenses (e.g., qualified residence interest, property taxes, homeowners insurance, utilities), are these expenses otherwise deductible? Some are (property taxes), and some are not (homeowners insurance). But even the expenses that are deductible (property taxes) may be subject to various limitations placed on itemized deductions (see Chapter 10).
- The simplified method, being limited to a maximum of $1,500, does not offer a very generous result. In most cases, the regular method will yield a larger deduction.
- Unlike the regular method, under the simplified method, a taxpayer is not allowed to carry over unused deductions.
- Once a taxpayer has made a choice for a year, the election is irrevocable and cannot be changed.

Example 54	Tyler, a calendar year taxpayer, prepared and filed his own tax return for 2013. Being in a hurry, he chose and used the simplified method of computing his deduction for an office in the home. In March 2015, Tyler seeks tax advice and learns how much he could have saved by using the regular method. Tyler cannot file an amended return for 2013, but he can switch to the regular method for 2014.

REFOCUS ON THE BIG PICTURE

THE FIRST JOB

© iStockphoto.com/Svetikd

The first issue that might arise as a result of Morgan's new job is the dependency exemption possibility. If Morgan was living at home and accepted the job late in the year, she could qualify as a dependent of her parents. If so, they might also be able to claim the qualified tuition deduction (or the lifetime learning credit). If, however, her employment began early in the year, she could not be a qualifying child (due to the self-supporting limitation) or a qualifying relative (due to the gross income limitation)—see Chapter 3.

Although Morgan's "extensive search" for employment indicates that she may have incurred job hunting expenses, such expenses are not deductible in a *first job* setting (see Example 47). Her qualified moving expenses, however, are not so restricted. Moving expenses are deductions *for* AGI (see Example 29).

Morgan is justified in claiming an office in the home deduction. She can use either the regular (actual expense) method or the simplified (safe harbor) method. Under the regular method, the deduction would include a portion of the rent and utilities paid and related maintenance costs (e.g., janitorial service). The safe harbor method would allow Morgan $5 per square foot for business space, but not more than 300 square feet, or $1,500. Under either method, she would also be allowed depreciation (or expensing) of office equipment and furnishings (e.g., computer, copier, desk, file cabinet). She must be careful, however, not to violate the "exclusive use" restriction (see Examples 43, 45, and 46) regardless of which method she uses.

As she is required to travel as part of her job, Morgan will use her car for business. Thus, she will need to make a choice between the automatic mileage method and the actual cost method (see Example 11). Because her tax home is in her apartment, she will have no nondeductible commuting expenses (see Example 9).

If she renders an adequate accounting (and has to return any excess) to Kite Corporation, then her allowance need not be reported on her Federal income tax return. Nonreimbursed amounts, however, will have to be allocated between meals and entertainment (subject to the 50 percent cutback adjustment) and other employment-related expenses. The balance is an itemized deduction subject to the 2 percent-of-AGI floor.

If she does not render an adequate accounting, the full allowance is included in her gross income. All of the meals and entertainment expenses are subject to the 50 percent cutback adjustment, and the total of all employment-related expenses is an itemized deduction subject to the 2 percent-of-AGI floor.

If Morgan started the job with Kite Corporation late in the year, it is unlikely that she will be in a position to itemize her deductions *from* AGI. Instead, she will claim the standard deduction.

Morgan must maintain adequate substantiation regarding all of these employment-related transactions. Detailed records are particularly important in arriving at the office in the home deduction (if the regular method is used) and the business use of an automobile (under the actual cost method). If Morgan does not render an accounting to Kite, records are crucial in supporting the travel and entertainment expenses.

Key Terms

Accountable plan, 9-28

Automatic mileage method, 9-6

Deduction for qualified tuition and related expenses, 9-16

Education expenses, 9-14

Entertainment expenses, 9-19

Independent contractor, 9-2

Moving expenses, 9-12

Nonaccountable plan, 9-29

Office in the home expenses, 9-23

Roth IRA, 9-27

Statutory employees, 9-4

Traditional IRA, 9-27

Transportation expenses, 9-4

Travel expenses, 9-8

Discussion Questions

1. **LO.1, 9** Sophia and Jacob are married and file a joint return. The return for 2013 included a Form 2106 for each of them. The return for 2014, however, included a Form 2106 and a Schedule C. In terms of employment status, what could have changed?

   Issue ID

2. **LO.1, 9** Yolanda is employed but is not reimbursed by her employer for her job-related expenses. If Yolanda always claims the standard deduction, she can never deduct any of these expenses. Do you agree with this conclusion? Explain.

   Issue ID

3. **LO.1** Mason performs services for Isabella. In determining whether Mason is an employee or an independent contractor, comment on the relevance of each of the factors listed below.
   a. Mason performs services only for Isabella and does not work for anyone else.
   b. Mason sets his own work schedule.
   c. Mason reports his job-related expenses on a Schedule C.
   d. Mason obtained his job skills from Isabella's training program.
   e. Mason performs the services at Isabella's business location.
   f. Mason is paid based on time worked rather than on task performed.

Decision Making

4. **LO.1** Bernard operates a hair styling salon as a sole proprietor. Because his shop has several extra workstations that are not being used, he is considering renting them to other stylists, but he wants to avoid any employer-employee relationship with them. Advise Bernard on the type of working arrangement he should set up to ensure that any new stylists will be classified as independent contractors and not as employees.

Issue ID

5. **LO.1, 11** In mid-2014, Madison goes to work for Knot Corporation. In January 2015, she receives a Form 1099 from Knot reflecting her classification as an independent contractor. Madison disagrees with this classification.
   a. Why does she disagree?
   b. Does Madison have any recourse on the issue of her employment status? Explain

6. **LO.1** In terms of characteristics, how are statutory employees similar to common law employees? To independent contractors?

7. **LO.1** The IRS presumes that two types of workers should be classified as independent contractors. Who are these workers, and why is the automatic classification justified?

Issue ID

8. **LO.2** Milton is a resident of Mobile (AL) and is employed by Scaup Corporation. Because Scaup closed its Mobile office, Milton no longer has any nondeductible commuting expenses although he continues to work for Scaup. Explain why.

Issue ID

9. **LO.2** In 2012, Emma purchased an automobile, which she uses for both business and personal purposes. Although Emma does not keep records as to operating expenses (e.g., gas, oil, and repairs), she can prove the percentage of business use and the miles driven each year. In March 2014, Emma seeks your advice as to what income tax benefit, if any, she can derive from the use of her automobile. What would you suggest?

10. **LO.2, 3** Explain the difference between *travel* expenses and *transportation* expenses.

11. **LO.3** Lance, who practices law in New York City, leaves his office on Tuesday at 4:00 A.M., flies to Los Angeles, makes a court appearance at 1:00 P.M., and flies back to New York that same day.
    a. Was Lance away from home for income tax purposes? Why or why not?
    b. What difference does it make?

12. **LO.3** The lodging expense of an employee who is not away from home overnight can never be deductible. Do you agree with this statement? Explain.

Issue ID

13. **LO.3** Dr. Werner is a full-time professor of accounting at Pelican University. During the year, he teaches continuing education programs for CPA groups in several cities. He also serves as an expert witness in numerous lawsuits involving accounting fraud. Comment on the possible tax treatment of Dr. Werner's job-related expenses.

14. **LO.3** Bill and Jean Wilder attend a three-day seminar in Chicago on current developments in taxation. Bill is a partner in a law firm in Memphis specializing in tax practice, while his wife, Jean, is a paralegal with the same firm. Comment on the deductibility of the Wilders' expenses in attending the seminar.

Decision Making

15. **LO.3** Rick is scheduled to go to London on business and would like to do some sightseeing while there. A colleague advises him that to maximize his deductible expenses, he should plan the business and personal portions of the trip carefully to make effective use of weekends and holidays. What is meant by this advice?

16. **LO.4** To qualify for the moving expense deduction, a taxpayer must satisfy a time test.
    a. What is the time test?
    b. When might the taxpayer be excused from satisfying the time test?
    c. What reporting procedure should be followed when the taxpayer has to file a return *after* the moving expenses have been incurred but *before* the time test requirement is met?

17. **LO.4** Emma, who lives and works in Wisconsin, is planning to retire and move to Costa Rica. She has heard that when you retire and move to a foreign country, all moving expenses are deductible. Does Emma have a correct grasp of the rules involved? Explain.

18. **LO.5, 10** Jamie has an undergraduate degree in finance and is employed full-time by a bank. She is taking courses at a local university leading to an MBA degree.
    a. Is the cost of this education deductible to her?
    b. If so, what limitations are imposed on the deduction?

19. **LO.5, 10** In connection with § 222 (deduction for qualified tuition and related expenses), comment on the relevance of the following:
    a. The standard deduction is claimed.
    b. Enrollment at a college does not require the payment of a student activity fee.
    c. Miscellaneous itemized deductions are less than 2% of AGI.
    d. The taxpayer is married and files a separate return.
    e. A father pays the tuition on behalf of a daughter who does not qualify as his dependent.
    f. The taxpayer is single and has MAGI of $80,001.
    g. The lifetime learning credit is claimed.
    h. The taxpayer, a CPA, pays for tuition and course materials to attend law school.

20. **LO.6** In each of the following situations, indicate whether there is a cutback adjustment.
    a. Each year, the employer awards its top salesperson an all-expense-paid trip to Jamaica.
    b. The employer has a cafeteria for its employees where meals are furnished at cost.
    c. The employer sponsors an annual Labor Day picnic for its employees.
    d. Every Christmas, the employer gives each employee a fruitcake.
    e. The taxpayer, an airline pilot, pays for meals and lodging during a layover between flights.
    f. The taxpayer pays a cover charge to take key clients to a nightclub.
    g. The taxpayer gives business gifts to her clients at Christmas.
    h. The taxpayer purchases tickets to take clients to an athletic event.

21. **LO.6** At the last minute, a law firm purchases 10 tickets to the Super Bowl to entertain certain key clients. Comment on some possible tax ramifications of this situation. *Issue ID*

22. **LO.7** In connection with the office in the home deduction, comment on the following:
    a. The exclusive use requirement.
    b. The distinction between *direct* and *indirect* expenses.
    c. The effect of the taxpayer's work status (i.e., employed or self-employed) on the deduction.
    d. The ownership status of the residence (i.e., owned or rented).
    e. The tax treatment of office furnishings (e.g., desk, chairs, and file cabinets).
    f. The treatment of expenses that exceed the gross income from the business.

23. **LO.7** Review the advantages and disadvantages of the new simplified method for determining the office in the home deduction.

24. **LO.4, 7** Trent, a resident of Florida, attends Rice University. After graduation, he moves to Dallas, where he begins a job search. Shortly thereafter, he accepts a position with a local TV station as a reporter. Trent's college degree is in accounting. Presuming no reimbursement, what employment-related expenses might Trent be eligible to deduct? *Issue ID*

25. **LO.8** Regarding the tax implications of various retirement plans, comment on the following:
    a. The difference between Keogh (H.R. 10) and traditional deductible IRA plans.
    b. The difference between traditional IRA and Roth IRA plans.

26. **LO.9** What tax return reporting procedures must be followed by an employee under the following circumstances?
    a. Expenses and reimbursements are equal under an accountable plan.
    b. Reimbursements at the appropriate Federal per diem rate exceed expenses, and an adequate accounting is made to the employer.
    c. Expenses exceed reimbursements under a nonaccountable plan.

27. **LO.10** Comment on the deductibility of each of the following items:
    a. Club dues for the Coronado Club. Taxpayer, a lawyer, uses the luncheon club exclusively for business.
    b. Cost of dry cleaning uniforms (including alterations by a tailor). Taxpayer is the doorman at a New York City hotel.
    c. Expenses incurred by taxpayer, a member of the Maine National Guard, to participate in a two-day training session conducted in New Jersey.
    d. Union dues paid by a self-employed carpenter.
    e. Cost of CPA exam review course paid by a self-employed accountant.

f. Fee paid to a real estate appraiser to determine the value of land a taxpayer is donating to charity.

g. Contribution to an IRA sponsored by taxpayer's employer.

h. Cost of school supplies purchased by a high school teacher.

Problems

28. **LO.2, 3** During the year, Olivia holds two jobs. After an eight-hour day at the first job, she works three hours at the second job. On Fridays of each week, she returns home for dinner before going to the second job. On the other days (Monday through Thursday), she goes directly from the first job to the second job, stopping along the way for a meal. The mileage involved is as follows:

Home to first job	15
First job to second job	18
Home to second job	20

a. Assuming that Olivia works 48 weeks during the year, how much of her mileage is deductible?

b. Can Olivia deduct the dinners she purchased? Why or why not?

29. **LO.2, 5** William is employed by an accounting firm and uses his automobile in connection with his work. During the month of October 2014, he works at the office for 4 days and participates in the audit of a key client for 19 days. In the audit situation, William goes directly from his home to the client's office. On all other days, he drives to his employer's office. On four Saturdays in October, he drives from his home to a local university where he attends classes in a part-time MBA program. Relevant mileage is as follows:

Home to office	12
Office to audit client	13
Home to audit client	14
Home to university	10

Using the automatic mileage method, what is William's deduction for the month?

30. **LO.2** Ella is the regional sales manager for a fast-food chain. She starts her work day by driving from home to the regional office, works there for several hours, and then visits the three sales outlets in her region. Relevant mileage is as follows:

Home to regional office	10
Regional office to sales outlet 1	13
Sales outlet 1 to sales outlet 2	11
Sales outlet 2 to sales outlet 3	9
Sales outlet 3 to home	15

If Ella uses the automatic mileage method and works 240 days in 2014, what is her deduction for the year?

31. **LO.2** Jackson uses his automobile 90% for business and during 2014 drove a total of 14,000 miles. Information regarding his car expenses is listed below.

Business parking	$ 140
Auto insurance	1,300
Auto club dues (includes towing service)	180
Toll road charges (business-related)	200
Oil changes and engine tune-ups	210
Repairs	160
Depreciation allowable	2,850
Fines for traffic violations (incurred during business use)	320
Gasoline purchases	2,800

What is Jackson's deduction in 2014 for the use of his car if he uses:

a. The actual cost method?

b. The automatic mileage method?

32. **LO.2** On July 1, 2010, Rex purchases a new automobile for $40,000. He uses the car 80% for business and drives the car as follows: 8,000 miles in 2010, 19,000 miles in 2011, 20,000 miles in 2012, and 15,000 miles in 2013. Determine Rex's basis in the auto as of January 1, 2014, under the following assumptions.

    a. Rex uses the automatic mileage method.
    b. Rex uses the actual cost method. [Assume that no § 179 expensing is claimed and that 200% declining-balance cost recovery with the half-year convention is used—see Chapter 8. The recovery limitation for an auto placed in service in 2010 is as follows: $3,060 (first year), $4,900 (second year), $2,950 (third year), and $1,775 (fourth year).]

33. **LO.3** Kristen, the regional manager for a national hardware chain, is based in Atlanta. During March and April of this year, she has to replace temporarily the district manager in Jackson (Mississippi). During this period, Kristen flies to Jackson on Sunday night, spends the week at the district office, and returns home to Atlanta on Friday afternoon. The cost of returning home is $550, while the cost of spending the weekend in Jackson would have been $490.

    a. Presuming no reimbursement by her employer, how much, if any, of these weekend expenses may Kristen deduct?
    b. Would your answer in (a) change if the amounts involved are reversed (i.e., the trip home cost $490; staying in Jackson would have been $550)? Explain.

34. **LO.3, 6** In June of this year, Dr. and Mrs. Bret Spencer traveled to Denver to attend a three-day conference sponsored by the American Society of Implant Dentistry. Bret, a practicing oral surgeon, participated in scheduled technical sessions dealing with the latest developments in surgical procedures. On two days, Mrs. Spencer attended group meetings where various aspects of family tax planning were discussed. On the other day, she went sightseeing. Mrs. Spencer does not work for her husband, but she does their tax returns and handles the family investments. Expenses incurred in connection with the conference are summarized below.

Airfare (two tickets)	$2,000
Lodging (single and double occupancy are the same rate—$250 each day)	750
Meals ($200 × 3 days)*	600
Conference registration fee (includes $120 for Family Tax Planning sessions)	620
Car rental	300

*Split equally between Dr. and Mrs. Spencer.

How much, if any, of these expenses can the Spencers deduct?

35. **LO.1, 3, 6** Kim works for a clothing manufacturer as a dress designer. She travels to New York City to attend five days of fashion shows and then spends three days sightseeing. Her expenses are as follows;

Airfare	$1,500
Lodging (8 nights)	1,920
Meals (8 days)	1,440
Airport transportation	120

[Assume that lodging/meals are the same amount for the business and personal portion of the trip (e.g., $180 per day for meals).]

    a. Presuming no reimbursement, how much can Kim deduct as to the trip?
    b. Would the tax treatment of Kim's deduction differ if she was an independent contractor (rather than an employee)? Explain.

36. **LO.3** On Thursday, Justin flies from Baltimore (his home office) to Cadiz (Spain). He conducts business on Friday and Tuesday; vacations on Saturday, Sunday, and Monday (a legal holiday in Spain); and returns to Baltimore on Thursday. Justin was scheduled to return home on Wednesday, but all flights were canceled due to bad weather. Therefore, he spent Wednesday watching floor shows at a local casino.

a. For tax purposes, what portion of Justin's trip is regarded as being for business?

b. Suppose Monday was not a legal holiday. Would this change your answer to (a)? Explain.

c. Under either (a) or (b), how much of Justin's airfare qualifies as a deductible business expense?

Decision Making

37. **LO.3** Monica travels from her office in Boston to Lisbon, Portugal, on business. Her absence of 13 days was spent as follows:

Thursday	Depart for and arrive at Lisbon
Friday	Business transacted
Saturday and Sunday	Vacationing
Monday through Friday	Business transacted
Saturday and Sunday	Vacationing
Monday	Business transacted
Tuesday	Depart Lisbon and return to office in Boston

a. For tax purposes, how many days has Monica spent on business?

b. What difference does it make?

c. Could Monica have spent more time than she did vacationing on the trip without loss of existing tax benefits? Explain.

38. **LO.4** Caden, a financial planner, decides to quit his job with an investment bank in Charleston, South Carolina, and establish a private practice in Santa Fe, New Mexico. In connection with the move, he incurs the following expenses:

Moving van charge	$4,500
Lodging during move	540
Meals during move	410
Loss on sale of residence in Charleston	9,000
Mileage for personal autos	3,500 miles

How much of these expenses, if any, can Caden deduct?

39. **LO.4, 7** Upon losing his job as a plant manager in Quincy (Massachusetts), Anthony incurs $6,200 in job search expenses. Having no success in finding new employment in the same type of work, Anthony moves to Clearwater (Florida) in 2014 and begins a charter boat business. His expenses in connection with the move are summarized below.

Penalty for breaking lease on Quincy rented residence	$2,800
Forfeiture of membership in Quincy Country Club	2,200
Packing and moving van charges	7,100
Lodging during move (3 nights)	380
Meals during move	360
Mileage (for two automobiles)	2,400 miles

How much of these expenses may Anthony deduct?

40. **LO.4** After being downsized by his former employer in November 2013, Wayne moves from Minnesota to Alabama to accept a new job. When filing his Federal income tax return for 2013, Wayne deducts the $14,000 in moving expenses he incurred (none of which were reimbursed by either his former or new employer). On June 6, 2014, Wayne's employment terminates. What are the tax consequences if the termination occurred because:

a. Wayne was killed by a drunk driver?

b. Wayne was downsized by the new employer?

c. Wayne was fired by the new employer because he assaulted a client?

d. Wayne quit because he inherited a large amount of money and decided he did not want to work anymore?

41. **LO.5** Elijah is employed as a full-time high school teacher. The school district where he works recently instituted a policy requiring all of its teachers to start working on a master's degree. Pursuant to this new rule, Elijah spent most of the summer of 2014 taking graduate courses at an out-of-town university. His expenses are as follows:

Tuition	$6,600
Books and course materials	1,500
Lodging	1,700
Meals	2,200
Laundry and dry cleaning	200
Campus parking	300

In addition, Elijah drove his personal automobile 2,200 miles in connection with the education. He uses the automatic mileage method.
a. How much, if any, of these expenses might qualify as deductions *for* AGI?
b. How much, if any, of these expenses might qualify as deductions *from* AGI?

42. **LO.5** In each of the following independent situations, determine how much, if any, qualifies as a deduction *for* AGI under § 222 (qualified tuition and related expenses):
a. Lily is single and is employed as an architect. During 2014, she spends $4,100 in tuition to attend law school at night. Her MAGI is $64,000.
b. Liam is single and is employed as a pharmacist. During 2014, he spends $2,400 ($2,100 for tuition and $300 for books) to take a course in herbal supplements at a local university. His MAGI is $81,000.
c. Hailey is married and is employed as a bookkeeper. She spends $5,200 for tuition and $900 for books and supplies pursuing a bachelor's degree in accounting. Her MAGI is $40,000 on the separate return she files.
d. John spends $6,500 of his savings on tuition to attend Carmine State College. John is claimed as a dependent by his parents.
e. How much, if any, of the above amounts *not allowed under* § 222 might otherwise qualify as a deduction *from* AGI?

43. **LO.6, 9** Eric is a licensed commercial pilot who works for Snipe Charter Jet Service. Typically, Eric, who lives near the airport, flies a charter out of Tupelo (MS) to either Las Vegas or Reno, spends several nights there, and then returns home with the same group. Snipe provides Eric with a travel allowance of $1,800 per month but requires no accountability. For the current calendar year, Eric had the following job-related expenses:

Meals	$ 7,000
Lodging	10,000
Transportation (taxis, limos)	500
Uniforms	1,300
Dry cleaning of uniforms	400
Annual physical exam	1,500

The uniforms are required to be worn on the job. The Federal Aviation Administration requires the annual physical exam for the maintenance of a commercial pilot's license. How may Eric treat these expenses for Federal income tax purposes?

44. **LO.6** Stork Associates paid $60,000 for a 20-seat skybox at Veterans Stadium for eight professional football games. Regular seats to these games range from $80 to $250 each. At one game, an employee of Stork entertained 18 clients. Stork furnished food and beverages for the event at a cost of $1,300. The game was preceded by a bona fide business discussion, and all expenses are adequately substantiated.
a. How much may Stork deduct for this event?
b. What, if any, is the deduction if no representative from Stork attended the game?
c. What if there was no bona fide business discussion either before or after the event?

45. **LO.6** During the current year, Paul, the vice president of a bank, made gifts in the following amounts:

To Sarah (Paul's personal assistant) at Christmas	$36
To Darryl (a key client)—$3 was for gift wrapping	53
To Darryl's wife (a homemaker) on her birthday	20
To Veronica (Paul's boss) at Christmas	30

In addition, on professional assistants' day, Paul takes Sarah to lunch at a cost of $82. Presuming that Paul has adequate substantiation and is not reimbursed, how much can he deduct?

46. **LO.7** Melanie is employed full-time as an accountant for a national hardware chain. She recently started a private consulting practice, which provides tax advice and financial planning to the general public. For this purpose, she maintains an office in her home. Expenses relating to her home for 2014 are as follows:

Real property taxes	$3,600
Interest on home mortgage	3,800
Operating expenses of home	900

Melanie's residence cost $350,000 (excluding land) and has living space of 2,000 square feet, of which 20% (400 square feet) is devoted to business. The office was placed in service in February 2013, and under the regular method, Melanie had an unused office in the home deduction of $800 for 2013. Presuming sufficient net income from her consulting practice, what is Melanie's office in the home deduction under the:
a. Regular method.
b. Simplified method.

47. **LO.7** Christine is a full-time teacher of the fourth grade at Vireo Academy. During the current year, she spends $1,400 for classroom supplies. On the submission of adequate substantiation, Vireo reimburses her for $500 of these expenses—the maximum reimbursement allowed for supplies under school policy. [The reimbursement is not shown as income (Box 1) of Form W–2 given to Christine by Vireo.] What are the income tax consequences of the $1,400 if Christine:
a. Itemizes her deductions *from* AGI?
b. Chooses the standard deduction?

48. **LO.3, 6, 9** Charles has AGI of $94,000 during the year and the following expenses related to his employment:

Lodging while in travel status	$5,000
Meals during travel	4,000
Business transportation	6,000
Entertainment of clients	3,800
Professional dues and subscriptions	800

Charles is reimbursed $14,000 under his employer's accountable plan. What are his deductions *for* and *from* AGI?

Decision Making   49. **LO.3, 6, 9** During the year, Brenda has the following expenses related to her employment:

Airfare	$8,500
Meals	4,000
Lodging	4,900
Transportation while in travel status (taxis and limos)	940
Entertainment of clients	8,000

Although Brenda renders an adequate accounting to her employer, she is reimbursed for only $12,000 of the above expenses. What are Brenda's tax consequences based on the following assumptions?
a. The $12,000 reimbursement does not designate which expenses are covered.
b. The reimbursement specifically covers *only* the meals and entertainment expenses.
c. The reimbursement covers any of the expenses *other than* meals and entertainment.
d. If Brenda has a choice of reimbursement procedures [parts (a), (b), or (c) above], which should she select? Why?

50. **LO.6, 9, 10** Audry, age 38 and single, earns a salary of $59,000. She has interest income of $1,600 and has a $2,000 long-term capital loss from the sale of a stock investment. Audry incurs the following employment-related expenses during the year:

Transportation	$5,500
Meals	2,800
Lodging	4,200
Entertainment of clients	2,200
Professional dues and subscriptions	300

Under an accountable plan, Audry receives reimbursements of $4,500 from her employer. Calculate her AGI and itemized employee business expenses.

51. **LO.6, 9, 10, 11** Ava recently graduated from college and is interviewing for a position in marketing. Gull Corporation has offered her a job as a sales representative that will require extensive travel and entertainment but provide valuable experience. Under the offer, she has two options: a salary of $53,000 and she absorbs all expenses; a salary of $39,000 and Gull reimburses for all expenses. Gull assures Ava that the $14,000 difference in the two options will be adequate to cover the expenses incurred. What issues should have an impact on Ava's choice?

Decision Making

52. **LO.5, 7, 10** B. J. and Carolyn Grace are full-time employees. B. J. is an elementary school teacher, and Carolyn is a registered nurse at a hospital. During the year, they incur the following employment-related expenses:

School supplies for use in the classroom	$1,400
Emergency room uniforms	800
Union dues (teachers association)	200
Job hunting expenses (Carolyn obtained another nursing position but decided not to change jobs)	1,300
Continuing education correspondence courses (required to maintain nursing license)	380
Professional dues and subscriptions	1,100

None of these expenses are reimbursed by the employers.

For the year, the Graces file a joint return reflecting salary income of $90,000. They also have gambling income of $6,000 and gambling losses of $7,000 (fully substantiated). They pay $400 to have their tax return prepared. They have other itemized deductions (i.e., interest on home mortgage, property taxes on personal residence, state income taxes, and charitable contributions) of $14,500. Determine the total amount of itemized deductions allowed to the Graces.

53. **LO.1, 2, 4, 5, 7, 10** Complete the following table by classifiying each of the independent expenditures (assume that no reimbursement takes place).

	Expense Item	Deductible *for* AGI	Deductible *from* AGI	Not Deductible
a.	Moving expense of an employee	___	___	___
b.	Tax return preparation fee incurred by an employed plumber	___	___	___
c.	Safety glasses purchased by an employed pipefitter	___	___	___
d.	Dues to auto club (e.g., AAA) for taxpayer who uses the automatic mileage method	___	___	___
e.	Nursing refresher course for taxpayer who retired from nursing five years ago	___	___	___
f.	Gambling loss *not* in excess of gambling gain by a self-employed architect	___	___	___
g.	Contribution to Roth IRA by a self-employed attorney	___	___	___
h.	Business travel expenses by a statutory employee	___	___	___
i.	Job hunting expense by an elementary school teacher seeking a position as an elementary school principal	___	___	___
j.	Cost of bar exam review course taken by a recent law school graduate	___	___	___

Cumulative Problems

Tax Return Problem

H&R BLOCK
TAX SOFTWARE

54. David R. and Ella M. Cole (ages 39 and 38, respectively) are husband and wife who live at 1820 Elk Avenue, Denver, CO 80202. David is a regional sales manager for Wren Industries, a national wholesaler of plumbing and heating supplies, and Ella is a part-time dental hygienist for a chain of dental clinics.

- David is classified by Wren as a statutory employee with compensation for 2013 (based on commissions) of $95,000. He is expected to maintain his own office and pay for all business expenses from this amount. Wren does not require him to render any accounting as to the use of these funds. It does not withhold Federal and state income taxes but does withhold and account for the payroll taxes incurred (e.g., Social Security and Medicare). David is covered by Wren's noncontributory medical plan but has chosen not to participate in its § 401(k) retirement plan.

   David's employment-related expenses for 2013 are summarized below:

Airfare	$8,800
Lodging	5,000
Meals (during travel status)	4,800
Entertainment	3,600
Ground transportation (e.g., limos, rental cars, and taxis)	800
Business gifts	900
Office supplies (includes postage, overnight delivery, and copying)	1,500

   The entertainment involved business meals for purchasing agents, store owners, and building contractors. The business gifts consisted of $50 gift certificates to a national restaurant. These were sent by David during the Christmas holidays to 18 of his major customers.

   In addition, David drove his 2011 Ford Expedition 11,000 miles for business and 3,000 for personal use during 2013. He purchased the Expedition on August 15, 2010, and has always used the automatic (standard) mileage method for tax purposes. Parking and tolls relating to business use total $340 in 2013.

- When the Coles purchased their present residence in April 2010, they devoted 450 of the 3,000 square feet of living space to an office for David. The property cost $440,000 ($40,000 of which is attributable to the land) and has since appreciated in value. Expenses relating to the residence in 2013 (except for mortgage interest and property taxes; see below) are as follows:

Insurance	$2,600
Repairs and maintenance	900
Utilities	4,700
Painting office area; area rugs and plants (in the office)	1,800

   In terms of depreciation, the Coles use the MACRS percentage tables applicable to 39-year nonresidential real property. As to depreciable property (e.g., office furniture), David tries to avoid capitalization and uses whatever method provides the fastest write-off for tax purposes.

- Ella works part-time as a substitute for whichever hygienist is ill or on vacation or when one of the clinics is particularly busy (e.g., prior to the beginning of the school year). Besides her transportation, she must provide and maintain her own uniforms. Her expenses for 2013 appear below.

Uniforms	$690
State and city occupational licenses	380
Professional journals and membership dues in the American Dental Hygiene Association	340
Correspondence study course (taken online) dealing with teeth whitening procedures	420

   Ella's salary for the year is $42,000, and her Form W–2 for the year shows income tax withholdings of $4,000 (Federal) and $1,000 (state) and the proper amount of Social Security and Medicare taxes. Because Ella is a part-time employee, she is not included in her employer's medical or retirement plans.

- Besides the items already mentioned, the Coles had the following receipts during 2013.

Interest income—		
State of Colorado general purpose bonds	$2,500	
IBM bonds	800	
Wells Fargo Bank CD	1,200	$ 4,500
Federal income tax refund for year 2012		510
Life insurance proceeds paid by Eagle Assurance Corporation		200,000
Inheritance of savings account from Sarah Cole		50,000
Sales proceeds from two ATVs		9,000

For several years, the Coles's household has included David's divorced mother, Sarah, who has been claimed as their dependent. In late November 2013, Sarah unexpectedly died of coronary arrest in her sleep. Unknown to Ella and David, Sarah had a life insurance policy and a savings account (with David as the designated beneficiary of each). In 2012, the Coles purchased two ATVs for $14,000. After several near mishaps, they decided that the sport was too dangerous. In 2013, they sold the ATVs to their neighbor.

- Additional expenditures for 2013 include:

Funeral expenses for Sarah		$ 4,500
Taxes—		
Real property taxes on personal residence	$6,400	
Colorado state income tax due (paid in April 2013 for tax year 2012)	310	6,710
Mortgage interest on personal residence		6,600
Paid church pledge		2,400
Contributions to traditional IRAs for Ella and David ($5,500 + $5,500)		11,000

In 2013, the Coles made quarterly estimated tax payments of $1,400 (Federal) and $500 (state) for a total of $5,600 (Federal) and $2,000 (state).

Part 1—Tax Computation

Using the appropriate forms and schedules, compute the Coles's Federal income tax for 2013. Disregard the alternative minimum tax (AMT) and various education credits as these items are not discussed until later in the text (Chapters 12 and 13). Relevant Social Security numbers are:

David Cole	123-45-6788
Ella Cole	123-45-6787
Sarah Cole	123-45-6799

The Coles do not want to contribute to the Presidential Election Campaign Fund. Also, they want any overpayment of tax refunded to them and *not* applied toward next year's tax liability. Suggested software: H&R BLOCK Tax Software.

Part 2—Follow-Up Advice

Ella has always wanted to pursue a career in nursing. To this end, she has earned a substantial number of college credits on a part-time basis. With Sarah no longer requiring home care, Ella believes that she can now complete her degree by attending college on a full-time basis.

David would like to know how Ella's plans will affect their income tax position. Specifically, he wants to know:

- How much Federal income tax they will save if Ella quits her job.
- Any tax benefits that might be available from the cost of the education.

Write a letter to David addressing these concerns. Note: In making your projections, assume that David's salary and expenses remain the same. Also disregard any consideration of the educational tax credits (i.e., American Opportunity and lifetime learning) as they are not discussed until Chapter 13.

Tax Computation Problem   55. Addison Parker, single and age 32, lives at 3218 Columbia Drive, Spokane, WA 99210. She is employed as regional sales manager by VITA Corporation, a manufacturer and distributor of vitamins and food supplements. Addison is paid an annual salary of $83,000 and a separate travel allowance of $24,000. As to the travel allowance, VITA does not require any accounting on the part of Addison.

- Addison participates in VITA's contributory health and § 401(k) plans. During 2014, she paid $3,500 for the medical insurance and contributed $11,000 to the § 401(k) retirement plan.
- Addison uses her automobile 70% for business and 30% for personal. The automobile, a Toyota Avalon, was purchased new on June 30, 2012, for $37,000 (no trade-in was involved). Depreciation has been claimed under MACRS 200% declining balance method, and no § 179 election was made in the year of purchase. (For depreciation information, see the IRS Instructions for Form 4562, Part V). During 2014, Addison drove 15,000 miles and incurred and paid the following expenses relating to the automobile:

Gasoline	$3,100
Insurance	2,900
Auto club dues	240
Interest on car loan	1,100
Repairs and maintenance	1,200
Parking (during business use)	600
Traffic fines (during business use)	500

- Because VITA does not have an office in Spokane, the company expects Addison to maintain one in her home. Out of 1,500 square feet of living space in her apartment, Addison has set aside 300 square feet as an office. Expenses for 2014 relating to the office are listed below.

Rent	$18,000
Utilities	4,000
Insurance (renter's casualty and theft coverage)	1,600
Carpet replacement (office area only)	1,200

- Addison's employment-related expenses (except for the trip to Korea) for 2014 are summarized below.

Airfare	$4,100
Lodging	3,200
Meals	2,800
Entertainment (business lunches)	2,400
Transportation (taxis and airport limos)	300
Business gifts	540
Continuing education	400
Professional journals	140

Most of Addison's business trips involve visits to retail outlets in her region. Store managers and their key employees, as well as some suppliers, were the parties entertained. The business gifts were boxes of candy costing $30 ($25 each plus $5 for wrapping and shipping) sent to 18 store managers at Christmas. The continuing education was a noncredit course dealing with improving management skills that Addison took online.

- In July 2014, Addison traveled to Korea to investigate a new process that is being developed to convert fish parts to a solid consumable tablet form. She spent one week checking out the process and then took a one-week vacation tour of the country. The round-trip airfare was $3,600, while her expenses relating to business were $2,100 for lodging ($300 each night), $1,470 for meals, and $350 for transportation. Upon returning to the United States, Addison sent her findings about the process to her employer. VITA was so pleased with her report that it gave her an employee achievement award of $10,000. The award was sent to Addison in January 2015.
- Addison provides more than 50% of the support of her parents (Gordon and Anita Parker), who live in Seattle. In addition to modest Social Security benefits, her parents receive a small amount of interest on municipal bonds and nontaxable retirement income.

- Besides the items already mentioned, Addison had the following receipts in 2014:

Interest income—		
City of Tacoma general purpose bonds	$ 350	
Olympia State Bank	400	$ 750
Proceeds from property sales—		
City lot	$13,000	
Sailboat	18,000	31,000
Cash found at airport		5,000

Regarding the city lot (located in Vancouver), Addison purchased the property in 2000 for $16,000 and held it as an investment. Unfortunately, the neighborhood where the lot was located deteriorated, and property values declined. In 2014, Addison decided to cut her losses and sold the property for $13,000. The sailboat was used for pleasure and was purchased in 2010 for $16,500. Addison sold the boat because she purchased a new and larger model (see below). While at the Spokane airport, Addison found an unmarked envelope containing $5,000 in $50 bills. As no mention of any lost funds was noted in the media, Addison kept the money.

- Addison's expenditures for 2014 (not previously noted) are summarized below.

Medical (not covered by insurance)	$7,000
State and local general sales tax	3,300
Church pledge (2013 and 2014)	5,600
Fee paid for preparation of 2013 income tax return	500
Contribution to mayor's reelection campaign fund	200
Premiums on life insurance policy	2,100
Contribution to a Coverdell Education Savings account (on behalf of a favorite nephew)	2,000

Most of the medical expenses Addison paid were for her mother's dental implants. Addison keeps careful records regarding sales taxes. In 2014, the sales tax total was unusually high due to the purchase of a new sailboat. In 2014, Addison decided to pay her church pledge for both 2013 and 2014. The insurance premium was on a policy covering her father's life. (Addison is the designated beneficiary under the policy.)

Relevant Social Security numbers are 123-45-6785 (Addison), 123-45-6783 (Gordon), and 123-45-6784 (Anita). Addison's employer withheld $5,600 for Federal income tax purposes, and she applied her $800 overpayment for 2013 toward the 2014 tax liability.

Compute Addison's Federal income tax payable (or refund) for 2014. In making the calculation, use the Tax Rate Schedule and disregard the application of the alternative minimum tax (AMT), which is not discussed until Chapter 12.

Research Problems

Note: Solutions to Research Problems can be prepared by using the **Checkpoint®** **Student Edition** online research product, which is available to accompany this text. It is also possible to prepare solutions to the Research Problems by using tax research materials found in a standard tax library.

THOMSON REUTERS
CHECKPOINT®

Research Problem 1. Aaron, a resident of Minnesota, has been a driver for Green Delivery Service for the past six years. For this purpose, he leases a truck from Green, and his compensation is based on a percentage of the income resulting from his pickup and delivery services. Green allows its drivers to choose their 10-hour shifts and does not exercise any control on how these services are carried out (e.g., the route to be taken or the order in which parcels are delivered or picked up). Under Green's operating agreement with its drivers, Green can terminate the arrangement after 30 days' notice. In practice, however, Green allows its truckers to quit immediately without giving advance notice. The agreement also labels the drivers as independent contractors. Green maintains no health or retirement plans for its drivers, and each year it reports their income by issuing Forms

1099–MISC (and not Forms W–2). Green requires its drivers to maintain a commercial driver's license and be in good standing with the state highway law enforcement division.

Citing the employment tax Regulations in §§ 31.3121(d)–1(c)(2) and 31.3306(i)–1(b), an IRS agent contends that Aaron is an independent contractor and, therefore, is subject to the self-employment tax. Based on *Peno Trucking, Inc.* (93 TCM 1027, T.C.Memo. 2007–66), Aaron disagrees and contends that he is an employee (i.e., not self-employed). Who is correct? Why?

Research Problem 2. Your client, a large construction firm organized as a C corporation, allows certain employees (including the president of the corporation) to use its company-owned airplane for nonbusiness flights. The employees include the value of the flights in their income. Your client is uncertain about how to treat the expenses related to these nonbusiness flights. In certain situations, the expenses of operating the plane are more than the income imputed to the employees, and in certain circumstances, the expenses are less. In doing some of its own research, your client found *Sutherland Lumber-Southwest, Inc.* (114 T.C .197 (2000)), which suggests that as long as the employee imputes income, the full amount of the related expenses can be deducted. [The decision in the case was affirmed on appeal, *Sutherland Lumber-Southwest, Inc. v. Comm.*, 2001–2 USTC ¶50,503, 88 AFTR 2d 2001–5026, 255 F.3d 495 (CA–8, 2001).] Should your client follow the approach in *Sutherland*?

Research Problem 3. Tony Martin has worked for many years as a mechanic for Eagle Airlines in its repair facility at the Minneapolis-Saint Paul airport. In early 2011, Eagle downsized its Minnesota staff and eliminated Tony's job. Using his union seniority, Tony was able to obtain a similar position by "bumping" a mechanic in Chicago. A few months later, Eagle continued the downsizing and Tony ended up at LaGuardia (New York). After one final "bump" to Anchorage, Tony ran out of seniority and was finally terminated by Eagle.

During his work assignment in Chicago, New York, and Anchorage, Tony kept his family and residence in the Minneapolis area. Consequently, he deducted all of his out-of-town expenses (e.g., meals and lodging) as being work-related. Is this the correct approach? In other words, are Tony's travel expenses incurred while he is considered to be away from home? Explain.

Communications

Research Problem 4. Rick Beam has been an independent sales representative for various textile manufacturers for many years. His products consist of soft goods, such as tablecloths, curtains, and drapes. Rick's customers are clothing store chains, department stores, and smaller specialty stores. The employees of these companies who are responsible for purchasing merchandise are known as buyers. These companies generally prohibit their buyers from accepting gifts from manufacturers' sales representatives.

Each year, Rick gives cash gifts (never more than $25) to most of the buyers who are his customers. Generally, he cashes a large check in November and gives the money personally to the buyers around Christmas. Rick says, "This is one of the ways I maintain my relationship with my buyers." He maintains adequate substantiation of all of the gifts.

Rick's deductions for these gifts have been disallowed by the IRS, based on § 162(c)(2). Rick is confused and comes to you, a CPA, for advice.

a. Write a letter to Rick concerning his tax position on this issue. Rick's address is 948 Octavia Street, Baton Rouge, LA 70821.
b. Prepare a memo for your files supporting the advice you have given.

Internet Activity

Use the tax resources of the Internet to address the following questions. Do not restrict your search to the Web, but include a review of newsgroups and general reference materials, practitioner sites and resources, primary sources of the tax law, chat rooms and discussion groups, and other opportunities.

Research Problem 5. What are the guidelines regarding the deductibility of luxury water travel (e.g., cruise ships) for business purposes? Refer to Chapter 1 of IRS Publication 463.

Research Problem 6. In reporting the transactions of a self-employed taxpayer, when can a Schedule C–EZ be used instead of the regular Schedule C of Form 1040?

Research Problem 7. Retrieve IRS Form 8919 (Uncollected Social Security and Medicare Tax on Wages). According to the instructions, who should file this form?

CHAPTER

10

Deductions and Losses: Certain Itemized Deductions

LEARNING OBJECTIVES: *After completing Chapter 10, you should be able to:*

LO.1 Distinguish between deductible and nondeductible personal expenses.

LO.2 Define medical expenses and compute the medical expense deduction.

LO.3 Contrast deductible taxes with nondeductible fees, licenses, and other charges.

LO.4 Explain the Federal income tax treatment of state and local income taxes and sales taxes.

LO.5 Distinguish between deductible and nondeductible interest and apply the appropriate limitations to deductible interest.

LO.6 Recognize charitable contributions and identify their related measurement problems and percentage limitations.

LO.7 List the business and personal expenditures that are deductible either as miscellaneous itemized deductions or as other itemized deductions.

LO.8 Recognize the limitation on certain itemized deductions applicable to high-income taxpayers.

LO.9 Identify tax planning strategies that can maximize the benefit of itemized deductions.

CHAPTER OUTLINE

THE BIG PICTURE   Tax Solutions for the Real World

IMPACT OF ITEMIZED DEDUCTIONS ON MAJOR PURCHASES

John and Susan Williamson, a young professional couple, have been renting an apartment in Atlanta, Georgia, since they were married. Their income has grown as they've become more established in their careers, and they now believe that the time has come to purchase their own home. In addition, their desire to buy a home now may be coming at a good time, because John's mother, Martha, needs to move in with them due to her declining health and their current apartment is too small to accommodate her. John and Susan's current monthly rent is $2,000, but they are willing to spend $2,500 per month on an after-tax basis if necessary for their first home.

After months of house hunting, they have found the perfect home, but they fear it may be too expensive. If they acquire a standard mortgage to finance the purchase of the home, the total cash outlay during the first year of ownership will be $43,000 ($2,000 principal payments, $37,000 interest payments, and $4,000 real estate taxes). Alternatively, if they use their retirement and taxable investments to secure the home financing, they can qualify for a lower interest rate and thereby reduce the interest charge from $37,000 to $35,000. They expect their Federal AGI to be $200,000 and their taxable income to range between $160,000 and $185,000 for the year. John and Susan have not itemized their deductions in prior years because the amount of their qualifying personal expenditures has fallen just short of the standard deduction amount. Assume that the Williamsons' marginal income tax rate under Georgia law is 6 percent.

Can John and Susan Williamson afford to pursue their dream of home ownership?

Read the chapter and formulate your response.

FRAMEWORK 1040
Tax Formula for Individuals

This chapter covers the boldfaced portions of the Tax Formula for Individuals that was introduced in Figure 3.1 on p. 3-3. Below those portions are the sections of Form 1040 where the results are reported.

Income *(broadly conceived)*	$xx,xxx
Less: Exclusions	(x,xxx)
Gross income	$xx,xxx
Less: Deductions for adjusted gross income	(x,xxx)
Adjusted gross income	$xx,xxx
Less: The greater of total **itemized deductions** *or* the standard deduction	(x,xxx)

FORM 1040 (p. 2)

40 **Itemized deductions** (from Schedule A) **or** your **standard deduction** (see left margin) . .

Personal and dependency exemptions	(x,xxx)
Taxable income	$xx,xxx
Tax on taxable income *(see Tax Tables or Tax Rate Schedules)*	$ x,xxx
Less: Tax credits *(including income taxes withheld and prepaid)*	(xxx)
Tax due *(or refund)*	$ xxx

LO.1

Distinguish between deductible and nondeductible personal expenses.

As a general rule, a deduction for personal expenditures is disallowed by § 262 of the Code. However, Congress has chosen to allow certain personal expenditures to be deducted as itemized deductions. Personal expenditures that are deductible as itemized deductions include medical expenses, certain taxes, mortgage interest, investment interest, and charitable contributions. These expenditures and other personal expenditures that are allowed as itemized deductions are covered in this chapter. Although certain exceptions exist (e.g., alimony and traditional IRA contributions are deductible *for* AGI), personal expenditures not specifically allowed as itemized deductions by the tax law are nondeductible.

Allowable itemized deductions are deductible *from* AGI in arriving at taxable income if the taxpayer elects to itemize. The election to itemize is appropriate when total itemized deductions exceed the standard deduction based on the taxpayer's filing status.[1]

THE BIG PICTURE

Example 1

Return to the facts of *The Big Picture* on p. 10-1. John and Susan Williamson will discover that with the purchase of a home, they will be able to itemize their deductions for the first time instead of claiming the standard deduction. Assuming that the home mortgage interest expense and real estate taxes meet the requirements discussed in this chapter, they will be deducted *from* AGI because their total would exceed the amount of the standard deduction for a married couple filing a joint return. Further, other qualifying expenditures, such as state income taxes and charitable contributions, likewise will be deductible as itemized deductions, providing an explicit tax benefit to the Williamsons.

---

[1]See §§ 63(c) and (d), respectively, for the definitions of the terms *standard deduction* and *itemized deductions*.

TAX IN THE NEWS **The Debate Continues Over the Future of Itemized Deductions**

In an era of huge government deficits and debt ceiling debates, many have concluded that the Federal government needs to learn to live within its means. In simplest of terms, to bring the government's spending in line with its revenues, more revenues must be raised, expenditures must be decreased, or some combination of the two must occur. During these debates, some continue to argue that "tax reform" should occur simultaneously with the search for increased tax revenues, and such reform should lead to certain tax deductions being either repealed or scaled back. They observe that if the tax code were simplified by no longer allowing certain popular itemized deductions, billions of dollars of additional tax revenue would be collected because taxable income would be higher.

Currently, popular tax deductions "cost" the government billions by virtue of the fact that they reduce taxable income. These deductions are often referred to as "tax expenditures." Recently, the Joint Committee on Taxation estimated the cost during 2015 of allowing the following itemized deductions for individuals:

Deduction	Cost in Billions of Dollars
Mortgage interest on owner-occupied housing	$75.0
Charitable contributions	45.1
State and local income, sales, and personal property taxes	54.9
Property tax on real property	30.4

Arguably, by repealing these deductions, government revenues would increase by significant amounts. While repealing all of these deductions may not be feasible for political, economic, or other reasons, be aware that certain politicians or policy wonks will push to reform, limit, or scale back these deductions to all or certain taxpayers in the future.

Source: The Joint Committee on Taxation, "Estimates of Federal Tax Expenditures for Fiscal Years 2012–2017," (JCS-1-13), February 1, 2013, Table 1.

© iStockphoto.com/Andrey Prokhorov

10-1 MEDICAL EXPENSES

Medical expenses paid for the care of the taxpayer, spouse, and dependents are allowed as an itemized deduction to the extent the expenses are not reimbursed. The **medical expense** deduction is limited to the amount by which such expenses *exceed* a threshold percentage of the taxpayer's AGI. Beginning in 2013, the threshold percentage is 10 percent for most taxpayers. For taxpayers age 65 and older, however, the threshold is 7.5 percent of AGI until 2017, when it increases to 10 percent.[2]

LO.2

Define medical expenses and compute the medical expense deduction.

THE BIG PICTURE

Example 2

Return to the facts of *The Big Picture* on p. 10-1. Because the Williamsons' AGI for the year is $200,000, they must itemize their deductions and have more than $20,000 ($200,000 × 10%) in unreimbursed medical expenses to receive a tax benefit from those expenses.

10-1a Medical Expenses Defined

The term *medical care* includes expenditures incurred for the "diagnosis, cure, mitigation, treatment, or prevention of disease, or for the purpose of affecting any structure or function of the body."[3] A *partial* list of deductible and nondeductible medical items appears in Exhibit 10.1.

A medical expense does not have to relate to a particular ailment to be deductible. Because the definition of medical care is broad enough to cover preventive

---

[2]Prior to 2013, the percentage threshold for regular income tax purposes was 7.5 percent of AGI for all taxpayers.

[3]§ 213(d)(1)(A).

TAX IN THE NEWS   The President and Vice President Itemize

Approximately two-thirds of all individual taxpayers take the standard deduction each year rather than itemize. President Barack H. Obama and Vice President Joseph R. Biden are among the one-third who itemize. Both the President and the Vice President, who file joint returns with their wives, released their 2012 income tax returns to the public in 2013. Their itemized deductions, along with certain other information from their tax returns, are shown below.

	President Obama	Vice President Biden
Gross income	$662,076	$385,072
Adjusted gross income	$608,611	$385,072
Itemized deductions:		
Medical expenses	$ –0–	$ –0–
Taxes	63,305	28,521
Interest	45,046	26,679
Charitable contributions	150,034	7,190
Job expenses and other miscellaneous deductions	–0–	–0–
Total itemized deductions	$258,385	$ 62,390

measures, the cost of periodic physical and dental exams qualifies even for a taxpayer in good health.

Amounts paid for unnecessary *cosmetic surgery* are not deductible medical expenses. However, if cosmetic surgery is deemed necessary, it is deductible as a medical expense. Cosmetic surgery is necessary when it improves the effects of (1) a deformity arising from a congenital abnormality, (2) a personal injury, or (3) a disfiguring disease.

EXHIBIT 10.1	Examples of Deductible and Nondeductible Medical Expenses

Deductible	Nondeductible
Medical (including dental, mental, and hospital) care	Funeral, burial, or cremation expenses
Prescription drugs and insulin	Nonprescription drugs (except insulin)
Special equipment	Bottled water
Wheelchairs	Toiletries, cosmetics
Crutches	Diaper service, maternity clothes
Artificial limbs	Programs for the *general* improvement of health
Eyeglasses (including contact lenses)	Weight reduction
Hearing aids	Health spas
Transportation for medical care	Social activities (e.g., dancing and swimming lessons)
Medical and hospital insurance premiums	Unnecessary cosmetic surgery
Long-term care insurance premiums (subject to limitations)	
Cost of alcohol and drug rehabilitation	
Certain costs to stop smoking	
Weight reduction programs related to obesity	

> **Example 3**
>
> Art, a calendar year taxpayer, paid $21,000 to a plastic surgeon for a face-lift. Art, age 75, merely wanted to improve his appearance. The $21,000 does not qualify as a medical expense because the surgery was unnecessary. In contrast, Marge's face is disfigured as a result of a serious automobile accident. The cost of restorative cosmetic surgery is deductible as a medical expense.

The cost of care in a *nursing home or home for the aged*, including meals and lodging, can be included in deductible medical expenses if the primary reason for being in the home is to get medical care. If the primary reason for being there is personal, any costs for medical or nursing care can be included in deductible medical expenses, but the cost of meals and lodging must be excluded.[4]

> **Example 4**
>
> Norman has a chronic heart ailment. In October, his family decides to place Norman in a nursing home equipped to provide medical and nursing care. Total nursing home expenses amount to $35,000 during the year. Of this amount, $20,000 is directly attributable to medical and nursing care. Because Norman is in need of significant medical and nursing care and is placed in the facility primarily for this purpose, all $35,000 of the nursing home costs are deductible (subject to the AGI floor, explained earlier).

Tuition expenses of a dependent at a special school may be deductible as a medical expense. The cost of medical care can include the expenses of a special school for a mentally or physically handicapped individual. The deduction is allowed if a principal reason for sending the individual to the school is the school's special resources for alleviating the infirmities. In this case, the cost of meals and lodging, in addition to the tuition, is a proper medical expense deduction.[5]

> **Example 5**
>
> Jason's daughter Marcia attended public school through the seventh grade. Because Marcia was a poor student, she was examined by a psychiatrist who diagnosed a problem that created a learning disability. Upon the recommendation of the psychiatrist, Marcia is enrolled in a private school so that she can receive individual attention. The school has no special program for students with learning disabilities and does not provide special medical treatment. The expense related to Marcia's attendance is not deductible as a medical expense. The cost of any psychiatric care, however, qualifies as a medical expense.

Example 5 shows that the recommendation of a physician does not automatically make the expenditure deductible.

ETHICS & EQUITY   Pigging Out to Get a Deduction

Michael has always been overweight, and now he has decided to do something about it. He recently read in a news story that the IRS allows a medical expense deduction for the cost of certain weight reduction programs. He scheduled an appointment with his doctor to discuss enrolling in the clinic's weight reduction program and mentioned that he was happy that he would be able to deduct the cost. His doctor, who was familiar with the IRS's position, informed Michael that he was 10 pounds below the weight considered obese under the IRS guidelines and would not be able to take the medical expense deduction. Michael scheduled another appointment and proceeded to eat much more than usual for the next month. He returned 20 pounds heavier than at the first appointment and joked with the doctor that he now qualified for the medical expense deduction. Discuss whether Michael is justified in deducting the cost of the weight reduction program.

© iStockphoto.com/LdF

---

[4]Reg. § 1.213–1(e)(1)(v).

[5]*Donald R. Pfeifer*, 37 TCM 816, T.C.Memo. 1978–189. Also see Rev.Rul. 78–340, 1978–2 C.B. 124.

10-1b Capital Expenditures for Medical Purposes

When capital expenditures are incurred for medical purposes, they must be deemed medically necessary by a physician, the facility must be used primarily by the patient alone, and the expense must be reasonable. Examples of such expenditures include dust elimination systems,[6] elevators,[7] and vans specially designed for wheelchair-bound taxpayers. Other examples of expenditures that may qualify are swimming pools if the taxpayer does not have access to a neighborhood pool and air conditioners if they do not become permanent improvements (e.g., window units).[8]

Both a capital expenditure for a permanent improvement and expenditures made for the operation or maintenance of the improvement may qualify as medical expenses. The allowable cost of such qualified medical expenditures is deductible in the year incurred. Although depreciation is required for most other capital expenditures, it is not required for those qualifying for medical purposes.

A permanent capital improvement that ordinarily would not have a medical purpose qualifies as a medical expense if it is directly related to prescribed medical care and is deductible to the extent that the expenditure *exceeds* the increase in value of the related property. Appraisal costs related to capital improvements are also deductible, but not as medical expenses. These costs are classified as expenses incurred in the determination of the taxpayer's tax liability.[9]

Example 6	Fred is afflicted with heart disease. His physician advises him to install an elevator in his residence so that he will not be required to climb the stairs. The cost of installing the elevator is $10,000, and the increase in the value of the residence is determined to be only $4,000. Therefore, $6,000 ($10,000 − $4,000) is deductible as a medical expense. Additional utility costs to operate the elevator and maintenance costs are deductible as medical expenses as long as the medical reason for the capital expenditure continues to exist.

The full cost of certain home-related capital expenditures incurred to enable a *physically handicapped* individual to live independently and productively qualifies as a medical expense. Qualifying costs include expenditures for constructing entrance and exit ramps to the residence, widening hallways and doorways to accommodate wheelchairs, installing support bars and railings in bathrooms and other rooms, and adjusting electrical outlets and fixtures.[10] These expenditures are subject to the AGI percentage limitation only, and the increase in the home's value is deemed to be zero.

10-1c Medical Expenses Incurred for Spouse and Dependents

In computing the medical expense deduction, a taxpayer may include medical expenses for a spouse and for a person who was a dependent at the time the expenses were paid or incurred. Of the requirements that normally apply in determining dependency status,[11] neither the gross income nor the joint return test applies in determining dependency status for medical expense deduction purposes.

Example 7	Ernie (age 22) is married and a full-time student at a university. During the year, Ernie incurred medical expenses that were paid by Karen (Ernie's mother). She provided more than half of Ernie's support for the year. Even if Ernie files a joint return with his wife, Karen may claim the medical expenses she paid for him. Karen would combine Ernie's expenses with her own before applying the AGI floor.

[6]Ltr.Rul. 7948029.

[7]*Riach v. Frank*, 62–1 USTC ¶9419, 9 AFTR 2d 1263, 302 F.2d 374 (CA–9, 1962).

[8]Reg. § 1.213–1(e)(1)(iii).

[9]§ 212(3).

[10]For a complete list of the items that qualify, see Rev.Rul. 87–106, 1987–2 C.B. 67.

[11]Refer to Chapter 3 for discussion of these requirements.

For *divorced persons* with children, a special rule applies to the noncustodial parent. The noncustodial parent may claim any medical expenses he or she pays even though the custodial parent claims the children as dependents.

Example 8

Irv and Joan were divorced last year, and Joan was awarded custody of their child, Keith. During the current year, Irv pays $2,500 of Keith's medical bills. Together, Irv and Joan provide more than half of Keith's support. Even though Joan claims Keith as a dependent, Irv can combine the $2,500 of medical expenses that he pays for Keith with his own when calculating his medical expense deduction.

10-1d Transportation, Meal, and Lodging Expenses for Medical Treatment

Payments for transportation to and from a point of treatment for medical care are deductible as medical expenses (subject to the AGI floor). These costs include bus, taxi, train, or plane fare; charges for ambulance service; and out-of-pocket expenses for the use of an automobile. A mileage allowance of 23.5 cents per mile[12] for 2014 may be used instead of actual out-of-pocket automobile expenses. Whether the taxpayer chooses to claim out-of-pocket automobile expenses or the 23.5 cents per mile automatic mileage option, related parking fees and tolls can also be deducted. Also included are transportation expenditures for someone such as a parent or nurse who must accompany the patient. The cost of meals while en route to obtain medical care is not deductible.

A deduction is allowed for lodging while away from home for medical care if the following requirements are met:[13]

- The lodging is primarily for and essential to medical care.
- Medical care is provided by a doctor in a licensed hospital or a similar medical facility (e.g., a clinic).
- The lodging is not lavish or extravagant under the circumstances.
- There is no significant element of personal pleasure, recreation, or vacation in the travel away from home.

The deduction for lodging expenses included as medical expenses cannot exceed $50 *per* night for *each* person. The deduction is allowed not only for the patient but also for anyone who must travel with the patient.

THE BIG PICTURE

Example 9

Return to the facts of *The Big Picture* on p. 10-1. John's mother, Martha, eventually moves in with the Williamsons because of her disabilities, and she becomes their dependent. John is advised by his family physician that Martha needs specialized treatment for her heart condition. Consequently, John and Martha fly to Cleveland, Ohio, where Martha receives the therapy at a heart clinic on an outpatient basis. Expenses in connection with the trip are as follows:

Round-trip airfare ($250 each)	$500
Lodging in Cleveland for two nights ($120 each per night)	480

Assuming that the Williamsons itemize their deductions, the medical expense deduction for transportation is $500 and the medical expense deduction for lodging is $200 ($50 per night per person). Because Martha is disabled, it is assumed that John's accompanying her is justified.

---

[12]This amount is adjusted periodically. The allowance was 24 cents per mile for 2013.   [13]§ 213(d)(2).

No deduction is allowed for the cost of meals unless they are part of the medical care and are furnished at a medical facility. When allowable, such meals are not subject to the 50 percent limit applicable to business meals.

10-1e Amounts Paid for Medical Insurance Premiums

Medical insurance premiums are included with other medical expenses subject to the AGI floor. Premiums paid by the taxpayer under a group plan or an individual plan are included as medical expenses. If an employer pays all or part of the taxpayer's medical insurance premiums, the amount paid by the employer is not included in gross income by the employee. Likewise, the premium is not included in the employee's medical expenses. However, the medical insurance premiums paid by the employer are deductible as business expenses on the employer's tax return (see Chapter 6).

If a taxpayer is *self-employed*, insurance premiums paid for medical coverage are deductible as a *business* expense (*for* AGI).[14] The deduction *for* AGI is allowed for premiums paid on behalf of the taxpayer, the taxpayer's spouse, and dependents of the taxpayer. The deduction is not allowed to any taxpayer who is eligible to participate in a subsidized health plan maintained by any employer of the taxpayer or of the taxpayer's spouse.

THE BIG PICTURE

Example 10

Return to the facts of *The Big Picture* on p. 10-1. John Williamson is the sole practitioner in his unincorporated accounting firm. During the year, he paid health insurance premiums of $8,000 for his own coverage and $7,000 for coverage for his wife, Susan. John can deduct $15,000 as a business deduction (*for* AGI) in computing their taxable income.

Taxpayers may also include premiums paid on qualified long-term care insurance contracts in medical expenses, subject to limitations based on the age of the insured. For 2014, the per-person limits range from $370 for taxpayers age 40 and under to $4,660 for taxpayers over age 70. See IRS Publication 502 for details relating to requirements for deducting costs associated with qualified long-term care insurance contracts.[15]

10-1f Year of Deduction

Regardless of a taxpayer's method of accounting, medical expenses are deductible only in the year *paid*. In effect, this places all individual taxpayers on a cash basis as far as the medical expense deduction is concerned. One exception, however, is allowed for deceased taxpayers. If the medical expenses are paid within one year from the day following the day of death, they can be treated as being paid at the time they were *incurred*. Thus, such expenses may be reported on the final income tax return of the decedent or on earlier returns if incurred before the year of death.

No current deduction is allowed for payment for medical care to be rendered in the future unless the taxpayer is under an obligation to make the payment. Whether an obligation to make the payment exists depends upon the policy of the physician or the institution furnishing the medical care.

Example 11

Upon the recommendation of his regular dentist, in December 2014, Gary consults Dr. Smith, a prosthodontist, who specializes in crown and bridge work. Dr. Smith tells Gary that he can do the restorative work for $12,000 and that he requires all new

---

[14]§ 162(l).

[15]The amounts for 2013 were $360 for taxpayers age 40 and under and $4,550 for taxpayers over age 70.

patients to prepay 40% of the total cost of the procedure. Accordingly, Gary pays $4,800 in December 2014. The balance of $7,200 is paid when the work is completed in January 2015. Under these circumstances, the qualifying medical expense deductions are $4,800 for 2014 and $7,200 in 2015. The result would be the same even if Gary prepaid the full $12,000 in 2014.

10-1g Reimbursements

If medical expenses are reimbursed in the same year as paid, no problem arises. The reimbursement merely reduces the amount that would otherwise qualify for the medical expense deduction. But what happens if the reimbursement occurs in a later year than the expenditure? In computing casualty losses, any reasonable prospect of recovery must be considered (refer to Chapter 7). For medical expenses, however, any expected reimbursement is disregarded in measuring the amount of the deduction. Instead, the reimbursement is accounted for separately in the year in which it occurs.

Under the *tax benefit rule*, a taxpayer who receives an insurance reimbursement for medical expenses deducted in a previous year must include the reimbursement in income up to the amount of the deductions that decreased taxable income in the earlier year. A taxpayer who did not itemize deductions in the year the expenses were paid did not receive a tax benefit and is *not* required to include a reimbursement in gross income.

Example 12

Homer (age 50) had AGI of $45,000 for 2014. He was injured in a car accident and paid $4,300 for hospital expenses and $700 for doctor bills. Homer also incurred medical expenses of $600 for his dependent child. In 2015, Homer was reimbursed $650 by his insurance company for the medical expenses attributable to the car accident. His deduction for medical expenses in 2014 is computed as follows:

Hospitalization	$ 4,300
Bills for doctor's services	700
Medical expenses for dependent	600
Total	$ 5,600
Less: 10% of $45,000	(4,500)
Medical expense deduction (assuming that Homer itemizes his deductions)	$ 1,100

Assume that Homer would have elected to itemize his deductions even if he had no medical expenses in 2014. If the reimbursement for medical care had occurred in 2014, the medical expense deduction would have been only $450 [$5,600 (total medical expenses) − $650 (reimbursement) − $4,500 (floor)] and Homer would have paid more income tax.

Because the reimbursement was made in a subsequent year, Homer will include $650 in gross income for 2015. If Homer had not itemized in 2014, he would *not* have included the $650 reimbursement in 2015 gross income because he would have received no tax benefit for the medical expenses in 2014.

10-1h Health Savings Accounts

Qualifying individuals may make deductible contributions to a **Health Savings Account (HSA)**. An HSA is a qualified trust or custodial account administered by a qualified HSA trustee, which can be a bank, an insurance company, or another IRS-approved trustee.[16] A taxpayer can use an HSA in conjunction with a high-deductible medical insurance policy to help reduce the overall cost of medical coverage. Converting from a low-deductible to a high-deductible plan can generally save an individual a considerable amount in premiums. The high-deductible policy

---

[16]§ 223.

provides coverage for extraordinary medical expenses (in excess of the deductible), and expenses not covered by the policy can be paid with funds withdrawn tax-free from the HSA.

Example 13

Sanchez, who is married and has three dependent children, carries a high-deductible medical insurance policy with a deductible of $4,400. He establishes an HSA and contributes the maximum allowable amount to the HSA in 2014. During 2014, the Sanchez family incurs medical expenses of $7,000. The high-deductible policy covers $2,600 of the expenses ($7,000 expenses − $4,400 deductible). Sanchez may withdraw $4,400 from the HSA to pay the medical expenses not covered by the high-deductible policy.

High-Deductible Plans

High-deductible policies are less expensive than low-deductible policies, so taxpayers with low medical costs can benefit from the lower premiums and use funds from the HSA to pay costs not covered by the high-deductible policy. A plan must meet two requirements to qualify as a high-deductible plan.[17]

1. The annual deductible in 2014 is not less than $1,250 for self-only coverage ($2,500 for family coverage).
2. The annual limit in 2014 on total out-of-pocket costs (excluding premiums) under the plan does not exceed $6,350 for self-only coverage ($12,700 for family coverage).

Tax Treatment of HSA Contributions and Distributions

To establish an HSA, a taxpayer contributes funds to a tax-exempt trust.[18] As illustrated in the preceding example, funds can be withdrawn from an HSA to pay medical expenses that are not covered by the high-deductible policy. The following general tax rules apply to HSAs:

1. Contributions made by the taxpayer to an HSA are deductible from gross income to arrive at AGI (deduction *for* AGI). Thus, the taxpayer does not need to itemize to take the deduction.
2. Earnings on HSAs are not subject to taxation unless distributed, in which case taxability depends on the way the funds are used.[19]
   - Distributions from HSAs are excluded from gross income if they are used to pay for medical expenses not covered by the high-deductible policy.
   - Distributions that are not used to pay for medical expenses are included in gross income and are subject to an additional 20 percent penalty if made before age 65, death, or disability. Such distributions made by reason of death or disability and distributions made after the HSA beneficiary becomes eligible for Medicare are taxed but not penalized.

HSAs have at least two other attractive features. First, an HSA is portable. Taxpayers who switch jobs can take their HSAs with them. Second, anyone under age 65 who has a high-deductible plan and is not covered by another policy that is not a high-deductible plan can establish an HSA.

Deductible Amount

The annual deduction for contributions to an HSA is limited to the sum of the monthly limitations. The monthly limitation is calculated for each month the individual is an eligible individual. The monthly deduction is not allowed after the individual becomes eligible for Medicare coverage.

---

[17]§ 223(c)(2).
[18]§ 223(d).

[19]§ 223(f).

TAX IN THE NEWS The Far-Reaching Effect of Health Care Reform

One of the marquee (and controversial) accomplishments of the Obama administration has been the enactment of sweeping health care legislation, the Patient Protection and Affordable Care Act (PPACA), in March 2010. Upon being challenged, the Supreme Court later ruled that this politically charged legislation is constitutional. Consequently, it seems clear that the legislation will become fully effective over the next several years unless Congress chooses to change the law.

The revenues the Federal government needs to cover the cost of providing health care benefits to millions of previously uninsured Americans are generated in a multitude of ways, including additional taxes and reduced deductions—and the associated provisions are scattered throughout the tax law and other Federal statutes. Some of the more common provisions arising from PPACA that have a direct bearing on medical care planning and could have a costly effect on taxpayers include the following:

- The threshold that limits the deductibility of medical expenses for regular income tax purposes increased

for most taxpayers from 7.5 percent of AGI to 10 percent of AGI beginning in 2013. For taxpayers 65 and older, the 7.5 percent threshold will remain in effect through 2016.

- An annual cap of $2,500 (indexed for inflation) limits contributions that may be made to a health Flexible Spending Account (FSA), while previously a larger amount could have been sheltered.
- Nonprescribed over-the-counter drugs (with the exception of insulin) are no longer qualified medical expenses for purposes of an FSA or a Health Savings Account (HSA).
- The penalty tax increased from 10 percent to 20 percent on distributions from an HSA that are not used for qualified medical expenses.

These examples reflect only the "tip of the iceberg." In fact, PPACA gathers needed resources from taxpayers in many other ways. Unfortunately, some of these provisions will not become apparent to affected taxpayers until they are surprised with an unexpectedly high tax bill.

© iStockphoto.com/Andrey Prokhorov

The amount of the monthly limitation for an individual who has self-only coverage in 2014 is one-twelfth of $3,300, while the monthly limitation for an individual who has family coverage in 2014 is one-twelfth of $6,550. These amounts are subject to annual cost-of-living adjustments.[20] An eligible taxpayer who has attained age 55 by the end of the tax year may make an additional annual contribution in 2014 of up to $1,000. This additional amount is referred to as a *catch-up* contribution.

Liu, who is married and self-employed, carries a high-deductible medical insurance policy with family coverage and an annual deductible of $4,000. In addition, he has established an HSA. Liu's maximum annual contribution to the HSA in 2014 is $6,550.	**Example 14**

During 2014, Adam, who is self-employed, made 12 monthly payments of $1,200 for an HSA contract that provides medical insurance coverage with a $3,600 deductible. The plan covers Adam, his wife, and two children. Of the $1,200 monthly fee, $675 was for the high-deductible policy and $525 was deposited into an HSA. The deductible monthly contribution to the HSA is calculated as follows:	**Example 15**

Maximum annual deduction for family coverage	$ 6,550
Monthly limitation (1/12 of $6,550)	$545.83

Because Adam is self-employed, he can deduct $8,100 of the amount paid for the high-deductible policy ($675 per month × 12 months) as a deduction *for* AGI (refer to Example 10). In addition, he can deduct the $6,300 ($525 × 12) paid to the HSA as a deduction *for* AGI. Note that the $6,300 HSA deduction does not exceed the $6,550 ceiling.

---

[20]§ 223(b)(2). The annual limits were $3,250 and $6,450 in 2013.

EXHIBIT 10.2	Deductible and Nondeductible Taxes

Deductible	Nondeductible
State, local, and foreign real property taxes	Federal income taxes
	FICA taxes imposed on employees
State and local personal property taxes	Employer FICA taxes paid on domestic household workers
State and local income taxes *or* sales/use taxes*	Estate, inheritance, and gift taxes
Foreign income taxes	Federal, state, and local excise taxes (e.g., gasoline, tobacco, and spirits)
	Foreign income taxes if the taxpayer chooses the foreign tax credit option
	Taxes on real property to the extent such taxes are to be apportioned and treated as imposed on another taxpayer

* The sales/use tax alternative is available through 2013. Many tax professionals expect Congress to extend this provision.

10-2 TAXES

LO.3

Contrast deductible taxes with nondeductible fees, licenses, and other charges.

A deduction is allowed for certain state and local taxes paid or accrued by a taxpayer.[21] The deduction was created to relieve the burden of multiple taxes upon the same source of revenue.

10-2a Deductibility as a Tax

A distinction must be made between a tax and a fee, because fees are not deductible unless incurred as an ordinary and necessary business expense or as an expense in the production of income. The IRS has defined a tax as follows:

> A tax is an enforced contribution exacted pursuant to legislative authority in the exercise of taxing power, and imposed and collected for the purpose of raising revenue to be used for public or governmental purposes, and not as payment for some special privilege granted or service rendered. Taxes are, therefore, distinguished from various other contributions and charges imposed for particular purposes under particular powers or functions of the government. In view of such distinctions, the question whether a particular contribution or charge is to be regarded as a tax depends upon its real nature.[22]

Accordingly, fees for dog licenses, automobile inspections, automobile titles and registration, hunting and fishing licenses, bridge and highway tolls, driver's licenses, parking meter deposits, and postage are not deductible if personal in nature. Deductible and nondeductible taxes are summarized in Exhibit 10.2.

10-2b Property Taxes

State, local, and foreign taxes on real property are generally deductible only by the person upon whom the tax is imposed. Deductible personal property taxes must be *ad valorem* (assessed in relation to the value of the property). Therefore, a motor vehicle tax based on weight, model, year, and horsepower is not an ad valorem tax. However, a tax based on value and other criteria may qualify in part.

---

[21]Most deductible taxes are listed in § 164, while nondeductible items are included in § 275.

[22]Rev.Rul. 57–345, 1957–2 C.B. 132, and Rev.Rul. 70–622, 1970–2 C.B. 41.

Example 16

Return to the facts of *The Big Picture* on p. 10-1. Assuming that the Williamsons proceed with the purchase of a home, the real estate taxes they pay will be deductible *from* AGI because they qualify to itemize their deductions. However, if they also pay a personal property tax on their automobile, the payment may be only partially deductible. Assume that in their state, the government imposes a motor vehicle registration tax on 2% of the value of the vehicle plus 40 cents per hundredweight. The Williamsons own a car having a value of $20,000 and weighing 3,000 pounds. They pay an annual registration tax of $412. Of this amount, $400 (2% of $20,000) is deductible as a personal property tax. The remaining $12, based on the weight of the car, is not deductible.

Assessments for Local Benefits

As a general rule, real property taxes do not include taxes assessed for local benefits because such assessments tend to increase the value of the property (e.g., special assessments for streets, sidewalks, curbing, and other similar improvements). A taxpayer was denied a deduction for the cost of a new sidewalk (relative to a personal residence), even though the construction was required by the city and the sidewalk may have provided an incidental benefit to the public welfare.[23] Such assessments are added to the adjusted basis of the taxpayer's property.

Apportionment of Real Property Taxes between Seller and Purchaser

Real estate taxes for the entire year are apportioned between the buyer and seller on the basis of the number of days the property was held by each during the real property tax year. This apportionment is required whether the tax is paid by the buyer or the seller or is prorated according to the purchase agreement. The apportionment determines who is entitled to deduct the real estate taxes in the year of sale. The required apportionment prevents the shifting of the deduction for real estate taxes from the buyer to the seller, or vice versa. In making the apportionment, the assessment date and the lien date are disregarded.[24]

Example 17

A county's real property tax year runs from January 1 to December 31. Susan, the owner on January 1 of real property located in the county, sells the real property to Bob on June 30 (assume that this year is not a leap year). Bob owns the real property from June 30 through December 31. The tax for the real property tax year, January 1 through December 31, is $3,650. The portion of the real property tax treated as imposed upon Susan, the seller, is $1,800 [(180/365) × $3,650, January 1 through June 29], and $1,850 [(185/365) × $3,650, June 30 through December 31] of the tax is treated as imposed upon Bob, the purchaser.

If the actual real estate taxes are not prorated between the buyer and seller as part of the purchase agreement, adjustments are required. The adjustments are necessary to determine the amount realized by the seller and the adjusted basis of the property to the buyer. If the buyer pays the entire amount of the tax, he or she has, in effect, paid the seller's portion of the real estate tax and has therefore paid more for the property than the actual purchase price. Thus, the amount of real estate tax that is apportioned to the seller (for Federal income tax purposes) and paid by the buyer is added to the buyer's adjusted basis. The seller must increase the amount realized on the sale by the same amount.

---

[23]*Erie H. Rose*, 31 TCM 142, T.C.Memo. 1972–39; Reg. § 1.164–4(a).

[24]For most years, the apportionment is based on a 365-day year. However, in a leap year (i.e., a year that is evenly divisible by 4, such as 2012), the taxes are prorated over 366 days. In making the apportionment, the date of sale counts as a day the property is owned by the buyer.

Global Tax Issues

Deductibility of Foreign Taxes

Josef, a citizen of the United States who works primarily in New York, also works several months each year in Austria. He owns a residence in Austria and pays income taxes to Austria on the income he earns there. Both the property tax he pays on his Austrian residence and the income tax he pays on his Austrian income are deductible in computing U.S. taxable income. However, if Josef deducts the Austrian income tax, he may not claim the foreign tax credit with respect to this tax (see Chapter 13).

Example 18

Seth sells real estate on October 3 for $400,000. The buyer, Wilma, pays the real estate taxes of $3,650 for the calendar year, which is the real estate property tax year. Assuming that this is not a leap year, $2,750 (for 275 days) of the real estate taxes is apportioned to and is deductible by the seller, Seth, and $900 (for 90 days) of the taxes is deductible by Wilma. The buyer has, in effect, paid Seth's real estate taxes of $2,750 and has therefore paid $402,750 for the property. Wilma's basis is increased to $402,750, and the amount realized by Seth from the sale is increased to $402,750.

The opposite result occurs if the seller (rather than the buyer) pays the real estate taxes. In this case, the seller reduces the amount realized from the sale by the amount that has been apportioned to the buyer. The buyer is required to reduce his or her adjusted basis by a corresponding amount.

Example 19

Ruth sells real estate to Butch for $400,000 on October 3. While Ruth held the property, she paid the real estate taxes of $3,650 for the calendar year, which is the real estate property tax year. Although Ruth paid the entire $3,650 of real estate taxes, $900 of that amount is apportioned to Butch, based on the number of days he owned the property, and is therefore deductible by him. The effect is that the buyer, Butch, has paid only $399,100 ($400,000 − $900) for the property. The amount realized by Ruth, the seller, is reduced by $900, and Butch reduces his basis in the property to $399,100.

10-2c State and Local Income Taxes and Sales Taxes

LO.4

Explain the Federal income tax treatment of state and local income taxes and sales taxes.

The position of the IRS is that state and local income taxes imposed upon an individual are deductible only as itemized deductions, even if the taxpayer's sole source of income is from a business, rents, or royalties.

Cash basis taxpayers are entitled to deduct state income taxes withheld by the employer in the year the taxes are withheld. In addition, estimated state income tax payments are deductible in the year the payment is made by cash basis taxpayers even if the payments relate to a prior or subsequent year.[25] If the taxpayer overpays state income taxes because of excessive withholdings or estimated tax payments, the refund received is included in gross income of the following year to the extent the deduction reduced taxable income in the prior year.

Example 20

Leona, a cash basis, unmarried taxpayer, had $800 of state income tax withheld during 2014. Also in 2014, Leona paid $100 that was due when she filed her 2013 state income tax return and made estimated payments of $300 on her 2014 state income tax. When Leona files her 2014 Federal income tax return in April 2015, she elects to itemize deductions, which amount to $7,500, including the $1,200 of state income tax payments and withholdings, all of which reduce her taxable income.

As a result of overpaying her 2014 state income tax, Leona receives a refund of $200 early in 2015. She will include this amount in her 2015 gross income in computing her Federal income tax. It does not matter whether Leona received a check from the state for $200 or applied the $200 toward her 2015 state income tax.

---

[25]Rev.Rul. 71–190, 1971–1 C.B. 70. See also Rev.Rul. 82–208, 1982–2 C.B. 58, where a deduction is not allowed when the taxpayer cannot, in good faith, reasonably determine that there is additional state income tax liability.

Itemized Deduction for Sales Taxes Paid

Individuals can elect to deduct either their state and local income taxes *or* their sales/use taxes paid as an itemized deduction on Schedule A of Form 1040. The annual election can reflect actual sales/use tax payments *or* an amount from an IRS table (see Appendix A). The amount from the table may be increased by sales tax paid on the purchase of motor vehicles, boats, and other specified items. Most likely, the sales tax deduction will be elected by those living in states with no individual income tax. At the time of this writing, this deduction alternative was available through 2013. However, many tax professionals believe that Congress will extend this provision.

10-3 INTEREST

A deduction for interest has been allowed since the income tax law was enacted in 1913. Despite its long history of congressional acceptance, the interest deduction has been one of the most controversial areas in the tax law. The controversy centered around the propriety of allowing the deduction of interest charges for the purchase of consumer goods and services and interest on borrowings used to acquire investments (investment interest). Currently, personal (consumer) interest is not deductible. This includes credit card interest; interest on car loans; and other types of interest. However, interest on qualified student loans, qualified residence (home mortgage) interest, and investment interest continue to be deductible, subject to the limits discussed on the following pages.

LO.5

Distinguish between deductible and nondeductible interest and apply the appropriate limitations to deductible interest.

10-3a Allowed and Disallowed Items

The Supreme Court has defined *interest* as compensation for the use or forbearance of money.[26] The general rule permits a deduction for interest paid or accrued within the taxable year on indebtedness.

Interest on Qualified Student Loans

Taxpayers who pay interest on a qualified student loan may be able to deduct the interest as a deduction *for* AGI. The deduction is allowable only to the extent that the proceeds of the loan are used to pay qualified education expenses. Such payments must be made to qualified educational institutions. See IRS Publication 970, *Tax Benefits for Education*, for details.

The maximum annual deduction for qualified student loan interest is $2,500. However, in 2014, the deduction is phased out for taxpayers with modified AGI (MAGI) between $65,000 and $80,000 ($130,000 and $160,000 on joint returns). The deduction is not allowed for taxpayers who are claimed as dependents or for married taxpayers filing separately.[27]

The numerator in the phaseout computation is equal to MAGI minus the floor of the phaseout range (i.e., $65,000 or $130,000, depending on filing status). The denominator is equal to the amount of the phaseout range (e.g., $160,000 − $130,000 = $30,000 for married taxpayers filing jointly).

Example 21

In 2014, Curt and Rita, who are married and file a joint return, paid $3,000 of interest on a qualified student loan. Their MAGI was $137,500. Their maximum potential deduction for qualified student loan interest is $2,500, but it must be reduced by $625 as a result of the phaseout rules.

$2,500 interest × ($137,500 MAGI − $130,000 phaseout floor)/
$30,000 phaseout range = $625 reduction

Curt and Rita would be allowed a student loan interest deduction of $1,875 ($2,500 maximum deduction − $625 reduction = $1,875 deduction *for* AGI).

---

[26]*Old Colony Railroad Co. v. Comm.*, 3 USTC ¶880, 10 AFTR 786, 52 S.Ct. 211 (USSC, 1932).

[27]§ 221. See § 221(b)(2)(C) for the definition of MAGI. For 2013, the MAGI threshold amounts were $60,000 and $75,000 ($125,000 and $155,000 on joint returns).

Qualified Residence Interest

Qualified residence interest is interest paid or accrued during the taxable year on indebtedness (subject to limitations) *secured* by any property that is a qualified residence of the taxpayer. Qualified residence interest falls into two categories: (1) interest on acquisition indebtedness and (2) interest on home equity loans. Before discussing each of these categories, however, the term *qualified residence* must be defined.

A *qualified residence* includes the taxpayer's principal residence and one other residence of the taxpayer or spouse. The *principal residence* is one that meets the requirement for nonrecognition of gain upon sale under § 121 (see Chapter 15). The *one other residence*, or second residence, refers to one that is used as a residence if not rented or, if rented, meets the requirements for a personal residence under the rental of vacation home rules (refer to Chapter 6). A taxpayer who has more than one second residence can make the selection each year as to which one is the qualified second residence. A residence includes, in addition to a house in the ordinary sense, cooperative apartments, condominiums, and mobile homes and boats that have living quarters (sleeping accommodations and toilet and cooking facilities).

Although in most cases interest paid on a home mortgage is fully deductible, there are limitations.[28] Interest paid or accrued during the tax year on aggregate **acquisition indebtedness** of $1 million or less ($500,000 for married persons filing separate returns) is deductible as qualified residence interest. *Acquisition indebtedness* refers to amounts incurred in acquiring, constructing, or substantially improving a qualified residence of the taxpayer.

THE BIG PICTURE

Example 22

Return to the facts of *The Big Picture* on p. 10-1. Because John and Susan Williamson will need to borrow at least a portion of the purchase price of a new home, a standard mortgage likely will qualify as acquisition indebtedness because the borrowed funds are used to acquire a principal residence. However, the interest on the acquisition indebtedness will be fully deductible only if the amount of the mortgage is $1 million or less (assuming that John and Susan file a joint return) and the mortgage is secured by the home, which is the typical case. Recall that the Williamsons are also considering what appears to be a less expensive route of using their retirement and taxable investments to secure the debt. If they choose this alternative, the interest will not be deductible as qualified residence interest because the loan would not be acquisition indebtedness (i.e., the loan would not be secured by the home).

Qualified residence interest also includes interest on **home equity loans**. These loans utilize the personal residence of the taxpayer as security, typically in the form of a second mortgage. Because the funds from home equity loans can be used for personal purposes (e.g., auto purchases and medical expenses), what would otherwise have been nondeductible personal interest becomes deductible qualified residence interest.

However, interest is deductible only on the portion of a home equity loan that does not exceed the *lesser of*:

- The fair market value of the residence, reduced by the acquisition indebtedness, *or*
- $100,000 ($50,000 for married persons filing separate returns).

Example 23

Larry owns a personal residence with a fair market value of $450,000 and an outstanding first mortgage of $420,000. Therefore, his equity in his home is $30,000 ($450,000 − $420,000). Larry issues a second mortgage on the residence and in return borrows $15,000 to purchase a new family automobile. All interest on the $435,000 of first and second mortgage debt is treated as qualified residence interest.

---

[28]§ 163(h)(3).

TAX IN THE NEWS   Don't Allow the Tax Tail to Wag the Dog

Sometimes taxpayers are lulled into the belief that it is always a good idea to maximize their tax deductions. After all, higher income tax deductions reduce taxable income, which leads to a lower tax payment to Uncle Sam. However, taxpayers who follow this approach without evaluating broader economic considerations often regret their decisions.

The deduction for interest paid on home equity line debt has become very popular over the years. Home equity debt is considered "good debt" while credit card debt is considered "bad debt" because the after-tax cost of interest on home equity debt is typically much lower than interest on credit cards. Further, not long ago when home valuations were at record highs, many taxpayers saw no measurable risk in borrowing against the equity in their homes. However, many taxpayers now regret having consumed too much of their home equity and using their home equity as a "piggy bank" to pay for expensive vacations and fancy new cars. With the downturn in the economy and the real estate bubble having popped, a substantial percentage of homeowners find that their homes are worth less than the debt they owe on their homes. Apparently, the easy borrowing terms amid high home valuations of yesteryear were too much of an attraction to turn down. Perhaps they wish now that they hadn't tapped their home equity to finance the expensive vacation that now is but a memory. As home values have dropped, even though they have recovered some, many of these taxpayers are finding it difficult to get back on their feet.

© iStockphoto.com/Andrey Prokhorov

Example 24

Leon and Pearl, married taxpayers, took out a mortgage on their home for $290,000 in 1997. In March of the current year, when the home has a fair market value of $400,000 and they owe $195,000 on the mortgage, Leon and Pearl take out a home equity loan for $120,000. They use the funds to purchase a boat to be used for recreational purposes. The boat, which does not have living quarters, does not qualify as a personal residence. On a joint return, Leon and Pearl can deduct all of the interest on the first mortgage because it is acquisition indebtedness. Of the $120,000 home equity loan, only the interest on the first $100,000 is deductible. The interest on the remaining $20,000 is not deductible because it exceeds the statutory ceiling of $100,000.

Interest Paid for Services

Mortgage loan companies commonly charge a fee, often called a loan origination fee, for finding, placing, or processing a mortgage loan. Loan origination fees are typically nondeductible amounts included in the basis of the acquired property. Other fees, sometimes called **points** and expressed as a percentage of the loan amount, are paid to reduce the interest rate charged over the term of the loan. Essentially, the payment of points is a prepayment of interest and is considered compensation to a lender solely for the use or forbearance of money. To be deductible, points must be in the nature of interest and cannot be a form of service charge or payment for specific services.[29]

Points must be capitalized and are amortized and deductible ratably over the life of the loan. A special exception, however, permits the purchaser of a principal residence to deduct qualifying points in the year of payment.[30] The exception also covers points paid to obtain funds for home improvements.

Points paid to *refinance* an existing home mortgage cannot be immediately deducted, but must be capitalized and amortized as an interest deduction over the life of the new loan.[31]

Example 25

Sandra purchased her residence many years ago, obtaining a 30-year mortgage at an annual interest rate of 8%. In the current year, Sandra refinances the mortgage to reduce the interest rate to 4%. To obtain the refinancing, she has to pay points of $2,600. The $2,600, which is considered prepayment of interest, must be capitalized and amortized over the life of the mortgage.

---

[29]Rev.Rul. 69–188, 1969–1 C.B. 54.

[30]§ 461(g)(2).

[31]Rev.Rul. 87–22, 1987–1 C.B. 146.

Points paid by the seller for a buyer are, in effect, treated as an adjustment to the price of the residence, and the buyer is treated as having used cash to pay the points that were paid by the seller. A buyer may deduct seller-paid points in the tax year in which they are paid if several conditions are met. Refer to Revenue Procedure 94–27 for a complete list of these conditions and additional aspects of this arrangement.[32]

Mortgage Insurance Payments

Mortgage insurance is an additional cost that some taxpayers incur when purchasing a home. To protect their interests, mortgage lenders may require this coverage if the homebuyer cannot afford to, or chooses not to, make a down payment of at least 20 percent of the purchase price. The borrower pays the premiums on the policy, but the lender is the beneficiary that receives reimbursement in the event of foreclosure. Under current law, mortgage insurance premiums may be deductible as interest if they relate to a qualified residence of the taxpayer. However, the deduction begins to phase out for taxpayers with AGI in excess of $100,000 ($50,000 for married taxpayers filing separately).[33]

Prepayment Penalty

When a mortgage or loan is paid off in full in a lump sum before its term (early), the lending institution may require an additional payment of a certain percentage applied to the unpaid amount at the time of prepayment. This is known as a prepayment penalty and is considered to be interest (e.g., personal, qualified residence, or investment) in the year paid. The general rules for deductibility of interest also apply to prepayment penalties.

Interest Paid to Related Parties

Nothing prevents the deduction of interest paid to a related party as long as the payment actually took place and the interest meets the requirements for deductibility. Recall from Chapter 6 that a special rule for related taxpayers applies when the debtor uses the accrual basis and the related creditor is on the cash basis. If this rule is applicable, interest that has been accrued but not paid at the end of the debtor's tax year is not deductible until payment is made and the income is reportable by the cash basis recipient.

Investment Interest

Taxpayers frequently borrow funds they use to acquire investment assets. Congress, however, has limited the deductibility of interest on funds borrowed for the purpose of purchasing or continuing to hold investment property. Under this limitation, the deduction for investment interest expense may not exceed the net investment income for the year. A complete discussion of investment interest occurs in Chapter 11 in the context of the limitations taxpayers face when dealing with assets held for investment purposes.

Tax-Exempt Securities

The tax law provides that no deduction is allowed for interest on debt incurred to purchase or carry tax-exempt securities.[34] A major problem for the courts has been to determine what is meant by the words *to purchase or carry*. Refer to Chapter 6 for a detailed discussion of these issues.

---

[32]Rev.Proc. 94–27, 1994–1 C.B. 613.

[33]§§ 163(h)(3)(E)(i) and (ii). The deduction is fully phased out when AGI exceeds $109,000 ($54,500 for married taxpayers filing separately). The deduction thresholds are not subject to indexation for inflation. This

provision expired at the end of 2013. At the time of this writing, Congress has not extended this deduction.

[34]§ 265(a)(2).

10-3b Restrictions on Deductibility and Timing Considerations

Even if the interest expense qualifies as a type that is deductible (e.g., qualified residence interest), a current deduction still may not be available unless certain additional conditions described below are met.

Taxpayer's Obligation

Allowed interest is deductible if the related debt represents a bona fide obligation for which the taxpayer is liable.[35] Thus, for interest to be deductible, both the debtor and the creditor must intend for the loan to be repaid. Intent of the parties can be especially crucial between related parties such as a shareholder and a closely held corporation. In addition, an individual may not deduct interest paid on behalf of another taxpayer. For example, a shareholder may not deduct interest paid by the corporation on his or her behalf.[36] Likewise, a husband may not deduct interest paid on his wife's property if he files a separate return, except in the case of qualified residence interest. If both husband and wife consent in writing, either the husband or the wife may deduct the allowed interest on the principal residence and one other residence.

Time of Deduction

Generally, interest must be paid to secure a deduction unless the taxpayer uses the accrual method of accounting. Under the accrual method, interest is deductible ratably over the life of the loan.

On November 1, 2014, Ramon borrows $1,000 to purchase appliances for a rental house. The loan is payable in 90 days at 12% interest. On the due date in late January 2015, Ramon pays the $1,000 note and interest amounting to $30. Ramon can deduct the accrued portion ($2/3 \times \$30 = \$20$) of the interest in 2014 only if he is an accrual basis taxpayer. Otherwise, the entire amount of interest ($30) is deductible in 2015.

Example 26

Prepaid Interest

Accrual method reporting is imposed on cash basis taxpayers for interest prepayments that extend beyond the end of the taxable year.[37] Such payments must be allocated to the tax years to which the interest payments relate. These provisions are intended to prevent cash basis taxpayers from *manufacturing* tax deductions before the end of the year by prepaying interest.

10-3c Classification of Interest Expense

Whether interest is deductible *for* AGI or as an itemized deduction (*from* AGI) depends on whether the indebtedness has a business, investment, or personal purpose. If the indebtedness is incurred in relation to a business (other than performing services as an employee) or for the production of rent or royalty income, the interest is deductible *for* AGI. If the indebtedness is incurred for personal use, such as qualified residence interest, any deduction allowed is taken *from* AGI and is reported on Schedule A of Form 1040 if the taxpayer elects to itemize. Note, however, that interest on a student loan is a deduction *for* AGI. If the taxpayer is an employee who incurs debt in relation to his or her employment, the interest is considered to be personal, or consumer, interest and is not deductible. Business expenses appear on Schedule C of Form 1040, and expenses related to rents or royalties are reported on Schedule E.

If a taxpayer deposits money in a certificate of deposit (CD) that has a term of one year or less and the interest cannot be withdrawn without penalty, the full amount of the interest must still be included in income, even though part of the

---

[35]*Arcade Realty Co.*, 35 T.C. 256 (1960).
[36]*Continental Trust Co.*, 7 B.T.A. 539 (1927).

[37]§ 461(g)(1).

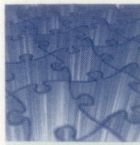

CONCEPT SUMMARY 10.1

Deductibility of Personal, Student Loan, Mortgage, and Investment Interest

Type	Deductible	Comments
Personal (consumer) interest	No	Includes any interest that is not qualified residence interest, qualified student loan interest, investment interest, or business interest. Examples include interest on car loans and credit card debt.
Qualified student loan interest	Yes	Deduction *for* AGI; subject to limitations.
Qualified residence interest on acquisition indebtedness	Yes	Deductible as an itemized deduction; limited to indebtedness of $1 million.
Qualified residence interest on home equity indebtedness	Yes	Deductible as an itemized deduction; limited to indebtedness equal to lesser of $100,000 or FMV of residence minus acquisition indebtedness.
Investment interest (*not* related to rental or royalty property)	Yes	Itemized deduction; limited to net investment income for the year; disallowed interest can be carried over to future years. See Chapter 11 for a complete discussion of investment interest.
Investment interest (related to rental or royalty property)	Yes	Deduction *for* AGI; limited to net investment income for the year; disallowed interest can be carried over to future years. See Chapter 11 for a complete discussion of investment interest.

interest is forfeited due to an early withdrawal. However, the taxpayer will be allowed a deduction *for* AGI as to the forfeited amount.

See Concept Summary 10.1 for a summary of the interest deduction rules.

10-4 CHARITABLE CONTRIBUTIONS

LO.6

Recognize charitable contributions and identify their related measurement problems and percentage limitations.

Section 170 allows individuals and corporations to deduct contributions made to qualified *domestic* organizations. Contributions to qualified charitable organizations serve certain social welfare needs and thus relieve the government of the cost of providing these needed services to the community.

The **charitable contribution** provisions are among the most complex in the tax law. To determine the amount deductible as a charitable contribution, several important questions must be answered:

- What constitutes a charitable contribution?
- Was the contribution made to a qualified organization?
- When is the contribution deductible?
- What record-keeping and reporting requirements apply to charitable contributions?
- How is the value of donated property determined?
- What special rules apply to contributions of property that has increased in value?
- What percentage limitations apply to the charitable contribution deduction?
- What rules apply to amounts in excess of percentage limitations (carryovers)?

These questions are addressed in the sections that follow.

10-4a Criteria for a Gift

A *charitable contribution* is defined as a gift made to a qualified organization.[38] The major elements needed to qualify a contribution as a gift are a donative intent, the absence of consideration, and acceptance by the donee. Consequently, the

---

[38]§ 170(c).

taxpayer has the burden of establishing that the transfer was made from motives of *disinterested generosity* as established by the courts.[39] This test is quite subjective and has led to problems of interpretation (refer to the discussion of gifts in Chapter 5).

Benefit Received Rule

When a donor derives a tangible benefit from a contribution, he or she cannot deduct the value of the benefit.

Ralph purchases a ticket at $100 for a special performance of the local symphony (a qualified charity). If the price of a ticket to a symphony concert is normally $35, Ralph is allowed only $65 as a charitable contribution. Even if Ralph does not attend the concert, the deduction is limited to $65. However, if Ralph does not accept the ticket from the symphony, he can deduct the full $100.

Example 27

An exception to this benefit rule provides for the deduction of an automatic percentage of the amount paid for the right to purchase athletic tickets from colleges and universities.[40] Under this exception, 80 percent of the amount paid to or for the benefit of the institution qualifies as a charitable contribution deduction.

Example 28

Janet donates $1,000 to State University's athletic department. The payment guarantees that she will have preferred seating on the 50-yard line at football games. Subsequently, Janet buys four $50 game tickets. Under the exception to the benefit rule, she is allowed an $800 (80% of $1,000) charitable contribution deduction for the taxable year.

If, however, Janet's $1,000 donation includes four $50 tickets, that portion [$200 ($50 × 4)] and the remaining portion of $800 ($1,000 − $200) are treated as separate amounts. Thus, Janet is allowed a charitable contribution deduction of $640 (80% of $800).

Contribution of Services

No deduction is allowed for a contribution of one's services to a qualified charitable organization. However, unreimbursed expenses related to the services rendered may be deductible. For example, the cost of a uniform (without general utility) that is required to be worn while performing services may be deductible, as are certain out-of-pocket transportation costs incurred for the benefit of the charity. In lieu of these out-of-pocket costs for an automobile, a standard mileage rate of 14 cents per mile is allowed.[41] Deductions are permitted for transportation, reasonable expenses for lodging, and the cost of meals while away from home that are incurred in performing the donated services. The travel expenses are not deductible if the travel involves a significant element of personal pleasure, recreation, or vacation.[42]

Example 29

Grace, a delegate representing her church in Miami, Florida, travels to a two-day national meeting in Denver, Colorado, in February. After the meeting, Grace spends two weeks at a nearby ski resort. Under these circumstances, none of the transportation, meals, or lodging is deductible because the travel involved a significant element of personal pleasure, recreation, or vacation.

Nondeductible Items

In addition to the benefit received rule and the restrictions placed on contributions of services, the following items may *not* be deducted as charitable contributions:

- Dues, fees, or bills paid to country clubs, lodges, fraternal orders, or similar groups.
- Cost of raffle, bingo, or lottery tickets.

---

[39]*Comm. v. Duberstein*, 60–2 USTC ¶9515, 5 AFTR 2d 1626, 80 S.Ct. 1190 (USSC, 1960).

[40]§ 170(l).

[41]§ 170(i).

[42]§ 170(j).

- Cost of tuition.
- Value of blood given to a blood bank.
- Donations to homeowners associations.
- Gifts to individuals.
- Rental value of property used by a qualified charity.

10-4b Qualified Organizations

To be deductible, a contribution must be made to one of the following organizations:[43]

- A state or possession of the United States or any subdivisions thereof.
- A corporation, trust, community chest, fund, or foundation that is situated in the United States and is organized and operated exclusively for religious, charitable, scientific, literary, or educational purposes or for the prevention of cruelty to children or animals.
- A veterans' organization.
- A fraternal organization operating under the lodge system.
- A cemetery company.

The IRS publishes a list of organizations that have applied for and received tax-exempt status under § 501 of the Code.[44] This publication is updated frequently and may be helpful in determining whether a gift has been made to a qualifying charitable organization.

Because gifts made to needy individuals are not deductible, a deduction will not be permitted if a gift is received by a donee in an individual capacity rather than as a representative of a qualifying organization.

ETHICS & EQUITY An Indirect Route to a Contribution Deduction

In July, a plane crashed into a residential community in Middleboro, destroying and damaging many homes. Chloe's church, a qualified charitable organization, initiated a fund-raising drive to help the Middleboro citizens whose homes had been affected. Chloe donated $50,000 to First Middleboro Church and suggested to the pastor that $25,000 of her contribution should be given to her sister, Rebecca, whose home had suffered extensive damage. The pastor appointed a committee to award funds to needy citizens. The committee solicited applications from the community and awarded Rebecca $15,000. Discuss whether Chloe is justified in deducting $50,000 as a charitable contribution.

10-4c Time of Deduction

A charitable contribution generally is deducted in the year the payment is made. This rule applies to both cash and accrual basis individuals. A contribution is ordinarily deemed to have been made on the delivery of the property to the donee. For example, if a gift of securities (properly endorsed) is made to a qualified charitable organization, the gift is considered complete on the day of delivery or mailing. However, if the donor delivers the certificate to his or her bank or broker or to the issuing corporation, the gift is considered complete on the date the stock is transferred on the books of the corporation.

A contribution made by check is considered delivered on the date of mailing. Thus, a check mailed on December 31, 2014, is deductible on the taxpayer's 2014 tax return. If the contribution is charged on a credit card, the date the charge is made determines the year of deduction.

---

[43]§ 170(c).
[44]Although this *Cumulative List of Organizations*, IRS Publication 78, may be helpful, qualified organizations are not required to be listed. Not all organizations that qualify are listed in this publication. The list is available at **www.irs.gov**.

TAX IN THE NEWS Complying with Documentation Requirements is Critical, Even for IRS Agents

The income tax law is clear that a taxpayer bears the burden to show that he or she is entitled to claim a deduction for a gift made to a qualified charity. Some may argue that the documentation and substantiation rules written by the IRS are overly strict. Nonetheless, if a taxpayer wants to take a deduction for charitable gifts, the best recommendation would be to follow the rules carefully and be able to provide credible support if requested by the IRS.

One taxpayer, a 28-year employee of the IRS, was denied charitable deductions in two recent years because she was unable to provide convincing evidence that she had made cash gifts of over $20,000 to a New York church (*Margaret*

Payne, T.C. Summary Opinion 2013–64). The evidence Payne provided to support the deduction, a statement on church letterhead, was characterized as a "cut and paste job" that was apparently signed by one of Payne's children. The Tax Court ultimately denied the deduction stating that the "record was full of inconsistencies, contradicting testimony, fabricated documents, and simple untruths."

So if any lessons can be gleaned from this experience, they may be that tax rules apply equally to IRS agents and regular citizens alike, and if a cash gift is made to one's favorite charity, whether it be for $20,000 or $20, legitimate and convincing documentation must be gathered to support it.

10-4d Record-Keeping and Valuation Requirements

Recall that income tax deductions allowed by law are a matter of legislative grace, but a taxpayer still bears the burden of showing that he or she is entitled to claim the deduction. Not surprisingly, the IRS provides specific documentation requirements that must be met if a charitable contribution deduction is to be protected.

Record-Keeping Requirements

No deduction is allowed for a charitable contribution made to a qualified organization unless the taxpayer gathers (and, in some cases, supplies to the IRS) the appropriate documentation and substantiation. The specific type of documentation required depends on the amount of the contribution and whether the contribution is made in cash or noncash property.[45] In addition, special rules may apply to gifts of certain types of property (e.g., used automobiles) where Congress has noted taxpayer abuse in the past. Further, for certain gifts of noncash property, Form 8283 (Noncash Charitable Contributions) must be attached to the taxpayer's return.

The required substantiation must be obtained before the earlier of (1) the due date (including extensions) of the return for the year the contribution is claimed or (2) the date the return is filed. Failure to comply with the reporting rules may result in disallowance of the charitable contribution deduction. In addition, significant overvaluation exposes the taxpayer to stringent penalties.

Common documentation and substantiation requirements are summarized in Concept Summary 10.2.

Valuation Requirements

Property donated to a charity is generally valued at fair market value at the time the gift is made. The Code and Regulations give very little guidance on the measurement of the fair market value except to say, "The fair market value is the price at which the property would change hands between a willing buyer and a willing seller, neither being under any compulsion to buy or sell and both having reasonable knowledge of relevant facts."

Generally, charitable organizations do not attest to the fair market value of the donated property. Nevertheless, as noted in Concept Summary 10.2, the taxpayer must maintain reliable written evidence of the donation.

---

[45]The specific documentation thresholds and requirements are provided in § 170(f).

CONCEPT SUMMARY 10.2

Documentation and Substantiation Requirements for Charitable Contributions

Cash gifts	• A deduction is allowed only if the taxpayer has a proper receipt (e.g., bank record such as a canceled check or written statement from the charity) showing the name of the charitable organization and the date and amount of the contribution.
	• A written statement from the charity is required if a payment is for more than $75 and is partly a contribution and partly for goods or services. The statement must provide an estimate of the value of the goods and services received by the donor.
Noncash gifts (e.g., household items)	• A receipt from the charity must be kept for any gift of property other than money. Clothes or other household items are deductible if they are in "good used condition or better" at the time of the gift.
	• If the items are not in good used condition or better and their value is $500 or more, a deduction is allowed if a "qualified appraisal" is included with the return.
Used automobiles	• The deduction is generally limited to the amount the charity receives on the sale of the car. The taxpayer should obtain a statement from the charity documenting the sales price of the automobile.
Cash or noncash gifts of $250 or more	• Written acknowledgment from the charity (or certain payroll records in the case of gifts made by payroll deductions) is required to deduct a single cash or property contribution of $250 or more. The acknowledgment must include the amount of money and a description of any other property contributed, whether the charity provided any goods or services in return for the contribution, and a description and estimated value of the goods or services provided.
Noncash gifts of more than $500	• Additional substantiation (e.g., how the property was acquired and its basis) is required on the tax return if donated noncash property is valued at more than $500. Qualified appraisals may be required if noncash contributions exceed $5,000 in value.
Antiques, paintings, jewelry, and other "tangible personal property"	• The deduction is equal to the property's appreciated FMV only if the charity puts the property to "a use related to its tax-exempt purpose." Otherwise, the deduction is limited to the property's cost. The taxpayer should obtain a statement from the charity documenting the property's use.

10-4e Limitations on Charitable Contribution Deduction

The potential charitable contribution deduction is the total of all donations, both money and property, that qualify for the deduction. After this determination is made, the actual amount of the charitable contribution deduction that is allowed for individuals for the tax year is limited as follows:

- If the qualifying contributions for the year total 20 percent or less of AGI, they are fully deductible.
- If the qualifying contributions are more than 20 percent of AGI, the deductible amount may be limited to 20 percent, 30 percent, or 50 percent of AGI, depending on the type of property given and the type of organization to which the donation is made.
- In any case, the maximum charitable contribution deduction may not exceed 50 percent of AGI for the tax year.

To understand the complex rules for computing the amount of a charitable contribution deduction, it is necessary to understand the distinction between capital gain property and ordinary income property. In addition, it is necessary to understand when the 50 percent, 30 percent, and 20 percent limitations apply. If a taxpayer's contributions for the year exceed the applicable percentage limitations, the excess contributions may be carried forward and deducted

Choose the Charity Wisely

Aiko, a U.S. citizen of Japanese descent, was distressed by the damage caused by a major earthquake in Japan. She donated $100,000 to the Earthquake Victims' Relief Fund, a Japanese charitable organization that was set up to help victims of the earthquake. Kaito, also a U.S. citizen of Japanese descent, donated $100,000 to help with the relief effort. However, Kaito's contribution went to his church, which sent the proceeds of a fund drive to the Earthquake Victims' Relief Fund in Japan. Aiko's contribution is not deductible, but Kaito's is. Why? Contributions to charitable organizations are not deductible unless the organization is a U.S. charity.

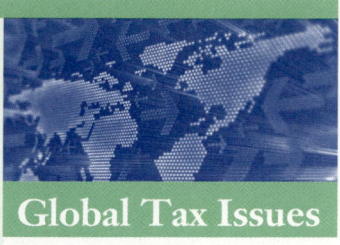

Global Tax Issues

© iStockphoto.com/Andrey Prokhorov

during a five-year carryover period. These topics are discussed in the sections that follow.

Ordinary Income Property

Ordinary income property is any property that, if sold, will result in the recognition of ordinary income. The term includes inventory for sale in the taxpayer's trade or business, a work of art created by the donor, and a manuscript prepared by the donor. It also includes, *for purposes of the charitable contribution calculation*, a capital asset held by the donor for less than the required holding period for long-term capital gain treatment (long-term is a period longer than one year). To the extent that disposition of property results in the recognition of ordinary income due to the recapture of depreciation, it is ordinary income property.[46]

If ordinary income property is contributed, the deduction is equal to the fair market value of the property less the amount of ordinary income that would have been reported if the property were sold. In most instances, the deduction is limited to the adjusted basis of the property to the donor.

Example 30

Tim donates stock in White Corporation to a university on May 1, 2014. Tim had purchased the stock for $2,500 on March 3, 2014, and the stock had a value of $3,600 when he made the donation. Because he had not held the property long enough to meet the long-term capital gain requirement, Tim would have recognized a short-term capital gain of $1,100 if he had sold the property. Because short-term capital gain property is treated as ordinary income property for charitable contribution purposes, Tim's charitable contribution deduction is limited to the property's adjusted basis of $2,500 ($3,600 − $1,100).

In Example 30, suppose the stock had a fair market value of $2,300 (rather than $3,600) when it was donated to charity. Because the fair market value now is less than the adjusted basis, the charitable contribution deduction is $2,300.

Capital Gain Property

Capital gain property is any property that would have resulted in the recognition of long-term capital gain or § 1231 gain if the property had been sold by the donor.[47] As a general rule, the deduction for a contribution of capital gain property is equal to the fair market value of the property.

Three major exceptions disallow the deductibility of the appreciation on capital gain property. One exception concerns certain private foundations. Private

---

[46]For a more complete discussion of the difference between ordinary income and capital gain property, see Chapter 16.

[47]See General Scheme of Taxation in Chapter 16 for a discussion of holding periods.

foundations are organizations that traditionally do not receive their funding from the general public (e.g., the Bill and Melinda Gates Foundation). Generally, foundations fall into two categories: operating and nonoperating. A private *operating* foundation spends substantially all of its income in the active conduct of the charitable undertaking for which it was established. Other private foundations are *nonoperating* foundations. Often, only the private foundation knows its status (operating or nonoperating) for sure, and the status can change from year to year.

If capital gain property is contributed to a private *nonoperating* foundation, the taxpayer must reduce the contribution by the long-term capital gain that would have been recognized if the property had been sold at its fair market value. The effect of this provision is to limit the deduction to the property's adjusted basis.[48]

Example 31

Walter purchased land for $8,000 on January 1, 2001, and has held it as an investment since then. This year, when the land is worth $20,000, he donates it to a private nonoperating foundation. Walter's charitable contribution is $8,000 ($20,000 − $12,000), the land's basis.

If, in Example 31, Walter had donated the land to either a public charity or a private operating foundation, his charitable contribution would have been $20,000, the fair market value of the land.

A second exception applying to capital gain property relates to *tangible personalty*. Tangible personalty is all property that is not realty (land and buildings) and does not include intangible property such as stock or securities. If tangible personalty is contributed to a public charity such as a museum, church, or university, the charitable deduction may have to be reduced. The amount of the reduction is the long-term capital gain that would have been recognized if the property had been sold for its fair market value. In general, the reduction is required if the property is put to an *unrelated use*. The term *unrelated use* means a use that is unrelated to the exempt purpose or function of the charitable organization. For example, artwork donated to the American Red Cross is unlikely to be put to a related use. Instead, the Red Cross would likely sell the art to generate funds that would then be used to support its mission of providing assistance to individuals who have been struck by disasters.

This reduction generally will not apply if the property is, in fact, not put to an unrelated use or if, at the time of the contribution, it was reasonable to anticipate that the property would not be put to an unrelated use by the donee.[49]

Example 32

Myrtle contributes a Picasso painting, for which she paid $20,000, to a local museum. She had owned the painting for four years. It had a value of $30,000 at the time of the donation. The museum displays the painting for five years and subsequently sells it for $50,000. The charitable contribution is $30,000. It is not reduced by the unrealized appreciation because the painting is not put to an unrelated use even though it is later sold by the museum.

A third exception applying to capital gain property disallows a deduction for the appreciation on several types of intellectual property. Patents, certain copyrights, trademarks, trade names, trade secrets, know-how, and some software are subject to this rule, which limits the contribution to the lesser of the taxpayer's basis in the property or the property's fair market value. As a consequence of this exception, if many of these types of intellectual property are donated by their creator, the charitable contribution deduction will be relatively small because the creator usually has a low basis for them.

---

[48]§ 170(e)(1)(B)(ii). However, § 170(e)(5) provides that taxpayers who donate *qualified appreciated stock* to private nonoperating foundations may deduct the fair market value of the stock. Qualified appreciated stock is stock for which market quotations are readily available on an established securities market.

[49]§ 170(e)(1)(B)(i) and Reg. § 1.170A–4(b)(3)(ii)(b). In certain situations, if the donee disposes of the property within three years of the contribution, the donor is required to recapture the appreciation element of the deduction unless the donee certifies that it put the property to a related use or intended to put the property to a related use.

Fifty Percent Ceiling

Contributions made to public charities may not exceed 50 percent of an individual's AGI for the year. The 50 percent ceiling on contributions applies to public charities such as churches; schools; hospitals; and Federal, state, or local governmental units. The 50 percent ceiling also applies to contributions to private operating foundations and certain private nonoperating foundations.

In the remaining discussion of charitable contributions, public charities and private foundations (both operating and nonoperating) that qualify for the 50 percent ceiling will be referred to as *50 percent organizations*.

Thirty Percent Ceiling

A 30 percent ceiling applies to contributions of cash and ordinary income property to private nonoperating foundations that are not 50 percent organizations. The 30 percent ceiling also applies to contributions of appreciated capital gain property to 50 percent organizations unless the taxpayer makes a special election (see below).

In the event the contributions for any one tax year involve both 50 percent and 30 percent property, the allowable deduction comes first from the 50 percent property.

> **Example 33**
>
> During the year, Lisa makes the following donations to her church: cash of $2,000 and unimproved land worth $30,000. Lisa had purchased the land four years ago for $22,000 and held it as an investment. Therefore, it is capital gain property. Lisa's AGI for the year is $60,000. Disregarding percentage limitations, Lisa's potential deduction is $32,000 [$2,000 (cash) + $30,000 (fair market value of land)].
>
> In applying the percentage limitations, however, the *current* deduction for the land is limited to $18,000 [30% (limitation applicable to capital gain property) × $60,000 (AGI)]. Thus, the total current deduction is $20,000 ($2,000 cash + $18,000 land). Note that the total deduction does not exceed $30,000, which is 50% of Lisa's AGI.

Under a special election, a taxpayer may choose to permanently forgo a deduction of the appreciation on capital gain property. Referred to as the *reduced deduction election*, this enables the taxpayer to move from the 30 percent limitation to the 50 percent limitation.

> **Example 34**
>
> Assume the same facts as in Example 33, except that Lisa makes the reduced deduction election. Now the deduction becomes $24,000 [$2,000 (cash) + $22,000 (basis in land)] because both donations fall under the 50% limitation. Thus, by making the election, Lisa has increased her current charitable contribution deduction by $4,000 [$24,000 − $20,000 (Example 33)].

Although the reduced deduction election appears attractive, it should be considered carefully. The election sacrifices a deduction for the appreciation on capital gain property that might eventually be allowed. Note that in Example 33, the potential deduction was $32,000, yet in Example 34, only $24,000 is allowed. The reason the potential deduction is decreased by $8,000 ($32,000 − $24,000) is that no carryover is allowed for the amount sacrificed by the election.

Twenty Percent Ceiling

A 20 percent ceiling applies to contributions of appreciated capital gain property to private nonoperating foundations that are not 50 percent organizations.

Concept Summary 10.3 summarizes limitations on the deductibility of charitable gifts.

Contribution Carryovers

Contributions that exceed the percentage limitations for the current year can be carried over for five years. In the carryover process, such contributions do not lose

CONCEPT SUMMARY 10.3

Determining the Deduction for Contributions of Appreciated Property by Individuals

If the Type of Property Contributed Is:	And the Property Is Contributed to:	The Contribution Is Measured by:	But the Deduction Is Limited to:
1. Capital gain property	A 50% organization	Fair market value of the property	30% of AGI
2. Ordinary income property	A 50% organization	The basis of the property*	50% of AGI
3. Capital gain property (and the property is tangible personal property put to an unrelated use by the donee)	A 50% organization	The basis of the property*	50% of AGI
4. Capital gain property (and the reduced deduction is elected)	A 50% organization	The basis of the property	50% of AGI
5. Capital gain property	A private nonoperating foundation that is not a 50% organization	The basis of the property*	The lesser of: 1. 20% of AGI 2. 50% of AGI minus other contributions to 50% organizations

*If the fair market value of the property is less than the adjusted basis (i.e., the property has declined in value instead of appreciating), the fair market value is used.

their identity for limitation purposes. Thus, if the contribution originally involved 30 percent property, the carryover will continue to be classified as 30 percent property in the carryover year.

Example 35

Assume the same facts as in Example 33. Because only $18,000 of the $30,000 value of the land is deducted in the current year, the balance of $12,000 may be carried over to the following year. But the carryover will still be treated as capital gain property and is subject to the 30%-of-AGI limitation.

In applying the percentage limitations, current charitable contributions must be claimed first before any carryovers can be considered. If carryovers involve more than one year, they are utilized in a first-in, first-out order.

10-5 MISCELLANEOUS ITEMIZED DEDUCTIONS

LO.7

List the business and personal expenditures that are deductible either as miscellaneous itemized deductions or as other itemized deductions.

In general, no deduction is allowed for personal, living, or family expenses.[50] However, a taxpayer may incur a number of expenditures related to employment. If an employee or outside salesperson incurs unreimbursed business expenses or expenses that are reimbursed under a nonaccountable plan, including travel and transportation, the expenses are deductible as **miscellaneous itemized deductions**.[51] Certain other expenses also fall into the special category of miscellaneous itemized deductions. Some are deductible only if, in total, they exceed 2 percent of the taxpayer's AGI. These miscellaneous itemized deductions include (but are not limited to) the following:

- Professional dues to membership organizations.
- Cost of uniforms or other clothing that cannot be used for normal wear.

---

[50]§ 262.

[51]Actors and performing artists who meet certain requirements are not subject to this rule. See § 62(a)(2)(B).

- Fees incurred for the preparation of one's tax return or fees incurred for tax litigation before the IRS or the courts.
- Job-hunting costs.
- Fee paid for a safe deposit box used to store papers and documents relating to taxable income-producing investments.
- Investment expenses that are deductible under § 212 as discussed in Chapter 6.
- Appraisal fees to determine the amount of a casualty loss or the fair market value of donated property.
- Hobby losses up to the amount of hobby income (refer to Chapter 6).
- Unreimbursed employee expenses (refer to Chapter 9).

Certain employee business expenses that are reimbursed are not itemized deductions, but are deducted *for* AGI. Employee business expenses are discussed in depth in Chapter 9.

10-6 OTHER MISCELLANEOUS DEDUCTIONS

Certain expenses and losses do not fall into any category of itemized deductions already discussed but are nonetheless deductible. The following expenses and losses are deductible on line 28 of Schedule A as Other Miscellaneous Deductions. These are not subject to the 2 percent-of-AGI floor.

- Gambling losses up to the amount of gambling winnings.
- Impairment-related work expenses of a handicapped person.
- Federal estate tax on income in respect of a decedent.
- Deduction for repayment of amounts under a claim of right if more than $3,000 (discussed in Chapter 18).
- The unrecovered investment in an annuity contract when the annuity ceases by reason of death, discussed in Chapter 4.

10-7 COMPREHENSIVE EXAMPLE OF SCHEDULE A

Harry and Jean Brown (ages 42 and 43, respectively), married filing jointly, had the following transactions for 2013:

Medicines that required a prescription	$ 430
Doctor and dentist bills paid and not reimbursed	2,120
Medical insurance premium payments	1,200
Contact lenses	170
Transportation for medical purposes on March 1, 2013 (221 miles × 24 cents/mile + $10.00 parking)	63
State income tax withheld (This amount exceeds the sales tax from the sales tax table.)	3,900
Real estate taxes	1,580
Interest paid on qualified residence mortgage	2,340
Qualifying charitable contributions paid by check	860
Transportation in performing charitable services (800 miles × 14 cents/mile + $7.00 parking and tolls)	119
Unreimbursed employee expenses (from Form 2106)	870
Tax return preparation	150
Safe deposit box (used for keeping investment documents and tax records)	170

The Browns' AGI is $40,000. Their completed 2013 Schedule A on the following page reports itemized deductions totaling $10,172. Schedule A for 2013 is used for illustration purposes because the 2014 form was not available at the date of this printing.

SCHEDULE A
(Form 1040)

Department of the Treasury
Internal Revenue Service (99)

Itemized Deductions

▶ Information about Schedule A and its separate instructions is at *www.irs.gov/schedulea*.
▶ Attach to Form 1040.

OMB No. 1545-0074

2013

Attachment
Sequence No. **07**

Name(s) shown on Form 1040

Harry and Jean Brown

Your social security number

111 11 1111

Medical and Dental Expenses		**Caution.** Do not include expenses reimbursed or paid by others.			
	1	Medical and dental expenses (see instructions)	**1**	3,983	
	2	Enter amount from Form 1040, line 38 **2** 40,000			
	3	Multiply line 2 by 10% (.10). But if either you or your spouse was born before January 2, 1949, multiply line 2 by 7.5% (.075) instead	**3**	3,000	
	4	Subtract line 3 from line 1. If line 3 is more than line 1, enter -0-	**4**		983
Taxes You Paid	5	State and local (**check only one box**):			
	a	☒ Income taxes, **or**	**5**	3,900	
	b	☐ General sales taxes			
	6	Real estate taxes (see instructions)	**6**	1,580	
	7	Personal property taxes	**7**		
	8	Other taxes. List type and amount ▶ _____			
			8		
	9	Add lines 5 through 8	**9**		5,480
Interest You Paid	10	Home mortgage interest and points reported to you on Form 1098	**10**	2,340	
	11	Home mortgage interest not reported to you on Form 1098. If paid to the person from whom you bought the home, see instructions and show that person's name, identifying no., and address ▶			
Note. Your mortgage interest deduction may be limited (see instructions).		_____	**11**		
	12	Points not reported to you on Form 1098. See instructions for special rules	**12**		
	13	Mortgage insurance premiums (see instructions)	**13**		
	14	Investment interest. Attach Form 4952 if required. (See instructions.)	**14**		
	15	Add lines 10 through 14	**15**		2,340
Gifts to Charity	16	Gifts by cash or check. If you made any gift of $250 or more, see instructions	**16**	860	
If you made a gift and got a benefit for it, see instructions.	17	Other than by cash or check. If any gift of $250 or more, see instructions. You **must** attach Form 8283 if over $500	**17**	119	
	18	Carryover from prior year	**18**		
	19	Add lines 16 through 18	**19**		979
Casualty and Theft Losses	20	Casualty or theft loss(es). Attach Form 4684. (See instructions.)	**20**		
Job Expenses and Certain Miscellaneous Deductions	21	Unreimbursed employee expenses—job travel, union dues, job education, etc. Attach Form 2106 or 2106-EZ if required. (See instructions.) ▶ _____	**21**	870	
	22	Tax preparation fees	**22**	150	
	23	Other expenses—investment, safe deposit box, etc. List type and amount ▶ *Safe deposit box* _____	**23**	170	
	24	Add lines 21 through 23	**24**	1,190	
	25	Enter amount from Form 1040, line 38 **25** 40,000			
	26	Multiply line 25 by 2% (.02)	**26**	800	
	27	Subtract line 26 from line 24. If line 26 is more than line 24, enter -0-	**27**		390
Other Miscellaneous Deductions	28	Other—from list in instructions. List type and amount ▶ _____			
			28		
Total Itemized Deductions	29	Is Form 1040, line 38, over $150,000?			
		☐ **No.** Your deduction is not limited. Add the amounts in the far right column for lines 4 through 28. Also, enter this amount on Form 1040, line 40.	**29**		10,172
		☐ **Yes.** Your deduction may be limited. See the Itemized Deductions Worksheet in the instructions to figure the amount to enter.			
	30	If you elect to itemize deductions even though they are less than your standard deduction, check here ▶ ☐			

For Paperwork Reduction Act Notice, see Form 1040 instructions.   Cat. No. 17145C   Schedule A (Form 1040) 2013

TAX IN THE NEWS   The First Family and Itemized Deduction Phaseouts

In 2010, President Barack H. and Michelle L. Obama itemized deductions on their 2009 tax return. Because of their income level, their itemized deductions were reduced by $53,386 as required by the law at that time (see below).

Because the marginal rate of 35 percent applied to the Obamas' taxable income in 2009, the phaseout of itemized deductions cost them $18,685 in additional Federal income tax ($53,386 reduction × 35% marginal tax rate). Over the years, phaseouts such as this have been a popular way to raise tax revenues without increasing tax rates.

Although this phaseout provision expired after 2009, Congress chose to bring it back beginning in 2013. It will be interesting to see the cost of the phaseout to the Obamas for 2013 once they release their income tax return for that year.

10-8 OVERALL LIMITATION ON CERTAIN ITEMIZED DEDUCTIONS

LO.8

Recognize the limitation on certain itemized deductions applicable to high-income taxpayers.

In the American Taxpayer Relief Act of 2012, Congress reinstated several provisions limiting tax benefits for high-income taxpayers. The limitations include the exemption phaseout (refer to Chapter 3) and a phaseout of itemized deductions. During the 2010–2012 period, these two phaseouts did not apply. However, beginning with 2013, these phaseouts returned, and the phaseout of itemized deductions (also referred to as a *cutback adjustment*) applies to married taxpayers filing jointly whose 2014 AGI exceeds $305,050 ($254,200 for single filers).[52] Phaseouts of this type are sometimes referred to as "stealth taxes." The "Tax in the News" above reports the effect of the limitation on President and Mrs. Obamas' 2009 income tax return, which required them to pay $18,685 more in Federal income taxes than they would have paid had their itemized deductions been fully deductible.

The limitation applies to the following frequently encountered itemized deductions:

- Taxes.
- Home mortgage interest, including points.
- Charitable contributions.
- Unreimbursed employee expenses subject to the 2 percent-of-AGI floor.
- All other expenses subject to the 2 percent-of-AGI floor.

The following are *not* subject to the limitation on itemized deductions:

- Medical expenses.
- Investment interest expense.
- Nonbusiness casualty and theft losses.
- Gambling losses.

Taxpayers subject to the limitation must reduce itemized deductions by the *lesser* of:

- 3 percent of the amount by which AGI exceeds $305,050 ($254,200 if single).
- 80 percent of itemized deductions that are affected by the limit.

The overall limitation is applied after applying all other limitations to those itemized deductions that are affected by the overall limitation. For example, other limitations apply to charitable contributions, certain meals and entertainment expenses, and certain miscellaneous itemized deductions.

---

[52]§ 68. The AGI thresholds are $279,650 for heads of household and $152,525 for married taxpayers filing separately. In 2013, the phaseouts applied to married taxpayers filing jointly whose AGI exceeded $300,000 ($250,000 for single taxpayers, $275,000 for heads of household, and $150,000 for married taxpayers filing separately).

Example 36

Gavin, who is single and age 45, had AGI of $275,000 for 2014. He incurred the following expenses and losses during the year:

Medical expenses before 10%-of-AGI limitation	$29,500
State and local income taxes	3,200
Real estate taxes	2,800
Home mortgage interest	7,200
Charitable contributions	2,000
Casualty loss before 10% limitation (after $100 floor)	29,000
Unreimbursed employee expenses (subject to 2%-of-AGI limitation)	5,800
Gambling losses (Gavin had $3,000 of gambling income)	7,000

Gavin's itemized deductions *before* the overall limitation are computed as follows:

Medical expenses [$29,500 − (10% × $275,000)]	$ 2,000
State and local income taxes	3,200
Real estate taxes	2,800
Home mortgage interest	7,200
Charitable contributions	2,000
Casualty loss [$29,000 − (10% × $275,000)]	1,500
Unreimbursed employee expenses [$5,800 − (2% × $275,000)]	300
Gambling losses ($7,000 loss limited to $3,000 of gambling income)	3,000
Total itemized deductions before overall limitation	$22,000

Gavin's itemized deductions subject to the overall limitation are as follows:

State and local income taxes	$ 3,200
Real estate taxes	2,800
Home mortgage interest	7,200
Charitable contributions	2,000
Unreimbursed employee expenses	300
Total	$15,500

Gavin must reduce the amount by the smaller of the following:

• 3% × ($275,000 AGI − $254,200)	$ 624
• 80% of itemized deductions subject to limitation ($15,500 × .80)	12,400

Therefore, the amount of the reduction is $624, and Gavin has $21,376 of deductible itemized deductions, computed as follows:

Deductible itemized deductions subject to overall limitation ($15,500 − $624)	$14,876
Itemized deductions not subject to overall limitation:	
Medical expenses	2,000
Casualty loss	1,500
Gambling losses	3,000
Deductible itemized deductions	$21,376

ETHICS & EQUITY   Between a Rock and a Hard Place

Robert Ryan, a candidate for governor, has released his income tax return to the public. As Ryan's former tax adviser, you examine the return closely and realize that a considerable amount of his income was not reported on the return. You confide to a friend in the tabloid newspaper business that you are aware that a candidate for high public office has filed a fraudulent tax return. Your friend assures you that you will be able to sell your story for at least $25,000 to a tabloid and still remain anonymous. Another friend, a CPA, argues that you should inform Ryan and give him an opportunity to correct the problem. You tell your friend that you are concerned that Ryan will be very vindictive if you approach him about the issue. Which course of action will you choose?

10-9 TAX PLANNING

10-9a Effective Utilization of Itemized Deductions

LO.9

Identify tax planning strategies that can maximize the benefit of itemized deductions.

Because an individual may use the standard deduction in one year and itemize deductions in another year, it is frequently possible to obtain maximum benefit by shifting itemized deductions from one year to another. For example, if a taxpayer's itemized deductions and the standard deduction are approximately the same for each year of a two-year period, the taxpayer should use the standard deduction in one year and shift itemized deductions (to the extent permitted by law) to the other year. The individual could, for example, prepay a church pledge for a particular year to shift the deduction to the current year or avoid paying end-of-the-year medical expenses to shift the deduction to the following year.

10-9b Utilization of Medical Deductions

When a taxpayer anticipates that medical expenses will approximate the percentage floor, much might be done to generate a deductible excess. Any of the following procedures can help build a deduction by the end of the year:

*   Incur the obligation for needed dental work or have needed work carried out.[53]
*   Have elective remedial surgery that may have been postponed from prior years.
*   Incur the obligation for capital improvements to the taxpayer's personal residence recommended by a physician (e.g., an air filtration system to alleviate a respiratory disorder).

As an aid to taxpayers who may experience temporary cash-flow problems at the end of the year, the use of credit cards is deemed to be payment for purposes of timing the deductibility of charitable and medical expenses.

On December 13, 2014, Marge (a calendar year taxpayer) purchases two pairs of prescription contact lenses and one pair of prescribed orthopedic shoes for a total of $450. These purchases are separately charged to Marge's credit card. On January 6, 2015, Marge receives her statement containing these charges and makes payment shortly thereafter. The purchases are deductible as medical expenses in the year charged (2014) and not in the year the account is settled (2015).	**Example 37**

Recognizing which expenditures qualify for the medical deduction also may be crucial to exceeding the percentage limitations.

Ethan employs Lana (an unrelated party) to care for his incapacitated and dependent mother. Lana is not a trained nurse but spends approximately one-half of the time performing nursing duties (e.g., administering injections and providing physical therapy) and the rest of the time doing household chores. An allocable portion of Lana's wages that Ethan pays (including the employer's portion of FICA taxes) qualifies as a medical expense.	**Example 38**

10-9c Timing the Payment of Deductible Taxes

It is sometimes possible to defer or accelerate the payment of certain deductible taxes, such as state income tax, real property tax, and personal property tax. For

---

[53]Prepayment of medical expenses does not generate a current deduction unless the taxpayer is under an obligation to make the payment.

instance, the final installment of estimated state income tax is generally due after the end of a given tax year. Accelerating the payment of the final installment could result in larger itemized deductions for the current year.

Example 39

Jenny, who is single, expects to have itemized deductions of $5,500 in 2014 and $2,500 in 2015. She plans to pay $900 as the final installment on her 2014 estimated state income tax, which is due on January 15, 2015. The standard deduction for 2014 is $6,200 for single taxpayers. If Jenny does not pay the final installment until 2015, she will not itemize in either 2014 or 2015. However, if she pays the final installment in December 2014, her itemized deductions will be $6,400 ($5,500 + $900) in 2014 and she will benefit from itemizing.

10-9d Protecting the Interest Deduction

Although the deductibility of prepaid interest by a cash basis taxpayer has been severely restricted, a notable exception allows a deduction for points paid by the buyer to obtain financing for the purchase or improvement of a principal residence in the year of payment. However, such points must actually be paid by the taxpayer obtaining the loan and must represent a charge for the use of money. It has been held that points paid from the mortgage proceeds do not satisfy the payment requirement.[54] Also, the portion of the points attributable to service charges does not represent deductible interest.[55] Taxpayers financing home purchases or improvements usually should direct their planning toward avoiding these two hurdles to immediate deductibility.

In rare instances, a taxpayer may find it desirable to forgo the immediate expensing of points in the year paid. Instead, it could prove beneficial to capitalize the points and write them off as interest expense over the life of the mortgage.

Example 40

Gerald purchases a home on December 15, 2014, for $380,000 with $120,000 cash and a 15-year mortgage of $260,000 financed by the Greater Metropolis National Bank. Gerald pays two points in addition to interest allocated to the period from December 15 until December 31, 2014, at an annual rate of 4%. Because Gerald does not have enough itemized deductions to exceed the standard deduction for 2014, he should elect to capitalize the points and amortize them over 15 years. In this instance, Gerald would deduct $346.67 for 2015, as part of his qualified residence interest expense [$5,200 (two points) divided by 15 years], if he elects to itemize that year.

Because personal (consumer) interest is not deductible, taxpayers should consider making use of home equity loans. Recall that these loans utilize the personal residence of the taxpayer as security. The funds from these loans can be used for personal purposes (e.g., auto purchases and vacations). By making use of home equity loans, therefore, what would have been nondeductible personal interest becomes deductible qualified residence interest.

10-9e Ensuring the Charitable Contribution Deduction

For a charitable contribution deduction to be available, the recipient must be a qualified charitable organization. Sometimes the mechanics of how the contribution is carried out can determine whether a deduction results.

---

[54]*Alan A. Rubnitz*, 67 T.C. 621 (1977). Seller-paid points may also be deductible by the buyer under the provisions of Rev.Proc. 94–27, cited in footnote 32.

[55]*Donald L. Wilkerson*, 70 T.C. 240 (1978).

Example 41

Fumiko wants to donate $5,000 to her church's mission in Kobe, Japan. In this regard, she considers three alternatives:

1. Send the money directly to the mission.
2. Give the money to her church in Charlotte with the understanding that it is to be passed on to the mission.
3. Give the money directly to the missionary in charge of the mission who is currently in the United States on a fund-raising trip.

If Fumiko wants to obtain a deduction for the contribution, she should choose alternative 2. A direct donation to the mission (alternative 1) is not deductible because the mission is a foreign charity. A direct gift to the missionary (alternative 3) does not comply because an individual cannot be a qualified charity for income tax purposes.[56]

A clearly established rule provides that a donor may not claim a charitable contribution to the extent that a benefit is received in return. For example, if $100 is paid to attend a charity ball and a reasonable value of that privilege is $35, the charitable contribution is $65. However, consider the following circumstances.

Example 42

In response to a solicitation from the University Medical Association, Rich and Lucile pay $200, which allows them to attend a fund-raising benefit event. The charity mails them a ticket and a statement indicating that for a contribution at the $200 level, $140 may be deducted because the value of the benefit provided to the donor equals $60. If Rich and Lucile accept the ticket, whether or not they attend the benefit, their deduction is $140. However, if they *return* the ticket to the charity for resale (e.g., they know their schedule will prevent them from attending), the charitable contribution deduction equals the entire amount paid for the ticket.

When making noncash donations, the type of property chosen can have decided implications in determining the amount, if any, of the deduction.

Example 43

Sam wants to give $60,000 in value to his church in some form other than cash. In this connection, he considers four alternatives:

1. Stock held for two years as an investment with a basis of $100,000 and a fair market value of $60,000.
2. Stock held for five years as an investment with a basis of $10,000 and a fair market value of $60,000.
3. The rent-free use for a year of a building that normally leases for $5,000 a month.
4. A valuable stamp collection held as an investment and owned for 10 years with a basis of $10,000 and a fair market value of $60,000. The church plans to sell the collection if and when it is donated.

Alternative 1 is ill-advised as the subject of the gift. Even though Sam would obtain a deduction of $60,000, he would forgo the potential loss of $40,000 that would be recognized if the property were sold.[57] Alternative 2 makes good sense because the deduction still is $60,000 and none of the $50,000 of appreciation that has occurred must be recognized as income. Alternative 3 yields no deduction at all and is not a wise choice. Alternative 4 involves tangible personalty that the recipient does not plan to use. As a result, the amount of the deduction is limited to $10,000, the stamp collection's basis.[58]

For property transfers (particularly real estate), the ceiling limitations on the amount of the deduction allowed in any one year (50 percent, 30 percent, or 20 percent of AGI, as the case may be) could be a factor to take into account. With proper planning, donations can be controlled to stay within the limitations and therefore avoid the need for a carryover of unused charitable contributions.

---

[56]*Thomas E. Lesslie*, 36 TCM 495, T.C.Memo. 1977–111.

[57]*LaVar M. Withers*, 69 T.C. 900 (1978).

[58]No reduction of appreciation is necessary in alternative 2 because stock is intangible property and not tangible personalty.

Example 44

Andrew wants to donate a tract of unimproved land held as an investment to Eastern University (a qualified charitable organization). The land has been held for six years and has a current fair market value of $300,000 and a basis to Andrew of $50,000. Andrew's AGI for the current year is estimated to be $200,000, and he expects much the same for the next few years. In the current year, he deeds (transfers) an undivided one-fifth interest in the real estate to the university.

What has Andrew in Example 44 accomplished for income tax purposes? In the current year, he will be allowed a charitable contribution deduction of $60,000 ($\frac{1}{5} \times$ $300,000), which will be within the applicable limitation of AGI (30% × $200,000). Presuming no other charitable contributions for the year, Andrew has avoided the possibility of a carryover. In future years, Andrew can arrange donations of undivided interests in the real estate to stay within the bounds of the percentage limitations. The only difficulty with this approach is the need to revalue the real estate each year before the donation, because the amount of the deduction is based on the fair market value of the interest contributed at the time of the donation.

Example 45

Tiffany dies in October 2014. In completing her final income tax return for 2014, Tiffany's executor determines the following information: AGI of $104,000 and a donation by Tiffany to her church of stock worth $60,000. Tiffany had purchased the stock two years ago for $50,000 and held it as an investment. Tiffany's executor makes the reduced deduction election and, as a consequence, claims a charitable contribution deduction of $50,000. With the election, the potential charitable contribution deduction of $50,000 ($60,000 − $10,000) is less than the 50% ceiling of $52,000 ($104,000 × 50%). If the executor had not made the election, the potential charitable contribution deduction of $60,000 would have been reduced by the 30% ceiling to $31,200 ($104,000 × 30%). No carryover of the $28,800 ($60,000 − $31,200) would have been available because Tiffany's 2014 income tax return is her final return.

REFOCUS ON THE BIG PICTURE

ITEMIZED DEDUCTIONS CAN REDUCE THE AFTER-TAX COST OF MAJOR PURCHASES

Because the Federal tax law provides that qualified residence interest and real estate taxes are deductible by individual taxpayers, the after-tax cost of a home purchase will be reduced by the tax savings associated with these itemized tax deductions (see Example 1). Given the Williamsons' projected taxable income, they are in the 28 percent Federal tax bracket and the 6 percent state tax bracket (i.e., aggregate marginal tax bracket of 34 percent). As a result, the after-tax cost of financing the purchase of the home will be:

Nondeductible principal payments	$ 2,000
Deductible qualified residence interest and real estate taxes [($37,000 + $4,000) × (1 − .34)]	27,060
Total	$29,060
After-tax monthly cost ($29,060 ÷ 12)	$ 2,422

Because the Williamsons will be able to itemize their deductions if they purchase a new home and will be able to deduct most of their monthly house payment, the home purchase will be affordable (see Examples 16 and 22).

What If?

What if the Williamsons use the less expensive route to finance the purchase of their home by using their retirement and taxable portfolio as security for the loan? What may at first appear to be a cost-effective approach ends up being more costly

when considering the impact of the tax law. With this approach, the interest expense is not deductible because it is not qualified residence interest (see Example 22); further, it is not deductible as investment interest (see Chapter 11). Therefore, the after-tax cost of financing the home using this approach makes the home unaffordable.

Nondeductible principal and interest payments	$37,000
Deductible real estate taxes [$4,000 × (1 − .34)]	2,640
Total	$39,640
After-tax monthly cost ($39,640 ÷ 12)	$ 3,303

Key Terms

Acquisition indebtedness, 10-16	Home equity loans, 10-16	Ordinary income property, 10-25
Capital gain property, 10-25	Medical expense, 10-3	Points, 10-17
Charitable contribution, 10-20	Miscellaneous itemized deductions, 10-28	Qualified residence interest, 10-16
Health Savings Account (HSA), 10-9		

Discussion Questions

1. **LO.1, 2** Dan, a self-employed individual taxpayer, prepared his own income tax return for the past year and has asked you to check it for accuracy. Your review indicates that Dan failed to claim certain business entertainment expenses.
   a. Will the correction of this omission affect the amount of medical expenses Dan can deduct? Explain.
   b. Would it matter if Dan were employed rather than self-employed? Explain.

2. **LO.2** Barbara incurred the following expenses during the year: $840 dues at a health club she joined at the suggestion of her physician to improve her general physical condition, $240 for multiple vitamins and antioxidant vitamins, $500 for a smoking cessation program, $240 for nonprescription nicotine gum, $600 for insulin, and $7,200 for funeral expenses for her mother who passed away in June. Which of these expenses may be included in computing the medical expense deduction?

3. **LO.2** Joe was in an accident and required cosmetic surgery for injuries to his nose. He also had the doctor do additional surgery to reshape his chin, which had not been injured. Will the cosmetic surgery to Joe's nose qualify as a medical expense? Will the cosmetic surgery to Joe's chin qualify as a medical expense? Explain.

4. **LO.2, 9** Jerry and Ernie are comparing their tax situations. Both are paying all of the nursing home expenses of their parents. Jerry can include the expenses in computing his medical expense deduction, but Ernie cannot. What explanation can you offer for the difference?

5. **LO.2** During the current year, Pauline and her three dependent children had annual physical exams, which cost $750, and dental checkups for all four of them, which cost $420. In addition, Pauline paid $800 for medically supervised treatments to enable her to stop smoking. After she stopped smoking, she began to gain weight and incurred $1,200 in costs for a medically supervised weight loss program. Which of these expenses qualify for the medical expense deduction?

Issue ID

6. **LO.2** Caroyl incurred $8,700 of medical expenses in November 2014. On December 5, the clinic where she was treated mailed her the insurance claim form it had prepared for her with a suggestion that she sign and return the form immediately to receive her reimbursement from the insurance company by December 31. What tax issues should Caroyl consider in deciding whether to sign and return the form in December 2014 or January 2015?

7. **LO.2** David, a sole proprietor of a bookstore, pays a $7,500 premium for medical insurance for him and his family. Joan, an employee of a small firm that doesn't provide her with medical insurance, pays medical insurance premiums of $8,000 for herself. How does the tax treatment differ for David and Joan?

8. **LO.2** Arturo, a calendar year taxpayer, paid $16,000 in medical expenses and sustained a $20,000 casualty loss in 2014. He expects $12,000 of the medical expenses and $14,000 of the casualty loss to be reimbursed by insurance companies in 2015. Before considering any limitations on these deductions, how much can Arturo include in determining his itemized deductions for 2014?

9. **LO.2** Hubert, a self-employed taxpayer, is married and has two children. He has asked you to explain the tax and nontax advantages of creating a Health Savings Account (HSA) for him and his family.

Issue ID

10. **LO.2** A local ophthalmologist's advertising campaign included a certificate for free LASIK eye surgery for the lucky winner of a drawing. Ahmad held the winning ticket, which was drawn in December 2013. Ahmad had no vision problems and was uncertain what he should do with the prize. In February 2014, Ahmad's daughter, who lives with his former wife, was diagnosed with a vision problem that could be treated with either prescription glasses or LASIK surgery. The divorce decree requires that Ahmad pay for all medical expenses incurred for his daughter. Identify the relevant tax issues for Ahmad.

Issue ID

11. **LO.3** In 2014, a state issued checks to homeowners as a rebate of property taxes. Funds for the rebate were available because of unexpectedly high state tax revenues due to a new law that legalized gambling in the state. In December 2014, Edward received a $290 rebate check from the state. In January 2015, he returned the check to the governor because he thought it was improper for the state to spend the money in this manner. Edward, a dedicated opponent of gambling and other "games of chance," attached a letter to the governor indicating his desire to have the $290 spent on a campaign to educate youth about the financial and nonfinancial dangers of gambling. List some of the tax issues relevant to Edward's situation.

Decision Making

12. **LO.5, 9** Diane owns a principal residence in Georgia, a townhouse in San Francisco, and a yacht in Cape Cod. All of the properties have mortgages on which Diane pays interest. What are the limitations on Diane's mortgage interest deduction? What strategy should Diane consider to maximize her mortgage interest deduction?

Issue ID

13. **LO.5, 9** Mason Gregg's car was destroyed by a flood. Unfortunately, his insurance had lapsed two days before he incurred the loss. Mason uses his car for both business and personal use. Mason, who is self-employed, does not have adequate savings to replace the car and must borrow money to purchase a new car. He is considering taking out a home equity loan, at a 5% interest rate, to obtain funds for the purchase. Margaret, his wife, would prefer not to do so because they paid off their mortgage recently and she does not want to incur any obligations related to their home. She would prefer to sell some of their stock in Bluebird, Inc., to raise funds to purchase the new car. Mason does not want to sell the stock because it has declined in value since they purchased it and he is convinced that its price will increase in the next two years. Mason has suggested that they obtain conventional financing for the purchase from their bank, which charges 7% interest on car loans. Identify the tax issues related to each of the three alternatives Mason and Margaret are considering.

14. **LO.5** Commercial Bank has initiated an advertising campaign that encourages customers to take out home equity loans to pay for purchases of automobiles. Are there any tax advantages related to this type of borrowing? Explain.

15. **LO.5** Thomas purchased a personal residence from Rachel. To sell the residence, Rachel agreed to pay $5,500 in points related to Thomas's mortgage. Discuss the deductibility of the points.

16. **LO.5** Ellen borrowed $50,000 from her parents for a down payment on the purchase of a new home. She paid interest of $3,200 in 2012, $0 in 2013, and $9,000 in 2014. The IRS disallowed the deduction. What explanation can you offer for the disallowance?

17. **LO.6** The city of Lawrence was hit by a tornado in April 2014, leaving many families in need of food, clothing, shelter, and other necessities. Betty contributed $500 to a family whose home was completely destroyed by the tornado. Jack contributed $700 to the family's church, which gave the money to the family. Discuss the deductibility of these contributions.

18. **LO.6** Mike purchased four $100 tickets to a fund-raising dinner and dance sponsored by the public library, a qualified charitable organization. In its advertising for the event, the library indicated that the cost of the tickets would be deductible for Federal income tax purposes. Comment on the library's assertion.

19. **LO.6** Nancy, who is a professor at State University, does some of her writing and class preparation at home at night. Her department provides faculty members with a $1,500 allowance for a desktop computer for use at school, but does not ordinarily provide computers for use at home. To have a computer for use at school and at home, Nancy has asked the department to provide her with a notebook computer that costs $2,500. The head of her department is willing to provide the standard $1,500 allowance and will permit Nancy to purchase the $2,500 notebook computer if she makes a donation of $1,000 to the department. If she acquires the notebook computer, Nancy's home use of the computer will be approximately 60% for business and 40% for personal use not related to her job. Discuss the tax issues that Nancy should consider in deciding whether to acquire the notebook computer under these conditions.   *Issue ID*

20. **LO.6** Susan traveled to rural Tennessee during the year to do volunteer work for one week for Habitat for Humanity. She normally receives $2,000 salary per week at her job and is planning to deduct the $2,000 as a charitable contribution. In addition, Susan incurred the following costs in connection with the trip: $300 for transportation, $700 for lodging, and $250 for meals. What is Susan's deduction associated with this charitable activity?

21. **LO.6, 9** William, a high school teacher, earns about $50,000 each year. In December 2014, he won $1 million in the state lottery. William plans to donate $100,000 to his church. He has asked you, his tax adviser, whether he should donate the $100,000 in 2014 or 2015. Identify the tax issues related to William's decision.   *Issue ID*

22. **LO.6, 9** Nate, whose combined Federal and state income tax rates total 40% in 2014, expects to retire in 2015 and have a combined tax rate of 30%. He plans to donate $100,000 to his church. Because he will not have the cash available until 2015, Nate donates land (long-term capital gain property) with a basis of $20,000 and fair market value of $100,000 to the church in December 2014. He reacquires the land from the church for $100,000 in February 2015. Discuss Nate's tax objectives and all tax issues related to his actions.   *Issue ID*

23. **LO.6, 9** Megan decided to have a garage sale to get rid of a number of items she no longer needed, including books, old computer equipment, clothing, bicycles, and furniture. She scheduled the sale for Friday and Saturday, but was forced to close at noon on Friday because of a torrential downpour. She had collected $500 for the items she sold before closing. The heavy rains continued through the weekend, and Megan was unable to continue the sale. She had not enjoyed dealing with the people who came to the sale on Friday morning, so she donated the remaining items to several local organizations. Megan has asked your advice on how she should treat these events on her tax return. List some of the tax issues you would discuss with her.   *Issue ID*

Problems

Communications

24. **LO.2** Emma Doyle, age 55, is employed as a corporate attorney. For calendar year 2014, she had AGI of $100,000 and paid the following medical expenses:

Medical insurance premiums	$3,700
Doctor and dentist bills for Bob and April (Emma's parents)	6,800
Doctor and dentist bills for Emma	5,200
Prescription medicines for Emma	400
Nonprescription insulin for Emma	350

Bob and April would qualify as Emma's dependents except that they file a joint return. Emma's medical insurance policy does not cover them. Emma filed a claim for reimbursement of $2,800 of her own expenses with her insurance company in December 2014 and received the reimbursement in January 2015. What is Emma's maximum allowable medical expense deduction for 2014? Prepare a memo for your firm's tax files in which you document your conclusions.

25. **LO.2** Reba, who is single and age 45, does a lot of business entertaining at home. Lawrence, Reba's 84-year-old dependent grandfather, lived with Reba until this year, when he moved to Lakeside Nursing Home because he needs medical and nursing care. During the year, Reba made the following payments on behalf of Lawrence:

Room at Lakeside	$11,000
Meals for Lawrence at Lakeside	2,200
Doctor and nurse fees at Lakeside	1,700
Cable TV service for Lawrence's room at Lakeside	380
Total	$15,280

Lakeside has medical staff in residence. Disregarding the 10% of AGI floor, how much, if any, of these expenses qualifies for a medical expense deduction by Reba?

26. **LO.2** Paul, age 62, suffers from emphysema and severe allergies and, upon the recommendation of his physician, has a dust elimination system installed in his personal residence. In connection with the system, Paul incurs and pays the following amounts during 2014:

Doctor and hospital bills	$ 2,500
Dust elimination system	10,000
Increase in utility bills due to the system	450
Cost of certified appraisal	300

In addition, Paul pays $750 for prescribed medicines.

The system has an estimated useful life of 20 years. The appraisal was to determine the value of Paul's residence with and without the system. The appraisal states that his residence was worth $350,000 before the system was installed and $356,000 after the installation. Paul's AGI for the year was $50,000. How much of the medical expenses qualify for the medical expense deduction in 2014?

27. **LO.2** For calendar year 2014, Jean was a self-employed consultant with no employees. She had $80,000 of net profit from consulting and paid $7,000 in medical insurance premiums on a policy covering 2014. How much of these premiums may Jean deduct as a deduction *for* AGI? How much may she deduct as an itemized deduction (subject to the AGI floor)?

28. **LO.2** During 2014, Susan, age 49, incurred and paid the following expenses for Beth (her daughter), Ed (her father), and herself:

Surgery for Beth	$4,500
Red River Academy charges for Beth:	
Tuition	5,100
Room, board, and other expenses	4,800
Psychiatric treatment	5,100
Doctor bills for Ed	2,200
Prescription drugs for Susan, Beth, and Ed	780
Insulin for Ed	540
Nonprescription drugs for Susan, Beth, and Ed	570
Charges at Heartland Nursing Home for Ed:	
Medical care	5,000
Lodging	2,700
Meals	2,650

Beth qualifies as Susan's dependent, and Ed would also qualify except that he receives $7,400 of taxable retirement benefits from his former employer. Beth's psychiatrist recommended Red River Academy because of its small classes and specialized psychiatric treatment program that is needed to treat Beth's illness. Ed, who is a paraplegic and diabetic, entered Heartland in October. Heartland offers the type of care that he requires.

Upon the recommendation of a physician, Susan has an air filtration system installed in her personal residence. She suffers from severe allergies. In connection with this equipment, Susan incurs and pays the following amounts during the year:

Filtration system and cost of installation	$6,500
Increase in utility bills due to the system	700
Cost of certified appraisal	360

The system has an estimated useful life of 10 years. The appraisal was to determine the value of Susan's residence with and without the system. The appraisal states that the system increased the value of Susan's residence by $2,200. Ignoring the 10% floor, what is the total of Susan's expenses that qualifies for the medical expense deduction?

29. **LO.2** In May, Rebecca's daughter, Susan, sustained a serious injury that made it impossible for her to continue living alone. Susan, who is a novelist, moved back into Rebecca's home after the accident. Susan has begun writing a novel based on her recent experiences. To accommodate Susan, Rebecca incurred significant remodeling expenses (widening hallways, building a separate bedroom and bathroom, and making kitchen appliances accessible to Susan). In addition, Rebecca had an indoor swimming pool constructed so that Susan could do rehabilitation exercises prescribed by her physician.   *Issue ID*

In September, Susan underwent major reconstructive surgery in Denver. The surgery was performed by Dr. Rama Patel, who specializes in treating injuries of the type sustained by Susan. Rebecca drove Susan from Champaign, Illinois, to Denver, a total of 1,100 miles, in Susan's specially equipped van. They left Champaign on Tuesday morning and arrived in Denver on Thursday afternoon. Rebecca incurred expenses for gasoline, highway tolls, meals, and lodging while traveling to Denver. Rebecca stayed in a motel near the clinic for eight days while Susan was hospitalized. Identify the relevant tax issues based on this information and prepare a list of questions you would need to ask Rebecca and Susan to advise them as to the resolution of any issues you have identified.

30. **LO.2** In 2014, Roger pays a $3,000 premium for high-deductible medical insurance for him and his family. In addition, he contributed $2,600 to a Health Savings Account.
    a. How much may Roger deduct if he is self-employed? Is the deduction *for* AGI or *from* AGI?
    b. How much may Roger deduct if he is an employee? Is the deduction *for* AGI or *from* AGI?

31. **LO.3** Alicia sold her personal residence to Rick on June 30 for $300,000. Before the sale, Alicia paid the real estate tax of $4,380 for the calendar year. For income tax purposes, the deduction is apportioned as follows: $2,160 to Alicia and $2,220 to Rick. What is Rick's basis in the residence?

32. **LO.4** Norma, who uses the cash method of accounting, lives in a state that imposes an income tax. In April 2014, she files her state income tax return for 2013 and pays an additional $1,000 in state income taxes. During 2014, her withholdings for state income tax purposes amount to $7,400, and she pays estimated state income tax of $700. In April 2015, she files her state income tax return for 2014, claiming a refund of $1,800. Norma receives the refund in August 2015.

    a. Assuming that Norma itemized deductions in 2014, how much may she claim as a deduction for state income taxes on her Federal return for calendar year 2014 (filed April 2015)?

    b. Assuming that Norma itemized deductions in 2014, how will the refund of $1,800 that she received in 2015 be treated for Federal income tax purposes?

    c. Assume that Norma itemized deductions in 2014 and that she elects to have the $1,800 refund applied toward her 2015 state income tax liability. How will the $1,800 be treated for Federal income tax purposes?

    d. Assuming that Norma did not itemize deductions in 2014, how will the refund of $1,800 received in 2015 be treated for Federal income tax purposes?

33. **LO.5** In 2005, Roland, who is single, purchased a personal residence for $340,000 and took out a mortgage of $200,000 on the property. In May of the current year, when the residence had a fair market value of $440,000 and Roland owed $140,000 on the mortgage, he took out a home equity loan for $220,000. He used the funds to purchase a recreational vehicle, which he uses 100% for personal use. What is the maximum amount on which Roland can deduct home equity interest?

34. **LO.5** Malcolm owns 60% and Buddy owns 40% of Magpie Corporation. On July 1, 2014, each lends the corporation $30,000 at an annual interest rate of 10%. Malcolm and Buddy are not related. Both shareholders are on the cash method of accounting, and Magpie Corporation is on the accrual method. All parties use the calendar year for tax purposes. On June 30, 2015, Magpie repays the loans of $60,000 together with the specified interest of $6,000.

    a. How much of the interest can Magpie Corporation deduct in 2014? In 2015?

    b. When is the interest included in Malcolm and Buddy's gross income?

35. **LO.6** Nadia donates $4,000 to Eastern University's athletic department. The payment guarantees that Nadia will have preferred seating near the 50-yard line.

    a. Assume that Nadia subsequently buys four $100 game tickets. How much can she deduct as a charitable contribution to the university's athletic department?

    b. Assume that Nadia's $4,000 donation includes four $100 tickets. How much can she deduct as a charitable contribution to the university's athletic department?

36. **LO.6** Liz had AGI of $130,000 in 2014. She donated Bluebird Corporation stock with a basis of $10,000 to a qualified charitable organization on July 5, 2014.

    a. What is the amount of Liz's deduction assuming that she purchased the stock on December 3, 2013, and the stock had a fair market value of $17,000 when she made the donation?

    b. Assume the same facts as in (a), except that Liz purchased the stock on July 1, 2011.

    c. Assume the same facts as in (a), except that the stock had a fair market value of $7,500 (rather than $17,000) when Liz donated it to the charity.

Decision Making

Communications

37. **LO.6, 9** Pedro contributes a painting to an art museum in October of this year. He has owned the painting for 12 years, and it is worth $130,000 at the time of the donation. Pedro's adjusted basis for the painting is $90,000, and his AGI for the year is $250,000. Pedro has asked you whether he should make the reduced deduction election for this contribution. Write a letter to Pedro Valdez at 1289 Greenway Avenue, Foster City, CA 94404 and advise him on this matter.

38. **LO.6** During the year, Ricardo made the following contributions to a qualified public charity:

Cash	$220,000
Stock in Seagull, Inc. (a publicly traded corporation)	280,000

Ricardo acquired the stock in Seagull, Inc., as an investment five years ago at a cost of $120,000. Ricardo's AGI is $840,000.

    a. What is Ricardo's charitable contribution deduction?

    b. How are excess amounts, if any, treated?

39. **LO.6** Ramon had AGI of $180,000 in 2014. He contributed stock in Charlton, Inc. (a publicly traded corporation), to the American Heart Association, a qualified charitable organization. The stock was worth $105,000 on the date it was contributed. Ramon had acquired it as an investment two years ago at a cost of $84,000.

    Decision Making

    a. Assuming that Ramon carries over any disallowed contribution from 2014 to future years, what is the total amount he can deduct as a charitable contribution?
    b. What is the maximum amount Ramon can deduct as a charitable contribution in 2014?
    c. What factors should Ramon consider in deciding how to treat the contribution for Federal income tax purposes?
    d. Assume that Ramon dies in December 2014. What advice would you give the executor of his estate with regard to possible elections that can be made relative to the contribution?

40. **LO.6** On December 27, 2014, Roberta purchased four tickets to a charity ball sponsored by the city of San Diego for the benefit of underprivileged children. Each ticket cost $200 and had a fair market value of $35. On the same day as the purchase, Roberta gave the tickets to the minister of her church for personal use by his family. At the time of the gift of the tickets, Roberta pledged $4,000 to the building fund of her church. The pledge was satisfied by a check dated December 31, 2014, but not mailed until January 3, 2015.

    a. Presuming that Roberta is a cash basis and calendar year taxpayer, how much can she deduct as a charitable contribution for 2014?
    b. Would the amount of the deduction be any different if Roberta was an accrual basis taxpayer? Explain.

41. **LO.6, 9** In December each year, Eleanor Young contributes 10% of her gross income to the United Way (a 50% organization). Eleanor, who is in the 28% marginal tax bracket, is considering the following alternatives for satisfying the contribution.

    Decision Making

    Communications

	Fair Market Value
(1) Cash donation	$23,000
(2) Unimproved land held for six years ($3,000 basis)	23,000
(3) Blue Corporation stock held for eight months ($3,000 basis)	23,000
(4) Gold Corporation stock held for two years ($28,000 basis)	23,000

    Eleanor has asked you to help her decide which of the potential contributions listed above will be most advantageous taxwise. Evaluate the four alternatives and write a letter to Eleanor to communicate your advice to her. Her address is 2622 Bayshore Drive, Berkeley, CA 94709.

42. **LO.2, 3, 4, 5, 7, 9** Bart and Susan Forrest, both age 47, are married and have no dependents. They have asked you to advise them whether they should file jointly or separately in 2014. They present you with the following information:

    Decision Making

    Communications

	Bart	Susan	Joint
Salary	$38,000		
Business net income		$110,000	
Interest income	400	1,200	$2,200
Deductions *for* AGI	2,400	14,000	
Medical expenses	10,427	3,358	
State income tax	800	1,800	
Real estate tax			3,800
Mortgage interest			4,200
Unreimbursed employee expenses	1,200		

    If they file separately, Bart and Susan will split the real estate tax and mortgage interest deductions equally. Write Bart and Susan a letter in which you make and explain a recommendation on filing status for 2014. Bart and Susan reside at 2003 Highland Drive, Durham, NC 27707.

43. **LO.2, 3, 4, 5, 6, 7, 8** Linda, age 37, who files as a single taxpayer, had AGI of $280,000 for 2014. She incurred the following expenses and losses during the year:

Medical expenses before the 10%-of-AGI limitation	$33,000
State and local income taxes	4,500
State sales tax	1,300
Real estate taxes	4,000
Home mortgage interest	5,000
Automobile loan interest	750
Credit card interest	1,000
Charitable contributions	7,000
Casualty loss before 10% limitation (after $100 floor)	34,000
Unreimbursed employee expenses subject to the 2%-of-AGI limitation	7,600

Calculate Linda's allowable itemized deductions for the year.

44. **LO.2, 3, 4, 5, 6, 7, 8** For calendar year 2014, Stuart and Pamela Gibson file a joint return reflecting AGI of $350,000. Their itemized deductions are as follows:

Casualty loss after $100 floor (not covered by insurance)	$48,600
Home mortgage interest	19,000
Credit card interest	800
Property taxes on home	16,300
Charitable contributions	28,700
State income tax	18,000
Tax return preparation fees	1,200

Calculate the amount of itemized deductions the Gibsons may claim for the year.

Cumulative Problems

Tax Return Problem

Decision Making

TAX SOFTWARE

45. Alice J. and Bruce M. Byrd are married taxpayers who file a joint return. Their Social Security numbers are 123-45-6789 and 111-11-1111, respectively. Alice's birthday is September 21, 1966, and Bruce's is June 27, 1965. They live at 473 Revere Avenue, Lowell, MA 01850. Alice is the office manager for Lowell Dental Clinic, 433 Broad Street, Lowell, MA 01850 (employer identification number 98-7654321). Bruce is the manager of a Super Burgers fast-food outlet owned and operated by Plymouth Corporation, 1247 Central Avenue, Hauppauge, NY 11788 (employer identification number 11-1111111).

The following information is shown on their Wage and Tax Statements (Form W–2) for 2013.

Line	Description	Alice	Bruce
1	Wages, tips, other compensation	$58,000	$62,100
2	Federal income tax withheld	4,500	6,300
3	Social Security wages	58,000	62,100
4	Social Security tax withheld	3,596	3,850
5	Medicare wages and tips	58,000	62,100
6	Medicare tax withheld	841	900
15	State	Massachusetts	Massachusetts
16	State wages, tips, etc.	58,000	62,100
17	State income tax withheld	2,950	3,100

The Byrds provide over half of the support of their two children, Cynthia (born January 25, 1989, Social Security number 123-45-6788) and John (born February 7, 1993, Social Security number 123-45-6786). Both children are full-time students and live with the Byrds except when they are away at college. Cynthia earned $4,200 from a summer internship in 2013, and John earned $3,800 from a part-time job.

During 2013, the Byrds furnished 60% of the total support of Bruce's widower father, Sam Byrd (born March 6, 1937, Social Security number 123-45-6787). Sam lived alone and covered the rest of his support with his Social Security benefits. Sam died in November, and Bruce, the beneficiary of a policy on Sam's life, received life insurance proceeds of $800,000 on December 28.

The Byrds had the following expenses relating to their personal residence during 2013:

Property taxes	$5,000
Qualified interest on home mortgage	8,800
Repairs to roof	5,750
Utilities	4,100
Fire and theft insurance	1,900

The following facts relate to medical expenses for 2013:

Medical insurance premiums	$4,500
Doctor bill for Sam incurred in 2012 and not paid until 2013	7,600
Operation for Sam	8,500
Prescription medicines for Sam	900
Hospital expenses for Sam	3,500
Reimbursement from insurance company, received in 2013	3,600

The medical expenses for Sam represent most of the 60% that Bruce contributed toward his father's support.

Other relevant information follows:

- When they filed their 2012 state return in 2013, the Byrds paid additional state income tax of $900.
- During 2013, Alice and Bruce attended a dinner dance sponsored by the Lowell Police Disability Association (a qualified charitable organization). The Byrds paid $300 for the tickets. The cost of comparable entertainment would normally be $50.
- The Byrds contributed $5,000 to Lowell Presbyterian Church and gave used clothing (cost of $1,200 and fair market value of $350) to the Salvation Army. All donations are supported by receipts, and the clothing is in very good condition.
- In 2013, the Byrds received interest income of $2,750, which was reported on a Form 1099–INT from Second National Bank.
- Alice's employer requires that all employees wear uniforms to work. During 2013, Alice spent $450 on new uniforms and $225 on laundry charges.
- Bruce paid $400 for an annual subscription to the *Journal of Franchise Management*.
- Neither Alice's nor Bruce's employer reimburses for employee expenses.
- The Byrds do not keep the receipts for the sales taxes they paid and had no major purchases subject to sales tax.
- Alice and Bruce paid no estimated Federal income tax. Neither Alice nor Bruce wants to designate $3 to the Presidential Election Campaign Fund.

Part 1—Tax Computation
Compute net tax payable or refund due for Alice and Bruce Byrd for 2013. If they have overpaid, they want the amount to be refunded to them. If you use tax forms for your computations, you will need Forms 1040 and 2106 and Schedules A and B. Suggested software: H&R BLOCK At Home.

Part 2—Tax Planning
Alice and Bruce are planning some significant changes for 2014. They have provided you with the following information and asked you to project their taxable income and tax liability for 2014.

The Byrds will invest the $800,000 of life insurance proceeds in short-term certificates of deposit (CDs) and use the interest for living expenses during 2014. They expect to earn total interest of $32,000 on the CDs.

Bruce has been promoted to regional manager, and his salary for 2014 will be $88,000. He estimates that state income tax withheld will increase by $4,000 and the Social Security tax withheld will be $5,456.

Alice, who has been diagnosed with a serious illness, will take a leave of absence from work during 2014. The estimated cost for her medical treatment is $15,400, of which $6,400 will be reimbursed by their insurance company in 2014. Their medical insurance premiums will increase to $9,769.

John will graduate from college in December 2013 and will take a job in New York City in January 2014. His starting salary will be $46,000.

Assume that all of the information reported in 2013 will be the same in 2014 unless other information has been presented above.

Tax Computation Problem

46. Paul and Donna Decker are married taxpayers, ages 44 and 42, respectively, who file a joint return for 2014. The Deckers live at 1121 College Avenue, Carmel, IN 46032. Paul is an assistant manager at Carmel Motor Inn, and Donna is a teacher at Carmel Elementary School. They present you with W–2 forms that reflect the following information:

	Paul	Donna
Salary	$68,000	$56,000
Federal tax withheld	6,770	6,630
State income tax withheld	900	800
FICA (Social Security and Medicare) withheld	5,202	4,284
Social Security numbers	111-11-1111	123-45-6789

Donna is the custodial parent of two children from a previous marriage who reside with the Deckers through the school year. The children, Larry and Jane Parker, reside with their father, Bob, during the summer. Relevant information for the children follows:

	Larry	Jane
Age	17	18
Social Security numbers	123-45-6788	123-45-6787
Months spent with Deckers	9	9

Under the divorce decree, Bob pays child support of $150 per month per child during the nine months the children live with the Deckers. Bob says that he spends $200 per month per child during the three summer months they reside with him. Donna and Paul can document that they provide $2,000 support per child per year. The divorce decree is silent as to which parent can claim the exemptions for the children.

In August, Paul and Donna added a suite to their home to provide more comfortable accommodations for Hannah Snyder (123-45-6786), Donna's mother, who had moved in with them in February 2013 after the death of Donna's father. Not wanting to borrow money for this addition, Paul sold 300 shares of Acme Corporation stock for $50 per share on May 3, 2014, and used the proceeds of $15,000 to cover construction costs. The Deckers had purchased the stock on April 29, 2009, for $25 per share. They received dividends of $750 on the jointly owned stock a month before the sale.

Hannah, who is 66 years old, received $7,500 in Social Security benefits during the year, of which she gave the Deckers $2,000 to use toward household expenses and deposited the remainder in her personal savings account. The Deckers determine that they have spent $2,500 of their own money for food, clothing, medical expenses, and other items for Hannah. They do not know what the rental value of Hannah's suite would be, but they estimate it would be at least $300 per month.

Interest paid during the year included the following:

Home mortgage interest (paid to Carmel Federal Savings & Loan)	$7,890
Interest on an automobile loan (paid to Carmel National Bank)	1,660
Interest on Citibank Visa card	620

In July, Paul hit a submerged rock while boating. Fortunately, he was uninjured after being thrown from the boat and landing in deep water. However, the boat, which was uninsured, was destroyed. Paul had paid $25,000 for the boat in June 2013, and its value was appraised at $18,000 on the date of the accident.

The Deckers paid doctor and hospital bills of $10,700 and were reimbursed $2,000 by their insurance company. They spent $640 for prescription drugs and medicines and $5,904 for premiums on their health insurance policy. They have filed additional claims of $1,200 with their insurance company and have been told they will receive payment for that amount in January 2015. Included in the amounts paid for doctor and hospital bills were payments of $380 for Hannah and $850 for the children.

Additional information of potential tax consequence follows:

Real estate taxes paid	$3,850
Sales taxes paid (per table)	1,379
Contributions to church	1,950
Appraised value of books donated to public library	740
Paul's unreimbursed employee expenses to attend hotel management convention:	
Airfare	340
Hotel	170
Meals	95
Registration fee	340
Refund of state income tax for 2013 (the Deckers itemized on their 2013 Federal tax return)	1,520

Compute net tax payable or refund due for the Deckers for 2014. Ignore the child tax credit in your computations. If the Deckers have overpaid, the amount is to be credited toward their taxes for 2015.

Research Problems

Note: Solutions to Research Problems can be prepared by using the **Checkpoint®** **Student Edition** online research product, which is available to accompany this text. It is also possible to prepare solutions to the Research Problems by using tax research materials found in a standard tax library.

THOMSON REUTERS
CHECKPOINT®

Research Problem 1. Jane suffers from a degenerative spinal disorder. Her physician said that swimming could help prevent the onset of permanent paralysis and recommended the installation of a swimming pool at her residence for her use. Jane's residence had a market value of approximately $500,000 before the swimming pool was installed. The swimming pool was built, and an appraiser estimated that the value of Jane's home increased by $98,000 because of the addition.

The pool cost $194,000, and Jane claimed a medical expense deduction of $96,000 ($194,000 − $98,000) on her tax return. Upon audit of the return, the IRS determined that an adequate pool should have cost $70,000 and would increase the value of her home by only $31,000. Thus, the IRS claims that Jane is entitled to a deduction of only $39,000 ($70,000 − $31,000).

a. Is there any ceiling limitation on the amount deductible as a medical expense? Explain.
b. Can capital expenditures be deductible as medical expenses? Explain.
c. What is the significance of a "minimum adequate facility"? Should aesthetic or architectural qualities be considered in the determination? Why or why not?

Research Problem 2. Ken and Mary Jane Blough, your neighbors, have asked you for advice after receiving correspondence in the mail from the IRS. You learn that the IRS is asking for documentation in support of the itemized deductions the Bloughs claimed on a recent tax return. The Bloughs tell you that their income in the year of question was $75,000. Because their record-keeping habits are poor, they felt justified in claiming itemized deductions equal to the amounts that represent the average claimed by other taxpayers in their income bracket. These averages are calculated and reported by the IRS annually based on actual returns filed in an earlier year. Accordingly, they claimed medical expenses of $7,102, taxes of $6,050, interest of $10,659, and charitable contributions of $2,693. What advice do you give the Boughs?

Partial list of research aids:
Cheryl L. de Werff, T.C. Summary Opinion, 2011–29.

Communications

Research Problem 3. In January, Ron, a firefighter, was injured in the line of duty as a result of interference by a homeowner. He incurred medical expenses of $6,500 related to his injuries. Ron sued the homeowner and was awarded damages of $26,500 in December. The court indicated that $6,500 of the award was for payment of Ron's medical expenses and $20,000 was for punitive damages. Ron has prepared his income tax return for the year and has asked you to review it. You notice that Ron has not reported any part of the award as income and has included the medical expenses in computing his itemized deductions. Write a brief memorandum for the tax files that summarizes the advice you should give Ron.

Research Problem 4. Tom and Mary Smith, whose son was found murdered in a parking garage, offered a $100,000 reward for the city police to use to obtain information leading to the arrest and conviction of the murderer. As a result of the reward, a person who had overheard the murderer telling a friend about the crime reported the conversation to the police. The murderer was arrested and convicted, and the Smiths contributed the money to the police department, which gave the reward to the informant. Can the Smiths treat the payment as an itemized deduction? Explain.

Communications

Research Problem 5. Marcia, a shareholder in a corporation with stores in five states, donated stock with a basis of $10,000 to a qualified charitable organization in 2013. Although the stock of the corporation was not traded on a public stock exchange, many shares had been sold over the past several years. Based on the average selling price for the stock in 2013, Marcia deducted $95,000 on her 2013 tax return. Marcia received a notice from the IRS that the $95,000 deduction had been reduced to $10,000 because she had not obtained a qualified appraisal or attached a summary of her appraisal to her tax return. Marcia has asked you to advise her on this matter. Write a letter containing your conclusions to Ms. Marcia Meyer, 1311 Santos Court, San Bruno, CA 94066.

Partial list of research aids:
Reg. § 1.170A–13(c)(2).

Internet Activity

Use the tax resources of the Internet to address the following questions. Do not restrict your search to the Web, but include a review of newsgroups and general reference materials, practitioner sites and resources, primary sources of the tax law, chat rooms and discussion groups, and other opportunities.

Research Problem 6. The cutback adjustment that limits the amount of itemized deductions for some taxpayers is otherwise known as the Pease limitation. This limitation is named after former Congressman Donald Pease and was first in effect for tax years after December 31, 1990. The purpose of this limitation is to raise additional tax revenue by limiting some popular and common itemized deductions incurred by high-income taxpayers. One such deduction is the charitable contribution deduction. Search Google or a business press database to see what tax law analysts speculated the consequences would be of limiting charitable contribution deductions. Also determine whether such speculation has materialized.

Research Problem 7. Use the IRS's website to determine if taxpayers who are not U.S. residents can claim itemized deductions when calculating their taxable income.

Investor Losses

LEARNING OBJECTIVES: *After completing Chapter 11, you should be able to:*

LO.1 Explain the tax shelter problem and the reasons for at-risk and passive loss limitations.

LO.2 Explain the at-risk limitation.

LO.3 Describe how the passive loss rules limit deductions for losses and identify the taxpayers subject to these restrictions.

LO.4 Explore the elements required for an activity to be treated as passive and review the rules for identifying an activity.

LO.5 Identify the tests for material participation.

LO.6 Describe the nature of rental activities under the passive loss rules.

LO.7 Determine the relationship between the at-risk and passive loss limitations.

LO.8 Recognize the special treatment available to real estate activities.

LO.9 Determine the proper tax treatment upon the disposition of a passive activity.

LO.10 Identify restrictions placed on the deductibility of other investor losses and deductions, including those that apply to investment interest.

LO.11 Suggest tax planning strategies to minimize the effect of the passive loss and investment interest limitations.

THE BIG PICTURE Tax Solutions for the Real World

Investor Loss Limitations Affect the Viability of Certain Investment Opportunities

Trudy and Jim Reswick are considering ways to enhance their financial security. In fact, they are willing to borrow a substantial sum so that they can make an appropriate investment.

Currently, Trudy and Jim's sole source of income is their salaries, totaling $100,000, from their full-time jobs. Their most significant asset is their personal residence (fair market value of $500,000 with a mortgage of $350,000). The Reswicks' broker suggests that they borrow $100,000 at 8 percent and use the proceeds to make *one* of the following investments:

- A high-growth, low-yield portfolio of marketable securities. The portfolio's value is expected to grow 10 percent each year.
- An interest in a limited partnership that owns and operates orange groves in Florida. The limited partnership interest is expected to generate tax losses of $25,000 in each of the next five years, after which profits are expected. The broker predicts that after taking into account the tax benefit from the losses, the Reswicks would average an annual 10 percent return over a 10-year period.
- An interest in a local limited partnership that owns and rents apartments to college students. This limited partnership interest also would generate losses of $25,000 per year for five years, after which profits would follow. These expected profits and losses would produce an average annual total return of 10 percent over a 10-year period.

Trudy and Jim want to choose the alternative that produces the best after-tax return over a 10-year planning horizon. They are aware, however, that tax restrictions may limit the advantages of some of these investment options. In this connection, evaluate each option.

Read the chapter and formulate your response.

FRAMEWORK 1040

Tax Formula for Individuals

This chapter covers the boldfaced portions of the Tax Formula for Individuals that was introduced in Figure 3.1 on p. 3-3. Below those portions are the sections of Form 1040 where the results are reported.

Income *(broadly conceived)*	$xx,xxx
Less: Exclusions	(x,xxx)
Gross income	$xx,xxx
Less: Deductions for adjusted gross income	(x,xxx)

FORM 1040 (p. 1)

12	Business income or (loss). Attach Schedule C or C-EZ	
13	Capital gain or (loss). Attach Schedule D if required. If not required, check here ▶ ☐	
14	Other gains or (losses). Attach Form 4797	
17	Rental real estate, royalties, partnerships, S corporations, trusts, etc. Attach Schedule E	

Adjusted gross income	$xx,xxx
Less: The greater of total **itemized deductions** *or* the standard deduction	(x,xxx)

FORM 1040 (p. 2)

40	**Itemized deductions** (from Schedule A) **or** your **standard deduction** (see left margin)

Personal and dependency exemptions	(x,xxx)
Taxable income	$xx,xxx
Tax on taxable income *(see Tax Tables or Tax Rate Schedules)*	$ x,xxx
Less: Tax credits *(including income taxes withheld and prepaid)*	(xxx)
Tax due *(or refund)*	$ xxx

A s discussed in Chapter 6, a tax deduction for an expense or a loss is not allowed unless specifically provided for by Congress. For example, losses can be recognized and deducted in the case of certain unprofitable investments only because the Code so provides. Such losses can arise from the operation of an activity or upon its ultimate disposition. For most individual taxpayers, deductible investor losses come within the scope of § 165(c)(2) relating to transactions entered into for profit.[1] But what happens if the investment is mostly motivated by the tax loss it generates and the profit objective is not controlling? Or what if the investment generates expenses that offset ordinary income and it later is expected to produce appreciation taxed at capital gain rates? This chapter addresses these tax minimization procedures and the Code provisions enacted to restrict their use.

11-1 THE TAX SHELTER PROBLEM

LO.1

Explain the tax shelter problem and the reasons for at-risk and passive loss limitations.

Before Congress enacted legislation to reduce their effectiveness, **tax shelters** provided a popular way to avoid or defer taxes, as they could generate deductions and other benefits to offset income from other sources. Because of the tax avoidance potential of many tax shelters, they were attractive to wealthy taxpayers in high-income tax brackets. Many tax shelters merely provided an opportunity for "investors" to buy deductions and credits in ventures that were not expected to generate a profit, even in the long run.

Although it may seem odd that a taxpayer would intentionally invest in an activity that was designed to produce losses, there is a logical explanation. The typical tax shelter operated as a partnership and relied heavily on nonrecourse financing.[2]

---

[1]If the losses are incurred in connection with a trade or business, § 165(c)(1) applies.

[2]Nonrecourse debt is an obligation for which the borrower is not personally liable. An example of nonrecourse debt is a liability on real estate acquired by a partnership without the partnership or any of the partners assuming any liability for the mortgage. The acquired property generally is pledged as collateral for the loan.

Accelerated depreciation and interest expense deductions generated large losses in the early years of the activity. At the very least, the tax shelter deductions deferred the recognition of any net income from the venture until the activity was sold. In the best of situations, the investor could realize additional tax savings by offsetting other income (e.g., salary, interest, dividends) with deductions flowing from the tax shelter. Ultimately, the sale of the investment would result in capital gain. The following example illustrates what was possible *before* Congress enacted legislation to curb tax shelter abuses.

Example I

Bob, who earned a salary of $400,000 as a business executive and dividend income of $15,000, invested $20,000 for a 10% interest in a cattle-breeding tax shelter. Through the use of $800,000 of nonrecourse financing and available cash of $200,000, the partnership acquired a herd of an exotic breed of cattle costing $1 million. Depreciation, interest, and other deductions related to the activity resulted in a loss of $400,000, of which Bob's share was $40,000. Bob was allowed to deduct the $40,000 loss even though he had invested and stood to lose only $20,000 if the investment became worthless. The net effect of the $40,000 deduction from the partnership was that a portion of Bob's salary and dividend income was "sheltered," and as a result, he was required to calculate his tax liability on only $375,000 of income [$415,000 (salary and dividends) − $40,000 (deduction)] rather than $415,000. If this deduction were available under current law and if Bob was in a combined Federal and state income tax bracket of 40%, this deduction would generate a tax savings of $16,000 ($40,000 × 40%) in the first year alone!

A review of Example 1 shows that the taxpayer took a *two-for-one* write-off ($40,000 deduction, $20,000 amount invested). In the heyday of these types of tax shelters, promoters often promised tax deductions for the investor well in excess of the amount invested.

The first major provision aimed at tax shelters was the **at-risk limitation**. Its objective is to limit a taxpayer's deductions to the amount "at risk," which is the amount the taxpayer stands to lose if the investment becomes worthless. Thus, in Example 1, the at-risk rule limits Bob's loss to $20,000—the amount at risk.

The second major attack on tax shelters came with the passage of the **passive loss** rules. The passive loss rules require the taxpayer to segregate all income and losses into three categories: active, portfolio, and passive. (These categories are defined in Section 11-3.) In general, the passive loss limits disallow the deduction of passive losses against active or portfolio income even when the taxpayer is at risk to the extent of the loss. In general, passive losses can only offset passive income.

Thus, in Example 1, the passive loss rules disallow a current deduction for any of the loss. The loss from the tax shelter is a passive loss because Bob does not materially participate in the activity. Therefore, the $20,000 loss that is allowed under the at-risk rules is disallowed under the passive loss rules because Bob does not report any passive income for the year—he reports only active and portfolio income. Consequently, Bob's current-year income must reflect his nonpassive income of $415,000. As explained later in the chapter, the disallowed $20,000 passive loss is suspended and may be deducted in a future year under certain conditions.

The nature of the at-risk limits and the passive activity loss rules and their impact on investors are discussed in the pages that follow. An interesting consequence of these rules is that now investors evaluating potential investments must consider mainly the economics of the venture instead of the tax benefits or tax avoidance possibilities that an investment may generate.

11-2 AT-RISK LIMITS

The at-risk provisions limit the deductibility of losses from business and income-producing activities. These provisions, which apply to individuals and closely held corporations, are designed to prevent taxpayers from deducting losses in excess of their actual economic investment in an activity. In the case of an S corporation or a

LO.2

Explain the at-risk limitation.

partnership, the at-risk limits apply at the owner level. Under the at-risk rules, a taxpayer's deductible loss from an activity for any taxable year is limited to the amount the taxpayer has at risk at the end of the taxable year (the amount the taxpayer could actually lose in the activity).

While the amount at risk generally vacillates over time, the initial amount considered at risk consists of the following:[3]

- The amount of cash and the adjusted basis of property contributed to the activity by the taxpayer.
- Amounts borrowed for use in the activity for which the taxpayer is personally liable or has pledged as security property not used in the activity.

This amount generally is increased each year by the taxpayer's share of income and is decreased by the taxpayer's share of losses and withdrawals from the activity. In addition, because general partners are jointly and severally liable for recourse debts of the partnership, their at-risk amounts are increased when the partnership increases its debt and are decreased when the partnership reduces its debt. However, a taxpayer generally is not considered at risk with respect to borrowed amounts if either of the following is true:

- The taxpayer is not personally liable for repayment of the debt (e.g., nonrecourse debt).
- The lender has an interest (other than as a creditor) in the activity.

An important exception provides that in the case of an activity involving the holding of real property, a taxpayer is considered at risk for his or her share of any *qualified nonrecourse financing* that is secured by real property used in the activity.[4]

Subject to the passive activity rules discussed later in the chapter, a taxpayer may deduct a loss as long as the at-risk amount is positive. However, once the at-risk amount is exhausted, any remaining loss cannot be deducted until a later year. Any losses disallowed for any given taxable year by the at-risk rules may be deducted in the first succeeding year in which the rules do not prevent the deduction—that is, when there is, and to the extent of, a positive at-risk amount.

THE BIG PICTURE

Example 2

Return to the facts of *The Big Picture* on p. 11-1. In addition to the three investment options presented to the Reswicks, in 2014, they invest $40,000 in an oil partnership that incurs a first-year net loss, of which $60,000 is their share. Assume that the Reswicks' interest in the partnership is subject to the at-risk limits but is not subject to the passive loss limits. Because the Reswicks have only $40,000 of capital at risk, they cannot deduct more than $40,000 against their other income and must reduce their at-risk amount to zero ($40,000 at-risk amount − $40,000 loss deducted). The nondeductible loss of $20,000 ($60,000 loss generated − $40,000 loss allowed) can be carried over to 2015.

THE BIG PICTURE

Example 3

In 2015, the Reswicks in the preceding example have taxable income of $15,000 from the oil partnership and invest an additional $10,000 in the venture. Their at-risk amount is now $25,000 ($0 beginning balance + $15,000 taxable income + $10,000 additional investment). This enables them to deduct the carryover loss and requires them to reduce their at-risk amount to $5,000 ($25,000 at-risk amount − $20,000 carryover loss allowed).

---

[3]§ 465(b)(1).

[4]Section 465(b)(6) defines qualified nonrecourse financing.

TABLE 11.1	Calculation of At-Risk Amount

Increases to a taxpayer's at-risk amount:	Decreases to a taxpayer's at-risk amount:
• Cash and the adjusted basis of property contributed to the activity. • Amounts borrowed for use in the activity for which the taxpayer is personally liable or has pledged as security property not used in the activity. • Taxpayer's share of amounts borrowed for use in the activity that are qualified nonrecourse financing. • Taxpayer's share of the activity's income.	• Withdrawals from the activity. • Taxpayer's share of the activity's deductible loss. • Taxpayer's share of any reductions of debt for which recourse against the taxpayer exists or any reductions of qualified nonrecourse debt.

Complicating the at-risk rule is the fact that previously allowed losses must be recaptured to the extent the at-risk amount is reduced below zero.[5] That is, previous losses that were allowed must be offset by the recognition of enough income to bring the at-risk amount up to zero. This rule applies in situations such as those when the amount at risk is reduced below zero by distributions to the taxpayer or when the status of indebtedness changes from recourse to nonrecourse.

Calculation of at-risk amount is reviewed in Table 11.1.

11-3 PASSIVE LOSS LIMITS

This section identifies and explains a number of key issues that are pertinent when applying the passive loss limits.

LO.3

Describe how the passive loss rules limit deductions for losses and identify the taxpayers subject to these restrictions.

- The limits apply only to passive losses incurred by certain types of taxpayers.
- Losses are limited under these rules only if they are generated by a passive activity.
- Special rules exist for interests in real estate activities.
- Benefits may arise when a disposition of a passive activity occurs.

11-3a Classification and Impact of Passive Income and Losses

The passive loss rules operate by requiring taxpayers to classify their income and losses into various categories. Then the rules limit the extent to which losses in the passive category can be used to offset income in the other categories.

Classification

The passive loss rules require income and losses to be classified into one of three categories: active, portfolio, or passive. **Active income** includes the following:

- Wages, salary, commissions, bonuses, and other payments for services rendered by the taxpayer.
- Profit from a trade or business in which the taxpayer is a material participant.
- Gain on the sale or other disposition of assets used in an active trade or business.
- Income from intangible property if the taxpayer's personal efforts significantly contributed to the creation of the property.

Portfolio income includes the following:

- Interest, dividends, annuities, and royalties not derived in the ordinary course of a trade or business.

---
[5]§ 465(e).

- Gain or loss from the disposition of property that produces portfolio income or is held for investment purposes.

Section 469 provides that passive income or loss arises from activities that are treated as passive, which include:

- Any trade or business or income-producing activity in which the taxpayer does not materially participate.
- Subject to certain exceptions, all rental activities, whether the taxpayer materially participates or not.

Although the Code defines rental activities as passive activities, several exceptions allow losses from certain real estate rental activities to offset nonpassive (active or portfolio) income. These exceptions are discussed under Special Passive Activity Rules for Real Estate Activities later in the chapter.

General Impact

Losses or expenses generated by passive activities can be deducted only to the extent of income from all of the taxpayer's passive activities. Any excess may not be used to offset income from active sources or portfolio income. Instead, any unused passive losses are suspended and carried forward to future years to offset passive income generated in those years. Otherwise, suspended losses may be used only when a taxpayer disposes of his or her entire interest in an activity. In that event, all current and suspended losses related to the activity may offset active and portfolio income.

THE BIG PICTURE

Example 4

Return to the facts of *The Big Picture* on p. 11-1. In addition to their salaries of $100,000 from full-time jobs, assume that the Reswicks receive $12,000 in dividends and interest from various portfolio investments. Further, assume that they decide to invest $100,000 in the orange grove limited partnership, which produces a $25,000 loss for the Reswicks this year. Because their at-risk basis in the partnership is $100,000, the current $25,000 loss is not limited by the at-risk rules. However, because the loss is a passive loss, it is not deductible against their other income. The loss is suspended and carried over to the future. If the Reswicks have passive income from this investment or from other passive investments in the future, they can offset the suspended loss against that passive income. If they do not have passive income to offset this suspended loss in the future, they will be allowed to offset the loss against other types of income when they eventually dispose of their investment in the passive activity.

Impact of Suspended Losses

When a taxpayer disposes of his or her entire interest in a passive activity, the actual economic gain or loss from the investment, including any suspended losses, can finally be determined. As a result, under the passive loss rules, upon a fully taxable disposition, any overall loss realized from the taxpayer's activity is recognized and can be offset against any income.

A fully taxable disposition generally involves a sale of the property to a third party at arm's length and thus, presumably, for a price equal to the property's fair market value. As presented in the following example, a gain recognized upon the transfer of an interest in a passive activity generally is treated as passive and is first offset by the suspended losses from that activity.

Example 5

Rex sells an apartment building, a passive activity, with an adjusted basis of $100,000 for $180,000. In addition, he has suspended losses of $60,000 associated with the building. His total gain, $80,000, and his taxable gain, $20,000, are calculated as follows:

Net sales price	$ 180,000
Less: Adjusted basis	(100,000)
Total gain	$ 80,000
Less: Suspended losses	(60,000)
Taxable gain (passive)	$ 20,000

If current and suspended losses of the passive activity exceed the gain realized or if the sale results in a realized loss, the amount of

- any loss from the activity for the tax year (including losses suspended in the activity disposed of)

in excess of

- net income or gain for the tax year from all passive activities (without regard to the activity disposed of)

is treated as a loss that is not from a passive activity. In computing the loss from the activity for the year of disposition, any gain or loss recognized is included.

Example 6

Dean sells an apartment building, a passive activity, with an adjusted basis of $100,000 for $150,000. In addition, he has current and suspended losses of $60,000 associated with the building and has no other passive activities. His total gain of $50,000 and his deductible loss of $10,000 are calculated as follows:

Net sales price	$ 150,000
Less: Adjusted basis	(100,000)
Total gain	$ 50,000
Less: Suspended losses	(60,000)
Deductible loss (not passive)	($ 10,000)

The $10,000 deductible loss is offset against Dean's active and portfolio income. Even if the building is sold for a loss (i.e., the adjusted basis exceeds the sales price), the total loss, including the suspended losses, is deductible as a nonpassive loss.

Carryovers of Suspended Losses

The preceding examples assumed that the taxpayer had an interest in only one passive activity; as a result, the suspended loss was related exclusively to the activity that was disposed of. However, taxpayers often own interests in more than one activity, in which case any suspended losses must be allocated among those passive activities. The allocation to an activity is made by multiplying the disallowed passive activity loss from all activities using the following fraction:

$$\frac{\text{Loss from one passive activity}}{\text{Sum of losses for taxable year from all passive activities having losses}}$$

Example 7

Diego has investments in three passive activities with the following income and losses for 2013:

Activity A	($30,000)
Activity B	(20,000)
Activity C	25,000
Net passive loss	($25,000)
Net passive loss allocated to:	
Activity A ($25,000 × $30,000/$50,000)	($15,000)
Activity B ($25,000 × $20,000/$50,000)	(10,000)
Total suspended losses	($25,000)

Suspended losses are carried over indefinitely and are offset in the future against any passive income from the activities to which they relate.[6]

Example 8

Assume that the facts are the same as in Example 7 and that Activity A produces $10,000 of income in 2014. Of the suspended loss of $15,000 from 2013 for Activity A, $10,000 is offset against the income from this activity. If Diego sells Activity A in early 2015, the remaining $5,000 suspended loss is used to determine his taxable gain or loss.

Passive Credits

Credits (such as the low-income housing credit and rehabilitation credit—discussed in Chapter 13) that arise from passive activities are limited in much the same way as passive losses. Passive credits can be utilized only against regular tax attributable to passive income,[7] which is calculated by comparing the tax on all income (including passive income) with the tax on income excluding passive income.

Example 9

Sam owes $50,000 of tax, disregarding net passive income, and $80,000 of tax, considering both net passive and other taxable income (disregarding the credits in both cases). The amount of tax attributable to the passive income is $30,000.

In the preceding example, Sam can claim a maximum of $30,000 of passive activity credits; the excess credits are carried over. These passive activity credits can be used only against the *regular* tax attributable to passive income. If a taxpayer has a net loss from passive activities during a given year, no credits can be used.

Carryovers of Passive Credits

Tax credits attributable to passive activities can be carried forward indefinitely much like suspended passive losses. Unlike passive losses, however, passive credits are lost forever when the activity is disposed of in a taxable transaction where loss is recognized. Credits are allowed on dispositions only when there is sufficient tax on passive income to absorb them.

Example 10

Alicia sells a passive activity for a gain of $10,000. The activity had suspended losses of $40,000 and suspended credits of $15,000. The $10,000 gain is offset by $10,000 of the suspended losses, and the remaining $30,000 of suspended losses is deductible against Alicia's active and portfolio income. The suspended credits are lost forever because the sale of the activity did not generate any tax.

Example 11

If Alicia in Example 10 had realized a $100,000 gain on the sale of the passive activity, the suspended credits could have been used to the extent of the regular tax attributable to the net passive income.

Gain on sale	$100,000
Less: Suspended losses	(40,000)
Taxable gain	$ 60,000

If the tax attributable to the taxable gain of $60,000 is $15,000 or more, the entire $15,000 of suspended credits can be used. If the tax attributable to the gain is less than $15,000, the excess of the suspended credits over the tax attributable to the gain is lost forever.

When a taxpayer has sufficient regular tax liability from passive activities to trigger the use of suspended credits, the credits lose their character as passive credits. They are reclassified as regular tax credits and made subject to the same limits as other credits (discussed in Chapter 13).

---

[6]§ 469(b).   [7]§ 469(d)(2).

Passive Activity Changes to Active

If a formerly passive activity becomes an active one, suspended losses are allowed to the extent of income from the now active business.[8] If any of the suspended loss remains, it continues to be treated as a loss from a passive activity. The excess suspended loss can be deducted from passive income or carried over to the next tax year and deducted to the extent of income from the now active business in the succeeding year(s). The activity must continue to be the same activity.

Rebecca has owned an interest in a passive activity for several years, which has produced losses of $80,000 during that period. Because she did not have passive income from other sources, she could not deduct any of the activity's passive losses. In the current year, she becomes a material participant in the activity and her share of the business profits total $25,000. As a result, she may use $25,000 of the suspended passive loss to offset the current business profits. Rebecca's remaining suspended passive loss from the activity is $55,000 ($80,000 − $25,000), which is carried over to future years.	**Example 12**

11-3b Taxpayers Subject to the Passive Loss Rules

The passive loss rules apply to individuals, estates, trusts, personal service corporations, and closely held C corporations.[9] Passive income or loss from investments in S corporations or partnerships (see Chapter 20) flows through to the owners, and the passive loss rules are applied at the owner level.

Personal Service Corporations

Application of the passive loss limitations to personal service corporations is intended to prevent taxpayers from sheltering personal service income by creating personal service corporations and acquiring passive activities at the corporate level.

Two tax accountants who earn an aggregate of $200,000 a year in their individual practices agree to work together in a newly formed personal service corporation. Shortly after its formation, the corporation invests in a passive activity that produces a $200,000 loss during the year. Because the passive loss rules apply to personal service corporations, the corporation may not deduct the $200,000 passive loss against the $200,000 of active income.	**Example 13**

Determination of whether a corporation is a **personal service corporation** is based on rather broad definitions. A personal service corporation is a regular (or C) corporation that meets *both* of the following conditions:

- The principal activity is the performance of personal services.
- Such services are substantially performed by employee-owners.

Generally, personal service corporations include those in the fields of health, law, engineering, architecture, accounting, actuarial science, performing arts, and consulting.[10] A corporation is treated as a personal service corporation if more than 10 percent of the stock (by value) is held by employee-owners.[11] An employee is treated as an employee-owner if he or she owns stock on *any day* during the taxable year.[12] For these purposes, shareholder status and employee status do not have to occur on the same day.

Closely Held C Corporations

Application of the passive loss rules to closely held (non-personal service) C corporations is also intended to prevent individuals from incorporating to avoid the passive loss limitations. A corporation is classified as a **closely held corporation** if at any time during the taxable year more than 50 percent of the value of its outstanding stock is owned, directly or indirectly, by or for five or fewer individuals. Closely held

---

[8]§ 469(f).
[9]§ 469(a).
[10]§ 448(d)(2)(A).

[11]§ 469(j)(2).
[12]§ 269A(b)(2).

C corporations (other than personal service corporations) may use passive losses to offset *active* income but not portfolio income.

Silver Corporation, a closely held (non-personal service) C corporation, has $500,000 of passive losses from a rental activity, $400,000 of active income, and $100,000 of portfolio income. The corporation may offset $400,000 of the $500,000 passive loss against the $400,000 of active business income but may not offset the remainder against the $100,000 of portfolio income. Thus, $100,000 of the passive loss is suspended ($500,000 passive loss − $400,000 offset against active income).

Application of the passive loss limitations to closely held C corporations prevents taxpayers from transferring their portfolio investments to such corporations to offset passive losses against portfolio income.

11-3c Working with the Definition of Passive Activities

LO.4

Explore the elements required for an activity to be treated as passive and review the rules for identifying an activity.

As noted earlier, the following types of activities are treated as passive:

- Any trade or business or income-producing activity in which the taxpayer does not materially participate.
- Subject to certain exceptions pertaining to real estate (discussed later), all rental activities.

To understand the meaning of the term *passive activity* and the impact of the rules, one must address the following issues, each of which is the subject of statutory or administrative guidance:

- What constitutes an activity?
- What is meant by material participation?
- When is an activity a rental activity?

Even though guidance is available to help the taxpayer deal with these issues, their resolution is anything but simple.

Identification of an Activity

Identifying what constitutes an activity is a necessary first step in applying the passive loss limitations. Taxpayers who are involved in complex business operations need to determine whether a given segment of their overall business operations constitutes a separate activity or is to be treated as part of a single activity. Proper treatment is necessary to determine whether income or loss from an activity is active or passive.

Example 15

Ben owns a business with two separate departments. Department A generates net income of $120,000, and Department B generates a net loss of $95,000. Ben participates 700 hours in the operations of Department A and 100 hours in Department B. If Ben is allowed to treat the departments as components of a single activity, he can offset the $95,000 loss from Department B against the $120,000 of income from Department A.

Example 16

Assume the same facts as in the previous example. If Ben is required to treat each department as a separate activity, the tax result is not as favorable. Because he is a material participant in Department A (having devoted 700 hours to it), the $120,000 profit is active income. Assuming Ben is not considered a material participant in Department B (100 hours), the $95,000 loss is a passive loss. Therefore, Ben cannot offset the $95,000 passive loss from Department B against the $120,000 of active income from Department A. (A complete discussion of the material participation rules follows.)

Recall that on the disposition of a passive activity, a taxpayer is allowed to offset suspended losses from the activity against other types of income. Therefore, as illustrated in the following example, identifying what constitutes an activity is of crucial importance for this purpose too.

© iStockphoto.com/Andrey Prokhorov

TAX IN THE NEWS   If You Can't Trust Your Tax Preparer, Who Can You Trust?

Many taxpayers choose to remain ignorant of the tax law because they assume that by paying a "professional" to complete their returns, they have shifted all responsibility to someone else. But they do so at their own risk. Failure to have at least a general understanding of the tax rules that apply to one's return can be a big mistake and can lead to various tax penalties.

One such taxpayer invested in several partnerships that engaged in horse activities in California. Being fully employed in New York, he did not participate in the partnerships' activities and had no knowledge of their business operations. When he received the tax information from the partnerships about his investments, he simply turned over the statements to his tax preparer, who included the information on the return filed. Essentially, the tax return reflected the taxpayer's losses from the horse activities even though they are disallowed under the passive loss rules.

When the IRS discovered the error, the taxpayer pleaded ignorance and blamed the tax preparer. The taxpayer claimed that he had been "duped by a charlatan" and pleaded for mercy. The Tax Court showed no compassion and held that he owed additional taxes, interest, and penalties (*Ralph P. Cunningham,* 98 TCM 143, T.C.Memo. 2009–194). Perhaps the result would have been different if the taxpayer had had a better understanding of the tax law in general and the passive activity rules in particular. Reliance on a tax preparer is not an excuse for blindly signing a tax return without understanding its content.

> **Example 17**
>
> Linda owns a business with two departments. Department A has a net loss of $125,000 in the current year, and Department B has a $70,000 net loss. She disposes of Department B at the end of the year. Assuming Linda is allowed to treat the two departments as separate passive activities, she can offset the passive loss from Department B against other types of income in the following order: gain from disposition of the passive activity, other passive income, and nonpassive income. This treatment leaves her with a suspended loss of $125,000 from Department A. If Departments A and B are treated as components of the same activity, however, upon the disposal of Department B, its $70,000 net loss would be suspended along with the other $125,000 of suspended loss of the activity.

The rules used to delineate what constitutes an activity for purposes of the passive loss limitations are provided in the Regulations.[13] These guidelines state that, in general, a taxpayer can treat one or more trade or business activities or rental activities as a single activity if those activities form an *appropriate economic unit* for measuring gain or loss. To determine what ventures form an appropriate economic unit, all of the relevant facts and circumstances must be considered. Taxpayers may use any reasonable method in applying the facts and circumstances. The following example, adapted from the Regulations, illustrates the application of the general rules for grouping activities.[14]

> **Example 18**
>
> George owns a men's clothing store and an Internet café in Chicago. He also owns a men's clothing store and an Internet café in Milwaukee. Reasonable methods of applying the facts and circumstances test may result in any of the following groupings:
>
> - All four activities may be grouped into a single activity because of common ownership and control.
> - The clothing stores may be grouped into an activity, and the Internet cafés may be grouped into a separate activity.
> - The Chicago activities may be grouped into an activity, and the Milwaukee activities may be grouped into a separate activity.
> - Each of the four activities may be treated as a separate activity.

Regrouping of Activities Taxpayers should carefully consider all tax factors when deciding how to group their activities. Once activities have been grouped, they cannot be

---

[13]Reg. § 1.469–4.   [14]Reg. § 1.469–4(c)(3).

regrouped unless the original grouping was clearly inappropriate or there has been a material change in the facts and circumstances. The Regulations also grant the IRS the right to regroup activities when both of the following conditions exist:[15]

- The taxpayer's grouping fails to reflect one or more appropriate economic units.
- One of the primary purposes of the taxpayer's grouping is to avoid the passive loss limitations.

Special Grouping Rules for Rental Activities   Two rules deal specifically with the grouping of rental activities. These provisions are designed to prevent taxpayers from grouping rental activities, which are generally passive, with other businesses in a way that would result in a tax advantage.

First, a rental activity may be grouped with a trade or business activity only if one activity is insubstantial in relation to the other. That is, the rental activity must be insubstantial in relation to the trade or business activity, or the trade or business activity must be insubstantial in relation to the rental activity. The Regulations provide no clear guidelines as to the meaning of "insubstantial."[16]

Example 19	Schemers, a firm of CPAs, owns a building in downtown Washington, D.C., in which it conducts its public accounting practice. The firm also rents space on the street level of the building to several retail establishments, which generally is considered a passive activity. Of the total revenue generated by the firm, 95% is associated with the public accounting practice and 5% is related to the rental operation. It is likely that the rental activity would be considered insubstantial relative to the accounting practice and the two ventures could be grouped as one nonrental activity. This grouping could be advantageous to the firm, particularly if the rental operation generates a loss! Alternatively, treating the rental operation as a *separate* activity may be advantageous if this operation produces (passive) income. The passive income could then be used to absorb otherwise nondeductible passive losses.

Second, taxpayers generally may not treat an activity involving the rental of real property and an activity involving the rental of personal property as a single activity.

Material Participation

LO.5

Identify the tests for material participation.

As indicated previously, if an individual taxpayer materially participates in a nonrental trade or business activity, any loss from that activity is treated as an active loss that can offset active or portfolio income. (Participation is defined later in the chapter.) If a taxpayer does not materially participate, however, the loss is treated as a passive loss, which can only offset passive income. Therefore, controlling whether a particular activity is treated as active or passive is an important part of the tax strategy of a taxpayer who owns an interest in one or more businesses. Consider the following examples.

Example 20	Dewayne, a corporate executive, earns a salary of $600,000 per year. In addition, he owns a separate business in which he participates. The business produces a loss of $100,000 during the year. If Dewayne materially participates in the business, the $100,000 loss is an active loss that may offset his active income from his corporate employer. If he does not materially participate, the loss is passive and is suspended. Dewayne may use the suspended loss in the future only when he has passive income or disposes of the activity.

Example 21	Kay, an attorney, earns $350,000 a year in her law practice. In addition, she owns interests in two activities, A and B, in which she participates. Activity A, in which she does *not* materially participate, produces a loss of $50,000. Kay has not yet met the material participation standard, described below, for Activity B, which produces income of $80,000. However, she can meet the material participation standard if she spends an additional 50 hours in Activity B during the year. Should Kay attempt to meet the

material participation standard for Activity B? If she continues working in Activity B and becomes a material participant, the $80,000 of income from the activity is *active*, and the $50,000 passive loss from Activity A must be suspended. A more favorable tax strategy is for Kay *not to meet* the material participation standard for Activity B, thus making the income from that activity passive. This enables her to offset the $50,000 passive loss from Activity A against most of the passive income from Activity B.

It is possible to devise numerous scenarios in which the taxpayer could control the tax outcome by increasing or decreasing his or her participation in different activities. Examples 20 and 21 demonstrate some of the possibilities. The conclusion reached in most analyses of this type is that taxpayers will benefit by having profitable activities classified as passive so that any passive losses can be used to offset that passive income. If the activity produces a loss, however, the taxpayer will benefit if it is classified as active so that the loss is not subject to the passive loss limitations.

As discussed previously, a nonrental trade or business in which a taxpayer owns an interest must be treated as a passive activity unless the taxpayer materially participates. As the Staff of the Joint Committee on Taxation explained, a material participant is one who has "a significant nontax economic profit motive" for taking on activities and selects them for their economic value. In contrast, a passive investor mainly seeks a return from a capital investment (including a possible reduction in taxes) as a supplement to an ongoing source of livelihood.[17] Even if the concept or the implication of being a material participant is clear, the precise meaning of the term **material participation** can be vague. As enacted, § 469 requires a taxpayer to participate on a *regular, continuous, and substantial* basis to be a material participant. In many situations, however, it is difficult or impossible to gain any assurance that this nebulous standard is met.

In response to this dilemma, Temporary Regulations[18] provide seven tests that are intended to help taxpayers cope with these issues. Material participation is achieved by meeting any *one* of the tests. These tests are listed in Table 11.2 and can be divided into the following three categories:

- Tests based on current participation.
- Tests based on prior participation.
- Test based on facts and circumstances.

Participation Defined Participation generally includes any work done by an individual in an activity that he or she owns. Participation does not include work if it is of a type not customarily done by owners *and* if one of its principal purposes is to avoid the disallowance of passive losses or credits. Also, work done in an individual's capacity as an investor (e.g., reviewing financial reports in a nonmanagerial capacity) is not counted in applying the material participation tests. However, participation by an owner's spouse counts as participation by the owner.[19]

Tom, who is a partner in a CPA firm, owns a computer store that operated at a loss during the year. To offset this loss against the income from his CPA practice, Tom would like to avoid having the computer business classified as a passive activity. During the year, he worked 480 hours in the business in management and selling activities and 30 hours doing janitorial chores. In addition, Tom's wife participated 40 hours as a salesperson. It is likely that Tom's 480 hours of participation in management and selling activities will count as participation in work customarily done by owners, but the 30 hours spent doing janitorial chores will not. However, the 40 hours of participation by his wife will count. Assuming none of the participation's principal purposes is to avoid the disallowance of passive losses or credits, Tom will qualify as a material participant under the more-than-500-hour rule (480 + 40 = 520).	**Example 22**

---

[17] *General Explanation of the Tax Reform Act of 1986* ("Blue Book"), prepared by The Staff of the Joint Committee on Taxation, May 4, 1987, H.R. 3838, 99th Cong., p. 212.

[18] Temp.Reg. § 1.469–5T(a). The Temporary Regulations are also Proposed Regulations. Temporary Regulations have the same effect as final Regulations. Refer to Chapter 2 for a discussion of the different categories of Regulations.

[19] § 469(h)(5) and Temp.Reg. § 1.469–5T(f)(3).

TABLE 11.2	Tests to Determine Material Participation

Tests Based on Current Participation

1. The individual participates in the activity for more than 500 hours during the year.
2. The individual's participation in the activity for the taxable year constitutes substantially all of the participation in the activity of all individuals (including nonowner employees) for the year.
3. The individual participates in the activity for more than 100 hours during the year, and this participation is not less than that participation of any other individual (including nonowner employees) for the year.
4. The activity is a **significant participation activity** (where the person's participation *exceeds* 100 hours during the year), and the aggregate of all significant participation activities during the year is more than 500 hours.

Tests Based on Prior Participation

5. The individual materially participated in the activity for any 5 taxable years during the 10 taxable years that immediately precede the current taxable year.
6. The activity is a personal service activity, and the individual materially participated in the activity for any three preceding taxable years.

Test Based on Facts and Circumstances

7. Based on all of the facts and circumstances, the individual participates in the activity on a regular, continuous, and substantial basis during the year.

Limited Partners A *limited* partner is a partner whose liability to third-party creditors of the partnership is limited to the amount the partner has invested in the partnership. Such a partnership must have at least one *general* partner, who is fully liable in an individual capacity for the debts of the partnership to third parties. Generally, a *limited partner* is not considered a material participant unless he or she qualifies under Test 1, 5, or 6 as shown in Table 11.2. However, a *general partner* may qualify as a material participant by meeting any of the seven tests. If a general partner also owns a limited interest in the same limited partnership, all interests are treated as a general interest.[20]

Rental Activities Defined

LO.6

Describe the nature of rental activities under the passive loss rules.

Subject to certain exceptions, all rental activities are to be treated as passive activities.[21] A **rental activity** is defined as any activity where payments are received principally for the use of tangible (real or personal) property.[22] Importantly, an activity that is classified as a rental activity is subject to the passive activity loss rules even if the taxpayer involved is a material participant.

> **Example 23**
>
> Sarah owns a fleet of automobiles that are held for rent, and she spends an average of 60 hours a week in the activity. Assuming that her automobile business is classified as a rental activity, it is automatically subject to the passive activity rules even though Sarah spends more than 500 hours a year in its operation.

Temporary Regulations, however, provide exceptions for certain situations where activities involving rentals of real and personal property are *not* to be *treated* as rental activities.[23] Consider the following example.

> **Example 24**
>
> Dan owns a bicycle rental business at a nearby resort. Because the average period of customer use is seven days or less, Dan's business is not treated as a rental activity.

This exception is based on the presumption that a person who rents property for seven days or less is generally required to provide significant services to the customer. Providing such services supports a conclusion that the person is engaged in a service business rather than a rental business.

The fact that Dan's business in the previous example is not treated as a rental activity does not necessarily mean that it is classified as a nonpassive activity.

---

[20]§ 469(h)(2) and Temp.Reg. § 1.469–5T(e)(3)(ii).
[21]§ 469(c)(2).

[22]§ 469(j)(8).
[23]Temp.Reg. § 1.469–1T(e)(3).

© iStockphoto.com/Andrey Prokhorov

TAX IN THE NEWS   The Passive Loss Rules Are a Trap for the Novice Landlord

Most sophisticated investors are well aware of the passive loss rules. Such investors are not surprised when the rules apply and have learned how to minimize their negative effect.

The real damage caused by the passive loss rules often falls on taxpayers who have never heard of them and hold passive activities "on the side" only as secondary ventures. Suppose, for example, that Taylor just inherited her aunt's furnished residence. Rather than sell the house in a depressed market, she is attracted by the regular cash flow provided by rent income. Although Taylor knows to expect a tax benefit from the paper loss that may result from rental property, does she know about the passive loss limitations? Unlike the professional, most novice landlords are surprised by these rules on an after-the-fact basis.

Instead, the business is treated as a trade or business activity subject to the material participation standards listed in Table 11.2. If Dan is a material participant, the business is treated as active. If he is not a material participant, it is treated as a passive activity. For additional discussion of the rental exceptions, see IRS Publication 925 (*Passive Activity and At-Risk Rules*).

11-3d Interaction of the At-Risk and Passive Loss Limits

LO.7

Determine the relationship between the at-risk and passive loss limitations.

The determination of whether a loss is suspended under the passive loss rules is made *after* application of the at-risk rules, as well as other provisions relating to the measurement of taxable income. A loss that is not allowed for the year because the taxpayer is not at risk with respect to it is suspended under the at-risk provision, not under the passive loss rules. Further, a taxpayer's at-risk basis is reduced by the losses (but not below zero) even if the deductions are not currently usable because of the passive loss rules. The following examples illustrate these points.

Example 25

Jack's adjusted basis in a passive activity is $10,000 at the beginning of 2013. His loss from the activity in 2013 is $4,000. Because Jack has no passive activity income, the $4,000 cannot be deducted. At year-end, Jack has an adjusted basis and an at-risk amount of $6,000 in the activity and a suspended passive loss of $4,000.

Example 26

Jack in Example 25 has a loss of $9,000 in the activity in 2014. Because the $9,000 exceeds his at-risk amount ($6,000) by $3,000, that $3,000 loss is disallowed by the at-risk rules. If Jack has no passive activity income, the remaining $6,000 is suspended under the passive activity rules. At year-end, he has:

- A $3,000 loss suspended under the at-risk rules.
- $10,000 of suspended passive losses ($4,000 from 2013 and $6,000 from 2014).
- An adjusted basis and an at-risk amount in the activity of zero.

Example 27

Jack in Example 26 realizes $1,000 of passive income from the activity in 2015. Because the $1,000 increases his at-risk amount, $1,000 of the $3,000 unused loss from 2014 is reclassified as a passive loss. If he has no other passive income, the $1,000 income is offset by $1,000 of suspended passive losses. At the end of 2015, Jack has:

- No taxable passive income.
- $2,000 ($3,000 − $1,000) of unused losses under the at-risk rules.
- $10,000 of (reclassified) suspended passive losses ($10,000 + $1,000 of reclassified unused at-risk losses − $1,000 of passive losses offset against passive income).
- An adjusted basis and an at-risk amount in the activity of zero.

TAX IN THE NEWS   Caution Is Needed in the Classification of Owners in LLCs and LLPs as Material Participants

When the passive loss rules were enacted in the mid-1980s, LLCs and LLPs had not developed as entity forms that could be used to operate businesses. But as their popularity increased, the impact of the passive loss rules on its owners became a matter of conflict between taxpayers and the IRS.

In general, § 469(h)(2) states that limited partners are treated as not materially participating and, as a consequence, are subject to the passive loss restrictions. Similarly, the IRS treated owners who had limited liability protection in other business forms (i.e., LLCs and LLPs) in like fashion. In other words, the only way an LLC member or an LLP partner could be considered a material participant was by meeting the requirements under Test 1, 5, or 6 in Table 11.2.

In recent years, numerous courts have assigned material participation status to owners in LLCs and LLPs (over the objections of the IRS) based on the rights to participate in the management of their businesses. Ultimately, the IRS reversed its position with the release of Prop.Reg. § 1.469–5. The new holding eliminates limited liability as the determinant of material participation status and makes the status dependent on an investor's general involvement in the business.

Nonetheless, the new rules remain tentative until the Proposed Regulations (or some variation thereof) become final. In the meantime, owners of LLCs and LLPs should operate with caution.

Example 28

In 2016, Jack has no gain or loss from the activity in Example 27. He contributes $5,000 more to the passive activity. Because the $5,000 increases his at-risk amount, the $2,000 of losses suspended under the at-risk rules is reclassified as passive. Jack gets no passive loss deduction in 2016. At year-end, he has:

- No suspended losses under the at-risk rules.
- $12,000 of suspended passive losses ($10,000 + $2,000 of reclassified suspended at-risk losses).
- An adjusted basis and an at-risk amount of $3,000 ($5,000 additional investment − $2,000 of reclassified losses).

THE BIG PICTURE

Example 29

Return to the facts of *The Big Picture* on p. 11-1. If the Reswicks invest in the orange grove limited partnership, the at-risk rules will not limit the deductibility of the $25,000 losses until after year 4. Ample at-risk basis will exist until the close of that year (i.e., the at-risk basis is reduced from $100,000 by $25,000 over each of the first four years of the investment). However, the passive loss rules prohibit deductions for the losses in the first four years of the investment (assuming that the Reswicks do not have passive income from other sources). Therefore, based on the facts provided, none of the suspended losses would be deductible until year 6, when the orange grove is expected to begin producing profits.

11-3e Special Passive Activity Rules for Real Estate Activities

LO.8

Recognize the special treatment available to real estate activities.

The passive loss limits contain two exceptions related to real estate activities. These exceptions allow all or part of real estate rental losses to offset active or portfolio income even though the activity otherwise is defined as a passive activity.

Material Participation in a Real Property Rental Trade or Business

The first exception relates to a special rule for material participation in a real estate rental trade or business. Losses from real estate rental activities are *not*

TAX IN THE NEWS   Full-Time Employees May Face Difficulty Showing Real Estate Professional Status

To qualify as a real estate professional, a taxpayer must devote more than 50 percent of his or her personal services to real property trades or businesses. This requirement typically would make it very difficult for a person with a full-time job to qualify for this status because the efforts as an employee likely would comprise the bulk of the taxpayer's labor.

If you were a judge, how reasonable would a taxpayer's assertion be that he worked more time on his real estate properties than his full-time, 40-hour-a-week job? One taxpayer, who faced such a challenge before the Tax Court (*Mohammad Hassanipour* 105 TCM 1542, T.C.Memo. 2013–88), was unable to convince the judge. Consequently, he was required to pay additional taxes and penalties—over $45,000—for inappropriately claiming deductions as a real estate professional.

Essentially, the taxpayer reported that he worked 1,936 hours for his employer and was not able to persuade the judge that he spent more than this working on his real estate properties. In the end, the Tax Court stated that the taxpayer's testimony was undermined by "his questionable claims about the contemporaneous calendar, and by the vagueness and inherent improbability of his estimates."

A basic premise of tax compliance illustrated by the case is that a taxpayer should never claim a deduction unless it can be supported with adequate and convincing documentation.

treated as passive losses for certain real estate professionals.[24] To qualify for nonpassive treatment, a taxpayer must satisfy both of the following requirements:

- More than half of the personal services that the taxpayer performs in trades or businesses are performed in real property trades or businesses in which the taxpayer materially participates.
- The taxpayer performs more than 750 hours of services in these real property trades or businesses as a material participant.

Taxpayers who do not satisfy the above requirements must continue to treat losses from real estate rental activities as passive losses.

> **Example 30**
>
> During the current year, Della performs personal service activities as follows: 900 hours as a personal financial planner, 550 hours in a real estate development business, and 600 hours in a real estate rental activity. Any loss Della incurs in either real estate activity will not be subject to the passive loss rules. Being a nonrental business, the development business is deemed active under the more-than-500-hour rule. The real estate rental activity is active because more than 50% of her personal services are devoted to real property trades or businesses (i.e., the development and rental businesses) and her material participation in those real estate activities exceeds 750 hours. Thus, any losses from either real estate activity can offset active and portfolio sources of income.

As discussed earlier, a spouse's work is taken into consideration in satisfying the material participation requirement. However, the hours worked by a spouse are *not* taken into account when ascertaining whether a taxpayer has worked for more than 750 hours in real property trades or businesses during a year.[25] Services performed by an employee are not treated as being related to a real estate trade or business unless the employee performing the services owns more than a 5 percent interest in the employer. In addition, a closely held C corporation may also qualify for the passive loss relief if more than 50 percent of its gross receipts for the year are derived from real property trades or businesses in which it materially participates.

---

[24]§ 469(c)(7).

[25]§ 469(c)(7)(B) and Reg. § 1.469–9.

ETHICS & EQUITY   Punching the Time Clock at Year-End

As the end of the tax year approaches, Ralph, a successful full-time real estate developer and investor, recognizes that his income tax situation for the year could be bleak. Unless he and his wife are able to generate more hours of participation in one of his real estate rental activities, they will not reach the material participation threshold. Consequently, the tax losses from the venture will not be deductible. To ensure deductibility, Ralph suggests the following plan:

• He will document the time he spends "thinking" about his rental activities.
• During the week, his wife will visit the apartment building to oversee (in a management role) the operations of the rentals.

• On weekends, he and his wife will visit the same units to further evaluate the operations.
• Also on the weekends, while they are doing their routine household shopping, they will be on the lookout for other rental properties to buy. Ralph plans to count both his and his wife's weekend hours toward the tally of total participation.

Ralph contends that the law clearly allows the efforts of one's spouse to count for purposes of the material participation tests. Likewise, nothing in the tax law requires taxpayers to be efficient in their hours of participation. How do you react?

© iStockphoto.com/LdF

Real Estate Rental Activities

The second exception is more significant in that it is not restricted to real estate professionals. This exception allows individuals to deduct up to $25,000 of losses from real estate rental activities against active and portfolio income.[26] The potential annual $25,000 deduction is reduced by 50 percent of the taxpayer's AGI in excess of $100,000. Thus, the entire deduction is phased out at $150,000 of AGI. If married individuals file separately, the $25,000 deduction is reduced to zero unless they lived apart for the entire year, in which case the loss amount is $12,500 each and the phaseout begins at $50,000. AGI for purposes of the phaseout is calculated without regard to IRA deductions, Social Security benefits, interest deductions on education loans, and net losses from passive activities.

To qualify for the $25,000 exception, a taxpayer must meet both of the following requirements:[27]

• Actively participate in the real estate rental activity.
• Own 10 percent or more (in value) of all interests in the activity during the entire taxable year (or shorter period during which the taxpayer held an interest in the activity).

The difference between *active participation* and *material participation* is that the former can be satisfied without regular, continuous, and substantial involvement in operations as long as the taxpayer participates in making management decisions in a significant and bona fide sense. In this context, relevant management decisions include decisions such as approving new tenants, deciding on rental terms, and approving capital or repair expenditures.

THE BIG PICTURE

Example 31

Return to the facts of *The Big Picture* on p. 11-1. If the Reswicks invest in the apartment rental limited partnership, their $25,000 loss would be deductible under the real estate rental activities exception. This assumes that they actively participate and own at least a 10% interest in the partnership. The loss will be deductible in each of the first four years of their investment before their at-risk basis has been exhausted (as explained earlier, the Reswick's original at-risk basis of $100,000 will be reduced to $0 over four years) even if they do not have passive income from other sources.

---

[26]§ 469(i).   [27]§ 469(i)(6).

TAX IN THE NEWS Refocused IRS Audits and New Reporting Requirements Expected to Produce Increased Tax Collections

In an August 2008 report, the Government Accountability Office (GAO) estimated that "at least 53 percent of individual taxpayers with rental real estate activity . . . misreported their rental real estate activity." With the current tax gap being measured in the hundreds of billions of dollars, targeting areas of intentional or unintentional noncompliance seems to make sense.

The GAO's report was followed by the release of a study in December 2010 conducted by the Treasury Inspector General for Tax Administration (TIGTA). In its report, TIGTA indicated that tax assessments of $27.3 million over a five-year period could result if the IRS were to audit more tax returns that reflect losses from rental real estate activity. The Treasury Inspector also recommended that taxpayers with losses from rental activity be required to report more information about these activities on their tax returns.

The IRS is taking these reports and recommendations to heart. As a result, taxpayers owning rental real estate should see additional tax compliance requirements soon. In addition, such investors should not be surprised to find themselves the target of an IRS audit in the future. TIGTA makes the point that even though the potential benefit of about $27 million is relatively small in light of the huge tax gap, even small improvements in the IRS's examination procedures "can increase the public confidence in the IRS's ability to enforce tax laws in a fair, equitable, and consistent manner."

Sources: "Actions Are Needed in the Identification, Selection, and Examination of Individual Tax Returns With Rental Real Estate Activity," Treasury Inspector General for Tax Administration, December 20, 2010, Reference Number: 2011-30-005; "Tax Gap: Actions That Could Improve Rental Real Estate Reporting Compliance," Government Accountability Office, August 2008, GAO-08-956.

The $25,000 allowance is available after all active participation rental losses and gains are netted and applied to other passive income. If a taxpayer has a real estate rental loss in excess of the amount that can be deducted under the real estate rental exception, that excess is treated as a passive loss.

Example 32

Brad, who has $90,000 of AGI before considering rental activities, has $85,000 of losses from a real estate rental activity in which he actively participates. He also actively participates in another real estate rental activity from which he has $25,000 of income. He has other passive income of $36,000. Of the net rental loss of $60,000 ($85,000 − $25,000), $36,000 is absorbed by the passive income, leaving $24,000 that can be deducted against active or portfolio income because of the availability of the $25,000 allowance.

The $25,000 offset allowance is an aggregate of both deductions and credits in deduction equivalents. The deduction equivalent of a passive activity credit is the amount of deductions that reduces the tax liability for the taxable year by an amount equal to the credit.[28] A taxpayer with $5,000 of credits and a tax bracket of 25 percent would have a deduction equivalent of $20,000 ($5,000 ÷ 25%).

If the total deduction and deduction equivalent exceed $25,000, the taxpayer must allocate the allowance on a pro rata basis, first among the losses (including real estate rental activity losses suspended in prior years) and then to credits in the following order: (1) credits other than rehabilitation and low-income housing credits, (2) rehabilitation credits, and (3) low-income housing credits.

Example 33

Kevin is an active participant in a real estate rental activity that produces $8,000 of income, $26,000 of deductions, and $1,500 of credits. Kevin, who is in the 25% tax bracket, may deduct the net passive loss of $18,000 ($8,000 − $26,000). After deducting the loss, he has an available deduction equivalent of $7,000 ($25,000 − $18,000 passive loss). Therefore, the maximum amount of credits he may claim is $1,750 ($7,000 × 25%). Because the actual credits are less than this amount, Kevin may claim the entire $1,500 credit.

---

[28]§ 469(j)(5).

Example 34

Kelly, who is in the 25% tax bracket, is an active participant in three separate real estate rental activities. The relevant tax results for each activity are as follows:

- Activity A: $20,000 of losses.
- Activity B: $10,000 of losses.
- Activity C: $4,200 of credits.

Kelly's deduction equivalent from the credits is $16,800 ($4,200 ÷ 25%). Therefore, the total passive deductions and deduction equivalents are $46,800 ($20,000 + $10,000 + $16,800), which exceeds the maximum allowable amount of $25,000. Consequently, Kelly must allocate pro rata first from among losses and then from among credits. Deductions from losses are limited as follows:

- Activity A {$25,000 × [$20,000 ÷ ($20,000 + $10,000)]} = $16,667.
- Activity B {$25,000 × [$10,000 ÷ ($20,000 + $10,000)]} = $8,333.

Because the amount of passive deductions exceeds the $25,000 maximum, the deduction balance of $5,000 and passive credits of $4,200 must be carried forward. Kelly's suspended losses and credits by activity are as follows:

	Total	Activity A	Activity B	Activity C
Allocated losses	$ 30,000	$ 20,000	$10,000	$ –0–
Allocated credits	4,200	–0–	–0–	4,200
Utilized losses	(25,000)	(16,667)	(8,333)	–0–
Suspended losses	5,000	3,333	1,667	–0–
Suspended credits	4,200	–0–	–0–	4,200

11-3f Dispositions of Passive Interests

LO.9

Determine the proper tax treatment upon the disposition of a passive activity.

Recall from an earlier discussion that if a taxpayer disposes of an entire interest in a passive activity, any suspended losses (and in certain cases, suspended credits) may be utilized when calculating the final economic gain or loss on the investment. In addition, if a loss ultimately results, that loss can offset other types of income. However, the consequences may differ if the activity is disposed of in a transaction that is other than a fully taxable transaction. The following sections discuss the treatment of suspended passive losses in other types of dispositions.

Disposition of a Passive Activity at Death

When a transfer of a taxpayer's interest occurs because of the taxpayer's death, suspended losses are allowed (to the decedent) to the extent they exceed the amount, if any, of the allowed step-up in basis.[29] Suspended losses that are equal to or less than the amount of the basis increase are, however, lost. The losses allowed generally are reported on the final return of the deceased taxpayer.

Example 35

Alyson dies with passive activity property having an adjusted basis of $40,000, suspended losses of $10,000, and a fair market value at the date of her death of $75,000. The increase (i.e., step-up) in basis (see Chapter 14) is $35,000 (fair market value at date of death in excess of adjusted basis). None of the $10,000 suspended loss is deductible on Alyson's final return or by the beneficiary. The suspended losses ($10,000) are lost because they do not exceed the step-up in basis ($35,000).

---

[29]§ 469(g)(2).

Example 36

Assume the same facts as in the previous example except that the property's fair market value at the date of Alyson's death is $47,000. Because the step-up in basis is only $7,000 ($47,000 − $40,000), the suspended losses allowed are limited to $3,000 ($10,000 suspended loss at time of death − $7,000 increase in basis). The $3,000 loss available to Alyson is reported on her final income tax return.

Disposition of a Passive Activity by Gift

In a disposition of a taxpayer's interest in a passive activity by gift, the suspended losses are added to the basis of the property.[30] As such, the suspended losses become permanently nondeductible to both the donor and the donee. Nonetheless, a tax *benefit* may be available to the donee for another reason. Due to the increase in the property's basis, greater depreciation deductions can result, and there will be less gain (or more loss) on a subsequent sale of the property. The side benefits of increased basis do not materialize if the recipient is a charity, as such organizations generally are not subject to income taxation.

Example 37

Carlton makes a gift to Yolanda of passive activity property having an adjusted basis of $40,000, suspended losses of $10,000, and a fair market value at the date of the gift of $100,000. Carlton cannot deduct the suspended losses in the year of the disposition. However, the suspended losses transfer with the property and are added to the adjusted basis of the property, thus becoming $50,000 in Yolanda's hands. Assuming Yolanda is able to sell the property for $105,000 soon after she receives the gift, her taxable gain would be $55,000 ($105,000 − $50,000), which reflects the benefit from the increased basis.

Installment Sale of a Passive Activity

An installment sale of a taxpayer's entire interest in a passive activity triggers recognition of the suspended losses.[31] The losses are allowed in each year of the installment obligation in the ratio that the gain recognized in each year bears to the total gain on the sale.

Example 38

Stan sells his entire interest in a passive activity for $100,000. His adjusted basis in the property is $60,000. If he uses the installment method, his gross profit ratio is 40% ($40,000/$100,000). If Stan receives a $20,000 down payment, he will recognize a gain of $8,000 (40% of $20,000). If the activity has a suspended loss of $25,000, Stan will deduct $5,000 [($8,000 ÷ $40,000) × $25,000] of the suspended loss in the first year.

The general rules relating to passive activity losses are reviewed in Concept Summary 11.1.

11-4 INVESTMENT INTEREST LIMITATION

As just described, well-to-do investors tried to use the Code for many years to generate deductible tax losses. As a result, Congress imposed special rules placing limitations on losses where the taxpayer was not at risk or where the losses were from passive activities. Another approach in using the tax law to create wealth involved the use of the interest deduction. By borrowing to purchase investments that would appreciate in the future, the interest on the debt was claimed as an ordinary deduction when paid. Later, when the asset was sold at a gain, only a capital gains tax was due on the appreciation. Thus, today's interest deduction could lead to tomorrow's capital gain.

LO.10

Identify restrictions placed on the deductibility of other investor losses and deductions, including those that apply to investment interest.

11-4a Limitation Imposed

In response, Congress has limited the deductibility of **investment interest**, which is interest paid on debt borrowed for the purpose of purchasing or continuing to

---

[30]§ 469(j)(6). [31]§ 469(g)(3).

CONCEPT SUMMARY 11.1

Passive Activity Loss Rules: Key Issues and Answers

What is the fundamental passive activity rule?	Passive activity losses may be deducted only against passive activity income and gains. Losses not allowed are suspended and used in future years.
Who is subject to the passive activity rules?	Individuals. Estates. Trusts. Personal service corporations. Closely held C corporations.
What is a passive activity?	Trade or business or income-producing activity in which the taxpayer does not materially participate during the year, or rental activities, subject to certain exceptions, regardless of the taxpayer's level of participation.
What is an activity?	One or more trade or business or rental activities that comprise an appropriate economic unit.
How is an appropriate economic unit determined?	Based on a reasonable application of the relevant facts and circumstances.
What is material participation?	In general, the taxpayer participates on a regular, continuous, and substantial basis. More specifically, when the taxpayer meets the conditions of one of the seven tests provided in the Regulations.
What is a rental activity?	In general, an activity where payments are received for the use of tangible property. Special rules apply to rental real estate.

hold investment property. The deduction for investment interest allowed during the tax year is limited to the lesser of the investment interest paid or net investment income.[32]

THE BIG PICTURE

Example 39

Return to the facts of *The Big Picture* on p. 11-1. If the Reswicks invest in the high-growth, low-yield portfolio of marketable securities, most of the investment return will consist of appreciation, which will not be taxed until the securities are sold. Relatively little of the current return will consist of currently taxable interest and dividend income. Assume that the interest and dividend income for the year from these securities equals $500 and that all of it is treated as investment income. If the investment interest expense on the $100,000 loan is $8,000, only $500 of this interest will be deductible this year (i.e., the deduction for the investment interest is limited to the $500 of net investment income).

Investment Income and Expenses

Net investment income, which serves as the ceiling on the deductibility of investment interest, is the excess of investment income over investment expenses. **Investment income** includes gross income from interest, annuities, and royalties not derived in the ordinary course of a trade or business.[33] However, investment

---

[32]§ 163(d)(1).   [33]§ 163(d)(4)(B).

income does not include any income taken into account when calculating income or loss from a passive activity.

Investment expenses are those deductible expenses directly connected with the production of investment income, such as brokerage and investment counsel fees. Investment expenses do not include interest expense.

11-4b Computation of Allowable Deduction

After net investment income is determined, the allowable deductible investment interest expense is calculated.

Example 40

Ethan's financial records for the year reflect the following:

Interest income from bank savings account	$10,000
Taxable annuity receipts	5,500
Investment counsel fee	1,100
Safe deposit box rental (to hold annuity documents)	200
Investment interest expense	17,000

Ethan's investment income amounts to $15,500 ($10,000 + $5,500) and investment expenses total $1,300 ($1,100 + $200). Therefore, his net investment income is $14,200 ($15,500 − $1,300). Consequently, the investment interest deduction is limited to $14,200, the lesser of investment interest paid or net investment income.

The amount of investment interest disallowed is carried over to future years. In Example 40, therefore, the amount that is carried over to the following year is $2,800 ($17,000 investment interest expense − $14,200 allowed). No limit is placed on the length of the carryover period.[34] The investment interest expense deduction is determined by completing Form 4952. (Investment Interest Deduction).

11-5 OTHER INVESTMENT LOSSES

The investment activities summarized below are discussed elsewhere in this text (see the references provided).

- Sales of securities held as investments for less than basis result in capital losses. These losses can offset capital gains. In the case of individual taxpayers, excess losses are applied against ordinary income up to $3,000 (§ 1211). Any remaining excess capital losses are carried over for use in future years (§ 1212). See Chapter 16 for additional discussion.
- Securities held as an investment that become worthless produce capital losses. The losses are usually long-term because they are treated as occurring on the last day of the year in which the securities become worthless [§ 165(g)(1)]. Because the securities must be completely worthless, determining the year when this takes place is often difficult. See Chapter 7 for additional discussion.
- Losses on small business stock (i.e., stock that qualifies under § 1244) are treated as ordinary losses up to a maximum of $100,000. Thus, the limitations placed on capital losses (see above) are avoided. See Chapter 7 for additional discussion.
- As discussed in Chapter 6, vacation homes that are rented for part of the year may generate investment losses depending on the extent of the rental period as compared to time devoted to personal use (§ 280A). If sufficient rental activity takes place, the facility may be treated as rental property. As such, any losses could be subject to the passive loss rules. See the discussion earlier in this chapter.
- When an activity is classified as a hobby, any losses resulting are limited to the income from the activity [§ 183(b)(2)]. If the activity is not a hobby (i.e., a profit motive controls), however, full deduction of the losses is allowed [§§ 162 and 212(2)]. See the relevant discussion of hobby losses in Chapter 6.

---

[34]§ 163(d)(2).

11-6 TAX PLANNING

11-6a Utilizing Passive Losses

LO.11

Suggest tax planning strategies to minimize the effect of the passive loss and investment interest limitations.

Perhaps the biggest challenge individuals face with the passive loss rules is to recognize the potential impact of the rules and then to structure their affairs to minimize this impact. Taxpayers who have passive activity losses (PALs) should adopt a strategy of generating passive activity income that can be sheltered by existing passive losses. One approach is to buy an interest in a passive activity that is generating income (referred to as passive income generators, or PIGs). Then the PAL can offset income from the PIG. From a tax perspective, it would be foolish to buy a loss-generating passive activity unless one has other passive income to shelter or the activity is rental real estate that can qualify for the $25,000 exception or the exception available to real estate professionals.

If a taxpayer does invest in an activity that produces losses subject to the passive loss rules, the following strategies may help minimize the loss of current deductions:

- If money is borrowed to finance the purchase of a passive activity, the associated interest expense is generally treated as part of any passive loss. Consequently, by using more available (i.e., not borrowed) cash to purchase the passive investment, the investor will need less debt and will incur less interest expense. By incurring less interest expense, a possible suspended passive loss deduction is reduced.
- If the investor does not have sufficient cash readily available for the larger down payment, it can be obtained by borrowing against the equity in his or her personal residence. The interest expense on such debt will be deductible under the qualified residence interest provisions (see Chapter 10) and will not be subject to the passive loss limitations. Thus, the taxpayer avoids the passive loss limitation and secures a currently deductible interest expense.

As explained earlier, unusable passive losses often accumulate and provide no current tax benefit because the taxpayer has no passive income. When the taxpayer disposes of the entire interest in a passive activity, however, any suspended losses from that activity are used to reduce the taxable gain. If any taxable gain still remains, it can be offset by losses from other passive activities. As a result, the taxpayer should carefully select the year in which to dispose of a passive activity. It is to the taxpayer's advantage to wait until sufficient passive losses have accumulated to offset any gain recognized on the asset's disposition.

Example 41	Bill, a calendar year taxpayer, owns interests in two passive activities: Activity A, which he plans to sell in December of this year at a gain of $100,000, and Activity B, which he plans to keep indefinitely. Current and suspended losses associated with Activity B total $60,000, and Bill expects losses from the activity to be $40,000 next year. If Bill sells Activity A this year, the $100,000 gain can be offset by the current and suspended losses of $60,000 from Activity B, producing a net taxable gain of $40,000. However, if Bill delays the sale of Activity A until January of next year, the $100,000 gain will be fully offset by the $100,000 of losses generated by Activity B ($60,000 current and prior losses + $40,000 next year's loss). Consequently, by postponing the sale by one month, he could avoid recognizing $40,000 of gain that would otherwise result.

Taxpayers with passive losses should consider the level of their involvement in all other trades or businesses in which they have an interest. If they show that they do not materially participate in a profitable activity, the activity becomes a passive activity. Any income generated by the profitable business then could be sheltered by current and suspended passive losses. Family partnerships in which certain members do not materially participate would qualify. The silent partner in any general partnership engaged in a trade or business would also qualify.

Example 42

Gail has an investment in a limited partnership that produces annual passive losses of approximately $25,000. She also owns a newly acquired interest in a convenience store where she works. Her share of the store's income is $35,000. If she works enough to be classified as a material participant, her $35,000 share of income is treated as active income. This results in $35,000 being subject to tax every year, while her $25,000 loss is suspended. However, if Gail reduces her involvement at the store so that she is not a material participant, the $35,000 of income receives passive treatment. Consequently, the $35,000 of income can be offset by the $25,000 passive loss, resulting in only $10,000 being subject to tax. Thus, by reducing her involvement, Gail ensures that the income from the profitable trade or business receives passive treatment and can then be used to absorb passive losses from other passive activities.

The impact of the passive loss rules often extend to other seemingly unrelated Code sections. For example, because of the restrictive nature of the passive activity loss rules, it may be advantageous for a taxpayer to use a vacation home enough to convert it to a second residence. This would enable all of the qualified interest and real estate taxes to be deducted without limitation. However, this strategy would lead to the loss of other deductions, such as repairs, maintenance, and insurance. See Examples 25 and 28 and the related discussion in Chapter 6.

As this chapter has shown, the passive loss rules can have a dramatic effect on a taxpayer's ability to claim passive losses currently. As a result, it is important to keep accurate records of all sources of income and losses, particularly any suspended passive losses and credits and the activities to which they relate, so that their potential tax benefit will not be lost.

11-6b Planning with Investment Interest Limitation

The term *investment income* includes net capital gain and qualified dividend income only if the taxpayer *elects* to treat them as such. For this purpose,

- net capital gain includes gain attributable to property held for investment and
- qualified dividend income includes dividends that are taxed at the same marginal rate that is applicable to a net capital gain.

By electing to include net capital gain and qualified dividend income as components of investment income, the amount of investment interest deductible in a particular year likewise increases. Form 4952 is used to make such an election. However, the election comes with a cost and is available only if the taxpayer agrees to reduce amounts qualifying for the preferential rates that otherwise apply to net capital gain (see Chapter 16) and qualified dividends (refer to Chapter 4) by an equivalent amount.[35]

Example 43

Terry incurred $13,000 of interest expense related to her investments during the year. Her investment income included $4,000 of interest, $2,000 of qualified dividends, and a $5,000 net capital gain on the sale of investment securities. If Terry does not make the election to include the net capital gain and qualified dividends in investment income, her investment income for purposes of computing the investment income limitation is $4,000 (interest income). If she does make the election, her investment income is $11,000 ($4,000 interest + $2,000 qualified dividends + $5,000 net capital gain). In that case, $11,000 of her interest expense, rather than $4,000, is deductible currently.

Should Terry in the previous example make the election to include the additional $7,000 of qualified dividends and net capital gain as investment income? By doing so, the current year investment interest deduction increases by $7,000, and the investment interest deduction potentially carried forward to future years is reduced by the same amount. That is, the election allows for an acceleration of the investment interest deduction. As Terry evaluates her decision, she should consider the following points:

---

[35]Reg. §1.163(d)–1.

- The election would make sense only if her marginal ordinary income tax rate exceeds the applicable capital gains rate.
- Using time value of money concepts, she should compare the tax cost of postponing the interest deduction to a subsequent year with the impact of losing the benefit from the preferential capital gains rate. In performing this analysis, consideration should be given to the length of the deferral of the investment interest deduction and the current and future years' tax brackets.

11-6c Effect of Medicare Contribution Surtax on Net Investment Income

As if the passive loss and investment interest limitations are not complicated enough, beginning in 2013, individuals, estates, and trusts are subject to a 3.8 percent surtax on net investment income. This new tax provision arose as a part of the Federal health care reform enacted in 2010.[36] Net investment income *for this purpose* generally includes amounts such as interest, dividends, long- and short-term capital gains, royalties, rents, and income from passive activities. The tax is levied at the flat 3.8 percent rate on the lesser of the taxpayer's net investment income or the excess of modified AGI over a threshold amount. The threshold amounts for individuals are $250,000 for surviving spouses and taxpayers filing a joint return, $125,000 for married taxpayers filing separate returns, and $200,000 for all other individual taxpayers. As a consequence, this tax is aimed at higher-income taxpayers. Unfortunately, this tax could very well come as a surprise to taxpayers, potentially increasing the marginal capital gain tax rate to 23.8 percent (from 20 percent) and the marginal ordinary income tax bracket to 43.4 percent (from 39.6 percent). See Chapter 13 for a complete discussion of this surtax.

REFOCUS ON THE BIG PICTURE

INVESTOR LOSS LIMITATIONS CAN SIGNIFICANTLY AFFECT INVESTMENT RETURNS

© Rido/Shutterstock.com

The objective for most investors should be to maximize after-tax wealth from among investment alternatives. This requires an understanding of the relevant tax restrictions that apply to certain expenses and losses arising from various investment choices. The after-tax returns from the three alternatives the Reswicks are considering may be affected by the at-risk, passive activity, and investment interest limitations.

The high-growth, low-yield portfolio is expected to generate very little, if any, current interest and dividend income (i.e., investment income). Nonetheless, if the broker's prediction is correct, the market value of the securities will grow by approximately 10 percent a year. However, the annual $8,000 interest expense on the debt incurred to purchase the securities may not be deductible as investment interest due to the lack of investment income. Unless investment income is generated from this or some other source, the interest will not be deductible until the securities are sold (see Example 39). In addition, to the extent that any capital gain from the portfolio's sale is treated as investment income, the gain will not be subject to preferential capital gains rates (see Example 43). As a result, the net after-tax return will be impaired because of the investment interest limitation.

The net returns from the other two investment choices will be diminished by the at-risk and passive activity loss rules in addition to the investment interest limitation. The projected 10 percent return is apparently contingent on the investor being able to utilize the current tax losses as they arise. These benefits will be deferred because the at-risk and passive activity loss rules delay the timing of the deductions. For example, in the case of the orange grove investment, none of the

---

[36]§ 1411.

passive losses are deductible until year 6, when the investment is expected to produce passive income (see Example 29). In the real estate rental venture, however, Jim and Trudy could deduct the $25,000 passive loss under the exception for rental real estate for the first four years (see Example 31); the at-risk rules would limit any additional losses in year 5 to the at-risk amount. Consequently, because the at-risk and passive loss rules limit the tax losses flowing to the Reswicks, the after-tax return will not be nearly as high as their broker predicts.

What If?

If the Reswicks decide that the investment in marketable securities is their best option, could they modify their plan so that they avoid the restriction imposed by the investment interest limitation? Jim and Trudy's net after-tax return would improve if the interest cost of financing their investment could be deducted as incurred. They could finance their investment by borrowing up to $100,000 against the equity in their home (see Chapter 10). The interest on the home equity loan would be fully deductible; consequently, the after-tax return from their investment would increase. Furthermore, any gain recognition would be deferred until the securities are sold, and the tax on the gain would be subject to the preferential capital gains rate.

Key Terms

Active income, 11-5

At-risk limitation, 11-3

Closely held corporation, 11-9

Investment income, 11-22

Investment interest, 11-21

Material participation, 11-13

Net investment income, 11-22

Passive loss, 11-3

Personal service corporation, 11-9

Portfolio income, 11-5

Rental activity, 11-14

Significant participation activity, 11-14

Tax shelters, 11-2

Discussion Questions

1. **LO.1** Identify two provisions designed to limit the tax benefits a taxpayer may obtain from a tax shelter investment. Describe how these rules reduce or defer the recognition of tax losses.

2. **LO.2** Ken invested $200,000 for a 30% interest in a partnership in which he is a material participant. The partnership borrowed $250,000 from a bank and used the proceeds to acquire equipment. What is Ken's at-risk amount if the $250,000 was borrowed on a nonrecourse loan? How could Ken's at-risk amount differ if the partnership's business involved a real estate development activity and the debt was secured by land the partnership owns?

3. **LO.2** List some events that increase or decrease an investor's at-risk amount. What are some strategies that a taxpayer can employ to increase the at-risk amount to claim a higher deduction for losses?

4. **LO.2, 3** Roberto invested $18,000 in a chicken production operation. Using nonrecourse notes, the business purchases $120,000 worth of grain to feed the chickens. If Roberto's share of the expense is $26,000, how much can he deduct?

5. **LO.3** Explain the meaning of the terms *active income*, *portfolio income*, and *passive income*.

6. **LO.3** Carlos owns an interest in an activity that produces a $100,000 loss during the year. Would he prefer to have the activity classified as active or passive? Explain.

7. **LO.3** Kim owns an interest in an activity that produces $100,000 of income during the year. Would Kim prefer to have the activity classified as active or passive? Discuss.

8. **LO.3** Pamela owns a passive activity acquired several years ago that has incurred losses since its acquisition. This is the only passive activity she has ever owned. How will these passive losses affect Pamela's tax computation when she disposes of the activity?

9. **LO.3** Upon a taxable disposition of a passive activity, the taxpayer can utilize any suspended losses and credits related to that activity. Do you agree? Explain.

10. **LO.3** Discuss whether the passive loss rules apply to the following: individuals, closely held C corporations, S corporations, partnerships, and personal service corporations.

11. **LO.3** New-Tech Services, Inc., is owned by four engineers, all of whom work full-time for the corporation. The corporation has eight other full-time employees, all on the clerical staff. New-Tech provides consulting services to inventors. The corporation has invested in a passive activity that produces a $60,000 loss this year. Can New-Tech deduct the loss in the current year? Explain.

12. **LO.3** Bronze Corporation has $100,000 of active income, $55,000 of portfolio income, and a $55,000 passive loss. Under what circumstances is Bronze prohibited from deducting the loss? Allowed to deduct the loss?

13. **LO.4** Discuss what constitutes a passive activity.

14. **LO.4** Under what circumstances may the IRS regroup activities in a different way than the taxpayer?

15. **LO.5** What is the significance of the term *material participation*? Why is the extent of a taxpayer's participation in an activity important in determining whether a loss from the activity is deductible or nondeductible?

16. **LO.5** How many hours must a participant work in a nonrental activity to be guaranteed material participation status?

Decision Making   17. **LO.5** Suzanne owns interests in a bagel shop, a lawn and garden store, and a convenience store. Several full-time employees work at each of the enterprises. As of the end of November of the current year, Suzanne has worked 150 hours in the bagel shop, 250 hours at the lawn and garden store, and 70 hours at the convenience store. In reviewing her financial records, you learn that she has no passive investments that are generating income and that she expects these three ventures collectively to produce a loss. What recommendation would you offer Suzanne as she plans her activities for the remainder of the year?

18. **LO.5, 11** John, an engineer, operates a separate business that he acquired eight years ago. If he participates 85 hours in the business and it incurs a loss of $34,000, under what circumstances can John claim an active loss?

Issue ID   19. **LO.2, 3, 5** Rita retired from public accounting after a long and successful career of 45 years. As part of her retirement package, she continues to share in the profits and losses of the firm, albeit at a lower rate than when she was working full-time. Because Rita wants to stay busy during her retirement years, she has invested and works in a local hardware business, operated as a partnership. Unfortunately, the business has recently gone through a slump and has not been generating profits. Identify relevant tax issues for Rita.

20. **LO.5** Some types of work are counted in applying the material participation standards, and some types are not counted. Discuss and give examples of each type.

Issue ID   21. **LO.5** Last year Alan's accountant informed him that he could not claim any of his passive activity losses on his income tax return because of his lack of material participation. To circumvent the tax problem this year, Alan tells his wife that she may have to put in some time at the various businesses. Identify the tax issues that Alan faces.

22. **LO.5** Sean, a limited partner in Ivy Nursery, is informed that his portion of the entity's current loss is $18,000. As a limited partner, can Sean assume that his share of the partnership loss is a passive loss? Explain.

23. **LO.6** Explain why some rental activities may not be *treated* as such under the passive loss rules.

24. **LO.4, 5, 6** How is *passive activity* defined in the Code? What aspects of the definition have been clarified by final or Temporary Regulations?

25. **LO.6** What is a *real estate professional?* Why could qualifying for this status be beneficial under the passive loss rules?

26. **LO.8** Caroline owns a real estate rental activity that produces a loss of $65,000 during the current year. Under what circumstances can Caroline treat the entire loss as nonpassive?

27. **LO.2, 3, 4, 5, 6, 7** In the current year, David and Debbie Wayland, both successful physicians, made a cash investment for a limited partnership interest in a California berry farm. In addition to the cash obtained from the investors, management borrowed a substantial sum to purchase assets necessary for the farm's operations. The Waylands' investment adviser told them that their share of the tax loss in the first year alone would be in excess of their initial cash investment. This would be followed by several more years of losses. They feel confident that their interest in the berry farm is a sound investment. Identify the tax issues facing the Waylands.   *Issue ID*

28. **LO.4** Since his college days, Charles has developed an entrepreneurial streak. After working in his family's grocery business, he starts several ventures on his own. Even though Charles is independently wealthy, he is looking forward to working in each of the ventures. He plans to "drop in" on the businesses from time to time between personal trips to Europe and the Caribbean. As of the end of the year, he has established computer software stores in Dayton (Ohio), Austin, and Seattle; bagel bakeries in Albany, Athens (Georgia), and Tallahassee; and mountain bike and ski rental shops in small towns in Vermont, West Virginia, Colorado, and California. Identify the tax issues facing Charles.   *Issue ID*

29. **LO.5, 8** Elizabeth owns an interest in a dress shop that has three full-time employees; during the year, she works 450 hours in the shop. Elizabeth also owns an apartment building with no employees in which she works 1,200 hours a year. Is either activity a passive activity? Explain.

30. **LO.8** Brad owns a small townhouse complex that generates a loss during the year. Under what circumstances can Brad deduct a loss from the rental activity? What limitations apply?

31. **LO.8** In connection with passive activities, what is a *deduction equivalent* and how is it computed?

32. **LO.8, 11** Betty and Steve plan to use some of an inheritance for a beach-related investment. They identify two possibilities that seem worthwhile. First, they would purchase a beach cottage and use it for both personal and rental purposes. Second, they would pool their money with Steve's brother and purchase several cottages. One of the cottages would be held for personal use, while the others would be held for rental use. Identify the tax issues facing Betty and Steve.   *Issue ID*

33. **LO.10** What is *investment interest expense?* Describe the basic rules that may limit its deductibility.

Problems

34. **LO.2** In 2013, Fred invested $50,000 in a general partnership. Fred's interest is not considered to be a passive activity. If his share of the partnership losses is $35,000 in 2013 and $25,000 in 2014, how much can he deduct in each year?

35. **LO.2** In the current year, Bill Parker (54 Oak Drive, St. Paul, MN 55164) is considering making an investment of $60,000 in Best Choice Partnership. The prospectus provided by Bill's broker indicates that the partnership investment is not a passive activity and that Bill's share of the entity's loss in the current year will likely be $40,000, while his share of the   *Communications*

partnership loss next year will probably be $25,000. Write a letter to Bill in which you indicate how the losses would be treated for tax purposes in the current year and the following year.

Decision Making

36. **LO.2, 11** Heather wants to invest $40,000 in a relatively safe venture and has discovered two alternatives that would produce the following reportable ordinary income and loss over the next three years:

Year	Alternative 1 Income (Loss)	Alternative 2 Income (Loss)
1	($20,000)	($48,000)
2	(28,000)	32,000
3	72,000	40,000

She is interested in the after-tax effects of these alternatives over a three-year horizon. Assume that Heather's investment portfolio produces sufficient passive income to offset any potential passive loss that may arise from these alternatives, that her cost of capital is 6% (the present value factors are .9434, .8900, and .8396), that she is in the 25% tax bracket, that each investment alternative possesses equal growth potential, and that each alternative exposes her to comparable financial risk. In addition, assume that in the loss years for each alternative, there is no cash flow from or to the investment (i.e., the loss is due to depreciation), while in those years when the income is positive, cash flows to Heather equal the amount of the income. Based on these facts, compute the present value of these two investment alternatives and determine which option Heather should choose.

37. **LO.1, 3** Dorothy acquired a 100% interest in two passive activities: Activity A in January 2009 and Activity B in 2010. Through 2012, Activity A was profitable, but it produced losses of $200,000 in 2013 and $100,000 in 2014. Dorothy has passive income from Activity B of $20,000 in 2013 and $40,000 in 2014. After offsetting passive income, how much of the net losses may she deduct?

38. **LO.1, 3** A number of years ago, Kay acquired an interest in a partnership in which she is not a material participant. Kay's basis in her partnership interest at the beginning of 2013 is $40,000. Kay's share of the partnership loss is $35,000 in 2013, while her share of the partnership income is $15,000 in 2014. How much may Kay deduct in 2013 and 2014, assuming she owns no other passive activities?

39. **LO.3** Mike, an attorney, earns $200,000 from his law practice and receives $45,000 in dividends and interest during the year. In addition, he incurs a loss of $50,000 from an investment in a passive activity acquired three years ago. What is Mike's net income for the current year after considering the passive investment?

Decision Making

40. **LO.3, 11** Emily has $100,000 that she wants to invest and is considering the following two options:

- Option A: Investment in Redbird Mutual Fund, which is expected to produce interest income of $8,000 per year.
- Option B: Investment in Cardinal Limited Partnership (buys, sells, and operates wine vineyards). Emily's share of the partnership's ordinary income and loss over the next three years would be as follows:

Year	Income (Loss)
1	($ 8,000)
2	(2,000)
3	34,000

Emily is interested in the after-tax effects of these alternatives over a three-year horizon. Assume that Emily's investment portfolio produces ample passive income to offset any passive losses that may be generated. Her cost of capital is 8% (the present value factors are .92593, .85734, and .79383), and she is in the 28% tax bracket. The two investment alternatives possess equal growth potential and comparable financial risk. Based on these facts, compute the present value of these two investment alternatives and determine which option Emily should choose.

41. **LO.3** Ray acquired an activity several years ago, and in the current year, it generates a loss of $50,000. Ray has AGI of $140,000 before considering the loss from the activity. If the activity is a bakery and Ray is not a material participant, what is his AGI?

42. **LO.3, 11** Jorge owns two passive investments, Activity A and Activity B. He plans to dispose of Activity A in the current year or next year. Juanita has offered to buy Activity A this year for an amount that would produce a taxable passive gain to Jorge of $115,000. However, if the sale, for whatever reason, is not made to Juanita, Jorge believes that he could find a buyer who would pay about $7,000 less than Juanita. Passive losses and gains generated (and expected to be generated) by Activity B follow:

Decision Making

Two years ago	($35,000)
Last year	(35,000)
This year	(8,000)
Next year	(30,000)
Future years	Minimal profits

All of Activity B's losses are suspended. Should Jorge close the sale of Activity A with Juanita this year, or should he wait until next year and sell to another buyer? Jorge is in the 28% tax bracket.

43. **LO.3** Sarah has investments in four passive activity partnerships purchased several years ago. Last year the income and losses were as follows:

Activity	Income (Loss)
A	$ 30,000
B	(30,000)
C	(15,000)
D	(5,000)

In the current year, she sold her interest in Activity D for a $10,000 gain. Activity D, which had been profitable until last year, had a current loss of $1,500. How will the sale of Activity D affect Sarah's taxable income in the current year?

44. **LO.3** Leon sells his interest in a passive activity for $100,000. Determine the tax effect of the sale based on each of the following independent facts:
   a. Adjusted basis in this investment is $35,000. Losses from prior years that were not deductible due to the passive loss restrictions total $40,000.
   b. Adjusted basis in this investment is $75,000. Losses from prior years that were not deductible due to the passive loss restrictions total $40,000.
   c. Adjusted basis in this investment is $75,000. Losses from prior years that were not deductible due to the passive loss restrictions total $40,000. In addition, suspended credits total $10,000.

45. **LO.3** Ash, Inc., a closely held personal service corporation, has $100,000 of passive losses. In addition, Ash has $80,000 of active business income and $20,000 of portfolio income. How much of the passive loss may Ash use to offset the other types of income?

46. **LO.3** In the current year, White, Inc., earns $400,000 from operations and receives $36,000 in dividends and interest from various portfolio investments. White also pays $150,000 to acquire a 20% interest in a passive activity that produces a $200,000 loss.
   a. Assuming that White is a personal service corporation, how will these transactions affect its taxable income?
   b. Same as (a), except that White is closely held but not a personal service corporation.

47. **LO.2, 3, 7, 11** Kristin Graf (123 Baskerville Mill Road, Jamison, PA 18929) is trying to decide how to invest a $10,000 inheritance. One option is to make an additional investment in Rocky Road Excursions in which she has an at-risk basis of $0, suspended losses under the at-risk rules of $7,000, and suspended passive losses of $1,000. If Kristin makes this investment, her share of the expected profits this year will be $8,000. If her investment stays the same, her share of profits from Rocky Road Excursions will be $1,000. Another option is to invest $10,000 as a limited partner in the Ragged Mountain Winery;

Decision Making

Communications

this investment will produce passive income of $9,000. Write a letter to Kristin to review the tax consequences of each alternative. Kristin is in the 28% tax bracket.

Decision Making

48. **LO.2, 3, 7, 11** The end of the year is approaching, and Maxine has begun to focus on ways of minimizing her income tax liability. Several years ago she purchased an investment in Teal Limited Partnership, which is subject to the at-risk and the passive activity loss rules. (Last year Maxine sold a different investment that was subject to these rules and that produced passive income.) She believes that her investment in Teal has good long-term economic prospects. However, it has been generating tax losses for several years in a row. In fact, when she was discussing last year's income tax return with her tax accountant, he said that unless "things change" with respect to her investments, she would not be able to deduct losses this year.
    a. What was the accountant referring to in his comment?
    b. You learn that Maxine's current at-risk basis in her investment is $1,000 and that her share of the current loss is expected to be $13,000. Based on these facts, how will her loss be treated?
    c. After reviewing her situation, Maxine's financial adviser suggests that she invest at least an additional $12,000 in Teal to ensure a full loss deduction in the current year. How do you react to his suggestion?
    d. What would you suggest Maxine consider as she attempts to maximize her current-year deductible loss?

49. **LO.2, 3, 7** A number of years ago, Lee acquired a 20% interest in the BlueSky Partnership for $60,000. The partnership was profitable through 2013, and Lee's amount at risk in the partnership interest was $120,000 at the beginning of 2014. BlueSky incurred a loss of $400,000 in 2014 and reported income of $200,000 in 2015. Assuming that Lee is not a material participant, how much of his loss from BlueSky Partnership is deductible in 2014 and 2015? Consider the at-risk and passive loss rules, and assume Lee owns no other passive investments.

50. **LO.2, 3, 5, 7** Grace acquired an activity four years ago. The loss from the activity is $50,000 in the current year (at-risk basis of $40,000 as of the beginning of the year). Without considering the loss from the activity, she has gross income of $140,000. If the activity is a convenience store and Grace is a material participant, what is the effect of the activity on her taxable income?

51. **LO.2, 3, 5, 7** Jonathan, a physician, earns $200,000 from his practice. He also receives $18,000 in dividends and interest from various portfolio investments. During the year, he pays $45,000 to acquire a 20% interest in a partnership that produces a $300,000 loss. Compute Jonathan's AGI, assuming that:
    a. He does not participate in the operations of the partnership.
    b. He is a material participant in the operations of the partnership.

52. **LO.2, 3, 7** Five years ago Gerald invested $150,000 in a passive activity, his sole investment venture. On January 1, 2013, his amount at risk in the activity was $30,000. His shares of the income and losses were as follows:

Year	Income (Loss)
2013	($40,000)
2014	(30,000)
2015	50,000

How much can Gerald deduct in 2013 and 2014? What is his taxable income from the activity in 2015? Consider the at-risk rules as well as the passive loss rules.

Communications

53. **LO.3, 8** Several years ago Benny Jackson (125 Hill Street, Charleston, WV 25311) acquired an apartment building that currently generates a loss of $60,000. Benny's AGI is $130,000 before considering the loss. The apartment building is in an exclusive part of the city, and Benny is an active participant. Write a letter to Benny explaining what effect the loss will have on his AGI.

54. **LO.3, 8** This year Maria works 1,200 hours as a computer consultant, 320 hours in a real estate development business, and 400 hours in real estate rental activities. Juan, her husband, works 250 hours in the real estate development business and 180 hours in the real estate rental business. Maria earns $60,000 as a computer consultant, while she and

Juan lost $18,000 in the real estate development business and $26,000 in the real estate rental business. How should they treat the losses?

55. **LO.3, 8, 11** Bonnie and Jake (ages 35 and 36, respectively) are married with no dependents and live in Montana (not a community property state). Because Jake has large medical expenses, they seek your advice about filing separately to save taxes. Their income and expenses for 2014 are as follows:

Decision Making

Bonnie's salary	$ 42,500
Jake's salary	26,000
Interest income (joint)	1,500
Rental loss from actively managed rental property	(23,000)
Jake's unreimbursed medical expenses	8,500
All other itemized deductions:*	
Bonnie	9,000
Jake	3,400

*None subject to limitations

Determine whether Bonnie and Jake should file jointly or separately for 2014.

56. **LO.3, 8, 11** Mary and Charles have owned a beach cottage on the New Jersey shore for several years and have always used it as a family retreat. When they acquired the property, they had no intentions of renting it. Because family circumstances have changed, they are considering using the cottage for only two weeks a year and renting it for the remainder of the year. Their AGI approximates $80,000 per year, and they are in the 32% tax bracket (combined Federal and state). Interest and real estate taxes total $8,000 per year and are expected to continue at this level in the foreseeable future. If Mary and Charles rent the property, their *incremental* revenue and expenses are projected to be:

Decision Making

Rent income	$ 22,000
Rental commissions	(4,000)
Maintenance expenses	(9,000)
Depreciation expense	(10,000)

If the cottage is converted to rental property, they plan to be actively involved in key rental and maintenance decisions. Given the tax effects of converting the property to rental use, would the cash flow from renting the property be enough to meet the $12,000 annual mortgage payment? Explain.

57. **LO.3, 8** During the current year, Gene, a CPA, performs services as follows: 1,800 hours in his tax practice and 50 hours in an apartment leasing operation in which he has a 15% interest. Because of his oversight duties, Gene is considered to be an active participant. He expects that his share of the loss realized from the apartment leasing operation will be $30,000 and that his tax practice will show a profit of approximately $80,000. Gene is single and has no other income. Discuss the character and treatment of the income and losses generated by these activities.

58. **LO.3, 8** Ida, who has AGI of $80,000 before considering rental activities, is active in three separate real estate rental activities and is in the 28% tax bracket. She has $12,000 of losses from Activity A, $18,000 of losses from Activity B, and income of $10,000 from Activity C. She also has $2,100 of tax credits from Activity A. Calculate the deductions and credits that she is allowed and the suspended losses and credits.

59. **LO.8** Ella has $105,000 of losses from a real estate rental activity in which she actively participates. She has other rental income of $25,000 and other passive income of $32,000. How much rental loss can Ella deduct against active and portfolio income (ignoring the at-risk rules)? Does she have any suspended losses to carry over? Explain.

60. **LO.9** At death, Francine owns an interest in a passive activity property (adjusted basis of $160,000, suspended losses of $16,000, and fair market value of $170,000). What is deductible on Francine's final income tax return?

61. **LO.9** In the current year, Abe gives an interest in a passive activity to his daughter, Andrea. The value of the interest at the date of the gift is $25,000, and its adjusted basis

to Abe is $13,000. During the time that Abe owned the investment, losses of $3,000 could not be deducted because of the passive loss limitations. What is the tax treatment of the suspended passive activity losses to Abe and Andrea?

62. **LO.9** Tonya sells a passive activity in the current year for $150,000. Her adjusted basis in the activity is $50,000, and she uses the installment method of reporting the gain. The activity has suspended losses of $12,000. Tonya receives $60,000 in the year of sale. What is her gain? How much of the suspended losses can she deduct?

Decision Making

Communications

63. **LO.10, 11** In 2014, Kathleen Tweardy incurs $30,000 of interest expense related to her investments. Her investment income includes $7,500 of interest, $6,000 of qualified dividends, and a $12,000 net capital gain on the sale of securities. Kathleen asks you to compute the amount of her deduction for investment interest, taking into consideration any options she might have. In addition, she wants your suggestions as to any tax planning alternatives that are available. Write a letter to her that contains your advice. Kathleen lives at 11934 Briarpatch Drive, Midlothian, VA 23113.

64. **LO.10** Helen borrowed $150,000 to acquire a parcel of land to be held for investment purposes. During 2014, she paid interest of $12,000 on the loan. She had AGI of $90,000 for the year. Other items related to Helen's investments include the following:

Investment income	$11,000
Long-term capital gain on sale of stock	3,500
Investment counsel fees	200

Helen is unmarried and does not itemize her deductions.
a. Determine Helen's investment interest deduction for 2014.
b. Discuss the treatment of the portion of Helen's investment interest that is disallowed in 2014.

Research Problems

THOMSON REUTERS

CHECKPOINT®

Note: Solutions to Research Problems can be prepared by using the **Checkpoint®** **Student Edition** online research product, which is available to accompany this text. It is also possible to prepare solutions to the Research Problems by using tax research materials found in a standard tax library.

Research Problem 1. Carol is a successful physician who owns 100% of her incorporated medical practice. She and her husband, Dick, are considering the purchase of a commercial office building located near the local community hospital. If they purchase the building, Carol will move her medical practice to the new location and rent space for an arm's length price. The rent income Carol and Dick receive will be available to absorb passive losses generated by other passive activities they own. The net effect of this arrangement is a reduction in their income tax liability. Will Carol and Dick's plan work? Why or why not?

Research Problem 2. Five years ago Bridget decided to purchase a limited partnership interest in a fast-food restaurant conveniently located near the campus of Southeast State University. The general partner of the restaurant venture promised her that the investment would prove to be a winner. During the process of capitalizing the business, $2 million was borrowed from Northside Bank; however, each of the partners was required to pledge as collateral personal assets to satisfy the bank loan in the event the restaurant defaulted. Bridget pledged shares of publicly traded stock (worth $200,000, basis of $75,000) to satisfy the bank's requirement.

The restaurant did a good business until just recently, when flagrant health code violations were discovered and widely publicized by the media. As a result, business has declined to a point where the restaurant's continued existence is doubtful. In addition, the $2 million loan is now due for payment. Because the restaurant cannot pay, the bank has called for the collateral provided by the partners to be used to satisfy the debt. Bridget sells the pledged stock for $200,000 and forwards the proceeds to the bank. Bridget believes that her share of the restaurant's current and suspended passive losses can offset the $125,000 gain from the stock sale. As a result, after netting the passive losses against the gain, none of the gain is subject to tax.

How do you react to Bridget's position?

Research Problem 3. David Drayer (2632 Holkham Drive, Lewisburg, PA 17837) is the lead partner in a local accounting firm whose practice consists of tax consulting and compliance. The firm also serves clients by providing write-up and payroll processing services. As his firm has grown, David has developed various ways to build its business.

Communications

David and his wife, Judy, created DJ Partnership to purchase an office building where David moved his practice. Because the building is larger than what the practice currently needs, space is rented to other tax practitioners. In addition to providing office space, the partnership offers professional and administrative services on an exclusive basis to the tenants. These services include secretarial support, telephone answering service, tax professionals available for special projects, access to a tax research library, computer hardware technology, and miscellaneous administrative support. DJ Partnership considers its primary activity to be providing professional and administrative services to its tenants rather than being a lessor.

Because of the attractiveness of the services offered to its tenants, the building is fully leased. In the first year, Judy works full-time at the partnership and David commits about 550 hours to its operations. For the first year, the partnership incurs a tax loss of $60,000. Without considering the impact of the loss, David and Judy's AGI is $175,000. Write a letter to David in which you advise him on the deductibility of the $60,000 loss for Federal income tax purposes. Because David is a tax professional, your letter can include technical language and references to tax law sources.

Partial list of research aids:
Reg. § 1.469–1T(e)(3)(ii).

Research Problem 4. Ida Ross has decided to purchase a new home in a retirement community for $400,000. She has $50,000 in cash for the down payment but needs to borrow the remaining $350,000 to finance the purchase. Her financial adviser, Marc, suggests that rather than seeking a conventional mortgage, she should borrow the funds from State Bank using her portfolio of appreciated securities as collateral. Selling the securities to generate $350,000 in cash would lead to a substantial tax on the capital gain recognized. Therefore, a better strategy would be to borrow against her securities and then claim a deduction for the interest paid on the loan. How do you react to the financial adviser's strategy?

Partial list of research aids:
Temp.Reg. § 1.163–8T(c).

Use the tax resources of the Internet to address the following questions. Do not restrict your search to the Web, but include a review of newsgroups and general reference materials, practitioner sites and resources, primary sources of the tax law, chat rooms and discussion groups, and other opportunities.

 Internet Activity

Research Problem 5. In a recent Tax Court decision, a taxpayer argued that he met the 750-hour requirement for materially participating in his rental real estate activities. The taxpayer, James Moss, asserted that because the time he spent "on call" related to his rental properties, the hours should be included in the 750-hour calculation. Moss claimed that whenever he was not at his regular job, he was on call because he could have been called to deal with a problem at the rental properties at any time.

Go to the U.S. Tax Court (**www.ustaxcourt.gov**) website and find the *Moss* decision. What did the Tax Court conclude about including "on-call" hours in the 750-hour requirement?

Research Problem 6. Investment advisers and tax professionals are continuously striving to create sophisticated transactions and investment vehicles (i.e., tax-advantaged investments) that are designed to provide economic benefits to investors by reducing their taxes. These professionals might like to patent such schemes. Identify whether patenting a tax strategy is a legal possibility.

part 4

SPECIAL TAX COMPUTATION METHODS, PAYMENT PROCEDURES, AND TAX CREDITS

Part 4 presents several topics that relate to the theme of tax liability determination. The taxpayer must calculate the tax liability not only in accordance with the basic tax formula, but also in accordance with the tax formula for the alternative minimum tax (AMT). The basic tax formula was presented in Part 1, and the AMT formula is covered here. A wide variety of tax credits can be used to reduce the tax liability. However, these credits are not always available and are subject to certain monetary limitations. As part of arriving at overall tax liability, payroll taxes (including the self-employment tax) must be taken into account. The specific procedures for the timing of the payment of tax liability are also discussed.

CHAPTER

12 Alternative Minimum Tax

LEARNING OBJECTIVES: *After completing Chapter 12, you should be able to:*

LO.1 Explain the rationale for the alternative minimum tax (AMT).

LO.2 List and explain the formula for computing the AMT for individuals.

LO.3 Identify the adjustments made in calculating AMTI.

LO.4 Identify the preferences that are included in calculating AMTI.

LO.5 Compute the AMT and complete Form 6251.

LO.6 Describe and illustrate the role of the AMT credit in the alternative minimum tax structure.

LO.7 Compare the individual AMT calculation with the corporate AMT calculation.

LO.8 Identify and apply various tax planning opportunities to minimize the AMT.

CHAPTER OUTLINE

THE BIG PICTURE   Tax Solutions for the Real World

THE PRESENCE OR ABSENCE OF THE AMT

Bob and Carol are unmarried individuals who have been engaged for four months. They work for the same employer and earn identical compensation. They have the same amount of gross income, including the same amount of investment income, which consists solely of interest income; they have similar investments in tax-exempt bonds that produce identical amounts of interest income. They also have the same amount of deductions.

Bob's tax return is prepared by Adam, and Carol's tax return is prepared by Ava. While discussing their tax liability one day at lunch, Carol is dismayed to learn that she paid $15,000 more in Federal income taxes than Bob did for the tax year. Carol meets with Ava that evening. Ava reviews Carol's tax return and assures her that her tax liability was properly calculated.

The above events raise a number of interesting questions for Bob and Carol that can be answered after completing this chapter. Why didn't Bob and Carol have the same tax liability? Were both tax returns properly prepared? Should Carol consider replacing her tax return preparer Ava with Adam? Is it possible and/or desirable for Carol to file an amended return? Should Bob do anything?

Read the chapter and formulate your response.

FRAMEWORK 1040
Tax Formula for Individuals

This chapter covers the boldfaced portions of the Tax Formula for Individuals that was introduced in Figure 3.1 on p. 3-3. Below those portions are the sections of Form 1040 where the results are reported.

Income *(broadly conceived)*	$xx,xxx
Less: Exclusions	(x,xxx)
Gross income	$xx,xxx
Less: Deductions for adjusted gross income	(x,xxx)
Adjusted gross income	$xx,xxx
Less: The greater of total **itemized deductions** *or* the standard deduction	(x,xxx)
Personal and dependency exemptions	(x,xxx)
Taxable income	$xx,xxx
Tax on taxable income *(see Tax Tables or Tax Rate Schedules)*	$ x,xxx
Less: Tax credits *(including income taxes withheld and prepaid)*	(xxx)
Tax due *(or refund)*	$ xxx

FORM 1040 (p. 2)

45   **Alternative minimum tax** (see instructions). Attach Form 6251 . . . .

LO.1

Explain the rationale for the alternative minimum tax (AMT).

The tax law contains many incentives that are intended to influence the economic and social behavior of taxpayers (refer to Chapter 1). Some taxpayers were able to take advantage of enough of these incentives to avoid or minimize any liability for Federal income tax. Although these taxpayers were reducing taxes legally, Congress became concerned about the inequity that results when taxpayers with substantial economic incomes can avoid paying any income tax.[1] To attempt to alleviate this inequity, the **alternative minimum tax (AMT)** was enacted. The goal of the AMT is to ensure that all taxpayers with more than modest economic income pay some minimum amount of tax.

The AMT applies to individuals, corporations, trusts, and estates. While the calculations involved are similar for all taxpayers subject to the AMT, some portions of the AMT formula are unique to particular taxpayers. The first part of this chapter presents a discussion of the individual AMT. Details of the corporate AMT are presented in the second part of the chapter. The AMT provisions specific to trusts and estates are not addressed.

12-1 INDIVIDUAL ALTERNATIVE MINIMUM TAX

LO.2

List and explain the formula for computing the AMT for individuals.

In theory, all individual taxpayers subject to the Federal income tax are subject to AMT. As will be seen in this chapter, whether a taxpayer has an AMT liability depends on a number of factors, including the taxpayer's income, geographic location, and family situation as well as the exclusions, deductions, and credits utilized in the calculation of their regular Federal income tax liability.

---

[1] *General Explanation of the Tax Reform Act of 1986 ("Blue Book")*, prepared by The Staff of the Joint Committee on Taxation, May 4, 1987, H.R. 3838, 99th Cong., pp. 432–433.

12-1a Alternative Minimum Taxable Income (AMTI)

The tax base used to determine AMT liability is referred to as the alternative minimum taxable income (AMTI) amount (Figure 12.1). The calculation of AMTI does not follow the direct approach taken in the calculation of the tax-payer's regular taxable income.[2] In calculating regular taxable income, gross income is reduced by deductions to arrive at taxable income. However, in calculating AMTI, the tax law provides for an indirect approach. Rather than having taxpayers recalculate the components of the individual income tax formula using a different set of rules, the calculation of AMTI *begins* with regular taxable income as shown in Figure 12.1. In other words, the AMT calculation requires a taxpayer to reconcile taxable income to AMTI.

Part of the reason for this indirect approach may be that many items of income and expense are treated the same way for both regular income tax and AMT purposes. For example, a taxpayer's salary is included in computing taxable income and is also included in AMTI. Alimony paid and certain itemized deductions, such as charitable contributions and gambling losses, also are allowed for both regular income tax and AMT purposes.

While many amounts are left unchanged, the tax law provides that certain income and expense items are treated differently for regular income tax and AMT purposes. In some cases, the income or expense amount is reconsidered in aggregate. For example, interest income on bonds issued by state, county, or local governments is excluded in computing taxable income. However, if such bonds are private activity bonds, the interest on them is included in computing AMTI. The deduction for personal and dependency exemptions allowed for regular income tax purposes is disallowed for AMT purposes.

In other cases, the income or expense amount is considered in both the regular income tax and AMT computations, but the amount differs. For example, the completed contract method can be used to report income from some long-term contracts for regular income tax purposes, but the percentage of completion method is required for AMT purposes. Thus, in the tax year, the amount of income from the contract included in taxable income will differ from the amount included in AMTI. Similarly, medical expenses are deductible in calculating both taxable

FIGURE 12.1	Alternative Minimum Tax Formula for Individuals

Taxable income (increased by any standard deduction and personal or dependency exemptions)

Plus or minus: Adjustments

Plus: Preferences

Equals: Alternative minimum taxable income (AMTI)

Minus: Exemption

Equals: Alternative minimum tax (AMT) base

Multiplied by: 26% or 28% rate

Equals: Tentative minimum tax before foreign tax credit

Minus: AMT foreign tax credit

Equals: Tentative minimum tax (TMT)

Minus: Regular tax liability (less any foreign tax credit)

Equals: AMT (if TMT > regular tax liability)

---

[2]§ 55(b)(2).

income and AMTI, but the floor for the deduction under the regular income tax is lower where taxpayers are older than 65.[3]

As shown in Figure 12.1, differences between regular tax and AMT income and expense amounts are categorized as either adjustments or preferences. Most adjustments relate to timing differences that arise because of different regular income tax and AMT treatments. Adjustments that are caused by timing differences will eventually reverse; that is, positive adjustments will be offset by negative adjustments in the future, and vice versa.[4]

Depreciation provides a good example of a timing difference. In general, AMT depreciation methods are slower than regular tax depreciation methods. Initially then, there will be less depreciation for AMT purposes than for tax purposes. This difference will result in positive timing differences until AMT depreciation is larger than regular tax depreciation, when the timing difference will become negative. However, over time, the same amount of depreciation will be deducted for regular tax and AMT purposes because the basis for regular tax and AMT depreciation is the same.

In contrast, in the reconciliation of taxable income to AMTI, preference items will always serve to increase the taxable income amount.[5] Certain deductions and exclusions allowed to taxpayers for regular income tax purposes provide significant tax savings. The AMT is designed to take back all or part of the tax benefit derived through the use of preferences in the calculation of regular taxable income. This is why preference items serve only to increase taxable income, which is the starting point in computing AMTI. The effect of adding these preference items is to disallow them for AMT purposes. Examples of preferences include percentage depletion in excess of the property's adjusted basis and excess intangible drilling costs. Both adjustments and preferences are discussed in more detail later in the chapter.

ETHICS & EQUITY   Impact of the AMT on Accelerating Expenses

Maurice, a single, cash method taxpayer, projects his taxable income for 2014 to be about $300,000. For AMT purposes, he has positive adjustments and tax preferences of $200,000. He anticipates that his taxable income and positive adjustments and preferences will be about the same for 2015. He is evaluating several proposed transactions that could affect his 2014 tax liability.

One proposal involves an office building for which he is currently negotiating a lease. The lease has a starting date of July 1, 2014, provides for annual rent of $24,000, and carries an 18-month prepayment clause. Although Maurice favors a five-year lease, his tax adviser has suggested an 18-month period with an option to renew for 42 months. The adviser points out the tax advantage of being able to deduct the $36,000 of rent at the inception of the lease. The projected tax liability under each option would be as follows:

	18-Month Lease	5-Year Lease
Regular income tax liability	$ 70,978	$ 78,898
AMT	55,292	54,092
Total	$126,270	$132,990

After comparing these results, Maurice takes his adviser's suggestion.

Is it appropriate for Maurice to avoid taxes in this manner? Is it wise?

---

[3]§ 213(f).

[4]§ 56.

[5]§ 57.

TAX IN THE NEWS   The AMT—Then and Now

The AMT was enacted to target wealthy individuals who, because of numerous legitimate tax minimization strategies, paid little or no Federal income tax. However, over time, more and more middle-class taxpayers were subject to the AMT. According to the Tax Policy Center, the number of taxpayers in AMT grew from about 20,000 in 1970 to nearly 4 million in 2011. What explains the increased numbers of middle-class taxpayers subject to the AMT?

When enacted, the AMT exemption amount was not indexed to inflation. As a result, as incomes increased and the exemption amount stayed the same, more taxpayers were subject to the AMT. To try to limit the reach of the AMT to wealthy taxpayers, Congress had regularly increased the AMT exemption amount. Usually very near the end of the year and using what was often referred to

as the AMT "patch," Congress would increase the individual exemption amount to prevent inflation from subjecting taxpayers to the AMT. As part of the tax legislation that emerged in 2012 to moderate the effects of the fiscal cliff, a patch will no longer be needed. Beginning in 2013, both the exemption amount and the dollar amount dividing the 26 and 28 percent tax rates are permanently indexed to inflation.

From a tax revenue perspective, indexing the exemption amount to inflation is not free. The Joint Committee on Taxation estimates that indexing the exemption to inflation will cost $1.8 billion over the next decade.

Sources: www.taxpolicycenter.org/taxtopics/AMT.cfm; The Joint Committee on Taxation Report: JCX-1-13.

12-1b AMT Formula: Other Components

Calculating AMTI is the first step in the determination of whether a taxpayer will have an alternative minimum tax liability. To complete the AMT calculation, as shown in Figure 12.1, the exemption, rates, credit, and regular tax liability must all be considered.

Exemption Amount

After calculating AMTI, the taxpayer determines the AMT **exemption amount**. Tax law provides for exemption amounts in both the regular tax and AMT liability calculations. The exemption amounts for AMT are higher than the exemption amounts for regular tax liability purposes. The AMT exemption amount can be thought of as a materiality provision. Taxpayers with few or minimal positive adjustments and preferences will avoid being subject to the AMT as a result of the exemption.

The initial exemption amount in 2014 is $82,100 for married taxpayers filing joint returns, $52,800 for single taxpayers, and $41,050 for married taxpayers filing separate returns.[6] However, the exemption is phased out at a rate of 25 cents on the dollar when AMTI exceeds certain amounts (see Example 1). These amounts are tied to the taxpayer's filing status. The exemption phaseout is an application of the wherewithal to pay concept. Congress believes that as a taxpayer's AMTI increases, so does the taxpayer's ability to pay income taxes.

Harry, who is single, has AMTI of $192,500 for the year. His $52,800 initial exemption amount is reduced by $18,800 [($192,500 − $117,300) × 25% phaseout rate]. Harry's AMT exemption is $34,000 ($52,800 exemption − $18,800 reduction).

Example 1

---

[6]Beginning with the 2013 tax year, the exemption amounts are indexed to inflation. § 55(d)(4)(A).

The exemption and phaseout amounts are as follows:

Status	Exemption	Phaseout Begins at	Phaseout Ends at
Married, joint	$82,100	$156,500	$484,900
Single or head of household	52,800	117,300	328,500
Married, separate	41,050	78,250	242,450

Once AMTI equals the end of the phaseout range, a taxpayer's exemption amount will equal zero. Example 1 explains the calculation of the phaseout of the AMT exemption.

AMT Liability

After the exemption amount is calculated, a taxpayer's AMT liability can be determined. As shown in Figure 12.1, AMTI less the exemption amount equals the taxpayer's tentative minimum tax (TMT). The relationship between the regular tax liability and the TMT is key to the AMT calculation. If the regular tax liability exceeds the TMT, the taxpayer's AMT liability is zero. However, if the TMT exceeds the regular tax liability, the excess is the taxpayer's AMT liability. Technically, the AMT is a surtax; both tax law and the Form 6251 categorize this excess of TMT over the taxpayer's regular tax liability as the AMT amount.[7] For practical purposes, the taxpayer will pay whichever tax liability is greater—that calculated using the regular income tax rules or that calculated using the AMT rules.

A graduated, two-tier AMT rate schedule applies to noncorporate taxpayers. A 26 percent rate applies on an AMT base up to $182,500 ($91,250 for married, filing separately), and a 28 percent rate applies to an AMT base of $182,500 and above.[8] Any net capital gain or qualified dividend income included in the AMT base is taxed at the favorable alternative tax rates for capital gains (0 percent, 15 percent, or 20 percent) rather than at the AMT statutory rates. See the discussion of the alternative tax on capital gains in Chapter 16.

Example 2

Anna, an unmarried individual, has regular taxable income of $100,000. She has positive adjustments of $40,000 and preferences of $25,000. Anna's regular tax liability for 2014 is $21,176. Her AMT in 2014 is calculated as follows:

Taxable income (TI)	$100,000
Plus: Adjustments	40,000
Plus: Preferences	25,000
Equals: AMTI	$165,000
Minus: AMT exemption ($52,800 − $11,925)	40,875
Equals: AMT base	$124,125
Times: AMT rate of 26%	× .26
Equals: TMT	$ 32,273
Minus: Regular tax liability	21,176
Equals: AMT	$ 11,097

Anna will pay the IRS a total of $32,273, consisting of her regular tax liability of $21,176 plus her AMT of $11,097.

Credits against regular tax liability (see Chapter 13) are allowed to some taxpayers depending on their economic circumstances or the type of business activity in which they engage. Historically, the only credit allowed for AMT purposes was the Foreign Tax Credit (FTC). In that case, the AMT is equal to the tentative minimum tax (TMT) less any AMT FTC minus the regular tax liability less any regular tax FTC. However, beginning in 2012, personal nonrefundable credits (e.g., Adoption Credit, Lifetime Learning Credit, and Retirement Savings Contribution

---

Credit) are allowed to offset any AMT liability as well as any regular tax liability, as is shown in Example 3.[9]

> Michael has total personal nonrefundable credits of $11,000, regular tax liability of $33,000, and tentative minimum tax of $26,000. Prior to 2012, he could claim only $7,000 of the nonrefundable credits in the current year ($33,000 − $26,000 = $7,000). However, beginning in 2012, the entire $11,000 credit is available to offset Michael's $33,000 tax liability.

Example 3

12-1c AMT Adjustments

As discussed previously, **adjustments** relate to timing differences that arise because of differences in how an item is treated for regular income tax and AMT purposes. As a result, it is necessary to determine not only what the amount of an adjustment is but also whether the adjustment is positive or negative.

LO.3

Identify the adjustments made in calculating AMTI.

Remember that the AMTI calculation begins with the regular taxable income amount. Thus, these adjustments are being made to the regular taxable income amount. Where the regular tax and AMT treatment of an item of expense (or deduction) differ, the direction of the adjustment is determined as follows:

| Regular tax deduction | > | AMT deduction | = | Positive AMT adjustment |
| Regular tax deduction | < | AMT deduction | = | Negative AMT adjustment |

Conversely, the direction of an adjustment attributable to a revenue (or income item) can be determined as follows:

| Regular tax income | > | AMT income | = | Negative AMT adjustment |
| Regular tax income | < | AMT income | = | Positive AMT adjustment |

Depreciation of Post-1986 Real Property

As discussed in Chapter 8, for regular income tax purposes, real property is depreciated using the straight-line method. The cost of residential real property is recovered over 27.5 years, and the cost of all other real property is recovered over 39 years.[10] Whether an AMT adjustment is required for real property depreciation depends on when the property was placed in service.

For real property placed in service after 1986 (MACRS property) and before January 1, 1999, AMT depreciation is computed using the straight-line method, but the alternative depreciation system (ADS) recovery period of 40 years is used (see Table 8.7 in Chapter 8). Any difference in the depreciation amounts results in an AMT adjustment. Note that these adjustments will be positive during the regular income tax recovery period of the real property because the cost is written off over a shorter period for regular income tax purposes. For example, for residential real property, during the 27.5 year regular tax recovery period, the regular income tax depreciation will exceed the AMT depreciation because AMT depreciation is computed over a 40-year period. These adjustments will be negative once the asset is fully depreciated for regular tax purposes, as additional depreciation will be allowed for AMT purposes.

For real property placed in service after December 31, 1998, no AMT adjustment is required.[11] As a result of tax law changes, post 1998, real property depreciation is the same for both AMT and regular tax purposes. In other words, because straight-line depreciation and the same recovery period (see Table 8.6 in Chapter 8) are used for both regular tax and AMT purposes, no AMT adjustment is necessary for real property depreciation.

[9]§ 26(a)(2).
[10]The 39-year life generally applies to nonresidential real property placed in service on or after May 13, 1993.
[11]§ 56(a)(1)(A).

Depreciation of Post-1986 Personal Property

For most personal property that is MACRS property, the depreciation deduction for regular income tax purposes is calculated using the 200 percent declining-balance method with a switch to straight-line depreciation when that method produces a larger depreciation deduction. The MACRS recovery period is the general depreciation system (GDS) prescribed recovery period (see Table 8.1 in Chapter 8). Similar to the real property calculations, for AMT purposes, the depreciation calculation and the resulting adjustment depend on when the property was placed in service.

For property placed in service after 1986 (MACRS property) and before January 1, 1999, the taxpayer calculates depreciation for AMT using the 150 percent declining-balance method with a similar switch to straight-line depreciation. In addition, the recovery period is the ADS prescribed recovery period rather than the GDS recovery period.[12] (See Table 8.4 in Chapter 8.) Thus, for property placed in service prior to January 1, 1999, the difference between regular income tax depreciation and AMT depreciation is caused by both longer recovery periods (GDS recovery period versus ADS recovery period) and a larger accelerated depreciation percentage (200 percent declining balance versus 150 percent declining balance).

For property placed in service after December 31, 1998, the taxpayer continues to calculate AMT depreciation using the 150 percent declining-balance method with the switch to straight-line depreciation. However, the recovery period is the GDS recovery period for both AMT and regular tax purposes.[13] (See Table 8.4 in Chapter 8.) Thus, for personal property placed in service after December 31, 1998, the difference between regular income tax depreciation and AMT depreciation is caused only by a larger accelerated depreciation percentage (200 percent declining balance versus 150 percent declining balance). Example 4 illustrates the adjustments required where a three-year asset is depreciated.

Example 4

Sawyer placed an $8,000 breeding hog, a prime breeder sow, in service in 2012. The MACRS recovery period for breeding hogs is three years. Regular tax (using 200% declining balance) and AMT depreciation (using 150% declining balance) amounts over the recovery period of the asset are as follows:

	Regular Income Tax Deduction	AMT Deduction	AMT Adjustment
2012	$2,666	$2,000	$666
2013	3,556	3,000	556
2014	1,185	2,000	(815)
2015	593	1,000	(407)

As is shown in Example 4, the same conventions are used for regular tax and AMT depreciation. Thus, the asset is fully depreciated over four years for both regular tax and AMT purposes because the same recovery period is used and the half-year convention applies for both calculations. The AMT depreciation deduction is initially smaller because of the lesser declining balance percentage used for AMT purposes. As a result, the adjustments in 2012 and 2013 are positive; taxable income will be increased by these amounts to arrive at the AMT depreciation amount. In the last two years of the asset's life, the AMT adjustment is negative. Taxable income will be decreased by these amounts to arrive at the AMT depreciation amount. In total, the same amount of depreciation will be taken for both regular tax and AMT purposes.

Whether prior to January 1, 1999, or after December 31, 1998, all personal property placed in service may be taken into consideration in computing one net AMT depreciation adjustment. Using this netting process, the AMT adjustment for a tax year is the difference between the total regular tax depreciation for all personal

---

[12]§ 56(a)(1)(A)(i).   [13]§ 56(a)(1)(A)(ii).

property and the total depreciation computed for that property for AMT purposes. The same principles that apply in Example 4 apply in aggregate.

Finally, a taxpayer may elect to use the AMT depreciation method for personal property for regular income tax purposes. If this election is made, no AMT adjustment is required because the depreciation deduction is the same for regular income tax and for the AMT. This election eliminates the necessity to maintain two sets of tax depreciation records.

Additional First-Year Depreciation

As discussed in Chapter 8, for regular tax purposes, an additional first-year depreciation deduction equal to 50 percent of the unadjusted depreciable basis of qualified property is available for property placed in service after December 31, 2011, and before January 1, 2014. For property to which this additional first-year depreciation deduction (also known as bonus depreciation) is elected, no depreciation adjustment for AMT purposes is required.[14]

Pollution Control Facilities

To encourage private industry to abate pollution, tax law provides beneficial amortization provisions for certified pollution control facilities in lieu of depreciation. For regular income tax purposes, a taxpayer may elect to amortize the cost of certified facilities over 60 months. For AMT purposes, such amortization is not allowed. Instead, the cost of certified pollution control facilities is recovered through depreciation. Similar to the depreciation provisions discussed previously, the method is dictated by when the facility was placed in service.

Facilities placed in service after 1986 and before January 1, 1999, are depreciated using the alternative depreciation system (ADS) method. Thus, costs are recovered using the straight-line method over 40 years if the property is real property or over the class life if the property is personal property.[15] For facilities placed in service after December 31, 1998, depreciation for AMT purposes is calculated using the straight line method over the recovery period that would be used for regular tax (MACRS) purposes. Irrespective of when the property was placed in service, the adjustment for AMTI is equal to the difference between the regular tax amortization deduction and the AMT depreciation amount. The adjustment may be positive or negative.

Circulation Expenditures

Circulation expenditures are expenses incurred to establish, maintain, or increase the circulation of a newspaper, a magazine, or another periodical. For regular income tax purposes, circulation expenditures, other than those the taxpayer elects to charge to a capital account, may be expensed in the year incurred.[16] For AMT purposes, circulation expenditures are not deductible in the year incurred. In computing AMTI, these expenditures must be capitalized and amortized ratably over the three-year period beginning in the year the expenditures were made.[17]

The AMT adjustment for circulation expenditures is calculated by comparing the amount expensed for regular income tax purposes with the amount that can be amortized for AMT purposes. In general, in the year the circulation expenditures are incurred, the adjustment will be positive; more circulation expenditures are deducted for regular tax purposes than are allowed for AMT purposes. In the second and third years, the adjustment will be negative; a deduction is allowed for AMT purposes that was taken in the first year for regular tax purposes.

---

[14]§ 168(k).
[15]§ 56(a)(5).

[16]§ 173(a).
[17]§ 56(b)(2)(A)(i).

Example 5

In 2013, Lindsay's sole proprietorship incurred $30,000 of circulation expenditures. These expenditures were deducted in full for regular tax purposes but amortized over three years for AMT purposes. Thus, in 2014, Lindsay will not have a regular tax deduction for circulation expenditures, but will be allowed to deduct $10,000 of circulation expenditures for AMT purposes. As a result, a negative AMT adjustment is required in 2014.

2014 taxable income		$ 95,000
Plus or minus: AMT adjustments		
Circulation expenditures deducted for regular income tax purposes	$ –0–	
Circulation expenditures allowed for AMT purposes	(10,000)	
Negative adjustment		(10,000)
Plus: AMT preferences		–0–
AMTI		$ 85,000

Analysis of this computation shows that the allowable AMT deduction is $10,000 more than the allowable regular income tax deduction. Therefore, AMTI is $10,000 less than taxable income. This result is obtained by making a negative AMT adjustment of $10,000.

Note that a taxpayer can avoid an AMT adjustment for circulation expenditures by electing to write off the expenditures over a three-year period for regular income tax purposes.[18]

Expenditures Requiring 10-Year Write-Off for AMT Purposes

Certain expenditures that may be deducted in the year incurred for regular income tax purposes must be written off over a 10-year period for AMT purposes. These rules apply to (1) mining exploration and development costs and (2) research and experimental expenditures.

In computing taxable income, taxpayers are allowed to deduct expenditures paid or incurred during the taxable year for exploration (ascertaining the existence, location, extent, or quality of a deposit or mineral) and for development of a mine or other natural deposit, other than an oil or gas well.[19] Mining development expenditures are expenses paid or incurred after the existence of ores and minerals in commercially marketable quantities has been disclosed.

For AMT purposes, however, mining exploration and development costs must be capitalized and amortized ratably over a 10-year period.[20] Although circulation expenditures are recoverable over a three-year period for AMT purposes, the calculation of the adjustment for mining exploration and development costs is similar in spirit to that for circulation expenditures. The AMT adjustment is calculated by comparing the amount of mining exploration and development costs expensed (if any) for regular tax purposes with the AMT amortization for the year. In general, the adjustment will be positive in the year these expenses are incurred and negative thereafter. This provision does not apply to costs relating to an oil or gas well.

Example 6

In 2014, Audrey incurs $150,000 of mining exploration expenditures and deducts this amount for regular income tax purposes. For AMT purposes, these mining exploration expenditures must be amortized over a 10-year period. Audrey must make a positive adjustment for AMTI of $135,000 ($150,000 allowed for regular income tax − $15,000 for AMT) for 2014, the year the expenses were incurred. For AMT purposes, in each of the next nine years, Audrey is required to make a negative adjustment of $15,000 ($0 allowed for regular income tax − $15,000 for AMT).

---

[18] § 59(e)(2)(A).

[19] §§ 617(a) and 616(a).

[20] § 56(a)(2).

To avoid the AMT adjustments for mining exploration and development costs, a taxpayer may elect to write off the expenditures over a 10-year period for regular income tax purposes.[21]

Similarly, rather than capitalize the costs of research and experimentation, a taxpayer can choose to deduct those costs in the year incurred. For AMT purposes, such costs must be amortized over a 10-year time period. As a result, the calculation of the adjustment for research and experimental expenditures is similar to the mining development and exploration costs adjustment and similar in spirit to the adjustment for circulation expenditures.

Use of Completed Contract Method of Accounting

For a long-term contract, taxpayers are required to use the percentage of completion method for AMT purposes.[22] However, in limited circumstances, taxpayers can use the completed contract method for regular income tax purposes.[23] Thus, where the percentage of completion method is not used for regular tax purposes, a taxpayer recognizes a different amount of income for regular income tax purposes than for AMT purposes. The resulting AMT adjustment is equal to the difference between income reported under the percentage of completion method and the amount reported using the completed contract method. The adjustment can be either positive or negative, depending on the amount of income recognized under the different methods.

Similar to many of the other adjustments discussed previously, a taxpayer can avoid an AMT adjustment on long-term contracts by using the percentage of completion method for regular income tax purposes rather than the completed contract method.

Incentive Stock Options

Like other compensatory options, **incentive stock options (ISOs)** are granted by employers to help attract new personnel and retain those already employed. The rationale underlying this type of compensation contract is to provide employees an incentive to behave in ways that will increase the employer's stock price, which should then benefit both the employer and the employee.

At the time an ISO is granted, the option will not have value. The employer corporation grants the option either at the money (where the exercise price equals the stock's price on the date of grant) or out of the money (where the exercise price is greater than the stock's price on the date of grant). If the value of the stock increases during the option period, the employee can obtain stock at a favorable price by exercising the option. For regular tax purposes, because the option does not have value at issuance, no income is recognized at the date of grant for regular tax purposes. For AMT purposes, no adjustment is required on the date of grant.

For regular tax purposes the exercise of an ISO does not increase regular taxable income.[24] However, for AMT purposes, the excess of the fair market value of the stock over the exercise price (the *spread* or the *bargain element*) is treated as an adjustment in the taxable year in which the option is exercised.[25]

> **Example 7**
>
> In January 2014, Manuel exercised an ISO that had been granted by his employer, Gold Corporation, in March 2010. Manuel acquired 1,000 shares of Gold stock for the option price of $20 per share. The fair market value of the stock at the date of exercise was $50 per share. The transaction does not affect regular taxable income in either 2010 or 2014. For AMT purposes, Manuel has a positive adjustment of $30,000 ($50,000 fair market value − $20,000 option price) for 2014.

As a result of this adjustment, the regular income tax basis of the stock acquired through the exercise of ISOs is different from the AMT basis. The regular income

---

[21]§§ 59(e)(2)(D) and (E).

[22]§ 56(a)(3).

[23]See Chapter 18 for a detailed discussion of the completed contract and percentage of completion methods of accounting.

[24]§ 421(a).

[25]§ 56(b)(3).

tax basis of the stock is equal to its cost, the exercise price of the option, whereas the AMT basis is equal to the fair market value of the stock on the date the option is exercised. Consequently, the amount of any gain or loss upon disposition of the stock will likely differ for regular income tax and AMT purposes.

Example 8	Assume the same facts as in the previous example and assume that Manuel sells the stock acquired with the option for $60,000 in December 2015. His gain for regular income tax purposes is $40,000 ($60,000 amount realized − $20,000 regular income tax basis). For AMT purposes, the gain is $10,000 ($60,000 amount realized − $50,000 AMT basis). Therefore, Manuel will make a $30,000 negative adjustment in computing AMT in 2015. Because the gain on sale was larger for regular tax purposes, the gain reflected in taxable income is decreased by $30,000 ($40,000 regular income tax gain − $10,000 AMT gain) to reflect the $10,000 AMT gain. Note that this $30,000 negative adjustment upon disposition in 2015 offsets the $30,000 positive adjustment made in the year of exercise.

An employee may be restricted as to when he or she can dispose of stock acquired under an ISO. In other words, the stock acquired with the option may not be freely transferable until some specified period has passed (see Chapter 19 for further discussion of ISOs). If there were some restriction, then the employee would not make the AMT adjustment until the stock was freely transferable.

Example 9	In January 2014, Manuel exercised an ISO that had been granted by his employer, Gold Corporation, in March 2010. Manuel acquired 1,000 shares of Gold stock for the option price of $20 per share, when the fair market value of the stock was $50 per share. The stock became freely transferable in February 2015, when the fair market value was $55 per share. For AMT purposes, Manuel will make a positive adjustment of $30,000 ($50,000 fair market value − $20,000 option price) in 2015. The transaction does not affect regular taxable income in 2010, 2014, or 2015.

Finally, if the taxpayer exercises the ISO and disposes of the stock in the same tax year, otherwise known as a disqualifying disposition, the bargain element is reported as income for regular tax purposes, which means no AMT adjustment is required for that option.

Adjusted Gain or Loss

When property is sold or disposed of during the year, gain or loss reported for regular income tax may differ from gain or loss determined for AMT purposes. This difference occurs because the adjusted basis of the property for AMT purposes must reflect any current and prior AMT adjustments for the following:[26]

- Depreciation.
- Circulation expenditures.
- Research and experimental expenditures.
- Mining exploration and development costs.
- Amortization of certified pollution control facilities.

Remember that the AMT calculation begins with regular taxable income. The amount of the adjustment should reflect the difference between the regular tax and AMT gain or loss amount. A negative gain or loss adjustment is required if:

- Any gain for AMT purposes is less than the gain for regular income tax purposes,
- Any loss for AMT purposes is more than the loss for regular income tax purposes, or
- A loss is computed for AMT purposes and a gain is computed for regular income tax purposes.

Where the relationship between the regular tax and the AMT amount is reversed, the AMT gain or loss adjustment is positive.

---

[26] § 56(a)(6).

Assume that Sawyer sells the breeding hog he placed in service in 2012 (Example 4) on September 1, 2014, for $12,500. When Sawyer sells the animal, two AMT adjustments result: the depreciation adjustment for 2014 and any gain (or loss) adjustment resulting from the sale.

> **Example 10**

The regular income tax depreciation for 2014 is $593 [$8,000 cost × 14.81% (Chapter 8, Table 8.6) × 0.5]. AMT depreciation for 2014 is $1,000 [$8,000 × 25% (Chapter 8, Table 8.7) × 0.5]. Sawyer's negative AMT adjustment for 2014, reflecting the additional depreciation for AMT purposes, is $407 ($593 regular income tax depreciation − $1,000 AMT depreciation).

In computing gain (or loss) as a result of the sale, the adjusted basis in the animal is different for regular income tax and AMT purposes because of the depreciation. The adjusted basis for each purpose is determined as follows:

	Regular Income Tax	AMT
Cost	$ 8,000	$ 8,000
Less: Depreciation for 2012–2013 (see Example 4)	(6,222)	(5,000)
Depreciation for 2014 (see prior paragraph)	(593)	(1,000)
Adjusted basis	$ 1,185	$ 2,000

Having determined the adjusted basis, the recognized gain for regular tax and AMT purposes is calculated as follows:

	Regular Income Tax	AMT
Amount realized	$12,500	$12,500
Adjusted basis	(1,185)	(2,000)
Recognized gain	$11,315	$10,500

Because the regular income tax gain is greater than the AMT gain on the sale of the animal, Sawyer will make a negative AMT adjustment of $815 ($11,315 regular income tax gain − $10,500 AMT gain) in 2014. Note that this negative adjustment offsets the prior and current year adjustments for depreciation.

Passive Activity Losses

Losses on passive activities are not deductible in computing either the regular income tax or AMTI. However, the rules for computing taxable income differ from the rules for computing AMTI. It follows, then, that the rules for computing a loss for regular income tax purposes differ from the AMT rules for computing a loss. For example, where a passive activity involves depreciable assets, if the amount of depreciation differs for regular tax and AMT purposes, the amount of loss disallowed for AMT purposes will be larger or smaller than the loss disallowed for regular tax purposes. Therefore, as is seen in Example 11, any *passive loss* computed for regular income tax purposes may differ from the passive loss computed for AMT purposes.[27]

> **Example 11**

Matt acquired two passive activities in 2014. He received net passive income of $10,000 from Activity A and had no AMT adjustments or preferences in connection with the activity. Activity B had gross income of $27,000 and operating expenses (not affected by AMT adjustments or preferences) of $19,000. Matt claimed MACRS depreciation of $20,000 for Activity B; AMT depreciation totaled $15,000. In addition, Matt deducted $10,000 of percentage depletion in excess of basis (an AMT preference).

---

[27]See Chapter 11.

The following comparison illustrates the differences in the computation of the passive loss for regular income tax and AMT purposes for Activity B.

	Regular Income Tax	AMT
Gross income	$27,000	$27,000
Deductions:		
Operating expenses	(19,000)	(19,000)
Depreciation	(20,000)	(15,000)
Depletion	(10,000)	–0–
Passive loss	($22,000)	($ 7,000)

Because of the $5,000 adjustment for depreciation and the preference for depletion (see the discussion of AMT preferences later in the chapter), the regular income tax passive activity loss of $22,000 for Activity B is reduced, resulting in a passive activity loss of $7,000 for AMT purposes.

For regular income tax purposes, Matt would offset the $10,000 of net passive income from Activity A with $10,000 of the passive loss from Activity B. For AMT purposes, he would offset the $10,000 of net passive income from Activity A with the $7,000 passive activity loss allowed from Activity B, resulting in passive activity income of $3,000. Thus, in computing AMTI, Matt makes a positive passive loss adjustment of $3,000 [$10,000 (passive activity loss allowed for regular income tax) − $7,000 (passive activity loss allowed for the AMT)]. To avoid duplication, the AMT adjustment for depreciation and the AMT preference for depletion are *not* reported separately. They are accounted for in determining the AMT passive loss adjustment. Also note that differences in regular tax and AMT passive loss amounts in the current year will affect the amount of suspended losses carried forward to future tax years.

Example 12

Assume the same facts as in the previous example. For regular income tax purposes, Matt has a suspended passive loss of $12,000 [$22,000 (amount of loss) − $10,000 (used in 2014)]. This suspended passive loss can offset passive income in the future or can offset active or portfolio income when Matt disposes of the loss activity (refer to Chapter 11). For AMT purposes, Matt's suspended passive loss is $0 [$7,000 (amount of loss) − $7,000 (amount used in 2014)].

Alternative Tax Net Operating Loss Deduction

In computing taxable income, taxpayers are allowed to deduct net operating loss (NOL) carryovers and carrybacks (refer to Chapter 7). While the NOL deduction is allowed for AMT purposes, the regular income tax NOL must be modified to correctly compute AMTI.

The starting point in computing the **alternative tax NOL deduction (ATNOLD)** is the NOL computed for regular income tax purposes. The regular income tax NOL is then modified for AMT adjustments and tax preferences with the result being the ATNOLD. Thus, preferences and adjustment items that have benefited the taxpayer in computing the regular income tax NOL (in other words, the adjustments and preferences that have increased the regular tax NOL) are added back, thereby reducing or eliminating the ATNOLD.[28]

---

[28]§ 56(a)(4).

> **Example 13**
>
> In 2014, Max incurred an NOL of $400,000. Max owns an item of MACRS five-year property, placed in service on March 15, 2014, at a cost of $1,000,000. Regular tax depreciation is $200,000 ($1,000,000 × .20), and AMT depreciation is $150,000 ($1,000,000 × .15). Max's deductions also include tax preferences of $80,000. His ATNOLD carryback to 2012 is $320,000 ($400,000 regular income tax NOL − $80,000 tax preferences deducted in computing the NOL). Because the adjustment for depreciation was positive, the depreciation adjustment does not affect the ATNOLD.

In Example 13, if the regular income tax NOL was not adjusted, the $80,000 in tax preference items deducted in 2014 would have the effect of reducing AMTI in the year (or years) the 2014 NOL is utilized. This occurs despite the fact that this amount was disallowed in the calculation of AMTI. Such an outcome is contradictory to the purpose of the AMT.

Finally, in keeping with the goal of ensuring that taxpayers with economic income pay some minimum amount of tax, a ceiling exists on the amount of the ATNOLD that can be deducted in the carryback or carryforward year. The deduction is limited to 90 percent of AMTI (before the ATNOLD) for the carryback or carryforward year.[29]

> **Example 14**
>
> Assume the same facts as in the previous example except Max's AMTI (before the ATNOLD) in 2012 is $190,000. Therefore, of the $320,000 ATNOLD carried back to 2012 from 2014, only $171,000 ($190,000 × 90%) can be used in recalculating the 2012 AMT. The unused $149,000 of 2014 ATNOLD is now carried to 2013 for use in recalculating the 2013 AMT.

A taxpayer who has an ATNOLD that is carried back or over to another year must use the ATNOLD against AMTI in the carryback or carryforward year even if the taxpayer is not subject to the AMT. This can result in the loss of an ATNOLD, even when the taxpayer does not have an AMT liability.

> **Example 15**
>
> Emily's ATNOLD for 2014 (carried over from 2013) is $10,000. AMTI in 2014, before considering the ATNOLD, is $25,000. If Emily's regular income tax exceeds the TMT, the AMT does not apply. Nevertheless, Emily's ATNOLD of $10,000 is "used up" in 2014 and is not available for carryover to a later year.

For regular income tax purposes, the NOL generally can be carried back 2 years and forward 20 years. However, the taxpayer may elect to forgo the 2-year carryback. These rules generally apply to the ATNOLD as well, except that the election to forgo the 2-year carryback is available for the ATNOLD only if the taxpayer elected it for the regular income tax NOL.

Itemized Deductions

Most of the itemized deductions that are allowed for regular income tax purposes are allowed for AMT purposes. As discussed below, for AMT purposes, the itemized deduction for certain taxes, miscellaneous itemized deductions, medical expenses, and interest requires adjustment. The itemized deduction phaseout also triggers an AMT adjustment.

Taxes and Miscellaneous Itemized Deductions State, local, and foreign income taxes, sales taxes, and property taxes are not allowed as a deduction in computing AMTI.[30] Miscellaneous itemized deductions that are subject to the 2 percent-of-AGI floor also are not allowed in computing AMTI.[31] A positive AMT adjustment equal to the total amount of the regular income tax deduction for each is required.

Also remember that under the tax benefit rule, a tax refund is included in regular taxable income to the extent the taxpayer obtained a tax benefit by deducting the tax in a prior year. If the taxpayer's gross income includes the recovery of any tax deducted as an itemized deduction for regular income tax purposes, a negative

---

[29]§ 56(d)(1)(A)(i)(II).
[30]§ 56(b)(1)(A).
[31]§ 56(b)(1)(A).

AMT adjustment in the amount of the recovery is allowed for AMTI purposes.[32] For example, state, local, and foreign income taxes can be deducted for regular income tax purposes but cannot be deducted in computing AMTI. Because of this, any refund of such taxes from a prior year that would be included in the calculation of regular taxable income is not included in AMTI.

Medical Expenses For regular income tax purposes, medical expenses are deductible to the extent they exceed 10 percent of AGI, except for taxpayers and their spouses who are age 65 and older. For these taxpayers, from 2013–2016, medical expenses that exceed 7.5 percent of AGI are deductible. However, for AMT purposes, regardless of the taxpayer's age, medical expenses are deductible only to the extent they exceed 10 percent of AGI.[33]

Example 16

Joann, age 66, incurred uninsured medical expenses of $16,000 in 2014. She had AGI of $100,000 for the year. Her AMT adjustment for medical expenses is computed as follows:

	Regular Income Tax	AMT
Medical expenses incurred	$16,000	$ 16,000
Less reduction:		
$100,000 AGI × 7.5%	(7,500)	
$100,000 AGI × 10%		(10,000)
Medical expense deduction	$ 8,500	$ 6,000

Joann's AMT adjustment for medical expenses is $2,500 ($8,500 regular income tax deduction − $6,000 AMT deduction).

Interest in General The AMT itemized deduction allowed for interest expense includes only qualified housing interest[34] and investment interest[35] to the extent of net investment income that is included in the determination of AMTI. Any interest that is deducted in calculating the regular income tax that is not permitted in calculating AMTI is treated as a positive adjustment.

In computing regular taxable income, taxpayers who itemize can deduct the following types of interest (refer to Chapter 10):

- Qualified residence interest.
- Investment interest, subject to the investment interest limitations (discussed under Investment Interest, which follows).

Housing Interest Under current regular income tax rules, taxpayers who itemize can deduct *qualified residence interest* on up to two residences. The deduction is limited to interest on acquisition indebtedness up to $1 million and home equity indebtedness up to $100,000. Acquisition indebtedness is debt that is incurred in acquiring, constructing, or substantially improving a qualified residence of the taxpayer and is secured by the residence. Home equity indebtedness is indebtedness secured by a qualified residence of the taxpayer, but does not include acquisition indebtedness.

The mortgage interest deduction for AMT purposes is limited to *qualified housing interest*, rather than *qualified residence interest*. Qualified housing interest includes only interest incurred to acquire, construct, or substantially improve the taxpayer's principal residence and such interest on one other qualified dwelling used for personal purposes. Thus, interest on a home equity loan is deductible for AMT purposes only if the home equity loan meets the definition of qualified housing interest, which is not always the case.

---

[32]§ 56(b)(1)(D).

[33]§ 56(b)(1)(B) and § 213(f). In the case of any taxable year beginning after December 31, 2012, and ending before January 1, 2017, subsection (a) shall be applied with respect to a taxpayer by substituting "7.5 percent" for "10 percent" if such taxpayer or such taxpayer's spouse has attained age 65 before the close of such taxable year.

[34]§ 56(b)(1)(C)(i).

[35]§ 56(b)(1)(C)(v).

TAX IN THE NEWS   AMT versus the Buffett Rule

Warren Buffett's disclosure that his secretary's tax rate is higher than his resulted in much media coverage and debate. One effect is the creation of the Buffett Rule. Under this suggested provision, taxpayers making more than $1 million would be subject to an average tax rate of at least 30 percent.

A legislative proposal called the Pay a Fair Share Act contains the same $1 million and 30 percent provisions. According to the nonpartisan Tax Policy Center, the provision would raise $20 billion in 2015 from 116,000 taxpayers. The revenue estimate is based on the unlikely assumption that there would be no change in taxpayer behavior.

How does this relate to the AMT? A logical result of the enactment of the Pay a Fair Share Act would be the repeal of the AMT. In terms of revenue production, however, this makes no sense as the AMT has been raising $40 billion a year from about 4 million taxpayers. Besides keeping the AMT, another alternative that prevents a loss of revenue would be to expand the fair share tax to apply a broader taxpayer base (e.g., $200,000 for a single taxpayer and $250,000 for a couple).

Sources: Based on Laura Saunders, "Tax Report: More Uncertainty for 2013," *Wall Street Journal*, February 18–19, 2012, p. B9; "The Buffett Alternative Tax," *Wall Street Journal*, September 20, 2011, p. A14.

© iStockphoto.com/Andrey Prokhorov

When additional mortgage interest is incurred (e.g., a mortgage refinancing), interest paid is deductible as qualified housing interest for AMT purposes only if:

- The proceeds are used to acquire or substantially improve a qualified residence,
- Interest on the prior loan was qualified housing interest, and
- The amount of the loan was not increased.

A positive AMT adjustment is required in the amount of the difference between qualified *residence* interest allowed as an itemized deduction for regular income tax purposes and qualified *housing* interest allowed in the determination of AMTI.

Investment Interest   Investment interest is deductible for regular income tax purposes and for AMT purposes to the extent of qualified net investment income.

However, because the categorization of interest as investment interest may differ for regular tax and AMT purposes an adjustment is required if the amount of investment interest deductible for regular income tax purposes differs from the amount deductible for AMT purposes. For example, an adjustment will arise if proceeds from a home equity loan are used to purchase investments. Interest on a home equity loan is deductible as qualified residence interest for regular income tax purposes, but is not deductible for AMT purposes unless the proceeds are used to acquire or substantially improve a qualified residence. For AMT purposes, however, interest on a home equity loan is deductible as investment interest expense if proceeds from the loan are used for investment purposes.

To determine the AMT adjustment for investment interest expense, it is necessary to compute the investment interest deduction for both regular income tax and AMT purposes.

Example 17

Tom had $20,000 interest income from corporate bonds and $5,000 dividends from preferred stock. He reported the following amounts of investment income for regular income tax and AMT purposes:

	Regular Income Tax	AMT
Corporate bond interest	$20,000	$20,000
Preferred stock dividends	5,000	5,000
Net investment income	$25,000	$25,000

Tom incurred investment interest expense of $10,000 related to the corporate bonds. He also incurred $4,000 interest on a home equity loan and used the proceeds of the loan to purchase preferred stock. For regular income tax purposes, this $4,000 is deductible as qualified residence interest. His *investment* interest expense for regular income tax and AMT purposes is computed below.

	Regular Income Tax	AMT
To carry corporate bonds	$10,000	$10,000
On home equity loan to carry preferred stock	–0–	4,000
Total investment interest expense	$10,000	$14,000

Investment interest expense is deductible to the extent of net investment income. Because the amount deductible for regular income tax purposes ($10,000) differs from the amount deductible for AMT purposes ($14,000), an AMT adjustment is required. The adjustment is computed as follows:

AMT deduction for investment interest expense	$ 14,000
Regular income tax deduction for investment interest expense	(10,000)
Negative AMT adjustment	$ 4,000

As discussed subsequently under AMT Preferences, the interest on private activity bonds usually is a tax preference for AMT purposes. Such interest can also affect the calculation of the AMT investment interest deduction in that it is included in the calculation of net investment income.

Cutback Adjustment The 3 percent/80 percent cutback adjustment that applies to regular income tax itemized deductions of certain high-income taxpayers (refer to Chapter 10) serves to disallow a portion of the taxpayer's itemized deductions for regular income tax purposes. This cutback does not apply in computing AMTI.[36] As a result, a negative adjustment is made for the amount of the cutback taken into consideration in the taxable income calculation.

Unlike many other AMT adjustments, a taxpayer cannot mitigate the impact of the itemized deduction adjustments by electing to treat the amounts the same for regular income tax and AMT purposes. Also note that because the starting point of the AMT computation is regular taxable income, a taxpayer who elects the standard deduction for regular tax purposes cannot claim itemized deductions for AMT purposes.[37]

Other Adjustments

Neither the standard deduction nor the personal and dependency exemption are allowed in the calculation of AMTI. Thus, these amounts also give rise to AMT adjustments.[38] However, these adjustments enter the AMTI calculation indirectly by adjusting the taxable income amount that begins the AMTI calculation. If a taxpayer itemizes deductions, then the starting point for the AMTI calculation is adjusted gross income (AGI) less itemized deductions. If a taxpayer does not itemize, but takes the standard deduction, the starting point for the AMTI calculation is AGI. Thus, any standard deduction or personal exemption amount taken in the calculation of regular taxable income is accounted for by adjusting the starting point of the AMTI calculation. As discussed later in the chapter, a separate exemption (see Exemption Amount) is allowed for AMT purposes.

---

[36]§ 56(b)(1)(F).

[37]Service Center Advice 200103073.

[38]§ 56(b)(1)(E).

Michael is single and has no dependents. He earned a salary of $110,000 in 2014, and his itemized deductions totaled $18,000. Based on this information, Michael's taxable income for 2014 is $88,050 ($110,000 − $18,000 itemized deductions− $3,950 exemption). However, Michael's taxable income starting point for the AMTI calculation would be $92,000, as the adjustment for the personal exemption is made to the taxable income amount that starts the AMTI calculation. Any adjustments required for itemized deductions are made in the AMTI calculation.

Example 18

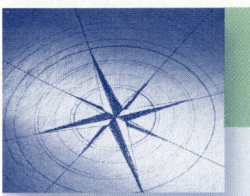

ETHICS & EQUITY Large Families and the AMT

The taxpayers claimed 12 personal and dependency exemptions (taxpayer, spouse, and 10 children) on their Federal income tax return. The taxpayers' itemized deductions included medical and dental expenses and state and local income and property taxes.

Under the regular income tax calculation, the taxpayers' taxable income was a negative amount. However, applying the AMT adjustments for personal and dependency exemptions, medical and dental expenses, and state and local income and property taxes resulted in the taxpayers being subject to the AMT.

The taxpayers are members of a religious denomination that encourages large families. The tax return they filed showed a $0 Federal income tax liability and did not include a Form 6251. According to the taxpayers, the AMT should not apply to them for the following reasons:

- Congress did not intend for a large family in itself to be a causative factor producing an AMT.
- They had no tax preferences.
- The AMT burdened the taxpayers' free exercise of religion.
- The AMT violated their equal protection and due process rights.

Both the Tax Court and the Third Circuit Court of Appeals rejected these arguments and held that the taxpayers were subject to the AMT.

Should taxpayers who have large families and no tax preferences be subject to the AMT? Was this the intended objective of the AMT?

Source: Based on *Klaassen v. Comm.*, 99–1 USTC ¶50,418, 83 AFTR 2d 99–1750, 182 F.3d 932 (CA–3, 1999), *aff'g* 76 TCM 20, T.C.Memo. 1998–241.

© iStockphoto.com/LdF

12-1d AMT Preferences

Unlike adjustments, which can be positive or negative, AMT **preferences** are always positive. In other words, preferences must be added back to taxable income in the calculation of AMTI. The following section discusses preferences for individual taxpayers.

LO.4

Identify the preferences that are included in calculating AMTI.

Percentage Depletion

Congress enacted the percentage depletion rules to provide taxpayers with incentives to invest in the development of specified natural resources. Percentage depletion is computed by multiplying a rate specified in the Code by the gross income from the property (refer to Chapter 8).[39] The rate is based on the type of mineral involved. The basis of the property is reduced by the amount of depletion taken until the basis reaches zero. However, because percentage depletion is based on gross income, rather than the investment in the property, taxpayers are allowed to continue taking percentage depletion deductions even after the basis of the property reaches zero. Thus, over the life of the property, depletion deductions may greatly exceed the cost of the property.

The percentage depletion preference is equal to the excess of the regular income tax deduction for percentage depletion over the adjusted basis of the property at the end of the taxable year.[40] Note that the end-of-year basis is determined

[39]§ 613(a).

[40]§ 57(a)(1). Note that the preference label does not apply to percentage depletion on oil and gas wells or to independent producers and royalty owners as defined in § 613A(c).

without regard to the depletion deduction for the taxable year. This preference is calculated separately for each mineral property owned by the taxpayer.[41] As a result, a taxpayer cannot use basis in one property to reduce the preference for excess depletion on another property.

Example 19	Kim owns a mineral property that qualifies for a 22% depletion rate. The basis of the property at the beginning of the year, prior to any current year depletion deduction, is $10,000. Gross income from the property for the year is $100,000. For regular income tax purposes, Kim's percentage depletion deduction (assume that it is not limited by taxable income from the property) is $22,000. For AMT purposes, Kim has a tax preference of $12,000 ($22,000 − $10,000).

Intangible Drilling Costs

In computing the regular income tax, taxpayers are allowed to deduct certain intangible drilling and development costs in the year incurred, although such costs are normally capital in nature (refer to Chapter 8). The deduction is allowed for costs incurred in connection with oil and gas wells and geothermal wells.

For AMT purposes, excess intangible drilling costs (IDC) for the year are treated as a preference.[42] The excess IDC preference is computed as follows:

> **IDC expensed in the year incurred**
> **Minus:** Deduction if IDC were capitalized and amortized over 10 years
> **Equals:** Excess of IDC expense over amortization
> **Minus:** 65% of net oil and gas or geothermal income
> **Equals:** Tax preference item

The IDC preference is computed separately for oil and gas wells and geothermal wells.

Example 20	Ben, who incurred IDC of $50,000 during the year, elected to expense that amount. His net oil and gas income for the year was $60,000. Currently, Ben has no income from geothermal wells. Ben's preference for IDC is $6,000 [($50,000 IDC − $5,000 amortization) − (65% × $60,000 income)].

A taxpayer can avoid the preference for IDC by electing to write off the expenditures over a 10-year period for regular income tax purposes.

Interest on Private Activity Bonds

Like interest income earned on other municipal bonds, income from private activity bonds is not included in taxable income, and expenses related to carrying such bonds are not deductible for regular income tax purposes. However, interest on private activity bonds usually is considered a preference in computing AMTI. As a result, expenses incurred in carrying the bonds are offset against the interest income in computing the preference amount.[43] Note that to encourage the economic recovery, interest on private activity bonds issued after December 31, 2008, and before January 1, 2011, is not treated as a preference.

The Code contains a lengthy, complex definition of private activity bonds.[44] In general, **private activity bonds** are bonds issued by states or municipalities with more than 10 percent of the proceeds being used for private business use. For example, a bond issued by a city whose proceeds are used to construct a factory that is leased to a private business at a favorable rate is a private activity bond.

The vast majority of tax-exempt bonds issued by states and municipalities are not classified as private activity bonds. Therefore, the interest income from such bonds does not regularly create a preference for AMT purposes for most individuals.

---

[41]§ 614(a).
[42]§ 57(a)(2).

[43]§ 57(a)(5).
[44]§ 141.

TAX IN THE NEWS   AMT Liabilities by State

Each year, as part of the Statistics of Income (SOI) program, the IRS provides interested citizens with information about how the U.S. Federal tax system works. The statistics provided as a part of the SOI program include information about tax revenues collected, number of returns filed, number of audits undertaken, hours worked by IRS personnel, and more. The Tax Policy Center uses the information in the SOI database to compile a profile of AMT liabilities by state. The states with the highest and lowest percentages of taxpayers in AMT are as follows:

States with Highest Number of Returns in AMT (% of returns)	States with Lowest Number of Returns in AMT (% of returns)
1. New Jersey (9.20)	50. Alaska (1.69)
2. Connecticut (8.20)	49. South Dakota (1.79)
3. New York (8.12)	48. Wyoming (1.84)
4. District of Columbia (7.85)	47. Tennessee (1.88)
5. California (7.05)	46. Nevada (1.91)

What explains the variance by state? Given that the AMT is intended to target wealthy taxpayers, some of the variance may have to do with income levels in a particular state. However, remember that the AMT disallows state and local tax deductions. According to the Tax Policy Center, this disallowed deduction, along with disallowed dependency exemptions, accounts for nearly 80 percent of the difference between the TMT and regular income tax amounts. Note that of the states at the bottom of the list, only Tennessee has an income tax (and even then, Tennessee's income tax is quite limited). As a consequence, living in high-tax states may make a taxpayer more likely to owe AMT.

Sources: State percentages: http://taxpolicycenter.org/taxfacts/displayafact.cfm?DocID=536; Causes of AMT: www.taxpolicycenter.org/upload/Elements/II-4KEYELEMENTS_AlternativeMinimumTax.final.pdf.

THE BIG PICTURE

Example 21

Return to the facts of *The Big Picture* on p. 12-1. Bob and Carol both have invested substantial amounts in private activity bonds. All of the private activity bonds that each of them owns were issued in 2010. Consequently, a tax preference does not result for either Carol or Bob.

Depreciation

For real property and leased personal property placed in service before 1987, there is an AMT preference for the excess of accelerated depreciation over straight-line depreciation.[45] However, examination of the cost recovery tables for pre-1987 real property (refer to Chapter 8) reveals that from the eighth year on, accelerated depreciation will not exceed straight-line depreciation. Consequently, taxpayers no longer have preferences attributable to pre-1987 real property.

Fifty Percent Exclusion for Certain Small Business Stock

Fifty percent of the gain on the sale of certain small business stock normally is excludible from gross income for regular income tax purposes. However, for 2009 and 2010, the 50 percent is increased to 75 percent. For qualified small business stock acquired after September 2, 2010, and before January 1, 2014, 100 percent of the gain is excluded from regular taxable income.[46]

For AMT purposes, 7 percent of the excluded gain amount is a preference.[47] Thus, in a year where 100 percent of the gain can be excluded from regular taxable income, 7 percent of the gain would be added back to taxable income in the calculation of AMTI.

---

[45] § 57(a)(6).
[46] § 1202(a)(4)(A).
[47] § 57(a)(7).

12-1e Illustration of the AMT Computation

LO.5

Compute the AMT and complete Form 6251.

The computation of the AMT is illustrated in the following example. Note that because the 2014 Form 6251 was not available at the time of printing, the 2013 AMT exemption amounts and tax brackets are used in the following example.

Example 22

Molly Seims, who is single and age 66, had taxable income for 2013 as follows:

Salary		$ 92,000
Interest		8,000
Adjusted gross income		$100,000
Less itemized deductions:		
Medical expenses ($17,500 − 7.5% of $100,000 AGI)[a]	$10,000	
State income taxes	4,000	
Interest[b]		
Home mortgage (for qualified housing)	20,000*	
Investment interest	3,300*	
Contributions (cash)	5,000*	
Casualty losses ($14,000 − 10% of $100,000 AGI)	4,000*	(46,300)
		$ 53,700
Less personal exemption		(3,900)
Taxable income		$ 49,800

[a] Total medical expenses were $17,500, reduced by 7.5% of AGI, as the taxpayer is older than 65. This results in an itemized deduction of $10,000. For AMT purposes, the reduction is 10%, irrespective of the age of the taxpayer, which leaves an AMT itemized deduction of $7,500 ($17,500 − 10% of $100,000 AGI). Therefore, an adjustment of $2,500 ($10,000 − $7,500) is required for medical expenses disallowed for AMT purposes.

[b] In this illustration, all interest is deductible in computing AMTI. Qualified housing interest is deductible without adjustment. Investment interest ($3,300) is deductible to the extent of net investment income included in AMTI. For this purpose, the $8,000 of interest income is treated as net investment income.

Deductions marked with an asterisk are allowed for AMT purposes. Thus, adjustments are required for state income taxes and for medical expenses to the extent the medical expenses deductible for regular income tax purposes are calculated using a 7.5% floor rather than the 10% AMT floor (see note [a]). In addition, Molly earned $40,000 of interest income on private activity bonds issued in 2012. She also exercised ISOs in 2013. The spread (the difference between the exercise price and the fair market value on the date of exercise) was $35,000. Molly's regular tax liability is calculated using the Tax Table method (see Chapter 3). AMTI is computed as follows:

Taxable income[c]	$ 53,700
Plus: Adjustments	
State income taxes	4,000
Medical expenses (see note [a])	2,500
Incentive stock options	35,000
Plus: Preference (interest on private activity bonds)	40,000
Equals: AMTI	$135,200
Minus: AMT exemption[d]	(46,950)
Equals: Minimum tax base	$ 88,250
Multiplied by: AMT tax rate	× 26%
Equals: Tentative minimum tax (TMT)	$ 22,945
Minus: Regular income tax on taxable income	(8,379)
Equals: AMT	$ 14,566

[c] Note that although the personal exemption is technically an adjustment, the Code and the Form 6251 add the personal exemption to the taxable income amount used to start the AMTI calculation, rather than include the personal exemption with the other adjustments.

[d] Because Molly's AMTI exceeds the $115,400 exemption phaseout amount, she is not entitled to the maximum 2013 exemption amount of $51,900. Her exemption amount is $46,950 [$51,900 − .25($135,200 − $115,400)].

The solution to Example 22 is also presented on Form 6251.

Form 6251

Department of the Treasury
Internal Revenue Service (99)

Alternative Minimum Tax—Individuals

▶ Information about Form 6251 and its separate instructions is at *www.irs.gov/form6251*.
▶ **Attach to Form 1040 or Form 1040NR.**

OMB No. 1545-0074

2013

Attachment
Sequence No. **32**

Name(s) shown on Form 1040 or Form 1040NR

Molly Seims

Your social security number

111-11-1111

Part I   Alternative Minimum Taxable Income (See instructions for how to complete each line.)

1	If filing Schedule A (Form 1040), enter the amount from Form 1040, line 41, and go to line 2. Otherwise, enter the amount from Form 1040, line 38, and go to line 7. (If less than zero, enter as a negative amount.)	**1**	*53,700*
2	Medical and dental. If you or your spouse was 65 or older, enter the **smaller** of Schedule A (Form 1040), line 4, **or** 2.5% (.025) of Form 1040, line 38. If zero or less, enter -0-	**2**	*2,500*
3	Taxes from Schedule A (Form 1040), line 9	**3**	*4,000*
4	Enter the home mortgage interest adjustment, if any, from line 6 of the worksheet in the instructions for this line	**4**	
5	Miscellaneous deductions from Schedule A (Form 1040), line 27	**5**	
6	If Form 1040, line 38, is $150,000 or less, enter -0-. Otherwise, see instructions	**6** (	)
7	Tax refund from Form 1040, line 10 or line 21	**7** (	)
8	Investment interest expense (difference between regular tax and AMT)	**8**	
9	Depletion (difference between regular tax and AMT)	**9**	
10	Net operating loss deduction from Form 1040, line 21. Enter as a positive amount	**10**	
11	Alternative tax net operating loss deduction	**11** (	)
12	Interest from specified private activity bonds exempt from the regular tax	**12**	*40,000*
13	Qualified small business stock (7% of gain excluded under section 1202)	**13**	
14	Exercise of incentive stock options (excess of AMT income over regular tax income)	**14**	*35,000*
15	Estates and trusts (amount from Schedule K-1 (Form 1041), box 12, code A)	**15**	
16	Electing large partnerships (amount from Schedule K-1 (Form 1065-B), box 6)	**16**	
17	Disposition of property (difference between AMT and regular tax gain or loss)	**17**	
18	Depreciation on assets placed in service after 1986 (difference between regular tax and AMT)	**18**	
19	Passive activities (difference between AMT and regular tax income or loss)	**19**	
20	Loss limitations (difference between AMT and regular tax income or loss)	**20**	
21	Circulation costs (difference between regular tax and AMT)	**21**	
22	Long-term contracts (difference between AMT and regular tax income)	**22**	
23	Mining costs (difference between regular tax and AMT)	**23**	
24	Research and experimental costs (difference between regular tax and AMT)	**24**	
25	Income from certain installment sales before January 1, 1987	**25** (	)
26	Intangible drilling costs preference	**26**	
27	Other adjustments, including income-based related adjustments	**27**	
28	**Alternative minimum taxable income.** Combine lines 1 through 27. (If married filing separately and line 28 is more than $238,550, see instructions.)	**28**	*135,200*

Part II   Alternative Minimum Tax (AMT)

29 Exemption. (If you were under age 24 at the end of 2013, see instructions.)

IF your filing status is . . .	AND line 28 is not over . . .	THEN enter on line 29 . . .		
Single or head of household	$115,400	$51,900		
Married filing jointly or qualifying widow(er)	153,900	80,800	**29**	*46,950*
Married filing separately	76,950	40,400		

If line 28 is **over** the amount shown above for your filing status, see instructions.

30	Subtract line 29 from line 28. If more than zero, go to line 31. If zero or less, enter -0- here and on lines 31, 33, and 35, and go to line 34	**30**	*88,250*
31	• If you are filing Form 2555 or 2555-EZ, see instructions for the amount to enter. • If you reported capital gain distributions directly on Form 1040, line 13; you reported qualified dividends on Form 1040, line 9b; **or** you had a gain on both lines 15 and 16 of Schedule D (Form 1040) (as refigured for the AMT, if necessary), complete Part III on the back and enter the amount from line 60 here. • **All others:** If line 30 is $179,500 or less ($89,750 or less if married filing separately), multiply line 30 by 26% (.26). Otherwise, multiply line 30 by 28% (.28) and subtract $3,590 ($1,795 if married filing separately) from the result.	**31**	*22,945*
32	Alternative minimum tax foreign tax credit (see instructions)	**32**	
33	Tentative minimum tax. Subtract line 32 from line 31	**33**	*22,945*
34	Tax from Form 1040, line 44 (minus any tax from Form 4972 and any foreign tax credit from Form 1040, line 47). If you used Schedule J to figure your tax, the amount from line 44 of Form 1040 must be refigured without using Schedule J (see instructions)	**34**	*8,379*
35	**AMT.** Subtract line 34 from line 33. If zero or less, enter -0-. Enter here and on Form 1040, line 45	**35**	*14,566*

For Paperwork Reduction Act Notice, see your tax return instructions.   Cat. No. 13600G   Form **6251** (2013)

12-1f AMT Credit

LO.6

Describe and illustrate the role of the AMT credit in the alternative minimum tax structure.

As was illustrated in several of the examples in this chapter, timing differences that give rise to AMT adjustments eventually reverse. To provide equity for taxpayers, a tax credit is created in a year in which a taxpayer pays AMT as a result of these timing differences.[48]

This credit, known as the **alternative minimum tax credit**, is created only by the AMT liability that results from timing differences.[49] A credit is not created or increased by AMT exclusions, which represent permanent differences between the regular income tax liability and the AMT. These AMT exclusions include the following amounts:

- The standard deduction.
- Personal exemptions.
- Medical expenses, to the extent deductible for regular income tax purposes but not deductible in computing AMTI.
- Other itemized deductions not allowable for AMT purposes, including miscellaneous itemized deductions, taxes, and interest expense.
- Excess percentage depletion.
- Tax-exempt interest on specified private activity bonds.

Example 23

Patrick, who is single, has zero taxable income for 2014. He also has positive timing adjustments of $300,000 and AMT exclusions of $100,000. Because of the amount of his AMTI, the exemption is phased out completely and his AMT base is $400,000. Patrick's TMT is $108,350 [($182,500 × 26% AMT rate) + ($217,500 × 28% AMT rate)].

To determine the amount of AMT credit to carry over, the AMT must be recomputed to reflect only the effect of timing differences, as shown in Example 24.

Example 24

Assume the same facts as in the previous example. If there had been no positive timing adjustments for the year, Patrick's TMT would have been $12,272 [($100,000 AMT exclusions − $52,800 exemption) × 26% AMT rate]. Patrick may carry over an AMT credit of $96,078 ($108,350 AMT − $12,272 related to AMT exclusions) to 2015 and subsequent years.

The adjustments and preferences to taxable income in arriving at AMTI are set forth in Concept Summary 12.1.

12-2 CORPORATE ALTERNATIVE MINIMUM TAX

LO.7

Compare the individual AMT calculation with the corporate AMT calculation.

The AMT calculation for corporations is similar to that for individual taxpayers. However, there are several important differences:

- The corporate AMT rate is 20 percent versus the 26 and 28 percent rates for individuals.[50]
- The AMT exemption for corporations is $40,000 reduced by 25 percent of the amount by which AMTI exceeds $150,000 and has not historically been indexed to inflation.[51]
- While there are some differences, most of the adjustments and preferences applicable to individual taxpayers also are applicable to corporate taxpayers.

---

[48]§ 53.
[49]S Rept No. 99–313 (PL 99–514) p. 536.

[50]§ 55(b)(1)(B).
[51]§§ 55(d)(2) and (3).

CONCEPT SUMMARY 12.1

AMT Adjustments and Preferences for Individuals

Adjustments	Positive	Negative	Both*
Adjusted gain or loss on property dispositions			X
Alternative tax NOL deduction (ATNOLD)			X
Circulation expenditures			X
Completed contract method			X
Depreciation of post-1986 personal property			X
Depreciation of post-1986 real property			X
Incentive stock options	X**		
Itemized deductions:			
Medical expenses	X		
Miscellaneous itemized deductions	X		
Private activity bond interest that is AMT investment interest		X	
Property tax on personalty	X		
Property tax on realty	X		
Qualified interest on student loans	X		
Qualified residence interest that is AMT investment interest		X	
Qualified residence interest that is not qualified housing interest	X		
State income taxes	X		
Tax benefit rule for state income tax refund		X	
Mining exploration and development costs			X
Passive activity losses			X
Personal and dependency exemptions	X		
Pollution control facilities			X
Research and experimental expenditures			X
Standard deduction	X		
Preferences			
§ 1202 exclusion for certain small business stock	X		
Depreciation on pre-1987 leased personal property	X		
Intangible drilling costs	X		
Percentage depletion in excess of adjusted basis	X		
Private activity bond interest income	X***		

* Timing differences.

** While the adjustment is a positive adjustment, the AMT basis for the stock is increased by the amount of the positive adjustment.

*** Interest on private activity bonds issued after December 31, 2008, and before January 1, 2011, is not treated as a tax preference.

Although there are computational differences, the corporate AMT and the individual AMT have the identical objective: to try to ensure that taxpayers who have economic income pay some income tax. The formula for determining the corporate AMT appears in Figure 12.2.

12-2a Small Corporations and the AMT

Two provisions exist that allow small corporations to avoid the AMT. For these purposes, a corporation is classified as a small corporation based on the amount of its annual gross receipts.

In its first tax year of existence, a corporation will automatically be classified as a small corporation, which means that a new corporation will not be subject to AMT in its first year of existence.[52]

---

[52]§ 55(e)(1)(C).

FIGURE 12.2	AMT Formula for Corporations

Taxable income prior to any regular tax NOL deduction

Plus or minus: Adjustments

Plus: Preferences

Equals: Pre-ACE alternative minimum taxable income (AMTI)

Plus or minus: ACE adjustment

Equals: AMTI before ATNOLD

Minus: ATNOLD (limited to 90% of AMTI before ATNOLD)

Equals: AMTI

Minus: Exemption

Equals: Alternative minimum tax (AMT) base

Multiplied by: 20%

Equals: Tentative minimum tax before AMT foreign tax credit

Minus: AMT foreign tax credit

Equals: Tentative minimum tax (TMT)

Minus: Regular tax liability (less any foreign tax credit)

Equals: AMT (if TMT > regular tax liability)

For each succeeding tax year, the prior year's average annual gross receipts must be less than a certain threshold for the corporation to continue to be exempt from AMT. In its second year of operations, if a corporation's annual average gross receipts in the prior year were less than $5 million, the corporation is not subject to AMT. For each succeeding year of operations (i.e., the third year and after), if the corporation's average annual gross receipts for the three-year period ending before the current tax year do not exceed $7.5 million, the corporation continues to be exempt from AMT. However, if a corporation ever fails the gross receipts test, it is ineligible for small corporation classification in any future tax year.[53]

12-2b AMT Adjustments

Similar to individuals, adjustments in the corporate AMT calculation relate to timing differences. Adjustments are differences that arise because the provisions in the regular tax law for a particular item differ from the AMT tax law provisions. The following adjustments that were discussed in connection with the individual AMT also apply to the corporate AMT calculation:

- Excess of MACRS over AMT depreciation on real and personal property placed in service after 1986.
- Pollution control facilities placed in service after 1986.
- Mining and exploration expenditures.
- Income from long-term contracts.
- Adjusted gain or loss on the dispositions of assets.

While the NOL deduction must be recalculated for AMT purposes, the deduction is allowed in the corporate AMT calculation. In addition, the corporate ATNOLD cannot exceed 90 percent of AMTI before the deduction for the ATNOLD.[54]

---

[53]§§ 55(e)(1)(A) and (B). An estimated 3 million corporations (95% of incorporated businesses) qualify for this exemption.

[54]§ 56(d).

ETHICS & EQUITY   AMT and Small Corporations

Abigail is the controller of a medium-size company specializing in the construction of single-family homes. As such, she prepares the corporate tax return.

The corporation expects its gross revenue in each of its first three years of operations to be approximately $15 million and to increase thereafter by 15 percent annually.

Abigail is aware that the corporation is eligible for the small corporation exception to the AMT in its first year but will not be thereafter.

The corporation uses the completed contract method of accounting for 2014. After 2014, however, Abigail has the corporation switch to the percentage of completion method. Evaluate what Abigail has done.

© iStockphoto.com/LdF

Adjustment Applicable Only to Corporations

An AMT adjustment applicable only to corporations is the adjusted current earnings (ACE) adjustment.[55] This **ACE adjustment** differs from those discussed previously because the ACE amount is intended to approximate a corporation's economic income and, as a result, the corporation's true tax-paying ability. In other words, the ACE adjustment is intended to limit the benefits of certain tax provisions that the other adjustments, by their nature, cannot limit. Thus, a corporation may incur AMT not only because of specifically targeted adjustments and preferences but also as a result of any methods that cause ACE to exceed AMTI before the ACE adjustment.

Note that although the ACE calculation results in an adjustment amount, it is not made in the same place as the other AMT adjustments. The starting point for computing ACE is pre-ACE AMTI. As shown in Figure 12.2, pre-ACE AMTI is defined as regular taxable income after AMT adjustments (other than the ACE or ATNOLD adjustments) and preferences. This income amount is adjusted for various amounts to arrive at ACE. The ACE calculation is not addressed in detail in this chapter.[56] Although not identical, in spirit, the ACE calculation is similar to the earnings and profits calculation (see Chapter 20).

The ACE amount is not the ACE adjustment. The adjustment is equal to 75 percent of the excess of ACE over pre-ACE AMTI.[57] The ACE adjustment can be either a positive or negative amount. In other words, AMTI is increased by 75 percent of the excess of ACE over unadjusted AMTI or AMTI is reduced by 75 percent of the excess of unadjusted AMTI over ACE. The negative adjustment is limited to the aggregate of the positive adjustments under ACE for prior years, reduced by the previously claimed negative adjustments.[58] See Concept Summary 12.2 relating to the determination of the ACE adjustment.

Example 25

A calendar year corporation has the following data:

	2013	2014	2015
Pre-adjusted AMTI	$3,000	$3,000	$3,100
Adjusted current earnings	4,000	3,000	2,000

In 2013, because ACE exceeds unadjusted AMTI by $1,000, $750 (75% × $1,000) is included as a positive adjustment to AMTI. No adjustment is necessary for 2014. As unadjusted AMTI exceeds ACE by $1,100 in 2015, there is a potential negative adjustment to AMTI of $825 ($1,100 × 75%). Because the total increases to AMTI for prior years equal $750 and there are no previously claimed negative adjustments, only $750 of the potential negative adjustment reduces AMTI for 2015. Further, $75 of the negative amount is lost forever.

---

[55]§ 56(c).

[56]For additional coverage of the calculation of ACE, refer to Chapter 3 in *South-Western Federal Taxation: Corporations, Partnerships, Estates & Trusts.* The instructions for Form 4626 illustrate the ACE adjustment and provide a worksheet for its computation.

[57]§ 56(g).

[58]§§ 56(g)(1) and (2).

CONCEPT SUMMARY 12.2

Determining the ACE Adjustment*

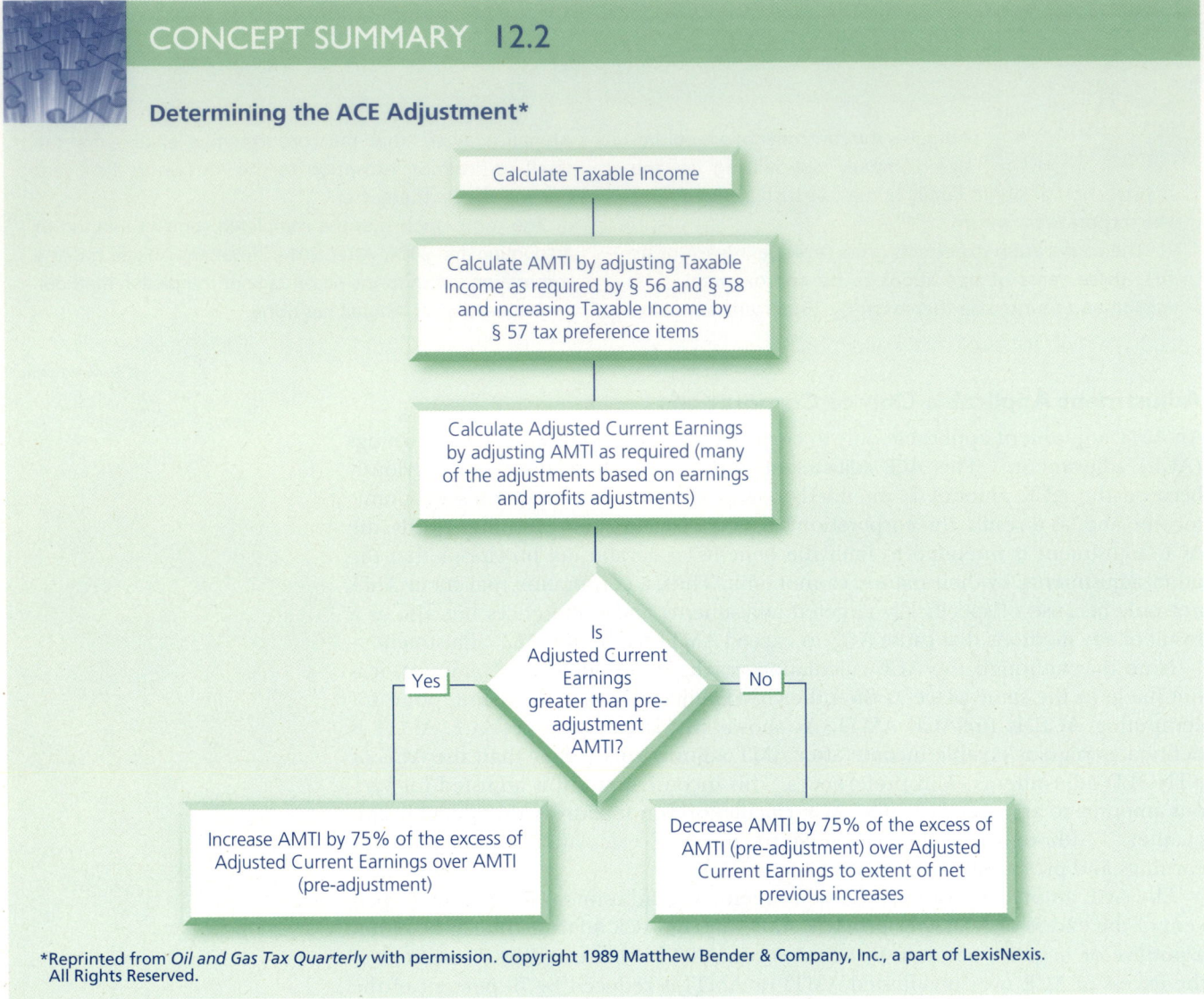

*Reprinted from *Oil and Gas Tax Quarterly* with permission. Copyright 1989 Matthew Bender & Company, Inc., a part of LexisNexis. All Rights Reserved.

© iStockphoto.com/Andrey Prokhorov

12-2c AMT Preferences

As is shown in Figure 12.2, the corporate AMTI calculation also includes preferences. The preference items discussed in the individual AMTI calculation also apply to corporations.

Example 26	The following information applies to Brown Corporation (a calendar year taxpayer) for 2014:	
	Taxable income	$4,000,000
	Mining exploration costs	500,000
	Percentage depletion claimed (the property has a zero adjusted basis)	2,600,000
	Brown Corporation's AMTI for 2014 is determined as follows:	
	Taxable income	$4,000,000
	Plus or minus: Adjustment:	
	Excess mining exploration costs [$500,000 (amount expensed) − $50,000 (amount allowed over a 10-year amortization period)]	450,000
	Plus: Preference:	
	Excess depletion	2,600,000
	AMTI	$7,050,000

TAX IN THE NEWS   Evaluating the AMT

The fact that the AMT is a parallel tax system adds complexity to an already complicated tax system. This complexity is exacerbated because many amounts are not disallowed in total for AMT purposes, but limited in some way for those who make too much use of them. As more taxpayers are subject to AMT and faced with its complexity, calls to abolish the AMT have increased. However, the AMT may actually present a road map for tax reform. One possibility might be to eliminate the parallel system approach and incorporate the best practices and principles of the AMT into a new income tax system.

Theoretically, a good tax is fair, easy to administer, economically efficient, and adjusted for the impacts of inflation. The AMT has many of these characteristics. The tax base is broad and few deductions are allowed, which is consistent with low administrative costs. The rates are flat (or nearly so) and not tied to the number of dependents, which is consistent with fairness. The high exemption amount means low-income taxpayers have neither a tax liability nor significant compliance costs, which also eases the administrative burden.

The existing AMT is not a perfect tax. The exemption phases out, so a taxpayer's actual tax rate can be higher than the stated rate, and special breaks for capital gains and dividends are allowed. Additionally, the current tax code creates incentives for certain types of behavior (e.g., home ownership, charitable giving), which might diminish under an AMT-like tax system. Despite this, given the AMT is currently a part of the tax system, using it as the starting point for a better income tax system could simplify the lengthy and contentious process of tax reform.

Source: Based on Daniel S. Goldberg, "To Praise the AMT or to Bury It," *Virginia Tax Review*, Vol. 24, p. 835–861, 2005. Available at SSRN: **http://ssrn.com/abstract=734605**.

12-2d Exemption Amount

The corporate tentative minimum tax (TMT) is calculated at a rate of 20 percent of AMTI that exceeds the corporation's exemption amount. The exemption amount for a corporation is $40,000 reduced by a phaseout of 25 percent of the amount by which AMTI exceeds $150,000. Neither the exemption amount nor the exemption phaseout threshold is indexed to inflation.

> **Example 27**
>
> Blue Corporation has AMTI of $180,000. The exemption amount is reduced by $7,500 [25% × ($180,000 − $150,000)], and the amount remaining is $32,500 ($40,000 − $7,500). Thus, Blue Corporation's AMT base (refer to Figure 12.2) is $147,500 ($180,000 − $32,500).

Note that the exemption amount phases out entirely when AMTI reaches $310,000, which is why many corporations realize no benefit from the exemption amount in the calculation of AMT.

12-2e Other Aspects of the Corporate AMT

In a year in which the corporation is subject to the AMT, the AMT amount creates a minimum tax credit available for carryover to future years. Unlike the individual minimum tax credit calculation, the entire AMT amount is available for a corporation to carry over (no adjustment to the amount is required).

> **Example 28**
>
> As calculated in Example 26, Brown Corporation's TMT is $1,410,000 (20% of $7,050,000). If the corporation's regular income tax liability is $1,360,000, the 2014 AMT liability is $50,000 ($1,410,000 − $1,360,000). Brown's minimum tax credit is $50,000, available in future years to offset any excess of regular corporate income tax liability over TMT.

Note that the only credit available to offset a corporate taxpayer's TMT is the foreign tax credit. Unlike the individual AMT calculation, no other credits can reduce a corporate taxpayer's TMT. In addition, to the extent the corporation is allowed other credits, those are allowed only to offset the excess of any regular tax liability (after the foreign tax credit) over the TMT (after the foreign tax credit).

Form 4626 (Alternative Minimum Tax—Corporations) is the form corporations use to report AMT amounts to the IRS. Any AMT calculated is carried over to Schedule J of Form 1120 (U.S. Corporation Income Tax Return).

12-3 TAX PLANNING

12-3a Avoiding Preferences and Adjustments

LO.8

Identify and apply various tax planning opportunities to minimize the AMT.

One strategic approach to managing AMT liabilities is to avoid preference and adjustment amounts where possible.

- A taxpayer who expects to be subject to the AMT should not invest in private activity bonds unless doing so makes good investment sense. Any AMT triggered by interest on private activity bonds reduces the yield on an investment in such bonds.
- Many AMT adjustments (e.g., depreciation, circulation expenditures, mining exploration and development costs, and research and experimental expenditures) can be avoided if the taxpayer elects to use the AMT tax treatment for regular tax purposes.
- Neither property taxes nor real estate taxes are deductible for AMT if they are categorized as itemized deductions. However, taxes deductible as a part of business operations or rental activities are allowed for AMT purposes. Therefore, a taxpayer who could qualify for a home-office deduction would be able to deduct a portion of his or her home's real estate taxes as business expenses rather than as an itemized deduction.
- A taxpayer who expects to be subject to the AMT will not realize a tax benefit from using a home equity line of credit to buy a car. Although the interest may be deductible for regular tax purposes, an AMT adjustment will be required. A lower interest rate may be obtained from a regular car loan. In addition, if the car is used in the taxpayer's business, some of the interest on the car loan may be deductible as a trade or business expense.

12-3b Controlling the Timing of Preferences and Adjustments

If preference and adjustment amounts cannot be avoided, the timing of these amounts may help to mitigate AMT liabilities.

- The AMT exemption often keeps items of tax preference from being subject to the AMT. To use the AMT exemption effectively, taxpayers should attempt to control the timing of such preference items when possible.
- In a year that a taxpayer expects to be subject to the AMT, real estate or fourth-quarter estimated state tax payments should not be made in December. Any benefit received from the regular income tax deduction for these amounts will be offset by the AMT adjustment made.

12-3c Other AMT Tax Planning Strategies

A potential AMT liability can be reduced by decreasing adjusted gross income (AGI). Certain contributions to qualified retirement savings plans are excluded from gross income, which would result in a decreased AGI amount. Where a taxpayer participates in a § 401(k), § 457(b) plan, or SIMPLE IRA plan (see Chapter 19), the maximum allowable salary deferral contributions to such a plan would reduce AGI, which is beneficial for both regular tax and AMT purposes as well as for retirement planning.

REFOCUS ON THE BIG PICTURE

THE PRESENCE OR ABSENCE OF THE AMT

Bob contacts Adam, his tax return preparer, and explains in an excited voice that he believes that he underpaid his Federal income tax liability for 2014 by $15,000. He is worried about the negative effects of any underpayment if it is discovered during an IRS audit, including the effect on his future marriage to Carol. Adam reviews Bob's tax return and assures him that it was properly prepared. Bob indicates that Carol has provided him with a copy of her tax return. He asks Adam to compare the returns and then explain the tax liability difference to him. He faxes a copy of Carol's return to Adam.

Adam examines the two tax returns and discovers that the difference relates to the treatment of the interest earned on the tax-exempt bonds. Both Bob and Carol own tax-exempt bonds, including private activity bonds that usually are subject to the AMT. However, Carol's accountant, Ava, apparently overlooked the fact that interest on private activity bonds is not a tax preference for such bonds issued in 2010. So the $15,000 AMT that was reported on Carol's Form 6251 is in error. Bob texts the good news to Carol that she is eligible for a Federal income tax refund.

© wavebreakmedia ltd/Shutterstock.com

Key Terms

ACE adjustment, 12-27

Adjustments, 12-7

Alternative minimum tax (AMT), 12-2

Alternative minimum tax credit, 12-24

Alternative tax NOL deduction (ATNOLD), 12-14

Exemption amount, 12-5, 12-29

Incentive stock options (ISOs), 12-11

Preferences, 12-19

Private activity bonds, 12-20

Discussion Questions

1. **LO.1** Kelly was recently promoted and received a substantial raise. She talks to her tax adviser about potential tax ramifications. After making some projections, her adviser welcomes her to the AMT club. Kelly believes that it is unfair that she must pay more than the regular income tax, as she does not feel wealthy and has substantial college-related debts. Explain to Kelly the purpose of the AMT and why it applies to her.

2. **LO.2** How could the AMT be calculated without using regular taxable income as a starting point?

3. **LO.2** Both AMT adjustments and AMT preferences can cause AMTI to increase. Both AMT adjustments and AMT preferences can cause AMTI to decrease. Evaluate these statements.

4. **LO.2, 4** Identify which of the following are preferences:
   a. Seven percent of the exclusion associated with gains on the sale of certain small business stock.
   b. Exclusion on the receipt of property by gift or by inheritance.
   c. Exclusion associated with payment of premiums by the employer on group term life insurance for coverage not in excess of $50,000.
   d. Percentage depletion in excess of the property's adjusted basis.
   e. Exclusion of life insurance proceeds received as the result of death.
   f. Exclusion to the employee on the employer's payments of health insurance premiums for employees.
   g. Qualified dividends that are eligible for the 15% tax rate.

5. **LO.2, 4** Identify which of the following are preferences:
   a. Exclusion for qualified employee discount provided by employer.
   b. Exclusion to employee on the employer's contribution to the employee's pension plan.
   c. Excess of deduction for circulation expenditures for regular income tax purposes over the deduction for AMT purposes.
   d. Excess of amortization allowance over depreciation on pre-1987 certified pollution control facilities.
   e. Excess of accelerated over straight-line depreciation on real property placed in service before 1987.
   f. Real property taxes on the taxpayer's residence.

6. **LO.2** Explain the AMT calculation presented in Figure 12.1 using the figure as a guide for your explanation.

7. **LO.2** AMT liability results if the tentative minimum tax (TMT) exceeds the regular income tax liability. What happens if the regular income tax liability exceeds the TMT? Does this create a negative AMT amount that can be carried to other years? Explain.

8. **LO.2** Andrew and Monica, unrelated individuals, have the same filing status (head of household). However, Monica's AMT exemption amount is $52,800, while Andrew's is $0. Explain.

9. **LO.2** Alfred is single, and his AMTI of $350,000 consists of the following:

Ordinary income	$250,000
Long-term capital gains	70,000
Qualified dividends	30,000

   What tax rates are applicable in calculating Alfred's TMT?

10. **LO.2** Can any nonrefundable credits, other than the foreign tax credit, reduce the regular income tax liability below the amount of the TMT? Explain.

11. **LO.3** Tad, who owns and operates a business, acquired machinery and placed it in service in June 2005. The machinery is 10-year property. Does Tad need to make an AMT adjustment in 2005 or 2014 for the depreciation on the machinery? Explain.

12. **LO.3** Nell recently purchased a weekly newspaper that has been generating losses. Nell is convinced she can turn the newspaper around with a new editorial style and increased circulation expenditures. What are the tax benefits and potential tax pitfalls, if any, of increasing the circulation expenses?

13. **LO.3, 8** How can an individual taxpayer avoid having an AMT adjustment for mining exploration and development costs?

14. **LO.3** Certain taxpayers have the option of using either the percentage of completion method or the completed contract method for reporting profit on long-term contracts. What impact could the AMT have on this decision?

15. **LO.3** If the stock received under an incentive stock option (ISO) is sold in the year of exercise, there is no AMT adjustment. If the stock is sold in a later year, there will be an AMT adjustment. Evaluate the validity of these statements.

16. **LO.3** In 1998, Douglas purchased an office building for $500,000 to be used in his business. He sells the building in the current tax year. Explain why his recognized gain or loss for regular income tax purposes will be different from his recognized gain or loss for AMT purposes.

Issue ID

17. **LO.3, 8** Celine is going to be subject to the AMT in 2014. She owns an investment building and is considering disposing of it and investing in other realty. Based on an appraisal of the building's value, the realized gain would be $85,000. Ed has offered to purchase the building from Celine with the closing date being December 29, 2014. Ed wants to close the transaction in 2014 because certain beneficial tax consequences will result only if the transaction is closed prior to the beginning of 2015. Abby has offered to purchase the building with the closing date being January 2, 2015. The building has a $95,000 greater AMT adjusted basis than regular tax basis. For regular income tax purposes, Celine expects to be in the 25% tax bracket in 2014 and the 28% tax bracket in 2015. What are the relevant tax issues that Celine faces in making her decision?

18. **LO.3** Passive activity losses are not deductible in computing either taxable income or AMTI. Explain why an adjustment for passive activity losses may be required for AMT purposes.

19. **LO.3, 4** What effect do adjustments and preferences have on the calculation of the ATNOLD?

20. **LO.3** For which of the following itemized deductions is the tax treatment the same for regular income tax and AMT purposes?

    - Medical expenses.
    - Casualty losses.
    - Miscellaneous itemized deductions subject to the 2% floor.
    - State income taxes.
    - Real estate taxes.
    - Charitable contributions.
    - Gambling losses.

21. **LO.3, 4, 8** Matt, who is single, has always elected to itemize deductions rather than take the standard deduction. In prior years, his itemized deductions always exceeded the standard deduction by a substantial amount. As a result of paying off the mortgage on his residence, he projects that his itemized deductions for 2014 will exceed the standard deduction by only $500. Matt anticipates that the amount of his itemized deductions will remain about the same in the foreseeable future. Matt's AGI is $150,000. He is investing the amount of his former mortgage payment each month in tax-exempt bonds that were issued in 2007. A friend recommends that Matt buy a beach house to increase his itemized deductions with the mortgage interest deduction. What are the relevant tax issues for Matt?   *Issue ID*

22. **LO.3** How does the treatment of medical expenses differ for AMT and regular income tax purposes?

23. **LO.3** In computing the AMT itemized deduction for interest, it is possible that some interest allowed for regular income tax purposes will not be allowed in the calculation of AMTI. Explain.

24. **LO.3** In the calculation of AMTI, where is the adjustment for personal and dependency exemptions made and what is the reason for the adjustment?

25. **LO.4** Alex owns a mineral deposit that qualifies for a 15% depletion rate. Under what circumstances will the depletion deduction for regular income tax and AMT purposes not be the same?

26. **LO.4** During the year, Rachel earned $18,000 of interest income on private activity bonds that she had purchased in 2008. She also incurred interest expense of $7,000 in connection with amounts borrowed to purchase the bonds. What is the effect on Rachel's taxable income? On her AMT? Could there be a related beneficial effect in calculating AMTI? Explain.   *Decision Making*

27. **LO.6** What is the purpose of the AMT credit? Briefly describe how the credit is computed.

28. **LO.2, 7** What requirements must be satisfied for a corporation to be exempt from the AMT?

29. **LO.7** Comment on the validity of the following statement: Because the regular tax NOL deduction must be added back to the taxable income starting point of the corporate AMTI calculation, an NOL deduction is not allowed for corporate AMT purposes.

30. **LO.2, 8** Beige, Inc.'s regular income tax liability is $110,000, and its TMT is $120,000 for the current year. Under what, if any, circumstances would Beige want to accelerate $15,000 of income to the current year rather than delay it until next year?   *Issue ID*

Problems

31. **LO.2** Use the following data to calculate Chiara's AMT base in 2014:

Taxable income	$148,000
Positive AMT adjustments	73,000
Negative AMT adjustments	55,000
Preferences	30,000

Chiara will file as a single taxpayer.

Communications

32. **LO.2** Arthur Wesson, an unmarried individual who is age 68, has taxable income of $160,000 in 2014. He has positive AMT adjustments of $40,000 and preferences of $35,000.
    a. What is Arthur's AMT?
    b. What is the total amount of Arthur's tax liability?
    c. Draft a letter to Arthur explaining why he must pay more than the regular income tax liability. Arthur's address is 100 Colonel's Way, Conway, SC 29526.

33. **LO.2** Calculate the AMT for the following cases in 2014. The taxpayer has regular taxable income of $450,000 and does not have any credits.

	TMT	
Filing Status	**Case 1**	**Case 2**
Single	$200,000	$190,000
Married, filing jointly	200,000	190,000

34. **LO.2** Calculate the exemption amount for the following cases in 2014 for a single taxpayer, a married taxpayer filing jointly, and a married taxpayer filing separately.

Case	AMTI
1	$150,000
2	300,000
3	800,000

35. **LO.2** Lisa has nonrefundable credits of $65,000 for 2014. Her regular income tax liability before credits is $190,000, and her TMT is $150,000.
    a. What is the amount of Lisa's AMT?
    b. What is the amount of Lisa's regular income tax liability after credits?

Decision Making

36. **LO.2, 3, 8** Angela, who is single, incurs circulation expenditures of $153,000 during 2014. She is in the process of deciding whether to expense the $153,000 or to capitalize it and elect to deduct it over a three-year period. Angela already knows that she will be subject to the AMT for 2014 at both the 26% and 28% rates. Angela is in the 28% bracket for regular income tax purposes this year (has regular taxable income of $153,000 before considering the circulation expenses) and expects to be in the 28% bracket in 2015 and 2016. Advise Angela on whether she should elect the three-year write-off rather than expensing the $153,000 in 2014.

37. **LO.2, 3** Vito owns and operates a news agency (as a sole proprietorship). During 2013, he incurred expenses of $600,000 to increase circulation of newspapers and magazines that his agency distributes. For regular income tax purposes, he elected to expense the $600,000 in 2013. In addition, he incurred $120,000 in circulation expenditures in 2014 and again elected expense treatment. What AMT adjustments will be required in 2013 and 2014 as a result of the circulation expenditures?

38. **LO.3** Lonzo owns two apartment buildings. He acquired Forsythia Acres on February 21, 1998, for $300,000 ($90,000 allocated to the land) and Square One on November 12, 2014, for $800,000 ($100,000 allocated to the land). Neither apartment complex qualifies as low-income housing. If Lonzo elects to write off the cost of each building as quickly as possible, what is the effect of depreciation (cost recovery) on his AMTI for:
    a. 1998?
    b. 2014?

39. **LO.3, 8** In March 2014, Helen Carlon acquired used equipment for her business at a cost of $300,000. The equipment is five-year property for regular income tax purposes and for AMT purposes.

    a. If Helen depreciates the equipment using the method that will produce the greatest deduction for 2014 for regular income tax purposes, what is the amount of the AMT adjustment? Helen does not elect § 179 expensing or additional first-year depreciation.

    b. How can Helen reduce the AMT adjustment to $0? What circumstances would motivate her to do so?

    c. Draft a letter to Helen regarding the choice of depreciation methods. Helen's address is 500 Monticello Avenue, Glendale, AZ 85306.

Decision Making

Communications

40. **LO.3, 8** In 2014, Geoff incurred $900,000 of mining and exploration expenditures. He elects to deduct the expenditures as quickly as the tax law allows for regular income tax purposes.

    a. How will Geoff's treatment of mining and exploration expenditures affect his regular income tax and AMT computations for 2014?

    b. How can Geoff avoid having AMT adjustments related to the mining and exploration expenditures?

    c. What factors should Geoff consider in deciding whether to deduct the expenditures in the year incurred?

Decision Making

41. **LO.3** Rust Company is a real estate construction business with average annual gross receipts of $3 million. Rust uses the completed contract method on a particular contract that requires 16 months to complete. The contract is for $500,000, with estimated costs of $300,000. At the end of 2013, $180,000 of costs had been incurred. The contract is completed in 2014, with the total cost being $295,000. Determine the amount of adjustments for AMT purposes for 2013 and 2014.

42. **LO.3** Burt, the CFO of Amber, Inc., was granted incentive stock options in 2009. Burt exercised the stock options in February 2013 when the exercise price was $75,000 and the fair market value of the stock was $90,000. He sold the stock in September 2016 for $150,000. What are the regular income tax consequences and the AMT consequences for Burt in:

    a. 2009?
    b. 2013?
    c. 2016?

43. **LO.3** In 2014, Liza exercised an incentive stock option that had been granted by her employer, White Corporation. Liza acquired 100 shares of White stock for the option price of $190 per share. The fair market value of the stock at the date of exercise was $250 per share. Liza sells the stock for $340 per share in 2016.

    a. What is the amount of Liza's AMT adjustment in 2014? What is her recognized gain on the sale for regular income tax and for AMT purposes in 2016?

    b. How would your answers in (a) change if Liza had sold the stock in 2014 rather than 2016?

44. **LO.3** Alicia owns two investment properties that she acquired several years ago. Her adjusted basis for each is as follows:

	Regular Income Tax	AMT
Land	$100,000	$100,000
Apartment building	450,000	450,000

Alicia sells the land for $250,000 and the building for $800,000.

    a. Calculate Alicia's recognized gain or loss on the sale of each asset for regular income tax and AMT purposes.

    b. Determine the AMT adjustment on the sale of each asset.

45. **LO.3** Freda acquired a passive activity in 2014 for $870,000. Gross income from operations of the activity was $160,000. Operating expenses, not including depreciation, were $122,000. Regular income tax depreciation of $49,750 was computed under MACRS. AMT depreciation was $41,000. Compute Freda's passive loss deduction and passive loss suspended for regular income tax purposes and for AMT purposes.

46. **LO.3** Sammy and Monica, both age 67, incur and pay medical expenses in excess of insurance reimbursements during the year as follows:

For Sammy	$16,000
For Monica (spouse)	4,000
For Chuck (son)	2,500
For Carter (Monica's father)	5,000

Sammy and Monica's AGI is $130,000. They file a joint return. Chuck and Carter are Sammy and Monica's dependents.
   a. What is Sammy and Monica's medical expense deduction for regular income tax purposes?
   b. What is Sammy and Monica's medical expense deduction for AMT purposes?
   c. What is the amount of the AMT adjustment for medical expenses?

47. **LO.3** Wolfgang, who is age 33, has AGI of $125,000. He has the following itemized deductions for 2014:

Medical expenses [$15,000 − (10% × $125,000)]	$ 2,500
State income taxes	4,200
Charitable contributions	5,000
Home mortgage interest on his personal residence	6,000
Casualty loss (after $100 and 10% reductions)	1,800
Miscellaneous itemized deductions [$3,500 − 2%($125,000)]	1,000
	$20,500

   a. Calculate Wolfgang's itemized deductions for AMT purposes.
   b. What is the total amount of his AMT adjustments?

48. **LO.3** Walter, who is single, owns a personal residence in the city. He also owns a cabin near a ski resort in the mountains. He uses the cabin as a vacation home. In August 2014, he borrowed $60,000 on a home equity loan and used the proceeds to reduce credit card obligations and other debt. During 2014, he paid the following amounts of interest:

On his personal residence	$16,000
On the cabin	7,000
On the home equity loan	2,500
On credit card obligations	1,500
On the purchase of an SUV	1,350

What amount, if any, must Walter recognize as an AMT adjustment in 2014?

49. **LO.3, 4** During the current year, Yoon earned $10,000 in dividends on corporate stock and incurred $13,000 of investment interest expense related to the stock holdings. Yoon also earned $5,000 interest on private activity bonds that were issued in 2007 and incurred interest expense of $3,500 in connection with the bonds.
   a. How much investment interest expense can Yoon deduct for regular income tax and AMT purposes for the year?
   b. What is the adjustment for AMT purposes?

50. **LO.3, 4** Gabriel, age 40, and Emma, age 33, are married with two dependents. They had AGI of $110,000 in 2014 that included net investment income of $10,000 and gambling winnings of $2,500.
   They incurred the following expenses during the year (all of which resulted in itemized deductions for regular income tax purposes):

Medical expenses (before 10%-of-AGI floor)	$13,000
State income taxes	2,800
Personal property tax	900
Real estate tax	9,100
Interest on personal residence	8,600
Interest on home equity loan (proceeds were used to buy a new fishing boat)	1,800
Investment interest expense	2,600
Charitable contribution (cash)	4,200
Unreimbursed employee expenses (before 2%-of-AGI floor)	3,800

a. What is the amount of Gabriel and Emma's AMT adjustment for itemized deductions in 2014? Is it positive or negative?

b. Assume the same facts as above and assume that Gabriel and Emma also earned interest of $5,000 on private activity bonds that were issued in 2012. They borrowed money to buy these bonds and paid interest of $3,900 on the loan. Determine the effect on AMTI.

51. **LO.2, 3** Chuck is single, has no dependents, and does not itemize deductions. In 2014, he claims a personal exemption of $3,950 and has taxable income of $120,000. His tax preferences total $51,000. What is Chuck's AMTI for 2014?

52. **LO.3, 4** Emily owns a coal mine (basis of $12,000 at the beginning of the year) that qualifies for a 15% depletion rate. Gross income from the property was $140,000, and net income before the percentage depletion deduction was $60,000. What is Emily's tax preference for excess depletion?

53. **LO.4** Amos incurred and expensed intangible drilling costs (IDC) of $70,000. His net oil and gas income was $60,000. What is the amount of Amos's preference for IDC?

54. **LO.2, 3, 4** Jerry, who is single with no dependents and does not itemize, provides you with the following information for 2014:

Short-term capital loss	$ 7,000
Long-term capital gain	25,000
Municipal bond interest received on private activity bonds acquired in 1997	9,000
Dividends from Procter & Gamble	2,300
Excess of FMV over exercise price of ISOs (no restrictions apply to the stock)	35,000

What is the total amount of Jerry's tax preferences and AMT adjustments for 2014?

55. **LO.2, 3, 4** Pat, who is age 66 and single with no dependents, received a salary of $90,000 in 2014. She had interest income of $1,000, dividend income of $5,000, gambling winnings of $4,000, and interest income from private activity bonds (issued in 2006) of $40,000. The dividends are not qualified dividends. The following additional information is relevant:

Medical expenses (before 7.5%-of-AGI floor)	$12,000
State income taxes	4,100
Real estate taxes	2,800
Mortgage interest on residence	3,100
Investment interest expense	1,800
Gambling losses	5,100

Compute Pat's tentative minimum tax for 2014.

56. **LO.2, 5** Renee and Sanjeev, who are married, had taxable income of $273,000 for 2014. They had positive AMT adjustments of $38,000, negative AMT adjustments of $14,000, and tax preference items of $67,500.

a. Compute their AMTI for 2014.

b. Compute their tentative minimum tax for 2014.

57. **LO.2, 3, 4, 5** Farr, who is single, has no dependents and does not itemize. She has the following items relative to her tax return for 2014:

Bargain element from the exercise of an ISO (no restrictions apply to the stock)	$ 45,000
MACRS depreciation on shopping mall building acquired in 2010	49,000
Percentage depletion in excess of property's adjusted basis	50,000
Taxable income for regular income tax purposes	121,000

a. Determine Farr's AMT adjustments and preferences for 2014.

b. Calculate Farr's AMT for 2014.

58. **LO.2, 3, 4, 5** Lynn, age 45, is single and has no dependents. Her income and expenses for 2014 are as follows:

Income—	
Salary	$33,000
Taxable interest on corporate bonds	1,800
Dividend income	1,900
Business income	64,000
Expenditures—	
Medical expenses	12,000
State income taxes	6,000
Real estate taxes	8,500
Mortgage (qualified housing) interest	9,200
Investment interest	5,500
Cash contributions to various charities	2,900

The $64,000 business income is from Apex Office Supplies Company, a sole proprietorship that Lynn owns and operates. Apex claimed MACRS depreciation of $3,175 on real and personal property used in the business. AMT depreciation on the property would have been $2,500. Lynn received interest of $30,000 on City of Pensacola private activity bonds that were issued in 2011.

Based on the financial information presented above, compute Lynn's AMT for 2014.

59. **LO.5, 6** Bonnie, who is single, has taxable income of $0 in 2014. She has positive timing adjustments of $200,000 and AMT exclusion items of $100,000 for the year. What is the amount of Bonnie's AMT credit for carryover to 2015?

60. **LO.7** Aqua, Inc., a calendar year corporation, has the following gross receipts and taxable income for 2011–2014:

Year	Gross Receipts	Taxable Income
2011	$6,000,000	$1,400,000
2012	7,000,000	1,312,000
2013	7,500,000	985,000
2014	7,200,000	1,002,000

Aqua's first year of operations was 2011. Is Aqua exempt from AMT in any of its first four years of operation? Explain.

61. **LO.7** Gray Corporation (a calendar year corporation) reports the following information for the years listed below:

	2012	2013	2014
Unadjusted AMTI	$3,000	$2,000	$5,000
Adjusted current earnings	4,000	3,000	2,000

Compute the ACE adjustment for each year.

62. **LO.7** In each of the following independent situations, determine the TMT:

	AMTI (before the exemption amount)
Quincy Corporation	$150,000
Redland Corporation	160,000
Tanzen Corporation	320,000

63. **LO.7** Brown Corporation (a calendar year taxpayer) provides you with the following information:

Taxable income	$2,600,000
Depreciation for regular income tax purposes on realty placed in service in 2006	550,000
Excess amortization of certified pollution control facilities	450,000
Tax-exempt interest on private activity bonds	1,030,000
Percentage depletion in excess of the property's adjusted basis	60,000

The private activity bonds were issued in 2007.
a. Calculate Brown's regular income tax liability.
b. Calculate Brown's TMT.
c. Calculate Brown's AMT.

Cumulative Problems

64. Robert A. Kliesh, age 41, is single and has no dependents. Robert's Social Security number is 111-11-1111. His address is 201 Front Street, Missoula, MT 59812. He is independently wealthy as a result of having inherited sizable holdings in real estate and corporate stocks and bonds. Robert is a minister at First Presbyterian Church, but he accepts no salary from the church. However, he does reside in the church's parsonage free of charge. The fair rental value of the parsonage is $3,000 a month. The church also provides him with a cash grocery allowance of $200 a week. Examination of Robert's financial records provides the following information for 2013:

Tax Return Problem

a. On January 16, 2013, Robert sold 1,000 shares of stock for a gain of $10,000. The stock was acquired 14 months ago.
b. He received $30,000 of interest on private activity bonds that he had purchased in 2008. He also received $40,000 of interest on tax-exempt bonds that are not private activity bonds.
c. He received gross rent income of $190,000 from an apartment complex he owns. He qualifies as an active participant.
d. Expenses related to the apartment complex, which he acquired in 2007, were $225,000.
e. Robert's interest income (on CDs) totaled $23,000. Because he invests only in growth stocks, he has no dividend income.
f. He won $60,000 on the lottery.
g. On October 9, 2013, Robert exercised his rights under Falcon Corporation's incentive stock option plan. For an option price of $20,000, he acquired stock worth $75,000. There were no restrictions on the stock.
h. Robert was the beneficiary of an $800,000 life insurance policy on his uncle Jake. He received the proceeds in October.
i. Contributed $5,000 to his traditional IRA.
j. Robert had the following potential itemized deductions *from* AGI:

- $5,200 fair market value of stock contributed to Presbyterian Church (basis of stock was $3,000). He had owned the stock for two years.
- $4,200 interest on consumer purchases.
- $3,900 state and local income tax.
- $6,500 medical expenses (before 10% floor) for himself. He also paid $15,000 of medical expenses for a parishioner who died.
- $300 for a safe deposit box that is used to store investments and related legal documents.
- $5,000 paid for lottery tickets associated with playing the state lottery. Robert contributed $5,000 of his winnings to the church.
- Because Robert lived in Montana, he paid no sales tax.
- $750 contribution to the campaign of the Democratic candidate for governor.

k. Robert made estimated Federal tax payments of $27,500.

Use Forms 1040 and 6251 and Schedules A, B, D, and E to compute the tax liability (including AMT) for Robert A. Kliesh for 2013. Suggested software: H&R BLOCK Tax Software.

Tax Computation Problem

Communications

65. Jacob M. and Jane R. Brewster live at 1802 College Avenue, Carmel, IN 46032. Jacob is age 48, and Jane is age 37. They are married and file a joint return for 2014. The Brewsters have two dependent children, Ellen J. and Sean M., who are 10-year-old twins. Ellen's Social Security number is 123-45-6788, and Sean's is 123-45-6787. Jacob pays child support of $15,000 for Amy, his 17-year-old daughter from his previous marriage. Amy's Social Security number is 123-45-6786. According to the divorce decree, Margaret, Jacob's former wife, has legal custody of Amy. Margaret provides the balance of Amy's support (about $6,000).

Jacob (111-11-1111) is a factory supervisor, and Jane (123-45-6789) is a computer systems analyst. The Brewsters' W–2 Forms for 2014 reflect the following information:

	Jacob	Jane
Salary (Indiana Foundry, Inc.)	$95,000	
Salary (Carmel Computer Associates)		$103,000
Federal income tax withheld	24,750	27,000
State income tax withheld	5,000	5,400

In addition to their salaries, the Brewsters had the following income items in 2014:

Interest income (Carmel Sanitation District Bonds)	$19,500
Interest income (Carmel National Bank)	4,600
Qualified dividend income (Able Computer Corporation)	15,000
Gambling winnings	6,500
Gift from uncle Raymond to Jacob	27,000

Jane inherited $900,000 from her grandfather in January and invested the money in the Carmel Sanitation District Bonds, which are private activity bonds. These bonds were initially issued in April 2008. Jane was selected "Citizen of the Year" and received an award of $7,500. She used the $7,500 to pay credit card debt.

The Brewsters incurred the following expenses during 2014:

Medical expenses (doctor and hospital bills)	$23,900
Real property tax on personal residence	8,100
Mortgage interest on personal residence (reported on Form 1098)	9,400
Investment interest expense	3,500
Contributions	15,500
Gambling losses	6,800

On March 1, Jacob and Jane contributed Ace stock to the Carmel Salvation Army, a public charity. They had acquired the stock on February 9, 2001, for $6,500. The stock was listed on the New York Stock Exchange at a value of $12,000 on the date of the contribution. In addition, Jacob and Jane contributed $3,500 during the year to Second Church.

Jacob sold five acres of land to a real estate developer on October 12, 2014, for $100,000. He had acquired the land on May 15, 2008, for $86,000.

Compute the tax liability (including AMT) for Jacob and Jane Brewster for 2014. Write a letter to the Brewsters indicating whether they have a refund or balance due for 2014, and suggest possible tax planning strategies for 2015.

Note: Solutions to Research Problems can be prepared by using the **Checkpoint**® **Student Edition** online research product, which is available to accompany this text. It is also possible to prepare solutions to the Research Problems by using tax research materials found in a standard tax library.

THOMSON REUTERS
CHECKPOINT®

Research Problem 1. Samuel had worked for Pearl, Inc., for 35 years when he was discharged and his position filled by a much younger person. He filed and pursued a suit for age discrimination and received an award of $1.5 million. Under the contingent fee arrangement with his attorney, one-third of the award was paid directly to the attorney with the balance going to Samuel. Of the $1.5 million received, Samuel included $1 million on his income tax return but did not include the $500,000 paid to the attorney.

The IRS audited Samuel's return and included the $500,000 contingency fee in his gross income. In addition, Samuel was allowed a miscellaneous itemized deduction (subject to the 2% floor) for the fee paid to the attorney. The IRS adjustment caused a tax deficiency to be assessed for both the regular income tax and the AMT.

Evaluate the result reached.

Research Problem 2. Jolene receives tax-exempt interest of $33,000 on bonds that are classified as private activity bonds. She properly excludes the $33,000 from her gross income for regular income tax purposes [under §§ 103(a) and (b)(1)]. Jolene asks your advice on the treatment of the interest for AMT purposes. Locate the Code Section that covers this matter and advise Jolene accordingly.

Research Problem 3. Stuart is a columnist for a metropolitan newspaper. He has a degree in journalism from a major midwestern university.

For the past 10 years, Stuart has prepared his own income tax returns. He finds doing so to be challenging and stimulating and believes that he pays lower taxes than he would if he hired a tax return preparer.

His 2012 return is audited. Although it included an AMT form (Form 6251), Stuart had not prepared it properly. Data from his Form 1040 were transferred to the wrong line in several places. In other cases, positive adjustments were not included because Stuart had failed to calculate them (e.g., he did not recalculate itemized deductions for AMT purposes and did not have a positive adjustment for the personal exemption). Based on the IRS's calculation, a deficiency of $3,000 was assessed. Stuart's response to the IRS is that Form 6251 is ambiguous and misleading and, therefore, he should not be liable for the AMT. Evaluate Stuart's argument.

Partial list of research aids:
William M. Christine, 66 TCM 1025, T.C.Memo. 1993–473.

Research Problem 4. On his 2013 Federal income tax return, Walter deducted state income taxes of $8,000 for amounts withheld and estimated tax payments made in 2013. When he filed his 2013 state income tax return in April 2014, he discovered that he had overpaid his state income taxes by $1,500. Rather than having the $1,500 refunded to him, he treated it as a 2014 estimated tax payment. The year 2013 was not an AMT year for Walter.

In preparing his 2014 Federal income tax return, Walter is confused about how he should treat the $1,500 in calculating his Federal income tax liability. He knows that under the § 111 tax benefit rule, he should include the $1,500 in gross income in calculating his regular taxable income. However, because he is going to be subject to the AMT, he is uncertain as to how he should treat the $1,500 in calculating AMT. He thinks that the amount could be treated as a negative adjustment in converting taxable income to AMTI if 2013 had been an AMT year. Because it was not, Walter is unsure of the treatment.

Advise Walter on the appropriate treatment of the $1,500 in calculating his 2014 Federal income tax liability.

Research Problem 5. Margaret is the owner of a housing unit in a cooperative housing corporation. As a tenant-stockholder, she deducts $6,000 of real estate taxes (i.e., her proportionate share of the property taxes paid by the cooperative) as an itemized deduction. She claims the $6,000 under § 216(a)(1), rather than under § 164(a)(1), because she does not have direct ownership of the housing unit.

Margaret is aware that § 56(b)(1)(A)(ii) disallows the deduction for real estate property taxes in determining the AMT. In calculating her AMT, however, Margaret deducts the $6,000 (i.e., does not treat it as a positive adjustment) in converting regular taxable income to AMTI. Her justification for this treatment is the statutory language of § 56(b)(1)(A)(ii), which refers only to taxes deducted under § 164(a).

The IRS disagrees with Margaret's interpretation and assesses a tax deficiency. In its opinion, the disallowance of the deduction in calculating the AMT applies to real estate taxes deducted under either § 164(a)(1) or § 216(a)(1).

Who is right?

Internet Activity

Use the tax resources of the Internet to address the following questions. Do not restrict your search to the Web, but include a review of newsgroups and general reference materials, practitioner sites and resources, primary sources of the tax law, chat rooms and discussion groups, and other opportunities.

Research Problem 6. Eliminating the deduction for state and local taxes is a significant component of some tax reform proposals. Proponents claim that eliminating the deduction would allow the top tax rate to be lowered while also keeping tax rates progressive. Given what you have learned about the deduction for state and local taxes in the AMT calculation, think about the validity of this claim. See if you can find any analysis of this claim by tax policy groups that have given some consideration to the AMT treatment of state and local taxes in their analysis.

Research Problem 7. Ascertain whether your state's income tax has an AMT component. If your state does not levy an income tax, choose a contiguous state that does.

Tax Credits and Payment Procedures

LEARNING OBJECTIVES: *After completing Chapter 13, you should be able to:*

LO.1 Explain how tax credits are used as a tool of Federal tax policy.

LO.2 Distinguish between refundable and nonrefundable credits and understand the order in which they can be used by taxpayers.

LO.3 Describe various business-related tax credits.

LO.4 Describe various tax credits that are available primarily to individual taxpayers.

LO.5 Describe the tax withholding and payment procedures applicable to employers.

LO.6 Explain and illustrate the payment procedures applicable to self-employed persons.

LO.7 Explain the additional Medicare taxes assessed on high-income individuals.

LO.8 Identify tax planning opportunities related to tax credits and payment procedures.

CHAPTER OUTLINE

THE BIG PICTURE Tax Solutions for the Real World

EDUCATION TAX CREDITS

Tom and Jennifer Snyder have two children in college. Lora is a freshman, and her tuition and required fees in 2014 total $14,000. Lora has a partial scholarship amounting to $6,500, and the Snyders paid the balance of her tuition ($7,500), plus room and board of $8,500. Sam is a junior, and the Snyders paid $8,100 for his tuition, plus $7,200 for his room and board. Both students qualify as Tom and Jennifer's dependents.

The Snyders have AGI of $158,000. They would like to know what tax options are available to them related to these educational expenses. They have heard about education tax credits, but they believe that their income is too high for them to get any benefit. Are they correct?

Read the chapter and formulate your response.

FRAMEWORK 1040
Tax Formula for Individuals

This chapter covers the boldfaced portions of the Tax Formula for Individuals that was introduced in Figure 3.1 on p. 3-3. Below those portions are the sections of Form 1040 where the results are reported.

Income *(broadly conceived)*	$xx,xxx
Less: Exclusions	(x,xxx)
Gross income	$xx,xxx
Less: Deductions for adjusted gross income	(x,xxx)
Adjusted gross income	$xx,xxx
Less: The greater of total **itemized deductions** *or* the standard deduction	(x,xxx)
Personal and dependency exemptions	(x,xxx)
Taxable income	$xx,xxx
Tax on taxable income *(see Tax Tables or Tax Rate Schedules)*	$ x,xxx
Less: Tax credits *(including income taxes withheld and prepaid)*	(xxx)

FORM 1040 (p. 2)

47	Foreign tax credit. Attach Form 1116 if required	47	
48	Credit for child and dependent care expenses. Attach Form 2441	48	
49	Education credits from Form 8863, line 19	49	
50	Retirement savings contributions credit. Attach Form 8880	50	
51	Child tax credit. Attach Schedule 8812, if required . . .	51	
52	Residential energy credits. Attach Form 5695.	52	
53	Other credits from Form: a ☐ 3800 b ☐ 8801 c ☐ _____	53	
54	Add lines 47 through 53. These are your **total credits**		

Tax due *(or refund)* .... $ xxx

A s explained in Chapter 1, Federal tax law often serves purposes besides merely raising revenue for the government. Evidence of equity, social, and economic considerations, among others, is found throughout the tax law. These considerations also bear heavily in the area of **tax credits**. Consider the following examples.

Example 1

Paul and Peggy, husband and wife, are both employed outside the home. Their combined salaries are $50,000. However, after paying for child care expenses of $2,000 on behalf of their daughter, Polly, the net economic benefit from both spouses working is $48,000. The child care expenses are, in a sense, business-related because they would not have been incurred if both spouses did not work outside the home. If no tax benefits are associated with the child care expenditures, $50,000 is subject to tax.

Another couple, Alicia and Diego, also have a child, John. Diego stays home to care for John (the value of those services is $2,000) while Alicia earns a $48,000 salary. Because the value of Diego's services rendered is not subject to tax, only Alicia's earnings of $48,000 are subject to tax.

The credit for child and dependent care expenses mitigates the inequity felt by working taxpayers who must pay for child care services to work outside the home.

Example 2

Graham, age 66, is a retired taxpayer who receives $17,000 of Social Security benefits as his only source of income in 2014. His Social Security benefits are excluded from gross income. Therefore, Graham's income tax is $0. In 2014, Olga, a single taxpayer 66 years of age, has, as her sole source of income, $17,000 from a pension plan funded by her former employer. Assuming that Olga has no itemized deductions or deductions

for AGI, her income tax for 2014 (before credits) is $530, based on the following computation:

Pension plan benefits	$17,000
Less: Basic standard deduction	(6,200)
Additional standard deduction	(1,550)
Personal exemption	(3,950)
Taxable income	$ 5,300
Income tax (at 10%)	$ 530

The tax credit for elderly or disabled taxpayers was enacted to mitigate this inequity.

> Jane is a single parent who depends on the government's "safety net" for survival—she receives benefits under the Temporary Assistance to Needy Families program in the amount of $15,000 per year. However, she very much wants to work. Jane has located a job that will pay $15,500 per year and has found an individual to care for her child at no cost. But with the $1,185.75 ($15,500 × 7.65% in 2014) withholding for Social Security and Medicare taxes, the economic benefit from working is less than remaining reliant on the government ($14,314.25 versus $15,000).

Example 3

To help offset the effect of Social Security and Medicare taxes on wages of the working poor and to provide an incentive to work, the earned income credit is used to increase the after-tax earnings of qualified individuals. In addition, the earned income credit helps offset the regressive nature of certain taxes, such as the Social Security and Medicare taxes, which impose a relatively larger burden on low-income taxpayers than on more affluent taxpayers.

The credit for child and dependent care expenses, the credit for elderly and disabled taxpayers, the earned income credit, and many of the other important tax credits available to individuals and other types of taxpayers are a major focus of this chapter. The chapter begins by discussing important tax policy considerations relevant to tax credits. Tax credits are categorized as being either refundable or nonrefundable. The distinction between refundable and nonrefundable credits is important because it may affect the taxpayer's ability to enjoy a tax benefit from a particular credit.

Next, an overview of the priority of tax credits is presented. The chapter continues with a discussion of the credits available to businesses and to individual taxpayers and the ways in which credits enter into the calculation of the tax liability.

The Federal tax system has long been based on the pay-as-you-go concept. That is, taxpayers or their employers are required to make regular deposits with the Federal government during the year as payment toward the tax liability that will be determined at the end of the tax year. These deposits are, in effect, refundable credits. The chapter concludes with a brief discussion of employer withholding procedures, special problems encountered by self-employed persons when estimating their tax payments, penalties imposed on underpayments, and additional Medicare taxes on high-income individuals.

13-1 TAX POLICY CONSIDERATIONS

LO.1

Explain how tax credits are used as a tool of Federal tax policy.

Congress has generally used tax credits to achieve social or economic objectives or to promote equity among different types of taxpayers. For example, the disabled access credit was enacted to accomplish a social objective: to encourage taxpayers to renovate older buildings so that they would be in compliance with the Americans with Disabilities Act. This Act requires businesses and institutions to make their facilities more accessible to persons with various types of disabilities. As another example, the foreign tax credit, which has been a part of the law for decades, has as its purpose the economic and equity objectives of mitigating the burden of multiple taxation on a single stream of income.

A tax credit should not be confused with an income tax deduction. Certain expenditures of individuals (e.g., business expenses) are permitted as deductions from gross income in arriving at adjusted gross income (AGI). In addition, individuals are allowed to deduct certain nonbusiness and investment-related expenses *from* AGI. While the tax benefit received from a tax deduction depends on the tax rate, a tax credit is not affected by the tax rate of the taxpayer.

Example 4	Assume that Congress wants to encourage a certain type of expenditure. One way to accomplish this objective is to allow a tax credit of 25% for such expenditures. Another way is to allow an itemized deduction for the expenditures. Assume that Abby's tax rate is 15% and Bill's tax rate is 35% and that each itemizes deductions. In addition, assume that Carmen does not incur enough qualifying expenditures to itemize deductions. The following tax benefits are available to each taxpayer for a $1,000 expenditure:

	Abby	**Bill**	**Carmen**
Tax benefit if a 25% credit is allowed	$250	$250	$250
Tax benefit if an itemized deduction is allowed	150	350	–0–

As these results indicate, tax credits provide benefits on a more equitable basis than do tax deductions. Equally apparent is that the deduction approach in this case benefits only taxpayers who itemize deductions, while the credit approach benefits all taxpayers who make the specified expenditure.

For many years, Congress has used the tax credit provisions of the Code liberally in implementing tax policy. Although budget constraints and economic considerations often have dictated the repeal of some credits, other credits, such as those applicable to expenses incurred for child and dependent care, have been kept to respond to important social policy considerations. Still other credits, such as the one available to low-income workers, have been retained based on economic and equity considerations. Finally, as the myriad of tax proposals so frequently pending before Congress makes clear, the use of tax credits as a tax policy tool continues to evolve as economic and political circumstances change.

13-2 OVERVIEW AND PRIORITY OF CREDITS

13-2a Refundable versus Nonrefundable Credits

As illustrated in Exhibit 13.1, certain credits are refundable while others are nonrefundable. **Refundable credits** are paid to the taxpayer even if the amount of the credit (or credits) exceeds the taxpayer's tax liability.

LO.2

Distinguish between refundable and nonrefundable credits and understand the order in which they can be used by taxpayers.

> **Example 5**
>
> Ted, who is single, had taxable income of $21,000 in 2014. His income tax from the 2014 Tax Rate Schedule is $2,696. During 2014, Ted's employer withheld income tax of $3,200. Ted is entitled to a refund of $504 because the credit for tax withheld on wages is a refundable credit.

Nonrefundable credits are not paid if they exceed the taxpayer's tax liability.

> **Example 6**
>
> Tina is single, age 67, and retired. Her taxable income for 2014 is $1,320, and the tax on this amount is $132. Tina's tax credit for the elderly is $225. This credit can be used to reduce her net tax liability to zero, but it will not result in a refund, even though the credit ($225) exceeds Tina's tax liability ($132). This result occurs because the tax credit for the elderly is a nonrefundable credit.

Some nonrefundable credits, such as the foreign tax credit, are subject to carryover provisions if they exceed the amount allowable as a credit in a given year. Other nonrefundable credits, such as the tax credit for the elderly (refer to Example 6), are lost if they exceed the limitations. Because some credits are

---

EXHIBIT 13.1	**Partial Listing of Refundable and Nonrefundable Credits**

Refundable Credits

Taxes withheld on wages

Earned income credit

Nonrefundable Credits

General business credit, which includes the following:

- Tax credit for rehabilitation expenditures
- Work opportunity tax credit
- Research activities credit
- Low-income housing credit
- Disabled access credit
- Credit for small employer pension plan startup costs
- Credit for employer-provided child care

Credit for elderly and disabled

Foreign tax credit

Adoption expenses credit

Child tax credit*

Credit for child and dependent care expenses

Education tax credits**

Energy credits

Credit for certain retirement plan contributions

Small employer health insurance credit

*The credit is refundable to the extent of 15 percent of the taxpayer's earned income in excess of $3,000 for tax years through 2017. Parents with three or more qualifying children may compute the refundable portion using an alternative method.
**Forty percent of the American Opportunity credit is refundable.

refundable and others are not and because some credits are subject to carryover provisions while others are not, the order in which credits are offset against the tax liability can be important.[1]

13-2b General Business Credit

As shown in Exhibit 13.1, the **general business credit** is composed of a number of other credits, each of which is computed separately under its own set of rules. The general business credit combines these credits into one amount to limit the amount of business credits that can be used to offset a taxpayer's income tax liability. The idea behind combining the credits is to prevent a taxpayer from completely avoiding an income tax liability in any one year by offsetting it with business credits that would otherwise be available.

Two special rules apply to the general business credit. First, any unused credit must be carried back 1 year, then forward 20 years. Second, for any tax year, the general business credit is limited to the taxpayer's *net income tax* reduced by the greater of:[2]

- The *tentative minimum tax.*
- 25 percent of *net regular tax liability* that exceeds $25,000.[3]

To understand the general business credit limitation, several terms need defining:

- *Net income tax* is the sum of the regular tax liability and the alternative minimum tax reduced by certain nonrefundable tax credits.
- *Tentative minimum tax* for this purpose is reduced by the foreign tax credit allowed.
- *Regular tax liability* is determined from the appropriate tax table or tax rate schedule, based on taxable income. However, the regular tax liability does not include certain taxes (e.g., alternative minimum tax).
- *Net regular tax liability* is the regular tax liability reduced by certain nonrefundable credits (e.g., credit for child and dependent care expenses and foreign tax credit).

Example 7

Floyd's general business credit for the current year is $70,000. His net income tax is $150,000, tentative minimum tax is $130,000, and net regular tax liability is $150,000. He has no other tax credits. Floyd's general business credit allowed for the tax year is computed as follows:

Net income tax	$ 150,000
Less: The greater of	
$130,000 (tentative minimum tax)	
$31,250 [25% × ($150,000 − $25,000)]	(130,000)
Amount of general business credit allowed for tax year	$ 20,000

Floyd then has $50,000 ($70,000 − $20,000) of unused general business credits that may be carried back or forward as discussed below.

13-2c Treatment of Unused General Business Credits

Unused general business credits are initially carried back one year and are applied to reduce the tax liability during that year. Thus, the taxpayer may receive a tax refund as a result of the carryback. Any remaining unused credits are then carried forward 20 years.[4]

---

[1]Since the passage of the Tax Relief Reconciliation Act of 2001, the ordering rules and limitations applied when offsetting tax credits against both the regular income tax liability and the alternative minimum tax liability have become increasingly complex. In addition, different variations of these rules will apply over time as this legislation is fully implemented. Further discussion of the intricacies of these rules is beyond the scope of this chapter.

[2]§ 38(c).

[3]This amount is $12,500 for married taxpayers filing separately unless one of the spouses is not entitled to the general business credit.

[4]§ 39(a)(1).

A FIFO method is applied to the carrybacks, carryovers, and utilization of credits earned during a particular year. The oldest credits are used first in determining the amount of the general business credit. The FIFO method minimizes the potential for loss of a general business credit benefit due to the expiration of credit carryovers, because the earliest years are used before the current credit for the taxable year.

Example 8

This example illustrates the use of general business credit carryovers.

General business credit carryovers		
2011	$ 4,000	
2012	6,000	
2013	2,000	
Total carryovers	$12,000	
2014 general business credit		$ 40,000
Total credit allowed in 2014 (based on tax liability)	$50,000	
Less: Utilization of carryovers		
2011	(4,000)	
2012	(6,000)	
2013	(2,000)	
Remaining credit allowed in 2014	$38,000	
Applied against		
2014 general business credit		(38,000)
2014 unused amount carried forward to 2015		$ 2,000

13-3 SPECIFIC BUSINESS-RELATED TAX CREDIT PROVISIONS

Each component of the general business credit is determined separately under its own set of rules. Some of the more important credits that make up the general business credit are explained here in the order listed in Exhibit 13.1.

LO.3

Describe various business-related tax credits.

13-3a Tax Credit for Rehabilitation Expenditures

Taxpayers are allowed a tax credit for expenditures incurred to rehabilitate industrial and commercial buildings and certified historic structures. The **rehabilitation expenditures credit** is intended to discourage businesses from moving from older, economically distressed areas (e.g., inner cities) to newer locations and to encourage the preservation of historic structures. The current operating features of this credit follow.[5]

Rate of the Credit for Rehabilitation Expenses	Nature of the Property
10%	Nonresidential buildings and residential rental property, other than certified historic structures, originally placed in service before 1936
20%	Nonresidential and residential certified historic structures

When taking the credit, the basis of a rehabilitated building must be reduced by the full rehabilitation credit allowed.[6]

---

[5]§ 47. [6]§ 50(c).

Example 9

Juan spent $60,000 to rehabilitate a building (adjusted basis of $40,000) that had originally been placed in service in 1932. He is allowed a $6,000 (10% × $60,000) credit for rehabilitation expenditures. Juan then increases the basis of the building by $54,000 [$60,000 (rehabilitation expenditures) − $6,000 (credit allowed)]. If the building were a historic structure, the credit allowed would be $12,000 (20% × $60,000) and the building's depreciable basis would increase by $48,000 [$60,000 (rehabilitation expenditures) − $12,000 (credit allowed)].

To qualify for the credit, buildings must be substantially rehabilitated. A building has been *substantially rehabilitated* if qualified rehabilitation expenditures exceed the greater of:

- The adjusted basis of the property before the rehabilitation expenditures, or
- $5,000.

Qualified rehabilitation expenditures do not include the cost of acquiring a building, the cost of facilities related to a building (such as a parking lot), and the cost of enlarging an existing building.

Recapture of Tax Credit for Rehabilitation Expenditures

The rehabilitation credit taken must be recaptured if the rehabilitated property is disposed of prematurely or if it ceases to be qualifying property. The **rehabilitation expenditures credit recapture** is based on a holding period requirement of five years and is added to the taxpayer's regular tax liability in the recapture year. The recapture amount is also *added* to the adjusted basis of the rehabilitation expenditures for purposes of determining the amount of gain or loss realized on the property's disposition.

The portion of the credit recaptured is a specified percentage of the credit that was taken by the taxpayer. This percentage is based on the period the property was held by the taxpayer, as shown in Table 13.1.

Example 10

On March 15, 2011, Rashad placed in service $30,000 of rehabilitation expenditures on a building qualifying for the 10% credit. A credit of $3,000 ($30,000 × 10%) was allowed, and the basis of the building was increased by $27,000 ($30,000 − $3,000). The building was sold on December 15, 2014. Rashad must recapture a portion of the rehabilitation credit based on the schedule in Table 13.1. Because he held the rehabilitated property for more than three years but less than four, 40% of the credit, or $1,200, is added to his 2014 tax liability. Also, the adjusted basis of the rehabilitation expenditures is increased by the $1,200 recapture amount.

TABLE 13.1	Recapture Calculation for Rehabilitation Expenditures Credit
If the Property Is Held for	**The Recapture Percentage Is**
Less than 1 year	100
One year or more but less than 2 years	80
Two years or more but less than 3 years	60
Three years or more but less than 4 years	40
Four years or more but less than 5 years	20
Five years or more	0

ETHICS & EQUITY   The Rehabilitation Tax Credit

Your brother—who buys, modernizes, and sells buildings in a large metropolitan city—has come to you for advice. Given the recent credit market conditions, business has been tough, and he has sold only a few buildings. One of your brother's buildings is a certified historic structure that would qualify for the 20 percent rehabilitation tax credit. Based on several recent appraisals, the building is currently worth $400,000. The expenditures needed to rehabilitate the building would be about $250,000—and all of these expenses would qualify for the rehabilitation tax credit. Your brother has been approached by an individual who is interested in buying the building once the rehabilitation is complete. The customer has offered to pay your brother $350,000 for the building and $300,000 for the rehabilitation work. This approach would provide the customer with a larger tax credit ($300,000 × 20% versus $250,000 × 20%) and provide a needed sale for your brother's business. How do you respond?

© iStockphoto.com/LdF

13-3b Work Opportunity Tax Credit

The **work opportunity tax credit** was enacted to encourage employers to hire individuals from one or more of a number of targeted and economically disadvantaged groups.[7] Examples of such targeted persons include qualified ex-felons, high-risk youths, food stamp recipients, veterans, summer youth employees, and long-term family assistance recipients.

Computation of the Work Opportunity Tax Credit: General

The credit is generally equal to 40 percent of the first $6,000 of wages (per eligible employee) for the first 12 months of employment. Thus, the credit is not available for any wages paid to an employee after the *first year* of employment. If the employee's first year overlaps two of the employer's tax years, however, the employer may take the credit over two tax years. If the credit is taken, the employer's tax deduction for wages is reduced by the amount of the credit.

For an employer to qualify for the 40 percent credit, the employee must (1) be certified by a designated local agency as being a member of one of the targeted groups and (2) have completed at least 400 hours of service to the employer. If an employee meets the first condition but not the second, the credit rate is reduced to 25 percent provided the employee has completed a minimum of 120 hours of service to the employer.

In January 2014, Green Company hires four individuals who are certified to be members of a qualifying targeted group. Each employee works 800 hours and is paid wages of $8,000 during the year. Green Company's work opportunity credit is $9,600 [($6,000 × 40%) × 4 employees]. If the tax credit is taken, Green must reduce its deduction for wages paid by $9,600. No credit is available for wages paid to these employees after their first year of employment.	**Example 11**

On June 1, 2014, Maria, a calendar year taxpayer, hires Joe, a certified member of a targeted group. During the last seven months of 2014, Joe is paid $3,500 for 500 hours of work. Maria is allowed a credit of $1,400 ($3,500 × 40%) for 2014. Joe continues to work for Maria in 2015 and is paid $7,000 through May 31, 2015. Because up to $6,000 of first-year wages are eligible for the credit, Maria is allowed a 40% credit on $2,500 [$6,000 − $3,500 (wages paid in 2014)] of wages paid in 2015, or $1,000 ($2,500 × 40%). None of Joe's wages paid after May 31, the end of the first year of employment, are eligible for the credit.	**Example 12**

---

[7]§ 51. At the time of this writing, the credit is available only if qualifying employees start work by December 31, 2013. However, because Congress is expected to extend this credit, the examples that follow and the end-of-chapter materials assume this is the case.

Computation of the Work Opportunity Tax Credit: Qualified Summer Youth Employees

The credit for qualified summer youth employees is allowed on wages for services during any 90-day period between May 1 and September 15. The maximum wages eligible for the credit are $3,000 per summer youth employee. The credit rate is the same as the general work opportunity tax credit rate. If the employee continues employment after the 90-day period as a member of another targeted group, the amount of the wages eligible for the general work opportunity tax credit as a member of the new target group is reduced by the wages paid to the employee as a qualified summer youth employee.

A *qualified summer youth employee* must be age 16 or 17 on the hiring date. In addition, the individual's principal place of abode must be within an empowerment zone, an enterprise community, or a renewal community.

Computation of the Work Opportunity Tax Credit: Long-Term Family Assistance Recipient

The credit[8] is available to employers hiring individuals who have been long-term recipients of family assistance welfare benefits. In general, *long-term recipients* are those individuals who are certified by a designated local agency as being a member of a family receiving assistance under a public aid program for at least an 18-month period ending on the hiring date. Unlike the work opportunity credit for other targeted groups, which applies only to first-year wages paid to qualified individuals, the credit is available for qualified wages paid in the *first two years* of employment if the employee is a long-term family assistance recipient. If an employee's first and second work years overlap two or more of the employer's tax years, the employer may take the credit during the applicable tax years.

The credit is equal to 40 percent of the first $10,000 of qualified wages paid to an employee in the first year of employment, plus 50 percent of the first $10,000 of qualified wages paid in the second year of employment, resulting in a maximum credit per qualified employee of $9,000 [$4,000 (year 1) + $5,000 (year 2)]. The credit rate is higher for second-year wages to encourage employers to retain qualified individuals, thereby promoting the overall welfare-to-work goal.

Example 13	In April 2014, Blue Company hires four individuals who are certified as long-term family assistance recipients. Each employee is paid $9,000 during 2014. Three of the four individuals continue to work for Blue Company in 2015, earning $11,000 each during the year. Blue Company's work opportunity tax credit is $14,400 [(40% × $9,000) × 4 employees] for 2014 and $15,000 [(50% × $10,000) × 3 employees] for 2015. In each year, Blue must reduce its deduction for wages paid by the amount of the credit for that year.

13-3c Research Activities Credit

To encourage research and experimentation, usually described as research and development (R&D), a credit is allowed for certain qualifying expenditures paid or incurred by a taxpayer. The **research activities credit** is the *sum* of three components: an incremental research activities credit, a basic research credit, and an energy research credit.[9]

---

[8]Prior to 2007, this component of the work opportunity tax credit was the welfare-to-work credit, which was provided for under § 51A. Under current law, long-term family assistance recipients are a designated targeted group under the work opportunity tax credit [§ 51(d)(1)(I)], and the maximum credit is now slightly more generous than under prior law.

[9]§ 41. At the time of this writing, each component of the research credit is available only if qualifying expenditures are paid or incurred by December 31, 2013. However, because Congress is expected to extend this credit, the examples that follow and the end-of-chapter materials assume this is the case.

Incremental Research Activities Credit

The incremental research activities credit is equal to 20 percent of the *excess* of qualified research expenses for the taxable year over the base amount.[10]

In general, *research expenditures* qualify if the research relates to discovering technological information that is intended for use in the development of a new or improved business component of the taxpayer. Such expenses qualify fully if the research is performed in-house (by the taxpayer or employees). If the research is conducted by persons outside the taxpayer's business (under contract), only 65 percent of the amount paid qualifies for the credit.[11]

> **Example 14**
>
> George incurs the following research expenditures:
>
> | | |
> |---|---|
> | In-house wages, supplies, computer time | $50,000 |
> | Paid to Cutting Edge Scientific Foundation for research | 30,000 |
>
> George's qualified research expenditures are $69,500 [$50,000 + ($30,000 × 65%)].

Beyond the general guidelines described above, the Code does not give specific examples of qualifying research. However, the credit is *not* allowed for research that falls into certain categories, including the following:[12]

- Research conducted after the beginning of commercial production of the business component.
- Surveys and studies such as market research, testing, or routine data collection.
- Research conducted *outside* the United States (other than research undertaken in Puerto Rico or possessions of the United States).
- Research in the social sciences, arts, or humanities.

Determining the *base amount* involves a relatively complex series of computations meant to approximate recent historical levels of research activity by the taxpayer. Thus, the credit is allowed only for increases in research expenses. A discussion of these computations is beyond the scope of this presentation.

> **Example 15**
>
> Jack, a calendar year taxpayer, incurs qualifying research expenditures of $200,000 at the beginning of the year. Assuming that the base amount is $100,000, the incremental research activities credit is $20,000 [($200,000 − $100,000) × 20%].

Qualified research and experimentation expenditures are not only eligible for the 20 percent credit but also can be *deducted* in the year incurred.[13] In this regard, a taxpayer has two choices:[14]

- Use the full credit and reduce the expense deduction for research expenses by 100 percent of the credit.
- Retain the full expense deduction and reduce the credit by the product of the full credit times the maximum corporate tax rate (35 percent).

As an alternative to the expense deduction, the taxpayer may *capitalize* the research expenses and *amortize* them over 60 months or more. In this case, the amount capitalized and subject to amortization is reduced by the full amount of the credit *only* if the credit exceeds the amount allowable as a deduction.

> **Example 16**
>
> Assume the same facts as in Example 15, which shows that the potential incremental research activities credit is $20,000. In the current year, the expense that the taxpayer can deduct and the credit amount under each of the three choices are as follows:

---

[10]In lieu of determining the incremental research credit as described here, a taxpayer may elect to calculate the credit using an alternative simplified credit procedure. See §§ 41(c)(4) and (5).

[11]In the case of payments to a qualified research consortium, § 41(b)(3)(A) provides that 75% of the amount paid qualifies for the credit. In contrast, for amounts paid to an energy research consortium, § 41(b)(3)(D) allows the full amount to qualify for the credit.

[12]§ 41(d). See also Reg. §§ 1.41–1 through 1.41–7.

[13]§ 174. Also refer to the discussion of rules for deducting research and experimental expenditures in Chapter 7.

[14]§ 280C(c).

	Credit Amount	Deduction Amount
Full credit and reduced deduction		
$20,000 − $0	$20,000	
$200,000 − $20,000		$180,000
Reduced credit and full deduction		
$20,000 − [(100% × $20,000) × 35%]	13,000	
$200,000 − $0		200,000
Full credit and capitalize and elect to amortize costs over 60 months		
$20,000 − $0	20,000	
($200,000/60) × 12		40,000

ETHICS & EQUITY   When Does "Research" Qualify as R&D?

The research activities credit is designed to encourage taxpayers to engage in research related to the discovery of technological information for use in developing a new or improved business component of the taxpayer.

You are employed as a staff accountant for a privately held corporation that manufactures medical equipment. During the current year, the corporation purchases new communications software and related document-management systems with the goal of enhancing employee efficiency and productivity. To familiarize employees with these new systems, an outside firm is hired to conduct numerous training seminars during the first six months after the software is installed. Substantial costs are incurred in connection with these training seminars. Not surprisingly, the firm encounters various inefficiencies until the employees have had sufficient training and time to learn the new systems.

The corporation's new president, ever mindful of the company's profitability and tax position, urges you to claim the research activities credit with respect to the software training costs. The president justifies this position on the grounds that the employees were "researching" the new software and its use. How do you respond?

© iStockphoto.com/LdF

Basic Research Credit

Corporations (other than S corporations or personal service corporations) are allowed an additional 20 percent credit for basic research payments made in *excess* of a base amount. This credit is not available to individual taxpayers. *Basic research payments* are defined as amounts paid in cash to a qualified basic research organization such as a college or university or a tax-exempt organization operated primarily to conduct scientific research.

Basic research is defined generally as any original investigation for the advancement of scientific knowledge not having a specific commercial objective. The definition excludes basic research conducted outside the United States and basic research in the social sciences, arts, or humanities. This reflects the intent of Congress to encourage high-tech research in the United States.

The calculation of this additional credit for basic research expenditures is complex and is based on expenditures in excess of a specially defined base amount. The portion of the basic research expenditures not in excess of the base amount is treated as a part of the qualifying expenditures for purposes of the regular credit for incremental research activities.

Example 17

Orange Corporation, a qualifying corporation, pays $75,000 to a university for basic research. Assume that Orange's base amount for the basic research credit is $50,000. The basic research activities credit allowed is $5,000 [($75,000 − $50,000) × 20%]. The $50,000 of basic research expenditures that equal the base amount are treated as research expenses for purposes of the regular incremental research activities credit.

Energy Research Credit

This component of the research credit is intended to stimulate additional energy research. The calculation of the credit is relatively straightforward and is equal to 20 percent of the amounts paid or incurred by a taxpayer to an energy research consortium for energy research.

13-3d Low-Income Housing Credit

To encourage building owners to make affordable housing available for low-income individuals, Congress has made a credit available to owners of qualified low-income housing projects.[15]

More than any other, the **low-income housing credit** is influenced by nontax factors. For example, certification of the property by the appropriate state or local agency authorized to provide low-income housing credits is required. These credits are issued based on a nationwide allocation.

The amount of the credit is based on the qualified basis of the property. The qualified basis depends on the number of units rented to low-income tenants. Tenants are low-income tenants if their income does not exceed a specified percentage of the area median gross income. The amount of the credit is determined by multiplying the qualified basis by a credit rate.[16] The credit is allowed over a 10-year period if the property continues to meet the required conditions.

> **Example 18**
>
> Sarah spends $1 million to build a qualified low-income housing project that is completed on January 1 of the current year. The entire project is rented to low-income families. Assume that the credit rate for property placed in service during January is 7.38%. Sarah may claim a credit of $73,800 ($1,000,000 × 7.38%) in the current year and in each of the following nine years. Generally, first-year credits are prorated based on the date the project is placed in service. A full year's credit is taken in each of the next nine years, and any remaining first-year credit is claimed in the eleventh year.

Recapture of a portion of the credit may be required if the number of units set aside for low-income tenants falls below a minimum threshold, if the taxpayer disposes of the property or the interest in it, or if the taxpayer's amount at risk decreases.

ETHICS & EQUITY A "Win-Win" Situation?

Tom and Sarah Prentice rent an apartment in a complex owned by Steve Heatherton, who has been a close friend since high school. About a week ago, Steve told Tom about the tax savings he has received by claiming the low-income housing credit on all of his apartment complexes—including the one in which the Prentices live.

Initially, Tom was pleased that Steve had been able to use this government "subsidy" to reduce his tax burden because, in general, he believes that the government rarely uses its resources wisely. However, during the conversation, Steve inadvertently let slip the fact that the apartment complex in which the Prentices live qualifies for the credit only because he overstates the percentage of low-income tenants living in the facility. Steve admitted that by claiming that the Prentices are low-income tenants (even though they aren't), the percentage of low-income tenants is just enough for Steve to "qualify" for the credit on the complex. Steve said that because Tom and Sarah are his friends, he was passing along some of his tax savings to them in the form of lower rent.

Tom knows that if he were to report Steve to the IRS, Steve not only would lose the economic benefits of the credit but also would have legal troubles—and could be sentenced to prison. In addition, Tom and Sarah would see an increase in their rent. Tom has come to you for advice. What course of action would you recommend to Tom?

---

[15]§ 42.

[16]The rate is subject to adjustment every month by the IRS.

13-3e Disabled Access Credit

The **disabled access credit** is designed to encourage small businesses to make their facilities more accessible to disabled individuals. The credit is available for any eligible access expenditures paid or incurred by an eligible small business. The credit is calculated at the rate of 50 percent of the eligible expenditures that exceed $250 but do not exceed $10,250. Thus, the maximum amount for the credit is $5,000 ($10,000 × 50%).[17]

An *eligible small business* is a business that during the previous year either had gross receipts of $1 million or less or had no more than 30 full-time employees. An eligible business can include a sole proprietorship, a partnership, a regular corporation, or an S corporation.

Eligible access expenditures are generally any reasonable and necessary amounts that are paid or incurred to make certain changes to facilities. These changes must involve the removal of architectural, communication, physical, or transportation barriers that would otherwise make a business inaccessible to disabled and handicapped individuals. Examples of qualifying projects include installing ramps, widening doorways, and adding raised markings on elevator control buttons. However, eligible expenditures do *not* include amounts that are paid or incurred in connection with any facility placed in service after November 5, 1990 (the date of the credit's enactment).

To the extent a disabled access credit is available, no deduction or credit is allowed under any other provision of the tax law. The adjusted basis for depreciation is reduced by the amount of the credit.

Example 19

This year, Red, Inc., an eligible business, makes $11,000 of capital improvements to business realty that had been placed in service in June 1990. The expenditures are intended to make Red's business more accessible to the disabled and are considered eligible expenditures for purposes of the disabled access credit. The amount of the credit is $5,000 [($10,250 − $250) × 50%]. Although $11,000 of eligible expenditures are incurred, only the excess of $10,250 over $250 qualifies for the credit. Further, the depreciable basis of the capital improvement is $6,000 because the basis must be reduced by the amount of the credit [$11,000 (cost) − $5,000 (amount of the credit)].

13-3f Credit for Small Employer Pension Plan Startup Costs

Small businesses are entitled to a nonrefundable credit for administrative costs associated with establishing and maintaining certain qualified retirement plans.[18] While such costs (e.g., payroll system changes and consulting fees) generally are deductible as ordinary and necessary business expenses, the credit is intended to lower the after-tax cost of establishing a qualified retirement program and thereby encourage qualifying businesses to offer retirement plans for their employees. The **credit for small employer pension plan startup costs** is available for eligible employers at the rate of 50 percent of qualified startup costs. An eligible employer is one with fewer than 100 employees who have earned at least $5,000 of compensation. Qualified startup costs include ordinary and necessary expenses incurred in connection with establishing or maintaining an employer pension plan and retirement-related education costs.[19] The maximum credit is $500 (based on a maximum $1,000 of qualifying expenses), and the deduction for the startup costs incurred is reduced by the amount of the credit. The credit can be claimed for qualifying costs incurred in each of the three years beginning with the tax year in which the retirement plan becomes effective (maximum total credit over three years of $1,500).

---

[17]§ 44.
[18]§ 45E.

[19]§§ 45E(c)(1) and (d)(1).

Example 20

Maple Company decides to establish a qualified retirement plan for its employees. In the process, it pays consulting fees of $1,200 to a firm that will provide educational seminars to Maple's employees and will assist the payroll department in making necessary changes to the payroll system. Maple may claim a credit for the pension plan startup costs of $500 ($1,200 of qualifying costs, limited to $1,000 × 50%), and its deduction for these expenses is reduced to $700 ($1,200 − $500).

13-3g Credit for Employer-Provided Child Care

The scope of § 162 trade or business expenses includes an employer's expenditures incurred to provide for the care of children of employees as ordinary and necessary business expenses. Alternatively, employers may claim a credit for qualifying expenditures incurred while providing child care facilities to their employees during normal working hours.[20] The **credit for employer-provided child care**, limited annually to $150,000, is composed of the aggregate of two components: 25 percent of qualified child care expenses and 10 percent of qualified child care resource and referral services. *Qualified child care expenses* include the costs of acquiring, constructing, rehabilitating, expanding, and operating a child care facility. *Child care resource and referral services* include amounts paid or incurred under a contract to provide child care resource and referral services to an employee. Any qualifying expenses otherwise deductible by the taxpayer must be reduced by the amount of the credit. In addition, the taxpayer's basis for any property acquired or constructed and used for qualifying purposes is reduced by the amount of the credit. If within 10 years of being placed in service a child care facility ceases to be used for a qualified use, the taxpayer will be required to recapture a portion of the credit previously claimed.[21]

Example 21

During the year, Tan Company constructed a child care facility for $400,000 to be used by its employees who have preschool-aged children in need of child care services while their parents are at work. In addition, Tan incurred salaries for child care workers and other administrative costs associated with the facility of $100,000. As a result, Tan's credit for employer-provided child care is $125,000 [($400,000 + $100,000) × 25%]. Correspondingly, the basis of the facility is reduced to $300,000 ($400,000 − $100,000), and the deduction for salaries and administrative costs is reduced to $75,000 ($100,000 − $25,000).

13-4 OTHER TAX CREDITS

LO.4

Describe various tax credits that are available primarily to individual taxpayers.

13-4a Earned Income Credit

The **earned income credit**, which has been a part of the law for many years, consistently has been justified as a means of providing tax equity to the working poor. In addition, the credit has been designed to help offset regressive taxes, such as the gasoline tax, that impose a relatively larger burden on low-income taxpayers. Further, the credit is intended to encourage economically disadvantaged individuals to become contributing members of the workforce.[22]

The earned income credit is determined by multiplying a maximum amount of earned income by the appropriate credit percentage (see Table 13.2). Generally, earned income includes employee compensation and net earnings from self-employment but excludes items such as interest, dividends, pension benefits, nontaxable employee compensation, and alimony. If a taxpayer has children, the credit percentage used in the calculation depends on the number of qualifying children. From 2009 through 2017, Congress has increased the credit percentage for families with three or more children. Thus, in 2014, the maximum earned income credit

---

[20]§ 45F.
[21]§ 45F(d).

[22]§ 32. The earned income credit is not available if the taxpayer's unearned income (e.g., interest and dividends) exceeds $3,350 in 2014 ($3,300 in 2013). See § 32(i).

for a taxpayer with one qualifying child is $3,305 ($9,720 × 34%), $5,460 ($13,650 × 40%) for a taxpayer with two qualifying children, and $6,143 ($13,650 × 45%) for a taxpayer with three or more qualifying children. However, the maximum earned income credit is phased out completely if the taxpayer's earned income or AGI exceeds certain thresholds, as shown in Table 13.2.[23] Larger phaseout threshold amounts are provided for married taxpayers filing joint returns. To the extent that the greater of earned income or AGI exceeds $23,260 in 2014 for married taxpayers filing a joint return ($17,830 for other taxpayers), the difference, multiplied by the appropriate phaseout percentage, is subtracted from the maximum earned income credit.

Example 22

In 2014, Grace Brown, who is married, files a joint return and otherwise qualifies for the earned income credit. Grace receives wages of $26,000, and she and her husband have no other income. The Browns have one qualifying child. The current earned income credit is $3,305 ($9,720 × 34%) reduced by $438 [($26,000 − $23,260) × 15.98%]. Thus, the earned income credit is $2,867. If, instead, the Browns have three or more qualifying children, the calculation produces a credit of $6,143 ($13,650 × 45%) reduced by $577 [($26,000 − $23,260) × 21.06%]. Thus, the Browns' earned income credit is $5,566 if they have three or more children.

Earned Income Credit Table

It is not necessary to compute the credit as shown in Example 22. To simplify the compliance process, the IRS issues an Earned Income Credit Table for the determination of the appropriate amount of the credit. This table and a worksheet are included in the instructions available to individual taxpayers.

TABLE 13.2	Earned Income Credit and Phaseout Percentages						
Tax Year	Number of Qualifying Children	Earned Income Base Amount	Credit Percentage	Maximum Credit	Phaseout Base	Phaseout Percentage	Phaseout Ends at Income of
2014	*Married, Filing Jointly:*						
	No children	$ 6,480	7.65	$ 496	$13,540	7.65	$20,020
	One child	9,720	34.00	3,305	23,260	15.98	43,941
	Two children	13,650	40.00	5,460	23,260	21.06	49,186
	Three or more children	13,650	45.00	6,143	23,260	21.06	52,427
	Other Taxpayers:						
	No children	$ 6,480	7.65	$ 496	$ 8,110	7.65	$14,590
	One child	9,720	34.00	3,305	17,830	15.98	38,511
	Two children	13,650	40.00	5,460	17,830	21.06	43,756
	Three or more children	13,650	45.00	6,143	17,830	21.06	46,997
2013	*Married, Filing Jointly:*						
	No children	$ 6,370	7.65	$ 487	$13,310	7.65	$19,680
	One child	9,560	34.00	3,250	22,870	15.98	43,210
	Two children	13,430	40.00	5,372	22,870	21.06	48,378
	Three or more children	13,430	45.00	6,044	22,870	21.06	51,567
	Other Taxpayers:						
	No children	$ 6,370	7.65	$ 487	$ 7,970	7.65	$14,340
	One child	9,560	34.00	3,250	17,530	15.98	37,870
	Two children	13,430	40.00	5,372	17,530	21.06	43,087
	Three or more children	13,430	45.00	6,044	17,530	21.06	46,227

[23] § 32(a)(2)(B).

TAX IN THE NEWS   The Earned Income Credit: A Boost to the Working Poor and Merchants Too!

Since 1975, the earned income credit has helped keep millions of Americans from falling below the poverty line. Representing one of the nation's biggest antipoverty efforts, in 2012 the earned income credit benefited more than 30 million households (about one-fifth of all households) at a cost to the Federal government of approximately $56 billion. However, these benefits don't come without problems: fraudulent claims are believed to be common (the IRS estimates that over 30 percent of the benefits are paid in error), and compliance requirements are dauntingly complex (the IRS publication covering the earned income credit exceeds 50 pages).

The benefits from the earned income credit that flow to the working poor have also led to another problem.

Some merchants are targeting this group of taxpayers—and their tax refunds. Pawnshops, jewelers, and auto dealerships in low-income neighborhoods commonly offer to prepare tax returns, hoping to benefit in three ways: they collect fees for preparing the returns, they offer bridge loans at exorbitant interest rates before the tax refund arrives, and they sell high-priced goods to individuals expecting a windfall from their tax refunds. Needless to say, some of these merchants provide fair and valuable assistance to many needy taxpayers; however, many other merchants are in this niche for the sole purpose of lining their own pockets. The caveat "buyer beware" could never be more appropriate.

Eligibility Requirements

Eligibility for the credit depends not only on the taxpayer meeting the earned income and AGI thresholds but also on whether he or she has a qualifying child. The term *qualifying child* generally has the same meaning here as it does for purposes of determining who qualifies as a dependent (see Chapter 3).

In addition to being available for taxpayers with qualifying children, the earned income credit is also available to certain *workers without children.* However, this provision is available only to taxpayers ages 25 through 64 who cannot be claimed as a dependent on another taxpayer's return. As shown in Table 13.2, the credit for 2014 is calculated on a maximum earned income of $6,480 times 7.65 percent and reduced by 7.65 percent of earned income over $13,540 for married taxpayers filing a joint return ($8,110 for other taxpayers).

> **Example 23**
>
> Walt, who is single, is 28 years of age, and is not claimed as a dependent on anyone else's return, earns $8,400 during 2014. Even though he does not have any qualifying children, he qualifies for the earned income credit. His credit is $496 ($6,480 × 7.65%) reduced by $22 [($8,400 − $8,110) × 7.65%]. Thus, Walt's earned income credit is $474. If, instead, Walt's earned income is $7,000, his earned income credit is $496. In this situation, there is no phaseout of the maximum credit because his earned income is not in excess of $8,110.

13-4b Tax Credit for Elderly or Disabled Taxpayers

The credit for the elderly was originally enacted to provide tax relief on retirement income for individuals who were not receiving substantial benefits from tax-free Social Security payments.[24] Currently, the **tax credit for the elderly or disabled** applies to the following:

- Taxpayers age 65 or older.
- Taxpayers under age 65 who are retired with a **permanent and total disability** and who have disability income from a public or private employer on account of the disability. A person generally is considered permanently and totally disabled if he or she is unable to engage in any substantial gainful activity due to a physical or mental impairment for a period of at least 12 months (or lesser period if the disability results in death).

---

[24]§ 22. This credit is not subject to indexation.

TAX IN THE NEWS   What Are the Chances of an IRS Audit?

Even though most taxpayers try to comply with the rules, most also worry that their return may be audited by the IRS. Are these taxpayers worrying needlessly? What are the chances that a particular return will be selected for audit?

The IRS picks returns for audit on the basis of a "DIF" score. "DIF" stands for "discriminant function"—a statistical technique that assigns a score to each individual return after it has been processed. The higher a return's DIF score, the higher the likelihood it will be selected for audit. What generates a high DIF score? The biggest factor is the amount of deductions and credits claimed relative to income.

For most taxpayers, the chances of an audit are low. In 2011, only about 1 percent of Federal individual income tax returns were selected for audit. For the self-employed and those with complex returns or high income, however,

the odds increase. For example, the audit rate was about 4 percent for proprietorship returns showing total gross receipts between $100,000 and $200,000. For individual returns reporting total income of $1 million or more, the audit rate was about 12 percent.

But the IRS also devotes a great deal of attention to low-income taxpayers. Because there have been many fraudulent claims of the earned income credit in the past, taxpayers who claim the credit have a good chance of finding themselves under scrutiny. Taxpayers who claimed the earned income credit in 2011 had about a 36 percent chance of being audited.

Sources: Based on "Assessing the Risk of IRS Audit for Your Tax Return," *Dallas Morning News* (online), March 28, 2008; *IRS Data Book*, 2012.

The *maximum* allowable credit is $1,125 (15% × $7,500 of qualifying income), but the credit will be less for a taxpayer who receives Social Security benefits or has AGI exceeding specified amounts. Under these circumstances, the qualifying income base amount used in the credit computation is reduced. Many taxpayers receive Social Security benefits or have AGI high enough to reduce the base for the credit to zero. In addition, because the credit is nonrefundable, the allowable credit cannot exceed the taxpayer's tax liablity.

The eligibility requirements and the tax computation are somewhat complicated. Consequently, an individual may elect to have the IRS compute his or her tax and the amount of the tax credit.

The credit generally is based on a qualifying income amount (referred to as the *base amount*) and the filing status of the taxpayer in accordance with Table 13.3. To qualify for the credit, married taxpayers who live together must file a joint return. For taxpayers under age 65 who are retired on permanent and total disability, the base amounts could be less than those shown in Table 13.3 because these amounts are limited to taxable disability income.

This initial base amount is *reduced* by (1) Social Security, Railroad Retirement, and certain excluded pension benefits and (2) one-half of the taxpayer's AGI in excess of a threshold amount (see Table 13.3), which is a function of the taxpayer's filing status.

TABLE 13.3	Base and Threshold Amounts for Tax Credit for Elderly or Disabled Taxpayers	
Status	**Base Amount**	**Threshold Amount**
Single, head of household, or surviving spouse	$5,000	$ 7,500
Married, joint return, only one spouse qualifies	5,000	10,000
Married, joint return, both spouses qualify	7,500	10,000
Married, separate returns, spouses live apart the entire year (amount for each spouse)	3,750	5,000

Example 24

Paul and Peggy, husband and wife, are both over age 65 and receive Social Security benefits of $1,000 in the current year. On a joint return, they report AGI of $21,000.

Base amount (from Table 13.3)		$ 7,500
Less: Social Security benefits	$1,000	
One-half of excess of AGI over threshold amount (from Table 13.3) [($21,000 − $10,000) × ½]	5,500	
Total reductions		(6,500)
Remaining base amount		$ 1,000
Multiply remaining base amount by 15%—this is the tax credit allowed, subject to tax liability limitation		$ 150

Schedule R of Form 1040 is used to calculate and report the credit.

13-4c Foreign Tax Credit

Both individual taxpayers and corporations may claim a tax credit for foreign income tax paid on income earned and subject to tax in another country or a U.S. possession.[25] As an alternative, a taxpayer may claim a deduction instead of a credit.[26] In most instances, the **foreign tax credit (FTC)** is advantageous because it provides a direct offset against the tax liability.

The purpose of the FTC is to mitigate double taxation because income earned in a foreign country is subject to both U.S. and foreign taxes. However, the FTC is subject to an overall limitation. This limitation may result in some form of double taxation or taxation at rates in excess of U.S. rates when the foreign tax rates are higher than the U.S. rates. This is a distinct possibility because U.S. tax rates are lower than those of some foreign countries.

Other special tax treatments applicable to taxpayers working outside the United States include the foreign earned income exclusion (see Chapter 5) and limitations on deducting expenses of employees working outside the United States (see Chapter 9). Recall from the earlier discussion that a taxpayer may not take advantage of *both* the FTC and the foreign earned income exclusion.

Computation

Taxpayers are required to compute the FTC based upon an overall limitation.[27] The FTC allowed is the *lesser* of the foreign taxes imposed or the *overall limitation* determined according to the following formula:

$$\frac{\text{Foreign-source taxable income}}{\text{Worldwide taxable income}} \times \text{U.S. tax before FTC}$$

For individual taxpayers, worldwide taxable income in the overall limitation formula is determined *before* personal and dependency exemptions are deducted.

Example 25

In 2014, Carlos, a calendar year taxpayer, has $10,000 of income from Country Y, which imposes a 15% tax, and $20,000 from Country Z, which imposes a 50% tax. He has taxable income of $54,200 from within the United States, is married filing a joint return, and claims two dependency exemptions. Thus, although Carlos's taxable income for purposes of determining U.S. tax is $84,200, taxable income amounts used in the limitation formula are not reduced by personal and dependency exemptions. Thus, for this purpose, taxable income is $100,000 [$84,200 + (4 × $3,950)]. Assume that Carlos's U.S. tax before the credit is $12,763. Overall limitation:

$$\frac{\text{Foreign-source taxable income}}{\text{Worldwide taxable income}} \times \frac{\$30,000}{\$100,000} \times \$12,763 = \$3,829$$

In this case, $3,829 is allowed as the FTC because this amount is less than the $11,500 of foreign taxes imposed [$1,500 (Country Y) + $10,000 (Country Z)].

---

[25]Section 27 provides for the credit, but the qualifications and calculation procedure for the credit are contained in §§ 901–908.

[26]§ 164.

[27]§ 904.

Thus, the overall limitation may result in some of the foreign income being subjected to double taxation. Unused FTCs [e.g., the $7,671 ($11,500 − $3,829) from Example 25] can be carried back 1 year and forward 10 years.[28]

Only foreign income taxes, war profits taxes, and excess profits taxes (or taxes paid in lieu of such taxes) qualify for the credit.[29] In determining whether a tax is an income tax, U.S. criteria are applied. Thus, value added taxes (VAT), severance taxes, property taxes, and sales taxes do not qualify because they are not regarded as taxes on income. Such taxes may be deductible, however.

13-4d Adoption Expenses Credit

Adoption expenses paid or incurred by a taxpayer may give rise to the **adoption expenses credit**.[30] The provision is intended to assist taxpayers who incur nonrecurring costs directly associated with the adoption process, such as adoption fees, attorney fees, court costs, social service review costs, and transportation costs.

In 2014, up to $13,190 of costs incurred to adopt an eligible child qualify for the credit.[31] An eligible child is one who is:

- Under 18 years of age at the time of the adoption or
- Physically or mentally incapable of taking care of himself or herself.

A taxpayer may claim the credit in the year qualifying expenses were paid or incurred if they were paid or incurred *during or after* the tax year in which the adoption was finalized. For qualifying expenses paid or incurred in a tax year *prior* to the year when the adoption was finalized, the credit must be claimed in the tax year following the tax year during which the expenses are paid or incurred. A married couple must file a joint return.

Example 26

In late 2013, Sam and Martha pay $4,000 in legal fees, adoption fees, and other expenses directly related to the adoption of an infant daughter, Susan. In 2014, the year in which the adoption becomes final, they pay an additional $10,000. Sam and Martha are eligible for a $13,190 credit in 2014 (for expenses of $14,000, limited by the $13,190 ceiling, paid in 2013 and 2014).

The amount of the credit that is otherwise available is phased out for taxpayers whose AGI (modified for this purpose) exceeds $197,880 in 2014, and the credit is completely eliminated when AGI reaches $237,880. The resulting credit is calculated by reducing the allowable credit (determined without this reduction) by the allowable credit multiplied by the ratio of the excess of the taxpayer's AGI over $197,880 to $40,000.[32]

Example 27

Assume the same facts as in the previous example, except that Sam and Martha's AGI is $222,880 in 2014. As a result, their available credit in 2014 is reduced from $13,190 to $4,946 {$13,190 − [$13,190 × ($25,000/$40,000)]}.

The credit is nonrefundable and is available to taxpayers only in a year in which this credit and the other nonrefundable credits do not exceed the taxpayer's tax liability. However, any unused adoption expenses credit may be carried over for up to five years, being utilized on a first-in, first-out basis.

13-4e Child Tax Credit

The **child tax credit** provisions allow individual taxpayers to take a tax credit based solely on the *number* of their qualifying children. This credit is one of several

---

[28]§ 904(c) and Reg. § 1.904–2(g), Example 1. This treatment of unused FTCs applies to tax years ending after October 22, 2004. Prior law provided a two-year carryback and a five-year carryforward.

[29]Reg. § 1.901–1(a)(3)(i).

[30]§ 23.

[31]§ 23(b)(1). In 2013, the maximum amount of eligible costs was $12,970. Unique rules are used in calculating the credit when adopting "a child with special needs." See § 23(d)(3).

[32]§ 23(b)(2). The AGI threshold amount is indexed for inflation. In 2013, the phaseout of the credit began when AGI exceeded $194,580.

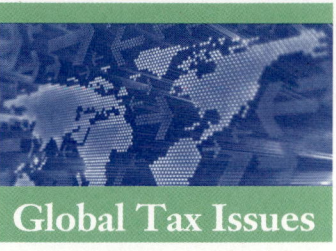

Sourcing Income in Cyberspace—Getting It Right When Calculating the Foreign Tax Credit

Global Tax Issues

© iStockphoto.com/Andrey Prokhorov

The overall limitation on the foreign tax credit (FTC) plays a critical role in restricting the amount of the credit available to a taxpayer. In the overall limitation formula, the taxpayer must characterize the year's taxable income as either earned (or sourced) inside the United States or earned from sources outside the United States. As a general rule, a relatively greater percentage of foreign-source income in the formula will lead to a larger FTC. Therefore, determining the source of various types of income is critical in the proper calculation of the credit. However, classifying income as either foreign or U.S. source is not always a simple matter.

For example, consumers and businesses are using the Internet to conduct more and more commerce involving both products and services. The problem is that the existing income-sourcing rules were developed long before the existence of the Internet, and taxing authorities are finding it challenging to apply these rules to Internet transactions. Where does a sale take place when the web server is in Scotland, the seller is in India, and the customer is in Illinois? Where is a service performed when all activities take place over the Net? These questions and more will have to be answered by the United States and its trading partners as the Internet economy grows in size and importance.

"family-friendly" provisions that currently are part of our tax law. To be eligible for the credit, the child must be under age 17, must be a U.S. citizen, and must be claimed as a dependent on the taxpayer's return.

Maximum Credit and Phaseouts

Under current law, the maximum credit available is $1,000 per child.[33] The available credit is phased out for higher-income taxpayers beginning when AGI reaches $110,000 for joint filers ($55,000 for married taxpayers filing separately) and $75,000 for single taxpayers. The credit is phased out by $50 for each $1,000 (or part thereof) of AGI above the threshold amounts.[34] Because the maximum credit amount available to taxpayers depends on the number of qualifying children, the income level at which the credit is phased out completely also depends on the number of children qualifying for the credit.[35]

> **Example 28**
>
> Juanita and Alberto are married and file a joint tax return claiming their two children, ages 6 and 8, as dependents. Their AGI is $122,400. Juanita and Alberto's maximum child tax credit is $2,000 ($1,000 × 2 children). Because Juanita and Alberto's AGI is in excess of the $110,000 threshold, the maximum credit must be reduced by $50 for every $1,000 (or part thereof) above the threshold amount {$50 × [($122,400 − $110,000)/$1,000]}. Thus, the credit reduction equals $650 [$50 × 13 (rounded from 12.4)]. Therefore, Juanita and Alberto's child tax credit is $1,350.

13-4f Credit for Child and Dependent Care Expenses

The **credit for child and dependent care expenses** mitigates the inequity felt by working taxpayers who must pay for child care services to work outside the home.[36]

---

[33]§ 24.

[34]AGI is modified for purposes of this calculation. The threshold amounts are *not* indexed for inflation. See §§ 24(a) and (b).

[35]The child tax credit is generally refundable to the extent of 15% of the taxpayer's earned income in excess of an inflation-adjusted amount. The

American Recovery and Reinvestment Tax Act of 2009 set this amount at $3,000 for 2009 and 2010, and subsequent legislation extends this modification through 2017. Prior to the ARRTA of 2009, the 2009 threshold was $12,550.

[36]§ 21.

This credit is a specified percentage of expenses incurred to enable the taxpayer to work or to seek employment. Expenses on which the credit for child and dependent care expenses is based are subject to limitations.

Eligibility

To be eligible for the credit, an individual must have either of the following:

- A dependent under age 13.
- A dependent or spouse who is physically or mentally incapacitated and who lives with the taxpayer for more than one-half of the year.

Generally, married taxpayers must file a joint return to obtain the credit.

Eligible Employment-Related Expenses

Eligible expenses include amounts paid for household services and care of a qualifying individual that are incurred to enable the taxpayer to be employed. Child and dependent care expenses include expenses incurred in the home, such as payments for a housekeeper. Out-of-the-home expenses incurred for the care of a dependent under the age of 13 also qualify for the credit. In addition, out-of-the-home expenses incurred for an older dependent or spouse who is physically or mentally incapacitated qualify for the credit if that person regularly spends at least eight hours each day in the taxpayer's household. This makes the credit available to taxpayers who keep handicapped older children and elderly relatives in the home instead of institutionalizing them. Out-of-the-home expenses incurred for services provided by a dependent care center will qualify only if the center complies with all applicable laws and regulations of a state or unit of local government.

Child care payments to a relative are eligible for the credit unless the relative is a child (under age 19) of the taxpayer.

Example 29	Wilma is an employed mother of an 8-year-old child. She pays her mother, Rita, $1,500 per year to care for the child after school. Wilma pays her daughter Eleanor, age 17, $900 for the child's care during the summer. Of these amounts, only the $1,500 paid to Rita qualifies as employment-related child care expenses.

Earned Income Ceiling

Qualifying employment-related expenses are limited to an individual's earned income. For married taxpayers, this limitation applies to the spouse with the *lesser* amount of earned income. Special rules are provided for taxpayers with nonworking spouses who are disabled or are full-time students. If a nonworking spouse is physically or mentally disabled or is a full-time student, he or she is *deemed* to have earned income for purposes of this limitation. The deemed amount is $250 per month if there is one qualifying individual in the household or $500 per month if there are two or more qualifying individuals in the household. In the case of a student-spouse, the student's income is *deemed* to be earned only for the months the student is enrolled on a full-time basis at an educational institution.[37]

Calculation of the Credit

In general, the credit is equal to a percentage of *unreimbursed* employment-related expenses up to $3,000 for one qualifying individual and $6,000 for two or more individuals. The credit rate varies between 20 percent and 35 percent, depending

---

[37]§ 21(d).

on the taxpayer's AGI. The following chart shows the applicable percentage for taxpayers as AGI increases:

Adjusted Gross Income		Applicable Rate of
Over	**But Not Over**	**Credit**
$ 0	$15,000	35%
15,000	17,000	34%
17,000	19,000	33%
19,000	21,000	32%
21,000	23,000	31%
23,000	25,000	30%
25,000	27,000	29%
27,000	29,000	28%
29,000	31,000	27%
31,000	33,000	26%
33,000	35,000	25%
35,000	37,000	24%
37,000	39,000	23%
39,000	41,000	22%
41,000	43,000	21%
43,000	No limit	20%

Example 30

Nancy, who has two children under age 13, worked full-time while her spouse, Ron, was attending college for 10 months during the year. Nancy earned $22,000 and incurred $6,200 of child care expenses. Ron is *deemed* to be fully employed and to have earned $500 for each of the 10 months (or a total of $5,000). Because Nancy and Ron have AGI of $22,000, they are allowed a credit rate of 31%. Nancy and Ron are limited to $5,000 in qualified child care expenses ($6,000 maximum expenses, limited to Ron's deemed earned income of $5,000). Therefore, they are entitled to a tax credit of $1,550 (31% × $5,000) for the year.

ETHICS & EQUITY   **Is This the Right Way to Use the Credit for Child and Dependent Care Expenses?**

Your friends, Tim and Susan, have hired a child care provider (Rebecca) to come into their home while they are at work to care for their two children. Rebecca charges $4,500 for her services for the year. Tim and Susan have discovered that up to $6,000 of qualifying expenditures will generate a credit for child and dependent care expenses and that qualifying expenditures can include payments for housecleaning services.

As a result, they ask Rebecca whether she would be interested in working several hours more per week, after Tim returns from work, for the sole purpose of cleaning the

house. Tim and Susan offer to pay Rebecca $1,500 for the additional work. For Tim and Susan, the net cost of the additional services would be $1,200 [$1,500 − ($1,500 × 20%)] due to the availability of the credit for child and dependent care expenses.

You learn of Tim and Susan's opportunity, but think it is unfair. If you hired someone to perform similar housecleaning services at the same price, your net cost would be $1,500, not $1,200, because you do not qualify for the credit. You are troubled by this inequity. Is your intuition correct?

© iStockphoto.com/LdF

Dependent Care Assistance Program

Recall from Chapter 5 that a taxpayer is allowed an exclusion from gross income for a limited amount reimbursed for child or dependent care expenses. However, the taxpayer is not allowed both an exclusion from gross income and a child and dependent care credit on the same amount. The $3,000 and $6,000 ceilings for allowable child and dependent care expenses are reduced dollar for dollar by the amount of reimbursement.[38]

Example 31	Assume the same facts as in Example 30, except that of the $6,200 paid for child care, Nancy was reimbursed $2,500 by her employer under a qualified dependent care assistance program. Under the employer's plan, the reimbursement reduces Nancy's taxable wages. Thus, Nancy and Ron have AGI of $19,500 ($22,000 − $2,500). The maximum amount of child care expenses for two or more dependents of $6,000 is reduced by the $2,500 reimbursement, resulting in a tax credit of $1,120 [32% × ($6,000 − $2,500)].

Reporting Requirements

The credit is claimed by completing and filing Form 2441, Credit for Child and Dependent Care Expenses.

13-4g Education Tax Credits

Two credits, the **American Opportunity credit** and the **lifetime learning credit**,[39] are available to help qualifying low- and middle-income individuals defray the cost of higher education. The credits are available for qualifying tuition and related expenses incurred by students pursuing undergraduate or graduate degrees or vocational training. Books and other course materials are eligible for the American Opportunity credit (but not the lifetime learning credit).[40] Room and board are ineligible for both credits.

Maximum Credit

The American Opportunity credit permits a maximum credit of $2,500 per year (100 percent of the first $2,000 of tuition expenses plus 25 percent of the next $2,000 of tuition expenses) for the *first four years* of postsecondary education.[41] The lifetime learning credit permits a credit of 20 percent of qualifying expenses (up to $10,000 per year) incurred in a year in which the American Opportunity credit is not claimed with respect to a given student. Generally, the lifetime learning credit is used for individuals who are beyond the first four years of postsecondary education.

Eligible Individuals

Both education credits are available for qualified expenses incurred by a taxpayer, taxpayer's spouse, or taxpayer's dependent. The American Opportunity credit is available per eligible student, while the lifetime learning credit is calculated per taxpayer. To be eligible for the American Opportunity credit, a student must take at least one-half the full-time course load for at least one academic term at a qualifying educational institution. No comparable requirement exists for the lifetime learning credit. Therefore, taxpayers who are seeking new job skills or maintaining existing skills through graduate training or continuing education are eligible for the lifetime learning credit. Taxpayers who are married must file a joint return to claim either education credit.

Income Limitations and Refundability

Both education credits are subject to income limitations, which differ for years after 2008.[42] In addition, the American Opportunity credit is partially refundable and may be used to offset a taxpayer's alternative minimum tax (AMT) liability (the lifetime learning credit is neither refundable nor an AMT liability offset).

The American Opportunity credit amount is phased out beginning when the taxpayer's AGI (modified for this purpose) reaches $80,000 ($160,000 for married

---

[38]§ 21(c).

[39]§ 25A. The HOPE scholarship credit was modified and renamed the American Opportunity tax credit by the American Recovery and Reinvestment Tax Act of 2009 for the 2009 and 2010 tax years. Subsequent legislation extends this credit through 2017. Without congressional intervention, the HOPE scholarship credit will return in 2018.

[40]§ 25A(i)(3).

[41]In years prior to 2009, the qualifying expense base for the HOPE scholarship credit was subject to inflation adjustment. The base was $1,200 in 2008, $1,100 in 2007 and 2006, and $1,000 for years prior to 2006.

[42]In 2008 and prior years, the HOPE scholarship and lifetime learning credits were combined and subject to a single modified AGI limitation.

TAX IN THE NEWS   Millions Are Wrongly Claiming Tax Credits

An estimated 2.1 million taxpayers may have received $3.2 billion in erroneous education credits, according to a report from the Treasury Inspector General for Tax Administration (TIGTA). The American Recovery and Reinvestment Act of 2009 created a refundable tax credit—the American Opportunity Tax Credit—to help taxpayers offset the cost of higher education. TIGTA found that 1.7 million taxpayers erroneously received an estimated $2.6 billion in education credits even though the Internal Revenue Service had no supporting documentation that these taxpayers had attended an eligible institution, defined as an accredited institution of higher learning. In addition, TIGTA found that almost 400,000 taxpayers received an estimated $550 million in education credits for which they were not eligible because they did not attend college for the required amount of time and/or were post-graduate students.

"Based on the results of our review, the IRS does not have effective processes to identify taxpayers who claim erroneous education credits," said J. Russell George, Treasury Inspector General for Tax Administration. "If not addressed, this could result in up to $12.8 billion in potentially erroneous refunds over four years," Mr. George added.

In a different report released in August 2013, TIGTA said that the IRS issued $11.6 billion to $13.6 billion in improper earned income tax credits in 2012, representing 21 to 25 percent of all payments in that category for the year. The numbers show an improvement of more than 15 percent compared with 2011, but they are still higher than the $11.2 billion to $13.3 billion range in 2009.

As part of their investigations, TIGTA made a number of recommendations to the IRS. In response, the IRS indicated that it has begun to take steps to increase monitoring and improve compliance.

Sources: Based on Stephen Dinan, "$3.2 Billion Wrongly Taken in Tuition Tax Credits," *Washington Times*, October 20, 2011; Bernie Becker, "Millions Are Wrongly Claiming Education Tax Credit," *The Hill*, October 20, 2011; Treasury Inspector General for Tax Administration Report 2013-40-084 (August 28, 2013).

taxpayers filing jointly).[43] The reduction is equal to the extent to which AGI exceeds $80,000 ($160,000 for married taxpayers filing jointly) as a percentage of a $10,000 phaseout range ($20,000 for married taxpayers filing jointly). As a result, the credit is completely eliminated when modified AGI reaches $90,000 ($180,000 for married taxpayers filing jointly). The entire credit allowed may be used to reduce a taxpayer's AMT liability. In addition, 40 percent of the American Opportunity credit is refundable.[44]

In 2014, the lifetime learning credit amount is phased out beginning when the taxpayer's AGI (modified for this purpose) reaches $54,000 ($108,000 for married taxpayers filing jointly).[45] The reduction is equal to the extent to which AGI exceeds $54,000 ($108,000 for married filing jointly) as a percentage of a $10,000 ($20,000 for married filing jointly) phaseout range. The credit is completely eliminated when AGI reaches $64,000 ($128,000 for married filing jointly).

THE BIG PICTURE

Example 32

Return to the facts of *The Big Picture* on p. 13-1. Recall that Tom and Jennifer Snyder are married; file a joint tax return; have modified AGI of $158,000; and have two children, Lora and Sam. The Snyders paid $7,500 of tuition and $8,500 for room and board for Lora (a freshman) and $8,100 of tuition plus $7,200 for room and board for Sam (a junior). Both Lora and Sam are full-time students and are Tom and Jennifer's dependents. Lora's tuition and Sam's tuition are qualified expenses for the American Opportunity credit. For 2014, Tom and Jennifer may claim a $2,500 American Opportunity credit for both Lora's and Sam's expenses [(100% × $2,000) + (25% × $2,000)]. So in total, they qualify for a $5,000 American Opportunity credit.

---

[43]These amounts are not adjusted for inflation.

[44]If the credit is claimed for a taxpayer subject to § 1(g) (the "kiddie tax"), the credit is not refundable.

[45]§ 25A(d). For 2013, the AGI bases were $53,000 and $107,000. § 25A(h)(2)(A).

THE BIG PICTURE

Example 33

Return to the facts of *The Big Picture* on p. 13-1. Now assume that Tom and Jennifer's modified AGI for 2014 is $172,000 instead of $158,000. Tom and Jennifer are eligible to claim a $2,000 American Opportunity credit for 2014. The potential $5,000 American Opportunity credit must be reduced because their AGI exceeds the $160,000 limit for married taxpayers. The percentage reduction is computed as the amount by which modified AGI exceeds the limit, expressed as a percentage of the phaseout range, or [($172,000 − $160,000)/$20,000)], resulting in a 60% reduction. Therefore, the maximum available credit for 2014 is $2,000 ($5,000 × 40% allowable portion).

THE BIG PICTURE

Example 34

Return to the facts of *The Big Picture* on p. 13-1. Now assume that Tom and Jennifer's modified AGI is $122,000. In addition, assume that Tom is going to school on a part-time basis to complete a graduate degree and pays qualifying tuition and fees of $4,000 during 2014. As Tom and Jennifer's modified AGI is below $160,000, a $5,000 American Opportunity credit is available to them ($2,500 for both Lora and Sam). In addition, Tom's qualifying expenses are eligible for the lifetime learning credit. The potential lifetime learning credit of $800 ($4,000 × 20%) must be reduced because their modified AGI exceeds the $108,000 limit for married taxpayers. As their modified AGI exceeds the $108,000 limit by $14,000 and the phaseout range is $20,000, their lifetime learning credit is reduced by 70%. Therefore, their lifetime learning credit for 2014 is $240 ($800 × 30%), and their total education credits amount to $5,240 ($5,000 American Opportunity credit and $240 lifetime learning credit).

Restrictions on Double Tax Benefit

Taxpayers are prohibited from receiving a double tax benefit associated with qualifying educational expenses. Therefore, taxpayers who claim an education credit may not deduct the expenses, nor may they claim the credit for amounts that are otherwise excluded from gross income (e.g., scholarships and employer-paid educational assistance). However, a taxpayer may claim an education tax credit and exclude from gross income amounts distributed from a Coverdell Education Savings Account as long as the distribution is not used for the same expenses for which the credit is claimed.

13-4h Energy Credits

The Internal Revenue Code contains a variety of credits for businesses and individuals to encourage the conservation of natural resources and the development of energy sources other than oil and gas. Exhibit 13.2 provides a summary of several of the more important energy tax credits.

13-4i Credit for Certain Retirement Plan Contributions

Taxpayers may claim a nonrefundable **credit for certain retirement plan contributions** based on eligible contributions of up to $2,000 to certain qualified retirement plans, such as traditional and Roth IRAs and § 401(k) plans.[46] This credit, sometimes referred to as the "saver's credit," is intended to encourage lower- and middle-income taxpayers to contribute to qualified retirement plans. The benefit provided

---

[46] § 25B.

EXHIBIT 13.2	**Energy Credits Summary**

Home Energy Efficiency Improvement Tax Credits

Consumers who purchase and install specific products, such as energy-efficient windows, insulation, doors, roofs, and heating and cooling equipment, in the home can receive a tax credit of up to $1,500 for property placed in service before January 1, 2014 (§ 25C). In addition, consumers who purchase photovoltaic, fuel cell, and/or solar water heating property can receive a credit equal to 30% of the purchase price. Improvements must be made to the taxpayer's principal residence and must be completed before January 1, 2017 (§ 25D).

Plug-in Electric Drive Motor Vehicles

Consumers who purchase new plug-in electric drive motor vehicles before January 1, 2015, can qualify for a credit of $2,500 plus $417 for each kilowatt-hour of battery capacity in excess of 5 kilowatt-hours. The maximum credit is $7,500 (§ 30D).

Business Energy Tax Credits

Businesses are eligible for tax credits for producing alternative fuels, constructing energy-efficient buildings, producing energy-efficient products, and producing energy using alternative means.

- *Biodiesel/Alternative Fuels—Small Producer Biodiesel and Renewable Diesel (§ 40) and Ethanol Credit (§ 40A).* Small agri-biodiesel producers are provided a tax credit measured in varying cents per gallon for producing these fuels (with varying maximums per year). The credit is available for sales through December 31, 2013.
- *Credit for Business Installation of Qualified Fuel Cells, Stationary Microturbine Power Plants, Solar, and Small Wind Energy Equipment.* A tax credit—based on the purchase price—is provided for installing qualified fuel cell power plants (a 30% credit), qualifying stationary microturbine power plants (a 10% credit), qualifying solar energy equipment (a 30% credit), and small wind energy equipment (a 30% credit). The credit applies to property placed in service before January 1, 2017 (§ 48).
- *Credit for Building Energy-Efficient New Homes.* A $2,000 tax credit is provided to eligible contractors for each qualified new energy-efficient home constructed through December 31, 2013. The credit applies to manufactured homes meeting ENERGY STAR® criteria and other homes (§ 45L).
- *Manufacturing Energy-Efficient Appliances.* A tax credit is provided to the manufacturer of energy-efficient dishwashers, clothes washers, and refrigerators. Credits vary depending on the efficiency of the unit and relate, generally, to production through December 31, 2013 (§ 45M).
- *Energy Credit for Producing Electricity via Wind, Solar, Geothermal, and Other Property.* A tax credit is provided for producing energy via qualified wind, solar, geothermal, and other property. The tax credit—based on the number of kilowatt-hours of electricity produced—applies to production through the end of 2013 (§ 45).

by this credit is in addition to any deduction or exclusion that otherwise is available due to the qualifying contribution. In calculating the credit, the qualifying contributions are reduced by taxable distributions from any of the qualifying plans received by the taxpayer and spouse during the tax year and the two previous tax years and during the period prior to the due date of the return.

The credit rate applied to the eligible expenses depends on the taxpayer's AGI[47] and filing status as shown in Table 13.4. However, the maximum credit allowed to an individual is $1,000 ($2,000 × 50%). As the taxpayer's AGI increases, the rate applied to contributions in calculating the credit is reduced, and once AGI exceeds the upper end of the applicable range, no credit is available. To qualify for the credit, the taxpayer must be at least 18 years of age and cannot be a dependent of another taxpayer or a full-time student.

> **Example 35**
>
> Earl and Josephine, married taxpayers, each contribute $2,500 to their respective § 401(k) plans offered through their employers. The AGI reported on their joint return is $45,000. The maximum amount of contributions that may be taken into account in calculating the credit is limited to $2,000 for Earl and $2,000 for Josephine. As a result, they may claim a credit for their retirement plan contributions of $400 [($2,000 × 2) × 10%]. They would not qualify for the credit if their AGI had exceeded $60,000.

---

[47]For years beginning after 2006, the AGI thresholds are indexed for inflation. The amounts shown in Table 13.4 are the relevant thresholds for 2014. For purposes of this credit, the AGI thresholds are modified to include certain excluded income items. See § 25B(e).

TABLE 13.4		"Saver's" Credit Rate and AGI Thresholds					
Joint Return		**Head of Household**		**All Other Cases**			
Over	Not Over	Over	Not Over	Over	Not Over	Applicable Percentage
$ 0	$36,000	$ 0	$27,000	$ 0	$18,000	50%
36,000	39,000	27,000	29,250	18,000	19,500	20%
39,000	60,000	29,250	45,000	19,500	30,000	10%
60,000		45,000		30,000		0%

13-4j   Small Employer Health Insurance Credit

Under the Affordable Care Act of 2010, a tax credit is provided for a qualified small employer for nonelective contributions to purchase health insurance for its employees.[48] To qualify for the credit in 2014, the employer must have no more than 25 full-time equivalent employees whose annual full-time wages average no more than $50,800 ($50,000 in 2013). The employer must pay at least half the cost of the health insurance premiums.[49] The credit is 50 percent of the health insurance premiums paid (35 percent in years from 2010 through 2013). It is subject to a phaseout if the employer has more than 10 full-time equivalent employees and/ or has annual full-time wages that average more than $25,400 ($25,000 in 2013).[50]

Concept Summary 13.1 provides an overview of the tax credits discussed in this chapter.

13-5 PAYMENT PROCEDURES

LO.5

Describe the tax withholding and payment procedures applicable to employers.

The tax law contains elaborate rules that require the prepayment of various Federal taxes. Consistent with the pay-as-you-go approach to the collection of taxes, these rules carry penalties for lack of compliance.[51] Prepayment procedures fall into two major categories: those applicable to employers and those applicable to self-employed persons. For employers, both payroll taxes (FICA and FUTA) and income taxes may be involved. With self-employed taxpayers, the focus is on the income tax and the self-employment tax.

13-5a   Procedures Applicable to Employers

Employment taxes include FICA (Federal Insurance Contributions Act) and FUTA (Federal Unemployment Tax Act). The employer usually is responsible for withholding the employee's share of FICA (commonly referred to as Social Security tax) and appropriate amounts for income taxes. In addition, the employer must match the FICA portion withheld and fully absorb the cost of FUTA. The sum of the employment taxes and the income tax withholdings must be paid to the IRS at specified intervals.

The key to employer compliance in this area involves the resolution of the following points:

- Ascertaining which employees and wages are covered by employment taxes and are subject to withholding for income taxes.
- Arriving at the amount to be paid and/or withheld.
- Reporting and paying employment taxes and income taxes withheld to the IRS on a timely basis through the use of proper forms and procedures.

---

[48]§ 45R; this credit began in 2010.

[49]§§ 45R(d)(1) and (4). The wage amount is indexed for inflation beginning in 2014.

[50]§ 45R(c). The credit percentage for tax-exempt employers is 25% in 2010 through 2013 and 35% in subsequent years.

[51]See, for example, § 3403 (employer liable for any taxes withheld and not paid over to the IRS), § 6656 (penalty on amounts withheld and not paid over), and § 6654 (penalty for failure by an individual to pay estimated income taxes).

CONCEPT SUMMARY 13.1

Tax Credits

Credit	Computation	Comments
Tax withheld on wages (§ 31)	Amount is reported to employee on Form W–2.	Refundable credit.
Earned income (§ 32)	Amount is determined by reference to Earned Income Credit Table published by IRS. Computations of underlying amounts in Earned Income Credit Table are illustrated in Example 22.	Refundable credit. A form of negative income tax to assist low-income taxpayers. Earned income and AGI must be less than certain threshold amounts. Generally, one or more qualifying children must reside with the taxpayer.
Child and dependent care (§ 21)	Rate ranges from 20% to 35% depending on AGI. Maximum base for credit is $3,000 for one qualifying individual, $6,000 for two or more.	Nonrefundable personal credit. No carryback or carryforward. Benefits taxpayers who incur employment-related child or dependent care expenses in order to work or seek employment. Eligible taxpayers must have a dependent under age 13 or a dependent (any age) or spouse who is physically or mentally incapacitated.
Elderly or disabled (§ 22)	15% of sum of base amount minus reductions for (1) Social Security and other nontaxable benefits, and (2) excess AGI. Base amount is fixed by law (e.g., $5,000 for a single taxpayer).	Nonrefundable personal credit. No carryback or carryforward. Provides relief for taxpayers not receiving substantial tax-free retirement benefits.
Adoption expenses (§ 23)	Up to $13,190 of costs incurred to adopt an eligible child qualify for the credit. Taxpayer claims the credit in the year qualified expenses were paid or incurred if they were paid or incurred during or after year in which adoption was finalized. For expenses paid or incurred in a year prior to when adoption was finalized, credit must be claimed in tax year following the tax year during which the expenses are paid or incurred.	Nonrefundable credit. Unused credit may be carried forward five years. Purpose is to assist taxpayers who incur nonrecurring costs associated with the adoption process.
Child (§ 24)	Credit is based on *number* of qualifying children under age 17. Maximum credit is $1,000 per child. Credit is phased out for higher-income taxpayers.	Generally a nonrefundable credit. Refundable in certain cases. Purpose is to provide tax relief for low- to moderate-income families with children.
Education (§ 25A)	American Opportunity credit is available for qualifying education expenses of students in first four years of postsecondary education. Maximum credit is $2,500 per year per eligible student. Credit is phased out for higher-income taxpayers.	Credit is partially refundable. Credit is designed to help defray costs of first four years of higher education for low- to middle-income families.
	Lifetime learning credit permits a credit of 20% of qualifying expenses (up to $10,000 per year) provided American Opportunity credit is not claimed with respect to those expenses. Credit is calculated per taxpayer, not per student, and is phased out for higher-income taxpayers.	Nonrefundable credit. Credit is designed to help defray costs of higher education beyond first four years and of costs incurred in maintaining or improving existing job skills for low- to middle-income taxpayers.
Credit for certain retirement plan contributions (§ 25B)	Calculation is based on amount of contribution multiplied by a percentage that depends on the taxpayer's filing status and AGI.	Nonrefundable credit. Purpose is to encourage contributions to qualified retirement plans by low- and middle-income taxpayers.
Foreign tax (§ 27)	Foreign taxable income/total worldwide taxable income × U.S. tax = overall limitation. Lesser of foreign taxes imposed or overall limitation.	Nonrefundable credit. Unused credits may be carried back 1 year and forward 10 years. Purpose is to prevent double taxation of foreign-source income.

Tax Credits—Continued

Credit	Computation	Comments
General business (§ 38)	May not exceed net income tax minus the greater of tentative minimum tax or 25% of net regular tax liability that exceeds $25,000.	Nonrefundable credit. Components include tax credit for rehabilitation expenditures, work opportunity tax credit, research activities credit, low-income housing credit, disabled access credit, credit for small employer pension plan startup costs, and credit for employer-provided child care. Unused credit may be carried back 1 year and forward 20 years. FIFO method applies to carrybacks, carryovers, and credits earned during current year.
Rehabilitation expenditures (§ 47)	Qualifying investment times rehabilitation percentage, depending on type of property. Regular rehabilitation rate is 10%; rate for certified historic structures is 20%.	Nonrefundable credit. Part of general business credit and therefore subject to same carryback, carryover, and FIFO rules. Purpose is to discourage businesses from moving from economically distressed areas to newer locations.
Research activities (§ 41)	Incremental credit is 20% of excess of computation year expenditures over the base amount. Basic research credit is allowed to certain corporations for 20% of cash payments to qualified organizations that exceed a specially calculated base amount. Energy research credit also available.	Nonrefundable credit. Part of general business credit and therefore subject to same carryback, carryover, and FIFO rules. Purpose is to encourage high-tech and energy research in the United States.
Low-income housing (§ 42)	Appropriate rate times eligible basis (portion of project attributable to low-income units). Credit is available each year for 10 years. Recapture may apply.	Nonrefundable credit. Part of general business credit and therefore subject to same carryback, carryover, and FIFO rules. Purpose is to encourage construction of housing for low-income individuals.
Disabled access (§ 44)	Credit is 50% of eligible access expenditures that exceed $250 but do not exceed $10,250. Maximum credit is $5,000. Available only to eligible small businesses.	Nonrefundable credit. Part of general business credit and therefore subject to same carryback, carryover, and FIFO rules. Purpose is to encourage small businesses to become more accessible to disabled individuals.
Credit for small employer pension plan startup costs (§ 45E)	Credit equals 50% of qualified startup costs incurred by eligible employers. Maximum annual credit is $500. Deduction for related expenses is reduced by the amount of the credit.	Nonrefundable credit. Part of general business credit and therefore subject to same carryback, carryover, and FIFO rules. Purpose is to encourage small employers to establish qualified retirement plans for their employees.
Credit for employer-provided child care (§ 45F)	Credit is equal to 25% of qualified child care expenses plus 10% of qualified expenses for child care resource and referral services. Maximum credit is $150,000. Deduction for related expenses or basis must be reduced by the amount of the credit.	Nonrefundable credit. Part of general business credit and therefore subject to same carryback, carryover, and FIFO rules. Purpose is to encourage employers to provide child care for their employees' children during normal working hours.
Work opportunity (§ 51)	Credit is limited to 40% of the first $6,000 of wages paid to each eligible employee. For long-term family assistance recipients, credit is limited to 40% of first $10,000 of wages paid to each eligible employee in first year of employment, plus 50% of first $10,000 of wages paid to each eligible employee in second year of employment.	Nonrefundable credit. Part of the general business credit and therefore subject to the same carryback, carryover, and FIFO rules. Purpose is to encourage employment of individuals in specified groups.

Coverage Requirements

IRS Publication 15, *Employer's Tax Guide* (Circular E), contains a listing of which employees and which wages require withholdings for income taxes and employment taxes. Excerpts from Publication 15 appear in Exhibit 13.3. In working with Exhibit 13.3, consider the following observations:

- The designation "Exempt" in the income tax withholding column does not mean the amount paid is nontaxable to the employee. It merely relieves the employer from having to withhold.

EXHIBIT 13.3	Withholding Classifications		

| Special Classes of Employment and Special Types of Payments | Treatment under Employment Taxes | | |
	Income Tax Withholding	Social Security and Medicare	Federal Unemployment
Employee business expense reimbursement:			
1. Accountable plan.			
a. Amounts not exceeding specified government rate for per diem or standard mileage.	Exempt	Exempt	Exempt
b. Amounts in excess of specified government rate for per diem or standard mileage.	Withhold	Taxable	Taxable
2. Nonaccountable plan.	Withhold	Taxable	Taxable
Family employees:			
1. Child employed by parent (or partnership in which each partner is a parent of the child).	Withhold	Exempt until age 18; age 21 for domestic service.	Exempt until age 21
2. Parent employed by child.	Withhold	Taxable if in course of the son's or daughter's business.	Exempt
3. Spouse employed by spouse.	Withhold	Taxable if in course of spouse's business.	Exempt
Household employees: Domestic service in private homes. Farmers see Publication 51 (Circular A).	Exempt (withhold if both employer and employee agree).	Taxable if paid $1,900 or more in cash in 2014. Exempt if performed by an individual under age 18 during any portion of the calendar year and is not the principal occupation of the employee.	Taxable if employer paid total cash wages of $1,000 or more in any quarter in the current or preceding calendar year.
Interns working in hospitals.	Withhold	Taxable	Exempt
Newspaper carriers under age 18.	Exempt (withhold if both employer and employee agree).	Exempt	Exempt
Salespersons:			
1. Common law employees.	Withhold	Taxable	Taxable
2. Statutory employees.	Exempt	Taxable	Taxable, except for full-time life insurance sales agents.
Scholarships and fellowship grants: [includible in income under § 117(c)].	Withhold	Taxability depends on the nature of the employment and the status of the organization.	Taxability depends on the nature of the employment and the status of the organization.
Severance or dismissal pay.	Withhold	Taxable	Taxable
Tips if less than $20 in a month.	Exempt	Exempt	Exempt
Worker's compensation.	Exempt	Exempt	Exempt

Example 36

Lee works for Yellow Corporation and has the type of job where tips are not common but do occur. If Lee's total tips amount to less than $20 per month, Yellow Corporation need not withhold Federal income taxes on the tips (see Exhibit 13.3). Nevertheless, Lee must include the tips in his gross income.

- In some cases, income tax withholding is not required but is voluntary. This is designated "Exempt (withhold if both employer and employee agree)."

Example 37

Pat is employed as a gardener by a wealthy family. In the past, he has encountered difficulty in managing his finances in order to be in a position to pay the income tax due every April 15. To ease the cash-flow problem that develops in April, Pat asks his employer to withhold income taxes from his wages.

- The Social Security and Medicare (FICA) column refers to the employer's share. The same is true of the Federal Unemployment (FUTA) column because the employee does not contribute to this tax.

Amount of FICA Taxes

The FICA tax has two components: Social Security tax (old age, survivors, and disability insurance) *and* Medicare tax (hospital insurance). The tax rates and wage base under FICA have increased substantially over the years. The base amount is adjusted each year for inflation. As Table 13.5 shows, the top base amount differs for the Medicare portion (unlimited since 1994) and for the Social Security portion. Table 13.5 represents the employee's share of the tax. The employer must match the employee's portion. For 2014 and 2013, the total Social Security tax rate is 12.4 percent (6.2 percent plus 6.2 percent). Legislation passed by Congress reduced the employee's (but not the employer's) Social Security tax rate from 6.2 percent to 4.2 percent for 2011 and 2012. A similar 2 percent reduction applied to self-employed taxpayers (discussed later in this chapter).

Withholdings from employees must continue until the maximum base amount is reached. In 2014, for example, FICA withholding ceases for the Social Security portion (6.2 percent) once the employee has earned wages subject to FICA in the amount of $117,000. For the Medicare portion (1.45 percent), however, the employer is required to withhold on all wages without limit. This contrasts with years prior to 1994 when a maximum base also existed for the Medicare portion.

TABLE 13.5				FICA Rates and Base				
	Social Security Tax				**Medicare Tax**			
	Percent	×	**Base Amount**	+	**Percent**	×	**Base Amount**	= **Maximum Tax**
2004	6.20%	×	87,900	+	1.45%	×	Unlimited	= Unlimited
2005	6.20%	×	90,000	+	1.45%	×	Unlimited	= Unlimited
2006	6.20%	×	94,200	+	1.45%	×	Unlimited	= Unlimited
2007	6.20%	×	97,500	+	1.45%	×	Unlimited	= Unlimited
2008	6.20%	×	102,000	+	1.45%	×	Unlimited	= Unlimited
2009	6.20%	×	106,800	+	1.45%	×	Unlimited	= Unlimited
2010	6.20%	×	106,800	+	1.45%	×	Unlimited	= Unlimited
2011	4.20%/6.20%	×	106,800	+	1.45%	×	Unlimited	= Unlimited
2012	4.20%/6.20%	×	110,100	+	1.45%	×	Unlimited	= Unlimited
2013	6.20%	×	113,700	+	1.45%**	×	Unlimited	= Unlimited
2014	6.20%	×	117,000	+	1.45%**	×	Unlimited	= Unlimited
2015 on	6.20%	×	*	+	1.45%**	×	Unlimited	= Unlimited

*Not yet determined.

**Does not include the additional Medicare taxes on high-income individuals.

TAX IN THE NEWS Will Social Security Be There for You When You Need It?

With an estimated 77 million baby boomers becoming eligible for Social Security over the next decade or so and with fewer employees paying into the system, a logical question for younger Americans who are just now entering the workforce is whether the Social Security system will be solvent when they reach their retirement years. This question often arises during political campaigns and is discussed in the news media as well as in hearings in Congress. Reality seems to suggest that with a burgeoning number of retirees drawing Social Security for a longer period of time because their life expectancies are increasing, the assets accumulated in the Social Security trust fund will be strained at some point in the future.

Things seem to be fine now, but beginning in about 2018, the Social Security Administration expects to be paying out more in benefits than it collects from the payroll tax. Interest income on the trust fund assets will help balance the books until about 2028, when the trust fund assets are expected to begin falling. Some suggest that by as early as 2042, the Social Security trust fund could run dry.

So do we have a crisis on our hands? Will benefits be cut, or will payroll taxes be increased? Will a "means test" be applied before retirees can receive their monthly checks? Will part or all of the Social Security contributions be "privatized"? The answers to these questions and the integrity of the system are issues that undoubtedly will take years to resolve.

Example 38

In 2014, Keshia earned a salary of $140,000 from her employer. Therefore, FICA taxes withheld from her salary are $7,254 ($117,000 × 6.2%) plus $2,030 ($140,000 × 1.45%) for a total of $9,284. In addition to paying the amount withheld from Keshia's salary to the government, her employer also has to pay $9,284.

In at least two situations, it is possible for an employee to have paid excess FICA taxes.

Example 39

During 2014, Kevin changed employers in the middle of the year and earned $60,000 (all of which was subject to FICA) from each job. As a result, each employer withheld $4,590 [(6.2% × $60,000) + (1.45% × $60,000)] for a total of $9,180. Although each employer acted properly, Kevin's total FICA tax liability for the year is only $8,994 [(6.2% × $117,000) + (1.45% × $120,000)]. Thus, Kevin has overpaid his share of FICA taxes by $186 [$9,180 (amount paid) − $8,994 (amount of correct liability)]. He should claim this amount as a tax credit when filing his income tax return for 2014. The tax credit will reduce any income tax Kevin might owe or possibly generate a tax refund.

Example 40

During 2014, Lori earned $94,000 from her regular job and $26,000 from a part-time job (all of which was subject to FICA). As a result, one employer withheld $7,191 [(6.2% × $94,000) + (1.45% × $94,000)] while the other employer withheld $1,989 [(6.2% × $26,000) + (1.45% × $26,000)] for a total of $9,180. Lori's total FICA tax liability for the year is only $8,994 [(6.2% × $117,000) + (1.45% × $120,000)]. Thus, Lori has overpaid her share of FICA taxes by $186 [$9,180 (amount paid) − $8,994 (amount of correct liability)]. She should claim this amount as a tax credit when filing her income tax return for 2014.

In Examples 39 and 40, the employee is subject to overwithholding. In both cases, however, the employee was able to obtain a credit for the excess withheld. The same result does not materialize for the portion paid by the employer. Because this amount is not refundable, in some situations, employers may pay more FICA taxes than the covered employees. The mere fact that a husband and wife are both employed does not, by itself, result in overwithholding of FICA taxes.

Example 41

During 2014, Jim and Betty (husband and wife) are both employed, and each earns wages subject to FICA of $60,000. Accordingly, each has $4,590 FICA withheld [(6.2% × $60,000) + (1.45% × $60,000)] for a total of $9,180. Because neither spouse paid FICA tax on wages in excess of $117,000 (the 2014 Social Security tax base), there is no overwithholding.

A spouse employed by another spouse is subject to FICA. However, children under the age of 18 who are employed in a parent's trade or business are exempted.

Amount of Income Tax Withholding

Arriving at the amount to be withheld for income tax purposes is not so simple. It involves three basic steps:

1. Have the employee complete Form W–4, Employee's Withholding Allowance Certificate.
2. Determine the employee's payroll period.
3. Compute the amount to be withheld, usually using either the wage-bracket tables or the percentage method.[52]

Form W–4 reflects the employee's marital status and **withholding allowances**. Generally, it need not be filed with the IRS and is retained by the employer as part of the payroll records.

The employer need not verify the number of exemptions claimed. Any misinformation on the form will be attributed to the employee. However, if the employer has reason to believe the employee made a false statement, the IRS should be notified. In the meantime, the Form W–4 should be honored. Employees are subject to both civil and criminal penalties for filing false withholding statements.

On the current Form W–4, an employee may claim *withholding allowances* for the following: personal exemptions for self and spouse and dependency exemptions. One *special withholding allowance* may be claimed if the employee is single and has only one job, if the employee is married and has only one job and the spouse is not employed, or if wages from a second job or a spouse's wages (or both) are $1,500 or less. An additional allowance is available if the employee expects to file using the head-of-household status or if the employee expects to claim a credit for child and dependent care expenses on qualifying expenditures of at least $2,000. A taxpayer qualifying for the child tax credit may claim one or two additional allowances for each eligible child. An employee who plans to itemize deductions or claim adjustments to income (e.g., alimony and deductible IRA contributions) should use the worksheet provided on page 2 of Form W–4 to determine the correct number of additional allowances.

To avoid having too little tax withheld, some employees may find it necessary to reduce their withholding allowances. This might be the case for an employee who has more than one job or who has other sources of income that are not subject to adequate withholding. Likewise, a married employee who has a working spouse or more than one job might want to claim fewer allowances.

If both spouses of a married couple are employed, they may allocate their total allowances between themselves as they see fit. The same allocation procedure is required if a taxpayer has more than one job. In no event should the same allowance be claimed more than once at the same time. It is permissible to declare *fewer* allowances than the taxpayer is entitled to in order to increase the amount of withholding. Doing so, however, does not affect the number of personal and dependency exemptions allowable on the employee's income tax return. An employee is also permitted to have the employer withhold a certain dollar amount in addition to the required amount. This additional dollar amount can be arbitrary or calculated in accordance with a worksheet on Form W–4.

---

[52]The withholding provisions are contained in §§ 3401 and 3402. IRS Publication 15, *Employer's Tax Guide* (Circular E), contains detailed information about the income tax withholding process along with examples illustrating the wage-bracket and percentage withholding methods, which are beyond the scope of this text.

Example 42

Carl G. and Carol D. Simmons live at 4886 Sycamore Lane, Elmhurst, IL 60126. Carl earns $90,000 as a software engineer, and Carol earns $60,000 as a marketing manager. They have three dependent children and will claim the standard deduction. Assume that they do not qualify to claim the child tax credit. Together they should be entitled to five allowances [2 (for personal exemptions) + 3 (for dependency exemptions)]. The special withholding allowance is not available because both spouses earn more than $1,500. If Carl is the spouse first employed and his Form W–4 reflects five allowances, Carol's Form W–4 should report none. They could, however, reallocate their allowances between them as long as the total claimed does not exceed five. A Form W–4 has been completed for Carl (see p. 13-36) assuming that he claims all three dependents and Carol claims herself on her Form W–4.

Reporting and Payment Procedures

Proper handling of employment taxes and income tax withholdings requires considerable compliance efforts by the employer. Among the Federal forms that have to be filed are the following:

Tax Form	Title
SS–4	Application for Employer Identification Number
W–2	Wage and Tax Statement
W–3	Transmittal of Wage and Tax Statements
940 or 940 EZ	Employer's Annual Federal Unemployment (FUTA) Tax Return
941	Employer's Quarterly Federal Tax Return

Form SS–4 is the starting point because it provides the employer with an identification number that must be used on all of the other forms filed with the IRS and the Social Security Administration. The number issued consists of nine digits and is hyphenated between the second and third digits (e.g., 98-7654321).

Form W–2 furnishes essential information to employees concerning wages paid, FICA, and income tax withholdings. Copies of Form W–2 are distributed to several parties for various purposes: to enable the employee to complete his or her income tax return, to inform the Social Security Administration of the amount of FICA wages earned by the employee, and to serve as a permanent record for the employer and employee of the payroll information contained on the form. Form W–2 (reporting information for the previous calendar year) must be furnished to an employee not later than January 31. If an employee leaves a place of employment before the end of the year, Form W–2 can be given to him or her at any time after employment ends but no later than the following January 31. However, if the terminated employee asks for Form W–2, it must be given to him or her within 30 days after the request or the final wage payment, whichever is later.

Form W–3 must accompany the copies of Forms W–2 filed by the employer with the Social Security Administration. Its basic purpose is to summarize and reconcile the amounts withheld for FICA and income taxes from *all* employees.

Form 940 (or Form 940 EZ) constitutes the employer's annual accounting for FUTA purposes. Generally, it must be filed on or before January 31 of the following year and must be accompanied by the payment of any undeposited FUTA due the Federal government.

Whether deposits[53] are required, most employers must settle their employment taxes every quarter. To do this, Form 941 must be filed on or before the last day of the month following the end of each calendar quarter.

---

[53]Deposit requirements are specified in IRS Publication 15, *Employer's Tax Guide* (Circular E). Under current rules, employers must make deposits on either a monthly or semiweekly basis.

Form W-4 (2014)

Purpose. Complete Form W-4 so that your employer can withhold the correct federal income tax from your pay. Consider completing a new Form W-4 each year and when your personal or financial situation changes.

Exemption from withholding. If you are exempt, complete **only** lines 1, 2, 3, 4, and 7 and sign the form to validate it. Your exemption for 2014 expires February 17, 2015. See Pub. 505, Tax Withholding and Estimated Tax.

Note. If another person can claim you as a dependent on his or her tax return, you cannot claim exemption from withholding if your income exceeds $1,000 and includes more than $350 of unearned income (for example, interest and dividends).

Exceptions. An employee may be able to claim exemption from withholding even if the employee is a dependent, if the employee:

• Is age 65 or older,

• Is blind, or

• Will claim adjustments to income; tax credits; or itemized deductions, on his or her tax return.

The exceptions do not apply to supplemental wages greater than $1,000,000.

Basic instructions. If you are not exempt, complete the **Personal Allowances Worksheet** below. The worksheets on page 2 further adjust your withholding allowances based on itemized deductions, certain credits, adjustments to income, or two-earners/multiple jobs situations.

Complete all worksheets that apply. However, you may claim fewer (or zero) allowances. For regular wages, withholding must be based on allowances you claimed and may not be a flat amount or percentage of wages.

Head of household. Generally, you can claim head of household filing status on your tax return only if you are unmarried and pay more than 50% of the costs of keeping up a home for yourself and your dependent(s) or other qualifying individuals. See Pub. 501, Exemptions, Standard Deduction, and Filing Information, for information.

Tax credits. You can take projected tax credits into account in figuring your allowable number of withholding allowances. Credits for child or dependent care expenses and the child tax credit may be claimed using the **Personal Allowances Worksheet** below. See Pub. 505 for information on converting your other credits into withholding allowances.

Nonwage income. If you have a large amount of nonwage income, such as interest or dividends, consider making estimated tax payments using Form 1040-ES, Estimated Tax for Individuals. Otherwise, you may owe additional tax. If you have pension or annuity income, see Pub. 505 to find out if you should adjust your withholding on Form W-4 or W-4P.

Two earners or multiple jobs. If you have a working spouse or more than one job, figure the total number of allowances you are entitled to claim on all jobs using worksheets from only one Form W-4. Your withholding usually will be most accurate when all allowances are claimed on the Form W-4 for the highest paying job and zero allowances are claimed on the others. See Pub. 505 for details.

Nonresident alien. If you are a nonresident alien, see Notice 1392, Supplemental Form W-4 Instructions for Nonresident Aliens, before completing this form.

Check your withholding. After your Form W-4 takes effect, use Pub. 505 to see how the amount you are having withheld compares to your projected total tax for 2014. See Pub. 505, especially if your earnings exceed $130,000 (Single) or $180,000 (Married).

Future developments. Information about any future developments affecting Form W-4 (such as legislation enacted after we release it) will be posted at *www.irs.gov/w4*.

Personal Allowances Worksheet (Keep for your records.)

A	Enter "1" for **yourself** if no one else can claim you as a dependent	**A**	*1*
B	Enter "1" if: { • You are single and have only one job; or • You are married, have only one job, and your spouse does not work; or • Your wages from a second job or your spouse's wages (or the total of both) are $1,500 or less. } . . .	**B**	
C	Enter "1" for your **spouse**. But, you may choose to enter "-0-" if you are married and have either a working spouse or more than one job. (Entering "-0-" may help you avoid having too little tax withheld.)	**C**	*3*
D	Enter number of **dependents** (other than your spouse or yourself) you will claim on your tax return	**D**	*3*
E	Enter "1" if you will file as **head of household** on your tax return (see conditions under **Head of household** above) . .	**E**	
F	Enter "1" if you have at least $2,000 of **child or dependent care expenses** for which you plan to claim a credit . . . (**Note.** Do **not** include child support payments. See Pub. 503, Child and Dependent Care Expenses, for details.)	**F**	
G	**Child Tax Credit** (including additional child tax credit). See Pub. 972, Child Tax Credit, for more information. • If your total income will be less than $65,000 ($95,000 if married), enter "2" for each eligible child; then **less** "1" if you have three to six eligible children or **less** "2" if you have seven or more eligible children. • If your total income will be between $65,000 and $84,000 ($95,000 and $119,000 if married), enter "1" for each eligible child . . .	**G**	
H	Add lines A through G and enter total here. (**Note.** This may be different from the number of exemptions you claim on your tax return.) ▶	**H**	*4*

For accuracy, complete all worksheets that apply.
{
• If you plan to **itemize** or **claim adjustments to income** and want to reduce your withholding, see the **Deductions and Adjustments Worksheet** on page 2.
• If you are **single and have more than one job** or are **married and you and your spouse both work** and the combined earnings from all jobs exceed $50,000 ($20,000 if married), see the **Two-Earners/Multiple Jobs Worksheet** on page 2 to avoid having too little tax withheld.
• If **neither** of the above situations applies, **stop here** and enter the number from line H on line 5 of Form W-4 below.
}

Separate here and give Form W-4 to your employer. Keep the top part for your records.

Form **W-4** Department of the Treasury Internal Revenue Service	**Employee's Withholding Allowance Certificate** ▶ **Whether you are entitled to claim a certain number of allowances or exemption from withholding is subject to review by the IRS. Your employer may be required to send a copy of this form to the IRS.**	OMB No. 1545-0074 **2014**

1 Your first name and middle initial	Last name	2 Your social security number
Carl G.	*Simmons*	*123-45-6789*

Home address (number and street or rural route)	
4886 Sycamore Lane	3 ☐ Single ☑ Married ☐ Married, but withhold at higher Single rate. **Note.** If married, but legally separated, or spouse is a nonresident alien, check the "Single" box.

City or town, state, and ZIP code	
Elmhurst, IL 60126	4 If your last name differs from that shown on your social security card, check here. You must call 1-800-772-1213 for a replacement card. ▶ ☐

5	Total number of allowances you are claiming (from line **H** above **or** from the applicable worksheet on page 2)	**5**	*4*
6	Additional amount, if any, you want withheld from each paycheck	**6**	$
7	I claim exemption from withholding for 2014, and I certify that I meet **both** of the following conditions for exemption. • Last year I had a right to a refund of **all** federal income tax withheld because I had **no** tax liability, **and** • This year I expect a refund of **all** federal income tax withheld because I expect to have **no** tax liability. If you meet both conditions, write "Exempt" here . . . . ▶	**7**	

Under penalties of perjury, I declare that I have examined this certificate and, to the best of my knowledge and belief, it is true, correct, and complete.

Employee's signature
(This form is not valid unless you sign it.) ▶ _____   Date ▶ _____

8 Employer's name and address (Employer: Complete lines 8 and 10 only if sending to the IRS.)	9 Office code (optional)	10 Employer identification number (EIN)

For Privacy Act and Paperwork Reduction Act Notice, see page 2.   Cat. No. 10220Q   Form **W-4** (2014)

Backup Withholding

Some types of payments made to individuals by banks or businesses are subject to backup withholding under certain conditions. Backup withholding is designed to ensure that income tax is collected on interest and other payments reported on a Form 1099. Backup withholding applies when the taxpayer does not give the business or bank his or her identification number in the required manner and in certain other situations.[54] If backup withholding applies, the payor must withhold 28 percent of the gross amount.

13-5b Procedures Applicable to Self-Employed Persons

Although the following discussion largely centers on self-employed taxpayers, some of the procedures may be applicable to employed persons. In many cases, for example, employed persons may be required to pay estimated tax if they have income other than wages that is not subject to withholding. An employee may conduct a second trade or business in a self-employment capacity. Depending on the circumstances, the second job may require the payment of a self-employment tax. In addition, taxpayers whose income consists primarily of rentals, dividends, or interest (this list is not all-inclusive) may be required to pay estimated tax.

LO.6

Explain and illustrate the payment procedures applicable to self-employed persons.

Estimated Tax for Individuals

Estimated tax is the amount of tax (including AMT and self-employment tax) an individual expects to owe for the year after subtracting tax credits and income tax withheld. Any individual who has estimated tax for the year of $1,000 or more *and* whose withholding does not equal or exceed the required annual payment (discussed below) must make quarterly payments.[55] Otherwise, a penalty may be assessed. No quarterly payments are required (and no penalty will apply on an

---

[54]§ 3406(a). The backup withholding rate is equal to the fourth lowest tax rate for single filers.

[55]§§ 6654(c)(1) and 6654(e)(1).

underpayment) if the taxpayer's estimated tax is under $1,000. No penalty will apply if the taxpayer had no tax liability for the preceding tax year *and* the preceding tax year was a taxable year of 12 months *and* the taxpayer was a citizen or resident for the entire preceding tax year. In this regard, having no tax liability is not the same as having no additional tax to pay.

The required annual payment must be computed first. This is the *smaller* of the following amounts:

- Ninety percent of the tax shown on the current year's return.
- One hundred percent of the tax shown on the preceding year's return (the return must cover the full 12 months of the preceding year). If the AGI on the preceding year's return exceeds $150,000 ($75,000 if married filing separately), the 100 percent requirement is increased to 110 percent.

In general, one-fourth of this required annual payment is due on April 15, June 15, and September 15 of the tax year and January 15 of the following year.

An equal part of withholding is deemed paid on each due date. Thus, the quarterly installment of the required annual payment reduced by the applicable withholding is the estimated tax to be paid. Payments are to be accompanied by the payment voucher for the appropriate date from Form 1040–ES.

Married taxpayers may make joint estimated tax payments even though a joint income tax return is not subsequently filed. In such event, the estimated tax payments may be applied against the separate return liability of the spouses as they see fit. If a husband and wife cannot agree on a division of the estimated tax payments, the Regulations provide that the payments are to be allocated in proportion to the tax liability on the separate returns.

Penalty on Underpayments

A nondeductible penalty is imposed on the amount of underpayment of estimated tax. The rate for this penalty is adjusted quarterly to reflect changes in the average prime rate.

An *underpayment* occurs when any installment (the sum of estimated tax paid and income tax withheld) is less than 25 percent of the required annual payment. The penalty is applied to the amount of the underpayment for the period of the underpayment.[56]

Example 43	

Marta made the following payments of estimated tax for 2014 and had no income tax withheld:

April 15, 2014	$1,400
June 16, 2014	2,300
September 15, 2014	1,500
January 15, 2015	1,800

Marta's actual tax for 2014 is $8,000, and her tax in 2013 was $10,000. Therefore, each installment should have been at least $1,800 [($8,000 × 90%) × 25%]. Of the payment on June 16, $400 will be credited to the unpaid balance of the first quarterly installment due on April 15,[57] thereby effectively stopping the underpayment penalty for the first quarterly period. Of the remaining $1,900 payment on June 16, $100 is credited to the September 15 payment, resulting in this third quarterly payment being $200 short. Then $200 of the January 15 payment is credited to the September 15 shortfall, ending the period of underpayment for that portion due. The January 15, 2015 installment is now underpaid by $200, and a penalty will apply from January 15, 2015, to April 15, 2015 (unless paid sooner). Marta's underpayments for the periods of underpayment are as follows:

1st installment due:	$400 from April 15 to June 16
2nd installment due:	Paid in full
3rd installment due:	$200 from September 15, 2014, to January 15, 2015
4th installment due:	$200 from January 15 to April 15, 2015

---

[56]§ 6654(b)(2).

[57]Payments are credited to unpaid installments in the order in which the installments are required to be paid. § 6654(b)(3).

Foreign "Withholding Tax" Performs an Important Role

Global Tax Issues

© iStockphoto.com/Andrey Prokhorov

Taxpayers in the United States are accustomed to having their employer withhold a portion of their salary or wages and then forward the amounts to the government in payment of their income tax liabilities. As a rule, other types of income, such as dividends, interest, and annuities, are not subject to withholding because the IRS has adequate mechanisms in place to ensure a high level of tax compliance. But for payments of U.S.-source income to foreign taxpayers, the IRS would not be as confident that it is getting its due were it not for the so-called withholding tax.

To ensure the collection of the income tax on amounts paid to nonresident aliens and foreign corporations, the person *paying* the income, rather than the recipient, is required to withhold and forward the appropriate payment to the government. Although the withholding rate is typically 30 percent, the rate can vary in certain situations. In some situations, this withholding mechanism also prevents the taxpayer from having to file an income tax return with the U.S. government.

If a possible underpayment of estimated tax is indicated, Form 2210 should be filed to compute the penalty due or to justify that no penalty applies.

Self-Employment Tax

The tax on self-employment income is levied to provide Social Security and Medicare benefits (old age, survivors, and disability insurance and hospital insurance) for self-employed individuals. Individuals with net earnings of $400 or more from self-employment are subject to the **self-employment tax**.[58] For 2014, the self-employment tax is 15.3 percent of self-employment income up to $117,000 and 2.9 percent of self-employment income in excess of $117,000. In other words, for 2014, the self-employment tax is 12.4 percent of self-employment earnings up to $117,000 (for the Social Security portion) *plus* 2.9 percent of the total amount of self-employment earnings (for the Medicare portion)—see Table 13.6.

Currently, self-employed taxpayers are allowed a deduction from net earnings from self-employment, at one-half of the self-employment rate, for purposes of determining self-employment tax[59] *and* an income tax deduction (normally, one-half of the amount of self-employment tax paid).[60]

Determining the amount of self-employment tax to be paid for 2014 involves completing the steps in Figure 13.1. The result of step 3 or 4 is the amount of self-employment tax to be paid. For *income tax purposes*, the amount to be reported is net earnings from self-employment before the deduction for the self-employment tax. Then the taxpayer is allowed a deduction *for* AGI of the appropriate amount of the self-employment tax.

---

[58] § 6017.

[59] § 1402(a)(12).

[60] § 164(f). For 2011 and 2012, the 2% Social Security rate reduction is not taken into account in determining the appropriate base for the self-employment tax [The Tax Relief Act of 2010, § 601(b)(1)]. In other words, the deduction to determine the self-employment tax base is 7.65%. Because of the 2% Social Security rate reduction that applied in 2011 and 2012, the income tax deduction allowed under § 164(f) in those years is computed at the rate of 59.6% of the Social Security tax paid plus one-half of the Medicare tax paid [The Tax Relief Act of 2010, § 601(b)(2)]. This revised percentage replaced the 50% deduction allowed under current law for 2011 and 2012 and allowed the taxpayer to deduct the full amount of the employer portion of Social Security taxes. The employer Social Security tax rate remained at 6.2%, whereas

the employee portion fell to 4.2% for 2011 and 2012. Thus, the employer share of total Social Security taxes is 6.2 divided by 10.4 (or 59.6%). To simplify this computation, the IRS used a blended factor (.5751) to compute the income tax deduction. The blended factor—which only applies to taxpayers using Section A of Schedule SE (Form 1040)—is computed as follows: Social Security tax (6.2%/10.4%) plus Medicare tax (1.45%/2.90%) = total self-employment tax (7.65%/13.3%); the resulting ratio is .575188, which the IRS rounded to .5751. Taxpayers using Section B of the Schedule SE (Form 1040) in 2011 or 2012 did not use this blended factor. Instead, the IRS provided a separate calculation for taxpayers with net earnings from self-employment in excess of $110,100 in 2012 ($106,800 in 2011). For 2012, the computation was 50% of the self-employment income plus $1,100; for 2011, the computation was 50% of the self-employment tax plus $1,067.

TABLE 13.6	Self-Employment Tax: Social Security and Medicare Portions		
Year		**Tax Rate**	**Ceiling Amount**
2014	Social Security portion	12.4%	$117,000
	Medicare portion	2.9%	Unlimited
	Aggregate rate	15.3%	
2013	Social Security portion	12.4%	$113,700
	Medicare portion	2.9%	Unlimited
	Aggregate rate	15.3%	

FIGURE 13.1	2014 Self-Employment Tax Worksheet

1. Net earnings from self-employment. _____
2. Multiply line 1 by 92.35%. _____
3. If the amount on line 2 is $117,000 or less, multiply the line 2 amount by 15.3%. This is the self-employment tax. _____
4. If the amount on line 2 is more than $117,000, multiply the excess of line 2 over $117,000 by 2.9% and add $17,901. This is the self-employment tax. _____

Example 44

Using the format in Figure 13.1, the self-employment tax is determined for two taxpayers with net earnings from self-employment for 2014 as follows: Ned, $55,000 and Terry, $135,000.

Ned's Self-Employment Tax Worksheet

1. Net earnings from self-employment. $55,000.00
2. Multiply line 1 by 92.35%. $50,792.50
3. If the amount on line 2 is $117,000 or less, multiply the line 2 amount by 15.3%. This is the self-employment tax. $ 7,771.25
4. If the amount on line 2 is more than $117,000, multiply the excess of line 2 over $117,000 by 2.9% and add $17,901. This is the self-employment tax. _____

Terry's Self-Employment Tax Worksheet

1. Net earnings from self-employment. $135,000.00
2. Multiply line 1 by 92.35%. $124,672.50
3. If the amount on line 2 is $117,000 or less, multiply the line 2 amount by 15.3%. This is the self-employment tax. _____
4. If the amount on line 2 is more than $117,000, multiply the excess of line 2 over $117,000 by 2.9% and add $17,901. This is the self-employment tax. $ 18,123.50

For income tax purposes, Ned has net earnings from self-employment of $55,000 and a deduction *for* AGI of $3,885.63 ($7,771.25 × 50%). Terry has net earnings from self-employment of $135,000 and a deduction *for* AGI of $9,061.75 ($18,123.50 × 50%). Both taxpayers benefit from the self-employment tax deduction.

For 2013, the self-employment tax computations are different from those for 2014, as the tax base was lower (see Table 13.6 and Figure 13.2).

FIGURE 13.2	2013 Self-Employment Tax Worksheet

1. Net earnings from self-employment. _____
2. Multiply line 1 by 92.35%. _____
3. If the amount on line 2 is $113,700 or less, multiply the line 2 amount by 13.3%. This is the self-employment tax. _____
4. If the amount on line 2 is more than $113,700, multiply the excess of line 2 over $113,700 by 2.9% and add $17,396.10. This is the self-employment tax. _____

If an individual also receives wages subject to the FICA tax, the ceiling amount of the Social Security portion on which the self-employment tax is computed is reduced. Thus, the self-employment tax may be reduced if a self-employed individual also receives FICA wages.

Example 45

In 2014, Kelly had $76,000 of net earnings from a bookkeeping services business she owns. During the year, she also received wages of $54,000 as an employee of a small accounting firm. The amount of Kelly's self-employment income subject to the Social Security portion (12.4%) is $63,000 ($117,000 − $54,000), producing a tax of $7,812.00 ($63,000 × 12.4%); note that $63,000 is less than $70,186 of net self-employment income.

	Social Security Portion
Ceiling amount	$117,000
Less: FICA wages	(54,000)
Net ceiling	$ 63,000
Net self-employment income ($76,000 × 92.35%)	$ 70,186
Lesser of net ceiling or net self-employment income	$ 63,000

Although there is a limit on Social Security taxes ($117,000 maximum base in 2014), no such limit exists for the Medicare portion of the self-employment tax. Therefore, all of Kelly's net self-employment earnings ($76,000 × .9235 = $70,186) are subject to the 2.9% Medicare portion of the self-employment tax. Thus, the self-employment tax on this portion is $2,035.39 ($70,186 × 2.9%). If Kelly's wages were only $30,000, then the net ceiling in the table above would be $87,000. Because her net self-employment income ($70,186) is less than this amount, she would compute her self-employment tax using the format in Figure 13.1.

Net earnings from self-employment includes gross income from a trade or business less allowable trade or business deductions, the distributive share of any partnership income or loss derived from a trade or business activity, and net income from rendering personal services as an independent contractor. Gain or loss from the disposition of property (including involuntary conversions) is excluded from the computation of self-employment income unless the property involved is inventory.

13-5c Additional Medicare Taxes on High-Income Individuals

The Affordable Care Act of 2010 and the Health Care Reconciliation Act of 2010 include two provisions that result in increased Medicare taxes for high-income individuals beginning in 2013: (1) an additional .9 percent tax on *wages* received in excess of specified amounts and (2) an additional 3.8 percent tax on *unearned income.*

LO.7

Explain the additional Medicare taxes assessed on high-income individuals.

Additional Tax on Wages

For tax years beginning after December 31, 2012, an additional .9 percent Medicare tax is imposed on wages received in excess of $250,000 for married taxpayers filing a joint return ($125,000 if married filing separately) and $200,000 for all other taxpayers.[61] Unlike the general 1.45 percent Medicare tax on wages, the additional tax on a joint return is on the *combined* wages of the employee and the employee's spouse. As a result, the Medicare tax rate will be:

1. 1.45 percent on the first $200,000 of wages ($125,000 on a married filing separate return; $250,000 of combined wages on a married filing joint return), and
2. 2.35 percent (1.45% + .9%) on wages in excess of $200,000 ($125,000 on a married filing separate return; $250,000 of combined wages on a married filing joint return).

Example 46

Jenna, who is single, earns wages of $500,000 in 2014. Jenna will pay $2,900 of Medicare taxes on the first $200,000 of her wages ($200,000 × 1.45%) and $7,050 of Medicare taxes on her wages in excess of $200,000 ($300,000 × 2.35%). In total, her Medicare tax will be $9,950, of which $2,700 ($300,000 × .9%) represents Jenna's additional Medicare tax.

Example 47

Patrick and Paula file a joint return in 2014. During the year, Patrick earns wages of $125,000, and Paula earns wages of $175,000—so their total wages are $300,000. Patrick and Paula will pay total Medicare taxes of $4,800 ($250,000 × 1.45% plus $50,000 × 2.35%), of which $450 ($50,000 × .9%) represents Patrick and Paula's additional Medicare tax.

Employers must withhold the additional .9% Medicare tax on wages paid in excess of $200,000.[62] An employer is not responsible for determining wages earned by an employee's spouse (and the implications of those wages on the total Medicare tax to be paid).

Example 48

Return to the facts of Example 47. In 2014, neither Patrick's nor Paula's employer will withhold the additional Medicare tax as both wage amounts are less than $200,000. Therefore, Paula will have $2,537.50 of Medicare tax withheld ($175,000 × 1.45%), and Patrick will have $1,812.50 of Medicare tax withheld ($125,000 × 1.45%). Total Medicare tax withheld is $4,350.00 ($2,537.50 + $1,812.50). Patrick and Paula will have to pay an additional $450.00 of Medicare taxes when they file their return.[63]

The additional Medicare tax also applies to self-employed individuals—with net earnings from self-employment being used for the threshold computations. As a result, the tax rate for the Medicare tax on self-employment income will be:

1. 2.9 percent on the first $200,000 of net earnings from self-employment ($125,000 on a married filing separate return; $250,000 on a married filing joint return), and
2. 3.8 percent (2.9% + .9%) on net earnings from self-employment in excess of $200,000 ($125,000 on a married filing separate return; $250,000 on a married filing joint return).

For married taxpayers, one of whom has wages and one of whom has self-employment income, the thresholds are reduced (but not below zero) by the amount of wages taken into account in determining the additional .9 percent Medicare tax on wages.[64] Although self-employed individuals are allowed an income tax deduction for part of the self-employment tax, this additional .9 percent Medicare tax will *not* create a deduction (i.e., the deduction is determined without regard to this additional tax).[65]

---

[61]§3101(b)(2). The base amounts are not indexed for inflation.

[62]§3102(f).

[63]Couples in this situation may have to make estimated tax payments to cover the additional Medicare taxes.

[64]§1401(b)(2)(B).

[65]§164(f).

Additional Tax on Unearned Income

For tax years beginning after December 31, 2012, an additional 3.8 percent Medicare tax is imposed on the unearned income of individuals, estates, and trusts.[66] For individuals, the tax is 3.8 percent of the lesser of:[67]

1. Net investment income, or
2. The excess of modified adjusted gross income over $250,000 for married taxpayers filing a joint return ($125,000 if married filing separately) and $200,000 for all other taxpayers.[68]

In general, "net investment income" includes interest, dividends, annuities, royalties, rents, and net gains from the sale of investment property less deductions allowed in generating that income.[69] Modified adjusted gross income (MAGI) is adjusted gross income (AGI) increased by any foreign earned income exclusion.[70] Thus, for individuals who don't have any excluded foreign earned income, MAGI is the same as AGI.

In 2014, Jill has net investment income of $50,000 and MAGI of $180,000 and files as a single taxpayer. As Jill's MAGI does not exceed $200,000, she will not have to pay the additional Medicare tax on unearned income.	**Example 49**

Now assume the same facts as in Example 49, except that Jill has net investment income of $85,000 and MAGI of $220,000. In this case, she will pay a Medicare tax on the lesser of (1) $85,000 (her net investment income) or (2) $20,000 (the amount by which her MAGI exceeds the $200,000 threshold). As a result, Jill's additional Medicare tax on unearned income will be $760 ($20,000 × 3.8%).	**Example 50**

Assume the same facts as Example 50, except that Jill's MAGI is $290,000. Because her MAGI exceeds the threshold amount by $90,000, she will pay a Medicare tax on the entire $85,000 of net investment income. As a result, Jill's additional Medicare tax on unearned income will be $3,230 ($85,000 × 3.8%).	**Example 51**

The 3.8 percent additional Medicare tax on unearned income is *in addition to* the additional .9 percent Medicare tax on wages or self-employment income. Taxpayers who have both high wages (or self-employment income) *and* high investment income may be subject to both taxes.

Assume the same facts as Example 51, except that Jill has MAGI of $325,000 (including $240,000 of wages and $85,000 of net investment income). In this case, in addition to her $3,230 additional Medicare tax on unearned income, Jill will also be subject to an additional Medicare tax on wages of $360 ($40,000 × .9%, her wages in excess of $200,000).	**Example 52**

13-6 TAX PLANNING

13-6a Foreign Tax Credit

A U.S. citizen or resident working abroad (commonly referred to as an *expatriate*) may elect to take either a foreign tax credit or the foreign earned income exclusion. In cases where the income tax of a foreign country is higher than the U.S. income tax, the credit choice usually is preferable. If the reverse is true, electing the foreign earned income exclusion probably reduces the overall tax burden.

LO.8

Identify tax planning opportunities related to tax credits and payment procedures.

---

[66]§1411.
[67]§1411(a)(1). For estates and trusts, the tax is 3.8% of the lesser of (1) undistributed net investment income or (2) the excess of AGI over the dollar amount at which the highest estate and trust income tax bracket begins.

[68]§1411(b). The base amounts are not indexed for inflation.
[69]§1411(c). Certain income, including qualified retirement plan distributions, tax-exempt income, and gain from the sale of a principal residence, are excluded from this definition.
[70]§1411(d).

Unfortunately, the choice between the credit and the earned income exclusion is not without some limitations. The election of the foreign earned income exclusion, once made, can be revoked for a later year. However, once revoked, the earned income exclusion will not be available for a period of five years unless the IRS consents to an earlier date. This will create a dilemma for expatriates whose job assignments over several years shift between low- and high-bracket countries.

Example 53

In 2013, Ira, a calendar year taxpayer, is sent by his employer to Saudi Arabia (a low-tax country). For 2013, therefore, Ira elects the foreign earned income exclusion. In 2014, Ira's employer transfers him to France (a high-tax country). Accordingly, he revokes the foreign earned income exclusion election for 2014 and chooses instead to use the foreign tax credit. If Ira is transferred back to Saudi Arabia (or any other low-tax country) within five years, he may not utilize the foreign earned income exclusion.

13-6b Credit for Child and Dependent Care Expenses

A taxpayer may incur employment-related expenses that also qualify as medical expenses (e.g., a nurse is hired to provide in-home care for an ill and incapacitated dependent parent). Such expenses may be either deducted as medical expenses (generally subject to the 10 percent of AGI limitation) or utilized in determining the credit for child and dependent care expenses. If the credit for child and dependent care expenses is chosen and the employment-related expenses exceed the limitation ($3,000, $6,000, or earned income, as the case may be), the excess may be considered a medical expense. If, however, the taxpayer chooses to deduct qualified employment-related expenses as medical expenses, any portion that is not deductible because of the percentage limitation may not be used in computing the credit for child and dependent care expenses.

Example 54

Alicia has the following tax position for the current year:

Adjusted gross income		$30,000
Potential itemized deductions *from* AGI—		
Other than medical expenses	$3,500	
Medical expenses	6,600	$10,100

All of Alicia's medical expenses were incurred to provide nursing care for her disabled father while she was working. Alicia's father lives with her and qualifies as her dependent.

What should Alicia do in this situation? One approach would be to use $3,000 of the nursing care expenses to obtain the maximum credit for child and dependent care expenses allowed of $810 (27% × $3,000). The balance of these expenses should be claimed as medical expenses. After a reduction of 10 percent of AGI, this would produce a medical expense deduction of $600 [$3,600 (remaining medical expenses) − (10% × $30,000)].

Another approach would be to claim the full $6,600 as a medical expense and forgo the credit for child and dependent care expenses. After the 10 percent adjustment of $3,000 (10% × $30,000), a deduction of $3,600 remains.

The choice, then, is between a credit of $810 plus a deduction of $600 or a credit of $0 plus a deduction of $3,600. Which is better, of course, depends on the relative tax savings involved, which in turn are dependent on the taxpayer's marginal tax rate.

One of the traditional goals of *family tax planning* is to minimize the total tax burden within the family unit. With proper planning and implementation, the credit for child and dependent care expenses can be used to help achieve this goal. For example, payments to certain relatives for the care of qualifying dependents and children qualify for the credit if the care provider is *not* a child (under age 19) of the taxpayer. Thus, if the care provider is in a lower tax bracket than the taxpayer, the following benefits result:

- Income is shifted to a lower-bracket family member.
- The taxpayer qualifies for the credit for child and dependent care expenses.

In addition, the goal of minimizing the family income tax liability can be enhanced in some other situations, but only if the credit's limitations are recognized and avoided. For example, tax savings may still be enjoyed even if the qualifying expenditures incurred by a cash basis taxpayer have already reached the annual ceiling ($3,000 or $6,000). To the extent that any additional payments can be shifted into future tax years, the benefit from the credit may be preserved on these excess expenditures.

> **Example 55**
>
> Andre, a calendar year and cash basis taxpayer, has spent $3,000 by December 1 on qualifying child care expenditures for his dependent 11-year-old son. The $250 that is due the care provider for child care services rendered in December does not generate a tax credit benefit if the amount is paid in the current year because the $3,000 ceiling has been reached. However, if the payment can be delayed until the next year, the total credit over the two-year period for which Andre is eligible may be increased.

A similar shifting of expenditures to a subsequent year may be wise if the potential credit otherwise generated would exceed the tax liability available to absorb the credit.

13-6c Adjustments to Increase Withholding

The penalty for underpayment of estimated tax by individuals is computed for each quarter of the tax year. A taxpayer can play *catch-up* to a certain extent. Each quarterly payment is credited to the unpaid portion of any previous required installment. Thus, the penalty stops on that portion of the underpayment for the previous quarter. However, because income tax withheld is assumed to have been paid evenly throughout the year and is allocated equally among the four installments in computing any penalty, a taxpayer who would otherwise be subject to a penalty for underpayment should increase withholdings late in the year. This can be done by changing the number of allowances claimed on Form W–4 or by special arrangement with the employer to increase the amount withheld.

A similar way to avoid (or reduce) a penalty for underpayment is to have the employer continue Social Security withholding beyond the base amount.

> **Example 56**
>
> Rose, a calendar year taxpayer, earns $130,000 from her job. In late October 2014, she realizes that she will be subject to a penalty for underpayment of estimated tax due to income from outside sources. Consequently, she instructs her employer to continue FICA withholdings for the rest of 2014. If this is done, an extra $13,000 [$130,000 (annual salary) − $117,000 (base amount of the Social Security portion for 2014)] will be subject to the 6.2% Social Security portion of the FICA tax [7.65% (total FICA rate) − 1.45% (Medicare portion of the FICA rate)]. Thus, Rose generates an additional $806.00 (6.2% × $13,000) that will be deemed withheld ratably during 2014.

13-6d Adjustments to Avoid Overwithholding

Publication 505, *Tax Withholding and Estimated Tax*, contains worksheets that taxpayers may use to take advantage of special provisions for avoiding overwithholding. Extra exemptions for withholding purposes are allowed if the taxpayer has unusually large itemized deductions, deductions *for* AGI, or tax credits. Net losses from Schedules C, D, E, and F may be considered in computing the number of extra withholding exemptions. Net operating loss carryovers may also be considered in the computation. A taxpayer who is entitled to extra withholding exemptions for any of these reasons should file a new Form W–4, Employee's Withholding Allowance Certificate, with his or her employer.

REFOCUS ON THE BIG PICTURE

EDUCATION TAX CREDITS

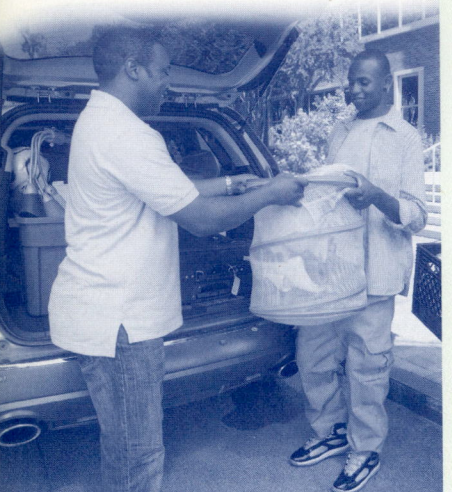

© Yellow Dog Productions/Lifesize/Jupiter Images

The American Opportunity tax credit (established by the American Recovery and Reinvestment Tax Act of 2009 and extended by the American Taxpayer Relief Act of 2012) provides some relief for Tom and Jennifer Snyder.

Both Lora and Sam qualify for the American Opportunity credit in 2014 as they are both in their first four years of postsecondary education. Lora and Sam both qualify for a $2,500 credit (100 percent of the first $2,000 and 25 percent of the next $2,000 of qualified expenses).

These credits phase out over a range of $20,000 once married taxpayers' AGI exceeds $160,000. As the Snyders' AGI ($158,000) is less than this amount, the total education credits available to them amount to $5,000, and they may claim this amount as a credit on their 2014 income tax return (see Example 32). Further, this credit may be used to offset any AMT liability, and 40 percent ($2,000) is refundable to the Snyders.

What If?

What if the Snyders' AGI is $188,000? In 2014, the Snyders would not qualify for any education credits (their income exceeds the limits for both the American Opportunity and the lifetime learning credits). Although a deduction *for* AGI is allowed for qualified tuition and related expenses involving higher education, their AGI exceeds the $160,000 maximum allowed for a deduction (see Chapter 9 for additional details).

Key Terms

Adoption expenses credit, 13-20

American Opportunity credit, 13-24

Child tax credit, 13-20

Credit for certain retirement plan contributions, 13-26

Credit for child and dependent care expenses, 13-21

Credit for employer-provided child care, 13-15

Credit for small employer pension plan startup costs, 13-14

Disabled access credit, 13-14

Earned income credit, 13-15

Employment taxes, 13-28

Estimated tax, 13-37

Foreign tax credit (FTC), 13-19

General business credit, 13-6

Lifetime learning credit, 13-24

Low-income housing credit, 13-13

Nonrefundable credits, 13-5

Permanent and total disability, 13-17

Refundable credits, 13-5

Rehabilitation expenditures credit, 13-7

Rehabilitation expenditures credit recapture, 13-8

Research activities credit, 13-10

Self-employment tax, 13-39

Tax credit for the elderly or disabled, 13-17

Tax credits, 13-2

Withholding allowances, 13-34

Work opportunity tax credit, 13-9

Discussion Questions

1. **LO.1** Would an individual taxpayer receive greater benefit from deducting an expenditure or from taking a credit equal to 25% of the expenditure? How would your response change if the item would only be deductible *from* AGI?

2. **LO.2** What is a refundable credit? Give examples. What is a nonrefundable credit? Give examples.

3. **LO.2** Tax credits are offset against the tax liability in a prescribed order. Explain why the order in which credits are utilized is important.

4. **LO.2, 3** Identify the components of the general business credit and discuss the treatment of unused general business credits.

5. **LO.2** Clint, a self-employed engineering consultant, is contemplating purchasing an old building for renovation. After the work is completed, Clint plans to rent out two-thirds of the floor space to businesses and to live and work in the remaining portion. Identify the relevant tax issues for Clint. *Issue ID*

6. **LO.3** Sonja is considering the purchase and renovation of an old building. She has heard about the tax credit for rehabilitation expenditures but does not know the specific rules applicable to the credit. Explain the most important and relevant provisions for her. *Issue ID*

7. **LO.3** Discuss the purpose of the work opportunity tax credit. Who receives the tax benefits from the credit? Give examples of the types of individuals who, if hired, give rise to the credit.

8. **LO.3** Explain the alternatives a taxpayer has in claiming the deduction and credit for research and experimentation expenditures.

9. **LO.3** Explain the purpose of the disabled access credit and identify several examples of the type of structural changes to a building that qualify for the credit.

10. **LO.4** Is the earned income credit a form of negative income tax? Why or why not?

11. **LO.4** Briefly discuss the requirements that must be satisfied for a taxpayer to qualify for the earned income credit.

12. **LO.4** Individuals who receive substantial Social Security benefits are usually not eligible for the tax credit for the elderly or disabled because these benefits effectively eliminate the base upon which the credit is computed. Explain.

13. **LO.4, 8** In general, when would an individual taxpayer find it more beneficial to use the foreign earned income exclusion rather than the foreign tax credit in computing his or her income tax liability?

14. **LO.4, 8** Tim was recently called into the partner's office and offered a two-year assignment in his public accounting firm's Shanghai office. Realizing that Tim will face incremental expenses while in Shanghai, such as foreign income taxes and rent, the firm will try to make him "whole" from a financial perspective by increasing his salary to help offset the expenses he will incur while living overseas. If Tim takes the assignment, he will likely rent his personal residence and sell several major tangible assets such as his personal automobile. Identify the relevant tax issues. *Issue ID*

15. **LO.4** Do all payments of foreign taxes qualify for the U.S. foreign tax credit? Explain.

16. **LO.4** Discuss, in general, the calculation of the adoption expenses credit.

17. **LO.4** Distinguish between the child tax credit and the credit for child and dependent care expenses.

18. **LO.3, 4** Discuss the rationale underlying the enactment of the following tax credits:
    a. Rehabilitation expenditures credit.
    b. Research activities credit.
    c. Low-income housing credit.
    d. Earned income credit.
    e. Foreign tax credit.

19. **LO.4, 8** Polly and her spouse, Leo, file a joint return and expect to report AGI of $75,000 in 2014. Polly's employer offers a child and dependent care reimbursement plan that allows up to $7,000 of qualifying expenses to be reimbursed in exchange for a $7,000 reduction in the employee's salary. Because Polly and Leo have two minor children requiring child care that costs $6,500 each year, Polly is wondering if she should sign up for the program instead of taking advantage of the credit for child and dependent care expenses. Assuming that Polly and Leo are in the 25% tax bracket, analyze the effect of the two alternatives. How would your answer differ if Polly and Leo's AGI was $25,000 instead of $75,000? Assume in this case that their marginal tax rate is 10%. *Decision Making*

20. **LO.4** Mark and Lisa are approaching an exciting time in their lives as their oldest son, Austin, graduates from high school and moves on to college. What are some of the tax issues Mark and Lisa should consider as they think about paying for Austin's college education? *Issue ID*

21. **LO.3, 4** Identify two tax credits enacted by Congress that are designed to encourage the establishment of or contributions to qualified retirement plans.

Issue ID   22. **LO.5** Elaborate rules exist that require employers to prepay various types of Federal taxes. Summarize the major issues that an employer must resolve if it is to comply with the requirements.

23. **LO.5** If an employer is not required to withhold income taxes on an item of income paid to an employee, does this mean the item is nontaxable? Explain.

24. **LO.5** Kathy, a sole proprietor, owns and operates a grocery store. Kathy's husband and her 16-year-old daughter work in the business and are paid wages. Will the husband and daughter be subject to FICA? Explain.

25. **LO.5** Under what circumstances will the special withholding allowance be allowed for purposes of determining income tax withholding?

26. **LO.6** Describe the exposure (i.e., wage base and tax rate) that a self-employed individual has to the self-employment tax for 2014.

27. **LO.7** Describe the two additional Medicare taxes that are assessed on high-income taxpayers beginning in 2013.

Problems

28. **LO.2** Charles has a tentative general business credit of $42,000 for the current year. His net regular tax liability before the general business credit is $107,000, and his tentative minimum tax is $88,000. Compute Charles's allowable general business credit for the year.

29. **LO.2** Oak Corporation has the following general business credit carryovers:

2010	$ 5,000
2011	15,000
2012	6,000
2013	19,000
Total carryovers	$45,000

If the general business credit generated by activities during 2014 equals $36,000 and the total credit allowed during the current year is $60,000 (based on tax liability), what amounts of the current general business credit and carryovers are utilized against the 2014 income tax liability? What is the amount of unused credit carried forward to 2015?

Decision Making   30. **LO.3, 8** In the current year, Paul Chaing (4522 Fargo Street, Geneva, IL 60134) acquires a qualifying historic structure for $350,000 (excluding the cost of the land) and

Communications   plans to substantially rehabilitate the structure. He is planning to spend either $320,000 or $380,000 on rehabilitation expenditures. Write a letter to Paul and a memo for the tax files explaining, for the two alternative expenditures, (1) the computation that determines the rehabilitation expenditures tax credit available to Paul, (2) the impact of the credit on Paul's adjusted basis in the property, and (3) (3) the cash-flow differences as a result of the tax consequences related to his expenditure choice.

31. **LO.3** Green Corporation hires six individuals on January 4, 2014, all of whom qualify for the work opportunity credit. Three of these individuals receive wages of $8,500 during 2014, and each individual works more than 400 hours during the year. The other three individuals work 300 hours and receive wages of $5,000 during the year.
    a. Calculate the amount of Green's work opportunity credit for 2014.
    b. If Green pays total wages of $140,000 to its employees during the year, how much of this amount is deductible in 2014 assuming that the work opportunity credit is taken?

32. **LO.3** In March 2014, Sparrow Corporation hired three individuals—Austin, Adam, and Angela—all of whom are certified as long-term family assistance recipients. Each of these individuals earned $11,000 during 2014. Only Adam continued to work for Sparrow in

2015, and he earned $13,500. In March 2015, Sparrow hired Sam, who is also certified as a long-term family assistance recipient. During 2015, Sam earned $12,000.

a. Compute Sparrow Corporation's work opportunity credit for 2014 and 2015.

b. If Sparrow Corporation pays total wages to its employees of $325,000 in 2014 and $342,000 in 2015, how much may Sparrow claim as a wage deduction in 2014 and 2015?

33. **LO.3, 8** Tom, a calendar year taxpayer, informs you that during the year, he incurs expenditures of $40,000 that qualify for the incremental research activities credit. In addition, it is determined that his base amount for the year is $32,800.

a. Determine Tom's incremental research activities credit for the year.

b. Tom is in the 25% tax bracket. Determine which approach to the research expenditures and the research activities credit (other than capitalization and subsequent amortization) would provide the greater tax benefit to Tom.

Decision Making

34. **LO.3** Ahmed Zinna (16 Southside Drive, Charlotte, NC 28204), one of your clients, owns two retail establishments in downtown Charlotte and has come to you seeking advice concerning the tax consequences of complying with the Americans with Disabilities Act. He understands that he needs to install various features at his stores (e.g., ramps, doorways, and restrooms that are handicap-accessible) to make them more accessible to disabled individuals. He asks whether any tax credits will be available to help offset the cost of the necessary changes. He estimates the cost of the planned changes to his facilities as follows:

Communications

Location	Projected Cost
Calvin Street	$22,000
Stowe Avenue	8,500

He reminds you that the Calvin Street store was constructed in 2004, while the Stowe Avenue store is in a building that was constructed in 1947. Ahmed operates his business as a sole proprietorship and has approximately eight employees at each location. Write a letter to Ahmed in which you summarize your conclusions concerning the tax consequences of his proposed capital improvements.

35. **LO.4** Which of the following individuals qualify for the earned income credit for 2014?

a. Thomas is single, is 21 years of age, and has no qualifying children. His income consists of $9,000 in wages.

b. Shannon, who is 27 years old, maintains a household for a dependent 11-year-old son and is eligible for head-of-household tax rates. Her income consists of $16,050 of salary and $50 of taxable interest (Shannon's AGI is $16,100).

c. Keith and Susan, both age 30, are married and file a joint return. Keith and Susan have no dependents. Their combined income consists of $28,500 of salary and $100 of taxable interest (their AGI is $28,600).

d. Colin is a 26-year-old, self-supporting, single taxpayer. He has no qualifying children and generates earnings of $9,000.

36. **LO.4** Jason, a single parent, lives in an apartment with his three minor children, whom he supports. Jason earned $27,400 during 2014, paid $800 in qualified moving expenses during 2014, and uses the standard deduction. Calculate the amount, if any, of Jason's earned income credit.

37. **LO.4, 8** Joyce, a widow, lives in an apartment with her two minor children (ages 8 and 10), whom she supports. Joyce earns $33,000 during 2014. She uses the standard deduction.

Decision Making

a. Calculate the amount, if any, of Joyce's earned income credit.

b. During the year, Joyce is offered a new job that has greater future potential than her current job. If she accepts the job offer, her earnings for the year will be $39,000; however, she is afraid she will not qualify for the earned income credit. Using after-tax cash-flow calculations, determine whether Joyce should accept the new job offer.

38. **LO.4** Robert, age 68, and Tanya, age 66, are married retirees who receive the following income and retirement benefits during the current year:

Fully taxable pension from Robert's former employer	$ 8,000
Dividends and interest	2,500
Social Security benefits	4,000
Total	$14,500

Assume that Robert and Tanya file a joint tax return, have no deductions *for* AGI, and use the standard deduction. Are they eligible for the tax credit for the elderly? If so, calculate the amount of the credit, assuming that the credit is not limited by their tax liability.

Decision Making

39. **LO.4, 8** Kim, a U.S. citizen and resident, owns and operates a novelty goods business. During 2014, Kim has taxable income of $100,000, made up of the following: $50,000 from foreign sources and $50,000 from U.S. sources. In calculating taxable income, the standard deduction is used. The income from foreign sources is subject to foreign income taxes of $26,000. For 2014, Kim files a joint return claiming his three children as dependents.
    a. Assuming that Kim chooses to claim the foreign taxes as an income tax credit, what is his income tax liability for 2014?
    b. Recently, Kim has become disenchanted with the location of his business and is considering moving his foreign operation to a different country. Based on his research, if he moves his business to his country of choice, all relevant revenues and costs would remain approximately the same except that the income taxes payable to that country would be only $8,000. Given that all of the foreign income taxes paid are available to offset the U.S. tax liability (whether he operates in a high-tax or a low-tax foreign jurisdiction), what impact will this have on his decision regarding the potential move?

40. **LO.4** Blue Horizons, Inc., a U.S. corporation, is a manufacturing concern that sells most of its products in the United States. It also does some business in the European Union through various branches. During the current year, Blue Horizons has taxable income of $700,000, of which $500,000 is U.S.-sourced and $200,000 is foreign-sourced. Foreign income taxes paid amounted to $45,000. Blue Horizons's U.S. income tax liability is $238,000. What is its U.S. income tax liability net of the allowable foreign tax credit?

41. **LO.4** Ann and Bill were on the list of a local adoption agency for several years, seeking to adopt a child. Finally, in 2013, good news comes their way, and an adoption seems imminent. They pay qualified adoption expenses of $4,000 in 2013 and $11,000 in 2014. Assume that the adoption becomes final in 2014. Ann and Bill always file a joint income tax return.
    a. Determine the amount of the adoption expenses credit available to Ann and Bill assuming that their combined annual income is $100,000. What year(s) will they benefit from the credit?
    b. Assuming that Ann and Bill's modified AGI in 2013 and 2014 is $200,000, calculate the amount of the adoption expenses credit.

42. **LO.4** Durell and Earline are married; file a joint return; and claim dependency exemptions for their two children, ages 5 years and 6 months. They also claim Earline's son from a previous marriage, age 18, as a dependent. Durell and Earline's combined AGI is $68,000.
    a. Compute Durell and Earline's child tax credit.
    b. Assume the same facts, except that Durell and Earline's combined AGI is $122,000. Compute their child tax credit.

43. **LO.4** Paul and Karen are married, and both are employed (Paul earns $44,000 and Karen earns $9,000 during 2014). Paul and Karen have two dependent children, both under the age of 13. So that they can work, Paul and Karen pay $3,800 to various unrelated parties to care for their children while they are working. Assuming that Paul and Karen file a joint return, what, if any, is their tax credit for child and dependent care expenses?

44. **LO.4** Jim and Mary Jean are married and have two dependent children under the age of 13. Both parents are gainfully employed and during 2014 earn salaries as follows: $16,000 (Jim) and $5,200 (Mary Jean). To care for their children while they work, they pay Eleanor (Jim's mother) $5,600. Eleanor does not qualify as a dependent of Jim and Mary. Assuming that Jim and Mary Jean file a joint tax return, what, if any, is their credit for child and dependent care expenses?

45. **LO.4, 8** Bernadette, a longtime client of yours, is an architect and the president of the local Rotary chapter. To keep up to date with the latest developments in her profession, she attends continuing education seminars offered by the architecture school at State University. During 2014, Bernadette spends $2,000 on course tuition to attend such seminars. She also spends another $400 on architecture books during the year. Bernadette's son is a senior majoring in engineering at the University of the Midwest. During the 2014 calendar year, Bernadette's son incurs the following expenses: $8,200 for tuition ($4,100 per semester) and $750 for books and course materials. Bernadette's son, whom she claims as a dependent, lives at home while attending school full-time. Bernadette is married, files a joint return, and has a combined AGI with her husband of $110,000.

    a. Calculate Bernadette's education tax credit for 2014.
    b. In her capacity as president of the local Rotary chapter, Bernadette has asked you to make a 30- to 45-minute speech outlining the different ways the tax law helps defray (1) the cost of higher education and (2) the cost of continuing education once someone is in the workforce. Prepare an outline of possible topics for presentation. A tentative title for your presentation is "How Can the Tax Law Help Pay for College and Continuing Professional Education?"

    Communications

46. **LO.4** Kathleen and Glenn decide that this is the year to begin getting serious about saving for their retirement by participating in their employers' § 401(k) plans. As a result, they each have $3,000 of their salary set aside in their qualified plans.

    a. Calculate the credit for certain retirement plan contributions available to Kathleen and Glenn if the AGI on their joint return is $35,000.
    b. Kathleen and Glenn persuade their dependent 15-year-old son, Joel, to put $500 of his part-time earnings into a Roth IRA during the year. What is the credit for certain retirement plan contributions available to Joel? His AGI is $7,000.

47. **LO.5** In each of the following independent situations, determine the amount of FICA that should be withheld from the employee's 2014 salary by the employer.

    a. Harry earns a $50,000 salary, files a joint return, and claims four withholding allowances.
    b. Hazel earns a $115,000 salary, files a joint return, and claims four withholding allowances.
    c. Tracy earns a $190,000 salary, files a joint return, and claims four withholding allowances.
    d. Alicia's 17-year-old son, Carlos, earns $10,000 at the family sole proprietorship.

48. **LO.5** During 2014, Greg Cruz (1401 Orangedale Road, Troy, MI 48084) works for Maple Corporation and Gray Company. He earns $80,000 at Maple Corporation, where he is a full-time employee. Greg also works part-time for Gray Company for wages of $45,000.

    a. Did Greg experience an overwithholding of FICA taxes? Write a letter to Greg and a memo for the tax files in which you explain your conclusion.
    b. Did Maple Corporation and Gray Company overpay the employer's portion of FICA? Explain.

    Communications

49. **LO.5** In each of the following independent situations, determine the maximum withholding allowances permitted Eli (an employee) on Form W–4.

    a. Eli is single with no dependents.
    b. Eli is married to a nonemployed spouse, and they have no dependents.
    c. Eli is married to Vera, an employed spouse who earns $25,000, and they have three dependent children. Eli and Vera do not qualify for the child tax credit. On the Form W–4 that she filed with the employer, Vera claimed zero allowances.
    d. Assume the same facts as in (c), except that Eli and Vera fully support Eli's mother, who lives with them. The mother (age 70 and blind) qualifies as their dependent. (Refer to Chapter 3.)
    e. Eli is single with no dependents but works for two employers, one on a full-time basis and the other on a part-time basis. The Form W–4 filed with the first employer (the full-time job) reflects two withholding exemptions. The wages from each job exceed $1,500.
    f. Assume the same facts as in (e), except that Eli is married to a nonemployed spouse.

Decision Making

50. **LO.5** Jane, who is expecting to finish college in May 2014, is fortunate to have already arranged full-time employment after graduation. She will begin work on July 1, 2014, as a staff accountant at a nearby professional services firm with a starting salary of $48,600 per year. Jane is married to Craig, who plans to be a full-time student throughout the year. They anticipate generating no income for the year other than the salary from her new position.

    a. How many withholding allowances would you expect Jane to claim on her Form W–4?

    b. Assuming that Jane and Craig use the standard deduction, calculate the Federal income tax liability on their projected taxable income for 2014. What advice would you give to Jane?

    c. What further changes should she make to her W–4 at the beginning of 2015?

51. **LO.6** Julie, being self-employed, is required to make estimated payments of her tax liability for the year. Her tax liability for 2013 was $25,000, and her AGI was less than $150,000. For 2014, Julie ultimately determines that her income tax liability is $18,000. During the year, however, she made the following payments, totaling $13,000:

April 15, 2014	$ 4,500
June 16, 2014	2,800
September 15, 2014	4,100
January 15, 2015	1,600
	$13,000

Because she prepaid so little of her ultimate income tax liability, she now realizes that she may be subject to the penalty for underpayment of estimated tax.

    a. Determine Julie's exposure to the penalty for underpayment of estimated tax.

    b. The same as (a), except that Julie's tax liability for 2013 was $15,960.

52. **LO.6** In 2014, Maria has self-employed earnings of $135,000. Using the format illustrated in the text, compute Maria's self-employment tax liability and the allowable income tax deduction for the self-employment tax paid.

Cumulative Problems

Tax Return Problem

H&R BLOCK

TAX SOFTWARE

53. Beth R. Jordan lives at 2322 Skyview Road, Mesa, AZ 85201. She is a tax accountant with Mesa Manufacturing Company, 1203 Western Avenue, Mesa, AZ 85201 (employer identification number 11-1111111). She also writes computer software programs for tax practitioners and has a part-time tax practice. Beth is single and has no dependents. Beth's birthday is July 4, 1972, and her Social Security number is 123-45-6789. She wants to contribute $3 to the Presidential Election Campaign Fund.

    The following information is shown on Beth's Wage and Tax Statement (Form W–2) for 2013:

Line	Description	Amount
1	Wages, tips, other compensation	$65,000.00
2	Federal income tax withheld	10,500.00
3	Social Security wages	65,000.00
4	Social Security tax withheld	4,030.00
5	Medicare wages and tips	65,000.00
6	Medicare tax withheld	942.50
15	State	Arizona
16	State wages, tips, etc.	65,000.00
17	State income tax withheld	1,650.00

    During 2013, Beth received interest of $1,300 from Arizona Federal Savings and Loan and $400 from Arizona State Bank. Each financial institution reported the interest income on a Form 1099–INT. She received qualified dividends of $800 from Blue Corporation, $750 from Green Corporation, and $650 from Orange Corporation. Each corporation reported Beth's dividend payments on a Form 1099–DIV.

Beth received a $1,100 income tax refund from the state of Arizona on April 29, 2013. On her 2012 Federal income tax return, she reported total itemized deductions of $8,200, which included $2,200 of state income tax withheld by her employer.

Fees earned from her part-time tax practice in 2013 totaled $3,800. She paid $600 to have the tax returns processed by a computerized tax return service.

On February 8, 2013, Beth bought 500 shares of Gray Corporation common stock for $17.60 a share. On September 12, 2013, Beth sold the stock for $14 a share.

Beth bought a used sport utility vehicle for $6,000 on June 5, 2013. She purchased the vehicle from her brother-in-law, who was unemployed and was in need of cash. On November 2, 2013, she sold the vehicle to a friend for $6,500.

On January 2, 2013, Beth acquired 100 shares of Blue Corporation common stock for $30 a share. She sold the stock on December 19, 2013, for $55 a share.

During 2013, Beth received royalties of $16,000 on a software program she had written. Beth incurred the following expenditures in connection with her software-writing activities:

Cost of personal computer	$7,000
Cost of printer	2,000
Furniture	3,000
Supplies	650
Fee paid to computer consultant	3,500

Beth elected to expense the maximum portion of the cost of the computer, printer, and furniture allowed under the provisions of § 179. These items were placed in service on January 15, 2013 and used 100% in her business.

Although her employer suggested that Beth attend a convention on current developments in corporate taxation, Beth was not reimbursed for the travel expenses of $1,420 she incurred in attending the convention. The $1,420 included $200 for the cost of meals.

During 2013, Beth paid $300 for prescription medicines and $2,875 for doctor bills and hospital bills. Medical insurance premiums were paid for her by her employer. Beth paid real property taxes of $1,766 on her home. Interest on her home mortgage was $3,845, and interest to credit card companies was $320. Beth contributed $30 each week to her church and $10 each week to the United Way. Professional dues and subscriptions totaled $350. Beth maintained her sales tax receipts. The total is $1,954.

Beth paid estimated taxes of $1,000.

Part 1—Tax Computation

Compute the net tax payable or refund due for Beth R. Jordan for 2013. If you use tax forms for your solution, you will need Forms 1040, 2106–EZ, and 4562 and Schedules A, B, C, D, and SE. Suggested software: H&R BLOCK Tax Software.

Part 2—Tax Planning

Beth is anticipating significant changes in her life in 2014, and she has asked you to estimate her taxable income and tax liability for 2014. She just received word that she has been qualified to adopt a 2-year-old daughter. Beth expects that the adoption will be finalized in 2014 and that she will incur approximately $2,000 of adoption expenses. In addition, she expects to incur approximately $3,500 of child and dependent care expenses relating to the care of her new daughter, which will enable her to keep her job at Mesa Manufacturing Company. However, with the additional demands on her time because of her daughter, she has decided to discontinue her two part-time jobs (i.e., the part-time tax practice and her software business), and she will cease making estimated income tax payments. In your computations, assume that all other income and expenditures will remain at approximately the same levels as in 2013.

Tax Computation Problem

54. Tim and Sarah Lawrence are married and file a joint return. Tim's Social Security number is 123-45-6789, and Sarah's Social Security number is 111-11-1111. They reside at 100 Olive Lane, Covington, LA 70434. They have two dependent children, Sean and Debra, ages 12 and 16, respectively. Sean's Social Security number is 123-45-6788, and Debra's Social Security number is 123-45-6787. Tim is a self-employed businessperson (sole

proprietor of an unincorporated business), and Sarah is a corporate executive. Tim has the following income and expenses from his business:

Gross income	$325,000
Business expenses	201,000

Records related to Sarah's employment provide the following information:

Salary	$145,000
Unreimbursed travel expenses (including $200 of meals)	1,100
Unreimbursed entertainment expenses	500

Other pertinent information relating to 2014 follows:

Proceeds from sale of stock acquired on July 15, 2014 (cost of $12,000), and sold on August 1, 2014	$ 9,800
Proceeds from sale of stock acquired on September 18, 2013 (cost of $5,000), and sold on October 5, 2014	3,800
Wages paid to full-time domestic worker for housekeeping and child supervision	10,000
Interest income received	7,000
Total itemized deductions (not including any potential deductions above)	27,900
Federal income tax withheld	31,850
Estimated payments of Federal income tax	34,000

Compute the net tax payable or refund due for Tim and Sarah Lawrence for 2014.

Research Problems

THOMSON REUTERS
CHECKPOINT®

Note: Solutions to Research Problems can be prepared by using the **Checkpoint®** **Student Edition** online research product, which is available to accompany this text. It is also possible to prepare solutions to the Research Problems by using tax research materials found in a standard tax library.

Research Problem 1. Ashby and Curtis, a young professional couple, have a 2-year-old son, Jason. Curtis works full-time as an electrical engineer, but Ashby has not worked outside the home since Jason was born. As Jason is getting older, Ashby thinks that Jason would benefit from attending nursery school several times a week, which would give her an opportunity to reinvigorate her love of painting at a nearby art studio. Ashby thinks that if she is lucky, the proceeds from the sale of her paintings will pay for the nursery school tuition. But in addition, she is planning to claim the credit for child and dependent care expenses because the care provided Jason at the nursery school is required for her to pursue her art. Can Ashby and Curtis claim the credit for child and dependent care expenses for the nursery school expenditure? Why or why not?

Communications

Research Problem 2. Your ophthalmologist, Dr. Hunter Francis (55 Wheatland Drive, Hampton, CT 06247), has been very pleased with the growth of his practice in the 15 years he has been in business. This growth has resulted, at least in part, because he has aggressively marketed his services and tried to accommodate clients with various needs. This year, Dr. Francis purchased a sophisticated piece of equipment that enables him to diagnose persons with mental handicaps, hearing impairments, and physical disabilities without having to go through a series of questions. In addition, he can treat his patients who are not disabled more accurately and efficiently by using this equipment. Since purchasing the machine this year for $9,500, Dr. Francis has used it on many occasions. Unfortunately, he has not been able to attract any disabled patients, even though previously he referred such people to other ophthalmologists who owned the necessary equipment. Therefore, the primary purpose for acquiring the equipment (i.e., to attract disabled patients) has not been realized, but he has put it to good use in treating other patients. Write a letter to Dr. Francis explaining whether he may claim the disabled access credit for this acquisition.

Research Problem 3. Erin is in graduate school to earn a master's degree in accounting. Her parents pay her tuition for the program. Early in 2014, Erin's dad left his job and took a few months off to relax and pursue his photography hobby. He started working at his new job in October. The resulting decrease in her parents' annual income means that their modified AGI will be well below the phaseout threshold for the lifetime learning credit. Thus, Erin's parents are considering prepaying Erin's 2015 spring semester tuition in December 2014, provided that the prepayment would qualify for their 2014 lifetime learning credit. Determine whether the prepayment qualifies for the credit.

Research Problem 4. During a recent Sunday afternoon excursion, Miriam, an admirer of early twentieth-century architecture, discovers a 1920s-era house in the countryside outside Mobile, Alabama. She wants not only to purchase and renovate this particular house but also to move the structure into Mobile so that her community can enjoy its architectural features. Being aware of the availability of the tax credit for rehabilitation expenditures, she wants to maximize her use of the provision, if it is available in this case, once the renovation work begins in Mobile. Miriam also informs you that she will pursue the purchase, relocation, and renovation of the house only if the tax credit is available. Comment on Miriam's decision and on whether any renovation expenditures incurred will qualify for the tax credit for rehabilitation expenditures.

Partial list of research aids:
George S. Nalle III v. Comm., 93–2 USTC ¶50,468, 72 AFTR 2d 93–5705, 997 F.2d 1134 (CA–5, 1993).

Use the tax resources of the Internet to address the following questions. Do not restrict your search to the Web, but include a review of newsgroups and general reference materials, practitioner sites and resources, primary sources of the tax law, chat rooms and discussion groups, and other opportunities.

Internet Activity

Research Problem 5. Find several news stories or government reports that document the incentive effects of any of the renewable energy credits (biodiesel/alternative fuels, solar, wind, geothermal, and/or electric).

Research Problem 6. Beginning in 2014, as a result of the Affordable Care Act, taxpayers who purchase health insurance coverage through the Health Insurance Marketplace may be eligible for the premium tax credit under § 36B. Use the IRS's website (**www.irs.gov**) to read about the credit and determine which taxpayers are eligible for this credit.

Research Problem 7. The IRS provides a web-based tool to help taxpayers determine whether they (or their clients) are eligible for the earned income tax credit. Locate this tool at the IRS website. Then apply the facts related to a hypothetical taxpayer and determine whether the earned income credit is available.

part 5

PROPERTY TRANSACTIONS

Part 5 presents the tax treatment of sales, exchanges, and other dispositions of property. Included are the determination of the realized gain or loss, recognized gain or loss, and the classification of the recognized gain or loss as capital or ordinary. The topic of basis is evaluated both in terms of its effect on the calculation of the gain or loss and in terms of the determination of the basis of any contemporaneous or related subsequent acquisitions of property.

Dennis Flaherty/Photographer's Choice/Getty Images

CHAPTER

14

Property Transactions: Determination of Gain or Loss and Basis Considerations

LEARNING OBJECTIVES: *After completing Chapter 14, you should be able to:*

LO.1 State and explain the computation of realized gain or loss on property dispositions.

LO.2 Distinguish between realized and recognized gain or loss.

LO.3 Review and illustrate how basis is determined for various methods of asset acquisition.

LO.4 Describe various loss disallowance provisions.

LO.5 Identify tax planning opportunities related to selected property transactions.

CHAPTER OUTLINE

Dennis Flaherty/Photographer's Choice/Getty Images

© Michael Courtney/iStockphoto.com

THE BIG PICTURE   Tax Solutions for the Real World

PROPOSED SALE OF A HOUSE AND OTHER PROPERTY TRANSACTIONS

Alice owns a house that she received from her mother seven months ago. Her mother's cost for the house was $275,000. Alice is considering selling the house to her favorite nephew, Dan, for $275,000. Alice anticipates that she will have no gain or loss on the transaction. She comes to you for advice.

As Alice's tax adviser, you need answers to the following questions:

- You are aware that Alice's mother died around the time Alice indicates that she received the house from her mother. Did Alice receive the house by gift prior to her mother's death? If so, what was the mother's adjusted basis? Did Alice instead inherit the house from her mother? If so, what was the fair market value of the house on the date of her mother's death?
- Has the house been Alice's principal residence during the period she has owned it? Was it her principal residence before she received it from her mother?
- How long did Alice's mother own the house?
- What is the current fair market value of the house?
- Does Alice intend for the transaction with Dan to be a sale or part sale and part gift?
- What does Alice intend to do with the sale proceeds?

Alice would also like to know the tax consequences of selling her boat, which she purchased for $22,000 four months ago and has used exclusively for personal use. She has been disappointed with its layout and capacity. Because it is a new model, there is significant demand for the boat, and based on listings in her area, she anticipates that she can sell it for $20,000 to $23,000.

In addition, earlier this year, Alice sold some stock at a realized loss and subsequently repurchased some shares of the same stock. She has also asked you about the tax consequences of these transactions.

Once you have more information, you can advise Alice on the tax consequences of these various transactions.

Read the chapter and formulate your response.

14-1

FRAMEWORK 1040

Tax Formula for Individuals

This chapter covers the boldfaced portions of the Tax Formula for Individuals that was introduced in Figure 3.1 on p. 3-3. Below those portions are the sections of Form 1040 where the results are reported.

Income *(broadly conceived)*...	$xx,xxx
Less: Exclusions	(x,xxx)
Gross income..	$xx,xxx
Less: Deductions for adjusted gross income..	(x,xxx)

FORM 1040 (p. 1)

12	Business income or (loss). Attach Schedule C or C-EZ	
13	Capital gain or (loss). Attach Schedule D if required. If not required, check here ▶	☐
14	Other gains or (losses). Attach Form 4797	

Adjusted gross income...	$xx,xxx
Less: The greater of total **itemized deductions** *or* the standard deduction	(x,xxx)
Personal and dependency exemptions...	(x,xxx)
Taxable income	$xx,xxx
Tax on taxable income *(see Tax Tables or Tax Rate Schedules)*	$ x,xxx
Less: Tax credits *(including income taxes withheld and prepaid)*..	(xxx)
Tax due *(or refund)*...	$ xxx

This chapter and the following three chapters are concerned with the income tax consequences of property transactions (the sale or other disposition of property). The following questions are considered with respect to the sale or other disposition of property:

- Is there a realized gain or loss?
- If so, is the gain or loss recognized?
- If the gain or loss is recognized, is it ordinary or capital?
- What is the basis of any replacement property that is acquired?

Chapters 14 and 15 discuss the determination of realized and recognized gain or loss and the basis of property. Chapters 16 and 17 cover the classification of the recognized gain or loss as ordinary or capital.

14-1 DETERMINATION OF GAIN OR LOSS

14-1a Realized Gain or Loss

LO.1

State and explain the computation of realized gain or loss on property dispositions.

Realized gain or loss is the difference between the amount realized from the sale or other disposition of property and the property's adjusted basis on the date of disposition. If the amount realized exceeds the property's adjusted basis, the result is a **realized gain**. Conversely, if the property's adjusted basis exceeds the amount realized, the result is a **realized loss**.[1]

Example 1

Tab sells Swan Corporation stock with an adjusted basis of $3,000 for $5,000. Tab's realized gain is $2,000. If Tab had sold the stock for $2,000, he would have had a realized loss of $1,000.

---

[1] § 1001(a) and Reg. § 1.1001–1(a).

Sale or Other Disposition

The term *sale or other disposition* is defined broadly in the tax law and includes virtually any disposition of property. Thus, transactions such as trade-ins, casualties, condemnations, thefts, and bond retirements are treated as dispositions of property. The most common disposition of property is through a sale or exchange. Usually, the key factor in determining whether a disposition has taken place is whether an identifiable event has occurred[2] as opposed to a mere fluctuation in the value of the property.[3]

> **Example 2**
>
> Lori owns Tan Corporation stock that cost $3,000. The stock has appreciated in value by $2,000 since Lori purchased it. Lori has no realized gain because mere fluctuation in value is not a disposition or an identifiable event for tax purposes. Nor would Lori have a realized loss if the stock declined in value by $2,000.

Amount Realized

The **amount realized** from a sale or other disposition of property is the sum of any money received plus the fair market value of other property received. The amount realized also includes any real property taxes treated as imposed on the seller that are actually paid by the buyer.[4] The reason for including these taxes in the amount realized is that by paying the taxes, the purchaser is, in effect, paying an additional amount to the seller of the property.

The amount realized also includes any liability on the property disposed of, such as a mortgage debt, if the buyer assumes the mortgage or the property is sold subject to the mortgage.[5] The amount of the liability is included in the amount realized even if the debt is nonrecourse and the amount of the debt is greater than the fair market value of the mortgaged property.[6]

> **Example 3**
>
> Barry sells property on which there is a mortgage of $20,000 to Cole for $50,000 cash. Barry's amount realized from the sale is $70,000 if Cole assumes the mortgage or takes the property subject to the mortgage.

The **fair market value** of property received in a sale or other disposition has been defined by the courts as the price at which property will change hands between a willing seller and a willing buyer when neither is compelled to sell or buy.[7] Fair market value is determined by considering the relevant factors in each case.[8] An expert appraiser is often required to evaluate these factors in arriving at fair market value. When the fair market value of the property received cannot be determined, the value of the property given up by the taxpayer may be used.[9]

In calculating the amount realized, selling expenses (such as advertising, commissions, and legal fees) relating to the disposition are deducted. The amount realized is the net amount the taxpayer received directly or indirectly, in the form of cash or anything else of value, from the disposition of the property.

Adjusted Basis

The **adjusted basis** of property disposed of is the property's original basis adjusted to the date of disposition.[10] Original basis is the cost or other basis of the property on the date the property is acquired by the taxpayer. Considerations involving original basis are discussed later in this chapter. *Capital additions* increase and *recoveries of capital* decrease the original basis so that on the date of disposition, the adjusted

---

[2]Reg. § 1.1001–1(c)(1).

[3]*Lynch v. Turrish,* 1 USTC ¶18, 3 AFTR 2986, 38 S.Ct. 537 (USSC, 1918).

[4]§ 1001(b) and Reg. § 1.1001–1(b). Refer to Chapter 10 for a discussion of this subject.

[5]*Crane v. Comm.,* 47–1 USTC ¶9217, 35 AFTR 776, 67 S.Ct. 1047 (USSC, 1947). Although a legal distinction exists between the direct assumption of a mortgage and the taking of property subject to a mortgage, the tax consequences in calculating the amount realized are the same.

[6]*Comm. v. Tufts,* 83–1 USTC ¶9328, 51 AFTR 2d 83–1132, 103 S.Ct. 1826 (USSC, 1983).

[7]*Comm. v. Marshman,* 60–2 USTC ¶9484, 5 AFTR 2d 1528, 279 F.2d 27 (CA–6, 1960).

[8]*O'Malley v. Ames,* 52–1 USTC ¶9361, 42 AFTR 19, 197 F.2d 256 (CA–8, 1952).

[9]*U.S. v. Davis,* 62–2 USTC ¶9509, 9 AFTR 2d 1625, 82 S.Ct. 1190 (USSC, 1962).

[10]§ 1011(a) and Reg. § 1.1011–1.

basis reflects the unrecovered cost or other basis of the property.[11] Adjusted basis is determined as follows:

Cost (or other adjusted basis) on date of acquisition
+ Capital additions
− Capital recoveries
= Adjusted basis on date of disposition

Capital Additions

Capital additions include the cost of capital improvements and betterments made to the property by the taxpayer. These expenditures are distinguishable from expenditures for the ordinary repair and maintenance of the property, which are neither capitalized nor added to the original basis (refer to Chapter 6). The latter expenditures are deductible in the current taxable year if they are related to business or income-producing property. Amounts representing real property taxes treated as imposed on the seller but paid or assumed by the buyer are part of the cost of the property.[12] Any liability on property that is assumed by the buyer is also included in the buyer's original basis of the property. The same rule applies if property is acquired subject to a liability. Amortization of the discount on bonds increases the adjusted basis of the bonds.[13]

Capital Recoveries

Capital recoveries decrease the adjusted basis of property. The prominent types of capital recoveries are discussed below.

Depreciation and Cost Recovery Allowances The original basis of depreciable property is reduced by the annual depreciation charges (or cost recovery allowances) while the property is held by the taxpayer. The amount of depreciation that is subtracted from the original basis is the greater of the *allowed* or *allowable* depreciation calculated on an annual basis.[14] In most circumstances, the allowed and allowable depreciation amounts are the same (refer to Chapter 8).

Casualties and Thefts A casualty or theft may result in the reduction of the adjusted basis of property.[15] The adjusted basis is reduced by the amount of the deductible loss. In addition, the adjusted basis is reduced by the amount of insurance proceeds received. However, the receipt of insurance proceeds may result in a recognized gain rather than a deductible loss. The gain increases the adjusted basis of the property.[16]

Example 4	An insured truck that Marvin used in his trade or business is destroyed in an accident. At the time of the accident, the adjusted basis was $8,000, and the fair market value was $6,500. Marvin receives insurance proceeds of $6,500. The amount of the casualty loss is $1,500 ($6,500 insurance proceeds − $8,000 adjusted basis). The truck's adjusted basis is reduced by the $1,500 casualty loss and the $6,500 of insurance proceeds received ($8,000 basis before casualty − $1,500 casualty loss − $6,500 insurance proceeds = $0 adjusted basis).

Example 5	An insured truck that Marvin used in his trade or business is destroyed in an accident. At the time of the accident, the adjusted basis was $6,500, and the fair market value was $8,000. Marvin receives insurance proceeds of $8,000. The amount of the casualty gain is $1,500 ($8,000 insurance proceeds − $6,500 adjusted basis). The truck's adjusted basis is increased by the $1,500 casualty gain and is reduced by the $8,000 of insurance proceeds received ($6,500 basis before casualty + $1,500 casualty gain − $8,000 insurance proceeds = $0 adjusted basis).

---

[11]§ 1016(a) and Reg. § 1.1016–1.

[12]Reg. §§ 1.1001–1(b)(2) and 1.1012–1(b). Refer to Chapter 10 for a discussion of this subject.

[13]See Chapter 16 for a discussion of bond discount and the related amortization.

[14]§ 1016(a)(2) and Reg. § 1.1016–3(a)(1)(i).

[15]Refer to Chapter 7 for the discussion of casualties and thefts.

[16]Reg. § 1.1016–6(a).

Certain Corporate Distributions A corporate distribution to a shareholder that is not taxable is treated as a return of capital, and it reduces the basis of the shareholder's stock in the corporation.[17] For example, if a corporation makes a cash distribution to its shareholders and has no earnings and profits, the distributions are treated as a return of capital. Once the basis of the stock is reduced to zero, the amount of any subsequent distributions is a capital gain if the stock is a capital asset. These rules are illustrated in Example 25 of Chapter 20.

Amortizable Bond Premium The basis in a bond purchased at a premium is reduced by the amortizable portion of the bond premium.[18] Investors in taxable bonds may *elect* to amortize the bond premium.[19] The amount of the amortized premium on taxable bonds is allowed as an interest deduction. Therefore, the election enables the taxpayer to take an annual interest deduction to offset ordinary income in exchange for a larger capital gain or smaller capital loss on the disposition of the bond. The amortization deduction is allowed for taxable bonds because the premium is viewed as a cost of earning the taxable interest from the bonds. The reason the basis of taxable bonds is reduced is that the amortization deduction is a recovery of the cost or basis of the bonds.

Unlike taxable bonds, the premium on tax-exempt bonds *must be* amortized (and the basis is reduced even though the amortization is not allowed as a deduction). No amortization deduction is permitted on tax-exempt bonds because the interest income is exempt from tax and the amortization of the bond premium merely represents an adjustment of the effective amount of such income.

> **Example 6**
>
> Antonio purchases Eagle Corporation taxable bonds with a face value of $100,000 for $110,000, thus paying a premium of $10,000. The annual interest rate is 7%, and the bonds mature 10 years from the date of purchase. The annual interest income is $7,000 (7% × $100,000). If Antonio elects to amortize the bond premium, the $10,000 premium is deducted over the 10-year period. Antonio's basis for the bonds is reduced each year by the amount of the amortization deduction. Note that if the bonds were tax-exempt, amortization of the bond premium and the basis adjustment would be mandatory. However, no deduction would be allowed for the amortization.

Easements An easement is the legal right to use another's land for a special purpose. Historically, easements were commonly used to obtain rights-of-way for utility lines, roads, and pipelines. In recent years, grants of conservation easements have become a popular means of obtaining charitable contribution deductions and reducing the value of real estate for transfer tax (i.e., estate and gift) purposes. Likewise, scenic easements are used to reduce the value of land as assessed for ad valorem property tax purposes.

If the taxpayer does not retain any right to the use of the land, all of the basis is assigned to the easement. However, if the use of the land is only partially restricted, an allocation of some of the basis to the easement is appropriate.

14-1b Recognized Gain or Loss

Recognized gain is the amount of the realized gain that is included in the taxpayer's gross income.[20] A **recognized loss**, on the other hand, is the amount of a realized loss that is deductible for tax purposes.[21] As a general rule, the entire amount of a realized gain or loss is recognized.[22]

Concept Summary 14.1 summarizes the realized gain or loss and recognized gain or loss concepts.

LO.2

Distinguish between realized and recognized gain or loss.

---

[17]§ 1016(a)(4) and Reg. § 1.1016–5(a).

[18]§ 1016(a)(5) and Reg. § 1.1016–5(b). The accounting treatment of bond premium amortization is the same as for tax purposes. The amortization results in a decrease in the bond investment account.

[19]§ 171(c).

[20]§ 61(a)(3) and Reg. § 1.61–6(a).

[21]§ 165(a) and Reg. § 1.165–1(a).

[22]§ 1001(c) and Reg. § 1.1002–1(a).

CONCEPT SUMMARY 14.1

Recognized Gain or Loss

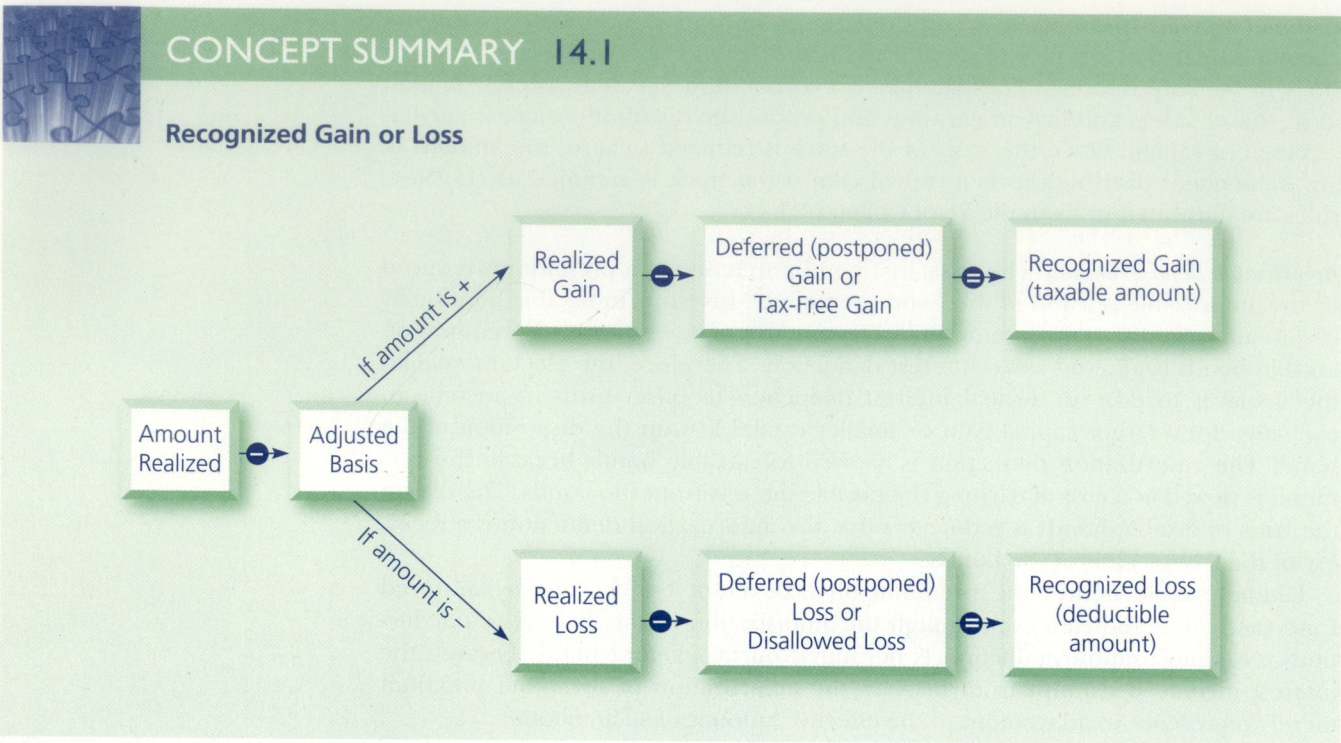

14-1c Nonrecognition of Gain or Loss

In certain cases, a realized gain or loss is not recognized upon the sale or other disposition of property. One such case involves nontaxable exchanges, which are covered in Chapter 15. Others include losses realized upon the sale, exchange, or condemnation of personal use assets (as opposed to business or income-producing property) and gains realized upon the sale of a residence (see Chapter 15). In addition, realized losses from the sale or exchange of business or income-producing property between certain related parties are not recognized.[23]

Sale, Exchange, or Condemnation of Personal Use Assets

A realized loss from the sale, exchange, or condemnation of personal use assets (e.g., a personal residence or an automobile not used at all for business or income-producing purposes) is not recognized for tax purposes. An exception exists for casualty or theft losses from personal use assets (see Chapter 7). In contrast, any gain realized from the sale or other disposition of personal use assets is, generally, fully taxable.

THE BIG PICTURE

Example 7

Return to the facts of *The Big Picture* on p. 14-1. Assume that Alice sells the boat, which she has held exclusively for personal use, for $23,000. Recall that her adjusted basis of the boat is $22,000. Alice has a realized and recognized gain of $1,000.

THE BIG PICTURE

Example 8

Assume that Alice sells the boat in Example 7 for $20,000. She has a realized loss of $2,000, but the loss is not recognized.

---

[23]§ 267(a)(1).

TAX IN THE NEWS   A Hard Way to Avoid the Disallowance of a Loss

One of the results of the bursting of the housing bubble has been to create "accidental landlords." These owners intended to sell but were unable to find a buyer for the "right price." Because of continuing low housing values in certain parts of the country, they have decided to rent their homes for the time being. By doing so, they hope the fair market value will increase so that a later sale will generate greater revenue, thereby avoiding any loss. Moreover, a loss on the sale of a personal residence is not deductible for Federal income tax purposes.

But such accidental landlords should be aware of the potential negative consequences that could result, including:

- The damage caused by unruly tenants.
- The legal responsibilities involved in being a landlord.

- The maintenance and repair costs associated with renting property.
- Other unforeseen headaches.

Perhaps the worst scenario is that the house does not increase in value and the homeowner eventually sells at a price that is the same as or less than could have been obtained originally. The only positive result of this situation is that any loss that occurs after the conversion to rental property is now deductible for tax purposes. Note that the loss that occurred prior to conversion to rental property is still nondeductible.

Source: Based on "Accidental Landlords," *Wall Street Journal,* December 12, 2011, p. R7; "Accidental Landlords: The Next Real Estate Nightmare or Effective Housing Solution?" *Forbes,* May 29, 2012.

14-2 BASIS CONSIDERATIONS

14-2a Determination of Cost Basis

LO.3

Review and illustrate how basis is determined for various methods of asset acquisition.

As noted earlier, the basis of property is generally the property's cost. Cost is the amount paid for the property in cash or other property.[24] This general rule follows logically from the recovery of capital doctrine; that is, the cost or other basis of property is to be recovered tax-free by the taxpayer.

A *bargain purchase* of property is an exception to the general rule for determining basis. A bargain purchase may result when an employer transfers property to an employee at less than the property's fair market value (as compensation for services) or when a corporation transfers property to a shareholder at less than the property's fair market value (a dividend). The amount included in income either as compensation for services or dividend income is the difference between the bargain purchase price and the property's fair market value. The basis of property acquired in a bargain purchase is the property's fair market value.[25] If the basis of the property were not increased by the bargain amount, the taxpayer would be taxed on this amount again at disposition.

Wade buys land from his employer for $10,000 on December 30. The fair market value of the land is $15,000. Wade must include the $5,000 difference between the cost and the fair market value of the land in gross income for the taxable year. The bargain element represents additional compensation to Wade. His basis for the land is $15,000, the land's fair market value.

Example 9

Identification Problems

Cost identification problems are frequently encountered in securities transactions. For example, the Regulations require that the taxpayer adequately identify the particular stock that has been sold (specific identification).[26] A problem arises

---

[24]§ 1012 and Reg. § 1.1012–1(a).

[25]Reg. §§ 1.61–2(d)(2)(i) and 1.301–1(j). See the discussion in Chapter 5 of the circumstances under which what appears to be a taxable bargain purchase is an excludible qualified employee discount.

[26]Reg. § 1.1012–1(c)(1).

TAX IN THE NEWS Brokers Provide Cost Basis Data to Taxpayers (and the IRS)

Brokers and others in similar enterprises are now required to provide investors with an annual report on the cost basis of their stocks sold during the year (to be included on Form 1099–B and reported to the IRS). The new reporting rules, part of the Emergency Economic Stabilization Act of 2008, are being phased in over several years: banks and brokers were required to begin tracking and reporting the cost basis of stocks purchased in 2011 or later years and held in taxable accounts (so, for example, IRAs or § 401(k) accounts are not covered). Mutual funds, dividend reinvestment plans, and certain exchange-traded funds are subject to the rules if purchased on or after January 1, 2012. Debt instruments, options, and other securities are covered if purchased on or after January 1, 2013.

According to the legislation, the primary reason for the requirement is to enable taxpayers to use the correct basis in calculating the gain or loss on the sale of the stock. In the simplest situation in which only a single lot of the stock was purchased, the taxpayer still may not have this information available when the stock is sold—perhaps many years later. Even if the investor maintains good records, nontaxable stock dividends, stock splits, and spin-offs may create confusion and result in unreliable data being used

to determine the basis. For the investor who has multiple purchases of a stock, the likelihood of making an incorrect determination of cost basis is even greater.

A secondary reason for the reporting requirement is to generate more revenue for the Treasury. The government believes that taxpayers are knowingly underreporting capital gains on the sale of securities. The Treasury believes that it will collect an additional $6 billion to $9 billion per year as a result of this requirement. Tax professionals will also benefit by providing consulting related to the requirements—some estimate the related compliance costs will exceed $500 million per year.

As a result of these requirements, the primary burden for determining cost basis is placed on the broker. As a practical matter, however, the ultimate responsibility for reporting the information correctly remains on the taxpayer (and his or her tax adviser).

Source: Based on "Cost Basis Reporting: Why Corporate Issuers (and Not Just Brokers) Should Care," *A&M Tax Advisor Weekly,* **www.taxand.com**, July 14, 2011; Laura Saunders, "When Your Broker 'Outs' You," *Wall Street Journal,* March 2, 2013, p. D3; Tara Siegel Bernard, "New Tax Laws Take Guesswork Out of Investment Tax Liability," *New York Times,* March 15, 2013.

when the taxpayer has purchased separate lots of stock on different dates or at different prices and cannot adequately identify the lot from which a particular sale takes place. In this case, the stock is presumed to come from the first lot or lots purchased (a FIFO presumption).[27] When securities are left in the custody of a broker, it may be necessary to provide specific instructions and receive written confirmation as to which securities are being sold.

Example 10

Polly purchases 100 shares of Olive Corporation stock on July 1, 2012, for $5,000 ($50 a share) and another 100 shares of Olive stock on July 1, 2013, for $6,000 ($60 a share). She sells 50 shares of the stock on January 2, 2014. The cost of the stock sold, assuming that Polly cannot adequately identify the shares, is $50 a share, or $2,500. This is the cost Polly will compare with the amount realized in determining the gain or loss from the sale.

Allocation Problems

When a taxpayer acquires *multiple assets in a lump-sum purchase*, the total cost must be allocated among the individual assets.[28] Allocation is necessary for several reasons:

- Some of the assets acquired may be depreciable (e.g., buildings), while others may not be (e.g., land).
- Only a portion of the assets acquired may be sold.
- Some of the assets may be capital or § 1231 assets that receive special tax treatment upon subsequent sale or other disposition.

The lump-sum cost is allocated on the basis of the fair market values of the individual assets acquired.

---

[27] *Kluger Associates, Inc.,* 69 T.C. 925 (1978). [28] Reg. § 1.61–6(a).

Example 11

Harry purchases a building and land for $800,000. Because of the depressed nature of the industry in which the seller was operating, Harry was able to negotiate a very favorable purchase price. Appraisals of the individual assets indicate that the fair market value of the building is $600,000 and that of the land is $400,000. Harry's basis for the building is $480,000 [($600,000/$1,000,000) × $800,000], and his basis for the land is $320,000 [($400,000/$1,000,000) × $800,000].

If a business is purchased and **goodwill** is involved, a special allocation rule applies. Initially, the purchase price is assigned to the assets, excluding goodwill, to the extent of their total fair market value. This assigned amount is allocated among the assets on the basis of the fair market value of the individual assets acquired. Goodwill is then assigned the residual amount of the purchase price. The resultant allocation is applicable to both the buyer and the seller.[29]

Example 12

Rocky sells his business to Paul. They agree that the values of the individual assets are as follows:

Inventory	$ 50,000
Building	500,000
Land	200,000
Goodwill	150,000

After negotiations, Rocky and Paul agree on a sales price of $1 million. Applying the residual method with respect to goodwill results in the following allocation of the $1 million purchase price:

Inventory	$ 50,000
Building	500,000
Land	200,000
Goodwill	250,000

The residual method requires that all of the excess of the purchase price over the fair market value of the assets ($1,000,000 − $900,000 = $100,000) be allocated to goodwill. Without this requirement, the purchaser could allocate the excess pro rata to all of the assets, including goodwill, based on their respective fair market values. This would have resulted in only $166,667 [$150,000 + ($150,000 ÷ $900,000 × $100,000)] being assigned to goodwill.

In the case of *nontaxable stock dividends,* the allocation depends on whether the dividend is a common stock dividend on common stock or a preferred stock dividend on common stock. If the stock dividend is common on common, the cost of the original common shares is allocated to the total shares owned after the dividend.[30]

Example 13

Susan owns 100 shares of Sparrow Corporation common stock for which she paid $1,100. She receives a 10% common stock dividend, giving her a new total of 110 shares. Before the stock dividend, Susan's basis was $11 per share ($1,100 ÷ 100 shares). The basis of each share after the stock dividend is $10 ($1,100 ÷ 110 shares).

If the nontaxable stock dividend is preferred stock on common, the cost of the original common shares is allocated between the common and preferred shares on the basis of their relative fair market values on the date of distribution.[31]

---

[29]§ 1060. The classification of the seller's recognized gain associated with the goodwill is discussed in Chapter 16.

[30]§§ 305(a) and 307(a).
[31]Reg. § 1.307–1(a).

TAX IN THE NEWS   Frequent-Flyer Miles and Basis

There are many ways to get frequent-flyer miles. Perhaps the most logical is to fly on an airplane, but staying in a hotel, renting a car, and using your credit card can also generate frequent-flyer miles. A more novel approach is to buy shares in a mutual fund.

Always watch out for the tax consequences, though. In a letter ruling, the IRS held that taxpayers who receive frequent-flyer miles for buying mutual fund shares must reduce their mutual fund basis by the fair market value of the miles received. The mutual fund must notify its shareholders of the fair market value, which is based on the cost of buying frequent-flyer miles from the airlines.

© iStockphoto.com/Andrey Prokhorov

Example 14

Fran owns 100 shares of Cardinal Corporation common stock for which she paid $1,000. She receives a nontaxable stock dividend of 50 shares of preferred stock on her common stock. The fair market values on the date of distribution of the preferred stock dividend are $30 a share for common stock and $40 a share for preferred stock.

Fair market value of common ($30 × 100 shares)	$3,000
Fair market value of preferred ($40 × 50 shares)	2,000
	$5,000
Basis of common: 3/5 × $1,000	$ 600
Basis of preferred: 2/5 × $1,000	$ 400

The basis per share for the common stock is $6 ($600/100 shares). The basis per share for the preferred stock is $8 ($400/50 shares).

The holding period for a nontaxable stock dividend, whether received in the form of common stock or preferred stock, includes the holding period of the original shares.[32] The significance of the holding period for capital assets is discussed in Chapter 16.

In the case of *nontaxable stock rights*, the basis of the rights is zero unless the taxpayer elects or is required to allocate a portion of the cost of the stock already held to the newly received stock rights. If the fair market value of the rights is 15 percent or more of the fair market value of the stock, the taxpayer is required to allocate. If the value of the rights is less than 15 percent of the fair market value of the stock, the taxpayer may elect to allocate.[33] When allocation is required or elected, the cost of the stock on which the rights are received is allocated between the stock and the rights on the basis of their relative fair market values.

Example 15

Donald receives nontaxable stock rights with a fair market value of $1,000. The fair market value of the stock on which the rights were received is $8,000 (cost $10,000). Donald does not elect to allocate. The basis of the rights is zero. If he exercises the rights, the basis of the new stock is the exercise (subscription) price.

Example 16

Assume the same facts as in Example 15, except that the fair market value of the rights is $3,000. Donald must allocate because the value of the rights ($3,000) is 15% or more of the value of the stock ($3,000/$8,000 = 37.5%).

- The basis of the stock is $7,273 [($8,000/$11,000) × $10,000].
- The basis of the rights is $2,727 [($3,000/$11,000) × $10,000].

If Donald exercises the rights, the basis of the new stock is the exercise (subscription) price plus the basis of the rights. If he sells the rights, he recognizes gain or loss

---

[32]§ 1223(5) and Reg. § 1.1223–1(e).   [33]§ 307(b).

equal to the difference between the amount realized and the basis of the rights. This allocation rule applies only when the rights are exercised or sold. Therefore, if the rights are allowed to lapse (expire), they have no basis and the basis of the original stock is the stock's cost, $10,000.

The holding period of nontaxable stock rights includes the holding period of the stock on which the rights were distributed. However, if the rights are exercised, the holding period of the newly acquired stock begins with the date the rights are exercised.[34]

14-2b Gift Basis

When a taxpayer receives property as a gift, there is no cost to the donee (recipient). Thus, under the cost basis provision, the donee's basis would be zero. However, this would violate the statutory intent that gifts not be subject to the income tax.[35] With a zero basis, if the donee sold the property, all of the amount realized would be treated as realized gain. Therefore, a basis is assigned to the property received depending on the following:

- The date of the gift.
- The basis of the property to the donor.
- The amount of the gift tax paid.
- The fair market value of the property.

Gift Basis Rules If No Gift Tax Is Paid

Property received by gift can be referred to as *dual basis* property; that is, the basis for gain and the basis for loss might not be the same amount. The present basis rules for gifts of property are as follows:

- If the donee disposes of gift property in a transaction that results in a gain, the basis to the donee is the same as the donor's adjusted basis.[36] The donee's basis in this case is referred to as the *gain basis*. Therefore, a *realized gain* results if the amount realized from the disposition exceeds the donee's gain basis.

> **Example 17**
>
> Melissa purchased stock in 2013 for $10,000. She gave the stock to her son, Joe, in 2014, when the fair market value was $15,000. No gift tax is paid on the transfer, and Joe subsequently sells the property for $15,000. Joe's basis is $10,000, and he has a realized gain of $5,000.

- If the donee disposes of gift property in a transaction that results in a loss, the basis to the donee is the *lower* of the donor's adjusted basis or the fair market value on the date of the gift. The donee's basis in this case is referred to as the *loss basis*. Therefore, a *realized loss* results if the amount realized from the disposition is less than the donee's loss basis.

> **Example 18**
>
> Burt purchased stock in 2013 for $10,000. He gave the stock to his son, Cliff, in 2014, when the fair market value was $7,000. No gift tax is paid on the transfer. Cliff later sells the stock for $6,000. Cliff's basis is $7,000 (fair market value is less than donor's adjusted basis of $10,000), and the realized loss from the sale is $1,000 ($6,000 amount realized − $7,000 basis).

The amount of the loss basis will *differ* from the amount of the gain basis only if, at the date of the gift, the adjusted basis of the property exceeds the property's fair market value. Note that the loss basis rule prevents the donee from receiving a tax

---

[34]§ 1223(5) and Reg. §§ 1.1223–1(e) and (f).

[35]§ 102(a).

[36]§ 1015(a) and Reg. § 1.1015–1(a)(1). See Reg. § 1.1015–1(a)(3) for cases in which the facts necessary to determine the donor's adjusted basis are unknown. Refer to Example 21 for the effect of depreciation deductions by the donee.

benefit from a decline in value that occurred while the donor held the property. Therefore, in Example 18, Cliff has a loss of only $1,000 rather than a loss of $4,000. The $3,000 difference represents the decline in value that occurred while Burt held the property. Ironically, however, the gain basis rule may result in the donee being subject to income tax on the appreciation that occurred while the donor held the property, as illustrated in Example 17.

If the amount realized from a sale or other disposition is *between* the basis for loss and the basis for gain, no gain or loss is realized.

Example 19

Assume the same facts as in Example 18, except that Cliff sells the stock for $8,000. Application of the gain basis rule produces a loss of $2,000 ($8,000 − $10,000). Application of the loss basis rule produces a gain of $1,000 ($8,000 − $7,000). Because the amount realized is between the gain basis and the loss basis, Cliff recognizes neither a gain nor a loss.

Adjustment for Gift Tax

Because of the size of the unified estate and gift tax exemption ($5.34 million in 2014), basis adjustments for gift taxes paid are rare. If, however, gift taxes are paid by the donor, the portion of the gift tax paid that is related to any appreciation is taken into account in determining the donee's gain basis.[37]

For *gifts made before 1977*, the full amount of the gift tax paid is added to the donor's basis, with basis capped at the donor's fair market value at the date of the gift.

Holding Period

The **holding period** for property acquired by gift begins on the date the donor acquired the property if the gain basis rule applies.[38] The holding period starts on the date of the gift if the loss basis rule applies.[39] The significance of the holding period for capital assets is discussed in Chapter 16.

The following example summarizes the basis and holding period rules for gift property:

Example 20

Jill acquired 100 shares of Wren Corporation stock on December 30, 1996, for $40,000. On January 3, 2014, when the stock has a fair market value of $38,000, Jill gives it to Dennis and pays gift tax of $4,000. The basis is not increased by a portion of the gift tax paid because the property has not appreciated in value at the time of the gift. Therefore, Dennis's gain basis is $40,000. Dennis's basis for determining loss is $38,000 (fair market value) because the fair market value on the date of the gift is less than the donor's adjusted basis.

- If Dennis sells the stock for $45,000, he has a recognized gain of $5,000. The holding period for determining whether the capital gain is short-term or long-term begins on December 30, 1996, the date Jill acquired the property.
- If Dennis sells the stock for $36,000, he has a recognized loss of $2,000. The holding period for determining whether the capital loss is short-term or long-term begins on January 3, 2014, the date of the gift.
- If Dennis sells the property for $39,000, there is no gain or loss because the amount realized is less than the gain basis of $40,000 and more than the loss basis of $38,000.

Basis for Depreciation

The basis for depreciation on depreciable gift property is the donee's gain basis.[40] This rule is applicable even if the donee later sells the property at a loss and uses the loss basis rule in calculating the amount of the realized loss.

---

[37]§ 1015(d)(6) and Reg. § 1.1015–5(c)(2). Examples illustrating these rules can be found in Reg. § 1.1015–5(c)(5) and IRS Publication 551 (Basis of Assets), p. 9.

[38]§ 1223(2) and Reg. § 1.1223–1(b).
[39]Rev.Rul. 59–86, 1959–1 C.B. 209.
[40]§ 1011 and Reg. §§ 1.1011–1 and 1.167(g)–1.

Example 21

Vito gave a machine to Tina in 2014. At that time, the adjusted basis was $32,000 (cost of $40,000 − accumulated depreciation of $8,000), and the fair market value was $26,000. No gift tax was paid. Tina's gain basis at the date of the gift is $32,000, and her loss basis is $26,000. During 2014, Tina deducts depreciation (cost recovery) of $6,400 ($32,000 × 20%). (Refer to Chapter 8 for the cost recovery tables.) At the end of 2014, Tina's gain basis and loss basis are calculated as follows:

	Gain Basis	Loss Basis
Donor's basis or fair market value	$32,000	$26,000
Depreciation	(6,400)	(6,400)
	$25,600	$19,600

14-2c Property Acquired from a Decedent

General Rules

The basis of property acquired from a decedent is generally the property's fair market value at the date of death (referred to as the *primary valuation amount*).[41] The property's basis is the fair market value six months after the date of death if the executor or administrator of the estate *elects* the alternate valuation date for estate tax purposes. This amount is referred to as the *alternate valuation amount.*

Return to the facts of *The Big Picture* on p. 14-1. Alice and various other family members inherited property from Alice's mother, who died in 2013. At the date of death, the mother's adjusted basis for the property Alice inherited—her mother's house—was $275,000. The house's fair market value at the date of death was $475,000. The alternate valuation date was not elected. Alice's basis for income tax purposes is $475,000. This is commonly referred to as a *stepped-up basis.*

Assume the same facts as in Example 22, except that the house's fair market value at the date of the mother's death was $260,000. Alice's basis for income tax purposes is $260,000. This is commonly referred to as a *stepped-down basis.*

No estate tax return must be filed for estates below a threshold amount. In such cases, the alternate valuation date and amount are not available. Even if an estate tax return is filed and the executor elects the alternate valuation date, the six months after death date is available only for property that the executor has not distributed before this date. For any property distributed or otherwise disposed of by the executor during the six-month period preceding the alternate valuation date, the adjusted basis to the beneficiary will equal the fair market value on the date of distribution or other disposition.[42]

The alternate valuation date can be elected *only if*, as a result of the election, both the value of the gross estate and the estate tax liability are lower than they would have been if the primary valuation date had been used. This provision

---

[41]§§ 1014(a) and 1022.

[42]§ 2032(a)(1) and Rev.Rul. 56–60, 1956–1 C.B. 443.

prevents the alternate valuation election from being used to increase the basis of the property to the beneficiary for income tax purposes without simultaneously increasing the estate tax liability (because of estate tax deductions or credits).[43]

Example 24

Nancy inherited all of the property of her father, who died in 2013. Her father's adjusted basis for the property at the date of death was $650,000. The property's fair market value was $3,750,000 at the date of death and $3,760,000 six months after death. The alternate valuation date cannot be elected because the value of the gross estate has increased during the six-month period. Nancy's basis for income tax purposes is $3,750,000.

Example 25

Assume the same facts as in Example 24, except that the property's fair market value six months after death was $3,745,000. If the executor elects the alternate valuation date, Nancy's basis for income tax purposes is $3,745,000.

Example 26

Assume the same facts as in the previous example, except that the property is distributed four months after the date of the decedent's death. At the distribution date, the property's fair market value is $3,747,500. Because the executor elected the alternate valuation date, Nancy's basis for income tax purposes is $3,747,500.

For inherited property, both unrealized appreciation and decline in value are taken into consideration in determining the basis of the property for income tax purposes. Contrast this with the carryover basis rules for property received by gift.

Income in Respect of a Decedent

Income in respect of a decedent (IRD) is income earned by a decedent to the point of death but not reportable on the final income tax return under the method of accounting used. IRD is most frequently applicable to decedents using the cash basis of accounting. IRD also occurs, for example, when a taxpayer at the time of death held installment notes receivable on which the gain has been deferred. For both cash and accrual taxpayers, IRD includes most post-death distributions from retirement plans [e.g., traditional IRA, § 401(k), H.R. 10 (Keogh), § 403(b), and other qualified plans]. With the exception of Roth IRAs, distributions from retirement plans invariably contain an income component that has not yet been subject to income tax.

Example 27

George, age 58, was entitled to a salary payment of $18,000 and a bonus of $20,000 at the time of his death. In addition, George had been contributing to a traditional IRA for over 20 years. The IRA has a basis of $83,000 (due to some nondeductible contributions over the years) and a current value of $560,000. George's estate collects the salary and bonus payments, and George's wife (his only beneficiary) cashes in the IRA.

Both the estate and George's wife have income in respect of a decedent (IRD) and must include ordinary income in their computation of taxable income for the year. The estate has IRD of $38,000 (salary of $18,000 plus bonus of $20,000), and George's wife has IRD of $477,000 ($560,000 proceeds less $83,000 basis). A better outcome might be achieved for George's wife if she rolled over the inherited IRA into an IRA in her name and deferred receiving distributions until required. (Note: Only a surviving spouse can roll over an inherited IRA without tax consequences.[44])

IRD is included in the gross estate at its fair market value on the appropriate valuation date. Because IRD is not subject to the step-up or step-down rules applicable to property passed by death, the income tax basis of the decedent transfers to the estate or heirs.[45] Furthermore, the recipient of IRD must classify it in the same manner (e.g., ordinary income or capital gain) as the decedent would have.[46]

[43]§ 2032(c).

[44]See *South-Western Federal Taxation: Corporations, Partnerships, Estates, & Trusts,* 2015 Edition, Chapter 19, for additional information.

[45]§ 1014(c).

[46]§ 691(a)(3).

Survivor's Share of Property

Both the decedent's share and the survivor's share of *community property* have a basis equal to the fair market value on the date of the decedent's death.[47] This result applies to the decedent's share of the community property because the property is included in the estate and assumes a fair market value basis. Because the surviving spouse's share of the community property is treated as if it is acquired from the decedent, it also has a basis equal to the fair market value.

Example 28

Floyd and Vera are married and reside in a community property state. They own as community property 200 shares of Crow stock acquired in 1989 for $100,000. Floyd dies in 2014, when the securities are valued at $300,000. One-half of the Crow stock is included in Floyd's estate. If Vera inherits Floyd's share of the community property, the basis for gain or loss is $300,000, determined as follows:

Vera's one-half of the community property (stepped up from $50,000 to $150,000 due to Floyd's death)	$150,000
Floyd's one-half of the community property (stepped up from $50,000 to $150,000 due to inclusion in his gross estate)	150,000
Vera's new basis	$300,000

In a *common law* state, only one-half of jointly held property of spouses (tenants by the entirety or joint tenants with rights of survivorship) is included in the estate.[48] In such a case, no adjustment of the basis is permitted for the excluded property interest (the surviving spouse's share).

Example 29

Assume the same facts as in the previous example, except that the property is jointly held by Floyd and Vera who reside in a common law state. Floyd purchased the property and made a gift of one-half of the property to Vera when the stock was acquired. No gift tax was paid. Only one-half of the Crow stock is included in Floyd's estate. Vera's basis for determining gain or loss in the excluded half is not adjusted upward for the increase in value to date of death. Therefore, Vera's basis is $200,000, determined as follows:

Vera's one-half of the jointly held property (carryover basis of $50,000)	$ 50,000
Floyd's one-half of the jointly held property (stepped up from $50,000 to $150,000 due to inclusion in his gross estate)	150,000
Vera's new basis	$200,000

Holding Period of Property Acquired from a Decedent

The holding period of property acquired from a decedent is *deemed to be long-term* (held for the required long-term holding period). This provision applies regardless of whether the property is disposed of at a gain or at a loss.[49]

14-2d Disallowed Losses

Related Taxpayers

LO.4

Describe various loss disallowance provisions.

Section 267 provides that realized losses from sales or exchanges of property, directly or indirectly, between certain related parties are not recognized. This loss disallowance provision applies to several types of related-party transactions. The most common involve (1) members of a family and (2) an individual and a corporation in which the individual owns, directly or indirectly, more than 50 percent in value of the corporation's outstanding stock. Section 707 provides a similar loss disallowance provision where the related parties are a partner and a partnership in which the partner owns, directly or indirectly, more than 50 percent of the capital interests

---

[47]§ 1014(b)(6). See the listing of community property states in Chapter 4.   [49]§ 1223(11).
[48]§ 2040(b).

or profits interests in the partnership. The rules governing the relationships covered by § 267 were discussed in Chapter 6. See Chapter 15 for a discussion of the special rules under § 1041 for property transfers between spouses or incident to divorce.

If income-producing or business property is transferred to a related taxpayer and a loss is disallowed, the basis of the property to the recipient is the property's cost to the transferee. However, if a subsequent sale or other disposition of the property by the original transferee results in a realized gain, the amount of gain is reduced by the loss that was previously disallowed.[50] This *right of offset* is not applicable if the original sale involved the sale of a personal use asset (e.g., the sale of a personal residence between related taxpayers). Furthermore, the right of offset is available only to the original transferee (the related-party buyer).

Example 30	Pedro sells business property with an adjusted basis of $50,000 to his daughter, Josefina, for its fair market value of $40,000. Pedro's realized loss of $10,000 is not recognized.

- How much gain does Josefina recognize if she sells the property for $52,000? Josefina recognizes a $2,000 gain. Her realized gain is $12,000 ($52,000 less her basis of $40,000), but she can offset Pedro's $10,000 loss against the gain.
- How much gain does Josefina recognize if she sells the property for $48,000? Josefina recognizes no gain or loss. Her realized gain is $8,000 ($48,000 less her basis of $40,000), but she can offset $8,000 of Pedro's $10,000 loss against the gain. Note that Pedro's loss can only offset Josefina's gain. It cannot create a loss for Josefina.
- How much loss does Josefina recognize if she sells the property for $38,000? Josefina recognizes a $2,000 loss, the same as her realized loss ($38,000 less $40,000 basis). Pedro's loss does not increase Josefina's loss. His loss can be offset only against a gain. Because Josefina has no realized gain, Pedro's loss cannot be used and is never recognized. This part of the example assumes that the property is business or income-producing property to Josefina. If not, her $2,000 loss is personal and is not recognized.

The loss disallowance rules are designed to achieve two objectives. First, the rules prevent a taxpayer from directly transferring an unrealized loss to a related taxpayer in a higher tax bracket who could receive a greater tax benefit from recognition of the loss. Second, the rules eliminate a substantial administrative burden on the Internal Revenue Service as to the appropriateness of the selling price (fair market value or not). The loss disallowance rules are applicable even where the selling price is equal to the fair market value and can be validated (e.g., listed stocks).

The holding period of the buyer for the property is not affected by the holding period of the seller. That is, the buyer's *holding period* includes only the period of time he or she has held the property.[51]

Wash Sales

Section 1091 stipulates that in certain cases, a realized loss on the sale or exchange of stock or securities is not recognized. Specifically, if a taxpayer sells or exchanges stock or securities and within 30 days before *or* after the date of the sale or exchange acquires substantially identical stock or securities, any loss realized from the sale or exchange is not recognized because the transaction is a **wash sale**.[52] The term *acquire* means acquire by purchase or in a taxable exchange and includes an option to purchase substantially identical securities. *Substantially identical* means the same in all important particulars. Corporate bonds and preferred stock normally are not considered substantially identical to the corporation's common stock. However, if the bonds and preferred stock are convertible into common stock, they may be considered substantially identical under certain circumstances.[53] Attempts to avoid the application of the wash sales rules by having a related taxpayer repurchase the securities have been unsuccessful.[54] The wash sales provisions do *not* apply to gains.

[50]§ 267(d) and Reg. § 1.267(d)–1(a).

[51]§§ 267(d) and 1223(2) and Reg. § 1.267(d)–1(c)(3).

[52]§ 1091(a) and Reg. §§ 1.1091–1(a) and (f).

[53]Rev.Rul. 56–406, 1956–2 C.B. 523.

[54]*McWilliams v. Comm.*, 47–1 USTC ¶9289, 35 AFTR 1184, 67 S.Ct. 1477 (USSC, 1947).

Recognition of the loss is disallowed because the taxpayer is considered to be in substantially the same economic position after the sale and repurchase as before the sale and repurchase. This disallowance rule does not apply to taxpayers engaged in the business of buying and selling securities.[55] Investors, however, are not allowed to create losses through wash sales to offset income for tax purposes.

Realized loss that is not recognized is added to the *basis* of the substantially identical stock or securities whose acquisition resulted in the nonrecognition of loss.[56] In other words, the basis of the replacement stock or securities is increased by the amount of the unrecognized loss. If the loss were not added to the basis of the newly acquired stock or securities, the taxpayer would never recover the entire basis of the old stock or securities.

The basis of the new stock or securities includes the unrecovered portion of the basis of the formerly held stock or securities. Therefore, the *holding period* of the new stock or securities begins on the date of acquisition of the old stock or securities.[57]

THE BIG PICTURE

Example 31

Return to the facts of *The Big Picture* on p. 14-1. Alice owned 100 shares of Green Corporation stock (adjusted basis of $20,000). She sold 50 shares for $8,000. Ten days later, she purchased 50 shares of the same stock for $7,000. Alice's realized loss of $2,000 ($8,000 amount realized − $10,000 adjusted basis of 50 shares) is not recognized because it resulted from a wash sale. Alice's basis in the newly acquired stock is $9,000 ($7,000 purchase price + $2,000 unrecognized loss from the wash sale).

A taxpayer may acquire fewer shares than the number sold in a wash sale. In this case, the loss from the sale is prorated between recognized and unrecognized loss on the basis of the ratio of the number of shares acquired to the number of shares sold.[58]

ETHICS & EQUITY   Drying Out a Wash Sale

Webb owned 1,000 shares of Taupe, Inc. stock that he had purchased three years ago for $50,000. Due to financial problems, he sold the stock on October 5, 2014, for $48,000. Although the stock had declined in value, Webb viewed it as a good long-term investment. After he unexpectedly inherited $200,000 from an uncle, he reacquired 3,000 shares of Taupe stock on November 1, 2014, for $156,000.

In a conversation with a friend who is actively involved in day trading, Webb becomes aware of the wash sales rules. To avoid the disallowance of the $2,000 loss on the October 5 sale, on November 3, 2014, Webb sells 1,000 of the 3,000 shares purchased on November 1, 2014, for $53,000.

Webb intends to show a $2,000 ($48,000 − $50,000) capital loss and a $1,000 ($53,000 − $52,000) capital gain on his 2014 tax return. Evaluate Webb's treatment of these stock transactions.

14-2e Conversion of Property from Personal Use to Business or Income-Producing Use

As discussed previously, losses from the sale of personal use assets are not recognized for tax purposes, but losses from the sale of business and income-producing assets are deductible. Can a taxpayer convert a personal use asset that has declined in value to business or income-producing use and then sell the asset to recognize a business or income-producing loss? The tax law prevents this practice by specifying

---

[55]Reg. § 1.1091–1(a).
[56]§ 1091(d) and Reg. § 1.1091–2(a).
[57]§ 1223(4) and Reg. § 1.1223–1(d).
[58]§ 1091(b) and Reg. § 1.1091–1(c).

TAX IN THE NEWS   Triple the Misery!

Although short sales have traditionally involved stocks, today the term *short sale* also refers to the sale of a personal residence by a homeowner who is "underwater," owing more on the home than it is worth. In a short sale, the homeowner sells the residence for its fair market value, which is less than the mortgage (or mortgages) on the property. One possible result of this transaction is that the taxpayer incurs a realized loss—the selling price is less than his or her basis in the property. Unfortunately, the realized loss cannot be recognized because a residence is a personal use asset. To add to the trauma of losing the home in a nondeductible loss sale, the mortgage company may require the taxpayer to keep paying on the portion of the mortgage still outstanding (i.e., the amount of the mortgage in excess of the net sales price). Thus, the taxpayer has triple misery: no home, a nondeductible loss, and an outstanding debt to pay.

that the *original basis for loss* on personal use assets converted to business or income-producing use is the *lower* of the property's adjusted basis or fair market value on the date of conversion.[59] The *gain basis* for converted property is the property's adjusted basis on the date of conversion. The tax law is not concerned with gains on converted property because gains are recognized regardless of whether property is business, income-producing, or personal use.

Example 32

Diane's personal residence has an adjusted basis of $175,000 and a fair market value of $160,000. Diane converts the personal residence to rental property. Her basis for loss is $160,000 (lower of $175,000 adjusted basis and fair market value of $160,000). The $15,000 decline in value is a personal loss and can never be recognized for tax purposes. Diane's basis for gain is $175,000.

The basis for loss is also the *basis for depreciating* the converted property.[60] This is an exception to the general rule that the basis for depreciation is the gain basis (e.g., property received by gift). This exception prevents the taxpayer from recovering a personal loss indirectly through depreciation of the higher original basis. After the property is converted, both its basis for loss and its basis for gain are adjusted for depreciation deductions from the date of conversion to the date of disposition. These rules apply only if a conversion from personal to business or income-producing use has actually occurred.

Example 33

At a time when his personal residence (adjusted basis of $140,000) is worth $150,000, Keith converts one-half of it to rental use. Assume that the property is not MACRS recovery property. At this point, the estimated useful life of the residence is 20 years, and there is no estimated salvage value. After renting the converted portion for five years, Keith sells the property for $144,000. All amounts relate only to the building; the land has been accounted for separately. Keith has a $2,000 realized gain from the sale of the personal use portion of the residence and a $19,500 realized gain from the sale of the rental portion. These gains are computed as follows:

	Personal Use	Rental
Original basis for gain and loss—adjusted basis on date of conversion (fair market value is greater than the adjusted basis)	$70,000	$ 70,000
Depreciation—five years	(–0–)	(17,500)
Adjusted basis—date of sale	$70,000	$ 52,500
Amount realized	72,000	72,000
Realized gain	$ 2,000	$ 19,500

As discussed in Chapter 15, Keith may be able to exclude the $2,000 realized gain from the sale of the personal use portion of the residence under § 121. If the § 121 exclusion applies, only $17,500 (equal to the depreciation deducted) of the $19,500 realized gain from the rental portion is recognized.

Example 34

Assume the same facts as in the previous example, except that the fair market value on the date of conversion is $130,000 and the sales proceeds are $90,000. Keith has a $25,000 realized loss from the sale of the personal use portion of the residence and a $3,750 realized loss from the sale of the rental portion. These losses are computed as follows:

	Personal Use	Rental
Original basis for loss—fair market value on date of conversion (fair market value is less than the adjusted basis)	*	$ 65,000
Depreciation—five years	(–0–)	(16,250)
Adjusted basis—date of sale	$70,000	$ 48,750
Amount realized	45,000	45,000
Realized loss	($25,000)	($ 3,750)

*Not applicable.

The $25,000 loss from the sale of the personal use portion of the residence is not recognized. The $3,750 loss from the rental portion is recognized.

14-2f Additional Complexities in Determining Realized Gain or Loss

Amount Realized

The calculation of the amount realized may appear to be one of the least complex areas associated with property transactions. However, because numerous positive and negative adjustments may be required, this calculation can be complex and confusing. In addition, determining the fair market value of the items received by the taxpayer can be difficult. The following example provides insight into various items that can affect the amount realized.

Example 35

Ridge sells an office building and the associated land on October 1, 2014. Under the terms of the sales contract, Ridge is to receive $600,000 in cash. The purchaser is to assume Ridge's mortgage of $300,000 on the property. To enable the purchaser to obtain adequate financing, Ridge is to pay the $15,000 in points charged by the lender. The broker's commission on the sale is $45,000. The purchaser agrees to pay the $12,000 in property taxes for the entire year. The amount realized by Ridge is determined as follows:

Selling price		
Cash	$600,000	
Mortgage assumed by purchaser	300,000	
Seller's property taxes paid by purchaser ($12,000 × 9/12)	9,000	$909,000
Less		
Broker's commission	$ 45,000	
Points paid by seller	15,000	(60,000)
Amount realized		$849,000

Adjusted Basis

Three types of issues tend to complicate the determination of adjusted basis. First, the applicable tax provisions for calculating the adjusted basis depend on how the property was acquired (e.g., purchase, taxable exchange, nontaxable exchange, gift, or inheritance). Second, if the asset is subject to depreciation, cost recovery, amortization, or depletion, adjustments must be made to the basis during the time period the asset is held by the taxpayer. Upon disposition of the asset, the taxpayer's records for both of these items may be deficient. For example, the donee does not know the amount of the donor's basis or the amount of gift tax paid by the donor, or the taxpayer does not know how much depreciation he or she has deducted. Third, the complex positive and negative adjustments encountered in calculating the amount realized are also involved in calculating the adjusted basis.

Example 36

Jane purchased a personal residence in 2005. The purchase price and the related closing costs were as follows:

Purchase price	$325,000
Recording costs	140
Title fees and title insurance	815
Survey costs	225
Attorney's fees	750
Appraisal fee	250

Other relevant tax information for the house during the time Jane owned it is as follows:

- Constructed a swimming pool for medical reasons. The cost was $20,000, of which $5,000 was deducted as a medical expense.
- Added a solar heating system. The cost was $18,000.
- Deducted home office expenses of $6,000. Of this amount, $5,200 was for depreciation.

The adjusted basis for the house is calculated as follows:

Purchase price	$325,000
Recording costs	140
Title fees and title insurance	815
Survey costs	225
Attorney's fees	750
Appraisal fee	250
Swimming pool ($20,000 − $5,000)	15,000
Solar heating system	18,000
	$360,180
Less: Depreciation deducted on home office	(5,200)
Adjusted basis	$354,980

14-2g Summary of Basis Adjustments

Some of the more common items that either increase or decrease the basis of an asset appear in Concept Summary 14.2.

In discussing the topic of basis, a number of specific techniques for determining basis have been presented. Although the various techniques are responsive to and mandated by transactions occurring in the marketplace, they do possess enough common characteristics to be categorized as follows:

- The basis of the asset may be determined by reference to the asset's cost.
- The basis of the asset may be determined by reference to the basis of another asset.
- The basis of the asset may be determined by reference to the asset's fair market value.
- The basis of the asset may be determined by reference to the basis of the asset to another taxpayer.

CONCEPT SUMMARY 14.2

Adjustments to Basis

Item	Effect	Refer to Chapter	Explanation
Amortization of bond discount.	Increase	16	Amortization is mandatory for certain taxable bonds and elective for tax-exempt bonds.
Amortization of bond premium.	Decrease	14	Amortization is mandatory for tax-exempt bonds and elective for taxable bonds.
Amortization of covenant not to compete.	Decrease	8	Covenant must be for a definite and limited time period. The amortization period is a statutory period of 15 years.
Amortization of intangibles.	Decrease	8	Intangibles are amortized over a 15-year period.
Assessment for local benefits.	Increase	10	To the extent not deductible as taxes (e.g., assessment for streets and sidewalks that increase the value of the property versus one for maintenance or repair or for meeting interest charges).
Bad debts.	Decrease	7	Only the specific charge-off method is permitted.
Capital additions.	Increase	14	Certain items, at the taxpayer's election, can be capitalized or deducted (e.g., selected medical expenses).
Casualty.	Decrease	7	For a casualty loss, the amount of the adjustment is the sum of the deductible loss and the insurance proceeds received. For a casualty gain, the amount of the adjustment is the insurance proceeds received reduced by the recognized gain.
Condemnation.	Decrease	15	See casualty explanation.
Cost recovery.	Decrease	8	§ 168 is applicable to tangible assets placed in service after 1980 whose useful life is expressed in terms of years.
Depletion.	Decrease	8	Use the greater of cost or percentage depletion. Percentage depletion can still be deducted when the basis is zero.
Depreciation.	Decrease	8	§ 167 is applicable to tangible assets placed in service before 1981 and to tangible assets not depreciated in terms of years.
Easement.	Decrease	14	If the taxpayer does not retain any use of the land, all of the basis is allocable to the easement transaction. However, if only part of the land is affected by the easement, only part of the basis is allocable to the easement transaction.
Improvements by lessee to lessor's property.	Increase	5	Adjustment occurs only if the lessor is required to include the fair market value of the improvements in gross income under § 109.
Imputed interest.	Decrease	18	Amount deducted is not part of the cost of the asset.
Inventory: lower of cost or market.	Decrease	18	Not available if the LIFO method is used.
Limited expensing under § 179.	Decrease	8	Occurs only if the taxpayer elects § 179 treatment.
Medical capital expenditure permitted as a medical expense.	Decrease	10	Adjustment is the amount of the deduction (the effect on basis is to increase it by the amount of the capital expenditure net of the deduction).
Real estate taxes: apportionment between the buyer and seller.	Increase or decrease	10	To the extent the buyer pays the seller's pro rata share, the buyer's basis is increased. To the extent the seller pays the buyer's pro rata share, the buyer's basis is decreased.
Rebate from manufacturer.	Decrease		Because the rebate is treated as an adjustment to the purchase price, it is not included in the buyer's gross income.
Stock dividend.	Decrease	5	Adjustment occurs only if the stock dividend is nontaxable. While the basis per share decreases, the total stock basis does not change.
Stock rights.	Decrease	14	Adjustment to stock basis occurs only for nontaxable stock rights and only if the fair market value of the rights is at least 15% of the fair market value of the stock or, if less than 15%, the taxpayer elects to allocate the basis between the stock and the rights.
Theft.	Decrease	7	See casualty explanation.

14-3 TAX PLANNING

14-3a Cost Identification and Documentation Considerations

When multiple assets are acquired in a single transaction, the contract price must be allocated for several reasons. First, some of the assets may be depreciable, while others are not. From the different viewpoints of the buyer and the seller, this may produce a tax conflict that needs to be resolved. That is, the seller prefers a high allocation for nondepreciable assets, whereas the purchaser prefers a high allocation for depreciable assets (see Chapters 16 and 17). Second, the seller needs to know the amount realized on the sale of the capital assets and the ordinary income assets so that the recognized gains and losses can be classified as capital or ordinary. For example, an allocation to goodwill or to a covenant not to compete (see Chapters 8, 16, and 17) produces different tax consequences to the seller. Third, the buyer needs the adjusted basis of each asset to calculate the realized gain or loss on a subsequent sale or other disposition of each asset.

14-3b Selection of Property for Making Gifts

A donor can achieve several tax advantages by making gifts of appreciated property. The donor avoids income tax on the unrealized gain that would have occurred had the donor sold the property. A portion of this amount can be permanently avoided because the donee's adjusted basis is increased by part or all of any gift tax paid by the donor. Even without this increase in basis, the income tax liability on the sale of the property by the donee can be less than the income tax liability that would have resulted from the donor's sale of the property, if the donee is in a lower tax bracket than the donor. In addition, any subsequent appreciation during the time the property is held by the lower tax bracket donee results in a tax savings on the sale or other disposition of the property. Such gifts of appreciated property can be an effective tool in family tax planning.

Taxpayers should generally not make gifts of depreciated property (property that, if sold, would produce a realized loss) because the donor does not receive an income tax deduction for the unrealized loss element. In addition, the donee receives no benefit from this unrealized loss upon the subsequent sale of the property because of the loss basis rule. The loss basis rule provides that the donee's basis is the lower of the donor's basis or the fair market value at the date of the gift. If the donor anticipates that the donee will sell the property upon receiving it, the donor should sell the property and take the loss deduction, assuming the loss is deductible. The donor can then give the proceeds from the sale to the donee.

14-3c Selection of Property for Making Bequests

A taxpayer should generally make bequests of appreciated property in his or her will. Doing so enables both the decedent and the heir to avoid income tax on the unrealized gain because the recipient takes the fair market value as his or her basis.

Taxpayers generally should not make bequests of depreciated property (property that, if sold, would produce a realized loss) because the decedent does not receive an income tax deduction for the unrealized loss element. In addition, the heir will receive no benefit from this unrealized loss upon the subsequent sale of the property.

Example 37

On the date of her death in 2014, Marta owned land held for investment purposes. The land had an adjusted basis of $130,000 and a fair market value of $100,000. If Marta had sold the property before her death, the recognized loss would have been $30,000. If Roger inherits the property and later sells it for $90,000, the recognized loss is $10,000 (the decline in value since Marta's death). In addition, regardless of the period of time Roger holds the property, the holding period is long-term (see Chapter 16).

From an income tax perspective, it is preferable to transfer appreciated property as a bequest rather than as a gift. The reason is that inherited property receives a step-up in basis, whereas property received by gift has a carryover basis to the donee. However, in making this decision, the estate tax consequences of the bequest should also be weighed against the gift tax consequences of the gift.

14-3d Disallowed Losses

Section 267 Disallowed Losses

Taxpayers should be aware of the desirability of avoiding transactions that activate the loss disallowance provisions for related parties. This is so even in light of the provision that permits the related-party buyer to offset his or her realized gain by the related-party seller's disallowed loss. Even with this offset, several inequities exist. First, the tax benefit associated with the disallowed loss ultimately is realized by the wrong party (the related-party buyer rather than the related-party seller). Second, the tax benefit of this offset to the related-party buyer does not occur until the buyer disposes of the property. Therefore, the longer the time period between the purchase and disposition of the property by the related-party buyer, the less the economic benefit. Third, if the property does not appreciate to at least its adjusted basis to the related-party seller during the time period the related-party buyer holds it, part or all of the disallowed loss is permanently lost. Fourth, because the right of offset is available only to the original transferee (the related-party buyer), all of the disallowed loss is permanently lost if the original transferee subsequently transfers the property by gift or bequest.

Tim sells property with an adjusted basis of $35,000 to Wes, his brother, for $25,000, the fair market value of the property. The $10,000 realized loss to Tim is disallowed by § 267. If Wes subsequently sells the property to an unrelated party for $37,000, he has a recognized gain of $2,000 (realized gain of $12,000 reduced by disallowed loss of $10,000). Therefore, from the perspective of the family unit, the original $10,000 realized loss ultimately is recognized. However, if Wes sells the property for $29,000, he has a recognized gain of $0 (realized gain of $4,000 reduced by disallowed loss of $4,000 necessary to offset the realized gain). From the perspective of the family unit, $6,000 of the realized loss of $10,000 is permanently wasted ($10,000 realized loss − $4,000 offset permitted).

Example 38

Wash Sales

The wash sales provisions can be avoided if the security that was sold is replaced within the statutory time period with a similar rather than a substantially identical security. For example, a sale of Dell, Inc. common stock accompanied by a purchase of Hewlett-Packard common stock is not treated as a wash sale. Such a procedure can enable the taxpayer to use an unrealized capital loss to offset a recognized capital gain. The taxpayer can sell the security before the end of the taxable year, offset the recognized capital loss against the capital gain, and invest the sales proceeds in a similar security.

Because the wash sales provisions do not apply to gains, it may be desirable to engage in a wash sale before the end of the taxable year. The recognized capital gain may be used to offset capital losses or capital loss carryovers from prior years. Because the basis of the replacement stock or securities will be the purchase price, the taxpayer in effect has exchanged a capital gain for an increased basis for the stock or securities.

ETHICS & EQUITY   Washing a Loss Using an IRA

Sam owns 1,500 shares of Eagle, Inc. stock that he purchased over ten years ago for $80,000. Although the stock has a current market value of $52,000, Sam still views the stock as a solid long-term investment. He has sold other stock during the year with overall gains of $30,000, so he would like to sell the Eagle stock and offset the $28,000 loss against these gains—but somehow keep his Eagle investment. He has devised a plan to keep his Eagle investment by using funds in his traditional IRA to purchase 1,500 Eagle shares immediately after selling the shares he currently owns. Evaluate Sam's treatment of these stock transactions. Can his plan work?

REFOCUS ON THE BIG PICTURE

PROPOSED SALE OF A HOUSE AND OTHER PROPERTY TRANSACTIONS

Alice's tax adviser asked a number of questions to advise her on her proposed transaction for the house. Alice provided the following answers (refer to Example 22):

- Alice inherited the house from her mother. The fair market value of the house at the date of her mother's death, based on the estate tax return, was $475,000. Based on an appraisal, the house currently is worth $485,000. Alice's mother lived in the house for 38 years. According to the mother's attorney, her adjusted basis for the house was $275,000.
- As a child, Alice lived in the house for 10 years. She has not lived there during the 25 years she has been married.
- The house has been vacant during the seven months Alice has owned it. She has been trying to decide whether she should sell it for its fair market value or sell it to her nephew for $275,000. Alice has suggested a $275,000 price for the sale to Dan because she believes this is the amount at which she will have no gain or loss.
- Alice intends to invest the $275,000 in stock.

You advise Alice that her adjusted basis for the house is the $475,000 fair market value on the date of her mother's death. If Alice sells the house for $485,000 (assuming no selling expenses), she would have a recognized gain of $10,000 ($485,000 amount realized − $475,000 adjusted basis). The house is a capital asset, and Alice's holding period is long-term because she inherited the house. Thus, the gain would be classified as a long-term capital gain. If, instead, Alice sells the house to her nephew for $275,000, she will have a part sale and part gift. The realized gain on the sale of $5,670 is recognized.

© Michael Courtney/iStockphoto.com

Amount realized	$ 275,000
Less: Adjusted basis	(269,330)*
Realized gain	$ 5,670
Recognized gain	$ 5,670

*[($275,000/$485,000) × $475,000] = $269,330.

The gain is classified as a long-term capital gain. Alice is then deemed to have made a gift to Dan of $210,000 ($485,000 − $275,000). With this information, Alice can make an informed selection between the two options.

See Examples 7 and 8 for the tax consequences associated with Alice's questions regarding selling the boat. See Example 31 for the tax consequences associated with Alice's questions regarding the wash sale of the stock.

Key Terms

Adjusted basis, 14-3

Amount realized, 14-3

Fair market value, 14-3

Goodwill, 14-9

Holding period, 14-12

Realized gain, 14-2

Realized loss, 14-2

Recognized gain, 14-5

Recognized loss, 14-5

Wash sale, 14-16

Discussion Questions

1. **LO.1** Upon the sale or other disposition of property, what four questions should be considered for income tax purposes?

2. **LO.1** A realized gain occurs when the amount realized is greater than the adjusted basis, and a realized loss occurs when the adjusted basis is greater than the amount realized. Evaluate this statement.

3. **LO.1** In addition to sales and exchanges, what other transactions are treated as dispositions of property?

4. **LO.1** Ivan invests in land, and Grace invests in taxable bonds. The land appreciates by $8,000 each year, and the bonds earn interest of $8,000 each year. After holding the land and bonds for five years, Ivan and Grace sell them. There is a $40,000 realized gain on the sale of the land and no realized gain or loss on the sale of the bonds. Are the tax consequences to Ivan and Grace the same for each of the five years? Explain.

Decision Making

5. **LO.1** Carol and Dave each purchase 100 shares of stock of Burgundy, Inc., a publicly owned corporation, in July for $10,000 each. Carol sells her stock on December 31 for $8,000. Because Burgundy's stock is listed on a national exchange, Dave is able to ascertain that his shares are worth $8,000 on December 31. Does the tax law treat the decline in value of the stock differently for Carol and Dave? Explain.

6. **LO.1** If a taxpayer sells property for cash, the amount realized consists of the net proceeds from the sale. For each of the following, indicate the effect on the amount realized:
   a. The property is sold on credit.
   b. A mortgage on the property is assumed by the buyer.
   c. A mortgage on the property is assumed by the seller.
   d. The buyer acquires the property subject to a mortgage of the seller.
   e. Stock that has a basis to the purchaser of $6,000 and a fair market value of $10,000 is received by the seller as part of the consideration.

7. **LO.1** Sally owns real property for which the annual property taxes are $8,000. She sells the property to Shelley on February 28, 2014, for $550,000. Shelley pays the real property taxes for the entire year on October 1.
   a. How much of the property taxes can be deducted by Sally and how much by Shelley?
   b. What effect does the property tax apportionment have on Shelley's adjusted basis in the property?
   c. What effect does the apportionment have on Sally's amount realized from the sale?
   d. How would the answers in (b) and (c) differ if the taxes were paid by Sally?

8. **LO.1** Taylor is negotiating to buy some land. Under the first option, Taylor will give Ella $150,000 and assume her mortgage on the land for $100,000. Under the second option, Taylor will give Ella $250,000, and she will immediately pay off the mortgage. Taylor wants his basis for the land to be as high as possible. Given this objective, which option should Taylor select?

Decision Making

9. **LO.1** Melba purchases land from Adrian. Melba gives Adrian $225,000 in cash and agrees to pay Adrian an additional $400,000 one year later plus interest at 5%.
   a. What is Melba's adjusted basis for the land at the acquisition date?
   b. What is Melba's adjusted basis for the land one year later?

10. **LO.1** Marge owns land and a building (held for investment) with an adjusted basis of $75,000 and a fair market value of $250,000. The property is subject to a mortgage of $400,000. Because Marge is in arrears on the mortgage payments, the creditor is willing to accept the property in return for canceling the amount of the mortgage.
   a. How can the adjusted basis of the property be less than the amount of the mortgage?
   b. If the creditor's offer is accepted, what are the effects on the amount realized, the adjusted basis, and the realized gain or loss for Marge?
   c. Does it matter in (b) if the mortgage is recourse or nonrecourse? Explain.

11. **LO.1** Distinguish between the terms *allowed depreciation* and *allowable depreciation*. What effect does the difference have on adjusted basis?

12. **LO.1** On July 16, 2014, Logan acquires land and a building for $500,000 to use in his sole proprietorship. Of the purchase price, $400,000 is allocated to the building, and $100,000 is allocated to the land. Cost recovery of $4,708 is deducted in 2014 for the building (nonresidential real estate).
   a. What is the adjusted basis for the land and the building at the acquisition date?
   b. What is the adjusted basis for the land and the building at the end of 2014?

13. **LO.1** Auralia owns stock in Orange Corporation and Blue Corporation. She receives a $10,000 distribution from both corporations. The instructions from Orange state that the $10,000 is a dividend. The instructions from Blue state that the $10,000 is not a dividend. What could cause the instructions to differ as to the tax consequences?

14. **LO.1** On July 1, 2014, Katrina purchased tax-exempt bonds (face value of $75,000) for $82,000. The bonds mature in five years, and the annual interest rate is 6%. The market rate of interest is 2%.
    a. How much interest income and/or interest expense must Katrina report in 2014?
    b. What is Katrina's adjusted basis for the bonds on January 1, 2015?

Decision Making

15. **LO.2** Wanda is considering selling two personal use assets that she owns. One has appreciated in value by $20,000, and the other has declined in value by $17,000. Wanda believes that she should sell both assets in the same tax year so that the loss of $17,000 can offset the gain of $20,000.
    a. Advise Wanda regarding the tax consequences of her plan.
    b. Could Wanda achieve better tax results by selling the assets in different tax years? Explain.

Issue ID

16. **LO.2** Ron sold his sailboat for a $5,000 loss in the current year because he was diagnosed with skin cancer. His spouse wants him to sell his Harley-Davidson motorcycle because her brother broke his leg while riding his motorcycle. Because Ron no longer has anyone to ride with, he is seriously considering accepting his wife's advice. Because the motorcycle is a classic, Ron has received two offers. Each offer would result in a $5,000 gain. Joe would like to purchase the motorcycle before Christmas, and Jeff would like to purchase it after New Year's. Identify the relevant tax issues Ron faces in making his decision.

17. **LO.3** In the case of a bargain purchase, why is the adjusted basis to the buyer the fair market value of the property rather than the purchase price?

18. **LO.3** How is cost allocated when a taxpayer acquires multiple assets in a lump-sum purchase?

19. **LO.3** Discuss how the tax treatment differs when stock rights are allocated on a cost basis versus when no such allocation occurs. When must an allocation be made?

20. **LO.1, 2, 3** Explain how a donee can sell investment property received by gift and recognize neither gain nor loss when the selling price differs from the donee's adjusted basis.

Issue ID

21. **LO.1, 2, 3, 5** Simon owns stock that has declined in value since acquired. He has decided either to give the stock to his nephew, Fred, or to sell it and give Fred the proceeds. If Fred receives the stock, he will sell it to obtain the proceeds. Simon is in the 15% tax bracket, while Fred's bracket is 25%. In either case, the holding period for the stock will be short-term. Identify the tax issues relevant to Simon in deciding whether to give the stock or the sale proceeds to Fred.

22. **LO.3** Under what circumstances is it possible to recognize neither gain nor loss on the sale of an asset previously received as a gift?

23. **LO.3** Robin inherits 1,000 shares of Wal-Mart stock from her aunt in 2014. According to the information received from the executor of her aunt's estate, Robin's adjusted basis for the stock is $55,000. Albert, Robin's fiancé, receives 1,000 shares of Wal-Mart stock from his uncle as a gift in 2014. His uncle tells Albert that his adjusted basis for the Wal-Mart stock is $7,000. What could cause the substantial difference in the adjusted basis for Robin's and Albert's respective 1,000 shares of Wal-Mart stock?

24. **LO.3** Thelma inherited land from Sadie on June 7, 2014. The land appreciated in value by 100% during the six months it was owned by Sadie. The value has remained stable during the three months Thelma has owned it, and she expects it to continue to do so in the near future. Although she would like to sell the land now, Thelma has decided to postpone the sale for another three months. The delay is to enable the recognized gain to qualify for long-term capital gain treatment. Evaluate Thelma's understanding of the tax law.

Decision Making

25. **LO.4** Marilyn owns land that she acquired three years ago as an investment for $250,000. Because the land has not appreciated in value as she anticipated, she sells it to

her brother, Amos, for its fair market value of $180,000. Amos sells the land two years later for $240,000.

a. Explain why Marilyn's realized loss of $70,000 ($180,000 amount realized − $250,000 adjusted basis) is disallowed.

b. Explain why Amos has neither a recognized gain nor a recognized loss on his sale of the land.

c. Is the family unit treated fairly under the related-party disallowance rule under § 267? Explain.

d. Which party wins, and which party loses?

e. How could Marilyn have avoided the loss disallowance on her sale of the land?

26. **LO.4, 5** Comment on the following transactions:

Decision Making

a. Mort owns 500 shares of Pear, Inc. stock with an adjusted basis of $22,000. On July 28, 2014, he sells 100 shares for $3,000. On August 16, 2014, he purchases another 100 shares for $3,400. Mort's realized loss of $1,400 ($3,000 − $4,400) on the July 28 sale is not recognized, and his adjusted basis for the 100 shares purchased on August 16 is $4,800. Explain.

b. How would your answer in (a) change if Mort purchased the 100 shares on December 27, 2014, rather than on August 16, 2014?

Problems

27. **LO.1** Anne sold her home for $290,000 in 2014. Selling expenses were $17,400. She purchased it in 2008 for $200,000. During the period of ownership, Anne did the following:

- Deducted $50,500 office-in-home expenses, which included $4,500 in depreciation. (Refer to Chapter 9.)
- Deducted a casualty loss in 2010 for residential trees destroyed by a hurricane. The total loss was $19,000 (after the $100 floor and the 10%-of-AGI floor), and Anne's insurance company reimbursed her for $13,500. (Refer to Chapter 7.)
- Paid street paving assessment of $7,000 and added sidewalks for $8,000.
- Installed an elevator for medical reasons. The total cost was $20,000, and Anne deducted $13,000 as medical expenses. (Refer to Chapter 10.)

What is Anne's realized gain?

28. **LO.1** Kareem bought a rental house in March 2009 for $300,000, of which $50,000 is allocated to the land and $250,000 to the building. Early in 2011, he had a tennis court built in the backyard at a cost of $7,500. Kareem has deducted $30,900 for depreciation on the house and $1,300 for depreciation on the court. In January 2014, he sells the house and tennis court for $330,000 cash.

a. What is Kareem's realized gain or loss?

b. If an original mortgage of $80,000 is still outstanding and the buyer assumes the mortgage in addition to the cash payment, what is Kareem's realized gain or loss?

c. If the buyer takes the property subject to the $80,000 mortgage, rather than assuming it, what is Kareem's realized gain or loss?

29. **LO.1** Norm is negotiating the sale of a tract of his land to Pat. Use the following classification scheme to classify each of the items contained in the proposed sales contract:

Legend
DARN = Decreases amount realized by Norm
IARN = Increases amount realized by Norm
DABN = Decreases adjusted basis to Norm
IABN = Increases adjusted basis to Norm
DABP = Decreases adjusted basis to Pat
IABP = Increases adjusted basis to Pat

a. Norm is to receive cash of $50,000.

b. Norm is to receive Pat's note payable for $25,000, payable in three years.

c. Pat assumes Norm's mortgage of $5,000 on the land.

d. Pat agrees to pay the realtor's sales commission of $8,000.

e. Pat agrees to pay the property taxes on the land for the entire year. If each party paid his or her respective share, Norm's share would be $1,000 and Pat's share would be $3,000.

f. Pat pays legal fees of $500.

g. Norm pays legal fees of $750.

30. **LO.1** Nissa owns a building (adjusted basis of $600,000 on January 1, 2014) that she rents to Len, who operates a restaurant in the building. The municipal health department closed the restaurant for three months during 2014 because of health code violations. Under MACRS, the cost recovery deduction for 2014 would be $20,500. However, Nissa deducted cost recovery only for the nine months the restaurant was open because she waived the rent income during the three-month period the restaurant was closed.

a. What is the amount of the cost recovery deduction Nissa should report on her 2014 income tax return?

b. Calculate the adjusted basis of the building at the end of 2014.

31. **LO.1, 2** Pam owns a personal use boat that has a fair market value of $35,000 and an adjusted basis of $45,000. Pam's AGI is $100,000. Calculate the realized and recognized gain or loss if:

a. Pam sells the boat for $35,000.

b. Pam exchanges the boat for another boat worth $35,000.

c. The boat is stolen and Pam receives insurance proceeds of $35,000.

d. Would your answer in (a) change if the fair market value and the selling price of the boat were $48,000?

32. **LO.1** Ricky owns stock in Dove Corporation. His adjusted basis for the stock is $90,000. During the year, he receives a distribution from the corporation of $75,000 that is labeled a return of capital (i.e., Dove has no earnings and profits).

a. Determine the tax consequences to Ricky.

b. Assume instead that the amount of the distribution is $150,000. Determine the tax consequences to Ricky.

c. Assume instead in (a) that the $75,000 distribution is labeled a taxable dividend (i.e., Dove has earnings and profits of at least $75,000).

33. **LO.1, 2** Chee purchases Tan, Inc. bonds for $108,000 on January 2, 2014. The face value of the bonds is $100,000; the maturity date is December 31, 2018; and the annual interest rate is 5%. Chee will amortize the premium only if he is required to do so. Chee sells the bonds on July 1, 2016, for $106,000.

a. Determine the interest income Chee should report for 2014.

b. Calculate Chee's recognized gain or loss on the sale of the bonds in 2016.

34. **LO.1, 2** Which of the following results in a recognized gain or loss?

a. Kay sells her vacation cabin (adjusted basis of $100,000) for $150,000.

b. Adam sells his personal residence (adjusted basis of $150,000) for $100,000.

c. Carl's personal residence (adjusted basis of $65,000) is condemned by the city. He receives condemnation proceeds of $55,000.

d. Olga's land is worth $40,000 at the end of the year. She had purchased the land six months earlier for $25,000.

e. Vera's personal vehicle (adjusted basis of $22,000) is stolen. She receives $23,000 from the insurance company and does not plan to replace the automobile.

f. Jerry sells used clothing (adjusted basis of $500) to a thrift store for $50.

35. **LO.1, 2** Yancy's personal residence is condemned as part of an urban renewal project. His adjusted basis for the residence is $480,000. He receives condemnation proceeds of $460,000 and invests the proceeds in stocks and bonds.

a. Calculate Yancy's realized and recognized gain or loss.

b. If the condemnation proceeds are $505,000, what are Yancy's realized and recognized gain or loss?

c. What are Yancy's realized and recognized gain or loss in (a) if the house was rental property?

36. **LO.3** Buddy Morgan is a real estate agent for Coastal Estates, a residential real estate development. Because of his outstanding sales performance, Buddy is permitted to buy a lot for $300,000 that normally would sell for $500,000. Buddy is the only real estate agent for Coastal Estates who is permitted to do so. Communications
    a. Does Buddy have gross income from the transaction? Explain.
    b. What is Buddy's adjusted basis for the land?
    c. Write a letter to Buddy informing him of the tax consequences of his acquisition of the lot. His address is 100 Tower Road, San Diego, CA 92182.

37. **LO.1, 2, 3** Karen makes the following purchases and sales of stock:

Transaction	Date	Number of Shares	Company	Price per Share
Purchase	1-1-2012	300	MDG	$ 75
Purchase	6-1-2012	150	GRU	300
Purchase	11-1-2012	60	MDG	70
Sale	12-3-2012	200	MDG	80
Purchase	3-1-2013	120	GRU	375
Sale	8-1-2013	90	GRU	330
Sale	1-1-2014	150	MDG	90
Sale	2-1-2014	75	GRU	500

Assuming that Karen is unable to identify the particular lots that are sold with the original purchase, what is the recognized gain or loss on each type of stock as of the following dates:
    a. 7-1-2012.
    b. 12-31-2012.
    c. 12-31-2013.
    d. 7-1-2014.

38. **LO.1, 2, 3** Kevin purchases 1,000 shares of Bluebird Corporation stock on October 3, 2014, for $300,000. On December 12, 2014, Kevin purchases an additional 750 shares of Bluebird stock for $210,000. According to market quotations, Bluebird stock is selling for $285 per share on December 31, 2014. Kevin sells 500 shares of Bluebird stock on March 1, 2015, for $162,500.
    a. What is the adjusted basis of Kevin's Bluebird stock on December 31, 2014?
    b. What is Kevin's recognized gain or loss from the sale of Bluebird stock on March 1, 2015, assuming the shares sold are from the shares purchased on December 12, 2014?
    c. What is Kevin's recognized gain or loss from the sale of Bluebird stock on March 1, 2015, assuming Kevin cannot adequately identify the shares sold?

39. **LO.3** Rod Clooney purchases Agnes Mitchell's sole proprietorship for $990,000 on August 15, 2014. The assets of the business are as follows: Communications

Asset	Agnes's Adjusted Basis	FMV
Accounts receivable	$ 70,000	$ 70,000
Inventory	90,000	100,000
Equipment	150,000	160,000
Furniture and fixtures	95,000	130,000
Building	190,000	250,000
Land	25,000	75,000
Total	$620,000	$785,000

Rod and Agnes agree that $50,000 of the purchase price is for Agnes's five-year covenant not to compete.
    a. Calculate Agnes's realized and recognized gain.
    b. Determine Rod's basis for each of the assets.
    c. Write a letter to Rod informing him of the tax consequences of the purchase. His address is 300 Riverview Drive, Delaware, OH 43015.

40. **LO.3** Donna owns 800 shares of common stock in Macaw Corporation (adjusted basis of $40,000). She receives a 5% stock dividend when the stock is selling for $60 per share.
    a. How much gross income must Donna recognize because of the stock dividend?
    b. What is Donna's basis for her 840 shares of stock?

41. **LO.3** Paula owns stock in Yellow, Inc., which she purchased for $5,000. The stock has a fair market value of $6,000. Because Yellow is experiencing a cash flow problem, it chooses to distribute nontaxable stock rights instead of cash to its shareholders.
    a. What effect does this distribution have on Paula's basis in her Yellow stock if the fair market value of the stock rights is $1,000?
    b. What is Paula's basis for the nontaxable stock rights?
    c. What is Paula's recognized gain or loss if she sells the stock rights for $1,200?
    d. What is Paula's recognized gain or loss if she allows the stock rights to lapse?
    e. If the fair market value of the stock rights is $750 (not $1,000), how will this change the answers to parts (a) and (b)?

42. **LO.1, 2, 3** Roberto has received various gifts over the years. He has decided to dispose of the following assets he received as gifts:
    a. In 1951, he received land worth $32,000. The donor's adjusted basis was $35,000. Roberto sells the land for $95,000 in 2014.
    b. In 1956, he received stock in Gold Company. The donor's adjusted basis was $19,000. The fair market value on the date of the gift was $34,000. Roberto sells the stock for $40,000 in 2014.
    c. In 1962, he received land worth $15,000. The donor's adjusted basis was $20,000. Roberto sells the land for $9,000 in 2014.
    d. In 2003, he received stock worth $30,000. The donor's adjusted basis was $42,000. Roberto sells the stock for $38,000 in 2014.

    What is the recognized gain or loss from each of the preceding transactions? Assume for each of the gift transactions that no gift tax was paid.

43. **LO.1, 2, 3** Nicky receives a car from Sam as a gift. Sam paid $48,000 for the car. He had used it for business purposes and had deducted $10,000 for depreciation up to the time he gave the car to Nicky. The fair market value of the car is $33,000.
    a. Assuming that Nicky uses the car for business purposes, what is her basis for depreciation?
    b. Assume that Nicky deducts depreciation of $6,500 and then sells the car for $32,500. What is her recognized gain or loss?
    c. Assume that Nicky deducts depreciation of $6,500 and then sells the car for $20,000. What is her recognized gain or loss?

44. **LO.3** Margo receives a gift of real estate with an adjusted basis of $175,000 and a fair market value of $100,000. The donor paid gift tax of $15,000 on the transfer. If Margo later sells the property for $110,000, what is her recognized gain or loss?

45. **LO.3** On September 18, 2014, Gerald received land and a building from Frank as a gift. Frank's adjusted basis and the fair market value at the date of the gift are as follows:

Asset	Adjusted Basis	FMV
Land	$100,000	$212,000
Building	80,000	100,000

    No gift tax was paid on the transfer.
    a. Determine Gerald's adjusted basis for the land and building.
    b. Assume instead that the fair market value of the land was $87,000 and that of the building was $65,000. Determine Gerald's adjusted basis for the land and building.

Decision Making

Communications

46. **LO.1, 2, 3, 5** Ira Cook is planning to make a charitable contribution of Crystal, Inc. stock worth $20,000 to the Boy Scouts. The stock has an adjusted basis of $15,000. A friend has suggested that Ira sell the stock and contribute the $20,000 in proceeds rather than contribute the stock.
    a. Should Ira follow the friend's advice? Why or why not?
    b. Assume that the fair market value is only $13,000. In this case, should Ira follow the friend's advice? Why or why not?
    c. Rather than make a charitable contribution to the Boy Scouts, Ira is going to make a gift to Nancy, his niece. Advise Ira regarding (a) and (b).

d. Write a letter to Ira regarding whether in (a) he should sell the stock and contribute the cash or contribute the stock. He has informed you that he purchased the stock six years ago. Ira's address is 500 Ireland Avenue, DeKalb, IL 60115.

47. **LO.3** As sole heir, Dazie receives all of Mary's property (adjusted basis of $1,400,000 and fair market value of $3,820,000). Six months after Mary's death in 2014, the fair market value is $3,835,000.
    a. Can the executor of Mary's estate elect the alternate valuation date and amount? Explain.
    b. What is Dazie's basis for the property?
    c. Assume instead that the fair market value six months after Mary's death is $3.8 million. Respond to (a) and (b).

48. **LO.3** Dan bought a hotel for $2,600,000 in January 2010. In May 2014, he died and left the hotel to Ed. While Dan owned the hotel, he deducted $289,000 of cost recovery. The fair market value in May 2014 was $2,800,000. The fair market value six months later was $2,850,000.
    a. What is the basis of the property to Ed?
    b. What is the basis of the property to Ed if the fair market value six months later was $2,500,000 (not $2,850,000) and the objective of the executor was to minimize the estate tax liability?

49. **LO.3** Helene and Pauline are twin sisters who live in Louisiana and Mississippi, respectively. Helene is married to Frank, and Pauline is married to Richard. Frank and Richard are killed in an auto accident in 2014 while returning from a sporting event.
    Helene and Frank jointly owned some farmland in Louisiana (value of $940,000, cost of $450,000). Pauline and Richard jointly owned some farmland in Mississippi (value of $940,000, cost of $450,000). Assume that all of Frank's and Richard's property passes to their surviving wives.
    a. Calculate Helene's basis in the land.
    b. Calculate Pauline's basis in the land.
    c. What causes the difference?

50. **LO.3, 4** Sheila sells land to Elane, her sister, for the fair market value of $40,000. Six months later when the land is worth $45,000, Elane gives it to Jacob, her son. (No gift tax resulted.) Shortly thereafter, Jacob sells the land for $48,000.
    a. Assuming that Sheila's adjusted basis for the land is $24,000, what are Sheila's and Jacob's recognized gain or loss on the sales?
    b. Assuming that Sheila's adjusted basis for the land is $60,000, what are Sheila's and Jacob's recognized gain or loss on the sales?

51. **LO.1, 2, 3, 4** Louis owns three pieces of land with an adjusted basis as follows: parcel A, $75,000; parcel B, $125,000; and parcel C, $175,000. Louis sells parcel A to his uncle for $50,000, parcel B to his partner for $120,000, and parcel C to his mother for $150,000.
    a. What is the recognized gain or loss from the sale of each parcel?
    b. If Louis's uncle eventually sells his land for $90,000, what is his recognized gain or loss?
    c. If Louis's partner eventually sells his land for $130,000, what is his recognized gain or loss?
    d. If Louis's mother eventually sells her land for $165,000, what is her recognized gain or loss?

52. **LO.1, 2, 3, 4** Tyneka inherited 1,000 shares of Aqua, Inc. stock from Joe. Joe's basis was $35,000, and the fair market value on July 1, 2014 (the date of death) was $45,000. The shares were distributed to Tyneka on July 15, 2014. Tyneka sold the stock on July 30, 2015, for $33,000. After giving the matter more thought, she decides that Aqua is a good investment and purchases 1,000 shares for $30,000 on August 20, 2015.
    a. What is Tyneka's basis for the 1,000 shares purchased on August 20, 2015?
    b. Could Tyneka have obtained different tax consequences in (a) if she had sold the 1,000 shares on December 27, 2014, and purchased the 1,000 shares on January 5, 2015? Explain.

Decision Making

53. **LO.1, 2, 4** On December 28, 2014, Kramer sells 150 shares of Lavender, Inc. stock for $77,000. On January 10, 2015, he purchases 100 shares of the same stock for $82,000.

Decision Making

a. Assuming that Kramer's adjusted basis for the stock sold is $65,000, what is his recognized gain or loss? What is his basis for the new shares?

b. Assuming that Kramer's adjusted basis for the stock sold is $89,000, what is his recognized gain or loss? What is his basis for the new shares?

c. Advise Kramer on how he can avoid any negative tax consequences encountered in part (b).

54. **LO.1, 2, 4** Abby's home had a basis of $360,000 ($160,000 attributable to the land) and a fair market value of $340,000 ($155,000 attributable to the land) when she converted 70% of it to business use by opening a bed-and-breakfast. Four years after the conversion, Abby sells the home for $500,000 ($165,000 attributable to the land).

a. Calculate Abby's basis for gain, loss, and cost recovery for the portion of her personal residence that was converted to business use.

b. Calculate the cost recovery deducted by Abby during the four-year period of business use, assuming the bed-and-breakfast is opened on January 1 of year 1 and the house is sold on December 31 of year 4.

c. What is Abby's recognized gain or loss on the sale of the business use portion?

Decision Making

55. **LO.4, 5** Surendra's personal residence originally cost $340,000 (ignore land). After living in the house for five years, he converts it to rental property. At the date of conversion, the fair market value of the house is $320,000. As to the rental property, calculate Surendra's basis for:

a. Loss.

b. Depreciation.

c. Gain.

d. Could Surendra have obtained better tax results if he had sold his personal residence for $320,000 and then purchased another house for $320,000 to hold as rental property? Explain.

Decision Making

56. **LO.3, 5** Hun, age 93, has accumulated substantial assets during his life. Among his many assets are the following, which he is considering giving to Koji, his grandson.

Asset	Adjusted Basis	Fair Market Value
Silver Corporation stock	$900,000	$700,000
Red Corporation stock	70,000	71,000
Emerald Corporation stock	200,000	500,000

Hun has been in ill health for the past five years. His physician has informed him that he probably will not live for more than six months. Advise Hun on which of the stocks should be transferred as gifts and which as bequests.

Cumulative Problems

Tax Return Problem

57. Alton Newman, age 67, is married and files a joint return with his wife, Clair, age 65. Alton and Clair are both retired, and during 2013, they received Social Security benefits of $10,000. Alton's Social Security number is 111-11-1111, and Clair's is 123-45-6789. They reside at 210 College Drive, Columbia, SC 29201.

Alton, who retired on January 1, 2013, receives benefits from a qualified pension plan of $2,750 a month for life. His total contributions to the plan (none of which were deductible) were $168,250. In January 2013, he received a bonus of $2,000 from his former employer for service performed in 2012. Although the former employer accrued the bonus in 2012, it was not paid until 2013.

Clair, who retired on December 31, 2012, started receiving benefits of $1,400 a month on January 1, 2013. Her contributions to the qualified pension plan (none of which were deductible) were $74,100.

On September 27, 2013, Alton and Clair received a 10% stock dividend on 600 shares of stock they owned. They had bought the stock on March 5, 2006, for $20 a share. On December 16, 2013, they sold the 60 dividend shares for $55 a share.

On October 10, 2013, Clair sold the car she had used in commuting to and from work for $17,000. She had paid $31,000 for the car in 2007.

On July 14, 2005, Alton and Clair received a gift of 1,000 shares of stock from their son, Thomas. Thomas's basis in the stock was $35 a share (fair market value at the date of gift was $25). No gift tax was paid on the transfer. Alton and Clair sold the stock on October 8, 2013, for $24 a share.

On May 1, 2013, Clair's mother died, and Clair inherited her personal residence. In February 2013, her mother had paid the property taxes for 2013 of $2,100. The residence had a fair market value of $235,000 and an adjusted basis to the mother of $160,000 on the date of her death. Clair listed the house with a real estate agent, who estimated it was worth $240,000 as of December 31, 2013.

Clair received rent income of $6,000 on a beach house she inherited three years ago from her uncle Charles. She had rented the property for one week during the July 4 holiday and one week during the Thanksgiving holidays. Charles's adjusted basis in the beach house was $150,000, and its fair market value on the date of his death was $240,000. Clair and Alton used the beach house for personal purposes for 56 days during the year. Expenses associated with the house were $3,700 for utilities, maintenance, and repairs; $2,200 for property taxes; and $800 for insurance. There are no mortgages on the property.

Clair and Alton paid estimated Federal income tax of $3,100 and had itemized deductions of $6,800 (excluding any itemized deductions associated with the beach house). If they have overpaid their Federal income tax, they want the amount refunded. Both Clair and Alton want $3 to go to the Presidential Election Campaign Fund.

Compute their net tax payable or refund due for 2013. If you use tax forms for your computations, you will need Form 1040 and Schedule D. Suggested software: H&R BLOCK Tax Software.

58. John Benson, age 40, is single. His Social Security number is 111-11-1111, and he resides at 150 Highway 51, Tangipahoa, LA 70465.

John has a five-year-old child, Kendra, who lives with her mother, Katy. John pays alimony of $6,000 per year to Katy and child support of $12,000. The $12,000 of child support covers 65% of Katy's costs of rearing Kendra. Kendra's Social Security number is 123-45-6789, and Katy's is 123-45-6788.

John's mother, Sally, lived with him until her death in early September 2014. He incurred and paid medical expenses for her of $12,900 and other support payments of $11,000. Sally's only sources of income were $5,500 of interest income on certificates of deposit and $5,600 of Social Security benefits, which she spent on her medical expenses and on maintenance of John's household. Sally's Social Security number was 123-45-6787.

John is employed by the Highway Department of the State of Louisiana in an executive position. His salary is $95,000. The appropriate amounts of Social Security tax ($5,890) and Medicare tax ($1,378) were withheld. In addition, $9,500 was withheld for Federal income taxes, and $4,000 was withheld for state income taxes.

In addition to his salary, John's employer provides him with the following fringe benefits:

- Group term life insurance with a maturity value of $95,000. The cost of the premiums for the employer was $295.
- Group health insurance plan. John's employer paid premiums of $5,800 for his coverage. The plan paid $2,600 for John's medical expenses during the year.

Upon the death of his aunt Josie in December 2013, John, her only recognized heir, inherited the following assets:

Asset	Josie's Adjusted Basis	FMV at Date of Death
Car	$35,000	$ 19,000
Land—300 acres	90,000	175,000
IBM stock	15,000	40,000
Cash	10,000	10,000

Three months prior to her death, Josie gave John a mountain cabin. Her adjusted basis for the mountain cabin was $120,000, and the fair market value was $195,000. No gift taxes were paid.

During the year, John had the following transactions:

- On February 1, 2014, he sold for $45,000 Microsoft stock that he inherited from his father four years ago. His father's adjusted basis was $49,000, and the fair market value at the date of the father's death was $41,000.

Tax Computation Problem

Decision Making

Communications

● The car John inherited from Josie was destroyed in a wreck on October 1, 2014. He had loaned the car to Katy to use for a two-week period while the engine in her car was being replaced. Fortunately, neither Katy nor Kendra was injured. John received insurance proceeds of $16,000, the fair market value of the car on October 1, 2014.

● On December 28, 2014, John sold the 300 acres of land to his brother, James, for its fair market value of $160,000. James planned on using the land for his dairy farm.

Other sources of income for John were as follows:

Dividend income (qualified dividends)	$ 3,500
Interest income:	
Guaranty Bank	1,000
City of Kentwood water bonds	2,000
Award from state of Louisiana for outstanding suggestion for highway beautification	10,000

Potential itemized deductions for John, in addition to items already mentioned, were as follows:

Property taxes paid on his residence and cabin	$7,000
Property taxes paid on personalty	3,500
Estimated Federal income taxes paid	3,000
Charitable contributions	4,500
Mortgage interest on his residence	7,200
Orthodontic expenses for Kendra	4,000

Part 1—Tax Computation
Compute John's net tax payable or refund due for 2014.

Part 2—Tax Planning
Assume that rather than selling the land to James, John is considering leasing it to him for $12,000 annually with the lease beginning on October 1, 2014. James would prepay the lease payments through December 31, 2014. Thereafter, he would make monthly lease payments at the beginning of each month. What effect would this have on John's 2014 tax liability? What potential problem might John encounter? Write a letter to John in which you advise him of the tax consequences of leasing versus selling. Also prepare a memo for the tax files.

Research Problems

THOMSON REUTERS
CHECKPOINT®

Note: Solutions to Research Problems can be prepared by using the **Checkpoint**® **Student Edition** online research product, which is available to accompany this text. It is also possible to prepare solutions to the Research Problems by using tax research materials found in a standard tax library.

Research Problem 1. Inez Butler is the sole shareholder of Pelican, Inc., which owns car dealerships. Pelican purchases the assets of a Chevrolet dealership. The purchase price of $12 million is allocated to the purchased assets based on the fair market values. This includes $3.5 million that is allocated to goodwill.

In addition to the price of $12 million, Pelican incurred legal fees of $250,000 associated with the purchase. According to an itemized invoice provided by the attorney, 80% of the legal fees relate to the acquisition of inventory. Consequently, Pelican assigned $200,000 of the legal fees to inventory with the balance being capitalized as goodwill. The expectation is that 60% of the $200,000 will become part of cost of goods sold in the current year with the remaining 40% doing so in the following year.

The IRS has concluded that § 1060 limits the amount that may be assigned to the fair market value of the inventory. Therefore, the $200,000 of legal fees cannot be added to the basis of the inventory. Instead, it must be included in goodwill under the residual method.

Who is correct?

Research Problem 2. Terry owns real estate with an adjusted basis of $600,000 and a fair market value of $1.1 million. The amount of the nonrecourse mortgage on the property is $2.5 million. Because of substantial past and projected future losses associated with the real estate development (occupancy rate of only 37% after three years), Terry deeds the property to the creditor.

a. What are the tax consequences to Terry?

b. Assume that the data are the same, except that the fair market value of the property is $2,525,000. Therefore, when Terry deeds the property to the creditor, she also receives $25,000 from the creditor. What are the tax consequences to Terry?

Research Problem 3. Your client, Jacob, turned 66 years old this year. Jacob has no heirs and has decided that he would like to sell a life insurance policy to fund a trip to Africa that he has wanted to take.

Jacob knew that he could surrender the policy (a whole-life policy) back to the insurance company, but a friend told him he could get more for the policy if he sold it to a life settlement company. A life settlement company buys life insurance policies from policyholders who are not ill and who generally have a life expectancy of between 2 and 15 years. In return, the seller of the policy receives a lump-sum payment. The life settlement company either holds the policy to maturity or resells the policy to an investor.

The lump sum received depends on factors such as age, health, and the terms and conditions of the policy, but is generally more than the policy's cash surrender value (which would be received from the life insurance company upon surrender of the policy).

In November 2014, Jacob (who was not terminally or chronically ill) sold his policy to a life settlement company for $160,000. During the time he owned the policy, Jacob did not borrow against the policy or receive any distributions. Jacob also had paid premiums totaling $122,000 (of which $32,000 was paid for the provision of insurance before the sale of the policy).

How should Jacob calculate his basis in the life insurance policy to determine if he has a realized gain or loss on the surrender of the policy?

Research Problem 4. Ruth Ames died on January 10, 2014. In filing the estate tax return, her executor, Melvin Sims, elects the primary valuation date and amount (fair market value on the date of death). On March 12, 2014, Melvin invests $30,000 of cash that Ruth had in her money market account in acquiring 1,000 shares of Orange, Inc. ($30 per share). On January 10, 2014, Orange was selling for $29 per share. The stock is distributed to a beneficiary, Annette Rust, on June 1, 2014, when it is selling for $33 per share. Melvin wants you to determine the amount at which the Orange shares should appear on the estate tax return and the amount of Annette's adjusted basis for the stock. Write a letter to Melvin in which you respond to his inquiry and prepare a memo for the tax files. His address is 100 Center Lane, Miami, FL 33124.

Communications

Research Problem 5. Amanda purchased the following lots of stock of Pearl, Inc. (a pharmaceutical company) during 2011:

Date	Number of Shares	Cost per Share
February 1	100	$150
July 25	100	140
November 3	100	130

On December 20, 2013, Amanda sold the 300 shares for $145 each.

In early January 2014, the Food and Drug Administration granted approval for a new drug developed by Pearl. Expecting the stock to continue to increase in value, Amanda purchased 300 shares on January 5, 2014, for $175 per share.

Amanda calculated her recognized gain as $1,500 ($43,500 amount realized − $42,000 adjusted basis). The IRS contends that the transaction must be treated as the sale of three lots of stock because of the wash sale rules. As a result, the $500 realized gain on the sale of the second lot and the $1,500 realized gain on the sale of the third lot must be recognized, and the $500 realized loss on the sale of the first lot is disallowed under § 1091.

Who is correct?

**Internet
Activity**

Communications

Use the tax resources of the Internet to address the following questions. Do not restrict your search to the Web, but include a review of newsgroups and general reference materials, practitioner sites and resources, primary sources of the tax law, chat rooms and discussion groups, and other opportunities.

Research Problem 6. Many see the "step-up in basis at death" rule of § 1014 as an expensive tax loophole enjoyed by the wealthy. Find the latest estimates of the revenue loss to the Treasury that is attributable to this rule.

   a. How does Canada's tax law determine the basis of property acquired from a decedent?

   b. Send an e-mail message to a member of the House Ways and Means Committee expressing a preference for the preservation of the current § 1014 rule or the modifications made to it by the Tax Relief Reconciliation Act of 2001 and the Tax Relief Act of 2010.

Research Problem 7. The specific identification method is important when one invests in mutual funds. When taxpayers sell part of their holdings, the basis of the surrendered shares can be difficult to compute. Go to the site of an investment adviser or mutual fund to find instructions on how to compute the basis of the shares sold. What options are available to the taxpayer according to this information? Illustrate each of the alternatives.

Property Transactions: Nontaxable Exchanges

LEARNING OBJECTIVES: *After completing Chapter 15, you should be able to:*

LO.1 State and explain the rationale for nonrecognition (postponement) of gain or loss in certain property transactions.

LO.2 Apply the nonrecognition provisions and basis determination rules for like-kind exchanges.

LO.3 Explain the nonrecognition provisions available on the involuntary conversion of property.

LO.4 Describe the provision for the permanent exclusion of gain on the sale of a personal residence.

LO.5 Identify other nonrecognition provisions contained in the Code.

LO.6 Review and apply various tax planning opportunities related to the nonrecognition provisions discussed in the chapter.

CHAPTER OUTLINE

ALTERNATIVE USES OF PROPERTY

Recall the situation introduced in *The Big Picture* in Chapter 14. After 11 months, Alice has changed her mind about selling the house to her nephew for $275,000. As a result of a recent groundbreaking for an upscale real estate development nearby, the appraised value of the house has increased to $600,000. Alice has decided she needs to do something with the house other than let it remain vacant. She is considering the following options and has come to you for advice.

- Sell the house for approximately $600,000 using the services of a real estate agent. The real estate commission rate is 5 percent and her inherited basis is $475,000.
- Convert the house to a vacation home (100 percent personal use by Alice and her family); then sell it in two years.
- Convert the house to a vacation home (projected 40 percent rental use and 60 percent personal use); then sell it in two years.
- Sell her current home and move into the inherited house. She has owned and lived in the current home for 15 years, and her gain on the sale would be about $200,000. Because she is nearing retirement, she would live in the inherited house for only the required two-year minimum period and then sell it.

Alice expects the inherited house to continue to appreciate in value by about 5 percent per year. She plans on retiring from her job in two years and moving to a warmer climate. Until then, she is neutral as to which house she lives in. What advice can you offer Alice?

Read the chapter and formulate your response.

Income *(broadly conceived)*	$xx,xxx
Less: Exclusions	(x,xxx)
Gross income	$xx,xxx
Less: Deductions for adjusted gross income	(x,xxx)

FORM 1040 (p. 1)

12	Business income or (loss). Attach Schedule C or C-EZ	
13	Capital gain or (loss). Attach Schedule D if required. If not required, check here ▶	☐
14	Other gains or (losses). Attach Form 4797	

Adjusted gross income	$xx,xxx
Less: The greater of total **itemized deductions** *or* the standard deduction	(x,xxx)
Personal and dependency exemptions	(x,xxx)
Taxable income	$xx,xxx
Tax on taxable income *(see Tax Tables or Tax Rate Schedules)*	$ x,xxx
Less: Tax credits *(including income taxes withheld and prepaid)*	(xxx)
Tax due *(or refund)*	$ xxx

Chapter 14 was the first of a four-chapter sequence in Part 5 dealing with property transactions. In Chapter 14, the sale or exchange concept is explained along with how basis is determined. As noted in Concept Summary 14.1, the intermediate result is realized gain or loss. What happens to the realized gain or loss depends on the nature of the sale or exchange. Some or all of the gain or loss may be recognized, deferred, or even avoided. Chapter 15 concentrates on several types of sales or exchanges where the usual result is deferral or avoidance of recognizing realized gain or loss.

15-1 GENERAL CONCEPT OF A NONTAXABLE EXCHANGE

LO.1

State and explain the rationale for nonrecognition (postponement) of gain or loss in certain property transactions.

A taxpayer who is going to replace a productive asset (e.g., machinery) used in a trade or business may structure the transactions as a sale of the old asset and the purchase of a new asset. When this approach is used, any realized gain or loss on the asset sale is recognized. The basis of the new asset is its cost. Alternatively, the taxpayer may be able to trade the old asset for the new asset. This exchange of assets may produce beneficial tax consequences by qualifying for nontaxable exchange treatment.

The tax law recognizes that nontaxable exchanges result in a change in the *form* but not in the *substance* of the taxpayer's relative economic position. The replacement property received in the exchange is viewed as substantially a continuation of the old investment.[1] Additional justification for nontaxable exchange treatment is that this type of transaction does not provide the taxpayer with the wherewithal to pay the tax on any realized gain.

The nonrecognition provisions for nontaxable exchanges do not apply to realized losses from the sale or exchange of personal use assets. Such losses are not recognized (are disallowed) because they are personal in nature and not because of any nonrecognition provision.

---

[1]Reg. § 1.1002–1(c).

In a **nontaxable exchange**, realized gains or losses are not recognized. However, the nonrecognition is usually temporary. The recognition of gain or loss is *postponed* (deferred) until the property received in the nontaxable exchange is subsequently disposed of in a taxable transaction. This is accomplished by assigning a carryover basis to the replacement property.

> **Example 1**
>
> Debra completes a *nontaxable exchange* of property with an adjusted basis of $10,000 and a fair market value of $12,000 for property with a fair market value of $12,000. Debra has a realized gain of $2,000 ($12,000 amount realized − $10,000 adjusted basis). Her recognized gain is $0. Her basis in the replacement property is a carryover basis of $10,000. Assume that the replacement property is nondepreciable and Debra subsequently sells it for $12,000. Her realized and recognized gain will be the $2,000 gain that was postponed (deferred) in the nontaxable transaction. If the replacement property is depreciable, the carryover basis of $10,000 is used in calculating depreciation.

In some nontaxable exchanges, only part of the property involved in the transaction qualifies for nonrecognition treatment. If the taxpayer receives cash or other nonqualifying property, part or all of the realized gain from the exchange is recognized. In these instances, gain is recognized because the taxpayer has changed or improved his or her relative economic position and has the wherewithal to pay income tax to the extent of cash or other property received.

It is important to distinguish between a nontaxable disposition, as the term is used in the statute, and a tax-free transaction. First, a direct exchange is not required in all circumstances (e.g., replacement of involuntarily converted property). Second, as previously mentioned, the term *nontaxable* refers to postponement of recognition via a carryover basis. In a *tax-free* transaction, the nonrecognition is permanent (e.g., see the discussion later in the chapter of the § 121 exclusion of realized gain on the sale of a personal residence). Therefore, the basis of any property acquired in a tax-free transaction does not depend on the basis of the property disposed of by the taxpayer.

15-2 LIKE-KIND EXCHANGES—§ 1031

Section 1031 provides for nontaxable exchange treatment if the following requirements are satisfied:[2]

- The form of the transaction is an exchange.
- Both the property transferred and the property received are held either for productive use in a trade or business or for investment.
- The property is like-kind property.

Like-kind exchanges include business for business, business for investment, investment for business, and investment for investment property. Property held for personal use, inventory, and partnership interests (both limited and general) do not qualify under the like-kind exchange provisions. Securities, even though held for investment, do not qualify for like-kind exchange treatment.

The nonrecognition provision for like-kind exchanges is *mandatory* rather than elective. A taxpayer who wants to recognize a realized gain or loss will have to structure the transaction in a form that does not satisfy the statutory requirements for a like-kind exchange. This topic is discussed further under Tax Planning.

15-2a Like-Kind Property

"The words 'like-kind' refer to the nature or character of the property and not to its grade or quality. One kind or class of property may not … be exchanged for property of a different kind or class."[3]

The term *like-kind* is intended to be interpreted very broadly. However, three categories of exchanges are not included. First, livestock of different sexes do not qualify as like-kind property. Second, real estate can be exchanged only for other real estate, and

LO.2

Apply the nonrecognition provisions and basis determination rules for like-kind exchanges.

---

[2] § 1031(a) and Reg. § 1.1031(a)–1(a).
[3] Reg. § 1.1031(a)–1(b).

personalty can be exchanged only for other personalty. For example, the exchange of a machine (personalty) for an office building (realty) is not a like-kind exchange. *Real estate* (or realty) includes principally rental buildings, office and store buildings, manufacturing plants, warehouses, and land. It is immaterial whether real estate is improved or unimproved. Thus, unimproved land can be exchanged for an apartment house. Personalty includes principally machines, equipment, trucks, automobiles, furniture, and fixtures. Third, real property located in the United States exchanged for foreign real property (and vice versa) does not qualify as like-kind property.

Example 2

Wade made the following exchanges during the taxable year:

a. Inventory for a machine used in business.
b. Land held for investment for a building used in business.
c. Stock held for investment for equipment used in business.
d. A light-duty business truck for a light-duty business truck.
e. An automobile used for personal transportation for an automobile used in business.
f. Livestock for livestock of a different sex.
g. Land held for investment in New York for land held for investment in London.

Exchanges (b), investment real property for business real property, and (d), business personalty for business personalty, qualify as exchanges of like-kind property. The other exchanges do not qualify because they involve (a), inventory; (c), stock; (e), personal use automobile (not held for business or investment purposes); (f), livestock of different sexes; and (g), U.S. and foreign real estate.

Regulations dealing with § 1031 like-kind exchange treatment provide that if the exchange transaction involves multiple assets of a business (e.g., a television station for another television station), the determination of whether the assets qualify as like-kind property will not be made at the business level.[4] Instead, the underlying assets must be evaluated.

Special Rule for Depreciable Tangible Personal Property

The Regulations also provide for greater specificity in determining whether depreciable tangible personal property is of a like kind or class. Such property held for productive use in a business is of a like class only if the exchanged property is within the same *general business asset class* (as specified by the IRS in Revenue Procedure 87–57 or as subsequently modified) or the same *product class* (as specified by the Department of Commerce). Property included in a general business asset class is evaluated under this system rather than under the product class system.

The following are examples of general business asset classes:

- Office furniture, fixtures, and equipment.
- Information systems (computers and peripheral equipment).
- Airplanes.
- Automobiles and taxis.
- Buses.
- Light general-purpose trucks.
- Heavy general-purpose trucks.

These Regulations have made it more difficult for depreciable tangible personal property to qualify for § 1031 like-kind exchange treatment. For example, the exchange of office equipment for a computer does not qualify as an exchange of like-kind property. Even though both assets are depreciable tangible personal property, they are not like-kind property because they are in different general business asset classes.

15-2b Exchange Requirement

The transaction must involve a direct exchange of property to qualify as a like-kind exchange. The sale of old property and the purchase of new property, even though

---

[4]Reg. § 1.1031(j)–1.

like kind, is generally not an exchange. However, if the two transactions are mutually dependent, the IRS may treat them as a like-kind exchange. For example, if the taxpayer sells an old business machine to a dealer and purchases a new one from the same dealer, like-kind exchange treatment could result.[5]

The taxpayer may want to avoid nontaxable exchange treatment. Recognition of gain gives the taxpayer a higher basis for depreciation (see Example 31). To the extent that such gains would, if recognized, either receive favorable capital gain treatment or be passive activity income that could offset passive activity losses, it might be preferable to avoid the nonrecognition provisions through an indirect exchange transaction. For example, a taxpayer may sell property to one individual, recognize the gain, and subsequently purchase similar property from another individual. The taxpayer may also want to avoid nontaxable exchange treatment so that a realized loss can be recognized.

Time Limitations

Like-kind exchanges—especially those involving real estate—can be complex. Further, it can be extremely difficult to coordinate a simultaneous transaction if the properties being exchanged are located in different counties or states. As a result, delayed (nonsimultaneous) exchanges are allowed, but there are time limits on its completion. In a delayed like-kind exchange, one party fails to take immediate title to the new property because it has not yet been identified. The Code provides that the delayed swap will qualify as a like-kind exchange if the following requirements are satisfied:

- *Identification period.* The new property must be identified within 45 days of the date when the old property was transferred.
- *Exchange period.* The new property must be received by the earlier of the following:
  - Within 180 days of the date when the old property was transferred.
  - The due date (including extensions) for the tax return covering the year of the transfer.

Are these time limits firm, or can they be extended due to unforeseen circumstances? Indications are that the IRS will allow no deviation from either the identification period or the exchange period even when events outside the taxpayer's control preclude strict compliance. See the exception to strict compliance provided for in Revenue Procedure 2010–14 in the "Tax in the News" on the next page.

ETHICS & EQUITY A Delayed § 1031 Like-Kind Exchange: If At First You Don't Succeed, Try Again

Randall owns an office building (adjusted basis of $250,000) that he has been renting to a group of physicians. During negotiations over a new seven-year lease, the physicians offer to purchase the building for $900,000. Randall accepts the offer with the stipulation that the sale be structured as a delayed § 1031 transaction. Consequently, the sales proceeds are paid to a qualified third-party intermediary on the closing date of September 30, 2014.

On October 2, 2014, Randall properly identifies an office building that he would like to acquire. Unfortunately, on November 10, 2014, the property Randall selected is withdrawn from the market. Working with the intermediary, on November 12, 2014, Randall identifies another office building that meets his requirements. The purchase of this property closes on December 15, 2014, and the title is transferred to Randall.

Randall treats the transaction as a § 1031 like-kind exchange. Even though the original office building identified was not acquired, Randall concludes that in substance, he has satisfied the 45-day rule. He identified the acquired office building as soon as the negotiations ceased on his first choice. Should the IRS accept Randall's attempt to comply?

---

[5]Rev.Rul. 61–119, 1961–1 C.B. 395.

TAX IN THE NEWS   **What Happens to § 1031 Deferral If the Qualified Intermediary Defaults?**

Normally, the IRS takes the position that the provisions of § 1031 are to be interpreted narrowly with respect to delayed § 1031 like-kind exchanges. In Revenue Procedure 2010–14, however, the IRS has announced an exception to this strict compliance requirement.

The exception applies if the 180-day time requirement for a delayed § 1031 like-kind exchange is not satisfied because the qualified intermediary defaults due to a bankruptcy or receivership proceeding. In this situation, no gain is recognized by the taxpayer until a payment is received from the qualified intermediary or the bankruptcy trustee. As payments are received, gain is recognized using the gross profit ratio method.

15-2c Boot

If the taxpayer in a like-kind exchange gives or receives some property that is not like-kind property, recognition may occur. Property that is not like-kind property, including cash, is referred to as **boot**. Although the term *boot* does not appear in the Code, tax practitioners commonly use it rather than saying "property that is not like-kind property."

The *receipt* of boot will trigger recognition of gain if there is realized gain. The amount of the recognized gain is the *lesser* of the boot received or the realized gain (realized gain serves as the ceiling on recognition).

Example 3

Emily and Fran exchange machinery, and the exchange qualifies as like kind under § 1031. Because Emily's machinery (adjusted basis of $20,000) is worth $24,000 and Fran's machine has a fair market value of $19,000, Fran also gives Emily cash of $5,000. Emily's recognized gain is $4,000, the lesser of the realized gain ($24,000 amount realized − $20,000 adjusted basis = $4,000) or the fair market value of the boot received ($5,000).

Example 4

Assume the same facts as in the previous example, except that Fran's machine is worth $21,000 (not $19,000). Under these circumstances, Fran gives Emily cash of $3,000 to make up the difference. Emily's recognized gain is $3,000, the lesser of the realized gain of $4,000 ($24,000 amount realized − $20,000 adjusted basis) or the fair market value of the boot received of $3,000.

The receipt of boot does not result in recognition if there is realized loss.

Example 5

Assume the same facts as in Example 3, except that the adjusted basis of Emily's machine is $30,000. Emily's realized loss is $6,000 ($24,000 amount realized − $30,000 adjusted basis). The receipt of the boot of $5,000 does not trigger recognition. Therefore, the recognized loss is $0.

The *giving* of boot usually does not trigger recognition. If the boot given is cash, no realized gain or loss is recognized.

Example 6

Sarah and Gary exchange equipment in a like-kind exchange. Sarah receives equipment with a fair market value of $75,000 and transfers equipment worth $63,000 (adjusted basis of $45,000) and cash of $12,000. Sarah's realized gain is $18,000 ($75,000 amount realized − $45,000 adjusted basis − $12,000 cash). However, none of the realized gain is recognized.

If, however, the boot given is appreciated or depreciated property, gain or loss is recognized to the extent of the difference between the adjusted basis and the fair market value of the boot. For this purpose, *appreciated or depreciated property* is defined as property whose adjusted basis is not equal to the fair market value.

Example 7

Assume the same facts as in the previous example, except that Sarah transfers equipment worth $30,000 (adjusted basis of $36,000) and boot worth $45,000 (adjusted basis of $27,000). Sarah's net gain on this exchange is $12,000 [$75,000 less adjusted basis of $63,000 ($36,000 + $27,000)]. But she is transferring two pieces of property: equipment (like-kind property) with a built-in realized loss of $6,000 ($30,000 fair market value less $36,000 adjusted basis) and non-like-kind property (boot) with a built-in realized gain of $18,000 ($45,000 fair market value less $27,000 adjusted basis).

In this case, the $6,000 realized loss on the like-kind property is *deferred* (not recognized) and the $18,000 realized gain on the non-like-kind property is recognized. In other words, the realized loss on the like-kind property *cannot* be used to offset the realized gain on the boot given up as part of the transaction.

15-2d Basis and Holding Period of Property Received

If an exchange does not qualify as nontaxable under § 1031, gain or loss is recognized and the basis of property received in the exchange is the property's fair market value. If the exchange qualifies for nonrecognition, the basis of property received must be adjusted to reflect any postponed (deferred) gain or loss. The *basis of like-kind property* received in the exchange is the property's fair market value less postponed gain or plus postponed loss. If the exchange partially qualifies for nonrecognition (if recognition is associated with boot), the basis of like-kind property received in the exchange is the property's fair market value less postponed gain or plus postponed loss. The *basis* of any *boot* received is the boot's fair market value.

If there is a postponed loss, nonrecognition creates a situation in which the taxpayer has recovered *less* than the cost or other basis of the property exchanged in an amount equal to the unrecognized loss. If there is a postponed gain, the taxpayer has recovered *more* than the cost or other basis of the property exchanged in an amount equal to the unrecognized gain.

Example 8

Jaime exchanges a building (used in his business) with an adjusted basis of $30,000 and a fair market value of $38,000 for land with a fair market value of $38,000. The land is to be held as an investment. The exchange qualifies as like kind (an exchange of business real property for investment real property). Thus, the basis of the land is $30,000 (the land's fair market value of $38,000 less the $8,000 postponed gain on the building). If the land is later sold for its fair market value of $38,000, the $8,000 postponed gain is recognized.

Example 9

Assume the same facts as in the previous example, except that the building has an adjusted basis of $48,000 and a fair market value of only $38,000. The basis in the newly acquired land is $48,000 (fair market value of $38,000 plus the $10,000 postponed loss on the building). If the land is later sold for its fair market value of $38,000, the $10,000 postponed loss is recognized.

The Code provides an alternative approach for determining the basis of like-kind property received:

> Adjusted basis of like-kind property surrendered
> + Adjusted basis of boot given
> + Gain recognized
> − Fair market value of boot received
> − Loss recognized
> = *Basis of like-kind property received*

This approach is logical in terms of the recovery of capital doctrine. That is, the unrecovered cost or other basis is increased by additional cost (boot given) or decreased by cost recovered (boot received). Any gain recognized is included in the basis of the new property. The taxpayer has been taxed on this amount and is now entitled to recover it tax-free. Any loss recognized is deducted from the basis of the new property. The taxpayer has received a tax benefit on that amount.

The holding period of the property surrendered in the exchange carries over and *tacks on* to the holding period of the like-kind property received.[6] The holding period for boot received in a like-kind exchange begins with the date of the exchange. See Chapter 16 for a discussion of the relevance of the holding period.

Depreciation recapture potential carries over to the property received in a like-kind exchange.[7] See Chapter 17 for a discussion of this topic.

The following comprehensive example illustrates the like-kind exchange rules.

Example 10

Vicki exchanged the following old machines for new machines in five independent like-kind exchanges:

Exchange	Adjusted Basis of Old Machine	Fair Market Value of Old Machine	Fair Market Value of New Machine	Adjusted Basis of Boot Given	Fair Market Value of Boot Received
1	$4,000	$ 9,000	$9,000	$ –0–	$ –0–
2	4,000	6,000	9,000	3,000	–0–
3	4,000	3,000	9,000	6,000	–0–
4	4,000	12,000	9,000	–0–	3,000
5	4,000	3,800	3,500	–0–	300

Vicki's realized and recognized gains and losses and the basis of each of the like-kind properties received are as follows:

			New Basis Calculation					
Exchange	Realized Gain (Loss)	Recognized Gain (Loss)	Old Adj. Basis	+ Boot Given	+ Gain Recognized	– Boot Received	=	New Basis
1	$ 5,000	$–(0)–	$4,000	+ $ –0–	+ $ –0–	– $ –0–	=	$ 4,000*
2	2,000	–(0)–	4,000	+ 3,000	+ –0–	– –0–	=	7,000*
3	(1,000)	–(0)–	4,000	+ 6,000	+ –0–	– –0–	=	10,000**
4	8,000	3,000	4,000	+ –0–	+ 3,000	– 3,000	=	4,000*
5	(200)	–(0)–	4,000	+ –0–	+ –0–	– 300	=	3,700**

* Basis may be determined in gain situations under the alternative method by subtracting the gain not recognized from the fair market value of the new property:
$9,000 – $5,000 = $4,000 for exchange 1.
$9,000 – $2,000 = $7,000 for exchange 2.
$9,000 – $5,000 = $4,000 for exchange 4.

** In loss situations, basis may be determined by adding the loss not recognized to the fair market value of the new property:
$9,000 + $1,000 = $10,000 for exchange 3.
$3,500 + $200 = $3,700 for exchange 5.
The basis of the boot received is the boot's fair market value.

If the taxpayer either assumes a liability or takes property subject to a liability, the amount of the liability is treated as boot given. For the taxpayer whose liability

---

[6]§ 1223(1) and Reg. § 1.1223–1(a). For this carryover holding period rule to apply to like-kind exchanges after March 1, 1954, the like-kind property surrendered must have been either a capital asset or § 1231 property.

[7]Reg. §§ 1.1245–2(a)(4) and 1.1250–2(d)(1).

is assumed or whose property is taken subject to the liability, the amount of the liability is treated as boot received. Example 11 illustrates the effect of such a liability. In addition, the example illustrates the tax consequences for both parties involved in the like-kind exchange.

	Example 11

Jill Saunders and Rick Thompson exchange real estate investments. Jill gives up property with an adjusted basis of $250,000 (fair market value of $400,000) that is subject to a mortgage of $75,000 (assumed by Rick). In return for this property, Jill receives property with a fair market value $300,000 (Rick's adjusted basis in the property is $200,000) and cash of $25,000. Jill's and Rick's realized and recognized gains and their basis in the like-kind property received are computed as follows:[8]

	Jill	Rick
Compute Realized Gain (Loss)		
FMV of like-kind property received	$ 300,000	$ 400,000
+ FMV of other property received		
+ Cash received	25,000	
+ Debt relief	75,000	
− Cash paid		(25,000)
− Debt assumed		(75,000)
= Net Consideration Received	$ 400,000	$ 300,000
− Adjusted basis of property given	(250,000)	(200,000)
= Realized Gain (Loss)	$ 150,000	$ 100,000
Compute Boot Received		
Debt relief	$ 75,000	$ -0-
+ Cash received	25,000	
+ FMV of other property received		
= Boot Received	$ 100,000	$ -0-
Compute Recognized Gain		
Lesser of realized gain or boot received	$ 100,000	$ -0-
Compute Basis for New Property (Other Than Cash)		
Adjusted Basis of Property Given	$ 250,000	$ 200,000
+ Boot given (cash paid; debt assumed)	-0-	100,000
+ Gain recognized	100,000	-0-
− Boot received	(100,000)	-0-
= Basis of New Property	$ 250,000	$ 300,000

15-2e Reporting Considerations

Section 1031 transactions are reported on Form 8824 (Like-Kind Exchanges). Part III of Form 8824 has been completed based on the information provided for Jill Saunders's exchange.

This form should be used even though the like-kind exchange transaction results in no recognized gain or loss. It must be filed with the regular return for the tax year in which the taxpayer transfers property in a like-kind exchange.

If the like-kind exchange is with a related party, additional Forms 8824 must be filed for the following two years.

---

[8]Example (2) of Reg. § 1.1031(d)–2 illustrates a special situation in which both the buyer and the seller transfer liabilities that are assumed by the other party or both parties acquire property that is subject to a liability.

Form 8824 (2013)   Page **2**

Name(s) shown on tax return. Do not enter name and social security number if shown on other side. | Your social security number

Jill Saunders (Example 11)

Part III	**Realized Gain or (Loss), Recognized Gain, and Basis of Like-Kind Property Received**

Caution: *If you transferred **and** received (a) more than one group of like-kind properties or (b) cash or other (not like-kind) property, see* **Reporting of multi-asset exchanges** *in the instructions.*

Note: *Complete lines 12 through 14* **only** *if you gave up property that was not like-kind. Otherwise, go to line 15.*

12	Fair market value (FMV) of other property given up	**12**	
13	Adjusted basis of other property given up	**13**	
14	Gain or (loss) recognized on other property given up. Subtract line 13 from line 12. Report the gain or (loss) in the same manner as if the exchange had been a sale	**14**	
	Caution: *If the property given up was used previously or partly as a home, see* **Property used as home** *in the instructions.*		
15	Cash received, FMV of other property received, plus net liabilities assumed by other party, reduced (but not below zero) by any exchange expenses you incurred (see instructions)	**15**	100,000
16	FMV of like-kind property you received	**16**	300,000
17	Add lines 15 and 16	**17**	400,000
18	Adjusted basis of like-kind property you gave up, net amounts paid to other party, plus any exchange expenses **not** used on line 15 (see instructions)	**18**	250,000
19	**Realized gain or (loss).** Subtract line 18 from line 17	**19**	150,000
20	Enter the smaller of line 15 or line 19, but not less than zero	**20**	100,000
21	Ordinary income under recapture rules. Enter here and on Form 4797, line 16 (see instructions)	**21**	-0-
22	Subtract line 21 from line 20. If zero or less, enter -0-. If more than zero, enter here and on Schedule D or Form 4797, unless the installment method applies (see instructions)	**22**	100,000
23	**Recognized gain.** Add lines 21 and 22	**23**	100,000
24	Deferred gain or (loss). Subtract line 23 from line 19. If a related party exchange, see instructions	**24**	50,000
25	**Basis of like-kind property received.** Subtract line 15 from the sum of lines 18 and 23	**25**	250,000

15-3 INVOLUNTARY CONVERSIONS—§ 1033

LO.3

Explain the nonrecognition provisions available on the involuntary conversion of property.

Section 1033 provides that a taxpayer who suffers an involuntary conversion of property may postpone recognition of *gain* realized from the conversion. The objective of this provision is to provide relief to the taxpayer who has suffered hardship and does not have the wherewithal to pay the tax on any gain realized from the conversion. Postponement of realized gain is permitted to the extent that the taxpayer *reinvests* the amount realized from the conversion in replacement property. The rules for nonrecognition of gain are as follows:

- If the amount reinvested in replacement property *equals or exceeds* the amount realized, realized gain is *not recognized*.
- If the amount reinvested in replacement property is *less than* the amount realized, realized gain *is recognized* to the extent of the deficiency.

If a *loss* occurs on an involuntary conversion, § 1033 does not modify the normal rules for loss recognition. That is, if a realized loss would otherwise be recognized, § 1033 does not change the result.

15-3a Involuntary Conversion Defined

An **involuntary conversion** results from the destruction (complete or partial), theft, seizure, requisition or condemnation, or sale or exchange under threat or imminence of requisition or condemnation of the taxpayer's property.[9] To prove the existence of a threat or imminence of condemnation, the taxpayer must obtain confirmation that there has been a decision to acquire the property for public use. In addition, the taxpayer must have reasonable grounds to believe the property will

---

[9]§ 1033(a) and Reg. §§ 1.1033(a)−1(a) and −2(a).

be taken.[10] The property does not have to be sold to the authority threatening to condemn it to qualify for § 1033 postponement. If the taxpayer satisfies the confirmation and reasonable grounds requirements, he or she can sell the property to another party.[11] Likewise, the sale of property to a condemning authority by a taxpayer who acquired the property from its former owner with the knowledge that the property was under threat of condemnation also qualifies as an involuntary conversion under § 1033.[12] A voluntary act, such as a taxpayer destroying the property by arson, is not an involuntary conversion.[13]

15-3b Computing the Amount Realized

The amount realized from an involuntary conversion is normally any insurance proceeds received. In the case of the condemnation of property, the amount realized usually includes only the amount received as compensation for the property.[14] Any amount received that is designated as severance damages by both the government and the taxpayer is not included in the amount realized. *Severance awards* usually occur when only a portion of the property is condemned (e.g., a strip of land is taken to build a highway). Severance damages are awarded because the value of the taxpayer's remaining property has declined as a result of the condemnation. Such damages are a tax-free recovery of capital and reduce the basis of the property. However, if either of the following requirements is satisfied, the nonrecognition provision of § 1033 applies to the severance damages:

- The severance damages are used to restore the usability of the remaining property.
- The usefulness of the remaining property is destroyed by the condemnation, and the property is sold and replaced at a cost equal to or exceeding the sum of the condemnation award, severance damages, and sales proceeds.

The government condemns a portion of Ron's farmland to build part of an interstate highway. Because the highway denies his cattle access to a pond and some grazing land, Ron receives severance damages in addition to the condemnation proceeds for the land taken. Ron must reduce the basis of the property by the amount of the severance damages. If the amount of the severance damages received exceeds the adjusted basis, Ron recognizes gain.	**Example 12**
Assume the same facts as in the previous example, except that Ron uses the proceeds from the condemnation and the severance damages to build another pond and to clear woodland for grazing. Therefore, all of the proceeds are eligible for § 1033 treatment. There is no possibility of gain recognition as the result of the amount of the severance damages received exceeding the adjusted basis.	**Example 13**

15-3c Replacement Property

The requirements for replacement property generally are more restrictive than those for like-kind property under § 1031. The basic requirement is that the replacement property be similar or related in service or use to the involuntarily converted property.[15]

Different interpretations of the phrase *similar or related in service or use* apply depending on whether the involuntarily converted property is held by an *owner-user* or by an *owner-investor* (e.g., lessor). A taxpayer who uses the property in his or her trade or business is subject to a more restrictive test in terms of acquiring replacement property. For an owner-investor, the *taxpayer use* test applies, and for an

---

[10]Rev.Rul. 63–221, 1963–2 C.B. 332, and *Joseph P. Balistrieri*, 38 TCM 526, T.C.Memo. 1979–115.

[11]Rev.Rul. 81–180, 1981–2 C.B. 161.

[12]Rev.Rul. 81–181, 1981–2 C.B. 162.

[13]Rev.Rul. 82–74, 1982–1 C.B. 110.

[14]*Pioneer Real Estate Co.*, 47 B.T.A. 886 (1942), *acq.* 1943 C.B. 18.

[15]§ 1033(a) and Reg. § 1.1033(a)–1.

TAX IN THE NEWS   The Fight Goes On

Boxing fans know that a boxer can be knocked down and then get up off the canvas and win. It appears that this is what happened to a property owner in California named Community Youth Athletic Center (CYAC). CYAC owned and operated a gym (including a boxing ring) that it made available to at-risk kids. The local governmental authority (National City) approved a condo project that would allow a developer to acquire and demolish CYAC's gym. Under the now classic U.S. Supreme Court decision in *Kelo v. City of New London*, the power of eminent domain is available if used for the purpose of economic improvement. Without any change since *Kelo*, therefore, CYAC would lose its gym through a condemnation proceeding.

Because of the potential widespread effect on private property rights of *Kelo*, many states have enacted restrictions on the use of condemnation. In California, blight can be a justification, but only if there is "specific and quantifiable" evidence of such blight and it cannot be removed without the use of eminent domain. Although National City had asserted that the CYAC gym was in a blighted area, the California Superior Court found no such "specific and quantifiable" evidence. Thus, unlike *Kelo*, where the property owner was knocked out, in *CYAC v. National City*, the public authority was the loser.

Source: Based on "Property Rights Knockout," *Wall Street Journal*, May 2, 2011, p. A14.

owner-user, the *functional use test* applies. Furthermore, a special test applies in the case of involuntary conversions that result from condemnations.

Taxpayer Use Test

The taxpayer use test for owner-investors provides the taxpayer with more flexibility in terms of what qualifies as replacement property than does the functional use test for owner-users. Essentially, the properties must be used by the taxpayer (the owner-investor) in similar endeavors. For example, rental property held by an owner-investor qualifies if replaced by other rental property, regardless of the type of rental property involved. The test is met when an investor replaces a manufacturing plant with a wholesale grocery warehouse if both properties are held for the production of rent income.[16] The replacement of a rental residence with a personal residence does not meet the test.[17]

Functional Use Test

The functional use test applies to owner-users (e.g., a manufacturer whose manufacturing plant is destroyed by fire is required to replace the plant with another facility of similar functional use). Under this test, the taxpayer's use of the replacement property and of the involuntarily converted property must be the same. Replacing a manufacturing plant with a wholesale grocery warehouse does not meet this test. Replacing a rental residence with a personal residence also does not pass the test.

Special Rule for Condemnations

Under one set of circumstances, the broader replacement rules for like-kind exchanges are substituted for the narrow replacement rules normally used for involuntary conversions. This beneficial provision applies if business real property or investment real property is condemned. This provision gives the taxpayer substantially more flexibility in selecting replacement property. For example, improved real property can be replaced with unimproved real property.

The rules concerning the nature of replacement property are illustrated in Concept Summary 15.1.

---

[16]*Loco Realty Co. v. Comm.*, 62–2 USTC ¶9657, 10 AFTR 2d 5359, 306 F.2d 207 (CA–8, 1962).

[17]Rev.Rul. 70–466, 1970–2 C.B. 165.

CONCEPT SUMMARY 15.1

Involuntary Conversions: Replacement Property Tests

Type of Property and User	Taxpayer Use Test	Functional Use Test	Special Rule for Condemnations*
An investor's rented shopping mall is destroyed by fire; the mall may be replaced with other rental properties (e.g., an apartment building).	X		
A manufacturing plant is destroyed by fire; replacement property must consist of another manufacturing plant that is functionally the same as the property converted.		X	
Personal residence of a taxpayer is condemned by a local government authority; replacement property must consist of another personal residence.		X	
Land used by a manufacturing company is condemned by a local government authority.			X
Apartment and land held by an investor are sold due to the threat or imminence of condemnation.			X

*Applies the same test as in the case of like-kind exchanges.

© iStockphoto.com/Andrey Prokhorov

15-3d Time Limitation on Replacement

The taxpayer normally has a two-year period after the close of the taxable year in which gain is realized from an involuntary conversion to replace the property.[18] This rule affords as much as three years from the date of realization of gain to replace the property if the realization of gain took place on the first day of the taxable year.[19]

> **Example 14**
> Megan's building is destroyed by fire on December 16, 2013. The adjusted basis is $325,000. Megan receives $400,000 from the insurance company on January 10, 2014. She is a calendar year taxpayer. The latest date for replacement is December 31, 2016 (the end of the taxable year in which realized gain occurred plus two years). The critical date is not the date the involuntary conversion occurred, but rather the date of gain realization.

In the case of a condemnation of real property used in a trade or business or held for investment, a three-year period is substituted for the normal two-year period. In this case, the taxpayer can actually have as many as four years from the date of realization of gain to replace the property.

> **Example 15**
> Assume the same facts as in the previous example, except that Megan's building is condemned. Megan receives notification of the future condemnation on November 1, 2013. The condemnation occurs on December 16, 2013, with the condemnation proceeds being received on January 10, 2014. The latest date for replacement is December 31, 2017 (the end of the taxable year in which realized gain occurred plus three years).

The *earliest date* for replacement typically is the date the involuntary conversion occurs. However, if the property is condemned, it is possible to replace the condemned property before this date. In this case, the earliest date is the date of the threat or imminence of requisition or condemnation of the property. The purpose of this provision is to enable the taxpayer to make an orderly replacement of the condemned property.

> **Example 16**
> Assume the same facts as in Example 15. The earliest date that Megan can replace the building is November 1, 2013, which is the date of the condemnation of the building.

[18]§§ 1033(a)(2)(B) and (g)(4) and Reg. § 1.1033(a)–2(c)(3).
[19]The taxpayer can apply for an extension of this time period anytime before its expiration [Reg. § 1.1033(a)–2(c)(3)]. Also, the period for filing the application for extension can be extended if the taxpayer shows reasonable cause.

15-3e Nonrecognition of Gain

Nonrecognition of gain can be either mandatory or elective, depending on whether the conversion is direct (into replacement property) or indirect (into money).

Direct Conversion

If the conversion is directly into replacement property rather than into money, nonrecognition of realized gain is *mandatory*. In this case, the basis of the replacement property is the same as the adjusted basis of the converted property. Direct conversion is rare in practice and usually involves condemnations.

Example 17

Lupe's property, with an adjusted basis of $20,000, is condemned by the state. Lupe receives property with a fair market value of $50,000 as compensation for the property taken. Because the nonrecognition of realized gain is mandatory for direct conversions, Lupe's realized gain of $30,000 is not recognized and the basis of the replacement property is $20,000 (adjusted basis of the condemned property).

Conversion into Money

If the conversion is into money, the realized gain is recognized only to the extent the amount realized from the involuntary conversion exceeds the cost of the qualifying replacement property.[20] This is the usual case, and nonrecognition (postponement) is *elective*. If the election is not made, the realized gain is recognized.

The basis of the replacement property is the property's cost less any postponed (deferred) gain.[21] If the election to postpone gain is made, the holding period of the replacement property includes the holding period of the converted property.

Section 1033 applies *only to gains* and *not to losses*. Losses from involuntary conversions are recognized if the property is held for business or income-producing purposes. Personal casualty losses are recognized, but condemnation losses related to personal use assets (e.g., a personal residence) are neither recognized nor postponed.

Example 18

Walt's building (used in his trade or business), with an adjusted basis of $50,000, is destroyed by fire on October 5, 2014. Walt is a calendar year taxpayer. On November 17, 2014, he receives an insurance reimbursement of $100,000 for the loss. Walt invests $80,000 in a new building and uses the other $20,000 of insurance proceeds to pay off credit card debt.

- Walt has until December 31, 2016, to make the new investment and qualify for the nonrecognition election.
- Walt's realized gain is $50,000 ($100,000 insurance proceeds received − $50,000 adjusted basis of old building).
- Assuming that the replacement property qualifies as similar or related in service or use, Walt's recognized gain is $20,000. He reinvested $20,000 less than the insurance proceeds received ($100,000 proceeds − $80,000 reinvested). Therefore, his realized gain is recognized to that extent.
- Walt's basis in the new building is $50,000. This is the building's cost of $80,000 less the postponed gain of $30,000 (realized gain of $50,000 − recognized gain of $20,000).

Example 19

Assume the same facts as in the previous example, except that Walt receives only $45,000 of insurance proceeds. He has a realized and recognized loss of $5,000. The basis of the new building is the building's cost of $80,000.

If the destroyed building in Example 19 had been held for personal use, the recognized loss would have been subject to the following additional limitations.[22]

---

[20]§ 1033(a)(2)(A) and Reg. § 1.1033(a)–2(c)(1).
[21]§ 1033(b).

[22]§ 165(c)(3) and Reg. § 1.165–7.

The loss of $5,000 would have been limited to the decline in fair market value of the property, and the amount of the loss would have been reduced first by $100 and then by 10% of adjusted gross income (refer to Chapter 7).

15-3f Reporting Considerations

Involuntary conversions from casualty and theft are reported first on Form 4684, Casualties and Thefts. Casualty and theft losses on personal use property for the individual taxpayer are carried from Form 4684 to Schedule A of Form 1040. For other casualty and theft items, the Form 4684 amounts are generally reported on Form 4797, Sales of Business Property, unless Form 4797 is not required. In the latter case, the amounts are reported directly on the tax return involved.

Except for personal use property, recognized gains and losses from involuntary conversions other than by casualty and theft are reported on Form 4797. As stated previously, if the property involved in the involuntary conversion (other than by casualty and theft) is personal use property, any realized loss is not recognized. Any realized gain is treated as gain on a voluntary sale.

What procedure should be followed if the taxpayer intends to acquire qualifying replacement property but has not done so by the time the tax return is filed? The taxpayer should elect § 1033 and report all of the details of the transaction on a statement attached to the return. Although a tax form (Form 8824) is available for § 1031 like-kind exchanges, no special form is provided for § 1033 transactions. When the qualifying replacement property is acquired, the taxpayer should attach a statement to the tax return that contains relevant information on the replacement property.

An amended return must be filed if qualified replacement property is not acquired during the statutory time period allowed. An amended return also is required if the cost of the replacement property is less than the amount realized from the involuntary conversion. In this case, the return would recognize the portion of the realized gain that can no longer be deferred.

15-4 SALE OF A RESIDENCE—§ 121

A taxpayer's **personal residence** is a personal use asset. Therefore, a realized loss from the sale of a personal residence is not recognized.[23]

A realized gain from the sale of a personal residence is subject to taxation. However, favorable relief from recognition of gain is provided in the form of the **§ 121 exclusion**. Under this provision, a taxpayer can exclude up to $250,000 of realized gain on the sale of a taxpayer's principal residence.[24]

LO.4

Describe the provision for the permanent exclusion of gain on the sale of a personal residence.

15-4a Principal Residence

Whether property is the taxpayer's principal residence "depends upon all of the facts and circumstances in each case."[25] A residence does not have to be a house. For example, a houseboat, a house trailer, or a motor home can qualify.[26] Land, under certain circumstances, can qualify for exclusion treatment. The lot on which a house is built obviously qualifies. An adjacent lot can qualify if it is regularly used by the owner as part of the residential property. To qualify, the land must be sold along with the residence or within two years before or after the sale of the residence.

---

[23]§ 165(c).
[24]§ 121(b).

[25]Regulation § 1.121–1(b)(2) includes factors to be considered in determining a taxpayer's principal residence.
[26]Reg. § 1.1034–1(c)(3)(i).

Example 20

Mitch graduates from college and moves to Boston, where he is employed. He decides to rent an apartment in Boston because of its proximity to his place of employment. He purchases a beach condo in the Cape Cod area that he occupies most weekends. Mitch does not intend to live at the beach condo except on weekends. The apartment in Boston is his principal residence.

15-4b Requirements for Exclusion Treatment

To qualify for exclusion treatment, at the date of the sale, the residence must have been *owned* and *used* by the taxpayer as the principal residence for at least two years during the five-year period ending on the date of the sale.[27]

Example 21

Melissa sells her principal residence on September 18, 2014. She had purchased it on July 5, 2012, and lived in it since then. The sale of Melissa's residence qualifies for the § 121 exclusion.

The five-year window enables the taxpayer to qualify for the § 121 exclusion even though the property is not his or her principal residence at the date of the sale.

Example 22

Benjamin sells his former principal residence on August 16, 2014. He had purchased it on April 1, 2006, and lived in it until July 1, 2013, when he converted it to rental property. Even though the property is rental property on August 16, 2014, rather than Benjamin's principal residence, the sale qualifies for the § 121 exclusion.[28] During the five-year period from August 16, 2009, to August 16, 2014, Benjamin owned and used the property as his principal residence for at least two years.

Taxpayers might be tempted to make liberal use of the § 121 exclusion as a means of speculating when the price of residential housing is rising. Without any time restriction on its use, § 121 would permit the exclusion of realized gain on multiple sales of principal residences. The Code curbs this approach by denying the application of the § 121 exclusion to sales occurring within two years of its last use.[29]

Example 23

Mike sells his principal residence (the first residence) in June 2013 for $150,000 (realized gain of $60,000). He then buys and sells the following (all of which qualify as principal residences):

	Date of Purchase	Date of Sale	Amount Involved
Second residence	July 2013		$160,000
Second residence		April 2014	180,000
Third residence	May 2014		200,000

Because multiple sales have taken place within a period of two years, § 121 does not apply to the sale of the second residence. Thus, the realized gain of $20,000 [$180,000 (selling price) − $160,000 (purchase price)] must be recognized.

15-4c Exceptions to the Two-Year Ownership Rule

The two-year ownership and use requirement and the "only once every two years" provision could create a hardship for taxpayers in certain situations that are beyond their control. Thus, under the following special circumstances, the requirements are waived:[30]

- Change in place of employment.
- Health.
- To the extent provided in the Regulations, other unforeseen circumstances.

---

[27]§ 121(a). However, § 121(d)(10) provides that exclusion treatment does not apply if the residence was acquired in a like-kind exchange within the prior five years of the sale of the residence.

[28]However, any realized gain on the sale that is attributable to depreciation is not eligible for the § 121 exclusion. See Example 36.

[29]§ 121(b)(3).

[30]§ 121(c)(2)(B).

TAX IN THE NEWS   Living in a High-Crime Neighborhood

Normally, a taxpayer must satisfy the tax year ownership and use requirements and the only once-every-two-years provision to be eligible for the § 121 exclusion. However, under the unforeseen circumstances exception, a taxpayer who does not satisfy these three requirements may be eligible for a reduced § 121 exclusion.

In several letter rulings, the IRS has been sympathetic to crime victims. One ruling involved a taxpayer who was accosted leaving his home, driven to several locations, and forced to withdraw money from an ATM. In another ruling, the taxpayers and their son were hospitalized after being assaulted by neighbors. In both cases, the taxpayers sold their homes. Although the taxpayers had not satisfied the three time period requirements, the IRS held that they were eligible for reduced § 121 exclusion treatment under the unforeseen circumstances exception.

© iStockphoto.com/Andrey Prokhorov

These three exceptions have been amplified by Treasury Department Regulations and are discussed in the sections that follow.[31] Each of these exceptions provides a *partial* exclusion. The calculation of the partial exclusion is discussed later in this chapter (see Relief Provision in Section 15-4d).

Change in Place of Employment

For this exception to apply, the distance requirements applicable to the deductibility of moving expenses must be satisfied (see Chapter 9). Consequently, the location of the taxpayer's new employment must be at least 50 miles further from the old residence than the old residence was from the old job. The house must be used as the principal residence of the taxpayer at the time of the change in the place of employment. Employment includes the commencement of employment with a new employer, the continuation of employment with the same employer, and the commencement or continuation of self-employment.

> **Example 24**
>
> Assume the same facts as in the previous example, except that in March 2014, Mike's employer transfers him to a job in another state that is 400 miles away. Thus, the sale of the second residence and the purchase of the third residence were due to relocation of employment. Consequently, the § 121 exclusion is partially available on the sale of the second residence.

Health Considerations

For the health exception to apply, health must be the primary reason for the sale or exchange of the residence. A sale or exchange that is merely beneficial to the general health or well-being of the individual will not qualify. The health exception can be satisfied under either a general facts and circumstances approach or by a safe harbor established in the Regulations. The safe harbor applies if there is a physician's recommendation for a change of residence (1) to obtain, provide, or facilitate the diagnosis, cure, mitigation, or treatment of disease, illness, or injury or (2) to obtain or provide medical or personal care for an individual suffering from a disease, an illness, or an injury.

Unforeseen Circumstances

For the unforeseen circumstances exception to apply, the primary reason for the sale or exchange of the residence must be an event the taxpayer did not anticipate before purchasing and occupying the residence. This exception can be satisfied

---

[31] See Reg. § 1.121–3T and IRS Publication 523 (Selling Your Home) for further details and illustrations.

TAX IN THE NEWS   **A Tax Break for Those Who Serve**

To qualify for exclusion treatment on the gain from the sale of a principal residence, a two-year ownership and occupancy requirement during the five-year period preceding the sale must be satisfied. As satisfying this provision was difficult for those in the military, Congress enacted the Military Family Tax Relief Act of 2003 to provide some relief.

The two-out-of-five-years requirement still must be satisfied, but at the election of the taxpayer, the running of the five-year period can be suspended during any period the taxpayer or spouse is serving on qualified official extended duty in the military. Because this extension is limited to 10 years, the maximum period allowed is 15 years. This provision is retroactive to home sales after May 6, 1997.

under either a general facts and circumstances approach or by a safe harbor established in the Regulations. The safe harbor applies in any of the following instances:

- Involuntary conversion of the residence.
- Natural or human-made disasters or acts of war or terrorism resulting in a casualty to the residence.
- Death of a qualified individual.
- Cessation of employment that results in eligibility for unemployment compensation.
- Change in employment or self-employment that results in the taxpayer being unable to pay housing costs and reasonable basic living expenses for the taxpayer's household.
- Divorce or legal separation.
- Multiple births resulting from the same pregnancy.

Example 25

Debra and Roy are engaged and buy a house (sharing the mortgage payments) and live in it as their personal residence. Eighteen months after the purchase, they cancel their wedding plans, and Roy moves out of the house. Because Debra cannot afford to make the payments alone, they sell the house. While the sale does not fit under the safe harbor, the sale does qualify under the unforeseen circumstances exception.

15-4d Calculation of the Amount of the Exclusion

General Provisions

The amount of the available § 121 exclusion on the sale of a principal residence is $250,000.[32] If the realized gain does not exceed $250,000, there is no recognized gain.

Realized gain is calculated in the normal manner. The *amount realized* is the selling price less the selling expenses, which include items such as the cost of advertising the property for sale, real estate broker commissions, legal fees in connection with the sale, and loan placement fees paid by the taxpayer as a condition of arranging financing for the buyer. Repairs and maintenance performed by the seller to aid in selling the property are treated neither as selling expenses nor as adjustments to the taxpayer's adjusted basis for the residence.

THE BIG PICTURE

Example 26

Return to the facts of *The Big Picture* on p. 15-1. Recall that one of Alice's options is to sell her current house and move into the inherited house. Assume that Alice, who is single, sells her current personal residence (adjusted basis of $130,000) for $348,000. She has owned and lived in the house for 15 years. Her selling expenses are $18,000. Three weeks prior to the sale, Alice pays a carpenter and a painter $1,000 to make

---

[32]§ 121(b)(1).

some repairs and paint the two bathrooms. Her recognized gain would be calculated as follows:

Amount realized ($348,000 − $18,000)	$ 330,000
Adjusted basis	(130,000)
Realized gain	$ 200,000
§ 121 exclusion	(200,000)
Recognized gain	$ –0–

Because the available § 121 exclusion of $250,000 would exceed Alice's realized gain of $200,000, her recognized gain would be $0.

THE BIG PICTURE

Example 27

Continue with *The Big Picture* and the facts of Example 26, except that the selling price is $490,000.

Amount realized ($490,000 − $18,000)	$ 472,000
Adjusted basis	(130,000)
Realized gain	$ 342,000
§ 121 exclusion	(250,000)
Recognized gain	$ 92,000

Because the realized gain of $342,000 would exceed the § 121 exclusion amount of $250,000, Alice's recognized gain would be $92,000.

Effect on Married Couples

If a married couple files a joint return, the $250,000 amount is increased to $500,000 if the following requirements are satisfied:[33]

- Either spouse meets the at-least-two-years *ownership* requirement.
- Both spouses meet the at-least-two-years *use* requirement.
- Neither spouse is ineligible for the § 121 exclusion on the sale of the current principal residence because of the sale of another principal residence within the prior two years.

Example 28

Margaret sells her personal residence (adjusted basis of $150,000) for $650,000. She has owned and lived in the residence for six years. Her selling expenses are $40,000. Margaret is married to Ted, and they file a joint return. Ted has lived in the residence since they were married two and one-half years ago.

Amount realized ($650,000 − $40,000)	$ 610,000
Adjusted basis	(150,000)
Realized gain	$ 460,000
§ 121 exclusion	(460,000)
Recognized gain	$ –0–

Because the realized gain of $460,000 is less than the available § 121 exclusion amount of $500,000, no gain is recognized.

---

[33]§ 121(b)(2).

A surviving spouse can continue to use the $500,000 exclusion amount on the sale of a personal residence for the next two years following the deceased spouse's death. If the sale occurs in the year of death, however, a joint return must be filed by the surviving spouse.

Relief Provision

As discussed earlier in Exceptions to the Two-Year Ownership Rule, partial § 121 exclusion treatment may be available when not all of the statutory requirements are satisfied. Under the relief provision, the § 121 exclusion amount ($250,000 or $500,000) is multiplied by a fraction, the numerator of which is the number of qualifying months and the denominator of which is 24 months. The resulting amount is the excluded gain.[34]

Example 29

On October 1, 2013, Rich and Audrey, who file a joint return and live in Chicago, sell their personal residence, which they have owned and lived in for eight years. The realized gain of $325,000 is excluded under § 121. They purchase another personal residence for $525,000 on October 2, 2013. Audrey's employer transfers her to the Denver office in August 2014. Rich and Audrey sell their Chicago residence on August 2, 2014, and purchase a residence in Denver shortly thereafter. The realized gain on the sale is $300,000.

The $325,000 gain on the first Chicago residence is excluded under § 121. The sale of the second Chicago residence is within the two-year window of the prior sale, but because it resulted from a change in employment, Rich and Audrey can qualify for partial § 121 exclusion treatment as follows:

Realized gain	$ 300,000
§ 121 exclusion:	
$\dfrac{10 \text{ months}}{24 \text{ months}} \times \$500,000$	(208,333)
Recognized gain	$ 91,667

Basis of New Residence

Because § 121 is an exclusion provision rather than a postponement of gain provision, the basis of a new residence is its cost.[35]

15-4e Involuntary Conversion and Using §§ 121 and 1033

A taxpayer can use both the § 121 exclusion of gain provision and the § 1033 postponement of gain provision.[36] The taxpayer initially can elect to exclude realized gain under § 121 to the extent of the statutory amount. Then a qualified replacement of the residence under § 1033 can be used to postpone the remainder of the realized gain. In applying § 1033, the amount of the required reinvestment is reduced by the amount of the § 121 exclusion.

Example 30

Angel's principal residence is destroyed by a tornado. Her adjusted basis for the residence is $140,000. She receives insurance proceeds of $480,000.

If Angel does not elect to use the § 121 exclusion, her realized gain on the involuntary conversion of her principal residence is $340,000 ($480,000 amount realized − $140,000 adjusted basis). Thus, to postpone the $340,000 realized gain under § 1033, she would need to acquire qualifying property costing at least $480,000.

---

[34]§ 121(c)(1).
[35]§ 1012.

[36]§ 121(d)(5).

Using the § 121 exclusion enables Angel to reduce the amount of the required reinvestment for § 1033 purposes from $480,000 to $230,000. That is, by using § 121 in conjunction with § 1033, the amount realized, for § 1033 purposes, is reduced to $230,000 ($480,000 − $250,000 § 121 exclusion).

Note that if Angel does not acquire qualifying replacement property for § 1033 purposes, her recognized gain is $90,000 ($480,000 − $140,000 adjusted basis − $250,000 § 121 exclusion).

15-5 OTHER NONRECOGNITION PROVISIONS

The typical taxpayer experiences the sale of a personal residence or an involuntary conversion more frequently than the other types of nontaxable exchanges. Several less common nonrecognition provisions are treated briefly in the remainder of this chapter.

LO.5

Identify other nonrecognition provisions contained in the Code.

15-5a Exchange of Stock for Property—§ 1032

Under § 1032, a corporation does not recognize gain or loss on the receipt of money or other property in exchange for its stock (including treasury stock). In other words, a corporation does not recognize gain or loss when it deals in its own stock. This provision is consistent with the accounting treatment of such transactions.

15-5b Certain Exchanges of Insurance Policies—§ 1035

Under § 1035, no gain or loss is recognized from the exchange of certain insurance contracts or policies. The rules relating to exchanges not solely in kind and the basis of the property acquired are the same as under § 1031. Exchanges qualifying for nonrecognition include the following:

- The exchange of life insurance contracts.
- The exchange of a life insurance contract for an endowment or annuity contract.
- The exchange of an endowment contract for another endowment contract that provides for regular payments beginning at a date not later than the date payments would have begun under the contract exchanged.
- The exchange of an endowment contract for an annuity contract.
- The exchange of annuity contracts.

15-5c Exchange of Stock for Stock of the Same Corporation—§ 1036

Section 1036 provides that a shareholder does not recognize gain or loss on the exchange of common stock solely for common stock in the same corporation or from the exchange of preferred stock for preferred stock in the same corporation. Exchanges between individual shareholders as well as between a shareholder and the corporation are included. The rules relating to exchanges not solely in kind and the basis of the property acquired are the same as under § 1031. For example, a nonrecognition exchange occurs when common stock with different rights, such as voting for nonvoting, is exchanged. A shareholder usually recognizes gain or loss from the exchange of common for preferred or preferred for common even though the stock exchanged is in the same corporation.

15-5d Certain Reacquisitions of Real Property—§ 1038

Under § 1038, no loss is recognized from the repossession of real property sold on an installment basis. Gain is recognized to a limited extent.

15-5e Transfers of Property between Spouses or Incident to Divorce—§ 1041

Section 1041 provides that transfers of property *between spouses or former spouses incident to divorce* are nontaxable transactions. Therefore, the basis to the recipient is a carryover basis. To be treated as incident to the divorce, the transfer must be related to the cessation of marriage or occur within one year after the date on which the marriage ceases.

Section 1041 also provides for nontaxable exchange treatment on property transfers *between spouses during marriage*. The basis to the recipient spouse is a carryover basis.

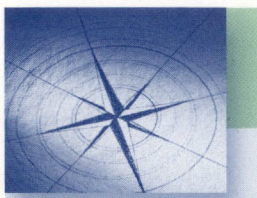

ETHICS & EQUITY Incident to Divorce or Not?

Randy and Judy are divorced on December 28, 2013, after being married for 10 years. Several years ago, they purchased a beach lot for $300,000 and planned to construct a beach house there for vacation purposes.

On December 21, 2014, Randy transfers his interest in the beach lot to Judy for $325,000 (i.e., 50 percent of the fair market value of $650,000). According to both Randy and Judy, the sale was not associated with the divorce but was made to enable Randy to invest the cash in a new business. They treat the transaction as the sale of Randy's one-half interest to Judy. Accordingly, Randy recognizes a capital gain of $175,000 ($325,000 − $150,000), which is eligible for the 15 percent alternative tax rate. Judy considers her adjusted basis to be $475,000 ($150,000 + $325,000).

Evaluate Randy and Judy's treatment of this transaction.

15-5f Rollovers into Specialized Small Business Investment Companies—§ 1044

A postponement opportunity is available for some sellers of publicly traded securities under § 1044. If the amount realized is reinvested in the common stock or partnership interest of a specialized small business investment company (SSBIC), the realized gain is not recognized. Any amount not reinvested will trigger recognition of the realized gain to the extent of the deficiency. The taxpayer must reinvest the proceeds within 60 days of the date of sale to qualify. Various statutory ceilings apply to the amount of realized gain that can be postponed and time limitations are also imposed.[37]

15-6 TAX PLANNING

15-6a Like-Kind Exchanges

LO.6

Review and apply various tax planning opportunities related to the nonrecognition provisions discussed in the chapter.

Because application of the like-kind exchange provisions is mandatory rather than elective, in certain instances, it may be preferable to avoid qualifying for § 1031 nonrecognition. To avoid the application of a deferral under § 1031, the taxpayer should structure the transaction so that at least one of the statutory requirements for a § 1031 like-kind exchange is not satisfied. If the like-kind exchange provisions do not apply, the end result may be the recognition of capital gain in exchange for a higher basis in the newly acquired asset. Also, the immediate recognition of gain may be preferable in certain

---

[37]See IRS Publication 550 (*Investment Income and Expenses*), Chapter 4, p. 66.

situations. Examples in which immediate recognition is beneficial include the following:

- Taxpayer has unused net operating loss carryovers.
- Taxpayer has unused general business credit carryovers.
- Taxpayer has suspended or current passive activity losses.

Alicia disposes of a machine (used in her business) with an adjusted basis of $3,000 for $4,000. She also acquires a new business machine for $9,000. If § 1031 applies, the $1,000 realized gain is not recognized and the basis of the new machine is reduced by $1,000 (from $9,000 to $8,000). If § 1031 does not apply, a $1,000 gain is recognized and may receive favorable capital gain treatment to the extent the gain is not recognized as ordinary income due to the depreciation recapture provisions (see Chapter 17). In addition, the basis for depreciation on the new machine is $9,000 rather than $8,000 because there is no unrecognized gain.

Example 31

The application of § 1031 nonrecognition treatment should also be avoided when the adjusted basis of the property being disposed of exceeds the fair market value.

Assume the same facts as in the previous example, except that the fair market value of the machine is $2,500. If § 1031 applies, the $500 realized loss is not recognized. To recognize the loss, Alicia should sell the old machine and purchase the new one. The purchase and sale transactions should be with different taxpayers.

Example 32

On the other hand, the like-kind exchange procedure can be utilized to control the amount of recognized gain.

Rex has property with an adjusted basis of $40,000 and a fair market value of $100,000. Sandra wants to buy Rex's property, but Rex wants to limit the amount of recognized gain on the proposed transaction. Sandra acquires other like-kind property (from an outside party) for $80,000. She then exchanges this property and $20,000 cash for Rex's property. Rex has a realized gain of $60,000 ($100,000 amount realized − $40,000 adjusted basis). His recognized gain is only $20,000, the lower of the $20,000 boot received or the $60,000 realized gain. Rex's basis for the like-kind property is $40,000 ($40,000 adjusted basis + $20,000 gain recognized − $20,000 boot received). If Rex had sold the property to Sandra for its fair market value of $100,000, the result would have been a $60,000 recognized gain ($100,000 amount realized − $40,000 adjusted basis) to him. It is permissible for Rex to identify the like-kind property that he wants Sandra to purchase.[38]

Example 33

In the present economic environment, however, there is another consideration. The beneficial result of tax deferral of realized gain could be more than offset by future tax rate increases. Some real estate investors who followed this approach, particularly with respect to undeveloped land, planned wisely. They were willing to accept current taxation at 15 percent to avoid the possibility of future taxation at a much higher rate (which turned out to be 20 percent for certain high-income taxpayers). Although turning down a tax deferral may sound like a strange strategy, it fits the notion of "pay a tax today to avoid a higher tax tomorrow."

15-6b Involuntary Conversions

In certain cases, a taxpayer may prefer to recognize gain from an involuntary conversion. Keep in mind that § 1033, unlike § 1031 (dealing with like-kind exchanges), generally is an elective provision.

---

[38]*Franklin B. Biggs*, 69 T.C. 905 (1978); Rev.Rul. 73–476, 1973–2 C.B. 300; and *Starker v. U.S.*, 79–2 USTC ¶9541, 44 AFTR 2d 79–5525, 602 F.2d 1341 (CA–9, 1979).

Example 34	Ahmad has a $40,000 realized gain from the involuntary conversion of an office building. He reinvests the entire proceeds of $450,000 in a new office building. He does not elect to postpone gain under § 1033, however, because of an expiring net operating loss carryover that is offset against the gain. Therefore, none of the realized gain of $40,000 is postponed. Because Ahmad did not elect § 1033 postponement, his basis in the replacement property is the property's cost of $450,000 rather than $410,000 ($450,000 reduced by the $40,000 realized gain).

15-6c Sale of a Principal Residence

Election to Forgo

The § 121 exclusion automatically applies if the taxpayer is eligible. That is, the taxpayer does not have to make an election. However, if the taxpayer wants to avoid § 121 exclusion treatment on an otherwise eligible sale, the taxpayer may elect to do so.[39]

Example 35	George owns two personal residences that satisfy the two-year ownership and use test with respect to the five-year window. The Elm Street residence has appreciated by $25,000, and the Maple Street residence has appreciated by $230,000. He intends to sell both of them and move into rental property. He sells the Elm Street residence in December 2014 and expects to sell the Maple Street residence early next year.
	Unless George elects not to apply the § 121 exclusion to the sale of the Elm Street residence, he will exclude the $25,000 realized gain on that residence in 2014. In 2015, however, he will have a recognized gain of $230,000 on the sale of the Maple Street residence.
	If George makes the election to forgo, he will report a recognized gain of $25,000 on the sale of the Elm Street residence in 2014. But by using the § 121 exclusion in 2015, he will eliminate the recognized gain of $230,000 on the sale of the Maple Street residence.

Negative Effect of Renting or Using as a Home Office

The residence does not have to be the taxpayer's principal residence at the date of sale to qualify for the § 121 exclusion. During part of the five-year window, it could have been rental property (e.g., either a vacation home or entirely rental property). In addition, the taxpayer can have used part of the principal residence as a qualifying home office. In either of these circumstances, the taxpayer may claim deductions for the expenses attributable to the rental or business use. But what effect, if any, do such deductions have on a later sale of the residence? Will the sales proceeds still qualify for nonrecognition of gain treatment under § 121?

Concern that the § 121 exclusion might be denied may have deterred some taxpayers from claiming legitimate deductions, particularly in the case of an office in the home. As noted below, however, the IRS has clarified its position regarding the effect of any such depreciation.

In either the rental or the home office setting, the taxpayer will have deducted depreciation. Any realized gain on the sale that is attributable to depreciation claimed after May 5, 1997, is not eligible for the § 121 exclusion.[40]

Example 36	On December 5, 2014, Amanda sells her principal residence, which qualifies for the § 121 exclusion. Her realized gain is $190,000. From January through November 2013, she was temporarily out of town on a job assignment in another city and rented the residence to a college student. For this period, she deducted MACRS cost recovery of $7,000. Without the depreciation provision, Amanda could exclude the $190,000 realized gain. However, the depreciation taken requires her to recognize $7,000 of the realized gain.

---

[39]§ 121(f).   [40]§ 121(d)(6).

Qualification for § 121 Exclusion

The key requirement for the § 121 exclusion is that the taxpayer must have *owned* and *used* the property as a principal residence for at least two years during the five-year window. As taxpayers advance in age, they quite frequently make decisions such as the following:

- Sell the principal residence and buy a smaller residence or rent the principal residence.
- Sell vacation homes they own.
- Sell homes they are holding as rental property.

These properties may have experienced substantial appreciation during the ownership period. Clearly, the sale of the principal residence is eligible for the § 121 exclusion. Less clear, however, is that proper planning can make it possible for a vacation home or rental property to qualify for the exclusion. Although this strategy may require taxpayers to be flexible about where they live, it can result in substantial tax savings.

Example 37

Thelma and David are approaching retirement. They have substantial appreciation on their principal residence and on a house they own at the beach (about two hours away). After retirement, they plan to move to Florida. They have owned and lived in the principal residence for 28 years and have owned the beach house for 9 years. If they sell their principal residence, it qualifies for the § 121 exclusion. At retirement, they could move into their beach house for two years and make it eligible for the exclusion. If the beach house were close enough, they could sell the principal residence now and move into the beach house to start the running of the two-year use period. Note that any realized gain on the beach house attributable to depreciation is not eligible for the § 121 exclusion. In addition, a reduction in the § 121 exclusion for prior use as a vacation home is required.[41]

Record Keeping

Because the amount of the available exclusion ($250,000 or $500,000) for most taxpayers will exceed the realized gain on the sale of the residence, the IRS has discontinued the form that previously was used to report the sale. IRS Publication 523 provides detailed worksheets that can be used to determine the gain (or loss) on the sale of a principal residence and any related § 121 exclusion. If the sale of the residence does result in a gain that is not excluded from gross income, the gain is reported on Schedule D of Form 1040 (Capital Gains and Losses).

However, it is a good idea for all taxpayers who own residences to continue to maintain records on the adjusted basis of the residence, including the original cost, any capital improvements, and any deductions that decrease basis (e.g., depreciation on a home office or on rental use) for the following reasons:

- The sale of the residence may not qualify for the § 121 exclusion.
- The realized gain may exceed the § 121 exclusion amount.
- The residence may be converted to rental or business use.
- If part of the residence has been rental or business use property (e.g., a qualifying home office) and depreciation has been deducted, the realized gain is recognized to the extent of the depreciation deducted.

Chapter 15 has covered certain situations in which realized gains or losses are not recognized (nontaxable exchanges). Chapters 16 and 17 are concerned with the *classification* of recognized gains and losses. That is, if a gain or loss is recognized, is it an ordinary or a capital gain or loss? Chapter 16 discusses the tax consequences of capital gains and losses.

---

[41]Additional information and examples of "nonqualified use" can be found on p. 15 of IRS Publication 523 (*Selling Your Home*).

REFOCUS ON THE BIG PICTURE

ALTERNATIVE USES OF PROPERTY

Alice needs to be aware of the different tax consequences of her proposals and whether there are any limits to these consequences.

- *Sale of the inherited house.* This is by far the simplest transaction for Alice. Based on the facts, her recognized gain would be:

Amount realized ($600,000 − $30,000)	$ 570,000
Adjusted basis	(475,000)
Recognized gain	$ 95,000

  Because the sale of the house is not eligible for the § 121 exclusion, the tax liability is $14,250 ($95,000 × 15%). So Alice's net cash flow would be $555,750 ($570,000 − $14,250).

- *Conversion into a vacation home with only personal use.* With this alternative, the only tax benefit Alice would receive is the deduction for property taxes as an itemized deduction. She would continue to incur upkeep costs (e.g., repairs, utilities, and insurance). At the end of the two-year period, the sales results are similar to those of a current sale. The sale of the house would not be eligible for the § 121 exclusion.

- *Conversion into a vacation home with partial personal use and partial rental use.* In this case, Alice would be able to deduct 40 percent of costs such as property taxes, the agent's management fee, depreciation, maintenance and repairs, utilities, and insurance. However, this amount cannot exceed the rent income generated. The remaining 60 percent of the property taxes can be claimed as an itemized deduction.

  At the end of the two-year period, the sales results would be similar to those of a current sale. In determining recognized gain, adjusted basis must be reduced by the amount of the depreciation claimed. The sale of the house would not be eligible for the § 121 exclusion.

- *Current sale of present home with sale of inherited home in two years.* The present sale of her current principal residence and the future sale of her inherited residence would enable Alice to qualify for the § 121 exclusion as to each sale (see Example 26). She would satisfy the two-year ownership requirement, the two-year use requirement, and the allowance of the § 121 exclusion only once every two years. Alice must be careful to occupy the inherited residence for at least two years. Also, the period between the sales of the first and second houses must be greater than two years. Qualifying for the § 121 exclusion of up to $250,000 would allow Alice to avoid any Federal income tax liability.

With this information, Alice can make an informed choice. In all likelihood, she probably will select the strategy of selling her current house now and the inherited house in the future. A noneconomic benefit of this option is that she will have to sell only one house at the time of her retirement.

Key Terms

Boot, 15-6	Like-kind exchanges, 15-3	Personal residence, 15-15
Involuntary conversion, 15-10	Nontaxable exchange, 15-3	Section 121 exclusion, 15-15

Discussion Questions

1. **LO.1** In most nontaxable exchanges, is the nonrecognition of the realized gain or loss temporary or permanent? Explain.

2. **LO.1** Distinguish between a loss that is not recognized on a nontaxable exchange and a loss that is not recognized on the sale or exchange of a personal use asset.

3. **LO.2** What are the three requirements that must be satisfied for a transaction to qualify for nontaxable exchange treatment under § 1031?

4. **LO.2** Karla exchanges personal use property for property to be held for productive use in her business. Can this transaction qualify for like-kind exchange treatment? Explain.

5. **LO.2, 6** Andrew owns a lathe (adjusted basis of $40,000) that he uses in his business. He exchanges the lathe and $20,000 in cash for a new lathe worth $50,000. May Andrew avoid like-kind exchange treatment to recognize his realized loss of $10,000? Explain.

6. **LO.2** Which of the following qualify as like-kind exchanges under § 1031?
   a. Improved for unimproved real estate.
   b. Vending machine (used in business) for inventory.
   c. Rental house for personal residence.
   d. Business equipment for securities.
   e. Warehouse for office building (both used for business).
   f. Truck for computer (both used in business).
   g. Rental house for land (both held for investment).
   h. Ten shares of stock in Blue Corporation for 10 shares of stock in Red Corporation.
   i. Office furniture for office equipment (both used in business).
   j. Unimproved land in Jackson, Mississippi, for unimproved land in Toledo, Spain.
   k. General partnership interest for a general partnership interest.

7. **LO.2** Melissa owns a residential lot in Spring Creek, Louisiana, that has appreciated substantially in value. She holds the lot for investment. She is considering exchanging the lot for a residential lot located in Paris, France, that she also will hold for investment. Identify the relevant tax issues for Melissa.   *Issue ID*

8. **LO.2** Ross would like to dispose of some land he acquired five years ago because he believes that it will not continue to appreciate. Its value has increased by $50,000 over the five-year period. He also intends to sell stock that has declined in value by $50,000 during the eight-month period he has owned it. Ross has four offers to acquire the stock and land: *Issue ID*

Buyer number 1:	Exchange land.
Buyer number 2:	Purchase land for cash.
Buyer number 3:	Exchange stock.
Buyer number 4:	Purchase stock for cash.

   Identify the tax issues relevant to Ross in disposing of this land and stock.

9. **LO.2** Sue exchanges a sport utility vehicle (adjusted basis of $16,000; fair market value of $19,500) for cash of $2,000 and a pickup truck (fair market value of $17,500). Both vehicles are for business use. Sue believes that her basis for the truck is $17,500. In calculating her basis, what has Sue failed to consider?

10. **LO.2** In connection with like-kind exchanges, discuss each of the following:
    a. Realized gain.
    b. Realized loss.
    c. Recognized gain.
    d. Recognized loss.
    e. Postponed gain.
    f. Postponed loss.
    g. Basis of like-kind property received.
    h. Basis of boot received.

11. **LO.2** Edith exchanges a machine used in her business for another machine and stock of Teal, Inc. If Edith had sold her machine, she would have had a realized gain. Explain why the new machine will have a different holding period than the stock.

12. **LO.2** Mortgaged real estate may be received in a like-kind exchange. If the taxpayer's mortgage is assumed, what effect does the mortgage have on the recognition of realized gain? On the basis of the real estate received?

13. **LO.3** What constitutes an involuntary conversion?

14. **LO.3** Sheila's appreciated property is involuntarily converted. She receives insurance proceeds equal to the fair market value of the property. What is the minimum amount Sheila must reinvest in qualifying property to defer recognition of realized gain?

15. **LO.3** Ed receives severance damages from the state government for a public road built across his property. Under what circumstances can the § 1033 involuntary conversion provision apply to prevent the recognition of gain?

16. **LO.3** Vera owns an office building that she leases to tenants. If the building is destroyed by a tornado, is the functional use test or the taxpayer use test applied as to replacement property? Explain the differences between the two tests.

17. **LO.3** On June 5, 2014, Brown, Inc., a calendar year taxpayer, receives cash of $750,000 from the county upon condemnation of its warehouse building (adjusted basis of $500,000 and fair market value of $750,000).
    a. What must Brown do to qualify for § 1033 postponement of gain treatment?
    b. How would your advice to Brown differ if the adjusted basis was $795,000?

18. **LO.3** Reba, a calendar year taxpayer, owns an office building that she uses in her business. The building is involuntarily converted on November 15, 2014. On January 5, 2015, Reba receives enough proceeds to produce a realized gain. What is the latest date she can replace the building and qualify for § 1033 postponement treatment if the conversion event is:
    a. A flood?
    b. A condemnation?
    c. A tornado?

19. **LO.3** Bob is notified by the city public housing authority on May 3, 2014, that his apartment building is going to be condemned as part of an urban renewal project. On June 1, 2014, Carol offers to buy the building from Bob. Bob sells the building to Carol on June 30, 2014. Condemnation occurs on September 1, 2014, and Carol receives the condemnation proceeds from the city. Assume that both Bob and Carol are calendar year taxpayers.
    a. What is the earliest date on which Bob can dispose of the building and qualify for § 1033 postponement treatment?
    b. Does the sale to Carol qualify as a § 1033 involuntary conversion? Why or why not?
    c. What is the latest date on which Carol can acquire qualifying replacement property and qualify for postponement of the realized gain?
    d. What type of property will be qualifying replacement property?

Issue ID

20. **LO.3** A warehouse owned by Martha and used in her business (i.e., to store inventory) is being condemned by the city to provide a right-of-way for a highway. The warehouse has appreciated by $180,000 based on Martha's estimate of its fair market value. In the negotiations, the city is offering $35,000 less than what Martha believes the property is worth. Alan, a real estate broker, has offered to purchase Martha's property for $20,000 more than the city's offer. Martha plans to invest the proceeds she will receive in an office building she will lease to various tenants.
    a. Identify the relevant tax issues for Martha.
    b. Would the answer in (a) change if Martha's warehouse was property being held for investment rather than being used in her business? Explain.

21. **LO.3** When does the holding period begin for replacement property acquired in an involuntary conversion?

22. **LO.4** What requirements must be satisfied to qualify for the § 121 exclusion on the sale of a principal residence?

23. **LO.4** Gary, who is single, sells his principal residence (owned and occupied by him for seven years) in November 2014 for a realized gain of $148,000. He had purchased a more expensive new residence eight months prior to the sale. He anticipates that he will occupy this new house as his principal residence for only about 18 additional months. He expects it to appreciate substantially while he owns it. Gary would like to recognize the realized gain on the 2014 sale to offset a large investment loss from the sale of stock. Can he recognize the realized gain of $148,000 on the sale of his principal residence in 2014? Explain.

24. **LO.4** Arnold, who is single, sold his principal residence on April 10, 2014, and excluded the realized gain under § 121 (exclusion on the sale of a principal residence). On April 12, 2014, he purchased another principal residence, which he sells on January 12, 2015, for a realized gain of $80,000. Can Arnold exclude the $80,000 realized gain on the January 2015 sale if his reason for selling was:
    a. His noisy neighbors? Explain.
    b. A job transfer to another city? Explain.

25. **LO.4** Explain how the following are determined on the sale or exchange of a principal residence:
    a. Realized gain.
    b. Recognized gain.
    c. Postponed gain.
    d. Basis of new residence.

26. **LO.4** To qualify for exclusion treatment on the sale of a principal residence, the residence must have been owned and used by the taxpayer for at least two years during the five-year period ending on the date of the sale. Are there any exceptions to this provision? Explain.

Problems

27. **LO.2** Katrina owns undeveloped land with an adjusted basis of $300,000. She exchanges it for undeveloped land worth $750,000.
    a. What are Katrina's realized and recognized gain or loss?
    b. What is Katrina's basis in the undeveloped land she receives?
    c. Would the answers in (a) and (b) change if Katrina exchanged the undeveloped land for land and a building? Explain.

28. **LO.2** Kareem owns a pickup truck that he uses exclusively in his business. The adjusted basis is $22,000, and the fair market value is $14,000. Kareem exchanges the truck for a truck that he will use exclusively in his business.
    a. What are Kareem's realized and recognized gain or loss?
    b. What is his basis in the new truck?
    c. What are the tax consequences to Kareem in (a) and (b) if he used the old truck and will use the new truck exclusively for personal purposes?

29. **LO.2** Tanya Fletcher owns undeveloped land (adjusted basis of $80,000 and fair market value of $92,000) on the East Coast. On January 4, 2014, she exchanges it with Lisa Martin (an unrelated party), for undeveloped land on the West Coast and $3,000 cash. Lisa has an adjusted basis of $72,000 for her land, and its fair market value is $89,000. As the real estate market on the East Coast is thriving, on September 1, 2015, Lisa sells the land she acquired for $120,000.

    Decision Making

    Communications

    a. What are Tanya's recognized gain or loss and adjusted basis for the West Coast land on January 4, 2014?
    b. What are Lisa's recognized gain or loss and adjusted basis for the East Coast land on January 4, 2014?
    c. What is Lisa's recognized gain or loss from the September 1, 2015 sale?
    d. What effect does Lisa's 2015 sale have on Tanya?
    e. Write a letter to Tanya advising her of the tax consequences of this exchange. Her address is The Corral, El Paso, TX 79968.

30. **LO.2** Sarah exchanges a yellow bus (used in her business) for Tyler's gray bus and some garage equipment (used in his business). The assets have the following characteristics:

	Adjusted Basis	Fair Market Value
Yellow bus	$6,000	$15,000
Gray bus	3,000	11,000
Equipment	2,000	4,000

a. What are Sarah's recognized gain or loss and basis for the gray bus and garage equipment?

b. What are Tyler's recognized gain or loss and basis for the yellow bus?

Decision Making

31. **LO.2, 6** In two unrelated transactions, Laura exchanges property that qualifies for like-kind exchange treatment. In the first exchange, Laura gives up office equipment purchased in May 2012 (adjusted basis of $20,000; fair market value of $17,000) in exchange for new office equipment (fair market value of $15,000) and $2,000 cash. In the second exchange, Laura receives a parking garage (to be used in her business) with a fair market value of $50,000 in exchange for a plot of land she had held for investment. The land was purchased in April 2006 for $12,000 and has a current fair market value of $48,000. In addition to transferring the land, Laura pays an additional $2,000 to the other party.

a. What is Laura's adjusted basis for the new office equipment?

b. When does the holding period begin?

c. What is Laura's adjusted basis for the parking garage?

d. When does the holding period begin?

e. How could Laura structure either of the transactions differently to produce better tax consequences?

32. **LO.2** Susan owns a car that she uses exclusively for personal purposes. Its original cost was $26,000, and the fair market value is $12,000. She exchanges the car and $18,000 cash for a new car.

a. Calculate Susan's realized and recognized gain or loss.

b. Calculate Susan's basis for the new car.

c. Determine when Susan's holding period for the new car begins.

33. **LO.2** Stephanie owns a machine (adjusted basis of $90,000; fair market value of $125,000) that she uses in her business. She exchanges it for another machine (worth $100,000) and stock (worth $25,000). Determine Stephanie's:

a. Realized and recognized gain or loss on the exchange.

b. Basis in the new machine.

c. Basis in the stock she received.

34. **LO.2** Ed owns investment land with an adjusted basis of $35,000. Polly has offered to purchase the land from Ed for $175,000 for use in a real estate development. The amount offered by Polly is $10,000 in excess of what Ed perceives as the fair market value of the land. Ed would like to dispose of the land to Polly but does not want to incur the tax liability that would result. He identifies an office building with a fair market value of $175,000 that he would like to acquire. Polly purchases the office building and then exchanges the office building for Ed's land.

a. Calculate Ed's realized and recognized gain on the exchange and his basis for the office building.

b. Calculate Polly's realized and recognized gain on the exchange and her basis in the land.

35. **LO.2** What is the basis of the new property in each of the following exchanges?

a. Apartment building held for investment (adjusted basis of $145,000) for office building to be held for investment (fair market value of $225,000).

b. Land and building used as a barbershop (adjusted basis of $190,000) for land and building used as a grocery store (fair market value of $350,000).

c. Office building (adjusted basis of $45,000) for bulldozer (fair market value of $42,000), both held for business use.

d. IBM common stock (adjusted basis of $20,000) for ExxonMobil common stock (fair market value of $28,000).

e. Rental house (adjusted basis of $90,000) for mountain cabin to be held for rental use (fair market value of $225,000).

f. General partnership interest (adjusted basis of $400,000) for a limited partnership interest (fair market value of $580,000).

36. **LO.2** Steve owns Machine A (adjusted basis of $12,000 and fair market value of $15,000), which he uses in his business. Steve sells Machine A for $15,000 to Aubry (a dealer) and then purchases Machine B for $15,000 from Joan (also a dealer). Machine B would normally qualify as like-kind property.

a. What are Steve's realized and recognized gain on the sale of Machine A?

b. What is Steve's basis for Machine B?

c. What factors would motivate Steve to sell Machine A and purchase Machine B rather than exchange one machine for the other?

d. Assume that the adjusted basis of Machine A is $15,000 and the fair market value of both machines is $12,000. Respond to (a) through (c).

37. **LO.2** Tab exchanges real estate used in his business along with stock for real estate to be held for investment. The stock transferred has an adjusted basis of $45,000 and a fair market value of $50,000. The real estate transferred has an adjusted basis of $85,000 and a fair market value of $190,000. The real estate acquired has a fair market value of $240,000.

a. What is Tab's realized gain or loss?

b. His recognized gain or loss?

c. The basis of the newly acquired real estate?

38. **LO.2, 6** Tom and Frank are brothers. Each owns investment property in the other's hometown. To make their lives easier, they decide to legally exchange the investment properties. Under the terms of the exchange, Frank will transfer realty (adjusted basis of $52,000; fair market value of $80,000) and Tom will exchange realty (adjusted basis of $60,000; fair market value of $92,000). Tom's property is subject to a mortgage of $12,000 that will be assumed by Frank.

Decision Making

a. What are Frank's and Tom's recognized gains?

b. What are their adjusted bases?

c. As an alternative, Frank has proposed that rather than assuming the mortgage, he will transfer cash of $12,000 to Tom. Tom would use the cash to pay off the mortgage. Advise Tom on whether this alternative would be beneficial to him from a tax perspective.

39. **LO.2** Determine the realized, recognized, and postponed gain or loss and the new basis for each of the following like-kind exchanges:

	Adjusted Basis of Old Machine	Boot Given	Fair Market Value of New Asset	Boot Received
a.	$ 7,000	$ –0–	$12,000	$4,000
b.	14,000	2,000	15,000	–0–
c.	3,000	7,000	8,000	500
d.	15,000	–0–	29,000	–0–
e.	10,000	–0–	11,000	1,000
f.	17,000	–0–	14,000	–0–

40. **LO.2** Shontelle owns an apartment house that has an adjusted basis of $760,000 but is subject to a mortgage of $192,000. She transfers the apartment house to Dave and receives from him $120,000 in cash and an office building with a fair market value of $780,000 at the time of the exchange. Dave assumes the $192,000 mortgage on the apartment house.

a. What is Shontelle's realized gain or loss?

b. What is her recognized gain or loss?

c. What is the basis of the newly acquired office building?

41. **LO.3** Howard's roadside vegetable stand (adjusted basis of $275,000) is destroyed by a tractor-trailer accident. He receives insurance proceeds of $240,000 ($300,000 fair market value less $60,000 coinsurance). Howard immediately uses the proceeds plus additional cash of $45,000 to build another roadside vegetable stand at the same location. What are the tax consequences to Howard?

42. **LO.3** Albert owns 100 acres of land on which he grows spruce Christmas trees. His adjusted basis for the land is $100,000. He receives condemnation proceeds of $10,000 when the city's new beltway takes 5 acres along the eastern boundary of his property. He also receives a severance award of $6,000 associated with the possible harmful effects of exhaust fumes on his Christmas trees. Albert invests the $16,000 in a growth mutual fund. Determine the tax consequences to Albert of the:
    a. Condemnation proceeds.
    b. Severance award.

43. **LO.3** For each of the following involuntary conversions, indicate whether the property acquired qualifies as replacement property, the recognized gain, and the basis for the property acquired:
    a. Frank owns a warehouse that is destroyed by a tornado. The space in the warehouse was rented to various tenants. The adjusted basis was $470,000. Frank uses all of the insurance proceeds of $700,000 to build a shopping mall in a neighboring community where no property has been damaged by tornadoes. The shopping mall is rented to various tenants.
    b. Ivan owns a warehouse that he uses in his business. The adjusted basis is $300,000. The warehouse is destroyed by fire. Because of economic conditions in the area, Ivan decides not to rebuild the warehouse. Instead, he uses all of the insurance proceeds of $400,000 to build a warehouse to be used in his business in another state.
    c. Ridge's personal residence is condemned as part of a local government project to widen the highway from two lanes to four lanes. The adjusted basis is $170,000. Ridge uses all of the condemnation proceeds of $200,000 to purchase another personal residence.
    d. Juanita owns a building that she uses in her retail business. The adjusted basis is $250,000. The building is destroyed by a hurricane. Because of an economic downturn in the area caused by the closing of a military base, Juanita decides to rent space for her retail outlet rather than replace the building. She uses all of the insurance proceeds of $300,000 to buy a four-unit apartment building in another city. A real estate agent in that city will handle the rental of the apartments for her.
    e. Susan and Rick's personal residence is destroyed by a tornado. They had owned it for 15 months. The adjusted basis was $170,000. Because they would like to travel, they decide not to acquire a replacement residence. Instead, they invest all of the insurance proceeds of $200,000 in a duplex, which they rent to tenants.
    f. Ellen and Harry's personal residence (adjusted basis of $245,000) is destroyed in a flood. They had owned it for 18 months. Of the insurance proceeds of $350,000, they reinvest $342,000 in a replacement residence four months later.

44. **LO.3** Mitchell, a calendar year taxpayer, is the sole proprietor of a fast-food restaurant. His adjusted basis for the building and the related land is $450,000. On March 12, 2014, state authorities notify Mitchell that his property is going to be condemned so that the highway can be widened. On June 20, Mitchell's property is officially condemned, and he receives an award of $625,000. Because Mitchell's business was successful in the past, he would like to reopen the restaurant in a new location.
    a. What is the earliest date Mitchell can acquire a new restaurant and qualify for § 1033 postponement?
    b. On June 30, Mitchell purchases land and a building for $610,000. Assuming that he elects postponement of gain under § 1033, what is his recognized gain?
    c. What is Mitchell's adjusted basis for the new land and building?
    d. If he does not elect § 1033, what are Mitchell's recognized gain and adjusted basis?
    e. Suppose he invests the $625,000 condemnation proceeds in the stock market on June 30. What is Mitchell's recognized gain?

45. **LO.3** Edith's warehouse (adjusted basis of $450,000) is destroyed by a hurricane in October 2014. Edith, a calendar year taxpayer, receives insurance proceeds of $525,000 in January 2015. Calculate Edith's realized gain or loss, recognized gain or loss, and basis for the replacement property if she:
    a. Acquires a new warehouse for $550,000 in January 2015.
    b. Acquires a new warehouse for $500,000 in January 2015.
    c. Does not acquire replacement property.

46. **LO.3** Cabel's warehouse, which has an adjusted basis of $380,000 and a fair market value of $490,000, is condemned by an agency of the Federal government to make way for a highway interchange. The initial condemnation offer is $425,000. After substantial negotiations, the agency agrees to transfer to Cabel a surplus warehouse that he believes is worth $490,000. Cabel is a calendar year taxpayer. The condemnation and related asset transfer occur during September 2014.

    a. What are the recognized gain or loss and the basis of the replacement warehouse if Cabel's objective is to recognize as much gain as possible?

    b. Advise Cabel regarding what he needs to do by what date to achieve his objective.

Decision Making

47. **LO.3** What are the *maximum* postponed gain or loss and the basis for the replacement property for the following involuntary conversions?

	Property	Type of Conversion	Amount Realized	Adjusted Basis	Amount Reinvested
a.	Drugstore (business)	Casualty	$160,000	$130,000	$110,000
b.	Apartments (investment)	Condemned	100,000	125,000	175,000
c.	Grocery store (business)	Casualty	400,000	300,000	450,000
d.	Residence (personal)	Casualty	16,000	18,000	17,000
e.	Vacant lot (investment)	Condemned	240,000	160,000	220,000
f.	Residence (personal)	Casualty	20,000	18,000	19,000
g.	Residence (personal)	Condemned	18,000	20,000	26,000
h.	Apartments (investment)	Condemned	150,000	100,000	200,000

48. **LO.3, 6** Wanda, a calendar year taxpayer, owned a building (adjusted basis of $250,000) in which she operated a bakery that was destroyed by fire in December 2014. She receives insurance proceeds of $290,000 for the building the following March. Wanda is considering two options regarding the investment of the insurance proceeds. First, she could purchase a local building (suitable for a bakery) that is for sale for $275,000. Second, she could buy a new home for $290,000 and go back to college and finish her degree.

    a. To minimize her tax liability, which of these alternatives should Wanda choose?

    b. What is the latest date on which Wanda can replace the involuntarily converted property to qualify for § 1033?

    c. What is the latest date on which Wanda can replace the involuntarily converted property to qualify for § 1033 if the involuntary conversion is a condemnation?

Decision Making

49. **LO.4, 6** Karl purchased his residence on January 2, 2013, for $260,000, after having lived in it during 2012 as a tenant under a lease with an option to buy clause. On August 1, 2014, Karl sells the residence for $315,000. On June 13, 2014, Karl purchases a new residence for $367,000.

    a. What is Karl's recognized gain? His basis for the new residence?

    b. Assume instead that Karl purchased his original residence on January 2, 2012 (rather than January 2, 2013). What is Karl's recognized gain? His basis for the new residence?

    c. In (a), what could Karl do to minimize his recognized gain?

Decision Making

50. **LO.4** Taylor has owned and occupied her personal residence (adjusted basis of $190,000) for four years. In April 2014, she sells the residence for $300,000 (selling expenses are $20,000). On the same day as the sale, Taylor purchases another house for $350,000. Because of noisy neighbors, she sells the new house after just 10 months. The selling price is $483,000 (selling expenses are $18,000).

    a. What is Taylor's recognized gain on the sale of the first residence?

    b. What is Taylor's basis for her second residence?

    c. What is Taylor's recognized gain on the sale of the second residence?

    d. Assume instead that the sale of the second residence was due to Taylor's job transfer to another state. What is her recognized gain on the sale of the second residence?

51. **LO.4** Wesley, who is single, listed his personal residence with a real estate agent on March 3, 2014, at a price of $390,000. He rejected several offers in the $350,000 range during the summer. Finally, on August 16, 2014, he and the purchaser signed a contract

to sell for $363,000. The sale (i.e., closing) took place on September 7, 2014. The closing statement showed the following disbursements:

Real estate agent's commission	$ 21,780
Appraisal fee	600
Exterminator's certificate	300
Recording fees	800
Mortgage to First Bank	305,000
Cash to seller	34,520

Wesley's adjusted basis for the house is $200,000. He owned and occupied the house for seven years. On October 1, 2014, Wesley purchases another residence for $325,000.
a. Calculate Wesley's recognized gain on the sale.
b. What is Wesley's adjusted basis for the new residence?
c. Assume instead that the selling price is $800,000. What is Wesley's recognized gain? His adjusted basis for the new residence?

52. **LO.4** Pedro, age 57, is the sole owner of his principal residence, which he has owned and occupied for 10 years. Maria, his spouse, has also lived there 10 years. He sells the house for a realized gain of $340,000.
a. Can Pedro use the § 121 exclusion if he and Maria file a joint return? If so, what are the available amount of the exclusion and the recognized gain?
b. Can Pedro use the § 121 exclusion if he files a separate return? If so, what are the available amount of the exclusion and the recognized gain?
c. Assume instead that the realized gain is $550,000 and a joint return is filed.
d. Assume instead that the realized gain is $550,000 and separate returns are filed.
e. Assume instead that Maria and Pedro have been married for only 18 months and that she has lived in his house only since their marriage. They file a joint return.

Communications   53. **LO.4** Nell, Nina, and Nora Sanders, who are sisters, sell their principal residence (owned as tenants in common) in which they have lived for the past 25 years. The youngest of the sisters is age 60. The selling price is $960,000, selling expenses and legal fees are $63,000, and the adjusted basis is $120,000 (the fair market value of the residence when inherited from their parents 25 years ago; they made no capital improvements during the time they held the residence). Because the sisters are going to live in rental housing, they do not plan to acquire another residence. Nell has contacted you on behalf of the three sisters regarding the tax consequences of the sale.
a. Write a letter to Nell advising her of the tax consequences and how taxes can be minimized. Nell's address is 100 Oak Avenue, Billings, MT 59101.
b. Prepare a memo for the tax files.

Decision Making   54. **LO.4** Lloyd owns a beach house (four years) and a cabin in the mountains (six years). His adjusted basis is $300,000 in the beach house and $315,000 in the mountain cabin. Llyod also rents a townhouse in the city where he is employed. During the year, he occupies each of the three residences as follows:

Townhouse	135 days
Beach house	155 days
Mountain cabin	75 days

The beach house is close enough to the city that he can commute to work during the spring and summer. While this level of occupancy may vary slightly from year to year, it is representative during the time period that Lloyd has owned the two residences.

As Lloyd plans on retiring in several years, he sells both the beach house and the mountain cabin. The mountain cabin is sold on March 3, 2014, for $540,000 (related selling expenses of $35,000). The beach house is sold on December 10, 2014, for $700,000 (related selling expenses of $42,000).
a. Calculate Lloyd's lowest recognized gain on the sale of the two residences.
b. Assume instead that both residences satisfy the two-year ownership and use tests as Lloyd's principal residence. Because the mountain cabin is sold first, is it possible for Lloyd to apply the § 121 exclusion to the sale of the beach house? Why or why not?

Decision Making   55. **LO.4, 6** Cisco, a calendar year taxpayer who is age 63, owns a residence in which he has lived for 21 years. The residence is destroyed by fire on August 8, 2014. The adjusted basis is $190,000, and the fair market value is $320,000. Cisco receives insurance proceeds of

$320,000 for the residence on September 1, 2014. He is trying to decide whether to purchase a comparable house. He anticipates that he will retire in two years and will move to a warmer climate, where he will rent in case he decides to live in different places.

a. Advise Cisco of the tax consequences of replacing versus not replacing the residence.

b. Which do you recommend to him?

c. How would your answer in (a) change if the fair market value and insurance proceeds received were $510,000?

56. **LO.4, 6** Missy, age 30, has owned her principal residence (adjusted basis of $225,000) for five years. During the first three years of ownership, she occupied it as her principal residence. During the past two years, she was in graduate school and rented the residence. After graduate school, Missy returned to the same location where she previously worked. At this point, she purchased another residence for $400,000 and listed her old residence for sale at $340,000. Due to a slow real estate market, 11 months later Missy finally receives an offer of $330,000.

Decision Making

a. What is Missy's recognized gain if she immediately accepts the $330,000 offer (i.e., 11 months after the listing date)? Selling expenses are $20,000.

b. What is Missy's recognized gain if she rejects the $330,000 offer and accepts another offer of $340,000 three months later (i.e., 14 months after the listing date)?

c. Advise Missy on which offer she should accept (assume that she is in the 28% tax bracket).

57. **LO.5** Roby and James have been married for 9 years. Roby sells Plum, Inc. stock that she has owned for four years to James for its fair market value of $180,000. Her adjusted basis is $200,000.

Decision Making

a. Calculate Roby's recognized gain or recognized loss.

b. Calculate James's adjusted basis for the stock.

c. How would the tax consequences in (a) and (b) differ if Roby had made a gift of the stock to James? Which form of the transaction would you recommend?

58. **LO.5** On September 1, 2014, Marsha sells stock in Orange, Inc., for $90,000. The stock is specialized small business investment company (SSBIC) stock and was purchased on August 16, 2013, for $60,000. On September 30, 2014, Marsha purchases $85,000 of Blue, Inc., also SSBIC stock.

a. What is Marsha's realized and recognized gain (or loss) on the sale of the Orange stock?

b. What is Marsha's basis in the Blue stock?

Cumulative Problems

59. Devon Bishop, age 45, is single. He lives at 1507 Rose Lane, Albuquerque, NM 87131. His Social Security number is 111-11-1111. Devon does not want $3 to go to the Presidential Election Campaign Fund.

Tax Return Problem

H&R BLOCK

TAX SOFTWARE

Devon's wife, Ariane, passed away in 2009. Devon's son, Tom, who is age 16, resides with Devon. Tom's Social Security number is 123-45-6788.

Devon owns a sole proprietorship for which he uses the accrual method of accounting and maintains no inventory. His revenues and expenses for 2013 are as follows:

Sales revenue	$740,000
Cost of goods sold (based on purchases for the year)	405,000
Salary expense	88,000
Rent expense	30,000
Utilities	8,000
Telephone	6,500
Advertising	4,000
Bad debts	5,000
Depreciation	21,000
Health insurance*	26,000
Accounting and legal fees	7,000
Supplies	1,000

*$18,000 for employees and $8,000 for Devon.

Other income received by Devon includes the following:

Dividend income (qualified dividends):

Swan, Inc.	$10,000
Wren, Inc.	2,000

Interest income:

First Bank	11,000
Second Bank	2,500
City of Asheville bonds	17,000

During the year, Devon and his sole proprietorship had the following property transactions:

a. Sold Blue, Inc. stock for $45,000 on March 12, 2013. He had purchased the stock on September 5, 2010, for $50,000.

b. Received an inheritance of $300,000 from his uncle, Henry. Devon used $200,000 to purchase Green, Inc. stock on May 15, 2013, and invested $100,000 in Gold, Inc. stock on May 30, 2013.

c. Received Orange, Inc. stock worth $9,500 as a gift from his aunt, Jane, on June 17, 2013. Her adjusted basis for the stock was $5,000. No gift taxes were paid on the transfer. Jane had purchased the stock on April 1, 2007. Devon sold the stock on July 1, 2013, for $22,000.

d. On July 15, 2013, Devon sold one-half of the Green, Inc. stock for $40,000.

e. Devon was notified on August 1, 2013, that Yellow, Inc. stock he purchased from a colleague on September 1, 2012, for $52,500 had become worthless. While he perceived that the investment was risky, he did not anticipate that the corporation would declare bankruptcy.

f. On August 15, 2013, Devon received a parcel of land in Phoenix worth $220,000 in exchange for a parcel of land he owned in Tucson. Because the Tucson parcel was worth $245,000, he also received $25,000 cash. Devon's adjusted basis for the Tucson parcel was $210,000. He originally purchased it on September 18, 2010.

g. On December 1, 2013, Devon sold the condominium in which he had been living for the past 20 years. The sales price was $480,000, selling expenses were $28,500, and repair expenses related to the sale were $9,400. Devon purchased the condominium for $180,000.

Devon's potential itemized deductions, exclusive of the aforementioned information, are as follows:

Medical expenses (before the 10% floor)	$ 9,500
Property taxes on residence	5,800
State income taxes	4,000
Charitable contributions	10,000
Mortgage interest on residence	9,900
Sales taxes paid	5,000

During the year, Devon makes estimated Federal income tax payments of $40,000.

Compute Devon's lowest net tax payable or refund due for 2013 assuming that he makes any available elections that will reduce the tax. If you use tax forms for your computations, you will need Forms 1040, 4562, 8332, and 8824 and Schedules A, B, C, D, and SE. Suggested software: H&R BLOCK Tax Software.

Tax Computation Problem

Decision Making

Communications

60. Tom and Alice Honeycutt, ages 35 and 36, live at 101 Glass Road, Delton, MI 49046. Tom is a county employee, and Alice is a self-employed accountant. Tom's Social Security number is 111-11-1111; Alice's Social Security number is 123-45-6789. The income and expenses associated with Alice's accounting practice for 2014 are as follows:

Revenues (cash receipts during 2014)	$185,000
Expenses	
Salaries	$ 45,000
Office supplies	3,200
Postage	2,900
Depreciation of equipment	42,000
Telephone	800
	$ 93,900

Because Alice is a cash method taxpayer, she does not record her receivables as revenue until she receives cash payment. At the beginning of 2014, her accounts receivable were $48,000, and the balance had decreased to $8,000 by the end of the year.

Alice used one room in their 10-room house as the office for her accounting practice (400 square feet out of a total square footage of 4,000). They paid the following expenses related to the house during 2014:

Utilities	$4,500
Insurance	2,100
Property taxes	5,200
Repairs	3,500

Tom and Alice purchased the house on September 1, 2013, for $400,000 (exclusive of land cost).

Tom and Alice have one child, Connor, age 16. Connor's Social Security number is 123-45-6788.

Tom received a salary of $50,000 during 2014. The appropriate amounts of Social Security tax and Medicare tax were withheld. In addition, $5,000 of Federal income taxes and $2,000 of state income taxes were withheld.

Alice provides part of the support of her father, age 69. Her father's Social Security number is 123-45-6787. The total support in 2014 for her father was as follows:

Social Security benefits	$5,200
From Alice	3,200
From Bob, Alice's brother	2,200
From Susan, Alice's sister	2,300

Bob and Susan have both indicated their willingness to sign a multiple support waiver form if it will benefit Alice.

Tom and Alice's allowable itemized deductions during 2014, excluding any itemized deductions related to the house, were $11,000. They made estimated tax payments of $25,000.

Part 1—Tax Computation
Compute Tom and Alice's lowest net tax payable or refund due for 2014.

Part 2—Tax Planning
Tom and Alice have 30 acres of prime farmland that they inherited from Tom's father several years ago. At that time, the fair market value of the land was $150,000 (which became their basis in the land). The Honeycutts have been holding the land as an investment. The property was recently appraised for $190,000, and there is an outstanding mortgage on the land of $28,000. They are considering trading this land for property in the mountains of southern Colorado. Ultimately, they would like to build a vacation home on the Colorado property. The Colorado property owner— who has significant land holdings in the area—has provided two options to Tom and Alice (in both cases, the Colorado property owner would assume the mortgage as part of the exchange):

1. 15 acres of property with a fair market value of $135,000 plus $27,000 of cash; or
2. 10 acres of property with a fair market value of $160,000 plus $2,000 of cash.

The Honeycutts have come to you for advice, believing either transaction to be a like-kind exchange that will allow them to defer any gain. Assume that Tom and Alice expect their marginal tax rate to remain the same for 2015. Write a letter to Tom and Alice that contains your advice on the proposed transactions. Also prepare a memo for the tax files.

Research Problems

THOMSON REUTERS
CHECKPOINT®

Note: Solutions to Research Problems can be prepared by using the **Checkpoint®** **Student Edition** online research product, which is available to accompany this text. It is also possible to prepare solutions to the Research Problems by using tax research materials found in a standard tax library.

Research Problem 1. Charlene and Alton Dutro had lived in their home for two and one-half years when they decided to enlarge and remodel the house. However, their architect advised them that more stringent building and permit restrictions had been imposed since the house was built 10 years earlier. So the Dutros decided to demolish the house and rebuild on the same site. Rather than occupying the new house, however, the Dutros sold it for a realized gain in excess of $500,000.

In calculating the recognized gain on their Federal income tax return, the Dutros reduced the realized gain of more than $500,000 by the $500,000 exclusion of § 121. The IRS has issued an income tax deficiency notice on the grounds that the Dutros did not satisfy the two-out-of-five-years requirement of § 121(a).

Who is correct?

Partial list of research aids:
§ 121(a)(1).
David A. Gates, 135 T.C. 1 (2010).

Research Problem 2. David acquired a house on Dauphin Island (off the coast of Alabama) in a tax-free like-kind exchange on January 1, 2009. David regularly vacations on the island and thought that a rental property there would be a good investment. The island is filled with beach lovers and fishermen throughout the year, which means that the house will not sit unoccupied. He has used the rental income to make additional contributions to tax-deferred retirement savings. At the time of acquisition, David's basis in the house was $200,000.

In 2009 and 2010, David rented the house for the entire year. On January 1, 2011, after retiring from his job as an engineer, he moved into the house and began to use it as his principal residence. Although he enjoyed receiving the rental income, he found that he enjoyed the island lifestyle more than he needed the additional income. David lived in the house until January 1, 2014, when he sold it to move closer to his children. The house sold for $900,000.

Given that the house was his principal residence, David would like to know if he can exclude any of the gain that he realized on the sale under the provisions of § 121.

Research Problem 3. April owned an annuity contract (cash balance of $250,000) issued by Teal Insurance Company. She decides to switch to an annuity contract issued by Brown Insurance Company. To make the change, April instructed Teal to cash out her annuity by issuing a check to Brown. Teal refused to do so and issued a check for $250,000 payable to April.

April intended that the exchange of annuity contracts qualify for tax deferral treatment under § 1035(a)(3). Consequently, rather than depositing or cashing the check from Teal, she endorsed it and sent it to Brown.

On audit, an IRS agent contends that the transaction does not qualify under § 1035(a)(3). For tax deferral to apply, the initial annuity contract must be directly exchanged for the new annuity contract. Evaluate the positions of the parties.

Research Problem 4. Ted and Marvin Brown purchased an apartment building in 2003 as equal tenants in common. After a hectic decade of co-ownership, the brothers decided that their business association should be terminated. This led to the sale of the apartment building and a division of the proceeds.

The realized gain on the sale of the apartment building for each brother was $350,000. Ted recognized gain on his share and used the net proceeds to invest in stock. Marvin wanted to defer any recognized gain, so he worked with a realtor to identify property that would be eligible for § 1031 like-kind exchange treatment. After one prospect failed, the realtor identified a single-family home on Lake Tahoe that was currently being rented by the owner. Marvin agreed with the choice and acquired the single-family house using the proceeds from the apartment building. Because the single-family house qualified as like-kind property, Marvin deferred all of his realized gain.

After attempting to rent the property for eight months without success, Marvin concluded that he could not continue to make the mortgage payments on his primary residence and this rental property. To ease his financial liquidity problem, Marvin sold his principal residence for a realized gain of $190,000 and moved into the Lake Tahoe house. He reported no recognized gain on the sale of his principal residence as the sale qualified for § 121 exclusion treatment.

The IRS issued a deficiency notice to Marvin associated with the sale of the apartment building. The position of the IRS was that Marvin did not hold the single-family residence for investment purposes as required by § 1031. Instead, his intention was personal—to use it as a replacement for his current residence that he planned on selling.

Who should prevail?

Research Problem 5. Taylor owns a 150-unit motel that was constructed in the late 1960s. It is located on 10 acres on the main highway leading into the city. Taylor renovated the motel three years ago.

Taylor's motel is condemned by the city, which is going to use 2 of the 10 acres for a small park. The other 8 acres are to be sold to a time-share developer who intends to build 400 units on the property. The developer has already secured approval from the city planning commission.

Taylor's attorney advises him not to contest the condemnation of the 2 acres for the park. Under the eminent domain provision, the city does have the right to take "private property for public use." However, the attorney advises Taylor to contest the condemnation of the remaining property. According to the attorney, the city does not have the right to take "private property for private use."

The city's position is that the condemnation will result in a substantial number of new jobs and additional tax revenue for the city.

Will Taylor be successful if he follows the attorney's advice? Explain.

Research Problem 6. Walter Albers, a physician, and his wife, Maud, owned and occupied a house in Hampton, Virginia, from 2008 through 2011. Dr. Albers's medical practice was located in a rental office building in Hampton.

In January 2012, Walter accepted employment in a medical practice in Richmond (75 miles from Hampton). During the same month, he and Maud purchased a home in Richmond that they occupied in February 2012. They did not sell the Hampton home because they planned to live there after retirement. Walter became dissatisfied with his employment in Richmond, so he quit and became a partner in a three-physician medical practice in West Point, Virginia (75 miles from Hampton and 30 miles from Richmond). Maud moved back to their Hampton residence. Walter commuted daily to his medical practice in West Point from either the residence in Richmond or the residence in Hampton. He normally spent four nights each week with Maud in the Hampton house and three nights each week by himself in the Richmond house. Maud occasionally spent a few nights at the Richmond residence during the periods Walter was there. They did not sell the Richmond house because it was closer to Walter's West Point office.

Even though Maud moved back to the Hampton house and Walter lived there part of the time, they retained the following associated with the Richmond house:

- Address listed on their Federal and state income tax returns.
- Address listed on their driver's licenses, automobile registrations, and voter registration cards.
- Address listed for their bills and correspondence.
- Location of their bank accounts.

They continued to use the Richmond address so that they would have a single address for all of their correspondence. Although Maud attended church in Hampton, Walter was not a member.

In October 2014, Walter retired, and the Albers moved to Tucson. They listed both houses for sale. The closing for the Hampton house was on December 15, 2014, and resulted in a realized gain of $650,000. On their 2014 Form 1040, they reported a recognized gain of $150,000 ($650,000 − $500,000 § 121 exclusion).

The IRS has concluded that the sale does not qualify for § 121 treatment because the Hampton house was not the principal residence of Walter and Maud for at least two years during the five-year period ending December 15, 2014. Evaluate the positions of the Albers and the IRS.

Internet Activity

Use the tax resources of the Internet to address the following questions. Do not restrict your search to the Web, but include a review of newsgroups and general reference materials, practitioner sites and resources, primary sources of the tax law, chat rooms and discussion groups, and other opportunities.

Research Problem 7. Find two newspaper stories about transactions to which you believe the involuntary conversion rules could apply. Do not limit your search to individual taxpayers.

Research Problem 8. In general, the 45-day identification period and the 180-day exchange period for like-kind exchanges cannot be extended. Does this rule change if the like-kind property or the taxpayer involved in the exchange is located in a Presidentially declared disaster area? Use the IRS's website (**www.irs.gov**) to find the answer.

Research Problem 9. The U.S. government has established various programs to help homeowners avoid foreclosure on the mortgage covering their principal residence. Locate a newspaper article that describes one of these programs.

16

Property Transactions: Capital Gains and Losses

LEARNING OBJECTIVES: *After completing Chapter 16, you should be able to:*

LO.1 Discuss the general scheme of taxation for capital gains and losses.

LO.2 Distinguish capital assets from ordinary assets.

LO.3 State and explain the relevance of a sale or exchange to classification as a capital gain or loss and apply the special rules for the capital gain or loss treatment of the retirement of corporate obligations, options, patents, franchises, and lease cancellation payments.

LO.4 Determine whether the holding period for a capital asset is long-term or short-term.

LO.5 Describe the beneficial tax treatment for capital gains and the detrimental tax treatment for capital losses for noncorporate taxpayers.

LO.6 Describe the tax treatment for capital gains and the detrimental tax treatment for capital losses for corporate taxpayers.

LO.7 Identify tax planning opportunities arising from the sale or exchange of capital assets.

CHAPTER OUTLINE

© auremar / Shutterstock.com

MANAGING CAPITAL ASSET TRANSACTIONS

Maurice has come to you for tax advice regarding his investments. He inherited $500,000 from his Uncle Joe. A financial adviser suggested that he make the following investments, which he did nine months ago.

- $5,000 for 100 shares of Eagle Company stock.
- $50,000 for a 50 percent interest in a patent that Kevin, a college roommate who is an unemployed inventor, obtained for a special battery he developed to power green cars. To date, Kevin has been unable to market the battery to an auto manufacturer or supplier, but he has high hopes of doing so given the current price of gasoline.
- $95,000 to purchase a franchise from Orange, Inc.
- $200,000 in the stock of Purple, a publicly held bank that follows a policy of occasionally paying dividends. At one time, the stock appreciated to $300,000, but now it is worth only $210,000. Maurice is considering unloading this stock.
- $50,000 in tax-exempt bonds. The interest rate on the bonds is only 3 percent. Maurice is considering moving this money into taxable bonds that pay 3.5 percent.
- $100,000 for a 10 percent ownership interest as a limited partner in a real estate development. Lots in the development are selling well.

Maurice read an article that talked about the beneficial tax rates for capital assets and dividends. He really liked the part about "costless" capital gains, although he did not understand it.

Maurice has retained his job as a toll booth supervisor at the municipal airport. His annual compensation is $35,000. He likes the job and has met some interesting people there.

Respond to Maurice's request for tax advice.

Read the chapter and formulate your response.

Income *(broadly conceived)*	$ xx,xxx
Less: Exclusions	(x,xxx)
Gross income	$xx,xxx
Less: Deductions for adjusted gross income	(x,xxx)

FORM 1040 (p. 1)

12	Business income or (loss). Attach Schedule C or C-EZ	
13	Capital gain or (loss). Attach Schedule D if required. If not required, check here ▶ ☐	
14	Other gains or (losses). Attach Form 4797	

Adjusted gross income	$ xx,xxx
Less: The greater of total **itemized deductions** *or* the standard deduction	(x,xxx)
Personal and dependency exemptions	(x,xxx)
Taxable income	$ xx,xxx
Tax on taxable income *(see Tax Tables or Tax Rate Schedules)*	$ x,xxx

FORM 1040 (p. 2)

44	**Tax** (see instructions). Check if any from: **a** ☐ Form(s) 8814 **b** ☐ Form 4972 **c** ☐ _____

Less: Tax credits *(including income taxes withheld and prepaid)*	(xxx)
Tax due *(or refund)*	$ xxx

Fourteen years ago, a taxpayer purchased 100 shares of IBM stock for $17 a share. This year, the taxpayer sells the shares for $186 a share. Should the $169 per share gain receive any special tax treatment? The $169 gain has built up over 14 years, so it may not be fair to tax it the same as income that was all earned this year.

What if the stock had been purchased for $186 per share and sold for $17 a share? Should the $169 loss be fully deductible? The tax law has an intricate approach to answering these investment activity-related questions.

As you study this chapter, keep in mind that how investment-related gains and losses are taxed can dramatically affect whether taxpayers make investments and which investments are made. Except for a brief discussion in Chapter 3, earlier chapters dwelt on how to determine the amount of gain or loss from a property disposition, but did not discuss the classification of gains and losses. This chapter will focus on that topic.

The tax law requires **capital gains** and **capital losses** to be separated from other types of gains and losses. There are two reasons for this treatment. First, long-term capital gains may be taxed at a lower rate than ordinary gains. The second reason the Code requires separate reporting of gains and losses and a determination of their tax character is that a net capital loss is subject to deduction limitations. For noncorporate taxpayers, a net capital loss is only deductible up to $3,000 per year. Any excess loss over the annual limit carries over and may be deductible in a future tax year.

For these reasons, capital gains and losses must be distinguished from other types of gains and losses. Most of this chapter and the next chapter describe the intricate rules for determining what type of gains and losses the taxpayer has.

As a result of the need to distinguish and separately match capital gains and losses, the individual tax forms include very extensive reporting requirements for capital gains and losses. This chapter explains the principles underlying the forms, which are illustrated with an example at the end of the chapter.

16-1 GENERAL SCHEME OF TAXATION

Recognized gains and losses must be properly classified. Proper classification depends upon three characteristics:

- The tax status of the property.
- The manner of the property's disposition.
- The holding period of the property.

The three possible tax statuses are capital asset, § 1231 asset, or ordinary asset. Property disposition may be by sale, exchange, casualty, theft, or condemnation.

There are two holding periods: short term and long term. The short-term holding period is one year or less. The long-term holding period is more than one year. (More explanation of the holding period is provided later in the chapter.)

The major focus of this chapter is capital gains and losses. Capital gains and losses usually result from the disposition of a capital asset. The most common disposition is a sale of the asset. Capital gains and losses can also result from the disposition of § 1231 assets, which is discussed in Chapter 17.

LO.1

Discuss the general scheme of taxation for capital gains and losses.

16-2 CAPITAL ASSETS

Personal use assets and investment assets are the most common capital assets owned by individual taxpayers. Personal use assets usually include items such as clothing, recreational equipment, a residence, and automobiles. Investment assets usually include investments in mutual funds, corporate stocks and bonds, government bonds, and vacant land. Remember, however, that losses from the sale or exchange of personal use assets are not recognized. Therefore, the classification of such losses as capital losses can be ignored.

The crux of capital asset determination hinges on whether the asset is held for personal use purposes (capital asset), investment purposes (capital asset), or business purposes (ordinary asset). The taxpayer's use of the property often provides objective evidence.

LO.2

Distinguish capital assets from ordinary assets.

Example 1

David buys an expensive painting.

- If David purchased the painting for personal use (as a decoration in his home) and it is not of investment quality, it is a capital asset, but any loss on its sale is not usable, whereas gain from its sale is taxable. Investment quality generally means that the painting is expected to appreciate in value.
- If the painting is used to decorate David's business office and is of investment quality, the painting is not depreciable and, therefore, is a capital asset.
- If David's business is buying and selling paintings, the painting is inventory and, therefore, an ordinary asset.
- If the painting is not of investment quality and the business did not purchase it for investment, the painting is an ordinary asset and it is depreciable even though it serves a decorative purpose in David's office.
- If David depreciates the painting, that is objective evidence that the painting is held for use in his business, is not being held for investment or as inventory, and is not a capital asset.

Due to the historical preferential treatment of capital gains, taxpayers have preferred that gains be capital gains rather than ordinary gains. As a result, a great many statutes, cases, and rulings have accumulated in the attempt to define what is and what is not a capital asset.

TAX IN THE NEWS Certainty over Capital Gain Rates

During the fall of 2012, President Obama proposed legislation that, starting in 2013, would increase capital gain rates on many high-income taxpayers. The proposed rates were not as favorable as the rates that applied to 2011 and 2012 tax returns of individual taxpayers. However, the American Taxpayer Relief Act of 2012 instead made the lower tax rates on long-term capital gains permanent. The current rates are discussed later in this chapter.

16-2a Definition of a Capital Asset (§ 1221)

Capital assets are not directly defined in the Code. Instead, § 1221(a) defines what is *not* a capital asset. A **capital asset** is property held by the taxpayer (when it is connected with the taxpayer's business) that is *not* any of the following:

- Inventory or property held primarily for sale to customers in the ordinary course of a business. The Supreme Court, in *Malat v. Riddell*, defined *primarily* as meaning "of first importance or principally."[1]
- Accounts and notes receivable acquired from the sale of inventory or acquired for services rendered in the ordinary course of business.
- Depreciable property or real estate used in a business.
- Certain copyrights; literary, musical, or artistic compositions; or letters, memoranda, or similar property held by (1) a taxpayer whose efforts created the property; (2) in the case of a letter, memorandum, or similar property, a taxpayer for whom it was produced; or (3) a taxpayer in whose hands the basis of the property is determined, for purposes of determining gain from a sale or exchange, in whole or in part by reference to the basis of such property in the hands of a taxpayer described in (1) or (2). When a sale or exchange involves musical compositions or copyrights in musical works either (1) created by the taxpayer's personal efforts or (2) having a basis determined by reference to the basis in the hands of a taxpayer whose personal efforts created the compositions or copyrights, the taxpayer may elect to treat the sale or exchange as the disposition of a capital asset.[2]
- U.S. government publications that are (1) received by a taxpayer from the U.S. government other than by purchase at the price at which they are offered for sale to the public or (2) held by a taxpayer whose basis, for purposes of determining gain from a sale or exchange, is determined by reference to a taxpayer described in (1).
- Supplies of a type regularly used or consumed in the ordinary course of a business.

The Code defines what is not a capital asset. From the preceding list, it is apparent that inventory, accounts and notes receivable, supplies, and most fixed assets of a business are not capital assets. Often, the only business asset that is a capital asset is goodwill. The following discussion provides further detail on each part of the capital asset definition.

Inventory

What constitutes inventory is determined by the taxpayer's business.

Example 2	Green Company buys and sells used cars. Its cars are inventory. Its gains from the sale of the cars are ordinary income.

Example 3	Soong sells her personal use automobile at a $500 gain. The automobile is a personal use asset and, therefore, a capital asset. The gain is a capital gain.

---

[1]66–1 USTC ¶9317, 17 AFTR 2d 604, 86 S.Ct. 1030 (USSC, 1966). [2]§ 1221(b)(3).

Accounts and Notes Receivable

Collection of an accrual basis account receivable usually does not result in a gain or loss because the amount collected equals the receivable's basis. The sale of an account or note receivable may generate a gain or loss, and the gain or loss is ordinary because the receivable is not a capital asset. The sale of an accrual basis receivable may result in a gain or loss because it will probably be sold for more or less than its basis. A cash basis account receivable has no basis. Sale of such a receivable generates a gain. Collection of a cash basis receivable generates ordinary income rather than a gain. A gain usually requires a sale of the receivable. See the discussion of Sale or Exchange later in this chapter.

> Oriole Company has accounts receivable of $100,000. Because Oriole needs working capital, it sells the receivables for $83,000 to a financial institution.
>
> If Oriole is an accrual basis taxpayer, it has a $17,000 ordinary loss. Revenue of $100,000 would have been recorded, and a $100,000 basis would have been established when the receivable was created.
>
> If Oriole is a cash basis taxpayer, it has $83,000 of ordinary income because it would not have recorded any revenue earlier; thus, the receivable has no tax basis.

Example 4

Business Fixed Assets

Depreciable personal property and real estate (both depreciable and nondepreciable) used by a business are not capital assets. Thus, *business fixed assets* are generally not capital assets.

The Code has a very complex set of rules pertaining to such property. One of these rules is discussed under Real Property Subdivided for Sale (§ 1237) later in this chapter; the remainder of the rules are discussed in Chapter 17. Although business fixed assets are not capital assets, a long-term capital gain can sometimes result from their sale. Chapter 17 discusses the potential capital gain treatment for business fixed assets under § 1231.

Copyrights and Creative Works

Generally, the person whose efforts led to the copyright or creative work has an ordinary asset, not a capital asset. *Creative works* include the works of authors, composers, and artists. Also, the person for whom a letter, a memorandum, or another similar property was created has an ordinary asset. Finally, a person receiving a copyright, creative work, a letter, a memorandum, or similar property by gift from the creator or the person for whom the work was created has an ordinary asset. Note the exception mentioned earlier that permits the taxpayer to elect to treat the sale or exchange of a musical composition or a copyright of a musical work as the disposition of a capital asset. (Patents are subject to special statutory rules discussed later in the chapter.)

> Wanda is a part-time music composer. A music publisher purchases one of her songs for $5,000. Wanda has a $5,000 ordinary gain from the sale of an ordinary asset unless she elects to treat the gain as a capital gain.

Example 5

Example 6

Ed received a letter from the President of the United States in 1982. In the current year, Ed sells the letter to a collector for $300. Ed has a $300 ordinary gain from the sale of an ordinary asset (because the letter was created for Ed).

Example 7

Isabella gives a song she composed to her son. The son sells the song to a music publisher for $5,000. The son has a $5,000 ordinary gain from the sale of an ordinary asset unless he elects to treat the gain as a capital gain. If the son inherits the song from Isabella, his basis for the song is its fair market value at Isabella's death. In this situation, the song is a capital asset because the son's basis is not related to Isabella's basis for the song.

ETHICS & EQUITY   Sculpture as a Capital Asset

Cynthia is a successful sculptor who created a work that is now worth $400,000 and has no tax basis. Cynthia forms a corporation and contributes the sculpture to it in exchange for the corporation's shares. Fourteen months later, she sells all the stock for $400,000. She wants to treat the sale of the stock as a long-term capital gain. Evaluate the propriety of Cynthia's actions.

U.S. Government Publications

U.S. government publications received from the U.S. government (or its agencies) for a reduced price are not capital assets. This prevents a taxpayer from later donating the publications to charity and claiming a charitable contribution equal to the fair market value of the publications. A charitable contribution of a capital asset generally yields a deduction equal to the fair market value. A charitable contribution of an ordinary asset generally yields a deduction equal to less than the fair market value. If such property is received by gift from the original purchaser, the property is not a capital asset to the donee. (For a more comprehensive explanation of charitable contributions of property, refer to Chapter 10.)

16-2b Effect of Judicial Action

Court decisions play an important role in the definition of capital assets. Because the Code only lists categories of what are *not* capital assets, judicial interpretation is sometimes required to determine whether a specific item fits into one of those categories. The Supreme Court follows a literal interpretation of the categories. For instance, corporate stock is not mentioned in § 1221. Thus, corporate stock is *usually* a capital asset. However, what if corporate stock is purchased for resale to customers? Then it is *inventory* and not a capital asset because inventory is one of the categories in § 1221. (See the discussion of Dealers in Securities that follows.)

A Supreme Court decision was required to distinguish between capital asset and non-capital asset status when a taxpayer who normally did not acquire stock for resale to customers acquired stock with the intention of resale.[3] The Court decided that because the stock was not acquired primarily for sale to customers (the taxpayer did not sell the stock to its regular customers), the stock was a capital asset.

Because of the uncertainty associated with capital asset status, Congress has enacted several Code Sections to clarify the definition. These statutory expansions of the capital asset definition are discussed in the following section.

---

[3]*Arkansas Best v. Comm.,* 88–1 USTC ¶9210, 61 AFTR 2d 88–655, 108 S.Ct. 971 (USSC, 1988).

TAX IN THE NEWS Losses on Home Mortgages

Banks and other financial institutions have taken huge financial accounting write-downs on securities that consist of "bundles" of home mortgages. If the financial institution held these securities as investments, they were capital assets. If the financial institution held these securities as inventory, they were ordinary assets. However, writing them down for financial accounting purposes does not mean the institution actually disposed of the securities. Therefore, the loss in value of the securities is not recognized for tax purposes until the securities are transferred in a sale or exchange.

16-2c Statutory Expansions

Congress has often expanded the § 1221 general definition of what is *not* a capital asset.

Dealers in Securities

As a general rule, securities (stocks, bonds, and other financial instruments) held by a dealer are considered to be inventory and are, therefore, not subject to capital gain or loss treatment. A *dealer in securities* is a merchant (e.g., a brokerage firm) that regularly engages in the purchase and resale of securities to customers. The dealer must identify any securities being held for investment. Generally, if a dealer clearly identifies certain securities as held for investment purposes by the close of business on the acquisition date, gain from the securities' sale will be capital gain. However, the gain will not be capital gain if the dealer ceases to hold the securities for investment prior to the sale. Losses are capital losses if at any time the securities have been clearly identified by the dealer as held for investment.[4]

> **Example 8**
>
> Tracy is a securities dealer. She purchases 100 shares of Swan stock. If Tracy takes no further action, the stock is inventory and an ordinary asset. If she designates in her records that the stock is held for investment, the stock is a capital asset. Tracy must designate the investment purpose by the close of business on the acquisition date. If Tracy maintains her investment purpose and later sells the stock, the gain or loss is capital gain or loss. If Tracy redesignates the stock as held for resale (inventory) and then sells it, any gain is ordinary, but any loss is capital loss.

Real Property Subdivided for Sale (§ 1237)

Substantial real property development activities may result in the owner being considered a dealer for tax purposes. Income from the sale of real estate property lots is treated as the sale of inventory (ordinary income) if the owner is considered to be a dealer. However, § 1237 allows real estate investors capital gain treatment if they engage *only* in *limited* development activities. To be eligible for § 1237 treatment, the following requirements must be met:

- The taxpayer may not be a corporation.
- The taxpayer may not be a real estate dealer.
- No substantial improvements may be made to the lots sold. *Substantial* generally means more than a 10 percent increase in the value of a lot. Shopping centers and other commercial or residential buildings are considered substantial, while filling, draining, leveling, and clearing operations are not.
- The taxpayer must have held the lots sold for at least 5 years, except for inherited property. The substantial improvements test is less stringent if the property is held at least 10 years.

---

[4]§§ 1236(a) and (b) and Reg. §§ 1.1236–1(a) and (b).

If the preceding requirements are met, all gain is capital gain until the tax year in which the *sixth* lot is sold. Sales of contiguous lots to a single buyer in the same transaction count as the sale of one lot. Beginning with the tax year the *sixth* lot is sold, some of the gain may be ordinary income. Five percent of the revenue from lot sales is potential ordinary income. That potential ordinary income is offset by any selling expenses from the lot sales. Practically, sales commissions often are at least 5 percent of the sales price, so none of the gain is treated as ordinary income.

Section 1237 does not apply to losses. A loss from the sale of subdivided real property is an ordinary loss unless the property qualifies as a capital asset under § 1221. The following example illustrates the application of § 1237.

Example 9

Jack owns a large tract of land and subdivides it for sale. Assume that Jack meets all of the requirements of § 1237 and during the tax year sells the first 10 lots to 10 different buyers for $10,000 each. Jack's basis in each lot sold is $3,000, and he incurs total selling expenses of $4,000 on the sales. Jack's gain is computed as follows:

Selling price (10 × $10,000)	$100,000	
Less: Selling expenses (10 × $400)	(4,000)	
Amount realized		$ 96,000
Basis (10 × $3,000)		(30,000)
Realized and recognized gain		$ 66,000
Classification of recognized gain:		
Ordinary income		
Five percent of selling price (5% × $100,000)	$ 5,000	
Less: Selling expenses	(4,000)	
Ordinary gain		1,000
Capital gain		$ 65,000

Nonbusiness Bad Debts

A loan not made in the ordinary course of business is classified as a nonbusiness receivable. In the year the receivable becomes completely worthless, it is a *nonbusiness bad debt*, and the bad debt is treated as a short-term capital loss. Even if the receivable was outstanding for more than one year, the loss is still a short-term capital loss. Chapter 7 discusses nonbusiness bad debts more thoroughly.

16-3 SALE OR EXCHANGE

LO.3

State and explain the relevance of a sale or exchange to classification as a capital gain or loss and apply the special rules for the capital gain or loss treatment of the retirement of corporate obligations, options, patents, franchises, and lease cancellation payments.

Recognition of capital gain or loss usually requires a sale or exchange of a capital asset. The Code uses the term **sale or exchange**, but does not define it. Generally, a property sale involves the receipt of money by the seller and/or the assumption by the purchaser of the seller's liabilities. An exchange involves the transfer of property for other property. Thus, an involuntary conversion (casualty, theft, or condemnation) is not a sale or exchange. In several situations, the determination of whether a sale or exchange has taken place has been clarified by the enactment of Code Sections that specifically provide for sale or exchange treatment.

Recognized gains or losses from the cancellation, lapse, expiration, or any other termination of a right or an obligation with respect to personal property (other than stock) that is or would be a capital asset in the hands of the taxpayer are capital gains or losses.[5] See the discussion under Options later in the chapter for more details.

16-3a Worthless Securities and § 1244 Stock

Occasionally, securities such as stock and, especially, bonds may become worthless due to the insolvency of their issuer. If such a security is a capital asset, the loss is deemed to have occurred as the result of a sale or exchange on the *last day* of the tax year.[6] This

---

[5]§ 1234A.

[6]§ 165(g)(1).

TAX IN THE NEWS Bankruptcy and Worthless Stock

During 2009, General Motors went into bankruptcy, was reorganized, and emerged from bankruptcy. However, the common shareholders of the General Motors that went into bankruptcy were not the common shareholders of the General Motors that emerged from bankruptcy. The original common shareholders lost their entire investment because their stock became worthless. The holding period of their stock ended for tax purposes on December 31, 2009,

because of the worthless stock rules. They had a capital loss equal to whatever their basis was for the worthless shares. The debtors of General Motors accepted common shares in the General Motors that emerged from bankruptcy. Generally, the exchange of debt for common shares in a bankruptcy reorganization is not a taxable transaction, and the basis of the debt becomes the basis for the shares.

© iStockphoto.com/Andrey Prokhorov

last-day rule may have the effect of converting what otherwise would have been a short-term capital loss into a long-term capital loss. (See Treatment of Capital Losses later in this chapter.) Worthless securities are discussed in Chapter 7 on pp. 7-7 and 7-27.

Section 1244 allows an ordinary deduction on disposition of stock at a loss. The stock must be that of a small business corporation, and the ordinary deduction is limited to $50,000 ($100,000 for married taxpayers filing jointly) per year. For a more detailed discussion, refer to Chapter 7, pp. 7-7 and 7-27.

16-3b Special Rule—Retirement of Corporate Obligations

A debt obligation (e.g., a bond or note payable) may have a tax basis in excess of or less than its redemption value because it may have been acquired at a premium or discount. Consequently, the collection of the redemption value may result in a loss or gain. Generally, the collection of a debt obligation is *treated* as a sale or exchange.[7] Therefore, any loss or gain can be a capital loss or capital gain because a sale or exchange has taken place. However, if the debt obligation was issued by an individual prior to June 9, 1997, and/or purchased by the taxpayer prior to June 9, 1997, the collection of the debt obligation is deemed not to be a sale or exchange.

> Fran acquires $1,000 of Osprey Corporation bonds for $980 in the open market. If the bonds are held to maturity, the $20 difference between Fran's collection of the $1,000 redemption value and her cost of $980 is treated as capital gain. If the obligation had been issued to Fran by an individual prior to June 9, 1997, her $20 gain would have been ordinary because she did not sell or exchange the debt.

Example 10

Original Issue Discount (§§ 1272–1288)

The benefit of the sale or exchange exception that allows a capital gain from the collection of certain obligations is reduced when the obligation has original issue discount. **Original issue discount (OID)** arises when the issue price of a debt obligation is less than the maturity value of the obligation. OID must generally be amortized over the life of the debt obligation using the effective interest method. The OID amortization increases the basis of the bond. Most new publicly traded bond issues do not carry OID because the stated interest rate is set to make the market price on issue the same as the bond's face amount. In addition, even if the issue price is less than the face amount, the difference is not considered to be OID if the difference is less than one-fourth of 1 percent of the redemption price at maturity multiplied by the number of years to maturity.[8]

In the case where OID does exist, it may or may not have to be amortized, depending upon the date the obligation was issued. When OID is amortized, the

---

[7]§ 1271. [8]§ 1273(a)(3).

amount of gain upon collection, sale, or exchange of the obligation is correspondingly reduced. The obligations covered by the OID amortization rules and the method of amortization are presented in §§ 1272–1275. Similar rules for other obligations can be found in §§ 1276–1288.

Example 11

Jerry purchases $10,000 of newly issued White Corporation bonds for $6,000. The bonds have OID of $4,000. Jerry must amortize the discount over the life of the bonds. The OID amortization *increases* his interest income. (The bonds were selling at a discount because the market rate of interest was greater than the bonds' stated interest rate.) After Jerry has amortized $1,800 of OID, he sells the bonds for $8,000. Jerry has a capital gain of $200 [$8,000 − ($6,000 cost + $1,800 OID amortization)].

The OID amortization rules prevent him from converting ordinary interest income into capital gain. Without the OID amortization, Jerry would have capital gain of $2,000 ($8,000 − $6,000 cost).

16-3c Options

Frequently, a potential buyer of property wants some time to make the purchase decision, but wants to control the sale and/or the sale price in the meantime. **Options** are used to achieve these objectives. The potential purchaser (grantee) pays the property owner (grantor) for an option on the property. The grantee then becomes the option holder. The option, which usually sets a price at which the grantee can buy the property, expires after a specified period of time.

Sale of an Option

A grantee may sell or exchange the option rather than exercising it or letting it expire. Generally, the grantee's sale or exchange of the option results in capital gain or loss if the option property is (or would be) a capital asset to the grantee.[9]

Example 12

Rosa wants to buy some vacant land for investment purposes. She cannot afford the full purchase price. Instead, Rosa (grantee) pays the landowner (grantor) $3,000 to obtain an option to buy the land for $100,000 anytime in the next two years. The option is a capital asset for Rosa because if she actually purchased the land, the land would be a capital asset.

Three months after purchasing the option, Rosa sells it for $7,000. She has a $4,000 ($7,000 − $3,000) short-term capital gain on this sale because she held the option for one year or less.

Failure to Exercise Options

If an option holder (grantee) fails to exercise the option, the lapse of the option is considered a sale or exchange on the option expiration date. Thus, the loss is a capital loss if the property subject to the option is (or would be) a capital asset in the hands of the grantee.

The grantor of an option on *stocks, securities, commodities, or commodity futures* receives short-term capital gain treatment upon the expiration of the option. Options on property other than stocks, securities, commodities, or commodity futures result in ordinary income to the grantor when the option expires. For example, an individual investor who owns certain stock (a capital asset) may sell a call option, entitling the buyer of the option to acquire the stock at a specified price higher than the value at the date the option is granted. The writer of the call receives a premium (e.g., 10 percent) for writing the option. If the price of the stock does not increase during the option period, the option will expire unexercised. Upon the expiration of the option, the grantor must recognize short-term capital gain (whereas the grantee recognizes a loss, the character of which depends on the underlying asset). These provisions do not apply to options held for sale to customers (the inventory of a securities dealer).

---

[9] § 1234(a) and Reg. § 1.1234–1(a)(1). Stock options are discussed in Chapter 19.

Exercise of Options by Grantee

If the option is exercised, the amount paid for the option is added to the optioned property's selling price. This increases the gain (or reduces the loss) to the grantor resulting from the sale of the property. The grantor's gain or loss is capital or ordinary depending on the tax status of the property. The grantee adds the cost of the option to the basis of the property purchased.

THE BIG PICTURE

Example 13

Return to the facts of *The Big Picture* on p. 16-1. On February 1, 2014, Maurice purchases 100 shares of Eagle Company stock for $5,000. On April 1, 2014, he writes a call option on the stock, giving the grantee the right to buy the stock for $6,000 during the following six-month period. Maurice (the grantor) receives a call premium of $500 for writing the call.

- If the call is exercised by the grantee on August 1, 2014, Maurice has $1,500 ($6,000 + $500 − $5,000) of short-term capital gain from the sale of the stock. The grantee has a $6,500 ($500 option premium+$6,000 purchase price) basis for the stock.
- Investors sometimes get nervous and want to "lock in" gains or losses. Assume that Maurice decides to sell his stock prior to exercise for $6,000 and enters into a closing transaction by purchasing a call on 100 shares of Eagle Company stock for $5,000. Because the Eagle stock is selling for $6,000, Maurice must pay a call premium of $1,000. He recognizes a $500 short-term capital loss [$1,000 (call premium paid) − $500 (call premium received)] on the closing transaction. On the actual sale of the Eagle stock, Maurice has a short-term capital gain of $1,000 [$6,000 (selling price) − $5,000 (cost)]. The grantee is not affected by Maurice's closing transaction. The original option is still in existence, and the grantee's tax consequences depend on what action the grantee takes—exercising the option, letting the option expire, or selling the option.
- Assume that the original option expired unexercised. Maurice has a $500 short-term capital gain equal to the call premium received for writing the option. This gain is not recognized until the option expires. The grantee has a loss from expiration of the option. The nature of the loss will depend upon whether the option was a capital asset or an ordinary asset.

Concept Summary 16.1 summarizes the rules for options.

16-3d Patents

Transfer of a **patent** is treated as the sale or exchange of a long-term capital asset when all substantial rights to the patent (or an undivided interest that includes all such rights) are transferred by a holder.[10] The transferor/holder may receive payment in virtually any form. Lump-sum or periodic payments are most common. The amount of the payments may also be contingent on the transferee/purchaser's productivity, use, or disposition of the patent. If the transfer meets these requirements, any gain or loss is *automatically a long-term* capital gain or loss. Whether the asset was a capital asset for the transferor, whether a sale or exchange occurred, and how long the transferor held the patent are not relevant.

This special long-term capital gain or loss treatment for patents is intended to encourage technological progress. Ironically, authors, composers, and artists are not eligible for capital gain treatment when their creations are transferred. Books, songs, and artists' works may be copyrighted, but copyrights and the assets they represent are not capital assets. Thus, the disposition of those assets by their creators usually results in ordinary gain or loss (unless the exception for musical compositions applies, as noted earlier). Example 14 illustrates the special treatment for patents.

---

[10]§ 1235.

CONCEPT SUMMARY 16.1

Options

Event	Effect on	
	Grantor	**Grantee**
Option is granted.	Receives value and has a contract obligation (a liability).	Pays value and has a contract right (an asset).
Option expires.	Has a short-term capital gain if the option property is stocks, securities, commodities, or commodity futures. Otherwise, gain is ordinary income.	Has a loss (capital loss if option property would have been a capital asset for the grantee).
Option is exercised.	Amount received for option increases proceeds from sale of the option property.	Amount paid for option becomes part of the basis of the option property purchased.
Option is sold or exchanged by grantee.	Result depends upon whether option later expires or is exercised (see above).	Could have gain or loss (capital gain or loss if option property would have been a capital asset for the grantee).

© iStockphoto.com/Andrey Prokhorov

Substantial Rights

To receive favorable capital gain treatment, all *substantial rights* to the patent (or an undivided interest in it) must be transferred. All substantial rights to a patent means all rights (whether then held by the grantor) that are valuable at the time the patent rights (or an undivided interest in the patent) are transferred. All substantial rights have not been transferred when the transfer is limited geographically within the issuing country or when the transfer is for a period less than the remaining life of the patent. The circumstances of the entire transaction, rather than merely the language used in the transfer instrument, are to be considered in deciding whether all substantial rights have been transferred.[11]

THE BIG PICTURE

Example 14

Return to the facts of *The Big Picture* on p. 16-1. Kevin transfers his 50% rights in the patent to the Green Battery Company, Inc., in exchange for a $1,000,000 lump-sum payment plus $.50 for each battery sold. Assuming that Kevin has transferred all substantial rights, the question of whether the transfer is a sale or exchange of a capital asset is not relevant. Kevin automatically has a long-term capital gain from both the $1 million lump-sum payment and the $.50 per battery royalty to the extent those proceeds exceed his basis for the patent. Kevin also had an automatic long-term capital gain when he sold 50% of his rights in the patent to Maurice, because Kevin transferred an undivided interest that included all substantial rights in the patent.

Whether Maurice gets long-term capital gain treatment depends upon whether Maurice is a holder. See the following discussion and Example 15.

Holder Defined

The *holder* of a patent must be an *individual* and is usually the invention's creator. A holder may also be an individual who purchases the patent rights from the creator before the patented invention is reduced to practice. However, the creator's employer and certain parties related to the creator do not qualify as holders. Thus, in the common situation where an employer has all rights to an employee's

---

[11]Reg. § 1.1235–2(b)(1).

inventions, the employer is not eligible for long-term capital gain treatment. More than likely, the employer will have an ordinary asset because the patent was developed as part of its business.

THE BIG PICTURE

Example 15

Return to the facts of *The Big Picture* on p. 16-1. Continuing with the facts of Example 14, Kevin is clearly a holder of the patent because he is the inventor and was not an employee when he invented the battery. When Maurice purchased a 50% interest in the patent nine months ago, he became a holder if the patent had not yet been reduced to practice. Because the patent apparently was not being utilized in the manufacturing process at the time of the purchase, it had not been reduced to practice.

Consequently, Maurice is also a holder, and he has an automatic long-term capital gain or loss if he transfers all substantial rights in his 50% interest to the Green Battery Company. Maurice's basis for his share of the patent is $50,000, and his proceeds equal $1 million plus $.50 for each battery sold. Thus, Maurice has a long-term capital gain even though he has not held his interest in the patent for more than one year.

16-3e Franchises, Trademarks, and Trade Names (§ 1253)

A mode of operation, a widely recognized brand name (trade name), and a widely known business symbol (trademark) are all valuable assets. These assets may be licensed (commonly known as franchising) by their owner for use by other businesses. Many fast-food restaurants (such as McDonald's and Taco Bell) are franchises. The franchisee usually pays the owner (franchisor) an initial fee plus a contingent fee. The contingent fee is often based upon the franchisee's sales volume.

For Federal income tax purposes, a **franchise** is an agreement that gives the franchisee the right to distribute, sell, or provide goods, services, or facilities within a specified area.[12] A franchise transfer includes the grant of a franchise, a transfer by one franchisee to another person, or the renewal of a franchise.

Section 1253 provides that a transfer of a franchise, trademark, or trade name is not a transfer of a capital asset when the transferor retains any significant power, right, or continuing interest in the property transferred.

Significant Power, Right, or Continuing Interest

Significant powers, rights, or continuing interests include control over assignment, quality of products and services, sale or advertising of other products or services, and the right to require that substantially all supplies and equipment be purchased from the transferor. Also included are the right to terminate the franchise at will and the right to substantial contingent payments. Most modern franchising operations involve some or all of these powers, rights, or continuing interests.

In the unusual case where no significant power, right, or continuing interest is retained by the transferor, a sale or exchange may occur, and capital gain or loss treatment may be available. For capital gain or loss treatment to be available, the asset transferred must qualify as a capital asset.

THE BIG PICTURE

Example 16

Return to the facts of *The Big Picture* on p. 16-1. Maurice sells for $210,000 to Mauve, Inc., the franchise purchased from Orange, Inc., nine months ago. The $210,000 received by Maurice is not contingent, and all significant powers, rights, and continuing interests are transferred. The $115,000 gain ($210,000 proceeds − $95,000 adjusted basis) is a short-term capital gain because Maurice has held the franchise for only nine months.

---

[12]§ 1253(b)(1).

Noncontingent Payments

When the transferor retains a significant power, right, or continuing interest, the transferee's noncontingent payments to the transferor are ordinary income to the transferor. The franchisee capitalizes the payments and amortizes them over 15 years. If the franchise is sold, the amortization is subject to recapture under § 1245.[13]

| Example 17 | Grey Company signs a 10-year franchise agreement with DOH Donuts. Grey (the franchisee) makes payments of $3,000 per year for the first 8 years of the franchise agreement—a total of $24,000. Grey cannot deduct $3,000 per year as the payments are made. Instead, Grey may amortize the $24,000 total over 15 years. Thus, Grey may deduct $1,600 per year for each of the 15 years of the amortization period.
| | The same result would occur if Grey made a $24,000 lump-sum payment at the beginning of the franchise period. Assuming that DOH Donuts (the franchisor) retains significant powers, rights, or a continuing interest, it will have ordinary income when it receives the payments from Grey. |

Contingent Payments

The contingent franchise payments are ordinary income for the franchisor and an ordinary deduction for the franchisee when the transferor retains a significant power, right, or continuing interest. For this purpose, a payment qualifies as a contingent payment only if the following requirements are met:

- The contingent amounts are part of a series of payments that are paid at least annually throughout the term of the transfer agreement.
- The payments are substantially equal in amount or are payable under a fixed formula.

| Example 18 | TAK, a spicy chicken franchisor, transfers an eight-year franchise to Otis. TAK retains a significant power, right, or continuing interest. Otis, the franchisee, agrees to pay TAK 15% of sales. This contingent payment is ordinary income to TAK and a business deduction for Otis as the payments are made. |

Sports Franchises

Professional sports franchises (e.g., the Detroit Tigers) are subject to § 1253.[14] Player contracts are usually one of the major assets acquired with a sports franchise. These contracts last only for the time stated in the contract. By being classified as § 197 intangibles, the player contracts and other intangible assets acquired in the purchase of the sports franchise are amortized over a statutory 15-year period.[15]

Concept Summary 16.2 summarizes the rules for franchises.

16-3f Lease Cancellation Payments

The tax treatment of payments received for canceling a lease depends on whether the recipient is the **lessor** or the **lessee** and whether the lease is a capital asset.

Lessee Treatment

Lease cancellation payments received by a lessee are treated as an exchange.[16] Thus, these payments are capital gains if the lease is a capital asset. Generally, a lessee's lease is a capital asset if the property (either personalty or realty) is used for the lessee's personal use (e.g., his or her residence). A lessee's lease is an ordinary asset if the property is used in the lessee's trade or business and the lease has existed for one year or less when it is canceled. A lessee's lease is a § 1231 asset if the property is used in the lessee's trade or business and the lease has existed for more than a year when it is canceled.[17]

---

[13]See Chapter 17 for a discussion of the recapture provisions.

[14]Section 1253(e) previously exempted sports franchises from § 1253, but was repealed for franchises acquired after October 22, 2004.

[15]§ 197(a).

[16]§ 1241 and Reg. § 1.1241–1(a).

[17]Reg. § 1.1221–1(b) and PLR 200045019.

CONCEPT SUMMARY 16.2

Franchises

Event	Effect on	
	Franchisor	**Franchisee**
Franchisor Retains Significant Powers and Rights		
Noncontingent payment	Ordinary income.	Capitalized and amortized over 15 years as an ordinary deduction; if franchise is sold, amortization is subject to recapture under § 1245.
Contingent payment	Ordinary income.	Ordinary deduction.
Franchisor Does *Not* Retain Significant Powers and Rights		
Noncontingent payment	Ordinary income if franchise rights are an ordinary asset; capital gain if franchise rights are a capital asset (unlikely).	Capitalized and amortized over 15 years as an ordinary deduction; if the franchise is sold, amortization is subject to recapture under § 1245.
Contingent payment	Ordinary income.	Ordinary deduction.

© iStockphoto.com/Andrey Prokhorov

> **Example 19**
>
> Mark owns an apartment building that he is going to convert into an office building. Vicki is one of the apartment tenants and receives $1,000 from Mark to cancel the lease. Vicki has a capital gain of $1,000 (which is long-term or short-term depending upon how long she has held the lease). Mark has an ordinary deduction of $1,000.

Lessor Treatment

Payments received by a lessor for a lease cancellation are always ordinary income because they are considered to be in lieu of rental payments.[18]

> **Example 20**
>
> Floyd owns an apartment building near a university campus. Hui-Fen is one of the tenants. Hui-Fen is graduating early and offers Floyd $800 to cancel the apartment lease. Floyd accepts the offer. Floyd has ordinary income of $800. Hui-Fen has a nondeductible payment because the apartment was personal use property.

16-4 HOLDING PERIOD

Property must be held more than one year to qualify for long-term capital gain or loss treatment.[19] Property not held for the required long-term period results in short-term capital gain or loss. To compute the **holding period**, start counting on the day after the property was acquired and include the day of disposition.

LO.4

Determine whether the holding period for a capital asset is long-term or short-term.

THE BIG PICTURE

> **Example 21**
>
> Return to the facts of *The Big Picture* on p. 16-1. Assume that Maurice purchased the Purple stock on January 15, 2013. If he sells it on January 16, 2014, Maurice's holding period is more than one year. If instead Maurice sells the stock on January 15, 2014, the holding period is exactly one year and the gain or loss is short-term.

---

[18]Reg. § 1.61–8(b).   [19]§ 1222(3).

To be held for more than one year, a capital asset acquired on the last day of any month must not be disposed of until on or after the first day of the thirteenth succeeding month.[20]

Example 22

Leo purchases a capital asset on February 28, 2013. If Leo sells the asset on February 28, 2014, the holding period is one year and Leo will have a short-term capital gain or loss. If Leo sells the asset on March 1, 2014, the holding period is more than one year and he will have a long-term capital gain or loss.

16-4a Review of Special Holding Period Rules

There are several special holding period rules.[21] The application of these rules depends upon the type of asset and how it was acquired.

Nontaxable Exchanges

The holding period of property received in a like-kind exchange includes the holding period of the former asset if the property that has been exchanged is a capital asset or a § 1231 asset. In certain nontaxable transactions involving a substituted basis, the holding period of the former property is *tacked on* to the holding period of the newly acquired property.

Example 23

On April 22, 2014, Vern exchanges a business truck he acquired on March 15, 2011 for another truck in a qualifying like-kind exchange. The holding period of the replacement truck begins March 15, 2011, because the holding period of the truck given up in the exchange *tacks* to the holding period of the replacement truck.

Certain Nontaxable Transactions Involving a Carryover of Another Taxpayer's Basis

A former owner's holding period is tacked on to the present owner's holding period if the transaction is nontaxable and the former owner's basis carries over to the present owner. These transactions are discussed in Chapter 14.

Example 24

Kareem acquires 100 shares of Robin Corporation stock for $1,000 on December 31, 2010. He transfers the shares by gift to Megan on December 31, 2013, when the stock is worth $2,000. Kareem's basis of $1,000 becomes the basis for determining gain or loss on a subsequent sale by Megan. Megan's holding period begins with the date the stock was acquired by Kareem.

Example 25

Assume the same facts as in Example 24, except that the fair market value of the shares is only $800 on the date of the gift. The holding period begins on the date of the gift if Megan sells the stock for a loss. The value of the shares on the date of the gift is used in the determination of her basis for loss. If she sells the shares for $500 on April 1, 2014, Megan has a $300 recognized capital loss and the holding period is from December 31, 2013, to April 1, 2014 (thus, the loss is short-term).

Certain Disallowed Loss Transactions

Under several Code provisions, realized losses are disallowed. When a loss is disallowed, there is no carryover of holding period. Losses can be disallowed under § 267 (sale or exchange between related taxpayers) and § 262 (sale or exchange of personal use assets) as well as other Code Sections. Taxpayers who acquire property in a disallowed loss transaction will have a new holding period begin and will have a basis equal to the purchase price.

---

[20]Rev.Rul. 66–7, 1966–1 C.B. 188.   [21]§ 1223.

Trading ADRs on U.S. Stock Exchanges

Many non-U.S. companies now have subsidiaries that were formerly U.S. companies. For instance, Chrysler Corporation is a subsidiary of Fiat. Shares in such foreign companies generally cannot be traded directly on U.S. stock exchanges. Instead, the foreign companies issue instruments called American Depository Receipts (ADRs) that can be traded on U.S. stock exchanges. Purchases and sales of ADRs are treated for tax purposes as though the ADRs were shares in the corporation that issued them.

Global Tax Issues

© iStockphoto.com/Andrey Prokhorov

Example 26

Janet sells her personal automobile at a loss. She may not deduct the loss because it arises from the sale of personal use property. Janet purchases a replacement automobile for more than the selling price of her former automobile. Janet has a basis equal to the cost of the replacement automobile, and her holding period begins when she acquires the replacement automobile.

Inherited Property

The holding period for inherited property is treated as long term no matter how long the property is actually held by the heir. The holding period of the decedent or the decedent's estate is not relevant for the heir's holding period.[22]

Example 27

Shonda inherits Blue Company stock from her father, who died in 2014. She receives the stock on April 1, 2014, and sells it on November 1, 2014. Even though Shonda did not hold the stock more than one year, she receives long-term capital gain or loss treatment on the sale.

16-4b Special Rules for Short Sales

General

The Code provides special rules for determining the holding period of property sold short.[23] A **short sale** occurs when a taxpayer sells borrowed property and repays the lender with substantially identical property either held on the date of the sale or purchased after the sale. Short sales usually involve corporate stock. The seller's objective is to make a profit in anticipation of a decline in the stock's price. If the price declines, the seller in a short sale recognizes a profit equal to the difference between the sales price of the borrowed stock and the price paid for the replacement stock.

Example 28

Chris does not own any shares of Brown Corporation. However, Chris sells 30 shares of Brown. The shares are borrowed from Chris's broker and must be replaced within 45 days. Chris has a short sale because he was short the shares he sold. He will *close* the short sale by purchasing Brown shares and delivering them to his broker.

If the original 30 shares were sold for $10,000 and Chris later purchases 30 shares for $8,000, he has a gain of $2,000. Chris's hunch that the price of Brown stock would decline was correct. Chris was able to profit from selling high and buying low.

If Chris had to purchase Brown shares for $13,000 to close the short sale, he would have a loss of $3,000. In this case, Chris would have sold low and bought high—not the result he wanted. Chris would be making a short sale against the box if he borrowed shares from his broker to sell and then closed the short sale by delivering other Brown shares he owned at the time he made the short sale.

A short sale gain or loss is a capital gain or loss to the extent that the short sale property constitutes a capital asset of the taxpayer. The gain or loss is not recognized until the short sale is closed. Generally, the holding period of the short sale property is determined by how long the property used to close the short sale was held. However, when

---

[22]The Federal estate tax has been the subject of substantial recent legislation that has raised numerous tax planning issues.

[23]§ 1233.

substantially identical property (e.g., other shares of the same stock) is held by the taxpayer, the holding period is determined as follows:

- The short sale *gain or loss* is *short-term* when, on the short sale date, the substantially identical property has been held *short term* (i.e., for one year or less). (See Examples 29 and 30.)
- The short sale *gain* is *long-term* when, on the short sale date, the substantially identical property has been held *long term* (i.e., for more than one year) *and* is used to close the short sale. If the long-term substantially identical property is not used to close the short sale, the short sale gain is *short-term*. (See Example 31.)
- The short sale *loss* is *long-term* when, on the short sale date, the substantially identical property has been held *long term* (i.e., for more than one year).
- The short sale *gain or loss* is *short-term* if the substantially identical property is acquired *after* the short sale date and on or before the closing date. (See Example 32.)

Concept Summary 16.3 summarizes the short sale rules. These rules are intended to prevent the conversion of short-term capital gains into long-term capital gains and long-term capital losses into short-term capital losses.

CONCEPT SUMMARY 16.3

Short Sales of Securities

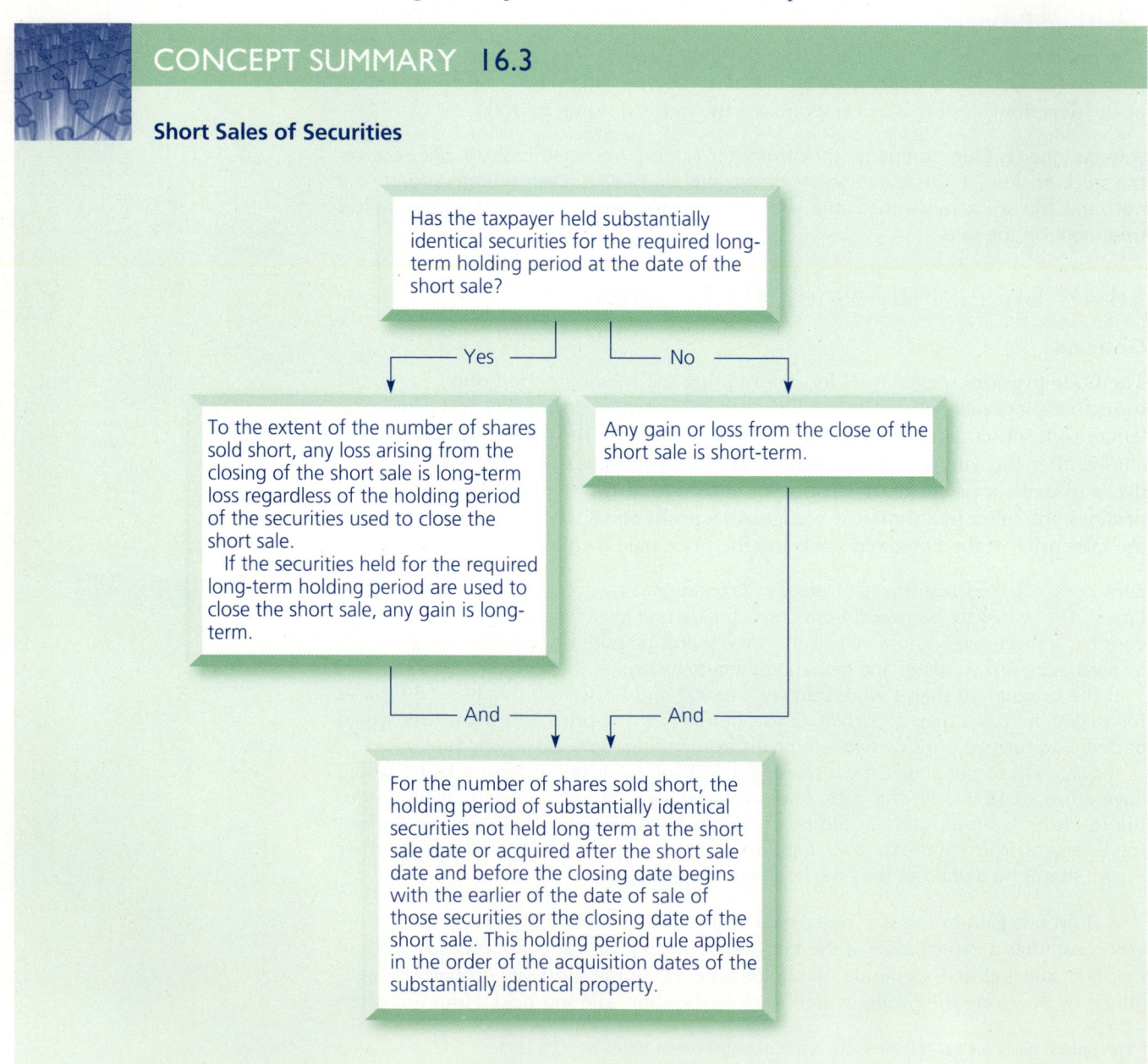

Has the taxpayer held substantially identical securities for the required long-term holding period at the date of the short sale?

Yes

To the extent of the number of shares sold short, any loss arising from the closing of the short sale is long-term loss regardless of the holding period of the securities used to close the short sale.

If the securities held for the required long-term holding period are used to close the short sale, any gain is long-term.

No

Any gain or loss from the close of the short sale is short-term.

And ... **And**

For the number of shares sold short, the holding period of substantially identical securities not held long term at the short sale date or acquired after the short sale date and before the closing date begins with the earlier of the date of sale of those securities or the closing date of the short sale. This holding period rule applies in the order of the acquisition dates of the substantially identical property.

Disposition Rules for Short Sales against the Box

A *short sale against the box* occurs when the stock is borrowed from a broker by a seller and the seller already owns the substantially identical securities on the short sale date or acquires them before the closing date.[24] To remove the taxpayer's flexibility as to when the short sale gain must be reported, a constructive sale approach is used. If the taxpayer has not closed the short sale by delivering the short sale securities to the broker *before* January 31 of the year following the short sale, the short sale is deemed to have been closed on the *earlier* of two events:

- On the short sale date if the taxpayer owned substantially identical securities at that time.
- On the date during the year of the short sale that the taxpayer acquired substantially identical securities.[25]

The basis of the shares in the deemed transfer of shares is used to compute the gain or loss on the short sale. As Examples 31 and 32 illustrate, when shares are *actually* transferred to the broker to close the short sale, there may be a gain or loss because the shares transferred will have a basis equal to the short sale date price and the value at the *actual* short sale closing date may be different from the short sale date price.

Illustrations

The following examples illustrate the treatment of short sales and short sales against the box.

On January 4, 2014, Donald purchases five shares of Osprey Corporation common stock for $100. On April 14, 2014, he engages in a short sale of five shares of the same stock for $150. On August 15, Donald closes the short sale by repaying the borrowed stock with the five shares purchased on January 4. Because his substantially identical shares were held short term as of the short sale date, Donald's $50 capital gain is short-term.	**Example 29**

Assume the same facts as in the previous example, except that Donald closes the short sale on January 28, 2015, by repaying the borrowed stock with five shares purchased on January 27, 2015, for $200. Because Donald's substantially identical property (purchased on January 4, 2014) was short-term property at the April 14, 2014 short sale date, his $50 capital loss ($200 cost of stock purchased on January 27, 2015, and a short sale selling price of $150) is short-term.	**Example 30**

On January 18, 2013, Rita purchases 200 shares of Owl Corporation stock for $1,000. On November 11, 2014, she sells short, for $1,300, 200 shares of Owl Corporation stock that she borrows from her broker. On February 10, 2015, Rita closes the short sale by delivering the 200 shares of Owl Corporation stock that she had acquired in 2013. On that date, Owl Corporation stock had a market price of $3 per share. Because Rita owned substantially identical stock on the date of the short sale and did not close the short sale before January 31, 2015, she is *deemed* to have closed the short sale on November 11, 2014 (the date of the short sale). On her 2014 tax return, she reports a $300 long-term capital gain ($1,300 short sale price − $1,000 basis). On February 10, 2015, Rita has a $700 short-term capital loss [$600 short sale closing date price (200 shares × $3 per share) − $1,300 basis] because the holding period of the shares used to close the short sale commences with the date of the short sale.	**Example 31**

---

[24]The "box" is the safe deposit box stock owners routinely used to keep stock certificates. Although stockbrokers today generally keep stock for their customers, the terminology *short sale against the box* is still used.

[25]§ 1259.

TAX IN THE NEWS   Short Sales in Real Estate

Recently, the term *short sale* has taken on a meaning in real estate transactions that is different from its use with regard to securities transactions. A short sale in real estate takes place when the mortgage on property exceeds the property's fair market value. A property owner in this predicament negotiates with the lender to allow the property to be sold at its fair market value with the lender accepting the sales price in full satisfaction of the mortgage. Lenders typically will not negotiate with such property owners until the owner has failed to make required mortgage payments and foreclosure by the lender is imminent. If the negotiations are successful, the property owner avoids foreclosure but may have debt cancellation income for the difference between the mortgage and the sales price.

© iStockphoto.com/Andrey Prokhorov

Example 32

Assume the same facts as in Example 31, except that Rita did not own any Owl Corporation stock on the short sale date and acquired the 200 shares of Owl Corporation stock for $1,000 on December 12, 2014 (after the November 11, 2014 short sale date). The *deemed* closing of the short sale is December 12, 2014, because Rita held substantially identical shares at the end of 2014 and did not close the short sale before January 31, 2015. Her 2014 short sale gain is a *short-term* gain of $300 ($1,300 short sale price − $1,000 basis), and she still has a short-term capital loss of $700 on February 10, 2015.

16-5 TAX TREATMENT OF CAPITAL GAINS AND LOSSES OF NONCORPORATE TAXPAYERS

LO.5

Describe the beneficial tax treatment for capital gains and the detrimental tax treatment for capital losses for noncorporate taxpayers.

All taxpayers net their capital gains and losses. Short-term gains and losses (if any) are netted against one another, and long-term gains and losses (if any) are netted against one another. The results will be net short-term gain or loss and net long-term gain or loss. If these two net positions are of opposite sign (one is a gain and one is a loss), they are netted against each other.

Six possibilities exist for the result after all possible netting has been completed. Three of these final results are gains, and three are losses. One possible result is a net long-term capital gain (NLTCG). Net long-term capital gains of noncorporate taxpayers are subject to beneficial treatment. A second possibility is a net short-term capital gain (NSTCG). Third, the netting may result in both NLTCG and NSTCG. The NLTCG portion of these results is eligible for an alternative tax calculation which is discussed later in the chapter under Alternative Tax on Net Capital Gain.

The American Taxpayer Relief Act of 2012 increased the maximum tax rate applied to net capital gain from 15 percent to 20 percent. This provision applies only to certain high-income taxpayers. The 20 percent applies when the taxpayer's regular tax bracket is 39.6 percent. In 2014, the taxpayer is subject to the 39.6 percent tax rate when taxable income exceeds $457,600 for married taxpayers filing jointly ($406,750 for single, $432,200 for head of household, and $228,800 for married taxpayers filing separately).

The last three results of the capital gain and loss netting process are losses. Thus, a fourth possibility is a net long-term capital loss (NLTCL). A fifth result is a net short-term capital loss (NSTCL). Finally, a sixth possibility includes both an NLTCL and an NSTCL. Neither NLTCLs nor NSTCLs are treated as ordinary losses. Treatment as an ordinary loss generally is preferable to capital loss treatment because ordinary losses are deductible in full while the deductibility of capital losses is subject to certain limitations. An individual taxpayer may deduct a maximum of $3,000 of net capital losses for a taxable year.[26]

---

[26]§ 1211(b).

16-5a Capital Gain and Loss Netting Process

Net short-term capital gain is not eligible for any special tax rate. It is taxed at the same rate as the taxpayer's other taxable income.

Net long-term capital gain is eligible for one or more of *five* alternative tax rates: 0 percent, 15 percent, 20 percent, 25 percent, and 28 percent. The 25 percent and 28 percent rates are used only in unique circumstances, so the discussion below concentrates more heavily on the other three rates. The net long-term capital gain components are referred to as the *0% / 15% / 20% gain*, the *25% gain*, and the *28% gain*.

The *25% gain* is technically called the **unrecaptured § 1250 gain** and is related to gain from disposition of § 1231 assets. Gains and losses from disposition of § 1231 assets are discussed in Chapter 17. In this chapter, the discussion will focus only on how the *25% gain* is taxed and not how it is determined. The *28% gain* relates to collectibles and § 1202 gain (see Chapter 5). Collectibles gain is discussed later in this chapter.

The *0% gain* portion of the *0% / 15% / 20% gain* applies when the taxable income (before taxing the *0% / 15% / 20% gain*) does not put the taxpayer out of the 15 percent bracket. Once the taxable income (including any portion of the *0% / 15% / 20% gain* taxed at 0 percent) puts the taxpayer above the 15 percent bracket, the remaining portion of the *0% / 15% / 20% gain* is taxed at 15 percent rather than at the regular tax rate until the taxable income reaches the 39.6 percent bracket. Once the taxable income (including any portion of the *0% / 15% / 20% gain* taxed at 0 percent or 15 percent) puts the taxpayer above the 35 percent bracket, the remaining portion of the *0% / 15% / 20% gain* is taxed at 20 percent rather than at the 39.6 percent regular tax rate. (In 2012 and earlier years, there was *0% / 15% gain*, but not *0% / 15% / 20% gain*. Thus, when the taxpayer's regular tax rate exceeded 15 percent, the 0 percent rate ended and the 15 percent rate began for the remainder of the *0% / 15% gain* included in taxable income.)

When the long-term capital gain exceeds short-term capital loss, a **net capital gain (NCG)** exists.[27] Net capital gain qualifies for beneficial alternative tax treatment (see the coverage later in the chapter).

Because there are both short- and long-term capital gains and losses and because the long-term capital gains may be taxed at various rates, an *ordering procedure* is required. The ordering procedure is intended to preserve the lowest long-term capital gain tax rate when there is a net long-term capital gain. This ordering procedure is explained in the following steps and then illustrated by several examples.

Step 1. Group all gains and losses into short term and 28%, 25%, and 0% / 15% / 20% long term.

Step 2. Net the gains and losses within each group.

Step 3. Offset the net 28% and net 25% amounts if they are of opposite sign.

Step 4. Offset the results after step 3 against the 0% / 15% / 20% amount if they are of opposite sign. If the 0% / 15% / 20% amount is a loss, offset it against the *highest-taxed gain first*. After this step, there is a net long-term capital gain or loss. If there is a net long-term capital gain, it may consist of only 28% gain, only 25% gain, only 0% / 15% / 20% gain, or some combination of all of these gains. If there is a net long-term capital loss, it is simply a net long-term capital loss.

Step 5. Offset the net short-term amount against the results of step 4 if they are of opposite sign. The netting rules offset net short-term capital loss against the *highest-taxed gain first*. Consequently, if there is a net short-term capital loss and a net gain from step 4, the short-term capital loss offsets first the 28% gain, then the 25% gain, and finally the 0% / 15% / 20% gain.

---

[27]§ 1222(11).

If the result of step 5 is *only* a short-term capital gain, the taxpayer is not eligible for a reduced tax rate. If the result of step 5 is a loss, the taxpayer may be eligible for a *capital loss deduction* (discussed later in this chapter). If there was no offsetting in step 5 because the short-term and step 4 results were both gains *or* if the result of the offsetting is a long-term gain, a net capital gain exists and the taxpayer may be eligible for a reduced tax rate. The net capital gain may consist of *28% gain, 25% gain,* and/or *0% / 15% / 20% gain.*

The five steps outlined above can have many unique final results. See Concept Summary 16.5 later in the chapter for a summary of the outcomes of the netting rules and how capital gains and losses are taxed. The following series of examples illustrates the capital gain and loss netting process.

Example 33

This example shows how a *net short-term capital gain* may result from the netting process.

Step	Short Term	28%	25%	0% / 15% / 20%	Comment
		Long-Term Gains and Losses			
1	$13,000	$ 12,000		$ 3,000	
	(2,000)	(20,000)			
2	$11,000	($ 8,000)		$ 3,000	
3					No 28% / 25% netting because no opposite sign.
4		3,000 →		(3,000)	Netted because of opposite sign.
		($ 5,000)		$ –0–	
5	(5,000) ←	5,000			The net short-term capital gain is taxed as ordinary income.
	$ 6,000	$ –0–			
	Net short-term capital gain				

Example 34

This example shows how a *net long-term capital gain* may result from the netting process.

Step	Short Term	28%	25%	0% / 15% / 20%	Comment
		Long-Term Gains and Losses			
1	$ 3,000	$15,000	$4,000	$ 3,000	
	(5,000)	(7,000)		(8,000)	
2	($ 2,000)	$ 8,000	$4,000	($ 5,000)	
3					No 28%/25% netting because no opposite sign.
4		(5,000)	←	5,000	Netted because of opposite sign. Net 0% / 15% / 20% loss is netted against 28% gain first.
		$ 3,000			
				$ –0–	
5	2,000 →	(2,000)			The net short-term capital loss is netted against 28% gain first. The net long-term capital gain is $5,000 ($1,000 + $4,000).
	$ –0–	$ 1,000	$4,000		
		Net 28% gain	Net 25% gain		

Example 35

This example shows how a *net long-term capital loss* may result from the netting process.

Step	Short Term	Long-Term Gains and Losses			Comment
		28%	25%	0% / 15% / 20%	
1	$ 3,000	$ 1,000		$ 3,000	
				(8,000)	
2	$ 3,000	$ 1,000		($ 5,000)	
3					No 28%/25% netting because no opposite sign.
4		(1,000)	→	1,000	Netted because of opposite sign.
		$ –0–		($ 4,000)	
5	(3,000)	→	→	3,000	The net short-term capital gain is netted against the net long-term capital loss, and the remaining loss is eligible for the capital loss deduction.
	$ –0–			($ 1,000)	
				Net long-term capital loss	

Use of Capital Loss Carryovers

A short-term capital loss carryover to the current year retains its character as short-term and is combined with the short-term items of the current year. A net long-term capital loss carries over as a long-term capital loss and is combined with the current-year long-term items. The long-term loss carryover is first offset with 28% gain of the current year, then 25% gain, and then 0% / 15% / 20% gain until it is absorbed.

Example 36

In 2014, Abigail has a $4,000 short-term capital gain, a $36,000 28% long-term capital gain, and a $13,000 0%/15%/20% long-term capital gain. She also has a $3,000 short-term capital loss carryover and a $2,000 long-term capital loss carryover from 2013. Thus, in 2014, Abigail has a $1,000 net short-term capital gain ($4,000 – $3,000), a $34,000 net 28% long-term capital gain ($36,000 – $2,000), and a $13,000 net 0%/15%/20% long-term capital gain.

ETHICS & EQUITY   Delaying a Marriage to Get a Tax Advantage

Jennifer and Fred are planning to marry on December 10. Jennifer has a very large stock portfolio that includes stocks that have substantially appreciated in value and have been held long term. Jennifer plans to sell the appreciated stocks and use the proceeds to purchase a home for Fred and herself. Jennifer's tax adviser has suggested that she sell these stocks before her wedding and that the wedding be postponed until next year. This tax strategy will result in significantly lower taxes for Jennifer because she will still be single at the end of the tax year in which she sells the stock. Fred thinks that postponing the wedding for such "commercial" reasons is not romantic and is unethical besides. What do you think?

Definition of Collectibles

Capital assets that are collectibles, even though they are held long term, are not eligible for the *0% / 15% / 20%* alternative tax rate. Instead, a 28 percent alternative tax rate applies.

For capital gain or loss purposes, **collectibles** include:[28]

- Any work of art.
- Any rug or antique.
- Any metal or gem.
- Any stamp.
- Any alcoholic beverage.
- Most coins.
- Any historical objects (documents, clothes, etc.).

16-5b Qualified Dividend Income

Dividends paid from current or accumulated earnings and profits of domestic and certain foreign corporations are eligible to be taxed at the 0% / 15% / 20% long-term capital gain rates if they are **qualified dividend income**. The question of which dividends constitute qualified dividend income is discussed more fully in Chapter 4. Here the discussion focuses on how the qualified dividend income is taxed.

THE BIG PICTURE

Example 37

Return to the facts of *The Big Picture* on p. 16-1. After holding the Purple stock for 10 months, Maurice receives $350 of dividends. If Purple is a domestic or qualifying foreign corporation, these are qualified dividends eligible for the 0%/15%/20% tax rate.

After the net capital gain or loss has been determined, the qualified dividend income is added to the net long-term capital gain portion of the net capital gain and is taxed as *0% / 15% / 20% gain*. If there is a net capital loss, the net capital loss is still deductible *for* AGI up to $3,000 per year with the remainder of the loss (if any) carrying forward. In this case, the qualified dividend income is still eligible to be treated as *0% / 15% / 20% gain* in the alternative tax calculation (it is *not* offset by the net capital loss).

Example 38

Refer to Example 34, but assume that there is qualified dividend income of $2,500 in addition to the items shown. The qualified dividend income is not netted against the capital gains and losses. Instead, the taxpayer has $1,000 of 28% gain, $4,000 of 25% gain, and $2,500 of qualified dividend income taxed at 0%/15%/20%.

Refer to Example 35, but assume that there is qualified dividend income of $2,500 in addition to the items shown. The qualified dividend income is not netted against the net capital loss. The taxpayer has a $1,000 capital loss deduction and $2,500 of qualified dividend income taxed at 0%/15%/20%.

16-5c Alternative Tax on Net Capital Gain

Section 1 contains the statutory provisions that enable the *net capital gain* to be taxed at special rates (0, 15, 20, 25, and 28 percent). This calculation is referred to as the **alternative tax** on net capital gain.[29] The alternative tax applies only if taxable income includes some long-term capital gain (there is net capital gain). Taxable income includes *all* of the net capital gain unless taxable income is less than the net capital gain. In addition, the net capital gain is taxed *last*, after other taxable income (including any short-term capital gain).

Example 39

Joan, an unmarried taxpayer, has 2014 taxable income of $108,000, including a $12,000 net capital gain. The last $12,000 of her $108,000 taxable income is the layer related to the net capital gain. The first $96,000 ($108,000 − $12,000) of her taxable income is not subject to any special tax rate, so it is taxed using the regular tax rates.

---

[28]§ 408(m)(2) and Reg. § 1.408–10(b).

[29]§ 1(h) Note: Examples 40, 41, and 42 use the 2014 Tax Rate Schedules rather than the 2014 Tax Tables (which are not yet available) to calculate the tax on the non-long-term capital gain portion of taxable income. This approach is used to better illustrate the concepts under discussion. The actual tax on the non-long-term portion of taxable income would be calculated using the Tax Tables because that income is less than $100,000.

Because the net capital gain may be made up of various *rate layers*, it is important to know in what order those layers will be taxed. (Review the five-step ordering procedure discussed on p. 16-21 and the examples that follow the discussion.) For *each* of the layers, the taxpayer compares the regular tax rate on that layer of income and the alternative tax rate on that portion of the net capital gain. The layers are taxed in the following order: *25% gain, 28% gain,* the 0 percent portion of the *0%/15%/20% gain,* the 15 percent portion of the *0%/15%/20% gain,* and then the 20 percent portion of the *0%/15%/20% gain.* As a result of this layering, the taxpayer will benefit from the 0 percent portion of the net capital gain if the taxpayer is still in the 10 percent or 15 percent regular rate bracket after taxing other taxable income and the 25 percent and 28 percent portions of the net capital gain. The taxpayer will benefit from the 15 percent portion of the net capital gain if the taxpayer is still in the 25 percent, 28 percent, 33 percent, or 35 percent regular rate bracket after taxing other taxable income and the 25 percent, 28 percent, and 0 percent portions of the net capital gain. The taxpayer benefits from the 20 percent portion of the net capital gain when taxable income reaches the 39.6 percent regular tax bracket.

Example 40

Assume that Joan's $12,000 net capital gain in Example 39 is made up of $10,000 *25% gain* and $2,000 *0%/15%/20% gain.* Examination of the 2014 tax rates reveals that $96,000 of taxable income for a single individual puts Joan at a marginal tax rate of 28%. Consequently, she will use the alternative tax on both the $10,000 gain and the $2,000 gain.

Her alternative tax liability for 2014 is $22,856 [$20,056 (tax on $96,000 of taxable income) + $2,500 ($10,000 × .25) + $300 ($2,000 × .15)]. Because the combination of the $96,000 taxable income and her $10,000 *25% gain* puts her above the 15% regular tax bracket, none of the $2,000 *0%/15%/20% gain* is taxed at 0%.

Her regular tax liability on $108,000 would be $23,416. Thus, Joan saves $560 ($23,416 − $22,856) by using the alternative tax calculation. Since none of Joan's taxable income puts her in the 39.6% bracket, none of her *0%/15%/20% gain* is taxed at the 20% alternative tax rate.

Example 41

Assume that Joan, an unmarried taxpayer, has 2014 taxable income of $25,000. Of this amount, $12,000 is net capital gain and $13,000 is other taxable income. The net capital gain is made up of $8,300 of *25% gain* and $3,700 of *0%/15%/20% gain* (including $1,000 of qualified dividend income).

Her alternative tax liability for 2014 is $2,741 [$1,496 (tax on $13,000 of taxable income) + $1,245 (tax on $8,300 *25% gain* at 15%) + $0 (tax on $3,700 *0%/15%/20% gain* at 0%)]. Because her marginal rate is still 15% after taxing the $13,000 of other taxable income, she uses the 15% regular tax rate rather than the 25% alternative tax rate on the $8,300 *25% gain.* After taxing the $13,000 and the $8,300, a total of $21,300 of the $25,000 taxable income has been taxed. Because her marginal rate is still 15%, she uses the 0% alternative rate for the $3,700 of *0%/15%/20% gain.* The $1,000 qualified dividend income is included in the $3,700 and, thus, is also taxed at 0%.

Joan's regular tax liability on $25,000 would be $3,296. Thus, she saves $555 ($3,296 − $2,741) by using the alternative tax calculation.

The alternative tax computation allows the taxpayer to receive the *lower of* the regular tax or the alternative tax on *each layer* of net capital gain or *portion of each layer* of net capital gain.

Example 42

Assume the same facts as in Example 41, except that Joan's taxable income is $38,000, consisting of $12,000 of net capital gain and $26,000 of other taxable income. Not all of the $3,700 of *0%/15%/20% gain* is taxed at 0% because Joan's taxable income exceeds $36,900, taking her out of the 15% bracket. Consequently, the last $1,100 ($38,000− $36,900) of the $3,700 of *0%/15%/20% gain* is taxed at 15% rather than 0%.

Her tax liability using the alternative tax computation is $4,856 [$3,446 (tax on $26,000 of taxable income) + $1,245 (tax on $8,300 *25% gain* at 15%) + $0 (tax on $2,600 of *0%/15%/20% gain* at 0%) + $165 (tax on $1,100 of *0%/15%/20% gain* at 15%)].

Joan's regular tax liability on $38,000 would be $5,356. Thus, she saves $500 ($5,356 − $4,856) by using the alternative tax calculation.

CONCEPT SUMMARY 16.4

Income Layers for Alternative Tax on Capital Gain Computation

Compute tax on:	Ordinary taxable income (including net short-term capital gain) using the regular tax rates.
Compute tax on:	Each of the layers below using the *lower* of the alternative tax rate or the regular tax rate for that layer (or portion of a layer) of taxable income.
+	25% long-term capital gain (unrecaptured § 1250 gain) portion of taxable income
+	28% long-term capital gain
+	0% long-term capital gain (portion of 0%/15%/20% capital gain that is taxed at 0%; available only if ordinary taxable income plus 25% and 28% capital gain layers do not put the taxpayer above the 15% bracket; 0% rate is no longer available once income including the portion of the gain taxed at 0% puts the taxpayer out of the 15% bracket)*
+	15% long-term capital gain (portion of 0%/15%/20% capital gain that is taxed at 15%; available only if ordinary taxable income plus the 25%, 28%, and 0% capital gain layers put the taxpayer above the 15% regular tax bracket, and only until ordinary taxable income plus the 25%, 28%, 0%, and 15% capital gain layers put the taxpayer above the 35% regular tax bracket)*
+	20% long-term capital gain (portion of 0%/15%/20% capital gain that is taxed at 20%; available when ordinary taxable income plus the 25%, 28%, 0%, and 15% capital gain layers put the taxpayer above the 35% regular tax bracket)*
=	Alternative tax on taxable income

*May include qualified dividend income.

Concept Summary 16.4 summarizes the alternative tax computation.

16-5d Treatment of Net Capital Losses

Computation of Net Capital Loss

A **net capital loss (NCL)** results if capital losses exceed capital gains for the year. An NCL may be all long-term, all short-term, or part long- and part short-term.[30] The characterization of an NCL as long or short term is important in determining the capital loss deduction (discussed next).

Example 43

Three different individual taxpayers have the following capital gains and losses during the year:

Taxpayer	LTCG	LTCL	STCG	STCL	Result of Netting	Description of Result
Robert	$1,000	($2,800)	$1,000	($ 500)	($1,300)	NLTCL
Carlos	1,000	(500)	1,000	(2,800)	(1,300)	NSTCL
Troy	400	(1,200)	500	(1,200)	(1,500)	NLTCL ($800)
						NSTCL ($700)

Robert's NCL of $1,300 is all long-term. Carlos's NCL of $1,300 is all short-term. Troy's NCL is $1,500, $800 of which is long-term and $700 of which is short-term.

---

[30]Section 1222(10) defines a net capital loss as the net loss after the capital loss deduction. However, that definition confuses the discussion of net capital loss. Therefore, net capital loss is used here to mean the result after netting capital gains and losses and before considering the capital loss deduction. The capital loss deduction is discussed later in this section.

TAX IN THE NEWS   Losses from Day Trading

Many investors were caught up with "Internet stock fever" during 2012. One such investor made *15,000* trades during the year. No stock was held more than one year; so each transaction resulted in a short-term capital gain or loss. Each trade had to be documented as to the basis for the stock sold, its holding period, and the selling price net of the sales commission. Unfortunately, there was a $75,000 net short-term capital loss after all transactions were accounted for. Only $3,000 of this loss was deductible in 2012 because the investor had no long-term capital gains to offset the loss and there is an annual $3,000 capital loss deduction limit. The $72,000 balance of the loss carried forward and could be deducted against capital gains of later years. However, the investor had no capital left to invest. Consequently, his annual loss deduction will be limited to $3,000 for many years to come.

© iStockphoto.com/Andrey Prokhorov

Capital Loss Deduction

An NCL is deductible from gross income to the extent of $3,000 per tax year.[31] Although there may or may not be beneficial treatment for capital gains, there is *unfavorable* treatment for capital losses in terms of the $3,000 annual limitation on deducting NCL against ordinary income. If the NCL includes both long-term and short-term capital loss, the short-term capital loss is counted first toward the $3,000 annual limitation.

> Burt has an NCL of $5,500, of which $2,000 is STCL and $3,500 is LTCL. Burt has a capital loss deduction of $3,000 ($2,000 of STCL and $1,000 of LTCL). He has an LTCL carryforward of $2,500 ($3,500 − $1,000).

Example 44

Carryovers

Taxpayers are allowed to carry over unused capital losses indefinitely. The short-term capital loss (STCL) retains its character as STCL. Likewise, the long-term capital loss retains its character as LTCL.

> In 2014, Mark incurred $1,000 of STCL and $11,000 of LTCL. In 2015, Mark has a $400 LTCG.
>
> - Mark's NCL for 2014 is $12,000. Mark deducts $3,000 ($1,000 STCL and $2,000 LTCL). He has $9,000 of LTCL carried forward to 2015.
> - Mark combines the $9,000 LTCL carryforward with the $400 LTCG for 2015. He has an $8,600 NLTCL for 2015. Mark deducts $3,000 of LTCL in 2015 and carries forward $5,600 of LTCL to 2016.

Example 45

When a taxpayer has both a capital loss deduction and negative taxable income, a special computation of the capital loss carryover is required.[32] Specifically, the capital loss carryover is the NCL minus the lesser of:

- The capital loss deduction claimed on the return.
- The negative taxable income increased by the capital loss deduction claimed on the return and the personal and dependency exemption deduction.

Without this provision, some of the tax benefit of the capital loss deduction would be wasted when the deduction drives taxable income below zero. However, the capital loss deduction is not reduced if taxable income before the exemption deduction is a positive number or zero. In that situation, it is the exemption deduction, and not the capital loss deduction, that is creating the negative taxable income.

---

[31]§ 1211(b)(1). Married taxpayers filing separate returns are limited to a $1,500 deduction per tax year.

[32]§ 1212(b).

Example 46

In 2014, Joanne has a $13,000 NCL (all long-term), a $3,950 personal exemption deduction, and $4,000 negative taxable income. The negative taxable income includes a $3,000 capital loss deduction. The capital loss carryover to 2015 is $10,100, computed as follows:

- The $4,000 negative taxable income is treated as a negative number, but the capital loss deduction and personal exemption deduction are treated as positive numbers.
- The normal ceiling on the capital loss deduction is $3,000.
- However, if the $3,000 capital loss deduction and the $3,950 exemption deduction are added back to the $4,000 negative taxable income, only $2,950 ($3,000 + $3,950 − $4,000) of the $3,000 capital loss deduction is needed to make taxable income equal to zero.
- Therefore, this special computation results in only $2,950 of the $13,000 NCL being consumed. The LTCL carryforward is $10,050 ($13,000 − $2,950).

Concept Summary 16.5 summarizes the rules for noncorporate taxpayers' treatment of capital gains and losses.

CONCEPT SUMMARY 16.5

Some Possible Final Results of the Capital Gain and Loss Netting Process and How They Are Taxed

Result	Maximum Tax Rate	Comments
Net short-term capital loss	—	Eligible for capital loss deduction ($3,000 maximum per year).
Net long-term capital loss	—	Eligible for capital loss deduction ($3,000 maximum per year).
Net short-term capital loss *and* net long-term capital loss	—	Eligible for capital loss deduction ($3,000 maximum per year). Short-term capital losses are counted first toward the deduction.
Net short-term capital gain	10 – 39.6%	Taxed as ordinary income.
Net long-term capital gain	0 – 28%	The net long-term capital gain may have as many as five tax rate components: 25%, 28%, and 0%/15%/20%.
• The net long-term capital gain is the *last* portion of taxable income.		The components are taxed in the following order: 25%, 28%, 0%, 15%, 20%. They are taxed *after* the non-long-term capital gain portion of taxable income has been taxed. The 0%/15%/20% component may include qualified dividend income.
• Each net long-term capital gain component of taxable income is taxed at the *lower* of the regular tax on that component or the alternative tax.		The alternative tax on net long-term capital gain can never increase the tax on taxable income, but it can reduce the tax on taxable income.
Net short-term capital gain *and* net long-term capital gain	10 – 39.6% on net short-term capital gain; 0 – 28% on net long-term capital gain	The net short-term capital gain is taxed as ordinary income; the net long-term capital gain is taxed as discussed above for just net long-term capital gain.

16-5e Reporting Procedures

The following example is used to discuss and illustrate the 2013 tax forms used for reporting because the 2014 tax forms were not available at the time of this writing.

> **Example 47**
>
> During 2013, Joan Rapson (Social Security number 123-45-6789) had the following sales of capital assets. In addition, she has other taxable income of $66,000, including $300 of qualified dividend income. Joan is single and has no dependents.
>
> | Description | Acquired On | Date Sold | Sales Price | Tax Basis | Gain or Loss | Character |
> |---|---|---|---|---|---|---|
> | 100 shares Blue stock | 1/21/13 | 11/11/13 | $11,000 | $17,000 | ($ 6,000) | STCL |
> | 100 shares Yellow stock | 9/12/08 | 10/12/13 | 36,000 | 20,000 | 16,000 | LTCG |
> | 100 shares Purple stock | 3/14/11 | 10/12/13 | 14,000 | 12,000 | 2,000 | LTCG |
>
> In 2013 there were *five* alternative tax rates: 25%, 28%, and 0%/15%/20%.
>
> Joan has a net capital gain of $12,000 ($16,000 0%/15% gain + $2,000 0%/15%/20% gain − $6,000 short-term capital loss). Consequently, all of the net capital gain is composed of 0%/15%/20% gain. Joan's $78,000 taxable income includes $65,700 ($66,000 − $300) of other taxable income.
>
> Joan's total stock sales were reported to her on Form 1099–B by her stockbroker, which showed the sales proceeds and adjusted basis of each of her transactions. Following a discussion of the reporting rules, Joan's completed forms and a worksheet are presented.

Capital gains and losses are reported on Schedule D of Form 1040 (Capital Gains and Losses). Part I of Schedule D is used to report short-term capital gains and losses. Part II of Schedule D is used to report long-term capital gains and losses. The information shown in Parts I and II comes from Form 8949 (Sales and Other Dispositions of Assets). Form 8949 is used to accumulate gains and losses from three sources:

- Capital gain and loss transactions for which a Form 1099-B (Proceeds from Broker and Barter Exchange Transactions) has been received and the provider of the form had information on the sales proceeds *and* the tax basis of the assets disposed of.
- Capital gain and loss transactions for which a Form 1099–B has been received and the provider of the form had information on the sales proceeds *but did not* have information on the tax basis of the assets disposed of.
- Capital gain and loss transactions for which a Form 1099–B was not received.

Part III of Form 1040 Schedule D summarizes the results of Parts I and II and indicates whether the taxpayer has a net capital gain or a net capital loss. Part III then helps determine which alternative tax worksheet is used to calculate the alternative tax on long-term capital gains and qualified dividends. If the taxpayer has a net long-term capital gain that does not include any 28% or 25% long-term capital gain, then the alternative tax is calculated using the Qualified Dividends and Capital Gain Worksheet from the Form 1040 instructions. If the taxpayer has a net long-term capital gain that does include either 28% or 25% long-term capital gain, then the alternative tax is calculated using the Schedule D Tax Worksheet from the Schedule D instructions. These worksheets do not have to be filed with the tax return, but are kept for the taxpayer's records.

SCHEDULE D (Form 1040) Department of the Treasury Internal Revenue Service (99)	**Capital Gains and Losses** ▶ Attach to Form 1040 or Form 1040NR. ▶ Information about Schedule D and its separate instructions is at *www.irs.gov/scheduled*. ▶ Use Form 8949 to list your transactions for lines 1b, 2, 3, 8b, 9, and 10.	OMB No. 1545-0074 20**13** Attachment Sequence No. **12**

Name(s) shown on return	Your social security number
Joan Rapson	*123 45 6789*

Part I Short-Term Capital Gains and Losses—Assets Held One Year or Less

See instructions for how to figure the amounts to enter on the lines below. This form may be easier to complete if you round off cents to whole dollars.	(d) Proceeds (sales price)	(e) Cost (or other basis)	(g) Adjustments to gain or loss from Form(s) 8949, Part I, line 2, column (g)	(h) Gain or (loss) Subtract column (e) from column (d) and combine the result with column (g)
1a Totals for all short-term transactions reported on Form 1099-B for which basis was reported to the IRS and for which you have no adjustments (see instructions). However, if you choose to report all these transactions on Form 8949, leave this line blank and go to line 1b .				
1b Totals for all transactions reported on Form(s) 8949 with **Box A** checked	*11,000*	*17,000*		*(6,000)*
2 Totals for all transactions reported on Form(s) 8949 with **Box B** checked				
3 Totals for all transactions reported on Form(s) 8949 with **Box C** checked				

4 Short-term gain from Form 6252 and short-term gain or (loss) from Forms 4684, 6781, and 8824 .	**4**	
5 Net short-term gain or (loss) from partnerships, S corporations, estates, and trusts from Schedule(s) K-1	**5**	
6 Short-term capital loss carryover. Enter the amount, if any, from line 8 of your **Capital Loss Carryover Worksheet** in the instructions	**6** (	)
7 **Net short-term capital gain or (loss).** Combine lines 1a through 6 in column (h). If you have any long-term capital gains or losses, go to Part II below. Otherwise, go to Part III on the back	**7**	*(6,000)*

Part II Long-Term Capital Gains and Losses—Assets Held More Than One Year

See instructions for how to figure the amounts to enter on the lines below. This form may be easier to complete if you round off cents to whole dollars.	(d) Proceeds (sales price)	(e) Cost (or other basis)	(g) Adjustments to gain or loss from Form(s) 8949, Part II, line 2, column (g)	(h) Gain or (loss) Subtract column (e) from column (d) and combine the result with column (g)
8a Totals for all long-term transactions reported on Form 1099-B for which basis was reported to the IRS and for which you have no adjustments (see instructions). However, if you choose to report all these transactions on Form 8949, leave this line blank and go to line 8b .				
8b Totals for all transactions reported on Form(s) 8949 with **Box D** checked	*50,000*	*32,000*		*18,000*
9 Totals for all transactions reported on Form(s) 8949 with **Box E** checked				
10 Totals for all transactions reported on Form(s) 8949 with **Box F** checked.				

11 Gain from Form 4797, Part I; long-term gain from Forms 2439 and 6252; and long-term gain or (loss) from Forms 4684, 6781, and 8824	**11**	
12 Net long-term gain or (loss) from partnerships, S corporations, estates, and trusts from Schedule(s) K-1	**12**	
13 Capital gain distributions. See the instructions	**13**	
14 Long-term capital loss carryover. Enter the amount, if any, from line 13 of your **Capital Loss Carryover Worksheet** in the instructions	**14** (	)
15 **Net long-term capital gain or (loss).** Combine lines 8a through 14 in column (h). Then go to Part III on the back	**15**	*18,000*

For Paperwork Reduction Act Notice, see your tax return instructions.   Cat. No. 11338H   **Schedule D (Form 1040) 2013**

Part III	**Summary**

16 Combine lines 7 and 15 and enter the result . . . . **16** | *12,000*

- If line 16 is a **gain,** enter the amount from line 16 on Form 1040, line 13, or Form 1040NR, line 14. Then go to line 17 below.
- If line 16 is a **loss,** skip lines 17 through 20 below. Then go to line 21. Also be sure to complete line 22.
- If line 16 is **zero,** skip lines 17 through 21 below and enter -0- on Form 1040, line 13, or Form 1040NR, line 14. Then go to line 22.

17 Are lines 15 and 16 **both** gains?
☒ **Yes.** Go to line 18.
☐ **No.** Skip lines 18 through 21, and go to line 22.

18 Enter the amount, if any, from line 7 of the **28% Rate Gain Worksheet** in the instructions . . ▶ **18** | *0*

19 Enter the amount, if any, from line 18 of the **Unrecaptured Section 1250 Gain Worksheet** in the instructions . . . . ▶ **19** | *0*

20 Are lines 18 and 19 **both** zero or blank?
☒ **Yes.** Complete the **Qualified Dividends and Capital Gain Tax Worksheet** in the instructions for Form 1040, line 44 (or in the instructions for Form 1040NR, line 42). **Do not** complete lines 21 and 22 below.

☐ **No.** Complete the **Schedule D Tax Worksheet** in the instructions. **Do not** complete lines 21 and 22 below.

21 If line 16 is a loss, enter here and on Form 1040, line 13, or Form 1040NR, line 14, the **smaller** of:

- The loss on line 16 or
- ($3,000), or if married filing separately, ($1,500) . . . . **21** |( )

Note. When figuring which amount is smaller, treat both amounts as positive numbers.

22 Do you have qualified dividends on Form 1040, line 9b, or Form 1040NR, line 10b?

☐ **Yes.** Complete the **Qualified Dividends and Capital Gain Tax Worksheet** in the instructions for Form 1040, line 44 (or in the instructions for Form 1040NR, line 42).

☐ **No.** Complete the rest of Form 1040 or Form 1040NR.

Schedule D (Form 1040) 2013

Form **8949**

Department of the Treasury
Internal Revenue Service

Sales and Other Dispositions of Capital Assets

▶ Information about Form 8949 and its separate instructions is at *www.irs.gov/form8949*.
▶ File with your Schedule D to list your transactions for lines 1b, 2, 3, 8b, 9, and 10 of Schedule D.

OMB No. 1545-0074

20**13**

Attachment
Sequence No. **12A**

Name(s) shown on return	Social security number or taxpayer identification number
Joan Rapson	*123 45 6789*

Most brokers issue their own substitute statement instead of using Form 1099-B. They also may provide basis information (usually your cost) to you on the statement even if it is not reported to the IRS. Before you check Box A, B, or C below, determine whether you received any statement(s) and, if so, the transactions for which basis was reported to the IRS. Brokers are required to report basis to the IRS for most stock you bought in 2011 or later.

Part I **Short-Term.** Transactions involving capital assets you held one year or less are short term. For long-term transactions, see page 2.

Note. You may aggregate all short-term transactions reported on Form(s) 1099-B showing basis was reported to the IRS and for which no adjustments or codes are required. Enter the total directly on Schedule D, line 1a; you are not required to report these transactions on Form 8949 (see instructions).

You *must* check Box A, B, *or* C below. Check only one box. If more than one box applies for your short-term transactions, complete a separate Form 8949, page 1, for each applicable box. If you have more short-term transactions than will fit on this page for one or more of the boxes, complete as many forms with the same box checked as you need.

☒ **(A)** Short-term transactions reported on Form(s) 1099-B showing basis was reported to the IRS (see **Note** above)
☐ **(B)** Short-term transactions reported on Form(s) 1099-B showing basis was **not** reported to the IRS
☐ **(C)** Short-term transactions not reported to you on Form 1099-B

(a) Description of property (Example: 100 sh. XYZ Co.)	**(b)** Date acquired (Mo., day, yr.)	**(c)** Date sold or disposed (Mo., day, yr.)	**(d)** Proceeds (sales price) (see instructions)	**(e)** Cost or other basis. See the **Note** below and see *Column (e)* in the separate instructions	**(f)** Code(s) from instructions	**(g)** Amount of adjustment	**(h)** Gain or (loss). Subtract column (e) from column (d) and combine the result with column (g)
100 Shares Blue Stock	*01/21/13*	*11/11/13*	*11,000*	*17,000*			*(6,000)*
2 Totals. Add the amounts in columns (d), (e), (g), and (h) (subtract negative amounts). Enter each total here and include on your Schedule D, **line 1b** (if **Box A** above is checked), **line 2** (if **Box B** above is checked), or **line 3** (if **Box C** above is checked) ▶			*11,000*	*17,000*			*(6,000)*

Note. If you checked Box A above but the basis reported to the IRS was incorrect, enter in column (e) the basis as reported to the IRS, and enter an adjustment in column (g) to correct the basis. See *Column (g)* in the separate instructions for how to figure the amount of the adjustment.

For Paperwork Reduction Act Notice, see your tax return instructions.   Cat. No. 37768Z   Form **8949** (2013)

Form 8949 (2013)   Attachment Sequence No. **12A**   Page **2**

Name(s) shown on return. (Name and SSN or taxpayer identification no. not required if shown on other side.)	Social security number or taxpayer identification number
Joan Rapson	*123 45 6789*

Most brokers issue their own substitute statement instead of using Form 1099-B. They also may provide basis information (usually your cost) to you on the statement even if it is not reported to the IRS. Before you check Box D, E, or F below, determine whether you received any statement(s) and, if so, the transactions for which basis was reported to the IRS. Brokers are required to report basis to the IRS for most stock you bought in 2011 or later.

Part II **Long-Term.** Transactions involving capital assets you held more than one year are long term. For short-term transactions, see page 1.

Note. You may aggregate all long-term transactions reported on Form(s) 1099-B showing basis was reported to the IRS and for which no adjustments or codes are required. Enter the total directly on Schedule D, line 8a; you are not required to report these transactions on Form 8949 (see instructions).

You *must* check Box D, E, *or* F below. Check only one box. If more than one box applies for your long-term transactions, complete a separate Form 8949, page 2, for each applicable box. If you have more long-term transactions than will fit on this page for one or more of the boxes, complete as many forms with the same box checked as you need.

- ☒ **(D)** Long-term transactions reported on Form(s) 1099-B showing basis was reported to the IRS (see **Note** above)
- ☐ **(E)** Long-term transactions reported on Form(s) 1099-B showing basis was **not** reported to the IRS
- ☐ **(F)** Long-term transactions not reported to you on Form 1099-B

1 (a) Description of property (Example: 100 sh. XYZ Co.)	(b) Date acquired (Mo., day, yr.)	(c) Date sold or disposed (Mo., day, yr.)	(d) Proceeds (sales price) (see instructions)	(e) Cost or other basis. See the **Note** below and see *Column (e)* in the separate instructions	(f) Code(s) from instructions	(g) Amount of adjustment	(h) Gain or (loss). Subtract column (e) from column (d) and combine the result with column (g)
100 Shares Yellow Stock	*09/12/08*	*10/12/13*	*36,000*	*20,000*			*16,000*
100 Shares Purple Stock	*03/14/11*	*10/12/13*	*14,000*	*12,000*			*2,000*
2 Totals. Add the amounts in columns (d), (e), (g), and (h) (subtract negative amounts). Enter each total here and include on your Schedule D, **line 8b** (if **Box D** above is checked), **line 9** (if **Box E** above is checked), or **line 10** (if **Box F** above is checked) ▶			*50,000*	*32,000*			*18,000*

Note. If you checked Box D above but the basis reported to the IRS was incorrect, enter in column (e) the basis as reported to the IRS, and enter an adjustment in column (g) to correct the basis. See *Column (g)* in the separate instructions for how to figure the amount of the adjustment.

Form **8949** (2013)

Qualified Dividends and Capital Gain Tax Worksheet—Line 44

Keep for Your Records

Before you begin:	✓ See the earlier instructions for line 44 to see if you can use this worksheet to figure your tax.
	✓ Before completing this worksheet, complete Form 1040 through line 43.
	✓ If you do not have to file Schedule D and you received capital gain distributions, be sure you checked the box on line 13 of Form 1040.

1. Enter the amount from Form 1040, line 43. However, if you are filing Form 2555 or 2555-EZ (relating to foreign earned income), enter the amount from line 3 of the Foreign Earned Income Tax Worksheet .... **1.** _78,000_

2. Enter the amount from Form 1040, line 9b* .... **2.** _300_

3. Are you filing Schedule D?*
   ☒ **Yes.** Enter the **smaller** of line 15 or 16 of Schedule D. If either line 15 or line 16 is blank or a loss, enter -0-
   ☐ **No.** Enter the amount from Form 1040, line 13 **3.** _12,000_

4. Add lines 2 and 3 .... **4.** _12,300_

5. If filing Form 4952 (used to figure investment interest expense deduction), enter any amount from line 4g of that form. Otherwise, enter -0- .... **5.** _____

6. Subtract line 5 from line 4. If zero or less, enter -0- .... **6.** _12,300_

7. Subtract line 6 from line 1. If zero or less, enter -0- .... **7.** _65,700_

8. Enter:
   $36,250 if single or married filing separately,
   $72,500 if married filing jointly or qualifying widow(er),
   $48,600 if head of household. **8.** _36,250_

9. Enter the smaller of line 1 or line 8 .... **9.** _36,250_

10. Enter the smaller of line 7 or line 9 .... **10.** _36,250_

11. Subtract line 10 from line 9. This amount is taxed at 0% .... **11.** _0_

12. Enter the smaller of line 1 or line 6 .... **12.** _12,300_

13. Enter the amount from line 11 .... **13.** _0_

14. Subtract line 13 from line 12 .... **14.** _12,300_

15. Enter:
    $400,000 if single,
    $225,000 if married filing separately,
    $450,000 if married filing jointly or qualifying widow(er),
    $425,000 if head of household. **15.** _400,000_

16. Enter the smaller of line 1 or line 15 .... **16.** _78,000_

17. Add lines 7 and 11 .... **17.** _65,700_

18. Subtract line 17 from line 16. If zero or less, enter -0- .... **18.** _12,300_

19. Enter the smaller of line 14 or line 18 .... **19.** _12,300_

20. Multiply line 19 by 15% (.15) .... **20.** _1,845_

21. Add lines 11 and 19 .... **21.** _12,300_

22. Subtract line 21 from line 12 .... **22.** _0_

23. Multiply line 22 by 20% (.20) .... **23.** _0_

24. Figure the tax on the amount on line 7. If the amount on line 7 is less than $100,000, use the Tax Table to figure the tax. If the amount on line 7 is $100,000 or more, use the Tax Computation Worksheet .... **24.** _12,360_

25. Add lines 20, 23, and 24 .... **25.** _14,205_

26. Figure the tax on the amount on line 1. If the amount on line 1 is less than $100,000, use the Tax Table to figure the tax. If the amount on line 1 is $100,000 or more, use the Tax Computation Worksheet .... **26.** _15,435_

27. **Tax on all taxable income.** Enter the **smaller** of line 25 or line 26. Also include this amount on Form 1040, line 44. If you are filing Form 2555 or 2555-EZ, do not enter this amount on Form 1040, line 44. Instead, enter it on line 4 of the Foreign Earned Income Tax Worksheet .... **27.** _14,205_

If you are filing Form 2555 or 2555-EZ, see the footnote in the Foreign Earned Income Tax Worksheet before completing this line.

16-6 Tax Treatment of Capital Gains and Losses of Corporate Taxpayers

The treatment of a corporation's net capital gain or loss differs from the rules for individuals. Briefly, the differences are as follows:

- There is an NCG alternative tax rate of 35 percent.[33] However, because the maximum corporate tax rate is 35 percent, the alternative tax is not beneficial.
- Capital losses offset only capital gains. No deduction of capital losses is permitted against ordinary taxable income (whereas a $3,000 deduction is allowed to individuals).[34]
- Corporations may carry back net capital losses (whether long-term or short-term) as short-term capital losses for three years; if losses still remain after the carryback, the remaining losses may be carried forward five years.[35] Individuals may carry forward unused capital losses indefinitely, but there is no carryback.

LO.6

Describe the tax treatment for capital gains and the detrimental tax treatment for capital losses for corporate taxpayers.

> **Example 48**
>
> Sparrow Corporation has a $15,000 NLTCL for the current year and $57,000 of ordinary taxable income. Sparrow may not offset the $15,000 NLTCL against its ordinary income by taking a capital loss deduction. The $15,000 NLTCL becomes a $15,000 STCL for carryback and carryover purposes. This amount may be offset against capital gains in the three-year carryback period or, if not absorbed there, offset capital gains in the five-year carryforward period.

The rules applicable to corporations are discussed in greater detail in Chapter 20.

16-7 Tax Planning

16-7a Importance of Capital Asset Status

Why is capital asset status important? Capital asset status enables the taxpayer to be eligible for the alternative tax on net capital gain. For a taxpayer in the 39.6 percent bracket, a 20 percent rate is available on capital assets held more than a year. For a taxpayer in the 25, 28, 33, or 35 percent regular tax bracket, a 15 percent rate is available on assets held longer than one year. For a taxpayer in the 10 or 15 percent regular tax bracket, a 0 percent rate is available on assets held longer than one year. Thus, individuals who can receive income in the form of long-term capital gains or qualified dividend income have an advantage over taxpayers who cannot receive income in these forms.

LO.7

Identify tax planning opportunities arising from the sale or exchange of capital assets.

Capital asset status is also important because capital gains must be offset by capital losses. If a net capital loss results, the maximum deduction is $3,000 per year.

Consequently, capital gains and losses must be segregated from other types of gains and losses and must be reported separately on Schedule D of Form 1040.

16-7b Planning for Capital Asset Status

It is important to keep in mind that capital asset status often is a question of objective evidence. Thus, property that is not a capital asset to one party may qualify as a capital asset to another party.

> **Example 49**
>
> Diane, a real estate dealer, transfers by gift a tract of land to Jeff, her son. The land was recorded as part of Diane's inventory (it was held for resale) and was therefore not a capital asset to her. Jeff, however, treats the land as an investment. The land is a capital asset in Jeff's hands, and any later taxable disposition of the property by him will yield a capital gain or loss.

---

[33]§ 1201.
[34]§ 1211(a).

[35]§ 1212(a)(1).

Capital Gain Treatment in the United States and Other Countries

The United States currently requires a very complex tax calculation when taxable income includes net long-term capital gain. However, the alternative tax on net long-term capital gain can generate tax savings even when the taxpayer is in the lowest regular tax bracket (10 percent) because there is an alternative tax rate of 0 percent. Many other countries do not have an alternative tax rate on long-term capital gains. Instead, those gains are taxed the same as other income. Consequently, even though the U.S. system is complex, it may be preferable because of the lower tax rates and because the lower rates are available to taxpayers in all tax brackets.

If proper planning is carried out, even a dealer may obtain long-term capital gain treatment on the sale of the type of property normally held for resale.

Example 50

Jim, a real estate dealer, segregates tract A from the real estate he regularly holds for resale and designates the property as being held for investment purposes. The property is not advertised for sale and is disposed of several years later. The negotiations for the subsequent sale were initiated by the purchaser and not by Jim. Under these circumstances, it would appear that any gain or loss from the sale of tract A should be a capital gain or loss.[36]

When a business is being sold, one of the major decisions usually concerns whether a portion of the sales price is for goodwill. For the seller, goodwill generally represents the disposition of a capital asset. Goodwill has no basis and represents a residual portion of the selling price that cannot be allocated reasonably to the known assets. The amount of goodwill thus represents capital gain.

From a legal perspective, the buyer may prefer that the residual portion of the purchase price be allocated to a covenant not to compete (a promise that the seller will not compete against the buyer by conducting a business similar to the one the buyer has purchased). Both purchased goodwill and a covenant not to compete are § 197 intangibles. Thus, both must be capitalized and can be amortized over a 15-year statutory period.

To the seller, a covenant produces ordinary income. Thus, the seller would prefer that the residual portion of the selling price be allocated to goodwill—a capital asset. If the buyer does not need the legal protection provided by a covenant, the buyer is neutral regarding whether the residual amount be allocated to a covenant or to goodwill. Because the seller would receive a tax advantage from labeling the residual amount as goodwill, the buyer should factor this into the negotiation of the purchase price.

Example 51

Marcia is buying Jack's dry cleaning proprietorship. An appraisal of the assets indicates that a reasonable purchase price would exceed the value of the known assets by $30,000. If the purchase contract does not specify the nature of the $30,000, the amount will be for goodwill and Jack will have a long-term capital gain of $30,000. Marcia will have a 15-year amortizable $30,000 asset.

If Marcia is paying the extra $30,000 to prevent Jack from conducting another dry cleaning business in the area (a covenant not to compete), Jack will have $30,000 of ordinary income. Marcia will have a $30,000 deduction over the statutory 15-year amortization period rather than over the actual life of the covenant (e.g., 5 years).

---

[36]*Toledo, Peoria & Western Railroad Co.,* 35 TCM 1663, T.C.Memo. 1976–366.

16-7c Effect of Capital Asset Status in Transactions Other Than Sales

The nature of an asset (capital or ordinary) is important in determining the tax consequences that result when a sale or exchange occurs. It may, however, be just as significant in circumstances other than a taxable sale or exchange. When a capital asset is disposed of, the result is not always a capital gain or loss. Rather, in general, the disposition must be a sale or exchange. Collection of a debt instrument having a basis less than the face value results in a capital gain if the debt instrument is a capital asset. The collection is a sale or exchange. Sale of the debt shortly before the due date for collection will produce a capital gain.[37] If selling the debt in such circumstances could produce a capital gain but collecting could not, the consistency of what constitutes a capital gain or loss would be frustrated. Another illustration of the sale or exchange principle involves a donation of certain appreciated property to a qualified charity. Recall that in certain circumstances, the measure of the charitable contribution is fair market value when the property, if sold, would have yielded a long-term capital gain [refer to Chapter 10 and the discussion of § 170(e)].

> **Example 52**
>
> Sharon wants to donate a tract of unimproved land (basis of $40,000 and fair market value of $200,000) held for the required long-term holding period to State University (a qualified charitable organization). However, Sharon currently is under audit by the IRS for capital gains she reported on certain real estate transactions during an earlier tax year. Although Sharon is not a licensed real estate broker, the IRS agent conducting the audit is contending that she has achieved dealer status by virtue of the number and frequency of the real estate transactions she has conducted.
>
> Under these circumstances, Sharon would be well advised to postpone the donation to State University until her status is clarified. If she has achieved dealer status, the unimproved land may be inventory (refer to Example 50 for another possible result) and Sharon's charitable contribution deduction would be limited to $40,000. If not and if the land is held as an investment, Sharon's deduction is $200,000 (the fair market value of the property).

16-7d Stock Sales

The following rules apply in determining the date of a stock sale:

- The date the sale is executed is the date of the sale. The execution date is the date the broker completes the transaction on the stock exchange.
- The settlement date is the date the cash or other property is paid to the seller of the stock. This date is *not* relevant in determining the date of sale.

> **Example 53**
>
> Lupe, a cash basis taxpayer, sells stock that results in a gain. The sale was executed on December 29, 2013. The settlement date is January 2, 2014. The date of sale is December 29, 2013 (the execution date). The holding period for the stock sold ends with the execution date.

16-7e Maximizing Benefits

Ordinary losses generally are preferable to capital losses because of the limitations imposed on the deductibility of net capital losses and the requirement that capital losses be used to offset capital gains. The taxpayer may be able to convert what would otherwise have been capital loss to ordinary loss. For example, business (but not nonbusiness) bad debts, losses from the sale or exchange of small business investment company stock, and losses from the sale or exchange of small business corporation stock all result in ordinary losses.[38]

Although capital losses can be carried over indefinitely, *indefinite* becomes definite when a taxpayer dies. Any loss carryovers not used by the taxpayer are

---

[37]§ 1271(b).

[38]§§ 166(d), 1242, and 1244. Refer to the discussion in Chapter 7.

permanently lost. That is, no tax benefit can be derived from the carryovers subsequent to death.[39] Therefore, the potential benefit of carrying over capital losses diminishes when dealing with older taxpayers.

It is usually beneficial to spread gains over more than one taxable year. In some cases, this can be accomplished through the installment sales method of accounting.

16-7f Year-End Planning

The following general rules can be applied for timing the recognition of capital gains and losses near the end of a taxable year:

- If the taxpayer already has recognized more than $3,000 of capital loss, sell assets to generate capital gain equal to the excess of the capital loss over $3,000.

Example 54

Kevin has already incurred a $7,000 STCL. Kevin should generate $4,000 of capital gain. The gain will offset $4,000 of the loss. The remaining loss of $3,000 can be deducted against ordinary income.

- If the taxpayer already has recognized capital gain, sell assets to generate capital loss equal to the capital gain. The gain will not be taxed, and the loss will be fully *deductible* against the gain.
- Generally, if the taxpayer has a choice between recognizing short-term capital gain or long-term capital gain, long-term capital gain should be recognized because it is subject to a lower tax rate.

REFOCUS ON THE BIG PICTURE

MANAGING CAPITAL ASSET TRANSACTIONS

You explain to Maurice that your area of expertise is tax, so you are providing tax advice and not investment advice. From an overall perspective, he is correct that certain capital gains and dividends are eligible for either a 0 percent, a 15 percent, or a 20 percent tax rate rather than the regular tax rates that go as high as 39.6 percent. You then discuss the potential tax consequences of each of his investments.

- *Purple stock and Eagle stock.* To qualify for the beneficial tax rate, the holding period for the stock must be longer than one year. From a tax perspective, Maurice should retain his stock investments for at least an additional three months and a day. To be eligible for the "costless" capital gains (i.e., capital gains taxed at 0%), his taxable income should not exceed $36,900 for 2014. The dividends received on the Purple stock are "qualified dividends" eligible for the *0% / 15% / 20%* alternative tax rate.
- *Patent.* Because he is a "holder" of the patent, it will qualify for the beneficial capital gain rate regardless of the holding period if the patent should produce income in excess of his $50,000 investment. However, if he loses money on the investment, he will be able to deduct only $3,000 of the loss per year against his ordinary income (assuming that there are no offsetting capital gains).
- *Tax-exempt bonds.* The after-tax return on the taxable bonds would be less than the 3 percent on the tax-exempt bonds. In addition, the interest on the taxable bonds would increase his taxable income, possibly moving it out of the desired 15 percent marginal tax rate into the 25 percent marginal tax rate.
- *Franchise rights.* The franchise rights purchased from Orange, Inc., probably require the payment of a franchise fee based upon the sales in the franchise business. Maurice should either start such a business or sell the franchise rights.

© auremar / Shutterstock.com

---

[39]Rev.Rul. 74–175, 1974–1 C.B. 52.

- *Partnership interest.* Whether Maurice receives capital or ordinary treatment associated with his partnership interest depends on whether he is reporting his share of profits or losses (ordinary income or ordinary loss) or is reporting recognized gain or loss from the sale of his partnership interest (capital gain or capital loss).

You conclude your tax advice to Maurice by telling him that whatever he does regarding his investments should make economic sense. There are no 100 percent tax rates. For example, disposing of the bank stock in the current market could be the wise thing to do.

Key Terms

Alternative tax, 16-24	Holding period, 16-15	Original issue discount (OID), 16-9
Capital asset, 16-4	Lessee, 16-14	Patent, 16-11
Capital gains, 16-2	Lessor, 16-14	Qualified dividend income, 16-24
Capital losses, 16-2	Net capital gain (NCG), 16-21	Sale or exchange, 16-8
Collectibles, 16-24	Net capital loss (NCL), 16-26	Short sale, 16-17
Franchise, 16-13	Options, 16-10	Unrecaptured § 1250 gain, 16-21

Discussion Questions

1. **LO.2, 4, 5** Sheila inherited 300 shares of stock, 100 shares of Magenta and 200 shares of Purple. She has a stockbroker sell the shares for her, uses the proceeds for personal expenses, and thinks nothing further about the transactions. What issues does she face when she prepares her Federal income tax return?   *Issue ID*

2. **LO.2** An individual taxpayer sells some used assets at a garage sale. Why are none of the proceeds taxable in most situations?   *Issue ID*

3. **LO.2, 4** Alison owns a painting that she received as a gift from her aunt 10 years ago. The aunt created the painting. Alison has displayed the painting in her home and has never attempted to sell it. Recently, a visitor noticed the painting and offered Alison $5,000 for it. If Alison decides to sell the painting, what tax issues does she face?   *Issue ID*

4. **LO.2** Is a song that is owned by its creator always an ordinary asset? Why or why not?

5. **LO.2** Is a note receivable that arose in the ordinary course of the taxpayer's retail business a capital asset? Why or why not?

6. **LO.2** Why do court decisions play an important role in the definition of capital assets?

7. **LO.2** Michel is a "bond trader" who buys and sells bonds regularly for his own account. His cousin, who purports to be a tax expert but is not a CPA, has told Michel that because the bonds Michel holds are inventory, they are ordinary assets and not capital assets. Is this always true? Explain.

8. **LO.2** Anwar owns vacant land that he purchased many years ago as an investment. After getting approval to subdivide it into 35 lots, he made minimal improvements and then sold the entire property to a real estate developer. Anwar's recognized gain on the sale was $1.2 million. Is this transaction eligible for the "real property subdivided for sale" provisions? Why or why not?

9. **LO.3** What is the difference between a "worthless security" and "§ 1244 stock"?

10. **LO.3** Gina purchased an original issue discount bond several years ago. She paid $138,000 for the $200,000 face value bond. She sold the bond this year for $173,000. Is all of Gina's gain long-term capital gain? Why or why not?

11. **LO.3** Tony receives $58,000 from a real estate developer for an option to purchase land Tony is holding for homesite development. Fourteen months later, the option expires unexercised. How is the $58,000 taxed to Tony?

Issue ID

12. **LO.3** Hubert purchases all of the rights in a patent from the inventor who developed the patented product. After holding the patent for two years, Hubert sells all of the rights in the patent for a substantial gain. What issues does Hubert face if he wants to treat the gain as a long-term capital gain?

13. **LO.3** Blue Corporation and Fuchsia Corporation are engaged in a contract negotiation over the use of Blue's trademarked name, DateSiteForSeniors. For a one-time payment of $45,000, Blue licensed Fuchsia to use the name DateSiteForSeniors, and the license requires that Fuchsia pay Blue a royalty every time a new customer signs up on Fuchsia's website. Blue is a developer of "website ideas" that it then licenses to other companies such as Fuchsia. Did Fuchsia purchase a franchise right from Blue, or did Fuchsia purchase the name DateSiteForSeniors from Blue?

Issue ID

14. **LO.4** Shen purchased corporate stock for $20,000 on April 10, 2012. On July 14, 2014, when the stock was worth $12,000, Shen died and his son, Mijo, inherited the stock. What has to happen to the value of the property while Mijo holds it if he is to tack Shen's holding period onto his own holding period?

15. **LO.4** At the date of a short sale, Sylvia has held substantially identical securities for more than 12 months. What is the nature of any gain or loss from the close of her short sale?

16. **LO.5** After netting all of her short-term and long-term capital gains and losses, Misty has a net short-term capital loss and a net long-term capital loss. Can she net these against each other? Why or why not?

17. **LO.2, 5** Charlie sells his antique farm tractor collection at a loss. He had acquired all of the tractors for his personal pleasure and sold all of them for less than he paid for them. What is the tax status of the tractors? Is his loss a 28% collectibles loss? Explain.

Issue ID

18. **LO.2, 5, 7** Near the end of 2014, Byron realizes that he has a net short-term capital loss of $13,000 for the year. Byron has taxable income (not including the loss) of $123,000 and is single. He owns numerous stocks that could be sold for a long-term capital gain. What should he do before the end of 2014?

Problems

19. **LO.2** During the year, Eugene had the four property transactions summarized below. Eugene is a collector of antique glassware and occasionally sells a piece to get funds to buy another. What are the amount and nature of the gain or loss from each of these transactions?

Property	Date Acquired	Date Sold	Adjusted Basis	Sales Price
Antique vase	06/18/03	05/23/14	$37,000	$42,000
Blue Growth Fund (100 shares)	12/23/05	11/22/14	22,000	38,000
Orange bonds	02/12/06	04/11/14	34,000	42,000*
Green stock (100 shares)	02/14/14	11/23/14	11,000	13,000

*The sales price included $750 of accrued interest.

Decision Making

20. **LO.2, 5** Rennie owns a video game arcade. He buys vintage video games from estates, often at much less than the retail value of the property. He usually installs the vintage video games in a special section of his video game arcade that appeals to players of "classic" video games. Recently, Rennie sold a classic video game that a customer "just had to have." Rennie paid $11,250 for it, owned it for 14 months, and sold it for $18,000. Rennie had suspected that this particular classic video game would be of interest to collectors; so he had it refurbished, put it on display in his video arcade, and listed it for sale on

the Internet. No customers in the arcade had played it other than those testing it before considering it for purchase. Rennie would like the gain on the sale of the classic video game to be a long-term capital gain. Did he achieve that objective? Why or why not?

21. **LO.2** George is the owner of numerous classic automobiles. His intention is to hold the automobiles until they increase in value and then sell them. He rents the automobiles for use in various events (e.g., antique automobile shows) while he is holding them. In 2014, he sold a classic automobile for $1.5 million. He had held the automobile for five years, and it had a tax basis of $750,000. Was the automobile a capital asset? Why or why not?

22. **LO.2, 4** Barbella purchased a wedding ring for $15 at a yard sale in May. She thought the ring was costume jewelry, but it turned out to be a real diamond ring. She is not in the business of buying and selling anything. She researched the ring on the Internet and discovered that it was worth at least $1,000. She sold it on an Internet auction site for $1,100 in July. Was the ring a capital asset? What were the amount and nature of the gain or loss from its sale by Barbella?

23. **LO.2** Puce is a corporation that buys and sells financial assets. It purchases notes receivable from manufacturers that need cash immediately and cannot wait to collect the notes. Puce pays about 88% of the face value of the receivables and then collects them. Because of the quality of the notes, Puce collected less than it paid for some of the notes. Does Puce have a capital loss when it collects the receivables for less than it paid for them? Explain.

24. **LO.2** Faith Godwin is a dealer in securities. She has spotted a fast-rising company and would like to buy and hold its stock for investment. The stock is currently selling for $2 per share, and Faith thinks it will climb to $40 a share within two years. Faith's coworkers have told her that there is "no way" she can get long-term capital gain treatment when she purchases stock because she is a securities dealer. Faith has asked you to calculate her potential gain and tell her whether her coworkers are right. Draft a letter to Faith responding to her request. Her address is 200 Catamon Drive, Great Falls, MT 59406.

Communications

25. **LO.2** Maria meets all of the requirements of § 1237 (subdivided realty). In 2014, she begins selling lots and sells four separate lots to four different purchasers. She also sells two contiguous lots to another purchaser. The sales price of each lot is $30,000. Maria's basis for each lot is $15,000. Selling expenses are $500 per lot.
   a. What are the realized and recognized gain?
   b. Explain the nature of the gain (i.e., ordinary income or capital gain).
   c. Would your answers change if, instead, the lots sold to the fifth purchaser were not contiguous? If so, how?

26. **LO.3, 5** Melaney has had a bad year with her investments. She lent a friend $8,000; the friend did not repay the loan when it was due and then declared bankruptcy. The loan is totally uncollectible. Melaney also was notified by her broker that the Oak corporate bonds she owned became worthless on October 13, 2014. She had purchased the bonds for $22,000 on November 10, 2013. Melaney also had a $60,000 loss on the disposition of § 1244 corporate stock that she purchased several years ago. Melaney is single.
   a. What are the nature and amount of Melaney's losses?
   b. What is Melaney's AGI for 2014 assuming that she has $65,000 of ordinary gross income from sources other than those discussed?
   c. What are the nature and amount of Melaney's loss carryforwards?

Decision Making

27. **LO.2, 3** Benny purchased $400,000 of Peach Corporation face value bonds for $320,000 on November 13, 2013. The bonds had been issued with $80,000 of original issue discount because Peach was in financial difficulty in 2013. On December 3, 2014, Benny sold the bonds for $283,000 after amortizing $1,000 of the original issue discount. What are the nature and amount of Benny's gain or loss?

28. **LO.3** Fred is an investor in vacant land. When he thinks he has identified property that would be a good investment, he approaches the landowner, pays the landowner for a "right of first refusal" to purchase the land, records this right in the property records, and then waits to see if the land increases in value. The right of first refusal is valid for

Decision Making

four years. Fourteen months ago, Fred paid a landowner $9,000 for a right of first refusal. The land was selected as the site of a new shopping center, and the landowner was offered $1 million for the land. In its title search on the land, the buyer discovered Fred's right of first refusal and involved him in the purchase negotiations. Ultimately, the landowner paid Fred $220,000 to give up his right of first refusal; the landowner then sold the land to the buyer for $4,220,000. Fred has a marginal tax rate of 39.6%.

a. What difference does it make whether Fred treats the right of first refusal as an option to purchase the land?

b. What difference does it make whether Fred is a "dealer" in land?

29. **LO.3** Carla was the owner of vacant land that she was holding for investment. She paid $2 million for the land in 2012. Raymond was an investor in vacant land. He thought Carla's land might be the site of an exit ramp from a new freeway. Raymond gave Carla $836,000 for an option on her land in 2013. The option was good for two years and gave Raymond the ability to purchase Carla's land for $4,765,000. The freeway was not approved by the government, and Raymond's option expired in 2014. Does Carla have $836,000 of long-term capital gain upon the expiration of the option? Explain.

30. **LO.3** Hilde purchased all of the rights to a patent on a new garden tool developed by a friend of hers who was an amateur inventor. The inventor had obtained the patent rights, set up a manufacturing company to produce and sell the garden tool, and produced substantial quantities of the tool, but he then became discouraged when no large garden company would agree to distribute the tool for him. Hilde purchased the patent rights (but not the manufacturing company) for $120,000 on October 24, 2013. Hilde had never engaged in such a transaction before, but she is a salesperson in the garden industry and thought she could succeed where her friend had failed. On June 27, 2014, she sold all of the patent rights to Garden Tool Company for $1,233,000. Garden Tool will manufacture the tool in its own factory and sell it to its customers. What is the nature of Hilde's gain from this transaction?

Decision Making
31. **LO.3, 4, 7** Mac, an inventor, obtained a patent on a chemical process to clean old aluminum siding so that it can be easily repainted. Mac has a $50,000 tax basis in the patent. Mac does not have the capital to begin manufacturing and selling this product, so he has done nothing with the patent since obtaining it two years ago. Now a group of individuals has approached him and offered two alternatives. Under one alternative, they will pay Mac $600,000 (payable evenly over the next 15 years) for the exclusive right to manufacture and sell the product. Under the other, they will form a business and contribute capital to it to begin manufacturing and selling the product; Mac will receive 20% of the company's shares of stock in exchange for all of his patent rights. Discuss which alternative is better for Mac.

32. **LO.3** Freys, Inc., sells a 12-year franchise to Reynaldo. The franchise contains many restrictions on how Reynaldo may operate his store. For instance, Reynaldo cannot use less than Grade 10 Idaho potatoes; must fry the potatoes at a constant 410 degrees; must dress store personnel in Freys-approved uniforms; and must have a Freys sign that meets detailed specifications on size, color, and construction. When the franchise contract is signed, Reynaldo makes a noncontingent $160,000 payment to Freys. During the same year, Reynaldo pays Freys $300,000—14% of Reynaldo's sales. How does Freys treat each of these payments? How does Reynaldo treat each of the payments?

Issue ID
33. **LO.3** Angie owns numerous strip malls. A major tenant of one of the strip malls wanted to cancel its lease because it was moving to another city. After lengthy negotiations, the tenant paid Angie $60,000 to cancel its obligations under the lease. If the tenant had fulfilled the lease terms, Angie would have received rent of $700,000. What factors should Angie consider to determine the amount and character of her income from these circumstances?

34. **LO.3** Consuela was a tenant in a campus apartment. She is a student at State University. Her lease began on August 1, 2014, and was due to expire on July 31, 2015. However, her landlord sold the building, and the new owner wanted to demolish it to build a retail building. Consuela's landlord paid her $1,000 to cancel the lease. Consuela received the $1,000 on November 30, 2014; moved out; and rented another apartment. How should Consuela treat the $1,000?

35. **LO.4** Maria held vacant land that qualified as an investment asset. She purchased the vacant land on April 10, 2010. She exchanged the vacant land for a rental house in a qualifying like-kind exchange on January 22, 2014. Maria was going to hold the house for

several years and then sell it. However, she got an "offer she could not refuse" and sold it on November 22, 2014, for a substantial gain. What was Maria's holding period for the house?

36. **LO.4** Roger inherited 100 shares of Periwinkle stock when his mother, Emily, died. Emily had acquired the stock for a total of $60,000 on November 15, 2010. She died on August 10, 2014, and the shares were worth a total of $55,000 at that time. Roger sold the shares for $36,000 on December 22, 2014. How much gain or loss does Roger recognize? What is the nature of that gain or loss?

37. **LO.4** Sarah received a gift of farmland from her father. The land was worth $4 million at the date of the gift, had been farmed by her father for 40 years, and had a tax basis for her father of $30,000. Sarah never farmed the land and sold it eight months after receiving it from her father for $4.2 million. What is Sarah's holding period for the farmland? What is the nature of the gain from its disposition?

38. **LO.5** Dennis sells short 100 shares of ARC stock at $20 per share on January 15, 2014. He buys 200 shares of ARC stock on April 1, 2014, at $25 per share. On May 2, 2014, he closes the short sale by delivering 100 of the shares purchased on April 1.
    a. What are the amount and nature of Dennis's loss upon closing the short sale?
    b. When does the holding period for the remaining 100 shares begin?
    c. If Dennis sells (at $27 per share) the remaining 100 shares on January 20, 2015, what will be the nature of his gain or loss?

39. **LO.5** Elaine Case (single with no dependents) has the following transactions in 2014:   Communications

AGI (exclusive of capital gains and losses)	$240,000
Long-term capital gain	22,000
Long-term capital loss	(8,000)
Short-term capital gain	19,000
Short-term capital loss	(23,000)

What is Elaine's net capital gain or loss? Draft a letter to Elaine describing how the net capital gain or loss will be treated on her tax return. Assume that Elaine's income from other sources puts her in the 39.6% bracket. Elaine's address is 300 Ireland Avenue, Shepherdstown, WV 25443.

40. **LO.3, 5** In 2014, Bertha Jarow (head of household with three dependents) had a   Communications
$28,000 loss from the sale of a personal residence. She also purchased from an individual inventor for $7,000 (and resold in two months for $18,000) a patent on a rubber bonding process. The patent had not yet been reduced to practice. Bertha purchased the patent as an investment. In addition, she had the following capital gains and losses from stock transactions:

Long-term capital loss	($ 6,000)
Long-term capital loss carryover from 2013	(12,000)
Short-term capital gain	21,000
Short-term capital loss	(7,000)

What is Bertha's net capital gain or loss? Draft a letter to Bertha explaining the tax treatment of the sale of her personal residence. Assume that Bertha's income from other sources puts her in the 28% bracket. Bertha's address is 1120 West Street, Ashland, OR 97520.

41. **LO.2, 4, 5** Bridgette is known as the "doll lady." She started collecting dolls as a child,   Issue ID
always received one or more dolls as gifts on her birthday, never sold any dolls, and eventually owned 600 dolls. She is retiring and moving to a small apartment and has decided to sell her collection. She lists the dolls on an Internet auction site and, to her great surprise, receives an offer from another doll collector of $45,000 for the entire collection. Bridgette sells the entire collection, except for five dolls she purchased during the last year. She had owned all of the dolls sold for more than a year. What tax factors should Bridgette consider in deciding how to report the sale?

42. **LO.5** Phil and Susan are married taxpayers, filing a joint return. The couple have two dependent children. Susan has wages of $34,000 in 2014. Phil does not work due to a disability, but he is a buyer and seller of stocks on the Internet. He generally buys and holds for long-term gain, but occasionally gets in and out of a stock quickly. The couple's 2014 stock transactions are detailed below. In addition, they have $2,300 of qualifying dividends. What is Phil and Susan's AGI?

Item	Date Acquired	Date Sold	Cost	Sales Price
Blue stock	11/10/13	03/12/14	$ 3,000	$ 6,000
Puce stock	12/13/12	05/23/14	36,000	32,000
Beige stock	12/14/09	07/14/14	13,000	14,500
Red stock	06/29/13	05/18/14	26,000	27,000
Black stock	05/15/13	10/18/14	67,000	67,800
Gray stock	04/23/12	10/18/14	89,000	88,200

43. **LO.5** Paul has the following long-term capital gains and losses for 2014: $62,000 28% gain, $21,000 28% loss, $18,000 25% gain, and $64,000 0% / 15% / 20% gain. He also has a $53,000 short-term loss and a $5,000 short-term gain. What is Paul's AGI from these transactions? If he has a net long-term capital gain, what is its makeup in terms of the alternative tax rates?

44. **LO.5** Helena has the following long-term capital gains and losses for 2014: $65,000 28% gain, $53,000 28% loss, $28,000 25% gain, and $24,000 0% / 15% / 20% loss. She also has a $33,000 short-term loss and a $65,000 short-term gain. What is Helena's AGI from these transactions? If she has a net long-term capital gain, what is its makeup in terms of the alternative tax rates?

45. **LO.5** For 2014, Ashley has gross income of $8,350 and a $5,000 long-term capital loss. She claims the standard deduction. Ashley is 35 years old and single with two dependent children. How much of Ashley's $5,000 capital loss carries over to 2015?

46. **LO.5** Jane and Blair are married taxpayers filing jointly and have 2014 taxable income of $97,000. The taxable income includes $5,000 of gain from a capital asset held five years, $2,100 of gain from a capital asset held seven months, and $13,000 of gain from a capital asset held four years. All of the capital assets were stock in publicly traded corporations. Jane and Blair also have qualified dividend income of $3,000. What is the couple's tax on taxable income?

47. **LO.5** For 2014, Wilma has properly determined taxable income of $36,000, including $3,000 of unrecaptured § 1250 gain and $8,200 of 0% / 15% / 20% gain. Wilma qualifies for head-of-household filing status. Compute Wilma's tax liability and the tax savings from the alternative tax on net capital gain.

48. **LO.5** Asok's AGI for 2014 is $133,050. Included in this AGI is a $45,000 25% long-term capital gain and a $13,000 0% / 15% / 20% long-term capital gain. Asok is single, uses the standard deduction, and has only his personal exemption. Compute his taxable income, the tax liability, and the tax savings from the alternative tax on net capital gain.

49. **LO.6** Gray, Inc., a C corporation, has taxable income from operations of $1,452,000 for 2014. It also has a net long-term capital loss of $355,000 from the sale of a subsidiary's stock. The year 2014 is the first year in the last 10 years that Gray has not had at least $500,000 per year of net long-term capital gains. What is Gray's 2014 taxable income? What, if anything, can it do with any unused capital losses?

Decision Making
50. **LO.2, 3, 7** Harriet, who is single, is the owner of a sole proprietorship. Two years ago, Harriet developed a process for preserving doughnuts that gives the doughnut a much longer shelf life. The process is not patented or copyrighted, but only Harriet knows how it works. Harriet has been approached by a company that would like to buy the process. Harriet insists that she receive a long-term employment contract with the acquiring company as well as be paid for the rights to the process. The acquiring company offers Harriet a choice of two options: (1) $650,000 in cash for the process and a 10-year covenant not to compete at $65,000 per year or (2) $650,000 in cash for a 10-year covenant not to compete and $65,000 per year for 10 years in payment for the process. Which option should Harriet accept? What is the tax effect on the acquiring company of each approach?

Tax Return Problem

H&R BLOCK

TAX SOFTWARE

51. Ashley Panda lives at 1310 Meadow Lane, Wayne, OH 43466, and her Social Security number is 123-45-6789. Ashley is single and has a 20-year-old son, Bill. His Social Security number is 111-11-1111. Bill lives with Ashley, and she fully supports him. Bill spent 2013 traveling in Europe and was not a college student. He had gross income of $4,655 in 2013.

Ashley owns Panda Enterprises, LLC sole proprietorship, a data processing service (98-7654321), which is located at 456 Hill Street, Wayne, OH 43466. The business activity code is 514210. Her 2013 Form 1040, Schedule C for Panda Enterprises shows revenues of $315,000, office expenses of $66,759, employee salary of $63,000, employee payroll taxes of $4,820, meals and entertainment expenses (before the 50% reduction) of $22,000, and rent expense of $34,000. The rent expense includes payments related to renting an office ($30,000) and payments related to renting various equipment ($4,000). There is no depreciation because all depreciable equipment owned has been fully depreciated in previous years. No fringe benefits are provided to the employee. Ashley personally purchases health insurance on herself and Bill. The premiums are $23,000 per year.

Ashley has an extensive stock portfolio and has prepared the following analysis:

Stock	Number of Shares	Date Purchased	Date Sold	Per Share Cost	Per Share Selling Price	Total Dividends
Beige	10	10/18/12	10/11/13	$80	$ 74	$30
Garland	30	10/11/06	10/11/13	43	157	70
Puce	15	3/10/13	8/11/13	62	33	45

NOTE: Ashley received a Form 1099–B from her stockbroker that included the adjusted basis and sales proceeds for each of her stock transactions. The per share cost includes commissions, and the per share selling price is net of commissions. Also, the dividends are the actual dividends received in 2013 and these are both ordinary dividends and qualified dividends.

Ashley had $800 of interest income from State of Ohio bonds and $600 of interest income on her Wayne Savings Bank account. She paid $25,000 of alimony to her former husband. His Social Security number is 123-45-6788.

Ashley itemizes her deductions and had the following items, which may be relevant to her return:

Item	Amount	Comment
Unreimbursed medical expenses for Ashley (all for visits to doctors)	$1,786	Does not include health insurance premiums.
State income taxes paid	1,830	
Real property taxes on personal residence	3,230	
Interest paid on home mortgage (Form 1098)	8,137	The loan is secured by the residence and was incurred when the home was purchased.
Charitable contributions	940	Cash paid to Ashley's church.
Sales taxes	619	Amount per sales tax table.

Ashley made a $30,000 estimated Federal income tax payment, does not want any of her taxes to finance presidential elections, has no foreign bank accounts or trusts, and wants any refund to be applied against her 2014 taxes.

Compute Ashley's net tax payable or refund due for 2013. If you use tax forms for your computations, you will need Form 1040 and its Schedules A, C, D, and SE and Form 8949. Suggested software: H&R BLOCK Tax Software.

52. Paul Barrone is a graduate student at State University. His 10-year-old son, Jamie, lives with him, and Paul is Jamie's sole support. Paul's wife died in 2013, and Paul has not remarried. Paul received $320,000 of life insurance proceeds (related to his wife's death) in early 2014 and immediately invested the entire amount as shown below:

Item	Date Acquired	Cost	Date Sold	Selling Price	Dividends/ Interest
1,000 shares Blue	01/23/14	$ 14,000	12/03/14	$ 3,500	None
400 shares Magenta	01/23/14	23,000			$750
600 shares Orange	01/23/14	230,000			$2,300
100 shares Brown	06/23/08	2,800	01/23/14	14,000	None
Green bonds	01/23/14	23,000			$1,200
Gold money market account	01/23/14	30,000			$600

Paul had $42,000 of taxable graduate assistant earnings from State University and received a $10,000 scholarship. He used $8,000 of the scholarship to pay his tuition and fees for the year and $2,000 for Jamie's day care. Jamie attended Little Kids Daycare Center, a state-certified child care facility. Paul received a statement related to the Green bonds saying that there was $45 of original issue discount amortization during 2014. Paul maintains the receipts for the sales taxes he paid of $735.

Paul lives at 1610 Cherry Lane, Bradenton, FL 34212, and his Social Security number is 111-11-1111. Jamie's Social Security number is 123-45-6789. The university withheld $3,000 of Federal income tax from Paul's salary. Paul is not itemizing his deductions.

Part 1—Tax Computation
Compute Paul's lowest tax liability for 2014.

Part 2—Tax Planning
Paul is concerned because the Green bonds were worth only $18,000 at the end of 2014, $5,000 less than he paid for them. He is an inexperienced investor and wants to know if this $5,000 is deductible. The bonds had original issue discount of $2,000 when he purchased them, and he is curious about how that affects his investment in the bonds. The bonds had 20 years left to maturity when he purchased them. Draft a brief letter to Paul explaining how to handle these items. Also prepare a memo for Paul's tax file.

Research Problems

Note: Solutions to Research Problems can be prepared by using the **Checkpoint®** **Student Edition** online research product, which is available to accompany this text. It is also possible to prepare solutions to the Research Problems by using tax research materials found in a standard tax library.

Research Problem 1. Ali owns 100 shares of Brown Corporation stock. He purchased the stock at five different times and at five different prices per share as indicated:

Share Block	Number of Shares	Per Share Price	Purchase Date
A	10	$60	10/10/97
B	20	20	8/11/98
C	15	15	10/24/99
D	35	30	4/23/00
E	20	25	7/28/00

On April 28, 2014, Ali will sell 40 shares of Brown stock for $40 per share. All of Ali's shares are held by his stockbroker. The broker's records track when the shares were purchased. May Ali designate the shares he sells? If so, which shares should he sell? Assume that Ali wants to maximize his gain because he has a capital loss carryforward.

Research Problem 2. Clean Corporation runs a chain of dry cleaners. Borax is used heavily in Clean's dry cleaning process and has been in short supply several times in the past. Clean Corporation buys a controlling interest in Dig Corporation—a borax mining concern. Clean's sole reason for purchasing the Dig stock is to ensure Clean of a continuous supply of borax if another shortage develops. Although borax must be refined before it is usable for dry cleaning purposes, a well-established commodities market exists for trading unrefined borax for refined borax. After owning the Dig stock for several years, Clean sells the stock at a loss because Dig is in financial straits. Clean no longer needs to own Dig because Clean has obtained an alternative source of borax. What is the nature of Clean's loss on the disposition of the Dig Corporation stock? Write a letter to the controller, Salvio Guitterez, that contains your advice and prepare a memo for the tax files. The mailing address of Clean Corporation is 4455 Whitman Way, San Mateo, CA 94404.

Communications

Research Problem 3. Clyde had worked for many years as the chief executive of Red Industries, Inc., and had been a major shareholder. Clyde and the company had a falling out, and Clyde was terminated. Clyde and Red executed a document under which Clyde's stock in Red would be redeemed and Clyde would agree not to compete against Red in its geographic service area. After extensive negotiations between the parties, Clyde agreed to surrender his Red stock in exchange for $600,000. Clyde's basis in his shares was $143,000, and he had held the shares for 17 years. The agreement made no explicit allocation of any of the $600,000 to Clyde's agreement not to compete against Red. How should Clyde treat the $600,000 payment on his 2014 tax return?

Research Problem 4. Siva Nathaniel owns various plots of land in Fulton County, Georgia. He acquired the land at various times during the last 20 years. About every fourth year, Siva subdivides into lots one of the properties he owns. He then has water, sewer, natural gas, and electricity hookups put in each lot and paves new streets. Siva has always treated his sales of such lots as sales of capital assets. His previous tax returns were prepared by an accountant whose practice you recently purchased. Has the proper tax treatment been used on the prior tax returns? Explain

Partial list of research aids:
§§ 1221 and 1237 and *Jesse W. and Betty J. English*, 65 TCM 2160, T.C.Memo. 1993–111.

Use the tax resources of the Internet to address the following questions. Do not restrict your search to the Web, but include a review of newsgroups and general reference materials, practitioner sites and resources, primary sources of the tax law, chat rooms and discussion groups, and other opportunities.

Internet Activity

Research Problem 5. Perform a Google search to find information about capital gains tax rates worldwide (and across U.S. states). Try searching for: "capital gains rate by country (state)". What jurisdiction has the highest capital gains tax rate? What U.S. states have high capital gains tax rates?

Research Problem 6. Find a website, other than the IRS website, that discusses the taxation of short sales of securities.

CHAPTER

17

Property Transactions: § 1231 and Recapture Provisions

LEARNING OBJECTIVES: *After completing Chapter 17, you should be able to:*

LO.1 State the rationale for and the nature and treatment of gains and losses from the disposition of business assets.

LO.2 Distinguish § 1231 assets from ordinary assets and capital assets and calculate the § 1231 gain or loss.

LO.3 Determine when § 1245 recapture applies and how it is computed.

LO.4 Determine when § 1250 recapture applies.

LO.5 Identify considerations common to §§ 1245 and 1250.

LO.6 Apply the special recapture provisions for related parties and intangible drilling costs (IDCs) and be aware of the special recapture provision for corporations.

LO.7 Describe and apply the reporting procedures for §§ 1231, 1245, and 1250.

LO.8 Identify tax planning opportunities associated with §§ 1231, 1245, and 1250.

CHAPTER OUTLINE

THE BIG PICTURE   Tax Solutions for the Real World

DEPRECIATION RECAPTURE

Hazel Brown (a sole proprietor filing a Form 1040 Schedule C) owns and operates a retail arts and crafts store. She has some 15-year-old snow removal equipment with a $1,000 tax basis. Next to her store is a small lot that she bought several years ago for $15,000 to expand the store's parking lot. In 2011, she remodeled the store and replaced the store's equipment (counters, display racks, etc.), at a cost of $450,000, with used equipment that she bought from a competitor. The equipment is 7-year MACRS property. That year, she claimed $250,000 of § 179 expense on it and depreciated the balance. She did not expense the entire $450,000 (the maximum § 179 deduction in 2011 was $500,000) because she expected to be in a higher tax bracket in later years and wanted to "save" some of the depreciation. As of June 30, 2014, the equipment has an adjusted basis of $74,960 ($450,000 cost − $250,000 § 179 expense − $125,040 of regular MACRS depreciation). Now Hazel is again planning on replacing the store's equipment, and she has determined that she can sell all of the existing equipment for $128,000.

If Hazel completes this transaction, what will be the impact on her 2014 tax return?

Read the chapter and formulate your response.

FRAMEWORK 1040
Tax Formula for Individuals

This chapter covers the boldfaced portions of the Tax Formula for Individuals that was introduced in Figure 3.1 on p. 3-3. Below those portions are the sections of Form 1040 where the results are reported.

Income *(broadly conceived)* .... $ xx,xxx
Less: Exclusions .... (x,xxx)
Gross income .... $ xx,xxx
Less: Deductions for adjusted gross income .... (x,xxx)

FORM 1040 (p. 1)		
12	Business income or (loss). Attach Schedule C or C-EZ	
13	Capital gain or (loss). Attach Schedule D if required. If not required, check here ▶	☐
14	Other gains or (losses). Attach Form 4797	

Adjusted gross income .... $ xx,xxx
Less: The greater of total itemized deductions *or* the standard deduction .... (x,xxx)
      Personal and dependency exemptions .... (x,xxx)
Taxable income .... $ xx,xxx
Tax on taxable income *(see Tax Tables or Tax Rate Schedules)* .... $ x,xxx

FORM 1040 (p. 2)	
44	**Tax** (see instructions). Check if any from: **a** ☐ Form(s) 8814 **b** ☐ Form 4972 **c** ☐ _____

Less: Tax credits *(including income taxes withheld and prepaid)* .... (xxx)
Tax due *(or refund)* .... $ xxx

G eneric Manufacturing, LLC (a limited liability company) sold machinery, office furniture, and unneeded production plants for $100 million last year. The company's disposition of these assets resulted in $60 million of gains and $13 million of losses. How are these gains and losses treated for tax purposes? Do any special tax rules apply? Could any of the gains and losses receive capital gain or loss treatment? This chapter answers these questions by explaining how to *classify* gains and losses from the disposition of assets that are used in the business rather than held for resale. Chapter 8 discussed how to *depreciate* such assets. Chapters 14 and 15 discussed how to determine the *adjusted basis* and the *amount* of gain or loss from their disposition.

A long-term capital gain was defined in Chapter 16 as the recognized gain from the sale or exchange of a capital asset held for the required long-term holding period.[1] Long-term capital assets are capital assets held more than one year.

This chapter is concerned with classification under § 1231, which applies to the sale or exchange of business properties and to certain involuntary conversions. Section 1221(a)(2) provides that such properties are not capital assets because they are depreciable and/or real property used in business or for the production of income. Nonetheless, these business properties may be held for long periods of time and may be sold at a gain.

Congress decided many years ago that such assets deserved *limited* capital gain-type treatment, which sometimes gives too much tax advantage when assets are eligible for depreciation (or cost recovery). Thus, certain recapture rules may prevent the capital gain treatment when depreciation is taken. This chapter covers the recapture provisions that tax as ordinary income certain gains that might otherwise qualify for long-term capital gain treatment.

---

[1] § 1222(3). To be eligible for any beneficial tax treatment, the holding period must be more than one year.

17-1 SECTION 1231 ASSETS

17-1a Relationship to Capital Assets

Because depreciable property and real property used in business are not capital assets[2], the recognized gains from the disposition of this property would appear to be ordinary income rather than capital gain. Due to § 1231, however, *net gain* from the disposition of this property is sometimes *treated* as *long-term capital gain*. A long-term holding period requirement must be met; the disposition must generally be from a sale, exchange, or involuntary conversion; and certain recapture provisions must be satisfied for this result to occur. Section 1231 may also apply to involuntary conversions of capital assets even though such a disposition, which is not a sale or exchange, normally would not result in a capital gain.

If the disposition of depreciable property and real property used in business results in a *net loss*, § 1231 *treats* the *loss* as an *ordinary loss* rather than as a capital loss. Ordinary losses are fully deductible *for* adjusted gross income (AGI). Capital losses are offset by capital gains, and if any loss remains, the loss is deductible to the extent of $3,000 per year for individuals and currently is not deductible at all by regular corporations. It seems, therefore, that § 1231 provides the *best* of both potential results: net gain may be treated as long-term capital gain, and net loss is treated as ordinary loss.

LO.1

State the rationale for and the nature and treatment of gains and losses from the disposition of business assets.

THE BIG PICTURE

Example 1

Return to the facts of *The Big Picture* on p. 17-1. If Hazel sells the parking lot for $25,000, she will have disposed of a § 1231 asset because it was property used in a trade or business and held for more than 12 months. Her gain will be $10,000 ($25,000 selling price − $15,000 adjusted basis). Because the asset is a § 1231 asset, all of the gain is § 1231 gain, and it may be treated as long-term capital gain.

THE BIG PICTURE

Example 2

Return to the facts of *The Big Picture* on p. 17-1. Assume that Hazel sells the snow removal equipment at a $1,000 loss and the business land at a $700 gain. Both properties were held for use in her business for the long-term holding period and, therefore, are § 1231 assets. Hazel's net § 1231 loss is $300, and that net loss is an ordinary loss.

The rules regarding § 1231 treatment do *not* apply to *all* business property. Important in this regard are the holding period requirements and the fact that the property must be either depreciable property or real estate used in business. Nor is § 1231 necessarily limited to business property. Transactions involving certain

---

[2]§ 1221(a)(2).

capital assets may fall into the § 1231 category. Thus, § 1231 singles out only some types of business property.

As discussed in Chapter 16, long-term capital gains receive beneficial tax treatment. Section 1231 requires netting of **§ 1231 gains and losses**. If the result is a gain, it may be treated as a long-term capital gain. The net gain is added to the "real" long-term capital gains (if any) and netted with capital losses (if any). Thus, the net § 1231 gain may eventually be eligible for beneficial capital gain treatment or help avoid the unfavorable net capital loss result. As noted earlier, if the § 1231 gain and loss netting results in a loss, it is an ordinary loss. Finally, § 1231 assets are treated the same as capital assets for purposes of the appreciated property charitable contribution provisions (refer to Chapter 10).

17-1b Justification for Favorable Tax Treatment

The favorable capital gain/ordinary loss treatment sanctioned by § 1231 can be explained by examining several historical developments. Before 1938, business property had been included in the definition of capital assets. Thus, if such property was sold for a loss (not an unlikely possibility during the depression years of the 1930s), a capital loss resulted. If, however, the property was depreciable and could be retained for its estimated useful life, much (if not all) of its costs could be recovered in the form of depreciation. Because the allowance for depreciation was fully deductible whereas capital losses were not, the tax law favored those who did not dispose of an asset. Congress recognized this inequity when it removed business property from the capital asset classification. During the period 1938–1942, therefore, all such gains and losses were ordinary gains and losses.

With the advent of World War II, two developments in particular forced Congress to reexamine the situation regarding business assets. First, the sale of business assets at a gain was discouraged because the gain would be ordinary income. Gains were common because the war effort had inflated prices. Second, taxpayers who did not want to sell their assets often were required to because the government acquired them through condemnation. Often, as a result of the condemnation awards, taxpayers who were forced to part with their property experienced large gains and were deprived of the benefits of future depreciation deductions. Of course, the condemnations constituted involuntary conversions, so taxpayers could defer the gain by timely reinvestment in property that was "similar or related in service or use." But where was such property to be found in view of wartime restrictions and other governmental condemnations? The end result did not seem equitable: a large ordinary gain due to government action and no possibility of deferral due to government restrictions.

In recognition of these conditions, in 1942, Congress eased the tax bite on the disposition of some business property by allowing preferential capital gain treatment. Thus, the present scheme of § 1231 and the dichotomy of capital gain/ordinary loss treatment evolved from a combination of economic considerations existing in 1938 and 1942.

17-1c Property Included

LO.2

Distinguish § 1231 assets from ordinary assets and capital assets and calculate the § 1231 gain or loss.

Section 1231 property generally includes the following assets if they are held for more than one year:

- Depreciable or real property used in business or for the production of income (principally machinery and equipment, buildings, and land).
- Timber, coal, or domestic iron ore to which § 631 applies.
- Livestock held for draft, breeding, dairy, or sporting purposes.
- Unharvested crops on land used in business.
- Certain *purchased* intangible assets (such as patents and goodwill) that are eligible for amortization.

These assets are ordinary assets until they have been held for more than one year. Only then do they become § 1231 assets.

17-1d Property Excluded

Section 1231 property generally does *not* include the following:

- Property not held for the long-term holding period. Because the benefit of § 1231 is long-term capital gain treatment, the holding period must correspond to the more-than-one-year holding period that applies to capital assets. Livestock must be held at least 12 months (24 months in some cases). Unharvested crops do not have to be held for the required long-term holding period, but the land must be held for the long-term holding period.
- Nonpersonal use property where casualty losses exceed casualty gains for the taxable year. If a taxpayer has a net casualty loss, the individual casualty gains and losses are treated as ordinary gains and losses.
- Inventory and property held primarily for sale to customers.
- Copyrights; literary, musical, or artistic compositions, etc.; and certain U.S. government publications.
- Accounts receivable and notes receivable arising in the ordinary course of the trade or business.

17-1e Special Rules for Certain § 1231 Assets

A rather diverse group of assets is included under § 1231. The following discussion summarizes the special rules for some of those assets.

Timber

Congress has provided preferential treatment relative to the natural growth value of timber, which takes a relatively long time to mature. Congress believed that this preferential treatment would encourage reforestation of timber lands. A taxpayer disposing of timber held for the long-term holding period has a long-term capital gain or loss if the timber was held for investment, has a § 1231 gain or loss if the timber was used in a trade or business, but, without special statutory treatment, would have ordinary income or loss if the timber was held as inventory. Section 631(a) allows the taxpayer to *elect* to treat the cutting of timber as a sale or exchange and, if the election is made, to treat the sale as the disposition of a § 1231 asset.[3]

The recognized § 1231 gain or loss is determined at the time the timber is cut and is equal to the difference between the timber's fair market value as of the *first day* of the taxable year and the adjusted basis for depletion. If a taxpayer sells the timber for more or less than the fair market value as of the first day of the taxable year in which it is cut, the difference is ordinary income or loss.

> Several years ago, Tom, a timber dealer, purchased a tract of land with a substantial stand of trees on it. The land cost $40,000, and the timber cost $100,000. On the first day of 2014, the timber was appraised at $250,000. In August 2014, Tom cut the timber and sold it for $265,000. Tom elects to treat the cutting as a sale or exchange under § 1231. He has a $150,000 § 1231 gain ($250,000 − $100,000) and a $15,000 ordinary gain ($265,000 − $250,000).
>
> What if the timber had been sold for $235,000? Tom would still have a $150,000 § 1231 gain, but he would also have a $15,000 ordinary loss. The price for computing § 1231 gain is the price at the beginning of the tax year. Any difference between that price and the sales price is ordinary gain or loss. Here, because the price declined by $15,000, Tom has an ordinary loss in that amount.

Example 3

Livestock

Cattle and horses must be held 24 months or more and other livestock must be held 12 months or more to qualify under § 1231.[4] The primary reason for enacting this

---

[3]§ 631(a) and Reg. § 1.631–1. To receive § 631 treatment, the holding period for the timber must be greater than one year.

[4]Note that the holding period is "12 months or more" and not "more than 12 months."

TAX IN THE NEWS   Timber Thinning Is Environmentally Sound and Good Business

Modern timber forests are regularly "thinned" to prevent the buildup of dry debris. Eliminating this dry debris helps prevent forest fires from spreading. Thinning also clears out smaller trees and allows the other trees to grow bigger and straighter.

The tax rules give favorable treatment to timber cutting and thus encourage this environmentally sound activity. Section 631(a) allows the taxpayer to elect to treat the cutting of timber as a sale or exchange and, if the election is made, to treat the sale as the disposition of a § 1231 asset.

provision was the considerable amount of litigation over the character of livestock [whether livestock was held primarily for sale to customers (ordinary income) or for use in a trade or business (§ 1231 property)]. Poultry is not livestock for purposes of § 1231.

ETHICS & EQUITY   Proper Classification of Animals

Willie is a CPA who prepares many farm returns. One of his clients is a notoriously sloppy record keeper. The farmer sold an animal this year, but the records provided to Willie did

not specify what type of animal was sold or how long it was held. Willie does determine that there is a loss on the sale and treats it on the farmer's return as an ordinary loss. Did Willie do the right thing?

Section 1231 Assets Disposed of by Casualty or Theft

When § 1231 assets are disposed of by casualty or theft, a special netting rule is applied. For simplicity, the term *casualty* is used to mean both casualty and theft dispositions. First, the casualty gains and losses from § 1231 assets *and* the casualty gains and losses from **long-term nonpersonal use capital assets** are determined. A nonpersonal use capital asset might be art held as an investment or a baseball card collection held by a nondealer.

Next, the § 1231 asset casualty gains and losses and the nonpersonal use capital asset casualty gains and losses are netted together (see Concept Summary 17.1 on p. 17-9). If the result is a *net loss*, the § 1231 casualty gains and the nonpersonal use capital asset casualty gains are treated as ordinary gains, the § 1231 casualty losses are deductible *for* AGI, and the nonpersonal use capital asset casualty losses are deductible *from* AGI subject to the 2 percent-of-AGI limitation.

If the result of the netting is a *net gain*, the net gain is treated as a § 1231 gain. Thus, a § 1231 asset disposed of by casualty may or may not get § 1231 treatment, depending on whether the netting process results in a gain or a loss. Also, a nonpersonal use capital asset disposed of by casualty may get § 1231 treatment or ordinary treatment, but it will not get capital gain or loss treatment.

Personal use property casualty gains and losses are not subject to the § 1231 rules. If the result of netting these gains and losses is a gain, the net gain is a capital gain. If the netting results in a loss, the net loss is a deduction *from* AGI to the extent it exceeds 10 percent of AGI.

Casualties, thefts, and condemnations are *involuntary conversions*. Involuntary conversion gains may be deferred if conversion proceeds are reinvested; involuntary conversion losses are recognized currently (refer to Chapter 15) regardless of whether the conversion proceeds are reinvested. Thus, the special netting process discussed previously for casualties and thefts would not include gains that are not currently recognizable because the insurance proceeds are reinvested.

The special netting process for casualties and thefts also does not include condemnation gains and losses. Consequently, a § 1231 asset disposed of by

TAX IN THE NEWS Loss from Cattle Rustling

A newspaper in "cattle country" reported that rustlers had stolen 20 head of prime milk cows from a local ranch. The rancher never recovered the cows. According to the article, the rancher had no insurance on the cows and was upset because he had no way of recovering his loss. A CPA might advise the rancher that he could be entitled to a special "theft loss" for tax purposes because the theft loss rules apply to § 1231 assets such as cattle held for 24 months or more.

condemnation will receive § 1231 treatment. This variation between recognized casualty and condemnation gains and losses sheds considerable light on what § 1231 is all about. Section 1231 has no effect on whether *realized* gain or loss is recognized. Instead, § 1231 merely dictates how such *recognized* gain or loss is *classified* (ordinary, capital, or § 1231) under certain conditions.

Personal use property condemnation gains and losses are not subject to the § 1231 rules. The gains are capital gains (because personal use property is a capital asset), and the losses are nondeductible because they arise from the disposition of personal use property.

17-1f General Procedure for § 1231 Computation

The tax treatment of § 1231 gains and losses depends on the results of a rather complex *netting* procedure. The steps in this netting procedure are as follows.

Step 1: Casualty Netting

Net all recognized long-term gains and losses from casualties of § 1231 assets and nonpersonal use capital assets. Casualty gains result when insurance proceeds exceed the adjusted basis of the property. This casualty netting is beneficial because if there is a net gain, the gain may receive long-term capital gain treatment. If there is a net loss, it receives ordinary loss treatment.

a. If the casualty gains exceed the casualty losses, add the excess to the other § 1231 gains for the taxable year.

b. If the casualty losses exceed the casualty gains, exclude all casualty losses and gains from further § 1231 computation. If this is the case, all casualty gains are ordinary income. Section 1231 asset casualty losses are deductible *for* AGI. Other casualty losses are deductible *from* AGI.

Step 2: § 1231 Netting

After adding any net casualty gain from step 1a to the other § 1231 gains and losses (including recognized § 1231 asset condemnation gains and losses), net all § 1231 gains and losses.

a. If the gains exceed the losses, the net gain is offset by the "lookback" nonrecaptured § 1231 losses (see step 3).

b. If the losses exceed the gains, all gains are ordinary income. Section 1231 asset losses are deductible *for* AGI. Other casualty losses are deductible *from* AGI.

Step 3: § 1231 Lookback Provision

The net § 1231 gain from step 2a is offset by the nonrecaptured net § 1231 losses for the five preceding taxable years (the **§ 1231 lookback** provision). For 2014, the lookback years are 2009, 2010, 2011, 2012, and 2013.

a. To the extent of the nonrecaptured net § 1231 loss, the current-year net § 1231 gain is ordinary income. The *nonrecaptured* net § 1231 losses are losses that have not already been used to offset net § 1231 gains.

b. Only the net § 1231 gain exceeding this net § 1231 loss carryforward is given long-term capital gain treatment.

Concept Summary 17.1 summarizes the § 1231 computational procedure. Examples 4 through 7 illustrate the application of the § 1231 computation procedure. Examples 6 and 7 illustrate the § 1231 lookback provision.

Example 4

During 2014, Ross had $125,000 of AGI before considering the following recognized gains and losses:

Capital Gains and Losses	
Long-term capital gain	$3,000
Long-term capital loss	(400)
Short-term capital gain	1,000
Short-term capital loss	(200)
Casualties	
Theft of diamond ring (owned four months)	($800)*
Fire damage to personal residence (owned 10 years)	(400)*
Gain from insurance recovery on fire loss to business building (owned two years)	200
§ 1231 Gains and Losses from Depreciable Business Assets Held Long Term	
Asset A	$ 300
Asset B	1,100
Asset C	(500)
Gains and Losses from Sale of Depreciable Business Assets Held Short Term	
Asset D	$ 200
Asset E	(300)

*As adjusted for the $100 floor on personal casualty losses.

Ross had no net § 1231 losses in tax years before 2014.

Disregarding the recapture of depreciation (discussed later in the chapter), Ross's gains and losses receive the following tax treatment:

- The diamond ring and the residence are personal use assets. Therefore, these casualties are not § 1231 transactions. The $800 (ring) plus $400 (residence) losses are potentially deductible *from* AGI. However, the total loss of $1,200 does not exceed 10% of AGI.
- **Step 1**: Only the business building (a § 1231 asset) casualty gain remains. The netting of the § 1231 asset and nonpersonal use capital asset casualty gains and losses contains only one item—the $200 gain from the business building. Consequently, there is a net gain, and that gain is treated as a § 1231 gain (and added to the § 1231 gains).
- **Step 1 (a)**: The gains from § 1231 transactions (Assets A and B and the § 1231 asset casualty gain) exceed the losses (Asset C) by $1,100 ($1,600 − $500). This excess is a long-term capital gain and is added to Ross's other long-term capital gains.
- **Step 2**: Ross's net long-term capital gain is $3,700 ($3,000 + $1,100 from § 1231 transactions − $400 long-term capital loss). Ross's net short-term capital gain is $800 ($1,000 − $200). The result is capital gain net income of $4,500. The $3,700 net long-term capital gain portion is eligible for beneficial capital gain treatment [assume that all of the gain is 0%/15%/20% gain (see the discussion in Chapter 16)]. The $800 net short-term capital gain is subject to tax as ordinary income.[5]

---

[5]Ross's taxable income (unless his itemized deductions and the personal and dependency exemptions are extremely large) will put him in at least the 28% bracket. Thus, the alternative tax computation will yield a lower tax. See Example 40 in Chapter 16.

CONCEPT SUMMARY 17.1

Section 1231 Netting Procedure

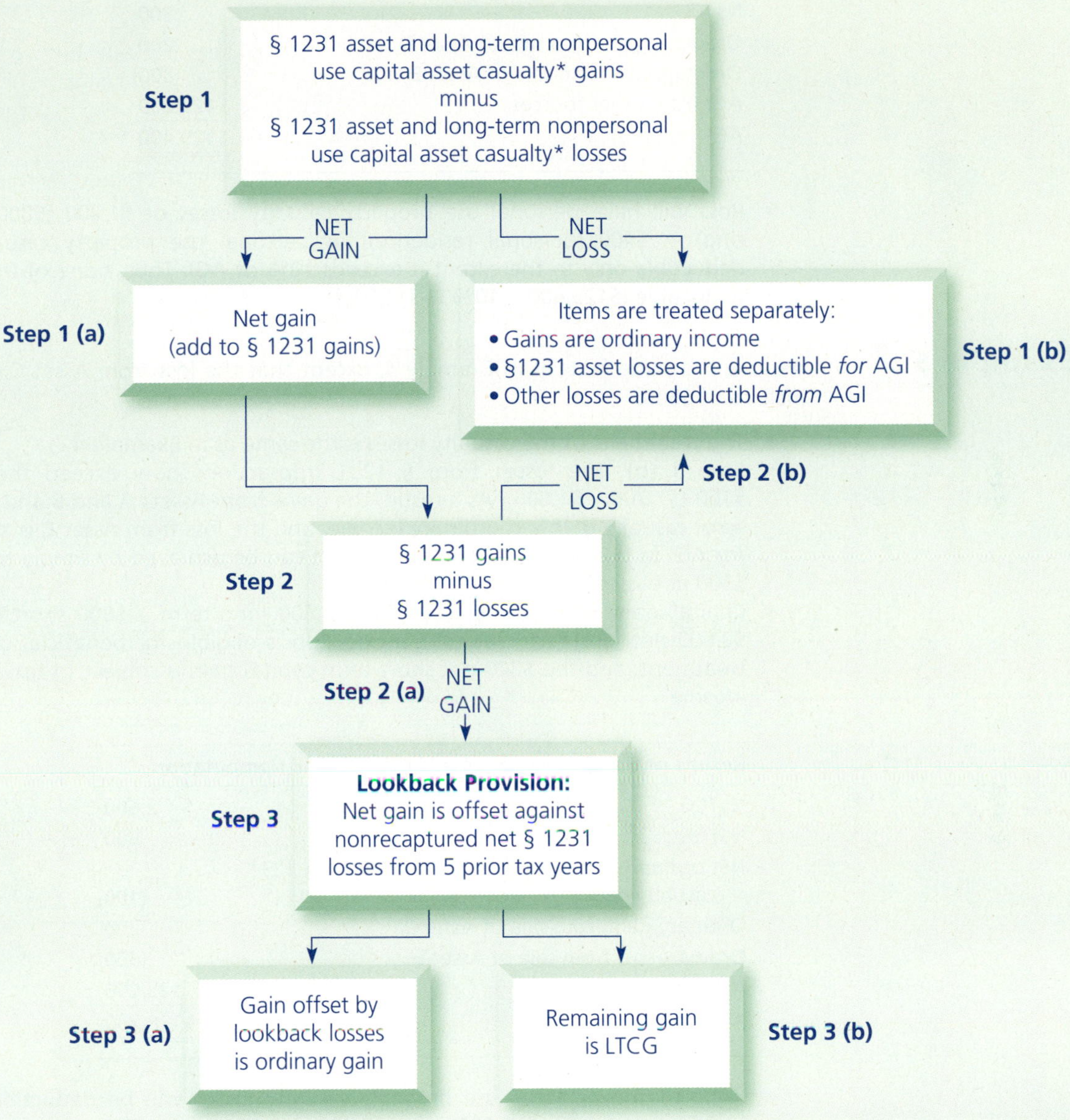

Step 1

§ 1231 asset and long-term nonpersonal
use capital asset casualty* gains
minus
§ 1231 asset and long-term nonpersonal
use capital asset casualty* losses

NET GAIN → **Step 1 (a)**
NET LOSS → **Step 1 (b)**

Step 1 (a)

Net gain
(add to § 1231 gains)

Step 1 (b)

Items are treated separately:
• Gains are ordinary income
• §1231 asset losses are deductible *for* AGI
• Other losses are deductible *from* AGI

Step 2

§ 1231 gains
minus
§ 1231 losses

NET LOSS → **Step 2 (b)**

NET GAIN **Step 2 (a)**

Step 3

Lookback Provision:
Net gain is offset against
nonrecaptured net § 1231
losses from 5 prior tax years

Step 3 (a)

Gain offset by
lookback losses
is ordinary gain

Step 3 (b)

Remaining gain
is LTCG

*Includes casualties and thefts.

© iStockphoto.com/Andrey Prokhorov

Canadian Slow Depreciation

A manufacturer has a division in Canada that manufactures auto components. The components are shipped to Detroit and become part of U.S.-manufactured automobiles. Due to slow auto sales, the manufacturer closes the Canadian plant and moves its machinery to the United States. Later, the manufacturer sells the machinery and has a tax loss because the machinery's adjusted basis is much higher than that of similar equipment that was used exclusively in the United States. The adjusted basis of the formerly Canadian equipment is higher because straight-line tax depreciation was required for the Canadian property (see Chapter 8).

Global Tax Issues

© iStockphoto.com/Andrey Prokhorov

- Ross treats the gain and loss from Assets D and E (depreciable business assets held for less than the long-term holding period) as ordinary gain and loss.

Results of the Gains and Losses on Ross's Tax Computation	
NLTCG	$ 3,700
NSTCG	800
Ordinary gain from sale of Asset D	200
Ordinary loss from sale of Asset E	(300)
AGI from other sources	125,000
AGI	$129,400

- Ross will have personal use property casualty losses of $1,200 [$800 (diamond ring) + $400 (personal residence)]. A personal use property casualty loss is deductible only to the extent it exceeds 10% of AGI. Thus, none of the $1,200 is deductible ($129,400 × 10% = $12,940).

Example 5

Assume the same facts as in Example 4, except that the loss from Asset C was $1,700 instead of $500.

- The treatment of the casualty losses is the same as in Example 4.
- **Step 1 (b)**: The losses from § 1231 transactions now exceed the gains by $100 ($1,700 − $1,600). As a result, the gains from Assets A and B and the § 1231 asset casualty gain are ordinary income, and the loss from Asset C is a deduction *for* AGI (a business loss). The same result can be achieved by simply treating the $100 net loss as a deduction *for* AGI.
- Capital gain net income is $3,400 ($2,600 long term + $800 short term). The $2,600 net long-term capital gain portion is eligible for beneficial capital gain treatment, and the $800 net short-term capital gain is subject to tax as ordinary income.

Results of the Gains and Losses on Ross's Tax Computation	
NLTCG	$ 2,600
NSTCG	800
Net ordinary loss on Assets A, B, and C and § 1231 casualty gain	(100)
Ordinary gain from sale of Asset D	200
Ordinary loss from sale of Asset E	(300)
AGI from other sources	125,000
AGI	$128,200

- None of the personal use property casualty losses will be deductible because $1,200 does not exceed 10% of $128,200.

Example 6

Assume the same facts as in Example 4, except that Ross has a $700 nonrecaptured net § 1231 loss from 2013.

- The treatment of the casualty losses is the same as in Example 4.
- **Step 3 (a)**: The 2014 net § 1231 gain of $1,100 is treated as ordinary income to the extent of the 2013 nonrecaptured § 1231 loss of $700.
- **Step 3 (b)**: The remaining $400 net §1231 gain is a long-term capital gain and is added to Ross's other long-term capital gains.
- Ross's net long-term capital gain is $3,000 ($3,000 + $400 from § 1231 transactions − $400 long-term capital loss). Ross's net short-term capital gain is still $800 ($1,000 − $200). The result is capital gain net income of $3,800. The $3,000 net long-term capital gain portion is eligible for beneficial capital gain treatment, and the $800 net short-term capital gain is subject to tax as ordinary income.

Results of the Gains and Losses on Ross's Tax Computation	
NLTCG	$ 3,000
NSTCG	800
Ordinary gain from recapture of § 1231 losses	700
Ordinary gain from sale of Asset D	200
Ordinary loss from sale of Asset E	(300)
AGI from other sources	125,000
AGI	$129,400

- None of the personal use property casualty losses will be deductible because $1,200 does not exceed 10% of $129,400.

Example 7

Assume the same facts as in Example 4, except that Ross had a net § 1231 loss of $2,700 in 2012 and a net § 1231 gain of $300 in 2013.

- The treatment of the casualty losses is the same as in Example 4.
- **Step 3 (a)**: The 2012 net § 1231 loss of $2,700 will have carried over to 2013 and been offset against the 2013 net § 1231 gain of $300. Thus, the $300 gain will have been classified as ordinary income, and $2,400 of nonrecaptured 2012 net § 1231 loss will carry over to 2014. The 2014 net § 1231 gain of $1,100 will be offset against this loss, resulting in $1,100 of ordinary income. The nonrecaptured net § 1231 loss of $1,300 ($2,400 − $1,100) carries over to 2015.
- Capital gain net income is $3,400 ($2,600 net long-term capital gain + $800 net short-term capital gain). The $2,600 net long-term capital gain portion is eligible for beneficial capital gain treatment, and the $800 net short-term capital gain is subject to tax as ordinary income.

Results of the Gains and Losses on Ross's Tax Computation	
NLTCG	$ 2,600
NSTCG	800
Ordinary gain from recapture of § 1231 losses	1,100
Ordinary gain from sale of Asset D	200
Ordinary loss from sale of Asset E	(300)
AGI from other sources	125,000
AGI	$129,400

- None of the personal use property casualty losses will be deductible because $1,200 does not exceed 10% of $129,400.

17-2 SECTION 1245 RECAPTURE

LO.3

Determine when § 1245 recapture applies and how it is computed.

Now that the basic rules of § 1231 have been introduced, it is time to add some complications. The Code contains two major *recapture* provisions—§§ 1245 and 1250. These provisions cause *gain* to be treated *initially* as ordinary gain. Thus, what may appear to be a § 1231 gain is ordinary gain instead. These recapture provisions may also cause a gain in a nonpersonal use casualty to be *initially* ordinary gain rather than casualty gain. Classifying gains (and losses) properly initially is important because improper initial classification may lead to incorrect mixing and matching of gains and losses. This section discusses the § 1245 recapture rules, and the next section discusses the § 1250 recapture rules.

Section 1245 requires taxpayers to treat all gain as ordinary gain unless the property is disposed of for more than its original cost. This result is accomplished by requiring that all gain be treated as ordinary gain to the extent of the depreciation taken on the property disposed of. The excess of the sales price over the original

TAX IN THE NEWS   Condemnation and § 1231

A farmer had owned his farmland for many years. A gravel road alongside the property was recently widened and paved. A strip of land 50-feet wide next to the road was condemned by the county as part of the road project, and the farmer was paid $50,000 for the land in a condemnation proceeding.

The farmer (with the help of his CPA) figured out that the basis of the land sold was $2,000. The land was a § 1231 asset because it was used in business (the farm) and held more than one year. The $48,000 gain from disposition of the land is a § 1231 gain.

cost is § 1231 gain. Section 1245 applies *primarily* to non-real-estate property such as machinery, trucks, and office furniture. Section 1245 does not apply if property is disposed of at a loss. Generally, the loss will be a § 1231 loss unless the form of the disposition is a casualty.

THE BIG PICTURE

Example 8

Refer to the facts of *The Big Picture* on p. 17-1. Hazel purchased the equipment for $450,000 and has taken $375,040 ($250,000 § 179 expense + $125,040 regular MACRS depreciation) of depreciation on it. The equipment's adjusted basis is $74,960.

If Hazel sells the equipment for $128,000, she will have a gain of $53,040 ($128,000 − $74,960). If it were not for § 1245, the $53,040 gain would be § 1231 gain. Section 1245 prevents this potentially favorable result by treating as ordinary income (not as § 1231 gain) any gain to the extent of depreciation taken. In this example, the entire $53,040 gain would be ordinary income.

If instead Hazel sold the equipment for $485,000, she would have a gain of $410,040 ($485,000 − $74,960 adjusted basis). The § 1245 gain would be $375,040 (equal to the depreciation taken), and the § 1231 gain would be $35,000 (equal to the excess of the sales price over the $450,000 original cost).

Section 1245 recapture provides, in general, that the portion of recognized gain from the sale or other disposition of § 1245 property that represents depreciation [including § 167 depreciation, § 168 cost recovery, § 179 immediate expensing, § 168(k) additional first-year depreciation, and § 197 amortization] is *recaptured* as ordinary income. Thus, in Example 8, $53,040 of the $375,040 depreciation taken is recaptured as ordinary income when the business equipment is sold for $128,000. Only $53,040 is recaptured rather than $375,040 because Hazel is only required to recognize § 1245 recapture ordinary gain equal to the lower of the depreciation taken or the gain recognized.

The method of depreciation (e.g., accelerated or straight-line) does not matter. All depreciation taken is potentially subject to recapture. Thus, § 1245 recapture is often referred to as *full recapture*. Any remaining gain after subtracting the amount recaptured as ordinary income will usually be § 1231 gain. If the property is disposed of in a casualty event, however, the remaining gain will be casualty gain. If the business equipment in Example 8 had been disposed of by casualty and the $128,000 received had been an insurance recovery, Hazel would still have a gain of $53,040 and the gain would still be recaptured by § 1245 as ordinary gain. The § 1245 recapture rules apply before there is any casualty gain. Because all of the $53,040 gain is recaptured, no casualty gain arises from the casualty.

The following examples illustrate the general application of § 1245.

Example 9

In the current year, Gary sold for $13,000 a machine acquired several years ago for $12,000. He had taken $10,000 of depreciation on the machine.

- The recognized gain from the sale is $11,000. This is the amount realized of $13,000 less the adjusted basis of $2,000 ($12,000 cost − $10,000 depreciation taken).
- Depreciation taken is $10,000. Therefore, because § 1245 recapture gain is the lower of depreciation taken or gain recognized, $10,000 of the $11,000 recognized gain is ordinary income, and the remaining $1,000 gain is § 1231 gain.
- The § 1231 gain of $1,000 is also equal to the excess of the sales price over the original cost of the property ($13,000 − $12,000 = $1,000 § 1231 gain).

Example 10

Assume the same facts as in the previous example, except that the asset is sold for $9,000 instead of $13,000.

- The recognized gain from the sale is $7,000. This is the amount realized of $9,000 less the adjusted basis of $2,000.
- Depreciation taken is $10,000. Therefore, because the $10,000 depreciation taken exceeds the recognized gain of $7,000, the entire $7,000 recognized gain is ordinary income.
- The § 1231 gain is zero. There is no § 1231 gain because the selling price ($9,000) does not exceed the original purchase price ($12,000).

Example 11

Assume the same facts as in Example 9, except that the asset is sold for $1,500 instead of $13,000.

- The recognized loss from the sale is $500. This is the amount realized of $1,500 less the adjusted basis of $2,000.
- Because there is a loss, there is no depreciation recapture. All of the loss is § 1231 loss.

If § 1245 property is disposed of in a transaction other than a sale, exchange, or involuntary conversion, the maximum amount recaptured is the excess of the property's fair market value over its adjusted basis. See the discussion under Considerations Common to §§ 1245 and 1250 later in the chapter.

17-2a Section 1245 Property

Generally, **§ 1245 property** includes all depreciable personal property (e.g., machinery and equipment), including livestock. Buildings and their structural components generally are not § 1245 property. The following property is *also* subject to § 1245 treatment:

- Amortizable personal property such as goodwill, patents, copyrights, and leaseholds of § 1245 property. Professional baseball and football player contracts are § 1245 property.
- Amortizable reforestation expenditures.
- Expensed costs to remove architectural and transportation barriers that restrict the handicapped and/or elderly.
- Immediately expensed depreciable tangible personal property costs under § 179.
- Elevators and escalators acquired before January 1, 1987.
- Certain depreciable tangible real property (other than buildings and their structural components) employed as an integral part of certain activities such as manufacturing and production. For example, a natural gas storage tank where the gas is used in the manufacturing process is § 1245 property.

TAX IN THE NEWS   Recapture and Casualty Loss

A fire completely destroyed an abandoned rental motor home. The local newspaper reported that the fire was "suspicious," meaning that it may have been deliberately set. The owner of the property was a local travel company with rental motor homes. The taxpayer, according to the newspaper article, had a $60,000 tax basis for the destroyed motor home and it was uninsured. The motor home was a § 1231 asset destroyed in a casualty event. There would be no § 1245 depreciation recapture because the motor home was disposed of at a loss—§ 1245 depreciation recapture only recaptures *gains*. Instead, the $60,000 loss is a *casualty loss*, not a *§ 1231 loss*, because it was disposed of by casualty, not by sale.

- Pollution control facilities, railroad grading and tunnel bores, on-the-job training, and child care facilities on which amortization is taken.
- Single-purpose agricultural and horticultural structures and petroleum storage facilities (e.g., a greenhouse or silo).
- Fifteen-year, 18-year, and 19-year nonresidential real estate for which accelerated cost recovery is used is subject to the § 1245 recapture rules, although it is technically not § 1245 property. Such property would have been placed in service after 1980 and before 1987.

Example 12

James acquired nonresidential real property on December 1, 1986, for $100,000. He used the statutory percentage method to compute the ACRS cost recovery. He sells the asset on January 15, 2014, for $120,000. The amount and nature of James's gain are computed as follows:

Amount realized		$120,000
Adjusted basis		
Cost	$ 100,000	
Less cost recovery: 1986–2009	(100,000)	
2010–2014	(–0–)	
January 15, 2014 adjusted basis		(–0–)
Gain realized and recognized		$120,000

The gain of $120,000 is treated as ordinary income to the extent of *all* depreciation taken because the property is 19-year nonresidential real estate for which accelerated depreciation was used. Thus, James reports ordinary income of $100,000 and § 1231 gain of $20,000 ($120,000 − $100,000).

17-2b Observations on § 1245

- In most instances, the total depreciation taken will exceed the recognized gain. Therefore, the disposition of § 1245 property usually results in ordinary income rather than § 1231 gain. Thus, generally, no § 1231 gain will occur unless the § 1245 property is disposed of for more than its original cost. Refer to Examples 9 and 10.
- Recapture applies to the total amount of depreciation allowed or allowable regardless of the depreciation method used.
- Recapture applies regardless of the holding period of the property. Of course, the entire recognized gain would be ordinary income if the property were held for less than the long-term holding period because § 1231 would not apply.
- Section 1245 does not apply to losses, which receive § 1231 treatment.
- Gains from the disposition of § 1245 assets may also be treated as passive activity gains (see Chapter 11).

17-3 SECTION 1250 RECAPTURE

Generally, **§ 1250 property** is depreciable real property (principally buildings and their structural components) that is not subject to § 1245.[6] Intangible real property, such as leaseholds of § 1250 property, is also included.

Section 1250 recapture rarely applies because only the amount of *additional depreciation* is subject to recapture. To have additional depreciation, accelerated depreciation must have been taken on the asset. Straight-line depreciation is not recaptured (except for property held one year or less). Because depreciable real property placed in service after 1986 can generally only be depreciated using the straight-line method, there will usually be *no § 1250 depreciation recapture* on such property. Nor does § 1250 apply if the real property is sold at a loss.

It is important to know what assets are defined as § 1250 property because even when there is no additional depreciation, the gain from such property may be subject to a special 25 percent tax rate. See the discussion of Unrecaptured § 1250 Gain (Real Estate 25% Gain) which follows.

LO.4

Determine when § 1250 recapture applies.

> **Example 13**
>
> Sanjay acquires a residential rental building on January 1, 2013, for $300,000. He receives an offer of $450,000 for the building in 2014 and sells it on December 23, 2014.
>
> - Sanjay takes $20,909 {($300,000 × .03485) + [$300,000 × .03636 × (11.5/12)] = $20,909} of total depreciation for 2013 and 2014, and the adjusted basis of the property is $279,091 ($300,000 − $20,909).
> - Sanjay's recognized gain is $170,909 ($450,000 − $279,091).
> - All of the gain is § 1231 gain.

17-3a Section 1250 Recapture Situations

In addition to residential real estate acquired before 1987 and nonresidential real estate acquired before 1981, accelerated depreciation may be taken on other types of real property. The § 1250 recapture rules apply to the following property for which accelerated depreciation was used:

- Additional first-year depreciation [§ 168(k)] exceeding straight-line depreciation taken on leasehold improvements, qualified restaurant property, and qualified retail improvement property.
- Immediate expense deduction [§ 179(f)] exceeding straight-line depreciation taken on leasehold improvements, qualified restaurant property, and qualified retail improvement property.
- Real property used predominantly outside the United States.
- Certain government-financed or low-income housing.[7]

Concept Summary 17.2 compares and contrasts the § 1245 and § 1250 depreciation recapture rules.

17-3b Unrecaptured § 1250 Gain (Real Estate 25% Gain)

This section explains what gain is eligible for the 25 percent tax rate on **unrecaptured § 1250 gain**. This gain is used in the alternative tax computation for net capital gain discussed in Chapter 16. Unrecaptured § 1250 gain (25% gain) is some or all of the § 1231 gain that is treated as long-term capital gain and relates to a sale of depreciable real estate.

---

[6]As noted above, in one limited circumstance, § 1245 does apply to nonresidential real estate. If the nonresidential real estate was placed in service after 1980 and before 1987 and accelerated depreciation was used, the § 1245 recapture rules rather than the § 1250 recapture rules apply.

[7]Described in § 1250(a)(1)(B).

TAX IN THE NEWS   Building or Tangible Personal Property?

Many taxpayers have "cost-segregated" their buildings. This means that an engineering study is done to determine whether some of a building's cost can be segregated into tangible personal property (generally a 5-year or 7-year MACRS life with accelerated depreciation) rather than real property (a 27.5-year or 39-year MACRS life with straight-line depreciation). The faster depreciation for the tangible personal property yields significant tax savings. However, there is a downside. When the property is sold, the tangible personal property gains are taxable as ordinary income due to § 1245 depreciation recapture, whereas the gain from the sale of the building is not subject to recapture, is a § 1231 gain, and may receive long-term capital gain treatment.

The maximum amount of this *25%* gain is the depreciation taken on real property sold at a recognized gain. That maximum amount is computed in one or more of the following ways:

- The recognized gain from disposition is more than the depreciation taken. The *25%* gain is equal to the depreciation taken. Refer to Example 13. The depreciation taken was $20,909, but the recognized gain was $170,909. Consequently, *some* of the recognized gain is potential *25% § 1231 gain.*

- The recognized gain from disposition is less than or equal to the depreciation taken. In this case, the *25%* gain is all of the recognized gain. Refer to Example 13, but assume the building sale price is $285,000. The recognized gain is $5,909 ($285,000 − $279,091), all of this gain is a § 1231 gain, and it is entirely a *25% § 1231 gain.*

- There is § 1250 recapture because there is additional first-year depreciation [§ 168(k)] exceeding straight-line depreciation taken on leasehold improvements, qualified restaurant property, and qualified retail property, and/or there is § 1250 recapture because there is immediate expense deduction [§ 179(f)] exceeding straight-line depreciation taken on leasehold improvements, qualified restaurant property, and qualified retail improvement property. The § 1250 recapture reduces the *25%* gain.

- There is § 1245 depreciation recapture because the property is nonresidential real estate acquired in 1981–1986 on which accelerated depreciation was taken. No *25% § 1231 gain* will be left because § 1245 will recapture all of the depreciation or the recognized gain, whichever is less. Refer to Example 12. Depreciation of $100,000 was taken, but all of it was recaptured as ordinary income by § 1245. Thus, there is no remaining potential *25% § 1231 gain.* The entire $20,000 § 1231 gain in Example 12 is potential *0% / 15% / 20%* gain.

- Section 1231 loss from disposition of other § 1231 assets held long term reduces the gain from real estate.

- Section 1231 lookback losses convert some or all of the potential *25% § 1231* gain to ordinary income.

Special 25% Gain Netting Rules

Where there is a § 1231 gain from real estate and that gain includes both potential *25%* gain and potential *0% / 15% / 20%* gain, any § 1231 loss from disposition of other § 1231 assets *first offsets* the *0% /15% / 20%* portion of the § 1231 gain and then offsets the *25%* portion of the § 1231 gain. Also, any § 1231 lookback loss *first recharacterizes* the *25%* portion of the § 1231 gain and then recharacterizes the *0% / 15% / 20%* portion of the § 1231 gain as ordinary income.

CONCEPT SUMMARY 17.2

Comparison of § 1245 and § 1250 Depreciation Recapture

	§ 1245	§ 1250
Property affected	All depreciable personal property, but also nonresidential real property acquired after December 31, 1980, and before January 1, 1987, for which accelerated cost recovery was used. Also includes miscellaneous items such as § 179 expense and § 197 amortization of intangibles such as goodwill, patents, and copyrights.	Nonresidential real property acquired after December 31, 1969, and before January 1, 1981, on which accelerated depreciation was taken. Residential rental real property acquired after December 31, 1975, and before January 1, 1987, on which accelerated depreciation was taken. Additional first-year depreciation [§ 168(k)] exceeding straight-line depreciation taken on leasehold improvements, qualified restaurant property, and qualified retail property. Immediate expense deduction [§ 179(f)] exceeding straight-line depreciation taken on leasehold improvements, qualified restaurant property, and qualified retail improvement property.
Depreciation recaptured	Potentially all depreciation taken. If the selling price is greater than or equal to the original cost, all depreciation is recaptured. If the selling price is between the adjusted basis and the original cost, only some depreciation is recaptured.	Normally, there is no depreciation recapture, but in the special situations listed above, there can be § 1250 depreciation recapture of additional depreciation (the excess of accelerated cost recovery over straight-line cost recovery or the excess of accelerated depreciation over straight-line depreciation).
Limit on recapture	Lower of depreciation taken or gain recognized.	Lower of additional depreciation or gain recognized.
Treatment of gain exceeding recapture gain	Usually § 1231 gain.	Usually § 1231 gain.
Treatment of loss	No depreciation recapture; loss is usually § 1231 loss.	No depreciation recapture; loss is usually § 1231 loss.

Net § 1231 Gain Limitation

The amount of unrecaptured § 1250 gain may not exceed the net § 1231 gain that is eligible to be treated as long-term capital gain. The unrecaptured § 1250 gain is the *lesser of* the unrecaptured § 1250 gain or the net § 1231 gain that is treated as capital gain. Thus, if there is a net § 1231 gain but it is all converted to ordinary income by the five-year § 1231 lookback loss provision, there is no surviving § 1231 gain or unrecaptured § 1250 gain.

Refer to Example 6. There was $200 of § 1231 gain from the building fire that would also be potential *25%* gain if at least $200 of depreciation was taken. The net § 1231 gain was $1,100 including the $200 building gain. (The $500 loss from Asset C would offset the potential *0%/15%/20%* § 1231 gain and not the potential *25%* gain, so all of the potential *25%* gain of $200 is in the $1,100 net § 1231 gain.) However, the $700 of § 1231 lookback losses would *first* absorb the $200 building gain, so the $400 of § 1231 gain that is treated as long-term capital gain includes no *25%* gain.

Section 1250 Property for Purposes of the Unrecaptured § 1250 Gain

Section 1250 property includes any real property (other than § 1245 property) that is or has been depreciable. Land is *not* § 1250 property because it is not depreciable.

Global Tax Issues

© iStockphoto.com/Andrey Prokhorov

Exchange for Foreign Property Yields Recognized Recapture Gain

Tangible personal property used in a trade or business may be the subject of a § 1031 like-kind exchange, and the postponed gain is most likely postponed § 1245 gain. However, tangible personal property used predominantly within the United States cannot be exchanged for tangible personal property used predominantly outside the United States. Thus, such an exchange would cause recognized gain, and as long as the fair market value of the property given up does not exceed its original cost, all of the gain is § 1245 depreciation recapture gain.

Example 14

Bill is a single taxpayer with 2014 taxable income of $120,000 composed of:

- $100,000 ordinary taxable income,
- $3,000 short-term capital loss,
- $15,000 long-term capital gain from sale of stock, and
- $8,000 § 1231 gain that is all unrecaptured § 1250 gain (the actual unrecaptured gain was $11,000, but net § 1231 gain is only $8,000).

Bill's net capital gain is $20,000 ($15,000 long-term capital gain + $8,000 unrecaptured § 1250 gain/net § 1231 gain − $3,000 short-term capital loss). The $3,000 short-term capital loss is offset against the $8,000 unrecaptured § 1250 gain, reducing that gain to $5,000 (see the discussion in Chapter 16 concerning netting of capital losses). Bill's adjusted net capital gain is $15,000 ($20,000 net capital gain − $5,000 unrecaptured § 1250 gain).

Bill's total tax (using the alternative tax calculation discussed in Chapter 16) is $24,676 [$21,176 (tax on $100,000 ordinary taxable income) + $1,250 ($5,000 unrecaptured § 1250 gain × 25%) + $2,250 ($15,000 adjusted net capital gain × 15%)].

ETHICS & EQUITY The Sale of a "Cost-Segregated" Building

Many taxpayers have "cost-segregated" their buildings. This means that an engineering study is done to determine whether some of a building's cost can be segregated into tangible personal property (generally a 5-year or 7-year MACRS life with accelerated depreciation) rather than real property (a 27.5-year or 39-year MACRS life with straight-line depreciation). The faster depreciation for the tangible personal property yields significant tax savings.

A CPA is determining the gain or loss from disposition of an office building. A sale document details the selling price of the land and building. However, the building was cost-segregated and the CPA finds records of cost and related depreciation for the tangible personal property that was part of the cost segregation. No mention of this tangible personal property was made in the sale agreement, but the building and all of its contents were sold. What should the CPA do?

© iStockphoto.com/LdF

17-4 CONSIDERATIONS COMMON TO §§ 1245 AND 1250

LO.5

Identify considerations common to §§ 1245 and 1250.

17-4a Exceptions

Gifts

The recapture potential carries over to the donee.[8]

---

[8]§§ 1245(b)(1) and 1250(d)(1) and Reg. §§ 1.1245–4(a)(1) and 1.1250–3(a)(1).

> **Example 15**
>
> Wade gives his daughter, Helen, § 1245 property with an adjusted basis of $1,000. The amount of recapture potential is $700. Helen uses the property in her business and claims further depreciation of $100 before selling it for $1,900. Helen's recognized gain is $1,000 ($1,900 amount realized − $900 adjusted basis), of which $800 is recaptured as ordinary income ($100 depreciation taken by Helen + $700 recapture potential carried over from Wade). The remaining gain of $200 is § 1231 gain. Even if Helen used the property for personal purposes, the $700 recapture potential would still be carried over.

Death

Although not a very attractive tax planning approach, death eliminates all recapture potential.[9] In other words, any recapture potential does not carry over from a decedent to an estate or heir.

> **Example 16**
>
> Assume the same facts as in Example 15, except that Helen receives the property as a result of Wade's death. The $700 recapture potential from Wade is extinguished. Helen has a basis for the property equal to the property's fair market value (assume $1,700) at Wade's death. She will have a $300 gain when the property is sold because the selling price ($1,900) exceeds the property's adjusted basis of $1,600 ($1,700 original basis to Helen − $100 depreciation) by $300. Because of § 1245, $100 is ordinary income. The remaining gain of $200 is § 1231 gain.

Charitable Transfers

The recapture potential reduces the amount of the charitable contribution deduction under § 170.[10]

> **THE BIG PICTURE**
>
> **Example 17**
>
> Return to the facts of *The Big Picture* on p. 17-1. If instead of selling the old equipment Hazel gives it to a charity, her charitable contribution is limited to zero. The potential § 1245 recapture on the equipment is $375,040 (the depreciation taken). When that amount is subtracted from the equipment's $128,000 fair market value, the result is zero because the charitable contribution cannot be less than zero.

Certain Nontaxable Transactions

In certain transactions, the transferor's adjusted basis of property carries over to the transferee.[11] The recapture potential also carries over to the transferee.[12] Included in this category are transfers of property pursuant to the following:

- Nontaxable incorporations under § 351.
- Certain liquidations of subsidiary companies under § 332.
- Nontaxable contributions to a partnership under § 721.
- Nontaxable reorganizations.

Gain may be recognized in these transactions if boot is received. If gain is recognized, it is treated as ordinary income to the extent of the recapture potential or recognized gain, whichever is lower.[13]

Like-Kind Exchanges (§ 1031) and Involuntary Conversions (§ 1033)

Realized gain will be recognized to the extent of boot received under § 1031. Realized gain also will be recognized to the extent the proceeds from an involuntary conversion are not

---

[9]§§ 1245(b)(2) and 1250(d)(2).

[10]§ 170(e)(1)(A) and Reg. § 1.170A–4(b)(1). In certain circumstances, § 1231 gain also reduces the amount of the charitable contribution. See § 170(e)(1)(B).

[11]§§ 1245(b)(3) and 1250(d)(3) and Reg. §§ 1.1245–4(c) and 1.1250–3(c).

[12]Reg. §§ 1.1245–2(a)(4) and −2(c)(2) and 1.1250–2(d)(1) and (3) and −3(c)(3).

[13]§§ 1245(b)(3) and 1250(d)(3) and Reg. §§ 1.1245–4(c) and 1.1250–3(c). Some of these special corporate problems are discussed in Chapter 20. Partnership contributions are also discussed in Chapter 20.

reinvested in similar property under § 1033. Such recognized gain is subject to recapture as ordinary income under §§ 1245 and 1250. The remaining recapture potential, if any, carries over to the property received in the exchange. Realized losses are not recognized in like-kind exchanges, but are recognized in involuntary conversions (see Chapter 15).

THE BIG PICTURE

Example 18

Refer to the facts of *The Big Picture* on p. 17-1. Rather than sell the equipment, Hazel could exchange it. If the equipment received in the exchange is worth $150,000, Hazel would have to pay $22,000 ($150,000 – the $128,000 fair market value of the equipment given up in the exchange) and would have a § 1031 like-kind exchange.

Her realized gain is $53,040 ($128,000 fair market value of the equipment given up – $74,960 adjusted basis of the equipment given up), but the gain is not recognized because boot was given (the $22,000 cash) and not received. The $375,040 of depreciation taken on the equipment given up carries over to the replacement equipment as potential § 1245 depreciation recapture.

17-4b Other Applications

Sections 1245 and 1250 apply notwithstanding any other provisions in the Code.[14] That is, the recapture rules under these Sections *override* all other Sections. Special applications include installment sales and property dividends.

Installment Sales

Recapture gain is recognized in the year of the sale regardless of whether gain is otherwise recognized under the installment method.[15] All gain is ordinary income until the recapture potential is fully absorbed. Nonrecapture (§ 1231) gain is recognized under the installment method as cash is received.

Gain is also recognized on installment sales in the year of the sale in an amount equal to the § 179 (immediate expensing) deduction taken with respect to the property sold.

THE BIG PICTURE

Example 19

Return to the facts of *The Big Picture* on p. 17-1. Assume that Hazel could sell the used equipment for $28,000 down and the balance in five yearly installments of $20,000 plus interest. She would have to recognize her entire $53,040 gain ($128,000 sale price – $74,960 adjusted basis) in 2014. All of the gain is § 1245 depreciation recapture gain because the $375,040 depreciation taken exceeds the $53,040 recognized gain.

Property Dividends

A corporation generally recognizes gain if it distributes appreciated property as a dividend. Recapture under §§ 1245 and 1250 applies to the extent of the lower of the recapture potential or the excess of the property's fair market value over the adjusted basis.[16]

Example 20

Emerald Corporation distributes § 1245 property as a dividend to its shareholders. The amount of the recapture potential is $300, and the excess of the property's fair market value over the adjusted basis is $800. Emerald recognizes $300 of ordinary income and $500 of § 1231 gain.

Concept Summary 17.3 integrates the depreciation recapture rules with the § 1231 netting process. It is an expanded version of Concept Summary 17.1.

---

[14]§§ 1245(d) and 1250(i).

[15]§ 453(i). The installment method of reporting gains on the sale of property is discussed in Chapter 18.

[16]§ 311(b) and Reg. §§ 1.1245–1(c) and –6(b) and 1.1250–1(a)(4), –1(b)(4), and –1(c)(2).

CONCEPT SUMMARY 17.3

Depreciation Recapture and § 1231 Netting Procedure

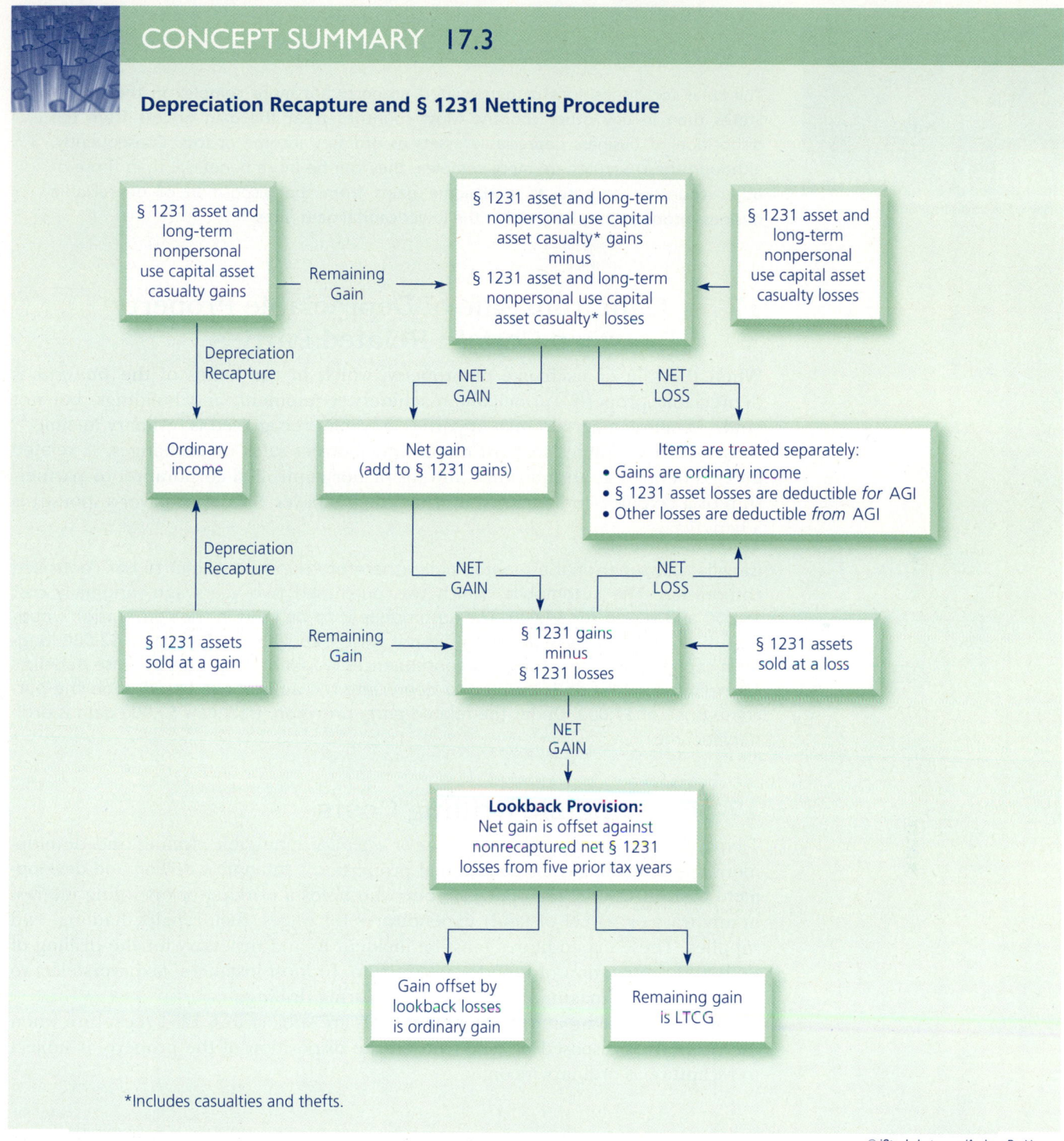

*Includes casualties and thefts.

© iStockphoto.com/Andrey Prokhorov

17-5 SPECIAL RECAPTURE PROVISIONS

17-5a Special Recapture for Corporations

Corporations selling depreciable real estate may have ordinary income in addition to that required by § 1250.[17] Under this provision, corporations selling depreciable real property are required to recapture as ordinary income the smaller of two amounts: (1) 20 percent of the recognized gain or (2) 20 percent of the depreciation taken. See the discussion of this topic in Chapter 20.

LO.6

Apply the special recapture provisions for related parties and intangible drilling costs (IDCs) and be aware of the special recapture provision for corporations.

[17]§ 291(a)(1).

Global Tax Issues

Depreciation Recapture in Other Countries

The rules for dispositions of depreciated property are more complex in the United States than in any other country. Most countries treat the gain or loss from the disposition of business depreciable assets as ordinary income or loss. Consequently, although the U.S. rules are more complex, they can be more beneficial than those of other countries because at least some gains from the disposition of depreciable business property may be taxed at the lower capital gain rates.

17-5b Gain from Sale of Depreciable Property between Certain Related Parties

When the sale or exchange of property, which in the hands of the *transferee* is depreciable property (principally machinery, equipment, and buildings, but not land), is between certain related parties, any gain recognized is ordinary income.[18] This provision applies to both direct and indirect sales or exchanges. A **related party** is defined as an individual and his or her controlled corporation or partnership or a taxpayer and any trust in which the taxpayer (or the taxpayer's spouse) is a beneficiary.

Example 21

Isabella sells a personal use automobile (therefore nondepreciable) to her controlled corporation. The automobile, which was purchased two years ago, originally cost $5,000 and is sold for $7,000. The automobile is to be used in the corporation's business. If the related-party provision did not exist, Isabella would realize a $2,000 long-term capital gain. The income tax consequences would be favorable because Isabella's controlled corporation is entitled to depreciate the automobile based upon the purchase price of $7,000. Under the related-party provision, Isabella's $2,000 gain is ordinary income.

17-5c Intangible Drilling Costs

Taxpayers may elect to either *expense or capitalize* intangible drilling and development costs for oil, gas, or geothermal properties.[19] **Intangible drilling and development costs (IDCs)** include operator (one who holds a working or operating interest in any tract or parcel of land) expenditures for wages, fuel, repairs, hauling, and supplies. These expenditures must be incident to and necessary for the drilling of wells and preparation of wells for production. In most instances, taxpayers elect to expense IDCs to maximize tax deductions during drilling.

Intangible drilling and development costs are subject to § 1254 recapture when the property is disposed of. The gain on the disposition of the property is subject to recapture as ordinary income.

17-6 REPORTING PROCEDURES

LO.7

Describe and apply the reporting procedures for §§ 1231, 1245, and 1250.

Noncapital gains and losses are reported on Form 4797, Sales of Business Property. Before filling out Form 4797, however, Form 4684, Casualties and Thefts, Part B, must be completed to determine whether any casualties will enter into the § 1231 computation procedure. Recall that recognized gains from § 1231 asset casualties may be recaptured by § 1245 or § 1250. These gains will not appear on Form 4684. The § 1231 gains and nonpersonal use long-term capital gains are netted against § 1231 losses and nonpersonal use long-term capital losses on Form 4684 to determine if there is a net gain to transfer to Form 4797, Part I.

---

[18]§ 1239.   [19]§ 263(c).

Because the 2014 tax forms were unavailable at this writing, 2013 tax forms are used in the remainder of the discussion.

Form 4797 is divided into four parts, summarized as follows:

Part	Function
I	To report regular § 1231 gains and losses [including recognized gains and losses from certain involuntary conversions (condemnations)].
II	To report ordinary gains and losses.
III	To determine the portion of the gain that is subject to recapture (e.g., §§ 1245 and 1250 gain).
IV	Computation of recapture amounts under §§ 179 and 280F when business use of depreciable property drops to 50% or less.

Generally, the best approach to completing Form 4797 is to start with Part III. Once the recapture amount has been determined, it is transferred to Part II. The balance of any gain remaining after the recapture has been accounted for is transferred from Part III to Part I. Also transferred to Part I is any net gain from certain casualties and thefts as reported on Form 4684, Part B (refer to the beginning of this section and Chapter 15). If the netting process in Form 4797, Part I, results in a gain, it is reduced by the nonrecaptured net § 1231 losses from prior years (line 8 of Part I). Any remaining gain is shifted to Schedule D, Capital Gains and Losses, of Form 1040. If the netting process in Part I of Form 4797 results in a loss, it goes to Part II to be treated as an ordinary loss.

The complex rules for the alternative tax on net capital gain for individuals, estates, and trusts affect the reporting of gains and losses from the disposition of business and rental assets. S corporations, partnerships, individuals, estates, and trusts that use Form 4797 must provide information sufficient to determine what portion of the gain surviving Form 4797, Part I (the gain that goes to Schedule D), is *28% gain, 25% gain,* or *0% / 15% / 20% gain.*

The process explained below is based upon an analysis of Form 1040, Schedule D, and Form 4797 and their instructions. One key point to remember is that all of the gains and losses that end up being treated as ordinary gains and losses (and therefore end up in Part II of Form 4797) are not eligible for any of the special tax rates for net capital gain. Another key point is that the gain that goes from Part I of Form 4797 to Schedule D will go to line 11 of Schedule D (long-term capital gains and losses). The entire gain from Form 4797 goes in column 11(f) of Schedule D.

The *25% gain* (if any) from Form 4797 is part of the Schedule D, line 11(f), gain. *Nothing on the face of Form 4797 or Schedule D identifies this gain.* Only when the alternative tax on net capital gain is computed is the *25% gain* portion of the Form 4797 net gain specifically mentioned on line 19.

Also remember that § 1231 assets are assets held more than one year. Therefore, no gain or loss is reportable on Form 4797, Part I or Part III, unless that holding period requirement is satisfied.

Example 22

For 2013, Troy Williams, a single taxpayer (Social Security number 111-11-1111), has taxable income of $133,000 *including* the following recognized gains and losses:

Sale of Depreciable Business Assets Held Long Term	
Asset A (Note 1)	$36,500
Asset B (Note 2)	20,126
Asset C (Note 3)	(880)

Sale of Depreciable Business Assets Held Short Term

Asset D (Note 4)	($ 600)

Capital Assets

Long-term gain (Note 5)	$3,000
Short-term loss (Note 6)	(200)

Note 1.   Asset A was acquired on June 23, 2010, for $50,000. It was five-year MACRS property, and four years' cost recovery allowances totaled $38,480. The property was sold for $48,020 on August 31, 2013.

Note 2.   Asset B was purchased on May 10, 2003, for $37,000. It was 27.5-year residential rental real estate, and straight-line depreciation totaled $14,126. Asset B was sold for $43,000 on November 10, 2013.

Note 3.   Asset C was purchased on December 9, 2010, for $16,000. It was five-year MACRS property, and four years' cost recovery totaled $12,314. The property was sold for $2,806 on December 30, 2013.

Note 4.   Asset D was purchased for $7,000 on July 27, 2013. It was five-year MACRS property but proved unsuitable to Troy's business. Troy sold it for $6,400 on November 3, 2013.

Note 5.   The LTCG resulted from the sale of 100 shares of Orange Corporation stock purchased for $10,000 on April 5, 2011. The shares were sold on October 21, 2013, for $13,223. Expenses of sale were $223.

Note 6.   The STCL resulted from the sale of 50 shares of Blue Corporation stock purchased for $350 on March 14, 2013. The shares were sold for $170 on August 20, 2013. Expenses of sale were $20.

The sale of asset A at a gain results in the recapture of cost recovery deductions. That recapture is shown in Part III of Form 4797. The gain from the sale of asset B is carried from line 32 to Part I, line 6, of Form 4797. On line 2, the loss from asset C appears. Part I is where the § 1231 netting process takes place. Assume that Troy Williams has no nonrecaptured net § 1231 losses from prior years. The net gain on line 7 is transferred to Schedule D, line 11. In Part II of Form 4797, the ordinary gains are accumulated. On line 13, the recapture from line 31 (Part III) is shown. On line 10, the loss from asset D is shown. The net gain on line 18 is ordinary income and is transferred to Form 1040, line 14.

Schedule D, Part I, line 1, reports the short-term capital loss from the Blue Corporation stock. It is assumed that the sale of the Blue Corporation stock was reported to Troy on a Form 1099–B that showed the adjusted basis and selling price of the stock. Part II of Schedule D has the net § 1231 gain transferred from Form 4797 on line 11 and the Orange Corporation gain on line 8. It is assumed that the sale of the Orange Corporation stock was reported to Troy on a Form 1099–B that showed the adjusted basis and selling price of the stock. The net capital gain is determined on line 16, Part III. The capital gain is then carried to line 13 of Form 1040.

In 2013 there were *five* alternative tax rates: 25%, 28%, and 0% / 15% / 20%. The 20% rate was enacted for tax years beginning in 2013.

On Form 4797, Part III, the $20,126 § 1231 gain from Asset B is made up of $14,126 (equals depreciation taken) of potential *25%* gain and $6,000 of potential *0% / 15% / 20%* gain. The $880 § 1231 loss from Form 4797, Part I, line 2, offsets the potential *0% / 15% / 20%* portion of the $20,126 § 1231 gain on Form 4797, Part I, line 6. Consequently, of the $19,246 § 1231 gain that goes from Form 4797, Part I, line 7, to Schedule D, line 11, $14,126 is *25%* gain and $5,120 is *0% / 15% / 20%* gain.

Schedule D, Part III, line 19, shows an unrecaptured § 1250 gain of $13,926. There is a worksheet in the Form 1040 Schedule D instructions to determine this amount. This gain results from the $14,126 *25%* gain being reduced by the $200 short-term capital loss from Schedule D, line 7.

Troy's 2013 tax liability is $29,060: $24,360 tax on ordinary taxable income of $110,954 ($133,000 taxable income − $22,046 net long-term capital gain), $3,482 tax on the *25%* gain ($13,926 × .25), and $1,218 tax on the *0% / 15% / 20%* gain ($8,120 × .15).

The 2013 tax form solution for Example 22 appears on the following pages.

Form **4797**	**Sales of Business Property** (Also Involuntary Conversions and Recapture Amounts Under Sections 179 and 280F(b)(2))	OMB No. 1545-0184

Department of the Treasury
Internal Revenue Service

▶ **Attach to your tax return.**
▶ **Information about Form 4797 and its separate instructions is at *www.irs.gov/form4797*.**

20**13**

Attachment
Sequence No. **27**

Name(s) shown on return	Identifying number
Troy Williams	*111 - 11 - 1111*

1 Enter the gross proceeds from sales or exchanges reported to you for 2013 on Form(s) 1099-B or 1099-S (or substitute statement) that you are including on line 2, 10, or 20 (see instructions) **1**

Part I Sales or Exchanges of Property Used in a Trade or Business and Involuntary Conversions From Other Than Casualty or Theft—Most Property Held More Than 1 Year (see instructions)

2	**(a) Description of property**	**(b) Date acquired (mo., day, yr.)**	**(c) Date sold (mo., day, yr.)**	**(d) Gross sales price**	**(e) Depreciation allowed or allowable since acquisition**	**(f) Cost or other basis, plus improvements and expense of sale**	**(g) Gain or (loss) Subtract (f) from the sum of (d) and (e)**
	Asset C	*12/09/10*	*12/30/13*	*2,806*	*12,314*	*16,000*	*(880)*

3	Gain, if any, from Form 4684, line 39	**3**	
4	Section 1231 gain from installment sales from Form 6252, line 26 or 37	**4**	
5	Section 1231 gain or (loss) from like-kind exchanges from Form 8824	**5**	
6	Gain, if any, from line 32, from other than casualty or theft	**6**	*20,126*
7	Combine lines 2 through 6. Enter the gain or (loss) here and on the appropriate line as follows:	**7**	*19,246*

Partnerships (except electing large partnerships) and S corporations. Report the gain or (loss) following the instructions for Form 1065, Schedule K, line 10, or Form 1120S, Schedule K, line 9. Skip lines 8, 9, 11, and 12 below.

Individuals, partners, S corporation shareholders, and all others. If line 7 is zero or a loss, enter the amount from line 7 on line 11 below and skip lines 8 and 9. If line 7 is a gain and you did not have any prior year section 1231 losses, or they were recaptured in an earlier year, enter the gain from line 7 as a long-term capital gain on the Schedule D filed with your return and skip lines 8, 9, 11, and 12 below.

8	Nonrecaptured net section 1231 losses from prior years (see instructions)	**8**	
9	Subtract line 8 from line 7. If zero or less, enter -0-. If line 9 is zero, enter the gain from line 7 on line 12 below. If line 9 is more than zero, enter the amount from line 8 on line 12 below and enter the gain from line 9 as a long-term capital gain on the Schedule D filed with your return (see instructions)	**9**	

Part II Ordinary Gains and Losses (see instructions)

10 Ordinary gains and losses not included on lines 11 through 16 (include property held 1 year or less):

(a)	(b)	(c)	(d)	(e)	(f)	(g)
Asset D	*07/27/13*	*11/03/13*	*6,400*	*0*	*7,000*	*(600)*

11	Loss, if any, from line 7	**11** ( )
12	Gain, if any, from line 7 or amount from line 8, if applicable	**12**	
13	Gain, if any, from line 31	**13**	*36,500*
14	Net gain or (loss) from Form 4684, lines 31 and 38a	**14**	
15	Ordinary gain from installment sales from Form 6252, line 25 or 36	**15**	
16	Ordinary gain or (loss) from like-kind exchanges from Form 8824	**16**	
17	Combine lines 10 through 16	**17**	*35,900*

18 For all except individual returns, enter the amount from line 17 on the appropriate line of your return and skip lines a and b below. For individual returns, complete lines a and b below:

a If the loss on line 11 includes a loss from Form 4684, line 35, column (b)(ii), enter that part of the loss here. Enter the part of the loss from income-producing property on Schedule A (Form 1040), line 28, and the part of the loss from property used as an employee on Schedule A (Form 1040), line 23. Identify as from "Form 4797, line 18a." See instructions . . **18a**

b Redetermine the gain or (loss) on line 17 excluding the loss, if any, on line 18a. Enter here and on Form 1040, line 14 **18b** | *35,900*

For Paperwork Reduction Act Notice, see separate instructions.   Cat. No. 13086I   Form **4797** (2013)

Form 4797 (2013)   Page **2**

| Part III | Gain From Disposition of Property Under Sections 1245, 1250, 1252, 1254, and 1255 (see instructions) |

19	(a) Description of section 1245, 1250, 1252, 1254, or 1255 property:	(b) Date acquired (mo., day, yr.)	(c) Date sold (mo., day, yr.)
A	*Asset A*	06/23/10	08/31/13
B	*Asset B*	05/10/03	11/10/13
C			
D			

These columns relate to the properties on lines 19A through 19D. ▶		Property A	Property B	Property C	Property D
20	Gross sales price (**Note:** *See line 1 before completing.*)	**20**	48,020	43,000		
21	Cost or other basis plus expense of sale	**21**	50,000	37,000		
22	Depreciation (or depletion) allowed or allowable	**22**	38,480	14,126		
23	Adjusted basis. Subtract line 22 from line 21	**23**	11,520	22,874		
24	Total gain. Subtract line 23 from line 20	**24**	36,500	20,126		
25	**If section 1245 property:**					
a	Depreciation allowed or allowable from line 22	**25a**	38,480			
b	Enter the **smaller** of line 24 or 25a	**25b**	36,500			
26	**If section 1250 property:** If straight line depreciation was used, enter -0- on line 26g, except for a corporation subject to section 291.					
a	Additional depreciation after 1975 (see instructions)	**26a**				
b	Applicable percentage multiplied by the **smaller** of line 24 or line 26a (see instructions)	**26b**				
c	Subtract line 26a from line 24. If residential rental property **or** line 24 is not more than line 26a, skip lines 26d and 26e	**26c**				
d	Additional depreciation after 1969 and before 1976	**26d**				
e	Enter the **smaller** of line 26c or 26d	**26e**				
f	Section 291 amount (corporations only)	**26f**				
g	Add lines 26b, 26e, and 26f	**26g**		0		
27	**If section 1252 property:** Skip this section if you did not dispose of farmland or if this form is being completed for a partnership (other than an electing large partnership).					
a	Soil, water, and land clearing expenses	**27a**				
b	Line 27a multiplied by applicable percentage (see instructions)	**27b**				
c	Enter the **smaller** of line 24 or 27b	**27c**				
28	**If section 1254 property:**					
a	Intangible drilling and development costs, expenditures for development of mines and other natural deposits, mining exploration costs, and depletion (see instructions)	**28a**				
b	Enter the **smaller** of line 24 or 28a	**28b**				
29	**If section 1255 property:**					
a	Applicable percentage of payments excluded from income under section 126 (see instructions)	**29a**				
b	Enter the **smaller** of line 24 or 29a (see instructions)	**29b**				

Summary of Part III Gains. Complete property columns A through D through line 29b before going to line 30.

30	Total gains for all properties. Add property columns A through D, line 24	**30**	56,626
31	Add property columns A through D, lines 25b, 26g, 27c, 28b, and 29b. Enter here and on line 13	**31**	36,500
32	Subtract line 31 from line 30. Enter the portion from casualty or theft on Form 4684, line 33. Enter the portion from other than casualty or theft on Form 4797, line 6	**32**	20,126

| Part IV | Recapture Amounts Under Sections 179 and 280F(b)(2) When Business Use Drops to 50% or Less (see instructions) |

			(a) Section 179	(b) Section 280F(b)(2)
33	Section 179 expense deduction or depreciation allowable in prior years	**33**		
34	Recomputed depreciation (see instructions)	**34**		
35	Recapture amount. Subtract line 34 from line 33. See the instructions for where to report	**35**		

Form **4797** (2013)

SCHEDULE D
(Form 1040)

Department of the Treasury
Internal Revenue Service (99)

Capital Gains and Losses

► **Attach to Form 1040 or Form 1040NR.**
► **Information about Schedule D and its separate instructions is at *www.irs.gov/scheduled*.**
► **Use Form 8949 to list your transactions for lines 1b, 2, 3, 8b, 9, and 10.**

OMB No. 1545-0074

2013

Attachment
Sequence No. **12**

Name(s) shown on return	Your social security number
Troy Williams	*111-11-1111*

Part I   Short-Term Capital Gains and Losses—Assets Held One Year or Less

See instructions for how to figure the amounts to enter on the lines below. This form may be easier to complete if you round off cents to whole dollars.	**(d)** Proceeds (sales price)	**(e)** Cost (or other basis)	**(g)** Adjustments to gain or loss from Form(s) 8949, Part I, line 2, column (g)	**(h) Gain or (loss)** Subtract column (e) from column (d) and combine the result with column (g)
1a Totals for all short-term transactions reported on Form 1099-B for which basis was reported to the IRS and for which you have no adjustments (see instructions). However, if you choose to report all these transactions on Form 8949, leave this line blank and go to line 1b .	*170*	*370*		*(200)*
1b Totals for all transactions reported on Form(s) 8949 with **Box A** checked				
2 Totals for all transactions reported on Form(s) 8949 with **Box B** checked				
3 Totals for all transactions reported on Form(s) 8949 with **Box C** checked				

4 Short-term gain from Form 6252 and short-term gain or (loss) from Forms 4684, 6781, and 8824 .	**4**	
5 Net short-term gain or (loss) from partnerships, S corporations, estates, and trusts from Schedule(s) K-1	**5**	
6 Short-term capital loss carryover. Enter the amount, if any, from line 8 of your **Capital Loss Carryover Worksheet** in the instructions	**6** (	)
7 **Net short-term capital gain or (loss).** Combine lines 1a through 6 in column (h). If you have any long-term capital gains or losses, go to Part II below. Otherwise, go to Part III on the back	**7**	*(200)*

Part II   Long-Term Capital Gains and Losses—Assets Held More Than One Year

See instructions for how to figure the amounts to enter on the lines below. This form may be easier to complete if you round off cents to whole dollars.	**(d)** Proceeds (sales price)	**(e)** Cost (or other basis)	**(g)** Adjustments to gain or loss from Form(s) 8949, Part II, line 2, column (g)	**(h) Gain or (loss)** Subtract column (e) from column (d) and combine the result with column (g)
8a Totals for all long-term transactions reported on Form 1099-B for which basis was reported to the IRS and for which you have no adjustments (see instructions). However, if you choose to report all these transactions on Form 8949, leave this line blank and go to line 8b .	*13,223*	*10,223*		*3,000*
8b Totals for all transactions reported on Form(s) 8949 with **Box D** checked				
9 Totals for all transactions reported on Form(s) 8949 with **Box E** checked				
10 Totals for all transactions reported on Form(s) 8949 with **Box F** checked				

11 Gain from Form 4797, Part I; long-term gain from Forms 2439 and 6252; and long-term gain or (loss) from Forms 4684, 6781, and 8824	**11**	*19,246*
12 Net long-term gain or (loss) from partnerships, S corporations, estates, and trusts from Schedule(s) K-1	**12**	
13 Capital gain distributions. See the instructions	**13**	
14 Long-term capital loss carryover. Enter the amount, if any, from line 13 of your **Capital Loss Carryover Worksheet** in the instructions	**14** (	)
15 **Net long-term capital gain or (loss).** Combine lines 8a through 14 in column (h). Then go to Part III on the back	**15**	*22,246*

For Paperwork Reduction Act Notice, see your tax return instructions.   Cat. No. 11338H   **Schedule D (Form 1040) 2013**

Part III	**Summary**

16 Combine lines 7 and 15 and enter the result . . . . **16** | *22,046*

- If line 16 is a **gain,** enter the amount from line 16 on Form 1040, line 13, or Form 1040NR, line 14. Then go to line 17 below.
- If line 16 is a **loss,** skip lines 17 through 20 below. Then go to line 21. Also be sure to complete line 22.
- If line 16 is **zero,** skip lines 17 through 21 below and enter -0- on Form 1040, line 13, or Form 1040NR, line 14. Then go to line 22.

17 Are lines 15 and 16 **both** gains?
☒ **Yes.** Go to line 18.
☐ **No.** Skip lines 18 through 21, and go to line 22.

18 Enter the amount, if any, from line 7 of the **28% Rate Gain Worksheet** in the instructions . . ▶ **18** | *0*

19 Enter the amount, if any, from line 18 of the **Unrecaptured Section 1250 Gain Worksheet** in the instructions . . . . ▶ **19** | *13,926*

20 Are lines 18 and 19 **both** zero or blank?
☐ **Yes.** Complete the **Qualified Dividends and Capital Gain Tax Worksheet** in the instructions for Form 1040, line 44 (or in the instructions for Form 1040NR, line 42). **Do not** complete lines 21 and 22 below.

☒ **No.** Complete the **Schedule D Tax Worksheet** in the instructions. **Do not** complete lines 21 and 22 below.

21 If line 16 is a loss, enter here and on Form 1040, line 13, or Form 1040NR, line 14, the **smaller** of:

- The loss on line 16 or
- ($3,000), or if married filing separately, ($1,500)   } . . . . **21** |(|)

Note. When figuring which amount is smaller, treat both amounts as positive numbers.

22 Do you have qualified dividends on Form 1040, line 9b, or Form 1040NR, line 10b?

☐ **Yes.** Complete the **Qualified Dividends and Capital Gain Tax Worksheet** in the instructions for Form 1040, line 44 (or in the instructions for Form 1040NR, line 42).

☐ **No.** Complete the rest of Form 1040 or Form 1040NR.

ETHICS & EQUITY   Incorrect Depreciation and Recognized Gain

A staff accountant for a large international company is calculating the tax gain from disposition of business equipment. The equipment was seven-year MACRS property and has been fully depreciated for tax purposes. The staff accountant notices that the equipment was used in Germany, not the United States, although it is listed as an asset of the U.S.

company for which the staff accountant works. Because the property was used outside the United States, it should have been depreciated using straight-line over a nine-year life. Consequently, the tax depreciation has been overstated, and the tax basis should be greater than zero, causing a smaller gain. What should the staff accountant do?

© iStockphoto.com/LdF

17-7 TAX PLANNING

17-7a Timing of § 1231 Gain

Although §§ 1245 and 1250 recapture much of the gain from the disposition of business property, sometimes § 1231 gain is still substantial. For instance, land held as a business asset will generate either § 1231 gain or § 1231 loss. If the taxpayer already has a capital loss for the year, the sale of land at a gain should be postponed so that the net § 1231 gain is not netted against the capital loss. The capital loss deduction will therefore be maximized for the current tax year, and the capital loss carryforward (if any) may be offset against the gain when the land is sold. If the taxpayer already has a § 1231 loss, § 1231 gains might be postponed to maximize the ordinary loss deduction this year. However, the carryforward of unrecaptured § 1231 losses will make some or all of the § 1231 gain next year an ordinary gain.

In the examples below, the 2014 and 2015 long-term capital gain rates are assumed to be the same.

LO.8

Identify tax planning opportunities associated with §§ 1231, 1245, and 1250.

Example 23

Mark has a $2,000 net STCL for 2014. He could sell business land held 27 months for a $3,000 § 1231 gain. He will have no other capital gains and losses or § 1231 gains and losses in 2014 or 2015. He has no nonrecaptured § 1231 losses from prior years. Mark is in the 28% tax bracket in 2014 and will be in the 25% bracket in 2015. If he sells the land in 2014, he will have a $1,000 net LTCG ($3,000 § 1231 gain − $2,000 STCL) and will pay a tax of $150 ($1,000 × 15%).

If Mark sells the land in 2015, he will have a 2014 tax savings of $560 ($2,000 capital loss deduction × 28% tax rate on ordinary income). In 2015, he will pay tax of $450 ($3,000 × 15%).

By postponing the sale by a year, Mark gets the use of $710 ($560 + $150) of tax savings until he has to pay $450 in 2015, for a net savings of $260 between the two years without considering the time value of money and other factors.

Example 24

Beth has a $15,000 § 1231 loss in 2014. She could sell business equipment held 30 months for a $20,000 § 1231 gain and a $12,000 § 1245 gain. Beth is in the 28% tax bracket in 2014 and will be in the 25% bracket in 2015. She has no nonrecaptured § 1231 losses from prior years. If she sold the equipment in 2014, she would have a $5,000 net § 1231 gain and $12,000 of ordinary gain. Her tax would be $4,110 [($5,000 § 1231 gain × 15%) + ($12,000 ordinary gain × 28%)].

If Beth postponed the equipment sale until 2015, she would have a 2014 ordinary loss of $15,000 and tax savings of $4,200 ($15,000 × 28%). In 2015, she would have $5,000 of § 1231 gain (the 2014 § 1231 loss carries over and recaptures $15,000 of the 2015 § 1231 gain as ordinary income) and $27,000 of ordinary gain. Her tax would be $7,500 [($5,000 § 1231 gain × 15%) + ($27,000 ordinary gain × 25%)].

By postponing the sale of the § 1231 property until 2015, Beth gets the use of $8,310 ($4,200 + $4,110) of tax savings until she has to pay $7,500 in 2015, for a net savings of $810 between the two years without considering the time value of money and other factors.

17-7b Timing of Recapture

Because recapture is usually not triggered until the property is sold or disposed of, it may be possible to plan for recapture in low-bracket or loss years. If a taxpayer has net operating loss (NOL) carryovers that are about to expire, the recognition of ordinary income from recapture may be advisable to absorb the loss carryovers.

Example 25

Ahmad has a $15,000 NOL carryover that will expire this year. He owns a machine that he plans to sell in the early part of next year. The expected gain of $17,000 from the sale of the machine will be recaptured as ordinary income under § 1245. Ahmad sells the machine before the end of this year and uses the $15,000 NOL carryover to offset $15,000 of the ordinary income.

17-7c Postponing and Shifting Recapture

It is also possible to postpone recapture or to shift the burden of recapture to others. For example, recapture is avoided upon the disposition of a § 1231 asset if the taxpayer replaces the property by entering into a like-kind exchange. In this instance, recapture potential is merely carried over to the newly acquired property (refer to Example 18).

Recapture can be shifted to others through the gratuitous transfer of § 1245 or § 1250 property to family members. A subsequent sale of such property by the donee will trigger recapture to the donee rather than the donor (refer to Example 15). This procedure would be advisable only if the donee was in a lower income tax bracket than the donor.

17-7d Avoiding Recapture

The immediate expensing election (§ 179) is subject to § 1245 recapture. If the election is not made, the § 1245 recapture potential will accumulate more slowly (refer to Chapter 8). Because using the immediate expense deduction complicates depreciation and book accounting for the affected asset, not taking the deduction may make sense even though the time value of money might indicate that it should be taken.

REFOCUS ON THE BIG PICTURE

DEPRECIATION RECAPTURE

Even though Hazel did not maximize her depreciation deductions when she acquired the store equipment in 2011, she still has ordinary income when she sells the equipment in 2014. She has a basis lower than the store equipment's value due to the § 179 immediate expense deduction she took and the rapid seven-year MACRS depreciation. Section 1245 "recaptures" this gain as ordinary income.

One way Hazel could avoid currently recognizing the $53,040 ($128,000 − $74,960) gain would be to do a like-kind exchange of the equipment acquired in 2011 for the replacement equipment to be acquired in 2014 (see Example 18). She would likely have to give up the 2011 equipment plus cash to acquire the replacement equipment. Thus, there would be no "boot received" and, therefore, no current gain recognized. However, the depreciation recapture potential on the 2011 equipment would carry over to the replacement equipment.

Key Terms

Intangible drilling and development costs (IDCs), 17-22

Long-term nonpersonal use capital assets, 17-6

Related party, 17-22

Section 1231 gains and losses, 17-4

Section 1231 lookback, 17-7

Section 1231 property, 17-4

Section 1245 property, 17-13

Section 1245 recapture, 17-12

Section 1250 property, 17-15

Section 1250 recapture, 17-15

Unrecaptured § 1250 gain, 17-15

Discussion Questions

1. **LO.1, 2** Harriet, an organic farmer, has owned depreciable farm equipment for several years. Is the equipment a capital asset? Why or why not?   *Issue ID*

2. **LO.1** If there is a net loss from the sale of depreciable business property held long-term, what is the character of the loss? How is it deducted (*for* or *from* AGI)?

3. **LO.1** If there is a net gain from the sale of land used in a business, is it possible that the gain could be treated as a long-term capital gain? If so, how?

4. **LO.1** Why is a depreciable asset that was held 12 months or less when it was sold not a § 1231 asset?

5. **LO.1, 2** Nate, a farmer, is thinking about raising llamas. Llama milk is highly sought after because it is high in protein and low in saturated fat. Nate would like to know what tax issues he will face if he decides to raise llamas in addition to the pigs he is currently raising.   *Issue ID*

6. **LO.1, 2** Bernice, a sole proprietor, sold two business assets during the year. As a result, she has an ordinary loss and a § 1231 gain. The loss asset was office furniture that was held for eight months, and the gain asset is land that was held for five years. Why doesn't the ordinary loss offset the § 1231 gain?   *Issue ID*

7. **LO.1, 2** Hakim's rental building was not insured when it was destroyed by a hurricane. His adjusted basis for the building was substantial, but was less than he had paid for the building in 2010. The building was Hakim's only asset that was damaged by the hurricane. How should Hakim handle this situation?   *Issue ID*

8. **LO.2** As a result of a casualty event, Theresa disposed of tangible personal property (a § 1231 asset) at a realized and recognized loss. At the time of the casualty, the property was worth substantially less than Theresa had paid for it, but it still had an adjusted basis greater than zero. This was her only business casualty, and she has some § 1231 lookback loss. Is the resulting loss a casualty loss that can be offset against a long-term capital gain or a casualty loss deductible *for AGI* as an ordinary loss?   *Issue ID*

9. **LO.2** An individual taxpayer had a net § 1231 loss in 2014. Could any of this loss be treated as a long-term capital loss? Why or why not?

10. **LO.2** Steven established a sole proprietorship in 2009. He sold § 1231 assets at a loss in 2012 and 2013. He had only sold § 1231 assets at a gain before 2012. In 2014, he could sell a § 1231 asset at a gain and would like to have the gain taxed as a long-term capital gain. What issue is Steven facing?   *Issue ID*

11. **LO.2** Review Examples 4 and 6 in the text. In both examples, the taxpayer's AGI is $129,400 even though in Example 6 there is $700 of nonrecaptured § 1231 loss from 2013. Explain why the two AGI amounts are the same.

12. **LO.3** A taxpayer owns depreciable business real property held for the short-term holding period. What would have to be true for the real property to generate a § 1231 loss when it is sold?

13. **LO.3** A depreciable business dump truck has been owned for four years and is no longer useful to the taxpayer. What would have to be true for the disposition of the dump truck to generate at least some § 1231 loss?

Issue ID

14. **LO.1, 2, 3** Sissie owns two items of business equipment. They were both purchased in 2010 for $100,000, both have a seven-year recovery period, and both have an adjusted basis of $37,490. Sissie is considering selling these assets in 2014. One of them is worth $60,000, and the other is worth $23,000. Because both items were used in her business, Sissie simply assumes that the loss on one will be offset against the gain from the other and that the net gain or loss will increase or reduce her business income. Is she correct? Explain.

15. **LO.1, 3** If depreciable equipment used in a business is sold at a recognized gain on July 10, 2014, and it was purchased on August 21, 2013, does § 1245 depreciation recapture apply to the asset? Explain.

Issue ID

16. **LO.3** A professional football player's contract is sold at a gain after it has been held for two years. What issues should the team consider in determining the nature of this gain?

17. **LO.3** A retailer's store is destroyed by a tornado, but is insured for its replacement cost. Consequently, the retailer has a $40,000 gain after receiving the insurance proceeds. The store is not replaced because the retailer spends the insurance proceeds on additional inventory. What is the nature of the gain if the store originally cost $100,000 three years ago and had an adjusted basis of $82,000 at the time of its destruction?

18. **LO.4** Nonresidential real estate leasehold improvements are sold at a loss. In what circumstances would the loss be subject to § 1250 depreciation recapture?

19. **LO.4** An apartment building was acquired in 2006. The depreciation taken on the building was $123,000, and the building was sold for a $34,000 gain. What is the maximum amount of 25% gain?

20. **LO.4** In the current year, an individual taxpayer has net long-term capital gain from disposition of capital assets and has unrecaptured § 1250 gain. What would the circumstances have to be for the unrecaptured § 1250 gain to be taxed at 25%?

21. **LO.4** An individual taxpayer has $25,000 of § 1231 gain from the disposition of nonresidential real estate. Straight-line depreciation of $43,000 was deducted on the real estate. The taxpayer also has a § 1231 loss of $56,000 from the sale of equipment. How much of the § 1231 gain is taxed as unrecaptured § 1250 gain?

22. **LO.3, 5** Mary receives tangible personal property as a gift. The property was depreciated by the donor, and Mary will also depreciate it. At the date of the gift, the property was worth more than the donor's adjusted basis. What is the impact of these facts on Mary when she sells the property at a gain several years after she acquired it?

23. **LO.3, 5** Thomas receives tangible personal property as an inheritance from a decedent who died in 2014. The property was depreciated by the deceased, and Thomas will also depreciate it. At the date of the deceased's death, the property was worth more than the deceased's adjusted basis. What is the impact of these facts on Thomas when he sells the property at a gain several years after he acquired it?

24. **LO.3, 5** Dino contributes to charity some tangible personal property that he had used in his business and depreciated. At the date of the donation, the property has a fair market value greater than its adjusted basis, but less than the original cost. What is the impact of these facts on Dino's charitable contribution?

25. **LO.3, 5** Desiree contributes to her wholly owned corporation some tangible personal property that she had used in her sole proprietorship business and depreciated. At the date of the contribution, the property has a fair market value greater than its adjusted basis. What is the impact of these facts on the corporation?

26. **LO.3, 5** A corporation distributes a truck it has owned for three years to its sole shareholder. The shareholder will use the truck for personal use activity. The truck's fair market value at the time of the distribution is greater than its adjusted basis, but less than its original cost. Does the corporation recognize a gain? If so, what is the character of the gain?

27. **LO.6** A corporation distributes a truck it has owned for three years to its sole shareholder. The shareholder will use the truck for business activity. The truck's fair market value at the time of the distribution is greater than its adjusted basis, but less than its original cost. Does the corporation recognize a gain? If so, what is the character of the gain?

28. **LO.7** Refer to Form 4797 near the end of this chapter. Where would a § 1231 loss be entered on the form?

29. **LO.7** Refer to Form 4797 near the end of this chapter. Where would a § 1231 gain on the disposition of business land be entered on the form?

30. **LO.7** Refer to Form 4797 near the end of this chapter. Where would a § 1231 lookback loss be entered on the form?

Problems

31. **LO.I, 2** Jenny purchased timber on a 100-acre tract of land in South Dakota in March 2012 for $100,000. On January 1, 2014, the timber had a fair market value of $145,000. Because of careless cutting in November 2014, when the fair market value was $158,000, the wood was sold on January 30, 2015, for $98,000.
    a. What gain (loss) was recognized in 2013, 2014, and 2015 if Jenny elected to treat the cutting as a sale?
    b. What was the nature of the gains (losses) in (a)?
    c. Does the answer change if the timber was sold in December 2014? Why or why not?
    d. If the timber was worth only $58,000 on January 1, 2014, was cut in November when it was worth $33,000, and was sold in December for $59,000, how would the answers to (a) and (b) change?

32. **LO.2** Bob owns a farming sole proprietorship. During the year, Bob sold a milk cow that he had owned for 15 months and a workhorse that he had owned for 66 months. The cow had an adjusted basis of $38,000 and was sold for $55,000. The horse had an adjusted basis of $750 and was sold for $4,000. Bob also has a $200 long-term capital loss from the sale of corporate stock. He has $55,000 of other AGI (not associated with the items above) for the year. He has $4,000 nonrecaptured § 1231 losses from the previous five years. What is the nature of the gains or losses from the disposition of the farm animals? What is Bob's AGI for the year?

33. **LO.2** A sculpture that Korliss Kane held for investment was destroyed in a flood. The sculpture was insured, and Korliss had a $60,000 gain from this casualty. He also had a $17,000 loss from an uninsured antique vase that was destroyed by the flood. The vase was also held for investment. Korliss had no other property transactions during the year and has no nonrecaptured § 1231 losses from prior years. Both the sculpture and the vase had been held more than one year when the flood occurred. Compute Korliss's net gain or loss and identify how it would be treated. Also write a letter to Korliss explaining the nature of the gain or loss. Korliss's address is 2367 Meridian Road, Hannibal, MO 63401.

Communications

34. **LO.2** Keshara has the following net § 1231 results for each of the years shown. What would be the nature of the net gains in 2013 and 2014?

Tax Year	Net § 1231 Loss	Net § 1231 Gain
2009	$18,000	
2010	33,000	
2011	42,000	
2012		$41,000
2013		30,000
2014		41,000

35. **LO.2, 8** Jinjie owns two parcels of business land (§ 1231 assets). One parcel can be sold at a loss of $60,000, and the other parcel can be sold at a gain of $70,000. Jinjie has no nonrecaptured § 1231 losses from prior years. The parcels could be sold at any time because potential purchasers are abundant. Jinjie has a $35,000 short-term capital loss carryover from a prior tax year and no capital assets that could be sold to generate long-term capital gains. Both land parcels have been held more than one year. What should Jinjie do based upon these facts? (Assume that tax rates are constant and ignore the present value of future cash flow.)

Decision Making

36. **LO.I, 2, 3** Siena Industries (a sole proprietorship) sold three § 1231 assets during 2014. Data on these property dispositions are as follows:

Asset	Cost	Acquired	Depreciation	Sold for	Sold on
Rack	$100,000	10/10/10	$62,000	$85,000	10/10/14
Forklift	35,000	10/16/11	23,000	5,000	10/10/14
Bin	87,000	03/12/13	34,000	60,000	10/10/14

a. Determine the amount and the character of the recognized gain or loss from the disposition of each asset.

b. Assuming that Siena has no nonrecaptured net § 1231 losses from prior years, how much of the 2014 recognized gains is treated as capital gains?

37. **LO.2, 3** Amber Industries (a sole proprietorship) sold three § 1231 assets during 2014. Data on these property dispositions are as follows:

Asset	Cost	Acquired	Depreciation	Sold for	Sold on
Rack	$100,000	10/10/10	$100,000	$145,000	10/10/14
Forklift	35,000	10/16/11	23,000	3,000	10/10/14
Bin	87,000	03/12/13	31,000	60,000	10/10/14

a. Determine the amount and the character of the recognized gain or loss from the disposition of each asset.

b. Assuming that Amber has $5,000 nonrecaptured net § 1231 losses from the five prior years, how much of the 2014 recognized gains is treated as capital gains?

38. **LO.2, 3** Copper Industries (a sole proprietorship) sold three § 1231 assets during 2014. Data on these property dispositions are as follows:

Asset	Cost	Acquired	Depreciation	Sold for	Sold on
Rack	$110,000	10/10/11	$70,000	$55,000	10/10/14
Forklift	45,000	10/16/10	21,000	15,000	10/10/14
Bin	97,000	03/12/13	31,000	60,000	10/10/14

a. Determine the amount and the character of the recognized gain or loss from the disposition of each asset.

b. Assuming that Copper has $6,000 nonrecaptured net § 1231 losses from prior years, how much of the 2014 recognized gains is treated as capital gains?

Communications

39. **LO.2, 3** On December 1, 2012, Lavender Manufacturing Company (a corporation) purchased another company's assets, including a patent. The patent was used in Lavender's manufacturing operations; $49,500 was allocated to the patent, and it was amortized at the rate of $275 per month. On July 30, 2014, Lavender sold the patent for $95,000. Twenty months of amortization had been taken on the patent. What are the amount and nature of the gain Lavender recognizes on the disposition of the patent? Write a letter to Lavender discussing the treatment of the gain. Lavender's address is 6734 Grover Street, Boothbay Harbor, ME 04538. The letter should be addressed to Bill Cubit, Controller.

40. **LO.2, 4** On June 1, 2010, Skylark Enterprises (not a corporation) acquired a retail store building for $500,000 (with $100,000 being allocated to the land). The store building was 39-year real property, and the straight-line cost recovery method was used. The property was sold on June 21, 2014, for $385,000.

a. Compute the cost recovery and adjusted basis for the building using Table 8.6 from Chapter 8.

b. What are the amount and nature of Skylark's gain or loss from disposition of the building? What amount, if any, of the gain is unrecaptured § 1250 gain?

41. **LO.2, 3, 4** On May 2, 1987, Hannah acquired residential rental real estate for $450,000. Of the cost, $100,000 was allocated to the land and $350,000 to the building. On August 20, 2015, the building, which then had an adjusted basis of $0, was sold for $545,000 and the land for $200,000.
    a. Determine the amount and character of the recognized gain from the sale of the building.
    b. Determine the amount and character of the recognized gain from the sale of the land.

42. **LO.2, 3, 4** Larry is the sole proprietor of a trampoline shop. During 2014, the following transactions occurred:

    • Unimproved land adjacent to the store was condemned by the city on February 1. The condemnation proceeds were $15,000. The land, acquired in 1985, had an allocable basis of $40,000. Larry has additional parking across the street and plans to use the condemnation proceeds to build his inventory.
    • A truck used to deliver trampolines was sold on January 2 for $3,500. The truck was purchased on January 2, 2010, for $6,000. On the date of sale, the adjusted basis was zero.
    • Larry sold an antique rowing machine at an auction. Net proceeds were $4,900. The rowing machine was purchased as used equipment 17 years ago for $5,200 and is fully depreciated.
    • Larry sold an apartment building for $300,000 on September 1. The rental property was purchased on September 1, 2011, for $150,000 and was being depreciated over a 27.5-year life using the straight-line method. At the date of sale, the adjusted basis was $124,783.
    • Larry's personal yacht was stolen on September 5. The yacht had been purchased in August at a cost of $25,000. The fair market value immediately preceding the theft was $19,600. Larry was insured for 50% of the original cost, and he received $12,500 on December 1.
    • Larry sold a Buick on May 1 for $9,600. The vehicle had been used exclusively for personal purposes. It was purchased on September 1, 2010, for $20,800.
    • Larry's trampoline stretching machine (owned two years) was stolen on May 5, but the business's insurance company will not pay any of the machine's value because Larry failed to pay the insurance premium. The machine had a fair market value of $8,000 and an adjusted basis of $6,000 at the time of theft.
    • Larry had AGI of $102,000 from sources other than those described above.
    • Larry has no nonrecaptured § 1231 lookback losses.

    a. For each transaction, what are the amount and nature of recognized gain or loss?
    b. What is Larry's 2014 AGI?

43. **LO.2, 4** On January 1, 2005, Stephanie Bridges acquired depreciable real property for $50,000. She used straight-line depreciation to compute the asset's cost recovery. The asset was sold for $96,000 on January 3, 2014, when its adjusted basis was $38,000. **Communications**
    a. What are the amount and nature of the gain if the real property was residential?
    b. Stephanie is curious about how the recapture rules differ for tangible personal property and for residential rental real estate acquired in 1987 and thereafter. Write a letter to Stephanie explaining the differences. Her address is 2345 Westridge Street #23, Edna, KS 67342.

44. **LO.2, 3, 5, 8** Joanne is in the 28% tax bracket and owns depreciable business equipment that she purchased several years ago for $135,000. She has taken $100,000 of depreciation on the equipment, and it is worth $55,000. Joanne's niece, Susan, is starting a new business and is short of cash. Susan has asked Joanne to gift the equipment to her so that Susan can use it in her business. Joanne no longer needs the equipment. Identify the alternatives available to Joanne if she wants to help Susan and the tax effects of those alternatives. (Assume that all alternatives involve the business equipment in one way or another and ignore the gift tax.) **Decision Making**

45. **LO.2, 3, 5** Anna received tangible personal property with a fair market value of $65,000 as a gift in 2012. The donor had purchased the property for $77,000 and had taken $77,000 of depreciation. Anna used the property in her business. Anna sells the property for $23,000 in 2014. What are the tax status of the property and the nature of the recognized gain when she sells the property?

46. **LO.2, 3, 5** Miguel receives tangible personal property as an inheritance in 2012. The property was depreciated by the deceased (Miguel's father), and Miguel will also depreciate it. At the date of the deceased's death, the property was worth $532,000. The deceased had purchased it for $900,000 and had taken $523,000 of depreciation on the property. Miguel takes $223,000 of depreciation on the property before selling it for $482,000 in 2014. What are the tax status of the property and the nature of the recognized gain when Miguel sells the property?

47. **LO.5** David contributes to charity some tangible personal property that he had used in his business and depreciated. At the date of the donation, the property has a fair market value of $233,000 and an adjusted basis of zero; it was originally acquired for $400,000. What is the amount of David's charitable contribution?

48. **LO.2, 3, 5** Dedriea contributes to her wholly owned corporation some tangible personal property that she had used in her sole proprietorship business and depreciated. She had acquired the property for $566,000 and had taken $431,000 of depreciation on it before contributing it to the corporation. At the date of the contribution, the property had a fair market value of $289,000. The corporation took $100,000 of depreciation on the property and then sold it for $88,000 in 2014. What are the tax status of the property to the corporation and the nature of the recognized gain or loss when the corporation sells the property?

49. **LO.2, 3, 6** Tan Corporation purchased depreciable tangible personal property for $100,000 in 2012 and immediately expensed the entire cost under § 179. In 2014, when the property was worth $80,000, Tan distributed it as a dividend to the corporation's sole shareholder. What was the tax status of this property for Tan? What is the nature of the recognized gain or loss from the distribution of the property?

50. **LO.4, 7** Jeremiah is the tenant of a shopping center. In 2012, he installed $250,000 of capitalized leasehold improvements in his store at the mall. He took $250,000 of depreciation on the leasehold improvements before selling them for $220,000 to the lessee who took over his lease in 2014. Straight-line depreciation on the leasehold improvements up to the point of sale would have been $67,253. Jeremiah's depreciation was so much larger than straight-line depreciation because he took § 179 depreciation in 2012. What is Jeremiah's recognized gain? What is the nature of that gain? How is the transaction reported in 2014?

51. **LO.4** Jasmine owned rental real estate that she sold to her tenant in an installment sale. Jasmine acquired the property in 2002 for $400,000; took $178,000 of depreciation on it; and sold it for $210,000, receiving $25,000 immediately and the balance (plus interest at a market rate) in equal payments of $18,500 for 10 years. What is the nature of the recognized gain or loss from this transaction?

52. **LO.4, 7** Sasha and Tara are married, filing jointly. Their correctly determined 2014 taxable income is $127,000. This taxable income includes a $5,000 § 1231 gain from the sale of business land that was included in their $22,000 of net long-term capital gain. None of the net long-term capital gain was from collectibles.
    a. In addition to their Form 1040, what tax forms related to their property transactions would the couple include in their income tax return?
    b. Calculate the couple's tax on taxable income using the alternative tax on net capital gain method.

53. **LO.7** On August 10, 2012, Jasper purchased business equipment for $40,000. On his 2012 tax return, $40,000 of § 179 immediate expense was taken on the equipment. On July 14, 2013, Jasper sold the equipment for $12,000. What is the nature of disposition gain or loss? Where is it reported on the 2013 Form 4797?

54. **LO.7** Adrian has a 2013 Form 4797, line 9 gain of $56,000. He also has one transaction on his 2013 Form 1040 Schedule D, Part I—a loss of $58,000. What is Adrian's AGI from these events?

55. **LO.7** Theresa has a 2013 Form 1040 Schedule D, line 16 gain of $45,000. There is also a $45,000 gain on the form's line 19. What is the nature of the gain? What alternative tax rate applies to it?

56. **LO.3, 8** Jay sold three items of business equipment for a total of $300,000. None of the equipment was appraised to determine its value. Jay's cost and adjusted basis for the assets are as follows:

Decision Making

Asset	Cost	Adjusted Basis
Skidder	$230,000	$ 40,000
Driller	120,000	60,000
Platform	620,000	–0–
Total	$970,000	$100,000

Jay has been unable to establish the fair market values of the three assets. All he can determine is that combined they were worth $300,000 to the buyer in this arm's length transaction. How should Jay allocate the sales price and figure the gain or loss on the sale of the three assets?

Cumulative Problems

57. Justin Stone was an employee of DataCare Services, Inc. His salary was $45,000 through November 10, 2013, when he was laid off. He received $7,000 of unemployment compensation from November 11, 2013, through December 31, 2013. FICA withholdings were as follows: Social Security of $2,790 ($45,000 × 6.2%) and Medicare of $653 ($45,000 × 1.45%). Justin lives at 112 Green Road, Crown City, OH 45623. His Social Security number is 111-11-1111. Justin owned an apartment building until November 22, 2013, when he sold it for $200,000. For 2013, he had rent revenue of $33,000. He incurred and paid expenses as follows: $4,568 of repairs, $22,000 of mortgage interest, and $1,000 of miscellaneous expenses. He purchased the building on January 2, 2007, for $125,000. The building generated an operating profit each year that Justin owned it.
Other information follows:

Tax Return Problem

H&R BLOCK
TAX SOFTWARE

- On November 22, 2013, Justin sold for $3,500 equipment that had been used for repairing various items in the apartments. The equipment was purchased for $25,000 on July 10, 2006, and was fully depreciated prior to 2013.
- Justin has $3,000 of unrecaptured § 1231 losses from prior years.
- Justin is age 38; is single; is divorced; and has custody of his 9-year-old son, Flint. Justin provides more than 50% of Flint's support. Flint's Social Security number is 123-45-6789.
- Justin had $1,000 interest income from Blue Corporation bonds.
- Justin had $1,500 interest income from a State Bank certificate of deposit.
- Justin had a $2,000 *0%/15%/20%* long-term capital gain distribution from the Brown Stock Investment Fund.
- Justin had the following itemized deductions: $4,600 real estate taxes on his home; $8,900 mortgage interest on his home; $4,760 charitable contributions (all in cash, properly documented, and no single contribution exceeded $25); $4,300 state income tax withholding during 2013; $2,000 state estimated income tax payments during 2013; $2,600 sales taxes paid.
- Justin does not want to donate to the Presidential Election Campaign Fund.
- He had $12,000 of Federal income tax withholding during 2013 and made total Federal estimated income tax payments of $14,000 during 2013.

Compute Justin's 2013 net tax payable or refund due. If you use tax forms for your computations, you will need Form 1040 and Schedules A, B, D, and E. You will also need Form 4797. Suggested software: H&R BLOCK Tax Software.

58. Glen and Diane Okumura (both age 48) are married, file a joint return, and live at 39 Kaloa Street, Honolulu, HI 96815. Glen's Social Security number is 111-11-1111, and Diane's is 123-45-6789. The Okumuras have two dependent children, Amy (age 15) and John (age 9). Amy's Social Security number is 123-45-6788, and John's Social Security number is 123-45-6787. Glen works for the Hawaii Public Works Department, and Diane works in a retail dress shop. The Okumuras had the following transactions during 2014:

Tax Computation Problem

Communications

a. Glen earned $57,000 in wages and had Federal income tax withholding of $2,000.

b. Diane earned $38,000 in wages from the dress shop and had Federal income tax withholding of $1,000.

c. The Okumuras sold a small apartment building for $89,980 on November 15, 2014. The building was acquired in October 2008 for $200,000; cost recovery was $66,820.

d. The Okumuras received $3,000 in qualified dividends on various domestic corporation stocks that they own.

e. The Okumuras sold stock on November 5 for a $23,000 long-term capital gain and other stock on December 10 at a $2,000 short-term capital loss.

f. The Okumuras had the following itemized deductions: $12,895 unreimbursed medical expenses, $10,500 personal use real property taxes, $7,000 qualified residence interest, $1,500 of Glen's unreimbursed employee business expenses, $535 of investment-related expenses, $2,700 of state income taxes paid, and $1,061 of sales taxes from the sales tax table.

g. The Okumuras spent $3,000 on qualifying child care expenses during the year.

Compute the Okumuras' 2014 net tax payable or refund due. Also write a letter to the Okumuras describing how the sale of the apartment building affects their return.

Research Problems

THOMSON REUTERS
CHECKPOINT

Note: Solutions to Research Problems can be prepared by using the **Checkpoint**® **Student Edition** online research product, which is available to accompany this text. It is also possible to prepare solutions to the Research Problems by using tax research materials found in a standard tax library.

Communications

Research Problem 1. Sidney owns a professional football franchise. He has received an offer of $80 million for the franchise, all of the football equipment, the rights to concession receipts, the rights to a stadium lease, and the rights to all of the player contracts he owns. Most of the players have been with the team for a long time and have contracts that were signed several years ago. The contracts have been substantially depreciated. Sidney is concerned about potential § 1245 recapture when the contracts are sold. He has heard about "previously unrecaptured depreciation with respect to initial contracts" and would like to know more about it. Find a definition for that phrase and write an explanation of it.

Research Problem 2. Walter is both a real estate developer and the owner and manager of residential rental real estate. Walter is retiring and is going to sell both the land he is holding for future development and the rental properties he owns. Straight-line depreciation was used to depreciate the rental real estate. The rental properties will be sold at a substantial loss, and the development property will be sold at a substantial gain. What is the nature of these gains and losses?

Partial list of research aids:
§§ 1221 and 1231.
Zane R. Tollis, 65 TCM 1951, T.C.Memo. 1993–63.

Research Problem 3. Your client, Alternate Fuel, Inc. (a regular corporation), owns three sandwich shops in the Philadelphia area. In 2011, the year Alternate Fuel incorporated, it acquired land on the outskirts of Philadelphia with the hope of someday farming the land, to cultivate humanely harvested meat and grow organic fruits and vegetables to use in its sandwich shops. In 2013, Alternate Fuel drew up plans for the farm and began consulting with agricultural experts about the best locations for crops and the number of animals that could be sustained on the acreage. After reviewing those plans, Alternate Fuel's CEO decided that the plans are not currently financially feasible and would like to sell the land in 2014. The land has appreciated substantially in value and the company could use the cash infusion. Given that the land has not actually been used in the business, will any gain realized be categorized as a § 1231 gain or as a long-term capital gain?

Research Problem 4. In 2009, a taxpayer made leasehold improvements that were eligible for a 15-year MACRS life. Straight-line depreciation was taken on the improvements. Will these improvements be subject to either § 1245 or § 1250 depreciation recapture if they are eventually disposed of at a recognized gain? Explain.

Internet Activity

Use the tax resources of the Internet to address the following questions. Do not restrict your search to the Web, but include a review of newsgroups and general reference materials, practitioner sites and resources, primary sources of the tax law, chat rooms and discussion groups, and other opportunities.

Research Problem 5. Summarize tax planning strategies related to each of the following topics that are presented on the Internet by tax advisers looking for clients:
a. A strategy for maximizing gains that are eligible for the 0%/15%/20% alternative tax rate rather than the 25% rate.
b. A strategy for maximizing gains that are eligible for the 0%/15%/20% alternative tax rate rather than the 28% rate.

Research Problem 6. Search for the phrase "mortgage and real estate fraud" on the IRS's website (**www.irs.gov**). Read the articles you find and explain why this type of fraud is often unearthed by the IRS.

Research Problem 7. Find a state website that has tax forms and instructions for the state. Call that state "X." Find a discussion in those sources that reveals whether state X taxes gains from the sale of real estate that is located in state Y when the taxpayer is an individual and is a full-time resident of state X.

Dennis Flaherty/Photographer's Choice/Getty Images

part 6

ACCOUNTING PERIODS, ACCOUNTING METHODS, AND DEFERRED COMPENSATION

Part 6 provides a more comprehensive examination of the accounting periods and accounting methods that were introduced in Part 2. A discussion of special accounting methods is also included. Part 6 concludes with an analysis of the tax consequences of deferred compensation transactions.

LEARNING OBJECTIVES: *After completing Chapter 18, you should be able to:*

LO.1 State and explain the relevance of the accounting period concept, the different types of accounting periods, and the limitations on their use.

LO.2 Apply the cash method, accrual method, and hybrid method of accounting.

LO.3 Utilize the procedure for changing accounting methods.

LO.4 Determine when the installment method of accounting can be utilized and apply the related calculation techniques.

LO.5 Review and illustrate the alternative methods of accounting for long-term contracts (the completed contract method and the percentage of completion method), including the limitations on the use of the completed contract method.

LO.6 Recognize when accounting for inventories must occur, be aware of the types of costs that must be included in inventories, and apply the LIFO method.

LO.7 Identify tax planning opportunities related to accounting periods and accounting methods.

CHAPTER OUTLINE

© Tetra Images/Jupiter Images

THE BIG PICTURE   Tax Solutions for the Real World

ACCOUNTING PERIOD AND METHOD

Pearl, Inc. (a C corporation), Tweety, Inc. (an S corporation), and Belinda (an individual) are going to form a partnership (Silver Partnership). The ownership interests and tax years of the partners are as follows:

Partner	Partnership Interest	Tax Year Ends
Belinda	25%	December 31
Pearl, Inc.	35%	November 30
Tweety, Inc.	40%	June 30

The partnership will begin business on April 1, 2014. The partners have several issues they would like you to address.

- A potential conflict exists among the partners regarding when the tax year should end for Silver. Belinda and Pearl would like a year-end close to their own year-ends, while Tweety would like to have a June 30 year-end. Is this a decision Tweety can make because it owns more of the partnership than either of the other two partners? Is this a decision Belinda and Pearl can make because collectively they own more of the partnership than Tweety owns?
- Because Silver will begin business on April 1, 2014, will the first tax year be a "short" tax year or a "long" tax year? Will annualization of the net income of the partnership be required?
- How will the partners know when their share of Silver's net income or net loss should be reported on their respective income tax returns?
- Belinda is a cash basis taxpayer, and the other partners use the accrual method to report their incomes. What accounting method must be used to compute Belinda's share of the partnership income?

Read the chapter and formulate your response.

Income *(broadly conceived)*	$ xx,xxx
Less: Exclusions	(x,xxx)
Gross income	$xx,xxx

FORM 1040 (p. 1)

12	Business income or (loss). Attach Schedule C or C-EZ	

Less: Deductions for adjusted gross income	(x,xxx)
Adjusted gross income	$ xx,xxx
Less: The greater of total itemized deductions *or* the standard deduction	(x,xxx)
Personal and dependency exemptions	(x,xxx)
Taxable income	$ xx,xxx
Tax on taxable income *(see Tax Tables or Tax Rate Schedules)*	$ x,xxx
Less: Tax credits *(including income taxes withheld and prepaid)*	(xxx)
Tax due *(or refund)*	$ xxx

Tax practitioners must deal with the issue of *when* particular items of income and expense are recognized as well as the basic issue of *whether* the items are includible in taxable income. Earlier chapters discussed the types of income subject to tax (gross income and exclusions) and allowable deductions (the *whether* issue).[1] This chapter focuses on the related issue of the periods in which income and deductions are reported (the *when* issue). Generally, a taxpayer's income and deductions must be assigned to particular 12-month periods—calendar years or fiscal years.

Income and deductions are placed within particular years through the use of tax accounting methods. The basic accounting methods are the cash method, accrual method, and hybrid method. Other special purpose methods, such as the installment method and the methods used for long-term construction contracts, are available for specific circumstances or types of transactions.

Over the long run, the accounting period used by a taxpayer will not affect the aggregate amount of reported taxable income. However, taxable income for any particular year may vary significantly due to the use of a particular reporting period. Also, through the choice of accounting methods or accounting periods, it is possible to postpone the recognition of taxable income and to enjoy the benefits from deferring the related tax. This chapter discusses the taxpayer's alternatives for accounting periods and accounting methods.

LO.1

State and explain the relevance of the accounting period concept, the different types of accounting periods, and the limitations on their use.

18-1 ACCOUNTING PERIODS

Generally, an individual or a corporation that keeps adequate books and records may be permitted to elect a **fiscal year**, a 12-month period ending on the *last day* of a month other than December, for the **accounting period**. Otherwise, a *calendar year* must be used.[2] Frequently, corporations can satisfy the record-keeping requirements

---

[1]See Chapters 4, 5, and 6.

[2]§ 441(c) and Reg. § 1.441–1(b)(1)(ii).

and elect to use a fiscal year.[3] Often the fiscal year conforms to a natural business year (e.g., a summer resort's fiscal year may end on September 30, after the close of the season). Individuals seldom use a fiscal year because they do not maintain the necessary books and records and because complications can arise as a result of changes in the tax law (e.g., often the transition rules and effective dates differ for fiscal year taxpayers).

Generally, a taxable year may not exceed 12 calendar months. However, if certain requirements are met, a taxpayer may elect to use an annual period that varies from 52 to 53 weeks.[4] In that case, the year-end must be on the same day of the week (e.g., the Tuesday falling closest to September 30 or the last Tuesday in September). The day of the week selected for ending the year will depend upon business considerations. For example, a retail business that is not open on Sundays may end its tax year on a Sunday so that it can take an inventory without interrupting business operations.

> **Example 1**
>
> Wade is in the business of selling farm supplies. His natural business year terminates at the end of October with the completion of harvesting. At the end of the fiscal year, Wade must take an inventory, which is most easily accomplished on a Tuesday. Therefore, Wade could adopt a 52- to 53-week tax year ending on the Tuesday closest to October 31. If Wade selects this method, the year-end date may fall in the following month if that Tuesday is closer to October 31. The tax year ending in 2014 will contain 52 weeks beginning on Wednesday, October 30, 2013, and ending on Tuesday, October 28, 2014. The tax year ending in 2015 will have 53 weeks beginning on Wednesday, October 29, 2014, and ending on Tuesday, November 3, 2015.

18-1a Specific Provisions for Partnerships, S Corporations, and Personal Service Corporations

When a partner's tax year and the partnership's tax year differ, the partner will enjoy a deferral of income. This results because the partner reports his or her share of the partnership's income and deductions for the partnership's tax year ending within or with the partner's tax year.[5] For example, if the tax year of the partnership ends on January 31, a calendar year partner will not report partnership profits for the first 11 months of the partnership tax year until the following year. Therefore, partnerships are subject to special tax year requirements.

In general, the partnership tax year must be the same as the tax year of the majority interest partners. The **majority interest partners** are the partners who together own a greater-than-50 percent interest in the partnership capital and profits. If there are no majority interest partners, the partnership must adopt the same tax year as its principal partners. A **principal partner** is a partner with a 5 percent or more interest in the partnership capital or profits.[6]

> **Example 2**
>
> The RST Partnership is owned equally by Rose Corporation, Steve Corporation, and Tom. The partners have the following tax years:
>
> | | Partner's Tax Year Ending |
> | --- | --- |
> | Rose Corporation | June 30 |
> | Steve Corporation | June 30 |
> | Tom | December 31 |
>
> The partnership's tax year must end on June 30 because Rose Corporation and Steve Corporation together have a greater than 50% interest in the partnership. If Steve Corporation's as well as Tom's year ended on December 31, the partnership would be required to adopt a calendar year.

---

[3]Reg. § 1.441–1(e)(2).
[4]§ 441(f).

[5]Reg. § 1.706–1(a).
[6]§§ 706(b)(1)(B) and 706(b)(3).

If the principal partners do not all have the same tax year and no majority of partners have the same tax year, the partnership must use a year that results in the *least aggregate deferral* of income.[7] Under the **least aggregate deferral method**, the different tax years of the principal partners are tested to determine which produces the least aggregate deferral. This is calculated by first multiplying the combined percentages of the principal partners with the same tax year by the months of deferral for the test year. Once this is done for each set of principal partners with the same tax year, the resulting products are summed to produce the aggregate deferral. After the aggregate deferral is calculated for each of the test years, the test year with the smallest summation (the least aggregate deferral) is the tax year for the partnership.

THE BIG PICTURE

Example 3

Return to the facts of *The Big Picture* on p. 18-1. The Code and Regulations eliminate the need for the Silver partners to bargain among themselves over the tax year-end. The partnership's tax year must end on November 30 because using that year-end results in the least aggregate deferral of partnership income as demonstrated below.

		1	2	1 × 2
Test for Tax Year Ending December 31				
	Partner's Year-End	Profit Percentage	Months Income Deferred	Aggregate Months of Deferral
Belinda	12-31	25%	0	0
Pearl, Inc.	11-30	35%	11	3.85
Tweety, Inc.	6-30	40%	6	2.40
				6.25

		1	2	1 × 2
Test for Tax Year Ending November 30				
	Partner's Year-End	Profit Percentage	Months Income Deferred	Aggregate Months of Deferral
Belinda	12-31	25%	1	0.25
Pearl, Inc.	11-30	35%	0	0
Tweety, Inc.	6-30	40%	7	2.80
				3.05

		1	2	1 × 2
Test for Tax Year Ending June 30				
	Partner's Year-End	Profit Percentage	Months Income Deferred	Aggregate Months of Deferral
Belinda	12-31	25%	6	1.50
Pearl, Inc.	11-30	35%	5	1.75
Tweety, Inc.	6-30	40%	0	0
				3.25

---

[7]Reg. § 1.706–1(b)(3).

TAX IN THE NEWS The Federal Government's Fiscal Year

The U.S. government operates on a fiscal year ending September 30. Prior to 1976, the government's fiscal year ended each June 30. The change was made to allow Congress more time to arrive at a budget each year. The Federal fiscal year gives elected congressmen and congresswomen, who begin office in January, time to participate in the budget process for the next fiscal year. After they start office, the President submits the budget for the next year by the first Monday in February. Congress, including the newly elected officials, has until September 30 of that calendar year to approve the budget. Thus, the September 30 year-end is a natural business year during election years.

If a goal of financial reporting for the Federal government was to present a clear picture of the revenue, a fiscal year ending May 31 would be more appropriate. This is true because most individuals would have filed their income tax returns for the previous year, paid their taxes due, or received their refunds. With a fiscal year ending in September, much of the revenue collected in the current year is from taxpayers' income earned in the previous year, while much of the tax on current earnings will be collected in the following year. Moreover, refunds of prior years' taxes will be paid and will reduce revenue in the current year.

Source: Based on "Fiscal Year," Kimberly Amadeo, **useconomy** .about.com/od/fiscalpolicydefinitions/g/Fiscal_Year.htm.

© iStockphoto.com/Andrey Prokhorov

Generally, S corporations must adopt a calendar year.[8] However, partnerships and S corporations may *elect* an otherwise *impermissible year* under any of the following conditions:

- A business purpose for the year can be demonstrated.[9]
- The partnership's or S corporation's year results in a deferral of not more than three months' income, and the entity agrees to make required tax payments.[10]

Business Purpose

The only business purpose for a fiscal year the IRS has acknowledged is the need to conform the tax year to the natural business year of a company.[11] Generally, only seasonal businesses have a natural business year. For example, the natural business year for a department store may end on January 31, after Christmas returns have been processed and clearance sales have been completed.

Required Tax Payments

Under the required payments system, tax payments are due from a fiscal year partnership or S corporation by May 15 of each tax year.[12] The amount due is computed by applying the highest individual tax rate plus 1 percentage point to an estimate of the deferral period income. The deferral period runs from the close of the fiscal year to the end of the required year. Estimated income for this period is based on the average monthly earnings for the previous fiscal year. The amount due is reduced by the amount of required tax payments for the previous year.[13]

Example 4

Brown, Inc., an S corporation, timely elected a fiscal year ending September 30. Bob is the only shareholder and is a calendar year taxpayer. The "required" tax year ends on December 31, 2014, the major shareholder's year end, and the deferral period is the maximum of three months. For the fiscal year ending September 30, 2014, Brown earned $100,000. The required tax payment for the previous year was $5,000. The corporation must pay $5,150 by May 15, 2015, calculated as follows:

$$(\$100,000 \times {}^3/_{12} \times 40.6\%^*) - \$5,000 = \$5,150$$

*Maximum § 1 rate of 39.6% + 1%.

---

[8] §§ 1378(a) and (b).

[9] §§ 706(b)(1)(C) and 1378(b)(2).

[10] § 444. See Form 8716.

[11] Rev.Rul. 87–32, 1987–2 C.B. 396.

[12] §§ 444(c) and Reg. 1.7519–2T(a)(4)(ii). No payment is required if the calculated amount is $500 or less. See Form 8752.

[13] § 7519(b).

ETHICS & EQUITY   Who Benefits from the Change in Tax Year?

A public accounting sole practitioner has reached a breaking point. All of his clients use the calendar year to report income. Many of the clients are S corporations and partnerships. His workload the first four months of the year is so heavy that it is putting the quality of his work at risk. He is considering asking some of his S corporations and partnerships to switch to a fiscal year ending September 30. The accountant believes that he can convince the shareholders and partners to make the change. Although the shareholders and partners would be subject to the "required tax payments" rules, the accountant will sell the plan by promising better service. Evaluate the plan proposed by the accountant.

Personal Service Corporations

A **personal service corporation (PSC)** is a corporation whose shareholder-employees provide personal services (e.g., medical, dental, legal, accounting, engineering, actuarial, consulting, or performing arts). Generally, a PSC must use a calendar year.[14] However, a PSC can *elect* a fiscal year under any of the following conditions:

* A business purpose for the year can be demonstrated.
* The PSC year results in a deferral of not more than three months' income, the corporation pays the shareholder-employee's salary during the portion of the calendar year after the close of the fiscal year, and the salary for that period is at least proportionate to the shareholder-employee's salary received for the preceding fiscal year.[15]

Example 5

Nancy's corporation paid Nancy a salary of $120,000 during its fiscal year ending September 30, 2014. The corporation cannot satisfy the business purpose test for a fiscal year. The corporation can continue to use its fiscal year without any negative tax effects, provided Nancy receives at least $30,000 [(3 months/12 months) × $120,000] as salary during the period October 1 through December 31, 2014.

If the salary test is not satisfied, the PSC can retain the fiscal year, but the corporation's deduction for salary for its next fiscal year is limited to the following:

$$A + A(F/N)$$

Where A = Amount paid after the close of the fiscal year.

F = Number of months in the fiscal year minus number of months from the end of the fiscal year to the end of the ongoing calendar year.

N = Number of months from the end of the fiscal year to the end of the ongoing calendar year.

Example 6

Assume that the corporation in the previous example paid Nancy $10,000 of salary during the period October 1 through December 31, 2014. The deduction for Nancy's salary for the corporation's fiscal year ending September 30, 2015, is thus limited to $40,000 calculated as follows:

$$\$10,000 + \left[\$10,000\left(\frac{12-3}{3}\right)\right] = \$10,000 + \$30,000 = \$40,000$$

Salary payments in excess of the limitation are not allowed as an expense of the corporation for the year of the payment, but may be carried to a subsequent year and are subject to the limitation on deductions in the later year.

---

[14]§ 441(i).   [15]§§ 444 and 280H.

18-1b Selecting the Tax Year

A taxpayer elects to use a calendar year or, if eligible, a fiscal year by the timely filing of his or her initial tax return. For all subsequent tax years, the taxpayer must use this same period unless approval for change is obtained from the IRS.[16]

18-1c Changes in the Accounting Period

A taxpayer must obtain consent from the IRS before changing its tax year.[17] This power to approve or not to approve a change is significant in that it permits the IRS to issue authoritative administrative guidelines that must be met by taxpayers who want to change their accounting period. An application for permission to change tax years must be made on Form 1128, Application for Change in Accounting Period. The application must be filed on or before the fifteenth day of the second calendar month following the close of the short period that results from the change in accounting period.[18]

> **Example 7**
>
> Beginning in 2014, Gold Corporation, a calendar year taxpayer, would like to switch to a fiscal year ending March 31. The corporation must file Form 1128 by May 15, 2014.

IRS Requirements

The IRS will not grant permission for the change unless the taxpayer can establish a substantial business purpose for the request. One substantial business purpose is to change to a tax year that coincides with the *natural business year* (the completion of an annual business cycle). The IRS applies an objective gross receipts test to determine whether the entity has a natural business year. At least 25 percent of the entity's gross receipts for the 12-month period must be realized in the final two months of the 12-month period for three consecutive years.[19]

> **Example 8**
>
> A Virginia Beach motel had gross receipts as follows:
>
> | | 2012 | 2013 | 2014 |
> | --- | --- | --- | --- |
> | July–August receipts | $ 300,000 | $250,000 | $ 325,000 |
> | September 1–August 31 receipts | 1,000,000 | 900,000 | 1,250,000 |
> | Receipts for final 2 months divided by receipts for 12 months | 30.0% | 27.8% | 26.0% |
>
> Because it satisfies the natural business year test, the motel will be allowed to use a fiscal year ending August 31.

---

[16]Reg. §§ 1.441–1(b)(3) and 1.441–1(b)(4).

[17]§ 442. Under certain conditions, corporations are allowed to change tax years without obtaining IRS approval. See Reg. § 1.442–1(c)(1); Rev.Proc. 2006–45, 2006 C.B. 851.

[18]Reg. § 1.442–1(b)(1). In Example 7, the first period after the change in accounting period (January 1, 2014 through March 31, 2014) is less than a 12-month period and is referred to as a *short period*.

[19]Rev.Proc. 87–32, 1987–1 C.B. 131; Rev.Rul. 87–57, 1987–2 C.B. 117; and Rev.Proc. 2002–39, 2002–1 C.B. 1046.

The IRS usually establishes certain conditions that the taxpayer must accept if the approval for change is to be granted. In particular, if the taxpayer has a net operating loss (NOL) for the short period, the IRS requires that the loss be carried forward; the loss cannot be carried back to prior years.[20] Recall that NOLs are ordinarily carried back for 2 years and forward for 20 years (refer to Chapter 7). Denying a carryback is intended to prevent abuse of the change in tax year rules.

Example 9	Parrot Corporation, a manufacturer that is not an S Corporation, changed from a calendar year to a fiscal year ending September 30. The short-period return for the nine months ending September 30, 2014, reflected a $60,000 NOL. The corporation had taxable income for 2012 and 2013. As a condition for granting approval, the IRS requires Parrot to carry the loss forward rather than carrying the loss back to the two preceding years (the usual order for applying an NOL).

18-1d Taxable Periods of Less Than One Year

A **short taxable year** (or **short period**) is a period of less than 12 calendar months. A taxpayer may have a short year for (1) the first income tax return, (2) the final income tax return, or (3) a change in the tax year. If the short period results from a change in the taxpayer's annual accounting period, the taxable income for the period must be annualized. Due to the progressive tax rate structure, taxpayers could reap benefits from a short-period return if some adjustments were not required. Thus, the taxpayer is required to do the following:

1. Annualize the short-period income.

$$\text{Annualized income} = \text{Short-period income} \times \frac{12}{\substack{\text{Number of months} \\ \text{in the short period}}}$$

2. Compute the tax on the annualized income.
3. Convert the tax on the annualized income to a short-period tax.

$$\text{Short-period income} = \text{Tax on annualized income} \times \frac{\substack{\text{Number of months} \\ \text{in the short period}}}{12}$$

Example 10	Gray Corporation, a retailer that is not an S corporation, obtained permission to change from a calendar year to a fiscal year ending September 30, beginning in 2014. For the short period January 1 through September 30, 2014, the corporation's taxable income was $48,000. The relevant tax rates and the resultant short-period tax are as follows:

Amount of Taxable Income	Tax Rates
$1–$50,000	15% of taxable income
$50,001–$75,000	$7,500 plus 25% of taxable income in excess of $50,000

Calculation of Short-Period Tax

Annualized income
  ($48,000 × $^{12/9}$) = **$64,000**

Tax on annualized income
  $7,500 + .25 ($64,000 − $50,000) =
    $7,500 + $3,500 = **$11,000**

Short-period tax = ($11,000 × $^{9/12}$) = **$8,250**

Annualizing the income increased the tax by $1,050:

Tax with annualizing	$ 8,250
Tax without annualizing (.15 × $48,000)	(7,200)
	$ 1,050

[20]Rev.Proc. 2002–39, 2002–1 C.B. 1046.

Rather than annualize the short-period income, the taxpayer can (1) elect to calculate the tax for a 12-month period beginning on the first day of the short period and (2) convert the tax in (1) to a short-period tax as follows:[21]

$$\frac{\text{Taxable income for short period}}{\text{Taxable income for the 12-month period}} \times \text{Tax on the 12 months of income}$$

Example 11

Assume that Gray Corporation's taxable income for the calendar year 2014 was $60,000. The tax on the full 12 months of income would have been $10,000 [$7,500 + .25($60,000 − $50,000)]. The short-period tax would be $8,000 [($48,000/$60,000) × $10,000]. Thus, if the corporation utilized this option, the tax for the short period would be $8,000 (rather than $8,250, as calculated in Example 10).

The short year counts as a full year for purposes of the net operating carryback and carryforward.[22]

18-1e Mitigation of the Annual Accounting Period Concept

Several provisions in the Code are designed to give the taxpayer relief from the seemingly harsh results that may be produced by the combined effects of an arbitrary accounting period and a progressive rate structure. For example, except for the change in accounting period restriction explained earlier, under the NOL carryback and carryover rules, a loss in one year can be carried back and offset against taxable income for the preceding two years. Unused NOLs are then carried over for 20 years.[23] In addition, the Code provides special relief provisions for casualty losses pursuant to a disaster and for the reporting of insurance proceeds from destruction of crops.[24]

Farm Relief

Farmers and fishermen are often subject to wide fluctuations in income between years, some of which are due to the weather. Congress has provided these taxpayers with a special method of computing their tax on income from farming or fishing. In the high-income years, these taxpayers can elect to compute their tax on income from farming or fishing as though it were earned equally in the three previous years.[25] Thus, the tax on the farming or fishing income for the year is the sum of the additional tax that would have been due in the three previous years if one-third of the income had been earned in each of those years. This averaging system enables the taxpayer to avoid the higher marginal tax rates associated with a large amount of income received in one year.

The income pattern for farmers can also be disrupted by natural disasters that are covered by insurance. The disaster may occur and the **crop insurance proceeds** may be received in a year before the income from the crop would have been realized. Under these circumstances, the farmer can defer reporting the income until the year following the disaster. Similar relief is available when livestock must be sold on account of drought or other weather-related conditions.[26]

Restoration of Amounts Received under a Claim of Right

The court-made **claim of right doctrine** applies when the taxpayer receives property as income and treats it as his or her own but a dispute arises over the taxpayer's rights to the income.[27] According to the doctrine, the taxpayer must include the

---

[21]§§ 443(b)(1) and (2).

[22]Reg. § 1.172–4(a)(2).

[23]§ 172. Refer to Chapter 7.

[24]§§ 165(i) and 451(d). Refer to Chapter 7.

[25]§ 1301. The tax is calculated on Schedule J.

[26]Sections 451(d) and (e).

[27]*North American Consolidated Oil Co. v. Burnet*, 3 USTC ¶943, 11 AFTR 16, 52 S.Ct. 613 (USSC, 1932).

TAX IN THE NEWS   Executive Compensation Clawbacks

In recent years, there has been a public outcry over the compensation of executives. With many companies receiving taxpayer-funded bailouts, both taxpayers and shareholders have demanded that executives repay the excessive amounts to the corporation. If executives are required to repay a portion of their salaries and bonuses, an executive's marginal tax rate may be greater in the year the income was received than in the year of repayment. This appears to be a situation that § 1341 should address. However, when the original amount received was based on an existing contract, the compensation was received under the executive's actual rights and is not income received under a mere claim of right. Therefore, the amount of the "clawback" is not eligible for § 1341 treatment.

amount as income in the year of receipt. The rationale for the doctrine is that the Federal government cannot await the resolution of all disputes before exacting a tax. As a corollary to the doctrine, if the taxpayer is later required to repay the funds, generally, a deduction is allowed in the year of repayment.[28]

Example 12

In 2014, Pedro received a $5,000 bonus computed as a percentage of profits. In 2015, Pedro's employer determined that the 2014 profits had been incorrectly computed, and Pedro had to refund the $5,000 in 2015. Pedro was required to include the $5,000 in his 2014 gross income, but he can claim a $5,000 deduction in 2015.

In Example 12 the transactions were a wash; that is, the income and deduction were the same ($5,000). Suppose, however, that Pedro was in the 35 percent tax bracket in 2014 but in the 15 percent bracket in 2015. Without some relief provision, the mistake would be costly to Pedro. He paid $1,750 tax in 2014 (.35 × $5,000), but the deduction reduced his tax liability in 2015 by only $750 (.15 × $5,000). The Code does provide the needed relief in such cases. Under § 1341, when income that has been taxed under the claim of right doctrine must later be repaid, in effect, the taxpayer gets to apply to the deduction the tax rate of the year that will produce the greatest tax benefit. Thus, in Example 12, the repayment in 2015 would reduce Pedro's 2015 tax liability by the higher 2014 rate (.35) applied to the $5,000. However, relief is provided only in cases where the tax is significantly different; that is, when deduction for the amount previously included in income exceeds $3,000.

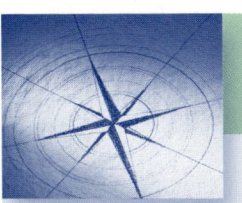

ETHICS & EQUITY   Special Tax Relief

A taxpayer who is required to report income in one year but must repay the income in a subsequent year is granted special tax relief. If the taxpayer is in a lower marginal tax bracket in the year the income is repaid than in the year it was received, the deduction reduces the tax for the year of repayment by using the higher tax rate that applied to the income when it was received.

In contrast, if a taxpayer takes a deduction in one year and receives a refund of the amount giving rise to the deduction in a subsequent year, the refund is taxed at the marginal tax rate in the year of refund. This is true even though the taxpayer's marginal tax rate in the year of receipt is higher than that in the year of the deduction.

Should both adjustments to income and adjustments to deductions receive the same tax relief? Or should neither situation be granted special relief?

---

[28]*U.S. v. Lewis,* 51–1 USTC ¶9211, 40 AFTR 258, 71 S.Ct. 522 (USSC, 1951).

18-2 ACCOUNTING METHODS

Accounting methods include overall methods such as cash or accrual. It also includes special accounting methods such as for farmers or prepaid income. These topics are explained in this section.

LO.2

Apply the cash method, accrual method, and hybrid method of accounting.

18-2a Permissible Methods

Section 446 requires the taxpayer to compute taxable income using the method of accounting regularly employed in keeping his or her books, provided the method clearly reflects income. The Code recognizes the following as generally permissible **accounting methods**:

- The cash receipts and disbursements method.
- The accrual method.
- A hybrid method (a combination of cash and accrual).

The Regulations refer to these alternatives as *overall methods* and add that the term *method of accounting* includes not only the taxpayer's overall method of accounting but also the accounting treatment of any item.[29]

Generally, any of the three methods of accounting may be used if the method is consistently employed and clearly reflects income. However, in most cases, the taxpayer is required to use the accrual method for sales and cost of goods sold if inventories are an income-producing factor to the business.[30] Other situations in which the accrual method is required are discussed later. Special methods are also permitted for installment sales, long-term construction contracts, and farmers.

A taxpayer who has more than one trade or business may use a different method of accounting for each trade or business activity. Furthermore, a taxpayer may use one method of accounting to determine income from a trade or business and use another method to compute nonbusiness items of income and deductions.[31]

> Linda operates a grocery store and owns stock and bonds. The sales and cost of goods sold from the grocery store must be computed by the accrual method because inventories are material. However, Linda can report her dividends and interest from the stocks and bonds under the cash method.

Example 13

The Code grants the IRS broad powers to determine whether the taxpayer's accounting method *clearly reflects income*. Thus, if the method employed does not clearly reflect income, the IRS has the power to prescribe the method to be used by the taxpayer.[32]

18-2b Cash Receipts and Disbursements Method—Cash Basis

Most individuals and many businesses use the cash basis to report income and deductions. The popularity of this method can largely be attributed to its simplicity and flexibility.

Under the **cash method**, income is not recognized until the taxpayer actually receives, or constructively receives, cash or its equivalent (e.g., the receipt of accounts receivable does not trigger income until collected). Cash is constructively received if it is available to the taxpayer.[33] Generally, a cash equivalent is anything

---

[29]Reg. § 1.446–1(a)(1).

[30]Reg. § 1.446–1(a)(4)(i). As discussed subsequently, as a matter of administrative convenience, the IRS will permit taxpayers to use the cash method even though inventory is a material income-producing factor if

average annual gross receipts are not more than $1 million for the most recent three-year period.

[31]§ 446(d) and Reg. § 1.446–1(c)(1)(iv)(b).

[32]§ 446(b).

[33]Reg. § 1.451–1(a). Refer to Chapter 4 for a discussion of constructive receipt.

TAX IN THE NEWS   Rescission Can Overcome Constructive Receipt

In many cases, a cash basis taxpayer has entered into an agreement to accept an amount at a certain date, but then decides it would be beneficial to defer the receipt of the payment until a subsequent year. If the payment is deferred when the funds are available, the taxpayer has a problem in that the payment may have actually or constructively been received when the payments became due.

The doctrine of rescission may be applied to remedy the taxpayer's problem. In a rescission, the original contract is set aside and the parties are returned to their former position (their position before the original transaction was undertaken). A new contract takes its place. When rescission occurs, the IRS ignores the original agreement and applies the tax law to the second agreement. However, the rescission and the return of any funds received must occur in the same tax year.

Source: Based on "Can Rescission Cure Constructive Receipt?" Robert W. Wood, *Tax Notes,* April 3, 2012.

with a fair market value, including any goods or services received in a barter transaction and a note receivable from a customer.

THE BIG PICTURE

Example 14

Return to the facts of *The Big Picture* on p. 4-1 in Chapter 4. Recall that Dr. Cliff Payne has opened a dental practice as a sole proprietorship and does not accept credit cards. In the second year of his business, he adopts a new policy of requiring that his patients either pay cash at the time the services are performed or give him a note receivable with interest at the market rate. Generally, the notes can be sold to the local banks for 95% of their face amount. At the end of the second year, Dr. Payne has $60,000 in notes receivable from patients. The notes receivable are a cash equivalent and have a fair market value of $57,000 ($60,000 × 95%). Therefore, Dr. Payne must include the $57,000 in his gross income for this year.

Deductions are generally permitted in the year of payment. Thus, year-end accounts payable and accrued expenses are not deducted in the determination of taxable income.

In many cases, a taxpayer using the cash method can choose the year in which a deduction is claimed simply by postponing or accelerating the payment of expenses. For fixed assets, however, the cash basis taxpayer claims deductions through depreciation or amortization, the same as an accrual basis taxpayer does. In addition, prepaid expenses must be capitalized and amortized if the life of the asset extends substantially beyond the end of the tax year.[34]

The Regulations have established a **one-year rule for prepaid expenses** that permits the taxpayer to deduct expenditures for rights that do not extend beyond the earlier of (1) 12 months after the first date on which the taxpayer realizes the right or (2) the end of the tax year following the year of payment. Both cash basis and accrual basis taxpayers are permitted to use the one-year rule.[35]

Restrictions on Use of the Cash Method

The cash method can distort income from a merchandising or manufacturing operation because the cost of goods sold is a function of when payments for the

---

[34]Reg. § 1.461–1(a)(1).

[35]Reg. § 1.263(a)–4(f). Refer to Chapter 6 for further discussion of the one-year rule.

Tax Accounting Methods as Well as Tax Rates in Foreign Countries Are Important Considerations

Global Tax Issues

When considering whether to conduct business in a foreign country, corporations must consider the accounting methods used to compute taxable income. Some countries have more generous depreciation and inventory valuation methods than others. Also, many countries permit expensing of start-up costs, whereas other countries (i.e., the United States) require capitalization.

goods were made rather than when they were sold. Thus, the Regulations require the accrual method to measure sales and cost of goods sold if inventories are material to the business. This prohibition on the use of the cash method is intended to ensure that annual income is clearly reflected.[36]

In addition, the following three types of taxpayers may not use the cash method (and must used the accrual method) for Federal income tax purposes regardless of whether inventories are material: (1) a corporation (other than an S corporation), (2) a partnership with a corporate partner (that is not an S corporation), and (3) a tax shelter. This accrual basis requirement has three exceptions:[37]

- A farming business.
- A qualified personal service corporation (a corporation that performs services in health, law, engineering, architecture, accounting, actuarial science, performing arts, or consulting and whose employees own substantially all of the stock).
- An entity that is not a tax shelter whose average annual gross receipts for the most recent three-year period are $5 million or less.

As a matter of administrative convenience, the IRS will permit any entity with average annual gross receipts of not more than $1 million for the most recent three-year period to use a modified form of the cash method even if the taxpayer is buying and selling inventory. Sales can be reported on the cash method, but the cost of the inventory is deductible only in the year of sale or in the year the taxpayer actually pays for the inventoriable items, whichever is later.

The IRS allows another exception. Companies whose principal business activity (the activity producing the largest percentage of gross receipts) does not include sales of goods, manufacturing, mining, and certain publishing activities and whose average annual gross receipts are greater than $1 million but are not more than $10 million for the most recent three-year period may use the cash method. However, under the $10 million exception, inventory on hand at the end of the tax year cannot be deducted until the inventory is sold (i.e., it must be capitalized). As already noted, C corporations, partnerships, and tax shelters must use the accrual method and, therefore, are not eligible for this exception unless they meet the exception noted earlier where average annual gross receipts for the prior three-year period do not exceed $5 million. The major beneficiaries of the $10 million exception are small construction companies and small service businesses that sell some goods in conjunction with the services provided.[38]

---

[36] Reg. § 1.446–1(a)(4)(i).

[37] §§ 448(a) and 448(b). For this purpose, the hybrid method of accounting is considered the same as the cash method.

[38] Rev.Proc. 2001–10, 2001–1 C.B. 272, and Rev.Proc. 2002–28, 2002–1 C.B. 815.

Special Rules for Small Farmers

The general tax accounting rules contain several exceptions specifically addressed to farmers. Athough inventories are material to farming operations and the accrual method would appear to be required, the IRS long ago created an exception to the general rule that allows small farmers to use the cash method of accounting.[39] The purpose of the exception is to relieve the small farmer from the bookkeeping burden of accrual accounting. Generally, this exception applies to unincorporated farms and closely held farming corporations with gross receipts for the year of less than $25 million.[40]

Nevertheless, cash method farmers must capitalize their costs of raising trees that have a preproduction period of more than two years.[41] For example, an apple farmer generally must capitalize the costs of raising the trees until they produce apples in merchantable quantities. However, to simplify the farmer's tax accounting, the cash method farmer is given an option: the preproduction cost of the trees can be expensed if the taxpayer elects to use the alternative depreciation system (refer to Chapter 8) for all of the farming assets.

Farmers who produce crops that take more than a year from planting to harvesting (e.g., pineapples) can elect to use the crop method to report the income. Under the **crop method**, the costs of raising the crop are capitalized as those costs are incurred and then deducted in the year the income from the crop is realized.[42] This method is analogous to the completed contract method used by contractors (discussed later in this chapter).

Generally, a cash basis farmer must capitalize the purchase price of an animal, whether it is acquired for sale or for breeding. However, the cost of raising the animal can be expensed.[43]

18-2c Accrual Method

The tax rules governing when an accrual method taxpayer reports income or claims deductions include an "all events test." The timing rules for deductions also include an "economic performance" requirement. These timing rules for income and deductions of accrual method taxpayers are explained below.

All Events Test for Income

Under the **accrual method**, an item is generally included in gross income for the year in which it is earned, regardless of when the income is collected. An item of income is earned when (1) all of the events have occurred to fix the taxpayer's right to receive the income and (2) the amount of income (the amount the taxpayer has a right to receive) can be determined with reasonable accuracy.[44]

Example 15

Andre Corporation, a calendar year taxpayer that uses the accrual basis of accounting, was to receive a bonus equal to 6% of Blue Corporation's net income for its fiscal year ending each June 30. For the fiscal year ending June 30, 2014, Blue Corporation had net income of $240,000, and for the six months ending December 31, 2014, the corporation's net income was $150,000. Andre Corporation will report $14,400 (.06 × $240,000) for 2014 because its right to the amount became fixed when Blue Corporation's year closed. However, Andre Corporation would not accrue income based on the corporation's profits for the last six months of 2014 because its right to the income does not accrue until the close of the corporation's tax year.

An accrual basis taxpayer's amount of income and the tax year the income is recognized are based on its right to receive the income. Thus, unlike in the case of a cash basis taxpayer, the fair market value of a receivable is irrelevant.

---

[39]Reg. § 1.61–4.
[40]See §§ 447(c) and 464.
[41]§ 263A(d).
[42]Reg. §§ 1.61–4 and 1.162–12(a).

[43]Reg. § 1.162–12(a).
[44]Reg. § 1.451–1(a). Refer to Chapter 4 for further discussion of the accrual basis.

TAX IN THE NEWS — Financial and Tax Accounting under Uncertainty

According to the Financial Accounting Standards Board's Accounting Standards Codification Project, § 605–10–25–4 follows the all events test used in tax accounting to determine when revenue is to be recognized. However, according to the financial accounting rules, when there is uncertainty as to whether the total selling price will be collected, the reporting entity may use the cost recovery method of reporting the income; that is, any amount collected from the sale will first be treated as a recovery of the cost of

the item sold, and gain is not recognized until the seller has recovered its total cost.

The tax accounting rules generally do not permit this cost recovery method. If uncertainty exists as to collectability of the selling price, the total selling price must nevertheless be included in gross income and the cost of the goods reduces the selling price in arriving at the gross profit. Any adjustment for collectability must run the rigors of qualifying for a bad debt deduction, which, in many cases, means that the deduction is recognized in a year subsequent to the year of sale.

© iStockphoto.com/Andrey Prokhorov

Example 16

Marcey Corporation, an accrual basis taxpayer, has provided services to clients and has the right to receive $60,000. The clients have signed notes receivable to Marcey that have a fair market value of $57,000. The corporation must include $60,000, the amount it has the right to receive, in its gross income, rather than the fair market value of the notes of $57,000.

If an accrual basis taxpayer receives prepayment of income for services that will not be fully earned by the end of the following year, the unearned amount at the end of the year of receipt must be allocated to the following year. (See Chapter 4.)

Example 17

Troy Corporation sells computers and two-year service contracts on the computers. On November 1, 2014, Troy Corporation sold a 24-month service contract and received $240. The corporation recognizes $20 gross income in 2014 ($240 $\times {}^{2}/_{24}$) and $220 ($240 − $20) in 2015.

However, prepaid income rental income and prepaid interest income must be recognized in the year of receipt and may not be deferred.[45]

In a situation where the accrual basis taxpayer's right to income is being contested and the income has not yet been collected, generally, no income is recognized until the dispute has been settled.[46] Before the settlement, "all of the events have not occurred that fix the right to receive the income."

All Events and Economic Performance Tests for Deductions

A three-part test is applied to determine when an accrual basis taxpayer considers an event as either an expense or a capital expenditure. The three parts are (1) **all events test**, (2) amount determinable with reasonable accuracy, and (3) **economic performance test**.[47]

As to when economic performance is met, that depends on the nature of the liability. For example, if an accrual method taxpayer owes money to another company that provided services to it, economic performance is met as the services are provided. Concept Summary 18.1 lists common types of liabilities covered by the economic performance Regulations (Reg. §1.461–4) and when economic performance is met for each liability.

One common liability illustrated in Example 18 is where a taxpayer has a liability because another party provided services.

[45]Rev.Proc. 2004–34, 2004–1 C.B. 991.

[46]*Burnet v. Sanford & Brooks Co.*, 2 USTC ¶636, 9 AFTR 603, 51 S.Ct. 150 (USSC, 1931).

[47]§ 461(h)(4).

CONCEPT SUMMARY 18.1

Accruals Under the Economic Performance Test

Event	Example	When Economic Performance Is Satisfied
The taxpayer's use of the owner's property	Rent	Ratably over the period used
Specific property provided to the taxpayer	A company's office supplies are purchased	When the taxpayer receives the supplies
Specific services provided to the taxpayer	The taxpayer contracts for repairs to be made to its equipment	When the repairs are made
Services to be provided for a specific time period	The taxpayer purchases a service contract, such as for cleaning services	Ratably over the contract period
Property or services provided by the taxpayer	A manufacturer contracts to customize a customer's van	When the manufacturer incurs costs under the contract
Rebates	Manufacturer rebates based on quantity of purchases	When the rebate is paid
Tort claims	Customers are awarded claims for harm caused by the taxpayer's product	When payment is made to the injured party; not eligible for the recurring item exception
State income tax	Taxes due when filing the return	When payment is made

© iStockphoto.com/Andrey Prokhorov

Example 18   An accrual basis calendar year taxpayer, JAB, Inc., promoted a boxing match held in the company's arena on December 31, 2014. CLN, Inc., had contracted to clean the arena for $5,000, but did not actually perform the work until January 1, 2015. JAB, Inc., did not pay the $5,000 until 2016. Although financial accounting rules would require JAB, Inc., to accrue the $5,000 cleaning expense in 2014 to match the revenues from the fight, the economic performance test was not satisfied until 2015, when CLN, Inc., performed the service. Thus, JAB, Inc., must deduct the expense in 2015.

If the taxpayer is obligated to provide property or services, economic performance occurs in the year the taxpayer provides the property or services, as illustrated in Example 19.

TAX IN THE NEWS   Payment Is Not Economic Performance

In recent pronouncements, the IRS has reiterated the point that when an accrual basis taxpayer has contracted to receive future services whose cost is deductible, the time for the deduction is when economic performance is satisfied. Moreover, economic performance can occur before or after the taxpayer pays for the services. Generally, economic performance is satisfied when the other party provides the services. If the taxpayer pays for the services before they are provided, the taxpayer has acquired an asset (prepaid expense). The deduction for the cost of the asset is not allowed until the services are actually received, unless the requirements for the recurring item exception are satisfied.

© iStockphoto.com/Andrey Prokhorov

FINANCIAL DISCLOSURE INSIGHTS   Tax Deferrals from Reserves

The tax law generally applies the economic performance test in determining when an expense is deductible. Accordingly, the use of reserves for financial accounting purposes does not carry over to the tax return. When a business creates a reserve, for example, to account for warranty obligations to customers or vacation pay for employees, book expenses are allowed, but the corresponding tax deduction usually is delayed until an expenditure is actually incurred. The temporary book-tax difference typically creates or adds to a deferred tax asset on the entity's balance sheet.

Deferred tax assets and liabilities are classified as *current* or *noncurrent* for balance sheet purposes. This classification is determined by the following:

- The nature of the underlying asset (e.g., deferral of a bad debt relates to an account receivable, typically a current asset).
- Any knowledge by the entity as to when the required expenditure will occur (e.g., as to the timing and amounts of a legal settlement or award).

For instance, suppose a software developer sells a program to a customer and agrees to provide free annual updates for the next three years. If the revenue from the sale is included in gross income in the year of sale, for financial accounting purposes, a reserve for the anticipated costs of the updates should be deducted and a reserve should be created in the year of the sale. In the simplest case, one-third of the costs associated with the contract are deductible in the year the contract is sold and used by the customer. Of the remaining warranty costs, one-half generates a current deferred tax asset (the costs will actually be incurred within the next tax year), and one-half generates a noncurrent deferred tax asset (for the third contract year).

Current versions of the related IFRS provisions eliminate the classification of deferred tax assets as current or noncurrent. Under IAS 1, all deferred tax assets are deemed to be noncurrent.

Example 19

Copper Corporation, an accrual basis taxpayer, is in the strip mining business. According to the contract with the landowner, the company must reclaim the land. The estimated cost of reclaiming land mined in 2014 was $500,000, but the land was not actually reclaimed until 2016. The all events test was satisfied in 2014. The obligation existed, and the amount of the liability could be determined with reasonable accuracy in 2014. However, the economic performance test was not satisfied until 2016 when Copper incurred costs to reclaim the land (it performed the work). Therefore, the deduction is not allowed until 2016.[48]

The economic performance test is waived, and thus year-end accruals can be deducted if all of the following conditions (i.e., the *recurring item exception*) are met:

- The obligation exists, and the amount of the liability can be reasonably estimated.
- Economic performance occurs within a reasonable period (but not later than $8\frac{1}{2}$ months after the close of the taxable year).
- The item is recurring in nature and is treated consistently by the taxpayer.
- Either the accrued item is not material or accruing it results in a better matching of revenues and expenses.

Example 20

Green Corporation often sells goods that are on hand but cannot be shipped for another week. The all events test for the sale are satisfied; therefore, the revenue is recognized although the goods have not been shipped at year-end. Green Corporation is obligated to pay shipping costs. Although the company's obligation for shipping costs can be determined with reasonable accuracy, economic performance is not satisfied until Green (or its agent) actually delivers the goods. However, accruing shipping costs on sold items will better match expenses with revenues for the period. Therefore, the company should be allowed to accrue the shipping costs on items sold but not shipped at year-end.

The economic performance test as set forth in the Code does not address all possible accrued expenses. That is, in some cases, the taxpayer incurs cost even

---

[48]See § 468 for an elective method for reporting reclamation costs.

though no property or services were received. In these instances, according to the Regulations, economic performance generally is not satisfied until the liability is paid. The following liabilities are cases in which payment is generally the only means of satisfying economic performance:[49]

1. Workers' compensation.
2. Torts.
3. Breach of contract.
4. Violation of law.
5. Rebates and refunds.
6. Awards, prizes, and jackpots.
7. Insurance, warranty, and service contracts.[50]
8. Taxes.

Example 21

Yellow Corporation sold defective merchandise that injured a customer. Yellow admitted liability in 2014, but did not pay the claim until January 2015. The customer's tort claim cannot be deducted until it is paid.

However, items (5) through (8) above are eligible for the aforementioned recurring item exception.

Example 22

Pelican Corporation filed its 2014 state income tax return in March 2015. At the time the return was filed, Pelican was required to pay an additional $5,000. The state taxes are eligible for the recurring item exception. Thus, the $5,000 of state income taxes can be deducted on the corporation's 2014 Federal tax return. The deduction is allowed because all of the events had occurred to fix the liability as of the end of 2014, the payment was made within 8½ months after the end of the tax year, the item is recurring in nature, and allowing the deduction in 2014 produces a good matching of revenues and expenses.

Reserves

Generally, the all events and economic performance tests will prevent the use of reserves (e.g., for product warranty expense) frequently used in financial accounting to match expenses with revenues. However, small banks are allowed to use a bad debt reserve.[51] Furthermore, an accrual basis taxpayer in a service business is permitted not to accrue revenue that appears uncollectible based on experience. In effect, this approach indirectly allows a reserve.[52]

18-2d Hybrid Method

A **hybrid method** of accounting involves the use of more than one method. For example, a taxpayer who uses the accrual basis to report sales and cost of goods sold but uses the cash basis to report other items of income and expense is employing a hybrid method. The Code permits the use of a hybrid method provided the taxpayer's income is clearly reflected.[53] A taxpayer who uses the accrual method for business expenses must also use the accrual method for business income.

Example 23

The Loyal Pet Clinic boards animals, provides veterinarian services, and sells pet supplies and medicines. The clinic's gross receipts are approximately $4 million per year, and 40 percent of the receipts are from sales of pet supplies. Under a hybrid method of accounting, the clinic would use the accrual method for the sales of supplies because inventories are an income-producing factor. However, the services income may be reported using the cash method.

---

[49]Reg. §§ 1.461–4(g)(2)–(6) and 1.461–5(c).

[50]This item applies to contracts the taxpayer enters into for his or her own protection, rather than the taxpayer's liability as insurer, warrantor, or service provider.

[51]§ 585.

[52]§ 448(d)(5).

[53]§ 446(c).

18-2e Change of Method

The taxpayer, in effect, makes an election to use a particular accounting method when an initial tax return is filed using that method. If a subsequent change in method is desired, the taxpayer must obtain the permission of the IRS. The request for change is made on Form 3115, Application for Change in Accounting Method. Generally, the form must be filed within the taxable year of the desired change.[54]

LO.3

Utilize the procedure for changing accounting methods.

As previously mentioned, the term *accounting method* encompasses not only the overall accounting method used by the taxpayer (the cash or accrual method) but also the treatment of any material item of income or deduction.[55] Thus, a change in the method of deducting property taxes from a cash basis to an accrual basis that results in a deduction for taxes in a different year constitutes a change in an accounting method. Another example of an accounting method change is a change involving the method or basis used in the valuation of inventories. However, a change in treatment resulting from a change in the underlying facts does not constitute a change in the taxpayer's method of accounting.[56] For example, a change in employment contracts so that an employee accrues one day of vacation pay for each month of service rather than 12 days of vacation pay for a full year of service is a change in the underlying facts and is therefore not an accounting method change.

Correction of an Error

A change in accounting method should be distinguished from the *correction of an error*. The taxpayer can correct an error (by filing amended returns) without permission, and the IRS can simply adjust the taxpayer's liability if an error is discovered on audit of the return. Some examples of errors are incorrect postings, errors in the calculation of tax liability or tax credits, deductions of business expense items that are actually personal, and omissions of income and deductions.[57] Unless the taxpayer or the IRS corrects the error within the statute of limitations, the taxpayer's total lifetime taxable income will be overstated or understated by the amount of the error.

Change from an Incorrect Method

An *incorrect accounting method* is the consistent (for at least two years) use of an incorrect rule to report an item of income or expense. The incorrect accounting method generally will not affect the taxpayer's total lifetime income (unlike the error). That is, an incorrect method has a self-balancing mechanism. For example, deducting freight on inventory in the year the goods are purchased, rather than when the inventory is sold, is an incorrect accounting method. The total cost of goods sold over the life of the business is not affected, but the year-to-year income is incorrect.[58]

If a taxpayer is employing an incorrect method of accounting, permission must be obtained from the IRS to change to a correct method. An incorrect method is not treated as a mechanical error that can be corrected by merely filing an amended tax return.

The tax return preparer as well as the taxpayer will be subject to penalties if the tax return is prepared using an incorrect method of accounting and permission for a change to a correct method has not been requested.[59]

Net Adjustments Due to Change in Accounting Method

In the year of a change in accounting method, some items of income and expense may have to be adjusted to prevent the change from distorting taxable income.

---

[54]See Rev.Proc. 2011–14, 2011–4 I.R.B. 330, which permits certain changes in methods requested with a timely filed return.

[55]Reg. § 1.446–1(a)(1).

[56]Reg. § 1.446–1(e)(2)(ii).

[57]Reg. § 1.446–1(e)(2)(ii)(b).

[58]But see *Korn Industries v. U.S.*, 76–1 USTC ¶9354, 37 AFTR 2d 76–1228, 532 F.2d 1352 (Ct.Cls., 1976).

[59]§ 446(f). See *South-Western Federal Taxation: Corporations, Partnerships, Estates, & Trusts*, Chapter 17.

Example 24

In 2014, White Corporation, with consent from the IRS, switched from the cash to the accrual basis for reporting sales and cost of goods sold. The corporation's accrual basis gross profit for the year was computed as follows:

Sales		$100,000
Beginning inventory	$ 15,000	
Purchases	60,000	
Less: Ending inventory	(10,000)	
Cost of goods sold		(65,000)
Gross profit		$ 35,000

At the end of the previous year, White Corporation had accounts receivable of $25,000 and accounts payable for merchandise of $34,000. The accounts receivable from the previous year in the amount of $25,000 were never included in gross income because White was on the cash basis and did not recognize the uncollected receivables. In the current year, the $25,000 was not included in the accrual basis sales because the sales were made in a prior year. Therefore, a $25,000 adjustment to income is required to prevent the receivables from being omitted from income.

The corollary of the failure to recognize a prior year's receivables is the failure to recognize a prior year's accounts payable. The beginning of the year's accounts payable were not included in the current or prior year's purchases. Thus, a deduction for the $34,000 was not taken in either year and is therefore included as an adjustment to income for the period of change.

An adjustment is also required to reflect the $15,000 beginning inventory that White deducted (due to the use of a cash method of accounting) in the previous year. In this instance, the cost of goods sold during the year of change was increased by the beginning inventory and resulted in a double deduction.

The net adjustment due to the change in accounting method is computed as follows:

Beginning inventory (deducted in prior and current year)	$ 15,000
Beginning accounts receivable (omitted from income)	25,000
Beginning accounts payable (omitted from deductions)	(34,000)
Net increase in taxable income	$ 6,000

Disposition of the Net Adjustment

Required changes in accounting methods can result from an IRS examination. The IRS usually will examine all years that are open under the statute of limitations. Generally, this means that the three preceding years are examined. The IRS will not require a change unless the net adjustment is positive. That adjustment generally must be included in gross income for the year of the change. Additional tax and interest on the tax will be due. However, if the adjustment is greater than $3,000, the taxpayer can elect to calculate the tax by spreading the adjustment over one or more previous years.[60] The election is beneficial if the taxpayer's marginal tax rate for the prior years is lower than the marginal tax rate for the year of the change.

To encourage taxpayers to *voluntarily* change (rather than wait for an IRS audit resulting in a required change) from incorrect methods and to facilitate changes from one correct method to another, the IRS generally allows the taxpayer to spread a positive adjustment into future years. One-fourth of the adjustment is applied to the year of the change, and one-fourth of the adjustment is applied to each of the next three taxable years. A negative adjustment can be deducted in the year of the change.[61]

---

[60]§ 481(b). See also Notice 98–31, 1998–1 C.B. 1165.

[61]Rev.Proc. 2002–9, 2002–1 C.B. 327, and Rev.Proc. 2002–18, 2002–1 C.B. 696.

Example 25

White Corporation in Example 24 voluntarily changed from an incorrect method (the cash basis was incorrect because inventories were material to the business) to a correct method. The company must add $1,500 ($1/4 \times \$6,000$ positive adjustment) to its 2014, 2015, 2016, and 2017 income.

ETHICS & EQUITY Change in Accounting Method

The IRS faces a difficult choice when it deals with taxpayers who use incorrect accounting methods. On the one hand, the taxpayer who has used an incorrect accounting method may be just as culpable as a person who has omitted income or taken an improper deduction. On the other hand, it is often difficult to discover that a taxpayer is using an incorrect accounting method. Therefore, the IRS relies to some extent on self-reporting by taxpayers. The Service encourages voluntary changes in incorrect accounting methods by waiving penalties for underpayment of prior years' taxes and permitting the taxpayer, in effect, to pay the related taxes over a four-year period. Is this equitable treatment?

© iStockphoto.com/LdF

18-3 SPECIAL ACCOUNTING METHODS

Generally, accrual basis taxpayers recognize income when goods are sold. Cash basis taxpayers generally recognize income from a sale on the collection of cash from the customer. The tax law provides special accounting methods for certain installment sales and long-term contracts. These special methods were enacted, in part, to ensure that the tax will be due when the taxpayer is best able to pay the tax.

LO.4

Determine when the installment method of accounting can be utilized and apply the related calculation techniques.

18-3a Installment Method

Under the general rule for computing the gain or loss from the sale of property, the taxpayer recognizes the entire amount of gain or loss upon the sale or other disposition of the property.

Example 26

Mark sells property to Fran for $10,000 cash plus Fran's note (fair market value and face amount of $90,000). Mark's basis for the property was $15,000. Gain or loss is computed under either the cash or accrual basis as follows:

Selling price	
Cash down payment	$ 10,000
Note receivable	90,000
	$100,000
Basis in the property	(15,000)
Realized gain	$ 85,000

In Example 26, the general rule for recognizing gain or loss requires Mark to pay a substantial amount of tax on the gain in the year of sale even though he received only $10,000 cash. Congress enacted the installment sales provisions to prevent this sort of hardship by allowing the taxpayer to spread the gain from installment sales over the collection period, when the taxpayer is best able to pay the tax. The installment method is a very important planning tool because of the tax deferral possibilities.

TAX IN THE NEWS   Seller Financing Is Popular in Troubled Times

As financial institutions are applying stringent loan requirements and real estate investors are anxious to sell, seller financing is becoming more common. In other words, instead of the financing being done by a financial institution, the seller of the property finances the transaction and receives a higher interest rate than could be earned from a bank. The seller receives a down payment and a mortgage for the balance on the contract. If the buyer turns out to be unable to pay, the seller regains ownership of the property. Thus, even under this worst-case scenario, the seller is still in a better position than if the original sale had not been made.

© iStockphoto.com/Andrey Prokhorov

Eligibility and Calculations

The **installment method** applies to *gains* (but not losses) from the sale of property by a taxpayer who will receive at least one payment *after* the year of sale. However, the installment method cannot be used for the following:[62]

- Gains on property held for sale in the ordinary course of business.
- Depreciation recapture under § 1245 or § 1250.
- Gains on stocks or securities traded on an established market.

As an exception to the first item, the installment method may be used to report gains from sales of the following:[63]

- Time-share units (e.g., the right to use real property for two weeks each year).
- Residential lots (if the seller is not to make any improvements).
- Any property used or produced in the trade or business of farming.

The Nonelective Aspect

As a general rule, eligible sales *must* be reported by the installment method.[64] A special election is required to report the gain by any other method of accounting (see the discussion in a subsequent section of this chapter).

Computing the Gain for Each Year Payments Are Received

The gain reported on each sale is computed using the following formula:

$$\frac{\text{Total gain}}{\text{Contract price}} \times \text{Payments received during the tax year} =$$

$$\text{Gain recognized in the tax year}$$

The taxpayer must compute each variable as follows:

1. *Total gain* is the selling price reduced by selling expenses and the adjusted basis of the property. The selling price is the total consideration received by the seller, including notes receivable from the buyer and the seller's liabilities assumed by the buyer.
2. *Contract price* is the selling price less the seller's liabilities that are assumed by the buyer. Generally, the contract price is the amount, other than interest, the seller will receive from the purchaser.
3. *Payments received* are the collections on the contract price received in each tax year. This generally is equal to the cash received less the interest income collected for the period. If the buyer pays any of the seller's expenses, the seller regards the amount paid as a payment received.[65]

---

[62]§§ 453(b), (i), and (l).
[63]§ 453(l)(2).

[64]§ 453(a).
[65]The gain is reported on Form 6252.

The seller is not a dealer, and the facts are as follows:

Example 27

Sales price		
Cash down payment	$ 1,000	
Seller's mortgage assumed	3,000	
Notes payable to the seller	13,000	$ 17,000
Selling expenses		(500)
Seller's basis		(10,000)
Total gain		$ 6,500

The contract price is $14,000 ($17,000 − $3,000). Assuming that the $1,000 is the only payment in the year of sale, the recognized gain in that year is computed as follows:

$$\frac{\$6{,}500 \text{ (total gain)}}{\$14{,}000 \text{ (contract price)}} \times \$1{,}000 = \$464 \text{ (gain recognized in year of sale)}$$

If the sum of the seller's basis and selling expenses is less than the liabilities assumed by the buyer, the difference must be added to the contract price and to the payments (treated as *deemed payments*) received in the year of sale.[66] This adjustment to the contract price is required so that the ratio of total gain to contract price will not be greater than one. The adjustment also accelerates the reporting of income from the deemed payments.

Assume the same facts as in Example 27, except that the seller's basis in the property is only $2,000. The total gain, therefore, is $14,500 [$17,000 − ($2,000 + $500)]. Payments in the year of sale are $1,500 and are calculated as follows:

Example 28

Down payment	$1,000
Excess of mortgage assumed over seller's basis and selling expenses ($3,000 − $2,000 − $500)	500
	$1,500

The contract price is $14,500 [$17,000 (selling price) − $3,000 (seller's mortgage assumed) + $500 (excess of mortgage assumed over seller's basis and selling expenses)]. The gain recognized in the year of sale is computed as follows:

$$\frac{\$14{,}500 \text{ (total gain)}}{\$14{,}500 \text{ (contract price)}} \times \$1{,}500 \text{ deemed payment received} =$$

$$\$1{,}500 \text{ (gain recognized in year of sale)}$$

In subsequent years, all amounts the seller collects on the note principal ($13,000) will be recognized gain ($13,000 × 100%).

As previously discussed, gains attributable to ordinary income recapture under §§ 1245 and 1250 are *ineligible* for installment reporting. Therefore, the § 1245 or § 1250 gain realized must be recognized in the year of sale, and the installment sale gain is the remaining gain.

Olaf sold an apartment building for $50,000 cash and a $75,000 note due in two years. Olaf's cost of the property was $90,000, and he had deducted depreciation of $65,000, $40,000 of which was in excess of what the straight-line amount would have been. Thus, the basis in the property was $25,000 ($90,000 − $65,000), and he recaptured $40,000 ordinary income under § 1250.

Example 29

---

[66]Temp.Reg. § 15a.453–1(b)(3)(i).

Olaf's realized gain is $100,000 ($125,000 − $25,000), and the $40,000 recapture must be recognized in the year of sale. Of the $60,000 remaining § 1231 gain, $24,000 must be recognized in the year of sale:

$$\frac{\text{§ 1231 gain}}{\text{Contract price}} \times \text{Payment received} = \frac{\$125,000 - \$25,000 - \$40,000}{\$125,000} \times \$50,000$$

$$= \frac{\$60,000}{\$125,000} \times \$50,000 = \$24,000$$

The remaining realized gain of $36,000 ($60,000 − $24,000) will be recognized as the $75,000 note is collected.

Character of the Gain on Depreciable Real Estate

As discussed in Chapter 17, an individual's recognized gain from the sale of depreciable real estate may be subject to a 25 percent tax rate. The gain to the extent of straight-line depreciation taken is subject to the special rate and is referred to as "unrecaptured § 1250 gain." The recognized gain in excess of the depreciation is a § 1231 gain eligible for the 15%/20% rate. Under the installment sale rules, when the sale results in both 25% gain and 15%/20% gain, the 25% gain is reported first and then the 15%/20% gain.

Example 30

Continuing with the facts in Example 29, the realized gain was $100,000, of which $40,000 was § 1250 ordinary income. The straight-line depreciation would have been $25,000 (total depreciation of $65,000 less excess depreciation of $40,000). Therefore, the unrecaptured § 1250 gain is $25,000. The recognized installment gain in the year of sale of $24,000 was less than the unrecaptured § 1250 gain of $25,000. Therefore, the $24,000 recognized gain in the year of sale is subject to the 25% tax rate.

Imputed Interest

If a deferred payment contract for the sale of property with a selling price greater than $3,000 does not contain a reasonable interest rate, a reasonable rate is imputed.[67] The imputing of interest effectively restates the selling price of the property to equal the sum of the payments at the date of the sale and the discounted present value of the future payments. The difference between the present value of a future payment and the payment's face amount is taxed as interest income, as discussed in the following paragraphs. Thus, the **imputed interest** rules prevent sellers of capital assets from increasing the selling price to reflect the equivalent of unstated interest on deferred payments and thereby converting ordinary (interest) income into long-term capital gains. In addition, the imputed interest rules are important because they affect the timing of income recognition.

Generally, if the contract does not charge at least the Federal rate, interest will be imputed at the Federal rate. The Federal rate is the interest rate the Federal government pays on new borrowing and is published monthly by the IRS.[68]

As a general rule, the buyer and seller must account for interest on the accrual basis with semiannual compounding.[69] Requiring the use of the accrual basis ensures that the seller's interest income and the buyer's interest expense are reported in the same tax year. The following example illustrates the calculation and amortization of imputed interest.

---

[67]§§ 483 and 1274.

[68]§ 1274(d)(1). There are three Federal rates: short-term (not over three years), midterm (over three years but not over nine years), and long-term (over nine years).

[69]§§ 1274(a), 1273(a), and 1272(a).

Example 31

Peggy, a cash basis taxpayer, sold land on January 1, 2014, for $200,000 cash and $6 million due on December 31, 2015, with 2% interest payable December 31, 2014, and December 31, 2015. At the time of the sale, the Federal rate was 4% (compounded semiannually). Because Peggy did not charge interest at least equal to the Federal rate, interest will be imputed at 4% (compounded semiannually).

Date	Payment	Present Value (at 4%) on 1/1/2014	Imputed Interest
12/31/2014	$ 120,000	$ 115,384	$ 4,616
12/31/2015	6,120,000	5,658,284	461,716
	$6,240,000	$5,773,668	$466,332

Thus, the selling price will be restated to $5,973,668 ($200,000 + $5,773,668) rather than $6,200,000 ($200,000 + $6,000,000), and Peggy will recognize interest income in accordance with the following amortization schedule:

	Beginning Balance	Interest (at 4%)*	Received	Ending Balance
2014	$5,773,668	$230,947	$ 120,000	$5,884,615
2015	5,884,615	235,385	6,120,000	–0–

*Compounded semiannually.

Congress has created several exceptions regarding the rate at which interest is imputed and the method of accounting for the interest income and expense. The general rules and exceptions are summarized in Concept Summary 18.2.

Related-Party Sales of Nondepreciable Property

If the Code did not contain special rules, a taxpayer could make an installment sale of property to a related party (e.g., a family member) who would obtain a basis in the property equal to the purchase price (the fair market value of the property). Then the purchasing family member could immediately sell the property to an unrelated party for cash with no recognized gain or loss (the amount realized would equal the basis). The related-party purchaser would not pay the installment note to the selling family member until a later year or years. The net result would be that the family has the cash, but no taxable gain is recognized until the intrafamily transfer of the cash (when the purchasing family member makes payments on the installment note).

Under special rules designed to combat the scheme described above, the proceeds from the subsequent sale (the second sale) by the purchasing family member are treated as though they were used to pay the installment note due the selling family member (the first sale). As a result, the recognition of gain from the original sale between the related parties is accelerated.[70]

However, even with these special rules, Congress did not eliminate the benefits of all related-party installment sales.

- Related parties include the first seller's brothers, sisters, ancestors, lineal descendants, controlled corporations, and partnerships, trusts, and estates in which the seller has an interest.[71]
- There is no acceleration if the second disposition occurs more than two years after the first sale.[72]

---

[70]§ 453(e).

[71]§ 453(f)(1), cross-referencing §§ 267(b) and 318(a). Although spouses are related parties, the exemption of gain between spouses (§ 1041)

makes the second-disposition rules inapplicable when the first sale was between spouses.

[72]§ 453(e)(2). But see § 453(e)(2)(B) for extensions of the two-year period.

CONCEPT SUMMARY 18.2

Interest on Installment Sales

	Imputed Interest Rate
General rule	Federal rate
Exceptions:	
• Principal amount not over $2.8 million.[1]	Lesser of Federal rate or 9%
• Sale of land (with a calendar year ceiling of $500,000) between family members (the seller's spouse, brothers, sisters, ancestors, or lineal descendants).[2]	Lesser of Federal rate or 6%

	Method of Accounting for Interest	
	Seller's Interest Income	**Buyer's Interest Expense**
General rule[3]	Accrual	Accrual
Exceptions:		
• Total payments under the contract are $250,000 or less.[4]	Taxpayer's overall method	Taxpayer's overall method
• Sale of a farm (sales price of $1 million or less).[5]	Taxpayer's overall method	Taxpayer's overall method
• Sale of a principal residence.[6]	Taxpayer's overall method	Taxpayer's overall method
• Sale for a note with a principal amount of not over $2 million, the seller is on the cash basis, the property sold is not inventory, and the buyer agrees to report expense by the cash method.[7]	Cash	Cash

[1]§ 1274A(b). This amount is adjusted annually for inflation. For 2014, the amount is $5,557,200.
[2]§§ 1274(c)(3)(F) and 483(e).
[3]§§ 1274(a) and 1272(a)(3).
[4]§§ 1274(c)(3)(C) and 483.
[5]§§ 1274(c)(3)(A) and 483.
[6]§§ 1274(c)(3)(B) and 483.
[7]§ 1274A(c). This amount is adjusted annually for inflation. For 2014, the amount is $3,969,500.

Thus, if the taxpayer can sell the property to an unrelated party (not a related party) or a patient family member, the intrafamily installment sale is still a powerful tax planning tool. Other exceptions also can be applied in some circumstances.[73]

Related-Party Sales of Depreciable Property

The installment method cannot be used to report a gain on the sale of depreciable property to a controlled entity. The purpose of this rule is to prevent the seller from deferring gain (until collections are received) while the related purchaser is enjoying a stepped-up basis for depreciation purposes.[74]

The prohibition on the use of the installment method applies to sales between the taxpayer and a partnership or corporation in which the taxpayer holds a more-than-50 percent interest. Constructive ownership rules are used in applying the ownership test (e.g., the taxpayer is considered to own stock owned by a spouse and certain other family members).[75] However, if the taxpayer can establish that tax avoidance was not a principal purpose of the transaction, the installment method can be used to report the gain.

[73]See §§ 453(e)(6) and (7).
[74]§ 453(g).
[75]§§ 1239(b) and (c).

Example 32

Alan purchased an apartment building from his controlled corporation, Emerald Corporation. Alan was short of cash at the time of the purchase (December 2014), but was to collect a large cash payment in January 2015. The agreement required Alan to pay the entire arm's length price in January 2015. Alan had good business reasons for acquiring the building. Emerald Corporation should be able to convince the IRS that tax avoidance was not a principal purpose for the installment sale because the tax benefits are not overwhelming. The corporation will report all of the gain in the year following the year of sale, and the building must be depreciated over 27.5 years (the cost recovery period).

18-3b Disposition of Installment Obligations

Generally, a taxpayer must recognize the deferred profit from an installment sale when the obligation is transferred to another party or otherwise relinquished. The rationale for accelerating the gain is that the deferral should continue for no longer than the taxpayer owns the installment obligation.[76]

The gift or cancellation of an installment note is treated as a taxable disposition by the donor. This discourages attempts to shift income among family members. The amount realized from the cancellation is the face amount of the note if the parties (obligor and obligee) are related to each other.[77]

Example 33

Liz cancels a note issued by Tina (Liz's daughter) that arose in connection with the sale of property. At the time of the cancellation, the note had a basis to Liz of $10,000, a face amount of $25,000, and a fair market value of $20,000. Presuming that the initial sale by Liz qualified as an installment sale, the cancellation results in gain of $15,000 ($25,000 − $10,000) to Liz.

Certain exceptions to the recognition of gain provisions are provided for transfers of installment obligations to the transferor's 80 percent controlled corporation, contributions of capital to a partnership, certain corporate liquidations, transfers due to the taxpayer's death, and transfers between spouses or incident to divorce.[78] In such situations, the deferred profit is merely shifted to the transferee, who is responsible for the payment of tax on the subsequent collections of the installment obligations. The exception to this rule is that in the case of a transfer of installment obligations to a partnership by a partner, the transferor partner is taxed on the income when the partnership collects on the installment receivables.

THE BIG PICTURE

Example 34

Return to the facts of *The Big Picture* on p. 18-1. Assume that Belinda's capital contribution to the partnership in 2014 was an installment obligation with a basis of $40,000 and a face amount of $100,000. In 2015, the partnership collected the $100,000. The transfer in 2014 was not a taxable disposition, but in 2015 when the receivable is collected, Belinda is required to recognize a gain of $60,000.

18-3c Interest on Deferred Taxes

With the installment method, the seller earns interest on the receivable. The receivable includes the deferred gain. Thus, one could argue that the seller is earning interest on the deferred taxes. Some commentators reason that the government is, in effect, making interest-free loans to taxpayers who report gains by the installment method. Following the argument that the amount of the

---

[76]§ 453B(a).
[77]§ 453B(f)(2).

[78]§§ 453B(c), (d), and (g). See Chapter 20 for a discussion of some of these subjects.

deferred taxes is a loan, the taxpayer is required to pay interest on the deferred taxes in some situations.[79]

The taxpayer is required to pay interest on the deferred taxes only if *both* of the following requirements are met:

- The installment obligation arises from the sale of property (other than farming property) for more than $150,000.
- The taxpayer's total installment obligations outstanding at the close of the tax year exceed $5 million.

Interest on the deferred taxes is payable only for the portion of the taxes that relates to the installment obligations in *excess* of $5 million. The interest is calculated using the underpayment rate in § 6621.

18-3d Electing Out of the Installment Method

A taxpayer can *elect not to use* the installment method. The election is made by reporting on a timely filed return the gain computed by the taxpayer's usual method of accounting (cash or accrual).[80] However, the Regulations provide that the amount realized by a cash basis taxpayer cannot be less than the fair market value of the property sold. This rule differs from the usual cash basis accounting rules (discussed earlier),[81] which measure the amount realized in terms of the fair market value of the property received. The net effect of the Regulations is to allow the cash basis taxpayer to report his or her gain as an accrual basis taxpayer. The election is frequently applied to year-end sales by taxpayers who expect to be in a higher tax bracket in the following year.

Example 35

On December 31, 2014, Kurt sold investment land to Jodie for $20,000 (fair market value). He had owned the land for seven years. The cash was to be paid on January 4, 2015. Kurt is a cash basis taxpayer, and his basis in the land is $8,000. Kurt has a large casualty loss that, when combined with his other income in 2014, puts him at a marginal tax rate of 15% in 2014. He expects his tax rate to increase to 35% in 2015.

The transaction constitutes an installment sale because a payment will be received in a tax year after the tax year of disposition. Jodie's promise to pay Kurt is an installment obligation, and under the Regulations, the value of the installment obligation is equal to the value of the property sold ($20,000). If Kurt elects out of the installment method, he will shift $12,000 of gain ($20,000 − $8,000) from the expected higher rate in 2015 of 15% to the 0% rate for long-term capital gains in 2014. The expected tax savings based on the rate differential may exceed the benefit of the tax deferral available with the installment method.

Permission of the IRS is required to revoke an election not to use the installment method.[82]

18-3e Long-Term Contracts

LO.5

Review and illustrate the alternative methods of accounting for long-term contracts (the completed contract method and the percentage of completion method), including the limitations on the use of the completed contract method.

A **long-term contract** is a building, installation, construction, or manufacturing contract that is entered into but not completed within the same tax year. However, a *manufacturing* contract is long-term *only* if the contract is to manufacture (1) a unique item not normally carried in finished goods inventory or (2) items that normally require more than 12 calendar months to complete.[83] An item is *unique* if it is designed to meet the customer's particular needs and is not suitable for use by others. A contract to perform services (e.g., auditing or legal services) is not considered a contract for this purpose and thus cannot qualify as a long-term contract.

---

[79]§ 453A.
[80]§ 453(d) and Temp.Reg. § 15a.453–1(d). See also Rev.Rul. 82–227, 1982–2 C.B. 89.

[81]Refer to Chapter 4, Example 6.
[82]§ 453(d)(3) and Temp.Reg. § 15a.453–1(d)(4).
[83]§ 460(f) and Reg. § 1.460–2(a).

Rocky, a calendar year taxpayer, entered into two contracts during the year. One contract was to construct a building foundation. Work was to begin in October 2014 and was to be completed by June 2015. The contract is long-term because it will not be entered into and completed in the same tax year. The fact that the contract requires less than 12 calendar months to complete is not relevant because the contract is not for manufacturing. The second contract was for architectural services to be performed over two years. These services will not qualify for long-term contract treatment because the taxpayer will not build, install, construct, or manufacture a product.

Generally, the taxpayer must accumulate all of the direct and indirect costs incurred under a contract. This means that the production costs must be accumulated and allocated to individual contracts. Furthermore, mixed services costs, costs that benefit contracts as well as the general administrative operations of the business, must be allocated to production. Exhibit 18.1 lists the types of costs that must be accumulated and allocated to contracts. The taxpayer must develop reasonable bases for cost allocations.[84]

Falcon, Inc., uses detailed cost accumulation records to assign labor and materials to its contracts in progress. The total cost of fringe benefits is allocated to a contract on the following basis:

$$\frac{\text{Labor on the contract}}{\text{Total salaries and labor}} \times \text{Total cost of fringe benefits}$$

Similarly, storage and handling costs for materials are allocated to contracts on the following basis:

$$\frac{\text{Contract materials}}{\text{Material purchases}} \times \text{Storage and handling costs}$$

The cost of the personnel operations, a mixed services cost, is allocated between production and general administration based on the number of employees in each function. The personnel cost allocated to production is allocated to individual contracts on the basis of the formula used to allocate fringe benefits.

The accumulated costs are deducted when the revenue from the contract is recognized. Generally, two methods of accounting are used in varying circumstances to determine when the revenue from a contract is recognized:[85]

- The completed contract method.
- The percentage of completion method.

The *completed contract method may be used* for (1) home construction contracts (contracts in which at least 80 percent of the estimated costs are for dwelling units in buildings with four or fewer units) and (2) certain other real estate construction contracts. Other real estate contracts can qualify for the completed contract method if the following requirements are satisfied:

- The contract is expected to be completed within the two-year period beginning on the commencement date of the contract.
- The contract is performed by a taxpayer whose average annual gross receipts for the three taxable years preceding the taxable year in which the contract is entered into do not exceed $10 million.

All other contractors must use the percentage of completion method.

Completed Contract Method

Under the **completed contract method**, no revenue from the contract is recognized until the contract is completed and accepted. Generally, the contract is completed

---

[84]Reg. §§ 1.460–5(b) and 1.263A–1(e).   [85]§ 460.

EXHIBIT 18.1	**Contract Costs, Mixed Services Costs, and Current Expense Items for Contracts**	

	Contracts Eligible for the Completed Contract Method	Other Contracts
Contract costs:		
Direct materials (a part of the finished product).	Capital	Capital
Indirect materials [consumed in production but not in the finished product (e.g., grease and oil for equipment)].	Capital	Capital
Storage, handling, and insurance on materials.	Expense	Capital
Direct labor (worked on the product).	Capital	Capital
Indirect labor [worked in the production process but not directly on the product (e.g., a construction supervisor)].	Capital	Capital
Fringe benefits for direct and indirect labor (e.g., vacation, sick pay, unemployment, and other insurance).	Capital	Capital
Pension costs for direct and indirect labor:		
Current cost.	Expense	Capital
Past service costs.	Expense	Capital
Depreciation on production facilities:		
For financial statements.	Capital	Capital
Tax depreciation in excess of financial statements.	Expense	Capital
Depreciation on idle facilities.	Expense	Expense
Property taxes, insurance, rent, and maintenance on production facilities.	Capital	Capital
Bidding expenses—successful.	Expense	Capital
Bidding expenses—unsuccessful.	Expense	Expense
Interest to finance real estate construction.	Capital	Capital
Interest to finance personal property:		
Production period of one year or less.	Expense	Expense
Production period exceeds one year and costs exceed $1 million.	Capital	Capital
Production period exceeds two years.	Capital	Capital
Mixed services costs:		
Personnel operations.	Expense	Allocate
Data processing.	Expense	Allocate
Purchasing.	Expense	Allocate
Selling, general, and administrative expenses (including an allocated share of mixed services).	Expense	Expense
Losses.	Expense	Expense

when it is accepted by the customer or the customer begins using the subject matter of the contract.[86]

In some situations, the original contract price may be disputed, or the buyer may want additional work to be done on a long-term contract. If the disputed amount is substantial (it is not possible to determine whether a profit or loss will ultimately be realized on the contract), the Regulations provide that no amount of income or loss is recognized until the dispute is resolved. In all other cases, the profit or loss (reduced by the amount in dispute) is recognized in the current period upon completion of the contract. However, additional work may need to be performed with respect to the disputed contract. When the amount in dispute is less than the net profit on the contract before the estimated additional cost, the taxpayer must report in the year of completion the profit as reduced by the estimated additional cost.[87]

---

[86]Reg. § 1.460–1(c)(3).

[87]Reg. §§ 1.451–3(d)(2)(ii)–(vii), Example 2.

Example 38

Ted, a calendar year taxpayer utilizing the completed contract method of accounting, constructed a building for Brad under a long-term contract. The gross contract price was $500,000. Ted finished construction in 2014 at a cost of $475,000. When Brad examined the building, he insisted that the building be repainted or the contract price be reduced. The estimated cost of repainting is $10,000. Because under the terms of the contract Ted is assured of a profit of at least $15,000 ($500,000 − $475,000 − $10,000) even if the dispute is ultimately resolved in Brad's favor, Ted must include $490,000 ($500,000 − $10,000) in gross income and is allowed deductions of $475,000 for 2014.

In 2015, Ted and Brad resolve the dispute, and Ted repaints certain portions of the building at a cost of $6,000. Ted must include $10,000 in 2015 gross income and may deduct the $6,000 expense in that year.

If the net profit less the estimated additional cost results in a loss, the loss is deferred until the dispute is resolved.

Example 39

Assume the same facts as in the previous example, except that the estimated cost of repainting the building is $50,000. Because the resolution of the dispute completely in Brad's favor would mean a net loss on the contract for Ted ($500,000 − $475,000 − $50,000 = $25,000 loss), Ted does not recognize any income or loss until the year the dispute is resolved.

Frequently, a contractor receives payment at various stages of completion. For example, when the contract is 50 percent complete, the contractor may receive 50 percent of the contract price less a retainage. The taxation of these payments is generally governed by Regulation § 1.451–5, "advance payments for goods and long-term contracts" (discussed in Chapter 4). Generally, contractors are permitted to defer the advance payments until the payments are recognized as income under the taxpayer's method of accounting.

Percentage of Completion Method

Under the **percentage of completion method**, a portion of the gross contract price is included in income during each period as the work progresses. The revenue accrued each period (except for the final period) is computed as follows:[88]

$$\frac{C}{T} \times P$$

Where C = Contract costs incurred during the period
T = Estimated total cost of the contract
P = Contract price

All of the costs allocated to the contract during the period are deductible from the accrued revenue.[89] The revenue reported in the final period is simply the unreported revenue from the contract. Because T in this formula is an estimate that frequently differs from total actual costs, which are not known until the contract has been completed, the profit on a contract for a particular period may be overstated or understated.

Example 40

Tan, Inc., entered into a contract that was to take two years to complete, with an estimated cost of $2,250,000. The contract price was $3,000,000. Costs of the contract for 2013, the first year, totaled $1,350,000. The gross profit reported by the percentage of completion method for 2013 was $450,000 [($1,350,000/$2,250,000 × $3,000,000) − $1,350,000]. The contract was completed at the end of 2014 at a total cost of $2,700,000. In retrospect, 2013 profit should have been $150,000 [($1,350,000/$2,700,000 × $3,000,000) − $1,350,000]. Thus, taxes were overpaid for 2013.

A *de minimis* rule enables the contractor to delay the recognition of income for a particular contract under the percentage of completion method. If less than 10 percent of the estimated contract costs have been incurred by the end of the

---

[88]§ 460(b)(1)(A).   [89]Reg. § 1.451–3(c)(3).

taxable year, the taxpayer can elect to defer the recognition of income and the related costs until the taxable year in which cumulative contract costs are at least 10 percent of the estimated contract costs.[90]

Lookback Provisions

In the year a contract is completed, a *lookback* provision requires the recalculation of annual profits reported on the contract under the percentage of completion method. Interest is paid to the taxpayer if taxes were overpaid, and interest is payable by the taxpayer if there was an underpayment.[91] For a corporate taxpayer, the lookback interest paid by the taxpayer is deductible, but for an individual taxpayer, it is nondeductible personal interest associated with a tax liability.

Example 41	Assume that Tan, Inc., in Example 40, was in the 35% tax bracket in both years and the relevant interest rate was 10%. For 2013, the company paid excess taxes of $105,000 [($450,000 − $150,000) × .35]. When the contract is completed at the end of 2014, Tan, Inc., should receive interest of $10,500 for one year on the tax overpayment ($105,000 × .10).

ETHICS & EQUITY The Deferring of Income from Foreign Subsidiaries

Generally, a U.S. parent corporation is not required to include in its taxable income the earnings of its foreign subsidiaries until the parent receives the income in the form of a dividend. That is, the parent and the subsidiary are viewed as separate entities, and the parent does not realize income until the dividends are received from the subsidiary. But deferring the income provides an incentive to move operations (and jobs) to foreign subsidiaries.

Recently, changes in the tax law have been introduced that would tax the dividends from the foreign subsidiary at a reduced rate (15% rather than the 35% corporate rate) to encourage the parent to bring the income back to the United States to be reinvested here. Opponents to these changes argue that the better solution would be to tax the parent on its worldwide income—including the income of the subsidiaries—as it is earned, rather than waiting until it is repatriated. However, there is justifiable concern that such a system would cause a flight of capital as corporations change their domicile. Which of the proposed changes should be enacted?

18-4 INVENTORIES

LO.6

Recognize when accounting for inventories must occur, be aware of the types of costs that must be included in inventories, and apply the LIFO method.

The use of inventories is necessary to clearly reflect income of any business engaged in the production, purchase, or sale of merchandise.[92] Generally, tax accounting and financial accounting for inventories are much the same:

- The use of inventories is necessary to clearly reflect the income of any business engaged in the production and sale or purchase and sale of goods.[93]
- The inventories should include all finished goods, goods in process, and raw materials and supplies that will become part of the product (including containers).
- Inventory rules must give effect to the *best* accounting practice of a particular trade or business, and the taxpayer's method should be consistently followed from year to year.
- All items included in inventory should be valued at either (1) cost or (2) the lower of cost or market value.

---

[90]§ 460(b)(5).

[91]§§ 460(b)(2) and (6). The taxpayer can elect not to apply the lookback method in situations where the cumulative taxable income as of the close of each prior year is within 10% of the correct income for each prior year.

[92]Reg. § 1.471–1.

[93]§ 471(a) and Reg. §§ 1.471–1 and −2.

The following are *not* acceptable methods or practices in valuing inventories:

* A deduction for a reserve for anticipated price changes.
* The use of a constant price or nominal value for a so-called normal quantity of materials or goods in stock (e.g., the base stock method).
* The inclusion in inventory of stock in transit to which title is not vested in the taxpayer.
* The direct costing approach (excluding fixed indirect production costs from inventory).
* The prime costing approach (excluding all indirect production costs from inventory).

The reason for the similarities between tax and financial accounting for inventories is that § 471 sets forth what appears to be a two-prong test. Under this provision, "inventories shall be taken … on such basis … as conforming as nearly as may be to the *best accounting practice* in the trade or business and as most *clearly reflecting the income.*" The best accounting practice is synonymous with generally accepted accounting principles (GAAP). However, the IRS determines whether an inventory method clearly reflects income.

In *Thor Power Tool Co. v. Comm.*, there was a conflict between the two tests.[94] The taxpayer's method of valuing obsolete parts was in conformity with GAAP. The IRS, however, successfully argued that the clear reflection of income test was not satisfied because the taxpayer's procedures for valuing its inventories were contrary to the Regulations. Under the taxpayer's method, inventories for parts in excess of estimated future sales were written off (expensed), although the parts were kept on hand and their asking prices were not reduced. [Under Regulation § 1.471–4(b), inventories cannot be written down unless the selling prices also are reduced.] The taxpayer contended that conformity to GAAP creates a presumption that the method clearly reflects income. The Supreme Court disagreed, concluding that the clear reflection of income test was *paramount.* Moreover, it is the opinion of the IRS that controls in determining whether the method of inventory clearly reflects income. Thus, the best accounting practice test was rendered practically meaningless. It follows that the taxpayer's method of inventory must strictly conform to the Regulations regardless of what GAAP may require.

18-4a Determining Inventory Cost

For merchandise purchased, cost is the invoice price less trade discounts plus freight and other handling charges.[95] Cash discounts approximating a fair interest rate can be deducted or capitalized at the taxpayer's option, provided that the method used is consistently applied.

Uniform Capitalization (UNICAP)

Section 263A provides that for inventory and property produced by the taxpayer, "(A) the direct cost of such property, and (B) such property's share of those indirect costs (including taxes) part or all of which are allocable to such property" must be capitalized. The Committee Reports observe that Congress is attempting to achieve a set of capitalization rules that will apply to all types of businesses: contractors, manufacturers, farmers, wholesalers, and retailers.[96] Congress has labeled the system the **uniform capitalization (UNICAP) rules**, and practitioners refer to the rules as a *super-full absorption costing system.*

---

[94]79–1 USTC ¶9139, 43 AFTR 2d 79–362, 99 S.Ct. 773 (USSC, 1979). See, Chapter 4, Section 4-1d for the Supreme Court's discussion of the differences between tax and financial accounting.

[95]Reg. § 1.471–3(b).

[96]H. Rep. 99–841, 99th Cong., 2nd Sess., 1986, pp. 302–309. See also Reg. § 1.263A–1(a).

Global Tax Issues

Inventory Acquired from a Foreign Subsidiary

Generally, a parent corporation and its foreign subsidiaries are treated as separate corporations. If a foreign subsidiary is producing goods in a country whose tax rates are lower than the U.S. tax rates, tax savings can accrue to the group if the foreign subsidiary's prices to the U.S. parent are as high as permissible. This will increase the income in the foreign country, but will reduce taxable income subject to the higher U.S. rates. Section 482 is the IRS's weapon against such income shifting. Under § 482, the prices charged on transactions between related parties must be equal to an "arm's length price."

To value inventory under the UNICAP rules, a *producer* must apply the following steps:[97]

- Classify all costs into three categories: (1) production, (2) general administrative expense, and (3) mixed services.
- Allocate mixed services costs to production and general administrative expenses.[98]
- Allocate the production costs between the cost of goods sold and the ending inventory.

Exhibit 18.1 (see the "Other Contracts" column) lists typical items that are included in the three classes of costs. The mixed services costs should be allocated to production on a rational basis. For example, the costs of operating the personnel department may be allocated between production and general administration based on the number of applications processed or the number of employees. In lieu of allocating each mixed services cost, the taxpayer can elect a *simplified method* whereby the total of all mixed services costs is allocated to production as follows:[99]

$$\text{MSP} = \frac{\text{TP}}{\text{TC}} \times \text{TMS}$$

Where MSP = Mixed services costs allocated to production

TP = Total production costs, other than interest and mixed services

TC = Total costs, other than interest; state, local, or foreign income taxes; and mixed services costs

TMS = Total mixed services costs

The usual cost accounting techniques (e.g., average cost per equivalent unit) can be used to allocate the costs between the cost of goods sold and the ending inventory.

Alternatively, the producer can elect to allocate mixed services costs to production on the basis of labor charges only (production labor as a percentage of total labor costs).

The costs included in the inventory of *wholesalers and retailers* are comparable to those of the producer. However, many of these costs are captured in the price these taxpayers pay for the goods. The following additional costs must be capitalized by these taxpayers:

- All storage costs for wholesalers.
- Off-site storage costs for retailers.
- Purchasing costs (e.g., buyers' wages or salaries).
- Handling, processing, assembly, and repackaging.
- The portion of mixed services costs allocable to these functions.

---

[97]Reg. § 1.263A–1(c).

[98]Producers with mixed services costs of less than $200,000 for the year are not required to allocate mixed services costs if the simplified method is used to allocate their production costs. Reg. § 1.263A–1(b)(12).

[99]Reg. § 1.263A–1(h)(5).

Mixed services costs must be allocated to off-site storage, purchasing, and packaging on the basis of direct labor costs of these departments as a percentage of total payroll. Thus, the storage, purchasing, and packaging costs allocated to ending inventory include some mixed services costs.

The UNICAP rules may result in some costs being capitalized for tax purposes but not for financial accounting purposes. For example, a wholesaler's or a manufacturer's storage costs are generally expensed for financial reporting purposes but are capitalized for tax purposes. Also, the taxpayer may capitalize straight-line depreciation of production equipment for financial accounting purposes, but the total tax depreciation must be capitalized under uniform capitalization.

Exemption from UNICAP

Taxpayers with average annual gross receipts of less than $10 million (calculated over the previous three years) are not required to apply the UNICAP rules to their inventories of merchandise purchased and held for resale. If the small business engages in production as well as reselling, UNICAP must be applied to the goods the taxpayer produces, with limited exceptions.[100]

A farmer who is permitted to use the cash method is not required to apply the UNICAP rules to (1) any animals or (2) any plants with a preproduction period of two years or less that the farmer produces. In exchange for this concession, the farmer is required to use the alternative depreciation system (see Chapter 8) for property used in the farming business.[101]

Lower of Cost or Market

Except for those taxpayers who use the LIFO method, inventories may be valued at the **lower of cost or market (replacement cost)**.[102] Taxpayers using LIFO must value inventory at cost. However, the write-down of damaged or shopworn merchandise and goods that are otherwise unsalable at normal prices is not considered to be an application of the lower of cost or market method. Such items should be valued at bona fide selling price less direct cost of disposal.[103]

In the case of excess inventories (as in *Thor Power Tool Co.*, discussed previously), the goods can be written down only to the taxpayer's offering price. If the offering price on the goods is not reduced, the goods must be valued at cost.

Example 42

The Cardinal Publishing Company invested $50,000 in printing 10,000 copies of a book. Although only 7,000 copies were sold in the first 3 years and none in the next 5 years, management is convinced that the book will become a classic in 20 years. Cardinal leaves the price the same as it was when the book was first distributed ($15 per copy). The remaining 3,000 books must be valued at cost ($15,000). Note that the tax law provides an incentive for the taxpayer to destroy or abandon its excess inventory and obtain an immediate deduction rather than wait for the event of future sales.

In applying the lower of cost or market method, *each* item included in the inventory must be valued at the lower of its cost or market value.[104]

Example 43

The taxpayer's ending inventory is valued as follows:

Item	Cost	Market	Lower of Cost or Market
A	$5,000	$ 4,000	$4,000
B	3,000	2,000	2,000
C	1,500	6,000	1,500
	$9,500	$12,000	$7,500

Under the lower of cost or market method, the taxpayer's inventory is valued at $7,500 rather than $9,500.

---

[100]101 § 263A(b)(2) and Reg. 1.263A–3(a)(2).
[101]§§ 263A(d) and (e)(3).
[102]Reg. § 1.472–4.
[103]Reg. § 1.471–2(c).
[104]Reg. § 1.471–4(c).

Inventory Shrinkage

The difference between the inventory per physical count and according to the company's records is referred to as *inventory shrinkage*. Inventory shrinkage is the result of accidents, theft, and errors in recording. Many companies take physical inventories at times other than the last day of the tax year and adjust their inventory per books to agree with the physical count. The inventory of the last day of the tax year, which is used to compute cost of goods sold, is based on the perpetual records. Such companies often adjust the ending inventory for the estimated shrinkage that has occurred between the date of the physical inventory and the last day of the tax year. The adjustment is often based on the historical relationship between inventory shrinkage and sales.[105]

Determining Cost—Specific Identification, FIFO, and LIFO

In some cases, it is feasible to determine the cost of the particular item sold. For example, an automobile dealer can easily determine the specific cost of each automobile that has been sold. However, in most businesses, it is necessary to resort to a flow of goods assumption such as *first in, first out (FIFO)*, *last in, first out (LIFO)*, or an *average cost* method. A taxpayer may use any of these methods, provided the method selected is consistently applied from year to year.

During a period of rising prices, LIFO will generally produce a lower ending inventory valuation and will result in a greater cost of goods sold than would be obtained under the FIFO method. The following example illustrates how LIFO and FIFO affect the computation of the cost of goods sold.

Example 44

On January 1, 2014, the taxpayer opened a retail store to sell refrigerators. At least 10 refrigerators must be carried in inventory to satisfy customer demands. The initial investment in the 10 refrigerators is $5,000. During the year, 10 refrigerators were sold at $750 each and were replaced at a cost of $6,000 ($600 each). Gross profit under the LIFO and FIFO methods is computed as follows:

		FIFO		LIFO
Sales (10 × $750)		$ 7,500		$ 7,500
Beginning inventory	$ 5,000		$ 5,000	
Purchases	6,000		6,000	
	$11,000		$11,000	
Ending inventory				
10 × $600	(6,000)			
10 × $500			(5,000)	
Cost of goods sold		(5,000)		(6,000)
Gross profit		$ 2,500		$ 1,500

Dollar-Value LIFO

In the previous example, the taxpayer was buying and selling a single product, a particular model of a refrigerator. The taxpayer employed the specific goods LIFO technique. Under the specific goods approach, if the identical items are not on hand at the end of the period, the LIFO inventory is depleted and all of the deferred profit must be recaptured. Thus, taxpayers who frequently change the items carried in inventory would realize little benefit from LIFO. However, the dollar-value LIFO technique avoids the LIFO depletion problem associated with the specific goods technique.

Under **dollar-value LIFO**, each inventory item is assigned to a pool. A *pool* is a collection of similar items and is treated as a separate inventory. Determining whether items are similar involves considerable judgment. In general, however, the taxpayer would prefer broad pools so that when a particular item is sold out, it can be

---

[105]§ 471(b).

replaced with increases in other items in the same pool. Generally, all products man-ufactured at a particular plant can be treated as a pool.[106] A department store may have a separate pool for each department. An automobile dealer may have separate pools for new cars, lightweight trucks, heavy-duty trucks, and car and truck parts.

At the end of the period, the ending inventory must be valued at the current-year prices and then at the LIFO base period (the year LIFO was adopted). The ratio of the ending inventory at current prices to the ending inventory at base period prices is the *LIFO index*. If the total current inventory at base period prices is greater than the base period inventory at base period prices, a LIFO layer must be added. The LIFO index is applied to the LIFO layer to convert it to current prices.

Example 45

Black Company adopted LIFO effective January 1, 2014. The base LIFO inventory (from December 31, 2013) was $1,000,000. On December 31, 2014, the inventory was $1,320,000 at end-of-2014 prices and $1,200,000 at end-of-2013 (the base period) pri-ces. Thus, Black added a 2014 layer of $200,000 ($1,200,000 − $1,000,000) at base pe-riod prices. The layer must be converted to 2014 prices as follows:

$$\text{LIFO index} = \$1,320,000/\$1,200,000 = 1.10$$
$$\text{2014 layer} \times \text{LIFO index} = \$200,000 \times 1.10 = \$220,000$$

Therefore, the 2014 ending inventory is $1,000,000 + $220,000 = $1,220,000.

The inventory on December 31, 2015, is $1,325,000 using 2015 prices and $1,250,000 using base period prices. Thus, the LIFO index for 2015 is $1,325,000/ $1,250,000 = 1.06. The LIFO inventory is $1,273,000, computed as follows:

BLACK COMPANY
LIFO Inventory
December 31, 2015

	Base Period Cost	LIFO Index	LIFO Layers
Base inventory	$1,000,000	1.00	$1,000,000
2014 layer	200,000	1.10	220,000
2015 layer	50,000	1.06	53,000
	$1,250,000		$1,273,000

ETHICS & EQUITY   Preserving the LIFO Reserve

Blanch Corporation has been using the dollar-value LIFO inventory method for 20 years. The company maintains one inventory pool that includes raw materials, goods in process, and finished goods. The LIFO deferral is several million dollars. At the end of the current year, the corporation's inventory of finished goods was almost depleted because the company's major competitor had to recall a substantial portion of its products. Blanch's management is aware that if the inventory is not replenished, the corporation will be required to recognize income that has been deferred for the past 20 years. The controller has suggested that the company buy sufficient raw materials to substitute for the depleted finished goods. This will require having on hand at the end of the year the raw materials required for the next 18 months, when ordinarily the company has only a three-month supply on hand. The controller argues that the cost of carrying the additional inventory is much less than the additional taxes that will be due if the inventories are allowed to decrease.

The operations manager has suggested that the company buy the raw materials before the end of year and have the supplier store the materials. Furthermore, the supplier would act as Blanch's agent to sell the excess materials. This would minimize the actual investment in inventory. Do you think the corporation should follow either proposal?

---

[106]See, generally, Rég. § 1.472–8.

18-4b The LIFO Election

A taxpayer may adopt LIFO by merely using the method in the tax return for the year of the change and by attaching Form 970 (Application to Use LIFO Inventory Method) to the tax return. Thus, a taxpayer does not have to request approval for the change. Once the election is made, it cannot be revoked. However, a prospective change from LIFO to any other inventory method can be made only if the consent of the IRS is obtained.[107]

The beginning inventory valuation for the first year LIFO is used is computed by the costing method employed in the preceding year. Thus, the beginning LIFO inventory is generally the same as the closing inventory for the preceding year. Because lower of cost or market cannot be used in conjunction with LIFO, previous write-downs to market for items included in the beginning inventory must be restored to income. The amount the inventories are written up is an adjustment due to a change in accounting method.[108] However, the usual rules for disposition of the adjustments under Revenue Procedure 2011–14 are not applicable.[109] The taxpayer is allowed to spread the adjustment ratably over the year of the change and the two succeeding years.

Example 46	In 2013, Paul used the lower of cost or market FIFO inventory method. The FIFO cost of his ending inventory was $30,000, and the market value of the inventory was $24,000. Therefore, the ending inventory for 2013 was $24,000. Paul switched to LIFO in 2014 and was required to write up the beginning inventory to $30,000. Paul must add $2,000 ($6,000 ÷ 3) to his income for each of the years 2014, 2015, and 2016.

Congress added this provision to the Code to overrule the previous IRS policy of requiring the taxpayer to include the entire adjustment in income for the year preceding the change to LIFO.[110]

Once the LIFO election is made for tax purposes, the taxpayer's financial reports to owners and creditors must also be prepared on the basis of LIFO.[111] The original reason for the conformity requirement was to make the taxpayers stand by their argument that LIFO was necessary to clearly reflect income. The *conformity* of financial reports to tax reporting is specifically required by the Code and is strictly enforced by the IRS. However, the Regulations permit the taxpayer to make a footnote disclosure of the net income computed by another method of inventory valuation (e.g., FIFO).[112]

18-4c Special Inventory Methods Relating to Farming and Ranching

Farmers who do not use the cash method and therefore account for inventories may elect to use the **farm price method** or the **unit-livestock-price method** rather than one of the inventory methods discussed previously. Under the farm price method, the inventory is valued at its market price less disposition costs (e.g., transportation and selling expenses).[113] If the taxpayer uses the unit-livestock-price method, the animals are valued at a standard cost, which is based on the average cost of raising an animal with the characteristics of the animals included in the ending inventory.[114] The farmer can also elect to use the lower of cost or market inventory method.

---

[107]Reg. §§ 1.472–3(a) and 1.472–5 and Rev.Proc. 84–74, 1984–2 C.B. 736 at 742.

[108]Reg. § 1.472–2(c). In Rev.Rul. 76–282, 1976–2 C.B. 137, the IRS required the restoration of write-downs for damaged and shopworn goods when the taxpayer switched to LIFO.

[109]I.R.B. 2011–4.

[110]§ 472(d), overruling the IRS position cited in Footnote 109.

[111]§ 472(c).

[112]Reg. § 1.472–2(e).

[113]Reg. § 1.471–6(d).

[114]Reg. § 1.471–6(e). See also IRS Pub. 225 (*Farmers Tax Guide*), p. 7.

18-5 TAX PLANNING

The tax accounting period and method rules sometimes present opportunities for tax planning.

LO.7

Identify tax planning opportunities related to accounting periods and accounting methods.

18-5a Taxable Year

Under the general rules for tax years, partnerships and S corporations frequently will be required to use a calendar year. However, if the partnership or S corporation can demonstrate a business purpose for a fiscal year, the IRS will allow the entity to use the requested year. The advantage to a fiscal year is that the calendar year partners and S corporation shareholders may be able to defer from tax the income earned from the close of the fiscal year until the end of the calendar year. Tax advisers for these entities should apply the IRS's gross receipts test described in Revenue Procedure 87–32 to determine whether permission for the fiscal year will be granted.[115]

18-5b Cash Method of Accounting

The cash method of accounting gives the taxpayer considerable control over the recognition of expenses and some control over the recognition of income. This method can be used by proprietorships, partnerships, S corporations, and small C corporations (gross receipts of $5 million or less) that provide services (inventories are not material to the service business). Farmers (except certain farming corporations) can also use the cash method.

18-5c Installment Method

Unlike the cash and accrual methods, the installment method often results in an interest-free loan (of deferred taxes) from the government. The installment method is not available for the sale of inventory. Nevertheless, the installment method is an important tax planning technique and should be considered when a sale of eligible property is being planned. That is, if the taxpayer can benefit from deferring the tax, the terms of sale can be arranged so that the installment method rules apply. If, on the other hand, the taxpayer expects to be in a higher tax bracket when the payments will be received, he or she can elect not to use the installment method.

Related Parties

Intrafamily installment sales can still be a useful family tax planning tool. If the related party holds the property more than two years, a subsequent sale will not accelerate the gain from the first disposition. Patience and forethought are rewarded.

Disposition of Installment Obligations

A disposition of an installment obligation is also a serious matter. Gifts of the obligations will accelerate income to the seller. The list of taxable and nontaxable dispositions of installment obligations should not be trusted to memory. In each instance where transfers of installment obligations are contemplated, the practitioner should conduct research to make sure he or she knows the consequences.

18-5d Completed Contract Method

Small contractors (average annual gross receipts do not exceed $10 million) working on contracts that are completed within a two-year period can elect to use the completed contract method and defer profit until the year in which the contract is completed.

---

[115]See also Rev.Proc. 2002–38, 2002–1 C.B. 1037.

18-5e Inventories

A $1 reduction in ending inventory valuation decreases taxable income for the year by $1. The ending inventory valuation can be minimized and thus taxable income reduced by using elective accounting methods: (1) purchase prices can be stated net of cash discounts, (2) the lower of cost or market method may be applied, and (3) the LIFO method can be adopted during rising prices.

REFOCUS ON THE BIG PICTURE

ACCOUNTING PERIOD AND METHOD

Selection of a Tax Year

An entity's tax form will govern the rules for determining the entity's tax year. Because Silver is a partnership, the Code's provisions for partnerships are applicable.

In this case, Tweety's 40 percent ownership interest in Silver is not sufficient to enable it to control the selection of the partnership's tax year. Likewise, Belinda and Pearl's collective controlling interest will not allow them to control the selection of the tax year for the partnership.

The Code and related Regulations have a very precise set of rules regarding the selection of a tax year for a partnership. The partnership applies these rules in the following sequence:

- *Majority interest tax year.* The tax year of the partners who have a common year-end and collectively own a greater-than-50 percent interest in the partnership capital and profits.
- *Principal partners' tax year.* The tax year if all of the principal partners (5 percent or greater interest in capital or profits) have the same tax year.
- *Least aggregate deferral tax year.* The tax year of the principal partners (grouped by a common year-end) that produces the least aggregate deferral of income.

Alternatively, the partnership can select its tax year based on a business purpose for the tax year selected. However, this requires the approval of the IRS, which is unlikely to be granted. The only business purpose the IRS has acknowledged is the need to conform the tax year to the entity's natural business year.

Therefore, from the data provided, it appears that Silver will determine its tax year by using the least aggregate deferral method. Based on this method, Silver's tax year will end on November 30 (see the calculations in Example 3).

Short Tax Year

Silver will have a short tax year that begins on April 1, 2014, and ends on November 30, 2014, as determined by the least aggregate deferral method. Silver will not have to annualize the income reported on its first income tax return. Note, however, that annualization will be required if Silver ever changes its tax year.

Partner's Reporting of Share of Net Income

Each of the partners will receive a Schedule K–1 that reports the partner's share of net income. From a timing perspective, the partner will include the Schedule K–1 items on the partner's income tax return only if a partnership tax year ends within or with the partner's tax year.

Partnership's Accounting Method

Silver Partnership must use the accrual method to compute its income because one of its partners (Pearl, Inc.) is a C corporation within gross receipts of more than $5 million. Thus, even though Belinda is a cash basis taxpayer, her share of the partnership income will be computed by the accrual method.

Key Terms

Accounting methods, 18-11

Accounting period, 18-2

Accrual method, 18-14

All events test, 18-15

Cash method, 18-11

Claim of right doctrine, 18-9

Completed contract method, 18-29

Crop insurance proceeds, 18-9

Crop method, 18-14

Dollar-value LIFO, 18-36

Economic performance test, 18-15

Farm price method, 18-38

Fiscal year, 18-2

Hybrid method, 18-18

Imputed interest, 18-24

Installment method, 18-21

Least aggregate deferral method, 18-4

Long-term contract, 18-28

Lower of cost or market (replacement cost), 18-35

Majority interest partners, 18-3

One-year rule for prepaid expenses, 18-12

Percentage of completion method, 18-31

Personal service corporation (PSC), 18-6

Principal partner, 18-3

Short period, 18-8

Short taxable year, 18-8

Uniform capitalization (UNICAP) rules, 18-33

Unit-livestock-price method, 18-38

Discussion Questions

1. **LO.1** Would a tax year ending December 31 be appropriate for a Ski lodge? Why or why not?

2. **LO.1** Assume that a partnership is profitable and that its tax year ends on December 31 but one of the partners' tax year ends on September 30. Does the partner enjoy a tax benefit or detriment from the partnership's use of a December 31 tax year-end? Explain.

3. **LO.1** A law practice was incorporated on January 1, 2014, and expects to earn $25,000 per month before deducting the lawyer's salary. The lawyer owns 100% of the stock. The corporation and the lawyer both use the cash method of accounting. The corporation does not need to retain any of the earnings in the business; thus, the salary of the lawyer (a calendar year taxpayer) will equal the corporation's net income before salary expense. If the corporation could choose any tax year and pay the lawyer's salary at the time that would be most tax efficient (but at least once every 12 months), what tax year should the corporation choose? When should the salary be paid each year?   *Decision Making*

4. **LO.1** Art Funkel started his incorporated medical practice on June 1, 2014. He immediately made an S election for the corporation. Art would like the corporation to adopt a tax year ending May 31 so that a full 12 months of income would be included in the first tax year. Can the corporation elect a fiscal year ending May 31? Explain.

5. **LO.1** Fred, a cash basis taxpayer, received a $15,000 bonus from his employer in 2014. The bonus was based on the company's profits for 2013. In 2015, the company discovered that its 2013 profits were incorrectly computed. As a result, Fred received an additional $10,000 with respect to 2013 profits. Fred's marginal tax rate in 2014 was 15%, and it was 35% in 2015. Sue, also a cash basis taxpayer, received a $35,000 bonus in 2015 that was based on 2014 profits. In 2015, the company discovered that it had overstated its profits in 2014. As a result, Sue was required to repay $10,000 of her bonus in 2015. Sue was in the 35% marginal tax bracket in 2014 and in the 15% marginal bracket in 2015. What special tax treatment is available to Fred and Sue as a result of their employer's errors?   *Issue ID*

6. **LO.2** Under what conditions would the cash method of accounting be advantageous as compared with the accrual basis?

7. **LO.2** In December 2014, Nell, Inc., an accrual basis taxpayer, paid $12,000 for insurance premiums for her business for the 2015 calendar year. How much of the premiums can Nell, Inc., deduct in 2014?

WWW **For the latest in changes to tax legislation, visit www.cengagebrain.com**

8. **LO.2** In 2013, the taxpayer became ineligible to use the cash method of accounting. At the beginning of the year, accounts receivable totaled $240,000, accounts payable for merchandise totaled $80,000, and the inventory on hand totaled $320,000. What is the amount of the adjustment due to the change in accounting method?

9. **LO.2** Osprey Corporation, an accrual basis taxpayer, had taxable income for 2014 and paid $40,000 on its estimated state income tax for the year. During 2014, the company received a $4,000 refund upon filing its 2013 state income tax return. The company filed its 2014 state income tax return in August 2015 and paid the $7,000 state income tax due for 2014. In December 2014, the company received a notice from the state tax commission that an additional $6,000 of income tax was due for 2012 because of an error on the return. The company acknowledged the error in December 2014 and paid the additional $6,000 in tax in February 2015. What is Osprey's 2014 Federal income tax deduction for state income taxes?

10. **LO.2** Compare the cash and accrual methods of accounting for the following events:
    a. Purchased new equipment, paying $50,000 cash and giving a note payable for $30,000 due next year.
    b. Paid $3,600 for a three-year service contract on the new equipment.
    c. Collected $1,800 for services to be provided over the current and following years.
    d. Received a $3,000 note from a customer for services provided in the current year. The market value of the note was only $2,400.

Decision Making

11. **LO.2** Edgar uses the cash method to report the income from his software consulting business. A large publicly held corporation has offered to invest in Edgar's business as a limited partner. What tax accounting complications would be created if Edgar and the corporation became partners?

12. **LO.2** Samantha, an accrual basis taxpayer, subscribes to a service that updates a database used in her business. In December 2014, Samantha paid the $120,000 subscription for the period January 2014 through December 2015. What is Samantha's deduction for 2014?

13. **LO.2** Emerald Motors is an automobile dealer. The controller consults with you about the type of accounting used for a special offer to its new car customers. Emerald has offered to provide at no charge to the customer the first four recommended service visits (i.e., at 3,000, 6,000, 9,000, and 12,000 miles). It is a virtual certainty that all customers will exercise their rights to the service, and the cost of the services can be accurately estimated. The controller reasons that the estimated cost should be accrued when the sale of an automobile is made so that all of the costs of the sale can be matched with the revenue. How would you respond to the controller?

Decision Making

14. **LO.4, 7** Irene has made Sara an offer on the purchase of a capital asset. Irene will pay (1) $200,000 cash or (2) $50,000 cash and a 6% installment note for $150,000 guaranteed by City Bank of New York. If Sara sells for $200,000 cash, she will invest the after-tax proceeds in certificates of deposit yielding 6% interest. Sara's cost of the asset is $25,000. Why would Sara prefer the installment sale?

15. **LO.4** Arnold gave land to his son, Bruce. Arnold's basis in the land was $100,000, and its fair market value at the date of the gift was $150,000. Bruce borrowed $130,000 from a bank that he used to improve the property. He sold the property to Della for $360,000. Della paid Bruce $90,000 in cash, assumed his $120,000 mortgage, and agreed to pay $150,000 in two years. Bruce's selling expenses were $10,000. Della is going to pay adequate interest. What is Bruce's installment sale gain in the year of sale?

16. **LO.4** A seller and a buyer agree that the sales/purchase price for land is $1,500,000 down and two annual payments of $1,500,000 each to be made over the next two years. The buyer intends to construct a building on the land that will be used as the buyer's warehouse. It will be built over the next two years. The seller proposes that the contract should read that the total selling price is $4,300,000 and that the two deferred payments of $1,500,000 each include interest at 4%, which is the current Federal intermediate-term rate but is less than the interest rate on commercial real estate. The land is a capital asset to the seller, and the holding period is four years. Why should the seller and not the buyer be more concerned about the stated interest rate?

17. **LO.4, 7** On June 1, 2012, Father sold land to Son for $300,000. Father reported the gain by the installment method, with the gain to be spread over five years. In May 2014, Son received an offer of $400,000 for the land, to be paid over three years. What would be the tax consequences of Son's sale? How could the tax consequences be improved?

Decision Making

18. **LO.4, 7** In December 2014, Carl Corporation sold land it held as an investment. The corporation received $50,000 in 2014 and a note payable (with adequate interest) for $150,000 to be paid in 2016. Carl Corporation's cost of the land was $80,000. The corporation has a $90,000 net capital loss carryover that will expire in 2014. Should Carl Corporation report the sale in 2014 or use the installment method to report the income as payments are received?

Decision Making

19. **LO.2, 5** What are the similarities between the crop method used for farming and the completed contract method used for long-term construction?

20. **LO.5** Nathan uses the percentage of completion method to report income from his real estate construction contracts. A contract was begun in 2014 and completed in 2015. In 2014, Nathan reported gross income from the partial completion of the contract. In 2015, however, costs had increased above the original estimate. The contract was completed with the actual profit on the contract being less than the income from the contract reported in 2014. What mechanism should be used to correct for the overpayment of tax in 2014?

21. **LO.5** Neal uses the percentage of completion method to report his gross income from long-term contracts that were to begin in 2014. In 2015, he completes a contract for more than the estimate of total costs that was used in the prior year. What are the tax accounting implications of the incorrect estimate?

22. **LO.5** The Hawk Corporation builds yachts. The vessels it currently produces are practically identical and are completed in approximately 8 months. A customer has approached Hawk about constructing a larger yacht that would take approximately 15 months to complete. What are the tax implications of accepting the contract proposal?

23. **LO.6** Largo Company is an engineering consulting business that uses the accrual method of accounting for its services. Mango Company is a manufacturer of nuts and bolts that also uses the accrual method to account for its sales. Each company has a personnel department. How should the cost of personnel operations be treated by each of the two companies?

Issue ID

24. **LO.6** Amber Auto Parts adopted the dollar-value LIFO inventory method. The company has consistently used a retail price index when it should have used a producer's. As a result, its LIFO layers have been consistently undervalued. Why is the company's error exacerbated by the fact that the company uses the LIFO method instead of the FIFO method?

Issue ID

25. **LO.6** Opal, Inc., is about to make its first attempt to borrow from a local bank. The company uses LIFO for tax purposes, solely to defer taxes, and believes that income computed using the FIFO method would better reflect its income. The company also uses the double-declining balance method of depreciation for tax, although the straight-line method better reflects the actual depreciation. The company would like to present its financial position in the most favorable light. Therefore, Opal's CEO intends to provide the bank with an income statement prepared using the FIFO inventory method and straight-line depreciation. What types of problems will presenting the income statement to the bank in this fashion cause for Opal?

Issue ID

26. **LO.6** Blue is a retailer that uses the FIFO inventory method. Blue has consistently taken its physical inventory at the end of the day on the last day of its tax year, December 31. This practice is very unpopular with its employees, who do not like working on New Year's Eve. The company is considering taking the inventory at the end of November and adjusting for sales and purchases in the last month of the year. However, the CFO has raised the issue that by taking the inventory at the end of November, loss from theft and breakage in December will not be taken into account until the physical inventory is taken in the following year. Is the CFO's concern valid? Explain.

Issue ID

Problems

27. **LO.1** Red, White, and Blue are unrelated corporations engaged in real estate development. The three corporations formed a joint venture (treated as a partnership) to develop a tract of land. Assuming that the venture does not have a natural business year, what tax year must the joint venture adopt under the following circumstances?

		Tax Year Ending	Interest in Joint Venture
a.	Red	March 31	60%
	Blue	June 30	20%
	White	October 31	20%
b.	Red	October 31	30%
	White	September 30	40%
	Blue	January 31	30%

Decision Making

28. **LO.1, 7** The Cardinal Wholesale Company is an S corporation that began business on March 1, 2014. Robert, a calendar year taxpayer, owns 100% of the Cardinal stock. He has $400,000 taxable income from other sources each year. Robert will work approximately 30 hours a week for the corporation. Cardinal sells swimming pool supplies, and its natural business year ends in September. Approximately 80% of Cardinal's gross receipts occur in June through September.
    a. What tax year should Cardinal elect, assuming that Robert anticipates the company will produce a net profit for all years?
    b. What tax year should Cardinal elect, assuming that it will lose $10,000 a month for the first 12 months and an average of $5,000 a month for the next 12 months? In the third year, the corporation will earn taxable income.

Decision Making

29. **LO.1** Zorn conducted his professional practice through Zorn, Inc. The corporation uses a fiscal year ending September 30 even though the business purpose test for a fiscal year cannot be satisfied. For the year ending September 30, 2014, the corporation paid Zorn a salary of $180,000, and during the period January through September 2014, the corporation paid him a salary of $150,000.
    a. How much salary should Zorn receive during the period October 1 through December 31, 2014?
    b. Assume that Zorn received only $24,000 salary during the period October 1 through December 31, 2014. What would be the consequences to Zorn, Inc.?

30. **LO.1** Mauve Corporation began operations as a farm supplies business and used a fiscal year ending October 31. The company gradually went out of the farm supplies business and into the mail-order Christmas gifts business. The company has received permission from the IRS to change to a fiscal year ending January 31, effective for the year ending January 31, 2015. For the short period November 1, 2014, through January 31, 2015, Mauve earned $20,000. Calculate Mauve's tax liability for the short period November 1, 2014, through January 31, 2015.

31. **LO.1** In 2013, Juan entered into a contract to write a book. The publisher advanced Juan $50,000, which was to be repaid out of future royalties. If the book was not completed by the end of 2014, however, Juan would be required to repay the publisher for the advance. Juan did not complete the book in 2014, and in accordance with the agreement, he repaid the $50,000 to the publisher in 2015. Juan is a cash basis taxpayer. What are the tax consequences to Juan of the repayment under the following assumptions?
    a. Juan's marginal tax rate was 15% in 2013 and 35% in 2015.
    b. Juan's marginal tax rate was 35% in 2013 and 15% in 2015.

Communications

32. **LO.2** Gold, Inc., is an accrual basis taxpayer. In 2014, an employee accidentally spilled hazardous chemicals on leased property. The chemicals destroyed trees on neighboring property, resulting in $30,000 of damages. In 2014, the owner of the property sued Gold, Inc., for the $30,000. Gold's attorney believes that it is liable and that the only issue is whether the neighbor will also seek punitive damages that could be as much as three times the actual damages. In addition, as a result of the spill, Gold was in violation of its lease and was therefore required to pay the landlord $15,000. However, the amount due for the lease violation is not payable until the termination of the lease in 2017. None of

these costs were covered by insurance. Jeff Stuart, the president of Gold, Inc., is generally familiar with the accrual basis tax accounting rules and is concerned about when the company will be allowed to deduct the amounts the company is required to pay as a result of this environmental disaster. Write Mr. Stuart a letter explaining these issues. Gold's address is 200 Elm Avenue, San Jose, CA 95192.

33. **LO.2** Compute Mary's income or deductions for 2014 using (1) the cash basis and (2) the accrual basis for each of the following:
    a. In May 2014, Mary paid a license fee of $1,200 for the period June 1, 2014, through May 31, 2015.
    b. In December 2014, Mary collected $10,000 for January 2015 rents. In January 2015, Mary collected $2,000 for December 2014 rents.
    c. In June 2014, Mary paid $7,200 for an office equipment service contract for the period July 1, 2014, through December 31, 2015.
    d. In June 2014, Mary purchased office furniture for $273,000. She paid $131,000 in cash and gave a $142,000 interest-bearing note for the balance. The office furniture has an MACRS cost recovery period of seven years. Mary did not make the § 179 election and elected not to take additional first-year depreciation.

34. **LO.2, 5** What accounting method (cash or accrual) would you recommend for the following businesses?
    a. A gift shop with average annual gross receipts of $900,000.
    b. An accounting partnership with annual gross receipts of $12 million.
    c. A drywall subcontractor who works on residences and has annual gross receipts of $3 million.
    d. An incorporated insurance agency with annual gross receipts of $6 million.

35. **LO.2** Blue Company, an architectural firm, has a bookkeeper who maintains a cash receipts and disbursements journal. At the end of the year (2014), the company hires you to convert the cash receipts and disbursements into accrual basis revenues and expenses. The total cash receipts are summarized as follows:

Decision Making

Cash sales	$150,000
Collections on accounts receivable	350,000
Bank loan	90,000
Total cash receipts	$590,000

The accounts receivable from customers at the end of the year are $120,000. You note that the accounts receivable at the beginning of the year were $190,000. The cash sales included $30,000 of prepayments for services to be provided over the period January 1, 2014, through December 31, 2016.
    a. Compute the company's accrual basis gross income for 2014.
    b. Would you recommend that Blue use the cash method or the accrual method? Why?
    c. The company does not maintain an allowance for uncollectible accounts. Would you recommend that such an allowance be established for tax purposes? Explain.

36. **LO.2** How do the all events and economic performance requirements apply to the following transactions by an accrual basis taxpayer?
    a. The company guarantees its products for six months. At the end of 2014, customers had made valid claims for $600,000 that were not paid until 2015. Also, the company estimates that another $400,000 in claims from 2014 sales will be filed and paid in 2015.
    b. The accrual basis taxpayer reported $200,000 in corporate taxable income for 2014. The state income tax rate was 6%. The corporation paid $7,000 in estimated state income taxes in 2014 and paid $2,000 on 2013 state income taxes when it filed its 2013 state income tax return in March 2014. The company filed its 2014 state income tax return in March 2015 and paid the remaining $5,000 of its 2014 state income tax liability.
    c. An employee was involved in an accident while making a sales call. The company paid the injured victim $15,000 in 2014 and agreed to pay the victim $15,000 a year for the next nine years.

37. **LO.3** Ross Company is a computer consulting firm. The company also sells equipment to its clients. The sales of equipment account for approximately 40% of the company's gross receipts. The company has consistently used the cash method to report its income from services and the accrual method to report its income from the sale of inventory. In June of the current year, Ross's accountant discovered that as a small business, the company qualifies to use the cash method for all of its activities. The company is a calendar year taxpayer. As of the beginning of the current year, the company had $120,000 of inventory on hand and $90,000 of accounts receivable from the sales of equipment and $30,000 of receivables from the consulting services.
    a. Compute the adjustment due to the change in accounting method.
    b. Is the adjustment positive or negative? Explain.
    c. When can the adjustment be taken into account in computing taxable income?

Decision Making

38. **LO.2, 3** Raven Finance Company experiences bad debts of about 3% of its outstanding loans. At the end of the year, the company had outstanding receivables of $18 million. This balance included $2 million of accrued interest receivable. Raven's loan loss reserve for the year was computed as follows:

Balance, January 1, 2014	$500,000
Accounts written off as uncollectible	
Loans made in 2014	(20,000)
Loans made in prior years	(40,000)
Collections on loans previously written off	15,000
Adjustment to required balance	85,000
Balance, December 31, 2014	$540,000

    a. Determine the effects of the above on Raven's taxable income for 2014.
    b. Assume that Raven has used the reserve method to compute its taxable income for the 10 years the company has been in existence. In 2014, you begin preparing Raven's tax return. What should be done with regard to the reserve?

Communications

39. **LO.2, 3, 6** Jeffrey Boyd, the president of Eagle Furniture Company (average annual gross receipts of $4 million), has prepared the company's financial statements and income tax returns for the past 15 years. In July 2015, however, he hires you to prepare the 2014 corporate income tax return because he has not studied taxes for over 20 years and suspects that the rules may have changed. Eagle uses the accrual method of accounting. Based on an initial examination of Eagle's trial balance and some account analyses, you have determined that the following items may require adjustments:

- The company uses the FIFO inventory method, as valued at cost. However, all freight expenses on incoming merchandise have been expensed for the 15 years the company has been in business.
- The company experiences inventory shrinkage (due to breakage and theft) of about 1% of sales each year. The shrinkage is not taken into account until the company takes a physical inventory each October, but the corporation's fiscal year ends January 31.
- The company has used an allowance for uncollectible accounts, which has a balance of $60,000. In the past, the company has been able to accurately predict its actual bad debt expense.
- The company sells a three-year service contract on its appliances. The company treats $1/36$ of the contract price as earned each month. At the beginning of the year, the company had $120,000 in its account for unearned revenues from the service contracts.
- The company deducts its state income tax in the year paid. Thus, the 2014 state income tax expense includes the estimated taxes paid in 2014 and the additional amount paid in 2014 on 2013 taxes.

    Write a letter to Mr. Boyd explaining what adjustments will be required and how they will be implemented. The address of Eagle Furniture Company is 1000 East Maryland Street, Evansville, IL 47722.

Decision Making

40. **LO.4, 7** Floyd, a cash basis taxpayer, has received an offer to purchase his land. The cash basis buyer will pay him either $100,000 at closing or $50,000 at closing and $56,000 two years after the date of closing. If Floyd recognizes the entire gain in the current year, his marginal tax rate will be 25% (combined Federal and state rates). However, if he spreads the gain over the two years, his marginal tax rate on the gain will be only 20%. Floyd does not consider the buyer a credit risk, and he understands that

shifting the gain to next year with an installment sale will save taxes. But he realizes that the deferred payment will, in effect, earn only $6,000 for waiting two years for the other $50,000. Floyd believes he can earn a 10% before-tax rate of return on his after-tax cash. Floyd's adjusted basis for the land is $25,000, the buyer is also a cash basis taxpayer, and the short-term Federal rate is 4%. Floyd has asked you to evaluate the two alternatives on an after-tax basis.

41. **LO.4, 7** Ted purchased equipment and used materials to develop a patent. The development costs were deducted on prior returns. The bases and fair market values of the assets are presented below.

Decision Making

Assets	Fair Market Value		Basis
Equipment	$350,000	Cost	$ 350,000
		Less: Depreciation	(250,000)
Patent	250,000		–0–
	$600,000		$ 100,000

Sarah has made an offer to purchase the assets. Under one plan, she would pay $200,000 now and $400,000 plus interest at 5% (the Federal rate) in one year. Alternatively, Ted would incorporate the assets and then sell the stock to Sarah. Incorporating the assets would not be a taxable event to Ted, and his basis in the stock would equal his basis in the assets of $100,000. The corporation's basis in the assets would also be $100,000, the same as Ted's basis for the stock. Because the corporation would have a basis in the assets of less than the fair market value (and therefore, there would be less depreciation and amortization than with an asset sale by Ted), Sarah would pay $200,000 in the current year but only $350,000, plus interest at 5%, in one year. Assume that Ted's marginal tax rate is 35%.

a. What is Ted's gain in the year of sale from the installment sale of his assets?
b. Assuming that Ted's time value of money is 5%, would he prefer the sale of the assets or the sale of the stock? Why?

42. **LO.4** Kay, who is not a dealer, sold an apartment house to Polly during the current year (2014). The closing statement for the sale is as follows:

Total selling price		$ 190,000
Add: Polly's share of property taxes (6 months) paid by Kay		3,000
Less: Kay's 8% mortgage assumed by Polly	$55,000	
Polly's refundable binder ("earnest money") paid in 2014	1,000	
Polly's 8% installment note given to Kay	99,000	
Kay's real estate commissions and attorney's fees	8,000	(163,000)
Cash paid to Kay at closing		$ 30,000
Cash due from Polly = $30,000 + $8,000 expenses		$ 38,000

During 2014, Kay collected $9,000 in principal on the installment note and $2,000 of interest. Kay's basis in the property was $110,000 [$125,000 – $15,000 (depreciation)]. The Federal rate is 6%.
a. Compute the following:
   1. Total gain.
   2. Contract price.
   3. Payments received in the year of sale.
   4. Recognized gain in the year of sale and the character of such gain.

   (*Hint:* Think carefully about the manner in which the property taxes are handled before you begin your computations.)
b. Same as (a)(2) and (3), except that Kay's basis in the property was $35,000.

43. **LO.4** On June 30, 2014, Kelly sold property for $240,000 cash and a $960,000 note due on September 30, 2015. The note will also pay 6% interest, which is slighty higher than the Federal rate. Kelly's cost of the property was $400,000. She is concerned that Congress may increase the tax rate that will apply when the note is collected. Kelly's after-tax rate of return on investments is 6%.

Decision Making

a. What can Kelly do to avoid the expected higher tax rate?

b. Assuming that Kelly's marginal combined Federal and state tax rate is 25% in 2014, how much would the tax rates need to increase to make the option identified in (a) advisable?

Decision Making

44. **LO.4** On December 30, 2013, Maud sold land to her son, Charles, for $50,000 cash and a 7% installment note for $350,000, payable over 10 years. Maud's cost of the land was $150,000. In October 2015, after Charles had paid $60,000 on the principal of the note, he received an offer to sell the land for $500,000 cash. What advice can you provide Charles that will minimize the present value of the tax liability for Maud and him?

45. **LO.4** George sold land to an unrelated party in 2013. His basis in the land was $45,000, and the selling price was $120,000—$30,000 payable at closing and $30,000 (plus 10% interest) due January 1, 2014, 2015, and 2016. What would be the tax consequences of the following? [Treat each part independently and assume that (1) George did not elect out of the installment method and (2) the installment obligations have values equal to their face amounts. Ignore interest in your calculations.]

a. In 2014, George borrowed $40,000 from the bank. The loan was partially secured by the installment notes, but George was personally liable for the loan.

b. In 2014, George gave to his daughter the right to collect all future payments on the installment obligations.

c. On December 31, 2014, George received the payment due on January 1, 2015. On December 15, 2015, George died, and the remaining installment obligation was transferred to his estate. The estate collected the amount due on January 1, 2016.

46. **LO.5** The Wren Construction Company reports its income by the completed contract method. At the end of 2014, the company completed a contract to construct a building at a total cost of $800,000. The contract price was $1.2 million, and the customer paid Wren $900,000. However, the customer refused to accept the work and would not pay anything else on the contract because he claimed that the roof did not meet specifications. Wren's engineers estimated that it would cost $140,000 to bring the roof up to the customer's standards. In 2015, the dispute was settled in the customer's favor; the roof was improved at a cost of $150,000, and the customer accepted the building and paid the remaining $300,000.

a. What would be the effects of the above on Wren's taxable income for 2014 and 2015?

b. Same as (a), except that Wren had $1,100,000 of accumulated costs under the contract at the end of 2014.

Communications

47. **LO.5** Rust Company is a real estate construction company with average annual gross receipts of $4 million. Rust uses the completed contract method, and the contracts require 18 months to complete.

a. Which of the following costs would be allocated to construction in progress by Rust?

1. The payroll taxes on direct labor.

2. The current services pension costs for employees whose wages are included in direct labor.

3. Accelerated depreciation on equipment used on contracts.

4. Freight charges on materials assigned to contracts.

5. The past service costs for employees whose wages are included in direct labor.

6. Bidding expenses for contracts awarded.

b. Assume that Rust generally builds commercial buildings under contracts with the owners and reports the income using the completed contract method. The company is considering building a series of similar stores for a retail chain. The gross profit margin would be a low percentage, but the company's gross receipts would triple. Write a letter to your client, Rust Company, explaining the tax accounting implications of entering into these contracts. Rust's mailing address is P.O. Box 1000, Harrisonburg, VA 22807.

48. **LO.5** On March 31, 2012, Big Boats Company entered into a contract with Vacations Unlimited to produce a state-of-the-art cruise ship, to be completed within three years. Big Boats estimated the total cost of building the ship at $300 million. The contract price was $400 million. The ship was completed on February 15, 2015.

a. What tax accounting method must Big Boats use for the contract? Why?

b. Using the financial data provided relating to the contract's performance, complete the following schedule:

Date	Total Costs Incurred to Date	Total Percentage of Contract Completed	Current-Year Revenue Accrued	Current-Year Costs Deductible
12/31/12	$ 90 million	——	——	——
12/31/13	150 million	——	——	——
12/31/14	270 million	——	——	——
12/31/15	360 million	N/A	——	——

c. What are the consequences of the total cost of $360 million exceeding the estimated total cost of $300 million?

49. **LO.5** Ostrich Company makes gasoline storage tanks. Everything produced is under contract (that is, the company does not produce until it gets a contract for a product). Ostrich makes three basic models. However, the tanks must be adapted to each individual customer's location and needs (e.g., the location of the valves and the quality of the materials and insulation). Discuss the following issues relative to Ostrich's operations:

   a. An examining IRS agent contends that each of the company's contracts is to produce a "unique product." What difference does it make whether the product is unique or a "shelf item"?

   b. Producing one of the tanks takes over one year from start to completion, and the total cost is in excess of $1 million. What costs must be capitalized for this contract that are not subject to capitalization for a contract with a shorter duration and lower cost?

   c. What must Ostrich do with the costs of bidding on contracts?

   d. Ostrich frequently makes several cost estimates for a contract, using various estimates of materials costs. These costs fluctuate almost daily. Assuming that Ostrich must use the percentage of completion method to report the income from the contract, what will be the consequence if the company uses the highest estimate of a contract's cost and the actual cost is closer to the lowest estimated cost?

50. **LO.5, 7** Swallow Company is a large real estate construction company that has made a Subchapter S election. The company reports its income using the percentage of completion method. In 2015, the company completed a contract at a total cost of $4.8 million. The contract price was $7.2 million. At the end of 2014, the year the contract was begun, Swallow estimated that the total cost of the contract would be $5.4 million. Total accumulated cost on the contract at the end of 2014 was $1.8 million. The relevant tax rate is 35%, and the relevant Federal interest rate is 5%. Assume that all income tax returns were filed and taxes were paid on March 15 following the end of the calendar tax year.

   a. Compute the gross profit on the contract for 2014 and 2015.

   b. Compute the lookback interest due or receivable with the 2015 tax return.

   c. Before bidding on a contract, Swallow generally makes three estimates of total contract costs: (1) optimistic, (2) pessimistic, and (3) most likely (based on a blending of optimistic and pessimistic assumptions). The company has asked you to write a letter explaining which of these estimates should be used for percentage of completion purposes. In writing your letter, you should consider the fact that Swallow is incorporated and has made an S corporation election. Therefore, the income and deductions flow through to the shareholders who are all individuals in the 35% marginal tax bracket. The relevant Federal interest rate is 8%. Swallow's mailing address is 400 Front Avenue, Ashland, OR 97520.

Communications

51. **LO.6** Grouse Company is a furniture retailer whose average annual gross receipts for the three preceding years exceeded $10 million. In the current tax year, the company purchased merchandise with an invoice price of $15 million, less a 2% discount for early payment. However, the company had to borrow on a bank line of credit and paid $150,000 interest to take advantage of the discount for early payment. Freight on the merchandise purchased totaled $360,000. For September, Grouse agreed to pay the customer's freight on goods sold. The total cost of this freight-out was $70,000. The company has three stores and operates a warehouse where it stores goods. The cost of operating the warehouse was $240,000. The $240,000 includes labor, depreciation, taxes, and insurance on the building. The cost of the purchasing operations totaled $420,000.

The jurisdiction where the company operates imposes a tax on inventories on hand as of January 1. The inventory tax for this year is $24,000. The invoice cost of goods on hand at the end of the year is $3 million. Compute Grouse's ending inventory using the FIFO method.

Decision Making

52. **LO.6, 7** Lavender Manufacturing Company began business in the current year. The company uses the simplified method to allocate mixed services costs to production. The company's costs and expenses for the year were as follows:

Direct labor	$ 3,000,000
Direct materials	4,000,000
Factory supervision	800,000
Property tax on factory	100,000
Personnel department	400,000
Computer operations	250,000
General administration	550,000
Marketing	800,000
State income tax	200,000
	$10,100,000

a. Determine Lavender's total production costs for the year.

b. Assume that the hourly pay for direct labor is much lower than the hourly pay for employees in general administration and that the employee turnover is much higher for production employees than for general administration employees. How should these facts affect the company's decision to use the simplified mixed services method to allocate mixed services costs to production?

Issue ID

53. **LO.6** Silver Creek Ranch, LLC, is a small, family-owned cattle ranch that began operations in the current year. The ranch grows hay that will be fed to its purebred cattle. It will take approximately three years to build up the herd and to begin producing a positive cash flow. The owners' other income will equal their deductions, so they will not be able to utilize farm losses for the first three years. The owners have asked you to discuss the tax accounting issues related to their cattle business.

54. **LO.3, 6** In 2014, Gail changed from the lower of cost or market FIFO method to the LIFO inventory method. The ending inventory for 2013 was computed as follows:

Item	FIFO Cost	Replacement Cost	Lower of Cost or Market
A	$26,000	$15,000	$15,000
B	52,000	55,000	52,000
C	30,000	7,000	7,000
			$74,000

Item C was damaged goods, and the replacement cost used was actually the estimated selling price of the goods. The actual cost to replace item C was $32,000.

a. What is the correct beginning inventory for 2014 under the LIFO method?

b. What immediate tax consequences (if any) will result from the switch to LIFO?

55. **LO.6** At the end of 2015, Magenta Manufacturing Company discovered that construction cost had been capitalized as a cost of the factory building in 2010 when it should have been treated as a cost of production equipment installation costs. As a result of the misclassification, the depreciation through 2013 was understated by $110,000, and depreciation for 2014 was understated by $90,000. What would be the consequences of correcting for the misclassification of the property cost?

a. The taxpayer uses the FIFO inventory method, and 25% of goods produced during the period were included in the ending inventory.

b. The taxpayer uses the LIFO inventory method, and no new LIFO layer was added during 2014.

56. **LO.6** Amber Company has used the dollar-value LIFO technique for the past three years. The company has only one inventory pool. Its beginning inventory for the current year was computed as follows:

	Base Period Cost	LIFO Index	LIFO Layer
Base period inventory	$1,200,000	1 .00	$1,200,000
Year 1 layer	300,000	1.04	312,000
Year 2 layer	400,000	1.06	424,000
	$1,900,000		$1,936,000

a. The current-year ending inventory (end of year 3) at current prices is $2,124,000, and the LIFO index is 1.06. Determine the company's LIFO inventory as of the end of the current year.

b. Assume that the current-year ending inventory at current prices is $1,850,000. What is the end-of-the-current-year LIFO inventory value?

57. **LO.4, 7** Your client, Bob Young, is negotiating a sale of investment real estate for $12 million. Bob believes that the buyer would pay cash of $8 million and a note for $4 million or $3 million cash and a note for $9 million. The notes will pay interest at slightly above the market rate. Bob realizes that the second option involves more risks of collection, but he is willing to accept that risk if the tax benefits of the installment sale are substantial. Write a letter to Bob advising him of the tax consequences of choosing the lower down payment and larger note option, assuming that he has no other installment receivables. Bob's address is 200 Jerdone, Gettysburg, PA 17325.

Decision Making

Communications

Research Problems

Note: Solutions to Research Problems can be prepared by using the **Checkpoint®** **Student Edition** online research product, which is available to accompany this text. It is also possible to prepare solutions to the Research Problems by using tax research materials found in a standard tax library.

THOMSON REUTERS

CHECKPOINT®

Research Problem 1. Your client is not permitted to deduct a year-end accrual for vacation pay earned but not paid. This result occurs because the tax law considers this to be deferred compensation that is ineligible for the recurring item exception, unless it is paid by March 15 of the year following the accrual [see §§ 404(a)(5) and (6)]. Your client has asked whether the related accrued Social Security taxes on the vacation pay can be accrued under the general recurring item exception because these taxes will be paid by the fifteenth day of the ninth month after the close of the tax year.

Research Problem 2. Like most other airlines, your client, XYZ Airlines (an accrual basis, calendar year C corporation), sells more tickets for some flights than there are available seats on the flight. Historical experience dictates that passengers do not always use all of the tickets they purchased in advance. However, sometimes a flight is oversold and volunteers are sought to take an alternative flight. Most often, the airline also provides these volunteers with a voucher they can use to purchase (some portion or all of) another ticket in the future. The vouchers issued by XYZ Airlines expire if they are not used to purchase a ticket within one year of issuance.

For XYZ's financial accounting purposes, when a passenger purchases a ticket for a flight, revenue recognition is deferred until the passenger actually flies. In an oversell situation, where a passenger is reseated on another flight and receives a voucher, XYZ defers a portion of the revenue received for the original flight until the voucher is used or expires. For example, assume that on March 1, 2014, a passenger paid $200 for a November 2, 2014 flight. As a result of an oversell situation on November 2, 2014, the passenger was reseated on a later flight and received a $150 voucher that expired on November 1, 2015. For financial accounting purposes, XYZ records $114 revenue as earned on November 2, 2014 [($200/$350) × $200] and the remaining $85 as revenue earned when the flight purchased with the voucher is taken or when the voucher expires unused.

Your client suggests that this revenue also is properly deferred for tax purposes, as this method clearly reflects income. Is your client's conclusion correct?

Research Problem 3. Your client supplies water to a housing development. The company requires new customers to pay for the extension of the water lines to their homes. The water lines are the company's property. The company has consistently treated the amounts received from its customers as a nontaxable contribution to capital and used the amounts received as a reduction in the cost of the water lines for tax purposes. In recent decisions, the courts have consistently ruled that the payments received from the utility customers in similar circumstances should be treated as income from services, rather than as a contribution to capital. Your client has concluded that it is only a matter of time before the IRS applies the recent court decisions to the company. The client would like you to explain the tax consequences of the IRS's likely adjustments based on these decisions.

Research Problem 4. Your client is a manufacturer. For several years, the company buried empty paint cans on its property. The paint was used in the production process. Recently, a state environmental agency informed the company that it was required to dig up the paint cans and decontaminate the land. The company spent a substantial amount for this environmental cleanup in the current year. An IRS agent contends that the cost must be added to the basis in the land because the cleanup improved the land. The company's CFO has asked you to determine whether any authority exists that would support a current deduction for these costs.

Research Problem 5. In 2014, your client, Clear Corporation, changed from the cash to the accrual method of accounting for its radio station. The company had a positive § 481 adjustment of $2.4 million as a result of the change and began amortizing the adjustment in 2014. In 2015, Clear received an offer to purchase the assets of the radio station business (this would be considered a sale of a trade or business under § 1060). If the offer is accepted, Clear plans to purchase a satellite television business. Clear has asked you to explain the consequences of the sale of the radio station on the amortization of the § 481 adjustment.

Internet Activity

Use the tax resources of the Internet to address the following questions. Do not restrict your search to the Web, but include a review of newsgroups and general reference materials, practitioner sites and resources, primary sources of the tax law, chat rooms and discussion groups, and other opportunities.

Research Problem 6. Your client sold a capital asset in June 2012 for which payment is to be made in June 2014. He did not charge interest on the deferred payment, and you need to make the imputed interest computations. What was the applicable Federal rate for a mid-term obligation in June 2014?

Research Problem 7. President Obama and others have called for repeal of the LIFO method for tax purposes. Conduct an Internet search to find arguments for and against this proposal. Prepare a summary of these arguments.

Deferred Compensation

LEARNING OBJECTIVES: *After completing Chapter 19, you should be able to:*

LO.1 Distinguish between qualified (defined contribution and defined benefit) and nonqualified compensation arrangements.

LO.2 Identify the qualification requirements for qualified plans.

LO.3 Discuss the tax consequences of qualified plans.

LO.4 Calculate the limitations on contributions to and benefits from qualified plans.

LO.5 State and explain the qualified plan (Keogh plan) available to a self-employed person.

LO.6 Describe the benefits of the different types of Individual Retirement Accounts (IRAs).

LO.7 Review the rationale for nonqualified deferred compensation plans and the related tax treatment.

LO.8 Explain the value of restricted property plans.

LO.9 Differentiate the tax treatment of qualified and nonqualified stock options.

LO.10 Identify tax planning opportunities available with deferred compensation.

CHAPTER OUTLINE

Dennis Flaherty/Photographer's Choice/Getty Images

THE BIG PICTURE   Tax Solutions for the Real World

A Taxpayer Who Saves

Joyce is a junior finance major at State University. Recently, Dr. Sanchez, the professor in her finance class, delivered a lecture on retirement savings that emphasized the need for a long-term savings horizon and multiple retirement plans. Near the end of the lecture, Dr. Sanchez mentioned that she has four different retirement plans. Joyce was surprised to hear this because she knows that her father has only a single retirement plan that is provided by his employer (an automobile manufacturer).

Joyce drops in on the professor during office hours. Her goal is to find out more about how a person can have multiple retirement plans. What are some facts that would be helpful for Joyce?

Read the chapter and formulate your response.

ompensation is important in any type of organization. If you have not chosen a career, consider becoming a boxer, a football player, a baseball player, a basketball player, a racer, or a soccer player. Forbes's latest list of the top–50 World's Top-Earning Athletes included 10 football players, 12 baseball players, 9 basketball players, and 3 motorsports drivers. In order, the 5 top-earning world athletes were as follows:[1]

Rank	Athlete	Sport	Age	Earnings
1	Tiger Woods	Golf	37	$78.1 million
2	Roger Federer	Tennis	32	$71.5 million
3	Kobe Bryant	Basketball	35	$61.9 million
4	LeBron James	Basketball	28	$59.8 million
5	Drew Brees	Football	34	$51 million

For comparison, a second lieutenant in the U.S. Army receives approximately $47,000 (after factoring in the exclusion benefit for the meal and housing allowance), and an entry-level accountant earns approximately $55,000.

Before you decide to give up your future career in accounting, education, or the military and jump into major league sports, also consider the tax consequences. Depending on the sport, level of skill, and injury experience, a professional athlete's lifetime sports income is compressed into about 10 years. Yet income averaging is not allowed for Federal income tax purposes. As a result, the athlete will lose a larger portion of lifetime earned income in the form of taxes than someone with a comparable amount of earned income over a typical work/life cycle of 40 or more years. The athlete and others have a method, in the form of deferred compensation, available to reduce the Federal income tax liability.

This chapter discusses the various types of deferred compensation arrangements available to employees and self-employed individuals. With **deferred compensation**, an employee receives compensation for services in a later period than that in which the services were performed—quite often during retirement years. The tax law encourages employers to offer deferred compensation plans to their employees to supplement the Federal Social Security retirement system.

Qualified deferred compensation plans receive particularly favorable tax treatment. The amounts that may be deferred under these plans are limited, so they might not be perfect for highly paid athletes. For employers and more traditional employees, however, they provide helpful tax advantages. For example, contributors to qualified pension, profit sharing, or stock bonus plans receive four major tax advantages:

1. Contributions are immediately deductible by the employer.
2. Employees are not taxed until these funds are distributed to them.
3. Income earned by the plan trust, which has received the contributions, is not subject to tax until made available to the employees and thus grows at a tax-free rate.
4. Employer contributions to and benefits payable under qualified plans generally are not subject to FICA and FUTA taxes.

Compared to nonqualified plans, though, qualified plans have some disadvantages, including the following:

• The employer must make contributions for most employees on a nondiscriminatory basis.
• There are a number of limits on contributions to defined contribution plans and on benefits that may be paid under defined benefit plans.
• Qualified plans have higher startup and administrative costs.

[1]Based on "The World's Top Earning Athletes," *Forbes*, 2013, **www.therichest. org/sports/forbes-highest-paid-athletes**.

TAX IN THE NEWS Compensation and Performance

Do a large payroll and large paycheck necessarily guarantee success? In baseball, the high-payroll teams tend to make the play-offs and win the World Series (e.g., the New York Yankees).

Where one or several employees have huge salaries compared with other employees, the business may not succeed in achieving its mission. Matt Bloom, a management professor at the University of Notre Dame, says that the bigger the pay difference between a major league baseball team's stars and scrubs, the worse its record. According to Bloom, more parity in performance pay will result in a better baseball team. Big pay differentials sow the seeds of discord rather than promote team unity.

Professor Bloom's theory may not work in basketball. The Miami Heat beat the San Antonio Spurs in seven games to become the NBA champions in 2013. The Heat had three $17 million players, with the remaining players paid $6 million or less. The team had a payroll of $82 million, ranking third in the NBA.

The Spurs had a more staggered pay scale with a payroll of only $68 million, ranking twelfth. The Spurs paid $1,179,080 per regular season win. The Miami Heat was ranked eighth in efficiency ($1,251,957 per win).

Compare the efficiency of the Spurs and the Heat with the Orlando Magic, with a payroll of $73 million (ranking sixth), paying $3,665,613 per win. The Charlotte Bobcats was next to worst, with a cost per regular season win of $2,705,723. Notice that the top 12 more efficient teams made the play-offs.

Payroll Ranking (in Millions)	Regular Season Games Won	Lowest Cost per Regular Season Win	
1. Los Angeles Lakers ($99)	45	1. Indiana Pacers ($1,031,243)	Y
2. Brooklyn Nets ($84)	49	2. Oklahoma City Thunder ($1,105,117)	Z
3. Miami Heat ($82)	66	3. Houston Rockets ($1,120,743)	X
4. Philadelphia 76ers ($79)	34	4. Denver Nuggets ($1,141,400)	X
5. Chicago Bulls ($74)	45	5. San Antonio Spurs ($1,179,080)	Y
6. Orlando Magic ($73)	20	6. Atlanta Hawks ($1,206,569)	X
7. New York Knicks ($72)	54	7. Memphis Grizzlies ($1,246,814)	X
8. Portland Trail Blazers ($71)	33	8. Miami Heat ($1,251,957)	Z
9. Golden State Warriors ($70)	47	9. Los Angeles Clippers ($1,256,823)	Y
10. Los Angeles Clippers ($70)	56	10. New York Nicks ($1,351,649)	Y
11. Memphis Grizzlies ($69)	56	11. Boston Celtics ($1,475,133)	X
12. San Antonio Spurs ($68)	58	12. Golden State Warriors ($1,504,240)	X
13. Detroit Pistons ($67)	29	13. Utah Jazz ($1,513,438)	
20. Boston Celtics ($60)	41		
23. Charlotte Bobcats ($56)	21		

X: Clinched play-off berth
Y: Clinched division
Z: Clinched conference

Source: Based on Gordeon Fairclough, "Listen Up, Managers; Fat Paychecks Don't Always Guarantee Success," *Wall Street Journal,* March 23, 1999, p. B1; www.nba.com.

A variety of deferred compensation arrangements are being offered to employees, including the following:

- Qualified pension plans.
- Qualified profit sharing plans.
- Cash or deferred arrangement plans.
- SIMPLE IRAs and § 401(k) plans.
- Tax-deferred annuities.
- Incentive stock option plans.
- Nonqualified deferred compensation plans.
- Restricted property plans.
- Cafeteria benefit plans.
- Employee stock purchase plans.

19-1 QUALIFIED PENSION, PROFIT SHARING, STOCK BONUS, AND CASH BALANCE PLANS

LO.1

Distinguish between qualified (defined contribution and defined benefit) and nonqualified compensation arrangements.

To ensure that retired people will not be dependent solely on government programs, the Federal government encourages private pension and profit sharing plans. Therefore, the Federal tax law provides substantial tax benefits for plans that meet certain requirements (qualified plans). The major requirement for qualification is that a plan not discriminate in favor of highly compensated employees.

19-1a Types of Plans

Qualified plans can be conveniently divided into four groups: pension, profit sharing, stock bonus, and cash balance plans.

Pension Plans

A **pension plan** is a deferred compensation arrangement that provides for systematic payments of definitely determinable retirement benefits to employees who meet the requirements set forth in the plan. Employer contributions under a qualified pension plan must *not* depend on profits. A pension plan normally must pay out benefits as lifetime annuities to provide retirement income to retired employees.

There are basically two types of qualified pension plans: defined benefit plans and defined contribution plans.

A **defined benefit plan** includes a formula that defines the benefits employees are to receive.[2] Benefits are generally measured by and based on such factors as years of service and employee compensation. Under such a plan, an employer must make annual contributions based upon actuarial computations that will be sufficient to fund the retirement benefits. If a plan document permits, employees may make contributions to the pension fund. A separate account is not maintained for each participant. A defined benefit plan provides some sense of security for employees because the benefits may be expressed in fixed dollar amounts. In a defined benefit plan, the employer (not the employee) assumes the market risk because the employer promises to pay fixed benefits. Because an expense is not deductible for tax purposes until paid, there often will be a book-tax difference because the employer accounts for the expense on an accrual basis for accounting purposes.

A **defined contribution pension plan** (or money purchase plan) defines the amount the employer is required to contribute (e.g., a flat dollar amount, an amount based on a special formula, or an amount equal to a certain percentage of compensation). A separate account must be maintained for each participant. Benefits are based solely on (1) the amount contributed and (2) income from the fund that accrues to the participant's account.[3] Consequently, actuarial calculations are not required to determine the employer's annual contribution. Upon retirement, an employee's pension amount depends on the value of his or her account. Although it is not mandatory, a plan may require or permit employee contributions to the pension fund. Because employers record the expense for both tax and accounting purposes when funding an employee's account, book-tax differences do not often occur.

Example 1

The qualified pension plan of Rose Company calls for both the employer and the employee to contribute annually to the pension trust an amount equal to 5% of the employee's compensation. Because the employer's rate of contribution is fixed, this pension plan is a defined contribution plan. If the plan called for contributions sufficient to provide retirement benefits equal to 30% of the employee's average salary for the last five years of employment, it would be a defined benefit plan.

[2]§ 414(j).   [3]§ 414(i).

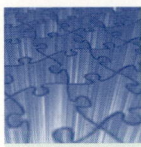

CONCEPT SUMMARY 19.1

Defined Benefit Plan and Defined Contribution Plan Compared

Defined Benefit Plan	Defined Contribution Plan
Includes a pension plan.	Includes profit sharing, stock bonus, money purchase, target benefit, qualified cash or deferred compensation, employee stock ownership plans, and some pension plans.
Determinable benefits based upon years of service and average compensation. Benefits calculated by a formula.	An account for each participant. Ultimate benefits depend upon contributions and investment performance.
Maximum annual *benefits* payable may not exceed the smaller of (1) $210,000 (in 2014)* or (2) 100% of the participant's average earnings in the three highest years of employment.	Maximum annual *contribution* to an account may not exceed the smaller of (1) $52,000** (in 2014) or (2) 100% of the participant's compensation (25% for a profit sharing plan, money purchase plan, or stock bonus plan).
Employer bears the investment risk and reward.	Employee bears the investment risk and reward.
Forfeitures must reduce subsequent funding costs and cannot increase the benefits any participant can receive under the plan.	Forfeitures may be allocated to the accounts of remaining participants.
Subject to minimum funding requirement to avoid penalties.	Exempt from funding requirements.
Greater administrative and actuarial costs and greater reporting requirements.	Costs and reporting requirements less burdensome.
Subject to Pension Benefit Guaranty Corporation (PBGC) plan termination insurance rules.	Not subject to PBGC plan termination insurance rules.
More favorable to employees who are older when plan is adopted because it is possible to fund higher benefits over a shorter period.	More favorable to younger employees because, over a longer period, higher benefits may result.

*This amount is subject to indexing annually in $5,000 increments.
**This amount is subject to indexing annually in $1,000 increments.

Concept Summary 19.1 compares and contrasts a defined benefit plan and a defined contribution plan.

Profit Sharing Plans

A **profit sharing plan** is a deferred compensation arrangement established and maintained by an employer to provide for employee participation in the company's profits. Contributions are paid from the employer to a trustee and are commingled in a single trust fund. Despite the name, an employer does not have to have current or accumulated profits to make a contribution. The contribution formula can be based on compensation, earnings, gross sales, or any other measurement chosen by the employer.

In a profit sharing plan, a separate account is maintained for each participant. The plan must provide a definite, predetermined formula for allocating the contributions made to the trustee among the participants. Likewise, it must include a definite, predetermined formula for distributing the accumulated funds after a fixed number of years; on the attainment of a stated age; or on the occurrence of certain events such as illness, layoff, retirement, or termination of the plan. A company is not required to contribute a definite, predetermined amount to the plan every year, although substantial and recurring contributions must be made to meet the permanency requirement. Forfeitures arising under this plan may be used to increase the individual accounts of the remaining participants as long as these increases do not result in prohibited discrimination.[4] Benefits to employees may normally be distributed through lump-sum payouts in a profit sharing plan. A § 401(k) cash or deferred arrangement plan, explained later in this chapter, is the most common type of profit sharing plan.

---

[4]Reg. §§ 1.401–1(b) and 1.401–4(a)(1)(iii).

Stock Bonus Plans

A **stock bonus plan** is another form of deferred compensation. The employer establishes and maintains the plan to contribute shares of its stock. The contributions need not be dependent on the employer's profits. A stock bonus plan is subject to the same requirements as a profit sharing plan for purposes of allocating and distributing the stock among the employees.[5] Also, as with profit sharing plans, benefits are paid out of each separate account, and participants bear the investment risks and rewards. Any benefits of the plan normally are distributable in the form of stock of the employer company, except that distributable fractional shares may be paid in cash. Employee stock ownership plans (ESOPs) may be either profit sharing or stock bonus plans.

Cash Balance Plans

A **cash balance plan** is a controversial hybrid form of pension plan that is similar in many aspects to a defined benefit plan. These plans are funded by the employer, and the employer bears the investment risks and rewards. Thus, the employer bears the mortality risk if an employee elects to receive benefits in the form of a lifetime annuity and lives beyond normal life expectancy. But like defined contribution plans, a cash balance plan accrues benefits to individual accounts. The benefits for an employee depend on how much builds up over time in the employee's account and not on a formula based on years of service and preretirement pay. Cash balance plans are better for younger, mobile employees, and the companies save money by reducing pension payouts for older and longer-service employees.

ETHICS & EQUITY   Uneven Compensation Playing Field

The top five executives of publicly traded corporations are subject to a $1 million limit each on the corporate deductibility of compensation paid to them. Many other highly paid individuals are not subject to this $1 million cap on deductibility.

In closely held, private corporations, an employee's salary must be reasonable. If part of an employee's salary is unreasonable, an IRS agent can disallow that portion and treat it as a distribution (usually classified as a dividend to the shareholder). Any deduction for compensation by the corporation must reflect a reasonable allowance for salaries or other compensation for personal services,

reflecting what would ordinarily be paid for like services by like enterprises under like circumstances. Frequently, the permitted deduction to the corporation exceeds $1 million.

Among those to whom the cap does not apply are highly paid entertainers receiving royalties or other compensation (other than as an executive of a company). Annual earnings for entertainers, such as Lady Gaga, Katy Perry and Leonardo DiCaprio, may run from $5 million to over $100 million.

Discuss the fairness of tax policy that subjects the compensation of certain business executives to a limitation on deductibility by their corporate employers while allowing compensation paid to noncovered executives, entertainers, sport stars, and others to be exempted from this limitation.

LO.2

Identify the qualification requirements for qualified plans.

19-1b Qualification Requirements

To be *qualified*, and thereby to receive favorable tax treatment, a plan generally must satisfy the following requirements:

- Nondiscrimination requirements.
- Participation and coverage requirements.
- Vesting requirements.
- Distribution requirements.
- Minimum funding requirements.

These qualification rules are highly technical and numerous. As a result, the IRS maintains a staggered determination letter request process that allows plan sponsors

---

[5]Reg. § 1.401–1(b)(1)(iii).

to file a plan document with the IRS for approval. A favorable determination letter (similar to a letter ruling) indicates that the form of the plan meets the qualification requirements and that the form of the plan's trust meets the requirements for exemption. However, the ultimate qualification of the plan depends upon its actual administration and operations. Therefore, the operations of the plan should be reviewed periodically. Favorable determination letters have an expiration date with individually designed plans on a five-year schedule and preapproved plans on a six-year schedule.

The IRS has an Employee Plans Compliance Resolution System (EPCRS) that allows sponsors of retirement plans to correct failures to satisfy requirements for a period of time. By using this system to correct failures, plan sponsors can avoid disqualification and continue to provide employees with retirement benefits on a tax-favored basis. The components of EPCRS include the Self-Correction Program (SCP), the Voluntary Correction Program (VCP), and the Audit Closing Agreement Program (Audit CAP).

Nondiscrimination Requirements

As indicated earlier, the contributions and benefits under a plan must *not discriminate* in favor of highly compensated employees. A plan is not considered discriminatory merely because contributions and benefits are proportional to compensation.[6] For example, a pension plan that provides for the allocation of employer contributions based upon a flat 3 percent of each employee's compensation would not be discriminatory solely because highly paid employees receive greater benefits.

Participation and Coverage Requirements

A qualified plan must provide, at a minimum, that all employees in the covered group who are 21 years of age be eligible to participate after completing one year of service. A year of service is generally defined as the completion of 1,000 hours of service within a measuring period of 12 consecutive months. As an alternative, where the plan provides that 100 percent of an employee's accrued benefits will be vested upon entering the plan, the employee's participation may be postponed until the later of age 21 or two years from the date of employment. Once the age and service requirements are met, an employee must begin participating no later than the *earlier* of the following:

- The first day of the first plan year beginning after the date on which the requirements were satisfied.
- Six months after the date on which the requirements were satisfied.[7]

> **Example 2**
>
> Coffee Corporation has a calendar year retirement plan covering its employees. The corporation adopts the most restrictive eligibility rules permitted. Wilma, age 21, is hired on January 31, 2013, and meets the service requirement over the next 12 months (completes at least 1,000 hours by January 31, 2014). Wilma must be included in this plan no later than July 31, 2014, because the six-month limitation would be applicable. If the company had adopted the two-year participation rule, Wilma must be included in the plan no later than July 31, 2015.

Because a qualified plan must be primarily for the benefit of employees and be nondiscriminatory, the plan has to cover a reasonable percentage of the company employees. A plan will be qualified only if it satisfies one of the following tests:[8]

- The plan benefits a percentage of non-highly compensated employees equal to at least 70 percent of the percentage of highly compensated employees benefiting under the plan (the *ratio percentage test*). In other words, the plan must benefit a percentage of the non-highly paid employees, which is at least 70 percent of the highly paid employees who benefit under the same plan.
- The plan meets the *average benefits test,* described below.

---

[6] §§ 401(a)(4) and (5).
[7] §§ 410(a)(1)(A) and (B) and 410(a)(4).
[8] § 410(b).

If a company has no highly compensated employees, the retirement plan will automatically satisfy the coverage rules.

Example 3

Suppose a company has 2 highly paid employees (HPEs) and 20 non-highly paid employees (NHPEs). If this plan covers both of the HPEs, for the NHPEs to qualify, the plan must cover at least 14 of them (70% × 20). If the plan covers only one of the HPEs, the plan must cover 7 of the NHPEs (70% × 50% = 35% × 20).

To satisfy the *average benefits test*, the nondiscriminatory plan must benefit any employees who qualify under a classification set up by the employer. In addition, the average benefit percentage for non-highly compensated employees must be at least 70 percent of the average benefit percentage for highly compensated employees. The *average benefit percentage* means, with respect to any group of employees, the average of the benefit percentages calculated separately for each employee in the group. The term *benefit percentage* means the employer-provided contributions (including forfeitures) or benefits of an employee under all qualified plans of the employer, expressed as a percentage of that employee's compensation.

An employee is a **highly compensated employee** if, at any time during the year or the preceding year, the employee satisfies *either* of the following:[9]

- Was a 5 percent owner of the company.
- Received more than $115,000 (in 2014) in annual compensation from the employer *and* was a member of the top-paid group of the employer.[10] The top-paid group clause is applicable only if the employer elects to have it apply. An employee whose compensation is in the top 20 percent of all of the employees is a member of the top-paid group.

An additional *minimum participation test* must also be met for some plans. A plan must cover at least 40 percent of all employees or, if fewer, at least 50 employees on one representative day of the plan year. In determining all employees, nonresident aliens, certain union members, and employees not fulfilling the minimum age or years-of-service requirement of the plan may be excluded.[11]

Example 4

Assume that Rust Corporation's retirement plan automatically meets the 70% test (the ratio percentage test) because 70% of all non-highly compensated employees benefit. The company has 100 employees, but only 38 of these employees are covered by the plan. Therefore, this retirement plan does not meet the minimum participation requirement.

Vesting Requirements

The **vesting requirements** protect an employee who has worked a reasonable period of time for an employer from losing employer contributions because of being fired or changing jobs. An employee's right to accrued benefits derived from his or her own contributions to a defined benefit plan must be nonforfeitable from the date of contribution. The accrued benefits derived from employer contributions must be nonforfeitable in accordance with one of *two alternative minimum vesting schedules* or an even more generous vesting schedule.

To satisfy the *first alternative*, a participant must have a nonforfeitable right to 100 percent of his or her accrued benefits derived from employer contributions upon completion of not more than five years of service (five-year or cliff vesting). The *second alternative* is satisfied if a participant has a nonforfeitable right at least equal to a percentage of the accrued benefits derived from employer contributions as depicted in Table 19.1 (graded vesting). Of the two alternatives, cliff vesting minimizes administrative expenses for a company and provides more vesting for a long-term employee.

---

[9]§§ 401(a)(4) and 414(q).

[10]The $115,000 amount is indexed annually in $5,000 increments.

[11]§§ 401(a)(26) and 410(b)(3) and (4).

TABLE 19.1	Three- to Seven-Year Vesting for Defined Benefit Plans
Years of Service	**Nonforfeitable Percentage**
3	20%
4	40%
5	60%
6	80%
7 or more	100%

TABLE 19.2	Two- to Six-Year Vesting for Defined Contribution Plans
Years of Service	**Nonforfeitable Percentage**
2	20%
3	40%
4	60%
5	80%
6 or more	100%

Example 5

Mitch has six years of service completed as of February 2, 2014, his employment anniversary date. If his defined benefit plan has a five-year (cliff) vesting schedule, 100% of Mitch's accrued benefits are vested. If the plan uses the graded vesting rule, Mitch's nonforfeitable percentage is 80%.

Defined contribution plans also must satisfy one of the following minimum vesting schedules: two- to six-year graded vesting as shown in Table 19.2, three-year cliff vesting, or an even more generous vesting schedule.

Example 6

Millie has five years of service completed as of February 2, 2014, her employment anniversary date. If her defined contribution plan uses three-year cliff vesting, Millie must be 100% vested. Under a two- to six-year vesting plan, Millie must be 80% vested.

Distribution Requirements

Uniform *minimum distribution rules* exist for all qualified defined benefit and defined contribution plans, traditional Individual Retirement Accounts (IRAs) and annuities, unfunded deferred compensation plans of state and local governments and tax-exempt employers, and tax-sheltered custodial accounts and annuities. Distributions to a participant must begin by April 1 of the calendar year *following the later* of (1) the calendar year in which the employee attains age $70\frac{1}{2}$ or (2) the calendar year in which the employee retires. Thus, an employee can delay receiving distributions until retirement. However, distributions to a 5 percent owner or a traditional IRA holder must begin no later than April 1 of the calendar year *following* the year in which the 5 percent owner or the IRA holder reaches age $70\frac{1}{2}$.[12]

Minimum annual distributions must be made over the life of the participant or the lives of the participant and a designated individual beneficiary. The amount of the required minimum distribution for a particular year is determined by dividing the account balance as of December 31 of the prior year by the applicable life expectancy. The life expectancy of the owner and his or her beneficiary is based

---

[12]§ 401(a)(9). These distribution requirements do not apply to Roth IRAs.

TAX IN THE NEWS   Spiking Your Retirement Plan

"Spiking" is more than a baseball player injuring an opponent with the spikes on his shoes or a player sharply spiking a volleyball over the net. Spiking also refers to the practice of increasing one's salary just before retirement to boost pension payouts. Spiking has been common in California because of favorable terms in pension contracts negotiated by powerful unions.

For example, Ventura County, California Chief Executive Marty Robinson was earning $228,000 annually. By adding $34,000 in unused vacation pay, an $11,000 bonus for earning a graduate degree, and more than $24,000 in extra pension benefits, Robinson walked away with a pension of $272,000 for life. In Ventura County, 84 percent of the retirees receiving more than $100,000 a year are receiving pension payments in excess of what they made before retirement.

In many states, legislators are passing laws to stop this backloading of compensation to increase retirement benefits.

The Virginia state legislature has enacted a law with the primary intent of preventing spiking at the College of William and Mary. Previously, William and Mary had provided its retiring faculty members with 8 and 7 percent raises during their last two years of employment. The effect was to build retirement pay for those faculty members participating in the state's defined benefit plan, because the benefit formula looked at the final three years of employment.

Sources: Based on *Virginia Gazette,* June 26, 2010, p. A1; Michael B. Marois and James Nash, "California Takes Aim at Public Pension Spiking," Bloomberg, May 19, 2011; Ken Carlson, "County Workers 'Spike' Retirement Pay," *Modesto Bee,* July 28, 2010, **www.modbee .com/2010/07/27/1269715/county-workers-spike-retirement.htm**; Catherine Saillant, Maloy Moore, and Doug Smith, "Salary 'Spiking' Drains Public Pension Funds, Analysis Finds," **www.latimes.com/ news/local/la-me-county-pensions-20120303,0,6677861.story**.

upon the expected return multiples in the Regulations, using ages attained within the calendar year the participant reaches age 70½.[13]

Example 7

> Beth reaches age 70½ in 2014, and she will also be age 71 in 2014. Her retirement account has a balance of $120,000 on December 31, 2013. If Beth is retired, a 5% owner, or the holder of a traditional IRA, she must withdraw $7,843 ($120,000 ÷ 15.3) for the 2014 calendar year, assuming that her multiple is 15.3. This distribution need not be made until April 1, 2015, but a second distribution must be made by December 31, 2015.

Failure to make a minimum required distribution to a particular participant results in a *50 percent nondeductible excise tax* on the excess in any taxable year of the amount that should have been distributed over the amount that actually was distributed. The tax is imposed on the individual required to take the distribution (the payee).[14] The Secretary of the Treasury is authorized to waive the tax for a given taxpayer year if the taxpayer is able to establish that the shortfall is due to reasonable error and that reasonable steps are being taken to remedy the shortfall.

If a taxpayer receives an *early distribution* from a qualified retirement plan, a 10 percent additional tax is levied on the full amount of any distribution includible in gross income.[15] For this purpose, the term *qualified retirement plan* includes a qualified defined benefit plan or defined contribution plan, a tax-sheltered annuity or custodial account, or a traditional IRA. The following distributions, however, are *not* treated as early distributions:

- Distributions made on or after the date the employee attains age 59½.
- Distributions made to a beneficiary (or the estate of an employee) on or after the death of the employee.
- Distributions attributable to the employee's being disabled.
- Distributions made as part of a scheduled series of substantially equal periodic payments (made not less frequently than annually) for the life of the participant (or the joint lives of the participant and the participant's beneficiary).

---

[13]Reg. § 1.72–9. Refer to Chapter 4.
[14]§ 4974(a).

[15]§ 72(t). See Ltr.Rul. 8837071.

Pension Revolution

The United Kingdom (UK) is revolutionizing savings for retirement. Starting October 2012, employers are required to automatically enroll all eligible employees into a compliant pension plan. Without encouragement, the UK believes that employees have the tendency to do nothing or wait until they are older to begin a retirement program. Along with other countries such as Australia, New Zealand, and Sweden, the UK believes that once in a retirement program, employees are less likely to opt out.

Global Tax Issues

© iStockphoto.com/Andrey Prokhorov

Source: Based on Padraig Floyd, "Pension 'Revolution' Shifts Responsibility to Employees," Raconteur, *The Times*, September 12, 2012, p. 3.

- Distributions made to an employee after separation from service because of early retirement under the plan after attaining age 55. This exception to early distribution treatment does not apply to a traditional IRA.
- Distributions used to pay medical expenses to the extent the expenses are deductible under § 213 (determined regardless of whether the taxpayer itemizes deductions).
- IRA distributions that are used to pay qualified higher education expenses of the taxpayer, the spouse, or any child or grandchild of the taxpayer or the taxpayer's spouse.
- IRA distributions up to $10,000 that are used to pay expenses incurred by qualified first-time homebuyers.

Minimum Funding Requirements

Minimum funding requirements apply to defined benefit plans, money purchase plans, and target benefit plans to regulate the amount that an employer must contribute to ensure that the plan is properly funded. The amount of contributions required for a plan year is the amount needed to fund benefits earned during a plan year (e.g., normal costs) plus the portion of other liabilities that are amortized over a period of years (e.g., investment losses). A special account called a funding standard account is required, and contribution amounts are determined under one of several acceptable actuarial cost methods. A tax equal to 10 percent of the aggregate unpaid required contribution is imposed on a single-employer plan (5 percent for a multiemployer plan). If an accumulated funding deficit is not corrected, a 100 percent tax is imposed.[16]

19-1c Tax Consequences to the Employee and Employer

LO.3

Discuss the tax consequences of qualified plans.

Although employer contributions to qualified plans are generally deductible immediately (subject to contribution and deductibility rules), these amounts are not subject to taxation until distributed to employees.[17] If benefits are paid with respect to an employee (to a creditor of the employee, a child of the employee, etc.), the benefits paid are treated as if paid to the employee. When benefits are distributed to employees, or paid with respect to an employee, the employer does not receive another deduction.

The tax benefit to the employee amounts to a substantial tax deferral and may be viewed as an interest-free loan from the government to the trust fund. Another advantage of a qualified plan is that any income earned by the trust is not taxable to the trust.[18] Employees, in effect, are taxed on such earnings when they receive the retirement benefits.

---

[16]§ 412.
[17]§ 402(a)(1).

[18]§ 501(a).

TAX IN THE NEWS Bonuses as Incentives

When Kentucky's John Calipari beat Kansas in the 2012 NCAA basketball championship game, he added $600,000 to the $150,000 he had already secured from his Wildcats' Southeastern Conference regular season final win. Calipari's annual base pay is $4.5 million.

The highest salary in college basketball of $7.5 million is paid to the Louisville Cardinals' Rick Pitino, who lost to Kentucky in the Final Four. Pitino earned a bonus of $225,000 for making the Final Four, and he earned $1.43 million of non-university money.

Source: Based on "An Analysis of Salaries for College Basketball Coaches," *USA Today*, March 20 2011, **www.usatoday.com/sports/college/mensbasketball/2011-coaches-salary-database.htm**; Steve Berkowitz and Jodi Upton, "Wins Bring Coaches Windfalls," *USA Today*, March 21, 2012, p. 1A.

© iStockphoto.com/Andrey Prokhorov

The taxation of amounts received by employees in periodic or installment payments is generally subject to the annuity rules in § 72 (refer to Chapter 4). In any situation where employee contributions have been subject to tax previously, they are included in the employee's investment in the contract. Two other alternative options generally are available for benefit distributions. A taxpayer may (1) receive the distribution in a lump-sum payment or (2) roll over the benefits into an IRA or another qualified employer retirement plan.

Lump-Sum Distributions from Qualified Plans

A **lump-sum distribution** occurs when an employee receives his or her entire payout from a qualified plan in a single payment rather than receiving the amount in installments. The annuity rules do not apply to a lump-sum distribution. All such payments are thrown into one year. Because lump-sum payments have been accumulated over a number of years, bunching retirement benefits into one taxable year may impose a high tax burden because of progressive rates.

Rollover Treatment

A taxpayer who receives a distribution can avoid current taxation by rolling the distribution into another qualified employer retirement plan or into an IRA.[19] The taxation of the distribution is deferred until distributions are made from the recipient's qualified employer retirement plan or IRA. The rollover can be *direct* with the balance in the account going directly from a qualified employer retirement plan to another qualified employer retirement plan or an IRA (sometimes called a conversion). The rollover can be *indirect* with the proceeds going to the taxpayer who has 60 days to transfer the proceeds into another qualified employer retirement plan or an IRA. One can use an indirect rollover to borrow from an IRA, but the "loan" must be fully reinvested in another retirement plan or IRA within the 60-day window so that the amount will not be taxable. A benefit of the direct rollover is that it is not subject to the 20 percent withholding applicable to indirect rollovers.[20]

19-1d Limitations on Contributions to and Benefits from Qualified Plans

LO.4

Calculate the limitations on contributions to and benefits from qualified plans.

The annual limitations on contributions to and benefits from qualified plans appearing in § 415 must be written into a qualified plan. Section 404 sets the limits on deductibility applicable to the employer. These limits may have an impact on the amount the employer is willing to contribute. In fact, a defined benefit plan or

---

[19]§ 402(c). [20]§ 3405(c).

defined contribution plan is not allowed a deduction for the amount that exceeds the § 415 limitations.[21]

Defined Contribution Plans

Under a *defined contribution plan*, the annual addition to an employee's account cannot exceed the smaller of $52,000 (in 2014) or 100 percent of the employee's compensation.[22] However, this individual percentage limitation of 100 percent normally is not attainable for small plans because the employer's deduction limit cannot exceed 25 percent of eligible compensation for all participants. The $52,000 amount is indexed (in $1,000 increments).[23]

Defined Benefit Plans

Under a *defined benefit plan*, the annual benefit payable to an employee is limited to the smaller of $210,000 (in 2014)[24] or 100 percent of the employee's average compensation for the highest three years of employment. This benefit limit is subject to a $10,000 *de minimis* floor. The $210,000 limitation is reduced actuarially if the benefits begin before the Social Security normal retirement age (currently age 65 and 10 months) and is increased actuarially if the benefits begin after the Social Security normal retirement age. The dollar limit on annual benefits ($210,000) is reduced by one-tenth for each year of *participation* under 10 years by the employee. Furthermore, the 100 percent of compensation limitation and the $10,000 *de minimis* floor are reduced proportionately for a participant who has less than 10 years of *service* with the employer.[25]

Example 8

Return to the facts of *The Big Picture* on p. 19-1. The university has offered Joyce's professor, Dr. Sanchez, a choice between a defined benefit pension plan and a defined contribution plan. Dr. Sanchez expects to work at a number of universities during her career. A colleague has recommended that Dr. Sanchez choose the defined contribution plan because of its mobility (i.e., she can take the plan with her). So she needs to decide if this mobility factor is significant in making her choice and how much she can contribute annually to a defined contribution plan.

Example 9

Adam's average compensation for the highest three years of employment is $87,000. The defined benefit plan would not qualify if the plan provides for benefits in excess of the smaller of (1) $87,000 or (2) $210,000 for Adam in 2014 (assuming normal retirement age).

Example 10

Peggy has participated for four years in a defined benefit plan and has six years of service with her employer. Her average compensation for the three highest years is $60,000. Her four years of participation reduce her dollar limitation to $84,000 ($210,000 × 4/10). Her six years of service reduce her 100% of compensation limitation to 60%. Therefore, her limit on annual benefits is $36,000 ($60,000 × 60%).

When calculating the average of the three highest years of compensation, the amount of compensation that may be taken into account under any plan is limited to $260,000 (in 2014).[26] Thus, the benefits that highly compensated individuals receive may be smaller as a percentage of their pay than those received by non-highly compensated employees.

---

[21]§ 404(j).

[22]§§ 415(c) and (d).

[23]§ 415(d)(4).

[24]This amount is indexed annually in $5,000 increments.

[25]§ 415(b).

[26]§§ 401(a)(17) and 404(l). This amount is indexed in $5,000 increments.

Example 11

Swan Corporation has a defined contribution plan with a 10% contribution formula. An employee earning less than $260,000 in 2014 would not be affected by this includible compensation limitation. However, an employee earning $520,000 in 2014 would have only 5% of compensation allocated to his or her account because of the $260,000 limit on includible compensation (5% × $520,000 = $26,000).

The maximum deduction an employer is permitted for contributions to pension plans may be determined by either of two methods. First, an aggregate cost method allows an actuarially determined deduction based on a level amount, or a level percentage, of compensation over the remaining future service of covered participants. Second, the employer is permitted to deduct the so-called normal cost plus no more than 10 percent of the past service costs. The *normal cost* represents the estimated contribution required associated with work performed by employees in the current year. *Past service costs* are costs that relate to the inception of the plan and costs that result from changes in the retirement plan.

While its contributions are deductible in the tax year such amounts are allocated or credited to the pension trust, the employer may defer the actual payment of the contributions until its Federal income tax return filing date, including extensions.[27] In effect, the employer is allowed a deduction to the extent it is compelled to make such contributions to satisfy the funding requirement. If an amount in excess of the allowable amount is contributed in any tax year, the excess may be carried forward indefinitely and deducted in succeeding tax years (to the extent the carryover plus the succeeding year's contribution does not exceed the deductible limitation for that year).[28]

Example 12

During 2014, Green Corporation contributes $17,500 to its qualified pension plan. Normal cost for this year is $7,200, and the amount necessary to pay retirement benefits on behalf of employee services before 2014 is $82,000 (past service costs). The corporation's maximum deduction is $15,400. This amount consists of the $7,200 normal cost plus 10% ($8,200) of the past service costs. The corporation has a $2,100 [$17,500 (contribution) − $15,400 (deduction)] contribution carryover.

Example 13

Assume in the previous example that Green Corporation has normal cost of $7,200 in 2015 and contributes $10,000 to the pension trust. The corporation's maximum deduction would be $15,400. Green Corporation may deduct $12,100, composed of this year's contribution ($10,000) plus the $2,100 contribution carryover.

A 10 percent excise tax is imposed on nondeductible contributions. The tax is levied on the employer making the contribution. The tax applies to nondeductible contributions for the current year and any nondeductible contributions for the preceding year that have not been eliminated by the end of the current year (as a carryover or by being returned to the employer in the current year).[29]

Profit Sharing and Stock Bonus Plan Limitations

As described above, there are limits on the amounts an employer may deduct in a tax year for contributions to profit sharing and stock bonus plans. Any nondeductible excess, a so-called contribution carryover, may be carried forward indefinitely and deducted in subsequent years. The maximum deduction in any succeeding year is 25 percent of all compensation paid or accrued in the aggregate during that taxable year.[30]

---

[27]§§ 404(a)(1) and (6).
[28]§ 404(a)(1)(D).

[29]§ 4972.
[30]§§ 404(a)(3)(A) and (a)(7).

19-1e Section 401(k) Plans

A **§ 401(k) plan** allows participants to elect either to receive up to $17,500 (in 2014)[31] in cash (taxed currently) or to have a contribution made on their behalf to a profit sharing or stock bonus plan. The plan may also be in the form of a salary-reduction agreement under which a contribution will be made only if the participant elects to reduce his or her compensation or to forgo an increase in compensation.

Any employee-elected plan contributions are pretax amounts that are excluded from gross income in the year of the deferral and are 100 percent vested. Like employer plan contributions, employee contributions are tax-deferred until distributed, as are earnings on those contributions.

> Sam participates in a § 401(k) plan of his employer. The plan permits the participants to choose between a full salary or a reduced salary where the reduction becomes a before-tax contribution to a retirement plan. Sam elects to contribute 10% of his annual compensation of $30,000 to the plan. Income taxes are paid on only $27,000. No income taxes are paid on the $3,000—or on any earnings—until it is distributed from the plan to Sam. The main benefit of a § 401(k) plan is that Sam can shift a portion of his income to a later taxable year.

Example 14

The maximum annual elective contribution to a § 401(k) plan is reduced dollar for dollar by other salary-reduction contributions to tax-sheltered annuities, simplified employee pension plans, and § 401(k) plans. Annual elective contributions are also limited by complicated nondiscrimination requirements designed to encourage participation by non-highly compensated employees and by the general defined contribution plan limitations.

A person who has attained age 50 by the end of the tax year can make catch-up contributions of $5,500.[32]

THE BIG PICTURE

Example 15

> Return to the facts of *The Big Picture* on p. 19-1. Although Dr. Sanchez is not eligible to participate in a § 401(k) plan, she does participate in a § 403(b) tax-deferred annuity plan for employees of § 501(c)(3) not-for-profit organizations (similar in many respects to a § 401(k) plan). Dr. Sanchez indicates that because she is age 51, she is eligible to make catch-up contributions to her § 403(b) annuity.

---

[31]§§ 402(g)(1) and (4).

[32]The $5,000 amount is indexed in $500 increments in 2007 and thereafter. For 2007 and 2008, the amount remained at $5,000. For 2009, the amount increased to $5,500. For 2010, the amount remained at $5,500. For 2011, the amount remained at $5,500. For 2012, 2013, and 2014, the amount remained at $5,500.

TAX IN THE NEWS   Money Is Not Everything

Would you walk away from a guaranteed $12 million baseball contract? Gil Meche, a starting pitcher for the Kansas City Royals, did just that. The Louisiana native walked away.

Meche said, "Once I started to realize I wasn't earning my money, I felt bad. I was making a crazy amount of money for not even pitching. Honestly, I didn't feel like I deserved it. I didn't want to have those feelings again." In four years with the Royals, he won 29 games and lost 39.

Alfonso Soriano signed an eight-year $136 million contract in 2007 (the highest in the Chicago Cubs' history), but he has batted .226 in five seasons with the Cubs. He says it is difficult because all people see is the money and not the talent and the work you put in. He says: "The most fun I ever had in baseball was when I was with the Yankees (2001–2003). I was making $600,000 and just enjoying the game."

Maybe Soriano should give up his high-salary contract and accept $600,000 again so that he can enjoy the game again. The decrease in pressure might increase his batting average.

Sources: Based on Greg Wilson, "Baseball Player Quits, Says 'I Don't Deserve $12M,'" NBC Washington, January 27, 2011; **www.nbcbayarea.com/news/sports/Baseball-Player-Quits-Says-I-Dont-Deserve-12M-114712809.html**; Bob Nightengale, "MLB's Big-Bucks Busts Pay Emotional Toll," *USA Today*, March 27, 2012, pp. 1C and 2C; **usatoday30.usatoday.com/SPORTS/usaedition/2012-03-27-Baseball-free-agents-cover-0327ART_CV_U.htm**.

Elective contributions in excess of the maximum limitation are taxable in the year of deferral. These amounts may be refunded from the plan tax-free before April 15 of the following year. Excess amounts not timely distributed will be double-taxed because they will be taxable in the year of distribution, even though they were included in income in the year of deferral. A 10 percent excise tax is imposed on the employer for excess elective deferral contributions not withdrawn from the plan within $2\frac{1}{2}$ months after the close of the plan year. The plan may lose its qualified status if these excess contributions (and any related income) are not withdrawn by the end of the plan year following the plan year in which the excess contributions were made.[33]

Example 16

Carmen, age 36, is an employee of a manufacturing corporation. She defers $19,500 in a § 401(k) plan in 2014. The $2,000 excess over the $17,500 limit, along with the appropriate earnings, must be returned to Carmen by April 15, 2015. This $2,000 excess amount plus related income is taxable to her in 2014 and will be taxed again upon distribution (if made after April 15, 2015). There will be a 10% tax on Carmen's employer on any excess contributions not returned within 2½ months after the close of the plan year.

Beginning in 2008, there is a qualified automatic enrollment arrangement (QAEA), whereby companies may automatically enroll employees in a § 401(k) plan with a prescribed percentage (not to exceed 10 percent) of the employee's pay automatically withdrawn from each paycheck (unless the employee elects otherwise). This stated percentage must be applied uniformly to all eligible employees.

If certain requirements are met, the plan administrator may choose the investments for the participants and be protected from liability involving investment choices. A § 401(k) plan consisting solely of contributions made under a QAEA also is exempt from the top-heavy rules.[34] Since 2010, small employers may establish a combined defined benefit/§ 401(k) plan (a DB/K plan); the § 401(k) component of the DB/K plan must have automatic enrollment, with an employee being treated as having elected to make deferrals of 4 percent of pay, and must provide a minimum match of 50 percent of elective deferrals up to 4 percent of pay.[35]

---

[33]§ 4979(a).
[34]§§ 401(a)(3)(G), 401(k)(8)(E), 401(k)(13), 401(m)(6)(A), 401(m)(12), and 414(w).

[35]§ 414(x) and ERISA § 210(e).

SIMPLE Plans

Employers with 100 or fewer employees who do not maintain another qualified retirement plan may establish a *savings incentive match plan for employees* (SIMPLE plan).[36] The plan can be in the form of a § 401(k) plan or an IRA. A SIMPLE § 401(k) plan is not subject to the nondiscrimination rules that are normally applicable to § 401(k) plans.

All employees who received at least $5,000 in compensation from the employer during any two preceding years and who reasonably expect to receive at least $5,000 in compensation during the current year must be eligible to participate in the plan. The decision to participate is up to the employee. A self-employed individual also may participate in the plan.

The contributions made by the employee (a salary-reduction approach) must be expressed as a percentage of compensation rather than as a fixed dollar amount. The SIMPLE plan must not permit the SIMPLE elective employee contribution for the year to exceed $12,000 (in 2014).[37] The SIMPLE elective deferral limit is increased under the catch-up provision for employees age 50 and over. The amount is $2,500 and is indexed for inflation in $500 increments (at present, it remains at $2,500).

Generally, the employer must either match elective employee contributions up to 3 percent of the employee's compensation or provide nonmatching contributions of 2 percent of compensation for each eligible employee. Thus, the maximum amount that may be contributed to the plan for an employee under age 50 for 2014 is $19,800 [$12,000 employee contributions + $ 7,800 ($260,000 compensation ceiling × 3 %) employer match].

No other contributions may be made to the plan other than the employee elective contribution and the required employer matching contribution (or nonmatching contribution under the 2 percent rule). All contributions are fully vested. An employer is required to make the required matching or nonmatching contributions to a SIMPLE § 401(k) plan once it is established, whereas an employer's contributions to a traditional § 401(k) plan generally may be discretionary.

An employer's deduction for contributions to a SIMPLE § 401(k) plan is limited to the greater of 25 percent of the compensation paid or accrued or the amount that the employer is required to contribute to the plan. Thus, an employer may deduct contributions to a SIMPLE § 401(k) plan in excess of 25 percent of the $260,000 salary cap. A traditional § 401(k) plan is limited to 25 percent of the total compensation of plan participants for the year (excluding age 50 catch-ups).

An employer is allowed a deduction for matching contributions only if the contributions are made by the due date (including extensions) for the employer's tax return. Contributions to a SIMPLE plan are excludible from the employee's gross income, and the SIMPLE plan is tax-exempt.

The Mauve Company has a SIMPLE plan for its employees under which it provides non-matching contributions of 2% of compensation for each eligible employee. The maximum amount that can be added to each participant's account in 2014 is $17,200, composed of the $12,000 employee salary reduction plus an employer contribution of $5,200 ($260,000 × 2%).	**Example 17**

Distributions from a SIMPLE plan are taxed under the IRA rules. Tax-free rollovers can be made from one SIMPLE account to another. A SIMPLE account can be rolled over to an IRA tax-free after the expiration of a two-year period since the individual first participated in the plan. Withdrawals of contributions during the two-year period beginning on the date an employee first participates in the SIMPLE plan are subject to a 25 percent early withdrawal tax rather than the 10 percent early withdrawal tax that otherwise would apply.

---

[36]§ 408(p). [37]§ 408(p)(2)(E)(i).

TAX IN THE NEWS   Cubemates Determine Your Bonus

Would you like your peers to determine your bonuses? This market-style bonus system is being used in businesses such as Coffee & Power. Its 15 full- and part-time employees are able to distribute 1,200 stock options to coworkers in whatever way they choose. The workers cannot reward themselves, nor give the option to company founders. They can give all of their options to one person or spread them among a group. Employees will only know what bonuses they receive. They do not learn who allocated the options.

Source: Based on Rachel E. Silverman, "My Colleague, My Paymaster," *Wall Street Journal*, April 4, 2012, p. B1.

Designated Roth Contributions

Section 401(k) plans and § 403(b) plans may be amended to permit employees to irrevocably designate some or all of their future salary deferral contributions as Roth § 401(k) or Roth § 403(b) contributions.[38] These designated amounts are currently includible in the employee's gross income and are maintained in a separate plan account. The earnings on these elective contributions build up in the plan on a tax-free basis. Future qualified distributions made from designated contributions are excludible from gross income. The adjusted gross income (AGI) limitation (discussed later in the chapter) does not apply to these designated contributions, so a Roth § 401(k) should be attractive to highly paid officers and employees.

Roth § 401(k)s must comply with the nondiscrimination requirements. The contributions are treated like regular § 401(k) contributions for other purposes and may not exceed the annual limitation ($17,500 in 2014) without regard to any catch-up contributions. A person should be able to roll a designated Roth contributions (DRCs) account into another designated Roth account or into a Roth IRA (explained later in the chapter) to preserve the tax-free nature of the account after age 70$\frac{1}{2}$ and to avoid the minimum distribution requirements. A "qualified distribution" from a designated Roth account is a distribution that is made after the person has participated for five years and that occurs on or after the date the person attains age 59$\frac{1}{2}$, dies, or becomes disabled. If a distribution is not a qualified distribution, such a distribution is taxable to the participant (or a beneficiary) to the extent it consists of earnings (in a pro rata manner).

Example 18

A designated Roth account has $18,800 of DRCs and $1,200 of earnings. If a qualified distribution of $10,000 is made to the participant, the entire amount is excluded from gross income. However, if the distribution is not a qualified distribution, $9,400 is a return of capital (excluded from gross income), but a pro rata amount of $600 is included in gross income [($10,000 ÷ $20,000) × $1,200].

19-2 RETIREMENT PLANS FOR SELF-EMPLOYED INDIVIDUALS AND THEIR EMPLOYEES

LO.5

State and explain the qualified plan (Keogh plan) available to a self-employed person.

Self-employed individuals (e.g., partners and sole proprietors) and their employees are eligible to receive qualified retirement benefits under the SIMPLE plans described previously or under what are known as **H.R. 10 (Keogh) plans**. Because of contribution limitations and other restrictions, self-employed plans previously were less attractive than corporate plans. Contributions and benefits of a self-employed person now are subject to the general corporate provisions, putting self-employed

---

[38]§ 402A.

persons on a parity with corporate employees. Consequently, Keogh plans can provide a self-employed person with an adequate retirement base.

A variety of funding vehicles can be used for Keogh investments, such as mutual funds, annuities, real estate shares, certificates of deposit, debt instruments, commodities, securities, and personal properties. Investment in most collectibles is not allowed in a self-directed plan. When an individual decides to make all investment decisions, a self-directed retirement plan is established. However, the individual may prefer to invest the funds with a financial institution such as a broker, a bank, or a savings and loan institution.

19-2a Coverage Requirements

Generally, the corporate coverage rules apply to Keogh plans. Thus, the ratio percentage and average benefits tests previously discussed also apply to self-employed plans.[39] An individual covered under a qualified corporate plan as an employee may also establish a Keogh plan for earnings from self-employment.

19-2b Contribution Limitations

A self-employed individual may annually contribute the smaller of $52,000 (in 2014) or 100 percent of earned income to a *defined contribution* Keogh plan.[40] However, if the defined contribution plan is a profit sharing plan or stock bonus plan, a 25 percent deduction limit applies. Under a *defined benefit* Keogh plan, the annual benefit payable to an employee is limited to the smaller of $210,000 (in 2014) or 100 percent of the employee's average compensation for the three highest years of employment.[41] An employee includes a self-employed person.

A defined *benefit* Keogh plan requires an actuary to calculate the amount to contribute each year. Thus, the annual actuarial fees and the required IRS reports can be expensive.

THE BIG PICTURE

Example 19

Return to the facts of *The Big Picture* on p. 19-1. Joyce's professor, Dr. Sanchez, has a forensic consulting practice in addition to her position at the university. Also, she receives book royalties from a textbook. Therefore, because she is self-employed (she will report her earnings on a Schedule C), she is able to establish a Keogh plan.

Earned income refers to net earnings from self-employment as defined in § 1402(a).[42] Net earnings from self-employment means the gross income derived by an individual from any trade or business carried on by that individual, less appropriate deductions, plus the distributive share of income or loss from a partnership.[43] Earned income is reduced by contributions to a Keogh plan on the individual's behalf and by 50 percent of any self-employment tax.[44]

Example 20

Pat, a partner, has earned income of $150,000 in 2014 (after the deduction for one-half of self-employment tax). The maximum contribution Pat may make to a defined contribution Keogh plan is $52,000, the lesser of $150,000 or $52,000.

For discrimination purposes, the 25 percent limitation on the employee contribution to a profit sharing plan or stock bonus plan is computed on the first $260,000 (in 2014) of earned income. Thus, the maximum contribution in 2014 is $52,000 ($260,000 − .25X = X; X = $208,000). Therefore, $260,000 − $208,000 = $52,000. Alternatively, this can be calculated by multiplying $260,000 by 20 percent.

---

[39]§ 401(d).
[40]§ 415(c)(1).
[41]§ 415(b)(1). This amount is indexed annually.

[42]§ 401(c)(2).
[43]§ 1402(a).
[44]§§ 401(c)(2)(A)(v) and 164(f).

Example 21

Terry, a self-employed accountant, has a profit sharing plan with a contribution rate of 15% of compensation. Terry's earned income after the deduction of one-half of self-employment tax, but before the Keogh contribution, is $260,000. Terry's contribution is limited to $33,913 ($260,000 − .15X = X), because X = $226,087 and .15 × $226,087 = $33,913.

Although a Keogh plan must be established before the end of the year in question, contributions may be made up to the normal filing date for that year.

19-3 INDIVIDUAL RETIREMENT ACCOUNTS (IRAs)

LO.6

Describe the benefits of the different types of Individual Retirement Accounts (IRAs).

Individual Retirement Accounts, or IRAs, are a fairly well-known type of retirement plan. They can be simple to create and maintain. There are several tax rules to be aware of, though, that govern deductible contributions, taxable distributions, age requirements, and possible penalties for early withdrawals or excess contributions. Several of these rules are covered in this section.

19-3a General Rules

An individual can contribute to a traditional **Individual Retirement Account (IRA)** assuming the person (or spouse) receives taxable income and is under 70½. These contributions may be deductible, depending upon income level and access to another work-related retirement plan. For 2014, the contribution ceiling is the smaller of $5,500 (or $11,000 for spousal IRAs) or 100 percent of compensation.[45] The contribution ceiling applies to all types of IRAs (traditional deductible, traditional nondeductible, and Roth). An individual who attains the age of 50 by the end of the tax year can make additional catch-up IRA contributions of up to $1,000 in 2014. The maximum contribution limit is increased by $1,000 each year.

The amount accumulated in an IRA can be substantial. For example, if a husband and wife each contribute only $4,000 annually to an IRA from age 25 to age 65 (and earn 6 percent annually), their account balances together would be approximately $1.4 million at retirement. If the taxpayer is an *active participant* in a qualified plan, the traditional IRA deduction limitation is phased out *proportionately* between certain AGI ranges, as shown in Table 19.3.[46] If AGI is above the phaseout range, no IRA deduction is allowed.

AGI is calculated taking into account any § 469 passive losses and § 86 taxable Social Security benefits and ignoring any § 911 foreign income exclusion, § 135 savings bonds interest exclusion, and the IRA deduction. There is a $200 floor on the IRA deduction limitation for individuals whose AGI is not above the phaseout range.

Example 22

Dan, who is single, has compensation income of $66,000 in 2014. He is an active participant in his employer's qualified retirement plan. Dan contributes $5,500 to a traditional IRA. The deductible amount is reduced from $5,500 by $3,300 because of the phaseout mechanism:

$$\frac{\$6,000}{\$10,000} \times \$5,500 = \$3,300 \text{ reduction}$$

Therefore, of the $5,500 contribution, Dan can deduct only $2,200 ($5,500−$3,300).

---

[45]§§ 219(b)(1) and (c)(2). The limit is adjusted annually for inflation in $500 increments.

[46]§ 219(g).

TABLE 19.3	Phaseout of IRA Deduction of an Active Participant in 2014	
AGI Filing Status	**Phaseout Begins***	**Phaseout Ends**
Single and head of household	$60,000	$ 70,000
Married, filing joint return	96,000	116,000
Married, filing separate return	–0–	10,000

*These amounts are indexed annually for inflation.

Example 23

Ben, an unmarried individual, is an active participant in his employer's qualified retirement plan in 2014. With AGI of $69,800, he would normally have an IRA deduction limit of $110 {$5,500 − [($69,800 − $60,000)/$10,000 × $5,500]}. However, because of the special floor provision, Ben is allowed a $200 IRA deduction.

An individual is not considered an active participant in a qualified plan merely because the individual's spouse is an active participant in such a plan for any part of a plan year. Thus, even when filing jointly, the nonparticipating individual may take a full $5,500 deduction regardless of the participation status of his or her spouse, unless the couple has AGI above $181,000. If their AGI is above $181,000, the phaseout of the deduction begins at $181,000 and ends at $191,000 (phaseout over the $10,000 range) rather than beginning and ending at the phaseout amounts in Table 19.3.[47]

Example 24

Nell is covered by a qualified employer retirement plan at work. Her husband, Nick, is not an active participant in a qualified plan. If Nell and Nick's combined AGI is $135,000, Nell cannot make a deductible IRA contribution because she exceeds the income threshold for an active participant in Table 19.3. However, because Nick is not an active participant and their combined AGI does not exceed $181,000, he can make a fully deductible contribution of $5,500 to an IRA.

To the extent an individual is ineligible to make a deductible contribution to an IRA, *nondeductible contributions* can be made to separate accounts.[48] The nondeductible contributions are subject to the same dollar limits as deductible contributions ($5,500 of earned income, $11,000 for a spousal IRA). Income in the account accumulates tax-free until distributed. Only the account earnings are taxed upon distribution because the account basis equals the contributions made by the taxpayer. A taxpayer may elect to treat deductible IRA contributions as nondeductible. If an individual has no taxable income for the year after taking into account other deductions, the election will be beneficial. The election is made on the individual's tax return for the taxable year to which the designation relates. A taxpayer may be entitled to a nonrefundable credit for contributions to an IRA or elective deferrals for a § 401(k) plan (see Chapter 13).

For distributions made in tax years 2006 through 2013, an exclusion from gross income was available for traditional IRA distributions made to charity.[49] The amount of the distribution that is eligible for this beneficial exclusion treatment is limited to $100,000 each year. This provision may be extended by Congress.

---

[47]§ 219(g)(7). However, a special rule in § 219(g)(4) allows a married person filing a separate return to avoid the phaseout rules even though the spouse is an active participant. The individual must live apart from the spouse at all times during the taxable year and must not be an active participant in another qualified plan.

[48]§ 408(o).
[49]§ 408(d)(8)(A).

Example 25

Amber has a traditional deductible IRA, so her basis is $0 (see the later discussion under Taxation of Benefits). Therefore, in 2013, she can have an IRA distribution of $100,000 made to a charity and exclude the $100,000 from her gross income. Assume instead that Amber has a traditional nondeductible IRA with a basis of $75,000. If she has a $100,000 IRA distribution made to a charity, she can exclude $25,000 ($100,000 − $75,000) from her gross income.

Roth IRAs

Introduced by Congress to encourage individual savings, a **Roth IRA** is a *nondeductible* alternative to the traditional deductible IRA. Earnings inside a Roth IRA are not taxable, and all qualified distributions from a Roth IRA are tax-free.[50] The maximum allowable annual contribution to a Roth IRA for 2014 is the smaller of $5,500 ($11,000 for spousal IRAs) or 100 percent of the individual's compensation for the year. Contributions to a Roth IRA must be made by the due date (excluding extensions) of the taxpayer's tax return. Roth IRAs are not subject to the minimum distribution rules that apply to traditional IRAs. Contributions to a Roth IRA (unlike a traditional IRA) may continue beyond age $70\frac{1}{2}$ so long as the person generates compensation income and is not barred by the AGI limits.

A taxpayer can make tax-free withdrawals from a Roth IRA after an initial five-year holding period if any of the following requirements is satisfied:

- The distribution is made on or after the date on which the participant attains age $59\frac{1}{2}$.
- The distribution is made to a beneficiary (or the participant's estate) on or after the participant's death.
- The participant becomes disabled.
- The distribution is used to pay for qualified first-time homebuyer's expenses (statutory ceiling of $10,000).

Example 26

Edith establishes a Roth IRA at age 42 and contributes $5,000 per year for 20 years. The account is now worth $149,400, consisting of $100,000 of nondeductible contributions and $49,400 in accumulated earnings that have not been taxed. Edith may withdraw the $149,400 tax-free from the Roth IRA because she is over age 59½ and has met the five-year holding period requirement.

If the taxpayer receives a distribution from a Roth IRA and does not satisfy the aforementioned requirements, the distribution may be taxable. If the distribution represents a return of capital, it is not taxable. Conversely, if the distribution represents a payout of earnings, it is taxable. Under the ordering rules for Roth IRA distributions, distributions are treated as first made from contributions (return of capital).

Example 27

Assume the same facts as in the previous example, except that Edith is only age 50 and receives a distribution of $55,000. Because her adjusted basis for the Roth IRA is $100,000 (contributions made), the distribution is tax-free and her adjusted basis is reduced to $45,000 ($100,000 − $55,000).

Roth IRAs are subject to income limits. In 2014, the maximum annual contribution of $5,500 is phased out beginning at AGI of $114,000 for single taxpayers and $181,000 for married couples who file a joint return. The phaseout range is $10,000 for married filing jointly and $15,000 for single taxpayers. For a married taxpayer filing separately, the phaseout begins with AGI of $0 and is phased out over a $10,000 range.[51]

---

[50]§ 408A.

[51]The income limits for Roth IRA contributions are indexed for tax years after 2006.

Example 28

Bev, who is single, would like to contribute $5,500 to her Roth IRA. However, her AGI is $124,000, so her contribution is limited to $1,833 ($5,500 − $3,667) calculated as follows:

$$\frac{\$10,000}{\$15,000} \times \$5,500 = \$3,667 \text{ reduction}$$

THE BIG PICTURE

Example 29

Return to the facts of *The Big Picture* on p. 19-1. Joyce's professor, Dr. Sanchez, also contributes annually to a traditional IRA. She would prefer a Roth IRA, but her AGI exceeds the phaseout limit.

As with a traditional IRA, an exclusion from gross income is available for Roth IRA distributions made to charity.[52] This exclusion treatment is beneficial for Roth IRA distributions that otherwise are not eligible for Roth IRA exclusion treatment.

Coverdell Education Savings Accounts (CESAs)

Distributions from a **Coverdell Education Savings Account (CESA)** to pay for qualified education expenses receive favorable tax treatment.[53] (See Chapter 9.) Qualified education expenses include tuition, fees, books, supplies, and related equipment. Room and board qualify if the student's course load is at least one-half of the full-time course load. If the CESA is used to pay the qualified education expenses of the designated beneficiary, the withdrawals are tax-free. To the extent the distributions during a tax year exceed qualified education expenses, part of the excess is treated as a return of capital (the contributions) and part is treated as a distribution of earnings under the § 72 annuity rules. Thus, the distribution is presumed to be pro rata from each category. The exclusion for the distribution of earnings part is calculated as follows:

$$\frac{\text{Qualified education expenses}}{\text{Total distributions}} \times \text{Earnings} = \text{Exclusion}$$

Example 30

Meg receives a $2,500 distribution from her CESA. She uses $2,000 to pay for qualified education expenses. On the date of the distribution, Meg's CESA balance is $10,000, $6,000 of which represents her contributions. Because 60% ($6,000/$10,000) of her account balance represents her contributions, $1,500 ($2,500 × 60%) of the distribution is a return of capital and $1,000 ($2,500 × 40%) is a distribution of earnings. The excludible amount of the earnings is calculated as follows:

$$\frac{\$2,000}{\$2,500} \times \$1,000 = \$800$$

Thus, Meg must include $200 ($1,000 − $800) in her gross income.

The maximum amount that can be contributed annually to a CESA for a beneficiary is $2,000. A beneficiary must be an individual and cannot be a group of children or an unborn child. The contributions are not deductible. A CESA is subject to income limits. The maximum annual contribution is phased out beginning at $95,000 for single taxpayers and $190,000 for married couples who file a joint return. The phaseout range is $30,000 for married filing jointly and $15,000 for single taxpayers. Contributions cannot be made to a CESA after the date on which the designated beneficiary attains age 18. Thus, a total of up to $36,000 can be contributed for each beneficiary—$2,000 in the year of birth and in each of the following

---

[52]§ 408(d)(8)(A).   [53]§ 530.

17 years. A 6 percent excise tax is imposed on excess contributions to a CESA. A 10 percent excise tax is imposed on any distributions that are included in gross income.

The balance in a CESA must be distributed within 30 days after the death of the beneficiary or within 30 days after the beneficiary reaches age 30. Any balance at the close of either 30-day period is considered to be distributed at such time, and the earnings portion is included in the beneficiary's gross income. Before a beneficiary reaches age 30, any balance can be rolled over tax-free into another CESA for a member of the beneficiary's family who is under age 30.

The CESA exclusion may be available in a tax year in which the beneficiary claims the American Opportunity credit or the lifetime learning credit (see Chapter 13). However, any excluded amount of the CESA distribution cannot be used for the same educational expenses for which the American Opportunity credit or the lifetime learning credit is claimed.

Contributions cannot be made to a beneficiary's CESA during any year in which contributions are made to a qualified tuition program on behalf of the same beneficiary (see Chapter 5).

Simplified Employee Pension Plans

An employer may contribute to an IRA covering an employee an amount equal to the lesser of $52,000 (in 2014) or 25 percent of the employee's earned income. In such a plan, the employer must make contributions for *each* employee who has reached age 21, has performed service for the employer during the calendar year and at least three of the five preceding calendar years, and has received at least $550 (in 2014) in compensation from the employer for the year.[54] Known as **simplified employee pension (SEP) plans**, these plans are subject to many of the same restrictions applicable to qualified plans (e.g., age and period-of-service requirements, and nondiscrimination limitations). Concept Summary 19.2 compares a SEP with a Keogh plan.

> **Example 31**
>
> In 2014, Ryan's compensation before his employer's contribution to a SEP is $30,000. Ryan's employer may contribute and deduct up to $7,500 ($30,000 × 25%) for 2014.

The amounts contributed to a SEP by an employer on behalf of an employee and the elective deferrals of an employee under a SEP are excludible from the employee's gross income. Elective deferrals under a SEP are subject to a statutory ceiling of $17,500 (in 2014),[55] which is increased under the catch-up provision for employees at least 50 years of age by the end of the tax year. Only $260,000 (in 2014) in compensation may be taken into account in making the SEP computation. An employer is permitted to elect to use its taxable year rather than the calendar year for purposes of determining contributions to a SEP.[56]

Simple IRA

A SIMPLE plan can be in the form of an IRA. See the earlier discussion under SIMPLE Plans.

Spousal IRA

For a married couple, each spouse may establish an IRA individually and deduct contributions of up to $5,500 if the combined compensation of both spouses is at least equal to the total contributed amount. Thus, if only one spouse is employed or if both are employed but one has compensation of less than $5,500, each of them may contribute a maximum of $5,500 if their combined compensation is at

---

[54]§§ 408(j) and (k)(2). This amount is indexed annually.

[55]Elective deferrals by an employee were repealed by the Small Business Job Protection Act of 1996 effective after December 31, 1996. However, if the employer plan was established before January 1, 1997, contributions can continue to be made under the pre-repeal provisions.

[56]§ 404(h)(1)(A). The $17,500 and $260,000 amounts are indexed annually. The elective deferral amount was increased in $1,000 annual increments until it reached $15,000 and then became subject to indexing.

CONCEPT SUMMARY 19.2

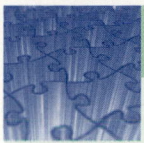

Keogh Plan and SEP Compared

	Keogh	SEP
Form	Trust.	IRA.
Establishment	By end of year.	By extension due date of employer.
Type of plan	Qualified.	Qualified.
Contributions to plan	By extension due date.	By extension due date of employer.
Vesting rules	Qualified plan rules.	100% immediately.
Participants' rules	Flexible.	Stricter.
Lump-sum distributions and averaging	Yes, favorable 10-year forward averaging.	No, ordinary income.
Deduction limitation	Varies.*	Smaller of $52,000 (in 2014) or 25% of earned income.**
Self as trustee	Yes.	No.

*For a defined contribution pension plan, the limit is the smaller of $52,000 (in 2014) or 100% of self-employment income (after one-half of self-employment tax is deducted). A defined contribution profit sharing plan has a 25% deduction limit. A defined benefit Keogh plan's limit is the smaller of $210,000 (in 2014) or 100% of the employee's average compensation for the highest three years of employment.

**Only $260,000 of income can be taken into consideration.

least $11,000. For the spousal IRA provision to apply, a joint return must be filed.[57] The spousal IRA deduction is also proportionately reduced for active participants whose AGI exceeds the above target ranges.

> **Example 32**
>
> Tony, who is married, is eligible to establish an IRA. He received $30,000 in compensation in 2014, and his spouse does not work outside the home. Tony can contribute up to $11,000 to two IRAs, to be divided in any manner between the two spouses, except that no more than $5,500 can be allocated to either spouse.

> **Example 33**
>
> Assume the same facts as in the previous example, except that Tony's wife has compensation income of $2,200. Without the spousal IRA provision, Tony could contribute $5,500 to his IRA, and his spouse could contribute only $2,200 to her IRA. With the spousal IRA provision, they both can contribute $5,500 to their IRAs.

Alimony is considered to be earned income for purposes of IRA contributions. Thus, a person whose only income is alimony can contribute to an IRA.

Timing of Contributions

Contributions (both deductible and nondeductible) can be made to an IRA anytime before the due date of the individual's tax return.[58] For example, an individual can establish and contribute to an IRA through April 15, 2015 (the return due date) and deduct this amount on his or her tax return for 2014. IRA contributions that are made during a tax return extension period do not satisfy the requirement of being made by the return due date. An employer can make contributions up until the time of the due date for filing the return (including extensions) and treat those amounts as a deduction for the prior year.[59] As noted earlier, a similar rule applies to Keogh plans. However, the Keogh plan must be established before the end of the tax year. Contributions to the Keogh plan may then be made anytime before the due date of the individual's tax return.

---

[57]§ 219(c).
[58]§ 219(f)(3).
[59]§ 404(h)(1)(B).

19-3b Penalty Taxes for Excess Contributions

A cumulative, nondeductible 6 percent excise penalty tax is imposed on the smaller of (1) any excess contributions or (2) the market value of the plan assets determined as of the close of the tax year. *Excess contributions* are any contributions that exceed the maximum limitation and contributions that are made to a traditional IRA during or after the tax year in which the individual reaches age 70$\frac{1}{2}$.[60] Contributions can be made to a Roth IRA during or after the tax year in which the individual reaches age 70$\frac{1}{2}$. A taxpayer is not allowed a deduction for excess contributions. If the excess is corrected by contributing less than the deductible amount for a later year, a deduction then is allowable in the later year as a *makeup* deduction.

An excess contribution is taxable annually until returned to the taxpayer or reduced by the underutilization of the maximum contribution limitation in a subsequent year. The 6 percent penalty tax can be avoided if the excess amounts are returned.[61]

Example 34	Nancy, age 45, establishes a traditional IRA in 2014 and contributes $5,800 in cash to the plan. She has earned income of $22,000. Nancy is allowed a $5,500 deduction *for* AGI for 2014. Assuming that the market value of the plan assets is at least $300, there is a nondeductible 6% excise penalty tax of $18 ($300 × 6%). The $300 may be subject to an additional penalty tax in future years if it is not returned to Nancy or reduced by underutilization of the $5,500 maximum contribution limitation (ignoring any catch-up contributions).

19-3c Taxation of Benefits

A participant has a zero basis in the *deductible* contributions of a traditional IRA because the contributions were deducted.[62] Therefore, all withdrawals from a deductible IRA are taxed as ordinary income in the year of receipt. They are not eligible for the 10-year averaging allowed for certain lump-sum distributions.

A participant has a basis equal to the contributions made for a *nondeductible* traditional IRA. Therefore, only the earnings component of withdrawals is included in gross income. Such amounts are taxed as ordinary income in the year of receipt and are not eligible for the 10-year averaging allowed for certain lump-sum distributions.

In addition to being included in gross income, payments from IRAs made to a participant before age 59$\frac{1}{2}$ are subject to a nondeductible 10 percent penalty tax on such actual, or constructive, payments.[63] However, an individual may make penalty-free withdrawals to pay for medical expenses in excess of 10 percent (7.5 percent if at least age 65) of AGI, to pay for qualified higher education expenses, and to pay for qualified first-time homebuyer expenses (up to $10,000). Note that a qualified first-time homebuyer is defined as an individual (and spouse) who has not owned a principal residence in the two-year period preceding the date of acquisition of a principal residence. Further, an individual who has received unemployment compensation for at least 12 consecutive weeks may use IRA withdrawals to pay for health insurance for himself or herself, the spouse, and dependents without incurring the 10 percent penalty tax.[64]

All traditional IRAs of an individual are treated as one contract, and all distributions during a taxable year are treated as one distribution. See the earlier discussion of the special rules for distributions from Roth IRAs and traditional IRAs. If an individual who previously made both deductible and nondeductible IRA contributions makes a withdrawal from a traditional IRA during a taxable year, the excludible amount must be calculated. The amount excludible from gross income for the

---

[60]§§ 4973(a)(1) and (b).

[61]§§ 408(d)(4) and 4973(b)(2).

[62]§ 408(d)(1).

[63]§ 72(t). There are limited exceptions to the penalty on early distributions.

[64]§§ 72(t)(2)(B), (D), (E), and (F). For purposes of the unemployment provision, a self-employed individual who otherwise would have been eligible for unemployment compensation will qualify.

taxable year is calculated by multiplying the amount withdrawn by a percentage. The percentage is calculated by dividing the individual's aggregate nondeductible IRA contributions by the aggregate balance of all of his or her traditional IRAs (including rollover IRAs and SEPs).[65]

> Carl, age 59, has a $12,000 deductible traditional IRA and a $2,000 nondeductible traditional IRA (without any earnings). Carl withdraws $1,000 from the nondeductible IRA. The excludible portion is $143 [($2,000/$14,000) × $1,000], and the includible portion is $857 [($12,000/$14,000) × $1,000]. Carl must also pay a 10% penalty tax on the prorated portion considered withdrawn from the deductible IRA and earnings in either type of IRA. Thus, the 10% penalty tax is $85.70 (10% × $857).

Example 35

Rollovers: General Provisions

As introduced earlier, an IRA may be the recipient of a rollover from another qualified plan, including another IRA. Such a distribution from a qualified plan is not included in gross income if it is transferred within 60 days of receipt to an IRA or another qualified plan. For a series of distributions that constitute a lump-sum distribution, the 60-day period does not begin until the last distribution. Amounts received from IRAs may be rolled over tax-free only once in a 12-month period. If a person has more than one IRA, the one-year waiting period applies separately to each IRA.[66]

> Nonemployer stock worth $60,000 is distributed to an employee from a qualified retirement plan. Hubert, the employee, sells the stock within 60 days for $60,000 and transfers one-half of the proceeds to a traditional IRA. Hubert has $30,000 of ordinary income, which is not eligible for 10-year forward averaging or for capital gain treatment under the pre-1987 rules. One-half of the distribution, or $30,000, does escape taxation because of the rollover.

Example 36

A tax-free rollover for distributions from qualified plans is an alternative to the taxable 10-year forward averaging technique. Any rollover amount in a traditional IRA may later be rolled over into another qualified plan if the IRA consists of only the amounts from the original plan and the receiving plan permits it. The amount of nondeductible employee contributions included in a distribution may not be rolled over, but that amount is tax-free because the contributions were made with after-tax dollars. Partial rollovers are allowed, but the maximum amount that may be rolled over may not exceed the portion of the distribution that is otherwise includible in gross income. Rollovers are not available for required distributions under the minimum distribution rules once age $70\frac{1}{2}$ is reached.

THE BIG PICTURE

> Return to the facts of *The Big Picture* on p. 19-1. Dr. Sanchez withdraws $15,000 from her traditional IRA on May 2, 2014, but she redeposits it in the same IRA on June 28, 2014. Although the withdrawal and redeposit was a partial rollover and Dr. Sanchez may have used the funds for a limited time, this is a tax-free rollover.[67]

Example 37

A rollover is different from a direct transfer of funds from a qualified plan to an IRA or another qualified plan by a trustee or an issuer. A direct transfer is not subject to the one-year waiting period and the withholding rules.[68] Further, in many states, IRA amounts are subject to claims of creditors, which is not the case for some employer plans.

---

[65]§ 408(d)(2).

[66]§ 408(d)(3)(B) and Reg. § 1.408–4(b)(4).

[67]Ltr.Rul. 9010007.

[68]Reg. § 35.3405–1.

CONCEPT SUMMARY 19.3

Comparison of IRAs

	Traditional			Coverdell Education Savings Account (CESA)
	Deductible IRA	**Nondeductible IRA**	**Roth IRA**	
Maximum contribution (per year)	$5,500*	$5,500*	$5,500*	$2,000
Tax-deductible contribution	Yes	No	No	No
Tax-free growth of income	Yes	Yes	Yes	Yes
Beginning of AGI phaseout for active participant (2014)	$60,000 single, $96,000 joint	N/A	$114,000 single, $181,000 joint	$95,000 single, $190,000 joint
Income tax on distributions	Yes, for entire distribution	Yes, for the earnings portion	No, if satisfy 5-year holding period**	No, if used for education expenses
50% excise tax: age 70½ insufficient distributions	Yes	Yes	No	No
10% early withdrawal penalty (before age 59½)	Yes, with exceptions†	Yes, with exceptions†	Yes, with exceptions†	Yes‡

* The total of deductible, nondeductible, and Roth IRA contributions may not exceed $5,500 per year.

** In addition, the distribution must satisfy one of the following: after age 59½, for qualified first-time homebuyer expenses, participant is disabled, or made to a beneficiary on or after the participant's death.

† Qualified education and first-time homebuyer costs (up to $10,000) avoid the 10% penalty.

‡ On early withdrawals not used for education costs. Qualified first-time homebuyer costs (up to $10,000) avoid 10% penalty.

An employer must withhold 20 percent of any lump-sum distributions unless the transfer is a direct transfer to an IRA or another qualified plan.[69]

Example 38

Kay receives a distribution from a qualified retirement plan. The amount of the distribution would have been $20,000, but Kay receives only $16,000 ($20,000 − $4,000) as a result of the 20% withholding provision. After several weeks, Kay decides to contribute $20,000 (the gross amount of the distribution) to her traditional IRA. Because she received only $16,000, she will need to contribute $4,000 from another source to make a $20,000 contribution. When she files her tax return for the year, Kay will be able to claim a refund for the $4,000 that was withheld.

Distributions from a traditional IRA are generally not eligible for 10-year averaging or capital gain treatment. An exception applies in the case of a *conduit IRA*, where the sole assets of a qualified plan are rolled over into an IRA and the assets are then rolled into a qualified plan. With a conduit IRA, the lump-sum distribution from the original plan is still eligible for the special tax treatments.

Rollovers and Conversions: Roth IRAs

A Roth IRA may be rolled over tax-free into another Roth IRA.

A traditional IRA may be rolled over or converted to a Roth IRA. A conversion occurs when the taxpayer notifies the IRA trustee that the IRA is now a Roth IRA. A rollover or conversion of a traditional IRA to a Roth IRA can occur only if the following requirements are satisfied:[70]

- The participant's AGI does not exceed $100,000 (excluding the amount included in gross income resulting from the rollover or conversion).
- The participant is not married filing a separate return.
- The rollover occurs within 60 days of the IRA distribution.

---

[69]§ 3405(c).

[70]§ 408A(c)(3)(B).

For 2010 only, the $100,000 AGI limitation for conversions and rollovers went away. In addition, while taxes were due on the conversion amount in 2010, taxpayers were allowed to spread the payment of those taxes over two years (2010 and 2011).[71] Further, unlike a traditional IRA, which requires withdrawals at age 70½, there are no required withdrawals from a Roth IRA. Thus, money can be accumulated over the taxpayer's lifetime and then passed to heirs without tax penalties.

When a traditional IRA is rolled over or converted to a Roth IRA, the tax consequences depend on whether the traditional IRA was deductible or nondeductible. If deductible, the basis for the IRA is zero. Thus, the entire amount of the rollover or conversion is included in gross income. If nondeductible, the basis for the IRA is equal to the sum of the contributions. Thus, only the IRA earnings included in the rollover or conversion are included in gross income. The 10 percent penalty tax will not apply in either case.[72]

Distributions from qualified retirement plans, § 403(b) annuities, and governmental § 457 plans also can be rolled over into a Roth IRA.[73] For these types of rollovers to be permitted, the $100,000 AGI limit must be satisfied.

19-4 NONQUALIFIED DEFERRED COMPENSATION PLANS

It should come as no surprise that if there are "qualified" plans, there are also "nonqualified" plans. Special rules relevant to employers and employees for these types of arrangements are discussed in this section.

LO.7

Review the rationale for nonqualified deferred compensation plans and the related tax treatment.

19-4a Underlying Rationale for Tax Treatment

Nonqualified deferred compensation (NQDC) plans provide a flexible way for taxpayers, particularly those in the 35 percent tax bracket (39.6 percent for certain high-income taxpayers), to defer income taxes on income payments until a potentially lower tax bracket year. When the deferred compensation is credited with annual earnings until payment, the entire deferred compensation, not just the after-tax amount, is generating investment income. Also, most NQDC plans do not have to meet the discrimination, funding, coverage, and other requirements of qualified plans. In addition to these advantages for the employee, the employer may not have a current cash outflow. The IRS will issue rulings on deferred compensation plans.

19-4b Tax Treatment to the Employer and Employee

Special rules apply to nonqualified arrangements that defer the receipt of compensation income to a year later than that in which it is earned. During a taxable year in which an NQDC plan does not meet certain conditions in § 409A or is not operating in accordance with these conditions, all amounts deferred under the arrangement will be included in the participant's gross income to the extent they are not subject to a substantial risk of forfeiture. In addition, a 20 percent penalty tax is imposed on such income along with interest at the underpayment rate plus 1 percent.[74]

A three-pronged analysis determines whether a plan to defer compensation faces these punitive actions. First, does the deferred compensation fall within the NQDC provisions under § 409A? Second, are the benefits subject to a substantial risk of forfeiture (SRF)? SRF is discussed later in this chapter under Restricted Property Plans, but the definition of SRF for NQDCs differs from the normal definition. For example, a covenant not to compete can never be an SRF under § 409A, nor will conditions under the discretionary control of the employee be an SRF under § 409A. Also, an elective extension of a forfeiture period will generally

---

[71]§ 408A(d)(3)(A).

[72]§ 408A(d)(3)(A)(ii).

[73]§ 402(c)(8)(B).

[74]§409A(a)(1).

be disregarded as an SRF unless there are substantial additional considerations for such an extension. Third, at the time the arrangement is not covered by an SRF, has the plan suffered a "plan failure"?

Compensation arrangements that do not fall within § 409A include a qualified employer plan, any bona fide vacation leave, sick leave, educational benefits, legal settlements, indemnification arrangements, compensatory time, disability pay, and a death benefit plan.[75] Excluded qualified employer plans include tax-qualified pension, profit sharing, or § 401(k) plans; a § 403(b) tax-deferred annuity; a simplified employee pension plan; or an eligible § 457(b) plan for state, government, or tax-exempt employees.

In general, a § 409A deferral occurs where an employee has a legally binding right to compensation that has been deferred to the future. The section casts a wide net and may even cover nonqualified stock options and stock appreciation rights (SARs). These rules do not cover restricted property under § 83, as well as nondiscounted stock options, nondiscounted SARs, and statutory stock options. Discounted stock options, discounted SARs, phantom stock, and restricted stock units are covered.

Generally, funded NQDC plans must be forfeitable to keep the compensation payments from being taxable immediately. In most instances, employees prefer to have some assurance that they will ultimately receive benefits from the NQDC (that the plan provides for nonforfeitable benefits). In such instances, the plan will have to be unfunded to prevent immediate taxation to the employee. Note that most funded NQDC plans are subject to many of the provisions that apply to qualified plans, including the nondiscrimination requirements, and are impractical as a result.

To be effective, an unfunded deferred compensation plan must meet and comply with the following requirements under § 409A.[76]

- The NQDC plan may not distribute the deferred compensation to the employee except in these six situations: separation of service, disability, death, specified time or fixed schedule, change in employer control, or unforeseeable emergency.
- The plan must not permit any participant to accelerate the time or scheduled date of distributions (subject to some exceptions).
- A participant must elect to postpone the compensation for the current year no later than the close of the preceding tax year (initial deferral election).
- The employee must decide on the form and time of the benefits (e.g., installment payments or lump sum) when the deferral election is made if the plan permits an election between alternatives, or the NQDC plan must specify the form and time of distribution when the deferral election is made.
- A participant must not change the time or form of benefits unless the employee does so at least 12 months before the scheduled distribution date and postpones the scheduled distribution date by at least five years.
- The plan should specify the amount payable (or the terms of the formula determining the amount), along with the payment schedule or triggering events that result in payment.
- Publicly held companies must provide for a six-month delay requirement for the top 50 officers with incomes of at least $130,000 (along with certain owner-employees).

Example 39

Eagle Corporation and Bill, a cash basis employee, enter into an employment agreement that provides an annual salary of $120,000 to Bill. Of this amount, $100,000 is paid in current monthly installments, and $20,000 is to be paid in 10 annual installments beginning at Bill's retirement or death. Although Eagle Corporation maintains a separate account for Bill, that account is not funded. Bill is merely an unsecured creditor of the corporation. The $20,000 is not considered constructively received and is deferred. Compensation of $100,000 is currently taxable to Bill and deductible to Eagle. The other $20,000 will be taxable and deductible when paid in future years.

---

[75]§409A(d)(1).   [76]§409A(a)(2),(3), and (4).

A deferred compensation arrangement occurs when an employee receives compensation after the $2^1/_2$-month period following the end of an employer's corporate tax year in which such services were performed.[77] An employer's deduction of NQDC must be delayed to match the employee's recognition of income regardless of the employer's method of accounting.[78]

> **Example 40**
>
> Beige, Inc., a calendar year employer, has an accrued NQDC liability of $300,000 on December 31, 2013. During 2014, the company accrues another $60,000 of NQDC. On February 13, 2015, the company pays the entire $360,000 to the employee. Because the $60,000 was paid within 2½ months after the end of 2014, only $300,000 ever met the requirement for deferred compensation. The entire $360,000 may be deducted by the company only in the year ending December 31, 2015, when the employee receives the cash and recognizes the income.

When to Use an NQDC Arrangement

As a general rule, NQDC plans are more appropriate for executives in a financially secure company. Because of the need for currently disposable income, such plans are usually not appropriate for young employees.

An NQDC plan can reduce an employee's overall tax payments by deferring the taxation of income to later years (possibly when the employee is in a lower tax bracket). In effect, these plans may produce a form of income averaging. Further, unfunded NQDC plans may discriminate in favor of shareholders, officers, specific highly compensated key employees, or a single individual.

Certain disadvantages should be noted, however. As mentioned earlier, nonqualified plans are usually required to be unfunded, which means that an employee has no assurance that funds ultimately will be available to pay the benefits. In other words, the deferred amounts are recorded as a liability on the company's books, and the employee will be an unsecured creditor in the event of the firm's bankruptcy.

Golden Parachute Arrangements

Golden parachute arrangements promise monetary benefits to key employees if they lose their jobs as a result of a change in ownership of the corporation. In essence, these are unfunded NQDC plans that do not vest until the change in ownership. These payments may be unreasonable or not really for services rendered. The term **golden parachute payments**, as used in the Code, means *excess severance pay*.

These excessive severance payments to employees are penalized. The Code denies a deduction to an employer who makes a payment of cash or property to an employee or independent contractor that satisfies both of the following conditions:

- The payment is contingent on a change of ownership of a corporation through a stock or asset acquisition.
- The aggregate present value of the payment equals or exceeds three times the employee's (or independent contractor's) average annual compensation.[79]

The disallowed amount is the excess of the payment over a statutory base amount (a five-year average of taxable compensation if the taxpayer was an employee for the entire five-year period). Further, a 20 percent excise tax is imposed on the recipient on the receipt of these parachute payments; the tax is withheld at the time of payment.[80]

> **Example 41**
>
> Irene, an executive, receives a golden parachute payment of $380,000 from her employer. Her average annual compensation for the most recent five tax years is $120,000. The corporation will be denied a deduction for $260,000 ($380,000 payment— $120,000 base amount). Irene's excise tax is $52,000 ($260,000 × 20%).

---

[77]Reg. § 1.409A–1(b)(4).
[78]§ 404(a)(5); Reg. § 1.404(a)–12(b)(1).

[79]§ 280G.
[80]§ 4999.

TAX IN THE NEWS   *Don't Feel Sorry for Conan O'Brien*

When Conan O'Brien was booted to make room for Jay Leno, NBC reportedly wrote O'Brien a nice severance check for $40 million. This tidy sum was nearly 15 times what the average American college graduate can expect to make over 40 years of full-time employment.

Consider these examples as well. Two-time Cy Young Award winner Johan Santana missed the entire 2011 baseball season after a shoulder injury, but he still received his $21.6 million salary from the New York Mets. Ann Curry was replaced as cohost of the NBC Today Show by Savannah Guthrie, but Curry was given $10 million. After one year on the job as CEO of Viacom, Thomas E. Freston was handed $100 million. John Corzine left behind approximately $12.1 million of golden parachute severance pay from MF Global when the firm went bankrupt.

When the Obama administration pushed out General Motors CEO Rick Wagoner in 2009, it was reported that Wagoner was scheduled to receive just over $8.2 million over five years and a lifetime annuity of roughly $75,000 plus other perks.

And ordinary employees worry about being fired.

Source: Based on David Grant, "How Does Conan O'Brien's Severance Stack Up on Wall Street?" *Christian Science Monitor,* January 19, 2010.

Golden parachute payments do not include payments to or from qualified pension, profit sharing, stock bonus, annuity, or simplified employee pension plans. Also excluded is the amount of the payment that, in fact, represents reasonable compensation for personal services actually rendered or to be rendered. Such excluded payments are not taken into account when determining whether the threshold (the aggregate present value calculation) is exceeded.

S corporations are not subject to the golden parachute rules. Generally, corporations that do not have stock that is readily tradable on an established securities market or elsewhere are also exempt.

Publicly Held Companies' Compensation Limitation

For purposes of both the regular income tax and the alternative minimum tax, the deductible compensation for the top five executives of publicly traded companies is limited to $1 million for each executive. A company is publicly held if the corporation has common stock listed on a national securities exchange.[81] This $1 million deduction limitation is decreased by any nondeductible golden parachute payments made to the employee during the same year. The $1 million deduction limitation becomes $500,000 during the period in which financial assistance under the Troubled Asset Relief Program (TARP) remains outstanding for a TARP participant company.

This deduction limitation applies when the compensation deduction would otherwise be taken. For example, in the case of a nonqualified stock option (NQSO), which is discussed later in this chapter, the deduction is normally taken in the year the NQSO is exercised, even though the option was granted with respect to services performed in a prior year.

Certain types of compensation are *not* subject to this deduction limit and are not taken into account in determining whether other compensation exceeds $1 million:

- Compensation payable on a commission basis.
- Compensation payable solely on account of the attainment of one or more performance goals when certain requirements involving the approval of outside directors and shareholders are met.
- Payments to a tax-qualified retirement plan (including salary-reduction contributions).
- Amounts that are excludible from an executive's gross income (such as employer-provided health benefits and miscellaneous fringe benefits).

---

[81]§ 162(m).

The most important exception is performance-based compensation. Compensation qualifies for this exception only if the following conditions are satisfied:

* The compensation is paid solely on account of the attainment of one or more performance goals.
* The performance goals are established by a compensation committee consisting solely of two or more outside directors.
* The material terms under which the compensation is to be paid (including the performance goals) are disclosed to and approved by the shareholders in a separate vote prior to payment.
* Prior to payment, the compensation committee certifies that the performance goals and any other material terms were in fact satisfied.

Disallowance of the compensation deduction can occur even where the employee's contract contains performance-based criteria if the employee also can receive compensation for employment that is terminated without cause or for voluntary retirement.

Compensation (other than stock options or other stock appreciation rights) is not treated as paid solely on account of the attainment of one or more performance goals unless the compensation is paid to the particular executive under a pre-established objective performance formula or standard that precludes discretion. In essence, a third party with knowledge of the relevant performance results could calculate the amount to be paid to the particular executive. A performance goal is broadly defined and includes, for example, any objective performance standard that is applied to the individual executive, a business unit (e.g., a division or a line of business), or the corporation as a whole. Performance standards could include increases in stock price, market share, sales, or earnings per share.

As part of the Affordable Care Act provisions enacted in 2010, a new compensation limit at § 162(m)(5) starts in 2013 for certain compensation payments in excess of $500,000 made by a covered health insurance provider.

19-5 RESTRICTED PROPERTY PLANS

LO.8

Explain the value of restricted property plans.

A **restricted property plan** is an arrangement whereby an employer transfers property (e.g., stock of the employer-corporation) to an employee or another provider of services at no cost or at a bargain price. The usual purpose of a restricted stock plan is to retain the services of key employees who might otherwise leave. The employer hopes that such compensation arrangements will encourage company growth and attainment of performance objectives. Section 83 was enacted in 1969 to provide rules for the taxation of incentive compensation arrangements, which previously were governed by judicial and administrative interpretations. Although the following discussion refers to an employee as the provider of the services, the services may be performed by an independent contractor.

As a general rule, if an employee performs services and receives property (e.g., stock), the fair market value of that property in excess of any amount paid by the employee is includible in his or her gross income. The time for inclusion is the earlier of (1) the time the property is no longer subject to a substantial risk of forfeiture or

(2) the time the property is transferable by the employee. The fair market value of the property is determined without regard to any restriction, except a restriction that by its terms will never lapse.[82] Because the amount of the compensation is determined at the date the restrictions lapse or when the property is transferable, the opportunity to generate capital gain treatment on the property is denied during a period when the ordinary income element is being deferred.

Example 42	On October 1, 2010, Blue Corporation sold 100 shares of its stock to Ahmad, an employee, for $10 per share. At the time of the sale, the fair market value of the stock was $100 per share. Under the terms of the sale, each share of stock was nontransferable and subject to a substantial risk of forfeiture (which was not to lapse until October 1, 2014). Evidence of these restrictions was stamped on the face of the stock certificates. On October 1, 2014, the fair market value of the stock was $250 per share. Because the stock was nontransferable and was subject to a substantial risk of forfeiture, Ahmad did not include any compensation in gross income during 2010 (assuming that no special election was made). Instead, Ahmad was required to include $24,000 of compensation in gross income [100 shares × ($250 − $10 per share)] during 2014. If for some reason the forfeiture had occurred (e.g., the plan required Ahmad to surrender the stock to the corporation if he voluntarily terminated his employment with the company before October 1, 2014) and Ahmad never received the stock certificates, he would have been allowed a capital loss of $1,000 (the extent of his investment).

19-5a Substantial Risk of Forfeiture

A **substantial risk of forfeiture (SRF)** exists if a person's rights to full enjoyment of property are conditioned upon the future performance, or the refraining from the performance, of substantial services by that individual.[83] For example, if an employee must return the property (receiving only his or her original cost, if any) should there be a failure to complete a substantial period of service (for any reason), the property is subject to an SRF. Another such situation exists when an employer can compel an employee to return the property due to a breach of a substantial covenant not to compete. Any SRF should be stated on the face of the stock certificates. Assuming that an SRF does not exist, the property received is valued at its fair market value, ignoring any restrictions, except for one instance dealing with closely held stock.

19-5b Special Election Available

An employee may elect within 30 days after the receipt of restricted property to recognize immediately as ordinary income the fair market value in excess of the amount paid for the property. Any appreciation in the value of the property after receipt is classified as capital gain instead of ordinary income. No deduction is allowed to the employee for taxes paid on the original amount included in income if the property is subsequently forfeited.[84] The employee is permitted to take a capital loss for any amounts that were actually paid for the property. Furthermore, in such a case, the employer must repay taxes saved by any compensation deduction taken in the earlier year.[85]

Any increase in value between the time the property is received and the time it becomes either nonforfeitable or transferable is taxed as ordinary income if the employee does not make this special election. However, if the employee elects to be taxed immediately on the difference between the cost and fair market value on the date of issue, any future appreciation is treated as capital gain. In determining whether the gain is long-term or short-term, the holding period starts when the employee is taxed on the ordinary income.[86]

[82]§ 83(a)(1); *Miriam Sakol*, 67 T.C. 986 (1977); *T. M. Horwith*, 71 T.C. 932 (1979).

[83]§ 83(c). Regulation § 1.83–3(c)(2) includes several examples of restricted property arrangements.

[84]§ 83(b).

[85]Reg. §§ 1.83–6(c) and 2(a).

[86]§ 1223(6).

Example 43

On July 1, 2004, Sparrow Company sold 100 shares of its preferred stock, worth $15 per share, to Diane (an employee) for $5 per share. The sale was subject to Diane's agreement to resell the preferred shares to the company for $5 per share if she terminated her employment during the following 10 years. The stock had a value of $25 per share on July 1, 2014, and Diane sold the stock for $30 per share on October 10, 2014. Diane made the special election to include the original spread (between the value of $15 in 2004 and the amount paid of $5) in income for 2004. Diane was required to recognize $1,000 of compensation income in 2004 ($15 − $5 = $10 × 100 shares), at which time her holding period in her stock began. Diane's tax basis in the stock was $1,500 ($1,000 + $500). When the preferred stock was sold in 2014, Diane recognized a $1,500 long-term capital gain ($30 × 100 shares − $1,500).

Example 44

Assume the same facts as in the previous example, except that Diane sells the stock in 2015 (rather than 2014). She would not recognize any gain in 2014 when the SRF lapses. Instead, Diane would recognize the $1,500 long-term capital gain in 2015.

This "gambler's choice" special provision is usually not elected because it results in an immediate recognition of income and adverse tax consequences result from a subsequent forfeiture. However, the special election may be attractive in the following situations:

- The bargain element is relatively small.
- Substantial appreciation is expected in the future.
- A high probability exists that the restrictions will be met.

19-5c Employer Deductions

At the time the employee is required to include the compensation in income, the employer is allowed a tax deduction for the same amount. The employer must withhold on this amount in accordance with § 3402. In the no-election situation, the deduction is limited to the fair market value of the restricted property (without regard to the restrictions) at the time the restrictions lapse, reduced by the amount originally paid for the property by the employee.[87] When the employee elects to be taxed immediately, the corporate deduction also is accelerated and deductible in like amount. In cases of deferred income recognition, the employer can receive a sizable deduction if the property has appreciated.

Example 45

On March 14, 2012, Gold Corporation sold to Harry, an employee, 10 shares of Gold common stock for $100 per share. Both the corporation and Harry were calendar year taxpayers. The common stock was subject to an SRF and was nontransferable; both conditions were to lapse on March 14, 2014. At the time of the sale, the fair market value of the common stock (without considering the restrictions) was $1,000 per share. On March 14, 2014, when the fair market value of the stock is $2,000 per share, the restrictions lapse. Harry did not make the special election. In 2014, Harry realizes ordinary income of $19,000 (10 shares at $2,000 per share less the $100 per share he had paid). Likewise, Gold Corporation is allowed a $19,000 compensation deduction in 2014.

Example 46

In the previous example, assume that Harry made the special election. Because he was taxed on $9,000 in 2012, the corporation was allowed to deduct a like amount in 2012. No deduction would be available in 2014.

---

[87]Reg. § 1.83–6(a).

19-6 STOCK OPTIONS

LO.9

Differentiate the tax treatment of qualified and nonqualified stock options.

Various equity types of stock option programs are available for an employee's compensation package. Some authorities believe that some form of *equity kicker* is needed to attract new management, convert key officers into *partners* by giving them a share of the business, and retain the services of executives who might otherwise leave. Encouraging the managers of a business to have a proprietary interest in its successful operation should provide executives with a key motive to expand the company and improve its profits. In addition, under certain conditions, stock options may fall outside the $1 million limitation on the salaries of the top five executives of publicly traded companies. Sometimes an executive's stock option income may far exceed cash salaries and bonuses. For example, Apple CEO Tim Cook had a salary of $900,017 in 2011. He also received 1 million restricted stock options worth around $377 million.

A **stock option** gives an individual the right to purchase a stated number of shares of stock from a corporation at a certain price within a specified period of time. The optionee must be under no obligation to purchase the stock, and the option may be revocable by the corporation. The option must be in writing, and its terms must be clearly expressed.[88]

19-6a Incentive Stock Options

An equity type of stock option called an *incentive stock option (ISO)* is available. An **incentive stock option (ISO)** is an option to purchase stock of a corporation granted to an individual for any reason connected with his or her employment that meets specific qualification requirements.[89] The option is granted by the employer-corporation or by a parent or subsidiary corporation of the employer-corporation.

There are no tax consequences for either the issuing corporation or the recipient when the option is granted. However, the *spread* (the excess of the fair market value of the share at the date of exercise over the option price)[90] is a positive tax preference item to the recipient for purposes of the alternative minimum tax. The determination of fair market value is made without regard to any lapse restrictions (a restriction that will expire after a period of time). After the option is exercised and when the stock is sold, any gain from the sale is taxed as a long-term capital gain if certain holding period requirements are met. For a gain to qualify as a long-term capital gain, the employee must not dispose of the stock within two years after the option is granted or within one year after the stock is acquired.[91] If the employee meets the holding period requirements, none of these transactions generates any business deduction for the employer.[92] If the employee pays anything for the option and does not exercise the option, any amount paid is recognized as a capital loss.

THE BIG PICTURE

Example 47

Return to the facts of *The Big Picture* on p. 19-1. Dr. Sanchez is on the board of directors of a medium-sized company, Wren Corporation. Wren Corporation granted an ISO for 100 shares of its stock to Dr. Sanchez on March 18, 2013, for service rendered. The option price was $100 and the fair market value was $100 on the date of the grant. Dr. Sanchez exercised the option on April 1, 2013, when the fair market value of the stock was $200 per share. She sells the stock on April 6, 2014, for $300 per share. Dr. Sanchez did not recognize any ordinary income on the date of the grant or the exercise date because the option qualified as an ISO. Wren received no compensation deduction. Dr. Sanchez has a $10,000 tax preference item on the exercise date. She has a long-term capital gain of $20,000 [($300 − $100) × 100] on the sale of the stock in 2014, because the one-year holding period and other requirements have been met.

---

[88]Reg. §§ 1.421–1(a)(1) and −7(a)(1).
[89]§ 422(b).
[90]§§ 422(a), 421(a)(1), 57(a)(3), and 1234(a)(1) and (2).
[91]§ 422(a)(1).
[92]§ 421(a)(2).

As a further requirement for ISO treatment, the option holder must be an employee of the issuing corporation from the date the option is granted until 3 months (12 months if disabled) before the date of exercise. The holding period and the employee-status rules just described (the one-year, two-year, and three-month requirements) are waived in the case of the death of an employee.[93]

THE BIG PICTURE
Example 48

Return to the facts in Example 47, except that Dr. Sanchez was not a service provider (or employee) of Wren Corporation for six months before the date she exercised the options. Dr. Sanchez must recognize $10,000 [($200 − $100) × 100] of ordinary income on the exercise date, to the extent of the spread, because she was not an employee of Wren Corporation at all times during the period beginning on the grant date and ending three months before the exercise date. Wren is allowed a deduction at the same time Dr. Sanchez reports the ordinary income.

If the holding period requirements are not satisfied but all other conditions are met, the tax is still deferred to the point of the sale. However, the difference between the option price and the value of the stock at the date the option was exercised is treated as ordinary income. The difference between the amount realized for the stock and the value of the stock at the date of exercise is short-term or long-term capital gain, depending on the holding period of the stock itself. The employer is allowed a deduction equal to the amount recognized by the employee as ordinary income. The employee does not have a tax preference for alternative minimum tax purposes.

THE BIG PICTURE
Example 49

Assume the same facts as in Example 47, except that Dr. Sanchez sells the stock on March 22, 2014, for $290 per share. Because Dr. Sanchez did not hold the stock for more than one year, $10,000 of the gain is treated as ordinary income in 2014 and Wren Corporation is allowed a $10,000 compensation deduction in 2014. The remaining $9,000 is short-term capital gain ($29,000 − $20,000).

Qualification Requirements for Incentive Stock Option Plans

An ISO plan may permit an employee to use company stock to pay for the exercise of the option without disqualifying the ISO plan.

For an option to qualify as an ISO, the terms of the option must identify it as an ISO and meet the following conditions:

- The option must be granted under a plan specifying the number of shares of stock to be issued and the employees or class of employees eligible to receive the options. The plan must be approved by the shareholders of the corporation within 12 months before or after the plan is adopted.
- The option must be granted within 10 years of the date the plan is adopted or of the date the plan is approved by the shareholders, whichever date is earlier.
- The option must by its terms be exercisable only within 10 years of the date it is granted.
- The option price must equal or exceed the fair market value of the stock at the time the option is granted. This requirement is deemed satisfied if there has been a good-faith attempt to value the stock accurately, even if the option price is less than the stock value.

---

[93]§§ 422(a)(2) and (c)(3). Exceptions are made for parent and subsidiary situations, corporate reorganizations, and liquidations. Also, in certain situations involving an insolvent employee, the holding period rules are modified.

- The option by its terms must be nontransferable other than at death and must be exercisable during the employee's lifetime only by the employee.
- The employee must not, immediately before the option is granted, own stock representing more than 10 percent of the voting power or value of all classes of stock in the employer-corporation or its parent or subsidiary. (Here, the attribution rules of § 267 are applied in modified form.) However, the stock ownership limitation will be waived if the option price is at least 110 percent of the fair market value (at the time the option is granted) of the stock subject to the option and the option by its terms is not exercisable more than five years from the date it is granted.[94]

An overall limitation is imposed on the amount of ISOs that can be first exercisable in one year by an employee. This limit is set at $100,000 per year based on the value of the stock determined at the time the option is granted. For example, an ISO plan may permit acquisition of up to $600,000 worth of stock if it provides that the options are exercisable in six installments, each of which becomes exercisable in a different year and does not exceed $100,000.

Because of these regulatory conditions and the fact that a company may never receive a tax deduction, employers may view ISOs less favorably than nonqualified stock options.

19-6b Nonqualified Stock Options

A **nonqualified stock option (NQSO)** does not satisfy the statutory requirements for ISOs. In addition, a stock option that otherwise would qualify as an ISO will be treated as an NQSO if the terms of the stock option provide that it is not an ISO. If the NQSO has a readily ascertainable fair market value (e.g., the option is traded on an established exchange), the value of the option must be included in the employee's income at the date of grant. Thereafter, capital gain or loss is recognized only upon the disposal of the optioned stock. The employee's basis is the amount paid for the stock plus any amount reported as ordinary income. The employer obtains a corresponding tax deduction at the same time and to the extent that ordinary income is recognized by the employee.[95]

Example 50

On February 1, 2013, Janet was granted an NQSO to purchase 100 shares of stock from her employer at $10 per share. On this date, the option was selling for $2 on an established exchange. Janet exercised the option on March 30, 2014, when the stock was worth $20 per share. On November 5, 2014, Janet sold the optioned stock for $22 per share.

- Janet must report ordinary income of $200 ($2 × 100 shares) on the date of grant (February 1, 2013), because the option has a readily ascertainable fair market value.
- Janet's adjusted basis for the stock is $1,200 ($1,000 cost + $200 recognized gain).
- Upon the sale of the stock (November 5, 2014), Janet must report a long-term capital gain of $1,000 [($22 − $12) × 100 shares].
- At the date of grant (February 1, 2013), the employer receives a tax deduction of $200, the amount of ordinary income reported by Janet.

If an NQSO does not have a readily ascertainable fair market value, an employee does not recognize income at the grant date. However, as a general rule, ordinary income must then be reported in the year of exercise (the difference between the fair market value of the stock at the exercise date and the option price).[96] The amount paid by the employee for the stock plus the amount reported as ordinary income becomes the basis. Any appreciation above that basis is taxed as a long-term

---

[94]§ 422(c)(5).
[95]Reg. §§ 1.421–6(c), (d), (e), and (f); Reg. § 1.83–7.

[96]Reg. § 1.83–7(a); Reg. § 1.421–6(d).

FINANCIAL DISCLOSURE INSIGHTS   Accounting for Executive Compensation

The recent crash of the financial sector of the U.S. economy has shed light on the high levels of bonuses, commissions, health care coverage, and other compensation devices that some firms use to attract and retain managerial talent. Payments to qualified retirement plans are limited in amount and timing, but other "IOUs" are made available to managers, typically as unfunded but enforceable promises to make large payments or stock transfers, for example, after the executive retires or works for the firm for a certain number of years. These arrangements embarrassed some of the employers who provided them while receiving bailouts from the Federal government, but the high levels of executive pay and deferred compensation live on today.

Bonus and retirement arrangements like these create a book-tax difference, as they represent compensation expenses for GAAP purposes, but no tax deduction is allowed until the compensation is paid or becomes fully funded and vested, for example, through a trust or an escrow account. Some firms do fund the deferred payments—no book-tax difference or deferred tax asset amount would result in that case. Usually, the employer also includes in this book-tax difference the amount by which current compensation paid to employees exceeds the tax law maximum deduction amount of §162(m).

Recent financial statements revealed the following amounts in the deferred tax asset accounts of the employer, using "deferred compensation" or "employee benefits and pay" as the line item in the tax footnote.

Employer	Deferred Tax Asset for Executive Compensation ($000)
Goldman Sachs	11,800
JPMorgan Chase	8,200
Citigroup	5,000
Bank of America	1,300
Cisco	1,200
Eli Lilly	1,150

capital gain upon disposition (assuming that the stock is held for the required long-term holding period after exercise). The corporation receives a corresponding tax deduction at the same time and to the extent that ordinary income is recognized by the employee.

> **Example 51**
>
> On February 3, 2012, Maria was granted an NQSO for 100 shares of common stock at $10 per share. On the date of the grant, there was no readily ascertainable fair market value for the option. Maria exercised the options on January 3, 2013, when the stock was selling for $15 per share. She sold one-half of the shares on April 15, 2013, and the other half on September 17, 2014. The sale price on both dates was $21 per share. Maria would not recognize any income on the grant date (February 3, 2012) but would recognize $500 ($1,500 − $1,000) of ordinary income on the exercise date (January 3, 2013). She would recognize a short-term capital gain of $300 on the sale of the first half in 2013 and a $300 long-term capital gain on the sale of the second batch of stock in 2014 [½($2,100 − $1,500)].

The major *advantages* of NQSOs can be summarized as follows:

- A tax deduction is available to the corporation without a cash outlay.
- The employee receives capital gain treatment on any appreciation in the stock starting either at the exercise date if the option does not have a readily ascertainable fair market value or at the date of grant if the option has a readily ascertainable fair market value.
- Options can be issued at more flexible terms than under ISO plans (e.g., longer exercise period and granted to nonemployees).

A major *disadvantage* is that the employee must recognize ordinary income on the exercise of the option or at the date of grant without receiving cash to pay the tax. Another negative factor is that the exercise price for NQSOs must not be lower than the underlying stock's fair market value on the grant date because of § 409A restrictions.

19-7 TAX PLANNING

A number of tax planning ideas are helpful for employers and employees.

19-7a Deferred Compensation

With the individual tax rate being as high as 35 percent (39.6 percent for certain high-income taxpayers) in 2014, taxpayers are motivated to try to lower their tax burden by participating in more deferred compensation arrangements. The $1 million annual limit on the compensation deduction for the top five executives of publicly traded companies may cause a shift into § 401(k) plans, qualified retirement plans, and especially nonqualified deferred compensation arrangements. However, only $255,000 of compensation can be taken into consideration for purposes of calculating contributions or benefits under a qualified pension or profit sharing plan. The $5,500 allowed for traditional IRAs and Roth IRAs should encourage more participation in retirement vehicles. The spousal IRA option should expand retirement coverage even further.

19-7b Qualified Plans

Qualified plans provide maximum tax benefits for employers, because the employer receives an immediate tax deduction for contributions to a plan's trust and the income that is earned on the contributions is not taxable to the employer. The employer's contributions and the trust earnings are not taxed to the employees until those funds are made available to them.

Qualified plans are most appropriate where it is desirable to provide benefits for a cross section of employees. In some closely held corporations, the primary objective is to provide benefits for the officer-shareholder group and other highly paid personnel. The nondiscrimination requirements that must be met in a qualified plan may prevent such companies from attaining these objectives. Thus, a nonqualified arrangement may be needed as a supplement to, or used in lieu of, the qualified plan.

Cash balance plans are better for younger, mobile employees, and the converting company saves money by reducing pension payouts for older and longer-service employees. If a participant moves or retires, he or she can roll over the lump-sum payment into an IRA or another qualified plan.

Although defined benefit plans are being eliminated by larger companies, many small-business owners with few or no employees (or a young, low-paid, transient staff) are adopting them.

19-7c Self-Employed Retirement Plans

A Keogh or traditional deductible IRA participant may make a deductible contribution for a tax year up to the time prescribed for filing the individual's tax return. A Keogh plan must have been established by the end of the tax year (e.g., December 31) to obtain a current deduction for the contribution made in the subsequent year. An individual can establish an IRA after the end of the tax year and still receive a current deduction for the contribution made in the subsequent year. However, because the deductibility of contributions to IRAs has been restricted for many middle-income and upper-income taxpayers, Keogh plans are likely to become more important.

19-7d Individual Retirement Accounts

Unlike a traditional IRA, which defers taxes on the entire account, a Roth IRA allows the earnings to accumulate completely tax-free. All ordinary income and capital gains earned inside a Roth IRA are never taxed (assuming that the five-year holding period provision is satisfied). Thus, a Roth IRA runs contrary to the general principle that it is usually better for a taxpayer to postpone the payment of any tax. In many situations, a retirement plan participant will earn more wealth with a Roth IRA than with a traditional IRA. This potential for tax-free growth is so

advantageous that taxpayers who have substantial traditional IRA balances and are eligible should evaluate converting at least some of their traditional IRA balances into a Roth IRA. A taxpayer does have to be careful because there can be a "big hit" in the year of conversion. Thus, timing is important.

19-7e Comparison of § 401(k) Plan with IRA

Most employees will find a § 401(k) plan more attractive than an IRA. Probably the biggest limitation of an IRA is the $5,500 maximum shelter in 2014 (ignoring the catch-up provision). Under § 401(k), employees are permitted to shelter compensation up to $17,500 (in 2014).[97] The restrictions on deducting contributions to IRAs for many middle-income and upper-income taxpayers may cause many employees to utilize § 401(k) plans more frequently.

Another difference between § 401(k) plans and IRAs is the manner in which the money is treated. Money placed in an IRA may be tax-deductible, whereas dollars placed in a § 401(k) plan are considered to be deferred compensation. Thus, a § 401(k) reduction may reduce profit sharing payments, group life insurance, and Social Security benefits. Finally, many employers "match or partially match" employee elective deferrals with employer money. Concept Summary 19.4 compares a § 401(k) plan with an IRA.

19-7f Nonqualified Deferred Compensation (NQDC) Plans

Nonqualified deferred compensation arrangements, such as restricted property plans, can be useful to attract executive talent or to provide substantial retirement benefits for executives. A restricted property plan may be used to retain a key employee of a closely held company when management continuity problems are anticipated. Without such employees, the untimely death or disability of one of the owners might cause a disruption of the business with an attendant loss in value for his or her heirs. Such plans may discriminate in favor of officers and other highly paid employees. The employer, however, does not receive a tax deduction until the employee is required to include the deferred compensation in income (upon the lapse of the restrictions).

The principal advantage of NQDC plans over current compensation is that the employee can defer the recognition of income to future periods when his or her

---

[97]These amounts are being increased through a phase-in approach. See Footnotes 33 and 48.

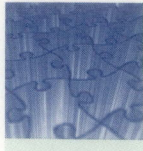

CONCEPT SUMMARY 19.4

Section 401(k) Plan and IRA Compared

	§ 401(k) Plan	IRA
Deduction limitation	Smaller of $17,500 (in 2014) or approximately 100% of total earnings. Limited by antidiscrimination requirements of § 401(k)(3).	$5,500 or 100% of compensation.
Distributions	Early withdrawal possible to take early retirement (55 or over) or to pay medical expenses.	10% penalty for early withdrawals, except for withdrawals to pay for certain medical expenses and health insurance, qualified education expenses, and qualified first-time homebuyer expenses.
Effect on gross earnings	Gross salary reduction, which may reduce profit sharing contributions, Social Security benefits, and group life insurance.	No effect.
Employer involvement	Must keep records; monitor for compliance with antidiscrimination test.	Minimal.
Lump-sum distributions	Favorable 10-year forward averaging under limited circumstances.	Ordinary income.
Timing of contribution	Within 30 days of plan year-end or due date of employer's return.*	Grace period up to due date of tax return (not including extensions).
Loans from plan	Yes.	No.

*Elective contributions must be made to the plan no later than 30 days after the end of the plan year and nonelective contributions no later than the due date of the tax return (including extensions).

© iStockphoto.com/Andrey Prokhorov

income tax bracket may be lower (e.g., during retirement years). The time value benefits from the deferral of income should also be considered. If the current tax rates continue, an executive with a deferred compensation arrangement entered into in a prior year might want to continue to delay the income into future years. However, if future rates are projected to rise, a different decision would be appropriate.

The principal disadvantage of NQDC plans could be the bunching effect that takes place on the expiration of the period of deferral. In some cases, planning can alleviate this result.

Example 52

During 2014, Kelly, an executive, enters into an agreement to postpone a portion of her payment for current services until retirement. The deferred amount is not segregated from the company's general assets and is subject to normal business risk. The entire payment, not the after-tax amount, is invested in securities and variable annuity contracts. Kelly is not taxed on the payment in 2014, and the company receives no deduction in 2014. If Kelly receives the deferred payment in a lump sum when she retires, the tax rates might be higher and more progressive than in 2014. Thus, Kelly may want to arrange for a number of payments to be made to her or a designated beneficiary over a number of years.

19-7g Stock Options

Rather than paying compensation in the form of corporate stock, a corporation may issue options to purchase stock at a specific price to an employee. Stock option plans are used more frequently by publicly traded companies than by closely held companies. This difference is due to the problems of determining the value of the stock of a company that is not publicly held, which is a practical requirement now to avoid negative treatment under § 409A.

Nonqualified stock options (NQSOs) are more flexible and less restrictive than incentive stock options (ISOs). For example, the holding period for an NQSO is not

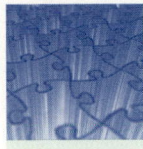

CONCEPT SUMMARY 19.5

Incentive Stock Options and Nonqualified Stock Options Compared

	ISO	NQSO
Granted at any price	No	Yes
May have any duration	No	Yes
Governing Code Section	§ 422	§ 83
Spread subject to alternative minimum tax	Yes	No
Deduction to employer for spread	No	Yes
Type of gain/loss on disposal	Capital	Capital
Statutory amount ($100,000) limitation	Yes	No

as long as that for an ISO. However, the option price of an NQSO cannot be less than the fair market value of the stock at the time the option is granted because of § 409A. An NQSO creates an employer deduction that lowers the cost of the NQSO to the employer. The employer may pass along this tax savings to the employee in the form of a cash payment. Both the employer and the employee may be better off by combining NQSOs with additional cash payments rather than using ISOs. Most stock options are nonqualified stock options. See Concept Summary 19.5.

For tax purposes, most companies are able to deduct the expense of options and thereby reduce their taxes. Generally, options carry an exercise price (strike price) equal to the fair market value on the date the options are approved by the board of directors. The Financial Accounting Standards Board (FASB) now requires stock options to be expensed, which lowers a company's earnings. Companies must measure the economic value of the options on the grant date and then amortize this cost equally over the vesting period of the options. Also, § 409A effectively forces stock options to be granted with an exercise price equal to the stock's fair market value.

Stock options are an effective compensation device as long as share prices are rising. When stock prices fall, the options become unexercisable and possibly worthless. In an upmarket, options are great. But during a downturn in the market, these underwater options can be ugly.

Stock options are likely to be a less dominant form of executive compensation in the future. The backdating scandals and the required expensing of stock options for financial statement purposes are causing businesses to turn to other forms of compensation. Performance-based bonuses and § 401(k) plans probably will become more popular.

19-7h Flexible Benefit Plans

Employees may be permitted to choose from a package of employer-provided fringe benefits.[98] In these so-called **cafeteria benefit plans**, some of the benefits chosen by an employee may be taxable, and some may be statutory nontaxable benefits (e.g., health and accident insurance and group term life insurance).

Under general tax rules, providing a choice to employees would result in all benefits (both taxable and nontaxable) under the cafeteria benefit plan to be taxable. However, if the cafeteria plan rules are met, a special provision applies to prevent this tax result from occurring.

Employer contributions made to a flexible plan are included in an employee's gross income only to the extent the employee actually elects the taxable benefits. Certain nondiscrimination standards with respect to coverage, eligibility for

---

[98]§ 125.

participation, contributions, and benefits must be met. Thus, such a plan must cover a fair cross section of employees. Also, a flexible plan cannot include an election to defer compensation, and a key employee is not exempt from taxation on the taxable benefits made available where more than 25 percent of the statutory nontaxable benefits are provided to key employees.

19-7i Liquidating Retirement Assets

If a person has funds from sources other than retirement assets, which retirement assets should an individual spend first? The most tax-efficient result is to postpone the income tax obligation for as long as possible. Generally, retirement assets should be taken from assets or accounts in the following order so that the tax-deferred growth continues:

1. Taxable accounts.
2. Section 457 accounts of government employees because no penalties apply once the employee is separated from employment.
3. Section 401(k) and nonprofit § 403(b) plans because the age 55 separation rule may apply.
4. Traditional IRAs because a taxpayer must be at least age 59½ to obtain penalty-free withdrawals.
5. Roth IRAs because no required minimum distribution rules apply.[99]

REFOCUS ON THE BIG PICTURE

A TAXPAYER WHO SAVES

From her discussion with Dr. Sanchez, Joyce learns that her professor has the following retirement plans:

- *Defined contribution plan.* The university offered its faculty members a choice between a defined benefit pension plan and a defined contribution plan. Dr. Sanchez expects to work at a number of universities during her career, so she chose the defined contribution plan because of its mobility (i.e., she can take the plan with her). The maximum annual contribution the university could make to the plan is $52,000 for 2014. Because the university contribution rate is 15 percent, the actual contribution is $22,500 ($150,000 × 15%).
- *§ 403 (b) annuity.* Dr. Sanchez makes contributions to a § 403(b) annuity [i.e., the equivalent of a § 401(k) plan, but available to educators]. The maximum annual contribution she can make in 2014 is $17,500, and Dr. Sanchez has the university deduct this total amount from her salary paychecks. In addition, because she is at least age 50 (i.e., she is age 51), she has the university deduct an additional $5,500 as a catch-up contribution.
- *Keogh (H.R. 10) plan.* In addition to her position at the university, Dr. Sanchez has a forensic consulting practice. Because she is self-employed, she is able to establish a Keogh defined contribution plan. She contributes 20 percent of her net earnings from the consulting practice, about $8,000 per year ($ 40,000 × 20%), to the plan.
- *IRA.* Dr. Sanchez also contributes annually to a traditional IRA. She would prefer a Roth IRA, but her AGI exceeds the $129,000 phaseout limit. Likewise, she cannot deduct her contribution of $5,500 (the maximum) because of the amount of her AGI. Because she cannot deduct her contributions, her basis in the IRA is the summation of her contributions. The $15,000 that Dr. Sanchez withdrew

---

[99]David M. Maloney and James E. Smith, "Distribution Options for Defined Contribution Plans, Part II," *The Tax Adviser,* June 2007, pp. 340 and 341.

from her traditional IRA is not subject to current taxation and does not reduce her basis for the IRA. This result occurs because Dr. Sanchez successfully completed a tax-free rollover (i.e., recontributed the $15,000 to her IRA within 60 days).

Dr. Sanchez explains that she wants to travel after retirement, so her goal is to retire by age 62 while she is still in good health. She anticipates that these plans will enable her to do so.

Key Terms

Cafeteria benefit plans, 19-43

Cash balance plan, 19-6

Coverdell Education Savings Account (CESA), 19-23

Deferred compensation, 19-2

Defined benefit plan, 19-4

Defined contribution pension plan, 19-4

Golden parachute payments, 19-31

H.R. 10 (Keogh) plans, 19-18

Highly compensated employee, 19-8

Incentive stock option (ISO), 19-36

Individual Retirement Account (IRA), 19-20

Lump-sum distribution, 19-12

Nonqualified deferred compensation (NQDC), 19-29

Nonqualified stock option (NQSO), 19-38

Pension plan, 19-4

Profit sharing plan, 19-5

Restricted property plan, 19-33

Roth IRA, 19-22

Section 401(k) plan, 19-15

Simplified employee pension (SEP) plans, 19-24

Stock bonus plan, 19-6

Stock option, 19-36

Substantial risk of forfeiture (SRF), 19-34

Vesting requirements, 19-8

Discussion Questions

1. **LO.1** What are the policy reasons for the advantages of qualified retirement plans?

2. **LO.1** List some disadvantages of qualified pension plans.

3. **LO.1** What are the two major types of qualified pension plans?

4. **LO.1** Determine whether each of the following independent statements best applies to a defined contribution plan *(DCP)*, a defined benefit plan *(DBP)*, both *(B)*, or neither *(N)*:
   a. The amount to be received at retirement depends on actuarial calculations.
   b. Forfeitures can be allocated to the remaining participants' accounts.
   c. Requires greater reporting requirements and more actuarial and administrative costs.
   d. Forfeitures can revert to the employer.
   e. More favorable to employees who are older at the time the plan is adopted.
   f. Employee forfeitures can be used to reduce future contributions by the employer.
   g. May exclude employees who begin employment within five years of normal retirement age.
   h. Annual addition to each employee's account may not exceed the smaller of $52,000 or 100% of the employee's salary.
   i. The final benefit to a participant depends upon investment performance.
   j. To avoid penalties, the amount of annual contributions must meet minimum funding requirements.

5. **LO.1** Indicate whether the following statements apply to a pension plan *(P)*, a profit sharing plan *(PS)*, both *(B)*, or neither *(N)*:
   a. Forfeited amounts can be used to reduce future contributions by the employer.
   b. Allocation of forfeitures may discriminate in favor of the prohibited group (highly compensated employees).
   c. Forfeitures can revert to the employer.
   d. Forfeitures can be allocated to participants and increase plan benefits.
   e. An annual benefit of $60,000 could be payable on behalf of a participant.
   f. More favorable to employees who are older at the time the qualified plan is adopted.

6. **LO.1** What is the maximum annual contribution that can be made to a defined contribution plan?

7. **LO.1** Who bears the investment risk and reward in a defined benefit plan? In a defined contribution plan?

8. **LO.1** What is a cash balance plan?

9. **LO.1, 4** What is the maximum annual benefit payable under a defined benefit plan?

10. **LO.2** A qualified retirement plan must meet what requirements?

Issue ID   11. **LO.2, 3, 6** Penny plans to retire in 2014 at age 70. Identify any issues that Penny faces with respect to distributions from her qualified retirement plan.

Issue ID   12. **LO.3, 6** Harvey Pehrson, who is age 71, is going to receive a lump-sum distribution from a qualified plan in 2014. He has asked you to provide him with a description of the alternatives available to him for taxing the lump-sum distribution. Draft a letter to Harvey in which you respond. He resides at 3000 East Glenn, Tulsa, OK 74104.

Communications

13. **LO.3** Which of the following would be considered a tax benefit or advantage of a qualified retirement plan?
    a. Certain lump-sum distributions may be subject to capital gain treatment.
    b. Employer contributions are deductible by the employer in the year of contribution.
    c. Employee contributions are deductible by the employee in the year of contribution.
    d. The qualified trust is tax deferred as to all income (other than unrelated business income).

Decision Making   14. **LO.3, 6** Donna is retiring and wants you to explain her alternatives for receiving payments from her qualified retirement plan.

15. **LO.5** Explain the contribution limitations for a defined contribution Keogh plan and for a defined benefit Keogh plan.

Decision Making   16. **LO.6, 10** Should a 31-year-old self-employed single woman establish a traditional deductible IRA, a traditional nondeductible IRA, or a Roth IRA? She has two children, ages 10 and 8.

17. **LO.6** Joey, who is single, is not covered by another qualified plan and earns $116,000 at his job in 2014. How much can he contribute to a traditional IRA or to a Roth IRA in 2014?

Communications   18. **LO.4** Scott Henry calls you and asks about a savings incentive match plan for employees (SIMPLE). Prepare a memo for the tax files about your response.

19. **LO.5** What funding vehicles are available for a Keogh plan?

20. **LO.6** Suppose an individual is 55 years old. How much of an additional catch-up IRA contribution can the person make?

Issue ID   21. **LO.7, 10** During his senior year in college, Sandy is drafted by the Los Angeles Dodgers. When he graduates, he expects to sign a five-year contract in the range of $1.7 million per year. Sandy plans to marry his girlfriend before he reports to the Dodger farm team in California. Identify the relevant tax issues facing this left-handed pitcher.

22. **LO.7** What conditions cause the golden parachute arrangement to be penalized?

23. **LO.8** What is the spread with respect to an incentive stock option? How is it treated under the tax law?

24. **LO.9** What are the major advantages of nonqualified stock options?

Problems

25. **LO.2** Blonde Corporation has a calendar year retirement plan covering its participants. William, age 21, is hired on January 31, 2013, and he meets the service requirement over the next 12 months (completes at least 1,000 hours by January 31, 2014).
    a. If the company adopts the most restrictive eligibility rules, William must be included in the plan by no later than what date?
    b. If the company adopts the two-year participation rule, William must be included in the plan by no later than what date?

26. **LO.2** Ben is a 4% owner of a title company. In the following situations, is he a highly compensated employee? Why or why not?
    a. Ben receives a total salary of $110,000 and is a member of the top-paid group in the company.
    b. Ben receives a total salary of $192,000, and his salary is in the top 30% of the employees.
    c. Ben receives a total salary of $113,500, which puts him in the top 15% of the employees.
    d. Ben receives a salary of $153,000, which puts him in the 25%–30% range of employees.

27. **LO.2** Sparrow, Inc., uses a three- to seven-year graded vesting approach in its retirement plan. Calculate the nonforfeitable percentage for each of the following participants based upon the years of service completed:

Participant	Years of Service
Mary	2
Sam	4
Peter	6
Heather	7

28. **LO.2** Mauve, Inc., uses a two- to six-year graded vesting approach in its retirement plan. Calculate the nonforfeitable percentage for each of the following participants based upon the years of service completed:

Participant	Years of Service
Caleb	3
Daniel	4
Sloane	5
Ryan	7

29. **LO.1, 4** Concept, Inc., has a profit sharing plan with some participants earning $260,000 or more. The company can maximize its participants' annual additions by using what percentage profit sharing contribution?

30. **LO.2** Sue has worked for Yellow Corporation for four and one-half years, but she has an offer to move to Red Corporation for a moderate increase in salary. Her average salary for Yellow has been $210,000, and she receives a 2% benefit for each year of service in her retirement plan. The company uses a five-year vesting schedule. Advise Sue as to this possible switch in jobs.

Decision Making

31. **LO.4** Heather has been an active participant in a defined benefit plan for 19 years. During her last 6 years of employment, Heather earned $42,000, $48,000, $56,000, $80,000, $89,000, and $108,000, respectively (representing her highest-income years).
    a. Calculate Heather's maximum allowable benefits from her qualified plan (assume that there are fewer than 100 participants).
    b. Assume that Heather's average compensation for her three highest years is $199,700. Calculate her maximum allowable benefits.

32. **LO.4** Determine the maximum annual benefits payable to a participant from a defined benefit plan in the following independent situations:
    a. Frank, age 66, has been a participant for 17 years, and his highest average compensation for 3 years is $127,300.
    b. Ellen, age 65, has been a participant for 9 years (11 years of service), and her highest average compensation for 3 years is $102,600.

33. **LO.4** In 2014, Magenta Corporation paid compensation of $45,300 to the participants in a profit sharing plan. During 2014, Magenta Corporation contributed $13,200 to the plan.
    a. Calculate Magenta's deductible amount for 2014.
    b. Calculate the amount of any contribution carryover from 2014.

Decision Making

34. **LO.4, 10** Amber's employer, Lavender, Inc., has a § 401(k) plan that permits salary deferral elections by its employees. Amber's salary is $99,000, and her marginal tax rate is 33%.
    a. What is the maximum amount Amber can elect for salary deferral treatment for 2014?
    b. If Amber elects salary deferral treatment for the amount in (a), how much can she save in taxes?
    c. What amount would you recommend that Amber elect for salary deferral treatment for 2014?

35. **LO.4** Shyam is a participant in a SIMPLE § 401(k) plan. He elects to contribute 4% of his $40,000 compensation to the account, while his employer contributes 3%. What amount will not vest immediately, if any?

36. **LO.2, 4, 5, 6** In 2014, Susan's sole proprietorship earns $300,000 of self-employment net income (after the deduction for one-half of self-employment tax).
    a. Calculate the maximum amount that Susan can deduct for contributions to a defined contribution Keogh plan.
    b. Suppose Susan contributes more than the allowable amount to the Keogh plan. What are the consequences to her?
    c. Can Susan retire and begin receiving Keogh payments at age 58 without incurring a penalty? Explain.

37. **LO.4, 5** Harvey is a self-employed accountant with earned income from the business of $120,000 (after the deduction for one-half of his self-employment tax). He has a profit sharing plan (e.g., defined contribution Keogh plan). What is the maximum amount Harvey can contribute to his retirement plan in 2014?

38. **LO.4, 6** Janet, age 29, is unmarried and is an active participant in a qualified retirement plan. Her modified AGI is $62,000 in 2014.
    a. Calculate the amount that Janet can contribute to a traditional IRA and the amount she can deduct.
    b. Assume instead that Janet is a participant in a SIMPLE IRA and that she elects to contribute 4% of her compensation to the account, while her employer contributes 3%. What amount will be contributed for 2014? What amount will be vested?

39. **LO.4, 6** Answer the following independent questions with respect to a deductible IRA and § 401(k) contributions for 2014:
    a. Govind, age 31, earns a salary of $26,000 and is not an active participant in any other qualified plan. His wife has $600 of compensation income. What is the maximum total deductible contribution to their IRAs?
    b. Danos is a participant in a SIMPLE § 401(k) plan. He contributes 6% of his salary of $42,000, and his employer contributes 3%. What amount will be contributed for the year? What amount will be vested?

40. **LO.6** Answer the following independent questions with respect to traditional IRA contributions for 2014:
    a. Juan, age 41, earns a salary of $28,000 and is not an active participant in any other qualified plan. His wife, Agnes, has no earned income. What is the maximum total deductible contribution to their IRAs? Juan wants to contribute as much as possible to his own IRA.
    b. Abby, age 29, has earned income of $25,000, and her husband, Sam, has earned income of $2,600. They are not active participants in any other qualified plan. What is the maximum contribution to their IRAs?
    c. Leo's employer makes a contribution of $3,500 to Leo's simplified employee pension plan. If Leo is single, has earned income of $32,000, and has AGI of $29,000, what amount, if any, can he contribute to an IRA?

41. **LO.6** Jimmy establishes a Roth IRA at age 47 and contributes a total of $89,600 over 18 years. The account is now worth $112,000. How much of these funds may Jimmy withdraw tax-free?

42. **LO.6** Dana, age 54, has a traditional deductible IRA with an account balance of $107,600, of which $77,300 represents contributions and $30,300 represents earnings. In 2014, she converts her traditional IRA into a Roth IRA. What amount must Dana include in her gross income for 2014?

43. **LO.6** Carri and Dane, ages 34 and 32, respectively, have been married for 11 years, and both are active participants in employer qualified retirement plans. Their total AGI in 2014 is $184,000, and they earn salaries of $87,000 and $95,000, respectively. What amount may Carri and Dane:
    a. Contribute to regular IRAs?
    b. Deduct for their contributions in (a)?
    c. Contribute to Roth IRAs?
    d. Deduct for their contributions in (c)?
    e. Contribute to Coverdell Education Savings Accounts for their three children?

44. **LO.4, 6** Louis is a participant in a SIMPLE IRA of his employer Brown, Inc. During 2014, he contributes 8% of his salary of $63,000, and his employer contributes 3%. What is the total amount that will be vested in his account at the end of 2014?

45. **LO.6** In 2015, Joyce receives a $4,000 distribution from her Coverdell Education Savings Account, which has a fair market value of $10,000. Total contributions to her CESA have been $7,000. Joyce's AGI is $25,000.
    a. Joyce uses the entire $4,000 to pay for qualified education expenses. What amount should she include in her gross income?
    b. Assume instead that Joyce uses only $2,500 of the $4,000 distribution for qualified education expenses. What amount should she include in her gross income?

46. **LO.6** Gene, age 34, and Beth, age 32, have been married for nine years. Gene, who is a college student, works part-time and earns $1,500. Beth is a high school teacher and earns a salary of $34,000. Their AGI is $37,000.
    a. What is the maximum amount Gene can contribute to an IRA in 2014?
    b. What is the maximum amount Beth can contribute to an IRA in 2014?

47. **LO.6** Samuel, age 32, loses his job in a corporate downsizing. As a result of his termination, he receives a distribution of the balance in his § 401(k) account of $20,000 ($25,000 − $5,000 withholding) on May 1, 2014. Samuel's marginal tax rate is 28%. *Decision Making*
    a. What effect will the distribution have on Samuel's gross income and tax liability if he invests the $20,000 received in a mutual fund?
    b. Same as (a) except that Samuel invests the $20,000 received in a traditional IRA within 60 days of the distribution.
    c. Same as (a) except that Samuel invests the $20,000 received in a Roth IRA within 60 days of the distribution.
    d. How could Samuel have received better tax consequences in (b)?

48. **LO.7** Dan, a professional basketball player, is to receive a bonus of $2 million for signing an employment contract. An NQDC plan is established to postpone the income beyond Dan's peak income years. In 2014, his employer transfers the bonus to an escrow agent, who then invests the funds in mutual funds. The funds are subject to the claims of the employer's creditors. The bonus is deferred for 10 years and becomes payable gradually in years 11 through 15. When is the bonus taxable to Dan and deductible by the employer?

49. **LO.7** Grace is an officer of a local bank that merges with a national bank, resulting in a change of ownership. She loses her job as a result of the merger, but she receives a cash settlement of $590,000 from her employer under her golden parachute. Her average annual compensation for the past five tax years was $200,000.
    a. What are the tax consequences to Grace and the bank of the $590,000 payment?
    b. Assume instead that Grace's five-year average annual compensation was $110,000 and that she receives $390,000 in the settlement. What are the tax consequences to Grace and the bank?

50. **LO.8** On February 20, 2009, Tom (an executive of Hawk Corporation) purchased 100 shares of Hawk stock (selling at $20 a share) for $10. A condition of the transaction was that Tom must resell the stock to Hawk at cost if he voluntarily leaves the company within five years of receiving the stock (assume that this represents a substantial risk of forfeiture). *Decision Making*
    a. Assuming that no special election is made under § 83(b), what amount, if any, is taxable to Tom in 2009?
    b. Five years later when the stock is selling for $40 a share, Tom is still employed by Hawk. What amount of ordinary income, if any, is taxable to Tom?

    c. Five years later, what amount, if any, is deductible by Hawk as compensation expense?

    d. Should Tom make the § 83(b) special election in 2009? Why or why not? What amount would be taxable in 2009 if he makes the special election?

    e. In (d), what amount would be deductible by Hawk five years later?

    f. Under (d), assume that Tom sold all of the stock six years later for $65 per share. How much capital gain is included in his gross income?

    g. In (d), what loss is available to Tom if he voluntarily resigns in 2013 before the five-year period and does not sell the stock back to the corporation?

    h. In (g), in the year Tom resigns, what amount, if any, would be taxable to Hawk Corporation?

51. **LO.8** On July 2, 2011, Black Corporation sold 1,000 of its common shares (worth $14 per share) to Earl, an employee, for $5 per share. The sale was subject to Earl's agreement to resell the shares to the corporation for $5 per share if his employment is terminated within the following four years. The shares had a value of $24 per share on July 2, 2015. Earl sells the shares for $31 per share on September 16, 2015. No special election under § 83(b) is made.

    a. What amount, if any, is taxed to Earl on July 2, 2011?

    b. On July 2, 2015?

    c. On September 16, 2015?

    d. What deduction, if any, will Black Corporation obtain? When?

    e. Assume the same facts, except that Earl makes an election under § 83(b). What amount, if any, will be taxed to Earl on July 2, 2011, July 2, 2015, and September 16, 2015?

    f. Will the assumption made in (e) have any effect on any deduction Black Corporation receives? Explain.

52. **LO.9** Rosa exercises ISOs for 100 shares of Copper Corporation common stock at the option price of $100 per share on May 21, 2014, when the fair market value is $120 per share. She sells the 100 shares of common stock three and one-half years later for $140.

    a. Calculate the long-term capital gain and the ordinary income on the sale.

    b. Assume that Rosa holds the stock only seven months and sells the shares for $140 per share. Calculate the capital gain and ordinary income on the sale.

    c. In (b), what amount can Copper Corporation deduct? When?

    d. Assume instead that Rosa holds the stock for two years and sells the shares for $115 per share. Calculate any capital gain and ordinary income on this transaction.

    e. In (a), assume that the options are nonqualified stock options with a nonascertainable fair market value on the date of the grant. Calculate the long-term capital gain and ordinary income on the date of the sale.

    f. In (e), assume that each option has an ascertainable fair market value of $10 on the date of the grant and that no substantial risk of forfeiture exists. Calculate the long-term capital gain and the ordinary income on the date of the sale.

53. **LO.9** On November 19, 2012, Rex is granted a nonqualified stock option to purchase 100 shares of Tan Company. On that date, the stock is selling for $8 per share, and the option price is $9 per share. Rex exercises the option on August 21, 2013, when the stock is selling for $10 per share. Five months later, Rex sells the shares for $11.50 per share.

    a. What amount is taxable to Rex in 2012?

    b. What amount is taxable to Rex in 2013?

    c. What amount and type of gain are taxable to Rex in 2014?

    d. What amount, if any, is deductible by Tan Company in 2013?

    e. What amount, if any, is recognized in 2013 if the stock is sold for $9.50 per share?

Decision Making

Communications

54. **LO.4, 5, 6, 10** Sara Reid, age 35, is the owner of a small business. She is trying to decide whether to go with a § 401(k) plan or a simplified employee pension plan. She is not interested in a SIMPLE § 401(k) plan. Her salary will be approximately $45,000, and she will have no employees. She asks you to provide her with information on the advantages and disadvantages of both types of plans and to give your recommendation. Draft a letter to Sara that contains your response. Her address is 1414 Canal Street, New Orleans, LA 70148.

55. **LO.10** Lou's employer provides a qualified cafeteria plan under which he can choose cash of $9,000 or health and accident insurance premiums worth approximately $7,000. Assuming that Lou is in the 35% tax bracket, advise him of his tax alternatives.

Decision Making

56. **LO.10** Zariat has the retirement assets listed below. She plans to retire and start withdrawing amounts on which to live. Rank the accounts in the order from which she should make withdrawals so that tax deferral is maximized.

Roth IRA	$923,408
Traditional IRA	118,120
§ 401(k) plan	837,010
§ 457 account	334,090

Research Problems

THOMSON REUTERS
CHECKPOINT®

Note: Solutions to Research Problems can be prepared by using the **Checkpoint®** **Student Edition** online research product, which is available to accompany this text. It is also possible to prepare solutions to the Research Problems by using tax research materials found in a standard tax library.

Research Problem 1. Your client, Casey Farber, is the CEO of a publicly traded corporation. This year, her compensation consisted of $600,000 in cash and $600,000 of stock. The stock received was part of a restricted stock grant. Casey was granted the restricted stock in 2010, when the stock's fair market value was $300,000. Casey did not make a Section 83(b) election. The restrictions on the stock lifted in the current year. The $600,000 was the stock's fair market value on the date the restrictions lifted, and Casey still owns the stock.

With respect to the compensation received by Casey this year, what will be the corporation's compensation expense deduction?

Partial list of research aids:
Regulation § 1.162–27.
Rev.Rul. 2012–19, 2012–28 I.R.B. 16.

Research Problem 2. John Curran and his wife own a construction company, and they want to set up two new corporations that will be owned by their Roth IRAs. The two Roth-owned corporations will then enter into contracts to provide services to their construction company. They believe that the Roth-owned businesses can benefit from the payments and then pay out dividends to each Roth up to $50,000 per year. The couple will continue to do all of the work for the construction company. Advise Mr. and Mrs. Curran about this strategy.

Research Problem 3. Frequently, a football or basketball coach moves to another university and incurs an obligation to make a payment to the former university under a buyout provision in his or her contract. In 2008, football coach Richard Rodriguez was required to pay $4 million to West Virginia when he moved from West Virginia University to the University of Michigan. Coach Rodriguez paid $1.5 million, and the University of Michigan paid $2.5 million (plus legal fees incurred). What were the tax consequences of these payments to Coach Rodriguez?

Research Problem 4. Jim Raby transfers one-half of his compensatory stock options (ISOs and nonqualified stock options) to his ex-wife as part of a divorce settlement. Discuss the tax aspects of this transfer.

Partial list of research aids:
FSA 200005006.
§§ 424(c)(4)(A) and (B).

Research Problem 5. Before Lemon Corporation was taken private in a transaction engineered by its largest stockholder, some of Lemon's employees had unexercised options to purchase stock of Lemon. Under an employee agreement, Lemon canceled the unexercised stock options by paying the employees the difference between the option price and the current fair market value of Lemon's stock. These employees reported this as ordinary income. Can Lemon Corporation deduct these payments to the employees, or are these termination payments treated as capital expenditures?

Internet Activity

Use the tax resources of the Internet to address the following questions. Do not restrict your search to the Web, but include a review of newsgroups and general reference materials, practitioner sites and resources, primary sources of the tax law, chat rooms and discussion groups, and other opportunities.

Research Problem 6. Some corporations offer their employees restricted stock whereas other corporations offer restricted stock units. Search the Internet to see if you can find the differences between these two types of restricted stock offerings.

Research Problem 7. Search the Internet for a U.S. 801(k) plan. Explain what it is.

Research Problem 8. Using newspapers, magazine articles, and other resources, prepare a report on stock appreciation rights to present to your class.

part 7

CORPORATIONS AND PARTNERSHIPS

CHAPTER **20**   **Corporations and Partnerships**

The primary orientation of this text is toward basic tax concepts and the individual taxpayer. Although many of these tax concepts also apply to corporations and partnerships, numerous tax concepts apply specifically to corporations or partnerships. An overview of these provisions is presented in Part 7. Comprehensive coverage of these topics appears in *South-Western Federal Taxation: Corporations, Partnerships, Estates & Trusts*.

LEARNING OBJECTIVES: *After completing Chapter 20, you should be able to:*

LO.1 Identify those entities that are treated as corporations for Federal income tax purposes.

LO.2 Contrast the income tax treatment of individuals with that applicable to corporations.

LO.3 Recognize and calculate the tax deductions available only to corporations.

LO.4 Calculate the corporate tax liability and comply with various procedural and reporting requirements.

LO.5 Describe the tax rules governing the formation of corporations.

LO.6 Explain the tax rules governing the operation of corporations.

LO.7 Assess the utility and effect of the Subchapter S election.

LO.8 Review the tax consequences of forming and operating a partnership.

LO.9 Identify the advantages and disadvantages of the various forms for conducting a business.

THE BIG PICTURE   Tax Solutions for the Real World

CHOICE OF BUSINESS ENTITY

The Todd sisters have decided to begin a catering business to handle private parties, weddings, anniversaries, and other large social events. As their parents previously owned several restaurants, the sisters are familiar with food service operations. All sisters will participate in the operation of the business and will provide the funds for capital acquisitions (e.g., delivery trucks, kitchen equipment, and food preparation facilities) and working capital needs. Due to the cost of the premiums, the sisters plan on minimal liability insurance coverage.

In the first few years of operation, the sisters anticipate losses. When and if the business becomes profitable, however, they would consider expansion. Any such expansion would require obtaining additional capital from outside sources.

In what type of entity should the Todd sisters conduct the business?

Read the chapter and formulate your response.

Until now, this text has concentrated on the Federal income taxation of individual taxpayers. In terms of conducting a business, an individual will often operate as a sole proprietorship. Although simple and straightforward—a mere Schedule C is involved—this may not be the best choice. Other forms of business organization are available and should be considered. Besides the sole proprietorship, the choices are:

- C corporation.
- S corporation.
- Limited liability company.
- Partnership.

To make an informed choice on what type of entity to select, familiarity with operational rules and the tax consequences of each is necessary. Starting with the corporate form, this chapter provides an overview of these rules and tax consequences. Limited liability companies are not discussed in depth because they are usually subject to sole proprietorship or partnership treatment, depending on the number of owners. The decision as to what type of entity to use for a business is referred to as a "choice of entity" question. This question arises when a business is first formed. In addition, it can arise again as a business grows or ownership changes. For example, an individual may start a business as a sole proprietorship and then convert it to a corporation if it grows and the owner seeks additional capital.

20-1 WHAT IS A CORPORATION?

LO.1

Identify those entities that are treated as corporations for Federal income tax purposes.

The classification of an entity as a corporation for Federal income tax purposes is controlled largely by state law and guidelines issued by the IRS. In this regard, criteria set forth by the courts have had a major impact.

20-1a Compliance with State Law

A company must comply with the specific requirements for corporate status under state law. For example, it is necessary to draft articles of incorporation and file them with the state regulatory agency, be granted a charter, and issue stock to shareholders.

Compliance with state law, although important, is not the only requirement that must be met to qualify for corporate *tax* status. For example, a corporation qualifying under state law may be disregarded as a taxable entity if it is a mere sham lacking in economic substance. The key consideration is the degree of business activity conducted at the corporate level.

| **Example 1** | Gene and Mike are joint owners of a tract of unimproved real estate that they want to protect from future creditors. Gene and Mike form Falcon Corporation and transfer the land to it in return for all of the corporation's stock. The corporation merely holds title to the land and conducts no other activities. In all respects, Falcon Corporation meets the legal requirements of a corporation under applicable state law. Nevertheless, Falcon might not be recognized as a separate entity for corporate tax purposes under these facts.[1] |

| **Example 2** | Assume the same facts as in Example 1. In addition to holding title to the land, Falcon Corporation leases the property, collects rents, and pays the property taxes. Falcon probably would be treated as a corporation for Federal income tax purposes because of the scope of its activities. |

---

[1]See *Paymer v. Comm.*, 45–2 USTC ¶9353, 33 AFTR 1536, 150 F.2d 334 (CA–2, 1945).

In some instances, the IRS has attempted to disregard (or collapse) a corporation to make the income taxable directly to the shareholders.[2] In other cases, the IRS has asserted that the corporation is a separate taxable entity so as to assess tax at the corporate level and to tax corporate distributions to shareholders as dividend income (double taxation).[3]

20-1b Entity Classification prior to 1997

Can an organization not qualifying as a corporation under state law still be treated as such for Federal income tax purposes? Yes. The tax law defines a corporation as including "associations, joint stock companies, and insurance companies."[4] As the Code contains no definition of an "association," the issue became the subject of frequent litigation.[5]

It was finally determined that an entity would be treated as a corporation if it had a majority of the characteristics common to corporations.[6] For this purpose, the relevant characteristics are:

- Continuity of life.
- Centralized management.
- Limited liability.
- Free transferability of interests.

These criteria did not resolve all of the problems that continued to arise over corporate classification. When a new type of business entity, the **limited liability company (LLC)**, was created by states, the IRS was deluged with inquiries about its tax status. As the LLC became increasingly popular with professional groups, all states enacted statutes allowing some form of this entity. The statutes invariably permitted the corporate characteristic of limited liability and often that of centralized management. Because continuity of life and free transferability of interests were absent, the hope was that the entity would be classified as a partnership. This treatment would avoid the double taxation result inherent in the corporate form.

20-1c Entity Classification after 1996

In late 1996, the IRS issued its so-called **check-the-box Regulations**.[7] Effective beginning in 1997, these Regulations enable taxpayers to classify a business entity for tax purposes without regard to its corporate (or noncorporate) characteristics. These rules have simplified tax administration considerably and eliminated the litigation that arose with regard to association (corporation) status.

Under the rules, an entity with more than one owner can elect to be classified as either a partnership or a corporation. An entity with only one owner can elect to be classified as a corporation or a sole proprietorship. In the event of default (no election is made), entities with multiple owners will be classified as partnerships and single-person businesses as sole proprietorships.

The election is not available to entities that are actually incorporated under state law or to entities that are required to be corporations under Federal law (e.g., certain publicly traded partnerships). LLCs not incorporated under state law can elect either corporation or partnership status for Federal tax purposes.

Eligible entities make the election as to tax status by filing Form 8832 (Entity Classification Election).[8] New elections are permitted, but only after a 60-month waiting period.

---

[2]*Floyd Patterson*, 25 TCM 1230, T.C.Memo. 1966–239, *aff'd* in 68–2 USTC ¶9471, 22 AFTR 2d 5810 (CA–2, 1968).

[3]*Raffety Farms Inc. v. U.S.*, 75–1 USTC ¶9271, 35 AFTR 2d 75–811, 511 F.2d 1234 (CA–8, 1975).

[4]§ 7701(a)(3).

[5]See, for example, *U.S. v. Kintner*, 54–2 USTC ¶9626, 46 AFTR 995, 216 F.2d 418 (CA–5, 1954).

[6]See Reg. § 301.7701–2(a) prior to repeal.

[7]Reg. §§ 301.7701–1 through –4 and –7.

[8]Reg. § 301.7701–3(c).

20-2 INCOME TAX CONSIDERATIONS

Some income tax rules apply differently for corporations versus other forms of business. This section provides some examples of both similarities and differences.

20-2a General Tax Consequences of Different Forms of Business Entities

A business operation may be conducted as a sole proprietorship, a partnership, an LLC, or a corporation.

- Sole proprietorships are not separate taxable entities. The owner of the business reports all business transactions on his or her individual income tax return.
- Partnerships are not subject to the income tax. Under the *conduit* concept, the various tax attributes of the partnership's operations flow through to the individual partners to be reported on their personal income tax returns. The tax treatment of limited liability companies (LLCs) usually follows that applicable to partnerships.
- The regular corporate form (known as a **C corporation**) of doing business carries with it the imposition of the corporate income tax. The corporation is recognized as a separate taxpaying entity. Income is taxed to the corporation as earned and taxed again to the shareholders as dividends when distributed.
- A regular corporation (C corporation) may elect to be taxed as an S corporation. This special treatment follows the conduit concept and is similar (although not identical) to the partnership rules. Income tax is generally avoided at the corporate level, and shareholders are taxed currently on the earnings of the S corporation.

Because they follow the conduit concept as to the treatment of their tax attributes, partnerships, LLCs, and S corporations are often referred to as pass-through entities.

A desirable characteristic of a business entity is that of limited liability. This means that the owners of the entity are not personally liable for its debts and obligations. Also beneficial is the existence of the conduit concept, which allows the entity to pass through to the owners certain favorable tax attributes (e.g., operating losses).

THE BIG PICTURE

Example 3

Return to the facts of *The Big Picture* on p. 20-1. It appears that the Todd sisters should consider a C or S corporation to obtain limited liability for their catering business. (An LLC also will provide this result.) On the other hand, the conduit effect of an S corporation or a partnership is needed to enable the sisters to take advantage of the initial losses anticipated for the business. Under the conduit concept, such losses could be deducted on their individual income tax returns.

20-2b Individuals and Corporations Compared—An Overview

LO.2

Contrast the income tax treatment of individuals with that applicable to corporations.

Similarities between Corporate and Individual Tax Rules

The gross income of a corporation is determined in much the same manner as for individuals. Both individuals and corporations are entitled to exclusions from gross income, such as interest on municipal bonds. Gains and losses from property transactions are also treated similarly. For example, whether a gain or loss is capital or ordinary depends on the nature and use of the asset rather than the type of tax-payer. Upon the sale or other taxable disposition of depreciable personalty, the recapture rules of § 1245 make no distinction between corporate and noncorporate taxpayers. In the case of the recapture of depreciation on real property (§ 1250), however, corporate taxpayers experience more severe tax consequences. As illustrated later, corporations must recognize as additional ordinary income 20 percent of the excess of the amount that would be recaptured under § 1245 over the amount recaptured under § 1250.

In cases involving nontaxable exchanges and certain transactions allowing the deferral of gain recognition, many of the rules are the same. Thus, both individuals and corporations can utilize the like-kind exchange provisions of § 1031 and the deferral allowed by § 1033 for involuntary conversions. In contrast, the § 121 exclusion for gain from the sale of a principal residence is a relief measure available only to individual taxpayers.

The business deductions of corporations parallel those available to individuals. Corporate deductions are allowed for all ordinary and necessary expenses paid or incurred in carrying on a trade or business. Corporations may also deduct interest, certain taxes, losses, bad debts, depreciation, cost recovery, charitable contributions subject to corporate limitation rules, net operating losses, research and experimental expenditures, and other less common deductions.

Many of the tax credits available to individuals, such as the foreign tax credit, can be claimed by corporations. Not available to corporations are certain credits that are personal in nature. Examples of credits not available to corporations include the credit for child and dependent care expenses, the credit for the elderly or disabled, and the earned income credit.

Corporations usually have the same choices of accounting periods as do individuals. Like an individual, a corporation may choose a calendar year or a fiscal year for reporting purposes. Corporations do enjoy greater flexibility in the election of a tax year. For example, corporations usually can have different tax years from those of their shareholders. Also, a newly formed corporation generally has a free choice of any approved accounting period without having to obtain the consent of the IRS. As noted in Chapter 18, however, personal service corporations are subject to severe restrictions on the use of a fiscal year.

In terms of methods of accounting, both individuals and corporations must use the *accrual* method in determining cost of goods sold if they maintain inventory for sale to customers. The *accrual* method must also be used by *large* corporations (annual gross receipts in excess of $5 million). The *cash method* of accounting, however, is available to *small* corporations and in the following additional situations:

- An S election is in effect.
- The trade or business is farming or timber.
- A qualified personal service corporation is involved.
- A qualified service provider (e.g., plumbing business) is involved, and annual gross receipts (for the past three years) do not exceed $10 million. This exception applies even if the service provider is buying and selling inventory.

Dissimilarities

Both noncorporate and corporate taxpayers are subject to progressive income tax rates. For individuals, the rates for 2014 are 10, 15, 25, 28, 33, 35, and 39.6 percent. For corporations, the rates are 15, 25, 34, and 35 percent. Corporate taxpayers lose the benefits of the lower brackets (using a phaseout approach) once taxable income reaches a certain level. Noncorporate taxpayers, however, continue to enjoy the benefits of the lower brackets even though they have reached the higher taxable income levels.

Starting in 2003, qualified dividends received by individual shareholders have been subject to preferential tax rates. For those shareholders in the top tax bracket (39.6 percent), the maximum rate of 20 percent applies; for the next four tax

Global Tax Issues

Are Corporate Taxes Too High?

A recent Treasury report shows that the average statutory corporate tax rate in the United States is 39 percent when both Federal and state income taxes are considered. In contrast, global average rates are 25 percent to 30 percent. The recent downward trend in corporate income tax rates has been particularly prevalent in European countries (e.g., from 34 to 33.33 percent in France, from 35 to 30 percent in Spain, and from 39 to 33.33 percent in Germany). Meanwhile, in the United States, the Federal tax rates on corporations have remained unchanged since they were substantially lowered in 1986.

brackets (25, 28, 33, and 35 percent), the rate is 15 percent; for those in the bottom two brackets (10 and 15 percent), the rate is 0 percent. As discussed later, corporate shareholders enjoy the alternative of the dividends received deduction.

Many corporate and all noncorporate taxpayers are subject to the alternative minimum tax (AMT). For AMT purposes, many adjustments and tax preference items are the same for both, but other adjustments and tax preferences apply only to corporations or only to individuals. The AMT is discussed at length in Chapter 12.

All allowable corporate deductions are treated as business expenses. The determination of adjusted gross income, so essential for individuals, has no relevance to corporations. Corporations need not be concerned with classifying deductions into *deduction for* and *deduction from* categories.

The similarities and dissimilarities between individuals and C corporations as to tax attributes are outlined in Concept Summary 20.1 later in the chapter.

20-2c Specific Provisions Compared

Corporate and individual tax rules also can vary in the following areas:

- Capital gains and losses.
- Recapture of depreciation.
- Charitable contributions.
- Domestic production activities deduction.
- Net operating losses.
- Special deductions for corporations.

Capital Gains and Losses

Both corporate and noncorporate taxpayers are required to aggregate gains and losses from the taxable sale or exchange of capital assets. (Refer to Chapter 16 for a description of the netting process that takes place after the aggregation has been completed.) For long-term capital gains (including gains from collectibles and unrecaptured § 1250 gain), individuals enjoy an advantage. Called the alternative tax, the maximum applicable tax rate is 28 percent for collectibles, 25 percent for unrecaptured § 1250 gain, and 20 percent for other capital gains. In the case of corporations, all capital gains are taxed using the rates for ordinary income. Therefore, the net long-term capital gain of a corporation could be taxed at a rate as high as 35 percent.

Example 4	In 2014, Rose has taxable income of $80,000, not including a long-term capital gain of $10,000. If Rose is an individual, the alternative tax yields a tax on the capital gain of $1,500 ($10,000 × 15%). If, however, Rose is a C corporation, the tax becomes $3,400 ($10,000 × 34%).

Significant differences exist in the treatment of capital losses for income tax purposes. Individuals, for example, can annually deduct up to $3,000 of net capital losses against ordinary income. If an individual has both net short-term and net long-term capital losses, the short-term capital losses are used first in arriving at the $3,000 ordinary loss deduction. While corporations may not use net capital losses to offset ordinary income, they may use net capital losses to offset past or future capital gains.[9] Unlike individuals, corporations are not allowed an unlimited carryover period for capital losses. Instead, they may carry back excess capital losses to the three preceding years, applying the losses initially to the earliest year. If not exhausted by the carryback, remaining unused capital losses may be carried forward for a period of five years from the year of the loss.[10]

When carried back or forward, *both* short-term capital losses and long-term capital losses are treated as short-term capital losses by corporate taxpayers. For noncorporate taxpayers, carryovers of capital losses retain their identity as short or long term.

Hawk Corporation, a calendar year taxpayer, incurs a long-term net capital loss of $5,000 for 2014. None of the capital loss may be deducted in 2014. Hawk may, however, carry the loss back to years 2011, 2012, and 2013 (in this order) and offset any capital gains recognized in these years. If the carryback does not exhaust the loss, the loss may be carried forward to 2015, 2016, 2017, 2018, and 2019 (in this order). Such capital loss carrybacks or carryovers are treated as short-term capital losses.	**Example 5**

Recapture of Depreciation

Corporations selling depreciable real estate may have ordinary income in addition to that required by § 1250. Under § 291, the additional ordinary income element is 20 percent of the excess of the § 1245 recapture potential over the § 1250 recapture. As a result, the § 1231 gain is correspondingly decreased by the additional recapture.

Under § 1250, the excess of accelerated depreciation over straight-line depreciation is recaptured as ordinary income as to real property. Because all real property purchased since 1986 is depreciated using only the straight-line method, after 2005, the § 1250 amount is zero because the depreciation period (19 years in 1986) has expired and such buildings are fully depreciated.

Example 6

Condor Corporation purchases residential real property on November 3, 2000, for $300,000. Straight-line cost recovery is taken in the amount of $143,624 (see Table 8.6 in Chapter 8) before the property is sold on January 6, 2014, for $250,000. (Neither the purchase nor the selling price includes any amount attributable to the land.)

First, determine the recognized gain:

Sales price		$ 250,000
Less adjusted basis:		
Cost of property	$ 300,000	
Less cost recovery	(143,624)	(156,376)
Recognized gain		$ 93,624

Second, determine the § 1245 recapture potential. This is the lesser of $93,624 (recognized gain) or $143,624 (cost recovery claimed).

Third, determine the § 1250 recapture amount:

Cost recovery taken	$ 143,624
Less straight-line cost recovery	(143,624)
§ 1250 ordinary income	$ –0–

Fourth, because the taxpayer is a corporation, determine the additional § 291 amount:

§ 1245 recapture potential	$ 93,624
Less § 1250 recapture amount	(–0–)
Excess § 1245 recapture potential	$ 93,624
Apply § 291 percentage	× 20%
Additional ordinary income under § 291	$ 18,725

---

[9] §§ 1211(a) and (b).   [10] § 1212(a).

Condor Corporation's recognized gain of $93,624 is accounted for as follows:

Ordinary income under § 1250	$ –0–
Ordinary income under § 291	18,725
§ 1231 gain	74,899
Total recognized gain	$93,624

Charitable Contributions

Generally, a charitable contribution deduction is allowed only for the tax year in which the payment is made. However, an important exception is made for accrual basis corporations. The deduction may be claimed in the tax year *preceding* payment if the following conditions are satisfied:

- The contribution is authorized by the board of directors by the end of that tax year *and*
- The contribution is paid on or before the fifteenth day of the third month of the next tax year.[11]

Example 7	On December 26, 2014, the board of directors of Dove Corporation, a calendar year, accrual basis taxpayer, authorizes a $20,000 donation to a qualified charity. The donation is paid on March 12, 2015. Dove Corporation may claim the $20,000 donation as a deduction for 2014. As an alternative, Dove may claim the deduction in 2015 (the year of payment).

Like individuals, corporations are not permitted an unlimited charitable contribution deduction. In any one year, a corporate taxpayer is limited to 10 percent of taxable income. For this purpose, taxable income is computed without regard to the charitable contribution deduction, any net operating loss carryback or capital loss carryback, or the dividends received deduction (discussed later in this chapter).[12] Any contributions in excess of the 10 percent limitation are carried forward to the five succeeding tax years. Any carryover must be added to subsequent contributions and is subject to the 10 percent limitation. In applying the limitation, the most recent contributions must be deducted first.[13]

Example 8	During 2014, Eagle Corporation (a calendar year taxpayer) had the following income and expenses:

Income from operations	$140,000
Expenses from operations	110,000
Dividends received	10,000
Charitable contributions made in 2014	5,000

For purposes of the 10% limitation only, Eagle's taxable income is $40,000 ($140,000 − $110,000 + $10,000). Consequently, the allowable charitable contribution deduction for 2014 is $4,000 (10% × $40,000). The $1,000 unused portion of the contribution is carried forward to 2015, 2016, 2017, 2018, and 2019 (in that order) until exhausted.

Example 9	Assume the same facts as in Example 8. In 2015, Eagle Corporation has taxable income (after adjustments) of $50,000 and makes a charitable contribution of $4,800. The maximum deduction allowed for 2015 is $5,000 (10% × $50,000). The first $4,800 of the allowed deduction must be allocated to the 2015 contribution, and the $200 excess is allocated to the carryover from 2014. The remaining $800 of the 2014 contribution is carried over to 2016, etc.

---

[11]§ 170(a)(2).
[12]§ 170(b)(2).

[13]§ 170(d)(2).

As noted in Chapter 10, the deduction for charitable contributions of ordinary income property is limited to the lesser of the fair market value or the adjusted basis of the property. A special rule provides an exception that permits a corporation to contribute inventory (ordinary income property) to certain charitable organizations and receive a deduction equal to the adjusted basis plus one-half of the difference between the fair market value and the adjusted basis of the property. In no event, however, may the deduction exceed twice the adjusted basis of the property. To qualify for this exception, the inventory must be used by the charity in its exempt purpose for the care of *children*, the *ill*, or the *needy*.[14]

In the current year, Robin Company (a retail clothier) donates sweaters and overcoats to Sheltering Arms (a qualified charity caring for the homeless). The clothing is inventory and has a basis of $10,000 and a fair market value of $14,000. If Robin is a corporation, the charitable contribution that results is $12,000 [$10,000 (basis) + $2,000 (50% of the appreciation of $4,000)]. In contrast, if Robin is not a corporation, the charitable contribution is limited to $10,000 (basis).	**Example 10**

Domestic Production Activities Deduction

As noted in Chapter 7, § 199 was designed to replace various export tax benefits that our world trading partners deemed discriminatory. Known as the domestic production activities deduction (DPAD), the provision is equally applicable to C corporations. In the case of C corporations, however, the limitation is based on taxable income, rather than AGI (both computed without considering the deduction). Thus, the DPAD is 9 percent of the *lesser* of qualified production activities income (QPAI) or taxable income. (The DPAD was 6 percent prior to 2010.) As with individual taxpayers, the DPAD cannot exceed 50 percent of the W–2 wages involved (those subject to withholding plus certain elective deferrals). Domestic gross receipts from manufacturing activities are a major source of QPAI. These gross receipts are adjusted by cost of goods sold and other assignable expenses to arrive at QPAI.

For corporations that are members of an affiliated group (based on 50 percent common control), the deduction is determined by treating the group as a single taxpayer. In effect, therefore, each member of the group is treated as being engaged in the activities of every other member. The deduction is then allocated among the members in proportion to each member's respective amount of QPAI.[15]

Mallard and Pintail Corporations are members of an affiliated group but do not file a consolidated return. Mallard manufactures a machine at a cost of $3,000 and sells it to Pintail for $5,000. Pintail incurs additional cost of $2,000 for marketing and then sells the machine to an unrelated customer for $9,000. The QPAI deduction is based on $4,000 ($9,000 − $3,000 − $2,000) even though the seller (Pintail) did not perform any manufacturing.[16] Note that this is the same result that would have been reached if Pintail had not been involved and Mallard had conducted its own marketing function.	**Example 11**

Assume the same facts as in Example 11, except that the parties are not related. Under these circumstances, Mallard has QPAI of $2,000 ($5,000 − $3,000) and Pintail has none. Pintail's activities, when considered alone, are not QPAI because they involve marketing and not manufacturing.	**Example 12**

In the case of pass-through entities (e.g., partnerships, S corporations, and LLCs), special rules apply for handling the DPAD.[17] Because the deduction is determined at the owner level, each partner or shareholder must make the computation separately. Thus, the entity allocates to each owner his or her share of QPAI.

---

[14]The inventory exception is prescribed by § 170(e)(3).
[15]§ 199(d)(4).
[16]Reg. § 1.199–7(c).
[17]§ 199(d)(1).

The QPAI that is passed through is then combined with any qualifying activities that the owner has from other sources (e.g., a partner also conducts a manufacturing activity on his or her own).

The DPAD can be claimed in computing the alternative minimum tax (including adjusted current earnings). The deduction allowed is the lesser of QPAI or alternative minimum taxable income (AMTI). In the case of an individual taxpayer, AGI is substituted for AMTI in determining the limitation on the amount allowed as a deduction.[18]

Net Operating Losses

The computation of a net operating loss (NOL) for individuals was discussed in Chapter 7. Corporations are not subject to the complex adjustments required for individuals because a corporation's loss more clearly approximates a true economic loss. Artificial deductions (e.g., personal and dependency exemptions) that merely generate paper losses are not permitted for corporations.

In computing the NOL of a corporation, the dividends received deduction (discussed below) can be claimed in determining the amount of the loss. Generally, NOLs may be carried back 2 years and forward 20 years (or taxpayers may elect to forgo the carryback period) to offset taxable income for those years.[19]

Example 13	In 2014, Wren Corporation has gross income of $200,000 and deductions of $300,000, excluding the dividends received deduction. Wren received taxable dividends of $100,000 from ExxonMobil stock. Wren has an NOL of $170,000, computed as follows:

Gross income (including ExxonMobil dividends)		$ 200,000
Less: Business deductions	$300,000	
Dividends received deduction (70% × $100,000)	70,000	(370,000)
Taxable income (loss)		($ 170,000)

Example 14	Assume the same facts as in Example 13 and assume that Wren Corporation had taxable income of $40,000 in 2012. The NOL of $170,000 is carried back to 2012 (unless Wren elects not to carry back the loss to that year). The carryover to 2013 is $130,000, computed as follows:

Taxable income for 2012	$ 40,000
Less: NOL carryback from 2014	(170,000)
Carryover of unabsorbed 2014 loss	($ 130,000)

In Example 14, the carryback to 2012 might have been ill-advised if Wren Corporation had little, if any, taxable income in 2012 and 2013 and if it anticipated large amounts of taxable income in the immediate future. In that case, the *election to forgo* the carryback might generate greater tax savings. In this regard, three points should be considered. First, the time value of the tax refund that is lost by not using the carryback procedure must be considered. Second, the election to forgo an NOL carryback is irrevocable. Thus, it cannot be changed later if the future high profits do not materialize. Third, future increases or decreases in corporate income tax rates that can reasonably be anticipated should be considered.

20-2d Deductions Available Only to Corporations

Dividends Received Deduction

The purpose of the **dividends received deduction** is to prevent triple taxation. Without the deduction, income paid to a corporation in the form of a dividend

LO.3

Recognize and calculate the tax deductions available only to corporations.

[18]§ 199(d)(6).   [19]§ 172(b).

TAX IN THE NEWS   Variations in Mitigating the Effect of Multiple Taxation

When a corporation receives a dividend from another corporation, multiple taxation of the same income is eased (or avoided) by allowing the corporate shareholder a dividends received deduction. But what happens when these funds are later passed through to the individual shareholders? In the past, such distributions were fully taxed as ordinary income.

This problem of double taxation of corporate distributions at the individual shareholder level was addressed by Congress in 2003. The solution arrived at, however, is different from that used for corporate shareholders. Instead of allowing a deduction for some (or all) of the dividends received, relief is provided through the application of a lower tax rate. Thus, qualified dividends are taxed at the same preferential tax rate available to net capital gains.

In summary, the possible triple taxation of corporate-source income is mitigated by the combination of a deduction (available to corporate shareholders) and a lower tax rate (available to individual shareholders).

would be subject to taxation for a second time (after being taxed first to the distributing corporation) with no corresponding deduction to the distributing corporation. A third level of tax would be assessed on the shareholders when the recipient corporation distributed the income to its shareholders. Because the dividends received deduction may be less than 100 percent, the law provides only partial relief.

The amount of the dividends received deduction depends upon the percentage of ownership the recipient corporate shareholder holds in the corporation making the dividend distribution.[20] For dividends received or accrued, the *deduction percentage* is summarized as follows:

Percentage of Ownership by Corporate Shareholder	Deduction Percentage
Less than 20%	70%
20% or more (but less than 80%)	80%
80% or more	100%

The dividends received deduction may be limited to a percentage of the taxable income of a corporation computed without regard to the NOL deduction, the dividends received deduction, the DPAD, or any capital loss carryback. The percentage of taxable income limitation corresponds to the deduction percentage. Thus, if a corporate shareholder owns less than 20 percent of the stock in the distributing corporation, the dividends received deduction is limited to 70 percent of taxable income (as previously defined). However, this limitation does not apply if the corporation has an NOL for the current taxable year.[21]

In working with these myriad rules, the following steps need to be taken:

1. Multiply the dividends received by the deduction percentage.
2. Multiply the taxable income (as previously defined) by the deduction percentage.
3. The deduction is limited to the lesser of step 1 or step 2, unless subtracting the amount derived from step 1 from taxable income (as previously defined) generates a negative number. If so, the amount derived in step 1 should be used.

---

[20]§ 243(a).   [21]§ 246(b).

Example 15

Crane, Osprey, and Gull Corporations, three unrelated calendar year corporations, have the following transactions for 2014:

	Crane Corporation	Osprey Corporation	Gull Corporation
Gross income from operations	$ 400,000	$ 320,000	$ 260,000
Expenses from operations	(340,000)	(340,000)	(340,000)
Dividends received from domestic corporations (less than 20% ownership)	200,000	200,000	200,000
Taxable income before the dividends received deduction	$ 260,000	$ 180,000	$ 120,000

In determining the dividends received deduction, use the step procedure just described:

	Crane Corporation	Osprey Corporation	Gull Corporation
Step 1: (70% × $200,000)	$140,000	$140,000	$140,000
Step 2:			
70% × $260,000 (taxable income)	$182,000		
70% × $180,000 (taxable income)		$126,000	
70% × $120,000 (taxable income)			$ 84,000
Step 3:			
Lesser of step 1 or step 2	$140,000	$126,000	
Generates an NOL			$140,000

Osprey Corporation is subject to the 70 percent of taxable income limitation. It does not qualify for the loss rule treatment because subtracting $140,000 (step 1) from $180,000 does not yield a loss. Gull Corporation qualifies for the loss rule treatment because subtracting $140,000 (step 1) from $120,000 does yield a loss. In summary, each corporation has the following dividends received deduction for 2014: $140,000 for Crane, $126,000 for Osprey, and $140,000 for Gull. If a corporation already has an NOL before any dividends received deduction is claimed, the full dividends received deduction (as calculated in step 1) is allowed.

Deduction of Organizational Expenditures

A corporation may elect to amortize organizational expenses over a period of 15 years or more. A special exception allows the corporation to immediately expense the first $5,000 of these costs in addition to the first year's amortization amount.[22] The exception, however, is phased out on a dollar-for-dollar basis when these expenses exceed $50,000.

Example 16

Kingbird Corporation, a calendar year taxpayer, is formed on June 1, 2014. In connection with its formation, it incurs organizational expenditures of $52,000. If Kingbird wants to claim as much of these expenses as soon as possible, its deduction for 2014 is as follows:

$$\text{Expense: } \$5,000 - (\$52,000 - \$50,000) = \$3,000$$

$$\text{Amortization: } \frac{\$52,000 - \$3,000}{180 \text{ months}} \times 7 \text{ (months)} = \$1,906$$

Kingbird deducts a total of $4,906 ($3,000 + $1,906) for 2014.

[22]§ 248.

Taxing the Income of Foreign Corporations

Are foreign corporations subject to the U.S. corporate income tax? If the income is from U.S. sources, the answer is *yes*! This presumes that the income is not insulated from U.S. taxation by a provision in a tax treaty between the United States and the country of incorporation.

The manner of taxation depends upon the nature of the income involved. If the income is fixed, determinable, annual, or periodic (known as FDAP income), it is taxed at 30 percent on the *gross* amount. The tax is collected by virtue of required withholding imposed on the payor. FDAP income generally includes passive income (e.g., dividends, interest, rents, royalties, and annuities) that is not effectively connected with a U.S. trade or business.

If, however, the income comes from the conduct of a U.S. trade or business, it is taxed at *net* in much the same manner as the income of domestic corporations. Any FDAP income effectively connected with the trade or business is taxed in the same manner as the business *net* income.

Global Tax Issues

© iStockphoto.com/Andrey Prokhorov

If the election is not made on a timely basis, the expenditures cannot be deducted until the corporation ceases to conduct business and liquidates. The election is made in a statement attached to the corporation's return for its first taxable year. The election covers all qualifying expenses *incurred* in the corporation's first tax year. Thus, a cash basis taxpayer need not have paid the expenses as long as they were incurred.

Organizational expenditures include the following:

- Legal services incident to organization (e.g., drafting the corporate charter, bylaws, minutes of organizational meetings, and terms of original stock certificates).
- Necessary accounting services.
- Expenses of temporary directors and of organizational meetings of directors and shareholders.
- Fees paid to the state of incorporation.

Expenditures connected with issuing or selling shares of stock or other securities (e.g., commissions, professional fees, printing costs) or with the transfer of assets to a corporation do not qualify. These expenditures are generally added to the capital account and are not subject to amortization.

20-2e Determination of Corporate Tax Liability

Income Tax Rates

LO.4

Calculate the corporate tax liability and comply with various procedural and reporting requirements.

The income tax rates for corporations are reproduced in Table 1.[23] Note that the income tax rates begin by being progressive—compare the marginal tax rate applicable to the first $50,000 (taxed at 15 percent) with that on taxable income over $50,000 (taxed at 25 percent). But the phaseout of these lower rates starts with the $100,001 to $335,000 bracket (taxed at 39 percent) and continues with the $15,000,001 to $18,333,333 bracket (taxed at 38 percent). Once taxable income reaches $18,333,334, the progression disappears (i.e., the lower brackets have been phased out) and the marginal rate on every dollar becomes 35 percent. Thus, the tax on $20 million is $7 million (35% × $20,000,000).

Example 17

A calendar year corporation has taxable income of $90,000 for the current year. The income tax liability is $18,850, determined as follows: $7,500 (15% × $50,000) + $6,250 (25% × $25,000) + $5,100 (34% × $15,000).

---

[23]§ 11(b).

TABLE 20.1	Income Tax Rates—Corporations

Taxable Income	Tax Rate
Not over $50,000	15%
Over $50,000 but not over $75,000	25%
Over $75,000 but not over $100,000	34%
Over $100,000 but not over $335,000	39%*
Over $335,000 but not over $10,000,000	34%
Over $10,000,000 but not over $15,000,000	35%
Over $15,000,000 but not over $18,333,333	38%**
Over $18,333,333	35%

*Five percent of this rate represents a phaseout of the benefits of the lower tax rates on the first $75,000 of taxable income.

**Three percent of this rate represents a phaseout of the benefits of the lower tax rate (34% rather than 35%) on the first $10 million of taxable income.

Qualified personal service corporations are taxed at a flat 35 percent rate on all taxable income. They do not enjoy the tax savings of the lower brackets. For this purpose, a *qualified* **personal service corporation** is a corporation that is substantially employee-owned and engages in one of the following activities: health, law, engineering, architecture, accounting, actuarial science, performing arts, or consulting.

Alternative Minimum Tax

Corporations are subject to an alternative minimum tax (AMT) that has the same objective and is structured in the same manner as that applicable to individuals. The AMT defines a more expansive tax base than for the regular tax. Like individuals, corporations are required to apply a minimum tax rate to the expanded base and pay the difference between the tentative AMT liability and the regular tax. Although many of the adjustments and tax preference items necessary to arrive at alternative minimum taxable income (AMTI) are the same for individuals and corporations, the rate and exemptions are different. As noted in Chapter 12, certain small business corporations are effectively exempt from the corporate AMT.

20-2f Corporate Filing Requirements

A corporation must file a return whether it has taxable income or not.[24] A corporation that was not in existence throughout an entire annual accounting period is required to file a return for the fraction of the year during which it was in existence. In addition, the corporation must file a return even though it has ceased to do business if it has valuable claims for which it will bring suit. It is relieved of filing returns once it ceases business and dissolves.

The corporate return is filed on Form 1120. Corporations making the S corporation election (discussed later in the chapter) file on Form 1120S.

Corporations with less than $250,000 of gross receipts and less than $250,000 in assets do not have to complete Schedule L (balance sheet) and Schedules M–1 and M–2 (see the next section) of Form 1120. Similar omissions are allowed for Form 1120S. These rules are intended to ease the compliance burden on small business.

The return must be filed on or before the fifteenth day of the third month following the close of the corporation's tax year. Corporations can receive an automatic extension of six months for filing the corporate return by filing Form 7004 by the due date of the return. However, the IRS may terminate an extension by mailing a 10-day notice to the taxpayer corporation.[25]

[24]§ 6012(a)(2).

[25]§ 6081.

TAX IN THE NEWS Many Corporations Escape the Income Tax

The Government Accountability Office (GAO) issued a report on a study of corporate tax liability during the period from 1998 to 2005. The GAO found that approximately 60 percent of all U.S. corporations reported no Federal income tax liability. For *large* corporations, however, the percentage with no liability was much lower—about 25 percent in 2005. (Large corporations are those with assets of at least $250 million or gross receipts of at least $50 million.)

Except to note that some of the absence of tax liability may be due to the carryover of losses and credits from prior years, the study did not explore other possible causal factors.

Source: Comparison of the Reported Tax Liabilities of Foreign- and U.S. Controlled Corporations, 1998–2005, U.S. Government Accountability Office, June 2008.

A corporation must make payments of estimated tax unless its tax liability can reasonably be expected to be less than $500. The payments must equal the lesser of 100 percent of the corporation's final tax or 100 percent of the last year's tax. These payments may be made in four installments due on or before the fifteenth day of the fourth, sixth, ninth, and twelfth months of the corporate taxable year.[26] The full amount of the unpaid tax is due on the date of the return. Failure to make the required estimated tax prepayments will result in a nondeductible penalty being imposed on the corporation. The penalty can be avoided, however, if any of various exceptions apply.[27]

20-2g Reconciliation of Corporate Taxable Income and Accounting Income

Taxable income and accounting net income are seldom the same amount. For example, a difference may arise if the corporation uses accelerated depreciation for tax purposes and straight-line depreciation for accounting purposes.

Many items of income for accounting purposes, such as proceeds from a life insurance policy on the death of a corporate officer and interest on municipal bonds, may not be includible in calculating taxable income. Some expense items for accounting purposes, such as expenses to produce tax-exempt income, estimated warranty reserves, a net capital loss, and Federal income taxes, are not deductible for tax purposes.

Schedule M–1 on the last page of Form 1120 is used to reconcile accounting net income (net income after Federal income taxes) with taxable income (as computed on the corporate tax return before the deduction for an NOL and the dividends received deduction). In the left-hand column of Schedule M–1, net income per books is added to the following: the Federal income tax liability for the year, the excess of capital losses over capital gains (which cannot be deducted in the current year), income for tax purposes that is not income in the current year for accounting purposes, and expenses recorded on the books that are not deductible on the tax return. In the right-hand column, income recorded on the books that is not currently taxable or is tax-exempt and deductions for tax purposes that are not expenses for accounting purposes are totaled and subtracted from the left-hand column total to arrive at taxable income (before the NOL or dividends received deductions).

---

[26]§ 6655(f). Corporations must use electronic funds transfers to make all Federal tax deposits, including estimated tax, through either the Electronic Federal Tax Payment System (EFTPS) or third-party providers.

[27]See § 6655 for the penalty involved and the various exceptions.

FINANCIAL DISCLOSURE INSIGHTS   Deferred Taxes on the Balance Sheet

A business entity that follows GAAP, whether it is incorporated or not, typically records deferred tax assets and liabilities on its Statement of Financial Position (the "balance sheet"). The differences between the entity's total tax expense and its current tax expense can represent sizable amounts on the balance sheet. Because certain transactions result in deferred tax assets and others result in deferred tax liabilities, many balance sheets include dollar amounts for both accounts. For example, some recent financial reports included the following estimates:

	Deferred Tax Liabilities ($000)	Deferred Tax Assets ($000)
General Electric	$34,200	$22,000
ExxonMobil	30,200	11,200
Berkshire Hathaway	22,500	4,300
Ford Motor	14,500	15,000

© iStockphoto.com/Pali Rao

As deferred tax amounts "reverse" themselves into the Statement of Earnings and Comprehensive Income (the "income statement"), shareholders and investment analysts must determine whether and how the tax deferrals indicate the current and future profitability of the entity. This can be difficult in situations such as the following:

- The taxpayer wins or loses an audit or other appeal with a taxing jurisdiction, creating an unusual amount due or refund.
- Tax rates change, and the amounts of the tax deferrals change accordingly.
- A multinational entity deals with countries outside the United States that apply a different mix of taxes and rates.

Much of the public information regarding tax deferrals is found in the footnotes to the entity's financial statements, but these data can be difficult to interpret for large businesses with complex legal structures.

Example 18

During the current year, Crow Corporation had the following transactions:

Net income per books (after tax)	$92,400
Taxable income	50,000
Federal income tax liability (15% × $50,000)	7,500
Interest income from tax-exempt bonds	5,000
Interest paid on loan, the proceeds of which were used to purchase the tax-exempt bonds	500
Life insurance proceeds received as a result of the death of a key employee	50,000
Premiums paid on key employee life insurance policy	2,600
Excess of capital losses over capital gains	2,000

For book and tax purposes, Crow determines depreciation under the straight-line method. Crow's Schedule M–1 for the current year follows:

Schedule M-1	**Reconciliation of Income (Loss) per Books With Income per Return**				
colspan note	*Note:* Schedule M-3 required instead of Schedule M-1 if total assets are $10 million or more—see instructions				
1	Net income (loss) per books	92,400	7	Income recorded on books this year not included on this return (itemize):	
2	Federal income tax per books	7,500			
3	Excess of capital losses over capital gains .	2,000		Tax-exempt interest $ 5,000	
4	Income subject to tax not recorded on books this year (itemize): _____			*Life insurance proceeds on key employee $50,000*	55,000
	_____		8	Deductions on this return not charged against book income this year (itemize):	
5	Expenses recorded on books this year not deducted on this return (itemize):		a	Depreciation . . $ _____	
a	Depreciation . . . . $ _____		b	Charitable contributions $ _____	
b	Charitable contributions . $ _____				
c	Travel and entertainment . $ _____			_____	
	Prem.–life ins. $2,600; Int.–exempt bonds $500	3,100	9	Add lines 7 and 8	55,000
6	Add lines 1 through 5	105,000	10	Income (page 1, line 28)—line 6 less line 9	50,000

Schedule M–2 reconciles unappropriated retained earnings at the beginning of the year with unappropriated retained earnings at year-end. Beginning balance plus net income per books, as entered on line 1 of Schedule M–1, less dividend distributions during the year equals ending retained earnings. Other sources of increases or decreases in retained earnings are also listed on Schedule M–2.

Example 19

Assume the same facts as in Example 18. Crow Corporation's beginning balance in unappropriated retained earnings is $125,000, and Crow distributed a cash dividend of $30,000 to its shareholders during the year. Based on these further assumptions, Crow has the following Schedule M–2 for the current year:

Schedule M-2	Analysis of Unappropriated Retained Earnings per Books (Line 25, Schedule L)				
1	Balance at beginning of year	125,000	5	Distributions: a Cash	30,000
2	Net income (loss) per books	92,400		b Stock	
3	Other increases (itemize):			c Property	
			6	Other decreases (itemize):	
			7	Add lines 5 and 6	30,000
4	Add lines 1, 2, and 3	217,400	8	Balance at end of year (line 4 less line 7)	187,400

Certain corporations must file **Schedule M–3**.[28] This schedule, designated "Net Income (Loss) Reconciliation for Corporations With Total Assets of $10 Million or More," is in lieu of Schedule M–1. It must be filed when the assets reported on Schedule L of Form 1120 total or exceed $10 million. Because it reveals significant differences between book and taxable income, Schedule M–3 will enable the IRS to more quickly identify possible abusive transactions (e.g., use of tax shelter schemes).

20-3 FORMING THE CORPORATION

20-3a Capital Contributions

LO.5

Describe the tax rules governing the formation of corporations.

The receipt of money or property in exchange for capital stock produces neither recognized gain nor loss to the recipient corporation.[29] Gross income of a corporation does not include shareholders' contributions of money or property to the capital of the corporation.[30] Contributions by nonshareholders are also excluded from the gross income of a corporation.[31] The basis of the property transferred by nonshareholders to the corporation is zero.

Example 20

A city donates land worth $900,000 to Cardinal Corporation as an inducement for it to locate in the city. The receipt of the land does not represent gross income. The land's basis to the corporation is zero.

Thin Capitalization

The advantages of capitalizing a corporation with debt may be substantial. Interest on debt is deductible by the corporation, while dividend payments are not. Further, the shareholders are not taxed on loan repayments unless the payments exceed basis.

In certain instances, the IRS will claim **thin capitalization** by holding that debt is really an equity interest and will deny the shareholders the tax advantages of debt financing. If the debt instrument has too many similarities to stock, it may be treated as a form of stock, with principal and interest payments treated as dividends.[32]

---

[28]Rev.Proc. 2004–45, 2004–2 C.B. 140. Schedule M–3 satisfies some of the disclosure requirements set forth in Reg. § 1.6011–4 when significant book-tax differences occur.

[29]§ 1032.

[30]§ 118.

[31]*Edwards v. Cuba Railroad Co.*, 1 USTC ¶139, 5 AFTR 5398, 45 S.Ct. 614 (USSC, 1925).

[32]Section 385 lists several factors that might be used to determine whether a debtor-creditor relationship or a shareholder-corporation relationship exists.

The form of the instrument will not ensure debt treatment, but failure to observe certain formalities in creating the debt may lead to an assumption that the purported debt is a form of stock. The debt should be in proper legal form, bear a legitimate rate of interest, have a definite maturity date, and be repaid on a timely basis. Payments should not be contingent upon earnings. Further, the debt should not be subordinated to other liabilities, and proportionate holdings of stock and debt should be avoided or minimized.

The preferential treatment allowed for qualified dividend income has added another dimension to the thin capitalization issue. Although a corporation would prefer to pay out profits in the form of interest (deductible as an expense) rather than as dividends (nondeductible), the shareholders have the opposite tax position. Interest income is ordinary income, while qualified dividends are subject to beneficial net capital gain rates. Nevertheless, the repayment of the debt is not taxed at all because it is a return of capital. Hence, the thin capitalization incentive will continue to exist.

Minimum Capitalization

With many small corporations, particularly nonmanufacturing personal service corporations, the capitalization is minimal. The corporation is formed with whatever investment in stock is required under applicable state law.

THE BIG PICTURE

Example 21

Return to the facts of *The Big Picture* on p. 20-1. Suppose the Todd sisters decide to conduct their catering business in the corporate form—either a C or S corporation. In forming the corporation, they should probably limit their capital investment to whatever state law requires. The sisters should consider acquiring the capital assets needed to operate the business (e.g., delivery trucks, kitchen equipment, location for food preparation) on their own and leasing them to the corporation. This would allow the sisters to claim the appropriate depreciation and would provide the corporation with a deduction for the rent paid. Although this strategy would force the sisters to recognize rent income rather than preferentially taxed dividends, no dividends will be forthcoming in the early loss years of the business.

20-3b Transfers to Controlled Corporations

Without special provisions in the Code, a transfer of property to a corporation in exchange for its stock would be a sale or exchange of property and would constitute a taxable transaction to the transferring shareholder. Section 351 provides for the nonrecognition of gain or loss upon such transfers of property if the transferors are in control of the corporation immediately after the transfer. Gain or loss is merely postponed in a manner similar to a like-kind exchange (see Chapter15). The following requirements must be met to qualify under § 351:

- The transferors must be in control of the corporation immediately after the exchange. *Control* is defined as ownership of at least 80 percent of the total combined voting power of all classes of stock entitled to vote and at least 80 percent of the total number of shares of all other classes of stock.[33]
- Realized gain (but not loss) is recognized to the extent that the transferors receive property other than stock. Such nonqualifying property is commonly referred to as *boot*.

If the requirements of § 351 are satisfied and no boot is involved, nonrecognition of gain or loss is *mandatory*.

---

[33]§ 368(c).

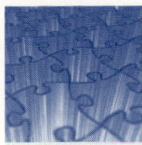

CONCEPT SUMMARY 20.1

Summary of Income Tax Consequences

	Individuals	Corporations
Computation of gross income	§ 61.	§ 61.
Computation of taxable income	§§ 62, 63(b) through (h).	§ 63(a). Concept of AGI has no relevance.
Deductions	Trade or business (§ 162); nonbusiness (§ 212); some personal and employee expenses (generally deductible as itemized deductions).	Trade or business (§ 162).
Charitable contributions	Limited in any tax year to 50% of AGI; 30% for long-term capital gain property unless election is made to reduce fair market value of gift; 20% for long-term capital gain property contributed to private nonoperating foundations.	Limited in any tax year to 10% of taxable income computed without regard to the charitable contribution deduction, net operating loss or capital loss carryback, and dividends received deduction.
	Time of deduction—year in which payment is made.	Time of deduction—year in which payment is made unless accrual basis taxpayer. Accrual basis corporation may take deduction in year preceding payment if contribution was authorized by board of directors by end of that year and contribution is paid by fifteenth day of third month of following year.
	Contribution of ordinary income property is limited to the lesser of adjusted basis or fair market value.	Contribution of certain ordinary income property can include one-half of any appreciation on the property.
	Excess charitable contributions can be carried over for a period of up to five years.	Excess charitable contributions can be carried over for a period of up to five years.
Casualty losses	$100 floor on nonbusiness casualty and theft losses; nonbusiness casualty and theft losses deductible only to extent losses exceed 10% of AGI.	Deductible in full.
Depreciation recapture for § 1250 property	Recaptured to extent accelerated depreciation exceeds straight-line.	20% of excess of amount that would be recaptured under § 1245 over amount recaptured under § 1250 is additional ordinary income under § 291.
Domestic production activities deduction	9% of the lesser of QPAI or AGI.	9% of the lesser of QPAI or taxable income.
Net operating loss	Adjusted for nonbusiness deductions over nonbusiness income and for personal and dependency exemptions.	Generally no adjustments.
Dividends received	Qualified dividends are taxed at the same rate applicable to net long-term capital gains.	Deduction allowed (70%, 80%, or 100%) as to dividends received.
Long-term capital gains	Generally taxed at a rate no higher than 15% (20% if taxpayer is in the 39.6% bracket and 0% if taxpayer is in the 15% or lower tax bracket).	Taxed using regular corporate rates.
Capital losses	Only $3,000 of capital loss can offset ordinary income; loss is carried forward indefinitely to offset capital gains or ordinary income up to $3,000; carryovers of short-term losses remain short term; long-term losses carry over as long term.	Can offset only capital gains; carried back three years and forward five years; carrybacks and carryovers are treated as short-term losses.

Summary of Income Tax Consequences—Continued

	Individuals	Corporations
Passive activity losses	Generally deductible only against income from passive activities.	For regular corporations, no limitation on deductibility. Personal service corporations and certain closely held corporations, however, are subject to same limitations as imposed on individuals. A closely held corporation is a corporation where five or fewer individuals own more than 50% of the stock either directly or indirectly.
Alternative minimum tax	Applied at a graduated rate schedule of 26% and 28% to AMT base (taxable income as modified by certain adjustments plus preference items minus exemption amount); exemption allowed depending on filing status; exemption phaseout begins when AMTI reaches a certain amount (e.g., $156,500 for married filing jointly).	Applied at a 20% rate to AMT base (taxable income as modified by certain adjustments plus preference items minus exemption amount); $40,000 exemption allowed but phaseout begins once AMTI reaches $150,000; adjustments and tax preference items similar to those applicable to individuals but also include 75% of adjusted current earnings (ACE) over AMTI. Certain small business corporations are exempt from the AMT.
Tax rates	Progressive with seven rates of 10%, 15%, 25%, 28%, 33%, 35%, and 39.6%.	Progressive with four rates of 15%, 25%, 34%, and 35%; lower brackets phased out at higher levels.

© iStockphoto.com/Andrey Prokhorov

Basis Considerations and Computation of Gain

The nonrecognition of gain or loss is accompanied by a carryover of basis. The basis of stock received in a § 351 transfer is determined as follows:

- Start with the adjusted basis of the property transferred by the shareholder.
- Add any gain recognized by the shareholder as a result of the transfer.
- Subtract the fair market value of any boot received by the shareholder from the corporation.[34]

Shareholders who receive noncash boot have a basis in the property equal to the fair market value.

The basis of properties received by the corporation is the basis in the hands of the transferor increased by the amount of any gain recognized to the transferring shareholder.[35]

Example 22

Ann and Lori form Bluejay Corporation. Ann transfers property with an adjusted basis of $30,000 and a fair market value of $60,000 for 50% of the stock. Lori transfers property with an adjusted basis of $40,000 and a fair market value of $60,000 for the remaining 50% of the stock. The realized gain ($30,000 for Ann and $20,000 for Lori) is not recognized on the transfer because the transfer qualifies under § 351. The basis of the stock to Ann is $30,000, and the basis of the stock to Lori is $40,000. Bluejay Corporation has a basis of $30,000 in the property transferred by Ann and a basis of $40,000 in the property transferred by Lori.

Example 23

Mike and John form Condor Corporation with the following investments: Mike transfers property (adjusted basis of $30,000 and fair market value of $70,000), and John transfers cash of $60,000. Each receives 50 shares of the Condor stock, but Mike also

---

[34]§ 358(a).   [35]§ 362(a).

receives $10,000 in cash. Assume that each share of the Condor stock is worth $1,200. Mike's realized gain is $40,000, determined as follows:

Value of the Condor stock received [50 (shares) × $1,200 (value per share)]	$ 60,000
Cash received	10,000
Amount realized	$ 70,000
Less basis of property transferred	(30,000)
Realized gain	$ 40,000

Mike's recognized gain is $10,000, the lesser of the realized gain ($40,000) or the fair market value of the boot received ($10,000). Mike's basis in the Condor stock is $30,000, computed as follows:

Basis in the property transferred	$ 30,000
Plus recognized gain	10,000
	$ 40,000
Less boot received	(10,000)
Basis to Mike of the Condor stock	$ 30,000

Condor Corporation's basis in the property transferred by Mike is $40,000 [$30,000 (basis of the property to Mike) + $10,000 (gain recognized by Mike)]. John neither realizes nor recognizes gain or loss and will have a basis of $60,000 in the Condor stock.

The receipt of stock for the performance of *services* always results in ordinary income to the transferring shareholder. An example might be an attorney who does not charge a fee for incorporating a business but instead receives the value equivalent in stock of the newly formed corporation. The basis of stock received for the performance of services is equal to the fair market value of the services.

ETHICS & EQUITY   Selective Incorporation

Miguel, a cash basis taxpayer, owns and operates a home renovation business that he decides to incorporate. In forming the corporation, he transfers *most* of the business, which includes unrealized receivables and inventory items.

However, he retains the land and building and the trade accounts payable.

For tax purposes, what is Miguel trying to accomplish by being selective in terms of what he transfers to the corporation? Will it work? Why or why not?

© iStockphoto.com/LdF

20-4 OPERATING THE CORPORATION

20-4a Dividend Distributions

Corporate distributions of cash or property to shareholders are treated as dividend income to the extent the corporation has accumulated *and/or* current earnings and profits (E & P).[36] In determining the source of the distribution, a dividend is deemed to have been made initially from current E & P.

LO.6

Explain the tax rules governing the operation of corporations.

Example 24

As of January 1, 2014, Teal Corporation has a deficit in accumulated E & P of $300,000. For tax year 2014, it has current E & P of $100,000. In 2014, the corporation distributes $50,000 to its shareholders. The $50,000 distribution is treated as a dividend because it is deemed to have been made from current E & P. This is the case even though Teal still has a deficit in its accumulated E & P at the end of 2014.

---

[36]§ 316. E & P is defined in the next section.

Global Tax Issues

Transferring Assets to Foreign Corporations— Forget § 351?

Tax-deferred transfers to controlled corporations under § 351 may generate current taxation when those transfers cross national borders. When a U.S. person transfers appreciated assets to a foreign corporation, the United States may lose its ability to tax the deferred gain on those assets (as well as the future income generated by the assets). To protect the U.S. taxing jurisdiction, § 367 provides that transfers of assets outside the U.S. tax net are generally taxable, in spite of the provisions of § 351.

Qualified dividend income is taxed like net long-term capital gain.[37] Consequently, the tax rate on such income cannot exceed 20 percent (0 percent for individual shareholders in the 15 percent or lower tax bracket).[38]

If a corporate distribution is not covered by E & P (either current or past), it is treated as a return of capital (refer to the discussion of the recovery of capital doctrine in Chapter 4). Because this treatment allows the shareholder to apply the amount of the distribution against the basis of the stock investment, the distribution represents a nontaxable return of capital. Any amount received in excess of the stock basis is classified as a capital gain (if the stock is a capital asset in the hands of the shareholder).

Example 25

When Mallard Corporation has no E & P (either current or accumulated), it distributes cash of $300,000 to its sole shareholder, Helen. The basis of Helen's stock investment is $200,000. Based on these facts, the $300,000 distribution Helen receives is accounted for as follows:

Return of capital (nontaxable)	$200,000
Capital gain	100,000
Total amount of distribution	$300,000

After the distribution, Helen has a basis of zero in her stock investment.

Concept of Earnings and Profits

The term **earnings and profits** is not defined in the Code, but § 312 does include certain transactions that affect E & P. Although E & P and the accounting concept of retained earnings have certain similarities, they differ in numerous respects. For example, a nontaxable stock dividend is treated as a capitalization of retained earnings for accounting purposes, yet it does not decrease E & P for tax purposes. Taxable dividends do reduce E & P but cannot yield a deficit. Referring to Example 25, after the distribution, Mallard Corporation's E & P remains zero rather than being a negative amount.

Accumulated E & P is the sum of the corporation's prior current E & P that has not been distributed as dividends. A more detailed discussion of the concept of E & P is beyond the scope of this chapter.

Property Dividends

A distribution of property to a shareholder is measured by the fair market value of the property on the date of distribution. The fair market value is also the shareholder's basis in the property.[39]

---

[37]Qualified dividend income is defined in § 1(h)(11)(B) and is discussed in Chapter 4.

[38]§ 1(h)(1). See the discussion in Chapter 3.
[39]§ 301.

> **Example 26**
>
> Drake Corporation has E & P of $60,000. It distributes land with a fair market value of $50,000 (adjusted basis of $30,000) to its sole shareholder, Art. Art has a taxable dividend of $50,000 and a basis in the land of $50,000.

A corporation that distributes appreciated property to its shareholders as a dividend must recognize the amount of the appreciation as gain.[40]

> **Example 27**
>
> Assume the same facts as in Example 26. Drake Corporation must recognize a gain of $20,000 on the distribution it made to Art.

However, if the property distributed has a basis in excess of its fair market value, the distributing corporation cannot recognize any loss.

Constructive Dividends

Many taxpayers mistakenly assume that dividend consequences do not take place unless the distribution carries the formalities of a dividend (declaration date, record date, and payment date). They further assume that dividends must be paid out to all shareholders on a pro rata basis. This may not be the case when closely held corporations are involved. Here, the key to dividend treatment depends upon whether the shareholders derive a benefit from the corporation that cannot be otherwise classified (e.g., as reasonable salary). The following are examples of **constructive dividends**:

- Salaries paid to shareholder-employees that are not reasonable (refer to Example 6 in Chapter 6).
- Interest on debt owed by the corporation to shareholders that is reclassified as equity because the corporation is thinly capitalized (refer to the earlier discussion in this chapter).
- Excessive rent paid by a corporation for the use of shareholder property. The arm's length standard is used to test whether the rent is excessive (refer to Example 28 in Chapter 1).
- Advances to shareholders that are not bona fide loans.
- Interest-free (or below-market) loans to shareholders. In this situation, the dividend component is the difference between the interest provided for, if any, and that calculated using the market rate.
- Shareholder use of corporate property for less than an arm's length rate.
- Absorption by the corporation of a shareholder's personal expenses.
- Bargain purchase of corporate property by shareholders.

ETHICS & EQUITY   Keeping It in the Family

Thrasher Company is a very profitable closely held C corporation owned and operated by the Fleming family. When its treasurer, Matilda Fleming, died, Michael Fleming was appointed as a temporary replacement. Although Matilda was 80 years old at death, she was a licensed CPA and had developed a competent accounting staff. Michael is the son of the CEO and major shareholder of Thrasher, but individually he owns no stock in the corporation. He just graduated from high school and plans to attend college full-time with a major in sports management. Thrasher Company will pay Michael the same salary Matilda was receiving. What are the parties trying to accomplish? Will they succeed? Why or why not?

Like regular dividends, constructive dividends must be covered by E & P to carry dividend income consequences to the shareholders. As noted previously,

---

[40]The tax consequences to a corporation of nonliquidating distributions to shareholders are covered in § 311.

however, constructive dividends need not be available to all shareholders on a pro rata basis.

Example 28

Return to the facts of *The Big Picture* on p. 20-1. Also recall the suggestions made in Example 21. If they choose the corporate form, the Todd sisters need to take the following into account:

- Any salaries the sisters pay themselves should satisfy the reasonableness test.
- Rent charged the corporation for the use of capital assets owned by the sisters should meet the arm's length standard.
- Loans made to the corporation for working capital purposes should provide for a market rate of interest to be charged.

Although the constructive dividend issue will not arise until the corporation becomes profitable (and has E & P), these procedures should be structured at the outset so that the parties will be prepared for a possible future challenge by the IRS.

Although dividends reduce the E & P of a corporation, they are not deductible for income tax purposes. In this regard, certain constructive dividends could have subtle tax consequences for all parties concerned.

Example 29

Grouse Corporation makes a loan to one of its shareholders, Hal. No interest is provided for, but application of the market rate would produce $20,000 of interest for the term of the loan. Presuming that the loan is bona fide, the following results occur:

- Hal has dividend income of $20,000.
- Grouse Corporation has interest income of $20,000.
- Hal might obtain an interest deduction of $20,000.

Not only does Grouse Corporation have to recognize income of $20,000, but it also obtains no income tax deduction for the $20,000 constructive dividend.

Example 30

Assume the same facts as in Example 29, except that the loan to Hal was not bona fide. In this event, the full amount of the loan is regarded as a dividend to Hal. Therefore, the interest element is not a factor because no bona fide loan ever existed.

20-4b Other Corporate Considerations

Complex tax provisions involving stock redemptions and corporate liquidations are beyond the scope of this text and are discussed in depth in *South-Western Federal Taxation: Corporations, Partnerships, Estates & Trusts.*

20-5 THE S ELECTION

LO.7

Assess the utility and effect of the Subchapter S election.

Numerous nontax reasons exist for operating a business in the corporate form (e.g., limited liability). Consequently, the existence of income tax disadvantages (e.g., double taxation of corporate income and shareholder dividends) should not deter businesspeople from using the corporate form. To prevent tax considerations from interfering with the exercise of sound business judgment, Congress enacted Subchapter S of the Code. The Subchapter S election enables taxpayers to use the corporate form for conducting a business without being taxed as a corporation.

20-5a Qualification for S Status

To achieve S corporation status, the corporation must meet certain requirements and make an effective election.

Qualifying for the Election

To qualify for **S corporation** status, the corporation must be a **small business corporation**. This includes any corporation that has the following characteristics:

- It is a domestic corporation.
- There are no more than 100 shareholders.
- Its shareholders are only individuals, estates, and certain trusts.
- No shareholder is a nonresident alien.
- It has only one class of stock outstanding.

These characteristics must continue to exist if an electing S corporation is to maintain S status.

The members of a family who own stock are treated as a single shareholder. Members of a family include all lineal descendants (e.g., children, grandchildren) of a shareholder and spouse (or ex-spouse) and the spouses (or ex-spouses) of such lineal descendants.[41]

Harry, a shareholder in an S corporation dies, and under his will, his stock is distributed among three children and eight grandchildren. The 11 new shareholders are treated as one shareholder for purposes of the 100-shareholder limitation.	**Example 31**

Making the Election

The election is made by filing Form 2553, and *all* shareholders must consent. For this purpose, husbands and wives are counted as a single shareholder.

To be effective for the current year, the election must be filed anytime during the preceding taxable year or on or before the fifteenth day of the third month of the current year.[42]

Heron, a calendar year taxpayer, is a regular corporation that wants to elect S status for 2014. If the election is filed anytime from January 1, 2013, through March 17, 2014, it will be effective for 2014.	**Example 32**

The IRS has the authority to waive invalid S elections (e.g., inadvertent failure to obtain all necessary shareholder consents to the original election) and to treat late elections as timely.

Loss of the Election

The S election may be terminated *voluntarily* (a majority of the shareholders file to revoke the election) or *involuntarily*. An involuntary termination may occur in *either* of the following ways:

- The corporation ceases to qualify as a small business corporation (e.g., the number of shareholders exceeds 100, or a partnership becomes a shareholder).
- The corporation has passive investment income (e.g., interest and dividends) in excess of 25 percent of gross receipts for a period of three consecutive years. This possibility applies only if the corporation was previously a regular corporation and has E & P from that period.

If the holders of a *majority* of the shares consent to a voluntary revocation of S status, the election to revoke must be made on or before the fifteenth day of the third month of the tax year to be effective for that year.

The shareholders of Stork Corporation, a calendar year S corporation, elect to revoke the election on January 3, 2014. Assuming that the election is duly executed and timely filed, Stork will become a regular corporation for calendar year 2014. If the election to revoke is not made until June 2014, Stork will not become a regular corporation until calendar year 2015.	**Example 33**

---

[41]§ 1361(c)(1).   [42]§ 1362.

Suppose the shareholders in Example 33 file the election to revoke on January 3, 2014, but do not want the revocation to take place until 2015. If the election so specifies, Stork Corporation will cease to have S status as of January 1, 2015.

In the case where S status is lost because of a disqualifying act (involuntarily), the loss of the election takes effect as of the date on which the event occurs.

Example 34	Crow Corporation has been a calendar year S corporation for several years. On August 13, 2014, one of its shareholders sells her stock to Kite Corporation. Because Crow Corporation no longer satisfies the definition of a small business corporation (it has another corporation as a shareholder), the election has been involuntarily terminated. For calendar year 2014, therefore, Crow will be an S corporation through August 12 and a regular corporation from August 13 through December 31, 2014.

Barring certain exceptions, the loss of the election places the corporation in a five-year holding period before S status can be reelected.

20-5b Operational Rules

The S corporation is primarily a tax-reporting rather than a taxpaying entity. In this respect, the entity is taxed much like a partnership.[43] Under the conduit concept, the taxable income and losses of an S corporation flow through to the shareholders who report them on their personal income tax returns.

To ascertain the annual tax consequences to each shareholder, it is necessary to carry out two steps at the S corporation level. First, all corporate transactions that will flow through to the shareholders on an *as is* basis under the conduit approach must be set aside. Second, what remains is aggregated as the taxable income of the S corporation and is allocated to each shareholder on a per-share and per-day of stock ownership basis.[44]

Separately Stated Items

Following are some of the items that do not lose their identity as they pass through the S corporation and are therefore picked up by each shareholder on an *as is* basis:

- Tax-exempt income.
- Long-term and short-term capital gains and losses.
- Section 1231 gains and losses.
- Charitable contributions.
- Domestic production activities deduction (DPAD).
- Qualified dividend income.
- Foreign tax credits.
- Depletion.
- Nonbusiness income or loss under § 212.
- Intangible drilling costs.
- Investment interest, income, and expenses covered under § 163(d).
- Certain portfolio income.
- Passive activity gains, losses, and credits under § 469.
- AMT adjustments and tax preference items.

In the case of the DPAD, the individual components needed to determine the deduction at the shareholder level must be broken out. These components include each shareholder's pro rata portion of QPAI and the W–2 wages paid by the corporation. This information is listed on Schedule K–1 (Form 1120S) and is picked up by the shareholder on lines 7 and 17 of his or her Form 8903 (Domestic Production Activities Deduction).

---

[43]This is not to imply that an S corporation is always free from the income tax. For example, a tax may be imposed on certain built-in gains or certain excessive passive investment income.

[44]§ 1366.

TAX IN THE NEWS   What Are Your Services Worth?

In an S corporation setting, the shareholder-employees tend to minimize the true value of their services. Why? Salaries are subject to payroll taxes, whereas a distribution of earnings is not. Unlike the case with C corporations where salaries generate a tax deduction, S corporations are indifferent about deductions because they are not subject to the income tax. Thus, the motivation is clear: keep salaries low and profits high.

The IRS is well aware of this ploy and is on the lookout for shareholder-employees with low self-esteem (and low salaries). In a recent case, the sole owner of a real estate brokerage firm found out that his services were worth more than $0. In a summary opinion, the Tax Court found that Sean McAlary was really worth a salary of $83,200. Considering the payroll taxes, interest, and penalties that resulted, Sean paid a steep price to learn that his services were not worthless.

In the preceding list, the items are separately stated because each may lead to a different tax result when combined with a particular shareholder's other transactions.

Example 35

Arnold and Jean are equal shareholders in Lark Corporation (an S corporation). For calendar year 2014, each must account for one-half of a corporate short-term capital gain of $6,000. Arnold has no other capital asset transactions, and Jean has a short-term capital loss of $3,000 from the sale of stock in IBM Corporation. In terms of overall effect, the difference between the two taxpayers is significant. Although both must report the short-term capital gain pass-through, Jean will neutralize its inclusion in gross income by offsetting it with the $3,000 short-term capital loss from the sale of the IBM stock. For Arnold, the short-term capital gain pass-through results in a $3,000 increase in his taxable income.

Taxable Income

After the separately stated items have been removed, the balance represents the taxable income of the S corporation. In arriving at taxable income, the dividends received deduction, the DPAD, and the NOL deduction are not allowed. An S corporation does come under the regular corporate rules, however, for purposes of amortization of organizational expenditures.

Once taxable income has been determined, it passes through to each shareholder as of the last day of the S corporation's tax year.

Example 36

Harrier Corporation, a calendar year S corporation, had the following transactions during the current year:

Sales		$ 400,000
Cost of goods sold		(230,000)
Other income		
*Tax-exempt interest	$ 3,000	
*Long-term capital gain	5,000	8,000
Other expenses		
*Charitable contributions	$ 4,000	
Advertising expense	15,000	
Other operating expenses	20,000	
*Short-term capital loss	1,500	(40,500)
Net income per books		$ 137,500

When the items that are to be separately stated [those preceded by an asterisk (*)] and shown *as is* by each shareholder are withdrawn, Harrier has the following taxable income:

Sales		$ 400,000
Cost of goods sold		(230,000)
Other expenses		
Advertising expense	$15,000	
Other operating expenses	20,000	(35,000)
Taxable income		$ 135,000

Example 37

If Oscar owned 10% of the stock in Harrier Corporation (refer to Example 36) during all of the current year, he must account for the following:

Separately stated items	
Tax-exempt interest	$ 300
Long-term capital gain	500
Charitable contributions	400
Short-term capital loss	150
Taxable income (10% of $135,000)	13,500

Some of the separately stated items (e.g., the tax-exempt interest) must be reported on Oscar's individual income tax return but may not lead to tax consequences. Oscar picks up his share of Harrier's taxable income ($13,500) as ordinary income.

Treatment of Losses

As previously noted, separately stated loss items (e.g., capital losses and § 1231 losses) flow through to the shareholders on an *as is* basis. Their treatment by a shareholder depends on the shareholder's individual income tax position. If the S corporation's taxable income determination results in an operating loss, it also passes through to the shareholders. As is the case with separately stated items, the amount of the loss each shareholder receives depends upon the stock ownership during the year.

Example 38

In 2014, Oriole Corporation (a calendar year S corporation) incurred an operating loss of $365,000. During 2014, Jason's ownership in Oriole was 20% for 200 days and 30% for 165 days. Jason's share of the loss is determined as follows:

[$365,000 × (200/365)] × 20% =	$40,000
[$365,000 × (165/365)] × 30% =	49,500
Total loss for Jason	$89,500

Presuming that the basis limitation does not come into play (see the following discussion), Jason deducts $89,500 in arriving at adjusted gross income.

THE BIG PICTURE

Example 39

Return to the facts of *The Big Picture* on p. 20-1. Recall that the Todd sisters anticipate losses in the early years of their catering business. If they form a C corporation, such losses will be of no benefit to the new corporation—no carryback will be available, and there will be only a potential for a delayed carryover. With an S election, however, losses pass through currently. Thus, the sisters will secure limited liability for their business and the immediate tax benefit of any losses.

Basis Determination

A shareholder's *basis* in the stock of an S corporation, like that of a regular corporation, is the original investment plus additional capital contributions less return of capital distributions. At this point, however, the symmetry disappears. Generally, basis is increased by the pass-through of income items (including those separately stated) and decreased by the loss items (including those separately stated).[45]

In 2014, Warbler Corporation is formed with an investment of $500,000, of which Janice contributed $100,000 for a 20% stock interest. A timely S election is made, and for 2014, Warbler earns taxable income of $50,000. Janice's basis in her stock investment now becomes $110,000 [$100,000 (original capital contribution) + $10,000 (the 20% share of the corporation's taxable income assigned to Janice)].	**Example 40**

Distributions by an S corporation reduce the basis of a shareholder's stock investment. However, if the amount of the distribution exceeds basis, the excess normally receives capital gain treatment.

As previously noted, operating losses of an S corporation pass through to the shareholders and reduce the basis in their stock investment. Because the basis of the stock cannot fall below zero, an excess loss is then applied against the basis of any loans the shareholder may have made to the corporation.

Flamingo Corporation, a calendar year S corporation, has an operating loss of $60,000 for 2014. Norman, a 50% shareholder, has an adjusted basis of $25,000 in his stock investment and has made loans to the corporation of $5,000. Based on these facts, Norman may take full advantage of the $30,000 loss (50% of $60,000) on his 2014 individual income tax return. Norman's basis in the stock and the loans must be reduced accordingly, and both will be zero after the pass-through.	**Example 41**

In the event the basis limitation precludes an operating loss from being absorbed, the loss can be carried forward and deducted when and if it is covered by basis.

Assume the same facts as in Example 41, except that Norman had not made any loans to Flamingo Corporation. Further assume that Flamingo has taxable income of $15,000 in the following year (2015). Norman's tax situation for 2014 and 2015 is summarized as follows:	**Example 42**

Ordinary loss for 2014 (limited to basis of investment)	$25,000
Income to be reported in 2015 (50% of $15,000)	7,500
Restoration of stock basis in 2015 (50% of $15,000)	7,500
Loss allowed for 2015 carried over from 2014:	
($30,000 − $25,000)	5,000
Basis in stock account after 2015 ($7,500 − $5,000)	2,500

Thus, Norman's unabsorbed loss of $5,000 from 2014 carries over to 2015 and is applied against the $7,500 of ordinary income for that year.

ETHICS & EQUITY   Income Tax Basis That Does Not Change?

In 2000, Howard purchased stock in Green, a C corporation, for $100,000. In 2006, Green made a valid election under Subchapter S. In 2014, Howard sells his stock in Green for $120,000.

Because he paid $100,000 for the stock, Howard plans to recognize a long-term capital gain of $20,000 as a result of the sale. Do you agree with Howard's proposed reporting?

---

[45]§ 1367.

20-6 PARTNERSHIPS

LO.8

Review the tax consequences of forming and operating a partnership.

Another choice of business entity to consider is a partnership. A partnership must have more than one owner. It has some similarities with corporations, particularly S corporations.

20-6a Nature of Partnership Taxation

Unlike corporations, partnerships are not considered separate taxable entities. Each member of a partnership is subject to income tax on the partner's distributive share of the partnership's income, even if an actual distribution is not made. The tax return (Form 1065) required of a partnership serves only to provide information necessary in determining the character and amount of each partner's distributive share of the partnership's income and expense. Because a partnership acts as a conduit, items that pass through to the partners do not lose their identity. For example, tax-exempt income earned by a partnership is picked up by the partners as tax-exempt income. In this regard, partnerships function in much the same fashion as S corporations, which also serve as conduits.

A partnership is considered a separate taxable entity for purposes of making various elections and selecting its taxable year, method of depreciation, and accounting method. A partnership is also treated as a separate legal entity under civil law with the right to own property in its own name and to transact business free from the personal debts of its partners.

20-6b Partnership Formation and Basis

Recognition of Gain or Loss

The general rule is that no gain or loss is recognized by a partnership or any of its partners on the contribution of property in exchange for a capital interest in the partnership.[46] This rule also applies to all subsequent contributions of property.

There are certain exceptions to the nonrecognition of gain or loss rule, including the following:

- If a partner transfers property to the partnership and receives money or other consideration (boot) as a result, the transaction will be treated as a sale or exchange rather than as a contribution of capital. Realized gain is recognized to the extent of the fair market value of the boot received.
- If a partnership interest is received in exchange for services rendered or to be rendered by the partner to the partnership, the fair market value of the transferred capital interest is regarded as compensation for services rendered. In such cases, the recipient of the capital interest must recognize the amount as ordinary income in the year actually or constructively received.
- If property that is subject to a liability in excess of its basis is contributed to a partnership, the contributing partner may recognize gain.

Basis of a Partnership Interest

The contributing *partner's basis* in the partnership interest received is the sum of money contributed plus the adjusted basis of any other property transferred to the partnership.[47]

Example 43

In return for the contribution of property (with a basis of $50,000 and a fair market value of $80,000) and cash of $10,000 to the Brown Partnership, Marcia receives a 10% capital interest worth $90,000. Although Marcia has a realized gain of $30,000 ($90,000 − $60,000) on the transfer, none of the gain is recognized. The basis of her interest in the Brown Partnership is $60,000 [$50,000 (basis of property contributed) + $10,000 (cash contribution)].

---

[46]§ 721.   [47]§ 722.

A partner's basis in the partnership interest is determined without regard to any amount reflected on the partnership's books as capital, equity, or a similar account.

> **Example 44**
>
> Marge and Clyde form the equal Blue Partnership with a cash contribution of $300,000 from Marge and a property contribution (adjusted basis of $180,000 and fair market value of $300,000) from Clyde. Although the books of the Blue Partnership may reflect a credit of $300,000 to each partner's capital account, only Marge has a tax basis of $300,000 in her partnership interest. Clyde's tax basis in his partnership interest is $180,000, the amount of his tax basis in the property contributed to the partnership.

After its initial determination, the basis of a partnership interest is subject to continuous fluctuations. A partner's basis is increased by additional contributions and the sum of his or her current and prior years' distributive share of the following:

- Taxable income of the partnership, including capital gains.
- Tax-exempt income of the partnership.
- The excess of the deductions for depletion over the basis of the partnership's property subject to depletion.[48]

Similarly, the basis of a partner's interest is decreased, but not below zero, by distributions of partnership property (including cash) and by the sum of the current and prior years' distributive share of the following:

- Partnership losses, including capital losses.
- Partnership expenditures that are not deductible in computing taxable income or loss and that are not capital expenditures.

Changes in the liabilities (including trade accounts payable and bank loans) of a partnership also affect the basis of a partnership interest. A partner's basis is increased by his or her assumption of partnership liabilities and by his or her pro rata share of liabilities incurred by the partnership. Likewise, the partner's basis is decreased by the amount of any personal liabilities assumed by the partnership and by the pro rata share of any decreases in the liabilities of the partnership.

> **Example 45**
>
> Tony, Martha, and Carolyn form the Orange Partnership with the following contributions: cash of $100,000 from Tony for a 50% interest in capital and profits, cash of $50,000 from Martha for a 25% interest, and property valued at $66,000 from Carolyn for a 25% interest. The property contributed by Carolyn has an adjusted basis of $30,000 and is subject to a mortgage of $16,000, which is assumed by the partnership. Carolyn's basis in her interest in the Orange Partnership is $18,000, determined as follows:
>
> | | |
> |---|---:|
> | Adjusted basis of Carolyn's contributed property | $ 30,000 |
> | Less portion of mortgage assumed by Tony and Martha and treated as a distribution of money to Carolyn (75% of $16,000) | (12,000) |
> | Basis of Carolyn's interest in Orange Partnership | $ 18,000 |

> **Example 46**
>
> Assuming the same facts as in Example 45, Tony and Martha have a basis in their partnership interests of $108,000 and $54,000, respectively.
>
> | | Tony | Martha |
> |---|---:|---:|
> | Cash contribution | $100,000 | $50,000 |
> | Plus portion of mortgage assumed and treated as an additional cash contribution: | | |
> | (50% of $16,000) | 8,000 | |
> | (25% of $16,000) | | 4,000 |
> | Basis of interest in Orange Partnership | $108,000 | $54,000 |

[48]§ 705(a).

Partnership's Basis in Contributed Property

The *basis of property* contributed to a partnership by a partner is the adjusted basis of the property to the contributing partner at the time of the contribution.[49] In addition, the holding period of the property for the partnership includes the period during which the property was held by the contributing partner. This is logical because the partnership's basis in the property is the same basis the property had in the hands of the partner.[50]

Example 47

In 2014, Roger contributed equipment with an adjusted basis of $100,000 and fair market value of $300,000 to the Red Partnership in exchange for a one-third interest in the partnership. No gain or loss is recognized by Roger. The Red Partnership's basis in the equipment is $100,000. If Roger had acquired the equipment in 2010, the partnership's holding period would include the period from 2010 through 2014.

20-6c Partnership Operation

Measuring and Reporting Partnership Income

Although a partnership is not subject to Federal income taxation, it is required to determine its taxable income and file an income tax return for information purposes.[51] The tax return, Form 1065, is due on the fifteenth day of the fourth month following the close of the taxable year of the partnership.

In measuring and reporting partnership income, certain transactions must be segregated and reported separately on the partnership return. Items such as charitable contributions, the domestic production activities deduction, capital gains and losses, qualified dividend income, and foreign taxes are excluded from partnership taxable income and are allocated separately to the partners.[52] These items must be segregated and allocated separately because they affect the computation of various exclusions, deductions, and credits at the individual partner level.

Similar to the procedure for an S corporation, the individual components needed to determine the DPAD at the partner level must be separated. These components include each partner's pro rata portion of QPAI and the W–2 wages paid by the partnership. This information is listed on Schedule K–1 (Form 1065) and is picked up by the partner on lines 7 and 17 of his or her Form 8903 (Domestic Production Activities Deduction).

The separate stating of certain attributes of the partnership is essential as they may result in differing tax consequences when passed through to the various partners.

Example 48

Alyssa, Madison, and Brad are equal partners in the Yellow Partnership. All parties use the calendar year for tax purposes. Among other transactions, Yellow had the following separately stated items for 2014: $30,000 in QPAI, $15,000 in long-term capital gains, and $6,000 in charitable contributions. The pass-through of these items generates the following results: Alyssa cannot use all of her $10,000 share of QPAI because of the AGI limitation; Madison's $5,000 long-term capital gain is not subject to tax (i.e., she is in a 15% or lower tax bracket); and Brad cannot benefit from his $2,000 share of the charitable contribution as he chooses not to itemize (i.e., claims the standard deduction). Thus, the pass-through of these separately stated items caused different tax consequences to the partners.

---

[49]§ 723.
[50]§ 1223(2).

[51]§ 6031.
[52]§ 702(a).

A second step in the measurement and reporting process is the computation of the partnership's ordinary income or loss. The taxable income of a partnership is computed in the same manner as the taxable income of an individual taxpayer. However, a partnership is not allowed the following deductions:[53]

- The deduction for personal and dependency exemptions.
- The deduction for taxes paid to foreign countries or possessions of the United States.
- The deduction for charitable contributions.
- The deduction for net operating losses.
- The additional itemized deductions allowed individuals in §§ 211 through 219.

The partnership's ordinary income or loss and each of the items requiring separate treatment are reported in the partnership's information return and allocated to the partners in accordance with their distributive shares.

Limitation on Partner's Share of Losses

A partner's deduction of the distributive share of partnership losses (including capital losses) could be limited. The limitation is the adjusted basis of the partnership interest at the end of the partnership year in which the losses were incurred.

The limitation for partnership loss deductions is similar to that applicable to losses of S corporations. Like S corporation losses, partnership losses may be carried forward by the partner and utilized against future increases in the basis of the partnership interest. Such increases might result from additional capital contributions to the partnership, from additional partnership liabilities, or from future partnership income. Unlike S corporations, however, loans to the entity cannot be utilized by a partner to absorb the pass-through of losses.

Florence and Donald do business as the Green Partnership, sharing profits and losses equally. All parties use the calendar year for tax purposes. As of January 1, 2014, Florence's basis in her partnership interest is $25,000. The partnership sustained an operating loss of $80,000 in 2014 and earned a profit of $70,000 in 2015. For the calendar year 2014, Florence may claim only $25,000 of her $40,000 distributive share of the partnership loss (one-half of the $80,000 loss). As a result, the basis in her partnership interest is reduced to zero as of January 1, 2015, and she must carry forward the remaining $15,000 of partnership losses.

Example 49

Assuming the same facts as in Example 49, what are the income tax consequences for Florence in 2015? Because the partnership earned a profit of $70,000 for the calendar year 2015, Florence reports income from the partnership of $20,000 ($35,000 distributive share of income for 2015 less the $15,000 loss not allowed for 2014). The adjusted basis of her partnership interest now becomes $20,000.

Example 50

Transactions between Partner and Partnership

A partner engaging in a transaction with the partnership is generally regarded as a nonpartner or an outsider. However, the Code includes certain exceptions to prevent unwarranted tax avoidance in related-party situations. For instance, losses from the sale or exchange of property are disallowed if they arise in either of the following cases:

- Between a partnership and a person whose direct or indirect interest in the capital or profits of the partnership is more than 50 percent.
- Between two partnerships in which the same persons own more than a 50 percent interest in the capital or profits.[54]

---

[53]§ 703(a).

[54]§ 707(b)(1).

An indirect interest includes those owned by family members (e.g., parents, children, brothers, and sisters).

Example 51

Michael, Samantha, and Sarah (brother and sisters) are equal partners in the Beige Partnership. For purposes of the 50% related-party rules described above, each partner indirectly owns the interests of the others. Thus, Michael has a 100% interest (i.e., his one-third *direct* interest plus the two-thirds *indirect* interests of his sisters) in the Beige Partnership.

In a related-party situation, if one of the purchasers later sells the property, any gain realized will be recognized only to the extent that it exceeds the loss previously disallowed.

Example 52

Pat owns a 60% interest in the capital and profits of the Rose Partnership. In the current year, Pat sells property with an adjusted basis of $50,000 to the partnership for its fair market value of $35,000. The $15,000 loss is not deductible because Pat's ownership interest is more than 50%. If the Rose Partnership later sells the property for $40,000, none of the $5,000 gain (sale price of $40,000 less adjusted basis to partnership of $35,000) will be recognized because it is offset by $5,000 of the previously disallowed loss of $15,000. The unused loss of $10,000, however, is of no tax benefit either to the partnership or to Pat.

Payments made by a partnership to one of its partners for services rendered or for the use of capital, to the extent they are determined without regard to the income of the partnership, are treated by the partnership in the same manner as payments made to a person who is not a partner. Referred to as **guaranteed payments**, these are generally deductible by the partnership as a business expense.[55] The payments must be reported as ordinary income by the receiving partner and do not affect the partner's basis in the partnership interest. Their deductibility distinguishes guaranteed payments from a partner's distributive share of income that is not deductible by the partnership.

Example 53

Under the terms of the Silver Partnership agreement, Kim is entitled to a fixed annual salary of $60,000 without regard to the income of the partnership. He is also to share in the profits and losses of the partnership as a one-third partner. After deducting the guaranteed payment, the partnership has $300,000 of ordinary income. Kim must include $160,000 as ordinary income on his income tax return for his tax year with or within which the partnership tax year ends ($60,000 guaranteed payment + $100,000 one-third distributive share of partnership income).

Other Partnership Considerations

Complex tax provisions involving liquidating and nonliquidating distributions and the sale of a partnership interest are beyond the scope of this text and are discussed in depth in *South-Western Federal Taxation: Corporations, Partnerships, Estates & Trusts.*

20-7 TAX PLANNING

LO.9

Identify the advantages and disadvantages of the various forms for conducting a business.

As with individuals, tax planning is important for corporations and partnerships to ensure proper application of the tax law and to avoid paying more tax than legally required.

---

[55]§ 707(c).

TAX IN THE NEWS   Tax Rates and Choice of Entity

Since enactment of the Tax Reform Act of 1986 (TRA86), there has been a slight decline in the number of C corporations and a steady increase in the number of pass-through entities. The graph produced here, provided by the congressional Joint Committee on Taxation, illustrates this trend. The graph is from a 2012 report, *Selected Issues Relating to Choice of Business Entity*, prepared for the House Ways and Means Committee for a hearing held on March 7, 2012, *Treatment of Closely-Held Businesses in the Context of Tax Reform*. Two key reasons underlie these trends. First, TRA86 lowered the top individual tax rate from 50 percent to 28 percent and the top corporate rate from

46 percent to 34 percent. This was the first time the top individual income tax rate was lower than the top corporate income tax rate, making the pass-through entity form more popular than the C corporation form for individual business owners. Second, since 1986, more states allow the LLC form of entity.

Related links:

- Full text of the JCT report: **www.jct.gov/publications.html?func=startdown&id=4402**.
- Video and testimony for the March 2012 hearing: **http://waysandmeans.house.gov/calendar/eventsingle.aspx?EventID=282644**.

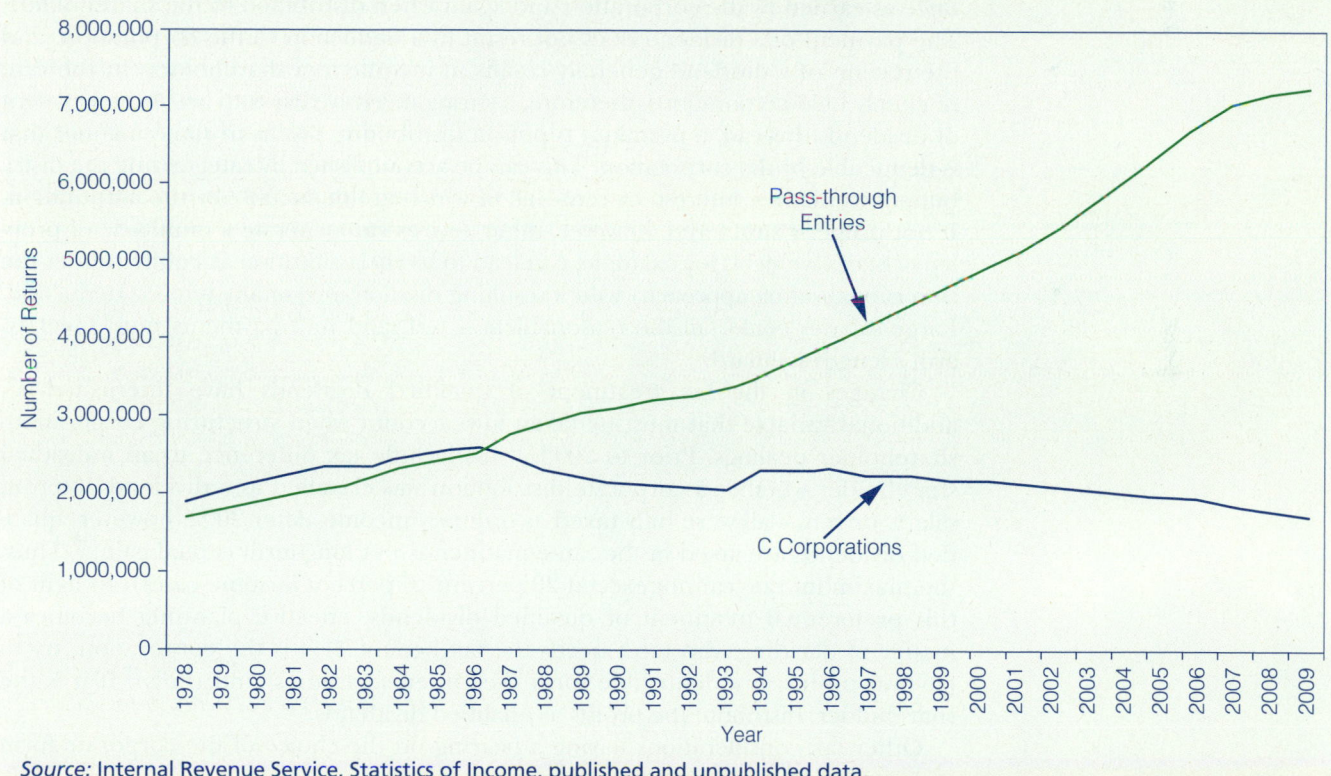

Number of C Corporation Returns Compared to the Sum of S Corporation and Partnership Returns, 1978–2009

Source: Internal Revenue Service, Statistics of Income, published and unpublished data.

20-7a Corporate versus Noncorporate Forms of Business Organization

Nontax Considerations

The decision of which entity to use in conducting a trade or business must be weighed carefully. Of prime importance are nontax considerations, including the legal attributes of the business entity chosen. For the corporate form, those commonly include limited liability, continuity of life, free transferability of interests, and centralized management. Many, if not all, of these attributes can also be obtained through the use of a limited liability company. When nontax considerations are evaluated, close attention must be paid to applicable state law. Many states, for example, place severe restrictions on the use of corporations to practice certain professions (e.g., medicine and law). Likewise, the legal attributes of an LLC may vary from one state to another and may not be identical to those of corporations.

Tax Considerations

The applicable income tax rates will affect the choice of the form of doing business. Because of the wide range of possibilities (10 to 39.6 percent for individuals in 2014 and 15 to 35 percent for corporations), this factor must be evaluated on a case-by-case basis. For example, the corporate form is very appealing if the anticipated taxable income falls within the 25 percent corporate bracket and the shareholder's individual bracket is 39.6 percent. Here, the time value of the taxes saved could make operating a business as a corporation advantageous. Do not, moreover, overlook the potential impact of state and local income taxes applicable to individuals and corporations. Also, in those states that do not have an income tax, a franchise tax can pose an added tax burden on corporations (see Chapter 1).

Unless an election is made under Subchapter S, operating as a corporation yields a potential double tax result. Corporate-source income will be taxed twice—once as earned by the corporation and again when distributed to the shareholders. The payment of a dividend does not result in a deduction to the corporation, and the receipt of a dividend generally results in income to a shareholder. In the case of closely held corporations, therefore, a strong incentive exists to avoid the payment of dividends. Instead, a premium is put on distributing profits in some manner that is deductible by the corporation. This can be accomplished by categorizing the distributions as salaries, interest, or rent—all of which are deductible by the corporation. If not properly structured, however, these devices can generate a multitude of problems. Excessive debt, for example, can lead to its reclassification as equity (under the thin capitalization approach) with a resulting disallowance of any interest deduction. Large salaries could fail the reasonableness test, and rent payments must meet an arm's length standard.

Changes in the tax treatment of qualified dividends have interjected an additional variable that must be taken into account when structuring corporation-shareholder dealings. Prior to 2003, it made little tax difference to an individual shareholder whether a corporate distribution was classified as a dividend, interest, salary, or rent—all were fully taxed as ordinary income. After 2002, however, qualified dividends are taxed in the same manner as net long-term capital gain.[56] Thus, the maximum rate cannot exceed 20 percent (0 percent in some cases). In light of this preferential treatment of qualified dividends, effective planning becomes a matter of deciding who most needs the tax benefit. If it is the corporation, try to pay out profits in a deductible form (i.e., interest, salaries, and rents). If it is the shareholder, distribute the profits as qualified dividends.[57]

Other tax considerations having a bearing on the choice of the corporate form to operate a business are summarized below:

- Corporate-source income loses its identity as it passes through the corporation to the shareholders. Thus, items possessing preferential tax treatment (e.g., interest on municipal bonds) are not taxed as such to the shareholders.
- As noted earlier, it may be difficult for shareholders to recover some or all of their investment in the corporation without a dividend income result. Recall that most corporate distributions are treated as dividends to the extent of the corporation's E & P. Structuring the capital of the corporation to include debt is a partial solution to this problem. Thus, the shareholder-creditor

---

[56] § 1(h)(3)(B).

[57] The 20% rate is applicable only to those in the 39.6% tax bracket. Most middle income taxpayers will be subject to a 15% rate.

could recoup part of his or her investment through the tax-free payment of principal. Too much debt, however, may lead to the debt being reclassified as equity.

- Corporate losses cannot be passed through to the shareholders.
- The domestic production activities deduction generated by the corporation is not available to its shareholders. The deduction has become even more attractive as the applicable rate has progressed from 6 to 9 percent.
- The liquidation of a corporation may generate tax consequences to both the corporation and its shareholders. Even when the corporation being liquidated does not sell its assets but distributes them in kind (i.e., "as is") to the shareholders, gain (or loss) is not avoided. The corporation must treat the distribution as a sale and recognize gain or loss measured by the fair market value of the assets involved.
- The corporate form provides the shareholders with the opportunity to be treated as employees for tax purposes if they render services to the corporation. This status makes a number of attractive tax-sheltered fringe benefits available (e.g., group term life insurance). These benefits are not available to partners and sole proprietors.

ETHICS & EQUITY   Making Good Use of the Statute of Limitations

In 2000, Mason purchased 1,000 shares of Goldfinch Corporation for $100,000. He planned to hold Goldfinch, a C corporation engaged in oil and gas exploration, as an investment. In 2001, Mason received a $20,000 distribution from Goldfinch, which was designated by the corporation as a "return of capital." However, upon audit of Goldfinch in 2008, the IRS determined that the 2001 distribution was not a return of capital but was a taxable dividend.

In the current year, Mason sells his 1,000 shares of Goldfinch for $250,000 and plans to recognize a long-term capital gain of $150,000. He believes that any adjustments normally required by the 2001 distribution and the 2008 IRS audit are barred by the statute of limitations. Is Mason correct? Why or why not?

20-7b Regular Corporation versus S Status

Due to the pass-through concept, the use of S status generally avoids the income tax at the corporate level, bringing the individual income tax into play. As noted in the previous section, the differential between the rates applicable to noncorporate and corporate taxpayers makes this a factor to be considered. The S election enables a business to operate in the corporate form; avoid the corporate income tax; and, depending on taxable income, possibly take advantage of the lower rates usually applicable to individuals. Also, losses incurred at the corporate level pass through to the shareholders, who will utilize them on their individual returns.

Electing S status can present several problems, however. First, the election is available only to small business corporations. Consequently, many corporations will not qualify for the election. Second, S corporations are subject to the rules governing regular corporations unless otherwise specified in the Code. For example, § 351 applies on the formation of an S corporation. Likewise, if the S corporation later carries out a stock redemption or is liquidated, the rules governing regular corporations apply. Third, a few states do not recognize S status for purposes of state and local taxation or recognize them but subject them to tax at both the entity and shareholder levels. Therefore, an S corporation might be subject to a state franchise tax or a state or local income tax.

20-7c Use of an Entity to Reduce the Family Income Tax Burden

One objective of tax planning is to keep the income from a business within the family unit but to disperse the income in such a manner as to minimize the overall tax burden. To the extent feasible, therefore, income should be shifted from higher-bracket to lower-bracket family members.

A recent legislative change, however, has raised major obstacles to shifting income to children. Beginning in 2008, the kiddie tax applies to all children under age 19 *and* to those who are full-time students under age 24.[58] As a result, shifting investment income (or capital gains) to a child provides no benefit to the extent that the income is taxed at the parents' tax rate.

Unfortunately, the income from property (a business) cannot be shifted to another without also transferring an interest in the property. If, for example, a father wants to assign income from his sole proprietorship to his children, he must form a partnership or incorporate the business. In either case, the transfer of the interest may be subject to the Federal gift tax. But any potential gift tax can be eliminated or controlled through judicious use of the annual exclusion, the election to split gifts (for married donors), and the unified tax credit (refer to the discussion of the Federal gift tax in Chapter 1).

Consequently, the first problem to be resolved becomes which form of business organization will best fit the objective of income shifting. For the partnership form, one major obstacle arises. Family partnership rules preclude the assignment of income to a family member unless capital is a material income-producing factor.[59] If not, the family member must contribute substantial or vital services. Ordinarily, capital is not a material income-producing factor if the income of the business consists principally of compensation for personal services performed by members or employees of the partnership. Conversely, capital is a material income-producing factor if the operation of the business entails a substantial investment in physical assets (e.g., inventory, plant, machinery, or equipment).

Income shifting through the use of a partnership, therefore, may be ineffectual if a personal service business is involved. In fact, it could be hopeless if the assignees are minors. The use of the corporate form usually involves no such impediment. Regardless of the nature of the business, a gift of stock carries with it the attributes of ownership. Thus, dividends paid on stock are taxed to the owner of the stock.

But what if the corporate form is utilized and the S election is made? A new hurdle arises. The Code authorizes the IRS to make adjustments in situations where shareholders are not being adequately compensated for the value of their services or capital provided to an S corporation in a family setting.[60] Thus, an S corporation suffers from the same vulnerability that exists with family partnerships.

A further factor that favors the corporate form (either a regular or an S corporation) as a device for income splitting is the ease with which it can be carried out. Presuming the entity already exists, the transfer of stock merely requires an entry in the corporation's stock ledger account. In contrast, a gift of a partnership interest probably requires an amendment to the articles of copartnership.

Regardless of the form of organization used for the business, income shifting will not take place unless the transfer is complete.[61] If the donor continues to exercise control over the interest transferred and does not recognize and protect the ownership rights of the donee, the IRS may argue that the transfer is ineffective for tax purposes. In that case, the income from the transferred interest continues to be taxed to the donor.

---

[58] The kiddie tax is restricted to *unearned* income (e.g., interest, dividends) and does not apply to *earned* income (e.g., wages, salaries). See the discussion of § 1(g) in Chapter 3.

[59] § 704(e).

[60] § 1366(e).

[61] *Ginsberg v. Comm.*, 74–2 USTC ¶9660, 34 AFTR 2d 74–5760, 502 F.2d 965 (CA–6, 1974), and *Michael F. Beirne*, 61 T.C. 268 (1973).

CHOICE OF BUSINESS ENTITY

A principal concern of the Todd sisters is limited liability. A food preparation business involves a high risk in terms of potential liability (e.g., litigation resulting from food poisoning). This hazard is further magnified by the sisters' intention to carry minimal liability insurance coverage. To obtain limited liability, therefore, the choice of entity cannot be a regular partnership—it must be a C or S corporation or a limited liability company (LLC). (Example 1)

The next concern is the pass-through of losses to the sisters in the early years of the business. This cannot be achieved with a C corporation and is only available with an S corporation or an LLC. (Examples 1 and 39)

In making the choice between a corporation and an LLC, the future must be considered. If the business is successful, the sisters could expand. This is more easily accomplished with a corporation than an LLC. A corporation can raise additional capital for expansion by issuing more stock—even going public if necessary. Issuing additional stock may cause the S corporation election to be lost, but by then, S status will have served its purpose (i.e., pass-through of losses).

When forming the corporation, the sisters should take the following into account:

- Key assets (e.g., food preparation facilities) might better be purchased by the sisters and leased to the corporation. This approach leads to a rent deduction for the corporation. (Example 21)
- A viable salary structure should be established for the services the sisters perform. This generates a salary deduction for the corporation. (Example 28)
- Interest should be charged for the funds the sisters loan to the corporation. This yields an interest deduction for the corporation. (Example 28)

If the S corporation becomes a C corporation, these rent, salary, and interest deductions will reduce the taxable income of the corporation and thereby lower any corporate income tax imposed.

© Gary Woods/Alamy

Key Terms

C corporation, 20-4	Guaranteed payments, 20-34	Schedule M–1, 20-15
Check-the-box Regulations, 20-3	Limited liability company (LLC), 20-3	Schedule M–3, 20-17
Constructive dividends, 20-23	Organizational expenditures, 20-13	Small business corporation, 20-25
Dividends received deduction, 20-10	Personal service corporation, 20-14	Thin capitalization, 20-17
Earnings and profits, 20-22	S corporation, 20-25	

Discussion Questions

1. **LO.1** What purpose is served by the check-the-box Regulations?

2. **LO.1, 9** Why are limited liability companies advantageous?

3. **LO.1** Presuming that no election is made under the check-the-box Regulations, how will the following businesses be treated for Federal income tax purposes?
   a. A one-person entity not incorporated under state law.
   b. A one-person entity incorporated under state law.
   c. A multi-owner entity not incorporated under state law and possessing all of the characteristics common to corporations (i.e., continuity of life, centralized management, limited liability, and free transferability of interests).

4. **LO.1** For calendar year 2011, Mario filed a Form 8332 and elected to treat his sole proprietorship as a C corporation. For 2014, he wants to revert back to a sole proprietorship for tax purposes.
   a. Why might Mario want to make the change?
   b. Is this change permitted under the check-the-box Regulations?

5. **LO.1** The Owen brothers have obtained financing to start a new venture. The business will be high-risk as to potential liability and is expected to incur losses before becoming profitable. What type of entity might the Owens consider using?

6. **LO.2, 3** Contrast the income taxation of individuals and C corporations as to each of the following:
   a. Alternative minimum tax.
   b. Dividend income.
   c. Use of the cash method of accounting.
   d. Accounting period used for tax purposes.
   e. Applicable tax rates.
   f. Due date of the tax return.

Issue ID
7. **LO.2** Brown purchased a stock investment on March 4, 2013. The investment has substantially appreciated in value, and Brown plans to sell and recognize the gain. The sale date would be either March 4, 2014, or March 5, 2014. What difference does the sale date make if Brown is:
   a. An individual?
   b. A C corporation?

Issue ID
8. **LO.2** A C corporation invests and trades in real estate. During the year, it sells a tract of land for a substantial loss. Because the land was held both for resale and as an investment, the loss could arguably be classified as ordinary or capital.
   a. In most cases, which classification will be preferable?
   b. Under what circumstances might the classification of the loss not make any immediate difference?

9. **LO.2, 7, 8** The taxpayer has excess capital losses (both short-term and long-term) for the current year. Discuss the income tax ramifications of the losses if the taxpayer is:
   a. An individual.
   b. A C corporation.
   c. An S corporation.
   d. A partnership.

10. **LO.2** In late December 2014, Gray Corporation (a calendar year C corporation) pledges a $50,000 donation to a local relief agency formed to fight AIDS in Africa. Although Gray's board of directors authorized the donation in 2014, the payment is not made until March 2015. What issues are involved?

11. **LO.2** If a C corporation donates ordinary income property to a qualified charity, the measure of the amount of the deduction is the adjusted basis of the property. Do you agree with this statement? Explain.

12. **LO.2** In connection with the domestic production activities deduction, what is the difference between individual and C corporation taxpayers?

13. **LO.2** Wren Corporation does no manufacturing but is engaged exclusively in marketing. Is it still possible that Wren may be able to claim a domestic production activities deduction (DPAD)? Explain.

14. **LO.2** Kite, a calendar year C corporation, incurs a net operating loss for 2014. What factors should be considered before Kite Corporation chooses to carry back the loss?

Issue ID
15. **LO.3** The dividends received deduction does not always completely eliminate the effect of taxation of dividend income at the corporate shareholder level. Explain this statement.

Issue ID
16. **LO.3** Two small C corporations have invested in the stock of IBM Corporation. Although they own the same number and type of shares, one corporation is able to claim a larger dividends received deduction than the other. Explain why this could be possible.

17. **LO.3** Some corporations may be able to avoid capitalizing and amortizing organizational expenditures. Explain.

18. **LO.3** Mallard Corporation was formed in December 2013 and plans to use the cash basis of accounting. Mallard incurred one-half of its organizational expenses in December 2013 and one-half in January 2014. The payment of these expenses also occurred in these two months. Do you recognize any income tax problem? Explain.

           Issue ID

19. **LO.4** Beige Corporation has lower taxable income than Drab Corporation. Yet Beige's marginal income tax rate is 39%, while Drab's marginal rate is 35%. Explain how this variance can occur.

           Issue ID

20. **LO.5** Small, closely held corporations are often formed with a minimum of capital investment. Key assets used in the business are then leased to the corporation by the shareholders. What are the advantages of this approach?

21. **LO.5** Cynthia and some associates want to form a corporation to develop and operate an industrial park. Cynthia is to contribute the land, which has significantly appreciated in value. She would like to recognize *some* of this gain to offset losses from other sources. In view of the rules governing the application of § 351, what do you suggest?

           Decision Making

22. **LO.6** Tom is one of the shareholders of Flamingo Corporation, a calendar year C corporation. During 2013, Tom receives a dividend distribution from Flamingo of $20,000. In early 2014, Flamingo notifies all of its shareholders that it incurred a net operating loss for 2013. How does the notification affect the tax treatment by Tom of the $20,000 he received in 2013?

           Issue ID

23. **LO.6** When a corporation distributes property as a dividend, what are the tax effects on the corporation and its shareholders under the following assumptions?
    a. The property has declined in value.
    b. The property has appreciated in value.

24. **LO.6** The stock of Grouse Corporation (a C corporation) is owned equally by a sister and two brothers: Mary, Rex, and Orson. During the year, the following transactions occur:
    a. Mary sells property to Grouse Corporation.
    b. Orson buys property from Grouse Corporation.
    c. Rex leases property from Grouse Corporation.
    d. Grouse Corporation pays for Orson's medical bills.
    e. All shareholders use an airplane owned by Grouse Corporation.
    f. Orson borrows money from Grouse Corporation.
    g. All shareholders are paid salaries by Grouse Corporation.
    h. All shareholders finance Grouse Corporation's capital acquisitions (e.g., machinery, equipment, land, and buildings) through the use of long-term debt.

           Issue ID

    Discuss any potential tax problems that these transactions might present.

25. **LO.7** A calendar year corporation has an election under Subchapter S. What will be the effect, if any, of the following events on its S status?
    a. The board of directors of the corporation revokes its S election in March of the current year.
    b. A shareholder who is a citizen of Mexico and works in San Antonio retires and moves back to Mexico.
    c. The corporation acquires an interest in a partnership.
    d. Because of the death of a shareholder, the total number of shareholders increases from 98 to 101.
    e. A shareholder transfers her stock to a newly formed LLC.

26. **LO.7** Roadrunner Corporation receives a dividend on its stock investment in General Electric Corporation. If Roadrunner is an S corporation, it cannot claim a dividends received deduction on the GE dividend. Therefore, the GE dividend will be subject to triple taxation. Comment on the accuracy of this last statement.

           Issue ID

27. **LO.7** Stork Corporation is a closely held C corporation that was formed several years ago. In 2010, Stork made an election to be treated as an S corporation. After obtaining

S status, Stork has consistently followed a practice of reducing the salaries of its share-holder employees. Could this practice be motivated by tax avoidance? Explain.

Issue ID   28. **LO.7** Alexis, Brayden, Brooke, and Charles are equal shareholders in Azul Corporation (a calendar year S corporation). During the year, Azul has a short-term capital loss, qualified dividend income, charitable contributions, and qualified production activities income (with related W–2 wages). Regarding these transactions, explain the following results:
   a. The short-term capital loss results in no additional tax benefit to Alexis.
   b. Brayden pays no tax on the qualified dividends.
   c. Brooke cannot claim a deduction for the charitable contributions.
   d. Charles cannot claim *all* of the domestic production activities deduction.

Issue ID   29. **LO.7** Cynthia and Doug are equal shareholders in Penguin, a calendar year S corporation. At the end of 2013, Penguin has an operating loss. Although Cynthia and Doug have the same basis in their Penguin stock, Cynthia can deduct all of her share of the corporation's loss, while Doug cannot. How can this result take place?

30. **LO.7, 8** S corporations and partnerships are categorized as "pass-through entities." Why?

31. **LO.8** Indicate whether each of the following will increase (+), decrease (−), or have no effect (*NE*) on a partner's basis in a partnership interest:
   a. Operating loss of the partnership.
   b. Capital gains of the partnership.
   c. Tax-exempt income of the partnership.
   d. Partnership expenditures that are not deductible in computing taxable income.
   e. Bank loans made to the partnership.
   f. The partnership pays off a mortgage on property it owns.
   g. Withdrawals by a partner that *are not* guaranteed payments.
   h. Withdrawals by a partner that *are* guaranteed payments.

Issue ID   32. **LO.8** Blaine, Cassie, and Kirstin are equal partners in the Maize Partnership. During the year, Maize has qualified dividends, charitable contributions, and a domestic production activities deduction. Explain the following results:
   a. Blaine pays less tax than Cassie and Kirstin on his share of the qualified dividends.
   b. Cassie cannot deduct any of her share of the charitable contributions.
   c. Kirstin has a larger domestic production activities deduction than either Blaine or Cassie.

Issue ID   33. **LO.8** Carlos and his parents are equal partners in the Puce Partnership. Carlos sells property to Puce for a realized loss. Puce later sells the property to a third party (i.e., an outsider) for a realized gain. Identify the issues involved.

34. **LO.8** What are guaranteed payments? When might such payments be used?

35. **LO.8** A guaranteed payment to one partner affects the operating income (or loss) that passes through to the other partners. Explain this statement.

Problems

36. **LO.2, 3, 4** Using the legend provided below, classify each statement.

Legend
I = Applies *only* to the income taxation of individuals
C = Applies *only* to the income taxation of C corporations
B = Applies to the income taxation of *both* individuals and C corporations
N = Applies to the income taxation of *neither* individuals nor C corporations

a. A foreign tax credit is not available.
b. The deduction of charitable contributions is subject to percentage limitation(s).
c. Excess charitable contributions can be carried forward for five years.
d. On the contribution of inventory to charity, the full amount of any appreciation can be claimed as a deduction.
e. Excess capital losses can be carried forward indefinitely.
f. Excess capital losses cannot be carried back.
g. A net short-term capital gain is subject to the same tax rate as ordinary income.
h. A domestic production activities deduction may be available.
i. A dividends received deduction is not available.
j. The like-kind provisions of § 1031 are available.
k. A taxpayer with a fiscal year of May 1–April 30 has a due date for filing a Federal income tax return of July 15.
l. Estimated Federal income tax payments may be required.

37. **LO.2** Garnet has the following capital asset transactions during 2014:

Long-term capital gain	$8,000
Short-term capital gain	3,000

Further, Garnet has an excess capital loss carryforward of $6,000 from 2013.
a. What are the tax consequences of these transactions if the $6,000 loss is long-term and Garnet is an individual? Garnet is a C corporation?
b. What are the tax consequences of these transactions if the $6,000 loss is short-term and Garnet is an individual? Garnet is a C corporation?

38. **LO.2, 7** Citron, a calendar year taxpayer, began business in January 2013. It had a long-term capital gain of $5,000 in 2013 and a long-term capital loss of $10,000 in 2014. For both years, Citron had an operating profit in excess of $100,000. How are these capital gain and loss transactions handled for income tax purposes if Citron is:
a. An individual?
b. A C corporation?
c. An S corporation?

39. **LO.2** Taupe, a calendar year taxpayer, has the following capital transactions for 2014: long-term capital loss of $4,000 and a short-term capital loss of $4,000. How are these items handled for tax purposes if Taupe is:
a. An individual?
b. A C corporation?

40. **LO.2, 7** Robin had the following capital transactions in 2014:

LTCG	$10,000
LTCL	8,000
STCG	2,000
STCL	–0–

Robin also had a net long-term capital loss in 2013 of $2,000, which it could not use. What are the tax consequences in 2014 if:
a. Robin is an individual.
b. Robin is a C corporation.
c. Robin is an S corporation.

41. **LO.2** On December 6, 2014, Kestrel Company (a calendar year taxpayer) authorizes a cash donation of $40,000 to the Memphis Public Library. The pledge is carried out as follows: $10,000 on December 12, 2014; $25,000 on February 13, 2015; and $5,000 on April 10, 2015. What are the alternatives for the year of the charitable contribution deduction if Kestrel is:
a. An accrual basis partnership?
b. An accrual basis C corporation?
c. What is the result under parts (a) and (b) if Kestrel is a cash basis taxpayer?

42. **LO.2** During 2014, Siskin Corporation (a C corporation) had the following transactions:

Income from operations	$500,000
Expenses from operations	425,000
Dividends from domestic corporations (less than 20% ownership)	40,000
Dividends received deduction (70% × $40,000)	28,000
Unused short-term capital loss from 2012 (there are no capital gains in 2013 and 2014)	2,500
NOL carryover from 2013	40,000

In June 2014, Siskin made a contribution to a qualified charitable organization of $10,500 in cash (not included in any of the items listed above).
   a. How much, if any, of the contribution can be claimed as a deduction for 2014?
   b. What happens to any portion not deductible for 2014?

43. **LO.2** Auburn Company manufactures and sells furnishings for hospitals (e.g., special needs bathroom fixtures). In the current year, it donates some of its inventory to a newly constructed hospice. The hospice is adjacent to a cancer treatment center and is intended to care for indigent and terminal patients. The property donated has an adjusted basis of $40,000 and a fair market value of $90,000. What is the amount of the charitable contribution deduction if Auburn is a:
   a. Sole proprietorship?
   b. C corporation?
   c. Would your answer to part (b) change if the fair market value of the property was $121,000 (not $90,000)?

44. **LO.2** For each of the following independent situations, determine the domestic production activities deduction (DPAD) for 2014.

Corporation	Qualified Production Activities Income	Taxable Income (without any DPAD)	Relevant W–2 Wages
Parula	$700,000	$600,000	$200,000
Knot	600,000	650,000	100,000
Junco	500,000	600,000	80,000

45. **LO.2** Tern Corporation manufactures a motor scooter at a cost of $5,000 and sells it to Snipe Corporation for $7,000. Snipe spends $2,000 marketing the scooter and sells it to the general public for $12,000. Presuming that the taxable income and W–2 wage limitations do not apply, what is the domestic production activities deduction (DPAD) if:
   a. Tern Corporation and Snipe Corporation are not members of the same affiliated group?
   b. Are members of the same affiliated group?

46. **LO.3** Determine the dividends received deduction for each of the following independent situations. Assume that the percentage of stock owned in the corporation paying the dividend is 30% for Green Corporation and less than 20% for Red Corporation and Blue Corporation.

	Red Corporation	Blue Corporation	Green Corporation
Income from operations	$3,000,000	$4,500,000	$8,000,000
Expenses of operations	2,700,000	4,800,000	8,400,000
Qualified dividends received	600,000	150,000	2,000,000

47. **LO.3** Puffin Corporation was formed on July 1, 2014, and incurred qualifying organizational expenditures. It uses a calendar year and wants to accelerate any deductions that are available. Based on this assumption, what is Puffin Corporation's deduction for 2014 if its organizational expenditures are:
   a. $3,000?
   b. $46,000?
   c. $52,000?
   d. $77,000?

48. **LO.4** In each of the following independent situations, determine the C corporation's Federal income tax liability for calendar year 2014.

Corporation	Taxable Income
Sparrow	$ 45,000*
Warbler	68,000**
Scaup	80,000
Ibis	126,000
Heron	390,000
Finch (a personal service corporation)	120,000

*Does not include a net short-term capital gain of $3,000.
**Does not include a net long-term capital loss of $4,000.

49. **LO.4** Puce, a calendar year C corporation, had the following Schedule M–1 transactions on its Form 1120 for 2014:

Taxable income	$100,000
Federal income tax	22,250
Excess capital losses over capital gains	4,000
Life insurance proceeds received on the death of Puce's vice president	100,000
Premiums paid on life insurance policy	1,000
Interest on tax-exempt bonds	10,000

What is Puce Corporation's net income per books for 2014?

50. **LO.5, 9** Doris, Walt, and Pat form Swan Corporation with the following investments:

	Basis to Transferor	Fair Market Value	Number of Shares Issued
From Doris—cash	$200,000	$200,000	200
From Walt—equipment	400,000	300,000	300
From Pat—land	550,000	600,000	500

In addition to the 500 shares of stock, Pat receives $100,000 in cash from Swan Corporation. Assume that each share of Swan stock is worth $1,000.
a. How much loss does Walt realize? Recognize?
b. What is Walt's basis in the Swan stock?
c. What is Swan Corporation's basis in the equipment?
d. How much gain does Pat realize? Recognize?
e. What is Pat's basis in the Swan stock?
f. What is Swan's basis in the land?
g. In terms of the answers to parts (a) through (f), does it matter whether Swan is formed as a C corporation or as an S corporation? Explain.

51. **LO.5** Elton, Neil, Courtney, and Zelma form Ecru Corporation with the following investments:

	Basis to Transferor	Fair Market Value	Number of Shares Issued
From Elton—cash	$ 200,000	$ 200,000	200
From Neil—inventory	230,000	270,000	260
From Courtney—machinery and equipment	400,000	370,000	350
From Zelma—land and building	1,270,000	1,300,000	1,200

In addition to its stock, Ecru distributes cash as follows: $10,000 to Neil, $20,000 to Courtney, and $100,000 to Zelma. Assume that each share of Ecru stock is worth $1,000. Regarding these transactions, provide the following information:
a. Neil's realized and recognized gain (or loss).
b. Neil's basis in the Ecru stock.
c. Ecru's basis in the inventory.
d. Courtney's realized and recognized gain (or loss).

    e. Courtney's basis in the Ecru stock.

    f. Ecru's basis in the machinery and equipment.

    g. Zelma's realized and recognized gain (or loss).

    h. Zelma's basis in the Ecru stock.

    i. Ecru's basis in the land and building.

52. **LO.6** Lily is the sole shareholder of Crimson Corporation (a C corporation). At a time when Crimson has a deficit in accumulated E & P of $100,000 and current E & P of $60,000, it distributes a cash dividend of $90,000. If Lily's basis in her stock is $10,000, what are the tax consequences of the distribution to:

    a. Lily?

    b. Crimson Corporation?

Issue ID

53. **LO.6** Harold, Marcia, and Richard are equal shareholders in Pelican Corporation, a calendar year C corporation. During the current year, Pelican makes a $150,000 distribution to its three shareholders. Of the $50,000 that each shareholder receives, the tax result is as follows:

- No income to Harold.
- $30,000 capital gain to Marcia.
- $50,000 capital gain to Richard.

Explain the variations in these tax consequences.

Decision Making

Communications

54. **LO.6, 9** The stock of Emerald Corporation is held equally by Barney and Faye. The shareholders would like to receive, as a dividend, value of $800,000 each. The corporation has the following assets that it can spare:

Asset	Adjusted Basis to Emerald Corporation	Fair Market Value
Unimproved land	$1,040,000	$800,000
Chevron stock	480,000	800,000

Both assets are held as investments. Emerald Corporation has a capital loss carryover from the previous year of $80,000 and has accumulated E & P in excess of $2 million.

    Barney and Faye have come to you for advice. Suggest an attractive tax plan to carry out what the parties want. Write a letter (addressed to Emerald Corporation at P.O. Box 940, Rochester, NY 14692) describing your plan and its tax consequences.

55. **LO.7** During 2014, Thrasher (a calendar year, accrual basis S corporation) has the following transactions:

Sales	$1,500,000
Cost of goods sold	900,000
Long-term capital gain	10,000
Short-term capital gain	5,000
Salaries	210,000
Qualified dividends from stock investments	30,000
Rent expense	170,000
Advertising expense	20,000
Interest on City of Trenton bonds	15,000
§ 1231 gain	25,000
Organizational expenditures	3,000
Charitable contributions	5,000
Bad debt (trade account receivable deemed to be uncollectible)	10,000
Cash dividend distributed to shareholders	120,000

    a. Determine Thrasher Corporation's separately stated items for 2014.

    b. Determine Thrasher's taxable income for 2014.

Communications

56. **LO.7** Assume the same facts as in Problem 55. Kirby Turner is a 20% shareholder in Thrasher Corporation. She is aware of the tax consequences of the various items listed on the Schedule K–1 (Form 1120S) she received but does not understand their effect on basis. She is considering selling her stock and wants to estimate the gain or loss that will result. In response to Kirby's request for assistance, write a letter to her (1120 Garden Way, Elizabeth, NJ 07207) summarizing the changes to stock basis that the 2014 transactions caused.

57. **LO.7, 9** Jim Olsen owns all of the stock in Drake, a calendar year S corporation. For calendar year 2014, Drake anticipates an operating loss of $160,000 and could, if deemed worthwhile, sell a stock investment that would generate a $10,000 long-term capital loss. Jim has an adjusted basis of $100,000 in the Drake stock. For the year, he has already realized a short-term capital gain of $7,000. He anticipates no other capital asset transactions and expects to be in the 33% tax bracket in 2014.

   Write a letter to Jim (470 Bay Avenue, Bedford, MA 01730) suggesting a course of action that could save him some income taxes.

Decision Making

Communications

58. **LO.7** Ida owns 30% of the stock in Mockingbird, a calendar year S corporation. Her basis in the stock as of January 1, 2014, is $120,000. Mockingbird has an operating loss of $500,000 in 2014 and an operating profit of $600,000 in 2015. Ida withdraws $70,000 in cash from the corporation in 2015.
   a. What are Ida's tax consequences in 2014?
   b. 2015?
   c. What is Ida's basis in her Mockingbird stock as of January 1, 2015?
   d. January 1, 2016?

59. **LO.8** Guy, Alma, and Kara form the Ivory Partnership. In exchange for a 30% capital interest, Guy transfers property (basis of $200,000; fair market value of $400,000) subject to a liability of $100,000. The liability is assumed by the partnership. Alma transfers property (basis of $350,000; fair market value of $300,000) for a 30% capital interest. Kara invests cash of $400,000 for the remaining 40% capital interest. Concerning these transactions, provide the following information:
   a. Guy's recognized gain.
   b. Guy's basis in the partnership interest.
   c. Alma's recognized loss.
   d. Alma's basis in the partnership interest.
   e. Kara's basis in the partnership interest.
   f. Ivory Partnership's basis in the property transferred by Guy and Alma.

60. **LO.8** The Pheasant Partnership had the following transactions in the current year:

Operating income		$700,000
Cost of goods sold		400,000
Capital gains—		
Long-term	$20,000	
Short-term	10,000	30,000
Salaries		60,000
Tax-exempt interest income		2,000
Rent		24,000
Dividend from IBM stock investment		3,000
Utilities		8,000
Donation to American Red Cross		1,000
Contribution to governor's reelection campaign		500

   a. What is Pheasant's ordinary income (or loss)?
   b. What are Pheasant's separately stated items?

61. **LO.8** Aiden has a 30% capital interest in the Oro Partnership and is entitled to a yearly guaranteed payment of $40,000. As of January 1, 2014, Aiden's basis in the partnership interest is $80,000. During tax year 2014, Oro had the following transactions:

Operating profit (after consideration of guaranteed payment)	$400,000
Interest income on City of Seattle bonds	20,000
Short-term capital loss	5,000
Long-term capital gain	7,000
Funds borrowed from bank to provide working capital	30,000

   During 2014, Aiden withdrew cash of $50,000 from Oro to help cover his living expenses. What is Aiden's basis in his partnership interest as of January 1, 2015?

Decision Making

62. **LO.8, 9** As of January 1, 2013, Norman has a basis of $90,000 in his 30% capital interest in the Plata Partnership. He and the partnership use the calendar year for tax purposes. The partnership incurs an operating loss of $450,000 for 2013 and a profit of $270,000 for 2014.
    a. How much, if any, loss may Norman recognize for 2013?
    b. How much income must Norman recognize for 2014?
    c. What basis will Norman have in his partnership interest as of January 1, 2014?
    d. What basis will Norman have in his partnership interest as of January 1, 2015?
    e. What year-end tax planning would you suggest to ensure that a partner could deduct all of his or her share of any partnership losses?

63. **LO.8** Brenda has a one-third capital interest in the Partridge Partnership; the other two-thirds is held by her brothers and sisters. In 2013, Brenda sells land (basis of $300,000) to Partridge for its fair market value of $295,000. In 2014, Partridge resells the land to a third party for $302,000. What are the tax consequences to:
    a. Brenda on the 2013 sale?
    b. Partridge on the 2014 sale?

Research Problems

THOMSON REUTERS
CHECKPOINT®

Note: Solutions to Research Problems can be prepared by using the **Checkpoint®
Student Edition** online research product, which is available to accompany this text. It is also possible to prepare solutions to the Research Problems by using tax research materials found in a standard tax library.

Communications

Research Problem 1. Tyler and Travis Best are brothers and equal shareholders in Maize Corporation, a calendar year C corporation. In 2012, they incurred travel and entertainment expenses on behalf of Maize Corporation. Because Maize was in a precarious financial condition, the brothers decided not to seek reimbursement for these expenditures. Instead, each brother deducted on his individual return (Form 1040) what he had spent on travel and entertainment expenses on behalf of the corporation. Upon audit of the returns filed by Tyler and Travis, the IRS disallowed these expenditures. Write a letter to Travis (140 Ridgeland Drive, Waynesburg, PA 15370) indicating whether he should challenge the IRS action. Explain your conclusions using nontechnical language.

Research Problem 2. Aaron and Leona (father and daughter) started Pottery Heaven in the late 1990s. Shortly after beginning business, Pottery Heaven was incorporated with stock issued as follows: 700 shares to Aaron and 300 shares to Leona. The business has prospered and by 2014 is in dire need of additional space for customer parking. Fortunately, Aaron owns land adjacent to the business, which he purchased many years ago (cost basis of $40,000 and current value of $200,000). To be suitable for parking, however, the property must be cleared, graded, and paved at a cost of $100,000. To carry out this objective, the parties are considering the following three alternatives:
    a. Aaron makes a capital contribution of the property to Pottery Heaven. To make the needed improvements, Pottery Heaven borrows $100,000 from a bank.
    b. Aaron transfers the property to Pottery Heaven in exchange for 200 shares of its stock. To make the improvements, Pottery Heaven borrows $100,000 from a bank.
    c. Aaron transfers the property to Pottery Heaven in exchange for 200 shares of its stock, while Leona invests cash of $100,000 for 100 shares.

Evaluate the tax ramifications of each of these alternatives.

Partial list of research aids:
§§ 118, 351, and 1032.
Reg. §§ 1.351–1(a)(1)(ii) and (b)(1).

Communications

Research Problem 3. During 2014, Jayden Steele received a distribution of $24,000 on stock he owns in Razorbill Corporation. He had planned to report this amount as dividend income until he talked to his father-in-law, Jim. According to Jim, who had examined Razorbill's financial statements, the company suffered an operating loss for the year. Consequently, Jim thinks that the distribution is a nontaxable return of capital. Because Jim is an accountant, Jayden is confused and seeks a second opinion from you. Write a letter to Jayden (1260 Pike Street, Eagle, ID 83616) explaining the possibilities involved.

Partial list of research aids:
Jason Michael Juha, 103 TCM 1338, T.C.Memo. 2012–68.

Research Problem 4. Scott and Brooke are the sole shareholders of Tanager Company, a calendar year Subchapter S corporation. After several loss years, in December 2013, Tanager is forced to borrow $300,000 for working capital purposes. Robin State Bank makes the loan to Tanager but only after Scott and Brooke personally guarantee the debt.

   Scott and Brooke deduct Tanager's $200,000 operating loss for 2013 on their individual income tax returns. Although they have a zero basis in their stock investment, they consider the guarantee of the bank loan to be debt within the meaning of § 1366(d)(1)(B).

   Are Scott and Brooke correct in their reasoning? Explain.

Partial list of research aids:
Milton T. Raynor, 50 T.C. 762 (1968).
William H. Maloof, 89 TCM 1022, T.C.Memo. 2005–75.

Use the tax resources of the Internet to address the following questions. Do not restrict your search to the Web, but include a review of newsgroups and general reference materials, practitioner sites and resources, primary sources of the tax law, chat rooms and discussion groups, and other opportunities.

Internet Activity

Research Problem 5. Does your state permit CPAs to practice public accounting in the corporate form? If not, can they form LLCs? What, if any, special restrictions are imposed?

Research Problem 6. Some C corporations are exempt from the application of the AMT. Review the Instructions to Form 4626 (Alternative Minimum Tax—Corporations) and be prepared to explain and illustrate the small corporation exemption.

Research Problem 7. Does your state recognize a Subchapter S election for state tax purposes? If so, does it treat out-of-state shareholders in the same way as resident shareholders?

Research Problem 8. To report its transactions for the year, a partnership must file a Form 1065 with the IRS.
   a. When is this return due?
   b. As is the case with individuals and corporations, can a partnership obtain an automatic six-month extension for filing the Form 1065?
   c. Does a partnership need to include a Schedule M–3 with its Form 1065? Explain.

Tax Rate Schedules and Tables

(The 2014 Tax Tables and 2014 Sales Tax Tables can be accessed at the IRS website: [**www.irs.gov**] when released.)

2013 Tax Rate Schedules

Single—Schedule X

If taxable income is: Over—	But not over—	The tax is:	of the amount over—
$ 0	$ 8,925	.........10%	$ 0
8,925	36,250	$ 892.50 + 15%	8,925
36,250	87,850	4,991.25 + 25%	36,250
87,850	183,250	17,891.25 + 28%	87,850
183,250	398,350	44,603.25 + 33%	183,250
398,350	400,000	115,586.25 + 35%	398,350
400,000	....	116,163.75 + 39.6%	400,000

Head of household—Schedule Z

If taxable income is: Over—	But not over—	The tax is:	of the amount over—
$ 0	$ 12,750	.........10%	$ 0
12,750	48,600	$ 1,275.00 + 15%	12,750
48,600	125,450	6,652.50 + 25%	48,600
125,450	203,150	25,865.00 + 28%	125,450
203,150	398,350	47,621.00 + 33%	203,150
398,350	425,000	112,037.00 + 35%	398,350
425,000	....	121,364.50 + 39.6%	425,000

Married filing jointly or Qualifying widow(er)—Schedule Y–1

If taxable income is: Over—	But not over—	The tax is:	of the amount over—
$ 0	$ 17,850	.........10%	$ 0
17,850	72,500	$ 1,785.00 + 15%	17,850
72,500	146,400	9,982.50 + 25%	72,500
146,400	223,050	28,457.50 + 28%	146,400
223,050	398,350	49,919.50 + 33%	223,050
398,350	450,000	107,768.50 + 35%	398,350
450,000	....	125,846.00 + 39.6%	450,000

Married filing separately—Schedule Y–2

If taxable income is: Over—	But not over—	The tax is:	of the amount over—
$ 0	$ 8,925	.........10%	$ 0
8,925	36,250	$ 892.50 + 15%	8,925
36,250	73,200	4,991.25 + 25%	36,250
73,200	111,525	14,228.75 + 28%	73,200
111,525	199,175	24,959.75 + 33%	111,525
199,175	225,000	53,884.25 + 35%	199,175
225,000	....	62,923.00 + 39.6%	225,000

2014 Tax Rate Schedules

Single—Schedule X

If taxable income is: Over—	But not over—	The tax is:	of the amount over—
$ 0	$ 9,075	.........10%	$ 0
9,075	36,900	$ 907.50 + 15%	9,075
36,900	89,350	5,081.25 + 25%	36,900
89,350	186,350	18,193.75 + 28%	89,350
186,350	405,100	45,353.75 + 33%	186,350
405,100	406,750	117,541.25 + 35%	405,100
406,750	....	118,118.75 + 39.6%	406,750

Head of household—Schedule Z

If taxable income is: Over—	But not over—	The tax is:	of the amount over—
$ 0	$ 12,950	.........10%	$ 0
12,950	49,400	$ 1,295.00 + 15%	12,950
49,400	127,550	6,762.50 + 25%	49,400
127,550	206,600	26,300.00 + 28%	127,550
206,600	405,100	48,434.00 + 33%	206,600
405,100	432,200	113,939.00 + 35%	405,100
432,200	....	123,424.00 + 39.6%	432,200

Married filing jointly or Qualifying widow(er)—Schedule Y–1

If taxable income is: Over—	But not over—	The tax is:	of the amount over—
$ 0	$ 18,150	.........10%	$ 0
18,150	73,800	$ 1,815.00 + 15%	18,150
73,800	148,850	10,162.50 + 25%	73,800
148,850	226,850	28,925.00 + 28%	148,850
226,850	405,100	50,765.00 + 33%	226,850
405,100	457,600	109,587.50 + 35%	405,100
457,600	....	127,962.50 + 39.6%	457,600

Married filing separately—Schedule Y–2

If taxable income is: Over—	But not over—	The tax is:	of the amount over—
$ 0	$ 9,075	.........10%	$ 0
9,075	36,900	$ 907.50 + 15%	9,075
36,900	74,425	5,081.25 + 25%	36,900
74,425	113,425	14,462.50 + 28%	74,425
113,425	202,550	25,382.50 + 33%	113,425
202,550	228,800	54,793.75 + 35%	202,550
228,800	....	63,981.25 + 39.6%	228,800

2013 Tax Table

See the instructions for line 44 to see if you must use the Tax Table below to figure your tax.

Example. Mr. and Mrs. Brown are filing a joint return. Their taxable income on Form 1040, line 43, is $25,300. First, they find the $25,300-25,350 taxable income line. Next, they find the column for married filing jointly and read down the column. The amount shown where the taxable income line and filing status column meet is $2,906. This is the tax amount they should enter on Form 1040, line 44.

Sample Table

At Least	But Less Than	Single	Married filing jointly *	Married filing separately	Head of a household
			Your tax is—		
25,200	25,250	3,338	2,891	3,338	3,146
25,250	25,300	3,345	2,899	3,345	3,154
25,300	25,350	3,353	(2,906)	3,353	3,161
25,350	25,400	3,360	2,914	3,360	3,169

If line 43 (taxable income) is— At least	But less than	Single	Married filing jointly *	Married filing separately	Head of a house-hold
			Your tax is—		
0	5	0	0	0	0
5	15	1	1	1	1
15	25	2	2	2	2
25	50	4	4	4	4
50	75	6	6	6	6
75	100	9	9	9	9
100	125	11	11	11	11
125	150	14	14	14	14
150	175	16	16	16	16
175	200	19	19	19	19
200	225	21	21	21	21
225	250	24	24	24	24
250	275	26	26	26	26
275	300	29	29	29	29
300	325	31	31	31	31
325	350	34	34	34	34
350	375	36	36	36	36
375	400	39	39	39	39
400	425	41	41	41	41
425	450	44	44	44	44
450	475	46	46	46	46
475	500	49	49	49	49
500	525	51	51	51	51
525	550	54	54	54	54
550	575	56	56	56	56
575	600	59	59	59	59
600	625	61	61	61	61
625	650	64	64	64	64
650	675	66	66	66	66
675	700	69	69	69	69
700	725	71	71	71	71
725	750	74	74	74	74
750	775	76	76	76	76
775	800	79	79	79	79
800	825	81	81	81	81
825	850	84	84	84	84
850	875	86	86	86	86
875	900	89	89	89	89
900	925	91	91	91	91
925	950	94	94	94	94
950	975	96	96	96	96
975	1,000	99	99	99	99

1,000

If line 43 (taxable income) is— At least	But less than	Single	Married filing jointly *	Married filing separately	Head of a house-hold
			Your tax is—		
1,000	1,025	101	101	101	101
1,025	1,050	104	104	104	104
1,050	1,075	106	106	106	106
1,075	1,100	109	109	109	109
1,100	1,125	111	111	111	111
1,125	1,150	114	114	114	114
1,150	1,175	116	116	116	116
1,175	1,200	119	119	119	119
1,200	1,225	121	121	121	121
1,225	1,250	124	124	124	124
1,250	1,275	126	126	126	126
1,275	1,300	129	129	129	129
1,300	1,325	131	131	131	131
1,325	1,350	134	134	134	134
1,350	1,375	136	136	136	136
1,375	1,400	139	139	139	139
1,400	1,425	141	141	141	141
1,425	1,450	144	144	144	144
1,450	1,475	146	146	146	146
1,475	1,500	149	149	149	149
1,500	1,525	151	151	151	151
1,525	1,550	154	154	154	154
1,550	1,575	156	156	156	156
1,575	1,600	159	159	159	159
1,600	1,625	161	161	161	161
1,625	1,650	164	164	164	164
1,650	1,675	166	166	166	166
1,675	1,700	169	169	169	169
1,700	1,725	171	171	171	171
1,725	1,750	174	174	174	174
1,750	1,775	176	176	176	176
1,775	1,800	179	179	179	179
1,800	1,825	181	181	181	181
1,825	1,850	184	184	184	184
1,850	1,875	186	186	186	186
1,875	1,900	189	189	189	189
1,900	1,925	191	191	191	191
1,925	1,950	194	194	194	194
1,950	1,975	196	196	196	196
1,975	2,000	199	199	199	199

2,000

If line 43 (taxable income) is— At least	But less than	Single	Married filing jointly *	Married filing separately	Head of a house-hold
			Your tax is—		
2,000	2,025	201	201	201	201
2,025	2,050	204	204	204	204
2,050	2,075	206	206	206	206
2,075	2,100	209	209	209	209
2,100	2,125	211	211	211	211
2,125	2,150	214	214	214	214
2,150	2,175	216	216	216	216
2,175	2,200	219	219	219	219
2,200	2,225	221	221	221	221
2,225	2,250	224	224	224	224
2,250	2,275	226	226	226	226
2,275	2,300	229	229	229	229
2,300	2,325	231	231	231	231
2,325	2,350	234	234	234	234
2,350	2,375	236	236	236	236
2,375	2,400	239	239	239	239
2,400	2,425	241	241	241	241
2,425	2,450	244	244	244	244
2,450	2,475	246	246	246	246
2,475	2,500	249	249	249	249
2,500	2,525	251	251	251	251
2,525	2,550	254	254	254	254
2,550	2,575	256	256	256	256
2,575	2,600	259	259	259	259
2,600	2,625	261	261	261	261
2,625	2,650	264	264	264	264
2,650	2,675	266	266	266	266
2,675	2,700	269	269	269	269
2,700	2,725	271	271	271	271
2,725	2,750	274	274	274	274
2,750	2,775	276	276	276	276
2,775	2,800	279	279	279	279
2,800	2,825	281	281	281	281
2,825	2,850	284	284	284	284
2,850	2,875	286	286	286	286
2,875	2,900	289	289	289	289
2,900	2,925	291	291	291	291
2,925	2,950	294	294	294	294
2,950	2,975	296	296	296	296
2,975	3,000	299	299	299	299

* This column must also be used by a qualifying widow(er).

(Continued)

2013 Tax Table—Continued

At least	But less than	Single	Married filing jointly *	Married filing separately	Head of a household
3,000					
3,000	3,050	303	303	303	303
3,050	3,100	308	308	308	308
3,100	3,150	313	313	313	313
3,150	3,200	318	318	318	318
3,200	3,250	323	323	323	323
3,250	3,300	328	328	328	328
3,300	3,350	333	333	333	333
3,350	3,400	338	338	338	338
3,400	3,450	343	343	343	343
3,450	3,500	348	348	348	348
3,500	3,550	353	353	353	353
3,550	3,600	358	358	358	358
3,600	3,650	363	363	363	363
3,650	3,700	368	368	368	368
3,700	3,750	373	373	373	373
3,750	3,800	378	378	378	378
3,800	3,850	383	383	383	383
3,850	3,900	388	388	388	388
3,900	3,950	393	393	393	393
3,950	4,000	398	398	398	398
4,000					
4,000	4,050	403	403	403	403
4,050	4,100	408	408	408	408
4,100	4,150	413	413	413	413
4,150	4,200	418	418	418	418
4,200	4,250	423	423	423	423
4,250	4,300	428	428	428	428
4,300	4,350	433	433	433	433
4,350	4,400	438	438	438	438
4,400	4,450	443	443	443	443
4,450	4,500	448	448	448	448
4,500	4,550	453	453	453	453
4,550	4,600	458	458	458	458
4,600	4,650	463	463	463	463
4,650	4,700	468	468	468	468
4,700	4,750	473	473	473	473
4,750	4,800	478	478	478	478
4,800	4,850	483	483	483	483
4,850	4,900	488	488	488	488
4,900	4,950	493	493	493	493
4,950	5,000	498	498	498	498
5,000					
5,000	5,050	503	503	503	503
5,050	5,100	508	508	508	508
5,100	5,150	513	513	513	513
5,150	5,200	518	518	518	518
5,200	5,250	523	523	523	523
5,250	5,300	528	528	528	528
5,300	5,350	533	533	533	533
5,350	5,400	538	538	538	538
5,400	5,450	543	543	543	543
5,450	5,500	548	548	548	548
5,500	5,550	553	553	553	553
5,550	5,600	558	558	558	558
5,600	5,650	563	563	563	563
5,650	5,700	568	568	568	568
5,700	5,750	573	573	573	573
5,750	5,800	578	578	578	578
5,800	5,850	583	583	583	583
5,850	5,900	588	588	588	588
5,900	5,950	593	593	593	593
5,950	6,000	598	598	598	598

At least	But less than	Single	Married filing jointly *	Married filing separately	Head of a household
6,000					
6,000	6,050	603	603	603	603
6,050	6,100	608	608	608	608
6,100	6,150	613	613	613	613
6,150	6,200	618	618	618	618
6,200	6,250	623	623	623	623
6,250	6,300	628	628	628	628
6,300	6,350	633	633	633	633
6,350	6,400	638	638	638	638
6,400	6,450	643	643	643	643
6,450	6,500	648	648	648	648
6,500	6,550	653	653	653	653
6,550	6,600	658	658	658	658
6,600	6,650	663	663	663	663
6,650	6,700	668	668	668	668
6,700	6,750	673	673	673	673
6,750	6,800	678	678	678	678
6,800	6,850	683	683	683	683
6,850	6,900	688	688	688	688
6,900	6,950	693	693	693	693
6,950	7,000	698	698	698	698
7,000					
7,000	7,050	703	703	703	703
7,050	7,100	708	708	708	708
7,100	7,150	713	713	713	713
7,150	7,200	718	718	718	718
7,200	7,250	723	723	723	723
7,250	7,300	728	728	728	728
7,300	7,350	733	733	733	733
7,350	7,400	738	738	738	738
7,400	7,450	743	743	743	743
7,450	7,500	748	748	748	748
7,500	7,550	753	753	753	753
7,550	7,600	758	758	758	758
7,600	7,650	763	763	763	763
7,650	7,700	768	768	768	768
7,700	7,750	773	773	773	773
7,750	7,800	778	778	778	778
7,800	7,850	783	783	783	783
7,850	7,900	788	788	788	788
7,900	7,950	793	793	793	793
7,950	8,000	798	798	798	798
8,000					
8,000	8,050	803	803	803	803
8,050	8,100	808	808	808	808
8,100	8,150	813	813	813	813
8,150	8,200	818	818	818	818
8,200	8,250	823	823	823	823
8,250	8,300	828	828	828	828
8,300	8,350	833	833	833	833
8,350	8,400	838	838	838	838
8,400	8,450	843	843	843	843
8,450	8,500	848	848	848	848
8,500	8,550	853	853	853	853
8,550	8,600	858	858	858	858
8,600	8,650	863	863	863	863
8,650	8,700	868	868	868	868
8,700	8,750	873	873	873	873
8,750	8,800	878	878	878	878
8,800	8,850	883	883	883	883
8,850	8,900	888	888	888	888
8,900	8,950	893	893	893	893
8,950	9,000	900	898	900	898

At least	But less than	Single	Married filing jointly *	Married filing separately	Head of a household
9,000					
9,000	9,050	908	903	908	903
9,050	9,100	915	908	915	908
9,100	9,150	923	913	923	913
9,150	9,200	930	918	930	918
9,200	9,250	938	923	938	923
9,250	9,300	945	928	945	928
9,300	9,350	953	933	953	933
9,350	9,400	960	938	960	938
9,400	9,450	968	943	968	943
9,450	9,500	975	948	975	948
9,500	9,550	983	953	983	953
9,550	9,600	990	958	990	958
9,600	9,650	998	963	998	963
9,650	9,700	1,005	968	1,005	968
9,700	9,750	1,013	973	1,013	973
9,750	9,800	1,020	978	1,020	978
9,800	9,850	1,028	983	1,028	983
9,850	9,900	1,035	988	1,035	988
9,900	9,950	1,043	993	1,043	993
9,950	10,000	1,050	998	1,050	998
10,000					
10,000	10,050	1,058	1,003	1,058	1,003
10,050	10,100	1,065	1,008	1,065	1,008
10,100	10,150	1,073	1,013	1,073	1,013
10,150	10,200	1,080	1,018	1,080	1,018
10,200	10,250	1,088	1,023	1,088	1,023
10,250	10,300	1,095	1,028	1,095	1,028
10,300	10,350	1,103	1,033	1,103	1,033
10,350	10,400	1,110	1,038	1,110	1,038
10,400	10,450	1,118	1,043	1,118	1,043
10,450	10,500	1,125	1,048	1,125	1,048
10,500	10,550	1,133	1,053	1,133	1,053
10,550	10,600	1,140	1,058	1,140	1,058
10,600	10,650	1,148	1,063	1,148	1,063
10,650	10,700	1,155	1,068	1,155	1,068
10,700	10,750	1,163	1,073	1,163	1,073
10,750	10,800	1,170	1,078	1,170	1,078
10,800	10,850	1,178	1,083	1,178	1,083
10,850	10,900	1,185	1,088	1,185	1,088
10,900	10,950	1,193	1,093	1,193	1,093
10,950	11,000	1,200	1,098	1,200	1,098
11,000					
11,000	11,050	1,208	1,103	1,208	1,103
11,050	11,100	1,215	1,108	1,215	1,108
11,100	11,150	1,223	1,113	1,223	1,113
11,150	11,200	1,230	1,118	1,230	1,118
11,200	11,250	1,238	1,123	1,238	1,123
11,250	11,300	1,245	1,128	1,245	1,128
11,300	11,350	1,253	1,133	1,253	1,133
11,350	11,400	1,260	1,138	1,260	1,138
11,400	11,450	1,268	1,143	1,268	1,143
11,450	11,500	1,275	1,148	1,275	1,148
11,500	11,550	1,283	1,153	1,283	1,153
11,550	11,600	1,290	1,158	1,290	1,158
11,600	11,650	1,298	1,163	1,298	1,163
11,650	11,700	1,305	1,168	1,305	1,168
11,700	11,750	1,313	1,173	1,313	1,173
11,750	11,800	1,320	1,178	1,320	1,178
11,800	11,850	1,328	1,183	1,328	1,183
11,850	11,900	1,335	1,188	1,335	1,188
11,900	11,950	1,343	1,193	1,343	1,193
11,950	12,000	1,350	1,198	1,350	1,198

* This column must also be used by a qualifying widow(er).

(Continued)

2013 Tax Table—Continued

If line 43 (taxable income) is—		And you are—			
At least	But less than	Single	Married filing jointly *	Married filing separately	Head of a house-hold
		Your tax is—			

12,000

At least	But less than	Single	MFJ *	MFS	HoH
12,000	12,050	1,358	1,203	1,358	1,203
12,050	12,100	1,365	1,208	1,365	1,208
12,100	12,150	1,373	1,213	1,373	1,213
12,150	12,200	1,380	1,218	1,380	1,218
12,200	12,250	1,388	1,223	1,388	1,223
12,250	12,300	1,395	1,228	1,395	1,228
12,300	12,350	1,403	1,233	1,403	1,233
12,350	12,400	1,410	1,238	1,410	1,238
12,400	12,450	1,418	1,243	1,418	1,243
12,450	12,500	1,425	1,248	1,425	1,248
12,500	12,550	1,433	1,253	1,433	1,253
12,550	12,600	1,440	1,258	1,440	1,258
12,600	12,650	1,448	1,263	1,448	1,263
12,650	12,700	1,455	1,268	1,455	1,268
12,700	12,750	1,463	1,273	1,463	1,273
12,750	12,800	1,470	1,278	1,470	1,279
12,800	12,850	1,478	1,283	1,478	1,286
12,850	12,900	1,485	1,288	1,485	1,294
12,900	12,950	1,493	1,293	1,493	1,301
12,950	13,000	1,500	1,298	1,500	1,309

13,000

At least	But less than	Single	MFJ *	MFS	HoH
13,000	13,050	1,508	1,303	1,508	1,316
13,050	13,100	1,515	1,308	1,515	1,324
13,100	13,150	1,523	1,313	1,523	1,331
13,150	13,200	1,530	1,318	1,530	1,339
13,200	13,250	1,538	1,323	1,538	1,346
13,250	13,300	1,545	1,328	1,545	1,354
13,300	13,350	1,553	1,333	1,553	1,361
13,350	13,400	1,560	1,338	1,560	1,369
13,400	13,450	1,568	1,343	1,568	1,376
13,450	13,500	1,575	1,348	1,575	1,384
13,500	13,550	1,583	1,353	1,583	1,391
13,550	13,600	1,590	1,358	1,590	1,399
13,600	13,650	1,598	1,363	1,598	1,406
13,650	13,700	1,605	1,368	1,605	1,414
13,700	13,750	1,613	1,373	1,613	1,421
13,750	13,800	1,620	1,378	1,620	1,429
13,800	13,850	1,628	1,383	1,628	1,436
13,850	13,900	1,635	1,388	1,635	1,444
13,900	13,950	1,643	1,393	1,643	1,451
13,950	14,000	1,650	1,398	1,650	1,459

14,000

At least	But less than	Single	MFJ *	MFS	HoH
14,000	14,050	1,658	1,403	1,658	1,466
14,050	14,100	1,665	1,408	1,665	1,474
14,100	14,150	1,673	1,413	1,673	1,481
14,150	14,200	1,680	1,418	1,680	1,489
14,200	14,250	1,688	1,423	1,688	1,496
14,250	14,300	1,695	1,428	1,695	1,504
14,300	14,350	1,703	1,433	1,703	1,511
14,350	14,400	1,710	1,438	1,710	1,519
14,400	14,450	1,718	1,443	1,718	1,526
14,450	14,500	1,725	1,448	1,725	1,534
14,500	14,550	1,733	1,453	1,733	1,541
14,550	14,600	1,740	1,458	1,740	1,549
14,600	14,650	1,748	1,463	1,748	1,556
14,650	14,700	1,755	1,468	1,755	1,564
14,700	14,750	1,763	1,473	1,763	1,571
14,750	14,800	1,770	1,478	1,770	1,579
14,800	14,850	1,778	1,483	1,778	1,586
14,850	14,900	1,785	1,488	1,785	1,594
14,900	14,950	1,793	1,493	1,793	1,601
14,950	15,000	1,800	1,498	1,800	1,609

15,000

At least	But less than	Single	MFJ *	MFS	HoH
15,000	15,050	1,808	1,503	1,808	1,616
15,050	15,100	1,815	1,508	1,815	1,624
15,100	15,150	1,823	1,513	1,823	1,631
15,150	15,200	1,830	1,518	1,830	1,639
15,200	15,250	1,838	1,523	1,838	1,646
15,250	15,300	1,845	1,528	1,845	1,654
15,300	15,350	1,853	1,533	1,853	1,661
15,350	15,400	1,860	1,538	1,860	1,669
15,400	15,450	1,868	1,543	1,868	1,676
15,450	15,500	1,875	1,548	1,875	1,684
15,500	15,550	1,883	1,553	1,883	1,691
15,550	15,600	1,890	1,558	1,890	1,699
15,600	15,650	1,898	1,563	1,898	1,706
15,650	15,700	1,905	1,568	1,905	1,714
15,700	15,750	1,913	1,573	1,913	1,721
15,750	15,800	1,920	1,578	1,920	1,729
15,800	15,850	1,928	1,583	1,928	1,736
15,850	15,900	1,935	1,588	1,935	1,744
15,900	15,950	1,943	1,593	1,943	1,751
15,950	16,000	1,950	1,598	1,950	1,759

16,000

At least	But less than	Single	MFJ *	MFS	HoH
16,000	16,050	1,958	1,603	1,958	1,766
16,050	16,100	1,965	1,608	1,965	1,774
16,100	16,150	1,973	1,613	1,973	1,781
16,150	16,200	1,980	1,618	1,980	1,789
16,200	16,250	1,988	1,623	1,988	1,796
16,250	16,300	1,995	1,628	1,995	1,804
16,300	16,350	2,003	1,633	2,003	1,811
16,350	16,400	2,010	1,638	2,010	1,819
16,400	16,450	2,018	1,643	2,018	1,826
16,450	16,500	2,025	1,648	2,025	1,834
16,500	16,550	2,033	1,653	2,033	1,841
16,550	16,600	2,040	1,658	2,040	1,849
16,600	16,650	2,048	1,663	2,048	1,856
16,650	16,700	2,055	1,668	2,055	1,864
16,700	16,750	2,063	1,673	2,063	1,871
16,750	16,800	2,070	1,678	2,070	1,879
16,800	16,850	2,078	1,683	2,078	1,886
16,850	16,900	2,085	1,688	2,085	1,894
16,900	16,950	2,093	1,693	2,093	1,901
16,950	17,000	2,100	1,698	2,100	1,909

17,000

At least	But less than	Single	MFJ *	MFS	HoH
17,000	17,050	2,108	1,703	2,108	1,916
17,050	17,100	2,115	1,708	2,115	1,924
17,100	17,150	2,123	1,713	2,123	1,931
17,150	17,200	2,130	1,718	2,130	1,939
17,200	17,250	2,138	1,723	2,138	1,946
17,250	17,300	2,145	1,728	2,145	1,954
17,300	17,350	2,153	1,733	2,153	1,961
17,350	17,400	2,160	1,738	2,160	1,969
17,400	17,450	2,168	1,743	2,168	1,976
17,450	17,500	2,175	1,748	2,175	1,984
17,500	17,550	2,183	1,753	2,183	1,991
17,550	17,600	2,190	1,758	2,190	1,999
17,600	17,650	2,198	1,763	2,198	2,006
17,650	17,700	2,205	1,768	2,205	2,014
17,700	17,750	2,213	1,773	2,213	2,021
17,750	17,800	2,220	1,778	2,220	2,029
17,800	17,850	2,228	1,783	2,228	2,036
17,850	17,900	2,235	1,789	2,235	2,044
17,900	17,950	2,243	1,796	2,243	2,051
17,950	18,000	2,250	1,804	2,250	2,059

18,000

At least	But less than	Single	MFJ *	MFS	HoH
18,000	18,050	2,258	1,811	2,258	2,066
18,050	18,100	2,265	1,819	2,265	2,074
18,100	18,150	2,273	1,826	2,273	2,081
18,150	18,200	2,280	1,834	2,280	2,089
18,200	18,250	2,288	1,841	2,288	2,096
18,250	18,300	2,295	1,849	2,295	2,104
18,300	18,350	2,303	1,856	2,303	2,111
18,350	18,400	2,310	1,864	2,310	2,119
18,400	18,450	2,318	1,871	2,318	2,126
18,450	18,500	2,325	1,879	2,325	2,134
18,500	18,550	2,333	1,886	2,333	2,141
18,550	18,600	2,340	1,894	2,340	2,149
18,600	18,650	2,348	1,901	2,348	2,156
18,650	18,700	2,355	1,909	2,355	2,164
18,700	18,750	2,363	1,916	2,363	2,171
18,750	18,800	2,370	1,924	2,370	2,179
18,800	18,850	2,378	1,931	2,378	2,186
18,850	18,900	2,385	1,939	2,385	2,194
18,900	18,950	2,393	1,946	2,393	2,201
18,950	19,000	2,400	1,954	2,400	2,209

19,000

At least	But less than	Single	MFJ *	MFS	HoH
19,000	19,050	2,408	1,961	2,408	2,216
19,050	19,100	2,415	1,969	2,415	2,224
19,100	19,150	2,423	1,976	2,423	2,231
19,150	19,200	2,430	1,984	2,430	2,239
19,200	19,250	2,438	1,991	2,438	2,246
19,250	19,300	2,445	1,999	2,445	2,254
19,300	19,350	2,453	2,006	2,453	2,261
19,350	19,400	2,460	2,014	2,460	2,269
19,400	19,450	2,468	2,021	2,468	2,276
19,450	19,500	2,475	2,029	2,475	2,284
19,500	19,550	2,483	2,036	2,483	2,291
19,550	19,600	2,490	2,044	2,490	2,299
19,600	19,650	2,498	2,051	2,498	2,306
19,650	19,700	2,505	2,059	2,505	2,314
19,700	19,750	2,513	2,066	2,513	2,321
19,750	19,800	2,520	2,074	2,520	2,329
19,800	19,850	2,528	2,081	2,528	2,336
19,850	19,900	2,535	2,089	2,535	2,344
19,900	19,950	2,543	2,096	2,543	2,351
19,950	20,000	2,550	2,104	2,550	2,359

20,000

At least	But less than	Single	MFJ *	MFS	HoH
20,000	20,050	2,558	2,111	2,558	2,366
20,050	20,100	2,565	2,119	2,565	2,374
20,100	20,150	2,573	2,126	2,573	2,381
20,150	20,200	2,580	2,134	2,580	2,389
20,200	20,250	2,588	2,141	2,588	2,396
20,250	20,300	2,595	2,149	2,595	2,404
20,300	20,350	2,603	2,156	2,603	2,411
20,350	20,400	2,610	2,164	2,610	2,419
20,400	20,450	2,618	2,171	2,618	2,426
20,450	20,500	2,625	2,179	2,625	2,434
20,500	20,550	2,633	2,186	2,633	2,441
20,550	20,600	2,640	2,194	2,640	2,449
20,600	20,650	2,648	2,201	2,648	2,456
20,650	20,700	2,655	2,209	2,655	2,464
20,700	20,750	2,663	2,216	2,663	2,471
20,750	20,800	2,670	2,224	2,670	2,479
20,800	20,850	2,678	2,231	2,678	2,486
20,850	20,900	2,685	2,239	2,685	2,494
20,900	20,950	2,693	2,246	2,693	2,501
20,950	21,000	2,700	2,254	2,700	2,509

* This column must also be used by a qualifying widow(er).

(Continued)

2013 Tax Table—Continued

At least	But less than	Single	Married filing jointly *	Married filing separately	Head of a house-hold
21,000					
21,000	21,050	2,708	2,261	2,708	2,516
21,050	21,100	2,715	2,269	2,715	2,524
21,100	21,150	2,723	2,276	2,723	2,531
21,150	21,200	2,730	2,284	2,730	2,539
21,200	21,250	2,738	2,291	2,738	2,546
21,250	21,300	2,745	2,299	2,745	2,554
21,300	21,350	2,753	2,306	2,753	2,561
21,350	21,400	2,760	2,314	2,760	2,569
21,400	21,450	2,768	2,321	2,768	2,576
21,450	21,500	2,775	2,329	2,775	2,584
21,500	21,550	2,783	2,336	2,783	2,591
21,550	21,600	2,790	2,344	2,790	2,599
21,600	21,650	2,798	2,351	2,798	2,606
21,650	21,700	2,805	2,359	2,805	2,614
21,700	21,750	2,813	2,366	2,813	2,621
21,750	21,800	2,820	2,374	2,820	2,629
21,800	21,850	2,828	2,381	2,828	2,636
21,850	21,900	2,835	2,389	2,835	2,644
21,900	21,950	2,843	2,396	2,843	2,651
21,950	22,000	2,850	2,404	2,850	2,659
22,000					
22,000	22,050	2,858	2,411	2,858	2,666
22,050	22,100	2,865	2,419	2,865	2,674
22,100	22,150	2,873	2,426	2,873	2,681
22,150	22,200	2,880	2,434	2,880	2,689
22,200	22,250	2,888	2,441	2,888	2,696
22,250	22,300	2,895	2,449	2,895	2,704
22,300	22,350	2,903	2,456	2,903	2,711
22,350	22,400	2,910	2,464	2,910	2,719
22,400	22,450	2,918	2,471	2,918	2,726
22,450	22,500	2,925	2,479	2,925	2,734
22,500	22,550	2,933	2,486	2,933	2,741
22,550	22,600	2,940	2,494	2,940	2,749
22,600	22,650	2,948	2,501	2,948	2,756
22,650	22,700	2,955	2,509	2,955	2,764
22,700	22,750	2,963	2,516	2,963	2,771
22,750	22,800	2,970	2,524	2,970	2,779
22,800	22,850	2,978	2,531	2,978	2,786
22,850	22,900	2,985	2,539	2,985	2,794
22,900	22,950	2,993	2,546	2,993	2,801
22,950	23,000	3,000	2,554	3,000	2,809
23,000					
23,000	23,050	3,008	2,561	3,008	2,816
23,050	23,100	3,015	2,569	3,015	2,824
23,100	23,150	3,023	2,576	3,023	2,831
23,150	23,200	3,030	2,584	3,030	2,839
23,200	23,250	3,038	2,591	3,038	2,846
23,250	23,300	3,045	2,599	3,045	2,854
23,300	23,350	3,053	2,606	3,053	2,861
23,350	23,400	3,060	2,614	3,060	2,869
23,400	23,450	3,068	2,621	3,068	2,876
23,450	23,500	3,075	2,629	3,075	2,884
23,500	23,550	3,083	2,636	3,083	2,891
23,550	23,600	3,090	2,644	3,090	2,899
23,600	23,650	3,098	2,651	3,098	2,906
23,650	23,700	3,105	2,659	3,105	2,914
23,700	23,750	3,113	2,666	3,113	2,921
23,750	23,800	3,120	2,674	3,120	2,929
23,800	23,850	3,128	2,681	3,128	2,936
23,850	23,900	3,135	2,689	3,135	2,944
23,900	23,950	3,143	2,696	3,143	2,951
23,950	24,000	3,150	2,704	3,150	2,959
24,000					
24,000	24,050	3,158	2,711	3,158	2,966
24,050	24,100	3,165	2,719	3,165	2,974
24,100	24,150	3,173	2,726	3,173	2,981
24,150	24,200	3,180	2,734	3,180	2,989
24,200	24,250	3,188	2,741	3,188	2,996
24,250	24,300	3,195	2,749	3,195	3,004
24,300	24,350	3,203	2,756	3,203	3,011
24,350	24,400	3,210	2,764	3,210	3,019
24,400	24,450	3,218	2,771	3,218	3,026
24,450	24,500	3,225	2,779	3,225	3,034
24,500	24,550	3,233	2,786	3,233	3,041
24,550	24,600	3,240	2,794	3,240	3,049
24,600	24,650	3,248	2,801	3,248	3,056
24,650	24,700	3,255	2,809	3,255	3,064
24,700	24,750	3,263	2,816	3,263	3,071
24,750	24,800	3,270	2,824	3,270	3,079
24,800	24,850	3,278	2,831	3,278	3,086
24,850	24,900	3,285	2,839	3,285	3,094
24,900	24,950	3,293	2,846	3,293	3,101
24,950	25,000	3,300	2,854	3,300	3,109
25,000					
25,000	25,050	3,308	2,861	3,308	3,116
25,050	25,100	3,315	2,869	3,315	3,124
25,100	25,150	3,323	2,876	3,323	3,131
25,150	25,200	3,330	2,884	3,330	3,139
25,200	25,250	3,338	2,891	3,338	3,146
25,250	25,300	3,345	2,899	3,345	3,154
25,300	25,350	3,353	2,906	3,353	3,161
25,350	25,400	3,360	2,914	3,360	3,169
25,400	25,450	3,368	2,921	3,368	3,176
25,450	25,500	3,375	2,929	3,375	3,184
25,500	25,550	3,383	2,936	3,383	3,191
25,550	25,600	3,390	2,944	3,390	3,199
25,600	25,650	3,398	2,951	3,398	3,206
25,650	25,700	3,405	2,959	3,405	3,214
25,700	25,750	3,413	2,966	3,413	3,221
25,750	25,800	3,420	2,974	3,420	3,229
25,800	25,850	3,428	2,981	3,428	3,236
25,850	25,900	3,435	2,989	3,435	3,244
25,900	25,950	3,443	2,996	3,443	3,251
25,950	26,000	3,450	3,004	3,450	3,259
26,000					
26,000	26,050	3,458	3,011	3,458	3,266
26,050	26,100	3,465	3,019	3,465	3,274
26,100	26,150	3,473	3,026	3,473	3,281
26,150	26,200	3,480	3,034	3,480	3,289
26,200	26,250	3,488	3,041	3,488	3,296
26,250	26,300	3,495	3,049	3,495	3,304
26,300	26,350	3,503	3,056	3,503	3,311
26,350	26,400	3,510	3,064	3,510	3,319
26,400	26,450	3,518	3,071	3,518	3,326
26,450	26,500	3,525	3,079	3,525	3,334
26,500	26,550	3,533	3,086	3,533	3,341
26,550	26,600	3,540	3,094	3,540	3,349
26,600	26,650	3,548	3,101	3,548	3,356
26,650	26,700	3,555	3,109	3,555	3,364
26,700	26,750	3,563	3,116	3,563	3,371
26,750	26,800	3,570	3,124	3,570	3,379
26,800	26,850	3,578	3,131	3,578	3,386
26,850	26,900	3,585	3,139	3,585	3,394
26,900	26,950	3,593	3,146	3,593	3,401
26,950	27,000	3,600	3,154	3,600	3,409
27,000					
27,000	27,050	3,608	3,161	3,608	3,416
27,050	27,100	3,615	3,169	3,615	3,424
27,100	27,150	3,623	3,176	3,623	3,431
27,150	27,200	3,630	3,184	3,630	3,439
27,200	27,250	3,638	3,191	3,638	3,446
27,250	27,300	3,645	3,199	3,645	3,454
27,300	27,350	3,653	3,206	3,653	3,461
27,350	27,400	3,660	3,214	3,660	3,469
27,400	27,450	3,668	3,221	3,668	3,476
27,450	27,500	3,675	3,229	3,675	3,484
27,500	27,550	3,683	3,236	3,683	3,491
27,550	27,600	3,690	3,244	3,690	3,499
27,600	27,650	3,698	3,251	3,698	3,506
27,650	27,700	3,705	3,259	3,705	3,514
27,700	27,750	3,713	3,266	3,713	3,521
27,750	27,800	3,720	3,274	3,720	3,529
27,800	27,850	3,728	3,281	3,728	3,536
27,850	27,900	3,735	3,289	3,735	3,544
27,900	27,950	3,743	3,296	3,743	3,551
27,950	28,000	3,750	3,304	3,750	3,559
28,000					
28,000	28,050	3,758	3,311	3,758	3,566
28,050	28,100	3,765	3,319	3,765	3,574
28,100	28,150	3,773	3,326	3,773	3,581
28,150	28,200	3,780	3,334	3,780	3,589
28,200	28,250	3,788	3,341	3,788	3,596
28,250	28,300	3,795	3,349	3,795	3,604
28,300	28,350	3,803	3,356	3,803	3,611
28,350	28,400	3,810	3,364	3,810	3,619
28,400	28,450	3,818	3,371	3,818	3,626
28,450	28,500	3,825	3,379	3,825	3,634
28,500	28,550	3,833	3,386	3,833	3,641
28,550	28,600	3,840	3,394	3,840	3,649
28,600	28,650	3,848	3,401	3,848	3,656
28,650	28,700	3,855	3,409	3,855	3,664
28,700	28,750	3,863	3,416	3,863	3,671
28,750	28,800	3,870	3,424	3,870	3,679
28,800	28,850	3,878	3,431	3,878	3,686
28,850	28,900	3,885	3,439	3,885	3,694
28,900	28,950	3,893	3,446	3,893	3,701
28,950	29,000	3,900	3,454	3,900	3,709
29,000					
29,000	29,050	3,908	3,461	3,908	3,716
29,050	29,100	3,915	3,469	3,915	3,724
29,100	29,150	3,923	3,476	3,923	3,731
29,150	29,200	3,930	3,484	3,930	3,739
29,200	29,250	3,938	3,491	3,938	3,746
29,250	29,300	3,945	3,499	3,945	3,754
29,300	29,350	3,953	3,506	3,953	3,761
29,350	29,400	3,960	3,514	3,960	3,769
29,400	29,450	3,968	3,521	3,968	3,776
29,450	29,500	3,975	3,529	3,975	3,784
29,500	29,550	3,983	3,536	3,983	3,791
29,550	29,600	3,990	3,544	3,990	3,799
29,600	29,650	3,998	3,551	3,998	3,806
29,650	29,700	4,005	3,559	4,005	3,814
29,700	29,750	4,013	3,566	4,013	3,821
29,750	29,800	4,020	3,574	4,020	3,829
29,800	29,850	4,028	3,581	4,028	3,836
29,850	29,900	4,035	3,589	4,035	3,844
29,900	29,950	4,043	3,596	4,043	3,851
29,950	30,000	4,050	3,604	4,050	3,859

* This column must also be used by a qualifying widow(er).

(Continued)

2013 Tax Table—*Continued*

30,000

At least	But less than	Single	Married filing jointly *	Married filing separately	Head of a household
			Your tax is—		
30,000	30,050	4,058	3,611	4,058	3,866
30,050	30,100	4,065	3,619	4,065	3,874
30,100	30,150	4,073	3,626	4,073	3,881
30,150	30,200	4,080	3,634	4,080	3,889
30,200	30,250	4,088	3,641	4,088	3,896
30,250	30,300	4,095	3,649	4,095	3,904
30,300	30,350	4,103	3,656	4,103	3,911
30,350	30,400	4,110	3,664	4,110	3,919
30,400	30,450	4,118	3,671	4,118	3,926
30,450	30,500	4,125	3,679	4,125	3,934
30,500	30,550	4,133	3,686	4,133	3,941
30,550	30,600	4,140	3,694	4,140	3,949
30,600	30,650	4,148	3,701	4,148	3,956
30,650	30,700	4,155	3,709	4,155	3,964
30,700	30,750	4,163	3,716	4,163	3,971
30,750	30,800	4,170	3,724	4,170	3,979
30,800	30,850	4,178	3,731	4,178	3,986
30,850	30,900	4,185	3,739	4,185	3,994
30,900	30,950	4,193	3,746	4,193	4,001
30,950	31,000	4,200	3,754	4,200	4,009

31,000

At least	But less than	Single	Married filing jointly *	Married filing separately	Head of a household
31,000	31,050	4,208	3,761	4,208	4,016
31,050	31,100	4,215	3,769	4,215	4,024
31,100	31,150	4,223	3,776	4,223	4,031
31,150	31,200	4,230	3,784	4,230	4,039
31,200	31,250	4,238	3,791	4,238	4,046
31,250	31,300	4,245	3,799	4,245	4,054
31,300	31,350	4,253	3,806	4,253	4,061
31,350	31,400	4,260	3,814	4,260	4,069
31,400	31,450	4,268	3,821	4,268	4,076
31,450	31,500	4,275	3,829	4,275	4,084
31,500	31,550	4,283	3,836	4,283	4,091
31,550	31,600	4,290	3,844	4,290	4,099
31,600	31,650	4,298	3,851	4,298	4,106
31,650	31,700	4,305	3,859	4,305	4,114
31,700	31,750	4,313	3,866	4,313	4,121
31,750	31,800	4,320	3,874	4,320	4,129
31,800	31,850	4,328	3,881	4,328	4,136
31,850	31,900	4,335	3,889	4,335	4,144
31,900	31,950	4,343	3,896	4,343	4,151
31,950	32,000	4,350	3,904	4,350	4,159

32,000

At least	But less than	Single	Married filing jointly *	Married filing separately	Head of a household
32,000	32,050	4,358	3,911	4,358	4,166
32,050	32,100	4,365	3,919	4,365	4,174
32,100	32,150	4,373	3,926	4,373	4,181
32,150	32,200	4,380	3,934	4,380	4,189
32,200	32,250	4,388	3,941	4,388	4,196
32,250	32,300	4,395	3,949	4,395	4,204
32,300	32,350	4,403	3,956	4,403	4,211
32,350	32,400	4,410	3,964	4,410	4,219
32,400	32,450	4,418	3,971	4,418	4,226
32,450	32,500	4,425	3,979	4,425	4,234
32,500	32,550	4,433	3,986	4,433	4,241
32,550	32,600	4,440	3,994	4,440	4,249
32,600	32,650	4,448	4,001	4,448	4,256
32,650	32,700	4,455	4,009	4,455	4,264
32,700	32,750	4,463	4,016	4,463	4,271
32,750	32,800	4,470	4,024	4,470	4,279
32,800	32,850	4,478	4,031	4,478	4,286
32,850	32,900	4,485	4,039	4,485	4,294
32,900	32,950	4,493	4,046	4,493	4,301
32,950	33,000	4,500	4,054	4,500	4,309

33,000

At least	But less than	Single	Married filing jointly *	Married filing separately	Head of a household
33,000	33,050	4,508	4,061	4,508	4,316
33,050	33,100	4,515	4,069	4,515	4,324
33,100	33,150	4,523	4,076	4,523	4,331
33,150	33,200	4,530	4,084	4,530	4,339
33,200	33,250	4,538	4,091	4,538	4,346
33,250	33,300	4,545	4,099	4,545	4,354
33,300	33,350	4,553	4,106	4,553	4,361
33,350	33,400	4,560	4,114	4,560	4,369
33,400	33,450	4,568	4,121	4,568	4,376
33,450	33,500	4,575	4,129	4,575	4,384
33,500	33,550	4,583	4,136	4,583	4,391
33,550	33,600	4,590	4,144	4,590	4,399
33,600	33,650	4,598	4,151	4,598	4,406
33,650	33,700	4,605	4,159	4,605	4,414
33,700	33,750	4,613	4,166	4,613	4,421
33,750	33,800	4,620	4,174	4,620	4,429
33,800	33,850	4,628	4,181	4,628	4,436
33,850	33,900	4,635	4,189	4,635	4,444
33,900	33,950	4,643	4,196	4,643	4,451
33,950	34,000	4,650	4,204	4,650	4,459

34,000

At least	But less than	Single	Married filing jointly *	Married filing separately	Head of a household
34,000	34,050	4,658	4,211	4,658	4,466
34,050	34,100	4,665	4,219	4,665	4,474
34,100	34,150	4,673	4,226	4,673	4,481
34,150	34,200	4,680	4,234	4,680	4,489
34,200	34,250	4,688	4,241	4,688	4,496
34,250	34,300	4,695	4,249	4,695	4,504
34,300	34,350	4,703	4,256	4,703	4,511
34,350	34,400	4,710	4,264	4,710	4,519
34,400	34,450	4,718	4,271	4,718	4,526
34,450	34,500	4,725	4,279	4,725	4,534
34,500	34,550	4,733	4,286	4,733	4,541
34,550	34,600	4,740	4,294	4,740	4,549
34,600	34,650	4,748	4,301	4,748	4,556
34,650	34,700	4,755	4,309	4,755	4,564
34,700	34,750	4,763	4,316	4,763	4,571
34,750	34,800	4,770	4,324	4,770	4,579
34,800	34,850	4,778	4,331	4,778	4,586
34,850	34,900	4,785	4,339	4,785	4,594
34,900	34,950	4,793	4,346	4,793	4,601
34,950	35,000	4,800	4,354	4,800	4,609

35,000

At least	But less than	Single	Married filing jointly *	Married filing separately	Head of a household
35,000	35,050	4,808	4,361	4,808	4,616
35,050	35,100	4,815	4,369	4,815	4,624
35,100	35,150	4,823	4,376	4,823	4,631
35,150	35,200	4,830	4,384	4,830	4,639
35,200	35,250	4,838	4,391	4,838	4,646
35,250	35,300	4,845	4,399	4,845	4,654
35,300	35,350	4,853	4,406	4,853	4,661
35,350	35,400	4,860	4,414	4,860	4,669
35,400	35,450	4,868	4,421	4,868	4,676
35,450	35,500	4,875	4,429	4,875	4,684
35,500	35,550	4,883	4,436	4,883	4,691
35,550	35,600	4,890	4,444	4,890	4,699
35,600	35,650	4,898	4,451	4,898	4,706
35,650	35,700	4,905	4,459	4,905	4,714
35,700	35,750	4,913	4,466	4,913	4,721
35,750	35,800	4,920	4,474	4,920	4,729
35,800	35,850	4,928	4,481	4,928	4,736
35,850	35,900	4,935	4,489	4,935	4,744
35,900	35,950	4,943	4,496	4,943	4,751
35,950	36,000	4,950	4,504	4,950	4,759

36,000

At least	But less than	Single	Married filing jointly *	Married filing separately	Head of a household
36,000	36,050	4,958	4,511	4,958	4,766
36,050	36,100	4,965	4,519	4,965	4,774
36,100	36,150	4,973	4,526	4,973	4,781
36,150	36,200	4,980	4,534	4,980	4,789
36,200	36,250	4,988	4,541	4,988	4,796
36,250	36,300	4,998	4,549	4,998	4,804
36,300	36,350	5,010	4,556	5,010	4,811
36,350	36,400	5,023	4,564	5,023	4,819
36,400	36,450	5,035	4,571	5,035	4,826
36,450	36,500	5,048	4,579	5,048	4,834
36,500	36,550	5,060	4,586	5,060	4,841
36,550	36,600	5,073	4,594	5,073	4,849
36,600	36,650	5,085	4,601	5,085	4,856
36,650	36,700	5,098	4,609	5,098	4,864
36,700	36,750	5,110	4,616	5,110	4,871
36,750	36,800	5,123	4,624	5,123	4,879
36,800	36,850	5,135	4,631	5,135	4,886
36,850	36,900	5,148	4,639	5,148	4,894
36,900	36,950	5,160	4,646	5,160	4,901
36,950	37,000	5,173	4,654	5,173	4,909

37,000

At least	But less than	Single	Married filing jointly *	Married filing separately	Head of a household
37,000	37,050	5,185	4,661	5,185	4,916
37,050	37,100	5,198	4,669	5,198	4,924
37,100	37,150	5,210	4,676	5,210	4,931
37,150	37,200	5,223	4,684	5,223	4,939
37,200	37,250	5,235	4,691	5,235	4,946
37,250	37,300	5,248	4,699	5,248	4,954
37,300	37,350	5,260	4,706	5,260	4,961
37,350	37,400	5,273	4,714	5,273	4,969
37,400	37,450	5,285	4,721	5,285	4,976
37,450	37,500	5,298	4,729	5,298	4,984
37,500	37,550	5,310	4,736	5,310	4,991
37,550	37,600	5,323	4,744	5,323	4,999
37,600	37,650	5,335	4,751	5,335	5,006
37,650	37,700	5,348	4,759	5,348	5,014
37,700	37,750	5,360	4,766	5,360	5,021
37,750	37,800	5,373	4,774	5,373	5,029
37,800	37,850	5,385	4,781	5,385	5,036
37,850	37,900	5,398	4,789	5,398	5,044
37,900	37,950	5,410	4,796	5,410	5,051
37,950	38,000	5,423	4,804	5,423	5,059

38,000

At least	But less than	Single	Married filing jointly *	Married filing separately	Head of a household
38,000	38,050	5,435	4,811	5,435	5,066
38,050	38,100	5,448	4,819	5,448	5,074
38,100	38,150	5,460	4,826	5,460	5,081
38,150	38,200	5,473	4,834	5,473	5,089
38,200	38,250	5,485	4,841	5,485	5,096
38,250	38,300	5,498	4,849	5,498	5,104
38,300	38,350	5,510	4,856	5,510	5,111
38,350	38,400	5,523	4,864	5,523	5,119
38,400	38,450	5,535	4,871	5,535	5,126
38,450	38,500	5,548	4,879	5,548	5,134
38,500	38,550	5,560	4,886	5,560	5,141
38,550	38,600	5,573	4,894	5,573	5,149
38,600	38,650	5,585	4,901	5,585	5,156
38,650	38,700	5,598	4,909	5,598	5,164
38,700	38,750	5,610	4,916	5,610	5,171
38,750	38,800	5,623	4,924	5,623	5,179
38,800	38,850	5,635	4,931	5,635	5,186
38,850	38,900	5,648	4,939	5,648	5,194
38,900	38,950	5,660	4,946	5,660	5,201
38,950	39,000	5,673	4,954	5,673	5,209

* This column must also be used by a qualifying widow(er).

(Continued)

2013 Tax Table—*Continued*

If line 43 (taxable income) is—		And you are—			
At least	But less than	Single	Married filing jointly *	Married filing separately	Head of a house-hold
		Your tax is—			

39,000

At least	But less than	Single	MFJ *	MFS	HoH
39,000	39,050	5,685	4,961	5,685	5,216
39,050	39,100	5,698	4,969	5,698	5,224
39,100	39,150	5,710	4,976	5,710	5,231
39,150	39,200	5,723	4,984	5,723	5,239
39,200	39,250	5,735	4,991	5,735	5,246
39,250	39,300	5,748	4,999	5,748	5,254
39,300	39,350	5,760	5,006	5,760	5,261
39,350	39,400	5,773	5,014	5,773	5,269
39,400	39,450	5,785	5,021	5,785	5,276
39,450	39,500	5,798	5,029	5,798	5,284
39,500	39,550	5,810	5,036	5,810	5,291
39,550	39,600	5,823	5,044	5,823	5,299
39,600	39,650	5,835	5,051	5,835	5,306
39,650	39,700	5,848	5,059	5,848	5,314
39,700	39,750	5,860	5,066	5,860	5,321
39,750	39,800	5,873	5,074	5,873	5,329
39,800	39,850	5,885	5,081	5,885	5,336
39,850	39,900	5,898	5,089	5,898	5,344
39,900	39,950	5,910	5,096	5,910	5,351
39,950	40,000	5,923	5,104	5,923	5,359

40,000

At least	But less than	Single	MFJ *	MFS	HoH
40,000	40,050	5,935	5,111	5,935	5,366
40,050	40,100	5,948	5,119	5,948	5,374
40,100	40,150	5,960	5,126	5,960	5,381
40,150	40,200	5,973	5,134	5,973	5,389
40,200	40,250	5,985	5,141	5,985	5,396
40,250	40,300	5,998	5,149	5,998	5,404
40,300	40,350	6,010	5,156	6,010	5,411
40,350	40,400	6,023	5,164	6,023	5,419
40,400	40,450	6,035	5,171	6,035	5,426
40,450	40,500	6,048	5,179	6,048	5,434
40,500	40,550	6,060	5,186	6,060	5,441
40,550	40,600	6,073	5,194	6,073	5,449
40,600	40,650	6,085	5,201	6,085	5,456
40,650	40,700	6,098	5,209	6,098	5,464
40,700	40,750	6,110	5,216	6,110	5,471
40,750	40,800	6,123	5,224	6,123	5,479
40,800	40,850	6,135	5,231	6,135	5,486
40,850	40,900	6,148	5,239	6,148	5,494
40,900	40,950	6,160	5,246	6,160	5,501
40,950	41,000	6,173	5,254	6,173	5,509

41,000

At least	But less than	Single	MFJ *	MFS	HoH
41,000	41,050	6,185	5,261	6,185	5,516
41,050	41,100	6,198	5,269	6,198	5,524
41,100	41,150	6,210	5,276	6,210	5,531
41,150	41,200	6,223	5,284	6,223	5,539
41,200	41,250	6,235	5,291	6,235	5,546
41,250	41,300	6,248	5,299	6,248	5,554
41,300	41,350	6,260	5,306	6,260	5,561
41,350	41,400	6,273	5,314	6,273	5,569
41,400	41,450	6,285	5,321	6,285	5,576
41,450	41,500	6,298	5,329	6,298	5,584
41,500	41,550	6,310	5,336	6,310	5,591
41,550	41,600	6,323	5,344	6,323	5,599
41,600	41,650	6,335	5,351	6,335	5,606
41,650	41,700	6,348	5,359	6,348	5,614
41,700	41,750	6,360	5,366	6,360	5,621
41,750	41,800	6,373	5,374	6,373	5,629
41,800	41,850	6,385	5,381	6,385	5,636
41,850	41,900	6,398	5,389	6,398	5,644
41,900	41,950	6,410	5,396	6,410	5,651
41,950	42,000	6,423	5,404	6,423	5,659

42,000

At least	But less than	Single	MFJ *	MFS	HoH
42,000	42,050	6,435	5,411	6,435	5,666
42,050	42,100	6,448	5,419	6,448	5,674
42,100	42,150	6,460	5,426	6,460	5,681
42,150	42,200	6,473	5,434	6,473	5,689
42,200	42,250	6,485	5,441	6,485	5,696
42,250	42,300	6,498	5,449	6,498	5,704
42,300	42,350	6,510	5,456	6,510	5,711
42,350	42,400	6,523	5,464	6,523	5,719
42,400	42,450	6,535	5,471	6,535	5,726
42,450	42,500	6,548	5,479	6,548	5,734
42,500	42,550	6,560	5,486	6,560	5,741
42,550	42,600	6,573	5,494	6,573	5,749
42,600	42,650	6,585	5,501	6,585	5,756
42,650	42,700	6,598	5,509	6,598	5,764
42,700	42,750	6,610	5,516	6,610	5,771
42,750	42,800	6,623	5,524	6,623	5,779
42,800	42,850	6,635	5,531	6,635	5,786
42,850	42,900	6,648	5,539	6,648	5,794
42,900	42,950	6,660	5,546	6,660	5,801
42,950	43,000	6,673	5,554	6,673	5,809

43,000

At least	But less than	Single	MFJ *	MFS	HoH
43,000	43,050	6,685	5,561	6,685	5,816
43,050	43,100	6,698	5,569	6,698	5,824
43,100	43,150	6,710	5,576	6,710	5,831
43,150	43,200	6,723	5,584	6,723	5,839
43,200	43,250	6,735	5,591	6,735	5,846
43,250	43,300	6,748	5,599	6,748	5,854
43,300	43,350	6,760	5,606	6,760	5,861
43,350	43,400	6,773	5,614	6,773	5,869
43,400	43,450	6,785	5,621	6,785	5,876
43,450	43,500	6,798	5,629	6,798	5,884
43,500	43,550	6,810	5,636	6,810	5,891
43,550	43,600	6,823	5,644	6,823	5,899
43,600	43,650	6,835	5,651	6,835	5,906
43,650	43,700	6,848	5,659	6,848	5,914
43,700	43,750	6,860	5,666	6,860	5,921
43,750	43,800	6,873	5,674	6,873	5,929
43,800	43,850	6,885	5,681	6,885	5,936
43,850	43,900	6,898	5,689	6,898	5,944
43,900	43,950	6,910	5,696	6,910	5,951
43,950	44,000	6,923	5,704	6,923	5,959

44,000

At least	But less than	Single	MFJ *	MFS	HoH
44,000	44,050	6,935	5,711	6,935	5,966
44,050	44,100	6,948	5,719	6,948	5,974
44,100	44,150	6,960	5,726	6,960	5,981
44,150	44,200	6,973	5,734	6,973	5,989
44,200	44,250	6,985	5,741	6,985	5,996
44,250	44,300	6,998	5,749	6,998	6,004
44,300	44,350	7,010	5,756	7,010	6,011
44,350	44,400	7,023	5,764	7,023	6,019
44,400	44,450	7,035	5,771	7,035	6,026
44,450	44,500	7,048	5,779	7,048	6,034
44,500	44,550	7,060	5,786	7,060	6,041
44,550	44,600	7,073	5,794	7,073	6,049
44,600	44,650	7,085	5,801	7,085	6,056
44,650	44,700	7,098	5,809	7,098	6,064
44,700	44,750	7,110	5,816	7,110	6,071
44,750	44,800	7,123	5,824	7,123	6,079
44,800	44,850	7,135	5,831	7,135	6,086
44,850	44,900	7,148	5,839	7,148	6,094
44,900	44,950	7,160	5,846	7,160	6,101
44,950	45,000	7,173	5,854	7,173	6,109

45,000

At least	But less than	Single	MFJ *	MFS	HoH
45,000	45,050	7,185	5,861	7,185	6,116
45,050	45,100	7,198	5,869	7,198	6,124
45,100	45,150	7,210	5,876	7,210	6,131
45,150	45,200	7,223	5,884	7,223	6,139
45,200	45,250	7,235	5,891	7,235	6,146
45,250	45,300	7,248	5,899	7,248	6,154
45,300	45,350	7,260	5,906	7,260	6,161
45,350	45,400	7,273	5,914	7,273	6,169
45,400	45,450	7,285	5,921	7,285	6,176
45,450	45,500	7,298	5,929	7,298	6,184
45,500	45,550	7,310	5,936	7,310	6,191
45,550	45,600	7,323	5,944	7,323	6,199
45,600	45,650	7,335	5,951	7,335	6,206
45,650	45,700	7,348	5,959	7,348	6,214
45,700	45,750	7,360	5,966	7,360	6,221
45,750	45,800	7,373	5,974	7,373	6,229
45,800	45,850	7,385	5,981	7,385	6,236
45,850	45,900	7,398	5,989	7,398	6,244
45,900	45,950	7,410	5,996	7,410	6,251
45,950	46,000	7,423	6,004	7,423	6,259

46,000

At least	But less than	Single	MFJ *	MFS	HoH
46,000	46,050	7,435	6,011	7,435	6,266
46,050	46,100	7,448	6,019	7,448	6,274
46,100	46,150	7,460	6,026	7,460	6,281
46,150	46,200	7,473	6,034	7,473	6,289
46,200	46,250	7,485	6,041	7,485	6,296
46,250	46,300	7,498	6,049	7,498	6,304
46,300	46,350	7,510	6,056	7,510	6,311
46,350	46,400	7,523	6,064	7,523	6,319
46,400	46,450	7,535	6,071	7,535	6,326
46,450	46,500	7,548	6,079	7,548	6,334
46,500	46,550	7,560	6,086	7,560	6,341
46,550	46,600	7,573	6,094	7,573	6,349
46,600	46,650	7,585	6,101	7,585	6,356
46,650	46,700	7,598	6,109	7,598	6,364
46,700	46,750	7,610	6,116	7,610	6,371
46,750	46,800	7,623	6,124	7,623	6,379
46,800	46,850	7,635	6,131	7,635	6,386
46,850	46,900	7,648	6,139	7,648	6,394
46,900	46,950	7,660	6,146	7,660	6,401
46,950	47,000	7,673	6,154	7,673	6,409

47,000

At least	But less than	Single	MFJ *	MFS	HoH
47,000	47,050	7,685	6,161	7,685	6,416
47,050	47,100	7,698	6,169	7,698	6,424
47,100	47,150	7,710	6,176	7,710	6,431
47,150	47,200	7,723	6,184	7,723	6,439
47,200	47,250	7,735	6,191	7,735	6,446
47,250	47,300	7,748	6,199	7,748	6,454
47,300	47,350	7,760	6,206	7,760	6,461
47,350	47,400	7,773	6,214	7,773	6,469
47,400	47,450	7,785	6,221	7,785	6,476
47,450	47,500	7,798	6,229	7,798	6,484
47,500	47,550	7,810	6,236	7,810	6,491
47,550	47,600	7,823	6,244	7,823	6,499
47,600	47,650	7,835	6,251	7,835	6,506
47,650	47,700	7,848	6,259	7,848	6,514
47,700	47,750	7,860	6,266	7,860	6,521
47,750	47,800	7,873	6,274	7,873	6,529
47,800	47,850	7,885	6,281	7,885	6,536
47,850	47,900	7,898	6,289	7,898	6,544
47,900	47,950	7,910	6,296	7,910	6,551
47,950	48,000	7,923	6,304	7,923	6,559

* This column must also be used by a qualifying widow(er).

(Continued)

2013 Tax Table—*Continued*

48,000–50,000

At least	But less than	Single	Married filing jointly *	Married filing separately	Head of a household
48,000					
48,000	48,050	7,935	6,311	7,935	6,566
48,050	48,100	7,948	6,319	7,948	6,574
48,100	48,150	7,960	6,326	7,960	6,581
48,150	48,200	7,973	6,334	7,973	6,589
48,200	48,250	7,985	6,341	7,985	6,596
48,250	48,300	7,998	6,349	7,998	6,604
48,300	48,350	8,010	6,356	8,010	6,611
48,350	48,400	8,023	6,364	8,023	6,619
48,400	48,450	8,035	6,371	8,035	6,626
48,450	48,500	8,048	6,379	8,048	6,634
48,500	48,550	8,060	6,386	8,060	6,641
48,550	48,600	8,073	6,394	8,073	6,649
48,600	48,650	8,085	6,401	8,085	6,659
48,650	48,700	8,098	6,409	8,098	6,671
48,700	48,750	8,110	6,416	8,110	6,684
48,750	48,800	8,123	6,424	8,123	6,696
48,800	48,850	8,135	6,431	8,135	6,709
48,850	48,900	8,148	6,439	8,148	6,721
48,900	48,950	8,160	6,446	8,160	6,734
48,950	49,000	8,173	6,454	8,173	6,746
49,000					
49,000	49,050	8,185	6,461	8,185	6,759
49,050	49,100	8,198	6,469	8,198	6,771
49,100	49,150	8,210	6,476	8,210	6,784
49,150	49,200	8,223	6,484	8,223	6,796
49,200	49,250	8,235	6,491	8,235	6,809
49,250	49,300	8,248	6,499	8,248	6,821
49,300	49,350	8,260	6,506	8,260	6,834
49,350	49,400	8,273	6,514	8,273	6,846
49,400	49,450	8,285	6,521	8,285	6,859
49,450	49,500	8,298	6,529	8,298	6,871
49,500	49,550	8,310	6,536	8,310	6,884
49,550	49,600	8,323	6,544	8,323	6,896
49,600	49,650	8,335	6,551	8,335	6,909
49,650	49,700	8,348	6,559	8,348	6,921
49,700	49,750	8,360	6,566	8,360	6,934
49,750	49,800	8,373	6,574	8,373	6,946
49,800	49,850	8,385	6,581	8,385	6,959
49,850	49,900	8,398	6,589	8,398	6,971
49,900	49,950	8,410	6,596	8,410	6,984
49,950	50,000	8,423	6,604	8,423	6,996
50,000					
50,000	50,050	8,435	6,611	8,435	7,009
50,050	50,100	8,448	6,619	8,448	7,021
50,100	50,150	8,460	6,626	8,460	7,034
50,150	50,200	8,473	6,634	8,473	7,046
50,200	50,250	8,485	6,641	8,485	7,059
50,250	50,300	8,498	6,649	8,498	7,071
50,300	50,350	8,510	6,656	8,510	7,084
50,350	50,400	8,523	6,664	8,523	7,096
50,400	50,450	8,535	6,671	8,535	7,109
50,450	50,500	8,548	6,679	8,548	7,121
50,500	50,550	8,560	6,686	8,560	7,134
50,550	50,600	8,573	6,694	8,573	7,146
50,600	50,650	8,585	6,701	8,585	7,159
50,650	50,700	8,598	6,709	8,598	7,171
50,700	50,750	8,610	6,716	8,610	7,184
50,750	50,800	8,623	6,724	8,623	7,196
50,800	50,850	8,635	6,731	8,635	7,209
50,850	50,900	8,648	6,739	8,648	7,221
50,900	50,950	8,660	6,746	8,660	7,234
50,950	51,000	8,673	6,754	8,673	7,246

51,000–53,000

At least	But less than	Single	Married filing jointly *	Married filing separately	Head of a household
51,000					
51,000	51,050	8,685	6,761	8,685	7,259
51,050	51,100	8,698	6,769	8,698	7,271
51,100	51,150	8,710	6,776	8,710	7,284
51,150	51,200	8,723	6,784	8,723	7,296
51,200	51,250	8,735	6,791	8,735	7,309
51,250	51,300	8,748	6,799	8,748	7,321
51,300	51,350	8,760	6,806	8,760	7,334
51,350	51,400	8,773	6,814	8,773	7,346
51,400	51,450	8,785	6,821	8,785	7,359
51,450	51,500	8,798	6,829	8,798	7,371
51,500	51,550	8,810	6,836	8,810	7,384
51,550	51,600	8,823	6,844	8,823	7,396
51,600	51,650	8,835	6,851	8,835	7,409
51,650	51,700	8,848	6,859	8,848	7,421
51,700	51,750	8,860	6,866	8,860	7,434
51,750	51,800	8,873	6,874	8,873	7,446
51,800	51,850	8,885	6,881	8,885	7,459
51,850	51,900	8,898	6,889	8,898	7,471
51,900	51,950	8,910	6,896	8,910	7,484
51,950	52,000	8,923	6,904	8,923	7,496
52,000					
52,000	52,050	8,935	6,911	8,935	7,509
52,050	52,100	8,948	6,919	8,948	7,521
52,100	52,150	8,960	6,926	8,960	7,534
52,150	52,200	8,973	6,934	8,973	7,546
52,200	52,250	8,985	6,941	8,985	7,559
52,250	52,300	8,998	6,949	8,998	7,571
52,300	52,350	9,010	6,956	9,010	7,584
52,350	52,400	9,023	6,964	9,023	7,596
52,400	52,450	9,035	6,971	9,035	7,609
52,450	52,500	9,048	6,979	9,048	7,621
52,500	52,550	9,060	6,986	9,060	7,634
52,550	52,600	9,073	6,994	9,073	7,646
52,600	52,650	9,085	7,001	9,085	7,659
52,650	52,700	9,098	7,009	9,098	7,671
52,700	52,750	9,110	7,016	9,110	7,684
52,750	52,800	9,123	7,024	9,123	7,696
52,800	52,850	9,135	7,031	9,135	7,709
52,850	52,900	9,148	7,039	9,148	7,721
52,900	52,950	9,160	7,046	9,160	7,734
52,950	53,000	9,173	7,054	9,173	7,746
53,000					
53,000	53,050	9,185	7,061	9,185	7,759
53,050	53,100	9,198	7,069	9,198	7,771
53,100	53,150	9,210	7,076	9,210	7,784
53,150	53,200	9,223	7,084	9,223	7,796
53,200	53,250	9,235	7,091	9,235	7,809
53,250	53,300	9,248	7,099	9,248	7,821
53,300	53,350	9,260	7,106	9,260	7,834
53,350	53,400	9,273	7,114	9,273	7,846
53,400	53,450	9,285	7,121	9,285	7,859
53,450	53,500	9,298	7,129	9,298	7,871
53,500	53,550	9,310	7,136	9,310	7,884
53,550	53,600	9,323	7,144	9,323	7,896
53,600	53,650	9,335	7,151	9,335	7,909
53,650	53,700	9,348	7,159	9,348	7,921
53,700	53,750	9,360	7,166	9,360	7,934
53,750	53,800	9,373	7,174	9,373	7,946
53,800	53,850	9,385	7,181	9,385	7,959
53,850	53,900	9,398	7,189	9,398	7,971
53,900	53,950	9,410	7,196	9,410	7,984
53,950	54,000	9,423	7,204	9,423	7,996

54,000–56,000

At least	But less than	Single	Married filing jointly *	Married filing separately	Head of a household
54,000					
54,000	54,050	9,435	7,211	9,435	8,009
54,050	54,100	9,448	7,219	9,448	8,021
54,100	54,150	9,460	7,226	9,460	8,034
54,150	54,200	9,473	7,234	9,473	8,046
54,200	54,250	9,485	7,241	9,485	8,059
54,250	54,300	9,498	7,249	9,498	8,071
54,300	54,350	9,510	7,256	9,510	8,084
54,350	54,400	9,523	7,264	9,523	8,096
54,400	54,450	9,535	7,271	9,535	8,109
54,450	54,500	9,548	7,279	9,548	8,121
54,500	54,550	9,560	7,286	9,560	8,134
54,550	54,600	9,573	7,294	9,573	8,146
54,600	54,650	9,585	7,301	9,585	8,159
54,650	54,700	9,598	7,309	9,598	8,171
54,700	54,750	9,610	7,316	9,610	8,184
54,750	54,800	9,623	7,324	9,623	8,196
54,800	54,850	9,635	7,331	9,635	8,209
54,850	54,900	9,648	7,339	9,648	8,221
54,900	54,950	9,660	7,346	9,660	8,234
54,950	55,000	9,673	7,354	9,673	8,246
55,000					
55,000	55,050	9,685	7,361	9,685	8,259
55,050	55,100	9,698	7,369	9,698	8,271
55,100	55,150	9,710	7,376	9,710	8,284
55,150	55,200	9,723	7,384	9,723	8,296
55,200	55,250	9,735	7,391	9,735	8,309
55,250	55,300	9,748	7,399	9,748	8,321
55,300	55,350	9,760	7,406	9,760	8,334
55,350	55,400	9,773	7,414	9,773	8,346
55,400	55,450	9,785	7,421	9,785	8,359
55,450	55,500	9,798	7,429	9,798	8,371
55,500	55,550	9,810	7,436	9,810	8,384
55,550	55,600	9,823	7,444	9,823	8,396
55,600	55,650	9,835	7,451	9,835	8,409
55,650	55,700	9,848	7,459	9,848	8,421
55,700	55,750	9,860	7,466	9,860	8,434
55,750	55,800	9,873	7,474	9,873	8,446
55,800	55,850	9,885	7,481	9,885	8,459
55,850	55,900	9,898	7,489	9,898	8,471
55,900	55,950	9,910	7,496	9,910	8,484
55,950	56,000	9,923	7,504	9,923	8,496
56,000					
56,000	56,050	9,935	7,511	9,935	8,509
56,050	56,100	9,948	7,519	9,948	8,521
56,100	56,150	9,960	7,526	9,960	8,534
56,150	56,200	9,973	7,534	9,973	8,546
56,200	56,250	9,985	7,541	9,985	8,559
56,250	56,300	9,998	7,549	9,998	8,571
56,300	56,350	10,010	7,556	10,010	8,584
56,350	56,400	10,023	7,564	10,023	8,596
56,400	56,450	10,035	7,571	10,035	8,609
56,450	56,500	10,048	7,579	10,048	8,621
56,500	56,550	10,060	7,586	10,060	8,634
56,550	56,600	10,073	7,594	10,073	8,646
56,600	56,650	10,085	7,601	10,085	8,659
56,650	56,700	10,098	7,609	10,098	8,671
56,700	56,750	10,110	7,616	10,110	8,684
56,750	56,800	10,123	7,624	10,123	8,696
56,800	56,850	10,135	7,631	10,135	8,709
56,850	56,900	10,148	7,639	10,148	8,721
56,900	56,950	10,160	7,646	10,160	8,734
56,950	57,000	10,173	7,654	10,173	8,746

* This column must also be used by a qualifying widow(er).

(Continued)

2013 Tax Table—Continued

If line 43 (taxable income) is—		And you are—			
At least	But less than	Single	Married filing jointly *	Married filing separately	Head of a household
		Your tax is—			

57,000

At least	But less than	Single	MFJ	MFS	HoH
57,000	57,050	10,185	7,661	10,185	8,759
57,050	57,100	10,198	7,669	10,198	8,771
57,100	57,150	10,210	7,676	10,210	8,784
57,150	57,200	10,223	7,684	10,223	8,796
57,200	57,250	10,235	7,691	10,235	8,809
57,250	57,300	10,248	7,699	10,248	8,821
57,300	57,350	10,260	7,706	10,260	8,834
57,350	57,400	10,273	7,714	10,273	8,846
57,400	57,450	10,285	7,721	10,285	8,859
57,450	57,500	10,298	7,729	10,298	8,871
57,500	57,550	10,310	7,736	10,310	8,884
57,550	57,600	10,323	7,744	10,323	8,896
57,600	57,650	10,335	7,751	10,335	8,909
57,650	57,700	10,348	7,759	10,348	8,921
57,700	57,750	10,360	7,766	10,360	8,934
57,750	57,800	10,373	7,774	10,373	8,946
57,800	57,850	10,385	7,781	10,385	8,959
57,850	57,900	10,398	7,789	10,398	8,971
57,900	57,950	10,410	7,796	10,410	8,984
57,950	58,000	10,423	7,804	10,423	8,996

58,000

At least	But less than	Single	MFJ	MFS	HoH
58,000	58,050	10,435	7,811	10,435	9,009
58,050	58,100	10,448	7,819	10,448	9,021
58,100	58,150	10,460	7,826	10,460	9,034
58,150	58,200	10,473	7,834	10,473	9,046
58,200	58,250	10,485	7,841	10,485	9,059
58,250	58,300	10,498	7,849	10,498	9,071
58,300	58,350	10,510	7,856	10,510	9,084
58,350	58,400	10,523	7,864	10,523	9,096
58,400	58,450	10,535	7,871	10,535	9,109
58,450	58,500	10,548	7,879	10,548	9,121
58,500	58,550	10,560	7,886	10,560	9,134
58,550	58,600	10,573	7,894	10,573	9,146
58,600	58,650	10,585	7,901	10,585	9,159
58,650	58,700	10,598	7,909	10,598	9,171
58,700	58,750	10,610	7,916	10,610	9,184
58,750	58,800	10,623	7,924	10,623	9,196
58,800	58,850	10,635	7,931	10,635	9,209
58,850	58,900	10,648	7,939	10,648	9,221
58,900	58,950	10,660	7,946	10,660	9,234
58,950	59,000	10,673	7,954	10,673	9,246

59,000

At least	But less than	Single	MFJ	MFS	HoH
59,000	59,050	10,685	7,961	10,685	9,259
59,050	59,100	10,698	7,969	10,698	9,271
59,100	59,150	10,710	7,976	10,710	9,284
59,150	59,200	10,723	7,984	10,723	9,296
59,200	59,250	10,735	7,991	10,735	9,309
59,250	59,300	10,748	7,999	10,748	9,321
59,300	59,350	10,760	8,006	10,760	9,334
59,350	59,400	10,773	8,014	10,773	9,346
59,400	59,450	10,785	8,021	10,785	9,359
59,450	59,500	10,798	8,029	10,798	9,371
59,500	59,550	10,810	8,036	10,810	9,384
59,550	59,600	10,823	8,044	10,823	9,396
59,600	59,650	10,835	8,051	10,835	9,409
59,650	59,700	10,848	8,059	10,848	9,421
59,700	59,750	10,860	8,066	10,860	9,434
59,750	59,800	10,873	8,074	10,873	9,446
59,800	59,850	10,885	8,081	10,885	9,459
59,850	59,900	10,898	8,089	10,898	9,471
59,900	59,950	10,910	8,096	10,910	9,484
59,950	60,000	10,923	8,104	10,923	9,496

60,000

At least	But less than	Single	MFJ	MFS	HoH
60,000	60,050	10,935	8,111	10,935	9,509
60,050	60,100	10,948	8,119	10,948	9,521
60,100	60,150	10,960	8,126	10,960	9,534
60,150	60,200	10,973	8,134	10,973	9,546
60,200	60,250	10,985	8,141	10,985	9,559
60,250	60,300	10,998	8,149	10,998	9,571
60,300	60,350	11,010	8,156	11,010	9,584
60,350	60,400	11,023	8,164	11,023	9,596
60,400	60,450	11,035	8,171	11,035	9,609
60,450	60,500	11,048	8,179	11,048	9,621
60,500	60,550	11,060	8,186	11,060	9,634
60,550	60,600	11,073	8,194	11,073	9,646
60,600	60,650	11,085	8,201	11,085	9,659
60,650	60,700	11,098	8,209	11,098	9,671
60,700	60,750	11,110	8,216	11,110	9,684
60,750	60,800	11,123	8,224	11,123	9,696
60,800	60,850	11,135	8,231	11,135	9,709
60,850	60,900	11,148	8,239	11,148	9,721
60,900	60,950	11,160	8,246	11,160	9,734
60,950	61,000	11,173	8,254	11,173	9,746

61,000

At least	But less than	Single	MFJ	MFS	HoH
61,000	61,050	11,185	8,261	11,185	9,759
61,050	61,100	11,198	8,269	11,198	9,771
61,100	61,150	11,210	8,276	11,210	9,784
61,150	61,200	11,223	8,284	11,223	9,796
61,200	61,250	11,235	8,291	11,235	9,809
61,250	61,300	11,248	8,299	11,248	9,821
61,300	61,350	11,260	8,306	11,260	9,834
61,350	61,400	11,273	8,314	11,273	9,846
61,400	61,450	11,285	8,321	11,285	9,859
61,450	61,500	11,298	8,329	11,298	9,871
61,500	61,550	11,310	8,336	11,310	9,884
61,550	61,600	11,323	8,344	11,323	9,896
61,600	61,650	11,335	8,351	11,335	9,909
61,650	61,700	11,348	8,359	11,348	9,921
61,700	61,750	11,360	8,366	11,360	9,934
61,750	61,800	11,373	8,374	11,373	9,946
61,800	61,850	11,385	8,381	11,385	9,959
61,850	61,900	11,398	8,389	11,398	9,971
61,900	61,950	11,410	8,396	11,410	9,984
61,950	62,000	11,423	8,404	11,423	9,996

62,000

At least	But less than	Single	MFJ	MFS	HoH
62,000	62,050	11,435	8,411	11,435	10,009
62,050	62,100	11,448	8,419	11,448	10,021
62,100	62,150	11,460	8,426	11,460	10,034
62,150	62,200	11,473	8,434	11,473	10,046
62,200	62,250	11,485	8,441	11,485	10,059
62,250	62,300	11,498	8,449	11,498	10,071
62,300	62,350	11,510	8,456	11,510	10,084
62,350	62,400	11,523	8,464	11,523	10,096
62,400	62,450	11,535	8,471	11,535	10,109
62,450	62,500	11,548	8,479	11,548	10,121
62,500	62,550	11,560	8,486	11,560	10,134
62,550	62,600	11,573	8,494	11,573	10,146
62,600	62,650	11,585	8,501	11,585	10,159
62,650	62,700	11,598	8,509	11,598	10,171
62,700	62,750	11,610	8,516	11,610	10,184
62,750	62,800	11,623	8,524	11,623	10,196
62,800	62,850	11,635	8,531	11,635	10,209
62,850	62,900	11,648	8,539	11,648	10,221
62,900	62,950	11,660	8,546	11,660	10,234
62,950	63,000	11,673	8,554	11,673	10,246

63,000

At least	But less than	Single	MFJ	MFS	HoH
63,000	63,050	11,685	8,561	11,685	10,259
63,050	63,100	11,698	8,569	11,698	10,271
63,100	63,150	11,710	8,576	11,710	10,284
63,150	63,200	11,723	8,584	11,723	10,296
63,200	63,250	11,735	8,591	11,735	10,309
63,250	63,300	11,748	8,599	11,748	10,321
63,300	63,350	11,760	8,606	11,760	10,334
63,350	63,400	11,773	8,614	11,773	10,346
63,400	63,450	11,785	8,621	11,785	10,359
63,450	63,500	11,798	8,629	11,798	10,371
63,500	63,550	11,810	8,636	11,810	10,384
63,550	63,600	11,823	8,644	11,823	10,396
63,600	63,650	11,835	8,651	11,835	10,409
63,650	63,700	11,848	8,659	11,848	10,421
63,700	63,750	11,860	8,666	11,860	10,434
63,750	63,800	11,873	8,674	11,873	10,446
63,800	63,850	11,885	8,681	11,885	10,459
63,850	63,900	11,898	8,689	11,898	10,471
63,900	63,950	11,910	8,696	11,910	10,484
63,950	64,000	11,923	8,704	11,923	10,496

64,000

At least	But less than	Single	MFJ	MFS	HoH
64,000	64,050	11,935	8,711	11,935	10,509
64,050	64,100	11,948	8,719	11,948	10,521
64,100	64,150	11,960	8,726	11,960	10,534
64,150	64,200	11,973	8,734	11,973	10,546
64,200	64,250	11,985	8,741	11,985	10,559
64,250	64,300	11,998	8,749	11,998	10,571
64,300	64,350	12,010	8,756	12,010	10,584
64,350	64,400	12,023	8,764	12,023	10,596
64,400	64,450	12,035	8,771	12,035	10,609
64,450	64,500	12,048	8,779	12,048	10,621
64,500	64,550	12,060	8,786	12,060	10,634
64,550	64,600	12,073	8,794	12,073	10,646
64,600	64,650	12,085	8,801	12,085	10,659
64,650	64,700	12,098	8,809	12,098	10,671
64,700	64,750	12,110	8,816	12,110	10,684
64,750	64,800	12,123	8,824	12,123	10,696
64,800	64,850	12,135	8,831	12,135	10,709
64,850	64,900	12,148	8,839	12,148	10,721
64,900	64,950	12,160	8,846	12,160	10,734
64,950	65,000	12,173	8,854	12,173	10,746

65,000

At least	But less than	Single	MFJ	MFS	HoH
65,000	65,050	12,185	8,861	12,185	10,759
65,050	65,100	12,198	8,869	12,198	10,771
65,100	65,150	12,210	8,876	12,210	10,784
65,150	65,200	12,223	8,884	12,223	10,796
65,200	65,250	12,235	8,891	12,235	10,809
65,250	65,300	12,248	8,899	12,248	10,821
65,300	65,350	12,260	8,906	12,260	10,834
65,350	65,400	12,273	8,914	12,273	10,846
65,400	65,450	12,285	8,921	12,285	10,859
65,450	65,500	12,298	8,929	12,298	10,871
65,500	65,550	12,310	8,936	12,310	10,884
65,550	65,600	12,323	8,944	12,323	10,896
65,600	65,650	12,335	8,951	12,335	10,909
65,650	65,700	12,348	8,959	12,348	10,921
65,700	65,750	12,360	8,966	12,360	10,934
65,750	65,800	12,373	8,974	12,373	10,946
65,800	65,850	12,385	8,981	12,385	10,959
65,850	65,900	12,398	8,989	12,398	10,971
65,900	65,950	12,410	8,996	12,410	10,984
65,950	66,000	12,423	9,004	12,423	10,996

* This column must also be used by a qualifying widow(er).

(Continued)

2013 Tax Table—*Continued*

If line 43 (taxable income) is— At least	But less than	And you are— Single	Married filing jointly *	Married filing separately	Head of a house-hold

66,000

At least	But less than	Single	Married filing jointly *	Married filing separately	Head of a household
66,000	66,050	12,435	9,011	12,435	11,009
66,050	66,100	12,448	9,019	12,448	11,021
66,100	66,150	12,460	9,026	12,460	11,034
66,150	66,200	12,473	9,034	12,473	11,046
66,200	66,250	12,485	9,041	12,485	11,059
66,250	66,300	12,498	9,049	12,498	11,071
66,300	66,350	12,510	9,056	12,510	11,084
66,350	66,400	12,523	9,064	12,523	11,096
66,400	66,450	12,535	9,071	12,535	11,109
66,450	66,500	12,548	9,079	12,548	11,121
66,500	66,550	12,560	9,086	12,560	11,134
66,550	66,600	12,573	9,094	12,573	11,146
66,600	66,650	12,585	9,101	12,585	11,159
66,650	66,700	12,598	9,109	12,598	11,171
66,700	66,750	12,610	9,116	12,610	11,184
66,750	66,800	12,623	9,124	12,623	11,196
66,800	66,850	12,635	9,131	12,635	11,209
66,850	66,900	12,648	9,139	12,648	11,221
66,900	66,950	12,660	9,146	12,660	11,234
66,950	67,000	12,673	9,154	12,673	11,246

67,000

At least	But less than	Single	Married filing jointly *	Married filing separately	Head of a household
67,000	67,050	12,685	9,161	12,685	11,259
67,050	67,100	12,698	9,169	12,698	11,271
67,100	67,150	12,710	9,176	12,710	11,284
67,150	67,200	12,723	9,184	12,723	11,296
67,200	67,250	12,735	9,191	12,735	11,309
67,250	67,300	12,748	9,199	12,748	11,321
67,300	67,350	12,760	9,206	12,760	11,334
67,350	67,400	12,773	9,214	12,773	11,346
67,400	67,450	12,785	9,221	12,785	11,359
67,450	67,500	12,798	9,229	12,798	11,371
67,500	67,550	12,810	9,236	12,810	11,384
67,550	67,600	12,823	9,244	12,823	11,396
67,600	67,650	12,835	9,251	12,835	11,409
67,650	67,700	12,848	9,259	12,848	11,421
67,700	67,750	12,860	9,266	12,860	11,434
67,750	67,800	12,873	9,274	12,873	11,446
67,800	67,850	12,885	9,281	12,885	11,459
67,850	67,900	12,898	9,289	12,898	11,471
67,900	67,950	12,910	9,296	12,910	11,484
67,950	68,000	12,923	9,304	12,923	11,496

68,000

At least	But less than	Single	Married filing jointly *	Married filing separately	Head of a household
68,000	68,050	12,935	9,311	12,935	11,509
68,050	68,100	12,948	9,319	12,948	11,521
68,100	68,150	12,960	9,326	12,960	11,534
68,150	68,200	12,973	9,334	12,973	11,546
68,200	68,250	12,985	9,341	12,985	11,559
68,250	68,300	12,998	9,349	12,998	11,571
68,300	68,350	13,010	9,356	13,010	11,584
68,350	68,400	13,023	9,364	13,023	11,596
68,400	68,450	13,035	9,371	13,035	11,609
68,450	68,500	13,048	9,379	13,048	11,621
68,500	68,550	13,060	9,386	13,060	11,634
68,550	68,600	13,073	9,394	13,073	11,646
68,600	68,650	13,085	9,401	13,085	11,659
68,650	68,700	13,098	9,409	13,098	11,671
68,700	68,750	13,110	9,416	13,110	11,684
68,750	68,800	13,123	9,424	13,123	11,696
68,800	68,850	13,135	9,431	13,135	11,709
68,850	68,900	13,148	9,439	13,148	11,721
68,900	68,950	13,160	9,446	13,160	11,734
68,950	69,000	13,173	9,454	13,173	11,746

69,000

At least	But less than	Single	Married filing jointly *	Married filing separately	Head of a household
69,000	69,050	13,185	9,461	13,185	11,759
69,050	69,100	13,198	9,469	13,198	11,771
69,100	69,150	13,210	9,476	13,210	11,784
69,150	69,200	13,223	9,484	13,223	11,796
69,200	69,250	13,235	9,491	13,235	11,809
69,250	69,300	13,248	9,499	13,248	11,821
69,300	69,350	13,260	9,506	13,260	11,834
69,350	69,400	13,273	9,514	13,273	11,846
69,400	69,450	13,285	9,521	13,285	11,859
69,450	69,500	13,298	9,529	13,298	11,871
69,500	69,550	13,310	9,536	13,310	11,884
69,550	69,600	13,323	9,544	13,323	11,896
69,600	69,650	13,335	9,551	13,335	11,909
69,650	69,700	13,348	9,559	13,348	11,921
69,700	69,750	13,360	9,566	13,360	11,934
69,750	69,800	13,373	9,574	13,373	11,946
69,800	69,850	13,385	9,581	13,385	11,959
69,850	69,900	13,398	9,589	13,398	11,971
69,900	69,950	13,410	9,596	13,410	11,984
69,950	70,000	13,423	9,604	13,423	11,996

70,000

At least	But less than	Single	Married filing jointly *	Married filing separately	Head of a household
70,000	70,050	13,435	9,611	13,435	12,009
70,050	70,100	13,448	9,619	13,448	12,021
70,100	70,150	13,460	9,626	13,460	12,034
70,150	70,200	13,473	9,634	13,473	12,046
70,200	70,250	13,485	9,641	13,485	12,059
70,250	70,300	13,498	9,649	13,498	12,071
70,300	70,350	13,510	9,656	13,510	12,084
70,350	70,400	13,523	9,664	13,523	12,096
70,400	70,450	13,535	9,671	13,535	12,109
70,450	70,500	13,548	9,679	13,548	12,121
70,500	70,550	13,560	9,686	13,560	12,134
70,550	70,600	13,573	9,694	13,573	12,146
70,600	70,650	13,585	9,701	13,585	12,159
70,650	70,700	13,598	9,709	13,598	12,171
70,700	70,750	13,610	9,716	13,610	12,184
70,750	70,800	13,623	9,724	13,623	12,196
70,800	70,850	13,635	9,731	13,635	12,209
70,850	70,900	13,648	9,739	13,648	12,221
70,900	70,950	13,660	9,746	13,660	12,234
70,950	71,000	13,673	9,754	13,673	12,246

71,000

At least	But less than	Single	Married filing jointly *	Married filing separately	Head of a household
71,000	71,050	13,685	9,761	13,685	12,259
71,050	71,100	13,698	9,769	13,698	12,271
71,100	71,150	13,710	9,776	13,710	12,284
71,150	71,200	13,723	9,784	13,723	12,296
71,200	71,250	13,735	9,791	13,735	12,309
71,250	71,300	13,748	9,799	13,748	12,321
71,300	71,350	13,760	9,806	13,760	12,334
71,350	71,400	13,773	9,814	13,773	12,346
71,400	71,450	13,785	9,821	13,785	12,359
71,450	71,500	13,798	9,829	13,798	12,371
71,500	71,550	13,810	9,836	13,810	12,384
71,550	71,600	13,823	9,844	13,823	12,396
71,600	71,650	13,835	9,851	13,835	12,409
71,650	71,700	13,848	9,859	13,848	12,421
71,700	71,750	13,860	9,866	13,860	12,434
71,750	71,800	13,873	9,874	13,873	12,446
71,800	71,850	13,885	9,881	13,885	12,459
71,850	71,900	13,898	9,889	13,898	12,471
71,900	71,950	13,910	9,896	13,910	12,484
71,950	72,000	13,923	9,904	13,923	12,496

72,000

At least	But less than	Single	Married filing jointly *	Married filing separately	Head of a household
72,000	72,050	13,935	9,911	13,935	12,509
72,050	72,100	13,948	9,919	13,948	12,521
72,100	72,150	13,960	9,926	13,960	12,534
72,150	72,200	13,973	9,934	13,973	12,546
72,200	72,250	13,985	9,941	13,985	12,559
72,250	72,300	13,998	9,949	13,998	12,571
72,300	72,350	14,010	9,956	14,010	12,584
72,350	72,400	14,023	9,964	14,023	12,596
72,400	72,450	14,035	9,971	14,035	12,609
72,450	72,500	14,048	9,979	14,048	12,621
72,500	72,550	14,060	9,989	14,060	12,634
72,550	72,600	14,073	10,001	14,073	12,646
72,600	72,650	14,085	10,014	14,085	12,659
72,650	72,700	14,098	10,026	14,098	12,671
72,700	72,750	14,110	10,039	14,110	12,684
72,750	72,800	14,123	10,051	14,123	12,696
72,800	72,850	14,135	10,064	14,135	12,709
72,850	72,900	14,148	10,076	14,148	12,721
72,900	72,950	14,160	10,089	14,160	12,734
72,950	73,000	14,173	10,101	14,173	12,746

73,000

At least	But less than	Single	Married filing jointly *	Married filing separately	Head of a household
73,000	73,050	14,185	10,114	14,185	12,759
73,050	73,100	14,198	10,126	14,198	12,771
73,100	73,150	14,210	10,139	14,210	12,784
73,150	73,200	14,223	10,151	14,223	12,796
73,200	73,250	14,235	10,164	14,236	12,809
73,250	73,300	14,248	10,176	14,250	12,821
73,300	73,350	14,260	10,189	14,264	12,834
73,350	73,400	14,273	10,201	14,278	12,846
73,400	73,450	14,285	10,214	14,292	12,859
73,450	73,500	14,298	10,226	14,306	12,871
73,500	73,550	14,310	10,239	14,320	12,884
73,550	73,600	14,323	10,251	14,334	12,896
73,600	73,650	14,335	10,264	14,348	12,909
73,650	73,700	14,348	10,276	14,362	12,921
73,700	73,750	14,360	10,289	14,376	12,934
73,750	73,800	14,373	10,301	14,390	12,946
73,800	73,850	14,385	10,314	14,404	12,959
73,850	73,900	14,398	10,326	14,418	12,971
73,900	73,950	14,410	10,339	14,432	12,984
73,950	74,000	14,423	10,351	14,446	12,996

74,000

At least	But less than	Single	Married filing jointly *	Married filing separately	Head of a household
74,000	74,050	14,435	10,364	14,460	13,009
74,050	74,100	14,448	10,376	14,474	13,021
74,100	74,150	14,460	10,389	14,488	13,034
74,150	74,200	14,473	10,401	14,502	13,046
74,200	74,250	14,485	10,414	14,516	13,059
74,250	74,300	14,498	10,426	14,530	13,071
74,300	74,350	14,510	10,439	14,544	13,084
74,350	74,400	14,523	10,451	14,558	13,096
74,400	74,450	14,535	10,464	14,572	13,109
74,450	74,500	14,548	10,476	14,586	13,121
74,500	74,550	14,560	10,489	14,600	13,134
74,550	74,600	14,573	10,501	14,614	13,146
74,600	74,650	14,585	10,514	14,628	13,159
74,650	74,700	14,598	10,526	14,642	13,171
74,700	74,750	14,610	10,539	14,656	13,184
74,750	74,800	14,623	10,551	14,670	13,196
74,800	74,850	14,635	10,564	14,684	13,209
74,850	74,900	14,648	10,576	14,698	13,221
74,900	74,950	14,660	10,589	14,712	13,234
74,950	75,000	14,673	10,601	14,726	13,246

* This column must also be used by a qualifying widow(er).

(Continued)

2013 Tax Table—*Continued*

If line 43 (taxable income) is—		And you are—			
At least	But less than	Single	Married filing jointly *	Married filing separately	Head of a household
		Your tax is—			

75,000

At least	But less than	Single	MFJ *	MFS	HoH
75,000	75,050	14,685	10,614	14,740	13,259
75,050	75,100	14,698	10,626	14,754	13,271
75,100	75,150	14,710	10,639	14,768	13,284
75,150	75,200	14,723	10,651	14,782	13,296
75,200	75,250	14,735	10,664	14,796	13,309
75,250	75,300	14,748	10,676	14,810	13,321
75,300	75,350	14,760	10,689	14,824	13,334
75,350	75,400	14,773	10,701	14,838	13,346
75,400	75,450	14,785	10,714	14,852	13,359
75,450	75,500	14,798	10,726	14,866	13,371
75,500	75,550	14,810	10,739	14,880	13,384
75,550	75,600	14,823	10,751	14,894	13,396
75,600	75,650	14,835	10,764	14,908	13,409
75,650	75,700	14,848	10,776	14,922	13,421
75,700	75,750	14,860	10,789	14,936	13,434
75,750	75,800	14,873	10,801	14,950	13,446
75,800	75,850	14,885	10,814	14,964	13,459
75,850	75,900	14,898	10,826	14,978	13,471
75,900	75,950	14,910	10,839	14,992	13,484
75,950	76,000	14,923	10,851	15,006	13,496

76,000

At least	But less than	Single	MFJ *	MFS	HoH
76,000	76,050	14,935	10,864	15,020	13,509
76,050	76,100	14,948	10,876	15,034	13,521
76,100	76,150	14,960	10,889	15,048	13,534
76,150	76,200	14,973	10,901	15,062	13,546
76,200	76,250	14,985	10,914	15,076	13,559
76,250	76,300	14,998	10,926	15,090	13,571
76,300	76,350	15,010	10,939	15,104	13,584
76,350	76,400	15,023	10,951	15,118	13,596
76,400	76,450	15,035	10,964	15,132	13,609
76,450	76,500	15,048	10,976	15,146	13,621
76,500	76,550	15,060	10,989	15,160	13,634
76,550	76,600	15,073	11,001	15,174	13,646
76,600	76,650	15,085	11,014	15,188	13,659
76,650	76,700	15,098	11,026	15,202	13,671
76,700	76,750	15,110	11,039	15,216	13,684
76,750	76,800	15,123	11,051	15,230	13,696
76,800	76,850	15,135	11,064	15,244	13,709
76,850	76,900	15,148	11,076	15,258	13,721
76,900	76,950	15,160	11,089	15,272	13,734
76,950	77,000	15,173	11,101	15,286	13,746

77,000

At least	But less than	Single	MFJ *	MFS	HoH
77,000	77,050	15,185	11,114	15,300	13,759
77,050	77,100	15,198	11,126	15,314	13,771
77,100	77,150	15,210	11,139	15,328	13,784
77,150	77,200	15,223	11,151	15,342	13,796
77,200	77,250	15,235	11,164	15,356	13,809
77,250	77,300	15,248	11,176	15,370	13,821
77,300	77,350	15,260	11,189	15,384	13,834
77,350	77,400	15,273	11,201	15,398	13,846
77,400	77,450	15,285	11,214	15,412	13,859
77,450	77,500	15,298	11,226	15,426	13,871
77,500	77,550	15,310	11,239	15,440	13,884
77,550	77,600	15,323	11,251	15,454	13,896
77,600	77,650	15,335	11,264	15,468	13,909
77,650	77,700	15,348	11,276	15,482	13,921
77,700	77,750	15,360	11,289	15,496	13,934
77,750	77,800	15,373	11,301	15,510	13,946
77,800	77,850	15,385	11,314	15,524	13,959
77,850	77,900	15,398	11,326	15,538	13,971
77,900	77,950	15,410	11,339	15,552	13,984
77,950	78,000	15,423	11,351	15,566	13,996

78,000

At least	But less than	Single	MFJ *	MFS	HoH
78,000	78,050	15,435	11,364	15,580	14,009
78,050	78,100	15,448	11,376	15,594	14,021
78,100	78,150	15,460	11,389	15,608	14,034
78,150	78,200	15,473	11,401	15,622	14,046
78,200	78,250	15,485	11,414	15,636	14,059
78,250	78,300	15,498	11,426	15,650	14,071
78,300	78,350	15,510	11,439	15,664	14,084
78,350	78,400	15,523	11,451	15,678	14,096
78,400	78,450	15,535	11,464	15,692	14,109
78,450	78,500	15,548	11,476	15,706	14,121
78,500	78,550	15,560	11,489	15,720	14,134
78,550	78,600	15,573	11,501	15,734	14,146
78,600	78,650	15,585	11,514	15,748	14,159
78,650	78,700	15,598	11,526	15,762	14,171
78,700	78,750	15,610	11,539	15,776	14,184
78,750	78,800	15,623	11,551	15,790	14,196
78,800	78,850	15,635	11,564	15,804	14,209
78,850	78,900	15,648	11,576	15,818	14,221
78,900	78,950	15,660	11,589	15,832	14,234
78,950	79,000	15,673	11,601	15,846	14,246

79,000

At least	But less than	Single	MFJ *	MFS	HoH
79,000	79,050	15,685	11,614	15,860	14,259
79,050	79,100	15,698	11,626	15,874	14,271
79,100	79,150	15,710	11,639	15,888	14,284
79,150	79,200	15,723	11,651	15,902	14,296
79,200	79,250	15,735	11,664	15,916	14,309
79,250	79,300	15,748	11,676	15,930	14,321
79,300	79,350	15,760	11,689	15,944	14,334
79,350	79,400	15,773	11,701	15,958	14,346
79,400	79,450	15,785	11,714	15,972	14,359
79,450	79,500	15,798	11,726	15,986	14,371
79,500	79,550	15,810	11,739	16,000	14,384
79,550	79,600	15,823	11,751	16,014	14,396
79,600	79,650	15,835	11,764	16,028	14,409
79,650	79,700	15,848	11,776	16,042	14,421
79,700	79,750	15,860	11,789	16,056	14,434
79,750	79,800	15,873	11,801	16,070	14,446
79,800	79,850	15,885	11,814	16,084	14,459
79,850	79,900	15,898	11,826	16,098	14,471
79,900	79,950	15,910	11,839	16,112	14,484
79,950	80,000	15,923	11,851	16,126	14,496

80,000

At least	But less than	Single	MFJ *	MFS	HoH
80,000	80,050	15,935	11,864	16,140	14,509
80,050	80,100	15,948	11,876	16,154	14,521
80,100	80,150	15,960	11,889	16,168	14,534
80,150	80,200	15,973	11,901	16,182	14,546
80,200	80,250	15,985	11,914	16,196	14,559
80,250	80,300	15,998	11,926	16,210	14,571
80,300	80,350	16,010	11,939	16,224	14,584
80,350	80,400	16,023	11,951	16,238	14,596
80,400	80,450	16,035	11,964	16,252	14,609
80,450	80,500	16,048	11,976	16,266	14,621
80,500	80,550	16,060	11,989	16,280	14,634
80,550	80,600	16,073	12,001	16,294	14,646
80,600	80,650	16,085	12,014	16,308	14,659
80,650	80,700	16,098	12,026	16,322	14,671
80,700	80,750	16,110	12,039	16,336	14,684
80,750	80,800	16,123	12,051	16,350	14,696
80,800	80,850	16,135	12,064	16,364	14,709
80,850	80,900	16,148	12,076	16,378	14,721
80,900	80,950	16,160	12,089	16,392	14,734
80,950	81,000	16,173	12,101	16,406	14,746

81,000

At least	But less than	Single	MFJ *	MFS	HoH
81,000	81,050	16,185	12,114	16,420	14,759
81,050	81,100	16,198	12,126	16,434	14,771
81,100	81,150	16,210	12,139	16,448	14,784
81,150	81,200	16,223	12,151	16,462	14,796
81,200	81,250	16,235	12,164	16,476	14,809
81,250	81,300	16,248	12,176	16,490	14,821
81,300	81,350	16,260	12,189	16,504	14,834
81,350	81,400	16,273	12,201	16,518	14,846
81,400	81,450	16,285	12,214	16,532	14,859
81,450	81,500	16,298	12,226	16,546	14,871
81,500	81,550	16,310	12,239	16,560	14,884
81,550	81,600	16,323	12,251	16,574	14,896
81,600	81,650	16,335	12,264	16,588	14,909
81,650	81,700	16,348	12,276	16,602	14,921
81,700	81,750	16,360	12,289	16,616	14,934
81,750	81,800	16,373	12,301	16,630	14,946
81,800	81,850	16,385	12,314	16,644	14,959
81,850	81,900	16,398	12,326	16,658	14,971
81,900	81,950	16,410	12,339	16,672	14,984
81,950	82,000	16,423	12,351	16,686	14,996

82,000

At least	But less than	Single	MFJ *	MFS	HoH
82,000	82,050	16,435	12,364	16,700	15,009
82,050	82,100	16,448	12,376	16,714	15,021
82,100	82,150	16,460	12,389	16,728	15,034
82,150	82,200	16,473	12,401	16,742	15,046
82,200	82,250	16,485	12,414	16,756	15,059
82,250	82,300	16,498	12,426	16,770	15,071
82,300	82,350	16,510	12,439	16,784	15,084
82,350	82,400	16,523	12,451	16,798	15,096
82,400	82,450	16,535	12,464	16,812	15,109
82,450	82,500	16,548	12,476	16,826	15,121
82,500	82,550	16,560	12,489	16,840	15,134
82,550	82,600	16,573	12,501	16,854	15,146
82,600	82,650	16,585	12,514	16,868	15,159
82,650	82,700	16,598	12,526	16,882	15,171
82,700	82,750	16,610	12,539	16,896	15,184
82,750	82,800	16,623	12,551	16,910	15,196
82,800	82,850	16,635	12,564	16,924	15,209
82,850	82,900	16,648	12,576	16,938	15,221
82,900	82,950	16,660	12,589	16,952	15,234
82,950	83,000	16,673	12,601	16,966	15,246

83,000

At least	But less than	Single	MFJ *	MFS	HoH
83,000	83,050	16,685	12,614	16,980	15,259
83,050	83,100	16,698	12,626	16,994	15,271
83,100	83,150	16,710	12,639	17,008	15,284
83,150	83,200	16,723	12,651	17,022	15,296
83,200	83,250	16,735	12,664	17,036	15,309
83,250	83,300	16,748	12,676	17,050	15,321
83,300	83,350	16,760	12,689	17,064	15,334
83,350	83,400	16,773	12,701	17,078	15,346
83,400	83,450	16,785	12,714	17,092	15,359
83,450	83,500	16,798	12,726	17,106	15,371
83,500	83,550	16,810	12,739	17,120	15,384
83,550	83,600	16,823	12,751	17,134	15,396
83,600	83,650	16,835	12,764	17,148	15,409
83,650	83,700	16,848	12,776	17,162	15,421
83,700	83,750	16,860	12,789	17,176	15,434
83,750	83,800	16,873	12,801	17,190	15,446
83,800	83,850	16,885	12,814	17,204	15,459
83,850	83,900	16,898	12,826	17,218	15,471
83,900	83,950	16,910	12,839	17,232	15,484
83,950	84,000	16,923	12,851	17,246	15,496

* This column must also be used by a qualifying widow(er).

(Continued)

2013 Tax Table—*Continued*

84,000

If line 43 (taxable income) is— At least	But less than	Single	Married filing jointly *	Married filing separately	Head of a household
84,000	84,050	16,935	12,864	17,260	15,509
84,050	84,100	16,948	12,876	17,274	15,521
84,100	84,150	16,960	12,889	17,288	15,534
84,150	84,200	16,973	12,901	17,302	15,546
84,200	84,250	16,985	12,914	17,316	15,559
84,250	84,300	16,998	12,926	17,330	15,571
84,300	84,350	17,010	12,939	17,344	15,584
84,350	84,400	17,023	12,951	17,358	15,596
84,400	84,450	17,035	12,964	17,372	15,609
84,450	84,500	17,048	12,976	17,386	15,621
84,500	84,550	17,060	12,989	17,400	15,634
84,550	84,600	17,073	13,001	17,414	15,646
84,600	84,650	17,085	13,014	17,428	15,659
84,650	84,700	17,098	13,026	17,442	15,671
84,700	84,750	17,110	13,039	17,456	15,684
84,750	84,800	17,123	13,051	17,470	15,696
84,800	84,850	17,135	13,064	17,484	15,709
84,850	84,900	17,148	13,076	17,498	15,721
84,900	84,950	17,160	13,089	17,512	15,734
84,950	85,000	17,173	13,101	17,526	15,746

85,000

At least	But less than	Single	Married filing jointly *	Married filing separately	Head of a household
85,000	85,050	17,185	13,114	17,540	15,759
85,050	85,100	17,198	13,126	17,554	15,771
85,100	85,150	17,210	13,139	17,568	15,784
85,150	85,200	17,223	13,151	17,582	15,796
85,200	85,250	17,235	13,164	17,596	15,809
85,250	85,300	17,248	13,176	17,610	15,821
85,300	85,350	17,260	13,189	17,624	15,834
85,350	85,400	17,273	13,201	17,638	15,846
85,400	85,450	17,285	13,214	17,652	15,859
85,450	85,500	17,298	13,226	17,666	15,871
85,500	85,550	17,310	13,239	17,680	15,884
85,550	85,600	17,323	13,251	17,694	15,896
85,600	85,650	17,335	13,264	17,708	15,909
85,650	85,700	17,348	13,276	17,722	15,921
85,700	85,750	17,360	13,289	17,736	15,934
85,750	85,800	17,373	13,301	17,750	15,946
85,800	85,850	17,385	13,314	17,764	15,959
85,850	85,900	17,398	13,326	17,778	15,971
85,900	85,950	17,410	13,339	17,792	15,984
85,950	86,000	17,423	13,351	17,806	15,996

86,000

At least	But less than	Single	Married filing jointly *	Married filing separately	Head of a household
86,000	86,050	17,435	13,364	17,820	16,009
86,050	86,100	17,448	13,376	17,834	16,021
86,100	86,150	17,460	13,389	17,848	16,034
86,150	86,200	17,473	13,401	17,862	16,046
86,200	86,250	17,485	13,414	17,876	16,059
86,250	86,300	17,498	13,426	17,890	16,071
86,300	86,350	17,510	13,439	17,904	16,084
86,350	86,400	17,523	13,451	17,918	16,096
86,400	86,450	17,535	13,464	17,932	16,109
86,450	86,500	17,548	13,476	17,946	16,121
86,500	86,550	17,560	13,489	17,960	16,134
86,550	86,600	17,573	13,501	17,974	16,146
86,600	86,650	17,585	13,514	17,988	16,159
86,650	86,700	17,598	13,526	18,002	16,171
86,700	86,750	17,610	13,539	18,016	16,184
86,750	86,800	17,623	13,551	18,030	16,196
86,800	86,850	17,635	13,564	18,044	16,209
86,850	86,900	17,648	13,576	18,058	16,221
86,900	86,950	17,660	13,589	18,072	16,234
86,950	87,000	17,673	13,601	18,086	16,246

87,000

At least	But less than	Single	Married filing jointly *	Married filing separately	Head of a household
87,000	87,050	17,685	13,614	18,100	16,259
87,050	87,100	17,698	13,626	18,114	16,271
87,100	87,150	17,710	13,639	18,128	16,284
87,150	87,200	17,723	13,651	18,142	16,296
87,200	87,250	17,735	13,664	18,156	16,309
87,250	87,300	17,748	13,676	18,170	16,321
87,300	87,350	17,760	13,689	18,184	16,334
87,350	87,400	17,773	13,701	18,198	16,346
87,400	87,450	17,785	13,714	18,212	16,359
87,450	87,500	17,798	13,726	18,226	16,371
87,500	87,550	17,810	13,739	18,240	16,384
87,550	87,600	17,823	13,751	18,254	16,396
87,600	87,650	17,835	13,764	18,268	16,409
87,650	87,700	17,848	13,776	18,282	16,421
87,700	87,750	17,860	13,789	18,296	16,434
87,750	87,800	17,873	13,801	18,310	16,446
87,800	87,850	17,885	13,814	18,324	16,459
87,850	87,900	17,898	13,826	18,338	16,471
87,900	87,950	17,912	13,839	18,352	16,484
87,950	88,000	17,926	13,851	18,366	16,496

88,000

At least	But less than	Single	Married filing jointly *	Married filing separately	Head of a household
88,000	88,050	17,940	13,864	18,380	16,509
88,050	88,100	17,954	13,876	18,394	16,521
88,100	88,150	17,968	13,889	18,408	16,534
88,150	88,200	17,982	13,901	18,422	16,546
88,200	88,250	17,996	13,914	18,436	16,559
88,250	88,300	18,010	13,926	18,450	16,571
88,300	88,350	18,024	13,939	18,464	16,584
88,350	88,400	18,038	13,951	18,478	16,596
88,400	88,450	18,052	13,964	18,492	16,609
88,450	88,500	18,066	13,976	18,506	16,621
88,500	88,550	18,080	13,989	18,520	16,634
88,550	88,600	18,094	14,001	18,534	16,646
88,600	88,650	18,108	14,014	18,548	16,659
88,650	88,700	18,122	14,026	18,562	16,671
88,700	88,750	18,136	14,039	18,576	16,684
88,750	88,800	18,150	14,051	18,590	16,696
88,800	88,850	18,164	14,064	18,604	16,709
88,850	88,900	18,178	14,076	18,618	16,721
88,900	88,950	18,192	14,089	18,632	16,734
88,950	89,000	18,206	14,101	18,646	16,746

89,000

At least	But less than	Single	Married filing jointly *	Married filing separately	Head of a household
89,000	89,050	18,220	14,114	18,660	16,759
89,050	89,100	18,234	14,126	18,674	16,771
89,100	89,150	18,248	14,139	18,688	16,784
89,150	89,200	18,262	14,151	18,702	16,796
89,200	89,250	18,276	14,164	18,716	16,809
89,250	89,300	18,290	14,176	18,730	16,821
89,300	89,350	18,304	14,189	18,744	16,834
89,350	89,400	18,318	14,201	18,758	16,846
89,400	89,450	18,332	14,214	18,772	16,859
89,450	89,500	18,346	14,226	18,786	16,871
89,500	89,550	18,360	14,239	18,800	16,884
89,550	89,600	18,374	14,251	18,814	16,896
89,600	89,650	18,388	14,264	18,828	16,909
89,650	89,700	18,402	14,276	18,842	16,921
89,700	89,750	18,416	14,289	18,856	16,934
89,750	89,800	18,430	14,301	18,870	16,946
89,800	89,850	18,444	14,314	18,884	16,959
89,850	89,900	18,458	14,326	18,898	16,971
89,900	89,950	18,472	14,339	18,912	16,984
89,950	90,000	18,486	14,351	18,926	16,996

90,000

At least	But less than	Single	Married filing jointly *	Married filing separately	Head of a household
90,000	90,050	18,500	14,364	18,940	17,009
90,050	90,100	18,514	14,376	18,954	17,021
90,100	90,150	18,528	14,389	18,968	17,034
90,150	90,200	18,542	14,401	18,982	17,046
90,200	90,250	18,556	14,414	18,996	17,059
90,250	90,300	18,570	14,426	19,010	17,071
90,300	90,350	18,584	14,439	19,024	17,084
90,350	90,400	18,598	14,451	19,038	17,096
90,400	90,450	18,612	14,464	19,052	17,109
90,450	90,500	18,626	14,476	19,066	17,121
90,500	90,550	18,640	14,489	19,080	17,134
90,550	90,600	18,654	14,501	19,094	17,146
90,600	90,650	18,668	14,514	19,108	17,159
90,650	90,700	18,682	14,526	19,122	17,171
90,700	90,750	18,696	14,539	19,136	17,184
90,750	90,800	18,710	14,551	19,150	17,196
90,800	90,850	18,724	14,564	19,164	17,209
90,850	90,900	18,738	14,576	19,178	17,221
90,900	90,950	18,752	14,589	19,192	17,234
90,950	91,000	18,766	14,601	19,206	17,246

91,000

At least	But less than	Single	Married filing jointly *	Married filing separately	Head of a household
91,000	91,050	18,780	14,614	19,220	17,259
91,050	91,100	18,794	14,626	19,234	17,271
91,100	91,150	18,808	14,639	19,248	17,284
91,150	91,200	18,822	14,651	19,262	17,296
91,200	91,250	18,836	14,664	19,276	17,309
91,250	91,300	18,850	14,676	19,290	17,321
91,300	91,350	18,864	14,689	19,304	17,334
91,350	91,400	18,878	14,701	19,318	17,346
91,400	91,450	18,892	14,714	19,332	17,359
91,450	91,500	18,906	14,726	19,346	17,371
91,500	91,550	18,920	14,739	19,360	17,384
91,550	91,600	18,934	14,751	19,374	17,396
91,600	91,650	18,948	14,764	19,388	17,409
91,650	91,700	18,962	14,776	19,402	17,421
91,700	91,750	18,976	14,789	19,416	17,434
91,750	91,800	18,990	14,801	19,430	17,446
91,800	91,850	19,004	14,814	19,444	17,459
91,850	91,900	19,018	14,826	19,458	17,471
91,900	91,950	19,032	14,839	19,472	17,484
91,950	92,000	19,046	14,851	19,486	17,496

92,000

At least	But less than	Single	Married filing jointly *	Married filing separately	Head of a household
92,000	92,050	19,060	14,864	19,500	17,509
92,050	92,100	19,074	14,876	19,514	17,521
92,100	92,150	19,088	14,889	19,528	17,534
92,150	92,200	19,102	14,901	19,542	17,546
92,200	92,250	19,116	14,914	19,556	17,559
92,250	92,300	19,130	14,926	19,570	17,571
92,300	92,350	19,144	14,939	19,584	17,584
92,350	92,400	19,158	14,951	19,598	17,596
92,400	92,450	19,172	14,964	19,612	17,609
92,450	92,500	19,186	14,976	19,626	17,621
92,500	92,550	19,200	14,989	19,640	17,634
92,550	92,600	19,214	15,001	19,654	17,646
92,600	92,650	19,228	15,014	19,668	17,659
92,650	92,700	19,242	15,026	19,682	17,671
92,700	92,750	19,256	15,039	19,696	17,684
92,750	92,800	19,270	15,051	19,710	17,696
92,800	92,850	19,284	15,064	19,724	17,709
92,850	92,900	19,298	15,076	19,738	17,721
92,900	92,950	19,312	15,089	19,752	17,734
92,950	93,000	19,326	15,101	19,766	17,746

* This column must also be used by a qualifying widow(er).

(Continued)

2013 Tax Table—Continued

93,000 / 94,000 / 95,000

If line 43 (taxable income) is—		And you are—			
At least	But less than	Single	Married filing jointly *	Married filing separately	Head of a household
		Your tax is—			
93,000					
93,000	93,050	19,340	15,114	19,780	17,759
93,050	93,100	19,354	15,126	19,794	17,771
93,100	93,150	19,368	15,139	19,808	17,784
93,150	93,200	19,382	15,151	19,822	17,796
93,200	93,250	19,396	15,164	19,836	17,809
93,250	93,300	19,410	15,176	19,850	17,821
93,300	93,350	19,424	15,189	19,864	17,834
93,350	93,400	19,438	15,201	19,878	17,846
93,400	93,450	19,452	15,214	19,892	17,859
93,450	93,500	19,466	15,226	19,906	17,871
93,500	93,550	19,480	15,239	19,920	17,884
93,550	93,600	19,494	15,251	19,934	17,896
93,600	93,650	19,508	15,264	19,948	17,909
93,650	93,700	19,522	15,276	19,962	17,921
93,700	93,750	19,536	15,289	19,976	17,934
93,750	93,800	19,550	15,301	19,990	17,946
93,800	93,850	19,564	15,314	20,004	17,959
93,850	93,900	19,578	15,326	20,018	17,971
93,900	93,950	19,592	15,339	20,032	17,984
93,950	94,000	19,606	15,351	20,046	17,996
94,000					
94,000	94,050	19,620	15,364	20,060	18,009
94,050	94,100	19,634	15,376	20,074	18,021
94,100	94,150	19,648	15,389	20,088	18,034
94,150	94,200	19,662	15,401	20,102	18,046
94,200	94,250	19,676	15,414	20,116	18,059
94,250	94,300	19,690	15,426	20,130	18,071
94,300	94,350	19,704	15,439	20,144	18,084
94,350	94,400	19,718	15,451	20,158	18,096
94,400	94,450	19,732	15,464	20,172	18,109
94,450	94,500	19,746	15,476	20,186	18,121
94,500	94,550	19,760	15,489	20,200	18,134
94,550	94,600	19,774	15,501	20,214	18,146
94,600	94,650	19,788	15,514	20,228	18,159
94,650	94,700	19,802	15,526	20,242	18,171
94,700	94,750	19,816	15,539	20,256	18,184
94,750	94,800	19,830	15,551	20,270	18,196
94,800	94,850	19,844	15,564	20,284	18,209
94,850	94,900	19,858	15,576	20,298	18,221
94,900	94,950	19,872	15,589	20,312	18,234
94,950	95,000	19,886	15,601	20,326	18,246
95,000					
95,000	95,050	19,900	15,614	20,340	18,259
95,050	95,100	19,914	15,626	20,354	18,271
95,100	95,150	19,928	15,639	20,368	18,284
95,150	95,200	19,942	15,651	20,382	18,296
95,200	95,250	19,956	15,664	20,396	18,309
95,250	95,300	19,970	15,676	20,410	18,321
95,300	95,350	19,984	15,689	20,424	18,334
95,350	95,400	19,998	15,701	20,438	18,346
95,400	95,450	20,012	15,714	20,452	18,359
95,450	95,500	20,026	15,726	20,466	18,371
95,500	95,550	20,040	15,739	20,480	18,384
95,550	95,600	20,054	15,751	20,494	18,396
95,600	95,650	20,068	15,764	20,508	18,409
95,650	95,700	20,082	15,776	20,522	18,421
95,700	95,750	20,096	15,789	20,536	18,434
95,750	95,800	20,110	15,801	20,550	18,446
95,800	95,850	20,124	15,814	20,564	18,459
95,850	95,900	20,138	15,826	20,578	18,471
95,900	95,950	20,152	15,839	20,592	18,484
95,950	96,000	20,166	15,851	20,606	18,496

96,000 / 97,000 / 98,000

If line 43 (taxable income) is—		And you are—			
At least	But less than	Single	Married filing jointly *	Married filing separately	Head of a household
		Your tax is—			
96,000					
96,000	96,050	20,180	15,864	20,620	18,509
96,050	96,100	20,194	15,876	20,634	18,521
96,100	96,150	20,208	15,889	20,648	18,534
96,150	96,200	20,222	15,901	20,662	18,546
96,200	96,250	20,236	15,914	20,676	18,559
96,250	96,300	20,250	15,926	20,690	18,571
96,300	96,350	20,264	15,939	20,704	18,584
96,350	96,400	20,278	15,951	20,718	18,596
96,400	96,450	20,292	15,964	20,732	18,609
96,450	96,500	20,306	15,976	20,746	18,621
96,500	96,550	20,320	15,989	20,760	18,634
96,550	96,600	20,334	16,001	20,774	18,646
96,600	96,650	20,348	16,014	20,788	18,659
96,650	96,700	20,362	16,026	20,802	18,671
96,700	96,750	20,376	16,039	20,816	18,684
96,750	96,800	20,390	16,051	20,830	18,696
96,800	96,850	20,404	16,064	20,844	18,709
96,850	96,900	20,418	16,076	20,858	18,721
96,900	96,950	20,432	16,089	20,872	18,734
96,950	97,000	20,446	16,101	20,886	18,746
97,000					
97,000	97,050	20,460	16,114	20,900	18,759
97,050	97,100	20,474	16,126	20,914	18,771
97,100	97,150	20,488	16,139	20,928	18,784
97,150	97,200	20,502	16,151	20,942	18,796
97,200	97,250	20,516	16,164	20,956	18,809
97,250	97,300	20,530	16,176	20,970	18,821
97,300	97,350	20,544	16,189	20,984	18,834
97,350	97,400	20,558	16,201	20,998	18,846
97,400	97,450	20,572	16,214	21,012	18,859
97,450	97,500	20,586	16,226	21,026	18,871
97,500	97,550	20,600	16,239	21,040	18,884
97,550	97,600	20,614	16,251	21,054	18,896
97,600	97,650	20,628	16,264	21,068	18,909
97,650	97,700	20,642	16,276	21,082	18,921
97,700	97,750	20,656	16,289	21,096	18,934
97,750	97,800	20,670	16,301	21,110	18,946
97,800	97,850	20,684	16,314	21,124	18,959
97,850	97,900	20,698	16,326	21,138	18,971
97,900	97,950	20,712	16,339	21,152	18,984
97,950	98,000	20,726	16,351	21,166	18,996
98,000					
98,000	98,050	20,740	16,364	21,180	19,009
98,050	98,100	20,754	16,376	21,194	19,021
98,100	98,150	20,768	16,389	21,208	19,034
98,150	98,200	20,782	16,401	21,222	19,046
98,200	98,250	20,796	16,414	21,236	19,059
98,250	98,300	20,810	16,426	21,250	19,071
98,300	98,350	20,824	16,439	21,264	19,084
98,350	98,400	20,838	16,451	21,278	19,096
98,400	98,450	20,852	16,464	21,292	19,109
98,450	98,500	20,866	16,476	21,306	19,121
98,500	98,550	20,880	16,489	21,320	19,134
98,550	98,600	20,894	16,501	21,334	19,146
98,600	98,650	20,908	16,514	21,348	19,159
98,650	98,700	20,922	16,526	21,362	19,171
98,700	98,750	20,936	16,539	21,376	19,184
98,750	98,800	20,950	16,551	21,390	19,196
98,800	98,850	20,964	16,564	21,404	19,209
98,850	98,900	20,978	16,576	21,418	19,221
98,900	98,950	20,992	16,589	21,432	19,234
98,950	99,000	21,006	16,601	21,446	19,246

99,000

If line 43 (taxable income) is—		And you are—			
At least	But less than	Single	Married filing jointly *	Married filing separately	Head of a household
		Your tax is—			
99,000					
99,000	99,050	21,020	16,614	21,460	19,259
99,050	99,100	21,034	16,626	21,474	19,271
99,100	99,150	21,048	16,639	21,488	19,284
99,150	99,200	21,062	16,651	21,502	19,296
99,200	99,250	21,076	16,664	21,516	19,309
99,250	99,300	21,090	16,676	21,530	19,321
99,300	99,350	21,104	16,689	21,544	19,334
99,350	99,400	21,118	16,701	21,558	19,346
99,400	99,450	21,132	16,714	21,572	19,359
99,450	99,500	21,146	16,726	21,586	19,371
99,500	99,550	21,160	16,739	21,600	19,384
99,550	99,600	21,174	16,751	21,614	19,396
99,600	99,650	21,188	16,764	21,628	19,409
99,650	99,700	21,202	16,776	21,642	19,421
99,700	99,750	21,216	16,789	21,656	19,434
99,750	99,800	21,230	16,801	21,670	19,446
99,800	99,850	21,244	16,814	21,684	19,459
99,850	99,900	21,258	16,826	21,698	19,471
99,900	99,950	21,272	16,839	21,712	19,484
99,950	100,000	21,286	16,851	21,726	19,496

$100,000 or over use the Tax Computation Worksheet

* This column must also be used by a qualifying widow(er).

2013 OPTIONAL SALES TAX TABLES

When Used

The election to deduct state and local general sales taxes requires that the taxpayer forgo any deduction for state and local income taxes. Whether this is advisable or not depends on a comparison of the amounts involved. In making the choice, however, the outcome could be influenced by the additional sales tax incurred due to certain "big ticket" purchases that were made. For example, a taxpayer who chose to deduct state and local income taxes for 2012 might well prefer the sales tax deduction in 2013 if a new boat was purchased or home improvements were made during the year. To make the sales tax election, the taxpayer must enter the amount on Schedule A, line 5, and check box b. Unless extended by Congress, the sales tax deduction will expire as to tax years after 2013.

If the sales tax election is made, the amount of the deduction can be determined by use of the *actual expense method* or the *optional sales tax tables* issued by the IRS. The actual expense method can be used only when the taxpayer has actual receipts to support the deduction claimed. In the absence of receipts, the usual case with most taxpayers, resorting to the optional sales tax tables is necessary. Under neither method, however, is the purchase of items used in a taxpayer's trade or business to be considered.

Adjustments Necessary

The optional sales tax tables are based on a number of assumptions that require adjustments to be made. As the starting point for the use of the tables is AGI, nontaxable receipts have not been included. Examples of receipts that should be added include: tax-exempt interest, veterans' benefits, nontaxable combat pay, public assistance payments, workers' compensation, nontaxable Social Security, and other retirement benefits. They do not include any large nontaxable items that are not likely to be spent. For example, a $100,000 inheritance should not be added if it was invested in a certificate of deposit.

The tables represent the sales tax on the average (and recurring) expenditures based on level of income by family size and do not include exceptional purchases. Therefore, add to the table amount any sales taxes on major purchases (such as motor vehicles, aircraft, boats, and home building materials, etc.).

When the optional sales tax tables are utilized, special adjustments may be needed when a taxpayer has lived in more than one taxing jurisdiction (e.g., state, county, city) during the year. The adjustments involve apportionment of taxes based on days involved and are illustrated in Instructions for Schedule A (Form 1040), pages A-3 to A-6.

Local Sales Taxes

Local sales taxes (i.e., those imposed by counties, cities, transit authorities) may or may not require a separate determination. In those states where they are not imposed, no further computations are necessary. This is also the case where the local taxes are uniform and are incorporated into the state sales tax table. In other situations, another step is necessary to arrive at the optional sales tax table deduction. Depending on where the taxpayer lives, one of two procedures needs to be used. In one procedure, the local sales tax is arrived at by using the **state table** amount—see the Example 1 worksheet. In the other procedure, special **local tables** issued by the IRS for enumerated state and local jurisdictions are modified (if necessary) and used—see the Example 2 worksheet.

Use Illustrated

EXAMPLE 1 The Archers file a joint return for 2013 reflecting AGI of $88,000 and claiming three exemptions. They have tax-exempt interest of $3,000, and during the year they incurred sales tax of $1,650 on the purchase of an automobile for their dependent teenage son. They live in Bellaire, Texas, where the general sales tax rates are 6.25% for state and 2% for local. Since the IRS *has not issued* optional local sales tax tables for Texas, use the Worksheet below to arrive at the Archers' general sales tax deduction of $3,085.

Sales Tax Deduction Worksheet
(To be used when *no* IRS Optional Local Sales Tax Table Available)

Adjusted Gross Income (AGI) as listed on line 38 of Form 1040		$88,000
Add nontaxable items		3,000
Table income to be used for purposes of line 1 below		$91,000
1. Use table income to determine table amount—go to state of residence and find applicable range of table income and exemption column* for *state* sales tax		$ 1,087
2a. Enter local general sales tax rate	2.0	
2b. Enter state general sales tax rate	6.25	
2c. Divide 2a by 2b	0.32	
2d. Multiply line 1 by line 2c for the local sales tax		348
3. Enter general sales tax on large purchases		1,650
4. Deduction for general sales tax (add lines 1 + 2d + 3) and report on line 5 of Schedule A of Form 1040		$ 3,085

*Use total of personal and dependency exemptions as reported in item 6d of Form 1040.

EXAMPLE 2 The Hardys file a joint return for 2013, reporting AGI of $40,000 and claiming four exemptions (two personal and two dependency). They received $30,000 in nontaxable pension benefits. Although the Hardys do not keep sales tax receipts, they can prove that they paid $4,800 in sales tax on the purchase of a new boat in 2013. The Hardys are residents of Georgia and live in a jurisdiction that imposes a 2% local sales tax. Since the IRS *has issued* optional local sales tax tables for Georgia, use the Worksheet below to arrive at the Hardys' general sales tax deduction of $5,679.

Sales Tax Deduction Worksheet
[To be used for Alaska, Arizona, Arkansas, Colorado, Georgia, Illinois, Louisiana, Missouri, New York, North Carolina, South Carolina, Tennessee, Utah, Virginia, and West Virginia]

Adjusted Gross Income (AGI) as listed on line 38 of Form 1040		$40,000
Add nontaxable income		30,000
Table income to be used for purposes of line 1 below		$70,000
1. Use the table income to determine *state* sales tax amount—go to table for state of residence and find applicable income range and exemption column*		$ 539
2a. Enter local general sales tax rate	2.0	
2b. Enter IRS *local* sales tax table amount (based on 1%)	$170	
2c. Multiply line 2b by 2a for the local sales tax		340
3. Enter general sales tax on large purchases		4,800
4. Deduction for general sales tax (add lines 1 + 2c + 3) and report on line 5 of Schedule A of Form 1040		$ 5,679

*Use total of personal and dependency exemptions as reported in item 6d of Form 1040.

2013 Optional State Sales Tax Tables (State Sales Tax Rate Shown Next to State Name)

Alabama[1] 4.0000%

Income At least	Income But less than	Exemptions 1	2	3	4	5	Over 5
$0	$20,000	217	256	282	302	319	343
20,000	30,000	329	387	426	456	482	517
30,000	40,000	384	451	497	532	561	602
40,000	50,000	431	506	556	596	628	674
50,000	60,000	472	554	609	652	687	737
60,000	70,000	509	597	656	702	741	794
70,000	80,000	544	638	701	750	790	848
80,000	90,000	576	675	741	793	836	897
90,000	100,000	606	710	780	834	879	942
100,000	120,000	646	755	830	887	935	1002
120,000	140,000	699	818	897	960	1011	1084
140,000	160,000	746	871	956	1022	1077	1154
160,000	180,000	792	924	1014	1084	1142	1223
180,000	200,000	833	972	1066	1139	1200	1285
200,000	or more	1034	1204	1319	1409	1483	1588

Arizona[2] 6.0137%

Income At least	Income But less than	Exemptions 1	2	3	4	5	Over 5
$0	$20,000	206	228	242	253	261	273
20,000	30,000	364	403	428	447	462	483
30,000	40,000	449	497	528	552	570	596
40,000	50,000	524	581	617	644	666	697
50,000	60,000	593	657	698	729	754	789
60,000	70,000	657	728	774	808	836	874
70,000	80,000	719	796	846	884	914	956
80,000	90,000	776	860	914	954	987	1032
90,000	100,000	831	921	979	1022	1058	1106
100,000	120,000	905	1002	1065	1113	1151	1204
120,000	140,000	1007	1116	1186	1239	1282	1340
140,000	160,000	1097	1216	1293	1350	1397	1461
160,000	180,000	1188	1317	1400	1463	1514	1583
180,000	200,000	1271	1410	1499	1566	1620	1694
200,000	or more	1697	1882	2001	2091	2164	2264

Arkansas[2] 6.2521%

Income At least	Income But less than	Exemptions 1	2	3	4	5	Over 5
$0	$20,000	273	304	324	339	351	367
20,000	30,000	461	513	547	572	593	621
30,000	40,000	559	623	664	695	720	754
40,000	50,000	644	718	766	801	830	870
50,000	60,000	722	805	858	898	931	976
60,000	70,000	793	885	943	987	1023	1072
70,000	80,000	861	960	1024	1072	1111	1164
80,000	90,000	924	1031	1099	1151	1193	1250
90,000	100,000	985	1098	1171	1226	1271	1332
100,000	120,000	1064	1187	1266	1326	1374	1441
120,000	140,000	1174	1310	1398	1464	1517	1590
140,000	160,000	1271	1419	1513	1585	1643	1722
160,000	180,000	1368	1527	1629	1706	1769	1854
180,000	200,000	1456	1625	1734	1816	1883	1974
200,000	or more	1900	2122	2264	2372	2459	2579

California[3] 7.5000%

Income At least	Income But less than	Exemptions 1	2	3	4	5	Over 5
$0	$20,000	257	282	298	309	319	331
20,000	30,000	446	489	516	536	553	575
30,000	40,000	547	599	632	657	677	705
40,000	50,000	635	696	735	764	787	819
50,000	60,000	716	785	828	861	887	923
60,000	70,000	791	866	915	951	980	1019
70,000	80,000	862	944	997	1036	1068	1111
80,000	90,000	928	1017	1074	1116	1151	1197
90,000	100,000	992	1087	1148	1193	1230	1280
100,000	120,000	1076	1180	1246	1295	1335	1389
120,000	140,000	1194	1308	1381	1436	1480	1540
140,000	160,000	1297	1422	1501	1561	1609	1674
160,000	180,000	1401	1536	1622	1686	1738	1809
180,000	200,000	1496	1640	1732	1800	1856	1931
200,000	or more	1978	2168	2290	2381	2454	2554

Colorado[2] 2.9000%

Income At least	Income But less than	Exemptions 1	2	3	4	5	Over 5
$0	$20,000	108	121	129	135	140	147
20,000	30,000	174	194	207	217	225	236
30,000	40,000	208	232	247	259	269	282
40,000	50,000	237	264	282	295	306	321
50,000	60,000	263	293	313	327	339	356
60,000	70,000	287	320	341	357	370	388
70,000	80,000	310	345	367	385	399	418
80,000	90,000	330	368	392	410	425	446
90,000	100,000	350	390	415	435	450	472
100,000	120,000	376	418	446	467	484	507
120,000	140,000	412	458	488	511	529	554
140,000	160,000	443	492	525	549	569	596
160,000	180,000	474	527	561	587	608	637
180,000	200,000	501	558	594	621	644	674
200,000	or more	640	711	757	792	821	859

Connecticut[4] 6.3500%

Income At least	Income But less than	Exemptions 1	2	3	4	5	Over 5
$0	$20,000	254	279	295	306	316	329
20,000	30,000	432	475	503	523	539	562
30,000	40,000	527	579	613	637	658	685
40,000	50,000	609	670	709	738	761	793
50,000	60,000	684	753	796	829	855	891
60,000	70,000	754	829	877	913	942	981
70,000	80,000	819	902	954	993	1025	1068
80,000	90,000	881	969	1026	1068	1102	1148
90,000	100,000	940	1034	1094	1139	1176	1225
100,000	120,000	1017	1120	1185	1234	1273	1327
120,000	140,000	1125	1239	1311	1365	1409	1468
140,000	160,000	1220	1343	1422	1481	1528	1593
160,000	180,000	1315	1449	1533	1597	1648	1718
180,000	200,000	1402	1544	1634	1702	1757	1831
200,000	or more	1840	2028	2147	2236	2309	2407

District of Columbia[4] 5.9370%

Income At least	Income But less than	Exemptions 1	2	3	4	5	Over 5
$0	$20,000	162	174	182	188	193	200
20,000	30,000	285	307	322	333	342	353
30,000	40,000	351	379	397	411	422	437
40,000	50,000	410	443	464	480	493	510
50,000	60,000	463	501	526	544	558	578
60,000	70,000	513	556	583	603	619	641
70,000	80,000	561	608	637	659	677	701
80,000	90,000	606	656	688	712	732	758
90,000	100,000	649	703	737	763	784	812
100,000	120,000	706	765	803	831	854	884
120,000	140,000	786	852	894	925	951	985
140,000	160,000	857	929	975	1009	1037	1074
160,000	180,000	928	1007	1056	1094	1124	1165
180,000	200,000	993	1077	1131	1171	1203	1247
200,000	or more	1327	1440	1513	1567	1610	1670

Florida[1] 6.0000%

Income At least	Income But less than	Exemptions 1	2	3	4	5	Over 5
$0	$20,000	230	252	267	277	286	298
20,000	30,000	396	435	459	478	493	514
30,000	40,000	484	532	562	585	603	629
40,000	50,000	562	617	652	678	700	729
50,000	60,000	632	694	734	764	788	821
60,000	70,000	697	766	810	843	869	906
70,000	80,000	759	834	882	918	947	987
80,000	90,000	817	898	949	988	1020	1063
90,000	100,000	872	958	1014	1055	1089	1135
100,000	120,000	946	1039	1099	1144	1181	1231
120,000	140,000	1047	1151	1218	1268	1308	1364
140,000	160,000	1137	1250	1323	1377	1421	1481
160,000	180,000	1227	1350	1428	1487	1534	1599
180,000	200,000	1309	1440	1523	1586	1637	1707
200,000	or more	1726	1898	2009	2092	2160	2252

Georgia[2] 4.0000%

Income At least	Income But less than	Exemptions 1	2	3	4	5	Over 5
$0	$20,000	146	163	173	181	188	196
20,000	30,000	241	267	285	298	308	323
30,000	40,000	290	321	342	358	370	388
40,000	50,000	332	368	392	410	424	444
50,000	60,000	370	410	436	456	472	494
60,000	70,000	404	449	477	499	517	541
70,000	80,000	437	485	516	539	558	584
80,000	90,000	468	519	552	577	597	625
90,000	100,000	497	551	586	613	634	663
100,000	120,000	535	593	631	660	683	714
120,000	140,000	587	652	693	724	749	784
140,000	160,000	634	703	747	781	808	845
160,000	180,000	679	753	801	837	866	906
180,000	200,000	721	799	850	888	919	962
200,000	or more	929	1029	1094	1143	1183	1237

Hawaii[1,7] 4.0000%

Income At least	Income But less than	Exemptions 1	2	3	4	5	Over 5
$0	$20,000	212	247	269	287	302	322
20,000	30,000	356	414	453	483	507	542
30,000	40,000	431	502	549	585	615	657
40,000	50,000	497	578	632	674	709	757
50,000	60,000	556	647	708	755	794	848
60,000	70,000	610	711	778	829	872	932
70,000	80,000	662	771	844	900	946	1011
80,000	90,000	710	827	905	965	1015	1085
90,000	100,000	756	880	964	1028	1081	1155
100,000	120,000	817	951	1041	1111	1168	1248
120,000	140,000	900	1049	1148	1225	1288	1377
140,000	160,000	974	1134	1242	1325	1394	1490
160,000	180,000	1047	1220	1336	1426	1500	1603
180,000	200,000	1114	1298	1421	1517	1595	1705
200,000	or more	1449	1690	1851	1976	2078	2222

Idaho[1] 6.0000%

Income At least	Income But less than	Exemptions 1	2	3	4	5	Over 5
$0	$20,000	327	385	424	454	480	515
20,000	30,000	501	588	647	693	731	784
30,000	40,000	587	688	757	810	854	916
40,000	50,000	660	773	850	909	959	1028
50,000	60,000	724	848	932	997	1051	1127
60,000	70,000	782	916	1006	1076	1134	1216
70,000	80,000	837	979	1075	1150	1212	1299
80,000	90,000	887	1037	1139	1218	1283	1375
90,000	100,000	934	1092	1199	1282	1351	1447
100,000	120,000	996	1164	1278	1366	1439	1541
120,000	140,000	1080	1262	1384	1479	1558	1669
140,000	160,000	1153	1346	1477	1578	1662	1780
160,000	180,000	1225	1430	1568	1675	1764	1889
180,000	200,000	1290	1505	1650	1762	1856	1987
200,000	or more	1607	1871	2050	2189	2304	2465

Illinois[2] 6.2500%

Income At least	Income But less than	Exemptions 1	2	3	4	5	Over 5
$0	$20,000	244	273	292	307	319	335
20,000	30,000	389	435	465	488	507	533
30,000	40,000	462	516	552	579	602	633
40,000	50,000	525	586	627	657	683	718
50,000	60,000	582	649	693	727	755	794
60,000	70,000	633	706	754	791	821	863
70,000	80,000	681	759	811	851	883	928
80,000	90,000	725	809	864	906	941	989
90,000	100,000	768	856	914	958	995	1045
100,000	120,000	823	917	979	1027	1066	1120
120,000	140,000	899	1001	1069	1121	1163	1222
140,000	160,000	965	1075	1147	1202	1248	1311
160,000	180,000	1031	1147	1225	1284	1332	1399
180,000	200,000	1090	1213	1294	1357	1408	1479
200,000	or more	1383	1538	1640	1718	1783	1872

Indiana[4] 7.0000%

Income At least	Income But less than	Exemptions 1	2	3	4	5	Over 5
$0	$20,000	279	312	333	349	361	379
20,000	30,000	448	500	534	559	579	607
30,000	40,000	534	596	635	665	690	723
40,000	50,000	607	677	723	757	784	822
50,000	60,000	673	751	801	838	869	911
60,000	70,000	733	817	872	913	946	992
70,000	80,000	789	880	939	983	1019	1068
80,000	90,000	841	938	1001	1048	1086	1138
90,000	100,000	890	993	1059	1109	1149	1205
100,000	120,000	955	1065	1136	1190	1233	1293
120,000	140,000	1044	1164	1242	1300	1347	1412
140,000	160,000	1121	1250	1333	1396	1447	1517
160,000	180,000	1198	1336	1425	1492	1546	1621
180,000	200,000	1267	1413	1507	1578	1635	1714
200,000	or more	1610	1796	1915	2005	2078	2178

Iowa[1] 6.0000%

Income At least	Income But less than	Exemptions 1	2	3	4	5	Over 5
$0	$20,000	237	264	281	293	304	318
20,000	30,000	408	454	484	506	524	549
30,000	40,000	498	555	592	619	642	672
40,000	50,000	578	644	687	719	745	781
50,000	60,000	651	725	773	810	839	879
60,000	70,000	718	800	853	893	926	971
70,000	80,000	781	872	930	974	1009	1058
80,000	90,000	841	939	1001	1048	1087	1139
90,000	100,000	898	1002	1069	1120	1161	1217
100,000	120,000	974	1087	1160	1215	1260	1321
120,000	140,000	1079	1205	1286	1347	1397	1465
140,000	160,000	1172	1309	1397	1464	1518	1592
160,000	180,000	1266	1414	1509	1581	1639	1719
180,000	200,000	1351	1509	1611	1687	1750	1835
200,000	or more	1783	1993	2128	2230	2313	2427

Kansas[1] 6.2244%

Income At least	Income But less than	Exemptions 1	2	3	4	5	Over 5
$0	$20,000	343	401	439	469	494	528
20,000	30,000	546	637	699	746	785	840
30,000	40,000	649	757	830	886	932	997
40,000	50,000	736	859	941	1005	1058	1132
50,000	60,000	815	950	1041	1112	1170	1252
60,000	70,000	886	1033	1132	1209	1272	1361
70,000	80,000	953	1111	1218	1300	1368	1464
80,000	90,000	1015	1183	1297	1384	1457	1559
90,000	100,000	1073	1252	1371	1464	1541	1648
100,000	120,000	1150	1341	1469	1569	1651	1766
120,000	140,000	1255	1463	1603	1712	1801	1927
140,000	160,000	1346	1570	1720	1836	1932	2067
160,000	180,000	1437	1676	1836	1960	2062	2206
180,000	200,000	1518	1771	1940	2071	2179	2331
200,000	or more	1922	2241	2455	2621	2758	2950

Kentucky[4] 6.0000%

Income At least	Income But less than	Exemptions 1	2	3	4	5	Over 5
$0	$20,000	227	253	270	283	294	308
20,000	30,000	371	414	442	462	479	503
30,000	40,000	445	496	530	554	575	603
40,000	50,000	509	568	605	634	657	689
50,000	60,000	567	632	673	705	731	766
60,000	70,000	619	690	736	770	798	837
70,000	80,000	669	745	794	832	862	904
80,000	90,000	715	797	849	889	921	966
90,000	100,000	759	845	901	943	977	1024
100,000	120,000	817	909	969	1014	1051	1102
120,000	140,000	896	997	1063	1112	1153	1208
140,000	160,000	965	1074	1145	1198	1241	1301
160,000	180,000	1034	1151	1226	1284	1330	1394
180,000	200,000	1097	1220	1300	1361	1410	1477
200,000	or more	1409	1566	1668	1746	1808	1895

Louisiana[2] 4.0000%

Income At least	Income But less than	Exemptions 1	2	3	4	5	Over 5
$0	$20,000	155	169	178	184	189	197
20,000	30,000	267	291	306	318	327	340
30,000	40,000	327	356	375	389	400	416
40,000	50,000	379	413	435	451	465	482
50,000	60,000	427	465	490	508	523	543
60,000	70,000	471	514	541	561	577	600
70,000	80,000	513	559	589	611	629	653
80,000	90,000	552	602	634	658	677	703
90,000	100,000	590	643	677	703	723	751
100,000	120,000	639	698	735	762	785	815
120,000	140,000	708	773	814	845	870	903
140,000	160,000	769	840	884	918	945	981
160,000	180,000	830	906	955	991	1020	1060
180,000	200,000	886	967	1019	1057	1089	1131
200,000	or more	1168	1276	1344	1396	1437	1493

Maine[4] 5.1260%

Income At least	Income But less than	Exemptions 1	2	3	4	5	Over 5
$0	$20,000	141	153	161	166	171	177
20,000	30,000	246	267	281	291	299	311
30,000	40,000	302	329	346	358	368	382
40,000	50,000	352	383	403	417	429	445
50,000	60,000	398	433	455	471	485	503
60,000	70,000	440	478	503	521	536	556
70,000	80,000	480	522	549	569	585	607
80,000	90,000	518	563	592	614	631	655
90,000	100,000	554	603	634	657	676	701
100,000	120,000	602	655	689	714	734	762
120,000	140,000	668	728	765	793	816	846
140,000	160,000	727	792	833	863	888	921
160,000	180,000	787	857	901	934	961	997
180,000	200,000	841	916	963	998	1027	1065
200,000	or more	1117	1216	1279	1326	1364	1416

Maryland[4] 6.0000%

Income At least	Income But less than	Exemptions 1	2	3	4	5	Over 5
$0	$20,000	200	221	235	246	254	266
20,000	30,000	344	380	404	422	437	458
30,000	40,000	420	464	494	516	534	560
40,000	50,000	486	538	572	598	619	649
50,000	60,000	547	605	644	673	697	730
60,000	70,000	603	667	710	742	768	805
70,000	80,000	656	726	773	808	837	876
80,000	90,000	706	782	831	869	900	943
90,000	100,000	753	834	887	928	961	1007
100,000	120,000	816	904	962	1006	1042	1092
120,000	140,000	903	1001	1065	1114	1154	1209
140,000	160,000	980	1086	1156	1209	1252	1312
160,000	180,000	1058	1172	1247	1305	1351	1416
180,000	200,000	1128	1250	1330	1391	1441	1511
200,000	or more	1484	1645	1751	1832	1898	1989

Massachusetts[4] 6.2500%

Income At least	Income But less than	Exemptions 1	2	3	4	5	Over 5
$0	$20,000	195	212	223	231	238	247
20,000	30,000	317	345	363	376	387	402
30,000	40,000	380	413	435	451	464	481
40,000	50,000	434	472	496	515	530	550
50,000	60,000	482	525	552	572	589	611
60,000	70,000	527	573	603	625	643	667
70,000	80,000	568	619	650	674	693	720
80,000	90,000	607	661	695	720	741	769
90,000	100,000	644	701	737	764	785	815
100,000	120,000	693	753	792	821	844	876
120,000	140,000	759	826	868	900	925	960
140,000	160,000	817	889	934	969	996	1034
160,000	180,000	875	952	1001	1037	1067	1107
180,000	200,000	928	1009	1060	1099	1130	1173
200,000	or more	1189	1292	1358	1407	1447	1501

Michigan[4] 6.0000%

Income At least	Income But less than	Exemptions 1	2	3	4	5	Over 5
$0	$20,000	219	243	258	269	279	291
20,000	30,000	357	395	419	438	453	473
30,000	40,000	427	473	502	524	542	567
40,000	50,000	488	540	573	598	619	647
50,000	60,000	543	600	637	665	688	719
60,000	70,000	593	655	696	726	751	785
70,000	80,000	640	708	751	784	810	847
80,000	90,000	684	756	802	837	865	904
90,000	100,000	725	802	851	888	918	959
100,000	120,000	780	862	915	954	987	1031
120,000	140,000	855	945	1003	1046	1081	1130
140,000	160,000	921	1017	1079	1126	1164	1216
160,000	180,000	986	1089	1156	1206	1246	1302
180,000	200,000	1045	1154	1225	1278	1320	1379
200,000	or more	1340	1479	1569	1636	1691	1766

Minnesota[1] 6.8750%

Income At least	Income But less than	Exemptions 1	2	3	4	5	Over 5
$0	$20,000	226	244	256	264	271	280
20,000	30,000	394	426	446	461	473	490
30,000	40,000	483	523	548	567	582	602
40,000	50,000	563	609	639	660	678	702
50,000	60,000	635	688	721	746	766	793
60,000	70,000	702	761	798	825	847	877
70,000	80,000	766	830	871	901	925	957
80,000	90,000	826	896	939	972	998	1033
90,000	100,000	884	958	1005	1040	1068	1105
100,000	120,000	960	1041	1092	1130	1161	1202
120,000	140,000	1066	1157	1214	1256	1290	1336
140,000	160,000	1161	1259	1321	1367	1404	1455
160,000	180,000	1255	1362	1429	1479	1520	1574
180,000	200,000	1342	1456	1528	1582	1625	1683
200,000	or more	1783	1936	2033	2105	2162	2241

Mississippi[1] 7.0000%

Income At least	Income But less than	Exemptions 1	2	3	4	5	Over 5
$0	$20,000	401	462	502	533	559	594
20,000	30,000	642	739	804	853	894	951
30,000	40,000	764	880	957	1016	1064	1131
40,000	50,000	869	1000	1087	1154	1209	1286
50,000	60,000	962	1108	1204	1279	1340	1424
60,000	70,000	1047	1206	1311	1392	1458	1550
70,000	80,000	1127	1298	1411	1498	1569	1669
80,000	90,000	1201	1383	1504	1596	1672	1778
90,000	100,000	1271	1464	1592	1689	1770	1882
100,000	120,000	1363	1570	1707	1812	1898	2018
120,000	140,000	1489	1715	1864	1979	2073	2205
140,000	160,000	1599	1841	2002	2125	2226	2367
160,000	180,000	1708	1967	2138	2270	2378	2529
180,000	200,000	1807	2080	2261	2400	2515	2674
200,000	or more	2293	2641	2871	3047	3192	3394

Missouri[2] 4.2250%

Income At least	Income But less than	Exemptions 1	2	3	4	5	Over 5
$0	$20,000	166	189	205	216	226	239
20,000	30,000	272	309	334	353	369	390
30,000	40,000	326	371	400	423	442	468
40,000	50,000	373	424	458	484	505	534
50,000	60,000	415	472	509	538	562	594
60,000	70,000	453	515	556	588	614	649
70,000	80,000	490	557	601	635	663	701
80,000	90,000	523	595	642	678	708	749
90,000	100,000	555	631	681	720	751	795
100,000	120,000	598	679	733	774	808	855
120,000	140,000	656	745	804	849	886	937
140,000	160,000	706	802	866	914	954	1009
160,000	180,000	757	860	928	980	1022	1081
180,000	200,000	803	912	983	1038	1083	1146
200,000	or more	1031	1170	1262	1332	1390	1470

Nebraska[1] 5.5000%

Income At least	Income But less than	Exemptions 1	2	3	4	5	Over 5
$0	$20,000	216	238	252	263	272	284
20,000	30,000	371	411	436	455	470	491
30,000	40,000	454	503	534	557	576	602
40,000	50,000	527	584	620	647	669	699
50,000	60,000	594	658	699	729	754	788
60,000	70,000	655	726	771	805	833	870
70,000	80,000	714	791	841	878	908	949
80,000	90,000	769	852	905	945	978	1022
90,000	100,000	821	910	967	1010	1045	1092
100,000	120,000	891	988	1050	1097	1134	1186
120,000	140,000	988	1095	1164	1216	1258	1315
140,000	160,000	1073	1190	1265	1322	1367	1430
160,000	180,000	1159	1286	1367	1428	1477	1545
180,000	200,000	1237	1373	1460	1525	1578	1650
200,000	or more	1635	1815	1931	2018	2088	2184

(Continued)

2013 Optional State Sales Tax Tables *(Continued)*

Nevada[5] 6.8500%

Income At least	But less than	1	2	3	4	5	Over 5
$0	$20,000	257	284	301	315	325	340
20,000	30,000	412	455	483	504	520	544
30,000	40,000	491	542	575	599	620	647
40,000	50,000	558	616	654	682	704	736
50,000	60,000	619	683	724	755	780	815
60,000	70,000	674	744	789	822	850	887
70,000	80,000	726	801	849	885	915	955
80,000	90,000	774	854	905	944	975	1018
90,000	100,000	820	904	958	999	1032	1077
100,000	120,000	880	970	1028	1072	1107	1156
120,000	140,000	962	1061	1124	1171	1210	1263
140,000	160,000	1034	1140	1207	1258	1300	1356
160,000	180,000	1105	1218	1290	1345	1389	1449
180,000	200,000	1169	1289	1365	1422	1469	1533
200,000	or more	1489	1639	1736	1808	1867	1948

New Jersey[4, 6] 7.0000%

Income At least	But less than	1	2	3	4	5	Over 5
$0	$20,000	239	257	268	276	283	292
20,000	30,000	413	444	463	478	490	505
30,000	40,000	505	544	568	586	600	620
40,000	50,000	587	631	659	680	697	720
50,000	60,000	661	711	743	767	786	812
60,000	70,000	729	785	820	847	868	896
70,000	80,000	795	856	894	923	946	977
80,000	90,000	856	922	963	994	1019	1053
90,000	100,000	914	985	1029	1063	1089	1126
100,000	120,000	992	1069	1117	1153	1182	1222
120,000	140,000	1100	1185	1239	1279	1312	1355
140,000	160,000	1195	1288	1347	1391	1426	1474
160,000	180,000	1291	1391	1455	1503	1541	1592
180,000	200,000	1378	1486	1554	1604	1645	1701
200,000	or more	1821	1965	2056	2123	2178	2251

New Mexico[1] 5.1250%

Income At least	But less than	1	2	3	4	5	Over 5
$0	$20,000	188	209	222	232	240	252
20,000	30,000	337	376	401	420	435	456
30,000	40,000	420	468	499	523	542	568
40,000	50,000	493	550	587	615	638	669
50,000	60,000	561	626	669	700	726	762
60,000	70,000	624	697	744	780	809	849
70,000	80,000	685	765	818	857	889	933
80,000	90,000	742	830	887	929	964	1012
90,000	100,000	797	892	953	999	1036	1088
100,000	120,000	871	975	1042	1092	1133	1190
120,000	140,000	975	1091	1166	1223	1269	1333
140,000	160,000	1067	1195	1277	1340	1390	1460
160,000	180,000	1160	1300	1390	1458	1513	1589
180,000	200,000	1246	1396	1493	1566	1626	1708
200,000	or more	1689	1895	2028	2129	2210	2323

New York[2] 4.0000%

Income At least	But less than	1	2	3	4	5	Over 5
$0	$20,000	139	149	155	160	164	169
20,000	30,000	239	257	268	276	283	292
30,000	40,000	292	314	328	338	347	358
40,000	50,000	339	364	381	393	402	416
50,000	60,000	381	410	429	442	453	468
60,000	70,000	421	453	473	488	500	517
70,000	80,000	458	493	516	532	545	563
80,000	90,000	493	531	555	573	587	607
90,000	100,000	527	567	593	612	628	648
100,000	120,000	571	616	643	664	681	704
120,000	140,000	633	682	713	736	755	780
140,000	160,000	688	741	775	800	820	848
160,000	180,000	742	800	837	864	886	916
180,000	200,000	792	854	893	923	946	978
200,000	or more	1046	1128	1180	1219	1250	1293

North Carolina[2] 4.7500%

Income At least	But less than	1	2	3	4	5	Over 5
$0	$20,000	213	242	261	276	288	304
20,000	30,000	350	398	429	453	472	499
30,000	40,000	421	478	515	544	567	599
40,000	50,000	481	547	590	622	649	686
50,000	60,000	536	609	657	693	723	764
60,000	70,000	586	666	718	758	790	835
70,000	80,000	633	720	776	819	854	902
80,000	90,000	677	769	830	876	913	965
90,000	100,000	719	817	881	930	969	1024
100,000	120,000	774	879	948	1001	1044	1103
120,000	140,000	849	965	1041	1098	1145	1210
140,000	160,000	915	1040	1122	1184	1234	1305
160,000	180,000	981	1115	1202	1269	1323	1399
180,000	200,000	1041	1183	1275	1346	1404	1483
200,000	or more	1338	1520	1640	1731	1805	1908

North Dakota[1] 5.0000%

Income At least	But less than	1	2	3	4	5	Over 5
$0	$20,000	182	204	218	229	238	251
20,000	30,000	295	330	353	371	385	406
30,000	40,000	353	394	422	443	460	485
40,000	50,000	402	450	481	505	525	552
50,000	60,000	447	499	534	561	583	613
60,000	70,000	487	545	583	612	635	669
70,000	80,000	526	587	628	659	685	721
80,000	90,000	561	627	671	704	731	769
90,000	100,000	595	665	711	746	775	815
100,000	120,000	639	714	763	801	832	876
120,000	140,000	700	782	836	877	911	958
140,000	160,000	753	841	899	943	980	1031
160,000	180,000	806	900	962	1009	1048	1103
180,000	200,000	854	953	1018	1069	1110	1167
200,000	or more	1092	1217	1301	1364	1417	1490

Ohio[1] 5.5836%

Income At least	But less than	1	2	3	4	5	Over 5
$0	$20,000	217	237	249	259	266	276
20,000	30,000	371	405	426	442	455	473
30,000	40,000	453	494	520	539	555	577
40,000	50,000	524	571	602	624	643	668
50,000	60,000	589	642	676	702	722	750
60,000	70,000	648	707	745	773	796	827
70,000	80,000	705	769	810	841	866	899
80,000	90,000	758	827	871	904	931	967
90,000	100,000	809	883	930	965	993	1032
100,000	120,000	876	956	1007	1045	1076	1118
120,000	140,000	968	1057	1114	1156	1190	1237
140,000	160,000	1050	1147	1208	1254	1291	1342
160,000	180,000	1132	1237	1303	1352	1392	1447
180,000	200,000	1207	1318	1389	1441	1484	1542
200,000	or more	1584	1731	1824	1893	1950	2026

Oklahoma[1] 4.5000%

Income At least	But less than	1	2	3	4	5	Over 5
$0	$20,000	235	270	294	312	327	348
20,000	30,000	379	435	473	502	526	560
30,000	40,000	452	519	564	599	628	668
40,000	50,000	515	592	643	682	715	761
50,000	60,000	572	656	713	757	793	843
60,000	70,000	623	715	777	824	864	919
70,000	80,000	672	771	837	888	931	990
80,000	90,000	717	822	893	948	993	1056
90,000	100,000	759	871	946	1004	1051	1118
100,000	120,000	815	935	1015	1077	1128	1200
120,000	140,000	892	1023	1110	1178	1234	1312
140,000	160,000	959	1099	1193	1266	1326	1410
160,000	180,000	1025	1175	1276	1354	1418	1508
180,000	200,000	1085	1244	1350	1433	1501	1595
200,000	or more	1384	1585	1720	1825	1911	2031

Pennsylvania[1] 6.0000%

Income At least	But less than	1	2	3	4	5	Over 5
$0	$20,000	187	203	213	220	226	234
20,000	30,000	319	346	363	376	387	401
30,000	40,000	389	422	443	459	472	489
40,000	50,000	450	488	513	531	546	566
50,000	60,000	505	548	576	597	614	636
60,000	70,000	556	604	634	657	676	701
70,000	80,000	604	657	690	715	735	763
80,000	90,000	650	706	742	769	791	821
90,000	100,000	693	753	792	820	844	876
100,000	120,000	750	816	857	889	914	948
120,000	140,000	830	902	948	983	1011	1049
140,000	160,000	900	978	1029	1066	1097	1139
160,000	180,000	970	1055	1109	1150	1183	1228
180,000	200,000	1033	1124	1182	1226	1261	1309
200,000	or more	1356	1476	1553	1611	1657	1721

Rhode Island[4] 7.0000%

Income At least	But less than	1	2	3	4	5	Over 5
$0	$20,000	247	270	284	294	303	315
20,000	30,000	397	433	455	472	486	504
30,000	40,000	473	515	542	562	579	601
40,000	50,000	538	586	617	640	658	683
50,000	60,000	596	649	683	709	729	757
60,000	70,000	649	707	744	772	794	824
70,000	80,000	698	761	801	831	855	888
80,000	90,000	745	812	854	886	911	946
90,000	100,000	788	859	904	938	965	1002
100,000	120,000	846	922	970	1006	1035	1075
120,000	140,000	924	1007	1060	1099	1131	1174
140,000	160,000	992	1082	1138	1181	1215	1261
160,000	180,000	1061	1156	1216	1262	1298	1348
180,000	200,000	1122	1223	1287	1334	1373	1425
200,000	or more	1426	1554	1635	1696	1745	1811

South Carolina[2] 6.0000%

Income At least	But less than	1	2	3	4	5	Over 5
$0	$20,000	225	248	263	274	283	295
20,000	30,000	386	426	451	470	485	505
30,000	40,000	471	520	550	573	592	617
40,000	50,000	546	602	638	664	686	715
50,000	60,000	613	677	717	747	772	805
60,000	70,000	676	746	790	824	850	887
70,000	80,000	736	812	860	896	926	966
80,000	90,000	791	873	926	965	996	1039
90,000	100,000	845	932	988	1030	1063	1109
100,000	120,000	915	1010	1071	1116	1152	1202
120,000	140,000	1013	1118	1185	1235	1276	1331
140,000	160,000	1099	1213	1286	1341	1385	1445
160,000	180,000	1185	1309	1388	1447	1494	1559
180,000	200,000	1264	1396	1480	1543	1593	1663
200,000	or more	1663	1837	1948	2031	2098	2189

South Dakota[1] 4.0000%

Income At least	But less than	1	2	3	4	5	Over 5
$0	$20,000	228	263	286	305	319	340
20,000	30,000	367	424	462	491	515	548
30,000	40,000	437	505	551	585	614	654
40,000	50,000	498	576	627	667	699	745
50,000	60,000	553	639	696	740	776	826
60,000	70,000	602	696	758	806	845	900
70,000	80,000	649	750	817	868	911	970
80,000	90,000	692	800	871	926	972	1035
90,000	100,000	733	847	923	981	1029	1096
100,000	120,000	787	909	991	1053	1105	1177
120,000	140,000	861	995	1084	1152	1208	1287
140,000	160,000	925	1069	1165	1238	1299	1383
160,000	180,000	989	1143	1245	1324	1389	1479
180,000	200,000	1047	1210	1318	1401	1470	1565
200,000	or more	1333	1541	1679	1785	1872	1994

Tennessee[2] 7.0000%

Income At least	But less than	1	2	3	4	5	Over 5
$0	$20,000	354	403	436	460	481	509
20,000	30,000	579	659	711	752	785	831
30,000	40,000	694	790	853	902	941	996
40,000	50,000	794	903	975	1031	1076	1139
50,000	60,000	884	1005	1085	1147	1197	1267
60,000	70,000	965	1098	1185	1253	1308	1384
70,000	80,000	1043	1186	1280	1353	1412	1494
80,000	90,000	1114	1267	1368	1445	1509	1597
90,000	100,000	1182	1345	1452	1534	1601	1694
100,000	120,000	1272	1446	1562	1650	1722	1822
120,000	140,000	1395	1586	1712	1809	1888	1998
140,000	160,000	1503	1709	1844	1948	2034	2152
160,000	180,000	1610	1830	1976	2087	2179	2306
180,000	200,000	1707	1940	2095	2213	2310	2444
200,000	or more	2190	2490	2687	2838	2962	3135

Texas[1] 6.2500%

Income At least	But less than	1	2	3	4	5	Over 5
$0	$20,000	246	273	291	304	315	330
20,000	30,000	419	467	497	521	539	565
30,000	40,000	511	569	607	635	658	690
40,000	50,000	591	659	703	736	763	799
50,000	60,000	664	741	790	827	857	899
60,000	70,000	732	816	871	912	945	991
70,000	80,000	796	888	947	992	1028	1078
80,000	90,000	856	955	1019	1067	1106	1160
90,000	100,000	913	1019	1087	1139	1181	1238
100,000	120,000	989	1104	1178	1234	1279	1342
120,000	140,000	1094	1222	1304	1366	1416	1485
140,000	160,000	1187	1325	1415	1482	1537	1612
160,000	180,000	1280	1430	1526	1599	1658	1739
180,000	200,000	1365	1524	1627	1705	1768	1855
200,000	or more	1793	2004	2141	2243	2327	2442

Utah[2] 4.7000%

Income At least	But less than	1	2	3	4	5	Over 5
$0	$20,000	228	259	279	294	307	324
20,000	30,000	376	426	459	484	505	533
30,000	40,000	452	512	552	582	607	641
40,000	50,000	518	587	632	667	695	734
50,000	60,000	578	654	705	743	775	818
60,000	70,000	632	716	771	813	847	895
70,000	80,000	683	774	833	879	916	968
80,000	90,000	731	828	892	940	980	1035
90,000	100,000	776	879	947	998	1041	1099
100,000	120,000	836	947	1020	1075	1121	1184
120,000	140,000	918	1040	1120	1181	1231	1300
140,000	160,000	990	1121	1208	1273	1327	1402
160,000	180,000	1062	1203	1295	1366	1423	1503
180,000	200,000	1127	1276	1374	1449	1510	1595
200,000	or more	1452	1643	1770	1866	1945	2054

Vermont[1] 6.0000%

Income At least	But less than	1	2	3	4	5	Over 5
$0	$20,000	158	168	175	180	184	189
20,000	30,000	253	270	281	288	295	303
30,000	40,000	302	322	334	343	351	361
40,000	50,000	343	366	380	391	399	410
50,000	60,000	380	405	421	433	442	455
60,000	70,000	414	441	459	471	481	495
70,000	80,000	446	475	494	507	518	533
80,000	90,000	475	507	526	541	552	568
90,000	100,000	503	536	557	573	585	601
100,000	120,000	540	575	598	614	627	645
120,000	140,000	590	629	653	671	686	705
140,000	160,000	633	675	702	721	736	757
160,000	180,000	677	722	750	770	787	809
180,000	200,000	716	763	793	815	832	856
200,000	or more	910	970	1008	1035	1058	1087

Virginia[2] 4.1512%

Income At least	But less than	1	2	3	4	5	Over 5
$0	$20,000	173	196	212	224	233	247
20,000	30,000	274	310	334	353	368	389
30,000	40,000	324	367	396	417	435	460
40,000	50,000	368	416	448	473	493	520
50,000	60,000	406	460	495	522	544	575
60,000	70,000	441	499	538	567	591	624
70,000	80,000	474	537	578	609	634	670
80,000	90,000	505	571	615	648	675	712
90,000	100,000	534	604	649	684	713	753
100,000	120,000	572	646	695	733	763	806
120,000	140,000	624	705	758	798	832	878
140,000	160,000	669	755	812	856	891	940
160,000	180,000	713	806	866	912	950	1003
180,000	200,000	754	851	915	964	1003	1059
200,000	or more	953	1075	1155	1216	1266	1335

Washington[1] 6.5000%

Income At least	But less than	1	2	3	4	5	Over 5
$0	$20,000	251	277	293	306	316	329
20,000	30,000	432	476	505	526	544	567
30,000	40,000	528	582	617	643	665	694
40,000	50,000	612	675	716	746	771	805
50,000	60,000	688	759	805	840	868	906
60,000	70,000	759	837	888	926	957	1000
70,000	80,000	826	912	967	1009	1042	1089
80,000	90,000	889	981	1041	1086	1122	1172
90,000	100,000	949	1048	1111	1159	1198	1252
100,000	120,000	1029	1136	1205	1257	1299	1357
120,000	140,000	1139	1258	1335	1393	1439	1504
140,000	160,000	1237	1366	1449	1512	1563	1633
160,000	180,000	1334	1474	1564	1632	1687	1762
180,000	200,000	1423	1573	1669	1741	1800	1880
200,000	or more	1875	2072	2199	2295	2373	2479

West Virginia[2] 6.0000%

Income At least	But less than	1	2	3	4	5	Over 5
$0	$20,000	241	269	287	301	312	327
20,000	30,000	413	461	493	516	535	562
30,000	40,000	504	564	602	631	655	687
40,000	50,000	584	653	698	732	759	797
50,000	60,000	657	735	785	823	854	897
60,000	70,000	724	810	866	908	942	989
70,000	80,000	788	882	943	989	1026	1077
80,000	90,000	848	949	1015	1064	1104	1160
90,000	100,000	905	1014	1083	1136	1179	1238
100,000	120,000	981	1099	1175	1232	1279	1343
120,000	140,000	1086	1217	1301	1365	1417	1488
140,000	160,000	1179	1321	1413	1482	1538	1616
160,000	180,000	1272	1426	1525	1600	1661	1744
180,000	200,000	1357	1521	1627	1707	1772	1861
200,000	or more	1787	2004	2144	2251	2337	2456

Wisconsin[1] 5.0000%

Income At least	But less than	1	2	3	4	5	Over 5
$0	$20,000	204	225	239	249	257	268
20,000	30,000	347	383	405	423	436	455
30,000	40,000	422	466	494	514	531	554
40,000	50,000	488	538	571	595	614	641
50,000	60,000	547	604	640	668	690	720
60,000	70,000	602	665	705	735	759	792
70,000	80,000	654	722	766	799	825	861
80,000	90,000	703	776	823	859	887	926
90,000	100,000	749	828	878	915	946	987
100,000	120,000	811	896	950	991	1024	1069
120,000	140,000	896	990	1050	1095	1132	1182
140,000	160,000	971	1073	1139	1187	1227	1281
160,000	180,000	1046	1157	1227	1280	1322	1381
180,000	200,000	1114	1232	1307	1364	1409	1471
200,000	or more	1460	1615	1714	1788	1848	1929

Wyoming[1] 4.0000%

Income At least	But less than	1	2	3	4	5	Over 5
$0	$20,000	155	169	178	184	190	197
20,000	30,000	266	290	305	317	326	339
30,000	40,000	325	354	373	387	399	414
40,000	50,000	376	411	433	449	462	480
50,000	60,000	423	462	487	505	520	541
60,000	70,000	466	509	537	557	574	596
70,000	80,000	508	554	584	606	624	649
80,000	90,000	546	597	629	653	672	698
90,000	100,000	583	637	671	697	717	746
100,000	120,000	632	690	727	755	778	808
120,000	140,000	699	764	805	836	861	895
140,000	160,000	759	829	874	908	935	972
160,000	180,000	819	895	943	979	1009	1049
180,000	200,000	873	954	1006	1045	1076	1118
200,000	or more	1149	1256	1325	1376	1417	1473

Note. Residents of **Alaska** do not have a state sales tax, but should follow the instructions on the next page to determine their local sales tax amount.

1 Use the Ratio Method to determine your local sales tax deduction, then add that to the appropriate amount in the state table. Your state sales tax rate is provided next to the state name.

2 Follow the instructions on the next page to determine your local sales tax deduction, then add that to the appropriate amount in the state table.

3 The California table includes the 1.25% uniform local sales tax rate in addition to the 6.25% state sales tax rate for a total of 7.50%. Some California localities impose a larger local sales tax. Taxpayers who reside in those jurisdictions should use the Ratio Method to determine their local sales tax deduction, then add that to the appropriate amount in the state table. The denominator of the correct ratio is 7.50%, and the numerator is the total sales tax rate minus 7.50%.

4 This state does not have a local general sales tax, so the amount in the state table is the only amount to be deducted.

5 The Nevada table includes the 2.25% uniform local sales tax rate in addition to the 4.6000% state sales tax rate for a total of 6.85%. Some Nevada localities impose a larger local sales tax. Taxpayers who reside in those jurisdictions should use the Ratio Method to determine their local sales tax deduction, then add that to the appropriate amount in the state table. The denominator of the correct ratio is 6.85%, and the numerator is the total sales tax rate minus 6.85%.

6 Residents of Salem County, New Jersey should deduct only half of the amount in the state table.

7 The 4.0% rate for Hawaii is actually an excise tax but is treated as a sales tax for purpose of this deduction.

Which Optional Local Sales Tax Table Should I Use?

IF you live in the state of...	AND you live in...	THEN use Local Table...
Alaska	Any locality	C
Arizona	Glendale, Mesa or Tucson	A
	Chandler, Gilbert, Peoria, Phoenix, Scottsdale, Tempe, Yuma, or any other locality	B
Arkansas	Any locality	B
Colorado	Adams County, Arapahoe County, Boulder County, Centennial, Colorado Springs, Denver City/Denver County, El Paso County, Jefferson County, Larimer County, Pueblo County, or any other locality	A
	Aurora, Lakewood, or Longmont	B
	Arvada, Boulder, Fort Collins, Greeley, Thornton, or Westminster	C
Georgia	Any locality	B
Illinois	Any locality	A
Louisiana	Ascension Parish, Bossier Parish, Caddo Parish, Calcasieu Parish, East Baton Rouge Parish, Iberia Parish, Jefferson Parish, Lafayette Parish, Lafourche Parish, Livingston Parish, Orleans Parish, Ouachita Parish, Rapides Parish, St. Bernard Parish, St. Landry Parish, St. Tammany Parish, Tangipahoa Parish, or Terrebonne Parish	C
	Any other locality	B
Missouri	Any locality	B
New York	Chautauqua County, Chenango County, Columbia County, Delaware County, Greene County, Hamilton County, Tioga County, Wayne County, New York City, or Norwich City	A
	Counties: Albany, Allegany, Broome, Cattaraugus, Cayuga, Chemung, Clinton, Cortland, Dutchess, Erie, Essex, Franklin, Fulton, Genesee, Herkimer, Jefferson, Lewis, Livingston, Madison, Monroe, Montgomery, Nassau, Niagara, Oneida, Onondaga, Ontario, Orange, Orleans, Oswego, Otsego, Putnam, Rensselaer, Rockland, St. Lawrence, Saratoga, Schenectady, Schoharie, Schuyler, Seneca, Steuben, Suffolk, Sullivan, Tompkins, Ulster, Warren, Washington, Westchester, Wyoming, or Yates	B
	Any other locality	D*
North Carolina	Any locality	A
South Carolina	Aiken County, Cherokee County, Chesterfield County, Darlington County, Dillon County, Horry County, Jasper County, Lexington County, Marlboro County, Newberry County, Orangeburg County, York County, or Myrtle Beach	A
	Bamberg County, Charleston County, Hampton County, Lee County, Marion County, or any other locality	B
Tennessee	Any locality	B
Utah	Any locality	A
Virginia	Any locality	C
West Virginia	Any locality	C

2013 Optional Local Sales Tax Tables for Certain Local Jurisdictions
(Based on a local sales tax rate of 1 percent)

Income		Exemptions						Exemptions						Exemptions						Exemptions					
At least	But less than	1	2	3	4	5	Over 5	1	2	3	4	5	Over 5	1	2	3	4	5	Over 5	1	2	3	4	5	Over 5
		Local Table A						Local Table B						Local Table C						Local Table D*					
$0	$20,000	37	42	45	47	49	51	47	55	60	64	67	71	53	61	66	70	73	78	35	37	39	40	41	42
20,000	30,000	60	67	72	75	78	82	74	86	93	99	104	111	85	97	105	112	117	124	60	64	67	69	71	73
30,000	40,000	72	80	85	89	93	97	87	101	110	117	123	131	101	116	126	133	139	148	73	79	82	85	87	90
40,000	50,000	82	91	97	102	106	111	99	114	125	133	139	148	115	132	143	151	158	168	85	91	95	98	101	104
50,000	60,000	91	101	108	113	117	123	109	126	137	146	153	164	127	146	158	168	175	186	95	103	107	111	113	117
60,000	70,000	99	110	117	123	127	134	118	137	149	159	166	177	139	159	172	183	191	203	105	113	118	122	125	129
70,000	80,000	106	119	126	132	137	144	127	147	160	170	179	190	149	171	186	197	206	218	115	123	129	133	136	141
80,000	90,000	114	126	135	141	146	154	135	156	170	181	190	202	159	182	198	210	219	233	123	133	139	143	147	152
90,000	100,000	120	134	143	149	155	163	143	165	179	191	200	213	169	193	209	222	232	246	132	142	148	153	157	162
100,000	120,000	129	144	153	160	166	174	153	176	192	204	214	228	181	207	225	238	249	264	143	154	161	166	170	176
120,000	140,000	141	157	167	175	182	191	166	192	209	222	233	248	198	226	245	260	272	289	158	171	178	184	189	195
140,000	160,000	152	169	180	188	195	205	178	205	224	238	249	266	212	243	264	279	292	310	172	185	194	200	205	212
160,000	180,000	162	180	192	201	209	219	190	219	238	253	266	283	227	260	282	298	312	331	186	200	209	216	222	229
180,000	200,000	172	191	203	213	221	231	200	231	251	267	280	298	240	275	298	315	330	350	198	214	223	231	237	245
200,000	or more	219	243	259	271	281	294	252	290	316	336	352	375	305	349	378	401	419	445	262	282	295	305	313	323

*Note. Local Table D is just 25% of the NY State table.

Appendix B

Tax Forms

*(Tax forms can be obtained from the IRS website: **http://www.irs.gov**)*

Form **1040**

Department of the Treasury—Internal Revenue Service   (99)

U.S. Individual Income Tax Return   **2013**   OMB No. 1545-0074   IRS Use Only—Do not write or staple in this space.

For the year Jan. 1–Dec. 31, 2013, or other tax year beginning _____, 2013, ending _____, 20___   See separate instructions.

Your first name and initial	Last name	Your social security number

If a joint return, spouse's first name and initial	Last name	Spouse's social security number

Home address (number and street). If you have a P.O. box, see instructions.   Apt. no.

▲ Make sure the SSN(s) above and on line 6c are correct.

City, town or post office, state, and ZIP code. If you have a foreign address, also complete spaces below (see instructions).

Presidential Election Campaign
Check here if you, or your spouse if filing jointly, want $3 to go to this fund. Checking a box below will not change your tax or refund. ☐ You ☐ Spouse

Foreign country name	Foreign province/state/county	Foreign postal code

Filing Status

Check only one box.

1 ☐ Single
2 ☐ Married filing jointly (even if only one had income)
3 ☐ Married filing separately. Enter spouse's SSN above and full name here. ▶
4 ☐ Head of household (with qualifying person). (See instructions.) If the qualifying person is a child but not your dependent, enter this child's name here. ▶
5 ☐ Qualifying widow(er) with dependent child

Exemptions

6a ☐ **Yourself.** If someone can claim you as a dependent, **do not** check box 6a . . . .
b ☐ **Spouse** . . . .

c **Dependents:**

(1) First name Last name	(2) Dependent's social security number	(3) Dependent's relationship to you	(4) ✓ if child under age 17 qualifying for child tax credit (see instructions)
			☐
			☐
			☐
			☐

If more than four dependents, see instructions and check here ▶ ☐

Boxes checked on 6a and 6b
No. of children on 6c who:
• lived with you
• did not live with you due to divorce or separation (see instructions)
Dependents on 6c not entered above
Add numbers on lines above ▶

d Total number of exemptions claimed . . . .

Income

Attach Form(s) W-2 here. Also attach Forms W-2G and 1099-R if tax was withheld.

If you did not get a W-2, see instructions.

7	Wages, salaries, tips, etc. Attach Form(s) W-2	**7**	
8a	**Taxable** interest. Attach Schedule B if required	**8a**	
b	**Tax-exempt** interest. **Do not** include on line 8a . . .	8b		
9a	Ordinary dividends. Attach Schedule B if required	**9a**	
b	Qualified dividends	9b		
10	Taxable refunds, credits, or offsets of state and local income taxes	**10**	
11	Alimony received	**11**	
12	Business income or (loss). Attach Schedule C or C-EZ	**12**	
13	Capital gain or (loss). Attach Schedule D if required. If not required, check here ▶ ☐	**13**	
14	Other gains or (losses). Attach Form 4797	**14**	
15a	IRA distributions .	15a		b Taxable amount . . .	**15b**	
16a	Pensions and annuities	16a		b Taxable amount . . .	**16b**	
17	Rental real estate, royalties, partnerships, S corporations, trusts, etc. Attach Schedule E	**17**	
18	Farm income or (loss). Attach Schedule F	**18**	
19	Unemployment compensation	**19**	
20a	Social security benefits	20a		b Taxable amount . . .	**20b**	
21	Other income. List type and amount _____	**21**	
22	Combine the amounts in the far right column for lines 7 through 21. This is your **total income** ▶	**22**	

Adjusted Gross Income

23	Educator expenses	23		
24	Certain business expenses of reservists, performing artists, and fee-basis government officials. Attach Form 2106 or 2106-EZ	24		
25	Health savings account deduction. Attach Form 8889 .	25		
26	Moving expenses. Attach Form 3903	26		
27	Deductible part of self-employment tax. Attach Schedule SE .	27		
28	Self-employed SEP, SIMPLE, and qualified plans .	28		
29	Self-employed health insurance deduction . . .	29		
30	Penalty on early withdrawal of savings	30		
31a	Alimony paid b Recipient's SSN ▶	31a		
32	IRA deduction	32		
33	Student loan interest deduction	33		
34	Tuition and fees. Attach Form 8917	34		
35	Domestic production activities deduction. Attach Form 8903	35		
36	Add lines 23 through 35	36	
37	Subtract line 36 from line 22. This is your **adjusted gross income** . . . . . . ▶	37	

For Disclosure, Privacy Act, and Paperwork Reduction Act Notice, see separate instructions.   Cat. No. 11320B   Form **1040** (2013)

Form 1040 (2013)   Page **2**

Tax and Credits	38	Amount from line 37 (adjusted gross income)	38	

Tax and Credits

39a	Check if: { ☐ **You** were born before January 2, 1949, ☐ Blind. } ☐ **Spouse** was born before January 2, 1949, ☐ Blind. **Total boxes checked** ▶ 39a		

Standard Deduction for—

• People who check any box on line 39a or 39b **or** who can be claimed as a dependent, see instructions.

• All others:

Single or Married filing separately, $6,100

Married filing jointly or Qualifying widow(er), $12,200

Head of household, $8,950

b	If your spouse itemizes on a separate return or you were a dual-status alien, check here ▶ 39b ☐	
40	**Itemized deductions** (from Schedule A) **or** your **standard deduction** (see left margin) . .	40
41	Subtract line 40 from line 38	41
42	**Exemptions.** If line 38 is $150,000 or less, multiply $3,900 by the number on line 6d. Otherwise, see instructions	42
43	**Taxable income.** Subtract line 42 from line 41. If line 42 is more than line 41, enter -0-	43
44	**Tax** (see instructions). Check if any from: **a** ☐ Form(s) 8814 **b** ☐ Form 4972 **c** ☐	44
45	**Alternative minimum tax** (see instructions). Attach Form 6251	45
46	Add lines 44 and 45 . . . . ▶	46

47	Foreign tax credit. Attach Form 1116 if required . . .	47	
48	Credit for child and dependent care expenses. Attach Form 2441	48	
49	Education credits from Form 8863, line 19	49	
50	Retirement savings contributions credit. Attach Form 8880	50	
51	Child tax credit. Attach Schedule 8812, if required . . .	51	
52	Residential energy credits. Attach Form 5695	52	
53	Other credits from Form: **a** ☐ 3800 **b** ☐ 8801 **c** ☐	53	
54	Add lines 47 through 53. These are your **total credits**	54	
55	Subtract line 54 from line 46. If line 54 is more than line 46, enter -0- . . . . . . ▶	55	

Other Taxes

56	Self-employment tax. Attach Schedule SE	56
57	Unreported social security and Medicare tax from Form: **a** ☐ 4137 **b** ☐ 8919 . .	57
58	Additional tax on IRAs, other qualified retirement plans, etc. Attach Form 5329 if required	58
59a	Household employment taxes from Schedule H	59a
b	First-time homebuyer credit repayment. Attach Form 5405 if required	59b
60	Taxes from: **a** ☐ Form 8959 **b** ☐ Form 8960 **c** ☐ Instructions; enter code(s)	60
61	Add lines 55 through 60. This is your **total tax** . . . . ▶	61

Payments

If you have a qualifying child, attach Schedule EIC.

62	Federal income tax withheld from Forms W-2 and 1099 . .	62	
63	2013 estimated tax payments and amount applied from 2012 return	63	
64a	**Earned income credit (EIC)**	64a	
b	Nontaxable combat pay election 64b		
65	Additional child tax credit. Attach Schedule 8812 . . .	65	
66	American opportunity credit from Form 8863, line 8 . . .	66	
67	Reserved	67	
68	Amount paid with request for extension to file	68	
69	Excess social security and tier 1 RRTA tax withheld . . .	69	
70	Credit for federal tax on fuels. Attach Form 4136 . . .	70	
71	Credits from Form: **a** ☐ 2439 **b** ☐ Reserved **c** ☐ 8885 **d** ☐	71	
72	Add lines 62, 63, 64a, and 65 through 71. These are your **total payments** . . . . . ▶	72	

Refund

Direct deposit? See instructions.

73	If line 72 is more than line 61, subtract line 61 from line 72. This is the amount you **overpaid**	73
74a	Amount of line 73 you want **refunded to you.** If Form 8888 is attached, check here . . ▶ ☐	74a
▶ b	Routing number ☐☐☐☐☐☐☐☐☐ ▶ c Type: ☐ Checking ☐ Savings	
▶ d	Account number ☐☐☐☐☐☐☐☐☐☐☐☐☐☐☐☐☐	
75	Amount of line 73 you want **applied to your 2014 estimated tax** ▶ 75	

Amount You Owe

76	**Amount you owe.** Subtract line 72 from line 61. For details on how to pay, see instructions ▶	76
77	Estimated tax penalty (see instructions) 77	

Third Party Designee

Do you want to allow another person to discuss this return with the IRS (see instructions)? ☐ **Yes. Complete below.** ☐ **No**

Designee's name ▶	Phone no. ▶	Personal identification number (PIN) ▶

Sign Here

Joint return? See instructions. Keep a copy for your records.

Under penalties of perjury, I declare that I have examined this return and accompanying schedules and statements, and to the best of my knowledge and belief, they are true, correct, and complete. Declaration of preparer (other than taxpayer) is based on all information of which preparer has any knowledge.

Your signature	Date	Your occupation	Daytime phone number
Spouse's signature. If a joint return, **both** must sign.	Date	Spouse's occupation	If the IRS sent you an Identity Protection PIN, enter it here (see inst.)

Paid Preparer Use Only

Print/Type preparer's name	Preparer's signature	Date	Check ☐ if self-employed	PTIN
Firm's name ▶			Firm's EIN ▶	
Firm's address ▶			Phone no.	

Form **1040** (2013)

SCHEDULE A
(Form 1040)

Department of the Treasury
Internal Revenue Service (99)

Itemized Deductions

▶ Information about Schedule A and its separate instructions is at *www.irs.gov/schedulea*.
▶ Attach to Form 1040.

OMB No. 1545-0074

20**13**

Attachment
Sequence No. **07**

Name(s) shown on Form 1040

Your social security number

Medical and Dental Expenses	**Caution.** Do not include expenses reimbursed or paid by others.	
	1 Medical and dental expenses (see instructions)	**1**
	2 Enter amount from Form 1040, line 38 **2**	
	3 Multiply line 2 by 10% (.10). But if either you or your spouse was born before January 2, 1949, multiply line 2 by 7.5% (.075) instead	**3**
	4 Subtract line 3 from line 1. If line 3 is more than line 1, enter -0-	**4**
Taxes You Paid	**5** State and local **(check only one box):**	
	a ☐ Income taxes, **or**	**5**
	b ☐ General sales taxes	
	6 Real estate taxes (see instructions)	**6**
	7 Personal property taxes	**7**
	8 Other taxes. List type and amount ▶ _____	
	_____	**8**
	9 Add lines 5 through 8	**9**
Interest You Paid

Note.
Your mortgage interest deduction may be limited (see instructions). | **10** Home mortgage interest and points reported to you on Form 1098 | **10** |
	11 Home mortgage interest not reported to you on Form 1098. If paid to the person from whom you bought the home, see instructions and show that person's name, identifying no., and address ▶ _____	**11**
	12 Points not reported to you on Form 1098. See instructions for special rules	**12**
	13 Mortgage insurance premiums (see instructions)	**13**
	14 Investment interest. Attach Form 4952 if required. (See instructions.)	**14**
	15 Add lines 10 through 14	**15**
Gifts to Charity

If you made a gift and got a benefit for it, see instructions. | **16** Gifts by cash or check. If you made any gift of $250 or more, see instructions . . . . | **16** |
	17 Other than by cash or check. If any gift of $250 or more, see instructions. You **must** attach Form 8283 if over $500 . . .	**17**
	18 Carryover from prior year	**18**
	19 Add lines 16 through 18	**19**
Casualty and Theft Losses	**20** Casualty or theft loss(es). Attach Form 4684. (See instructions.)	**20**
Job Expenses and Certain Miscellaneous Deductions	**21** Unreimbursed employee expenses—job travel, union dues, job education, etc. Attach Form 2106 or 2106-EZ if required. (See instructions.) ▶ _____	**21**
	22 Tax preparation fees	**22**
	23 Other expenses—investment, safe deposit box, etc. List type and amount ▶ _____	**23**
	24 Add lines 21 through 23	**24**
	25 Enter amount from Form 1040, line 38 **25**	
	26 Multiply line 25 by 2% (.02)	**26**
	27 Subtract line 26 from line 24. If line 26 is more than line 24, enter -0-	**27**
Other Miscellaneous Deductions	**28** Other—from list in instructions. List type and amount ▶ _____	
	_____	**28**
Total Itemized Deductions	**29** Is Form 1040, line 38, over $150,000?	
	☐ **No.** Your deduction is not limited. Add the amounts in the far right column for lines 4 through 28. Also, enter this amount on Form 1040, line 40.	**29**
	☐ **Yes.** Your deduction may be limited. See the Itemized Deductions Worksheet in the instructions to figure the amount to enter.	
	30 If you elect to itemize deductions even though they are less than your standard deduction, check here . . . . ▶ ☐	

For Paperwork Reduction Act Notice, see Form 1040 instructions.   Cat. No. 17145C   Schedule A (Form 1040) 2013

SCHEDULE B (Form 1040A or 1040) Department of the Treasury Internal Revenue Service (99)	Interest and Ordinary Dividends ▶ Attach to Form 1040A or 1040. ▶ Information about Schedule B (Form 1040A or 1040) and its instructions is at *www.irs.gov/scheduleb*.	OMB No. 1545-0074 20**13** Attachment Sequence No. **08**

Name(s) shown on return | Your social security number

Part I

Interest

(See instructions on back and the instructions for Form 1040A, or Form 1040, line 8a.)

Note. If you received a Form 1099-INT, Form 1099-OID, or substitute statement from a brokerage firm, list the firm's name as the payer and enter the total interest shown on that form.

		Amount
1	List name of payer. If any interest is from a seller-financed mortgage and the buyer used the property as a personal residence, see instructions on back and list this interest first. Also, show that buyer's social security number and address ▶	**1**
2	Add the amounts on line 1	**2**
3	Excludable interest on series EE and I U.S. savings bonds issued after 1989. Attach Form 8815	**3**
4	Subtract line 3 from line 2. Enter the result here and on Form 1040A, or Form 1040, line 8a . . . . ▶	**4**

Note. If line 4 is over $1,500, you must complete Part III.

Part II

Ordinary Dividends

(See instructions on back and the instructions for Form 1040A, or Form 1040, line 9a.)

Note. If you received a Form 1099-DIV or substitute statement from a brokerage firm, list the firm's name as the payer and enter the ordinary dividends shown on that form.

		Amount
5	List name of payer ▶	**5**
6	Add the amounts on line 5. Enter the total here and on Form 1040A, or Form 1040, line 9a . . . . ▶	**6**

Note. If line 6 is over $1,500, you must complete Part III.

Part III

Foreign Accounts and Trusts

(See instructions on back.)

You must complete this part if you **(a)** had over $1,500 of taxable interest or ordinary dividends; **(b)** had a foreign account; or **(c)** received a distribution from, or were a grantor of, or a transferor to, a foreign trust.

		Yes	No
7a	At any time during 2013, did you have a financial interest in or signature authority over a financial account (such as a bank account, securities account, or brokerage account) located in a foreign country? See instructions		
	If "Yes," are you required to file FinCEN Form 114, Report of Foreign Bank and Financial Accounts (FBAR), formerly TD F 90-22.1, to report that financial interest or signature authority? See FinCEN Form 114 and its instructions for filing requirements and exceptions to those requirements		
b	If you are required to file FinCEN Form 114, enter the name of the foreign country where the financial account is located ▶		
8	During 2013, did you receive a distribution from, or were you the grantor of, or transferor to, a foreign trust? If "Yes," you may have to file Form 3520. See instructions on back		

For Paperwork Reduction Act Notice, see your tax return instructions. Cat. No. 17146N Schedule B (Form 1040A or 1040) 2013

SCHEDULE C (Form 1040)	Profit or Loss From Business (Sole Proprietorship)	OMB No. 1545-0074

Department of the Treasury
Internal Revenue Service (99)

► For information on Schedule C and its instructions, go to *www.irs.gov/schedulec.*
► Attach to Form 1040, 1040NR, or 1041; partnerships generally must file Form 1065.

2013

Attachment Sequence No. **09**

Name of proprietor

Social security number (SSN)

A Principal business or profession, including product or service (see instructions)

B Enter code from instructions
►

C Business name. If no separate business name, leave blank.

D Employer ID number (EIN), (see instr.)

E Business address (including suite or room no.) ►
City, town or post office, state, and ZIP code

F Accounting method: **(1)** ☐ Cash **(2)** ☐ Accrual **(3)** ☐ Other (specify) ►

G Did you "materially participate" in the operation of this business during 2013? If "No," see instructions for limit on losses . ☐ Yes ☐ No

H If you started or acquired this business during 2013, check here . . . . ► ☐

I Did you make any payments in 2013 that would require you to file Form(s) 1099? (see instructions) . . . . . ☐ Yes ☐ No

J If "Yes," did you or will you file required Forms 1099? . . . . ☐ Yes ☐ No

Part I   Income

1	Gross receipts or sales. See instructions for line 1 and check the box if this income was reported to you on Form W-2 and the "Statutory employee" box on that form was checked . . . . ► ☐	1	
2	Returns and allowances	2	
3	Subtract line 2 from line 1	3	
4	Cost of goods sold (from line 42)	4	
5	**Gross profit.** Subtract line 4 from line 3	5	
6	Other income, including federal and state gasoline or fuel tax credit or refund (see instructions)	6	
7	**Gross income.** Add lines 5 and 6 . . . . ►	7	

Part II   Expenses   Enter expenses for business use of your home only on line 30.

8	Advertising	8		18	Office expense (see instructions)	18
9	Car and truck expenses (see instructions)	9		19	Pension and profit-sharing plans .	19
				20	Rent or lease (see instructions):	
10	Commissions and fees .	10		a	Vehicles, machinery, and equipment	20a
11	Contract labor (see instructions)	11		b	Other business property . . .	20b
12	Depletion	12		21	Repairs and maintenance . . .	21
13	Depreciation and section 179 expense deduction (not included in Part III) (see instructions)	13		22	Supplies (not included in Part III) .	22
				23	Taxes and licenses	23
				24	Travel, meals, and entertainment:	
14	Employee benefit programs (other than on line 19) . .	14		a	Travel	24a
15	Insurance (other than health)	15		b	Deductible meals and entertainment (see instructions) .	24b
16	Interest:			25	Utilities	25
a	Mortgage (paid to banks, etc.)	16a		26	Wages (less employment credits) .	26
b	Other	16b		27a	Other expenses (from line 48) . .	27a
17	Legal and professional services	17		b	Reserved for future use . . .	27b

28	**Total expenses** before expenses for business use of home. Add lines 8 through 27a . . . . . . ►	28	
29	Tentative profit or (loss). Subtract line 28 from line 7	29	
30	Expenses for business use of your home. Do not report these expenses elsewhere. Attach Form 8829 unless using the simplified method (see instructions). **Simplified method filers only:** enter the total square footage of: (a) your home: _____ and (b) the part of your home used for business: _____ . Use the Simplified Method Worksheet in the instructions to figure the amount to enter on line 30	30	
31	**Net profit or (loss).** Subtract line 30 from line 29.		

• If a profit, enter on both **Form 1040, line 12** (or **Form 1040NR, line 13**) and on **Schedule SE, line 2.** (If you checked the box on line 1, see instructions). Estates and trusts, enter on **Form 1041, line 3.**

• If a loss, you **must** go to line 32.

31	

32 If you have a loss, check the box that describes your investment in this activity (see instructions).

• If you checked 32a, enter the loss on both **Form 1040, line 12,** (or **Form 1040NR, line 13**) and on **Schedule SE, line 2.** (If you checked the box on line 1, see the line 31 instructions). Estates and trusts, enter on **Form 1041, line 3.**

• If you checked 32b, you **must** attach **Form 6198.** Your loss may be limited.

32a ☐ All investment is at risk.
32b ☐ Some investment is not at risk.

For Paperwork Reduction Act Notice, see the separate instructions.   Cat. No. 11334P   Schedule C (Form 1040) 2013

Schedule C (Form 1040) 2013   Page **2**

Part III	**Cost of Goods Sold** (see instructions)		

33 Method(s) used to
value closing inventory: **a** ☐ Cost   **b** ☐ Lower of cost or market   **c** ☐ Other (attach explanation)

34 Was there any change in determining quantities, costs, or valuations between opening and closing inventory?
If "Yes," attach explanation . . . .   ☐ Yes   ☐ No

35	Inventory at beginning of year. If different from last year's closing inventory, attach explanation . . .	**35**	
36	Purchases less cost of items withdrawn for personal use	**36**	
37	Cost of labor. Do not include any amounts paid to yourself	**37**	
38	Materials and supplies	**38**	
39	Other costs	**39**	
40	Add lines 35 through 39	**40**	
41	Inventory at end of year	**41**	
42	**Cost of goods sold.** Subtract line 41 from line 40. Enter the result here and on line 4	**42**	

Part IV	**Information on Your Vehicle.** Complete this part **only** if you are claiming car or truck expenses on line 9 and are not required to file Form 4562 for this business. See the instructions for line 13 to find out if you must file Form 4562.

43 When did you place your vehicle in service for business purposes? (month, day, year) ▶ _____ / _____ / _____

44 Of the total number of miles you drove your vehicle during 2013, enter the number of miles you used your vehicle for:

a Business _____   **b** Commuting (see instructions) _____   **c** Other _____

45 Was your vehicle available for personal use during off-duty hours? . . . .   ☐ Yes   ☐ No

46 Do you (or your spouse) have another vehicle available for personal use?. . . . .   ☐ Yes   ☐ No

47a Do you have evidence to support your deduction? . . . .   ☐ Yes   ☐ No

b If "Yes," is the evidence written? . . . .   ☐ Yes   ☐ No

Part V	**Other Expenses.** List below business expenses not included on lines 8–26 or line 30.

------------------------------------		
48 Total other expenses. Enter here and on line 27a	**48**	

Schedule C (Form 1040) 2013

SCHEDULE D (Form 1040) Department of the Treasury Internal Revenue Service (99)	**Capital Gains and Losses** ► **Attach to Form 1040 or Form 1040NR.** ► **Information about Schedule D and its separate instructions is at** *www.irs.gov/scheduled.* ► **Use Form 8949 to list your transactions for lines 1b, 2, 3, 8b, 9, and 10.**	OMB No. 1545-0074 20**13** Attachment Sequence No. **12**

Name(s) shown on return	Your social security number

Part I **Short-Term Capital Gains and Losses—Assets Held One Year or Less**

See instructions for how to figure the amounts to enter on the lines below. This form may be easier to complete if you round off cents to whole dollars.	**(d)** Proceeds (sales price)	**(e)** Cost (or other basis)	**(g)** Adjustments to gain or loss from Form(s) 8949, Part I, line 2, column (g)	**(h) Gain or (loss)** Subtract column (e) from column (d) and combine the result with column (g)
1a Totals for all short-term transactions reported on Form 1099-B for which basis was reported to the IRS and for which you have no adjustments (see instructions). However, if you choose to report all these transactions on Form 8949, leave this line blank and go to line 1b .				
1b Totals for all transactions reported on Form(s) 8949 with **Box A** checked				
2 Totals for all transactions reported on Form(s) 8949 with **Box B** checked				
3 Totals for all transactions reported on Form(s) 8949 with **Box C** checked				

4 Short-term gain from Form 6252 and short-term gain or (loss) from Forms 4684, 6781, and 8824 .	**4**	
5 Net short-term gain or (loss) from partnerships, S corporations, estates, and trusts from Schedule(s) K-1	**5**	
6 Short-term capital loss carryover. Enter the amount, if any, from line 8 of your **Capital Loss Carryover Worksheet** in the instructions	**6**	( )
7 **Net short-term capital gain or (loss).** Combine lines 1a through 6 in column (h). If you have any long-term capital gains or losses, go to Part II below. Otherwise, go to Part III on the back	**7**	

Part II **Long-Term Capital Gains and Losses—Assets Held More Than One Year**

See instructions for how to figure the amounts to enter on the lines below. This form may be easier to complete if you round off cents to whole dollars.	**(d)** Proceeds (sales price)	**(e)** Cost (or other basis)	**(g)** Adjustments to gain or loss from Form(s) 8949, Part II, line 2, column (g)	**(h) Gain or (loss)** Subtract column (e) from column (d) and combine the result with column (g)
8a Totals for all long-term transactions reported on Form 1099-B for which basis was reported to the IRS and for which you have no adjustments (see instructions). However, if you choose to report all these transactions on Form 8949, leave this line blank and go to line 8b .				
8b Totals for all transactions reported on Form(s) 8949 with **Box D** checked				
9 Totals for all transactions reported on Form(s) 8949 with **Box E** checked				
10 Totals for all transactions reported on Form(s) 8949 with **Box F** checked.				

11 Gain from Form 4797, Part I; long-term gain from Forms 2439 and 6252; and long-term gain or (loss) from Forms 4684, 6781, and 8824	**11**	
12 Net long-term gain or (loss) from partnerships, S corporations, estates, and trusts from Schedule(s) K-1	**12**	
13 Capital gain distributions. See the instructions	**13**	
14 Long-term capital loss carryover. Enter the amount, if any, from line 13 of your **Capital Loss Carryover Worksheet** in the instructions	**14**	( )
15 **Net long-term capital gain or (loss).** Combine lines 8a through 14 in column (h). Then go to Part III on the back	**15**	

For Paperwork Reduction Act Notice, see your tax return instructions.   Cat. No. 11338H   **Schedule D (Form 1040) 2013**

Part III	**Summary**

16 Combine lines 7 and 15 and enter the result **16**

> • If line 16 is a **gain,** enter the amount from line 16 on Form 1040, line 13, or Form 1040NR, line 14. Then go to line 17 below.
>
> • If line 16 is a **loss,** skip lines 17 through 20 below. Then go to line 21. Also be sure to complete line 22.
>
> • If line 16 is **zero,** skip lines 17 through 21 below and enter -0- on Form 1040, line 13, or Form 1040NR, line 14. Then go to line 22.

17 Are lines 15 and 16 **both** gains?
☐ **Yes.** Go to line 18.
☐ **No.** Skip lines 18 through 21, and go to line 22.

18 Enter the amount, if any, from line 7 of the **28% Rate Gain Worksheet** in the instructions . . ▶ **18**

19 Enter the amount, if any, from line 18 of the **Unrecaptured Section 1250 Gain Worksheet** in the instructions . . . . ▶ **19**

20 Are lines 18 and 19 **both** zero or blank?
☐ **Yes.** Complete the **Qualified Dividends and Capital Gain Tax Worksheet** in the instructions for Form 1040, line 44 (or in the instructions for Form 1040NR, line 42). **Do not** complete lines 21 and 22 below.

☐ **No.** Complete the **Schedule D Tax Worksheet** in the instructions. **Do not** complete lines 21 and 22 below.

21 If line 16 is a loss, enter here and on Form 1040, line 13, or Form 1040NR, line 14, the **smaller** of:

> • The loss on line 16 or
> • ($3,000), or if married filing separately, ($1,500) } . . . .   **21** (   )

Note. When figuring which amount is smaller, treat both amounts as positive numbers.

22 Do you have qualified dividends on Form 1040, line 9b, or Form 1040NR, line 10b?

☐ **Yes.** Complete the **Qualified Dividends and Capital Gain Tax Worksheet** in the instructions for Form 1040, line 44 (or in the instructions for Form 1040NR, line 42).

☐ **No.** Complete the rest of Form 1040 or Form 1040NR.

SCHEDULE E (Form 1040) Department of the Treasury Internal Revenue Service (99)	**Supplemental Income and Loss** (From rental real estate, royalties, partnerships, S corporations, estates, trusts, REMICs, etc.) ▶ Attach to Form 1040, 1040NR, or Form 1041. ▶ Information about Schedule E and its separate instructions is at *www.irs.gov/schedulee*.	OMB No. 1545-0074 20**13** Attachment Sequence No. **13**

Name(s) shown on return | Your social security number

Part I **Income or Loss From Rental Real Estate and Royalties** **Note.** If you are in the business of renting personal property, use **Schedule C** or **C-EZ** (see instructions). If you are an individual, report farm rental income or loss from **Form 4835** on page 2, line 40.

A Did you make any payments in 2013 that would require you to file Form(s) 1099? (see instructions) ☐ Yes ☐ No

B If "Yes," did you or will you file required Forms 1099? ☐ Yes ☐ No

1a	Physical address of each property (street, city, state, ZIP code)
A	
B	
C	

1b	Type of Property (from list below)	2	For each rental real estate property listed above, report the number of fair rental and personal use days. Check the **QJV** box only if you meet the requirements to file as a qualified joint venture. See instructions.		Fair Rental Days	Personal Use Days	QJV
A				A			☐
B				B			☐
C				C			☐

Type of Property:

1 Single Family Residence	3 Vacation/Short-Term Rental	5 Land	7 Self-Rental
2 Multi-Family Residence	4 Commercial	6 Royalties	8 Other (describe)

Income:	Properties:		A	B	C
3 Rents received	3				
4 Royalties received	4				
Expenses:					
5 Advertising	5				
6 Auto and travel (see instructions)	6				
7 Cleaning and maintenance	7				
8 Commissions.	8				
9 Insurance	9				
10 Legal and other professional fees	10				
11 Management fees	11				
12 Mortgage interest paid to banks, etc. (see instructions)	12				
13 Other interest.	13				
14 Repairs.	14				
15 Supplies	15				
16 Taxes	16				
17 Utilities	17				
18 Depreciation expense or depletion	18				
19 Other (list) ▶ ------------------------------------	19				
20 Total expenses. Add lines 5 through 19	20				
21 Subtract line 20 from line 3 (rents) and/or 4 (royalties). If result is a (loss), see instructions to find out if you must file **Form 6198**	21				
22 Deductible rental real estate loss after limitation, if any, on **Form 8582** (see instructions)	22	(	)(	)(	)

23a	Total of all amounts reported on line 3 for all rental properties	23a		
b	Total of all amounts reported on line 4 for all royalty properties	23b		
c	Total of all amounts reported on line 12 for all properties	23c		
d	Total of all amounts reported on line 18 for all properties	23d		
e	Total of all amounts reported on line 20 for all properties	23e		

24	**Income.** Add positive amounts shown on line 21. **Do not** include any losses	24	
25	**Losses.** Add royalty losses from line 21 and rental real estate losses from line 22. Enter total losses here	25	(	)
26	**Total rental real estate and royalty income or (loss).** Combine lines 24 and 25. Enter the result here. If Parts II, III, IV, and line 40 on page 2 do not apply to you, also enter this amount on Form 1040, line 17, or Form 1040NR, line 18. Otherwise, include this amount in the total on line 41 on page 2	26	

For Paperwork Reduction Act Notice, see the separate instructions.   Cat. No. 11344L   **Schedule E (Form 1040) 2013**

Schedule E (Form 1040) 2013
Attachment Sequence No. **13**
Page **2**

Name(s) shown on return. Do not enter name and social security number if shown on other side.

Your social security number

Caution. The IRS compares amounts reported on your tax return with amounts shown on Schedule(s) K-1.

Part II	**Income or Loss From Partnerships and S Corporations** **Note.** If you report a loss from an at-risk activity for which **any** amount is **not** at risk, you **must** check the box in column **(e)** on line 28 and attach **Form 6198.** See instructions.

27 Are you reporting any loss not allowed in a prior year due to the at-risk, excess farm loss, or basis limitations, a prior year unallowed loss from a passive activity (if that loss was not reported on Form 8582), or unreimbursed partnership expenses? If you answered "Yes," see instructions before completing this section.   ☐ **Yes**   ☐ **No**

28	**(a)** Name	**(b)** Enter **P** for partnership; **S** for S corporation	**(c)** Check if foreign partnership	**(d)** Employer identification number	**(e)** Check if any amount is not at risk
A			☐		☐
B			☐		☐
C			☐		☐
D			☐		☐

	Passive Income and Loss		Nonpassive Income and Loss		
	(f) Passive loss allowed (attach **Form 8582** if required)	**(g)** Passive income from **Schedule K–1**	**(h)** Nonpassive loss from **Schedule K–1**	**(i)** Section 179 expense deduction from **Form 4562**	**(j)** Nonpassive income from **Schedule K–1**
A					
B					
C					
D					
29a Totals					
b Totals					

30 Add columns (g) and (j) of line 29a **30**

31 Add columns (f), (h), and (i) of line 29b . . . . **31** ( )

32 **Total partnership and S corporation income or (loss).** Combine lines 30 and 31. Enter the result here and include in the total on line 41 below **32**

Part III	**Income or Loss From Estates and Trusts**

33	**(a)** Name	**(b)** Employer identification number
A		
B		

	Passive Income and Loss		Nonpassive Income and Loss	
	(c) Passive deduction or loss allowed (attach **Form 8582** if required)	**(d)** Passive income from **Schedule K–1**	**(e)** Deduction or loss from **Schedule K–1**	**(f)** Other income from **Schedule K–1**
A				
B				
34a Totals				
b Totals				

35 Add columns (d) and (f) of line 34a **35**

36 Add columns (c) and (e) of line 34b . . . . **36** ( )

37 **Total estate and trust income or (loss).** Combine lines 35 and 36. Enter the result here and include in the total on line 41 below **37**

Part IV	**Income or Loss From Real Estate Mortgage Investment Conduits (REMICs)—Residual Holder**

38	**(a)** Name	**(b)** Employer identification number	**(c)** Excess inclusion from **Schedules Q,** line 2c (see instructions)	**(d)** Taxable income (net loss) from **Schedules Q,** line 1b	**(e)** Income from **Schedules Q,** line 3b

39 Combine columns (d) and (e) only. Enter the result here and include in the total on line 41 below   **39**

Part V	**Summary**

40 Net farm rental income or (loss) from **Form 4835.** Also, complete line 42 below **40**

41 **Total income or (loss).** Combine lines 26, 32, 37, 39, and 40. Enter the result here and on Form 1040, line 17, or Form 1040NR, line 18 ▶   **41**

42 **Reconciliation of farming and fishing income.** Enter your **gross** farming and fishing income reported on Form 4835, line 7; Schedule K-1 (Form 1065), box 14, code B; Schedule K-1 (Form 1120S), box 17, code V; and Schedule K-1 (Form 1041), box 14, code F (see instructions) . .   **42**

43 **Reconciliation for real estate professionals.** If you were a real estate professional (see instructions), enter the net income or (loss) you reported anywhere on Form 1040 or Form 1040NR from all rental real estate activities in which you materially participated under the passive activity loss rules . .   **43**

Schedule E (Form 1040) 2013

SCHEDULE F
(Form 1040)

Department of the Treasury
Internal Revenue Service (99)

Profit or Loss From Farming

▶ Attach to Form 1040, Form 1040NR, Form 1041, Form 1065, or Form 1065-B.
▶ Information about Schedule F and its separate instructions is at *www.irs.gov/schedulef*.

OMB No. 1545-0074

20**13**

Attachment
Sequence No. **14**

Name of proprietor

Social security number (SSN)

A Principal crop or activity	B Enter code from Part IV ▶	C Accounting method: ☐ Cash ☐ Accrual	D Employer ID number (EIN), (see instr)

E Did you "materially participate" in the operation of this business during 2013? If "No," see instructions for limit on passive losses   ☐ Yes ☐ No

F Did you make any payments in 2013 that would require you to file Form(s) 1099 (see instructions)?   ☐ Yes ☐ No

G If "Yes," did you or will you file required Forms 1099? . . . .   ☐ Yes ☐ No

Part I   Farm Income—Cash Method. Complete Parts I and II (Accrual method. Complete Parts II and III, and Part I, line 9.)

1a	Sales of livestock and other resale items (see instructions)	**1a**	
b	Cost or other basis of livestock or other items reported on line 1a	**1b**	
c	Subtract line 1b from line 1a	**1c**	
2	Sales of livestock, produce, grains, and other products you raised	**2**	
3a	Cooperative distributions (Form(s) 1099-PATR) . **3a**	**3b** Taxable amount	**3b**	
4a	Agricultural program payments (see instructions) . **4a**	**4b** Taxable amount	**4b**	
5a	Commodity Credit Corporation (CCC) loans reported under election	**5a**	
b	CCC loans forfeited **5b**	**5c** Taxable amount	**5c**	
6	Crop insurance proceeds and federal crop disaster payments (see instructions)		
a	Amount received in 2013 . . . . **6a**	**6b** Taxable amount	**6b**	
c	If election to defer to 2014 is attached, check here ▶ ☐	**6d** Amount deferred from 2012	**6d**	
7	Custom hire (machine work) income	**7**	
8	Other income, including federal and state gasoline or fuel tax credit or refund (see instructions)	**8**	
9	**Gross income.** Add amounts in the right column (lines 1c, 2, 3b, 4b, 5a, 5c, 6b, 6d, 7, and 8). If you use the accrual method, enter the amount from Part III, line 50 (see instructions) . . . . ▶	**9**	

Part II   Farm Expenses—Cash and Accrual Method. Do not include personal or living expenses (see instructions).

10	Car and truck expenses (see instructions). Also attach **Form 4562**	**10**		**23** Pension and profit-sharing plans	**23**	
11	Chemicals	**11**		**24** Rent or lease (see instructions):		
12	Conservation expenses (see instructions)	**12**		**a** Vehicles, machinery, equipment	**24a**	
13	Custom hire (machine work) .	**13**		**b** Other (land, animals, etc.) . .	**24b**	
14	Depreciation and section 179 expense (see instructions) .	**14**		**25** Repairs and maintenance . .	**25**	
				26 Seeds and plants	**26**	
15	Employee benefit programs other than on line 23 . . .	**15**		**27** Storage and warehousing . .	**27**	
16	Feed	**16**		**28** Supplies	**28**	
17	Fertilizers and lime . . .	**17**		**29** Taxes	**29**	
18	Freight and trucking . . .	**18**		**30** Utilities	**30**	
19	Gasoline, fuel, and oil . . .	**19**		**31** Veterinary, breeding, and medicine	**31**	
20	Insurance (other than health)	**20**		**32** Other expenses (specify):		
21	Interest:			**a** _____	**32a**	
a	Mortgage (paid to banks, etc.)	**21a**		**b** _____	**32b**	
b	Other	**21b**		**c** _____	**32c**	
22	Labor hired (less employment credits)	**22**		**d** _____	**32d**	
				e _____	**32e**	
				f	**32f**	

33	**Total expenses.** Add lines 10 through 32f. If line 32f is negative, see instructions . . . . ▶	**33**	
34	**Net farm profit or (loss).** Subtract line 33 from line 9	**34**	

If a profit, stop here and see instructions for where to report. If a loss, complete lines 35 and 36.

35 Did you receive an applicable subsidy in 2013? (see instructions) . . . .   ☐ Yes ☐ No

36 Check the box that describes your investment in this activity and see instructions for where to report your loss.

a ☐ All investment is at risk.   **b** ☐ Some investment is not at risk.

For Paperwork Reduction Act Notice, see the separate instructions.   Cat. No. 11346H   **Schedule F (Form 1040) 2013**

Schedule F (Form 1040) 2013 Page **2**

Part III Farm Income—Accrual Method (see instructions).

					37	
37	Sales of livestock, produce, grains, and other products (see instructions)					
38a	Cooperative distributions (Form(s) 1099-PATR) .	**38a**		**38b** Taxable amount	38b	
39a	Agricultural program payments	**39a**		**39b** Taxable amount	39b	
40	Commodity Credit Corporation (CCC) loans:					
a	CCC loans reported under election				40a	
b	CCC loans forfeited	**40b**		**40c** Taxable amount	40c	
41	Crop insurance proceeds				41	
42	Custom hire (machine work) income				42	
43	Other income (see instructions)				43	
44	Add amounts in the right column for lines 37 through 43 (lines 37, 38b, 39b, 40a, 40c, 41, 42, and 43) . .				44	
45	Inventory of livestock, produce, grains, and other products at beginning of the year. Do not include sales reported on Form 4797	**45**				
46	Cost of livestock, produce, grains, and other products purchased during the year	**46**				
47	Add lines 45 and 46	**47**				
48	Inventory of livestock, produce, grains, and other products at end of year	**48**				
49	Cost of livestock, produce, grains, and other products sold. Subtract line 48 from line 47*				49	
50	**Gross income.** Subtract line 49 from line 44. Enter the result here and on Part I, line 9 . . . . . ▶				50	

*If you use the unit-livestock-price method or the farm-price method of valuing inventory and the amount on line 48 is larger than the amount on line 47, subtract line 47 from line 48. Enter the result on line 49. Add lines 44 and 49. Enter the total on line 50 and on Part I, line 9.

Part IV Principal Agricultural Activity Codes

⚠️ **CAUTION**

Do not file Schedule F (Form 1040) to report the following.
- *Income from providing agricultural services such as soil preparation, veterinary, farm labor, horticultural, or management for a fee or on a contract basis. Instead file Schedule C (Form 1040) or Schedule C-EZ (Form 1040).*
- *Income from breeding, raising, or caring for dogs, cats, or other pet animals. Instead file Schedule C (Form 1040) or Schedule C-EZ (Form 1040).*
- *Sales of livestock held for draft, breeding, sport, or dairy purposes. Instead file Form 4797.*

These codes for the Principal Agricultural Activity classify farms by their primary activity to facilitate the administration of the Internal Revenue Code. These six-digit codes are based on the North American Industry Classification System (NAICS).

Select the code that best identifies your primary farming activity and enter the six-digit number on line B.

Crop Production
111100   Oilseed and grain farming
111210   Vegetable and melon farming
111300   Fruit and tree nut farming
111400   Greenhouse, nursery, and floriculture production
111900   Other crop farming

Animal Production
112111   Beef cattle ranching and farming
112112   Cattle feedlots
112120   Dairy cattle and milk production
112210   Hog and pig farming
112300   Poultry and egg production
112400   Sheep and goat farming
112510   Aquaculture
112900   Other animal production

Forestry and Logging
113000   Forestry and logging (including forest nurseries and timber tracts)

SCHEDULE SE
(Form 1040)

Department of the Treasury
Internal Revenue Service (99)

Self-Employment Tax

▶ Information about Schedule SE and its separate instructions is at *www.irs.gov/schedulese.*

▶ **Attach to Form 1040 or Form 1040NR.**

OMB No. 1545-0074

20**13**

Attachment
Sequence No. **17**

Name of person with **self-employment** income (as shown on Form 1040)

Social security number of person
with **self-employment** income ▶

Before you begin: To determine if you must file Schedule SE, see the instructions.

May I Use Short Schedule SE or Must I Use Long Schedule SE?

Note. Use this flowchart **only if** you must file Schedule SE. If unsure, see *Who Must File Schedule SE* in the instructions.

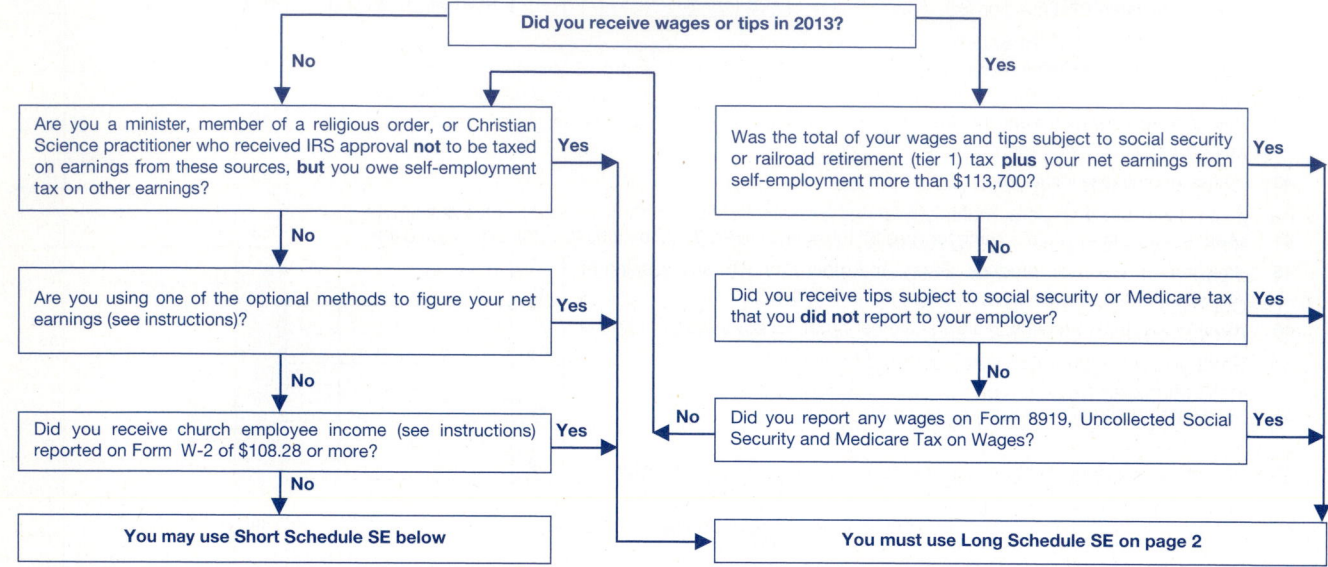

Section A—Short Schedule SE.   Caution. Read above to see if you can use Short Schedule SE.

1a	Net farm profit or (loss) from Schedule F, line 34, and farm partnerships, Schedule K-1 (Form 1065), box 14, code A	**1a**		
b	If you received social security retirement or disability benefits, enter the amount of Conservation Reserve Program payments included on Schedule F, line 4b, or listed on Schedule K-1 (Form 1065), box 20, code Z	**1b**	(	)
2	Net profit or (loss) from Schedule C, line 31; Schedule C-EZ, line 3; Schedule K-1 (Form 1065), box 14, code A (other than farming); and Schedule K-1 (Form 1065-B), box 9, code J1. Ministers and members of religious orders, see instructions for types of income to report on this line. See instructions for other income to report	**2**		
3	Combine lines 1a, 1b, and 2	**3**		
4	Multiply line 3 by 92.35% (.9235). If less than $400, you do not owe self-employment tax; **do not** file this schedule unless you have an amount on line 1b . . . . ▶	**4**		
	Note. If line 4 is less than $400 due to Conservation Reserve Program payments on line 1b, see instructions.			
5	**Self-employment tax.** If the amount on line 4 is:			
	• $113,700 or less, multiply line 4 by 15.3% (.153). Enter the result here and on **Form 1040, line 56,** or **Form 1040NR, line 54**			
	• More than $113,700, multiply line 4 by 2.9% (.029). Then, add $14,098.80 to the result. Enter the total here and on **Form 1040, line 56,** or **Form 1040NR, line 54**	**5**		
6	**Deduction for one-half of self-employment tax.** Multiply line 5 by 50% (.50). Enter the result here and on **Form 1040, line 27,** or **Form 1040NR, line 27**	**6**		

For Paperwork Reduction Act Notice, see your tax return instructions.   Cat. No. 11358Z   Schedule SE (Form 1040) 2013

Schedule SE (Form 1040) 2013   Attachment Sequence No. **17**   Page **2**

Name of person with **self-employment** income (as shown on Form 1040) | Social security number of person with **self-employment** income ▶

Section B—Long Schedule SE

| **Part I** | **Self-Employment Tax** |

Note. If your only income subject to self-employment tax is **church employee income,** see instructions. Also see instructions for the definition of church employee income.

A If you are a minister, member of a religious order, or Christian Science practitioner **and** you filed Form 4361, but you had $400 or more of **other** net earnings from self-employment, check here and continue with Part I . . . . ▶ ☐

1a Net farm profit or (loss) from Schedule F, line 34, and farm partnerships, Schedule K-1 (Form 1065), box 14, code A. **Note.** Skip lines 1a and 1b if you use the farm optional method (see instructions) | **1a** |

b If you received social security retirement or disability benefits, enter the amount of Conservation Reserve Program payments included on Schedule F, line 4b, or listed on Schedule K-1 (Form 1065), box 20, code Z | **1b** | (|) |

2 Net profit or (loss) from Schedule C, line 31; Schedule C-EZ, line 3; Schedule K-1 (Form 1065), box 14, code A (other than farming); and Schedule K-1 (Form 1065-B), box 9, code J1. Ministers and members of religious orders, see instructions for types of income to report on this line. See instructions for other income to report. **Note.** Skip this line if you use the nonfarm optional method (see instructions) . . . . | **2** |

3 Combine lines 1a, 1b, and 2 . . . . | **3** |

4a If line 3 is more than zero, multiply line 3 by 92.35% (.9235). Otherwise, enter amount from line 3 | **4a** |
Note. If line 4a is less than $400 due to Conservation Reserve Program payments on line 1b, see instructions.

b If you elect one or both of the optional methods, enter the total of lines 15 and 17 here . . | **4b** |

c Combine lines 4a and 4b. If less than $400, **stop;** you do not owe self-employment tax. **Exception.** If less than $400 and you had **church employee income,** enter -0- and continue ▶ | **4c** |

5a Enter your **church employee income** from Form W-2. See instructions for definition of church employee income . . . | **5a** |

b Multiply line 5a by 92.35% (.9235). If less than $100, enter -0- . . . . | **5b** |

6 Add lines 4c and 5b . . . . | **6** |

7 Maximum amount of combined wages and self-employment earnings subject to social security tax or the 6.2% portion of the 7.65% railroad retirement (tier 1) tax for 2013 . . . . . . | **7** | 113,700 | 00 |

8a Total social security wages and tips (total of boxes 3 and 7 on Form(s) W-2) and railroad retirement (tier 1) compensation. If $113,700 or more, skip lines 8b through 10, and go to line 11 | **8a** |

b Unreported tips subject to social security tax (from Form 4137, line 10) | **8b** |

c Wages subject to social security tax (from Form 8919, line 10) | **8c** |

d Add lines 8a, 8b, and 8c . . . . | **8d** |

9 Subtract line 8d from line 7. If zero or less, enter -0- here and on line 10 and go to line 11 . ▶ | **9** |

10 Multiply the **smaller** of line 6 or line 9 by 12.4% (.124) . . . . | **10** |

11 Multiply line 6 by 2.9% (.029) . . . . | **11** |

12 **Self-employment tax.** Add lines 10 and 11. Enter here and on **Form 1040, line 56,** or **Form 1040NR, line 54** | **12** |

13 **Deduction for one-half of self-employment tax.** Multiply line 12 by 50% (.50). Enter the result here and on **Form 1040, line 27,** or **Form 1040NR, line 27** . . . . . | **13** |

| **Part II** | **Optional Methods To Figure Net Earnings** (see instructions) |

Farm Optional Method. You may use this method **only** if **(a)** your gross farm income[1] was not more than $6,960, **or (b)** your net farm profits[2] were less than $5,024.

14 Maximum income for optional methods . . . . | **14** | 4,640 | 00 |

15 Enter the **smaller** of: two-thirds (²/₃) of gross farm income[1] (not less than zero) **or** $4,640. Also include this amount on line 4b above . . . . | **15** |

Nonfarm Optional Method. You may use this method **only** if **(a)** your net nonfarm profits[3] were less than $5,024 and also less than 72.189% of your gross nonfarm income,[4] **and (b)** you had net earnings from self-employment of at least $400 in 2 of the prior 3 years. **Caution.** You may use this method no more than five times.

16 Subtract line 15 from line 14 . . . . | **16** |

17 Enter the **smaller** of: two-thirds (²/₃) of gross nonfarm income[4] (not less than zero) **or** the amount on line 16. Also include this amount on line 4b above . . . . | **17** |

[1] From Sch. F, line 9, and Sch. K-1 (Form 1065), box 14, code B.

[2] From Sch. F, line 34, and Sch. K-1 (Form 1065), box 14, code A—minus the amount you would have entered on line 1b had you not used the optional method.

[3] From Sch. C, line 31; Sch. C-EZ, line 3; Sch. K-1 (Form 1065), box 14, code A; and Sch. K-1 (Form 1065-B), box 9, code J1.

[4] From Sch. C, line 7; Sch. C-EZ, line 1; Sch. K-1 (Form 1065), box 14, code C; and Sch. K-1 (Form 1065-B), box 9, code J2.

Schedule SE (Form 1040) 2013

Form **8949**

Department of the Treasury
Internal Revenue Service

Sales and Other Dispositions of Capital Assets

▶ Information about Form 8949 and its separate instructions is at *www.irs.gov/form8949.*
▶ File with your Schedule D to list your transactions for lines 1b, 2, 3, 8b, 9, and 10 of Schedule D.

OMB No. 1545-0074

2013

Attachment
Sequence No. **12A**

Name(s) shown on return	Social security number or taxpayer identification number

Most brokers issue their own substitute statement instead of using Form 1099-B. They also may provide basis information (usually your cost) to you on the statement even if it is not reported to the IRS. Before you check Box A, B, or C below, determine whether you received any statement(s) and, if so, the transactions for which basis was reported to the IRS. Brokers are required to report basis to the IRS for most stock you bought in 2011 or later.

Part I | **Short-Term.** Transactions involving capital assets you held one year or less are short term. For long-term transactions, see page 2.

Note. You may aggregate all short-term transactions reported on Form(s) 1099-B showing basis was reported to the IRS and for which no adjustments or codes are required. Enter the total directly on Schedule D, line 1a; you are not required to report these transactions on Form 8949 (see instructions).

You *must* check Box A, B, *or* C below. Check only one box. If more than one box applies for your short-term transactions, complete a separate Form 8949, page 1, for each applicable box. If you have more short-term transactions than will fit on this page for one or more of the boxes, complete as many forms with the same box checked as you need.

- ☐ **(A)** Short-term transactions reported on Form(s) 1099-B showing basis was reported to the IRS (see **Note** above)
- ☐ **(B)** Short-term transactions reported on Form(s) 1099-B showing basis was **not** reported to the IRS
- ☐ **(C)** Short-term transactions not reported to you on Form 1099-B

1 (a) Description of property (Example: 100 sh. XYZ Co.)	(b) Date acquired (Mo., day, yr.)	(c) Date sold or disposed (Mo., day, yr.)	(d) Proceeds (sales price) (see instructions)	(e) Cost or other basis. See the **Note** below and see *Column (e)* in the separate instructions	Adjustment, if any, to gain or loss. If you enter an amount in column (g), enter a code in column (f). See the separate instructions.		(h) Gain or (loss). Subtract column (e) from column (d) and combine the result with column (g)
					(f) Code(s) from instructions	(g) Amount of adjustment	
2 Totals. Add the amounts in columns (d), (e), (g), and (h) (subtract negative amounts). Enter each total here and include on your Schedule D, **line 1b** (if **Box A** above is checked), **line 2** (if **Box B** above is checked), or **line 3** (if **Box C** above is checked) ▶							

Note. If you checked Box A above but the basis reported to the IRS was incorrect, enter in column (e) the basis as reported to the IRS, and enter an adjustment in column (g) to correct the basis. See *Column (g)* in the separate instructions for how to figure the amount of the adjustment.

For Paperwork Reduction Act Notice, see your tax return instructions.   Cat. No. 37768Z   Form **8949** (2013)

Form 8949 (2013)

Name(s) shown on return. (Name and SSN or taxpayer identification no. not required if shown on other side.)	Social security number or taxpayer identification number

Most brokers issue their own substitute statement instead of using Form 1099-B. They also may provide basis information (usually your cost) to you on the statement even if it is not reported to the IRS. Before you check Box D, E, or F below, determine whether you received any statement(s) and, if so, the transactions for which basis was reported to the IRS. Brokers are required to report basis to the IRS for most stock you bought in 2011 or later.

Part II   **Long-Term.** Transactions involving capital assets you held more than one year are long term. For short-term transactions, see page 1.

Note. You may aggregate all long-term transactions reported on Form(s) 1099-B showing basis was reported to the IRS and for which no adjustments or codes are required. Enter the total directly on Schedule D, line 8a; you are not required to report these transactions on Form 8949 (see instructions).

You *must* check Box D, E, *or* F below. Check only one box. If more than one box applies for your long-term transactions, complete a separate Form 8949, page 2, for each applicable box. If you have more long-term transactions than will fit on this page for one or more of the boxes, complete as many forms with the same box checked as you need.

- ☐ **(D)** Long-term transactions reported on Form(s) 1099-B showing basis was reported to the IRS (see **Note** above)
- ☐ **(E)** Long-term transactions reported on Form(s) 1099-B showing basis was **not** reported to the IRS
- ☐ **(F)** Long-term transactions not reported to you on Form 1099-B

1	**(a)** Description of property (Example: 100 sh. XYZ Co.)	**(b)** Date acquired (Mo., day, yr.)	**(c)** Date sold or disposed (Mo., day, yr.)	**(d)** Proceeds (sales price) (see instructions)	**(e)** Cost or other basis. See the **Note** below and see *Column (e)* in the separate instructions	Adjustment, if any, to gain or loss. If you enter an amount in column (g), enter a code in column (f). See the separate instructions.		**(h)** Gain or (loss). Subtract column (e) from column (d) and combine the result with column (g)
						(f) Code(s) from instructions	**(g)** Amount of adjustment	

2 Totals. Add the amounts in columns (d), (e), (g), and (h) (subtract negative amounts). Enter each total here and include on your Schedule D, **line 8b** (if **Box D** above is checked), **line 9** (if **Box E** above is checked), or **line 10** (if **Box F** above is checked) ▶

Note. If you checked Box D above but the basis reported to the IRS was incorrect, enter in column (e) the basis as reported to the IRS, and enter an adjustment in column (g) to correct the basis. See *Column (g)* in the separate instructions for how to figure the amount of the adjustment.

Form **8949** (2013)

Form **8958**
(December 2012)
Department of the Treasury
Internal Revenue Service (99)

Allocation of Tax Amounts Between
Certain Individuals in Community Property States

▶ **Attach to Form 1040.**

OMB No. 1545-0074

Attachment
Sequence No. **72**

Your first name and initial	Your last name	Your social security number
Spouse's or partner's first name and initial	Spouse's or partner's last name	**Spouse's or partner's social security number**

	1 Total Income (Community/Separate)	2 Allocated to Spouse, RDP, or California Same-Sex Spouse SSN _____ - ___ - _____	3 Allocated to Spouse, RDP, or California Same-Sex Spouse SSN _____ - ___ - _____
1 Wages (each employer)			
2 Interest Income (each payer)			
3 Dividends (each payer)			
4 State Income Tax Refund			
5 Self-Employment Income (See instructions)			
6 Capital Gains and Losses			
7 Pension Income			
8 Rents, Royalties, Partnerships, Estates, Trusts			

For Paperwork Reduction Act Notice, see your tax return instructions.   Cat. No. 37779G   Form **8958** (12-2012)

Form 8958 (12-2012)   Page **2**

	1 Total Income (Community/Separate)	2 Allocated to Spouse, RDP, or California Same-Sex Spouse SSN _____ - ___ - _____	3 Allocated to Spouse, RDP, or California Same-Sex Spouse SSN _____ - ___ - _____
9 Deductible part of Self-Employment Tax (See instructions)			
10 Self-Employment Tax (See instructions)			
11 Taxes Withheld			
12 Other items such as: Social Security Benefits, Unemployment Compensation, Deductions, Credits, etc.			

Form **8958** (12-2012)

Form **8960**

Department of the Treasury
Internal Revenue Service (99)

Net Investment Income Tax—
Individuals, Estates, and Trusts

▶ Attach to Form 1040 or Form 1041.
▶ **Information about Form 8960 and its separate instructions is at** *www.irs.gov/form8960.*

OMB No. 1545-2227

2013

Attachment
Sequence No. **72**

Name(s) shown on Form 1040 or Form 1041

Your social security number or EIN

	Part I **Investment Income**	☐ Section 6013(g) election (see instructions)		
		☐ Regulations section 1.1411-10(g) election (see instructions)		
1	Taxable interest (Form 1040, line 8a; or Form 1041, line 1)		**1**	
2	Ordinary dividends (Form 1040, line 9a; or Form 1041, line 2a)		**2**	
3	Annuities from nonqualified plans (see instructions)		**3**	
4a	Rental real estate, royalties, partnerships, S corporations, trusts, etc. (Form 1040, line 17; or Form 1041, line 5)	**4a**		
b	Adjustment for net income or loss derived in the ordinary course of a non-section 1411 trade or business (see instructions)	**4b**		
c	Combine lines 4a and 4b		**4c**	
5a	Net gain or loss from disposition of property from Form 1040, combine lines 13 and 14; or from Form 1041, combine lines 4 and 7	**5a**		
b	Net gain or loss from disposition of property that is not subject to net investment income tax (see instructions)	**5b**		
c	Adjustment from disposition of partnership interest or S corporation stock (see instructions)	**5c**		
d	Combine lines 5a through 5c		**5d**	
6	Changes to investment income for certain CFCs and PFICs (see instructions)		**6**	
7	Other modifications to investment income (see instructions)		**7**	
8	Total investment income. Combine lines 1, 2, 3, 4c, 5d, 6, and 7		**8**	
	Part II **Investment Expenses Allocable to Investment Income and Modifications**			
9a	Investment interest expenses (see instructions)	**9a**		
b	State income tax (see instructions)	**9b**		
c	Miscellaneous investment expenses (see instructions)	**9c**		
d	Add lines 9a, 9b, and 9c		**9d**	
10	Additional modifications (see instructions)		**10**	
11	Total deductions and modifications. Add lines 9d and 10		**11**	
	Part III **Tax Computation**			
12	Net investment income. Subtract Part II, line 11 from Part I, line 8. Individuals complete lines 13– 17. Estates and trusts complete lines 18a–21. If zero or less, enter -0-		**12**	
	Individuals:			
13	Modified adjusted gross income (see instructions)	**13**		
14	Threshold based on filing status (see instructions)	**14**		
15	Subtract line 14 from line 13. If zero or less, enter -0-	**15**		
16	Enter the smaller of line 12 or line 15		**16**	
17	Net investment income tax for individuals. Multiply line 16 by 3.8% (.038). Enter here and on Form 1040, line 60		**17**	
	Estates and Trusts:			
18a	Net investment income (line 12 above)	**18a**		
b	Deductions for distributions of net investment income and deductions under section 642(c) (see instructions)	**18b**		
c	Undistributed net investment income. Subtract line 18b from 18a (see instructions)	**18c**		
19a	Adjusted gross income (see instructions)	**19a**		
b	Highest tax bracket for estates and trusts for the year (see instructions)	**19b**		
c	Subtract line 19b from line 19a. If zero or less, enter -0- . . .	**19c**		
20	Enter the smaller of line 18c or line 19c		**20**	
21	Net investment income tax for estates and trusts. Multiply line 20 by 3.8% (.038). Enter here and on Form 1041, Schedule G, line 4		**21**	

For Paperwork Reduction Act Notice, see your tax return instructions.   Cat. No. 59474M   Form **8960** (2013)

Appendix C

Glossary

The words and phrases in this glossary have been defined to reflect their conventional use in the field of taxation. The definitions may therefore be incomplete for other purposes.

A

Abandoned spouse. The abandoned spouse provision enables a married taxpayer with a dependent child whose spouse did not live in the taxpayer's home during the last six months of the tax year to file as a head of household rather than as married filing separately.

Accelerated cost recovery system (ACRS). A method in which the cost of tangible property is recovered over a prescribed period of time. Enacted by the Economic Recovery Tax Act (ERTA) of 1981 and substantially modified by the Tax Reform Act (TRA) of 1986 (the modified system is referred to as MACRS), the approach disregards salvage value, imposes a period of cost recovery that depends upon the classification of the asset into one of various recovery periods, and prescribes the applicable percentage of cost that can be deducted each year. § 168.

Accelerated death benefits. The amount received from a life insurance policy by the insured who is terminally ill or chronically ill. Any realized gain may be excluded from the gross income of the insured if the policy is surrendered to the insurer or is sold to a licensed viatical settlement provider. § 101(g).

Accelerated depreciation. Various methods of depreciation that yield larger deductions in the earlier years of the life of an asset than the straight-line method. Examples include the double declining-balance and the sum-of-the-years' digits methods of depreciation. § 167.

Accident and health benefits. Employee fringe benefits provided by employers through the payment of health and accident insurance premiums or the establishment of employer-funded medical reimbursement plans. Employers generally are entitled to a deduction for such payments, whereas employees generally exclude the fringe benefits from gross income. §§ 105 and 106.

Accountable plan. An accountable plan is a type of expense reimbursement plan that requires an employee to render an adequate accounting to the employer and return any excess reimbursement or allowance. If the expense qualifies, it will be treated as a deduction *for* AGI.

Accounting income. The accountant's concept of income is generally based upon the realization principle. Financial accounting income may differ from taxable income (e.g., accelerated depreciation might be used for Federal income tax and straight-line depreciation for financial accounting purposes). Differences are included in a reconciliation of taxable and accounting income on Schedule M–1 or Schedule M–3 of Form 1120 for corporations. Seventy-five percent of the excess of adjusted current earnings over alternative minimum taxable income is an adjustment for alternative minimum tax purposes for a corporation. See also *alternative minimum tax* and *economic income*.

Accounting method. The method under which income and expenses are determined for tax purposes. Major accounting methods are the cash basis and the accrual basis. Special methods are available for the reporting of gain on installment sales, recognition of income on construction projects (the completed contract and percentage of completion methods), and the valuation of inventories (last-in, first-out and first-in, first-out). §§ 446–474. See also *accrual method, cash receipts method, completed contract method, percentage of completion method*, etc.

Accounting period. The period of time, usually a year, used by a taxpayer for the determination of tax liability. Unless a fiscal year is chosen, taxpayers must determine and pay their income tax liability by using the calendar year (January 1 through December 31) as the period of measurement. An example of a fiscal year is July 1 through June 30. A change in accounting period (e.g., from a calendar year to a fiscal year) generally requires the consent of the IRS. A new taxpayer, such as a newly formed corporation or an estate created upon the death of an individual taxpayer, is free to select either a calendar or a fiscal year without the consent of the IRS. Limitations exist on the accounting period that may be selected by a partnership, an S corporation, and a personal service corporation. §§ 441–444.

Accrual basis. See *accrual method.*

Accrual method. A method of accounting that reflects expenses incurred and income earned for any one tax year. In contrast to the cash basis of accounting, expenses do not have to be paid to be deductible nor does income have to be received to be taxable. Unearned income (e.g., prepaid interest and rent) generally is taxed in the year of receipt regardless of the method of accounting used by the taxpayer. § 446(c)(2). See also *accounting method, cash receipts method,* and *unearned income.*

Accumulated earnings tax. A special tax imposed on corporations that accumulate (rather than distribute) their earnings beyond the reasonable needs of the business. The tax is imposed on accumulated taxable income and is imposed in addition to the corporate income tax. §§ 531–537.

ACE adjustment. See *adjusted current earnings (ACE) adjustment.*

Acquiescence. In agreement with the result reached. The IRS follows a policy of either acquiescing (*A, Acq.*) or nonacquiescing (*NA, Nonacq.*) in the results reached in certain judicial decisions.

Acquisition indebtedness. Debt incurred in acquiring, constructing, or substantially improving a qualified residence of the taxpayer. The interest on such loans is deductible as *qualified residence interest.* However, interest on such debt is deductible only on the portion of the indebtedness that does not exceed $1,000,000 ($500,000 for married persons filing separate returns). § 163(h)(3). See also *home equity loans.*

ACRS. See *accelerated cost recovery system.*

Active income. Active income includes wages, salary, commissions, bonuses, profits from a trade or business in which the taxpayer is a material participant, gain on the sale or other disposition of assets used in an active trade or business, and income from intangible property if the taxpayer's personal efforts significantly contributed to the creation of the property. The passive activity loss rules require classification of income and losses into three categories with active income being one of them.

Active participation. A term that is relevant for both the at-risk rules and the passive activity loss rules associated with rental real estate activities. For the at-risk rules, the following factors indicate active participation: (1) making decisions involving the operation or management of the activity, (2) performing services for the activity, and (3) hiring and discharging employees. For the passive activity loss rules, the taxpayer must participate in the making of management decisions in a significant and bona fide sense.

Ad valorem tax. A tax imposed on the value of property. The most familiar ad valorem tax is that imposed by states, counties, and cities on real estate. Ad valorem taxes can, however, be imposed upon personal property (e.g., a motor vehicle tax based on the value of an automobile). §§ 164(a)(1) and (2).

Additional depreciation. The excess of the amount of depreciation actually deducted over the amount that would have been deducted had the straight-line method been used. § 1250(b). See also *Section 1250 recapture.*

Additional first-year depreciation. See *fifty percent additional first-year depreciation* and *one hundred percent additional first-year depreciation.*

Adjusted basis. The cost or other basis of property reduced by depreciation (cost recovery) allowed or allowable and increased by capital improvements. See also *basis* and *realized gain or loss.*

Adjusted current earnings (ACE) adjustment. An adjustment in computing corporate alternative minimum taxable income (AMTI), computed at 75 percent of the excess of adjusted current earnings and profits computations over unadjusted AMTI. ACE computations reflect longer and slower cost recovery deductions and other restrictions on the timing of certain recognition events. Exempt interest, life insurance proceeds, and other receipts that are included in earnings and profits but not in taxable income also increase the ACE adjustment. If unadjusted AMTI exceeds adjusted current earnings and profits, the ACE adjustment is negative. The negative adjustment is limited to the aggregate of the positive adjustments under ACE for prior years, reduced by any previously claimed negative adjustments. See also *alternative minimum tax* and *earnings and profits.*

Adjusted gross income (AGI). A determination peculiar to individual taxpayers. Generally, it represents gross income less business expenses, expenses attributable to the production of rent or royalty income, the allowed capital loss deduction, and certain personal expenses (deductions *for* AGI). § 62. See also *gross income.*

Adoption expenses credit. A provision intended to assist taxpayers who incur nonrecurring costs directly associated with the adoption process such as legal costs, social service review costs, and transportation costs. Up to $13,190 ($13,190 for a child with special needs regardless of the actual adoption expenses) of costs incurred to adopt an eligible child qualify for the credit. A taxpayer may claim the credit in the year qualifying expenses are paid or incurred if the expenses are paid during or after the year in which the adoption is finalized. For qualifying expenses paid or incurred in a tax year prior to the year the adoption is finalized, the credit must be claimed in the tax year following the tax year during which the expenses are paid or incurred. § 23.

Advance payments. In general, prepayments for services or goods are includible in gross income upon receipt of the advance payments (for both accrual and cash basis taxpayers). However, Revenue Procedure 2004–34, 2004–1 C.B. 991, provides guidelines for the deferral of tax on certain advance payments providing specific conditions are met.

AFTR. Published by Research Institute of America (formerly by Prentice-Hall), *American Federal Tax Reports* contains all of the Federal tax decisions issued by the U.S. District Courts, U.S. Court of Federal Claims, U.S. Courts of Appeals, and U.S. Supreme Court.

AFTR 2d. The second series of the *American Federal Tax Reports.*

AFTR 3d. The third series of the *American Federal Tax Reports.*

Alimony and separate maintenance payments. Alimony and separate maintenance payments are includible in the gross income of the recipient and are deductible by the payor. The payments must be made in discharge of a legal obligation arising from a marital or family relationship. Child support and voluntary payments are not treated as alimony. Alimony is deductible *for* AGI. §§ 62(10), 71, and 215. See also *child support payments.*

Alimony recapture. The amount of alimony that previously has been included in the gross income of the recipient and deducted by the payor that now is deducted by the recipient and included in the gross income of the payor as the result of front-loading. § 71(f).

All events test. For accrual method taxpayers, income is earned when (1) all the events have occurred that fix the right to receive the income and (2) the amount can be determined with reasonable accuracy. Accrual of income cannot be postponed simply because a portion of the income may have to be returned in a subsequent period. The all events test also is utilized to determine when expenses can be deducted by an accrual basis taxpayer. The application of the test could cause a variation between the treatment of an item for accounting and for tax purposes. For example, a reserve for warranty expense may be properly accruable under generally accepted accounting principles but not be deductible under the Federal income tax law. Because of the application of the all events test, the deduction becomes available in the year the warranty obligation becomes fixed and the amount is determinable with reasonable certainty. See also *economic performance test.* Reg. §§ 1.446–1(c)(1)(ii) and 1.461–1(a)(2).

Alternate valuation date. Property passing from a person by reason of death may be valued for estate tax purposes as of the date of death or the alternate valuation date. The alternate valuation date is six months from the date of death or the date the property is disposed of by the estate, whichever comes first. To use the alternate valuation date, the executor or administrator of the estate must make an affirmative election. The election of the alternate valuation date is not available unless it decreases both the amount of the gross estate *and* the estate tax liability. §§ 1014(a) and 2032.

Alternative depreciation system (ADS). A cost recovery system that produces a smaller deduction than would be calculated under ACRS or MACRS. The alternative system must be used in certain instances and can be elected in other instances. § 168(g). See also *cost recovery allowance.*

Alternative minimum tax (AMT). The alternative minimum tax is imposed only to the extent it exceeds the regular income tax (in effect, the tax liability is the greater of the tax liability calculated using the AMT rules and that calculated using the regular income tax rules). The AMT rates (26 and 28 percent for the individual taxpayer and 20 percent for the corporate taxpayer) are applied to the AMT base. The AMT base is calculated by modifying taxable income as follows: (1) add tax preferences, (2) add certain adjustments, (3) deduct certain adjustments, and (4) deduct the exemption amount. §§ 55–59. See also *adjusted current earnings (ACE) adjustment.*

Alternative minimum tax credit. The AMT can result from timing differences that give rise to positive adjustments in calculating the AMT base. To provide equity for the taxpayer when these timing differences reverse, the regular tax liability may be reduced by a tax credit for prior year's minimum tax liability attributable to timing differences. § 53.

Alternative tax. An option that is allowed in computing the tax on net capital gain. For the corporate taxpayer, the rate is 35 percent (the same as the highest regular corporate tax rate). Thus, for corporate taxpayers, the alternative tax does not produce a beneficial result. For noncorporate taxpayers, the rate is usually 15 percent (but it is 25 percent for unrecaptured § 1250 gain and is

28 percent for collectibles and § 1202 gain). However, if the noncorporate taxpayer is in either the 10 percent or the 15 percent tax bracket, the alternative tax rate is 0 percent in 2008, 2009, 2010, 2011, 2012, and 2013 and 5 percent in 2007 and prior years (rather than 15 percent). Certain high-income taxpayers (i.e., in the 39.6 percent tax bracket) have an alternative tax rate of 20 percent. §§ 1(h) and 1201. See also *collectibles, net capital gain,* and *unrecaptured § 1250 gain (25 percent gain).*

Alternative tax NOL deduction (ATNOLD). In calculating the AMT, the taxpayer is allowed to deduct NOL carryovers and carrybacks. A special calculation, referred to as the ATNOLD, is required for this purpose. The regular income tax is modified for AMT adjustments and preferences to produce the ATNOLD. § 56(d).

American Opportunity credit. This credit replaces the HOPE scholarship credit for 2009 through 2017 and applies for qualifying expenses for the first four years of postsecondary education. Qualified expenses include tuition and related expenses and books and other course materials. Room and board are ineligible for the credit. The maximum credit available per student is $2,500 (100 percent of the first $2,000 of qualifying expenses and 25 percent of the next $2,000 of qualifying expenses). Eligible students include the taxpayer, taxpayer's spouse, and taxpayer's dependents. To qualify for the credit, a student must take at least one-half the full-time course load for at least one academic term at a qualifying educational institution. The credit is phased out for higher-income taxpayers. See also *HOPE scholarship credit* and *lifetime learning credit.* § 25A.

Amortization. The allocation (and charge to expense) of the cost or other basis of an intangible asset over a statutory period of 15 years. Examples of amortizable intangibles include patents, copyrights, covenants not to compete, acquired goodwill, and leasehold interests. See also *estimated useful life* and *goodwill.* § 197.

Amount realized. The amount received by a taxpayer on the sale or other disposition of property. The amount realized is the sum of the cash and the fair market value of any property or services received, plus any related debt assumed by the buyer. Determining the amount realized is the starting point for arriving at realized gain or loss. The amount realized is defined in § 1001(b) and the related Regulations. See also *realized gain or loss* and *recognized gain or loss.*

AMT adjustments. In calculating AMTI, certain adjustments are added to or deducted from taxable income. These adjustments generally reflect timing differences. § 56.

AMT exclusions. A credit that can be used to reduce the regular tax liability in future tax years is available in connection with the AMT (*AMT credit*). The credit is applicable only with respect to the AMT that results from timing differences. It is not available in connection with AMT exclusions, which include the standard deduction, personal exemptions, medical expenses deductible in calculating the regular income tax that are not deductible in computing the AMT, other itemized deductions that are not allowable for AMT purposes, excess percentage depletion, and tax-exempt interest on specified private activity bonds.

Annuity. A fixed sum payable to a person at specified intervals for a specific period of time or for life. Payments represent a partial return of capital and a return (interest) on the capital investment. Therefore, an exclusion ratio must be used to compute the amount of nontaxable income. The exclusion ratio is used until the annuitant has recovered his or her investment in the annuity contract. Thereafter, all of the annuity payments received are included in gross income. If the annuitant dies before his or her investment is recovered, a deduction is allowed. § 72. See also *qualified pension or profit sharing plan.*

Appellate court. For Federal tax purposes, appellate courts include the Courts of Appeals and the Supreme Court. If the party losing in the trial (or lower) court is dissatisfied with the result, the dispute may be carried to the appropriate appellate court. See also *Court of Appeals* and *trial court.*

Archer medical savings account. See *medical savings account.*

Arm's length transaction. The standard under which unrelated parties would determine an exchange price for a transaction. Suppose, for example, Cardinal Corporation sells property to its sole shareholder for $10,000. In testing whether the $10,000 is an "arm's length" price, one would ascertain the price that would have been negotiated between the corporation and an unrelated party in a bargained exchange.

Asset Depreciation Range (ADR) system. A system of estimated useful lives for categories of tangible assets prescribed by the IRS. The system provides a range for each category that extends from 20 percent above to 20 percent below the guideline class lives prescribed by the IRS.

Assignment of income. A procedure whereby a taxpayer attempts to avoid the recognition of income by assigning the property that generates the income to another. Such a procedure will not avoid the recognition of income by the taxpayer making the assignment if it can be said that the income was earned at the point of the transfer. In this case, usually referred to as an anticipatory assignment of income, the income will be taxed to the person who earns it.

Association. An organization treated as a corporation for Federal tax purposes even though it may not qualify as such under applicable state law. An entity designated as a trust or a partnership, for example, may be classified as an association if it clearly possesses corporate attributes. Corporate attributes include centralized management, continuity of life, free transferability of interests, and limited liability. When the check-the-box Regulations were finalized, the association Regulations were withdrawn. Thus, for most entities, reclassification as an association is unlikely. § 7701(a)(3). See also *check-the-box Regulations.*

At-risk limitation. Under the at-risk rules, a taxpayer's deductible losses from an activity for any taxable year are limited to the amount the taxpayer has at risk at the end of the taxable year. The initial amount considered at risk is generally the sum of the amount of cash and the adjusted basis of property contributed to the activity and amounts borrowed for use in the activity for which the taxpayer is personally liable or has pledged as security property not used in the activity. § 465.

Attribution. Under certain circumstances, the tax law applies attribution (construction ownership) rules to assign to one taxpayer the ownership interest of another taxpayer. If, for example, the stock of Gold Corporation is held 60 percent by Marsha and 40 percent by Sid, Marsha may be deemed to own 100 percent of Gold Corporation if she and Sid are mother and son. In that case, the stock owned by Sid is attributed to Marsha. See, for example, §§ 267 and 318.

Audit. Inspection and verification of a taxpayer's return or other transactions possessing tax consequences. See also *correspondence audit, field audit,* and *office audit.*

Automatic mileage method. See *automobile expenses.*

Automobile expenses. Automobile expenses are generally deductible only to the extent the automobile is used in business or for the production of income. Personal commuting expenses are not deductible. The taxpayer may deduct actual expenses (including depreciation and insurance), or the standard (automatic) mileage rate may be used (56.0 cents for 2014 and 56.5 cents for 2013). Automobile expenses incurred for medical purposes or in connection with job-related moving expenses are deductible to the extent of actual out-of-pocket expenses or at the rate of 23.5 cents per mile for 2014 and 24 cents for 2013. For charitable activities, the rate is 14 cents per mile. See also *transportation expenses.*

B

Bad debts. A deduction is permitted if a business account receivable subsequently becomes partially or completely worthless, providing the income arising from the debt previously was included in income. Available methods are the specific charge-off method and the reserve method. However, except for certain financial institutions, TRA of 1986 repealed the use of the reserve method for 1987 and thereafter. If the reserve method is used, partially or totally worthless accounts are charged to the reserve. A nonbusiness bad debt deduction is allowed as a short-term capital loss if the loan did not arise in connection with the creditor's trade or business activities. Loans between related parties (family members) generally are classified as nonbusiness. § 166. See also *nonbusiness bad debts.*

Basis. The acquisition cost assigned to an asset for income tax purposes. For assets acquired by purchase, the basis is the cost (§ 1012). Special rules govern the basis of property received by virtue of another's death (§ 1014) or by gift (§ 1015), the basis of stock received on a transfer of property to a controlled corporation (§ 358), the basis of the property transferred to the corporation (§ 362), and the basis of property received upon the liquidation of a corporation (§§ 334 and 338). See also *adjusted basis.*

Book value. The net amount of an asset after reduction by a related reserve. The book value of accounts receivable, for example, is the face amount of the receivables less the reserve for bad debts. The book value of a building is the cost less the accumulated depreciation.

Boot. Cash or property of a type not included in the definition of a nontaxable exchange. The receipt of boot will cause an otherwise nontaxable transfer to become taxable to the extent of the lesser of the fair market value of such boot or the realized gain on the transfer. Examples of nontaxable exchanges that could be partially or completely taxable due to the receipt of boot include transfers to controlled corporations [§ 351(b)] and like-kind exchanges [§ 1031(b)]. See also *realized gain or loss* and *recognized gain or loss*.

Bribes and illegal payments. Section 162 denies a deduction for bribes or kickbacks, fines, and penalties paid to a government official or employee for violation of law, and two-thirds of the treble damage payments made to claimants for violation of the antitrust law. Denial of a deduction for bribes and illegal payments is based upon the judicially established principle that allowing such payments would be contrary to public policy.

B.T.A. The Board of Tax Appeals was a trial court that considered Federal tax matters. This court is now the U.S. Tax Court.

Burden of proof. The requirement in a lawsuit to show the weight of evidence and thereby gain a favorable decision. Except in cases of tax fraud, the burden of proof in a tax case generally is on the taxpayer.

Business bad debt. A debt created or acquired in connection with a trade or business of the taxpayer, or a debt the loss from the worthlessness of which is incurred in the taxpayer's trade or business. A business bad debt is deducted as an ordinary deduction. § 166.

Business expenses. See *trade or business expenses*.

Business gifts. Business gifts are deductible only to the extent that each gift does not exceed $25 per person per year. Exceptions are made for gifts costing $4 or less and for certain employee awards. § 274(b).

C

C corporation. A corporation that has not elected conduit treatment under § 1361. See also *S corporation status*.

Cafeteria benefit plan. An employee benefit plan under which an employee is allowed to select from among a variety of employer-provided fringe benefits. Some of the benefits may be taxable and some may be statutory nontaxable benefits (e.g., health and accident insurance and group term life insurance). The employee is taxed only on the taxable benefits selected. A cafeteria benefit plan is also referred to as a flexible benefit plan. § 125.

Cafeteria plan. See *cafeteria benefit plan*.

Canons of taxation. Criteria used in the selection of a tax base that were originally discussed by Adam Smith in *The Wealth of Nations*. Canons of taxation include equality, convenience, certainty, and economy.

Capital asset. Broadly speaking, all assets are capital except those specifically excluded by the Code. Major categories of noncapital assets include property held for resale in the normal course of business (inventory), trade accounts and notes receivable, and depreciable property and real estate used in a trade or business (§ 1231 assets). § 1221. See also *capital gain* and *capital loss*.

Capital contributions. Various means by which a shareholder makes additional funds available to the corporation (placed at the risk of the business) without the receipt of additional stock. Such contributions are added to the basis of the shareholder's existing stock investment and do not generate income to the corporation. § 118.

Capital expenditure. An expenditure that should be added to the basis of the property improved. For income tax purposes, this generally precludes a full deduction for the expenditure in the year paid or incurred. Any capital recovery in the form of a tax deduction must come in the form of depreciation. § 263.

Capital gain. The gain from the sale or exchange of a capital asset. See also *capital asset* and *net capital gain*.

Capital gain net income. If the total capital gains for the tax year exceed the total capital losses, the result is capital gain net income. Note that the term does not distinguish between the long-term and short-term gains. § 1222(9). See also *net capital gain*.

Capital gain or loss holding period. The period of time that a capital asset is held by the taxpayer. To qualify for long-term treatment, the asset must be held for more than one year. If held for one year or less, the holding period is short term. See also *holding period*.

Capital gain property. Property contributed to a charitable organization that, if sold rather than contributed, would have resulted in long-term capital gain to the donor. See also *ordinary income property*.

Capital loss. The loss from the sale or exchange of a capital asset. See also *capital asset*.

Cash balance plan. A hybrid form of pension plan similar in some aspects to a defined benefit plan. Such a plan is funded by the employer, and the employer bears the investment risks and rewards. But like defined contribution plans, a cash balance plan establishes allocations to individual employee accounts, and the payout for an employee depends on investment performance.

Cash basis. See *accounting method* and *cash receipts method*.

Cash equivalent doctrine. Generally, a cash basis taxpayer does not report income until cash is constructively or actually received. Under the cash equivalent doctrine, cash basis taxpayers are required to report income if they receive the equivalent of cash (e.g., property is received) in a taxable transaction.

Cash method. See *cash receipts method*.

Cash receipts method. A method of accounting under which the taxpayer generally reports income when cash is collected and reports expenses when cash payments are made. However, for fixed assets, the cash basis taxpayer claims deductions through depreciation or amortization in the same manner as an accrual basis taxpayer. Prepaid expenses must be capitalized and amortized if the life of the asset extends "substantially beyond" the end of the tax year. See also *constructive receipt*.

Casualty loss. A casualty is defined as "the complete or partial destruction of property resulting from an identifiable event of a sudden, unexpected or unusual nature" (e.g., floods, storms, fires, auto accidents). Individuals may deduct a casualty loss only if the loss is incurred in a trade or business or in a transaction entered into for profit or arises from fire, storm, shipwreck, or other casualty or from theft. Individuals usually deduct personal casualty losses as itemized deductions subject to a $100 nondeductible amount and to an annual floor equal to 10 percent of adjusted gross income that applies after the $100 per casualty floor has been applied. Special rules are provided for the netting of certain casualty gains and losses. § 165. See also *disaster area loss* and *Section 1231 gains and losses*.

Cert. den. By denying the Writ of Certiorari, the U.S. Supreme Court refuses to accept an appeal from a U.S. Court of Appeals. The denial of certiorari does not, however, mean that the U.S. Supreme Court agrees with the result reached by the lower court.

Certiorari. Appeal from a U.S. Court of Appeals to the U.S. Supreme Court is by Writ of Certiorari. The Supreme Court does not have to accept the appeal and usually does not (*cert. den.*) unless there is a conflict among the lower courts that needs to be resolved or a constitutional issue is involved.

Change in accounting method. A change in the taxpayer's method of accounting (e.g., from FIFO to LIFO) generally requires prior approval from the IRS. Generally, a request must be filed within the taxable year of the desired change. In some instances, the permission for change will not be granted unless the taxpayer agrees to certain adjustments prescribed by the IRS.

Change in accounting period. A taxpayer must obtain the consent of the IRS before changing his or her tax year. Income for the short period created by the change must be annualized.

Charitable contributions. Contributions are deductible (subject to various restrictions and ceiling limitations) if made to qualified nonprofit charitable organizations. A cash basis taxpayer is entitled to a deduction solely in the year of payment. Accrual basis corporations may accrue contributions at year-end if payment is properly authorized before the end of the year and payment is made within two and one-half months after the end of the year. § 170.

Check-the-box Regulations. These Regulations enable taxpayers to classify the tax status of a business entity without regard to its corporate or noncorporate characteristics. An entity with more than one owner can elect to be classified either as a partnership or as a corporation. An entity with only one owner can elect to be classified as a sole proprietorship or as a corporation. These Regulations simplify tax administration and taxpayer compliance.

Child and dependent care expenses credit. A tax credit ranging from 20 percent to 35 percent of employment-related expenses (child and dependent care expenses) for amounts of up to $6,000 is available to individuals who are employed (or deemed to be employed) and maintain a household for a dependent child under age 13, disabled spouse, or disabled dependent. § 21.

Child support payments. Payments for child support do not constitute alimony and are therefore not includible in gross income by the recipient or deductible as alimony by the payor. Generally, none of the amounts paid are regarded as child support unless the divorce decree or separation agreement specifically calls for child support payments, However, if the amount of the payment to the former spouse would be reduced upon the happening of a contingency related to a child (e.g., the child attains age 21 or dies), the amount of the future reduction in the payment will be deemed child support for post-1984 agreements and decrees. § 71(c). See also *alimony and separate maintenance payments.*

Child tax credit. A tax credit based solely on the number of qualifying children under age 17. The maximum credit available is $1,000 per child through 2017. A qualifying child must be claimed as a dependent on a parent's tax return in order to qualify for the credit. Taxpayers who qualify for the child tax credit may also qualify for a supplemental credit. The supplemental credit is treated as a component of the earned income credit and is therefore refundable. The credit is phased out for higher-income taxpayers. § 24.

Circuit Court of Appeals. See *Court of Appeals.*

Circulation expenditures. Expenditures of establishing or increasing the circulation of a periodical that may be either expensed or capitalized. If such expenses are expensed, an adjustment will occur for AMT purposes, since the expenses are deducted over a three-year period for AMT purposes. Over the three-year period, both positive and negative AMT adjustments will be produced. § 173. See also *AMT adjustments.*

Citator. A tax research resource that presents the judicial history of a court case and traces the subsequent references to the case. When these references include the citing case's evaluations of the cited case's precedents, the research can obtain some measure of the efficacy and reliability of the original holding.

Claim of right doctrine. A judicially imposed doctrine applicable to both cash and accrual basis taxpayers that holds that an amount is includible in income upon actual or constructive receipt if the taxpayer has an unrestricted claim to the payment. For the tax treatment of amounts repaid when previously included in income under the claim of right doctrine, see § 1341.

Claims Court. One of three Federal trial courts that consider Federal tax controversies. Now known as the U.S. Court of Federal Claims, appeal from this court (formerly to the U.S. Supreme Court) now goes to the Court of Appeals for the Federal Circuit. See also *trial court.*

Clear reflection of income. The IRS has the authority to redetermine a taxpayer's income using a method that clearly reflects income if the taxpayer's method does not do so. § 446(b). In addition, the IRS may apportion or allocate income among various related businesses if income is not "clearly reflected." § 482.

Closely held corporation. A corporation where the stock ownership is not widely dispersed. Instead, a few shareholders are in control of corporate policy and are in a position to benefit personally from that policy.

Collectibles. A special type of capital asset, the gain from which is taxed at a maximum rate of 28 percent if the holding period is more than one year. Examples include art, rugs, antiques, gems, metals, stamps, some coins and bullion, and alcoholic beverages held for investment.

Community property. Louisiana, Texas, New Mexico, Arizona, California, Washington, Idaho, Nevada, and Wisconsin have community property systems. In Alaska, spouses can choose to have the community property rules apply. The rest of the states are classified as common law jurisdictions. The difference between common law and community property systems centers around the property rights possessed by married persons. In a common law system, each spouse owns whatever he or she earns. Under a community property system, one-half of the earnings of each spouse is considered owned by the other spouse. Assume, for example, Alice and Jeff are husband and wife and their only income is the $50,000 annual salary Jeff receives. If they live in New York (a common law state), the $50,000 salary belongs to Jeff. If, however, they live in Texas (a community property state), the $50,000 salary is divided equally, in terms of ownership, between Jeff and Alice. See also *separate property.*

Compensatory damages. Damages received or paid by the taxpayer can be classified as compensatory damages or as punitive damages. Compensatory damages are those paid to compensate one for harm caused by another. Compensatory damages are excludible from the recipient's gross income. See also *punitive damages*.

Completed contract method. A method of reporting gain or loss on certain long-term contracts. Under this method of accounting, gross income and expenses are recognized in the tax year in which the contract is completed. Reg. § 1.451–3. Limitations exist on a taxpayer's ability to use the completed contract method. § 460. See also *long-term contract* and *percentage of completion method*.

Component depreciation. The process of dividing an asset (e.g., a building) into separate components or parts for the purpose of calculating depreciation. The advantage of dividing an asset into components is to use shorter depreciation lives for selected components under § 167. Generally, the same cost recovery period must be used for all the components of an asset under § 168.

Condemnation. The taking of property by a public authority. The property is condemned as the result of legal action, and the owner is compensated by the public authority. The power to condemn property is known as the right of eminent domain.

Conduit concept. An approach assumed by the tax law in the treatment of certain entities and their owners. Specific tax characteristics pass through the entity without losing their identity. For example, items of income and expense, capital gains and losses, tax credits, etc., realized by a partnership pass through the partnership (a conduit) and are subject to taxation at the partner level. Also, in an S corporation, certain items pass through and are reported on the returns of the shareholders.

Constructive dividends. In addition to dividends formally declared by the board of directors of a corporation (i.e., declaration date, record date, and payment date), a shareholder may receive a distribution that does not have the formalities of a dividend but is treated as a dividend. Examples include salaries paid to shareholder-employees that are not reasonable and the shareholder use of corporate property for less than an arm's length rate.

Constructive ownership. See *attribution*.

Constructive receipt. If income is unqualifiedly available, it will be subject to the income tax even though it is not physically in the taxpayer's possession. An example is accrued interest on a savings account. Under the constructive receipt of income concept, the interest will be taxed to a depositor in the year it is available rather than the year actually withdrawn. The fact that the depositor uses the cash basis of accounting for tax purposes is irrelevant. See Reg. § 1.451–2.

Consumer interest. Interest expense of the taxpayer of a personal nature (not trade or business interest, investment interest, qualified residence interest, or passive activity interest) is not deductible. § 163(h). See also *interest on student loans* and *qualified residence interest*.

Contributions to the capital of a corporation. See *capital contributions*.

Convention expenses. Travel expenses incurred in attending a convention are deductible if the meetings are related to a taxpayer's trade or business or job-related activities. If, however, the convention trip is primarily for pleasure, no deduction is permitted for transportation expenses. Likewise, if the expenses are for attending a convention related to the production of income (§ 212), no deduction is permitted. Specific limitations are provided for foreign convention expenses. See § 274(n) for the limitations on the deductions for meals. § 274(h).

Correspondence audit. An audit conducted by the IRS by mail. Typically, the IRS writes to the taxpayer requesting the verification of a particular deduction, exemption, or credit. The completion of a special form or the remittance of copies of records or other support is all that is requested of the taxpayer. To be distinguished from a *field audit* or an *office audit*.

Cost depletion. Depletion that is calculated based on the adjusted basis of the asset. The adjusted basis is divided by the expected recoverable units to determine the depletion per unit. The depletion per unit is multiplied by the units sold during the tax year to calculate cost depletion. See also *percentage depletion*.

Cost recovery. The portion of the cost of an asset written off under ACRS (or MACRS), which replaced the depreciation system as a method for writing off the cost of an asset for most assets placed in service after 1980 (after 1986 for MACRS). § 168. See also *alternative depreciation system*, *fifty percent additional first-year depreciation*, and *one hundred percent additional first-year depreciation*.

Cost recovery period. A period specified in the Code for writing off the cost of an asset under ACRS or MACRS.

Court of Appeals. Any of 13 Federal courts that consider tax matters appealed from the U.S. Tax Court, U.S. Court of Federal Claims, or a U.S. District Court. Appeal from a U.S. Court of Appeals is to the U.S. Supreme Court by Writ of Certiorari. See also *appellate court*.

Court of Federal Claims. See *Claims Court*.

Court of original jurisdiction. The Federal courts are divided into courts of original jurisdiction and appellate courts. A dispute between a taxpayer and the IRS is first considered by a court of original jurisdiction (i.e., a trial court). The four Federal courts of original jurisdiction are the U.S. Tax Court, U.S. District Court, the Court of Federal Claims, and the Small Cases Division of the U.S. Tax Court. See also *Court of Appeals*.

Coverdell Education Savings Account (CESA). A savings account established to pay for qualified education expenses (i.e., tuition, fees, books, supplies, related equipment, room and board if the student's course load is at least one-half of the full-time course load). The maximum annual contribution to the savings account of a beneficiary is $2,000. The maximum annual contribution is subject to phaseout beginning at $95,000 for single taxpayers and $150,000 for married couples who file a joint return. Contributions are not deductible and cannot be made to a savings account once the beneficiary attains age 18. Distributions used to pay for qualified education expenses for a designated beneficiary are tax free. § 530.

Credit for certain retirement plan contributions. A nonrefundable credit is available based on eligible contributions of up to $2,000 to certain qualified retirement plans, such as traditional and Roth IRAs and § 401(k) plans, for taxable years beginning after 2001. The benefit provided by this credit is in addition to any deduction or exclusion that otherwise is available resulting from the qualifying contribution. The amount of the credit depends on the taxpayer's AGI and filing status. § 25B.

Credit for child and dependent care expenses. See *child and dependent care expenses credit*.

Credit for employer-provided child care. A nonrefundable credit is available to employers who provide child care facilities to their employees during normal working hours. The credit, limited to $150,000, is comprised of two components. The portion of the credit for qualified child care expenses is equal to 25 percent of these expenses while the portion of the credit for qualified child care resource and referral services is equal to 10 percent of these expenses. Any qualifying expenses otherwise deductible by the taxpayer must be reduced by the amount of the credit. In addition, the taxpayer's basis for any property used for qualifying purposes is reduced by the amount of the credit. § 45F.

Credit for small employer pension plan startup costs. A nonrefundable credit available to small businesses based on administrative costs associated with establishing and maintaining certain qualified plans. While such qualifying costs generally are deductible as ordinary and necessary business expenses, the availability of the credit is intended to lower the costs of starting a qualified retirement program, and therefore encourage qualifying businesses to establish retirement plans for their employees. The credit is available for eligible employers at the rate of 50 percent of qualified startup costs. The maximum credit is $500 (based on a maximum $1,000 of qualifying expenses). § 45E.

Crop insurance proceeds. The proceeds received when an insured crop is destroyed. Section 451(d) permits the farmer to defer reporting the income from the insurance proceeds until the tax year following the taxable year of the destruction.

Crop method. A method of accounting for agricultural crops that are planted in one year but harvested in a subsequent year. Under this method, the costs of raising the crop are accumulated as inventory and are deducted when the income from the crop is realized.

D

Death benefit. A payment made by an employer to the beneficiary or beneficiaries of a deceased employee on account of the death of the employee.

Death tax. See *estate tax*.

Declaration of estimated tax. A procedure whereby individuals and corporations are required to make quarterly installment payments of estimated tax. Individuals are required to make the declaration and file quarterly payments of the estimated tax if certain requirements are met.

Deduction for qualified tuition and related expenses. Taxpayers are allowed a deduction of up to $4,000 for higher education expenses. Certain taxpayers are not eligible for the deduction: those whose AGI exceeds a specified amount and those who can be claimed as a dependent by another taxpayer. These expenses are classified as a deduction *for* AGI and they need not be employment related. § 222.

Deductions for adjusted gross income. See *adjusted gross income*.

Deductions from adjusted gross income. See *itemized deductions*.

Deferred compensation. Compensation that will be taxed when received or upon the removal of certain restrictions on receipt and not when earned. Contributions by an employer to a qualified pension or profit sharing plan on behalf of an employee are an example. The contributions will not be taxed to the employee until the funds are made available or distributed to the employee (e.g., upon retirement). See also *qualified pension or profit sharing plan*.

Deficiency. Additional tax liability owed by a taxpayer and assessed by the IRS. See also *statutory notice of deficiency*.

Defined benefit plan. Qualified plans can be dichotomized into defined benefit plans and defined contribution plans. Under a defined benefit plan, a formula defines the benefits employees are to receive. The formula usually includes years of service, employee compensation, and some stated percentage. The employer must make annual contributions based on actuarial computations that will be sufficient to pay the vested retirement benefits. See also *defined contribution plan* and *pension plan*.

Defined contribution pension plan. See *defined contribution plan*.

Defined contribution plan. Qualified plans can be dichotomized into defined benefit plans and defined contribution plans. Under a defined contribution plan, a separate account is maintained for each covered employee. The employee's benefits under the plan are based solely on (1) the amount contributed and (2) income from the fund that accrues to the employee's account. The plan defines the amount the employer is required to contribute (e.g., a flat dollar amount, an amount based on a special formula, or an amount equal to a certain percentage of compensation). See also *defined benefit plan* and *pension plan*.

De minimis fringe. Benefits provided to employees that are too insignificant to warrant the time and effort required to account for the benefits received by each employee and the value of those benefits. Such amounts are excludible from the employee's gross income. § 132.

Dependency exemption. See *personal and dependency exemptions*.

Depletion. The process by which the cost or other basis of a natural resource (e.g., an oil or gas interest) is recovered upon extraction and sale of the resource. The two ways to determine the depletion allowance are the cost and percentage (or statutory) methods. Under the cost method, each unit of production sold is assigned a portion of the cost or other basis of the interest. This is determined by dividing the cost or other basis by the total units expected to be recovered. Under the percentage (or statutory) method, the tax law provides a special percentage factor for different types of minerals and other natural resources. This percentage is multiplied by the gross income from the interest to arrive at the depletion allowance. §§ 613 and 613A.

Depreciation. The deduction of the cost or other basis of a tangible asset over the asset's estimated useful life. § 167. For intangible assets, see *amortization*. For natural resources, see *depletion*. Also see *estimated useful life*. The depreciation system was replaced by ACRS for most assets placed in service after 1980 (by MACRS for most assets placed in service after 1986) but still applies for assets placed in service before 1981. See also *recapture of depreciation*.

Determination letter. Upon the request of a taxpayer, a District Director will comment on the tax status of a completed transaction. Determination letters are most frequently used to clarify employee versus self-employed status, to determine whether a pension or profit sharing plan qualifies under the Code, and to determine the tax-exempt status of certain nonprofit organizations.

Direct charge-off method. See *specific charge-off method.*

Disabled access credit. A tax credit designed to encourage small businesses to make their facilities more accessible to disabled individuals. The credit is equal to 50 percent of the eligible expenditures that exceed $250 but do not exceed $10,250. Thus, the maximum amount for the credit is $5,000. The adjusted basis for depreciation is reduced by the amount of the credit. To qualify, the facility must have been placed in service before November 6, 1990. § 44. See also *general business credit.*

Disaster area loss. A casualty sustained in an area designated as a disaster area by the President of the United States. In such an event, the disaster loss may be treated as having occurred in the taxable year immediately preceding the year in which the disaster actually occurred. Thus, immediate tax benefits are provided to victims of a disaster. § 165(i). See also *casualty loss.*

Dissent. To disagree with the majority. If, for example, Judge Brown disagrees with the result reached by Judges Charles and Davis (all of whom are members of the same court), Judge Brown could issue a dissenting opinion.

District Court. A Federal District Court is a trial court for purposes of litigating (among others) Federal tax matters. It is the only trial court where a jury trial can be obtained. See also *trial court.*

Dividends received deduction. A deduction allowed a shareholder that is a corporation for dividends received from a domestic corporation. The percentage applied in calculating the dividends received deduction varies according to the percentage of stock ownership. If the stock ownership percentage is less than 20 percent, the percentage is 70 percent of the dividends received. If the stock ownership percentage is at least 20 percent but less than 80 percent, the percentage is 80 percent. If the stock ownership percentage is at least 80 percent, the percentage is 100 percent. §§ 243–246A.

Dollar-value LIFO. An inventory technique that focuses on the dollars invested in the inventory rather than the particular items on hand each period. Each inventory item is assigned to a pool. A pool is a collection of similar items and is treated as a separate inventory. At the end of the period, each pool is valued in terms of prices at the time LIFO was adopted (base period prices), whether or not the particular items were actually on hand in the year LIFO was adopted, to compare with current prices to determine if there has been an increase or decrease in inventories.

Domestic production activities deduction (DPAD). See *production activities deduction (PAD).*

Domestic production gross receipts (DPGR). A key component in computing the domestic production activities deduction (DPAD). Includes receipts from the sale and other disposition of qualified production property produced in significant part within the United States. DPGR is defined in § 199(c)(4). See also *production activities deduction (PAD).*

E

Earned income. Income from personal services as distinguished from income generated by property. See §§ 32 and 911 and the related Regulations.

Earned income credit. A refundable tax credit designed to provide assistance to certain low-income individuals. To receive the most beneficial treatment, the taxpayer must have qualifying children. However, it is possible to qualify for the credit without having a child. See Chapter 13 for the computation procedure required in order to determine the amount of the credit allowed. § 32.

Earnings and profits. A tax concept peculiar to corporate taxpayers that measures economic capacity to make a distribution to shareholders that is not a return of capital. Such a distribution will result in dividend income to the shareholders to the extent of the corporation's current and accumulated earnings and profits.

Economic income. The change in the taxpayer's net worth, as measured in terms of market values, plus the value of the assets the taxpayer consumed during the year. Because of the impracticality of this income model, it is not used for tax purposes. See also *accounting income.*

Economic performance test. One of the requirements that must be satisfied in order for an accrual basis taxpayer to deduct an expense. The accrual basis taxpayer first must satisfy the all events test. That test is not deemed satisfied until economic performance occurs. This occurs when property or services are provided to the taxpayer or, in the case in which the taxpayer is required to provide property or services, whenever the property or services are actually provided by the taxpayer. See also *all events test.*

Education expenses. Employees may deduct education expenses that are incurred either (1) to maintain or improve existing job-related skills or (2) to meet the express requirements of the employer or the requirements imposed by law to retain employment status. The expenses are not deductible if the education is required to meet the minimum educational standards for the taxpayer's job or if the education qualifies the individual for a new trade or business. Reg. § 1.162–5. See also *American Opportunity credit, HOPE scholarship credit,* and *lifetime learning credit.*

Educational savings bonds. U.S. Series EE bonds whose proceeds are used for qualified higher educational expenses for the taxpayer, the taxpayer's spouse, or a dependent. The interest may be excluded from gross income, provided the taxpayer's adjusted gross income does not exceed certain amounts. § 135.

E-file. The electronic filing of a tax return. The filing is either direct or indirect. As to direct, the taxpayer goes online using a computer and tax return preparation software. Indirect filing occurs when a taxpayer utilizes an authorized IRS e-file provider. The provider often is the tax return preparer.

Employee expenses. The deductions *for* adjusted gross income include reimbursed expenses and certain expenses of performing artists. All other employee expenses are deductible *from* AGI. § 62. See also *trade or business expenses.*

Employment taxes. Employment taxes are those taxes that an employer must pay on account of its employees.

Employment taxes include FICA (Federal Insurance Contributions Act) and FUTA (Federal Unemployment Tax Act) taxes. Employment taxes are paid to the IRS in addition to income tax withholdings at specified intervals. Such taxes can be levied on the employees, the employer, or both. See also *FICA tax* and *FUTA tax.*

Entertainment expenses. These expenses are deductible only if they are directly related to or associated with a trade or business. Various restrictions and documentation requirements have been imposed upon the deductibility of entertainment expenses to prevent abuses by taxpayers. See, for example, the provision contained in § 274(n) that disallows 50 percent of entertainment expenses. § 274.

Estate tax. A tax imposed on the right to transfer property by reason of death. Thus, an estate tax is levied on the decedent's estate and not on the heir receiving the property. §§ 2001 and 2002. See also *inheritance tax.*

Estimated tax. The amount of tax (including alternative minimum tax and self-employment tax) an individual expects to owe for the year after subtracting tax credits and income tax withheld. The estimated tax must be paid in installments at designated intervals (e.g. for the individual taxpayer, by April 15, June 15, September 15, and January 15 of the following year).

Excise tax. A tax on the manufacture, sale, or use of goods or on the carrying on of an occupation or activity. Also, a tax on the transfer of property. Thus, the Federal estate and gift taxes are, theoretically, excise taxes.

Extraordinary personal services. These are services provided by individuals where the customers' use of the property is incidental to their receipt of the services. For example, a patient's use of a hospital bed is incidental to his or her receipt of medical services. This is one of the six exceptions to determine whether an activity is a passive rental activity. § 469.

F

Fair market value. The amount at which property would change hands between a willing buyer and a willing seller, neither being under any compulsion to buy or sell and both having reasonable knowledge of the relevant facts. Reg. §§ 1.1001–1(a) and 20.2031–1(b).

Farm price method. A method of accounting for agricultural crops. The inventory of crops is valued at its market price less the estimated cost of disposition (e.g., freight and selling expense.)

Federal district court. See *district court.*

FICA tax. An abbreviation for Federal Insurance Contributions Act, commonly referred to as the Social Security tax. The FICA tax is comprised of the Social Security tax (old age, survivors, and disability insurance) and the Medicare tax (hospital insurance) and is imposed on both employers and employees. The employer is responsible for withholding from the employee's wages the Social Security tax at a rate of 6.2 percent on a maximum wage base of $117,000 (for 2014) and the Medicare tax at a rate of 1.45 percent (no maximum wage base). The employer is required to match the employee's contribution. See also *employment taxes.*

Field audit. An audit by the IRS conducted on the business premises of the taxpayer or in the office of the tax practitioner representing the taxpayer. To be distinguished from a *correspondence audit* or an *office audit.*

Fifty percent additional first-year depreciation. This provision, which was effective for property acquired after December 31, 2007, and placed in service before January 1, 2014, provided for an additional cost recovery deduction of 50 percent in the tax year the qualified property is placed in service. Qualified property included most types of new property other than buildings. The taxpayer could elect to forgo this bonus depreciation. See also *cost recovery allowance* and *one hundred percent additional first-year depreciation.*

Finalized Regulation. See *regulations.*

Financial Accounting Standards Board (FASB). See *Generally accepted accounting principles (GAAP).*

First-in, first-out (FIFO). An accounting method for determining the cost of inventories. Under this method, the inventory on hand is deemed to be the sum of the cost of the most recently acquired units. See also *last-in, first-out (LIFO).*

Fiscal year. A fiscal year is a 12-month period ending on the last day of a month other than December. In certain circumstances, a taxpayer is permitted to elect a fiscal year instead of being required to use a calendar year. See also *accounting period* and *taxable year.*

Flat tax. In its pure form, it would replace the graduated income tax rates with a single rate (e.g., 17 percent). All deductions are eliminated, and a large personal exemption is allowed to remove low-income and many middle-income taxpayers from the application of the tax.

Flexible spending plan. An employee benefit plan that allows the employee to take a reduction in salary in exchange for the employer paying benefits that can be provided by the employer without the employee being required to recognize income (e.g., medical and child care benefits).

Foreign earned income exclusion. The foreign earned income exclusion is a relief provision that applies to U.S. citizens working in a foreign country. To qualify for the exclusion, the taxpayer must be either a bona fide resident of the foreign country or present in the country for 330 days during any 12 consecutive months. The exclusion is limited to $99,200 per year for 2014 ($97,600 in 2013). § 911.

Foreign tax credit (or deduction). Both individual taxpayers and corporations may claim a foreign tax credit on income earned and subject to tax in a foreign country or U.S. possession. As an alternative to the credit, a deduction may be taken for the foreign taxes paid. §§ 27, 164, and 901–905.

Franchise. An agreement that gives the transferee the right to distribute, sell, or provide goods, services, or facilities within a specified area. The cost of obtaining a franchise may be amortized over a statutory period of 15 years. In general, the franchisor's gain on the sale of franchise rights is an ordinary gain because the franchisor retains a significant power, right, or continuing interest in the subject of the franchise. §§ 197 and 1253.

Franchise tax. A tax levied on the right to do business in a state as a corporation. Although income considerations may come into play, the tax usually is based on the capitalization of the corporation.

Fringe benefits. Compensation or other benefits received by an employee that are not in the form of cash. Some fringe benefits (e.g., accident and health plans, group term life insurance) may be excluded from the employee's gross income and therefore are not subject to the Federal income tax.

Fruit and tree metaphor. The courts have held that an individual who earns income from property or services cannot assign that income to another. For example, a father cannot assign his earnings from commissions to his child and escape income tax on those amounts.

F.3d. An abbreviation for the Third Series of the *Federal Reporter*, the official series where decisions of the U.S. Claims Court (before October 1982) and the U.S. Courts of Appeals are published.

F.Supp. The abbreviation for the *Federal Supplement*, the official series where the reported decisions of the U.S. District Courts are published.

FUTA tax. An employment tax levied on employers. Jointly administered by the Federal and state governments, the tax provides funding for unemployment benefits. FUTA applies at a rate of 6.0 percent on the first $7,000 of covered wages paid during the year for each employee in 2014. The Federal government allows a credit for FUTA paid (or allowed under a merit rating system) to the state. The credit cannot exceed 5.4 percent of the covered wages. See also *employment taxes*.

G

General business credit. The summation of various nonrefundable business credits, including the tax credit for rehabilitation expenditures, business energy credit, work opportunity credit, research activities credit, low-income housing credit, and disabled access credit. The amount of general business credit that can be used to reduce the tax liability is limited to the taxpayer's net income tax reduced by the greater of (1) the tentative minimum tax or (2) 25 percent of the net regular tax liability that exceeds $25,000. Unused general business credits can be carried back 1 year and forward 20 years.

Generally accepted accounting principles (GAAP). Guidelines relating to how to construct the financial statements of enterprises doing business in the United States. Promulgated chiefly by the *Financial Accounting Standards Board (FASB)*.

Gift. A transfer of property for less than adequate consideration. Gifts usually occur in a personal setting (such as between members of the same family). Gifts are excluded from the income tax but may be subject to the *gift tax*.

Gift tax. A tax imposed on the transfer of property by gift. The tax is imposed upon the donor of a gift and is based upon the fair market value of the property on the date of the gift. §§ 2501–2524.

Golden parachute payment. A severance payment to employees that meets the following requirements: (1) the payment is contingent on a change of ownership of a corporation through a stock or asset acquisition and (2) the aggregate present value of the payment equals or exceeds three times the employee's average annual compensation. To the extent the severance payment meets these conditions, a deduction is disallowed to the employer for the excess of the payment over a statutory base amount (a five-year average of compensation if the taxpayer was an employee for the entire five-year period). In addition, a 20 percent excise tax is imposed on the employee who receives the excess severance pay. §§ 280G and 4999.

Goodwill. The ability of a business to generate income in excess of a normal rate on assets due to superior managerial skills, market position, new product technology, etc. In the purchase of a business, goodwill represents the difference between the purchase price and the fair market value of the net assets acquired. Goodwill is an intangible asset that possesses an indefinite life. However, since acquired goodwill is a § 197 intangible asset, it is amortized over a 15-year statutory period. Self-created goodwill cannot be amortized. Reg. § 1.167(a)–3. See also *amortization*.

Government bonds issued at a discount. Certain U.S. government bonds (Series EE) are issued at a discount and do not pay interest during the life of the bonds. Instead, the bonds are redeemable at increasing fixed amounts. Thus, the difference between the purchase price and the amount received upon redemption represents interest income to the holder. A cash basis taxpayer may defer recognition of gross income until the bonds are redeemed. For Series EE savings bonds issued after 1989, the interest otherwise taxable at redemption can be excluded if the bonds are qualified educational savings bonds. As an alternative to deferring recognition of gross income until the bonds are redeemed, the taxpayer may elect to include in gross income on an annual basis the annual increase in the value of the bonds. § 454.

Gross income. Income subject to the Federal income tax. Gross income does not include income for which the Code permits exclusion treatment (e.g., interest on municipal bonds). For a manufacturing or merchandising business, gross income means gross profit (gross sales or gross receipts less cost of goods sold). § 61 and Reg. § 1.61–3(a).

Group term life insurance. Life insurance coverage permitted by an employer for a group of employees. Such insurance is renewable on a year-to-year basis and does not accumulate in value (i.e., no cash surrender value is built up). The premiums paid by the employer on the insurance are not taxed to an employee on coverage of up to $50,000 per person. § 79 and Reg. § 1.79–1(a).

Guaranteed payments. Payments made by a partnership to one of its partners for services rendered or for the use of capital, to the extent the payments are determined without regard to the income of the partnership. Such payments generally are deductible by the partnership as a business expense and are reported as ordinary income by the recipient partner. § 707(c).

H

Half-year convention. The half-year convention is a cost recovery convention that assumes all property is placed in service at mid-year and thus provides for a half-year's cost recovery for that year.

Head of household. An unmarried individual who maintains a household for another and satisfies certain conditions set forth in § 2(b). Such status enables the taxpayer to use a set of income tax rates [see § 1(b)] that are lower than those applicable to other unmarried individuals [§ 1(c)] but higher than those applicable to surviving spouses and married persons filing a joint return [§ 1(a)]. See also *tax rate schedules*.

Health savings account (HSA). A medical savings account created in legislation enacted in December 2003 that is designed to replace and expand Archer Medical Savings Accounts. See also *medical savings account*.

Highly compensated employee. The employee group is generally divided into two categories for fringe benefit (including pension and profit sharing plans) purposes. These are (1) highly compensated employees and (2) non-highly compensated employees. For most fringe benefits, if the fringe benefit plan discriminates in favor of highly compensated employees, it will not be a qualified plan with respect, at a minimum, to the highly compensated employees.

Hobby loss. A nondeductible loss arising from a personal hobby as contrasted with an activity engaged in for profit. Generally, the law provides a rebuttable presumption that an activity is engaged in for profit if profits are earned during any three or more years during a five-year period. § 183. See also *vacation home*.

Holding period. The period of time property has been held for income tax purposes. The holding period is crucial in determining whether gain or loss from the sale or exchange of a capital asset is long term or short term. § 1223. See also *capital gain or loss holding period*.

Home equity loans. Loans that utilize the personal residence of the taxpayer as security. The interest on such loans is deductible as *qualified residence interest*. However, interest is deductible only on the portion of the loan that does not exceed the lesser of (1) the fair market value of the residence, reduced by the *acquisition indebtedness*, or (2) $100,000 ($50,000 for married persons filing separate returns). A major benefit of a home equity loan is that there are no tracing rules regarding the use of the loan proceeds. § 163(h)(3).

Home office expenses. See *office-in-the-home expenses*.

HOPE scholarship credit. A tax credit for qualifying expenses paid for the first two years of postsecondary education. Room, board, and book costs are ineligible for the credit. The maximum credit available is $1,800 per year per student, computed as 100 percent of the first $1,200 of qualifying expenses, plus 50 percent of the second $1,200 of qualifying expenses. Eligible students include the taxpayer, taxpayer's spouse, and taxpayer's dependents. To qualify for the credit, a student must take at least one-half the full-time course load for at least one academic term at a qualifying educational institution. The credit is phased out for higher-income taxpayers. For 2009, 2010, 2011, 2012, and 2013, the HOPE scholarship credit is replaced with the American Opportunity credit. § 25A.

H.R 10 (Keogh) plan. See *self-employment retirement plan*.

Hybrid method. A combination of the accrual and cash methods of accounting. That is, the taxpayer may account for some items of income on the accrual method (e.g., sales and cost of goods sold) and other items (e.g., interest income) on the cash method.

I

Imputed interest. For certain long-term sales of property, the IRS can convert some of the gain from the sale into interest income if the contract does not provide for a minimum rate of interest to be paid by the purchaser. The application of this procedure has the effect of forcing the seller to recognize less long-term capital gain and more ordinary income (interest income). §§ 483 and 1274 and the Regulations thereunder. In addition, interest income and interest expense are imputed (deemed to exist) on interest-free or below-market rate loans between certain related parties. § 7872. See also *interest-free loans*.

Incentive stock option (ISO). A type of stock option that receives favorable tax treatment. If various qualification requirements can be satisfied, there are no recognition tax consequences when the stock option is granted. However, the spread (the excess of the fair market value at the date of exercise over the option price) is a tax preference item for purposes of the alternative minimum tax. The gain on disposition of the stock resulting from the exercise of the stock option will be classified as long-term capital gain if certain holding period requirements are met (the employee must not dispose of the stock within two years after the option is granted or within one year after acquiring the stock). § 422. See also *nonqualified stock option (NQSO)*.

Income. For tax purposes, an increase in wealth that has been realized.

Independent contractor. A self-employed person as distinguished from one who is employed as an employee.

Indexation. A procedure whereby adjustments are made by the IRS to key tax components (e.g., standard deduction, tax brackets, personal and dependency exemptions) to reflect inflation. The adjustments usually are made annually and are based on the change in the consumer price index.

Individual retirement account (IRA). A type of retirement plan to which an individual with earned income can contribute a statutory maximum. The maximum amount is $5,500 in 2014. IRAs can be classified as traditional IRAs or Roth IRAs. With a traditional IRA, an individual can contribute and deduct a maximum of $5,500 per tax year in 2014. The deduction is a deduction *for* AGI. However, if the individual is an active participant in another qualified retirement plan, the deduction is phased out proportionally between certain AGI ranges (note that the phaseout limits the amount of the deduction and not the amount of the contribution). With a Roth IRA, an individual can contribute a maximum of $5,500 per tax year in 2014. No deduction is permitted. However, if a five-year holding period requirement is satisfied and if the distribution is a qualified distribution, the taxpayer can make tax-free withdrawals from a Roth IRA. The maximum annual contribution is phased out proportionally between certain AGI ranges. §§ 219 and 408A. See also *simplified employee pension plan*.

Inheritance tax. An excise tax levied on the heir based on the value of property received from a decedent. See also *estate tax*.

Installment method. A method of accounting enabling a taxpayer to spread the recognition of gain on the sale of property over the payout period. Under this procedure, the seller computes the gross profit percentage from the sale (the gain divided by the contract price) and applies it to each payment received to arrive at the gain to be recognized. §§ 453 and 453A.

Intangible drilling and development costs (IDC). Taxpayers may elect to expense or capitalize (subject to amortization) intangible drilling and development costs. However, ordinary income recapture provisions apply to oil and gas properties on a sale or other disposition if the expense method is elected. §§ 263(c) and 1254(a).

Interest-free loans. Bona fide loans that carry no interest (or a below-market rate). If made in a nonbusiness setting, the imputed interest element is treated as a gift from the lender to the borrower. If made by a corporation to a shareholder, a constructive dividend could result. In either event, the lender may recognize interest income, and the borrower may be able to deduct interest expense. § 7872.

Interest on student loans. A limited ability exists to deduct interest on student loans used to pay qualified higher education expenses (i.e., tuition, fees, books, supplies, room and board). The ceiling on the deduction is $2,500. The deduction is a deduction *for* AGI. § 221. See also *consumer interest.*

International Accounting Standards Board (IASB). The body that promulgates *International Financial Reporting Standards (IFRS).* Based in London, representing accounting standard setting bodies in over 100 countries, the IASB develops accounting standards that can serve as the basis for harmonizing conflicting reporting standards among nations.

International Financial Reporting Standards (IFRS). Produced by the *International Accounting Standards Board (IASB)*, guidelines developed since 2001 as to revenue recognition, accounting for business combinations, and a conceptual framework for financial reporting. IFRS provisions are designed so that they can be used by all entities, regardless of where they are based or conduct business. IFRS have gained widespread acceptance throughout the world, and the SEC is considering how to require U.S. entities to use IFRS in addition to, or in lieu of, the accounting rules of the *Financial Accounting Standards Board.*

Interpretive Regulation. A Regulation issued by the Treasury Department that purports to explain the meaning of a particular Code Section. An interpretive Regulation is given less deference than a legislative Regulation. See also *legislative regulation* and *procedural regulation.* § 7805.

Investigation of a new business. Expenditures incurred in the evaluation of prospective business activities by taxpayers who are not engaged in a trade or business (to acquire an existing business or enter into a new trade or business). If the expenditures are general, it is the position of the IRS that no deduction is permitted even if the investigation is abandoned because the taxpayer is not engaged in a trade or business. The courts, however, have permitted a loss deduction providing the expenditures were specific.

Investment income. Gross income from interest, dividends, annuities, and royalties not derived in the ordinary course of a trade or business. Net capital gain attributable to the disposition of property producing these types of income and qualified dividend income normally are not included in investment income. However, a taxpayer may elect to include the capital gains as investment income if the net capital gain qualifying for the *alternative tax* is reduced by an equivalent amount. A similar election can be made for qualified dividends. See also *investment interest.*

Investment indebtedness. If funds are borrowed by noncorporate taxpayers for the purpose of purchasing or continuing to hold investment property, some portion of the interest expense deduction may be disallowed. The interest deduction is generally limited to net investment income. Amounts that are disallowed may be carried forward and treated as investment interest of the succeeding year. § 163(d).

Investment interest. Payment for the use of funds used to acquire assets that produce investment income. The deduction for investment interest is limited to *net investment income* for the tax year. See also *investment income.*

Investment tax credit (ITC). A tax credit that usually was equal to 10 percent (unless a reduced credit was elected) of the qualified investment in tangible personalty used in a trade or business. If the tangible personalty had a recovery period of five years or more, the full cost of the property qualified for the credit. Only 60 percent of cost qualified for property with a recovery period of three years. However, the regular investment tax credit was repealed by TRA of 1986 for property placed in service after December 31, 1985. §§ 46–48. See also *general business credit* and *recapture of investment tax credit.*

Involuntary conversion. The loss or destruction of property through theft, casualty, or condemnation. Any gain realized on an involuntary conversion can, at the taxpayer's election, be postponed (deferred) for Federal income tax purposes if the owner reinvests the proceeds within a prescribed period of time in property that is similar or related in service or use. § 1033. See also *nontaxable exchange.*

IRA. See *individual retirement account.*

Itemized deductions. Certain personal expenditures allowed by the Code as deductions *from* adjusted gross income. Examples include certain medical expenses, interest on home mortgages, state income taxes, and charitable contributions. Itemized deductions are reported on Schedule A of Form 1040. Certain miscellaneous itemized deductions are reduced by 2 percent of the taxpayer's adjusted gross income. In addition, a taxpayer whose adjusted gross income exceeds a specified amount adjusted for inflation must reduce the itemized deductions by 3 percent of the excess. §§ 63(d), 67, and 68.

K

Keogh plan. See *self-employment retirement plan.*

Kiddie tax. To reduce the tax savings that result from shifting income from parents to children, the net unearned income of a child under age 19 (or under age 24 if a full-time student) is taxed at the marginal tax rate of the parent(s). For the provision to apply, the child must have at least one living parent and unearned income of more than $2,000 for the tax year. § 1(g). See also *unearned income.*

L

Last-in, first-out (LIFO). An accounting method for valuing inventories for tax purposes. Under this method, it is assumed that the inventory on hand is valued at the cost of the earliest acquired units. § 472 and the related Regulations. See also *first-in, first-out (FIFO).*

Least aggregate deferral method. An algorithm set forth in the Regulations to determine the tax year for a partnership with partners whose tax years differ. The tax year that produces the least aggregate deferral of income for the partners is selected.

Legislative Regulation. Some Code Sections give the Secretary of the Treasury or his delegate the authority to prescribe Regulations to carry out the details of administration or to otherwise complete the operating rules. Regulations issued pursuant to this type of authority truly possess the force and effect of law. In effect, Congress is almost delegating its legislative powers to the Treasury Department. See also *interpretive regulation* and *procedural regulation.*

Lessee. One who rents property from another. In the case of real estate, the lessee is also known as the tenant.

Lessor. One who rents property to another. In the case of real estate, the lessor is also known as the landlord.

Letter rulings. Issued upon a taxpayer's request, by the National Office of the IRS, they describe how the IRS will treat a proposed transaction for tax purposes. They apply only to the taxpayer who asks for and obtains the ruling, but post-1984 rulings may be substantial authority for purposes of avoiding the accuracy-related penalties. The IRS limits the issuance of letter rulings to restricted, preannounced areas of taxation.

Life insurance proceeds. Generally, life insurance proceeds paid to a beneficiary upon the death of the insured are exempt from Federal income tax. An exception is provided when a life insurance contract has been transferred for valuable consideration to another individual who assumes ownership rights. In that case, the proceeds are income to the assignee to the extent that the proceeds exceed the amount paid for the policy plus any subsequent premiums paid. Insurance proceeds may be subject to the Federal estate tax if the decedent retained any incidents of ownership in the policy before death or if the proceeds are payable to the decedent's estate. §§ 101 and 2042.

Lifetime learning credit. A tax credit for qualifying expenses for taxpayers pursuing education beyond the first two years of postsecondary education. Individuals who are completing their last two years of undergraduate studies, pursuing graduate or professional degrees, or otherwise seeking new job skills or maintaining existing job skills are all eligible for the credit. Eligible individuals include the taxpayer, taxpayer's spouse, and taxpayer's dependents. The maximum credit is 20 percent of the first $10,000 of qualifying expenses and is computed per taxpayer. The credit is phased out for higher-income taxpayers. § 25A.

Like-kind exchange. An exchange of property held for productive use in a trade or business or for investment (except inventory, stocks and bonds, and partnership interests) for other investment or trade or business property. Unless non-like-kind property is received (boot), the exchange will be nontaxable. § 1031. See also *boot* and *nontaxable exchange.*

Limited expensing. See *Section 179 expensing.*

Limited liability company (LLC). An organization that combines the corporate characteristic of limited liability with treatment as a partnership for Federal income tax purposes.

Liquidating distribution. A distribution of assets by a corporation associated with the termination of the business.

Listed property. The term listed property includes (1) any passenger automobile, (2) any other property used as a means of transportation, (3) any property of a type generally used for purposes of entertainment, recreation, or amusement, (4) any computer or peripheral equipment (with an exception for exclusive business use), (5) any cellular telephone (or other similar telecommunications equipment), and (6) any other property of a type specified in the Regulations. If listed property is predominantly used for business, the taxpayer is allowed to use the statutory percentage method of cost recovery. Otherwise, the straight-line cost recovery method must be used. § 280F.

Long-term care insurance. Insurance that helps pay the cost of care when the insured is unable to care for himself or herself. Such insurance is generally thought of as insurance against the cost of an aged person entering a nursing home. The employer can provide the insurance, and the premiums may be excluded from the employee's gross income. § 7702B.

Long-term contract. A building, installation, construction, or manufacturing contract that is entered into but not completed within the same tax year. A manufacturing contract is a long-term contract only if the contract is to manufacture (1) a unique item not normally carried in finished goods inventory or (2) items that normally require more than 12 calendar months to complete. The two available methods to account for long-term contracts are the percentage of completion method and the completed contract method. The completed contract method can be used only in limited circumstances. § 460. See also *completed contract method* and *percentage of completion method.*

Long-term nonpersonal use capital assets. Includes investment property with a long-term holding period. Such property disposed of by casualty or theft may receive § 1231 treatment. See also *Section 1231 gains and losses.*

Lower of cost or market. An elective inventory method, whereby the taxpayer may value inventories at the lower of the taxpayer's actual cost or the current replacement cost of the goods. This method cannot be used in conjunction with the LIFO inventory method.

Low-income housing. Low-income housing is rental housing that is a dwelling unit for low- or moderate-income individuals or families. Beneficial tax treatment is in the form of the *low-income housing credit.* § 42. See also *accelerated cost recovery system (ACRS).*

Low-income housing credit. Beneficial treatment to owners of low-income housing is provided in the form of a tax credit. The calculated credit is claimed in the year the building is placed in service and in the following nine years. § 42. See also *general business credit.*

Lump-sum distribution. Payment of the entire amount due at one time rather than in installments. Such distributions often occur from qualified pension or profit sharing plans upon the retirement or death of a covered employee. The recipient of a lump-sum distribution may recognize both long-term capital gain and ordinary income upon the receipt of the distribution. The ordinary income portion may be subject to a special 10-year income averaging provision. § 402(e).

M

MACRS. See *accelerated cost recovery system (ACRS).*

Majority interest partners. Partners who have more than a 50 percent interest in partnership profits and capital, counting only those partners who have the same taxable year, are referred to as majority interest partners. The term is of significance in determining the appropriate taxable year of a partnership. § 706(b). See also *accounting period* and *principal partner*.

Marital deduction. A deduction allowed upon the transfer of property from one spouse to another. The deduction is allowed under the Federal gift tax for lifetime (inter vivos) transfers or under the Federal estate tax for death (testamentary) transfers. §§ 2056 and 2523.

Marriage penalty. The additional tax liability that results for a married couple compared with what their tax liability would be if they were not married and filed separate returns.

Material participation. If an individual taxpayer materially participates in a nonrental trade or business activity, any loss from that activity is treated as an active loss that can be offset against active income. Material participation is achieved by meeting any one of seven tests provided in the Regulations. § 469(h).

Medical expenses. Medical expenses of an individual, spouse, and dependents are allowed as an itemized deduction to the extent that such amounts (less insurance reimbursements) exceed 10 percent (or 7.5 percent if at least age 65) of adjusted gross income. § 213.

Medical savings account. A plan available to employees of small firms (50 or fewer employees) with high-deductible health insurance. The employee can place money in the fund and then deduct the contributions (within limits) from gross income. If the employer contributes to the fund, the employee can exclude the contribution from gross income. Income earned from the fund and withdrawals for medical care are not subject to tax. §§ 106(b) and 220.

Mid-month convention. A cost recovery convention that assumes property is placed in service in the middle of the month that it is actually placed in service.

Mid-quarter convention. A cost recovery convention that assumes property placed in service during the year is placed in service at the middle of the quarter in which it is actually placed in service. The mid-quarter convention applies if more than 40 percent of the value of property (other than eligible real estate) is placed in service during the last quarter of the year.

Miscellaneous itemized deductions. A special category of itemized deductions that includes such expenses as professional dues, tax return preparation fees, job-hunting costs, unreimbursed employee business expenses, and certain investment expenses. Such expenses are deductible only to the extent they exceed 2 percent of adjusted gross income. § 67. See also *itemized deductions*.

Mitigation of the annual accounting period concept. Various tax provisions that provide relief from the effect of the finality of the annual accounting period concept. For example, the *net operating loss* provisions provide relief to a taxpayer whose business profits and losses for different taxable years fluctuate. See also *accounting period*.

Modified accelerated cost recovery system (MACRS). See *accelerated cost recovery system (ACRS)*.

Modified adjusted gross income. A key determinant in computing the domestic production activities deduction (DPAD) and certain other tax provisions (e.g., deduction for higher education tuition, exclusion of interest on education savings bonds). §§ 135, 144, and 199. See also *production activities deduction (PAD)*.

Moving expenses. A deduction *for* AGI is permitted to employees and self-employed individuals provided certain tests are met. The taxpayer's new job must be at least 50 miles farther from the old residence than the old residence was from the former place of work. In addition, an employee must be employed on a full-time basis at the new location for 39 weeks in the 12-month period following the move. Deductible moving expenses include the cost of moving the household and personal effects, transportation, and lodging expenses during the move. The cost of meals during the move are not deductible. Qualified moving expenses that are paid (or reimbursed) by the employer can be excluded from the employee's gross income. In this case, the related deduction by the employee is not permitted. §§ 62(a)(15), 132(a)(6), and 217.

Multiple support agreement. To qualify for a dependency exemption, the support test must be satisfied. This requires that over 50 percent of the support of the potential dependent be provided by the taxpayer. Where no one person provides more than 50 percent of the support, a multiple support agreement enables a taxpayer to still qualify for the dependency exemption. Any person who contributed more than 10 percent of the support is entitled to claim the exemption if each person in the group who contributed more than 10 percent files a written consent (Form 2120). Each person who is a party to the multiple support agreement must meet all the other requirements for claiming the dependency exemption. § 152(c). See also *personal and dependency exemptions*.

N

National sales tax. Intended as a replacement for the current Federal income tax. Unlike a value added tax (VAT), which is levied on the manufacturer, it would be imposed on the consumer upon the final sale of goods and services. To keep the tax from being regressive, low-income taxpayers would be granted some kind of credit or exemption.

Necessary. Appropriate and helpful in furthering the taxpayer's business or income-producing activity. §§ 162(a) and 212. See also *ordinary*.

Net capital gain (NCG). The excess of the net long-term capital gain for the tax year over the net short-term capital loss. The net capital gain of an individual taxpayer is eligible for the alternative tax. § 1222(11). See also *alternative tax*.

Net capital loss (NCL). The excess of the losses from sales or exchanges of capital assets over the gains from sales or exchanges of such assets. Up to $3,000 per year of the net capital loss may be deductible by noncorporate taxpayers against ordinary income. The excess net capital loss carries over to future tax years. For corporate taxpayers, the net capital loss cannot be offset against ordinary income, but it can be carried back three years and forward five years to offset net capital gains. §§ 1211, 1212, and 1221(10).

Net investment income. The excess of *investment income* over investment expenses. Investment expenses are those deductible expenses directly connected with the production of investment income. Investment expenses do not include investment interest. The deduction for *investment* *interest* for the tax year is limited to net investment income. § 163(d).

Net operating loss (NOL). To mitigate the effect of the annual accounting period concept, § 172 allows taxpayers to use an excess loss of one year as a deduction for certain past or future years. In this regard, a carryback period of 2 years and a carryforward period of 20 years are allowed. See also *mitigation of the annual accounting period concept.*

Net worth method. An approach used by the IRS to reconstruct the income of a taxpayer who fails to maintain adequate records. Under this approach, the gross income for the year is the increase in net worth of the taxpayer (assets in excess of liabilities) with appropriate adjustment for nontaxable receipts and nondeductible expenditures. The net worth method often is used when tax fraud is suspected.

Ninety-day letter. See *statutory notice of deficiency.*

No-additional-cost services. Services that the employer may provide the employee at no additional cost to the employer. Generally, the benefit is the ability to utilize the employer's excess capacity (vacant seats on an airliner). Such amounts are excludible from the recipient's gross income. § 132.

Nonaccountable plan. An expense reimbursement plan that does not have an accountability feature. The result is that employee expenses must be claimed as deductions *from* AGI. An exception is moving expenses, which are deductions *for* AGI. See also *accountable plan.*

Nonacquiescence. Announcement of disagreement by the IRS on the result reached in certain judicial decisions. Sometimes abbreviated *Nonacq.* or *NA.* See also *acquiescence.*

Nonbusiness bad debts. A bad debt loss not incurred in connection with a creditor's trade or business. The loss is deductible as a short-term capital loss and is allowed only in the year the debt becomes entirely worthless. In addition to family loans, many investor losses fall into the classification of nonbusiness bad debts. § 166(d). See also *bad debts.*

Nonqualified deferred compensation (NQDC). Compensation arrangements that are frequently offered to executives. Such plans may include stock options, restricted stock, etc. Often, an executive may defer the recognition of taxable income. The employer, however, does not receive a tax deduction until the employee is required to include the compensation in income. See also *restricted property plan.*

Nonqualified stock option (NQSO). A type of stock option that does not satisfy the statutory requirements of an incentive stock option. If the NQSO has a readily ascertainable fair market value (e.g., the option is traded on an established exchange), the value of the option must be included in the employee's gross income at the date of the grant. Otherwise, the employee does not recognize income at the grant date. Instead, ordinary income is recognized in the year of exercise of the option. See also *incentive stock option (ISO).*

Nonrecourse debt. An obligation on which the endorser is not personally liable. An example of a nonrecourse debt is a mortgage on real estate acquired by a partnership without the assumption of any liability on the mortgage by the partnership or any of the partners. The acquired property generally is pledged as collateral for the loan.

Nonrefundable credit. A nonrefundable credit is a credit that is not paid if it exceeds the taxpayer's tax liability. Some nonrefundable credits qualify for carryback and carryover treatment. See also *refundable credit.*

Nontaxable exchange. A transaction in which realized gains or losses are not recognized. The recognition of gain or loss is postponed (deferred) until the property received in the nontaxable exchange is subsequently disposed of in a taxable transaction. Examples are § 1031 like-kind exchanges and § 1033 involuntary conversions. See also *involuntary conversion* and *like-kind exchange.*

O

Occupational fee. A tax imposed on various trades or businesses. A license fee that enables a taxpayer to engage in a particular occupation.

Office audit. An audit by the IRS of a taxpayer's return that is conducted in the agent's office. To be distinguished from a *correspondence audit* or a *field audit.*

Office-in-the-home expenses. Employment and business-related expenses attributable to the use of a residence (e.g., den or office) are allowed only if the portion of the residence is exclusively used on a regular basis as a principal place of business of the taxpayer or as a place of business that is used by patients, clients, or customers. If the expenses are incurred by an employee, the use must be for the convenience of the employer as opposed to being merely appropriate and helpful. In computing the office-in-the-home expenses, a taxpayer can use either the regular method or simplified method. As a general rule, the regular method requires more effort and recordkeeping but results in a larger deduction. § 280A.

One hundred percent additional first-year depreciation. The Tax Relief Act of 2010 provides for a cost recovery deduction of 100 percent in the tax year qualified property is placed in service. Qualified property includes most types of new property other than buildings. This provision is effective for property acquired after December 31, 2010 and placed in service before January 1, 2012. See also *cost recovery allowance* and *fifty percent additional first-year depreciation.*

One-year rule for prepaid expenses. Taxpayers who use the cash method are required to use the accrual method for deducting certain prepaid expenses (i.e., must capitalize the item and can deduct only when used). If a prepayment will not be consumed or expire by the end of the tax year following the year of payment, the prepayment must be capitalized and prorated over the benefit period. Conversely, if the prepayment will be consumed by the end of the tax year following the year of payment, it can be expensed when paid. To obtain the current deduction under the one-year rule, the payment must be a required payment rather than a voluntary payment.

Open transaction. A judicially imposed doctrine that allows the taxpayer to defer all gain until he or she has collected an amount equal to the adjusted basis of assets transferred pursuant to an exchange transaction. This doctrine has been applied where the property received in an exchange has no ascertainable fair market value due to the existence of contingencies. The method is permitted only in very limited circumstances. See also *recovery of capital doctrine.*

Options. The sale or exchange of an option to buy or sell property results in capital gain or loss if the property is a capital asset. Generally, the closing of an option transaction results in short-term capital gain or loss to the writer of the call and the purchaser of the call option. § 1234.

Ordinary. Common and accepted in the general industry or type of activity in which the taxpayer is engaged. It comprises one of the tests for the deductibility of expenses incurred or paid in connection with a trade or business; for the production or collection of income; for the management, conservation, or maintenance of property held for the production of income; or in connection with the determination, collection, or refund of any tax. §§ 162(a) and 212. See also *necessary*.

Ordinary and necessary. See *necessary* and *ordinary*.

Ordinary income property. Property contributed to a charitable organization that, if sold rather than contributed, would have resulted in other than long-term capital gain to the donor (i.e., ordinary income property and short-term capital gain property). Examples are inventory and capital assets held for less than the long-term holding period.

Organizational expenditures. A corporation may elect to immediately expense the first $5,000 (subject to phaseout) of organizational expenses and generally amortize the balance over a period of 180 months. Certain expenses of organizing a company do not qualify for amortization (e.g., expenditures connected with issuing or selling stock or other securities). § 248.

Original issue discount (OID). The difference between the issue price of a debt obligation (e.g., a corporate bond) and the maturity value of the obligation when the issue price is *less than* the maturity value. OID represents interest and must be amortized over the life of the debt obligation using the effective interest method. The difference is not considered to be original issue discount for tax purposes when it is less than one-fourth of 1 percent of the redemption price at maturity multiplied by the number of years to maturity. §§ 1272 and 1273(a)(3).

Outside salesperson. An outside salesperson solicits business away from the employer's place of business on a full-time basis. The employment-related expenses of an outside salesperson are itemized deductions unless reimbursed by the employer. If reimbursed, such expenses are deductible *for* AGI.

P

Partnerships. A partnership is treated as a conduit and is not subject to taxation. Various items of partnership income, expenses, gains, and losses flow through to the individual partners and are reported on the partners' personal income tax returns. §§ 701 and 702.

Passive activity. A trade or business activity in which the taxpayer does not materially participate is subject to limitations on the deduction of losses and credits. Rental activities (subject to exceptions) and limited partnership interests are inherently passive. Relief from passive activity limitation treatment is provided in certain situations, such as for certain rental real estate, if the taxpayer actively participates in the activity. The annual ceiling on this rental real estate relief is $25,000. Relief also is provided for material participation in a real estate trade or business. § 469. See also *passive loss* and *portfolio income*.

Passive investment income. As defined in § 1362(d)(3)(D), passive investment income means gross receipts from royalties, certain rents, dividends, interest, annuities, and gains from the sale or exchange of stock and securities. Revocation of the S corporation election may occur in certain cases when the S corporation has passive investment income in excess of 25 percent of gross receipts for a period of three consecutive years.

Passive loss. Any loss from (1) activities in which the taxpayer does not materially participate or (2) rental activities (subject to certain exceptions). Net passive losses cannot be used to offset income from nonpassive sources. Rather, they are suspended until the taxpayer either generates net passive income (and a deduction of the losses is allowed) or disposes of the underlying property (at which time the loss deductions are allowed in full). One relief provision allows landlords who actively participate in the rental activities to deduct up to $25,000 of passive losses annually. However, a phaseout of the $25,000 amount commences when the landlord's AGI exceeds $100,000. Another relief provision applies for material participation in a real estate trade or business. See also *passive activity* and *portfolio income*.

Patent. A patent is an intangible asset that may be amortized over a statutory 15-year period as a § 197 intangible. The sale of a patent usually results in favorable long-term capital gain treatment. §§ 197 and 1235.

Pension plan. A type of deferred compensation arrangement that provides for systematic payments of definitely determinable retirement benefits to employees who meet the requirements set forth in the plan. See also *defined benefit plan* and *defined contribution plan*.

Percentage depletion. Percentage depletion is depletion based on a statutory percentage applied to the gross income from the property. The taxpayer deducts the greater of cost depletion or percentage depletion. § 613. See also *cost depletion*.

Percentage of completion method. A method of reporting gain or loss on certain long-term contracts. Under this method of accounting, the gross contract price is included in income as the contract is being completed. § 460 and Reg. § 1.451–3. See also *completed contract method* and *long-term contract*.

Permanent and total disability. A person is considered permanently and totally disabled if he or she is unable to engage in any substantial gainful activity due to a physical or mental impairment. In addition, this impairment must be one that can be expected to result in death or that has lasted or can be expected to last for a continuous period of not less than 12 months. The taxpayer generally must provide the IRS a physician's statement documenting this condition.

Personal and dependency exemptions. The tax law provides an exemption for each individual taxpayer and an additional exemption for the taxpayer's spouse if a joint return is filed. An individual may also claim a dependency exemption for each dependent, provided certain tests are met. The amount of the personal and dependency exemptions is $3,650 in 2010, $3,700 in 2011, $3,800 in 2012, $3,900 in 2013, and $3,950 in 2014. The amount is indexed for inflation. The exemption is subject to phaseout once adjusted gross income exceeds certain statutory threshold amounts. This phaseout provision is subject to partial phase-out beginning in 2012 and is increased each year. §§ 151 and 152. See also *qualifying child* and *qualifying relative.*

Personal casualty gain. The recognized gain from any involuntary conversion of personal use property arising from fire, storm, shipwreck, or other casualty, or from theft. See also *personal casualty loss.*

Personal casualty loss. The recognized loss from any involuntary conversion of personal use property arising from fire, storm, shipwreck, or other casualty, or from theft. See also *personal casualty gain.*

Personal exemption. See *personal and dependency exemptions.*

Personal expenses. Expenses of an individual for personal reasons that are not deductible unless specifically provided for under the tax law. § 262.

Personal property. Generally, all property other than real estate. It is sometimes referred to as personalty when real estate is termed realty. Personal property also can refer to property that is not used in a taxpayer's trade or business or held for the production or collection of income. When used in this sense, personal property can include both realty (e.g., a personal residence) and personalty (e.g., personal effects such as clothing and furniture).

Personal residence. See *sale of principal residence.*

Personal service corporation (PSC). A corporation the principal activity of which is the performance of personal services (e.g., health, law, engineering, architecture, accounting, actuarial science, performing arts, or consulting), with such services being substantially performed by the employee-owners. The 35 percent statutory rate applies to PSCs.

Personalty. All property other than realty (real estate). Personalty usually is categorized as tangible or intangible property. Tangible personalty includes such assets as machinery and equipment, automobiles and trucks, and office equipment. Intangible personalty includes stocks and bonds, goodwill, patents, trademarks, and copyrights. See also *personal property.*

Points. Loan origination fees that may be deductible as interest by a buyer of property. A seller of property who pays points reduces the selling price by the amount of the points paid for the buyer. While the seller is not permitted to deduct this amount as interest, the buyer may do so. See *prepaid interest* for the timing of the interest deduction.

Pollution control facilities. A certified pollution control facility, the cost of which may be amortized over a 60-month period if the taxpayer elects. § 169.

Portfolio income. The term is relevant in applying the limitation on passive activity losses and credits. Although normally considered passive in nature, for this purpose portfolio income is treated as nonpassive. Therefore, net passive losses and credits cannot be offset against portfolio income. Examples of portfolio income are interest, dividends, annuities, and certain royalties. § 469. See also *passive activity.*

Precedent. A previously decided court decision that is recognized as authority for the disposition of future decisions.

Prepaid expenses. Cash basis as well as accrual basis taxpayers usually are required to capitalize prepayments for rent, insurance, etc., that cover more than one year. Deductions are taken during the period the benefits are received.

Prepaid interest. In effect, the Code places cash basis taxpayers on an accrual basis for purposes of recognizing a deduction for prepaid interest. Thus, interest paid in advance is deductible as an interest expense only as it accrues. The one exception to this rule involves the interest element when a cash basis taxpayer pays points to obtain financing for the purchase of a principal residence (or to make improvements thereto) if the payment of points is an established business practice in the area in which the indebtedness is incurred and the amount involved is not excessive. § 461(g). See also *points.*

Principal partner. A partner with a 5 percent or greater interest in partnership capital or profits. § 706(b)(3). See also *majority interest partners.*

Private activity bond. Interest on state and local bonds is excludible from gross income. § 103. Certain such bonds are labeled private activity bonds. Although the interest on such bonds is excludible for regular income tax purposes, it is treated as a tax preference in calculating the AMT. See also *alternative minimum tax (AMT).*

Prizes and awards. The fair market value of a prize or award generally is includible in gross income. However, exclusion is permitted if the prize or award is made in recognition of religious, charitable, scientific, educational, artistic, literary, or civic achievement, and the recipient transfers the award to a qualified governmental unit or a nonprofit organization. In that case, the recipient must be selected without any action on his or her part to enter a contest or proceeding, and the recipient must not be required to render substantial future services as a condition of receiving the prize or award. § 74.

Procedural Regulation. A Regulation issued by the Treasury Department that is a housekeeping-type instruction indicating information that taxpayers should provide the IRS as well as information about the internal management and conduct of the IRS itself. See also *interpretive regulation* and *legislative regulation.*

Production activities deduction (PAD). A deduction based on 3 percent of the lesser of qualified production activities income (QPAI) or modified adjusted gross income but not to exceed 50 percent of the W–2 production wages paid. In the case of a corporate taxpayer, taxable income is substituted for modified AGI. The deduction rate increases to 6 percent for 2007 to 2009 and to 9 percent for 2010 and thereafter. § 199. See also *qualified production activities income (QPAI).*

Profit sharing plan. A deferred compensation plan established and maintained by an employer to provide for employee participation in the company's profits. Contributions are paid from the employer's current or accumulated profits to a trustee. Separate accounts are maintained for each participant employee. The plan must provide a definite, predetermined formula for allocating the contributions among the participants. It also must include a definite, predetermined formula for distributing the accumulated funds after a fixed number of years, on the attainment of a stated age, or on the occurrence of certain events such as illness, layoff, or retirement.

Proposed Regulation. A Regulation issued by the Treasury Department in proposed, rather than final, form. The interval between the proposal of a Regulation and its finalization permits taxpayers and other interested parties to comment on the propriety of the proposal. See also *regulations* and *temporary regulation.*

Public policy limitation. See *bribes and illegal payments.*

Punitive damages. Damages received or paid by the taxpayer can be classified as compensatory damages or as punitive damages. Punitive damages are those awarded to punish the defendant for gross negligence or the intentional infliction of harm. Such damages are includible in gross income. § 104. See also *compensatory damages.*

Q

Qualified dividend income. Dividends that are eligible for the beneficial 0 percent or 15 percent tax rate. The American Taxpayer Relief Act of 2012 increased the beneficial tax rate from 15 percent to 20 percent for certain high-income taxpayers (i.e., tax bracket is 39.6 percent). Excluded are certain dividends from foreign corporations, dividends from tax-exempt entities, and dividends that do not satisfy the holding period requirement. A dividend from a foreign corporation is eligible for qualified dividend status only if one of the following requirements are met: (1) the foreign corporation's stock is traded on an established U.S. securities market, or (2) the foreign corporation is eligible for the benefits of a comprehensive income tax treaty between its country of incorporation and the United States. To satisfy the holding period requirement, the stock on which the dividend is paid must have been held for more than 60 days during the 120-day period beginning 60 days before the ex-dividend date.

Qualified employee discounts. Discounts offered employees on merchandise or services that the employer ordinarily sells or provides to customers. The discounts must be generally available to all employees. In the case of property, the discount cannot exceed the employer's gross profit (the sales price cannot be less than the employer's cost). In the case of services, the discounts cannot exceed 20 percent of the normal sales price. § 132.

Qualified pension or profit sharing plan. An employer-sponsored plan that meets the requirements of § 401. If these requirements are met, none of the employer's contributions to the plan will be taxed to the employee until distributed to him or her (§ 402). The employer will be allowed a deduction in the year the contributions are made (§ 404). See also *annuity* and *deferred compensation.*

Qualified production activities income (QPAI). A key determinant in computing the domestic production activities deduction (DPAD). It consists of domestic production gross receipts (DPGR) reduced by cost of goods sold and other assignable expenses. Thus, QPAI represents the profit derived from production activities. § 199. See also *production activities deduction (PAD)* and *domestic production gross receipts (DPGR).*

Qualified real property business indebtedness. Indebtedness that was incurred or assumed by the taxpayer in connection with real property used in a trade or business and is secured by such real property. The taxpayer must not be a C corporation. For qualified real property business indebtedness, the taxpayer may elect to exclude some or all of the income realized from cancellation of debt on qualified real property. If the election is made, the basis of the property must be reduced by the amount excluded. The amount excluded cannot be greater than the excess of the principal amount of the outstanding debt over the fair market value (net of any other debt outstanding on the property) of the property securing the debt. § 108(c).

Qualified residence interest. A term relevant in determining the amount of interest expense the individual taxpayer may deduct as an itemized deduction for what otherwise would be disallowed as a component of personal interest (consumer interest). Qualified residence interest consists of interest paid on qualified residences (principal residence and one other residence) of the taxpayer. Debt that qualifies as qualified residence interest is limited to $1 million of debt to acquire, construct, or substantially improve qualified residences (acquisition indebtedness) plus $100,000 of other debt secured by qualified residences (home equity indebtedness). The home equity indebtedness may not exceed the fair market value of a qualified residence reduced by the acquisition indebtedness for that residence. § 163(h)(3). See also *consumer interest* and *home equity loans.*

Qualified transportation fringes. Transportation benefits provided by the employer to the employee. Such benefits include (1) transportation in a commuter highway vehicle between the employee's residence and the place of employment, (2) a transit pass, and (3) qualified parking. Qualified transportation fringes are excludible from the employee's gross income to the extent categories (1) and (2) above do not exceed $130 per month in 2014 and category (3) does not exceed $259 per month in 2014. These amounts are indexed annually for inflation. § 132.

Qualified tuition program. A program that allows college tuition to be prepaid for a beneficiary. When amounts in the plan are used, nothing is included in gross income provided they are used for qualified higher education expenses. § 529.

Qualified tuition reduction plan. A type of fringe benefit plan that is available to employees of nonprofit educational institutions. Such employees (and the spouse and dependent children) are allowed to exclude from gross income a tuition waiver pursuant to a qualified tuition reduction plan. The exclusion applies to undergraduate tuition. In limited circumstances, the exclusion also applies to the graduate tuition of teaching and research assistants. § 117(d).

Qualifying child. An individual who, as to the taxpayer, satisfies the relationship, abode, and age tests. To be claimed as a dependent, such an individual must also meet the citizenship and joint return tests and not be self-supporting. §§ 152(a)(1) and (c). See also *personal and dependency exemptions.*

Qualifying relative. An individual who, as to the taxpayer, satisfies the relationship, gross income, support, citizenship, and joint return tests. Such an individual can be claimed as a dependent of the taxpayer. §§ 152(a)(2) and (d). See also *personal and dependency exemptions.*

R

RAR. A Revenue Agent's Report, which reflects any adjustments made by the agent as a result of an audit of the taxpayer. The RAR is mailed to the taxpayer along with the 30-day letter, which outlines the appellate procedures available to the taxpayer.

Realized gain or loss. The difference between the amount realized upon the sale or other disposition of property and the adjusted basis of the property. § 1001. See also *adjusted basis* and *recognized gain or loss.*

Realty. All real estate, including land and buildings. Permanent improvements to a building (fixtures) become realty if their removal would cause significant damage to the property. An example of a fixture is the installation of a central air conditioning or heating system to a building. Thus, personalty can become realty through the fixture reclassification.

Reasonable needs of the business. See *accumulated earnings tax.*

Reasonableness. The Code includes a reasonableness requirement with respect to the deduction of salaries and other compensation for services. What constitutes reasonableness is a question of fact. If an expense is unreasonable, the amount that is classified as unreasonable is not allowed as a deduction. The question of reasonableness generally arises with respect to closely held corporations where there is no separation of ownership and management. § 162(a)(1).

Recapture. To recover the tax benefit of a deduction or a credit previously taken.

Recapture of depreciation. Upon the disposition of depreciable property used in a trade or business, gain or loss is measured by the difference between the consideration received (the amount realized) and the adjusted basis of the property. Before the enactment of the recapture of depreciation provisions of the Code, any such gain recognized could be § 1231 gain and usually qualified for long-term capital gain treatment. The recapture provisions of the Code (e.g., §§ 1245 and 1250) may operate to convert some or all of the previous § 1231 gain into ordinary income. The justification for recapture of depreciation is that it prevents a taxpayer from deducting depreciation at ordinary income rates and having the related gain on disposition taxed at capital gain rates. The recapture of depreciation rules do not apply when the property is disposed of at a loss. See also *residential rental property, Section 1231 gains and losses, Section 1245 recapture,* and *Section 1250 recapture.*

Recapture of investment tax credit. When investment tax credit property is disposed of or ceases to be used in the trade or business of the taxpayer, some or all of the investment tax credit claimed on the property may be recaptured as additional tax liability. The amount of the recapture is the difference between the amount of the credit originally claimed and what should have been claimed in light of the length of time the property was actually held or used for qualifying purposes. § 50. See also *investment tax credit.*

Recapture potential. Reference is to property that, if disposed of in a taxable transaction, would result in the recapture of depreciation (§§ 1245 or 1250) and/or of the investment tax credit (§ 50).

Recognized gain or loss. The portion of realized gain or loss that is considered in computing taxable income. See also *realized gain or loss.*

Recovery of capital doctrine. When a taxable sale or exchange occurs, the seller may be permitted to recover his or her investment (or other adjusted basis) in the property before gain or loss is recognized. See also *open transaction.*

Refundable credit. A refundable credit is a credit that is paid to the taxpayer even if the amount of the credit (or credits) exceeds the taxpayer's tax liability. See also *nonrefundable credit.*

Regulations. Treasury Department Regulations represent the position of the IRS as to how the Internal Revenue Code is to be interpreted. Their purpose is to provide taxpayers and IRS personnel with rules of general and specific application to the various provisions of the tax law. Regulations are published in the *Federal Register* and in all tax services. See also *interpretive regulation, legislative regulation, procedural regulation,* and *proposed regulation.*

Rehabilitation expenditures credit. A credit that is based on expenditures incurred to rehabilitate industrial and commercial buildings and certified historic structures. The credit is intended to discourage businesses from moving from older, economically distressed areas to newer locations and to encourage the preservation of historic structures. § 47. See also *rehabilitation expenditures credit recapture.*

Rehabilitation expenditures credit recapture. When property that qualifies for the rehabilitation expenditures credit is disposed of or ceases to be used in the trade or business of the taxpayer, some or all of the tax credit claimed on the property may be recaptured as additional tax liability. The amount of the recapture is the difference between the amount of the credit claimed originally and what should have been claimed in light of the length of time the property was actually held or used for qualifying purposes. § 50. See also *rehabilitation expenditures credit.*

Related party. Includes certain family members and controlled entities (i.e., partnerships and corporations). §§ 267, 707(b), and 1239. See also *related-party transactions.*

Related-party transactions. The tax law places restrictions upon the recognition of gains and losses between related parties because of the potential for abuse. For example, restrictions are placed on the deduction of losses from the sale or exchange of property between related parties. In addition, under certain circumstances, related-party gains that would otherwise be classified as capital gain are classified as ordinary income. §§ 267, 707(b), and 1239. See also *related party.*

Rental activity. Any activity where payments are received principally for the use of tangible property is a rental activity. Temporary Regulations provide that in certain circumstances activities involving rentals of real and personal property are not to be *treated* as rental activities. The Temporary Regulations list six exceptions.

Research activities credit. A tax credit whose purpose is to encourage research and development. It consists of three components: the incremental research activities credit, the basic research credit, and the energy credit. The incremental research activities credit is equal to 20 percent of the excess of qualified research expenditures over the base amount. The basic research credit is equal to 20 percent of the excess of basic research payments over the base amount. § 41. See also *general business credit.*

Research and experimental expenditures. The Code provides three alternatives for the tax treatment of research and experimentation expenditures. They may be expensed in the year paid or incurred, deferred subject to amortization, or capitalized. If the taxpayer does not elect to expense such costs or to defer them subject to amortization (over 60 months), the expenditures must be capitalized. § 174. Three types of research activities credits are available: the basic research credit, the incremental research activities credit and the energy credit. The rate for each type is 20 percent. § 41. See also *research activities credit*.

Reserve for bad debts. A method of accounting whereby an allowance is permitted for estimated uncollectible accounts. Actual write-offs are charged to the reserve, and recoveries of amounts previously written off are credited to the reserve. The Code permits only certain financial institutions to use the reserve method. § 166. See also *specific charge-off method*.

Reserve method. See *reserve for bad debts*.

Reserves for estimated expenses. Except in the limited case for bad debts, reserves for estimated expenses (e.g., warranty service costs) are not permitted for tax purposes even though such reserves are appropriate for financial accounting purposes. See also *all events test*.

Residential rental property. Buildings for which at least 80 percent of the gross rents are from dwelling units (e.g., an apartment building). This type of building is distinguished from nonresidential (commercial or industrial) buildings in applying the recapture of depreciation provisions. The term also is relevant in distinguishing between buildings that are eligible for a 27.5-year life versus a 39-year (or 31.5-year) life for MACRS purposes. Generally, residential buildings receive preferential treatment. §§ 168(e)(2) and 1250. See also *recapture of depreciation*.

Residential rental real estate. See *residential rental property*.

Restricted property plan. An arrangement whereby an employer transfers property (usually stock) to an employee at a bargain price (for less than the fair market value). If the transfer is accompanied by a substantial risk of forfeiture and the property is not transferable, no compensation results to the employee until the restrictions disappear. An example of a substantial risk of forfeiture would be a requirement that the employee return the property if his or her employment is terminated within a specified period of time. § 83. See also *nonqualified deferred compensation (NQDC) plans* and *substantial risk of forfeiture*.

Retirement of corporate obligations. The retirement of corporate and certain government obligations is considered to be a sale or exchange. Gain or loss, upon the retirement of a corporate obligation, therefore, is treated as capital gain or loss rather than as ordinary income or loss. §§ 1271–1275.

Return of capital doctrine. See *recovery of capital doctrine*.

Revenue neutrality. A description that characterizes tax legislation when it neither increases nor decreases the revenue result. Thus, any tax revenue losses are offset by tax revenue gains.

Revenue Procedure. A matter of procedural importance to both taxpayers and the IRS concerning the administration of the tax law is issued by the National Office of the IRS as a Revenue Procedure (abbreviated Rev.Proc.). A Revenue Procedure is first published in an *Internal Revenue Bulletin* (I.R.B.) and later transferred to the appropriate *Cumulative Bulletin* (C.B.). Both the *Internal Revenue Bulletin* and the *Cumulative Bulletin* are published by the U.S. Government Printing Office.

Revenue Ruling. A Revenue Ruling (abbreviated Rev.Rul.) is issued by the National Office of the IRS to express an official interpretation of the tax law as applied to specific transactions. It is more limited in application than a Regulation. A Revenue Ruling is first published in an *Internal Revenue Bulletin* (I.R.B.) and later transferred to the appropriate *Cumulative Bulletin* (C.B.). Both the *Internal*

Revenue Bulletin and the *Cumulative Bulletin* are published by the U.S. Government Printing Office.

Roth IRA. See *individual retirement account (IRA)*.

S

S corporation. See *S corporation status*.

S corporation status. An elective provision permitting certain small business corporations (§ 1361) and their shareholders to elect (§ 1362) to be treated for income tax purposes in accordance with the operating rules of §§ 1363–1379. Of major significance are the facts that S status avoids the corporate income tax and corporate losses can be claimed by the shareholders. See also *C corporation*.

Sale of principal residence. If a residence has been owned and used by the taxpayer as the principal residence for at least two years during the five-year period ending on the date of sale, up to $250,000 of realized gain is excluded from gross income. For a married couple filing a joint return, the $250,000 is increased to $500,000 if either spouse satisfies the ownership requirement and both spouses satisfy the use requirement. § 121.

Sale or exchange. A requirement for the recognition of capital gain or loss. Generally, the seller of property must receive money or relief from debt in order to have sold the property. An exchange involves the transfer of property for other property. Thus, collection of a debt is neither a sale nor an exchange. The term *sale or exchange* is not defined by the Code.

Sales tax. A transaction tax imposed upon the sale of goods. It usually is based on a specified percentage of the value of the property sold. A sales tax differs from an excise tax, in that a sales tax applies to a broad variety of commodities.

Salvage value. The estimated amount a taxpayer will receive upon the disposition of an asset used in the taxpayer's trade or business. Salvage value is relevant in calculating depreciation under § 167, but is not relevant in calculating cost recovery under § 168.

Schedule M-1. On the Form 1120, a reconciliation of book net income with Federal taxable income. Accounts for timing and permanent differences in the two computations, such as depreciation differences, exempt income, and nondeductible items. On Forms 1120S and 1065, the Schedule M-1 reconciles book income with the owners' aggregate ordinary taxable income.

Schedule M-3. An *expanded* reconciliation of book net income with Federal taxable income (refer to *Schedule M-1* above). Applies to corporations with total assets of $10 million or more.

Scholarships. Scholarships are generally excluded from the gross income of the recipient unless the payments are a disguised form of compensation for services rendered. However, the Code imposes restrictions on the exclusion. The recipient must be a degree candidate. The excluded amount is limited to amounts used for tuition, fees, books, supplies, and equipment required for courses of instruction. Amounts received for room and board are not eligible for the exclusion. § 117.

Section 121 exclusion. See *sale of principal residence*.

Section 179 expensing. The ability to deduct a capital expenditure in the year an asset is placed in service rather than over the asset's useful life or cost recovery period. The annual ceiling on the deduction is $500,000 for 2013 ($500,000 for 2012). However, the deduction is reduced dollar for dollar when § 179 property placed in service during the taxable year exceeds $2 million in 2013 ($2 million in 2012). A previously existing inflation adjustment for this provision has expired. Thus, in the absence of any activity on the part of Congress, for 2014, the original amounts ($25,000 and $200,000) will go into effect. In addition, the amount expensed under § 179 cannot exceed the aggregate amount of taxable income derived from the conduct of any trade or business by the taxpayer.

Section 401(k) plan. A cash or deferred arrangement plan that allows participants to elect to receive up to $17,500 in 2014 in cash (taxed currently) or to have a contribution made on their behalf to a profit sharing or stock bonus plan (excludible from gross income). The plan may also be in the form of a salary reduction agreement between the participant and the employer.

Section 1231 assets. Depreciable assets and real estate used in a trade or business and held for the required long-term holding period. Under certain circumstances, the classification also includes timber, coal, domestic iron ore, livestock (held for draft, breeding, dairy, or sporting purposes), and unharvested crops. § 1231(b).

Section 1231 gains and losses. If the net result of the combined gains and losses from the taxable dispositions of § 1231 assets plus the net gain from the involuntary conversion of nonpersonal use assets is a gain, the gains and losses from § 1231 assets are treated as long-term capital gains and losses. In arriving at § 1231 gains, however, the depreciation recapture provisions (e.g., §§ 1245 and 1250) are first applied to produce ordinary income. If the net result of the combination is a loss, the gains and losses from § 1231 assets are treated as ordinary gains and losses. § 1231(a). See also *recapture of depreciation*.

Section 1231 lookback. In order for gain to be classified as § 1231 gain, the gain must survive the § 1231 lookback. To the extent of nonrecaptured § 1231 losses for the five prior tax years, the gain is classified as ordinary income. § 1231(c).

Section 1231 property. See *Section 1231 assets*.

Section 1244 stock. Stock issued under § 1244 by qualifying small business corporations. If § 1244 stock is disposed of at a loss or becomes worthless, the shareholders may claim an ordinary loss rather than the usual capital loss. The annual ceiling on the ordinary loss treatment is $50,000 ($100,000 for married individuals filing jointly). See also *worthless securities*.

Section 1245 property. Property that is subject to the recapture of depreciation under § 1245. For a definition of § 1245 property, see § 1245(a)(3). See also *Section 1245 recapture*.

Section 1245 recapture. Upon a taxable disposition of § 1245 property, all depreciation claimed on the property is recaptured as ordinary income (but not to exceed the recognized gain from the disposition). See also *recapture of depreciation*.

Section 1250 property. Real estate that is subject to the recapture of depreciation under § 1250. For a definition of § 1250 property, see § 1250(c). See also *Section 1250 recapture*.

Section 1250 recapture. Upon a taxable disposition of § 1250 property, some or all of the additional depreciation claimed on the property may be recaptured as ordinary income. Various recapture rules apply depending upon the type of property (residential or nonresidential real estate) and the date acquired. Generally, the additional depreciation is recaptured in full to the extent of the gain recognized. See also *additional depreciation* and *recapture of depreciation*.

Self-employment retirement plan. A designation for retirement plans available to self-employed taxpayers. Also referred to as H.R. 10 and Keogh plans. Under such plans, in 2013, a taxpayer may deduct each year up to either 100 percent of net earnings from self-employment or $52,000, whichever is less. If the plan is a profit sharing plan, the percentage is 25 percent.

Self-employment tax. A tax of 12.4 percent is levied on individuals with net earnings from self-employment (up to $117,000 in 2014) to provide Social Security benefits (i.e., the old age, survivors, and disability insurance portion) for such individuals. In addition, a tax of 2.9 percent is levied on individuals with net earnings from self-employment (with no statutory ceiling) to provide Medicare benefits (i.e., the hospital insurance portion) for such individuals. If a self-employed individual also receives wages from an employer that are subject to FICA, the self-employment tax will be reduced if total income subject to Social Security is more than $117,000 in 2014. A partial deduction is allowed in calculating the self-employment tax. Individuals with net earnings of $400 or more from self-employment are subject to this tax. §§ 1401 and 1402.

Separate property. In a community property jurisdiction, separate property is the property that belongs entirely to one of the spouses. Generally, it is property acquired before marriage or acquired after marriage by gift or inheritance. See also *community property*.

Severance tax. A tax imposed upon the extraction of natural resources.

Short period. See *short taxable year*.

Short sale. A short sale occurs when a taxpayer sells borrowed property (usually stock) and repays the lender with substantially identical property either held on the date of the short sale or purchased after the sale. No gain or loss is recognized until the short sale is closed, and such gain or loss is generally short term. § 1233.

Short taxable year. A tax year that is less than 12 months. A short taxable year may occur in the initial reporting period, in the final tax year, or when the taxpayer changes tax years.

Significant participation activity. There are seven tests to determine whether an individual has achieved material participation in an activity, one of which is based on more than 500 hours of participation in significant participation activities. A significant participation activity is one in which the individual's participation exceeds 100 hours during the year. Temp.Reg. § 1.469–5T.

Simplified employee pension (SEP) plan. An employer may make contributions to an employee's IRA in amounts not exceeding the lesser of 15 percent of compensation or $52,000 per individual in 2014. These employer-sponsored simplified employee pensions are permitted only if the contributions are nondiscriminatory and are made on behalf of all employees who have attained age 21 and have worked for the employer during at least three of the five preceding calendar years. § 219(b). See also *individual retirement account (IRA)*.

Small business corporation. A corporation that satisfies the definition of § 1361(b), § 1244(c)(3), or both. Satisfaction of § 1361(b) permits an S corporation election, and satisfaction of § 1244 enables the shareholders of the corporation to claim an ordinary loss. See also *S corporation status* and *Section 1244 stock.*

Small business stock. See *small business corporation.*

Small cases division. A subsidiary division of the U.S. Tax Court. The jurisdiction of the Small Cases division is limited to small claims (i.e., claims of $50,000 or less). The proceedings of the Small Cases Division are informal, and the findings cannot be appealed.

Specific charge-off method. A method of accounting for bad debts in which a deduction is permitted only when an account becomes partially or completely worthless. See also *reserve for bad debts.*

Standard deduction. The individual taxpayer can either itemize deductions or take the standard deduction. The amount of the standard deduction depends on the taxpayer's filing status (single, head of household, married filing jointly, surviving spouse, or married filing separately). For 2014, the amount of the standard deduction ranges from $6,200 to $12,400. Additional standard deductions of either $1,200 (for married taxpayers) or $1,550 (for single taxpayers) are available if the taxpayer is either blind or age 65 or over. Limitations exist on the amount of the standard deduction of a taxpayer who is another taxpayer's dependent. The standard deduction amounts are adjusted for inflation each year. § 63(c).

Standard mileage rate. See *automatic mileage rate.*

Startup expenditures. Expenditures paid or incurred associated with the creation of a business prior to the beginning of business. Examples of such expenditures include advertising, salaries and wages, travel and other expenses incurred in lining up prospective distributors, suppliers, or customers, and salaries and fees to executives, consultants, and professional service providers. A taxpayer may elect to immediately expense the first $5,000 (subject to phaseout) of startup expenditures and generally amortize the balance over a period of 180 months.

Statute of limitations. Provisions of the law that specify the maximum period of time in which action may be taken on a past event. Code §§ 6501–6504 contain the limitation periods applicable to the IRS for additional assessments, and §§ 6511–6515 relate to refund claims by taxpayers.

Statutory employee. Statutory employees are considered self-employed independent contractors for purposes of reporting income and expenses on their tax returns. Generally, a statutory employee must meet three tests:

- It is understood from a service contract that the services will be performed by the person.
- The person does not have a substantial investment in facilities (other than transportation used to perform the services).
- The services involve a continuing relationship with the person for whom they are performed.

For further information on statutory employees, see Circular E, *Employer's Tax Guide,* IRS Publication 15.

Statutory notice of deficiency. Commonly referred to as the 90-day letter, this notice is sent to a taxpayer upon request, upon the expiration of the 30-day letter, or upon exhaustion by the taxpayer of his or her administrative remedies before the IRS. The notice gives the taxpayer 90 days in which to file a petition with the U.S. Tax Court. If a petition is not filed, the IRS will issue a demand for payment of the assessed deficiency. §§ 6211–6216. See also *thirty-day letter.*

Stock bonus plan. A type of deferred compensation plan in which the employer establishes and maintains the plan and contributes employer stock to the plan for the benefit of employees. The contributions need not be dependent on the employer's profits. Any benefits of the plan are distributable in the form of employer stock, except that distributable fractional shares may be paid in cash.

Stock option. The right to purchase a stated number of shares of stock from a corporation at a certain price within a specified period of time. §§ 421 and 422. See also *incentive stock option (ISO)* and *nonqualified stock option (NQSO).*

Stock redemption. The redemption of the stock of a shareholder by the issuing corporation is treated as a sale or exchange of the stock if the redemption is not a dividend. §§ 301 and 302.

Substantial risk of forfeiture (SRF). A term that is associated with a restricted property plan. Generally, an employee who receives property (e.g., stock of the employer-corporation) from the employer at a bargain price or at no cost must include the bargain element in gross income. However, the employee currently does not have to do so if there is a substantial risk of forfeiture. A substantial risk of forfeiture exists if a person's rights to full enjoyment of property are conditioned upon the future performance, or the refraining from the performance, of substantial services by the individual. § 83. See also *restricted property plan.*

Sunset provision. A provision attached to new tax legislation that will cause such legislation to expire at a specified date. Sunset provisions are attached to tax cut bills for long-term budgetary reasons in order to make their effect temporary. Once the sunset provision comes into play, the tax cut is rescinded and former law is reinstated. An example of a sunset provision is the one contained in the Tax Relief Reconciliation Act of 2001, which relates to the estate tax. After the estate tax was phased out in 2010, a sunset provision reinstated the estate tax as of January 1, 2011.

Super-full absorption costing rules. See *uniform capitalization rules.*

Surviving spouse. The joint return tax rates apply for a surviving spouse. Such rates apply for the two tax years after the tax year of the death of the spouse. To qualify as a surviving spouse, the taxpayer must maintain a household for a dependent child. § 2.

T

Targeted jobs tax credit. See *work opportunity tax credit.*

Taxable year. The annual period over which income is measured for income tax purposes. Most individuals use a calendar year, but many businesses use a fiscal year based on the natural business year. See also *accounting period* and *fiscal year.*

Tax avoidance. The minimization of one's tax liability by taking advantage of legally available tax planning opportunities. Tax avoidance can be contrasted with tax evasion, which entails the reduction of tax liability by illegal means.

Tax benefit rule. A provision that limits the recognition of income from the recovery of an expense or loss properly deducted in a prior tax year to the amount of the deduction that generated a tax benefit. § 111.

Tax Court. The U.S. Tax Court is one of three trial courts of original jurisdiction that decides litigation involving Federal income, estate, or gift taxes. It is the only trial court where the taxpayer need not first pay the deficiency assessed by the IRS. The Tax Court will not have jurisdiction over a case unless the statutory notice of deficiency (90-day letter) has been issued by the IRS and the taxpayer files the petition for hearing within the time prescribed.

Tax credit for the elderly or disabled. An elderly (age 65 and over) or disabled taxpayer may receive a tax credit amounting to 15 percent of $5,000 ($7,500 for qualified married individuals filing jointly). This amount is reduced by Social Security benefits, excluded pension benefits, and one-half of the taxpayer's adjusted gross income in excess of $7,500 ($10,000 for married taxpayers filing jointly). § 22.

Tax credits. Tax credits are amounts that directly reduce a taxpayer's tax liability. The tax benefit received from a tax credit is not dependent on the taxpayer's marginal tax rate, whereas the benefit of a tax deduction or exclusion is dependent on the taxpayer's tax bracket.

Tax-free exchange. Transfers of property specifically exempted from Federal income tax consequences. Examples are a transfer of property to a controlled corporation under §351(a) and a like-kind exchange under § 1031(a). The recognition of gain or loss is postponed, rather than being permanently excluded, through the assignment of a carryover basis to the replacement property. See also *nontaxable exchange.*

Tax home. Since travel expenses of an employee are deductible only if the taxpayer is away from home, the deductibility of such expenses rests upon the definition of tax home. The IRS position is that the tax home is the business location, post, or station of the taxpayer. If an employee is temporarily reassigned to a new post for a period of one year or less, the taxpayer's home should be his or her personal residence, and the travel expenses should be deductible. If the assignment is for more than two years, the IRS position is that it is indefinite or permanent and the taxpayer is therefore not in travel status. If the assignment is for between one and two years, the IRS position is that the location of the tax home will be determined on the basis of the facts and circumstances. The courts are in conflict regarding what constitutes a person's home for tax purposes. The taxpayer will not be treated as temporarily away from home if the employment period exceeds one year. Thus, in this situation, the tax home will be the place of employment. See also *travel expenses.*

Tax preferences. Those items set forth in § 57 that may result in the imposition of the alternative minimum tax. See also *alternative minimum tax (AMT).*

Tax rate schedules. Rate schedules appearing in Appendix A that are used by upper-income taxpayers and those not permitted to use the tax table. Separate rate schedules are provided for married individuals filing jointly, head of household, single taxpayers, estates and trusts, and married individuals filing separate returns. § 1.

Tax research. The method used to determine the best available solution to a situation that possesses tax consequences. Both tax and nontax factors are considered.

Tax shelters. The typical tax shelter generated large losses in the early years of the activity. Investors would offset these losses against other types of income and, therefore, avoid paying income taxes on this income. These tax shelter investments could then be sold after a few years and produce capital gain income, which is taxed at a lower rate than ordinary income. The passive activity loss rules and the at-risk rules now limit tax shelter deductions.

Tax table. A tax table appearing in Appendix A that is provided for taxpayers with less than $100,000 of taxable income. Separate columns are provided for single taxpayers, married taxpayers filing jointly, head of household, and married taxpayers filing separately. § 3.

Technical advice memoranda (TAMs). TAMs are issued by the National Office of the IRS in response to questions raised by IRS field personnel during audits. They deal with completed rather than proposed transactions and are often requested for questions related to exempt organizations and employee plans.

Temporary Regulation. A Regulation issued by the Treasury Department in temporary form. When speed is critical, the Treasury Department issues Temporary Regulations, which take effect immediately. These Regulations have the same authoritative value as final Regulations and may be cited as precedent for three years. Temporary Regulations are also issued as Proposed Regulations. See also *proposed regulation* and *regulations.*

Theft loss. A loss from larceny, embezzlement, and robbery. It does not include misplacement of items. See also *casualty loss.*

Thin capitalization. When debt owed by a corporation to its shareholders is large relative to its capital structure (stock and shareholder equity), the IRS may contend that the corporation is thinly capitalized. In effect, this means that some or all of the debt will be reclassified as equity. The immediate result is to disallow any interest deduction to the corporation on the reclassified debt. To the extent of the corporation's earnings and profits, interest payments and loan repayments on the reclassified debt are treated as dividends to the shareholders. § 385.

Thirty-day letter. A letter that accompanies a Revenue Agent's Report (RAR) issued as a result of an IRS audit of a taxpayer (or the rejection of a taxpayer's claim for refund). The letter outlines the taxpayer's appeal procedure before the IRS. If the taxpayer does not request any such procedures within the 30-day period, the IRS will issue a *statutory notice of deficiency* (the 90-day letter).

Timber. Special rules apply to the recognition of gain from the sale of timber. A taxpayer may elect to treat the cutting of timber that is held for sale or use in a trade or business as a sale or exchange. If the holding period requirements are met, the gain is recognized as § 1231 gain and may therefore receive long-term capital gain treatment. § 631.

Trade or business expenses. Deductions *for* AGI that are attributable to a taxpayer's business or profession. Some employee expenses may also be treated as trade or business expenses. See also *employee expenses.*

Traditional IRA. See *individual retirement account (IRA)*.

Transportation expenses. Transportation expenses for an employee include only the cost of transportation (taxi fares, automobile expenses, etc.) in the course of employment when the employee is not away from home in travel status. Commuting expenses are not deductible. See also *automobile expenses*.

Travel expenses. Travel expenses include meals (generally subject to a 50 percent disallowance) and lodging and transportation expenses while away from home in the pursuit of a trade or business (including that of an employee). See also *tax home*.

Trial court. The court of original jurisdiction; the first court to consider litigation. In Federal tax controversies, trial courts include U.S. District Courts, the U.S. Tax Court, and the U.S. Court of Federal Claims. See also *appellate court*.

U

Unearned income. Also referred to as investment income, it includes such income as interest, dividends, capital gains, rents, royalties, and pension and annuity income. See also *kiddie tax*.

Unearned (prepaid) income. For tax purposes, prepaid income (e.g., rent) is taxable in the year of receipt. In certain cases involving advance payments for goods and services, income may be deferred. See Revenue Procedure 2004–34 (2004–22 I.R.B. 13, 991) and Reg. § 1.451–5. See also *accrual method*.

Uniform capitalization (UNICAP) rules. Under § 263A, the Regulations provide a set of rules that all taxpayers (regardless of the particular industry) can use to determine the items of cost (and means of allocating those costs) that must be capitalized with respect to the production of tangible property.

Unit-livestock-price method. A method of accounting for the cost of livestock. The livestock are valued using a standard cost of raising an animal with the characteristics of that animal to the same age as the animals on hand.

Unreasonable compensation. Under § 162(a)(1), a deduction is allowed for "reasonable" salaries or other compensation for personal services actually rendered. To the extent compensation is excessive ("unreasonable"), no deduction will be allowed. The problem of unreasonable compensation usually is limited to closely held corporations where the motivation is to pay out profits in some form deductible to the corporation. Deductible compensation, therefore, becomes an attractive substitute for nondeductible dividends when the shareholders are also employees of the corporation.

Unrecaptured § 1250 gain (25 percent gain). Gain from the sale of depreciable real estate held more than one year. The gain is equal to or less than the depreciation taken on such property and is reduced by § 1245 gain and § 1250 gain. See also *alternative tax*.

U.S. Court of Federal Claims. See *Claims Court*.

U.S. Supreme Court. The highest appellate court or the court of last resort in the Federal court system and in most states. Only a small number of tax decisions of the U.S. Courts of Appeal are reviewed by the U.S. Supreme Court under its certiorari procedure. The Supreme Court usually grants certiorari to resolve a conflict among the Courts of Appeal (e.g., two or more appellate courts have assumed opposing positions on a particular issue) or when the tax issue is extremely important (e.g., size of the revenue loss to the Federal government).

U.S. Tax Court. See *Tax Court*.

Use tax. A use tax is an ad valorem tax, usually at the same rate as the sales tax, on the use or consumption of tangible personalty. The purpose of a use tax is to prevent the avoidance of a sales tax.

USTC. Published by Commerce Clearing House, *U.S. Tax Cases* contain all of the Federal tax decisions issued by the U.S. District Courts, U.S. Court of Federal Claims, U.S. Courts of Appeals, and the U.S. Supreme Court.

V

Vacation home. The Code places restrictions upon taxpayers who rent their residences or vacation homes for part of the tax year. The restrictions may result in a scaling down of expense deductions for the taxpayers. § 280A. See also *hobby loss*.

Value added tax (VAT). A national sales tax that taxes the increment in value as goods move through the production process. A VAT is much used in other countries, but has not yet been incorporated as part of the U.S. Federal tax structure.

Vesting requirements. A qualified deferred compensation arrangement must satisfy a vesting requirement. Under this provision, an employee's right to accrued plan benefits derived from employer contributions must be nonforfeitable in accordance with one of two vesting time period schedules (or two required alternate vesting schedules for certain employer matching contributions).

W

W–2 wages. The domestic production activities deduction (DPAD) cannot exceed 50 percent of the W–2 wages paid for any particular year. Prop.Reg. § 199–2(f)(2) provides several methods for calculating the W–2 wages, but the payments must involve common law employees. To qualify, the employees need to be involved in the production process. § 199. See also *production activities deduction (PAD)*.

Wash sale. A loss from the sale of stock or securities that is disallowed because the taxpayer within 30 days before or after the sale has acquired stock or securities that are substantially identical to those sold. § 1091.

Welfare-to-work credit. A tax credit available to employers hiring individuals who have been long-term recipients of family assistance welfare benefits. In general, long-term recipients are those individuals who are certified by a designated local agency as being members of a family receiving assistance under a public aid program for at least an 18-month period ending on the hiring date. The welfare-to-work credit is available for qualified wages paid in the first two years of employment. The maximum credit is equal to $9,000 per qualified employee, computed as 40 percent of the first $10,000 of qualified wages paid in the first year of employment, plus 50 percent of the first $10,000 of qualified wages paid in the second year of employment. Starting in 2007, the welfare-to-work credit became part of the work opportunity tax credit. § 51(e). See also *general business credit* and *work opportunity tax credit.*

Wherewithal to pay. This concept recognizes the inequity of taxing a transaction when the taxpayer lacks the means with which to pay the tax. Under it, there is a correlation between the imposition of the tax and the ability to pay the tax. It is particularly suited to situations in which the taxpayer's economic position has not changed significantly as a result of the transaction.

Withholding allowances. The number of withholding allowances serves as the basis for determining the amount of income taxes withheld from an employee's salary or wages. The more withholding allowances claimed, the less income tax withheld by an employer. An employee may claim withholding allowances for personal exemptions for self and spouse (unless claimed as a dependent of another person), dependency exemptions, and special withholding allowances.

Working condition fringe. A type of fringe benefit received by the employee that is excludible from the employee's gross income. It consists of property or services provided (paid or reimbursed) by the employer for which the employee could take a tax deduction if the employee had paid for them. § 132.

Work opportunity tax credit. Employers are allowed a tax credit equal to 40 percent of the first $6,000 of wages (per eligible employee) for the first year of employment. Eligible employees include certain hard-to-employ individuals (e.g., qualified ex-felons, high-risk youth, food stamp recipients, and veterans). For an employer to qualify for the 40 percent credit, the employees must (1) be certified by a designated local agency as being members of one of the targeted groups and (2) have completed at least 400 hours of service to the employer. For employees who meet the first condition but not the second, the credit rate is reduced to 25 percent provided the employees meet a minimum employment level of 120 hours of service to the employer. The employer's deduction for wages is reduced by the amount of the credit taken. For qualified summer youth employees, the 40 percent rate is applied to the first $3,000 of qualified wages. See the *welfare-to-work credit* for the calculation for long-term recipients of family assistance welfare benefits. §§ 51 and 52.

Worthless securities. A loss (usually capital) is allowed for a security that becomes worthless during the year. The loss is deemed to have occurred on the last day of the year. Special rules apply to securities of affiliated companies and small business stock. § 165. See also *Section 1244 stock.*

Writ of certiorari. See *certiorari.*

© iStockphoto.com/Pali Rao

Table of Code Sections Cited

[See Title 26 U.S.C.A.]

Table of Regulations Cited

© iStockphoto.com/Pali Rao

Table of Revenue Procedures and Revenue Rulings Cited

Appendix E

Practice Set Assignments—Comprehensive Tax Return Problems

PROBLEM 1

Will S. (age 42) and Mari N. (age 41) Frost are married and live at 426 East Twin Oaks Road, Sioux Falls, SD 57105. Will is the regional manager for a restaurant chain (Moveable Feast), and Mari is a self-employed architect. They are calendar-year, cash-basis taxpayers.

1. Will's annual salary from Moveable Feast is $82,000. He also earns an annual bonus. The amount is determined in late December, and Will receives it in January of the next year. Will's 2012 bonus was $6,000 (received in 2013), and his 2013 bonus was $7,000 (received in 2014). Will is also paid a flat travel allowance of $16,000 per year. The allowance is to cover his expenses in visiting restaurants in his region to conduct inspections, consult with the local managers, and recruit potential hires. Although Will maintains substantiation of his travel, he is not required to account for these expenses to Moveable Feast. Will participates in his employer's group health insurance plan to which he contributed $3,600 in 2013 for medical coverage. These contributions were made with after-tax dollars. The health plan covers Will, Mari, and their two dependent children. Moveable Feast does not provide any retirement benefits, but it has established a §401(k) plan to enable its employees to make voluntary contributions. Will contributed $10,000 to the plan in 2013. The company provides an office for Will's use that is located at 110 North Reid Street, Suite 217, Sioux Falls.

2. Besides the business use of his car (see item 3 below), Will's out-of-pocket employment-related expenses for 2013 are as follows:

Airfare	$2,600
Lodging	3,200
Meals	3,400
Entertainment	800
Car rentals, limos, taxis	600
Parking and tolls	300
Subscriptions to trade journals	120
Dues to trade association	80
Business gifts	550

While on business trips in his car, Will was cited for speeding several times and paid related fines totaling $620. Will presented the business gifts in late December to managers of the top 11 restaurants in his region, with each manager receiving a $50 gift card to a national retailer.

3. On March 5, 2012, Will purchased a new Ford Focus for use in his job. The car cost $24,000 (including sales tax), with no trade-in involved. The car was driven 14,000 miles in 2012 and 18,000 in 2013 with usage as follows: 20% for commuting to the office and 80% for business trips. The mileage for 2013 was evenly distributed throughout the year. Will uses the actual operating cost method, and for depreciation purposes, uses 200% declining-balance with a half-year convention. In addition, Will did not claim any §179 expensing or additional first-year depreciation last year when he bought the car. (See Table 3 of the Instructions to Form 4562.) Will's expenses related to operating the Ford Focus for 2013 are as follows:

Gasoline	$2,900
Oil change and lubrication	150
Auto insurance	1,800
Repairs	400
Auto club dues	160
License and registration	120
Interest on car loan	900

4. Mari Frost is a licensed architect who works part time on a consulting basis. Her professional activity code is 541310. Her major clients are real estate developers (both residential and commercial) for whom she prepares structural designs and construction plans. She also advises on building code requirements regarding the renovation and remodeling of existing structures. Mari collected $52,000 in consulting fees during 2013. This total includes a $3,000 payment for work she performed in 2012 and does not include $5,000 she billed in December for work performed in late 2013. In addition, Mari has an unpaid invoice for $6,000 from a client for work done in 2011. This client was convicted of arson in August 2013 and is now serving a five-year sentence in state prison. Mari feels certain that she will never collect the $6,000 she is owed.

Mari does her work at the client's premises or in her office at home (see item 5 below). Her business expenses for 2013 are as follows:

Drafting supplies	$4,800
Reproduction materials (e.g., molds, models, photos, blueprints, copies)	3,200
On-site work clothing (e.g., hip boots, safety glasses, safety helmet)	800
Professional license fee	400
Subscriptions to professional journals	250
Dues to professional organizations	240

In addition, Mari drove the family Acura (purchased on June 7, 2012) 940 miles on her job assignments. She uses the standard mileage method to deduct business costs related to the Acura. During 2013, Mari drove the car a total of 10,000 miles.

5. When the Frosts purchased their home on February 2, 2012, they set aside 300 square feet (out of a total of 2,400 square feet) of living space for Mari's office. As of January 1, 2013, the home had an adjusted basis of $240,000 for purposes of line 36 of Form 8829 (of which $40,000 is attributable to the land)—the fair market value of the property is in excess of this amount. Relevant information concerning the residence for all of 2013 follows:

Homeowner's insurance	$3,200
Repairs and maintenance	1,800
Utilities	6,200
Painting (office area only)	2,500

The cost of Mari's office furniture and equipment was previously deducted under §179 in the years these assets were acquired. On June 29, 2013, she purchased a fireproof file cabinet for $800 to safeguard the blueprints of her structural designs and construction plans. If possible, Mari prefers to avoid depreciating capital expenditures.

6. One of Mari's clients was interested in building a shopping center on a tract of land Mari owned in Lincoln County. Mari inherited the property from her uncle when he died on June 6, 1993. At that time, the land was worth $40,000. It has since been rezoned for commercial use and has a current value of $200,000. On February 10, 2013, Mari exchanged the Lincoln County parcel for a similar tract in Minnehaha County (worth $190,000) and cash of $10,000.

7. On September 2, 2013, Mari sold a tract of land in McCook County to a farmer who owned the adjoining property. The land was inherited from the same uncle who died in 1993 and was worth $30,000 on June 6, 1993. Under the terms of the sale, Mari received cash of $20,000 and four notes receivable (to be paid at one-year intervals) that each call for the payment of $25,000 plus simple interest of 8%. To the extent allowed by law, Mari wants to defer recognition of gain as long as possible.

8. In early 2012, Will learned that one of his restaurant managers, Carrie Jones, was suffering domestic abuse at the hands of her husband Steve. When Steve also started to abuse their 5-year-old daughter, Carrie decided it was time for her and her daughter to get away. Before they left on April 14, 2012, Will loaned Carrie $5,500 to help them relocate. Will had her sign an interest-free note due in one year. Will never heard from Carrie again. In late 2013, Will learned that Steve tracked down Carrie and their daughter and killed both of them before committing suicide. Given these tragic circumstances, Will has no expectation that the loan will ever be repaid.

9. On August 5, 2011, Will purchased 1,000 shares of Farmer's Markets America (FMA) common stock for $16 a share as part of its initial public offering. The corporation was formed to establish and operate farmers' markets in mid-size cities throughout the United States. Although some market locations were profitable, the venture as a whole proved to be a failure. In November 2013, FMA's remaining assets were seized by its creditors, and FMA stock became worthless.

10. Besides the items previously noted, the Frosts had the following receipts for 2013:

Interest income:		
City of Sioux Falls bonds	$1,400	
General Motors corporate bonds	1,900	
Castle Bank certificate of deposit	210	$ 3,510
Qualified dividends from MG&E Inc.		3,100
Refund from HomeStuff (received 1/13/13)		430
Loan repayment by Sarah Frost-Caine		4,500
Cash gifts from Mari's parents		32,000
Federal income tax refund (2012 return)		290

In December 2012, the Frosts made major purchases of household items (e.g., appliances, furniture) at HomeStuff (a discount big box store). They called the manager when they realized they did not receive the advertised sale price. Consequently, the store corrected the mistake and sent a $430 refund. Four years ago when his sister Sarah married, Will lent her $4,000 to help pay for her honeymoon. Will was pleasantly surprised when Sarah paid him back (plus interest of $500) on December 20, 2013. On March 20 of each year, Mari's parents send a generous gift of cash as a birthday present. Just as she has done for the past seven years, Mari immediately invested the cash in her kids' § 529 college savings plans.

11. In addition to the items already noted, the Frosts had the following expenditures for 2013:

Mari's contribution to her traditional IRA		$5,500
Net gambling loss		1,000
Life insurance premiums		2,700
Medical and dental expenses not covered by insurance		6,200
Taxes:		
Ad valorem taxes on personal residence	$4,800	
State and local sales taxes	3,200	8,000
Interest on home mortgage		4,000
Cash Contributions:		
Goodwill (Sioux Falls branch)	1,200	
South Dakota governor's election campaign fund	300	1,500

The $1,000 net gambling loss for 2013 is the difference between the Frosts' gambling winnings of $1,200 and losses of $2,200. The life insurance premiums relate to the universal life insurance policies that Will and Mari own. The first beneficiary on both policies is the other spouse, with the second beneficiaries being the children. Included in the medical expenses are $1,200 incurred in 2012, which was paid in early February 2013. The Frosts can substantiate the $3,200 in sales taxes paid based on their purchase receipts for the year. The local sales tax rate in Sioux Falls is 2%. [HINT: Be sure to check to see if the Optional Sales Tax Tables provide the Frosts with a greater deduction.] Mari contributed to the governor's campaign fund because she thinks his influence is key in getting the Lincoln County land rezoned for commercial use (see item 6 above).

12. The Frosts maintain a household that includes their two children, Austin (age 16) and Emma (age 19). Austin is a junior in high school and a talented wrestler. In hopes of competing at the state tournament, all of his free time is consumed with weight training and wrestling practices. Emma graduated from high school on June 7, 2013, and is undecided about college. Emma is an accomplished vocalist and during 2013 earned $7,200 performing at various events (e.g., weddings, funerals). She placed most of her earnings in a savings account and kept only a small amount to spend on herself.

13. Will's Form W–2 from Moveable Feast shows $13,800 withheld for Federal income tax. The Frosts have made total quarterly income tax payments of $4,000.

14. Relevant Social Security numbers are as follows:

Name	Social Security Number
Will S. Frost	111–11–1111
Mari N. Frost	123–45–6787
Emma J. Frost	123–45–6788
Austin W. Frost	123–45–6789

Requirements

Prepare an income tax return (with appropriate schedules) for the Frosts for 2013, using the following guidelines:

- The Frosts choose to file a joint income tax return.
- The Frosts do not wish to contribute to the Presidential Election Campaign Fund.
- The Frosts do not own any foreign bank accounts or other investments.
- The Frosts prefer to receive any refund of overpaid taxes.
- The taxpayers are preparing their own return (i.e., no preparer is involved).
- For the past several years, the Frosts have itemized their deductions from AGI instead of using the standard deduction.

- The taxpayers have the necessary substantiation (e.g., records, receipts) to support all transactions reported in their tax return.
- Make necessary assumptions for information not given in the problem but needed to complete the return.

PROBLEM 2

Matthew B. (age 42) and Shelli R. (age 48) Thomson are married and live at 7605 Walnut Street, Kansas City, MO 64114. Matthew is a chemist employed by Sargent Pharmaceuticals, Inc., and Shelli is a self-employed doctor of anesthesiology. They are calendar-year, cash-basis taxpayers.

1. Sargent Pharmaceuticals develops and produces injectable medicines used in chemotherapy treatments for cancer patients. Matthew manages the Kansas City facility for an annual salary of $90,000. Sargent makes contributions to a qualified defined contribution pension plan for all of its full-time employees. Although Matthew also has the opportunity to make contributions into the plan, he chose not to do so in 2013. Matthew participates in his employer's group health insurance plan to which he contributed $4,000 in 2013 for medical coverage. These contributions were made with after-tax dollars. The health plan covers Matthew, Shelli, and their two dependent children. Because of the risk associated with Matthew's work (i.e., processing of chemotherapy drugs), Sargent provides all of its employees with $200,000 of group term life insurance coverage. An additional $180 of income is included in Matthew's Form W–2 to report the taxable value of this insurance.

2. In late 2012, three employees at Sargent's Chicago facility were seriously injured while processing a customer order. While the injuries occurred in what the company described as a "freak accident," Matthew began to look for a safer job in the chemical industry. He incurred the following expenses during 2013:

Employment agency fee	$3,200
Vita consultation, preparation, and distribution	1,800
Expenses in connection with job interviews	4,100

   Matthew received several attractive offers but ultimately decided against changing jobs. Influential in his choice was a promotion to regional manager and a $20,000 pay raise (starting in 2014).

3. Sargent generally reimburses Matthew for expenses related to his work for the company. However, as a matter of policy, Sargent does not reimburse for the following:

Monthly dinner sessions of the Midwestern Chemists Association (11 meetings in 2013)	$825
Dues to professional organizations	240
Subscriptions to professional journals	180
MIA correspondence study course	230

   Each dinner involved the following costs: $40 (fee for speaker), $25 (price of meal), and $10 (parking). Matthew goes to the meeting from work and returns home the same night. The MIA (Management Institute of America) charge was for an online home study course on ways to improve safety measures and avoid accidents in the industrial workplace.

4. Shelli Thomson is a board-certified doctor of anesthesiology. She provides anesthesiology services at a handful of hospitals and surgical centers in the greater Kansas City area on a part-time basis. Shelli is well respected by the surgeons with whom she works. She uses her home as her business address. She keeps her records there and otherwise conducts business (e.g., accepts surgery appointments, renders professional advice, and bills patients) on the premises.

Because Shelli does not maintain a specific area for exclusive business use, she does not claim an office in the home for tax purposes. Shelli's receipts from her practice during 2013 were $245,000, $16,000 of which was for services performed in 2012. Not included in these amounts is $17,500 that she received in January 2014 for services rendered in December 2013. Shelli's professional activity code is 621111.

5. Shelli had the following business expenses in 2013:

Medical clothing (e.g., lab coats, surgical scrubs)	$2,200
Medical malpractice insurance	9,500
State medical license fee	450
Dues to professional organizations	350
Subscriptions to professional journals	340

In addition, she drove the family Suburban (purchased on March 2, 2012) 2,900 miles in connection with her work. She uses the standard mileage method. Total mileage for the Suburban is 9,000 miles for the year.

6. Matthew's widowed mother, Lucy, suffered a stroke on December 30, 2012, and died in the hospital on February 3, 2013. Most of Lucy's medical expenses were covered by Medicare, with Matthew paying the rest. On February 18, 2013, he paid $9,800 to the hospital, half of which was attributable to expenses incurred in 2012. At the same time, Matthew also paid the funeral expenses of $16,000. Although Lucy lived in her own home prior to the stroke, Matthew and Shelli have properly claimed her as a dependent for the past few years.

7. As Lucy's sole heir, Matthew inherited her home and its furnishings (located at 1420 Chickadee Lane, Topeka, KS 66546). The costs and values involved are as follows:

	Cost Basis	FMV on 2/3/13
Lot	$ 10,000	$ 30,000
House	110,000	250,000
Furnishings	55,000	25,000

Because the real estate market was depressed and the home was located in an attractive rental area, Matthew decided not to sell. Instead, he rented the property fully furnished on May 1, 2013. The terms of the lease (executed on April 30) provide for the following: one-year lease at $2,500 per month (payable on the first of each month), last month's rent payable in advance, and damage deposit of $3,000. In total, Matthew received $25,500 from the tenants in 2013 for their use of the property. Besides depreciation, his expenses were as follows:

Property taxes	$4,800
Insurance	3,900
Repairs	2,100
Real estate renter's location service	400

Matthew plans to use MACRS straight-line depreciation (mid-month convention) for the realty. Regarding the personalty, see Exhibit 8.1 in Chapter 8 of the text.

8. While walking the family dogs in late July, Shelli was struck by a delivery van and seriously injured. After being hospitalized for a week, she was released—bruised and sore, but with no permanent injuries. The driver of the van was arrested and ticketed by the police for reckless operation of a vehicle and was later prosecuted for drug use. To prevent adverse publicity related to a lawsuit, the owner of the delivery service paid for Shelli's medical expenses and sent her a check on August 16, 2013, for $90,000. The check was accompanied by a letter that stated: "This $90,000 is a settlement for physical injuries sustained by

Shelli Thomson." Shelli was represented in the negotiations with the delivery company by her brother, a practicing attorney. He did not charge the Thomsons for his services.

9. The Thomsons had the following property transactions during 2013:

   a. On October 5, the City Council condemned unimproved land owned by Matthew for the construction of a fire station. He purchased the land (two vacant lots at 3400 and 3402 Sycamore Lane) as an investment on May 25, 2007, for $14,000. In exchange for the lots, the city gave Matthew a large unimproved lot at 440 Genoa Street that was valued at $20,000. All in all, he was satisfied with the exchange because the Genoa Street property is in a better neighborhood and has a greater potential for appreciation.

   b. On November 22, Matthew sold a gun collection for $32,000 to an avid collector. The collection was a gift from Matthew's father on December 25, 2009, when it was worth $22,000. His father bought the collection in 1997 for $14,000. The sale was evidenced by a bill of sale.

   c. On November 9, they sold 3,000 shares of Dove Pharmaceuticals for $2,000. The stock was purchased by the Thomsons on December 4, 2012, for $25,000. The investment was motivated by the rumor that Dove was developing a new drug for infertility. After the FDA failed to approve the drug, the Thomsons decided to cut their losses. Their broker provided them with a Form 1009–B, which reported the gross proceeds from the sale and their basis in the stock.

10. The Thomsons have a long-term capital loss carryover of $1,500 from 2012.

11. In March 2013, the Thomsons were audited by the Missouri Department of Revenue for tax years 2010 and 2011. The audit proposed no changes for the 2010 tax return. However, the Thomsons were assessed $2,250 additional income tax for 2011 (no interest or penalties were included). The Thomsons agreed with the assessment and paid the $2,250 immediately.

12. During 2013, Matthew was called to serve on a jury. As a result of the service, he was paid $700 and incurred nonreimbursed expenses (e.g., parking) of $60. In conformance with company policy, Matthew remitted the $700 of fees to Sargent.

13. Besides the items already noted, the Thomsons had the following receipts in 2013:

Life insurance proceeds		$50,000
2012 Missouri state income tax refund		450
Proceeds from garage sale		2,600
Interest income—		
Kansas City general purpose bonds	$480	
CitiBank certificate of deposit	600	1,080

The insurance proceeds relate to a policy on Lucy's life, which paid Matthew as the designated beneficiary. At the garage sale, the Thomsons sold personal items (e.g., camper, furniture, hunting and fishing equipment) that belonged to Matthew's father and mother (i.e., Lucy). Matthew and Shelli estimated that the items they sold had cost $7,100. The garage sale proceeds were donated to the Alzheimer's Association (a qualified charity) in memory of Matthew's father.

14. The Thomsons had additional expenditures for 2013 as follows:

Dentist bills not covered by insurance	$3,100
Ad valorem property taxes on personal residence	4,100
Interest on home mortgage	2,600
Contributions to Goodwill (a qualified charity)	3,600

As part of a program sponsored by their church (a qualified charity), the Thomsons used the family Suburban to transport senior citizens to religious services for a total of 900 miles. The Suburban also was used for medical purposes (e.g., visits to an orthodontist) for 480 miles.

15. The Thomsons' household includes two dependent children: Ethan (age 15) and Bella (age 14), both of whom are full-time students. Relevant Social Security numbers follow:

Name	Social Security Number
Matthew B. Thomson	111–11–1111
Shelli R. Thomson	123–45–6786
Lucy E. Thomson	123–45–6787
Ethan M. Thomson	123–45–6788
Bella A. Thomson	123–45–6789

16. Matthew's Form W–2 from Sargent Pharmaceuticals reflects income tax withholdings of $6,500 (Federal) and $4,000 (state). The Thomsons made quarterly income tax payments of $20,000 (Federal) and $9,000 (state) for total payments of $80,000 (Federal) and $36,000 (state). They had their Federal income tax refund of $3,000 for 2012 applied toward their 2013 income tax.

Requirements

Prepare an income tax return (with appropriate schedules) for the Thomsons for 2013, using the following guidelines:

- The Thomsons choose to file a joint income tax return.
- The Thomsons do not wish to contribute to the Presidential Election Campaign Fund.
- The Thomsons do not own any foreign bank accounts or other investments.
- The Thomsons want to apply any federal tax refund to their 2014 tax liability.
- The taxpayers are preparing their own return (i.e., no preparer is involved).
- For the past several years, the Thomsons have itemized their deductions from AGI instead of using the standard deduction. In addition, the Thomsons have deducted state income taxes (not sales taxes) for the past several years.
- The taxpayers have the necessary substantiation (e.g., records, receipts) to support all transactions reported in their tax return.
- Make necessary assumptions for information not given in the problem but needed to complete the return.

Table of Cases Cited

© iStockphoto.com/Pali Rao

Depreciation and the Accelerated Cost Recovery System (ACRS)

INTRODUCTION

Cost recovery, amortization, and depletion are presented in Chapter 8. For most fixed assets (e.g., machinery, equipment, furniture, fixtures, buildings) placed in service after December 31, 1980, the Economic Recovery Tax Act of 1981 (ERTA) has replaced the depreciation system with the cost recovery system.[1] The general relationship between the depreciation system and the cost recovery system is summarized in Exhibit G.1.

Despite ERTA, a discussion of § 167 depreciation is still relevant for two reasons. First, assets that were placed in service prior to 1981 are still in use. Second, certain assets placed in service after 1980 are not eligible to use the cost recovery system (ACRS and MACRS) and therefore must be depreciated. They include property placed in service after 1980 whose life is not based on years (e.g., units-of-production method).

As to cost recovery, Chapter 8 focuses on the Modified Accelerated Cost Recovery System (MACRS). A brief summary of the Accelerated Cost Recovery System (ACRS) concludes this appendix.

EXHIBIT G.1	Depreciation and Cost Recovery: Relevant Time Periods
System	**Date Property Is Placed in Service**
§ 167 depreciation	Before January 1, 1981, and *certain* property placed in service after December 31, 1980.
Original accelerated cost recovery system (ACRS)	After December 31, 1980, and before January 1, 1987.
Modified accelerated cost recovery system (MACRS)	After December 31, 1986.

---

[1]Depreciation is covered in § 167, and cost recovery (ACRS and MACRS) is covered in § 168.

DEPRECIATION

Section 167 permits a depreciation deduction in the form of a reasonable allowance for the exhaustion, wear and tear, and obsolescence of business property and property held for the production of income (e.g., rental property held by an investor).[2] Obsolescence refers to normal technological change due to reasonably foreseeable economic conditions. If rapid or abnormal obsolescence occurs, a taxpayer may change to a shorter estimated useful life if there is a "clear and convincing basis for the redetermination." Depreciation deductions are *not* permitted for personal use property.

The taxpayer must adopt a reasonable and consistent plan for depreciating the cost or other basis of assets over the estimated useful life of the property (e.g., the taxpayer cannot arbitrarily defer or accelerate the amount of depreciation from one year to another). The basis of the depreciable property must be reduced by the depreciation allowed and by not less than the allowable amount.[3] The *allowed* depreciation is the depreciation actually taken, whereas the *allowable* depreciation is the amount that could have been taken under the applicable depreciation method. If the taxpayer does not claim any depreciation on property during a particular year, the basis of the property still must be reduced by the amount of depreciation that should have been deducted (the allowable depreciation).

Example 1

On January 1, Ted paid $7,500 for a truck to be used in his business. He chose a five-year estimated useful life, no salvage value, and straight-line depreciation. Thus, the allowable depreciation deduction was $1,500 per year. However, depreciation actually taken (allowed) was as follows:

Year 1	$1,500
Year 2	–0–
Year 3	–0–
Year 4	1,500
Year 5	1,500

The adjusted basis of the truck must be reduced by the amount of allowable depreciation of $7,500 ($1,500 × 5 years) even though Ted claimed only $4,500 depreciation during the five-year period. Therefore, if Ted sold the truck at the end of year 5 for $1,000, he would recognize a $1,000 gain, since the adjusted basis of the truck is zero.

QUALIFYING PROPERTY AND BASIS FOR DEPRECIATION

The use rather than the character of property determines whether a depreciation deduction is permitted. Property must be used in a trade or business or held for the production of income to qualify as depreciable.

Example 2

Carol is a self-employed CPA who maintains her office in a room in her home. The room, which is used exclusively for her business, comprises 20% of the square footage of her house. Carol is permitted a depreciation deduction only for the business use part of the house. No depreciation deduction is permitted for the 80% of the square footage of her house that is used as her residence.

The basis for depreciation generally is the adjusted cost basis used to determine gain if the property is sold or otherwise disposed of.[4] However, if personal use

---

[2] § 167(a) and Reg. § 1.167(a)–1.

[3] § 1016(a)(2) and Reg. § 1.167(a)–10(a).

[4] § 167(c).

assets are converted to business or income-producing use, the basis for depreciation *and* for loss is the *lower* of the adjusted basis or fair market value at the time of the conversion of the property.[5] As a result of this lower of basis rule, losses that occurred while the property was personal use property will not be recognized for tax purposes through the depreciation of the property.

Hans acquires a personal residence for $130,000. Four years later, when the fair market value is only $125,000, he converts the property to rental use. The basis for depreciation is $125,000, since the fair market value is less than the adjusted basis. The $5,000 decline in value is deemed to be personal (since it occurred while the property was held for personal use) and therefore nondeductible.	**Example 3**

The Regulations provide that tangible property is depreciable only to the extent that the property is subject to wear and tear, decay or decline from natural causes, exhaustion, and obsolescence.[6] Thus, land and inventory are not depreciable, but land improvements are depreciable (e.g., paved surfaces, fences, landscaping).

OTHER DEPRECIATION CONSIDERATIONS

In determining the amount of the depreciation deduction, the following additional considerations need to be addressed:

- The salvage value of the asset.
- The choice of depreciation methods.
- The useful life of the asset.

For property subject to depreciation under § 167, taxpayers generally must take into account the **salvage value** (assuming there is a salvage value) of an asset in calculating depreciation. An asset cannot be depreciated below its salvage value. However, the Code permits a taxpayer to disregard salvage value for amounts up to 10 percent of the basis in the property. This provision applies to tangible personal property (other than livestock) with an estimated useful life of three years or more.[7]

Green Company acquired a machine for $10,000 in 1980 with an estimated salvage value of $3,000 after 19 years. The company may disregard salvage value to the extent of $1,000 and compute the machine's depreciation based upon a cost of $10,000 less $2,000 salvage value. The adjusted basis may be reduced to $2,000 (depreciation of $8,000 may be taken) even though the actual salvage value is $3,000.	**Example 4**

This provision was incorporated into the law to reduce the number of IRS-taxpayer disputes over the amount of the salvage value that should be used.

Another consideration is the *choice of depreciation methods* from among the several allowed. The following alternative depreciation methods are permitted for property placed into service before January 1, 1981, and for the aforementioned property placed in service after December 31, 1980, for which cost recovery is not permitted:

- The straight-line (SL) method (cost basis less salvage value ÷ estimated useful life).
- The declining-balance method (DB) using a rate not to exceed twice the straight-line rate. Common methods include 200 percent DB (double-declining balance), 150 percent DB, and 125 percent DB. Salvage value is not taken into account under any of the declining-balance methods. However, no further depreciation can be claimed once net book value (cost minus depreciation) and salvage value are the same.

---

[5]Reg. § 1.167(g)–1.
[6]Reg. § 1.167(a)–2.

[7]Reg. §§ 1.167(a)–1(c) and (f)–1.

- The sum-of-the-years' digits method (SYD).
- Any other consistent method that does not result in greater total depreciation being claimed during the first two-thirds of the useful life than would have been allowable under the double-declining balance method. Permissible methods include machine hours and the units-of-production method.

Example 5

On January 1, 1980, Diego acquired a new machine to be used in his business. The asset cost $10,000 with an estimated salvage value of $2,000 and a four-year estimated useful life.[8] The following amounts of depreciation could be deducted, depending on the method of depreciation used:

	1980	1981	1982	1983
1. Straight-line:				
$10,000 cost less ($2,000 salvage value reduced by 10% of cost) ÷ 4 years	$2,250	$2,250	$2,250	$2,250
2. Double-declining balance:				
a. $10,000 × 50% (twice the straight-line rate)	5,000			
b. ($10,000 − $5,000) × 50%		2,500		
c. ($10,000 − $5,000 − $2,500) × 50%			1,250	
d. ($10,000 − $5,000 − $2,500 − $1,250) × 50%				250[9]
3. Sum-of-the-years' digits:*				
$10,000 cost less ($2,000 salvage value reduced by 10% of cost) or $9,000				
a. $9,000 × 4/10	3,600			
b. $9,000 × 3/10		2,700		
c. $9,000 × 2/10			1,800	
d. $9,000 × 1/10				900

*The formula for the sum-of-the-years' digits (SYD) method is

$$\text{Cost} - \text{Salvage value} \times \frac{\text{Remaining life at the beginning of the year}}{\text{Sum-of-the-years' digits of the estimated life}}$$

In this example, the denominator for SYD is $1 + 2 + 3 + 4$, or 10. The numerator is 4 for year 1 (the number of years left at the beginning of year 1), 3 for year 2, etc. The denominator can be calculated by the following formula:

$$S = \frac{Y(Y + 1)}{2} \text{ where } Y = \text{estimated useful life}$$

$$S = \frac{4(4 + 1)}{2} = 10$$

Example 6

Using the depreciation calculations in Example 5, the depreciation reserve (accumulated depreciation) and net book value at the end of 1983 are as follows:

	Cost	−	Depreciation	=	Net Book Value*
Straight-line	$10,000		$9,000		$1,000
Double-declining balance	10,000		9,000		1,000
Sum-of-the-years' digits	10,000		9,000		1,000

* Note that an asset may not be depreciated below its salvage value even when a declining-balance method is used.

---

[8] A four-year life is used to illustrate the different depreciation methods. Note that an asset placed in service in 1980 must have a useful life of at least 36 years in order for depreciation to be deducted in 2015.

[9] Total depreciation taken cannot exceed cost minus estimated salvage value ($1,000 in this example).

In 1969, Congress placed certain restrictions on the use of accelerated methods for new and used realty that are subject to the depreciation rules under § 167. These restrictions were imposed to reduce the opportunities for using real estate investments as tax shelters. The use of accelerated depreciation frequently resulted in the recognition of ordinary tax losses on economically profitable real estate ventures.

The following methods were permitted for residential and nonresidential real property:

	Nonresidential Real Property (Commercial and Industrial Buildings, Etc.)	**Residential Real Property (Apartment Buildings, Etc.)**
New property acquired after July 24, 1969, and generally before January 1, 1981	150% DB, SL	200% DB, SYD, 150% DB, or SL
Used property acquired after July 24, 1969, and generally before January 1, 1981	SL	125% DB (if estimated useful life is 20 years or greater) or SL

Congress chose to permit accelerated methods (200 percent declining-balance and sum-of-the-years' digits) for new residential rental property. Presumably, the desire to stimulate construction of new housing units justified the need for such accelerated methods.

Restrictions on the use of accelerated methods were not imposed on new tangible personalty (e.g., machinery, equipment, and automobiles). However, the 200 percent declining-balance and sum-of-the-years' digits methods were not permitted for used tangible personal property. The depreciation methods permitted for *used* tangible personal property were as follows:

	Useful Life of Three Years or More	**Useful Life of Less Than Three Years**
Used tangible personal property acquired after July 24, 1969, and generally before January 1, 1981	150% DB, SL	SL

Since the acquisition of used property does not result in any net addition to gross private investment in our economy, Congress chose not to provide as rapid accelerated depreciation for used property.

The determination of a *useful life* for a depreciable asset often led to disagreement between taxpayers and the IRS. One source of information was the company's previous experience and policy with respect to asset maintenance and utilization. Another source was the guideline lives issued by the IRS.[10] In 1971, the IRS guideline life system was modified and liberalized by the enactment of the **Asset Depreciation Range (ADR) system**.[11]

ACCELERATED COST RECOVERY SYSTEM (ACRS)

The major characteristics of the **accelerated cost recovery system (ACRS)** are listed in Exhibit G.2. Note that for personalty, except for 20-year property, the recovery period expired (i.e., all of the cost recovery basis has been recovered) prior to 2006. For 20-year property, the recovery period expired during 2006. For realty, the recovery period expired no later than 2005.

---

[10]Rev.Proc. 72–10, 1972–1 C.B. 721, superseded by Rev.Proc. 83–35, 1983–1 C.B. 745.   [11]Reg. § 1.167(a)–11.

EXHIBIT G.2	Characteristics of ACRS		
Property	**Accounting Convention**	**Life**	**Method**
Personalty	Half-year or mid-quarter	3, 5, 7, 10, 15, or 20 years	Accelerated or straight-line
Realty	Mid-month	15, 18, or 19 years	Accelerated or straight-line

Key Terms

Accelerated cost recovery system (ACRS), G-5

Asset Depreciation Range (ADR) system, G-5

Salvage value, G-3

Index

AMT Formula for Individuals

Taxable income (increased by any standard deduction and personal or dependency exemptions)

Plus or minus: Adjustments

Plus: Preferences

Equals: Alternative minimum taxable income (AMTI)

Minus: Exemption

Equals: Alternative minimum tax (AMT) base

Multiplied by: 26% or 28% rate

Equals: Tentative minimum tax before foreign tax credit

Minus: AMT foreign tax credit

Equals: Tentative minimum tax (TMT)

Minus: Regular tax liability (less any foreign tax credit)

Equals: AMT (if TMT > regular tax liability)

AMT Exemption Phaseout for Individuals for 2014

		Phaseout	
Filing Status	**Exemption**	**Begins at**	**Ends at**
Married, filing jointly	$82,100	$156,500	$484,900
Single or head of household	52,800	117,300	328,500
Married, filing separately	41,050	78,250	242,450